Systematics and the Economics of Culture

FREIBERGER BEITRÄGE ZUR INTERKULTURELLEN UND WIRTSCHAFTSKOMMUNIKATION

A Forum for General and Intercultural Business Communication

Herausgegeben von/Edited by
Michael B. Hinner

Band 5

PETER LANG
Frankfurt am Main · Berlin · Bern · Bruxelles · New York · Oxford · Wien

Victor Lux Tonn

Systematics and the Economics of Culture

PETER LANG
Internationaler Verlag der Wissenschaften

Bibliographic Information published by the Deutsche Nationalbibliothek
The Deutsche Nationalbibliothek lists this publication in the Deutsche Nationalbibliografie; detailed bibliographic data is available in the internet at <http://www.d-nb.de>.

ISSN 1612-989X
ISBN 978-3-631-57649-6

www.peterlang.de

Acknowledgement

To be able to finish writing this book, I am grateful for the inspiration and support rendered by my wife Viviana and my daughters Synthia and Regina.

In my decades of studying old ideas, fermenting new ideas and finally creating systematics and the economics of culture, many dear friends and great teachers have been encouraging and helpful. For this, I sincerely thank Professor Guo-ming Chen and Professor Hsi C. Li. Besides, I am thankful to, among others, Mr. James Chou, Professor Hirsh (advisor for my master thesis), Professor Eva S. M. Huang, Professor L. Dwight Israelson and late professor Pan-tai Liu.

Acknowledgement goes further to the insightful Professor Michael B. Hinner and to his students Mr. Xu Yejia and Mr. Christian Peter for converting my manuscript into the publisher's book form.

Author's Preface

This is essentially the English version of the book I have been working on for years (see Tonn [2008]) with the deletion of the portions of the systemic structures of the Y system (a proto-type model of the United States) and C system (a proto-type model of modern China). The study of systematics and that of the economics of culture constitute a twin endeavor in the frontier of human thinking and cultural inquiry. It has been an extraordinarily beautiful, extremely interesting and intellectually highly rewarding experience for this author to invent and advance these frontiers of cultural research in his life-long efforts of intensive research. It is a great relief for the author to see these adventures finally taking a proper step to be crystallized into this book.

In this book, the economy is studied from the perspective of culture. In actuality, this economic study is a cultural study, although it may not be perceived in any conventional sense. In contrast to the conventionally oriented mathematic methods, the systematic method provides simultaneously a cultural orientation and a "structural and qualitative" method in studying the fields of human, socio-political and economic activities in a "systematic" manner. One objective of this method of systematics (or xystematics) is to serve as the guiding principle in the studies of the cultural economies like those of the United States and China. In this book, an introduction to systematics is presented in the Appendices. It is hoped that this systemic method may be applied successfully to the study of natural sciences in the future.

Some day in the future, we hope to pursue a general approach to the economics of culture, i.e., a comprehensive approach to the study of the world economy as a whole. But currently in this book, our immediate goal is just to unfold a self-contained, though not yet entirely complete, framework of the economics of culture (established solidly on the foundations of micro and macro economic aspects) based on the structure of cultural systematics.

In light of the theory of systematics, the theory of multi-stage development and advancement of a modern cultural economy and the related theory of trade for a late-coming nation will also be emphasized. These multiple stages of development and advancement include the capital, technological, and cultural stages. Here, the pre-capital stages of economic development and growth are ignored just for simplicity of theoretical treatment.

In a related reasoning process, for a latecomer, the theory of modern trade also embodies several stages including the stages of import-substitution, export-substitution (or export promotion), and cultural substitution. Here, the stages other than the afore-mentioned ones are ignored as well for the simplicity of theoretical inquiry.

Essentially, we developed and have been advancing the idea that the current world is entering into the critical stage of cultural advancement--the cultural stage of economic development and growth and the stage of cultural creation and substitution in the arena of global trade even for advancing nations. The presentation of this theory is intended to be as comprehensive as possible, applicable to both countries of advancing cultures and nations of developing cultures.

Since the cultural direction is the key to the future of any economic development and advancement, a cultural growth model using techniques of mathematics will then be developed and the association between culture and economic growth will be examined in great detail. The long-term success of any cultural economy will fundamentally depend upon the critical aspect of cultural activity which is essentially the ultimate provider of the scientific and technological creativities of the human kind.

We hope this approach of the economics of culture would significantly increase the explanatory power of the mathematics-based economic analysis and eventually help promote the well-being of many, if not all, citizens of the world. By promoting cultural understanding of the multitude of people and nations, through our study of cultural systematics, we hope to remove some root causes of wars among nations (due to cultural misunderstanding and the inadequacy of reasoning process) and thereby contribute positively to inter-cultural justice and world peace as well.

V.L.T. September 2008, Middletown, R.I., U.S.A.

Editor's Preface

The *Freiberger Beiträge* are a series dedicated to highlight and spotlight the relevance of communication and culture in the world of business. When Victor Lux Tonn sought to publish his book, *Systematics and the economics of culture*, Peter Lang thought it would be a good addition to our series which is why this fifth volume is solely dedicated to Tonn's book. I am, therefore, very pleased that Victor Lux Tonn has consented to publish his book in our series.

In his book, Tonn attempts something quite unique: The quantification of culture in national economies. As an economist and an applied mathematician, Tonn is, in a sense, predestined to carry out such an undertaking. He always felt dissatisfied with the fact that economics usually does not focus on culture when attempting to analyze national economies. According to Tonn, differences in national economies do not seem to be fully explainable and understandable without taking human cultural variations into consideration. It seems that in addition to all the other economic factors, human culture does appear to play a role in national economies which is why Tonn commenced with his analysis.

While Tonn notes that human systems – and culture is such a human system – are not mathematical systems, the human element is part of the physical universe which in turn is mathematically verifiable. Consequently, Tonn sought to determine the influence of culture on the behavior of individuals in an attempt to quantify culture because culture can provide clues as to why and how people respond to certain situations. Tonn argues that with the quantification of culture, it ought to be possible to determine the relative significance of human resources among the other resources relevant in an economy. While other economic resources have been quantified, human resources have generally remained vague and intangible, Tonn notes.

It, thus, becomes clear that the fascination of this book is in a large part due to the attempt to compile a mathematical model that seeks to explain all the factors involved in a national economy, including culture and its subcomponents. Tonn is actually able to offer an explanation on the basis of culture as to why some national economies are relatively advanced and others are not. In his discussion, Tonn draws not only on conventional economics, but also on socio-politics, philosophy, and theology. It is this broad, eclectic blend of various academic disciplines which makes this book so fascinating. But then again, anyone who has studied culture realizes that culture is very complex and extremely interdisciplinary. So any attempt to quantify culture would have to include these disciplines. Tonn has set out to bring these very diverse disciplines into one model. In so doing, he actually manages to demonstrate mathematically that culture is a true economic resource that needs to be considered and nurtured by economic policy makers if a national economy is to flourish. Hence, the relevance and significance of culture can no longer be ignored in the analysis of an economy and in the world of business, Tonn argues.

What makes Tonn's book so fascinating is also the extension of the systematic framework to other disciplines. In fact, his comparison and contrast of Western and Eastern philosophy and theology create a very fascinating blend that in and by itself is already well worth reading. The same might be said of Tonn's translation of philosophical thought and theological exegesis into mathematical equations. In this, he is actually following a tradition that harkens back to classical philosophy and medieval theology which saw the universe grounded in numerology.

In the first half of his book, Tonn unfolds his theory step by step, adding one essential element after another to his model in order to encompass all essential elements and factors relevant to a national economy. The various components of the pertinent formulas and equations are then explained in detail in the second half of the book.

Such a systematic approach provides "simultaneously a cultural orientation and a 'structural and qualitative' method in studying the fields of human, socio-political and economic activities" Tonn notes. The reader will, therefore, encounter a very fascinating approach to the study of culture and economics in this book. An approach one might expect when an economist and mathematician sets out to study, analyze, and evaluate culture and its relevance in national economies.

"I must begin with rudiments of art;
To teach you gamut in a briefer sort,
More pleasant, pithy, and effectual,
Than hath been taught by any of my trade."

William Shakespeare
The Taming of the Shrew, III, 1.

Michael B. Hinner,
Editor

Victor Lux Tonn received his B.L. in Economics and B.A. in Foreign Languages and Literature from National Taiwan University. After teaching a few years in Taiwan, he went to study mathematics and economics in New York City. Later, he received a Ph.D. in Economics from Utah State University. In the 1980's, he developed a general interest in global culture, growing out of his love of philosophy and poetry. In 1986, he began taking courses in mathematics at the University of Rhode Island and in 1994 received his Ph.D. in Applied Mathematical Sciences. Since his first day of studying economics, he was entirely dissatisfied with the lack of comprehensive human foundations and the very limited characteristics of the equilibrium analysis in the traditional economic study. Furthermore, for decades he sensed that in human and social studies, there is no reason to be restricted to the methods of natural sciences. Eventually, from his works in late 1980's and 1990's, and to be stimulated by his association with several friends, he succeeded in creating *systematics*, to be somewhat parallel to mathematics in attempting to provide a general framework of research to be consistent with both aspirations of modernism and postmodernism and with both spirits of the East and the West, and in creating the initial form of the *economics of culture*, using systematics in addressing the culture-humanity foundations of economics. He is currently teaching Economics at Salve Regina University. One of his current research interests is in inquiring into the advancement frontiers of nations. He hopes in doing so the methods of systematics will further be refined.

Table of Contents

Chapter 1 - Introduction

This book is about the study of systematics and its applications in the economics of culture, both formally and simultaneously created in 1990 (for the earliest and yet informal ideas of systematics, see Tonn 1980, 1984, 1990b). **Systematics** (or **xystematics**, see Tonn [2008]) is defined as the study of systems of universal entities with a focus on the cultural underpinning of systems (for a preliminary definition of the system, see Chapter 2).

There are several cultural sources leading to the creation of systematics. To be specific, we may say that, among others, the development of systematics has been indirectly inspired by mathematics which is defined as the study of the structures or systems of numbers (especially in the context of economics). Furthermore, it is partially inspired by the thinking patterns of dialectic in the West and the YYWX thinking patterns (reasoning process of the scheme of yin-yang five elements) of classic China.

In the broad sense, the **economics of culture**, formerly called the cultural economics by this author, is defined as the study of economics, politics and culture with a focus on the interactions among them. Nevertheless, in the narrow sense, we shall define the economics of culture as the study of economics (i.e., the study of human activities in the areas of production, distribution and consumption with regard to material goods and services) in the interactive complex with the forces of politics and culture.

It is well known that cultural forces are indispensable in the operation of any cultural economy of the West. One's cultural inclination has a definite imprint on one's economic behavior. The role of religion, or more accurately the belief systems in Christianity, is a case in point. And yet, quite surprisingly, the cultural issue is never a focal point of study in the conventional economics developed in the West since the rise of the tide of the scientific revolution.

The economies of East Asia are different from those of the West, due to the difference in the underlying cultures. The difference in culture can be seen in the proto-type systems of human ways of thinking.

In the West, mathematics is a powerful tool of human reasoning. From mathematics, we see how the concept of group is defined. For a set of primitive (or undefined) elements G with an operation "$\circ$," it is defined as a **group** if the following conditions hold: (i) G is closed under "$\circ$": $\forall$ a, b $\in$ G, $a \circ b \in G$. (ii) $(a \circ b) \circ c = a \circ (b \circ c)$, $\forall a, b, c \in G$ (associative law). (iii) $\forall a \in G, \exists\, e \in G \ni e \circ a = a \circ e$, e is called an identity element. (iv) $\forall\, a \in G\ \exists\, {-a} \in G \ni a \circ (-a) = e$. Here "-a" is called the "inverse" of a (existence of the inverse in G).

Furthermore, in mathematics, the "ring" is defined as follows. For a set of primitive elements R with operations "+' and "$\times$," R is called a **ring** provided the following conditions hold: (i) Under the additive operation "+," R is a group. Note that under addition "+": $\forall a \in R, \exists\, 0 \in R \ni 0+a = a+0$, 0 is the additive identity; and $a + (-a) = (-a)+a = 0$ (-a is the additive inverse of a). (ii) Under the additive operation "+," R is commutative. (iii) R is a group under the multiplicative operation "x." Note that under multiplication "$\times$": $\forall a \in R, \exists\, 1 \in R \ni 1 \times a = a \times 1$, 1 is the multiplicative identity; and $a \times a^{-1} = a^{-1} \times a = 1$ (a^{-1} is the multiplicative inverse of a). (iv) Two distributive laws hold in R: $a \times (b+c) = a \times b + a \times c$, $(a+b) \times c = (a \times b) + (a \times c)$, $\forall\, a, b, c \in R$.

If we could use the theories of group, ring and dialectic together to present a few essential aspects of the proto-type thinking patterns of the West, we may use the following **yin-yang scheme** ("yin-yang superior-subject schemes," schemes of yin-yang balance-in-tranquility, or scheme of generative states) as an example of the simplified proto-type thinking patterns of East Asia. Note that dialectic is a scheme that transforms an element into its opposite and then the opposite is further transformed into the opposite of this opposite: thesis → anti-thesis → synthesis, where thesis, anti-thesis and synthesis represents the primitive (and undefined) element, the "opposite of the primitive element," and the opposite of the "opposite of the primitive element," respectively.

For simplicity, we have the following yin-yang schemes: Let {yin,yang} be a system (for the formal definition of a system, see Appendix A, Section A2, §A.2-2-2). Here a system roughly represents a collection, a combination, an event, a complex of events, or a group of elements or people with general or particular activities and specific relations connecting them into a comprehensive whole.

In a more elaborate manner, we would like to present the following schemes as simple manifestations of the afore-mentioned yin-yang scheme. There are nine levels of representations. We shall proceed to discuss each of them in the following.

The first level of yin-yang scheme is the one that yu is created from wu: wu → yu.

At the second level of yin-yang scheme, there are four types of systems: (1) yu → yin. (2) yin → $yin^?$, where "?" = growth, decline, no change, or vanishing. (3) Yin begetting yang: yin → {yin,yang}. This is a transformational process of tranquility. (4) Positive (element) begetting negative (element): positive → {positive,negative}. This is a transformational process of conflict.

The third level of yin-yang scheme concerns systems (or collections) of two elements. There are eleven types of operations associated with this first level scheme. (1) The scheme of **independence**. There is an absolute balance between these two elements and there is no central element. Note that we can write "v center" as the virtual center of this system so that the central force governing each element is virtually the same. (2) **Yin-yang balance**: {yin,yang} → {yin $\stackrel{*}{=}$ yang}. Here yin denotes yin- or implicit element, yang denotes the yang- or explicit element, "→" stands for transformation, creation or a related operation (later to be seen that: "→" ⊨ $\mathbb{H}$ is an impactor), and {yin=yang} refers to the state of yin-yang balance-in-tranquility. (3) **Yang-master and yin-subject**: {yin,yang} ↪ {yin | yang}. Here "↪" represents a force of operation (or an impactor), " | " refers to the convention that the element on the right-hand side of it represents the major force of operation and the element on the left-hand side of it represents the auxiliary force of the operation, and {yin | yang}represents the tranquil association, combination or integration of yin and yang in which yang is the master and yin serves as the subject. (4) **Yin-yang mutually beneficial operation** (mutual prosperity jointly created): {yin,yang} → {yin^+, $yang^+$}, where "→" stands for a mutually beneficial operation and "+" stands for a growth notation. (5) **Yin-yang mutually conflicting operation**: {yin,yang} → {yin^+, $yang^-$}, where "→" stands for a mutually beneficial operation and "+" stands for a growth notation. (6) **Yin-yang benefit-conflict operation** (in tranquility): {yin,yang} → {$yin^?$, $yang^?$}, where ".?" represents "-" (weaker, harmful), "." (no change), or "+" (stronger, growing), with "→" standing for a mutually beneficial operation. Note that (4) and (5) are special cases of (6). (7) **Yang-master and yin-slave**: {yin,yang} ↣ {yin | yang}={slave | master}. Here yang controls the system or operation, and yin is the one to be controlled. (8) **Holding two ends to meet the middle**: {left,right} ↦ {left ⇝ right}, where "left" denotes the left element which is actually any primitive element, "right" denotes the right element which is the primitive element to be in pair with the left element, the set "{left ⇝ right}" = "{left,right | center}" denotes the state of tranquility and balance between the left and right elements, with (i) "v center" being the virtual center so that the central force governing the left element is the same as the central force governing the right element and (ii) there is a balance between the right and left elements. (9) **Positive-negative conflicting operation** (in conflict): {pos,neg} → {pos$^?$, neg$^?$}, where "→" stands for a positive-negative operation, and pos, pos$^?$, neg, and neg$^?$ stand for the positive (or original) element, the negative element, the affected positive element (with the impact of the operation to be determined), and the affected negative element (with the impact of the operation to be determined), respectively. (10) (a) {yin,yang} → {yin$^?$} (yin changes while yang vanishes). (b) {yin,yang} → {yang$^?$} (yin vanishes while yang changes), where "$^?$" denotes "+" (stronger, growth), ."""(no change), or "-" (weaker, decline). (11) This is the same as (10) except the elements or roles of yin and yang are replaced by those of thesis and antithesis, respectively.

In general, these schemes involving one of the following operations: (1) independent operation, (2) yin-yang operation (mutually beneficial operations), either in a yin-yang pair per se (or implicit-explicit pair), an up-down pair, a left-right pair, an east-west pair (directional pair), or a south-north pair, and (3) positive-negative pair. Note that although the third operation is originally Western (i.e., the left-wing Western pattern of thinking), it is essentially in accordance with the thinking pattern of Legalism in classical China. Therefore it is included here for the completeness of our coverage.

For the fourth level, we have several schemes involving three elements. (1) The scheme of **independence**. There is an absolute balance among all three elements and there is no central element. Note that we can write "v center" as the virtual center of this system so that the central force governing each element is virtually the same. (2) The scheme of **yin-yang-he harmony**. In this scheme {(yin,yang)|he||tranquility}, yin and yang are non-central elements and "he" is the central element, whereas the culture of this system is that of tranquility. That is, yin and yang are in tranquility (or harmony), and between both "he" and yin and "he" and yang are also of the same relationship of tranquility. (3) The scheme of **thesis-antithesis-synthesis dialectic**. In this scheme {(thesis,antithesis)|synthesis||conflict}, thesis and anti-thesis are non-central elements while "synthesis" is the central element, whereas the culture of this system is that of conflict. That is, "thesis" and "antithesis" are in conflict; and between "thesis" and "synthesis" and between "synthesis" and "antithesis," there are also the same relationship of conflict. (4) **Yin-yang begetting a daughter**. {daughter|(yin, yang)}: a pair {yin,yang} ↭$^+$ {daughter,yin | yang}, where "daughter" is the junior or young-yin, and ↭$^+$ is an impactor. Here "yin" and "yang" represent co-centers, while "daughter" is a non-central element. (5) **Yin-yang begetting a son**. {son |(yin,yang)}: a pair {yin,yang} ↭$^-$ {son,yin | yang}, where "son" is the junior-yang and ↭$^+$ is an impactor. Here "yin" and "yang" represent co-centers, while "son" is a non-central element. (6) The scheme of **up-down-left**. In this scheme {left,down|up}, "left" is the non-central element, "down" is the secondary central element, and "up" is the major central element. Note that this scheme could be represented by {left|(down,up)}, {west,south|north}, or {west| (south,north)}}. (7) The scheme of **up-down-right**. In this scheme {right, down|up}, "right" is the non-central element, d"own" is the secondary central element, and "up" is the major central element. Note that this scheme could be represented by {right|(down,up)}, {east,south|north}, or {east|(south,north)}}. (8) The scheme of {common person|{gentry|master}} with common person ={peasant,worker, merchant}. In this system, the common person (i.e., the common people composed of peasants, artisans and merchants) is the non-central element, the gentry class (i.e., gentry) is the secondary center, and the master (i.e., king or emperor) is the center. In this special system, the master is also the center with respect to the gentry. That is, as a grand system, {gentry|master} is the center with the common person being the non-central element, whereas in central unit system {gentry|master}, master is the center with gentry being the non-central element.

Note that in (4) and (5), these {daughter|(yin,yang)} and {daughter, |(yin,yang)} constitute a yin-yang pair; and further, in (6) and (7), these {left,down|up)} and {right,down|up)} schemes constitute a yin-yang pair.

(9) **Positive-negative begetting positive junior**. This is the same as (4) except that "yin," "yang" and "daughter" are replaced by positive (element), negative (element) and junior positive (element), respectively. (10) **Positive-negative begetting negative junior**. This is the same as (5) except that "yin," "yang" and "son" are replaced by positive (element), negative (element) and junior negative (element), respectively.

For the fifth level, we have several schemes involving four elements. (1) The scheme of independence. This is the same as in the case of two or three elements. (2) The scheme of up-down-left-right = {(left,right,down)|up)}. This is a system in which "up" is the center, while all others are non-central elements. Note that this can be represented by a scheme of east-west-south-north. (3) The scheme of up-down-left-right = {(left,right)|(down,up)}. This is a system in which "(down,up)" is the center with both elements as co-centers, while all others are non-central elements. Similar to the above case (2), this can be represented by a scheme of east-west-south-north as well.

For the sixth level, we have several schemes involving four elements. (1) The scheme of independence. This is essentially the same as in the above cases. For example, we have the scheme of east-west-virtual center-south-north. In this system, the virtual center is the "center," while all others are non-centers. But if the virtual center vanishes, then there is no such thing as a center; and therefore all members in the system are neither central nor non-central elements. This is the same as (1) in the above fifth level. This is a 5-polar MFCE scheme with virtual center. (2) The scheme of east-west-south-north-center. This is a system in which "center" is the center, while all others are non-central elements. This is the prototype system of the multi-dimensional scheme, in which there is a balance between "east" and "west," and another one between "south" and "north." Later in Chapter 6, Section 6.2, this will be represented by the celebrated 5-polar MFCE scheme.

For the seventh level, (1) we have the scheme of **yin-yang begetting children**. In this scheme, at first there are two systems: {daughter|(yin1,yang1} and {son|(yin2,yang2)}. Then, these "daughter" and "son" leave their respective families to form a new family through marriage: {daughter,son} → {new yin, new yang}, {daughter|(yin1,yang1)} → {yin1,yang1}, {son|(yin2, yang2)} → {yin2,yang2} with the overlapping of "daughter" and "son" being taken cared of properly. Note that this scheme is one of tranquil culture which, in general, embodies a philosophical idea of human activism. In addition to the above scheme, we have (2) the scheme of **positive-negative begetting children**. This is the same as (1) in the above, except that the positions of "yin," "yang," "daughter" and "son" are replaces by "positive," "negative," "positive junior" and "negative junior," respectively. Note that this scheme is one of conflict culture.

For the eighth level, we have the **Yin-yang 5-polar MFCE scheme**. That is, $\{(x^-,y), (x,y^-), (x,y), (x,y^+), (x^+,y)\}$, where (x,y) is the central unit system, and all others are non-central unit systems, for y being "yin" and z being "yang " The graphical presentation is in Figure 1.1.

Figure 1.1
Yin-yang 5-polar MFCE scheme

$$\begin{array}{ccccc} & & (x,y^+) & & \\ & & \uparrow & & \\ (x^-,y) & \leftarrow & (x,y) & \rightarrow & (x^+,y) \\ & & \downarrow & & \\ & & (x,y^-) & & \end{array}$$

For the ninth level, we have the scheme of the Confucian doctrine of the overlapping center {e|{d|{c|{b|a}}}}, a (i.e., sincerity), b (i.e., noble mind), c (i.e., family in harmony), d (i.e., nation in order), e (i.e., world peace) ⊫ **U** (i.e., a, b, c, d, and e are "events" or complexes of human characteristics, human elements, and impactors. Here {b|a}, {c|{b|a}}, {d|{c|{b|a}}}, {e|{d|{c|{b|a}}}} ⊑ $(\Omega,\mathcal{Z}\circ,_{v}\mathcal{H},\{\mathbb{C}\})$, with a being the center of the system {a,b}, {b|a} the center of {a,b,c}, {c|{b|a}} the center of the system {a,b,c,d}, and {d|{c|{b|a}}} the center of the system {a,b,c,d,e}. In terms of a figure, we have Figure 1.2.

Figure 1.2
Confucian scheme of the overlapping circles with a core center

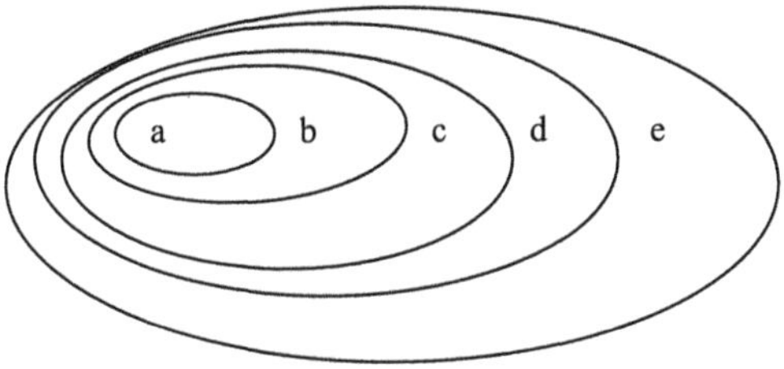

From this above presentation, one may see that the proto-type thinking patterns of the West are evidently inclining more toward the study of the motions and relationships between matters. It is seen that the associative and distributive laws present important keys to the understanding of the motions of matters. In contrast, the proto-type thinking paths of East Asia are inclining more prominently toward shaping the organizational structure of the human society. Furthermore, the proto-type thinking patterns of the West appear to be immersed either in the characterization of the individuality and independence of a human being or in the structural development of the relationships of conflict and conquest among unrelated individuals. As for the proto-type thinking paths of East Asia, they appear to express themselves in tranquil and harmonious relationships, perhaps developed in the patterns of "systemic dynamics," consensual harmony, middle-position (or "mediety") and controlled centrality.

In this book, we present and develop a frame of reference, in general, for studying the essential structures of systems; and, in particular, for studying the economics of culture with culture serving as the focal point. Culture is ultimately the very source of economic development and social advancement, and it is a major break through in human studies for this advancement.

It is well known that in terms of the methods of study, mathematics is used extensively in studying the market economy of capitalism, while dialectic is employed in studying the planning economy of the Soviet-type socialism. To study the Faziranist economy of ancient China, then, the MFCE scheme (multifactor cause-and-effect scheme) inspired by the scheme of YYWX (scheme of yin-yang five-elements) is a necessary tool. Thus, in order to develop an appropriate framework for the analysis of the modern cultural economy, one must draw inspirations from all of the afore-mentioned schemes and analytical methods.

In terms of cultural context, the cultural mix of Christianity and modern sciences has been providing the most precious humane foundations in the cultural fields of the economies of the capitalist West. As for the socialist or communist West, the most significant cultural foundation was provided by the culture of Marxism-Leninism, among others. When we turn to the continental East Asia, obviously throughout the history, we discovered that the cultures of Taoism, Confucianism, Legalism, Buddhism and Islam, with that of Christianity to a lesser degree, did contribute significantly to the establishment of the most essential cultural foundations of the various economies in this region.

The following chapters present both an introduction and a further development of the topics and themes of the economics of culture presented in Tonn (2001). Due to the limitation of space and time, a brand new approach to the ideas and structures of systematics and a refinement of the economics of culture will be left to the future (on the basis of the materials presented in Tonn 2006, 2007 and Tonn [2006]). Note that most of the ideas presented here in this book were originally developed for the preparatory draft of Tonn [2006], in which the theories have been developed in searching for a comprehensive framework to enable the author to engage in a comparative study of, among others, nations of the West and East Asia.

In this book, the objective of the economics of culture is to promote the meaning of life through studying various methods of wealth creation and distribution (Tonn 1980, 1981, 1984, 1989, 1990a, 1990b, 1991a, 1991b, 1993, 1994, 2001, 2003). Here, wealth is treated as the material foundation of the meaning of life for the human being. Simply stated, economics of culture is a field study of systematics applied to the fields of wealth creation and distribution. Another way to state this is that, the approach to the economics of culture is derived from the interactive points of view among the economic activities, the intellectuals and the civil servants. In other words, the economics of culture is the global economics in which the objective is to study the interactions among sciences and engineering, economic, political and cultural factors and structures, with a focus placed upon the process of creating and distributing products and services. Here, one of the long-term goals of this economics of culture (or global economics) is not only to integrate Marxian economics into its macro-foundation, but also to integrate business management into its micro-foundation; and then, to integrate the micro- and macro-foundations in a comprehensive and coherent whole.

Here by culture is meant an organic entity, being composed of knowledge, belief systems, arts, ethics and customs, etc. In this book, we may temporarily define **culture** in a narrow sense: the meta-systemic entity underlying knowledge, belief systems, arts, ethics and customs of law, information, technologies and politico-economic activities. This definition encompasses both a materialistic approach to society and a culture-philosophical approach to life.[1] Historically, the classical "economic tradition" of China since The Kuan Tzu may be thought of as the spiritual predecessor of the economics of culture (Tonn [1996]). In the West, we may say that the Roman Catholic Church's approach to economics in the medieval age was the predecessor of the economics of culture.

In our approach, the economics of culture is actually referred to the study of the operations of the economy, polity, culture and the interactions among them. As such, the economics of culture is not designed to study every aspect of the polity and culture; instead, culture and polity are studied in the context of the interactions with the economic forces.

The economics of culture is developed by employing the methods of systematics. The objective of the theory of systematics is to develop a new method of intellectual inquiry that would enable us to better investigate both natural phenomena and human institutions and interactive activities, in a spirit of a balance between the structural (or qualitative) approach and the quantitative (or mathematical) approach. While the starting points for the quantitative approach are the principles of independent development and general equilibrium in conflict, the foundations of the systematic methods and thereby those of the structural approach are the principle of centrality and the principle of balance, cooperation and mutual benefits in both cultures of tranquility and conflict. Here equilibrium means a state of constant conflict in which various forces within a system are balanced and equalized.

We mentioned in the above that one objective of this book is to apply the systematic methods to study economics. There are noted characteristics associated with this systematics. First, the underlying culture of this systematic study is comprehensive. This is especially true because the cultural foundations of systematics are more than the philosophy of utilitarianism, be it a Benthamic or an enlightened one. As such, the cultural foundations have gone beyond the philosophy of utilitarianism, both Western and East Asian (Legalist), and include those of Faziranism, Catholicism and others.[2]

Secondly, the political foundations of this approach go well beyond that of the social philosophy of democracy. Naturally, in its foundations, systematics entails those systems such as socialism, Catholicism, Islam, Hinduism, Faziranism and self-masterism as well.

Thirdly, the economic foundations of this approach go beyond capitalism. Since it is to be comprehensive, any economic system, either modern or archaic, is or will be absorbed as one of the theoretical bases of the economics of culture.

In sum, in the systematics of culture, to study the social systems of the West, the cultures of capitalism as well as those of Christianity and socialism must be brought in; to study East Asia, the traditional culture of Faziranism must be included; and to study the systems of the rest of world, ancient or modern, all other cultures (such as Islam and Hinduism) must be incorporated. Then based on a comprehensive framework formulated from all of these aforementioned cultural foundations, the study of a social system (of culture) could become truly global and meaningful.

The organization of this book is therefore set as follows. Chapter 1 is the introductory chapter. After that, we divide the rest of this book into two parts. PART I shall include five chapters as follows. In Chapter 2, we discuss the relationship between cultural foundations and modernization. In Chapter 3, we discuss cultural demand and supply curves and a few principles of firms and microeconomic management. In Chapter 4, we discuss the total demand and supply curves, cultural IS and LM curves and some macroeconomic aspects of national strategies of development. In Chapter 5, we shall discuss culture as it influences the development and trade stages of a modern economy. In Chapter 6, we shall study structural connections in a system with the concepts of Tcentrals presented as a central point of systemic study.

In PART II, five chapters will be included. In Chapter 7, the overall future development schemes of a cultural economy-polity will be discussed. In Chapter 8, we study schemes of strategic competition between nations. In Chapter 9, we study strategic spaces and economic-cultural models. In Chapter 10, brief accounts of the cultural economies of the United States and China (in the future context of East Asian Union) will be provided. Then in Chapter 11, summaries and conclusions will be provided.

In PART III, we introduce essential topics of systematics to make this book self-contained. In Appendix A, we shall study basic concepts of systematics: the structure of universe, basic concepts of systems, mind, cosmic structure of the system of "self-masterism," various "impactors" including the integration and decomposition impactors, and various schemes of systems like MFCE scheme. Appendix B is about the study of topics of the systemic-change "becomings." Appendix C is about the study of the topics of reversal construction of systems. Appendix D is a chapter about the study of the topics of dynamic CE balance. In Appendix E, we shall study the mind complex and MPFX-GPFX cycles. In Appendix F, we study several interrelated topics. The cs and cd curves of a microeconomy will be studied, topics of conflict and tranquil firms will be addressed, systematic organizations will also be studied. In Appendix F, TS-TD Model of macroeconomics is to be studied. In Appendix G, modern socioeconomic system of a mixed system will be discussed. In Appendix H, metaphysical systems of Y*(YX), Y+(YX)X- and N(B-HPh) will be presented. In Appendix I, topics of the distribution systems in the states of uncertainty will be focused. In Appendix J, classical concepts of yi-li TCentral will be uncovered. In Appendix K, we shall approach the structure of the society from the perspective of systematics. In Appendix L, we shall approach the structure of the polity from the perspective of systematics. In Appendix M, we shall present some human psychological schemes and the general symbolic structures of organization. In Appendix N, various philosophical systems of the East and the West through the perspective of systematics will be revealed. In Appendix O, we shall also approach various literary systems from the perspective of systematics. In Appendix P, we shall attempt to approach various belief systems by employing the methods of systematics. In Appendix Q, we shall present our discovery of a few historical systems from the perspective of systematics. In Appendix R, general structures of economic organizations will be formulated. Then in Appendix S, schemes of systemic distribution and the world of self-masterism are to be developed.

In PART IV, an introduction to the preliminary methods of "sysmetrics" is included. In PART V, a few additional topics are presented. And finally, a table of glossary and a list of symbols used in this book are provided to finish this book.

Remark 1.1 (yin-yang pair). Two entities (i.e., elements or systems, etc.) are said to form a **yin-yang pair** if and only if they have a relationship of "complementarity," contrast, or conflict, etc. In general, two entities in a yin-yang pair have an implicit-explicit relationship, such as the male-female, positive-negative, or master-subject relationships.

Remark 1.2. A scheme is a holistic presentation of an entity with embodied attributes or a set of entities with their relationships in systematics. In a more conventional terminology, a scheme may simply be considered as a model.

PART I THE ECONOMICS OF CULTURE

Chapter 2 - Cultural Foundations and Modernization

From one perspective, the philosophical foundation of the theory of systematics may be considered as basing on the scheme of self-organizing and self-mastering "systemism." This is essentially the philosophy of self-masterism (see Subsection §A.2-6 in Appendix A).[3] The commonly defined culture is related to the value and belief systems of the common people in a community. It is also shown in how people handle things on a daily basis. In general, culture as is commonly perceived encompasses the human will and rationality formulated over the entire history of the human kind, either consciously or subconsciously. The above-mentioned culture is called **culture in the narrow sense**. In the theory of systematics, culture and the organizational and strategic factors together are what is called the **culture in the broad sense**.

To go beyond the scope of conventional wisdom of equilibrium (in conflict) and scientific spirit, below we shall address the concepts of balance and centrality. The concept of systemic balance, or that of middle central, may be represented as a force of balance between two extremes.

Note that harmonious balance (or balance in tranquility) and consensual centrality can be derived from the concept of T central or specific "Tcentral" (to be formally defined in Chapter 6). In the classical sense, one may see the spirit of Tcentral through the human spirit associated with the self-generating life-will (or shengsheng life-will-to-creation) and yu-wu rationality (yu-wu rationality-to-creation). To be more specific, this human spirit of life-will entails (1) the spirit of self-creativity, (2) the spirit of self-existence, (3) the individual-group centrality and balance (or cooperation in harmony), and (4) the self-generating balance. It is obvious that, in the classical case of either the East or the West as well as in the modern Chinese case, this spirit of creativity, be it micro-, macro- or globally oriented, permeates the demand and supply sides of human activities. Note that, in the above, in the "tranquil sense," the self-generating life-will is a **life-will of mutuality** by which is meant the life-will that, amid the will to achieve the inner greatness of the self, helps promote the mutual benefits of all involved. Note that the life-will of mutuality is a sharp contrast to the life-will of individuality. Furthermore, although the latter is self-centered, it does have to be incompatible with the life-will of mutuality.

The afore-mentioned yu-wu rationality is closely associated with the classical Chinese culture. It is a systemic rationality or a rationality of yu-wu recursion which is a "self-immersing" process of reasoning and quest for knowledge and truth. Here by the **systemic rationality** is meant the macro-global rationality which is holistic, organic, and synthetic, and is flexible and easy to transform from one strict category into any other category. This is in a sharp contrast to the scientific rationality, a micro rationality, which is analytical and usually restricts itself to some fixed categories of quantitative reasoning. In addition, by the "self" (i.e., Self* as such, or Seemingly-Self) is meant the creativity-destructivity per se. In the old days of East Asia, this "self"-orientation of rationality once enlarged its scope of rationality under the influence of Buddhism, while at the modern time this rationality has been able to expand its horizon by absorbing the ideas of Western sciences and technology. This newly integrated rationality of the modern time, called the **self-existing systemic rationality-to-creation** (or self-deepening and wu-penetrating rationality) which includes dialectic rationality and others as well, is more comprehensive and even richer than both the original tao-rationality of East Asia and the being-rationality of the West.

Perhaps as is in the case of studying Latin America and other developing countries, in dealing with East Asia, one has to see through the light of this comprehensive systemic rationality in addressing the issues of the creativity of sciences and technology. That is equivalent to saying that, in addressing the foundations of human rationality, one has to go beyond the Western concept of scientific rationality.

Note that upon this systemic rationality lie the very cultural foundations of the economic sources of supply and the highly praised and valued activities of invention and innovation.

It goes without saying that it is the joint force of the newly developed self-creating and self-mastering life-will-to-creation and the self-existing and self-organizing systemic rationality-to-creation that undergirds the very cultural foundations of the new China's technological creativity in particular and its vitality in general.

In the above, these may be called the micro-aspects of culture. For the macro-global part of culture, other than dealing with the issues of the interactive relationships among individuals, communities and firms, one has to be properly concerned with the role of government.[4]

In terms of culture, as is related closely to economic development and advancement, common citizens' high spirit to advance their economic positions play a key role in laying down the human conditions from there the high saving rate and high investment rate are made possible. Then, the capital production frontier of the nation of those citizens is pushed outward.

To address the issues of human will and rationality, one has to pay close attention to the worlds of human compassion, aspiration and their dynamical strengths over time. Christian ideas of love, mercy and justice, Confucian ideas of humanity and righteousness, Taoist ideas of simplicity, self-service, mind-fasting and abstention, sitting-in-forgetfulness, and inaction, all great ideas of Buddhism, Hinduism and Islam, and such entities as revelation rationality and Buddhist rationality are also integrated parts of these worlds of human will and rationality. Due to the limitation of space, the details of these issues will be left to the agenda for future research.

To capture the above arguments in a nutshell, in the following, we develop a systematic scheme. For the background materials related to systems, see Appendix A. Simply stated, a *system* is the collection of universal or human elements (i.e., the basic players in the world of our study) together with necessary structures to support these elements and with self or mutual-relational operations of dynamical forces affecting these elements and structures over time. For the formal definition of a system and the related concepts of the universal and human elements, see Appendix A (§A.2-1-2 and §A.2-2).

In the following simple presentation, for X to be a system, we write $X \sqsubseteq (\Omega, \mathbb{Z}\circ,{}_{\vee}\mathbb{H}, \{\mathbb{C}\})$, where Ω denotes the collection of systems (composed of elements, structures and cultures) in question, and $\mathbb{Z}$ and $\mathbb{H}$ refer to the spaces of "self-impactors" and "mutual-impactors" (or "interactors"), respectively. Note that these impactors are systems as well. For a system X, we shall also write $X \sqsubseteq (\Omega, \mathbb{Z}\circ,{}_{\vee}\mathbb{H}, \{\mathbb{C}\})$ (or $(X,\Psi) \sqsubseteq (\Omega, \mathbb{Z}\circ,{}_{\vee}\mathbb{H}, \{\mathbb{C}\})$, Ψ being the set of impactors and $\mathbb{Z}\circ,{}_{\vee}\mathbb{H}$ being the collection of self-operating impactors and mutually operating interactors,), with $X = \chi \oplus < \mathbb{C}_X >$, for χ being the system's structural framework (or hierarchy-transformational structure) and $<\mathbb{C}_X>$ the system's cultural complex. Here, as the collection of all systems and the closure of their operations, $(\Omega,\mathcal{Z}\circ,{}_v\mathcal{H},\{\mathbb{C}\})$ is called the **space of systems**.

Now, for a cultural economy $X \sqsubseteq (\Omega,\mathcal{Z}\circ,{}_v\mathcal{H},\{\mathbb{C}\})$, we write

(2.1) $X = \varphi\{A_1(org,c,.|e)\text{-}A_2(tech,c,.|e)\}\_\psi\{D_1(K,c,.|e)\text{-}D_2(L,c,.|e)\} \oplus \mathcal{S}<\mathbb{C}_{x1},\mathbb{C}_{x2}>$

with φ, ψ, $\mathcal{S} \vDash \mathcal{Z}\circ,{}_v\mathcal{H}$ being "creative impactors," $A_1(org,c|.)\text{-}A_2(tech,c|.)$ being the "pure structures" of X, $D_1(K,c,.|e)\text{-}D_2(L,c,.|e)$ being the dynamical structure of X, and $<\mathbb{C}_{x1},\mathbb{C}_{x2}>$ being the cultural complex of X. Here c stands for the cultural factor affecting $A_.(.)$ and $D_.(.)$, and e stands for the environmental factor upon which the system X is conditioned. Note that all these $A_.(,)$, $D_.(.)$ and $\mathbb{C}_.$ are subsystems (or unit systems) of the grand system X.

Then, to account for the economic forces of growth and advancement, we may write $\{\varphi\{A_1(org,.|.),\psi\{D_1(K,.|.),\psi D_2(L,.|.),\varphi A_2(tech,.|.)|(\mathcal{S}\mathbb{C}_{x1},\mathcal{S}\mathbb{C}_{x2})\}$ as a 5-polar MFCE model (see Appendix A, A.4). Here the center is $(\mathcal{S}\mathbb{C}_{x1},\mathcal{S}\mathbb{C}_{x2})$, for $\mathcal{S}\mathbb{C}_{x1}$ and $\mathcal{S}\mathbb{C}_{x2}$ being the cultures of the elite and the common people, respectively. In addition, the organizational efficiency is represented by $\varphi\{A_1(org,.|.)$, the engineering-technological efficiency is represented by $\varphi\{A_2(tech,.|.)$, the capital force is represented by $\psi\{D_1(K,.|.)$, and the labor force is represented by $\psi\{D_2(L,.|.)$.

Note that one way to classify culture is to have a dichotomy between the culture of the East (or the culture of yu-wu recursion) and the culture of the West (or the culture of being penetration).

To account for cultures, in an explicit manner, let A_i and D_i be subsystems of X, B_i sub-subsystems of A_i, …, O_i residuals of X in the decomposition and s-t the notation for the spatiotemporal dimension. Then we have the following organization-cultural Bcm's (2.2) and (2.3):

(2.2)
$$\begin{aligned} X(s\text{-}t|\xi) = {} & \varphi_{a1}A_1(org,.,s\text{-}t|\xi_{a1}) + \varphi_{a2}A_2(tech,.,s\text{-}t|\xi_{a2}) + \ldots + \\ & \varphi_{b1}B_1(.,s\text{-}t|\xi_{b1}) + \varphi_{b2}B_2(.,s\text{-}t|\xi_{b2}) + \ldots + \\ & \psi_{d1}D_1(K,.,s\text{-}t|\xi_{d1}) + \psi_{d2}D_2(L,.,s\text{-}t|\xi_{d2}) + \ldots + \\ & H_{o1}O_1(.,s\text{-}t|\xi_{o1}) + H_{o2}O_2(.,s\text{-}t|\xi_{o2}) + \ldots + \zeta \end{aligned}$$

(2.3) $\zeta = \zeta(+,-;\Delta)$, $\Delta \Vdash Ш^{\Delta}$.

Here ζ represents the ultimate cultural forces, and ξ and $\xi_.$ represent the manifestations of this cultural creativity ζ in X and in X's various subsystems, respectively. Thus in Bcms. (2.2) and (2.3), we have the decomposition becoming of a system X. Here $(+,(\xi_.,\ldots)) \leftrightarrow \zeta$ (ζ denoting the impactor of interactions), by which is meant the interactions of composition-decomposition between ζ and $\xi_.$'s; and $\varphi_.$, $\psi_. \vDash \mathcal{Z}\circ,{}_v\mathcal{H}$ are the respective creative impactors. Note that "+" ("-") (associated with ζ) denotes the positive (negative) interactions between systems or elements, to be measured by the degree of positive interactions between these two sets. That is, by the notations "☆ and ⋆," we have: for systems X and Y, X ☆ Y = (X⋆Y) + X + Y; and for sets A and B (in mathematics): A☆B = (A⋆B)∪A∪B with "A⋆B" reading as X "interacting with" Y.

Here the function of Bcms. (2.2) and (2.3) is that, we can use them to decompose Bcm. (2.1).

Remark 2.1. In this book, for excluding the cultures of religion, we classify the general culture types into the **culture of conflict**, to be inclusive of scientific rationality and conquest life-will, and the **culture of tranquility**, to be inclusive of systemic rationality, self-adoptive, and/or self-mastering life-will (or self-creating life-will). For the cultural types of religion, we shall classify them into the culture of Buddhism with Buddhist rationality and Buddhist life-will, the culture of Christianity with revelation rationality and revelation life-will, the culture of Hinduism and the culture of Islam, etc.

The other useful way of classifying the culture is to have a dichotomy between the culture of individuality and the culture of mutuality. For the society dominated by a **culture of individuality-in-conflict**, it enjoys the efficiency of the technologies of individuality-in-conflict and the organizations of individuality-in-conflict. That is, the strengths of the society under this culture of individuality are derived from the science-based and individually-oriented technologies and the business-oriented organizations. As for the society dominated by a culture of mutuality-in-tranquility, it enjoys the efficiency of the technology of mutuality-in-tranquility and the mutuality-in-tranquility directed organizations. That is, the strengths of the society under this **culture of mutuality-in-tranquility** are derived from the technologies of mutuality-in-tranquility based on the "classic-systematics" and the family/polity-oriented organizations. One of the best examples of the classic-systemics-based technologies is the complex of technologies that classic China developed under the thinking patterns of the scheme of YYWX. For the classic Chinese technologies, one may see Temple (1986).

Notice that in the above, it is not to deny the existence of the technologies of individuality-in-tranquility and the organizations of individuality-in-tranquility. Actually, in a system of classical Faziranism, there are technologies of individuality-in-tranquility, and in a system of capitalism, there are some forms of mutuality-in-tranquility directed organizations.

The third way of dealing with the cultural types is to classify systems of the world into those of capitalism, Faziranism and socialism according to the categories of socio-economic systems and political ideologies.

So far for a non-systemic approach, the cultural types of the worlds may be classified into: America-Indian, Chinese, Indian, Islam, Japanese, other Asian, Russian, Sub-Saharan and Western Europe-North American cultures, etc. Note that, with appropriate steps being taken, these conventionally constructed cultural types can be developed into well defined systems.

To illustrate the use of these cultural types, we may say that, for a typical Western nation, it is composed of a conflict cultural unit (i.e., the unit system of the culture of conflict, Western style) and the Christian cultural unit (i.e., the unit system of the culture of Christianity). Note that here this Christian cultural unit plays the role of the tranquil cultural unit.

For classic China, it is composed of a conflict cultural unit (i.e., the unit system of the culture of conflict, Legalist style), a tranquil cultural unit (i.e., the unit system of the culture of Taoism-Confucianism), and a religious mix of (religious) Taoism, (Mahayana) Buddhism and Islam.

As for modern China, it is a mixed grand system of "three cultures," although in a simplified account, it may also be considered as a mix of the two cultures of the classic Chinese system and the modern Western system. This is definitely a sophisticated n-level system with the essential system core being played by the cultural chain complex constructed on the dual bases of the “modernized Taoist-Confucianist-Legalist system of tranquility” (or the Chinese cultural system of mutuality) and the Western culture of conflict (or the Western cultural system of individuality). In this modern Chinese cultural mix, the religious cultural unit which is actually composed of (religious) Taoism, (Mahayana) Buddhism, Christianity and Islam, appears to be less essential.

Chapter 3 - Culture and Microeconomics: Firms and Micro-management

3.1 Introduction

In this chapter, we discuss important topics of microeconomics and business management from the perspective of cultural systematics. To this end, first, we shall present the principles of CE (i.e., cause-and-effect) balance and CE imbalance. Later on, the ideas of yinyang becoming (YYBCM) will be introduced for the purpose of eventually been transformed into the culturally-determined supply and demand curves. Finally, to finish this Chapter, some management systems in the spirit of cultural systematics will also be introduced.

3.2 CE Systemic Balance–Centrality and CE Imbalance

In this section,we present the concepts of cause-effect (CE) balance and imbalance to facilitate the study of systematics in later chapters.

§3.2-1 Systemic Schemes – Scheme of Equicentrality and T continuity

Here we develop a systemic scheme (or scheme of equicentrality and T continuity). This is in general what is employed in the method of effective intra-inter systemic operations/T continuity (IISO/T scheme, or systemic optimality). To facilitate the discussion of the following sections, below we proceed to define the concept of "equicentrality."

Remark 3.2-1-1 (equicentrality, systemic balance-centrality). This is a new term used to designate the state of systemic balance-centrality among all related entities in a causal net (or network). That is, a system is said in a state of **equicentrality** if and only if the following conditions hold. (1) The system as a whole reaches a state of centrality. (2) Each member is "relatively independent" (i.e., independent and yet in well coordination with other members). (3) A state of CE balance in coordination is reached among all relevant entities in the system. (4) All relevant entities outside of this system are in a state of CE balance and centrality. (5) The system in question reaches the vicinity of a frontier entailing a partially-flexible ideal state. That is, the measure of the most essential aspect of the system in question can at best be marginally improved (or in a variational path) by any change in the system. A definition of equicentrality for an element can be provided in essentially the same manner.

Let two basic or grand systems X, Y $\sqsubseteq (\Omega, \mathcal{Z}\circ, {}_{v}\mathcal{H}, \{\mathbb{C}\})$ be:

(3.2-1-1) $X \Vdash \zeta(\xi(\tau)),\ \tau \Vdash (\mathfrak{I}, \text{Ш}^{\text{Д}}) \Vvdash \mathbb{T}\mathrm{zu}^*$,

(3.2-1-2) $Y \Vdash \zeta(\xi(\tau)),\ Y \Vdash \zeta(\tau),\ \tau \Vdash (\mathfrak{I}, \text{Ш}^{\text{Д}}) \Vvdash \mathbb{T}\mathrm{zu}^*$,

where $\zeta \sqsubseteq (\Omega, \mathcal{Z}\circ, {}_{v}\mathcal{H}, \{\mathbb{C}\})$ for $\zeta \equiv \{\zeta(\xi) \mid \xi = \xi(\tau) \leftsquigarrow \tau \Vdash (\mathfrak{I}, \text{Ш}^{\text{Д}})\}$ representing the underlying forces that unify the systems X and Y. Note that ζ is a force in the dynamical world $\text{Ш}^{\Delta} \equiv \text{Ш}^{\text{Д}}$ which is generated by the Ultimate Creativity-Destructivity of the universe (i.e., $\zeta \Vvdash \text{Ш}^{\Delta}(\tau) \leftsquigarrow \tau \Vdash (\mathfrak{I}, \text{Ш}^{\text{Д}}) \Vvdash \mathbb{T}\mathrm{zu}^*$.

Then, let the set {X,Y} reaches a **state of T continuity** (which is defined as the state that X and Y reach a state of momentarily systemic continuity and momentarily strategic continuity). In these states of equicentrality and T continuity, then it is said that there exists a solution to the following scheme: Under the system operation of systems X and Y,

(3.2-1-3) $\varphi\{X\} = X$,

(3.2-1-4) $\varphi\{Y\} = Y$,

(i.e., X and Y are in a state of systemic continuity, respectively), where $\varphi \vDash \mathcal{Z}_{\circ,v}\mathcal{H}$ is the impactor of the system, and these systems are under the constraint of the pure dynamic structure:

(3.2-1-5) $\Delta \sqsubseteq \Omega$.

To solve this scheme, let

(3.2-1-6) $T = \{X,Y\} \curlyvee \Delta$,

where $\curlyvee \vDash \mathcal{Z}_{\circ,v}\mathcal{H}$ is the interactor connecting X and Δ.

Note that this T depicts the target, be it an objective function/functional to be maximize in mathematical form, an entity at a satisfactory level (assuming it is measurable in a meaningful way), an entity (or system) in T continuity state, an irrational target level of the underlying systems {X,Y}, or any targeted objective. This is much broader than the mathematical formula of maximizing the "objective" {X,Y} with the "constraint" of Δ. For a human being just wanting to pursue a target level of the underlying system per se, for instance, a thing of beauty or a piece of mind in peace and leisure which is not quantifiable, this appears to work well. For more details about the reasoning of this solution, see Appendix D, D.2.

Suppose, this scheme is under the principle of effective intra-inter systemic operations and T continuity (IISO/T scheme). That is, the system is in a state entailing the operations of the X and Y in a state of T continuity and a state of systemic equicentrality, the latter concept being a state of equality and centrality of relevant entities (or variables) in terms of its carriage of energy, power or forces of vitality, holding all other things constant. Then we are able to write:

(3.2-1-7)
$$
\begin{aligned}
(\varphi\{T\})_{X,Y} &= (\varphi[\{X,Y\} \curlyvee \Delta])_{X,Y,I(x,y)} \\
&= (\varphi[\{X,Y,I(x,y)\},\Delta])_{X,Y} \ltimes \varphi[I(x,y),E] \\
&= \{\varphi[\{X,Y\},\Delta] \otimes \psi\{X,\Delta\}\} \\
&\quad \stackrel{\star}{=} \{\varphi[\{X,Y\},\Delta] \otimes \psi\{Y,\Delta\}\} \\
&\quad\ \ltimes \varphi[I(x,y),E].
\end{aligned}
$$

In the state of CE mediety-centrality, we have: $\varphi\{X\} = X$, $\varphi\{Y\} = Y$ and $\varphi[\{X,Y, I(x,y)\}]= \{X,Y,(I(x,y)\}$. And by removing $(\varphi\{T\})_{X,Y}$ and $(\varphi[\{X,Y\},\Delta])$ from both sides of bcm. (3.2-1-7) respectively, we derive the formula $(([\psi\{X,\Delta\} \stackrel{\star}{=} \psi\{Y,\Delta\}] \ltimes \psi\{I(x,y),E\} =< T^{CE}) \Subset Ш^{\Delta}$. That is, we derive the **principle of two-system CE systemic balance**:

(3.2-1-8) $\psi\{X,\Delta\} \stackrel{\star}{=} \psi\{Y,\Delta\}$.

This is a state of balance between two systems which are unified under a more fundamental system ζ.

To expand the above principle to the case of more than two systems, we shall have the **principle of multiple-system CE systemic balance**:

(3.2-1-9) $\psi\{X,\Delta\} \stackrel{\pm}{=} \psi\{Y,\Delta\} \stackrel{\pm}{=} \ldots \stackrel{\pm}{=} \psi\{Z,\Delta\}$,

(3.2-1-10) $Z \Vdash \zeta(\tau),\ \tau \Vdash (\mathfrak{I},\text{Ш}^{\text{Д}}) \Vvdash \mathbb{T}zu^*$,

for $Z \sqsubseteq (\Omega, \mathcal{Z}\circ, {}_{v}\mathcal{H}, \{\mathbb{C}\})$.

In the above, by $X \Vdash \zeta(\tau)$, $Y \Vdash \zeta(\tau)$, $\tau \Vdash (\mathfrak{I},\text{Ш}^{\text{Д}}) \Vvdash \mathbb{T}zu^*$ (Bcms 3.2-1-1, 3.2-1-2), we have

(3.2-1-11) $X \Lleftarrow \zeta$,

(3.2-1-12) $Y \Lleftarrow \zeta$.

Since X and Y are separately conditioned by ζ, we can write:

(3.2-1-13) $X(\xi) \Lleftarrow \zeta(\xi)$,

(3.2-1-14) $Y(\xi) \Lleftarrow \zeta(\xi)$,

where ξ is the force of creativity generated by $\mathbb{T}zu^*$ (Ultimate Creativity/ Destructivity Itself). Thus, from $\{X(\xi) \Lleftarrow \zeta(\xi)\}$ and $\{Y(\xi) \Lleftarrow \zeta(\xi)\}$, for $\tau \Vdash (\mathfrak{I},\text{Ш}^{\text{Д}}) \Vvdash \mathbb{T}zu^*$, $\tau \vDash \mathcal{Z}\circ, {}_{v}\mathcal{H}$, we can write

$$
\begin{aligned}
(3.2\text{-}1\text{-}15)\quad & \kappa\,[\{X(\xi) \Lleftarrow \zeta(\xi)\}, Y(\xi) \Lleftarrow \zeta(\xi)] \\
& = [\{X(\xi), Y(\xi)\} \Lleftarrow \zeta(\xi) \,|\, \xi = \xi(\tau),\ \tau \Vdash (\mathfrak{I},\text{Ш}^{\text{Д}}) \Vvdash \mathbb{T}zu^*] \\
& \Leftrightarrow [\{X,Y\} \Vdash \zeta \,|\, \zeta(\tau)]. \\
& \equiv \{X,Y\} \Vdash \zeta,\ \zeta = \zeta(\tau).
\end{aligned}
$$

Note that, for $\xi = \xi(\tau)$, $\tau \Vdash (\mathfrak{I},\text{Ш}^{\text{Д}}) \Vvdash \mathbb{T}zu^*$, and for this, we can also write $\zeta = \zeta(\tau) \backsim \tau \Vdash (\mathfrak{I},\text{Ш}^{\text{Д}}) \Vvdash \mathbb{T}zu^*$. That is, in the above, Bcm. (3.2-1-8) and Bcm. (3.2-1-9) can be replaced respectively by,

$$
\begin{aligned}
(3.2\text{-}1\text{-}16)\quad & \psi\{X,\Delta\} \stackrel{\pm}{=} \psi\{Y,\Delta\}, \\
& \{X,Y\} \Vdash \zeta,
\end{aligned}
$$

and

$$
\begin{aligned}
(3.2\text{-}1\text{-}17)\quad & \psi\{X,\Delta\} \stackrel{\pm}{=} \psi\{Y,\Delta\} \stackrel{\pm}{=} \ldots \stackrel{\pm}{=} \psi\{Z,\Delta\}, \\
& \{X,Y,\ldots,Z\} \Vdash \zeta,
\end{aligned}
$$

where, for X, Y,…, $Z \sqsubseteq (\Omega, \mathcal{Z}\circ, {}_{v}\mathcal{H}, \{\mathbb{C}\})$, we have:

$$
\begin{aligned}
(3.2\text{-}1\text{-}18)\quad & X(\xi) \Lleftarrow \zeta(\xi), \\
& Y(\xi) \Lleftarrow \zeta(\xi), \\
& \ldots \\
& Z(\xi) \Lleftarrow \zeta(\xi).
\end{aligned}
$$

Remark 3.2-1-2 (scheme of CE systemic imbalance). Similar to the above reasoning, let two basic or grand systems X, Y $\sqsubseteq (\Omega, \mathbb{Z}\circ,_{v}\mathbb{H}, \{\mathbb{C}\})$ be: X $\Vdash \zeta \Subset Ш^{\Delta}$ and Y $\Vdash \zeta \Subset Ш^{\Delta}$, where $\zeta \sqsubseteq (\Omega, \mathbb{Z}\circ,_{v}\mathbb{H}, \{\mathbb{C}\})$ is the underlying force unifying the systems X and Y. Then, for the set {X,Y}, we may also derive the following principle of the **multiple-system CE systemic imbalance**:

$$(3.2\text{-}1\text{-}19)\quad \psi\{X,\Delta\} \leqq \psi\{Y,\Delta\}.$$

Here Y dominates X.

§3.2-2 CE Systemic Balance, Imbalance, Centrality and Self-Masterism

For the simplicity of analysis and because of cultural complexity, a firm based on Western culture is assumed to behave conventionally, or to attain the firm's equilibrium position of price and output. That is, this firm is supposed to maximize profits, to maximize the wealth of stockholders, or to maximize the short-term stock value of the company.

By contrast, due to its complex culture mix and to be quite different from a typical Western firm, for the Chinese firm, from the way we understand, it shall follow the principle of CE balance. Before we turn to develop a formula for CE balance, note that, in East Asia as well in the West, culture affects the realms of business organizations, employee behavior, work ethics, and human resource development (also see Tai 1989, p. 19).

For this purpose, we shall elaborate a scheme of CE balance. Let a basic or grand system be: $X = \{X_1, X_2, \ldots, X_n\} \sqsubseteq (\Omega, \mathbb{Z}\circ,_{v}\mathbb{H}, \{\mathbb{C}\})$, X and $[Y_k, Y_j] \Leftarrow <\mathbb{C}_X>$, where $Y_j \equiv [(X_1, \mathbb{C}_{X1/Z}), (X_2, \mathbb{C}_{X2/Z}), \ldots, (X_n, \mathbb{C}_{Xn/Z}) | (C, \sigma(C))]$ (i.e., the forces of counter- dominance of the non-central elements or sub-systems), $Y_k \equiv [(C, \mathbb{C}_{C/Z} | ((X_1, \xi_1(X_1)), (X_2, \xi_2(X_2)), \ldots, (X_n, \xi_n(X_n)))]$ (i.e., the force of dominance of the central element or unit-system over the non-central elements or sub-systems), $\xi_i \vDash \mathbb{Z}\circ,_{v}\mathbb{H}$, $i = 1,2,\ldots,n$, Here these X_i, Y_j, Y_k are sub- or unit systems. Then, let $X = \chi \oplus <\mathbb{C}_X>$ reach a specific state of T continuity, and therefore there exists a solution to the following scheme. Then under the system operation of unit system X_i, for each i,

$$(3.2\text{-}2\text{-}1)\quad \varphi\{X\} = X$$

(i.e., X is in a state of systemic continuity), $i = 1, 2, \ldots, n$, $i \neq k, j$, where $\varphi \vDash \mathbb{Z}\circ,_{v}\mathbb{H}$ is the impactor of the system. This system is now under the constraint of the pure dynamic structure:

$$(3.2\text{-}2\text{-}2)\quad \Delta \Vdash \Omega.$$

To solve this scheme, let

$$(3.2\text{-}2\text{-}3)\quad T = X \curlyvee \Delta,$$

where $\curlyvee \vDash \mathbb{Z}\circ,_{v}\mathbb{H}$ is the interactor connecting X and Δ.

Suppose, under the *principle of effective intra-inter systemic operations/T continuity* (effective IISO/T scheme -- partition, modification, alternation, reorganization, and/or integration, etc.), this scheme entails the operations of the whole (or mutuality-entity per se) and individuality (or self-entity per se) in a joint state of equicentrality and T continuity. Then, at the state of CE systemic balance, we have:

(3.2-2-4a) $(\varphi\{T\})_{x_1,\ldots,x_n}$
$= (\varphi\{X \curlyvee \Delta\})_{x_1,\ldots,x_n,Ix}$
$= (\varphi\{X,\Delta\})_{x_1,\ldots,x_n} \ltimes \varphi\{Ix,E\}$
$= \varphi\{X\} \otimes (\psi\{X_1 \dot{\pm} X_2 \dot{\pm} \ldots \dot{\pm} X_n,\Delta\} \ltimes \varphi\{Ix,E\})$

(where $Ix \equiv I(x_1,x_2,\ldots,x_n)$, see Bcm. (3.2-1-7)) in the case of n-element (or unit) balance, or

(3.2-2-4b) $(\varphi\{T\})_{x_1,\ldots,x_n}$
$= (\varphi\{X \curlyvee \Delta\})_{x_1,\ldots,x_n,Ix}$
$= (\varphi\{X,\Delta\})_{x_1,\ldots,x_n} \ltimes \varphi\{Ix,E\}$
$= \varphi\{X\} \otimes (\psi\{Y_j \dot{\pm} Y_K,\Delta\} \ltimes \varphi\{Ix,E\})$

in the case of two-force balance, where E stands for environment system (as a subsystem of the comprehensive energy system). Here $(\varphi\{X,\Delta\})_i$ represents the operations of the whole of the individuality (or selfhood), while $\varphi\{Ix,E\}$ represents the interactive operations among different elements or units systems (or mutuality) and individuality (or selfhood). Note that $\ltimes \vDash \mathbb{Z}_{o,v}\mathbb{H}$ is the impactor connecting $\varphi\{X,\Delta\})_i$ with $\varphi\{Ix,E\}$, $\psi \vDash \mathbb{Z}_{o,v}\mathbb{H}$ is the impactor implementing the policy or strategy of "$X_1 \dot{\pm} X_2 \dot{\pm} \ldots \dot{\pm} X_n$" (in the case of n-element or unit balance) or "$Y_j \dot{\pm} Y_k$" (in case of a balance between two factors) under the influence of Δ, and $\otimes \vDash \mathbb{Z}_{o,v}\mathbb{H}$ is the impactor separating Δ from X. Here it is assumed that, after the separation, Δ operates together with "$X_1 \dot{\pm} \ldots \dot{\pm} X_n$" or "$Y_j \dot{\pm} Y_k$" and the contents of operations are determined by the interactions between Δ and X_i, for all i, with E being the external environment or "SELF" (i.e., Self*, Ultimate Creativity/Destructivity Itself, or Tzu*). Then, we obtain the solution under the condition of continuity: $\varphi\{T\} = \varphi\{X\}$ under the operation of X_i, for all i. That is, we have $(\varphi\{T\})_{x_1,\ldots,x_n} = (\varphi\{T\}) = \varphi\{X\}$, where $(\varphi\{T\})_{x_1,\ldots,x_n}$ is $\varphi\{T\}$ under the operation of X_i, for all i.

For $\varphi\{T\} = \varphi\{X \curlyvee \Delta\} = \varphi\{T\}$, the other route to derive this is as follows: let Δ be the central system ("identity system" or an "empty system" $\circ$, i.e., $\Delta = \circ$), like the zero or the empty set $\varnothing$ in mathematics: for any set $A \in R$ the set of real numbers, $A \cup \varnothing = A$; or $a + 0 = 0$, $a \in R$). At the same time, let the systems $\xi = \zeta$, $\Delta \equiv \xi\,\bar{}\,\zeta$, where $\Delta \equiv \xi\,\bar{}\,\zeta$ is an identity or empty system under the operation of X_i, for "$\bar{}$ " being the impactor eliminating the last term from the first term to set a stage for CE middle-centrality. In other words, φ is the central system or a nullifying impactor that makes Δ an empty system. Therefore, we have: $\varphi\{T\} = \varphi\{X \curlyvee \Delta\} = \varphi\{X\}$, X* being X in the state of CE middle-centrality. Without loss of generality, we write X for X*. Therefore, $\varphi\{T\} = \varphi\{X\}$.

Afterwards, under the operation of X_i, let the basic system reaches a state of CE balance and a state of system's continuity (i.e., T continuity) for X (or X = X*): $(\varphi\{T\})_{x_1,\ldots,x_n} = X = X^*$. Then, we have: $(\varphi\{T\})_{x_1,\ldots,x_n} = X$, and by replacing $(\varphi\{T\})_{x_1,\ldots,x_n}$ by X in the right hand side of Bcm. (3.2-2-4b), we get $X = \varphi\{X\} \otimes \{\psi\{Y_j \dot{\pm} Y_k,\Delta\} \ltimes \varphi\{Ix,E\})$. Because in the state of CE middle-centrality $\varphi\{X\} = X$, by removing X and $(\varphi\{T\})_{x_i}$ from each side of Bcm. (3.2-2-4b) respectively, we derive the formula $\{\psi\{Y_j \dot{\pm} Y_k,\Delta\} \ltimes \varphi\{Ix,E\}) =\!< T^{CE\text{-}T}\} \in Ш^{Д}$. Note that, for a system X, by writing $X =\!< T^{CE\text{-}T}$, we meant X is in a state of CE balance or T continuity. Hence we derive the **principle of CE systemic balance** (or **micro-management**) for two factors:

(3.2-2-5) $\psi\{Y_j \stackrel{\star}{=} Y_k, \Delta_i\} \overline{\barwedge}\ \tau,\ \tau \Vdash (\mathfrak{J}, Ш^{Д}) \Vvdash \mathbb{T}zu^*$,

where $\mathfrak{J}$ denotes the comprehensive energy directly generated by $\mathbb{T}zu^*$ (Ultimate Creativity/Destructivity Itself, or a form of manifestation of $\mathbb{T}zu^*$); or in the case of the balance among multiple elements or sub-systems:

(3.2-2-6) $\psi\{X_1 \stackrel{\star}{=} X_2 \stackrel{\star}{=} \ldots \stackrel{\star}{=} X_n, \Delta\} \overline{\barwedge}\ \tau$.

These above becomings or formulae can also be written as: $\psi\{Y_j \stackrel{\star}{=} Y_k, \Delta_i\} \overline{\barwedge}\ \tau$ (in the case of a balance between two factors), or $\psi\{X_1 \stackrel{\star}{=} X_2 \stackrel{\star}{=} \ldots \stackrel{\star}{=} X_n, \Delta_i\} \overline{\barwedge}\tau$ (in the case of a balance among n elements or unit systems), for each X_i, where

(3.2-2-7) $\Delta_i \equiv$ "$X_i \Lleftarrow \Delta$"

for "$X_i \Lleftarrow \Delta$" referring to X_i operating under the influence of the pure dynamical structure Δ_i ("$\Lleftarrow$" $\vDash Z\circ,_{v}H$ being a restrictive impactor) and "$\overline{\barwedge}$" $\vDash Z\circ,_{v}H$ an impactor connecting ψ and τ (or E being the energy complex or environments).

This means, for a modern firm of East Asian tradition, the objective is not just to maximize profits, but also to achieve a balance between organizational and technological approaches, and between profit maximization and market share maximization. This objective may also involve a determination to promote the technology, organizational efficiency and strategic effects.

Remark 3.2-1-1 (scheme of CE centrality). Note that in the above derivation, in Bcm. (3.2-2-4a), if it is instead at a state of EC imbalance, and then $\psi\{X_1 \stackrel{\star}{=} X_2 \stackrel{\star}{=} \ldots \stackrel{\star}{=} X_n, \Delta\}$ is to be replaced by $\psi\{X_1 \geq X_2 \geq \ldots \geq X_n, \Delta\}$. From there, we derive the **principle of unbalanced micro-management in the broad sense**:

(3.2-2-8) $\psi\{X_1 \geq X_2 \geq \ldots \geq X_n, \Delta\} \overline{\barwedge}\ \tau$.

Now, to have the principle of interconnectedness, in the above derivation (3.2-2-4a), replace the third term by: $(\varphi\{X\} \otimes \psi\{X_1 \risingdotseq X_2 \risingdotseq \ldots \risingdotseq X_n, \Delta\}) \ltimes \varphi\ \{Ix, E\}$ with "$\risingdotseq$" denoting the impactor of interconnectedness (i.e., one is closely connected to other in a reciprocal manner, like in the case of Taiwanese kuanhsi business group, Japanese keiretsu or South Korean chaebol. That is, at a state of CE interconnectedness, we have the **principle of interconnectedness**:

(3.2-2-9) $\psi\{X_1 \risingdotseq X_2 \risingdotseq \ldots \risingdotseq X_n, \Delta\} \overline{\barwedge}\ \tau$.

Note that in the context of a cultural (i.e. national) economy, this principle of connectedness may lead to the *economies of networking* (see Appendix D) and thereby the *cultural advantage* which may be expressed by the formula: $E(\mathfrak{C} \mid \psi\{v,\Delta\} \stackrel{\star}{=} \psi\{p,\Delta\}) = E[E\_P\_S(\xi), E\_F\_Eg(\xi), E\_\omega\text{-}\rho(\xi) \mid \xi \Vdash co(\mathfrak{C} \sqcap \mathbb{T}^*(\tau))]$ (see Bcm. (J.4) in Appendix J where v depicting righteousness and p depicting profits). Here $\mathbb{T}^*(\tau)$ is a form of $\mathbb{T}zu^*$.

Let X_i be a person, a thing, or an event, X_1 be the "self," or the target thing or event, and "$\geq$" $\vDash Z\circ,_{v}H$ as a relationship of strategic centrality. Let X_1^{Strg} be the X_1 with absolute strategic priority. That is, at a state of CE centrality, by modifying Bcm. (3.2-2-8), we derive the **principle of CE centrality**:

(3.2-2-10) $\psi\{X_1 \geq X_2 \geq \ldots \geq X_n, \Delta\} \;\overline{\barwedge}\; \tau.$

or $\psi\{X_1 = X_1{}^{Strg} \mid X_1 \Vdash (X_1, X_2, \ldots, X_n; \Delta) \Vdash \text{Ш}^{\Delta}\} \;\overline{\barwedge}\; \tau,$

Note that for the other type of CE centrality, see Bcm. (K.2-2).

Now let X_i be a person, a thing, or an event, X_1 be the "self," or the target thing or event, and $X_1{}^{Master}$ be the master of all X_i or the one with absolute strategic priority. That is, at a state of self-masterism, by modifying Bcm. (3.2-2-8), we derive the **principle of self-masterism**:

(3.2-2-11) $\psi\{X_1 = X_1{}^{Master} \mid X_1 \Vdash (X_1, X_2, \ldots, X_n; \Delta) \Vdash \text{Ш}^{\Delta}\} \;\overline{\barwedge}\; \tau,$

$\tau \Vdash (\mathfrak{J}, \text{Ш}^{\text{Д}}) \Vvdash \mathbb{T}zu^*.$

§3.2-3 Preliminary Concepts of Demand and Supply

For the conventional approach, on the foundation of the philosophy of utilitarianism, one may assume that: (1) demand curve is the graphical representation of the negative relationship between price and the quantity demanded of a commodity, ceteris paribus; and (2) supply curve is the graphical representation of the positive relationship between price and the quantity supplied of a commodity, ceteris paribus.

Inspired by the "conventional wisdom," our "demand and supply curves" are derived from the MOL-q becoming (MOL being the notation for the meaning of life). That is, from there we derive cs and cd, called the *cultural supply curve* and *cultural demand curve*, respectively.

On the demand side, by drawing the *will-to-use* and the *rationality-to-use* curves together and by shifting them, we derive the downward-sloping MOL-q *meaning-to-use curve* (MTU). Here we have: $\odot \approx^{B} \{\{[x_i(y_i, h_i^*, v_i, IRI_i(\rho, \omega),.), \ldots, x_n(y_n, h_n^*, v_n, IRI_n(\rho,\omega),.) \mid \varphi(MOL,q)] =< T^{B\Delta}\} \sqsubseteq \text{Ш}^{\text{Д}}\}$ (see §A.2-2-2), or in short $\odot \approx^{B} \{\{[(\rho,\omega) \mid \varphi(MOL,q)] =< T^{B\Delta}\} \sqsubseteq \text{Ш}^{\text{Д}}\}$ as a systematic expression of the meaning-to-use becoming in a *state of CE balance*. For the meaning of v_i and v_j, see the following Section3.3 YY BCM; here x_i and x_j are just universal elements with h_i^* and h_j^* being human characteristics, see Bcm. (A.2-1-2-1).

Then, from there, the cultural demand curve is derived by transforming the axis MOL into the price P. On the supply side, by drawing the *will-to-creation curve* and the *rationality-to-creation curve* together and by shifting them, we derive the upward-sloping MOL-q *meaning-to-creation curve* (MTC) which can be expressed as $\odot \approx^{B} \{\{[x_i(y_i, h_i^*, v_i, IRI_i(\rho,\omega),.), \ldots, x_n(y_n, h_n^*, v_n, IRI_n(\rho,\omega),.) \mid \varphi(MOL, q)] =< T^{B\Delta}\} \sqsubseteq \text{Ш}^{\text{Д}}\}$ (see §A.2-2-2) or in short $\odot \approx^{B} \{\{[(\rho,\omega) \mid \varphi(MOL,q)] =< T^{B\Delta}\} \sqsubseteq \text{Ш}^{\text{Д}}$, a systematic expression of the meaning-to-creation becoming in a state of CE balance.

Then, from there, the cultural supply curve can be derived by transforming the axis MOL into the price P.

Note that the firm can manipulate the cd and cs curves in carrying out its plan in order to achieve its goal. Because the cultural forces of will and rationality are underlying these cs and cd curves, the philosophical foundations of MOL are deeper than that of utilitarianism. Therefore, non-utilitarian concerns can be addressed naturally and endogenously in our formulation.

3.3 YY BCM

Let $u_1, u_2 \Vdash \mathbf{U}$ be "thinking elements" or the universal elements with a characteristic of being able to think like a human being (thinking element). That is, let u_1 and u_2 be the subjects of "consciousness/activity," "intentionality/activity toward outside," and "intentionality/ activity of outside toward oneself," where {intentionality/activity toward outside, intentionality/ activity of outside toward oneself} $\sqsubseteq (\Omega, \mathcal{Z}\circ, {}_{v}\mathcal{H}, \{\mathbb{C}\})$ constitutes a unit system (or a sub-system in the following v_1) in which consciousness is the center. From this, v_1 = {(intentionality toward outside, intentionality of outside toward self | consciousness)$|u_1\} \sqsubseteq (\Omega, \mathcal{Z}\circ, {}_{v}\mathcal{H}, \{\mathbb{C}\})$ constitutes a basic system. Here v_1 is one having interactions with its object v_2 (or having a mutually influencing force). Similarly, let v_2 = {(intentionality toward outside, intentionality of outside toward self | consciousness)$|u_2\} \sqsubseteq (\Omega, \mathcal{Z}\circ, {}_{v}\mathcal{H}, \{\mathbb{C}\})$, where $u_2 \Vdash \mathbf{U}$ is a thinking element, u_1 is the interactive object of u_2. Below, we denote the space of those elements v_1 and v_2 as **V**.

Note that in the above, the use of the concepts of consciousness/activity and intentionality/activity are understood in the sense of the existence proof in the real world (see §A.2-5, Appendix A). In the above presentation, the other piece of the existence proof, i.e., that which related to the indirect approach, which in turn relies essentially on the validity of the theory of coherence (Urban 1995), is omitted just for the simplicity of the presentation.

When v_1 and v_2 interact to each other in the state of **CE balance** ($T^{B\Delta}$), we write: $\{\varphi(v_1, v_2) =< T^{B\Delta}\} \sqsubseteq Ш^{Д}$, where $\varphi \vDash \mathbf{H}$ is an interactor. Here the so-called T^B is that both of the impact of v_1 on v_2 and that of v_2 on v_1 have reached a state of equilibrium-in-conflict or balance in tranquility. That is, $\{\{[(v_1,v_2)|\varphi] =< T^{B\Delta}\} \sqsubseteq Ш^{Д}\} \equiv \{(v_1 \approx^B v_2)|\varphi\}$ a system reaching $T^{B\Delta}$, φ is the interactor acting as the virtual center, and $v_1 \approx^B v_2$. Here, $\approx^B$, as a becoming of φ, is the symbol expressing the state of $T^{B\Delta}$. Thus for a_1 and $a_2 \sqsubseteq (\Omega, \mathcal{Z}\circ, {}_{v}\mathcal{H}, \{\mathbb{C}\})$ (i.e., a_1 and a_2 are systems, see §A.2-2-1), $\{[\varphi(a_1,a_2) =< T^{B\Delta}] \sqsubseteq Ш^{Д}\} \equiv \{\{[(a_1,a_2)|\varphi] =< T^{B\Delta}\} \sqsubseteq Ш^{Д}\} \equiv \{(a_1 \approx^B a_2|\varphi\}$ is called T^B **becoming structure** and is a system. Here by a system is meant a collection of elements (or universal and human elements, see §A.2-1-2) with certain structures (see §A.2-2-1). Thus it may be called a $T^{B\Delta}$ **system** (with no center) written as: $(a_1,a_2|R)$, where $R = (\varphi =< T^{B\Delta}) \sqsubseteq Ш^{Д}$.

Note that in business which is part of the economics of culture, a management structure $(x_1,x_2,\ldots,x_m|R_1,R_2,\ldots,R_n) \sqsubseteq (\Omega, \mathcal{Z}\circ, {}_{v}\mathcal{H}, \{\mathbb{C}\})$, for human elements $x_i(h_i^*, v_{k,\cdot}|(\rho,\omega)) \Vdash \mathbf{U}$ with $h_i^* \Vdash \mathbf{H}^*$ for $i, j \in \mathbb{N}$, $v_k \Vdash \mathbf{V}$, for $k \in \mathbb{N}$, and system relationships R_j (in **H**, the basis being-field and the will-and-rationality-to-creation-and-destruction entity) may be called a $T^{B\Delta}$ **management system** if it is a system of two or more human elements with CE balance or centrality. Here the *CE balance* may occur between the will-to-use and the rationality-to-use, between the will-to-creation and the rationality-to-creation of each of the human elements, and among other relationships. In particular, for $h_i^*(.|\omega,\rho) \Vdash \mathbf{H}^*$, $k \in \mathbb{N}$, $\{(\omega,\rho) =< T^{B\Delta}\} \sqsubseteq Ш^{Д}$.

Note that in general, for a management system we write it as a grand system in organization: $\{(\rho,\omega)|(\text{org-func})\} \equiv \lbrace\{[x_i(h_j^*, v_{n,\cdot}|(\rho,\omega))]|\ (\text{org-func}|\ R;O)\|(\mathbb{C},Z)\} =< T^{B\Delta}\} \sqsubseteq Ш^{Д}\rbrace$, $i, j, n \in \mathbb{N}$ (for more detail, see Section 3.7). Here for the sub-system "(org-func|R,O)," with (org-func|R,O) ≡ "(vd,hc,γ),[R,$R^D(e_k)$]," we refer to the part of the structure in Bcm. (A.2-2-1-5): $\lbrace\mathbf{x}(H^*)|\ \mathbf{x}(H^*) \Vdash \{(vd,hc,\gamma),[R,R^D(e_k)]\ |E(\{e_g\},Z)\}\rbrace$, where $\gamma(\tau,\mathfrak{C}) \backsim (\tau,\mathfrak{C})$, $(\tau,\mathfrak{C}) \Vdash (Ш^{\Delta}(\tau), <\mathbb{C}_X>) \Vvdash \mathbb{T}\mathrm{zu}^*$. Here $\mathfrak{C}$ represents the core of $\mathbb{C}$, and the notation "$\backsim$" means "to be generated by" or "being derived from."

In the above, in "$\{\varphi(v_i,v_j) =< T^{B\Delta}\} \sqsubseteq Ш^{Д}$," let v_i = {(self-to-outside consciousness /activity, outside-to-self consciousness/activity)$|u_j$}, v_j = {(self-to-outside conscious- ness/activity, outside-to-self consciousness/activity)$|u_i$}, for $v_j \Vdash \mathbf{V} \sqcup \mathbf{U}$ (**V** is the space containing all of the human elements v_i, in reality $\mathbf{V} \Subset \mathbf{U}$) be human elements of "action" or "practice." Then, v_i and v_j are in simple existence. By the Chinese philosophical tradition, u_i and u_j are elements in the unity of knowledge and action for which "to think or to be conscious of" is the same as "to act," and "the ability to think" is the same as "the ability to act."

Similarly, if u_1 and $u_2 \Vdash \mathbf{U}$ are universal elements, let a_1 = {(self-to-outside consciousness/ activity, outside-to-self consciousness/activity)$|u_1$}, a_2 = {(self-to-outside consciousness/ activity, outside-to-self consciousness/ activity)$|u_2$}, with $\{\varphi(a_1,a_2) =< T^{B\Delta}\} \sqsubseteq Ш^{Д}$ denoting the CE balanced state of the interactions between a_i and a_2. Then, a_1 is the generalized element of the afore-mentioned v_i, and a_2 is the generalized element of the afore-mentioned v_j.

In the above, a_1 and a_2 (or v_i, v_j) are in natural or simple existence. For simplicity, from the above argument, we shall set a_1, a_2 (and v_i, v_j) as in true existence through the argument of coherence theory.

Here we mention again that, in the case of decision-making, the above TC becoming structure is a management system.

In the following, let $\rhd_i \equiv (\{[x_1(h_\alpha^*,v_j,.|(\rho,\omega)),x_2(h_\beta^*,v_k,.|(\rho,\omega)),\ldots|\varphi(MOL,q)\|(\mathbb{C},Z)] =< T^{B\Delta}\} \sqsubseteq Ш^{Д})$, $i \in \mathbb{N}$, v_j, $v_k \Vdash \mathbf{V}$, (α, β are indexes), where MOL $\Vdash H^* \Subset \mathbf{U}$ is the "meaning of life," $q \Vdash \mathbf{U}$ is a general event, while MOL and q are general operating elements. Note that here, φ is the virtual center of the sub-system, $T^{B\Delta}$ is a becoming in a state of CE balance, and "$\|$" denotes the relationship that (MOL,q|φ) is conditioned upon the set $\{x_i(h_\alpha^*,v_j,.|(\rho,\omega))\}$ for all $i \in \mathbb{N}$. Hence, $\rhd_i \sqsubseteq (\Omega,\mathcal{Z}\circ,{}_v\mathcal{H},\{\mathbb{C}\}))$, $i \in \mathbb{N}$, is a system. Furthermore, let $(\rhd_i, \rhd_j) \Vdash$co-system (i.e., $\rhd_i$ is iso-systemic to $\rhd_j$, $i \neq j$). From here, we get $\rhd_i$-$\rhd_{i+1}$--- as a generating yang system, see "(yang) **right-up BCM**" in Figure 3.3-1.

Figure 3.3-1
Going-up BCM

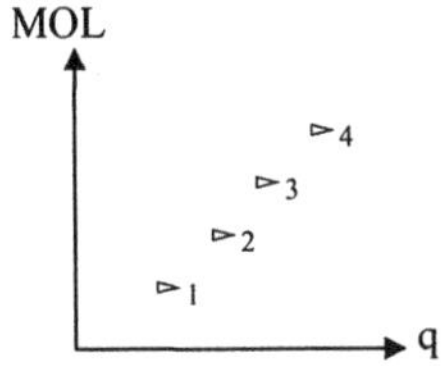

In the above $\rhd_i$-string: $\rhd_i$-$\rhd_{i+1}$---, we utilize the principle of CE balance (3.2-5) with positive relationship: $\psi\{X_1 \pm X_2,\Delta^+\} \mathrel{\bar{\wedge}} \tau$. That is, all other things being equal, the gain from MOL is equal to the cost of generating q. Similarly, we get $\rhd_i$-$\rhd_{i+1}$--- as a generating yin system, see "(yin) **right-down BCM**" in Figure 3.3-2.

In the above in describing the $\rhd_i$-string: $\rhd_i$-$\rhd_{i+1}$---, we employ the principle of causal-effect balance (Bcm. (3.2-2-5)) with negative relationship: $\psi\{X_1 \pm X_2,\Delta^-\} \mathrel{\bar{\wedge}} \tau$. That is, all other

things being equal, the loss of MOL is equal to the benefit received from consuming q and the more one gains in q, the lower the level of MOL will be.
Figure 3.3-2
Going-down BCM

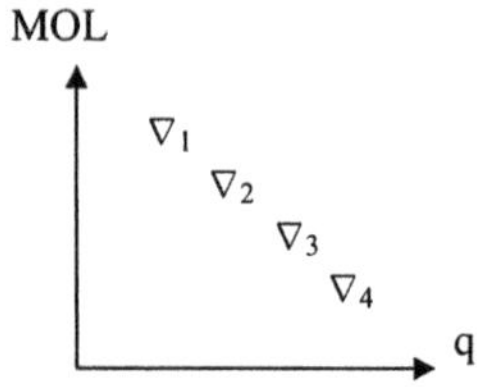

Note that for this $〔\{[\{x_1(h_1^*,v_{j,\cdot}|(\rho,\omega))\}|(MOL,q|\varphi)\|(\mathbb{C},Z)] =\!< T^{B\Delta}\} \sqsubseteq Ш^{Д}〕$ we may write it as: $\{\{[(X,Y)|\varphi] =\!< T^{B\Delta}\} \sqsubseteq Ш^{Д}\} \equiv \{(X \approx^{B} Y)|\varphi\}$ (with $\{z\}$ depicting the set of z and X and Y depicting relevant entities in question). In the case of a right-down BCM, it is a $T^{B\Delta}$ becoming structure and is thereby a system. As shown in the above, it is also a $T^{B\Delta}$ system : $(X,Y|R)$, where $R = (\varphi =\!< T^{B\Delta}) \sqsubseteq Ш^{Д}$.

3.4 Supply and Demand Becomings

From the above, we know that the supply becoming is in a state of CE centrality for the meaning to creation (see Bcm. (4.2-2) in Section 4.2): $\psi\{X_1 \geq X_2,\Delta\} \,\overline{\overline{\wedge}}\, \tau$, where X_1 is the will-to-creation system and X_2 is the rationality-to-creation system, and the supply is a grand system: $\{(\rho,\omega)|(P,q)^{+}\} \equiv 〔\{\{x_1(h_1^*,v_{j,\cdot}|(\rho,\omega))\}|(P,q|R^{+};O)\|(\mathbb{C},Z) =\!< T^{B\Delta}\} \sqsubseteq Ш^{Д}〕$, where R denotes the relationship between P (converted from MOL, a meaning of life measure) and q so that they are moving in the same direction (either both positive or both negative), given the condition O that all other variables being held constant. Note that the grand system $\{(\rho,\omega)|(P,q)^{+}\}$ is nothing but the Going-up BCM in the above Subsection 3.3.

Conventionally, in the system $\{(\rho,\omega)|(P,q)^{+}\} \sqsubseteq (\Omega,\mathcal{Z}\circ,{}_{v}\mathcal{H},\{\mathbb{C}\})\sqcap\mathbb{C}$ ($\mathbb{C}$ being the mathematical system of complex numbers), q is set as a function of P: $q = f(P)$. That is, to follow the conventional way of thinking, we must have $\{P,q\}^{+} \equiv \{(\rho,\omega)|(P,q)^{+}\} \equiv \{q|P\}^{+}$ as a grand system, in which P is treated as the central unit system, and q is the non-central unit system. In our systematic approach, this is not necessarily true. In our (mathematical) approach, $\{P,q\}^{+}$ is set as one-to-one function. That is, q is a function of P: $q = f(P)$ and P is a function of q: $P = f^{1}(q)$, or vice versa. That is, in the sense of a system, $\{P,q\}^{+}$ is a system without a center, and both are non-central units. It is obvious that this $\{P,q\}^{+} \equiv \{P,q|\mathbb{C}\}^{+}$ may be treated as a system with a virtual center (see Subsection A.2-3) being the cultural core underlying this system ($\mathfrak{C}$).

Similarly, we know that the demand becoming is in a state of CE centrality for the meaning to use system (see Bcm. (4.2-2) in the next section): $\psi\{X_1 \leq X_2,\Delta\} \,\overline{\overline{\wedge}}\, \tau$, where X_1 is the will-to-creation system and X_2 is the rationality-to-creation system, and the system of demand curve is a grand system: $\{P,q|R^{-};O'\} \equiv 〔\{\{x_1(h_1^*,v_{j,\cdot}|(\rho,\omega))\}|\ (P,q|R^{-};O)\|(\mathfrak{C},Z) =\!< T^{B\Delta}\} \sqsubseteq Ш^{Д}〕$, where R^{-} denotes the relationship between P (converted from MOL, a meaning of life measure) and q such that they are moving to the opposite directions (i.e., for one being in one direction and the other being in the opposite direction), given the condition O' which denotes all other variables (or elements) being held constant. Note that the grand system $\{P,q|R^{-};O\}$ is nothing but the going-down SBC in the above Subsection 3.3. Similar to the above case, in the grand system $\{P,q\}^- \equiv \{q|P\}^- \equiv \{(\rho,\omega)|(P,q)^-\} \equiv (\{\{x_1(h_1^*,v_{j,\cdot}|(\rho,\omega))\}|(P,q|R^-;O)\|(\mathbb{C},Z) =<T^{B\Delta}\} \sqsubseteq \text{Ш}^{\text{Д}}) \equiv \{P,q|C\}^-$, $C = (\mathbb{C},Z)$, $\{G:\mathbb{C}\}$, or $\{M:\mathbb{C}\}$ for G and M referring to the elements of government and market forces, respectively. In the macro case, this $\{P,q|C\}^-$ (and similarly for $\{P,q|C\}^+$) may also be treated as a system with the government (or market forces) serving as the center of the system and the cultural core underlying this system ($\mathfrak{C}$) serving as the virtual center. In terms of the system complex of will and rationality (i.e., W-R or $\{\omega,\rho\}$), the system of demand becoming is a system $\{\xi(\omega,\rho)\}$ in which ξ indicates the ability and willingness to purchase good(s) or service(s) for consumption.

Then the system of market equilibrium or balance is a state of CE balance: $\psi\{X_1 \pm X_2,\Delta\} \barwedge \tau$, where X_1 refers to the supply-curve system and X_2 the demand-curve system. Generally speaking, this system of market equilibrium is culture-specific. For the West, the system of market equilibrium: $\{\{\omega,\rho\}|DD{=}SS|\mathbb{C};Others\}$ is a grand system determined by the efficiency of sciences and technology, and its cultural system $\mathfrak{C}$ is itself a "grand system" in a state of CE imbalance: $\psi\{X_\alpha \leq X_\beta,\Delta\} \barwedge \tau$, where α represents a tranquil cultural system and β a conflict cultural system.

For classic East Asia, this state of CE balance: $\psi\{X_1 \pm X_2,\Delta\} \barwedge \tau$ may be called as one of *market balance* rather than one of market equilibrium, since the strength of this sytem is derived from the organizational efficiency and the underlying culture is more of a tranquil type than a conflict type (i.e., this cultural system $\mathfrak{C}$ is a "grand system" in a state of CE imbalance: $\psi\{X_\alpha \leq X_\beta,\Delta\} \barwedge \tau$, $\alpha \neq \beta$).

In terms of the scheme of the circular flow of a cultural economy, the output market in the conventional approach is replaced by our systematic complex in which the upper part is the collection of the macro-output markets, and the lower part is the collection of the micro-output markets composed of various interactions between households and those of inter-firm activities. Similarly, the input market in the conventional approach is replaced by our systematic complex in which the upper part is the collection of the micro-input markets composed of various interactions between firms and households and those of inter-firm activities, and the lower part is the collection of the macro-input markets

Note that this system of the circular flow can be regarded as a variation of the MFCE scheme presented in Appendix A, A.4.1. The way the forces of equilibrium/disequilibrium of an output market operate through the interactions of the demand and supply curve systems is the same as the way East and West together generate North in the MFCE scheme. Similarly, the forces of equilibrium/disequilibrium of an input market operate through the interactions of the demand and supply curve systems is the same as the way East and West together generate South.

For details of the derivations of the supply and demand curves, see Appendix F. For the simplicity of analysis, it is assumed that each firm (including the competitive one) faces a downward sloping demand curve and thereby incurs a level of positive normal profits except in the case of the long term equilibrium. Therefore the fund needed for R&D is always available and a surviving firm is always in a good position to engage in new capital formation and in promoting new technology. For the details of the downward-sloping cultural demand curve of a competitive firm, also see Appendix F.

For further discussions of the systems of business management, for example, a "virtue organization" or a capitalist firm, see Section F.3 of Appendix F. Before we leave this subsection, note that these demand and supply becomings are systems (also called demand and supply curve systems) and from there demand and supply curves may be derived by going through the assumed systematic transformations.

3.5 Classification of Households

In this section, we shall classify households into the categories of the household of leisure-pursuing and the household of material-pursuing. By a **household** is meant a group of human elements forming a system in making joint decisions about non-productive activities such as consumption and leisure.

Below we shall in turn define each type of these households.

Definition 3.5-1. A household as a system in $(\Omega,\mathbb{Z}\circ,_{v}\mathbb{H},\{\mathbb{C}\})$ is called **leisure-pursuing household** or spirituality-pursuing household if its major concerns are about the pursuit of leisure or spirituality rather than that of material satisfaction (or the satisfaction of basic needs in daily life).

Definition 3.5-2. A household as a system $(\Omega,\mathbb{Z}\circ,_{v}\mathbb{H},\{\mathbb{C}\})$ is called **material-pursuing household** if its major concerns are about the material satisfaction or the satisfaction of basic needs in daily life.

Note that this classification of households must also depend on the institutional settings (e.g., IRI chain, MPFX cycles and SIFP chain complex). And further, some schemes of systemic-change becoming systems may also be addressed for them.

3.6 Classification of Firms and Management

In this section and the next section, we discuss some aspects of an organization. Later in §A.2-10, we shall provide more details of the structures of an organization. There are several issues involved in our study of firms and management. According to the conventional approach, transactions costs, profit incentives and even institutional arrangements are perceived as among the major topics of any research on firm's behavior (for a summary of institutional approach, see Van Den Berg 2001). Naturally, in our approach of systematics, the issues of the structure-organization, technology, strategy and culture are keys to this study.

To a firm under the culture of conquest, conflict and scientific rationality, the promotion of efficiency may be achieved by two approaches. First, competition shall ensure the proper working of work ethics. This approach is suitable for a firm engaging in the businesses of low- to medium-levels of technology. Secondly, by combining the mechanism of competition with the method of scientific management, production, and R&D, the required efficiency shall be safeguarded. This second approach is suitable for firms engaging in the businesses of high- or advanced-levels of technology.

Although these above approaches create micro-efficiency, undesirable consequences of excessive competition may follow logically. In the first approach, communitarian ethics may be of great help in dealing with the lack of macro-efficiency. In the second approach, communitarian ethics and a certain kind of humane rationality may be necessary to ensure any level of the macro-efficiency. Scientific rationality alone may lead to fragmentation and compartmentalization of human rationality. This rationality needs to be balanced or even to be lead by a certain kind of qualitative and structural rationality. Then the bias of single-dimensional rationality in the information-evaluation_rational-decision-making_planning-implementation (IRI) chain of a firm may be corrected.

For a firm under the culture of tranquility (self-mastering life-will, yu-wu rationality, and life-oriented rationality), the economic efficiency may be promoted through the following desirable approaches. First, harmonious coordination within the system may ensure the macro-efficiency. This approach is suitable for a firm engaging in the businesses of low- to medium-levels of technology. Secondly, by combining the mechanism of harmonious coordination and networking with systemic management, production and R&D, macro-efficiency shall be achieved. This second approach is suitable for a firm engaging in the fields of businesses with high- or advanced-level of technology.

Certainly, these above approaches may not create micro-efficiency. Harmonious coordination may lead to complacence, systemic inertia and even corruption. In the first approach, strong self-motivation helps greatly for the remedy for the lack of micro-efficiency. In addition, the here-and-now-oriented scientific rationality and an appropriate degree of competition among members of the system will be of great help in correcting for the lack of micro-efficiency. In the second approach, competitive ethics and future-oriented scientific rationality may be necessary for correcting the inadequacy of micro-efficiency. Life-oriented or yu-wu rationality alone may fail to address the quantitative and experimental aspects of modern economic and business management in the areas of research, development, and production of new products and the distribution of income to members of the institution in a fair and efficient manner.

These management schemes may be represented by those schemes developed for studying structures of the polity and society (see schemes of polities 1 and 2 in Bcms. (L.3-4) and (L.3-8)).

Below we shall set up some criteria for the classification of firms. In general, there are several ways to classify firms. One could classify according to technological level involved, cultural orientation, strategic concerns, or other criteria.

(1) Cultural concerns. A firm can be classified according to whether it is of the culture type of tranquility or conflict, and whether it is of the type of individual decision making or consensual decision making. In this case, the issue of the bias in the IRI chain (in terms of will and rationality) needs to be addressed.

(2) Classification according to whether it is of the MPFX cycle or the GPFX cycle. An independent firm may base itself on the MPFX chain complex of capitalism, while a relational firm may have to base on the social relationship network GPFX cycle.

(3) Classification according to whether it is of the science-orientated SIFP chain complex or the YYWX-orientated YXSIFP chain complex.

(4) Classification according to whether it has political connection or not.

(5) Technological concerns: A firm can be classified according to the level of technology involved, i.e., whether it is of low-tech, medium-tech, high-tech or advanced-tech.

(6) Concerns in the area of structure-organization: whether it is centralized or decentralized.

(7) Strategic concerns: whether it is a system of D-, G-, S-,V-, or SC-strategy. That is, to classify a firm according to its strategic orientation. This involved basis-being field (in the narrow sense), social-PE net (in the narrow sense), and strategic space feasible to the firm (based upon the corporate culture).

i). Leap-strategic firm (D-strategic firm). Some of its characteristics are: decentralization, high content of R&D, high investment capacity, horizontal connection with other firms, and excellent ability of vertical command of its internal structure and elements.

ii). Golden-strategic firm (G-strategic firm).

iii). Stable-growth-strategic firm (S-strategic firm).

iv). Variational-strategic firm (V-strategic firm).

v). Continuity-strategic firm (C-strategic firm).

For example, for a D-strategic firm/organization, the system may be written as:

$$\text{(3.6-1)}\quad X = (\Delta 1\text{-}\Delta 2\text{-}\ldots\text{-}\Delta i)\text{-}(\boxtimes 1\sim\boxtimes 2\sim\boxtimes j) + (\langle\mathbb{C}_1\rangle\langle\mathbb{C}_2\rangle)\ldots\langle\mathbb{C}_n\rangle)$$
$$= \{\text{workers,Mgt}|\text{Ceo}\}\text{-}\{\text{Market,R\&D,Fin,Prod}|Z\}\sim\{D,G,S,V,sC\} \oplus \langle\mathbb{C}_X\rangle,$$

for $X \sqsubseteq (\Omega,\mathbb{Z}\circ,{}_v\mathbb{H},\{\mathbb{C}\})$ with (Δ1-Δ2-…-Δi) being the static structures and ($\boxtimes$1~$\boxtimes$2~$\boxtimes$j) being dynamic structures, where {workers,Managers|Ceo} is a "trisystem," {Market, R&D,Fin,Prod | $Z \Leftarrow \mathbb{C}_X \Vdash \mathbb{T}zu^*$} is a 5-polar MFCE system (with the cultural core serving as the virtual center; here the decision-making and strategic complex Z is not a center, but an imposed condition for this system), and {D,G,S,V,sC} is a 6-polar MFCE system (with the cultural core as the virtual center). If Y = {Market,R&D, Fin, Prod|Z}, then we have a solution for the systemic-change becoming in a state of the simple Tcentral (also see Appendix B):

$$\text{(3.6-2)}\quad Y = \{[\psi^{2^*}(y) \oplus \psi(y) \oplus y] \circledcirc Iy\} \circ F = \Phi .$$

where Market = Hf{R&D| Fin} = ψ^{2^*} {R&D|Fin}, Prod = ψ{R&D}, ψ being an Hf impactor, Iy the system-integrating factor, and F a factor of Fin.

Then a possible joint solution to this becoming is to find a solution of

$$\text{(3.6-3)}\quad Y = \{[\psi^{2^*}(y) \oplus \psi(y) \oplus y] \circledcirc Iy\} = \Phi .$$

Let Bcm. (3.6-4) be a possible solution of this new becoming in a state of simple Tcentral:

$$\text{(3.6-4)}\quad y(.) = [\alpha_{r\&d}y(\mathbb{H}_2;.)\oplus\xi_{prod}y(\mathbb{H}_1;.)\oplus\zeta_{mkt}y(\mathbb{H}_0;.)] \circledcirc Iy(\mathbb{H}_y;.)$$

for the system-integrating factor Iy, where the system-dynamical impactor $\alpha_{r\&d}$ representing the characteristics for R&D remaining essentially itself over time, the system-dynamical impactor ξ_{prod} representing the characteristics for R&D evolving into Prod, and the system-dynamical impactor ζ_{mkt} represents the characteristics for R&D evolving into Market over time assuming this can be achieved without the factor of Fin. Then a possible solution to Bcm. (3.6-2), which may be called the **externally constrained systemic-change becoming**, is:

(3.6-5) $y(.) = \{[\alpha_{r\&d}y(\mathbb{H}_2;.) \oplus \xi_{prod}y(\mathbb{H}_1;.) \oplus \zeta_{mkt}y(\mathbb{H}_0;.)] \circledast Iy(\mathbb{H}_y;.)\} \odot| F,$

for the system-integrating factor $Iy(\mathbb{H};.)$, where F is the constrained factor evolving essentially into Fin over time, $\circledast \vDash \mathcal{Z}\circ,v\mathcal{H}$, and "$\odot|$" $\vDash \mathcal{Z}\circ,v\mathcal{H}$ an impactor constrained by an external factor (or an impactor attaching an external factor to the original systemic-change becoming).

If E = {D,G,S,V,sC}, then we have a solution for the systemic-change becoming in a state of the Tcentral:

(3.6-6) $Y = \{[\eta^{4*}(y) \oplus \eta^3(y) \oplus \eta^2(y) \oplus \eta^2(y) \oplus y] \circledast Iy\} \odot| x = \Phi,$

where $D = \eta^{4*}\{sC|x\}$, $G = \eta^3\{sC\}$, $S = \eta^2\{sC\}$, $V = \eta\{sC\}$, $y = sC$, with $\eta = Hf$ being an impactor and $\eta^* \equiv \eta(.|x) = Hf$ an impactor constrained by the external factor x, and x a factor of D.

Then a possible joint solution to this becoming is:

(3.6-7) $y(.) = \{[\alpha_{sC}y(\mathbb{H}_{sC};.) \oplus \xi_V y(\mathbb{H}_V;.) \oplus \xi_S y(\mathbb{H}_V;.) \oplus \xi_G y(\mathbb{H}_G;.)] \circledast Iy(\mathbb{H}_G;.)\}$
$\odot| \zeta_{(D,x)}x(\mathbb{H}_D;.),$

with the system-dynamical impactor α_{sC} representing the characteristics for sC remaining essentially itself over time, the system-dynamical impactor ξ_V representing the characteristics for sC evolving into $V=\psi(sC)$, the system-dynamical impactor ξ_S represents the characteristics for sC evolving into $S=\psi^2(sC)$, the system-dynamical impactor ξ_G represents the characteristics for $G=\psi^3(sC)$, and the system-dynamical impactor $\zeta_{(D,x)}$ represents the characteristics for $D=\psi^{*4}(sC|x)$ (with ψ^{*4} being an impactor transformed from ψ^{*4} by placing constraint on the impactor ψ^{*4}).

For the cultural aspects of the D-strategic firm, let the system be $U = \{A(.|\mathcal{T}),X(.|\mathcal{K})|(\omega,\rho)^{TCentral}(\mathcal{T},\mathcal{K})\}$, for $\mathcal{T}$ and $\mathcal{K}$ be the cultural forces of tranquility and conflict, respectively and $(\omega,\rho)^{TCentral}(\mathcal{T},\mathcal{K})$ be the *culture of mediety and balance*, where $A = \{(a,b|c);\mathbb{C}^T\} \sqsubseteq (\Omega,\mathcal{Z}\circ,_v\mathcal{H},\{\mathbb{C}\})$ is a *standard Y-system* with $\mathbb{C}^T$ referring to the culture of tranquility and $X = \{(x,y|z);\mathbb{C}^K\} \sqsubseteq (\Omega,\mathcal{Z}\circ,_v\mathcal{H},\{\mathbb{C}\})$ is an *standard Hg-system* with $\mathbb{C}^K$ referring to the culture of conflict. Then, by letting $\varphi, \psi, \eta \vDash \mathcal{Z}\circ,_v\mathcal{H}$ be impactors, we may derive A and X by the following **static forms of systemic-change becomings**:

(3.6-8) $\{[\psi(a,\varphi(a)) \oplus \varphi(a) \oplus a] \circledast Ia\} = \Phi,$

(3.6-9) $\{[\eta^2(x) \oplus \eta(x) \oplus x] \circledast Ix\} = \Phi.$

A possible joint solution to these two becomings is then:

(3.6-10) $x(.) = [(\alpha_a \oplus \alpha_x)\, x(\mathbb{H}_2;.) \oplus (\xi_a \oplus \xi_x)\, x(\mathbb{H}_1;.) \oplus (\zeta_a \oplus \zeta_x) x(\mathbb{H}_0;.)] \circledast Ix(\mathbb{H}_x;.)$,

with the system-dynamical impactor α_a representing the characteristics for a remaining essentially a over time, the system-dynamical impactor ξ_a representing the characteristics for a evolving into φa, the system-dynamical impactor ζ_a represents the characteristics for $(a,\varphi(a))$ evolving into $\psi(a,\varphi(a))$, the system-dynamical impactor α_x represents the characteristics for x remaining essentially x over time, the system-dynamical impactor ξ_x represents the characteristics for x evolving into ηx, and the system-dynamical impactor ζ_x represents the characteristics for x evolving into $\eta^2 x$.

Note that, for a firm, we may write it as: X = Δ-⊠+<> = {R&D,PubProd,Gov,Fin,(PrivProd} -{consumption,production|central authority|Z} ⊕ <ℂX> ⊑ (Ω,𝒵○,ᵥ𝐻,{ℂ}), where

(3.6-11) $X = X(.|Z),\ Z = Z(.|\Omega^{Org} \sqcap \Omega^{Strg}) \Leftarrow \{\mathbb{C} \Leftarrow \mathbb{T}zu^*\}$,

with $\Omega^{Strg} = \{D,G^+,G,S,V,sC\} \equiv \{\Omega^D, \Omega^{Rh}, \Omega^H, \Omega^S, \Omega^V, \Omega^{sC}\}$ (see Bcm. (8.2-2)) being the space of strategies and Ω^{Org} being space of organizations. Following the principle of centrality-balance: centrality of the key element, CE balance among all targets, then, in the micro-concerns, the entrepreneur-planner can change the R&D mix, product mix, financial mix, marketing mix, advertising mix and its relationship with other firms (either firms in alliance or competitors), and thereby rotate and shift the cultural supply and demand curves. In the global concerns, he or she can change the profit target and the market share as well.

Further, as the background of business firms, the money-power-fame-sex cycle, S&T-investment-finance-production cycle, and the information-evaluation/rational decision-making/planning-implementation cycle of the society in their totality is affected by the culture:

(3.6-12) MPFX cycle $\Leftarrow \{\mathbb{C} \Leftarrow \mathbb{T}zu^*\}$, or MPFX($\tau$) ⇝ $\tau \Vdash \mathfrak{I} \Vvdash \mathbb{T}zu^*$,

(3.6-13) SIFP-Export chain complex $\Leftarrow \{\mathbb{C} \Leftarrow \mathbb{T}zu^*\}$,

(3.6-14) IRI chain $\Leftarrow \{\mathbb{C} \Leftarrow \mathbb{T}zu^*\}$.

Note that these MPFX cycle, SIFP chain complex and IRI chain are MFCE schemes. Here $\mathfrak{C}$ is the cultural variables nurtured by the force of Ultimate Creativity- Destructivity $\mathbb{T}zu^*$. As a point of reflection, note that in general, a firm is not in a position to change the culture of its employees. As for a nation, cultural change as a field of social engineering may even be well beyond the control of the national planners.

(8) Classification according to primary-secondary or tertiary activities or capital-technology-cultural intensity: natural resources-based firms – capital intensive firm; service-oriented firms, either high- or low-technological activities involved; low-tech agricultural business firms – labor intensive firm; medium-technological firm, capital-intensive firm; high-technological firm: niche-technological firms; advanced-technological firm: the leaders; the technology-followers: niche technological firm.

(9) Classification according to cultural orientation:

i). Tranquil culture or conflict culture.
ii). Either material/spiritual orientation or religious/secular culture.

(10) Classification according to functional areas: marketing, finance, manufacturing, production and R&D, etc.

(11) Classification according to geographic areas: Latin America, Middle East, Western Europe, East Asia, South Asia, and Russia, etc.

(12) Classification according to other factors: ethnicity (African American, Asian American, Hispanic, etc.), community, and so on.

3.7 Proto-type Systems of Organizations

Similar to the reasoning presented in Section 3.4, an organization can be written as a grand system: $\{(\rho,\omega)|(\text{org-func})\} \equiv \{\{\{x_1(h_1^*,v_{j},.|(\rho,\omega))\}|(\text{org-func}|R;O)\|(\mathfrak{C},Z)\} =< T^{B\Delta}\} \Subset Ш^{Д}\}$, where R denotes the relationship between various org-func (organization-operational roles or functions), given the condition O (i.e, all other relevant entities) being held constant.

Definition 3.7-1. For human elements x, y, $z \Vdash \mathbf{H} \Subset \mathbf{U}$, $\{x,y|z\} \sqsubseteq (\Omega,\mathcal{Z}\circ,{}_{v}H,\{\mathbb{C}\})$ is said to be a **C-weak system** if and only if the following conditions hold: (1) (x,y) forms a yin-yang pair of f-systemism or thesis-antithesis pair of Hf-systemism with x and y may be at the same stage of development, (2) ((x,y),z) forms a yin-yang pair of f-systemism or thesis-antithesis pair of Hf-systemism with z's stage development being higher than those of x and y (see Definition A.5-2-4b). (3) In the system {x,y|z}, the central element z exerts a weak force of dominance over the non-central elements x and y. (4) The underlying culture of this system is one of conflict culture.

Definition 3.7-2. For human elements x, y, $z \Vdash \mathbf{H} \Subset \mathbf{U}$, $\{x,y|z\} \sqsubseteq (\Omega,\mathcal{Z}\circ,{}_{v}H,\{\mathbb{C}\})$ is said to be a **C-strong system** if and only if the following conditions hold: (1) (x,y) forms a yin-yang pair of f-systemism or thesis-antithesis of Hf-systemism, with x and y may be at the same stage of development, (2) ((x,y),z) forms a yin-yang pair of f-systemism or thesis-antithesis pair of Hf-systemism with z's stage development being higher than those of x and y. (3) In the system {x,y|z}, the central element z exerts a strong force of dominance over the non-central elements x and y. (4) The underlying culture of this system is one of conflict culture.

Definition 3.7-3. For human elements x, y, $z \Vdash \mathbf{H} \Subset \mathbf{U}$, $\{x,y|z\} \sqsubseteq (\Omega,\mathcal{Z}\circ,{}_{v}H,\{\mathbb{C}\})$ is said to be a **T-weak system** if and only if the following conditions hold: (1) (x,y) forms a yin-yang pair of f-systemism or y-systemism with x and y may be at the same stage of development, (2) ((x,y),z) forms a yin-yang pair of f-systemism or y-systemism with z's stage development being higher than those of x and y. That is, $x \rightarrow z$ may be an h^L-systemism. (3) In the system {x,y|z}, the central element z exerts a weak force of dominance over the non-central elements x and y. (4) The underlying culture of this system is one of tranquil culture.

Definition 3.7-4. For human elements x, y, $z \Vdash \mathbf{H} \Subset \mathbf{U}$, $\{x,y|z\} \sqsubseteq (\Omega,\mathcal{Z}\circ,{}_{v}H,\{\mathbb{C}\})$ is said to be a **T-semistrong system** if and only if the following conditions hold: (1) (x,y) forms a yin-yang pair of f-systemism and y is at a stage of development higher than that of x. (2) (y,z) forms a yin-yang pair of f-systemism with z being at a stage higher than that of y. That is, $x \rightarrow z$ is an h^R-systemism. (3) In the system $\{x,y|z\}$, the central element z exerts a semi-strong force of dominance over the non-central elements x and y. (4) The underlying culture of this system is one of tranquil culture.

Definition 3.7-5. For human elements $x, y, z \Vdash \mathbf{H} \Subset \mathbf{U}$, $\{x,y|z\} \sqsubseteq (\Omega,\mathcal{Z}^{\circ},{}_{v}\mathcal{H},\{\mathbb{C}\})$ is said to be a **T-strong system** if and only if the following conditions hold: (1) (x,y) forms a yin-yang pair of f-systemism or y-systemism with y may be at a stage of development higher than that of x. (2) (y,z) forms a yin-yang pair of f-systemism with z may be at a stage higher than that of y. That is, $x \rightarrow z$ may be an h^R-systemism. (3) In the system $\{x,y|z\}$, the central element z exercises a strong force of dominance over the non-central elements x and y. (4) The underlying culture of this system is one of tranquil culture.

Below we shall introduce the IRI chain system, MPFX cycle, and SIFP chain complex system.

Figure 3.7-1
Incomplete Structure of {a,b,c}

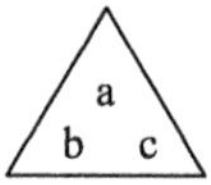

Definition 3.7-6. For $A = \{a_1,a_2,a_3\} \sqsubseteq (\Omega,\mathcal{Z}^{\circ},{}_{v}\mathcal{H},\{\mathbb{C}\})$ (Figure 3.7-1), suppose it can be written as:

$$(3.7\text{-}1)\quad A = a_1 \oplus a_2 \oplus a_3 = \sigma \Vdash \Sigma^{TC}$$

(at a state of simple Tcentral, see Definition B.1-1, where $a_2 = \varphi(a_1)$, $a_3 = \varphi^2(a_1)$, for $\varphi \vDash \mathcal{Z}^{\circ},{}_{v}\mathcal{H}$ being the impactor transforming a_1 into a_2) with the solution

$$(3.7\text{-}2)\quad x(.) = [\alpha_2 x(\mathbb{H}_2;.) \oplus \alpha_1 x(\mathbb{H}_1;.) \oplus \alpha_0 x(\mathbb{H}_0;.)],$$

where α_1 represents the characteristics for x evolving into φx and α_2 represents the characteristics for x evolving into $\varphi^2 x$ (see §8.4-3 for more details of these becomings). Then A is called the **small-org system**. This is true for a system of the culture of independence. And yet, in general, we may write this system as:

$$(3.7\text{-}3)\quad A = (a_3 \oplus a_1 \oplus a_0) \circledast Ia = \sigma \Vdash \Sigma^{TC}$$

for the integrating factor of A (Ia):

$$(3.7\text{-}4)\quad Ia = (I^-,I^+) = \circ.$$

That is, we suppose in this case that the positive and negative impact of integrating factor cancel out entirely. Note that for a system of the culture of conflict, we may approximate it with a small-org system.

Definition 3.7-7. Let $A = \{a_1,a_2,a_3\}$, $B = \{b_1,b_2,b_3\}$, $C = \{c_1,c_2,c_3\} \sqsubseteq (\Omega,\mathcal{Z}\circ,{}_v\mathcal{H},\{\mathbb{C}\})$, and suppose we can write, for $\circledast \vDash \mathcal{Z}\circ,{}_v\mathcal{H}$:

(3.7-5) $A = (a_1 \oplus a_2 \oplus a_3) \circledast Ia = \sigma \Vdash \Sigma^{TC}$

(at a state of simple Tcentral, where $a_2 = \varphi(a_1)$, $a_3 = \varphi^2(a_1)$, for $\varphi \vDash \mathcal{Z}\circ,{}_v\mathcal{H}$ being the impactor of transforming a_1 into a_2, and Ia being the integrating force of A with possibility of: $Ia = \circ$) with the solution

(3.7-6) $x(.) = [\alpha_1 x(\mathbb{H}_1;.) \oplus \alpha_2 x(\mathbb{H}_2;.) \oplus \alpha_3 x(\mathbb{H}_3;.)] \circledast Ix(\mathbb{H}_x;.)$,
where α_2 represents the characteristics for x evolving into φx, α_3 represents the characteristics for x evolving into $\varphi^2 x$, and $Ix(\mathbb{H};.)$ represents the integrating factor of x(.) (here we may have: $Ix(\mathbb{H};.) = \circ$). Further, suppose that we can write in a similar fashion that:

(3.7-7) $B = (b_1 \oplus b_2 \oplus b_3) \circledast Ib = \sigma \Vdash \Sigma^{TC}$,

(here we may have: $Ib = \circ$) with the solution:

(3.7-8) $y(.) = [\beta_1 y(\mathbb{H}_1;.) \oplus \beta_2 y(\mathbb{H}_2;.) \oplus \beta_3 y(\mathbb{H}_3;.)] \circledast Iy(\mathbb{H}_x;.)$,

(here we may have: $Iy(\mathbb{H}_x;.) = \circ$) and

(3.7-9) $C = [c_1 \oplus c_2 \oplus c_3] \circledast Ic = \sigma \Vdash \Sigma^{TC}$,

(here we may have: $Ic = \circ$) with the solution:

(3.7-10) $z(.) = [\gamma_1 z(\mathbb{H}_1;.) \oplus \gamma_2 z(\mathbb{H}_2;.) \oplus \gamma_3 z(\mathbb{H}_3;.)] \circledast Iz(\mathbb{H};.)$

(here we may have: $Iz(\mathbb{H};.) = \circ$).

Now for $X = \{A,B,C\} \sqsubseteq (\Omega,\mathcal{Z}\circ,{}_v\mathcal{H},\{\mathbb{C}\})$ (see Figure 3.7-2), with both of $(A \oplus B \oplus C)$ and $I_{.<C} \sqsubseteq (\Omega,\mathcal{Z}\circ,{}_v\mathcal{H},\{\mathbb{C}\})$, let us write:

Figure 3.7-2
Incomplete Structure of {A,B,C}

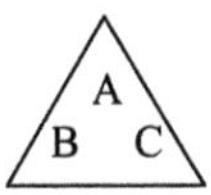

(3.7-11) $X = \{A,B|C\} = (A \oplus B \oplus C) \circledast I_{.<C} = \sigma \Vdash \Sigma^{TC}$,

(B as an Hf-systemism of A, C as a Hh-systemism of A , and I_X can not be an empty system) with the solution:

(3.7-12) $S(.) = [\sigma_1 S(\mathbb{H}_1;.) \oplus \sigma_2 S(\mathbb{H}_2;.) \oplus \sigma_3 S(\mathbb{H}_3;.)] \circledast I_S(\mathbb{H};.)$

with the same interpretations for σ_1, σ_2, σ_3 and $I_S(\mathbb{H};.)$ as in §8.4-3 (where $I_S(\mathbb{H};.)$ can not be an empty system) at the state of simple Tcentral. Then X is called the **large-complex-org system**.

IRI chain system. Here the cultural complex (ρ,ω) includes the incentive talked about often by the economists: the desire to reap financial benefits (for example, see Van Den Berg 2000). Here, ρ and ω represent thc life-will and human rationality, respectively. Actually the general incentive is about "feeling good and having fun in doing things," one ingredient in our sense of ethical foundations.

(i) For the system under the culture of independence, let IE be the mechanism of information-evaluation, RD the mechanism of rational-decision making, and PI the mechanism of planning and policy-implementation. Then, in the following, we have the information-evaluation_rational decision-making_ planning-implementation chain IRI as:

(3.7-13) $IRI = \{IE,RD,PI\} = IE(\rho,\omega) \oplus RD(\rho,\omega) \oplus PI(\rho,\omega)$,

(3.7-14) $x(.) = \alpha_1 x(\mathbb{H}_{IE};.) \oplus \alpha_2 x(\mathbb{H}_{RD};.) \oplus \alpha_3 x(\mathbb{H}_{PI};.)$

(ii) For the culture of conflict:

(3.7-15)
$$\begin{aligned} IRI &= \{IE,RD,PI\} \\ &= (IE \oplus RD \oplus PI)\ ] \circledcirc (I_{IRI}^-, I_{IRI}^+) \\ &= [IE(\rho,\omega) \oplus RD(\rho,\omega) \oplus PI(\rho,\omega)\ ] \circledcirc I_{IRI}(\rho,\omega), \end{aligned}$$

with $I_{IRI}(\rho,\omega) = (I_{\rho,\omega}^-, I_{\rho,\omega}^+)$ being "o" or a structure of negative force.

(iii) For the system under the culture of independence, let the IRI chain be: $IRI = \{IE,RD,PI\} = [(IE \oplus RD \oplus PI)] \circledcirc I_{IRI} = [IE(\rho,\omega) \oplus RD(\rho,\omega) \oplus PI(\rho,\omega)] \circledcirc I_{IRI}(\rho,\omega) = [\rho(IE,RD,PI) \oplus \omega(IE,RD,PI)] \circledcirc I_{IRI}(\rho,\omega)$ with $I_{IRI}(\rho,\omega)$ being a structure of positive force. Then we have:

(3.7-16) $x(.) = [\alpha_1 x(\mathbb{H}_{IE};.) \oplus \alpha_2 x(\mathbb{H}_{RD};.) \oplus \alpha_3 x(\mathbb{H}_{PI};.)] \circledcirc Ix(\mathbb{H};.)$

(3.7-17) $x_{IRI}(.) = [\beta_1 x(\mathbb{H}_\rho;.) \oplus \beta_2 x(\mathbb{H}_\omega;.)] \circledcirc Ix_{IRI}(\mathbb{H}_{\rho,\omega};.)$

MPFX cycle. See Section E.3, we have the cycle: phyK ⟷ (K : **M**)⟷ P ⟷ FS, or the MPFX cycle of capitalism: X = A-C-B-D, A = phyK, B = P, C = (K : **M**) and D = FS. Then we write $X = \{A,B,D|C\} = (A \oplus C \oplus B \oplus D) \circledcirc I_{.<C}$ with following solutions as a **leaf-shaped system** (also see Section E.3)

(3.7-18) $x(.) = [\alpha_1 x(\mathbb{H}_A;.) \oplus \alpha_2 x(\mathbb{H}_B;.) \oplus \alpha_3 x(\mathbb{H}_C;.) \oplus \alpha_4 x(\mathbb{H}_D;.)] \circledcirc Ix(\mathbb{H}_{.<C};.)$

(3.7-19) $x_{MPFX}(.) = [\beta_1 x(\mathbb{H}_\rho;.) \oplus \beta_2 x(\mathbb{H}_\omega;.)] \circledcirc Ix_{MPFX}(\mathbb{H}_{\rho,\omega};.)$

For a graphical presentation of this leaf-shaped system, see Figure E.3-3. As for the other kinds of MPFX cycles, we have:

SIFP chain complex system. Let S, I, F, and P stand for the saving, investment, finance and production functions of a cultural economy, respectively. For this SIFP chain complex, we write $X = \{S,I,P|F\} = (S \oplus I \oplus F \oplus P) \circledcirc I_{.<F}$ with following solutions:

(3.7-20) $x(.) = [\alpha_1 x(\mathbb{H}_S;.) \oplus \alpha_2 x(\mathbb{H}_I;.) \oplus \alpha_3 x(\mathbb{H}_F;.) \oplus \alpha_4 x(\mathbb{H}_P;.)] \circledcirc Ix(\mathbb{H}_{\cdot<F};.)$

(3.7-21) $x_{SIFP}(.) = [\beta_1 x(\mathbb{H}_\rho;.) \oplus \beta_2 x(\mathbb{H}_\omega;.)] \circledcirc Ix_{SIFP}(\mathbb{H}_{\rho,\omega};.)$.

For more details of organizational systems, see Appendix F, Section F.3.

Chapter 4 – Culture and Macroeconomics: Nations and Macro-management

4.1 Introduction

In this chapter we shall study the cultural macroeconomics more or less following the conventional macroeconomics.

Here we shall take the structure of a nation as given. Different nations have different sociopolitical structures. Due to the limitation of space, we basically treat the differences in these sociopolitical aspects as sufficiently manifested in the differences of their cultures.

The prototype nations in this chapter are those with cultures of centralization/ tranquility/ YYWX and decentralization/conflict/sciences.

4.2 CE Centrality and Strategic Centrality

By the convention of Western macroeconomics, one may say the goal of the government of a democratic capitalism is to achieve stability and full employment. While the goal of economic growth is desirable, this may be well beyond the mandate of the government, or beyond much of its ability to do so in the practical sense.

By contrast, for the economic planners of the nations of East Asia, due to the cultural complex being quite different from the culture of the West, the problem facing them is to employ the principles of systemic centrality and sectoral CE balance. Now we derive these principles. To this end, in the above of derivation of Bcm. (3.2-2-4b), we shall replace it by the following:

(4.2-1a)
$$\begin{aligned}&(\varphi\{T\})_{X1,\ldots,Xn}\\ &= (\varphi\{X \curlyvee \Delta\})_{X1,\ldots,Xn,Ix}\\ &= (\varphi\{X,\Delta\})_{X1,\ldots,Xn} \ltimes \varphi\{Ix,E\}\\ &= \varphi\{X\}\otimes(\psi\{Y_j \geq Y_K,\Delta\} \ltimes \varphi\{Ix,E\})\end{aligned}$$

in the case of two-factor dominance, or

(4.2-1b)
$$\begin{aligned}&(\varphi\{T\})_{X1,\ldots,Xn}\\ &= (\varphi\{X \curlyvee \Delta\})_{X1,\ldots,Xn,Ix}\\ &= (\varphi\{X,\Delta\})_{X1,\ldots,Xn} \ltimes \varphi\{Ix,E\}\\ &= \varphi\{X\}\otimes(\psi\{X_1 \stackrel{\star}{=} X_2 \stackrel{\star}{=} \ldots \stackrel{\star}{=} X_n,\Delta\} \ltimes \varphi\{Ix,E\})\end{aligned}$$

(with X_1 being the center) in the case of n-element (or unit) balance.

Then, under the operation of X_i, the basic or grand system reaches a state of CE centrality (or system's continuity) for X (or $X = X^*$): $(\varphi\{T\})_i = X = X^*$.

Consequently, $(\varphi\{T\})_i = X$, $X = \varphi\{X\}\otimes(\psi\{Y_j \geq Y_k,\Delta\} \ltimes \varphi\{Ix,E\})$ in the case of two sub-sectors or subsystems Y_j and Y_k. Then it follows that $\varphi\{X\} = X$, and we have $\{\psi\{Y_j \geq Y_k,\Delta\} \ltimes \varphi\{Ix,E\}) =< T^{CE/C}\} \Subset Ш^{\Delta}$. That is, we derive the **principle of CE centrality** (systemic, or sectoral centrality):

(4.2-2) For each X_i, $\psi\{Y_j>Y_k,\Delta_i\} \doublebarwedge \tau$,

where $\tau \Vdash \mathfrak{J} \Vvdash \mathbb{T}\mathrm{zu}^*$ ($\mathfrak{J}$ being the comprehensive energy directly generated by Ultimate Creativity-Destructivity $\mathbb{T}\mathrm{zu}^*$), or in the case of multiple factors,

(4.2-3) For all i and j, $\psi\{X_i \triangleq X_j,\Delta\} \doublebarwedge \tau$.

Note that, when combined these Bcms. (4.2-2) and (4.2-3) together, what we have is identical to Bcm. (3.2-2-8).

Now we come to the concept of strategic centrality. Let the grand system $X = \{X_1,X_2,\ldots,X_n|C\} \sqsubseteq (\Omega,\mathbb{Z}^{\circ},{}_{v}\mathbb{H},\{\mathbb{C}\})$, where C refers to the central system. Then from $T = X \curlyvee \Delta$, suppose this operation involves the concentration of power by the center, where $\curlyvee \vDash \mathbb{Z}^{\circ},{}_{v}\mathbb{H}$. Let $\mathcal{T} \vDash \mathbb{Z}^{\circ},{}_{v}\mathbb{H}$ be the strategic impactor of the center. Then, for $X_i \neq C$, i =1,2,…,n, we have:

$$
\begin{aligned}
\text{(4.2-4)}\quad TD^G: (\varphi\{T\})_{X1,\ldots,Xn} &= (\varphi\{X \curlyvee \Delta\})_{X1,\ldots,Xn,Ix} \\
&= (\varphi\{X,\Delta\})_{X1,\ldots,Xn} \ltimes \varphi\{Ix,E\} \\
&= \varphi\{X\} \otimes (\psi\{\mathcal{T}^*C>\mathcal{T}X_i,\Delta\} \ltimes \varphi\{Ix,E\}),
\end{aligned}
$$

with $\varphi, \otimes, \psi, \varphi \vDash \mathbb{Z}^{\circ},{}_{v}\mathbb{H}$. Here, by "$\mathcal{T}^*C > \mathcal{T}X_i$" is meant that $\mathcal{T}X_i \Vdash \mathcal{T}^*C$ or $\mathcal{T}X_i$ is part of $\mathcal{T}^*C$. This is due to the hypothesis of a state of CE centrality (or strategic centrality).

Now, for generality we assume that if $X_i \neq C$, then $(\varphi\{T\})_i = \varphi\{X\} \otimes (\psi\{\mathcal{T}^*C= \mathcal{T}C_i,\Delta\} \ltimes \varphi\{Ix,E\})$. Therefore the above becoming transforms into: $(\psi\{\mathcal{T}^*C>\mathcal{T}X_i,\Delta\} \ltimes \varphi\{X_i, E\}) =<T^{CE/C}\} \Subset \text{Ш}^{\Delta}$. Here, by "$\mathcal{T}^*C > \mathcal{T}X_i$" is meant $\mathcal{T}^*C > \mathcal{T}X_i$. Note that if $X_i = C$, then we have $\mathcal{T}^*C = \mathcal{T}C$. That is, for $X = \{X_1,X_2,\ldots,X_n|C\}$, $C = X_{n+1}$, i = 1, 2,…,n+1, the derived **principle of strategic centrality** is:

(4.2-5) For each X_i, $\psi\{\mathcal{T}^*C \geq \mathcal{T}X_i,\Delta_i\} \doublebarwedge \tau$,

or

(4.2-6) For each X_i, $\psi\{\mathcal{T}^*C \geq \mathcal{T}X_i,\Delta_i\} \doublebarwedge \tau$.

This means, for the national planners, the goal is to achieve systematic and strategic centralities of the cultural economy:

(1) To pursuit a strategic advantage of industrial development in order to reap substantial benefits of industrial linkage effects in the process of economic development and advancement.

(2) To pursuit a systematic advantage of global trade in order to create dynamic comparative advantages in global trade over time in a comprehensive manner. These advantages will definitely and uncompromisingly affect the nation's trade position which will in turn determine the common course of the culture at large as well as the technological and sociopolitical structures of that nation.

(3) To pursuit a cultural advantage in order to promote saving, investment and capital formation and to stimulate the growth of qualitative labor and cultural advancement.

Following the conventional wisdom of demand and supply curves and by deriving from the meaning of life becomings, we obtain TS and TD, called the total supply curve and total demand curve, respectively, as follows.

Note that the planners can manipulate TS and TD in carrying out their plans for attempting to achieve the goal of economic development and advancement. Because of the will-to-creation and rationality-to-creation systems underlying these TS and TD curves, the philosophical foundations of these TS and TD systems lie much deeper than that of utilitarianism. Therefore, non-utilitarian concerns can be addressed endogenously.

Below we turn to discuss these TS and TD curves.

Total demand curve. For the general price level φ and the real output y, let us define the multiple-dimensional total demand curve (TD^G) as:

(4.2-7) $\varphi = f(y) + a\mathfrak{C} + bO_d$,
$y = \Sigma_d + C + I^{pv} + I^{pb} + G + (EX\text{-}IM)$,

where a, b being real numbers, $\mathfrak{C}$ being the cultural factors, O_d being all other demand factors related to y, y being the real national income, Σ_d being the residual or inactive actors (or the saving factor) of the total demand, $C \equiv C(.|g)$ being the private sector's consumption demand (g is the government's strategic or policy factor), I^{pv} being the private sector's investment demand, G(.|g) being the government's consumption demand, I^{pb} being the government's or the public sector's investment demand, and EX-IM being the demand of the foreign sector. Here, the role of Σ_d is that as C, I^{pv}, I^{pb}, G or (EX-IM) increases, Σ_d may decrease simultaneously. This shall change the internal composition of TD and thereby releases a Keynesian-type multiplier that shall create a force of shifting the TD curve.

From here, we get the 2-dimensional total demand curve (TD):

(4.2-8) TD: $\varphi = f(y)$,
$y = \Sigma_d + C + I^{pv} + I^{pb} + G + (EX\text{-}IM)$,

Here, TD is assumed to be negatively sloped (also see Additional Topics 3).

Total supply curve. Let $h \equiv h(.)$ be a function of the real output y. For the general price level φ and real output y, let us define the multiple-dimensional total demand curve (TS^G):

(4.2-9) TS^G: $\varphi = h(y) + aO_s$,
$y = Q + \Sigma_s$,
$Q = AK^{\alpha}L^{\beta}\mathfrak{C}^{\gamma}$,

with a and A being parameters, $\mathfrak{C} = (\mathfrak{C}^*, \mathfrak{C}^T)$, $\mathfrak{C}^*$ being the cultural factor not related to technology, $\mathfrak{C}^T$ being the cultural factor underlie the strength of technology, O_s being the set of "other factors" on the supply side, $y = Q + \Sigma_s$ for Σ_s representing the set of residual or inactive factors on the supply side (or the "reserve" of (K,L,$\mathfrak{C}$), $Q = AK^{\alpha}L^{\beta}\mathfrak{C}^{\gamma}$ being the active production function and O_s being the set of "other factors" in the total supply curve. Here technology is the function of active K(.|g), active L(.|g) and $\mathfrak{C}$, and A is not the coefficient of technology. Note that the change in technology, culture and investment, organizational factors and the elements within O_s will cause the whole TS curve to shift. That is, with the TS and TD curves embodying cultural variables directly, the change in the composition of y (i.e., $y = Q + \Sigma_s$) will create a shift of TS curve. For this TS, also see Additional Topics 3.

From Eq. (4.2-6), by eliminating O_s, we obtain the 2-dimensional total supply curve (TS) as follows:

(4.2-10) TS:
$$\varphi = h(y),$$
$$y = Q + \Sigma_s,$$
$$Q = AK^{\alpha}L^{\beta}\mathfrak{C}^{\gamma}.$$

Here in TS and TD respectively, Q and y are functions of government's strategies. The planners play by the rules of systematic and strategic centralities, and TS and TD curves are affected accordingly. Note that by our definition, the cultural variable (or the chain complex of cultural variables) is the complex of the culture in general, organizational factors and strategic factors. Now the planners and the intellectuals of the nation may be in a position to work together to eventually create a new culture of technology that would raise the national income of the nation in a desirable fashion.

Note that we could derive the total supply and total demand curves as in the case of the cultural supply and demand curves. That is, the total supply becoming is in a state of CE centrality (similar to Bcm. (4.2-2) or (4.2-3)): If $\psi\{X_1 \leq X_2, \Delta\} \overline{\wedge} \kappa$, where X_1 is the will-to-creation system (in the macro-sense) and X_2 is the rationality-to-creation system (in the macro-sense), and the system of total supply curve is a grand system: $\{\varphi, y|R^+;O'\}$, where R^+ denotes the relationship between φ (converted from MOL, a meaning of life measure) and y so that they are moving in the same direction, given the condition O' which denotes all other variables being held constant. Note that this grand system $\{\varphi, y|R^+;O'\}$ is nothing but the Going-up BCM in the above Subsection 3.3. Further, in the grand system $\{\varphi, y|R^+;O'\}$, this $\{\varphi, y\} \equiv \{\varphi, y|C\}$, with $C = (G, \mathfrak{C}_{c0})$ may also be treated as a system with the government serving as the center and the cultural core underlying this system ($\mathfrak{C}_{c0}$) serving as the virtual center. Also note that this culture core $\mathfrak{C}$ differs for different countries due to differences in geographical conditions, historical forces and cultural heritage. Here the concept of supply becoming $\{\varphi(\omega,\rho), y(\omega,\rho)|C\}$ is defined as the ability and willingness to produce for sale.

Cultural development is important in developing indigenous technology and eventually exporting one's culture to the outside world. We shall come back to this topic in Chapter 5. Below in Appendix F (Section F.4), we present a TS-TD model to bridge a gap between our systematic approach and the conventional approach to macroeconomics.

Remark 4.2-1. A conventional way to define AS is as follows in the spirit of Mankiw (2003). On the first quadrant of the Cartesian coordinate system with vertical axis φ and horizontal axis y, we shall define the short run AS as a horizontal curve and the long run AS a vertical curve. Then, in order to derive the short run and long run equilibrium points of AD and AS, let the intersection point of the short run and long run AS curves be E. Then, in one case, let AD intersect AS on the left hand side of E and denote this point as A; and in the other case, let AD intersect AS on the right hand side of E and denote this point as B. In both cases, the economy will gradually move downward away from the disequilibrium points and will eventually reach some equilibrium points (see Figure 4.2-1). In Panels (c) and (d), the spirit of non-governmental intervention is very much there. In a free market, the equilibrium of the market (in actuality, the macro economy) will be automatically restored by the forces of price adjustment (i.e., deflation in the case of Panel (c) and inflation in the case of Panel (d)). Note that, in general, the case of Panel (c) may not match the reality of a modern macroeconomy since inflation occurs more often but deflation is rare in modern time.

Figure 4.2-1
Short and long run equilibrium of the macroeconomy: (a) and (b) under horizontal SRAS curve with no shift of AD curve; (c) and (d): shift of AD curve

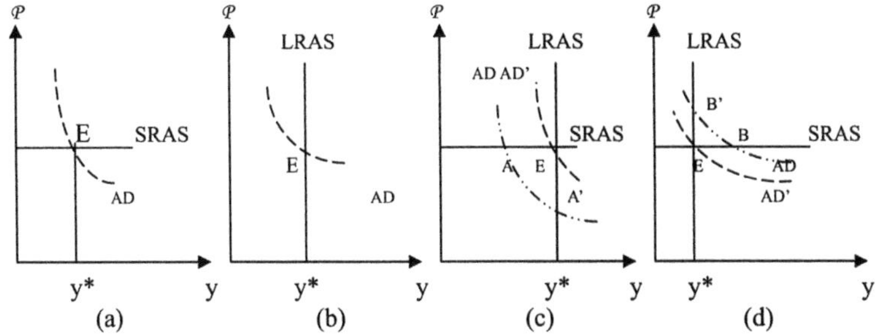

As an alternative to the above model, we may have as well an AS-AD model with an upward sloping SRAS curve (see Figure 4.2-2).

In the following, we define a few very useful concepts of macroeconomics. Unemployment is defined as not being able to find a job for a healthy person of eighteen year old or older who is actively searching for a job. Inflation is defined as a continuous rise in the general price level. The quantity theory of money is the one with the equation of exchange: MV = $\mathcal{P}$y. That is, the amount of money in circulation is identical to the total value of transactions in an economy. As for the process of money creation, it is a process of money expansion through the modern finance-banking system in an economy.

Figure 4.2-2
Upward-sloping SRAS curve: E = equilibrium point; Y_N = LR natural rate of the real national income

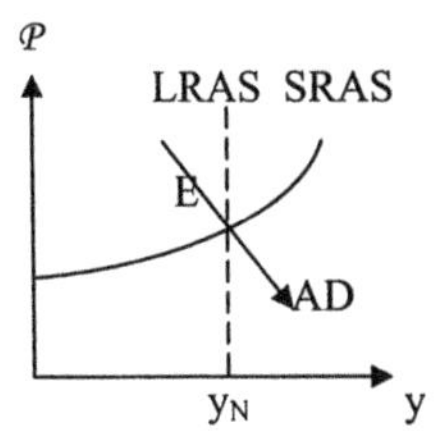

Remark 4.2-1. TS curve can be derived from a sum of cs curves with adjustment, and TD curve can also be derived from a sum of cd curves with adjustment. For an economy of conflict culture, the adjustment factor must be negative, while for an economy of tranquil

culture, the adjustment factor is expected to be less negative than in the case of conflict culture.

In the case of conflict culture, to go from cs system (see Section 3.4) to TS system, we have: TS = $\Phi\{cs_i,\}$, for Φ being an integrating impactor. Here, TS can be considered as a grand system with either the market (in the case of conflict culture) or the government (in the case of tranquil culture) as the virtual center. Then, by transforming from MOL to price (in the micro case) or prices (in the macro case), we have the aggregate macro variable derive from the micro variables.

Similarly, we can establish the relationship between the TD curve and the cd curves.

Remark 4.2-2 (T derivative). Note that T derivative is the "inverse" of T integral, and this adjustment factor in T derivative may be measured by the method of statistics (see Remark 4.2-4). For the original idea of this T integral, see Tonn (1994). This approach of T calculus may be called the mathematics of mutuality, in contrast to the conventional mathematics, the mathematics of (independence and) individuality.

Remark 4.2-3 (T derivative). To go from an element of system-creation to a system, in the case of culture of conflict, the whole system must be adjusted by an adversary factor. That is, in the system X = {a,b,c}, a being the system-creating element, Ψ being the system-creating impactor, and $X = \Phi\{a\} = (a \oplus b \oplus c) \circledast Ix$ with Ix being an adversary factor.

For a real number x, the regular formula of the integral of x in [a,b] is: $\int_{[a,b]} x dx = \lim_{i\to\infty} \Sigma_i x_i \Delta x_i$, Δx_i being the infinite partition of x in [a,b]. But our formula for the T integral would be: $(\int x dx)^T = \lim_{i\to\infty} (\Sigma_i x_i + \Sigma_{i\neq j} x_i \star x_j)\Delta x_i$, where $\star \vDash \mathbb{Z}\circ,_v\mathbb{H}$ is the interaction impactor in an operation of association impactor $\star \vDash \mathbb{Z}\circ,_v\mathbb{H}$ (with appropriate "mathematization," see Bcm (A.2-3-6-1)). In the case of mutually beneficial interactions (or under the culture of tranquility), this term $\Sigma_{i \neq j} x_i \star x_j$ will not vanish and be positive. Thus, $(\int x dx)^T > \int x dx$. In the case of the culture of conflict, we shall have: $(\int x dx)^T < \int x dx$. Hence, for a system under the culture of conflict, the value of the T integral must be smaller than the value of Riemann or Riemann-Stieljes integral. Conversely, the value of the T derivative must be greater than the value of Riemann or Riemann-Stieljes derivative. Naturally, the opposite is true in the case of tranquil culture.

For a system A = {u,v,w}, let a be the system-creating element and Φ be the system-creating impactor, with $A = \Phi\{u\} = (u \oplus v \oplus w) \circledast I_A$, for Ix being an integrating factor. Below let us set up the counter part of this system in mathematics as follows: For u, v, w being functions of x, $x \in (U,V,W)$, $u \in U$, $v \in V$, $w \in W$, the "integral" of A is:

$$(\int A dx)^T = \int u dx + \int v dx + \int w dx + \lim_{i\to\infty} [\Sigma_{i\neq j\neq k}\, u(x_i)\star v(x_j)\star w(x_k)]\Delta x_i,$$

where $[\Sigma_{i\neq j\neq k}\, u(x_i)\star v(x_j)\star w(x_k)]\Delta x_i$ (with a positive sign in the case of tranquil culture and a negative sign in the case of conflict culture underlying the system A) is the counter part of I_A in the system A. Note that the other expression of this "integral" is:

$$(\int A dx)^T = \int_{x\in U(x)} u dx + \int_{x\in V(x)} v dx + \int_{x\in W(x)} w dx + \int_{x\in(U,V,W)} y(x) dx,$$

where $\int_{x\in(U,V,W)} y(x) dx = \lim_{i\to\infty} [\Sigma_{i\neq j\neq k}\, u(x_i)\star v(x_j)\star w(x_k)]\Delta x_i$, for $y(x) = u(x)\star v(x)\star\, w(x)$. That is, $(\int A dx)^T$ is not equal to the conventionally defined integral:

$\int A dx \equiv \int_{x \in U(x)} u dx + \int_{x \in V(x)} v dx + \int_{x \in W(x)} w dx.$

Remark 4.2-4 (T statistics). Let X be a random variable, and let the mathematical expectation and variance of X be E[X] and Var[X], respectively. By using the association impactor (☆), we have E^T [X] (T mathematical expectation of X): $E^T[X] = E[X] + E[\Sigma_{i \neq j} X_i \star X_j]$, for X_i being the ith observation of X, i = 1,...,n, and $Var^T[X]$ (the T variance of X): $Var^T[X] = Var[X] + Var[\Sigma_{i \neq j} X_i \star X_j]$.

4.3 Culture-Determined IS and LM Curves

Below we shall derive the cultural IS curve first by fixing the levels of culture and technology. Then, by the introduction of cultural variable, we shall shift the curves.

Figure 4.3-1
Cultural IS Curve B'A" (r direction: r↓ ⇒ y⇈)

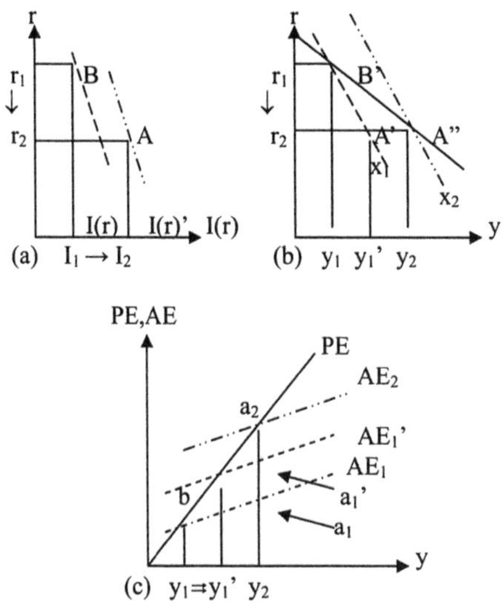

Cultural IS curve. (1) Let us proceed from the direction of a decrease in r that will cause Y to increase (i.e., r direction: r↓ ⇒ y↑, i.e., r↓ ⇒ y⇈). In Figure 4.3-1 presented below, in Panel (a), let the real interest rate r be reduced, then by allowing consumption and real national income to increase, the investment curve I shifts to the right (i.e., $I_1 \rightarrow I_2$) and, as r decreases, the equilibrium point B shifts to point A. In Panel (b), by allowing consumption and investment to increase, the curve X_1 shifts to the right and becomes X_2 curve, and as r decreases, the equilibrium point B' first shifts to point A' (b' → a') and then to point A". In Panel (c) of this Figure, the increase in investment without any concurrent increase in consumption causes AE_1 shifting upward to AE_1' curve; but if both of consumption and investment increase, then AE_1 curve shifts further upward to AE_2 curve. That is, the increase in consumption shifts AE_1'curve upward to AE_2 Curve. And as $r_1 \uparrow r_2$, the equilibrium point b moves to a_1, and then jumps to a_1', and finally to a_2.

In sum, as the whole cultural system changes, seeing from Figure 4.3-1 (Panels (a) and (c)), it causes I curve shifting to the right and AE curve shifting upward. But if only some micro-cultures change, while other micro-cultures kept intact, then (seeing from Figure (4.3-1), Panels (a) and (c)), both I and AE curves rotate and shift somewhat, depending on the specific situation. After all the concerns are addressed, then we derive the desirable cultural IS curve by connecting these points B' and A" on Panel (b) of Figure 4.3-1.

In the above derivation of the IS curve, see Panel (c) of Figure 4.3-1, if consumption is assumed to be constant, then, the increase in investment causes the real output to go up ($I\uparrow \rightarrow y\uparrow$), and by this, it is required to have an equilibrium condition: AE = PE. That is, with this equilibrium condition, $I\uparrow \rightarrow y\uparrow \Rightarrow b \rightarrow a_2$ (a_2 being on both curves AE_2 and PE). Without this equilibrium condition, we have $I\uparrow \rightarrow y\uparrow \Rightarrow b \rightarrow a_1$, or $b \rightarrow a_1$' (a_1 being on AE_1 curve, a_1' on AE_1' curve, and both not on PE curve), and the derivation of the IS curve fails.

Here the shift of $AE_1 \rightarrow AE_1$' is caused by favorable cultural conditions associated with the increase in I along the I(r) curve as r going down (see Panels (a) and (c)). To ensure the equilibrium, we must have: $AE_1 \rightarrow AE_2$, i.e., a further shift created by some even more favorable cultural conditions. By conventional approach, in order to close the disequilibrium gap, these shifts must be safeguarded by significant multiplier effects.

According to the economic logic, $I\uparrow \rightarrow y\uparrow \Rightarrow b \rightarrow a_1$', creates a disequilibrium: AE > AP. This desirable level of cultural total supply is greater than the desirable level of cultural total demand and this creates a logical break down. Certainly, if this error of margin is not big, then for the practical purpose, this logical problem may not be serious. Note that in the conventional approach, this gap is covered by the multiplier effect. But this is not consistent with the mathematical logic. Since Y = C + I + G + (EX-IM), any change in C, I or G will be taken care of by the change in Y itself. That is, in this case, C, I and G are not shift factors.

This possible inconsistency of logic may be removed by imposing a cultural solution to ensure the equilibrium condition (without tension): with appropriate cultural conditions, some changes in the cultural variables shift the AE curve and so that a new equilibrium is achieved. With the systematic reasoning, the consistency of the cultural IS curve is safeguarded. That is, with favorable cultural conditions, the slope of the cultural IS curve may be reasonable, i.e., neither very steep nor very flat. But with less favorable cultural conditions, the slope of the cultural IS curve may be very steep, and render it not very useful for policy purpose.

(2) In Figure 4.3-2, we proceed from the direction of an increase in national income Y which will then lower the real interest rate r (i.e., y direction: $y\uparrow \Rightarrow r\downarrow$, i.e., $y\uparrow \Rightarrow r\Downarrow$, an opposite direction to the above reasoning in Figure 4.3-1). In Panel (c), let the real national income increase. We see that, when investment increases but consumption is fixed, AE_1 curve shifts to AE_1' (i.e., $b \rightarrow a_1$' $\Leftrightarrow$ B' $\rightarrow$ A'); by allowing the consumption level to increases as investment increases, then AE_1 curve shifts to AE_2 (i.e., a_1' $\rightarrow a_2$).

That is, AE_1' curve shifts to AE_2 because consumption is also allowed to increase. In Panel (b), by allowing consumption and investment to increase, X_1 curve shifts to X_2 curve on the right (i.e., B' $\rightarrow$ A"). Seen from Panel (a) of Figure 4.3-1, this investment curve I shifts to the right ($I_1 \rightarrow I_2$) (i.e., B $\rightarrow$ A). The desirable cultural IS curve is derived by connecting these points B' and A".

Figure 4.3-2
Cultural IS Curve B'A" (y direction: $y\uparrow \Rightarrow r\downdownarrows$)

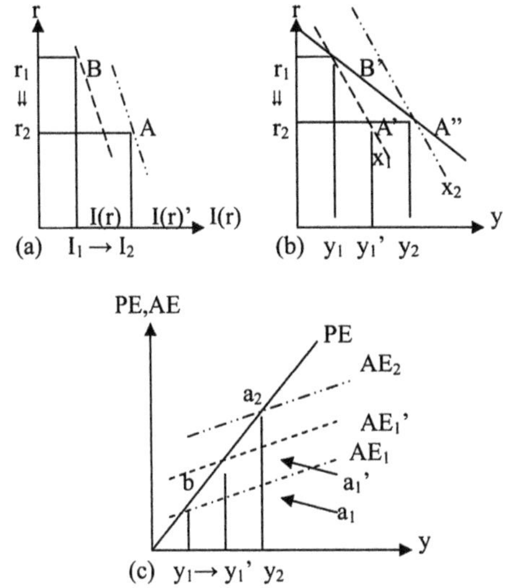

As the overall culture changes, in Figure 4.3-2, in Panels (a) and (c), I and AE curves both change, causing I curve to shift to the right. But if only a few micro cultures change, while most of the micro-cultures remain constant, then in Panels (a) and (c), I and AE curves may rotate and shift a bit, depending on specific situations.

In the above derivation of the cultural IS curve, consumption may be assumed to be fixed. Then for the increase in investment that would raise the level of real output ($I\uparrow \rightarrow y\uparrow$), an equilibrium condition is required: AE = PE, and therefore: $I\uparrow \rightarrow y\uparrow \Rightarrow b \rightarrow a_2$, but not $b \rightarrow a_1$' (the equilibrium point a_2 is on the intersection of AE_2 and PE; but the disequilibrium point a_1' is on AE_1' by assuming that the increase in I acts like a shift factor, not on AE). By the economic logic (but without imposing any additional equilibrium condition), $I\uparrow \rightarrow y\uparrow \Rightarrow b \rightarrow a_1$', creating a disequilibrium: AE < PE. Then, consumption is insufficient and the real output decreases: $b \nrightarrow a_2$, but $b \rightarrow a_1$', creating a possible inconsistency in economic logic. Note that if we proceed from the direction of $y\downarrow \Rightarrow r\uparrow$, then we would not have this problem of inconsistency. That is, the derivations of the cultural IS curve from these two directions are different: IS($r\downarrow \Rightarrow y\uparrow$) $\nLeftrightarrow$ IS($r\uparrow \Rightarrow y\downarrow$).

Note that the slope of the IS curve may be very steep at the time of recession or slow economic growth, essentially depending on the profitability of firms borrowing for expanding business, but then the effectiveness of fiscal and monetary policies based on this IS-LM approach may be limited. Further, as $r\downarrow$ or $r\uparrow$, if the business environment is not favorable (for the capitalist economy), the magnitude of the impact of this change in r on the investment (i.e., the increase or decrease in investment) and thereby the economy may be very limited. That is, unless the cultural variable works to the benefit of this model, the IS-LM theory may be ineffective in dealing with the macroeconomic problems. Since the definition of cultural variables includes the private and public policies and strategic activities, with favorable business expectation, enthusiastic entrepreneurial spirit, government fiscal policy, and national industrial and advancement policies, the derivation of the cultural IS curve is then complete. Note that under the theoretical conditions of definite derivation, without any help provided by the cultural variables, the slope of the derived cultural IS curve may rotate and become very steep, while with the incomplete assistance rendered by the cultural variables, the slope of the IS curve may still be relatively steep. For these concerns, we may call these the **rotation factors** of the cultural IS curve.

Cultural LM Model. (1) Let us proceed from the direction of an increase in Y which would be expected to raise r (i.e., $y\uparrow \Rightarrow r\uparrow$). In the following Figure 4.3.3, in Panel (a), let the real output y increase. Then, $L(r,y_1)$ shifts upward to $L(r,y_2)$ in equilibrium. The result is then: $r_1 \rightarrow r_2$, or an increase in the real interest on Panel (a) of Figure 4.3-3. Then on Panel (b), by connecting points A' and B', the cultural LM curve is derived.

Now, we have an equilibrium achieved in the financial market: $A \rightarrow B$ in Panel (a), where the desired level of the demand for real cash balances is equal to the desired level of the real supply of money (at point B).

Figure 4.3-3
Cultural LM Curve: $y \uparrow \Rightarrow r \uparrow$ with $m = M/\mathcal{P}$

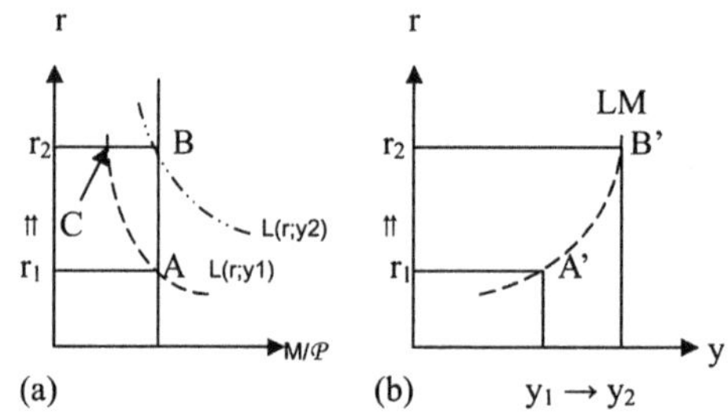

Note that, in the case of disequilibrium (see below), the logic under the derivation of the celebrated LM curve beaks down. But if the slope of the desired demand curve for real cash balances is very steep, then the error of margin in this derivation of the LM curve may be acceptable. As in the case of deriving the cultural IS curve, this disequilibrium gap can be closed by some changes in the cultural variables.

(2) Below, let us proceed from the direction of an increase in r which will then raise the level of national income y (i.e., $r\uparrow \Rightarrow y\uparrow$). In Panel (a) of Figure 4.3-3, let the real interest rises ($r_1 \rightarrow r_2$). Here we impose an equilibrium condition: as $y\uparrow$, $A \rightarrow B$, $A \nrightarrow C$. Then $L(r,y_1)$ shifts upward to $L(r,y_2)$. That is, $y_1 \rightarrow y_2$, or the real output y rises. In Panel (b), we connect the points A' and B' to reach the cultural LM curve.

Here, the equilibrium condition "r↑ ⇒ (A→B) ^ (A↛C)" may not be realistic. Because the rise in r just induces a movement along the demand for real cash balances curve. Then the economic activities remain the same: $y_1 \nrightarrow y_2$, or $y_1 \rightarrow y1$. This shall create a problem of inconsistency in the derivation of the conventional LM curve.

To remove the problem of inconsistency in deriving the IS and LM curves, let us define the cultural IS curve as, either (i) a downward sloping curve in the first quadrant of the Cartesian r-y coordinate system, or (ii) a vertical line. Then, the shift effect of the cultural variables is needed in case the cultural IS curve is vertical (i.e., in disequilibrium).

Figure 4.3-4
Cultural LM Curve: r↑⇒ y↑ with m = M/$\mathcal{P}$

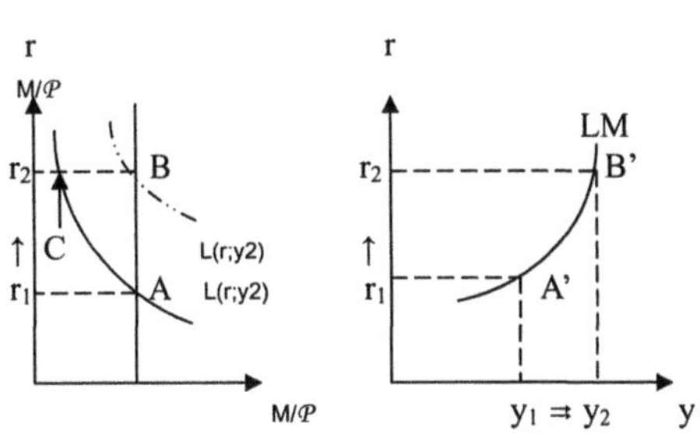

In contrast, for the cultural LM curve, first, assume that the cultural LM curve is either (i) an upward sloping curve in the first quadrant of the Cartesian r-y coordinate system, or (ii) a horizontal line. Noet that, the shapes (or slopes) of these cultural IS and LM curves are determined by the respective strengths of the cultural variables underlying these curves.

Below is an alternative way to remove the problem of inconsistency in the derivation of the cultural IS and LM curves. Suppose the original IS curve (i.e., the one without any concerns for the cultural variables) is a downward sloping curve on the first quadrant of the Cartesian r-y coordinate system.

Then, we take the following steps. (i) The cultural IS* curve is a downward sloping curve to be derived as follows. Let C_{AS} be a downward sloping curve on the first quadrant of the Cartesian r-y coordinate system as well. Here, this C_{AS} curve depicts the production-cultural curve under the assumption of diminishing marginal productivity. Then, with the operations of culture forces, both of these IS and C_{AS} curves shift, and the collection of the intersections of these two curves constitutes the downward sloping cultural IS* curve.

(ii) The cultural IS* curve is a vertical line on the first quadrant of the Cartesian r-y coordinate system, to be derived as follows. Let C_{AS} be a vertical line on the first quadrant of the Cartesian r-y coordinate system. With the operations of cultural forces, the original IS curve and the C_{AS} curve would both shift, and the collection of the intersections of these two curves constitutes the vertical cultural IS* curve.

(iii) The cultural IS* curve is an upward sloping curve on the first quadrant of the Cartesian r-y coordinate system, to be derived as follows. Let C_{AS} be an upward sloping curve on the first quadrant of the Cartesian r-y coordinate system. As the cultural forces exert their influence on the social economy, both of the original IS curve and the C_{AS} curve shift. Then the collection of the intersections of these two curves under various shifting conditions constitutes the upward sloping cultural IS* curve.

Similarly, we derive the cultural LM* curve in the following. (i) The cultural LM* curve is an upward sloping curve to be derived as follows. Let the original LM and C_{AD} curves be upward sloping on the first quadrant of the Cartesian r-y coordinate system, with the slope of C_{AD} be less than that of the original LM curve. Here, C_{AD} curve depicts the consumption cultural curve under the assumption of diminishing marginal MOL or utility. With cultural forces in operation, these two curves shift, and by collecting all the intersections points of these two curves sifting under various cultural conditions, the upward sloping cultural LM* curve is derived.

(ii) The cultural LM* curve is a vertical line to be derived as follows. Let the original LM curve be a downward sloping curve on the first quadrant of the Cartesian r-y coordinate system and C_{AD} curve be a horizontal line on the first quadrant of the Cartesian r-y coordinate system, with the slope of C_{AD} be less than that of the original LM curve. Here, C_{AD} curve depicts the consumption cultural curve under the assumption of constant marginal MOL or utility. With cultural forces in operation, these two curves shift, and by collecting all the intersections points of these two curves sifting under various cultural conditions, the vertical cultural LM* curve is then derived.

(iii) The cultural LM* curve is an downward sloping curve to be derived as follows. Let the original LM curve be an upward sloping curve on the first quadrant of the Cartesian r-y coordinate system and C_{AD} curve an upward sloping curve on the first quadrant of the Cartesian r-y coordinate system as well. Here, C_{AD} curve depicts the consumption cultural curve under the assumption of diminishing marginal MOL or utility. With cultural forces in operation, these two curves shift, and by collecting all the intersections points of these two curves sifting under various cultural conditions, the downward-sloping cultural LM* curve is then derived.

Related to the above analysis, the cultural IS* and LM* schemes can be written as $(I=S) \oplus \langle C_{I=S} \rangle$ and $(L=M) \oplus \langle C_{L=M} \rangle$, respectively. As for the interactions of the IS* and LM* schemes, they can be represented as the following becoming: $(I=S,L=M) \oplus \langle C_{I=S,L=M} \rangle$.

4.4 Production Function

Before leaving this Chapter, let us present a model of production function in terms of the upward sloping short-term TS curve (STTS) and the vertical long-term TS curve (STTS). Below, STTD and LTTD represent the short-term and long-term TD curves, respectively.

Seen in Figure 4.4-1, as K, L or $\mathfrak{C}$ grows, in the short term perspective, the real income will grow (i.e., the income effect, implied by the mathematical specification of $y = y(K,L,\mathfrak{C})^{+}$. That is, the (real) output level will grow from y to y' (i.e., A $\rightarrow$ B) given that the short-term total demand curve (STTD) curve will correspond automatically.

Figure 4.4-1
STTS, LTTS and Y

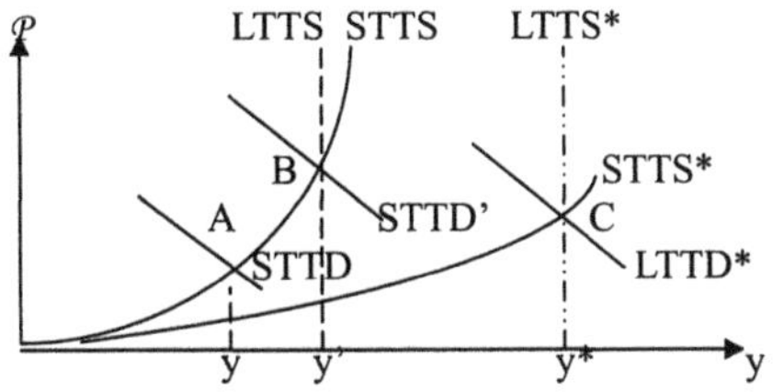

But in the long-term perspective, as K, L or ℭ grows, the long-term total supply curve (LTTS) will shift from LTTS to LTTS*, and correspondingly the short-term total supply curve will rotate from STTS to STTS*. Here it is assumed that the long-term total demand curve (LTTD) curve will correspond automatically to and hence reach the point of intersection between STTS* and LTTS*.

In the above, the forces of rotation and shift are jointly created by the organizational, strategic and cultural effects in the total supply side and by the multiplier effect in the total or aggregate demand side.

4.5 A Theory of Technological Change and Its Relationship with The IRI Chain

As a general rule, between different stages, we see discontinuity of technological change. But between any two consecutive phases within a stage, continuity of technological change may occur and a process of the accumulation of small changes in technology may be observed as well.

Technological adoption: take a link (i.e., the result of a stage of the technological development) without moving on the process of technological change (or changing the technology).

Technological imitation and modification: take a link of technology (i.e., the result of a stage of the technological development) and moving on to new phases of technological change without evolving into a new stage of technological change.

Technological change is a process of multiple-stage changes, presumably a multiple-pole MFCE scheme (for a 5-pole MFCE scheme, see Remark 6.2-2).

Now let us set up a 5-polar (or sub-system) MFCE scheme: {O, R, ℭ, T, and E}, where O stands for the unit system of observing the objects or events, R stands for that of reflection, ℭ stands for that of the cultural core as is existing in myself, T stands for that of theoretical formulation (or abstraction), and E stands for that of experimentation and confirmation of new technology. Due to the limitation of space, in terms of graphical presentation, we shall only have the O-R-ℭ sub-scheme in our discussion.

Figure 4.5-1
O-R-$\mathfrak{C}$ sub-scheme in the O-R-$\mathfrak{C}$-T-E scheme

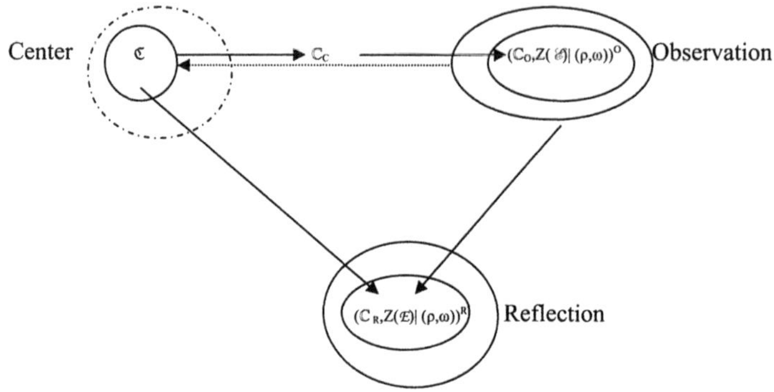

That is, from the center ($\mathfrak{C}$) of the O-R-$\mathfrak{C}$-T-E scheme, the energy ($\mathbb{C}_C$) is emitting from the center and then transfers itself into the O sub-scheme (i.e., the sub-system of Observation) and becomes $\mathbb{C}_O$ (the energy of O sub-system), and simultaneously, the center is receiving the feed-back energy going backward into it (i.e., from O sub-system). For the O sub-system, it is receiving the energy from the center while at the same time it is receiving the transforming energy from the E sub-system of the previous phase (or stage) as well. That is to say, the joint becoming process of the "energy from the center" and "the transforming energy from the Ec sub-system" generates the O sub-system (with the energy $\mathbb{C}_O$ of the system). Then moving forward to another node (or link) of the O-R-$\mathfrak{C}$-T-E scheme, we have the Reflection sub-system receiving the energy from the center while at the same time receiving the transforming energy from the O sub-system as well. That is to say, the joint becoming process of the "energy from the center" and "the transforming energy from the O sub-system" generates the Reflection sub-system (with the energy $\mathbb{C}_R$ of the system, see Figure 4.5-1). Here by a node (linkage) is meant an essential inter-connector in-between two parts or sections of a chain complex.

In the following, in terms of the regular MFCE scheme, we have:

$$(4.5\text{-}1)\quad \Phi^{O}\{<\mathbb{C}_{Axis/Z}>\} = <\frac{\mathbb{C}_O}{\mathfrak{C}_Z}> = \frac{<\mathbb{C}_O>}{Z(\mathcal{E})},$$

where Φ^O is the impactor in the process of generating the O system, and the Axis represents the core culture of the O-R-$\mathfrak{C}_{mc}$-T-Ec scheme (Axis $\equiv \mathfrak{C}_{co}$, or $\mathfrak{C}_{mc}$ in this case) which serves as the virtual center of the scheme-system. Then, by the operation of $\Phi^{-R} \equiv (\Phi^R)^{-1}$ (i.e., invertor of Φ^R) we get:

$$(4.5\text{-}2)\ \Phi^{-R}\ \{\frac{\langle \mathbb{C}_O \rangle}{Z(\mathcal{E})}\} = O,$$

where O depicts the O sub-system.

In this O-R-$\mathfrak{C}$-T-E scheme, let us suppose that each of O, R, T and E nodes are all becomings of the IRI chain. Then we come to the IRI scheme from which we derive the human-side energy of creativity in the process of technological development or advancement. From Bcm. (3.7-15), we have: IRI = {IE,RD,PI} = $[IE(\rho,\omega) \oplus RD(\rho,\omega) \oplus PI(\rho,\omega)\ ] \circledast I_{IRI}(\rho,\omega)$ for a general culture, and we have: IRI = {IE,RD,PI} = $[(IE \oplus RD \oplus PI)] \circledast I_{IRI} = [\rho(IE,RD,PI) \oplus \omega(IE,RD,PI)] \circledast I_{IRI}(\rho,\omega)$ (for a general culture).

Now let the IRI chain be a becoming of the "seed" of technological creativity of the human being. That is, we have IRI = $IRI[(\rho,\omega)_{(\tau)}]$, where $\tau \Vdash \mathfrak{I} \Vvdash \mathbb{T}zu^*$ is thought to be the seed of the ultimate human creativity.

Two micro-processes of technological change: (i) dialectical process:

$$(4.5\text{-}3)\ \kappa \rightarrow \varphi(\kappa) \Rightarrow \varphi^2(\kappa), \text{ and thus } x(\kappa) \rightarrow x(\varphi(\kappa)) = \psi(x) \Rightarrow x(\varphi^2(\kappa)) = \psi^2(x),$$

for the destructive or restraining force $\kappa \leadsto \tau$ ($\tau \Vdash \mathfrak{I} \Vvdash \mathbb{T}zu^*$) and some $\varphi, \psi \vDash Z_{O,\vee}\mathcal{H}$; and (ii) yinyang harmonious process:

$$(4.5\text{-}4)\ \sigma \rightarrow \xi(\sigma) \Rightarrow \zeta(\sigma,\xi(\sigma)),$$

$$(4.5\text{-}5)\ x(\sigma) \rightarrow x(\xi(\sigma)) = \alpha(x) \Rightarrow x(\zeta(\sigma,\xi(\sigma))) = \beta(x,\alpha(x)),$$

for the creative or generating force $\sigma \leadsto \tau$ ($\tau \Vdash \mathfrak{I} \Vvdash \mathbb{T}zu^*$) and some $\alpha, \beta, \xi, \xi \vDash Z_{O,\vee}\mathcal{H}$. Note that the seeds of technological creativity are products (becomings) of one's individual temperament, social culture, political structure, and national policies and strategies of technological development.

We may say that the creation of new technology involves these two processes just presented in the above. From one thing, one creates different thing. This is a positive step to develop technology. But then, in the next step, one is to find the similarity or sameness between these two different things in order to synthesize to a higher level. In mathematics, one sets out to find an isomorphism; that is, these two things are different from the ordinary perspective. And yet they share the same structure from a particular angle (i.e., in terms of algebraic structure).

Note that, in general, this IRI-related seed of creativity works to transform forces between different stages, between different phases and within a single phase of technological change. In particular, in the afore-mentioned 5-polar scheme, {O, R, $\mathfrak{C}$, T, and E}, this seed of creativity also works to form a link and then transfer energies in-between any two links. The forces of synthesis come from the center, and the forces of differentiation, opposition or development come mainly from each link (or node) itself.

Definition 4.5-1. The **culture of macro-tech/tranquility** is the culture of human-social tranquility so that the tempo of macro-technological development is fast and yet the tempo of micro-technological development is slow.

Definition 4.5-2. The **culture of micro-tech/conflict** is the culture of human-social conflict so that the tempo of micro-technological development is fast and yet the tempo of macro-technological development is slow.
Definition 4.5-3. The **culture of micro- and macro-tech/conflict** is the culture of human-social conflict so that the tempo of micro-technological development and that of macro-technological development are fast.

Below, we shall have more discussions about the IRI chain. To advance the idea of the will-rationality complex as a composite or integrated force of generation and restraint/destruction, let us write the IRI chain as follows:

$$
\begin{aligned}
(4.5\text{-}6)\quad & \mathrm{IRI} \\
&= \mathrm{IRI}[(\rho,\omega)_{(\tau)}] \\
&= \mathrm{IRI}[\sigma(\rho,\omega)_{(\tau)},\kappa(\rho,\omega)_{(\tau)}],
\end{aligned}
$$

where $\sigma(\rho,\omega)_{(\tau)}$ (or $\{\tau|(\rho,\omega)\}^{S}$) represents the force of generation and construction (sheng) and $\kappa(\rho,\omega)_{(\tau)}$ (or $\{\tau|(\rho,\omega)\}^{K}$) represents the force of restraint and destruction (ke).

Tranquil culture is one with a tendency toward seeking commonality among different elements or sub-systems. It is weaker in self-generative force, and yet very strong in a group force forging mutually reinforcing development. And if there is a strong consensus among all members of the system, then under this tranquil culture, a synthetic and even internally well integrated grand idea may be produced. The strength of this cultural system is therefore the great ability inherited and embodied in its systemic dynamics in creating a totally new idea of higher levels. But the weakness of this culture is obvious in that its way of thinking is not so clear, definite and logical (as compared with that in the culture of conflict, or actually the culture of sciences). Note that although the “systemic way of thinking,” both classical and especially modern, is not “logical and mathematical,” it is far more systematic and better fitted to the studies of human and social subject matters. One may argue that the weakness of the tranquil culture (actually that of the culture of classical systemic thinking) was caused by a strong and hard-to-subdue desire to formulate useful schemes in attempting to present the true state of affairs, events and things. This is a holistic view of treating subjects, in a sharp contrast to the micro-view of relying upon an impulse to penetrate deeply into the mathematical and quantitative worlds of things. The limitations of this holistic view in the classical systemic approach are obvious, because it is hard to develop new, different and even opposing ideas by following this approach.

There is no internal conflict in the IRI chain of a tranquil culture. For a system of the tranquil culture, in developing a new culture through the operations of its IRI chain, although it is more likely to choose a correct path (relative to the operations of the IRI chain of a system of conflict culture), the tempo and motion of the system may be less energetic. This may be due to the greater constraints of the IRI chain placed upon the developmental momentum for the system of tranquil culture. Nevertheless, the energy and scale of organizing operations of this system is far greater.

Here for the IE-RD-PI chain, in the IE link, due to the profound consensus among members of the system, all the information transmitting from it are of similar nature. Therefore, in the RD link, it is easy for the main body of the information to be communicated to the decision-maker, and it greatly facilitates the process of rational plan to be formulated. And in the PI link, effective execution of plans is made easy by the consensus reached among the members of the

RD link and those of the PI link. This is especially true because the decision-maker and those responsible for the implement of the plan have the same cultural orientation and the same benefit/cost measure. Nevertheless, the quality of the IRI chain may not be satisfactory due to the fact that diversity is lacking, accuracy is much desired, and more in-depth analysis may be needed in order to perfect this chain. In terms of the mechanisms of the IRI, for "∘" $\models \mathbb{Z}_{\circ,\vee}\mathbb{H}$ being an interactor, we have:

(4.5-7) IRI

$$= IRI[(\rho,\omega)_{(\tau)}]$$
$$= IRI[\sigma(\rho,\omega)_{(\tau)},\kappa(\rho,\omega)_{(\tau)}],$$
$$= IRI[\sigma(\rho,\omega)_{(\tau)},\kappa_M(\rho,\omega)_{(\tau)}],$$
$$= IE[\sigma_s(\rho,\omega)_{(\tau)},\sigma_M(\rho,\omega)_{(\tau)},\kappa_M(\rho,\omega)_{(\tau)}]\circ RD[\sigma_s(\rho,\omega)_{(\tau)}, \sigma_M(\rho,\omega)_{(\tau)},\kappa_M(\rho,\omega)_{(\tau)}]$$
$$\circ\, PI[\sigma_s(\rho,\omega)_{(\tau)},\sigma_M(\rho,\omega)_{(\tau)},\kappa_M(\rho,\omega)_{(\tau)}],$$

where $\sigma(\rho,\omega)_{(\tau)} \equiv (\sigma_s(\rho,\omega)_{(\tau)}, \sigma_M(\rho,\omega)_{(\tau)})$ with $\sigma_s(\rho,\omega)_{(\tau)}$ being the self-generating force, $\sigma_M(\rho,\omega)_{(\tau)}$ being the mutual-generating force, and $\kappa_{M3}(\rho,\omega)_{(\tau)}=\circ$. Note that all these $\sigma_s(\rho,\omega)_{(\tau)}$ are the same and all the $\sigma_M(\rho,\omega)_{(\tau)}$ are not much different either.

Our brief conclusion is that, the system of tranquil culture is strong in the mutual-generating force but slightly weaker in the self-generating force. And yet, by the very meditative nature of the tranquil culture, it is weak in excluding things foreign to its will-rationality complex. In any rate, the system of tranquil culture turns out to be quite adaptive and tends to be intrinsically energetic in absorbing foreign cultures when it is out of absolute necessity to do so. Therefore, in the future, a system based upon tranquil culture is definitely in a rock-solid position to perform superbly by integrating the strengths of conflict culture (with scientific rationality). And it goes without saying that this is a system of self-mastering will and self-creating rationality.

As for the culture of conflict, it is supposed to be a system which is strong in self-generating force, strong in differentiation of things, strong in conflicting to each other, but weak in having the right insight and in coordination and mutual reinforcement. In this culture, every one strives to reject the opinion of others, and even to reject one's own idea of the past. Consequently, under this culture, (relative to the system of tranquil culture) it is much easier to create new ideas (micro-ideas and therefore new ideas of technology, all other things except culture being equal). But it also tends to prevent comprehensive and higher-level grand ideas from emerging from within, all other things being equal.

For the IRI chain of a conflict culture, in terms of a scheme, we have:

(4-5-8) IRI

$$= IRI[(\rho,\omega)_{(\tau)}]$$
$$= IRI[\sigma(\rho,\omega)_{(\tau)},\kappa(\rho,\omega)_{(\tau)}]$$

and

(4-5-9) IRI

$$= IRI[(\rho,\omega)_{(\tau)}]$$
$$= IRI[\sigma(\rho,\omega)_{(\tau)},\kappa(\rho,\omega)_{(\tau)}]$$
$$= IE[\sigma_{s1}(\rho,\omega)_{(\tau)},\kappa_{M1}(\rho,\omega)_{(\tau)}]\circ RD[\sigma_{s2}(\rho,\omega)_{(\tau)},\kappa_{M2}(\rho,\omega)_{(\tau)}]$$
$$\circ\, PI[\sigma_{s3}(\rho,\omega)_{(\tau)},\kappa_{M3}(\rho,\omega)_{(\tau)}],$$

where "$\circ$" $\models \mathbb{Z}\circ,_v\mathcal{H}$ is an impactor, $\sigma_{si}(\rho,\omega)_{(\tau)}$ denoting the self-generating force with $\sigma_{si}(\rho,\omega)_{(\tau)} \neq \sigma_{sj}(\rho,\omega)_{(\tau)}$, for all $i \neq j$, and $\kappa_M(\rho,\omega)_{(\tau)}$ the mutual-destructive force with $\kappa_{Mi}(\rho,\omega)_{(\tau)} \neq \kappa_{Mj}(\rho,\omega)_{(\tau)}$, for all $i \neq j$. Note that each of these $\sigma_{si}(\rho,\omega)_{(\tau)}$ is distinctive (i.e., $\sigma_i \leftarrow\!|\!\rightarrow \sigma_j$, $\forall\ i \neq j$) and the $\kappa_{Mi}(\rho,\omega)_{(\tau)}$ are in conflict to each other (i.e., $\kappa_i \leftarrow\!|\!\rightarrow \kappa_j$, $\forall\ i \neq j$).

With regard to Bcm. (4.5-4), for a system of conflict culture, for the formation of the IRI chain, we have:

(4.5-10) $\sigma_1 \rightarrow \xi(\sigma_2) \Rightarrow \zeta(\sigma_1,\xi(\sigma_2)) \equiv \zeta(\sigma_3),\ \sigma_i \leftarrow\!|\!\rightarrow \sigma_j\ ,\ \forall\ i \neq j,$

where σ_i are distinct, for all i. That is, the seeds of conflict in the IE, RD and PI sub-systems are all distinct, and are in conflict to each other.

For the system of conflict culture, if its IRI chain is dominated by a few members within the system, then certain kind of unbalanced rationality chain may be stimulated which will then create unwarranted chain reaction of intellectual bias. It follows that, in the process of building up bias after bias, at times it leans toward one side, and at another time, it tilts inevitably toward the opposite side. This is because we assume that in this cultural system, the wisdom of mediety and moderation is lacking.

In sum, due to its internalized structure of competition and strong tendency of self-differentiation, in general, this system develops rapidly. And yet with the entropy of logical indulgence and quantification (of the members of the system), the self-contradiction fundamentally ingrained in the systemic dynamic may not be subject to any effective constraint from within. This cultural system may eventually get trapped in its self-induced intellectual imbalance. Historically, a purely natural science-oriented mind set may not be able to balance itself by any religious spirituality; and this may be the best witness of the system-imbalance of the conflict culture.

Here in the IE-RD-PI chain, in the IE link, due to the strong and divergent opinions of members, the information received and transmitted is full of confusion, self-contradiction and even distortion. In the RD link, on one side, correct and beneficial information is passed on to the center (i.e., the RD link); and on the other side, useless and even incorrect information is transmitted as well. Under the lopsided culture of decision making by the center, especially with the information not appropriately collected and faithfully transmitted, some irregularities and even irrational decision making are inevitable. Now in the PI link, the designs formulated and decreed by the center may not be as well implemented as was originally planned. This is because between the center and the unit of implementation there may have serious conflicts of interests. Under the capitalist system of the culture of conflict, there is a strong tendency of impersonal market and significant social progress, since the individuality of each members of the system is invigorated. And although each link develops well, the macro coordination of the system is apparently difficult.

In sum, the tendency for the self-deepening process of each member in the culture of conflict is strong, and the force to reject outside cultures is strong as well. Consequently, it is simply difficult to absorb other cultures. Under the culture of conflict, the IE-RD-PI chain is a system of relentless internal conflict among these three links. The internal limitation placed on the will-rationality complex under this IRI chain is significant. So far, the modern history of the system of the conflict culture did not displace any of this limitation, because the externally favorable factors were more than enough to compensate for the shortcomings of the IRI chain of this system. In the modern time, under factors such as colonial expansion, scientific development, competitive national environment, the absorption of macro-global cultures from outside and the weaknesses of other types of culture, the rapid economic and cultural developments of the system of conflict culture has self-corrected the weaknesses of the IRI chain. But in the future, the limitations of the IRI chain of this conflict cultural system may be revealed.

In the future, a system based on the culture of conflict may be difficult to absorb the merits of the tranquil cultural systems. This is because under the conquest will and scientific rationality, the necessary forces of integrating heterogeneous cultures are simply lacking. Hence, by following the above reasoning process, the potential for future development of a system of conflict culture appears to be relatively limited.

Classic China, due to its macro-tech/tranquility culture, eventually reached a plateau, the so-called high-level equilibrium trap. That is, the classical Chinese mind set is quick in synthesizing different technologies into a higher level technology and yet it is far slower in developing different or "opposing" technologies (except at the time of at war with the northern people while under a reasonable socio-political system). This may be related to the Chinese language which is more naturally connected in words and less clear and distinct between concepts which may be based on similar or closely related words than a typical alphabet-based Western language with a much larger reservoir of words. This may also be related to the Chinese tradition of slow in developing new mathematics, logic and quantifiable sciences.

Note that the methodology of a typical traditional Chinese researcher is that he (or she) would employ some scheme of yinyang five elements which are not precise and very often quite arbitrary, and in general he (or she) would not really try to quantify the studies of objects by going through a rigorous way of controlled-experiment. This may be one of the root causes of fact that the classical Chinese appears to be quick in synthesizing different technologies into a higher level technology and to be slower in developing different or "opposing" technologies. Related to this whole process of scientific development is the tendency that the traditional Chinese has paid far more attention to things of similarity than things of difference and distinction.

One solution to remove the deficiency in micro-technological development is to have a large scale import of the Western cultures: mathematics, natural sciences, various kinds of individual life styles, social and political structures. By so doing, modern China is in a process of developing a micro and macro-tech/tranquility culture. In terms of the human-side of will-rationality complex, this means in the IRI chain to develop the modern systemic rationality from the classical systemic rationality (or yu-wu rationality) and to develop the self-creating and self-mastering life-will from the shengsheng life-will.

Note that for the IRI chain in a static form, dynamical and even uncertain forms can be developed as well by employing a reasoning process which is, for example, similar to Bcm (3.7-17)): $x_{IRI}(.) = [\beta_1 x(\mathbb{H}_{\rho};.)\oplus\beta_2 x(\mathbb{H}_{\omega};.)] \circledast Ix_{IRI}(\mathbb{H}_{\rho,\omega};.)$.

Chapter 5 - Strategic Economics: Culture, Trade and Development Stages of A Modern Economy

5.1 Introduction

In the long-term perspective, culture in the broad sense plays the decisive role in any process of economic development, growth and advancement. In this chapter, we shall discuss topics of advancement models, development strategy and global trade. That is, we go beyond the so-called macroeconomics to address the interconnected issues between culture and economic development/advancement.

Today, for a developing economy, the growth model may need to focus on the role of labor-intensive activities. That is, it may center on the role of labor in the associated production function $F(L,K,\mathfrak{C})$, by keeping K and $\mathfrak{C}$ to be constant. For a developed economy, the role of capital stock in the associated production function $F(L,K,\mathfrak{C})$, as have been treated well in the conventional growth models, may be the key for economic growth. One of the few issues needed to be addressed in the conventional-type growth models is that it may be desirable to treat technological progress as a force to increase the steady-state equilibrium level of capital stock. This point will be well taken in the illustration. For this purpose, let us suppose that, following the conventional wisdom, the first order differential equation for capital stock per labor is:

$$\dot{k} = sf(k) + (\delta+n-\gamma)k,$$

where k, s, and δ stand for the capital stock per labor, saving rate per labor, depreciation rate of capital stock per labor, respectively, and γ is the coefficient for capital-augmenting technological progress.

As for an advancing economy, the cultural variables, i.e., the totality of the spirit-rationality of the intellectuals, entrepreneurship, and "plannership," strategic operations, organizational strengths, and others, shall be accounted for as is what is responsible for the manifestation of the human creativity that is ultimately the driving forces of economic advancement. This is the task that we shall tackle below. Note that a developing or developed economy can be an advancing economy at the same time.

To set the stage for a discussion of the impact of cultural strengths on the long-term advancement of an economy in the next section (i.e., Section 5.2), here in this section, we shall presents models of economic growth based on the accumulation of labor and capital, while holding culture constant.

Model of growth based on labor accumulation. Let the production function be:

$$(5.1\text{-}1)\quad Y = F(L,K,\mathfrak{C}),$$

where, as usual, Y, K, L, and $\mathfrak{C}$ denote the real output, raw labor, capital stock, and cultural variables, respectively. Note that through this $\mathfrak{C}$, national economic planning and business strategic management affect the level of output Y. Then the relationship between Y and the absolute level of raw labor, holding K and $\mathfrak{C}$ constant, is:

(5.1-2) $Y = F(L; \bar{K}, \acute{C})$,

where $\bar{K}$ and $\acute{C}$ depict the fixed levels of capital and culture (i.e., the cultural variables), respectively. By assuming F(.) as a concave function with respective to L, we have Figure 5.1-1.

Figure 5.1-1
A growth model with culture

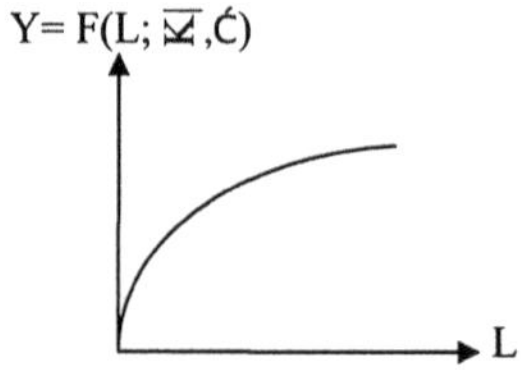

Model of growth based on capital accumulation. Let the production function be Eq. (5.1-1): $Y = F(L,K,\mathfrak{C})$. Then the relationship between Y and the absolute level of capital stock, holding L and $\mathfrak{C}$ constant, is:

(5.1-3) $Y = F(K; \acute{L}, \acute{C})$,

Figure 5.1-2
Output as a function of K, holding L and $\mathfrak{C}$ constant

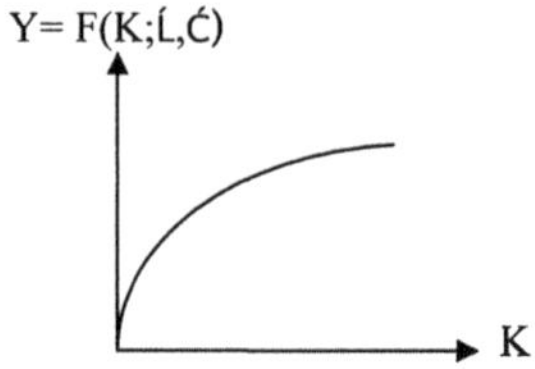

where $\acute{L}$ and $\acute{C}$ depict the fixed levels of raw labor and culture, respectively. By assuming F(.) as a concave function with respective to K, we have Figure 5.1-2.

Model of growth based on the accumulation of capital per labor unit. Let the production function be Eq. (5.1-1): $Y = F(L,K,\mathfrak{C})$. Then the relationship between Y per labor ($y = Y/L$) and K per labor (i.e., $k = K/L$), holding per $\mathfrak{C}$ constant ($c = \mathfrak{C}/L$), is:

(5.1-4) $y = F(1,k; \acute{c}) = f(k;\acute{c})$,

under the assumption of a linear homogeneous function of F(.), with $\acute{c}$ depicting the fixed level of culture per labor. By assuming f(.) as a concave function with respective to K, we have Figure 5.1-3.

Figure 5.1-3
A per-capita growth model with culture

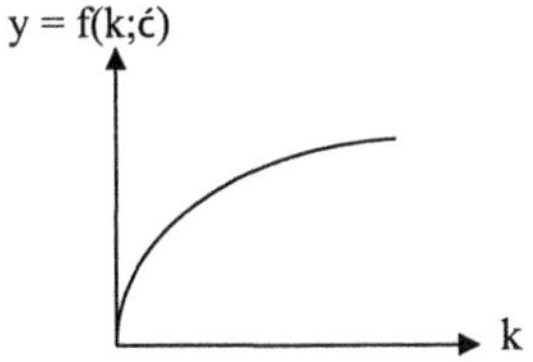

Note that by following conventional approaches, we can trace the steady-state equilibrium levels of k in both deterministic and uncertainty cases.

5.2 Strategic Economics of A Nation under Cultural Adaptation and Innovations

In this section, we study the relationships between culture and global trade in particular and between culture and the economic development in general.

§5.2-1 Advancement Model of A Cultural Economy

Now we shall present an advancing model for the cultural economy.

Advanced model of a cultural economy. Let $\mathcal{T}^{intl}$ be an impactor denoting the forces of the intellectuals. For a cultural economy, let the public-private strategic impactor be: $(\mathcal{T}^*,\mathcal{T})|t \equiv \{(\mathcal{T}^*,\mathcal{T}^{priv})\ (\mathcal{T}^*,\mathcal{T}^{intl})\}|_t$ with

(5.2-1-1) $$\{(\mathcal{T}^*,\mathcal{T}^{priv})(\mathcal{T}^*,\mathcal{T}^{intl})\}|_t$$
$$= [\{(\rho,\omega)^1,u^1,v^1\}_{t=1}\ \{(\rho,\omega)^2,u^2,v^2\}_{t=2}\ \ldots\ \{(\rho,\omega)^n,u^n,v^n\}_{t=n}]^T,$$

(where the subscripts, t = 1,2,…,n, refer the first, second, …, n^{th} stage, respectively) denotes the following *opening mechanism*:

(5.2-1-2) $$\{(\mathcal{T}^*,\mathcal{T}^{priv})(\mathcal{T}^*,\mathcal{T}^{intl})\}|_t$$
$$= [(\rho,\omega)^1,u^1,v^1]_t, \text{ for } t = 1,$$
$$= [(\rho,\omega)^2,u^2,v^2]_t, \text{ for } t = 2,$$
$$\ldots.$$
$$= [(\rho,\omega)^n,u^n,v^n]_t, \text{ for } t = n.$$

Let Q be the cultural production function, $\mathcal{T}(\rho,\omega) \equiv (\mathcal{T}^*,\mathcal{T})|_t$ the public-private strategic impactor under the opening mechanism, A a general coefficient or a stochastic variable, K the capital stock, L the raw-labor, u the utilization rate of capital stock in the total cultural (or non-directly productive) activities, v the labor participation rate (in the total cultural activities), r the coefficient of labor in pursuing leisure and α, β and γ the multipliers of culture (i.e., $\mathcal{T}(\rho,\omega)\mathfrak{C}$), "capital net of culture" (or capital less culture) and "raw-labor net of culture" (raw-labor less culture), respectively. Here, $\mathfrak{C}$ represents the core of a culture. Then we have the *cultural production function of a cultural economy*: $Q = A[\mathcal{T}(\rho,\omega)\mathfrak{C}uKvL]^{\alpha}[(1-u)K]^{\beta}[(1-v-$

r)L]$^{\gamma}$. Here, because the level of output is a function of the public-private strategies (i.e., $\{(\mathcal{T}^{*}, \mathcal{T}^{priv})(\mathcal{T}^{*},\mathcal{T}^{intl})\}|_{t}$) and the stages/phases of development.

Below, to facilitate the study of cultural stage of production, let:

$$
\begin{aligned}
(5.2\text{-}1\text{-}3)\ \{(\mathcal{T}^{*},\mathcal{T}^{priv})(\mathcal{T}^{*},\mathcal{T}^{intl})\}|_{t} &= \{(\rho,\omega)^{1},u^{1},v^{1}\}_{t=1} \quad \ldots \text{TC} \ldots 1^{st} \\
&= \{(\rho,\omega)^{2},u^{2},v^{2}\}_{t=2} \quad \ldots \text{CN} \ldots 2^{nd} \\
&\ldots \\
&= \{(\rho,\omega)^{n},u^{n},v^{n}\}_{t=n} \quad \ldots \text{MC} \ldots n^{th}
\end{aligned}
$$

where TC, CN and MC denote the traditional culture, cultural confusion, and triple (or multiple) cultures, respectively; while 1st, 2nd, ..., and nth denote the first, second,..., and nth cultural stages of production, respectively.

In the following, let us use China as an example to illustrate these points.

First stage. Tao-jen-Buddhist culture mix $\mathfrak{C}^{CLB} = (\rho,\omega)^{CLB}$. In this stage, the tao-jen culture ($\mathfrak{C}^{CL}$) created a grandiose civilization of the classical world with its yu-wu technology (yin-yang five-element technology (YYWX). This is the most glorious stage in the Eastern hemisphere of the pre-science world.

This cultural stage had five phases: pre-S&T(stone), low-level technology (fishing/ hunting/emerging agriculture and pottery), low/medium-level technology (former-agriculture and bronze), medium/high-tech (iron,paper), high-level technology (gun power, compass). In the classical world (or the world of pre-scientific agriculture), this culture ($\mathfrak{C}^{CLB}$) must be a high culture. But from today's perspective, the high-level technology of this cultural stage is only comparable to the pre-scientific level of the being-technology or the level of being-technology existed right before the industrial revolution of the eighteenth century in Western Europe.

These East Asian stages (i.e., five stages mentioned in the above) are closely associated and complementary to the systems of classic central planning, classic market, and classic human-relation network (or formal/semi-formal socio-political and economic structures), classic comprehensive systemic network and classic strategy-cultural set. This tao-jen-Buddhist cultural mix and its technological foundations are apparently different from the cultures of Western capitalism and socialism and the structures of their technologies. Capitalism of the West is a culture of individualism. Socialism of the West is a culture of collectivism (or one with collectivism in name). This tao-jen-Buddhist culture could be further decomposed into Taoist individualism, "Confucian family-based culture," Legalist collectivism, and secular Buddhist culture. The Confucian family-based culture is centered on the rationality of mediety-and-integration and a (classical) harmonic self-generating life-will, from which the cultures of classical individualism (i.e., Taoism) and classical collectivism (i.e., Legalism) can be incorporated into an integral whole. That is, the classical Chinese yu-wu technology covers a wide spectrum of individualistic technology (i.e., private handicraft technology), collectivist technology and family-based technology (family technology, or father-son or mother-daughter-in-law technology), with a distinctive feature of being essentially rooted in wood-mechanic technology rather than in metal-mechanic technology.

Second stage: Cultural confusion. In this stage, one's own culture was looked down upon and given up entirely with unsuccessful transplant of the alien being-culture.

This is what happened to China in the periods of the first half of the twentieth century. Today's Russia may get rapped in a similar situation like this.

Third stage: Triple or global cultural mix $\mathfrak{C}^{TPL} = \{(\rho,\omega)^{WLeft}, (\rho,\omega)^{CLB}, (\rho,\omega)^{WRight}\}$. In this stage, by firmly rooted in the traditional tao-jen-Buddhist culture, a new culture of zizhuism (i.e., self-masterism) is developed by absorbing the being culture and the culture of Marxism. In this approach, yu-wu rationality is set as the center to integrate scientific, dialectic and other rationalities, and the self-generating life-will is employed to integrate the will-to-conquest (or conflict, risk-taking and individualized will) and the will-to-transcending-the-daily-life, the material and the spiritual wills, and the biological and the super-biological and super-natural will, etc. This is a culture-intensive stage, with balances between humanity and technology and between spirituality and rationality been reached. Definitely, this culture mix shall incorporate the cultures of Hinduism and Islam and the cultures of others in an appropriate context.

In terms of technology, we shall classify it into four layers or phases: low (or low-tech), medium-low (or medium-low-tech), medium-high (or medium-high-tech) and high-tech (or high-technology) layers. For a catching up economy, these phases are corresponding to phases or stages of imitation, early imitation-creation, later imitation-creation and self-creation, respectively. Here we have the "complete production system" including these four layers of technology (corresponding to four phases of technological imitation-creation) : $\mathcal{P} = | \,|_{\Delta} \Delta^{up} \Delta_{down} \_\_ {}^{\Delta}|^{T}$.

This development of the afore-mentioned modern production system must be coordinated well with the organizations and operations of the modern central planning mechanism (for a Faziranist or socialist cultural economy), industrial policy mix (for a modern capitalist cultural economy of the twenty-first century like France, Japan and the United States, etc.), market, the socio-political and economic structure, the formal-informal human network (i.e., (vd,hc,γ) in a system $\mathfrak{C}^{TPL}$), the structure of systemic dynamics (i.e., structure-penetrating system $(R_M,R^{DM}(e_r))$, and the modern strategy-cultural complex ($[M^{I}\ M^{II}\ M^{III}\ M^{IV}]^{T}$-Z).

The triple/global cultural mix $\mathfrak{C}^{TPL}$ may have its technological foundations to be quite different from those of capitalism and socialism. In a simplified approach, the culture of pure capitalism in the West may be said to base essentially on the cultures of individualism, sciences and Christian religion. Similarly, the culture of socialism may be said to base essentially on the culture of dialectic collectivism and the nationalized culture of science. In contrast, the afore-mentioned global culture (in its complete or ideal form) is intended to be the culture of self-masterism, with its vertical axis lying in the systemic rationality and self-creating and self-mastering life-will mix, and its horizontal axis lying on a the system of small family/community. This is a system serving as the medium between the modern individualism the modern collectivism. In particular, this global system is one of the best choices facing nations of East Asia. This modern East Asian system is one suitable for developing the technologies of nationalism (military, educational, and basic research), the business technology (commercial and applied research and development to be divided into applied research and public and private product development), and the individual-based technologies. Among all these technologies, obviously, the individualistic and national technologies together constitute the technological complex of a modern cultural economy. It is apparent that this is the most vital technological system in the sense of being the very basis of the engine of modern technological development.

Under the operations of the public-private strategic impactors ($\mathcal{T}^*,\mathcal{T}^{priv}$), the public production sector develops rapidly and steeply (i.e., becoming more of a steep system), and the private production sector develops slowly and flatly (i.e., becoming more of a flat system), and R & D sector develops smoothly under the joint efforts of the national government, the intellectuals, and the business community. Under the operations of the government-intellectuals' strategic impactors ($\mathcal{T}^*,\mathcal{T}^{ntl}$), the system of government consumption goes up steeply, and the system of individual consumption goes up both steeply and flatly and converges eventually to a unitary system. (i.e., Δ-shaped balanced system).

Therefore, under the operations of the public-private strategic impactors $(\mathcal{T}^*,\mathcal{T})|t$, through the medium of economic planning, financial policy, educational policy (or cultural policy in general), and private industrial and commercial strategies, ηg shifts outward and γf shifts upward (see Figure 9.2-1-1 for the model of the steady-state equilibrium level of capital stock). Therefore, the old steady-state Tcentral equilibrium point K* shifts toward (or moves up to) the new steady-state Tcentral equilibrium point K**.

For the various stages of output in terms of culture-economic development, see Figure 5.2-1-1 below.

The cultural economic growth model in the above is studied from the angles of investments and capital accumulation. Below we shall continue the study of a cultural economy from the perspectives of input-output relationship. Let the input and output operations of a cultural economy be the functions of will-rationality mix (ρ,ω):

Figure 5.2-1-1
Stages of Output

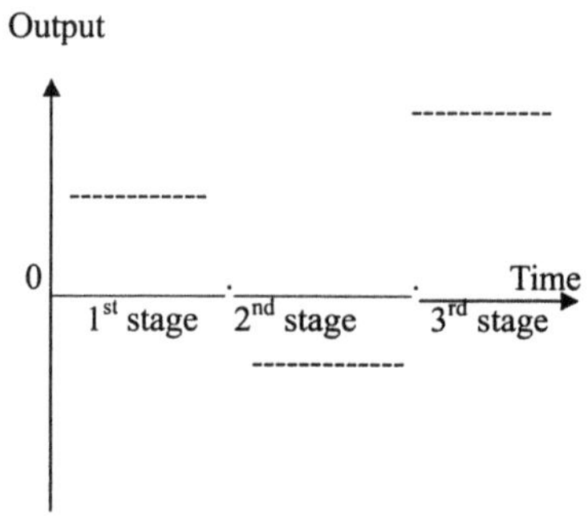

(5.2-1-4) $Y = TO_{nation} - TI_{nation}$,

where Y refers to the national income, TO_{nation} refers to the total output, TI_{nation} refers to the total input, f(L,K,ℭ) refers to the potential output, $(\mathcal{T}^*,\mathcal{T})|_t f(ℭ,K,L)$ refers to the actual level of "total revenue," X refers to the potential level of input (i.e., the maximal level of input, or the actual level of input plus the amount of input that has been wasted due to the inefficient operation of the cultural economy), and $(\mathcal{T}^*,\mathcal{T})|_t X$ refers to the actual level of input (i.e., "total costs").

Furthermore, let $\xi(\rho,\omega))f \equiv \xi(\rho,\omega))f(L,K) = (\mathcal{T}^*,\mathcal{T})|_t f(L,K,\mathfrak{C})$ and $\zeta(\rho,\omega)g \equiv \zeta(\rho,\omega)g(L,K) = (\mathcal{T}^*,\mathcal{T})|_t X$. To simplify the mathematical manipulation, the set of cultural variables including $(\mathcal{T}^*,\mathcal{T})|_t$ is treated as independent of Q. Then for $Y = (\mathcal{T}^*,\mathcal{T})|_t f(L,K,\mathfrak{C}) - (\mathcal{T}^*,\mathcal{T})|_t X$, the maximization of Y with respect to $Q = f(L,K|\mathfrak{C})$ at the state of cultural Tcentral leads to (by the first order condition):

$$(5.2\text{-}1\text{-}5)\quad \frac{dY}{dQ} = \frac{df(L,K|\mathfrak{C})}{dQ}(\mathcal{T}^*,\mathcal{T})|_t - \frac{dX}{dQ}(\mathcal{T}^*,\mathcal{T})|_t$$

$$= \xi(\rho,\omega)\frac{df(L,K;u,v|\mathfrak{C})}{dQ} - \zeta(\rho,\omega)\frac{dg(L,K;u,v|\mathfrak{C})}{dQ}$$

$$= \xi f' - \zeta g'$$

$$= 0,$$

where $f' = df(L,K;u,v|\mathfrak{C})/dQ$ (u, v being the operational coefficients of capital and raw labor, respectively), $g' = dg(L,K;u,v|\mathfrak{C})/dQ$, $\xi \equiv \xi(\rho,\omega)$, $\zeta \equiv \zeta(\rho,\omega)$. Here $\xi(\rho,\omega))f'$ denotes the marginal* output curve and $\zeta(\rho,\omega))g'$ denotes the marginal* input curve; and by the **marginal* curve** is meant the result of using T* derivative (see the K derivative in Tonn 1994, renamed later as T derivative).

In the above, $f(L,K,\mathfrak{C})(\mathcal{T}^*,\mathcal{T})|_t = \xi(\rho,\omega)f(L,K;.|\ \mathfrak{C})$ is derived from the manipulations below: Let $M^i(\mathcal{T}^*,\mathcal{T})|_t\mathfrak{C}$ and $\phi f(L,K,\mathfrak{C})(\mathcal{T}^*,\mathcal{T})|_t$ be reorganizable systems. In addition, let $M^i(\mathcal{T}^*,\mathcal{T})|_t\mathfrak{C} = \mathcal{M}^i$, i = I, II, III, IV. Here $\mathcal{M}^i$ is derived by reorganizing M^i, $(\mathcal{T}^*,\mathcal{T})|_t$ and $\mathfrak{C}$; and for reorganizable systems and impactors, see §A.2-11 and Tonn [2006]. Then we have:

$$(5.2\text{-}1\text{-}6)\quad \phi\, f(L,K,\mathfrak{C};.)(\mathcal{T}^*,\mathcal{T})|_t \approx \phi\,[M^I\, M^{II}\, M^{III}\, M^{IV}]^T(\mathcal{T}^*,\mathcal{T})|_t\,[L\ K\ \mathfrak{C}]^T$$
$$\Leftrightarrow [\mathcal{M}^I\, \mathcal{M}^{II}\, \mathcal{M}^{III}\, \mathcal{M}^{IV}]^T\,[LK]^T \approx \xi(\rho,\omega)f(L,K;.\ |\mathfrak{C}).$$

Here, M^I, M^{II}, M^{III}, and M^{IV} refer to the structures of ideas conceived in one's mind, the structure of interpersonal relationship conceived in one's mind, the structure of a society conceived in one's mind and the structure of matters conceived in one's mind, respectively, "≈" stands for the transformational operation between systematics and mathematics (which exists by our assertion), "⇔" denotes systemic operations and transformations, and ϕ stands for the reorganizing impactor.

So far, in the state of cultural T central, we derived the T central point of real national income as the intersection point of two curves introduced in the above. For simplicity, let us represent the T central income point in the state of cultural T central by the T central income point under the T central strategic impactor. In the Chinese cultural economy, T central culture $\mathfrak{C}^{TCentral}$ refers to $(\mathfrak{C}^{CLB})^{TCentral}$, or the culture of mediety and balance. In general, by the **culture of mediety and balance** is meant $\mathfrak{C}^{TCentral} \equiv \phi^H[\mathfrak{C}^{yin}\,\mathfrak{C}^M\mathfrak{C}^{yang}]^{TCentral}$, the integral whole of yin culture (inner-oriented culture of self-restraint and self-perfection), middle-culture (the culture between yin and yang cultures), yang culture (outer-oriented culture of conquest), the culture of self-entity-in-tranquility, and the culture of mutual-entity-in-tranquility (here $(\mathfrak{C}^{CLB})^{TCentral}$ is a command-reorganizing impactor, see ϕ^{Self} below). The **normal state of culture T central** is the normal state of culture which is operating in a state neither below nor above the long-term potential level of the cultural operation. Here, for the classical Chinese culture, there is $\mathfrak{C}^{CLB} \equiv \phi^{tao}[\mathbb{C}^{Legalism}\mathbb{C}^{GoldenMean}\mathbb{C}^{empty}]^{T}$, and for the modern Chinese culture, there is

$$(5.2\text{-}1\text{-}7)\quad \phi^{Self}[\mathbb{C}^{Wleft}\ \mathbb{C}^{CLB}\ \mathbb{C}^{Wright}]^{T} = \phi^{sys}\{\phi^{dial} * \phi^{tao} * \phi^{sci}\}\{[\circ \text{ Col Y+-i-c}]^{T}[\circ \text{ Zh-Mu-i-t } \circ]^{T}[\text{S-i-c} \circ \text{ Y+-i-c}]^{T}\} = [\text{Y- S-i-t Mu-i-t Y+}]^{T},$$

where $\phi^{Self} \equiv \phi^{sys}\{\phi^{dial} * \phi^{tao} * \phi^{sci}\}$ refers to the command-reorganizing impactor, ϕ^{sys} refers to the reorganizing impactor operating on the will-rationality mix, ϕ^{dial} refers to the dialectic-rationality-spirit impactor, ϕ^{tao} refers to the yu-wu rationality-spirit impactor, ϕ^{sci} refers to the scientific rationality-spirit impactor, * refers to a notation for a composite operation, "○" refers to an empty system, "S-i-c" refers to the self-entity-in-conflict, "Col" refers to the collective entity, "Zh-Mu-i-t" refers to the mediety/centrality-mutuality-in-tranquility, "Y+-i-c" refers to the yang-in-conquest entity, "Y-" refers to the yin entity, "Y+" refers to the yang entity, "S-i-t" refers to the self-entity in tranquility, and "Mu-i-t" refers to the mutual-entity in-tranquility. Bcm. (5.2-1-7) is a becoming referring to the operation of the rationality-spirituality of tao-wu with that of being-yu, centering on the culture of yu-Legalism/mediety/yin-emptiness in integrating the right- and left-wing cultures of the West in the transforming process of creating a new culture penetrating all aspects of yin, yang, selfhood and mutuality.

In a cultural economy, this T central culture simultaneously embodies cultures of market mechanism, central planning mechanism and Faziranist interpersonal network. Then by this culture again, people are able to reorganize and even integrate them into a comprehensive whole. By this approach, balances between humanities and technologies and between matters and spirituality can be reached by its internal dynamics of systematics. Hence, the choices of the public-private strategies are enlarged to the largest possible extent. That is, by the co-determination of environments, systemic structures and the strategic set, the system in question may operate in either normal or non-normal (or super-normal) state.

To show the Bcm. (5.2-1-7) by a graph, we have Figure 5.2-1-2.

Figure 5.2-1-2
Culture T central and super-T central under T central and non-T central strategic impactors; f' and g' are functions of u and v with: ξ (ρ,ω) = marginal*output curve; ζ (ρ,ω) = marginal*input curve

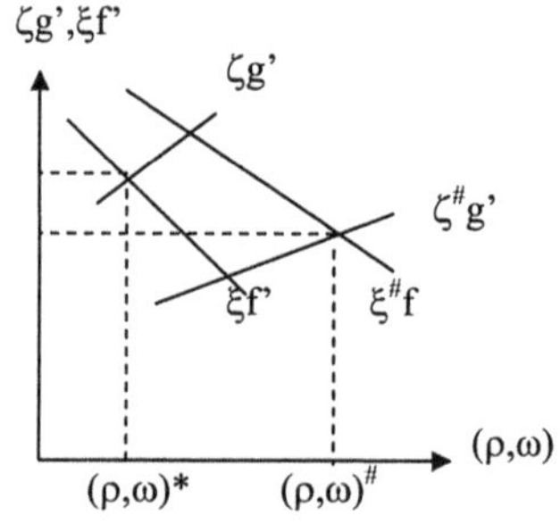

Under the T central or super-T central cultural operations, the steady-state equilibrium/balance level of (real) national income goes up from y* to y^{super*}. This is an evolution from a long-term equilibrium/balance y* (i.e., the intersection of the short-term total supply curve and the long-term total supply curve, under T central cultural operation, see Figure 5.2-1-3) into another long-term equilibrium/balance y^{super*} (i.e., the intersection of the short-run aggregate supply curve and the long-term total supply curve, under a super-T central cultural operation, see Figure 5.2-1-3). This process may last more than half a century, and it is really the first half part of a business cycle.

Figure 5.2-1-3
National Income under T central and super-T central cultural operations

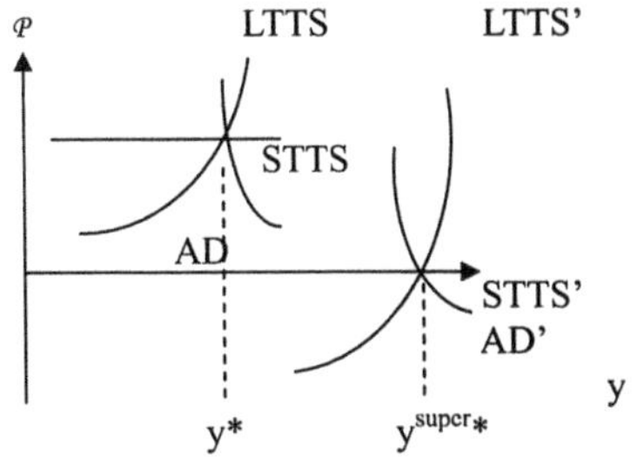

Note that this long-run aggregate supply curve must have a positive slope (and less than infinity). Thus, in the long run, every thing is changing; and in the short run, there is no infinite supply. This y* is not corresponding to any full-employment level of national income, but is the national income in the state of T central.

Super-normal state of culture. This is the state of super-normal operation of the cultural mix (ρ,ω) (or strategic impactors) (see Figure 5.2-1-2: $(\rho,\omega)^* \rightarrow (\rho,\omega)^{\#}$). Here $\xi(\rho,\omega)$ and $\zeta(\rho,\omega)$ move outward toward $\xi(\rho,\omega)^{\#}$ and $\zeta(\rho,\omega)^{\#}$, respectively. Thus, the income level under this super-normal level of culture is the super-normal national income. Hence, if culture (or technological culture) develops (or the efficiency of the culture develops) continuously, then real national income may rise without any limit. Therefore, the national income of a nation which develops its culture (or technological culture) continuously will be higher than that of those countries with stagnating culture. In the long term perspective, this difference will be extremely prominent.

Here as usual, although we shall not elaborate, the super or normal state of culture depends essentially on the culture-institutional arrangements of the IRI chain, the MPFX cycles and the SIFP chain complex of the specific society in question.

Now we turn to the discussion of the impact of a nation's culture on its national income. To simplify the manipulation, let $(\mathcal{T}^*,\mathcal{T})|_t$ be independent of the quantity of output Q. For $Y = (\mathcal{T}^*,\mathcal{T})|_t\, f(L,K,\mathfrak{C}) - (\mathcal{T}^*,\mathcal{T})|_t X$, $\max_{\{Q\}} Y$ implies (the first order condition) that the T derivative of the real national income must be set as zero so that, on the margin, the derivative of the actual output (i.e., total output under the strategic impactor) equals to the derivative of the actual output (i.e., total input under the strategic impactor):

$$(5.2\text{-}1\text{-}8)\quad \frac{dY}{dt} = \frac{df(L,K,\mathfrak{C})}{dQ}(\mathcal{T}^*,\mathcal{T})|_t \frac{dQ}{dt} - \frac{dX}{dQ}(\mathcal{T}^*,\mathcal{T})|_t \frac{dQ}{dt}$$

$$= \xi(\rho,\omega)\frac{df(L,K;u,v)}{dQ}Q^{\cdot} - \zeta(\rho,\omega)\frac{dg(L,K;u,v)}{dQ}Q^{\cdot}.$$

Hence, it yields

$$(5.2\text{-}1\text{-}9)\quad Y^{\cdot} = (\xi f' - \zeta g')Q^{\cdot},$$

where $Y^{\cdot} \equiv dY/dt$ and $Q^{\cdot} \equiv dQ/dt$. By setting a level of culture (ρ,ω), from $Y = (\mathcal{T}^*,\mathcal{T})|_t\, f(L,K,\mathfrak{C}) - (\mathcal{T}^*,\mathcal{T})|_t X = \xi(\rho,\omega)f(L,K) - \zeta(\rho,\omega)g(L,K)$, we derive Y (see Bcm. (5.2-1-9) and Figure 5.2-1-4).

Let us set up the following becoming:

$$(5.2\text{-}1\text{-}10)\quad (\rho,\omega)^{\cdot} = a(\rho,\omega) + b.$$

Then, we have Figure 5.2-1-5, with $(\rho,\omega)^{\cdot} \equiv d(\rho,\omega)/dt$.

Figure 5.2-1-4
Level of $Y^{\cdot}$ given a specific level of (ρ,ω)

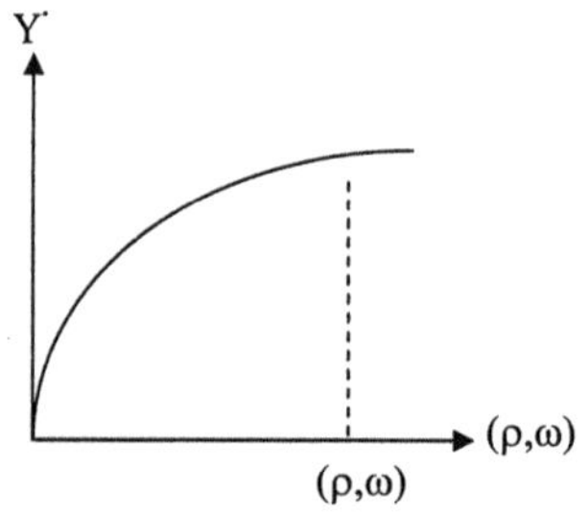

Figure 5.2-1-5
Dynamical CE centrality of (ρ,ω)

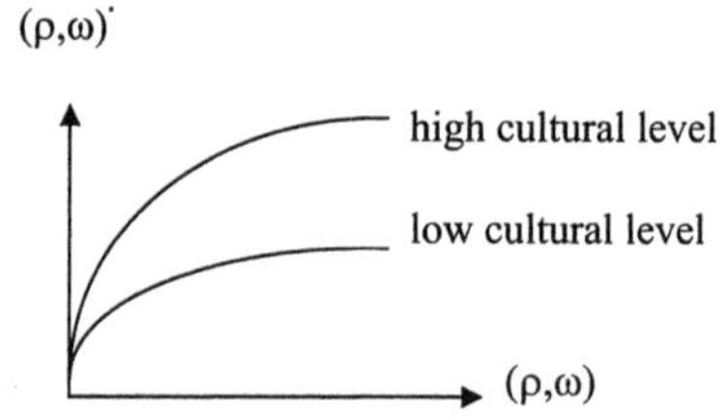

The cultural becoming. Before we proceed to the development of this cultural becoming, note that for the derivation of the becoming below, it is understood that the cultural variables involved are rooted in the backgrounds to be developed in Subsection §5.2-4. Now, let the cultural becoming be:

$$(5.2\text{-}1\text{-}11)\quad \dot{\mathfrak{C}} = \alpha\mathfrak{C} \otimes \{L,K\},$$

where $\mathfrak{C}$ refers to culture, $\dot{\mathfrak{C}} \equiv d\mathfrak{C}/dt$, and L, K and α stand for capital stock, raw labor and an impactor, respectively. This cultural becoming (5.2-1-11) represents the following ideas: (1) Culture, capital and labor affect each other. (2) The dynamics of culture is determined by the interactions of culture, capital and labor with $\otimes$ depicting the cultural impactor. Then we have:

$$(5.2\text{-}1\text{-}12)\quad \frac{\dot{\mathfrak{C}}}{\mathfrak{C}} = \alpha \otimes \frac{\{L,K\}}{\mathfrak{C}} = \alpha \otimes \{L,K\}_{\backslash\mathfrak{C}}.$$

In general, L and K are functions of culture. Suppose the term $\{L,K\}\backslash\mathfrak{C}$ is not a function of culture, then we write $\dot{\mathfrak{C}}/\mathfrak{C} = \alpha \otimes \{L,K\}_{\backslash\mathfrak{C}} \approx a + \{L,K\}_{\backslash\mathfrak{C}}$, where $\{L,K\}_{\backslash\mathfrak{C}}$ is the collection of capital and labor not affected by the cultural factor, for a being a parameter. Now, if we set $\{L,K\}\backslash\mathfrak{C} = \beta \otimes \{L,K\}_{\backslash\mathfrak{C}} \approx b + \{L,K\}_{\backslash\mathfrak{C}}$, where β is an impactor, then we have $\dot{\mathfrak{C}}/\mathfrak{C} = \alpha \otimes \{\beta \otimes \{L,K\}_{\backslash\mathfrak{C}}\} = \{\alpha \otimes \beta\} \otimes \{L,K\}_{\backslash\mathfrak{C}} \approx (a+b) + \{L,K\}_{\backslash\mathfrak{C}}$, where b is a parameter.

Figure 5.2-1-6
Dynamical CE centrality of $\mathfrak{C}$ ($\mathfrak{C}^*$)

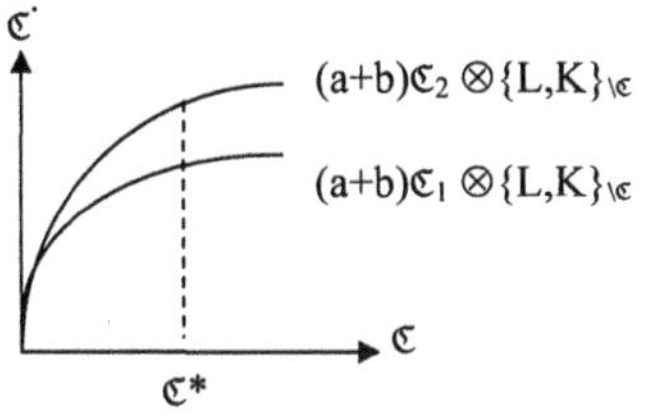

In a new frontier of cultural integration and innovation (or a new state of the integration and innovation of a set of strategic impactors), $\mathfrak{C} \equiv (\rho,\omega)$ operates super-normally. If we set $Y \propto Q = A[\mathcal{T}(\rho,\omega)\mathfrak{C}uLvK]^{\alpha}[(1\text{-}v\text{-}r)L]^{\beta}[(1\text{-}u)K]^{\gamma}$, where "$\propto$" refers to a positive relationship. Then we have Figure 5.2-1-7. Here $(\rho,\omega) \rightarrow (\rho,\omega)^*$ and $(\rho,\omega)^{\#}$, respectively, then $\mathfrak{C}$ shifts to $\mathfrak{C}^*$ and $\mathfrak{C}^{\#}$, respectively.

Thus, this is a super-normal level income. If culture (or culture of technology) advances forever (i.e., the efficiency of culture increases without ever ending), then real national income shall increase forever. Therefore, the national income of the nation of higher culture (especially in terms of technological efficiency) will be higher than that of the nation of lower culture. This is especially true for a prolonged period of time.

To address the long term dynamics of cultural advancement, first let:

(5.2-1-13) $\mathfrak{C}^{\cdot} = \mathfrak{C} \otimes \{L,K\}$.

Figure 5.2-1-7
CE T central income (Y*) and super-CE T central income (Y#)

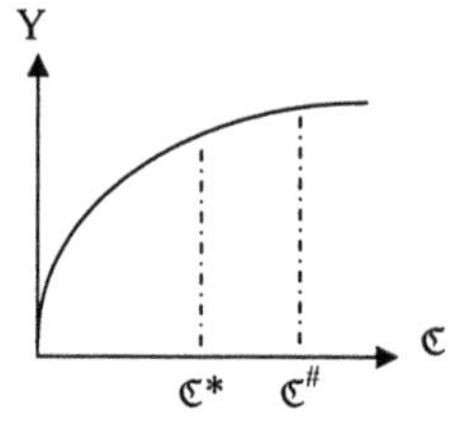

In addition, let ϕ be an IDR impactor, $\mathfrak{C} \otimes \{L,K\}$ be an IDR system (see Appendix A.2, Section §A.2-11). Suppose that:

(5.2-1-14) $\phi\mathfrak{C} \otimes \{L,K\} = |\{L,K\}_{\backslash\mathfrak{C}} \oplus c\mathfrak{C}|^{T} \otimes \{L,K,\mathfrak{C}\}_{-} \approx [\alpha(L,K) + c\mathfrak{C}] - \beta(L,K,\mathfrak{C})$,

for $\{L,K\}_{\backslash\mathfrak{C}} \equiv \alpha \equiv \alpha(L,K)$ being a function of K and L, $\{L,K,\mathfrak{C}\}_{-} \equiv -\beta(L,K,\mathfrak{C}) > 0$ a function of L, K and $\mathfrak{C}$. Here $|\{L,K\}_{\backslash\mathfrak{C}} \oplus c\mathfrak{C}|^{T}$ represents the driving force of culture, and $\{L,K,\mathfrak{C}\}_{-}$ is a term representing the negative forces of development. Consequently, we have

(5.2-1-15) $\mathfrak{C}^{\cdot} = (\alpha + c\mathfrak{C}) - \beta$.

From the above reasoning, we have Figure 5.2-1-8 representing the dynamical trajectory of culture, where $\mathfrak{C}^*$ and $\mathfrak{C}$'are steady state T central and steady state super-T central levels of culture, respectively. In this figure, it is seen that the trajectory from the origin O to $\mathfrak{C}$' lies above the trajectory from the origin to $\mathfrak{C}^*$.

Figure 5.2-1-8
Dynamical trajectories of culture

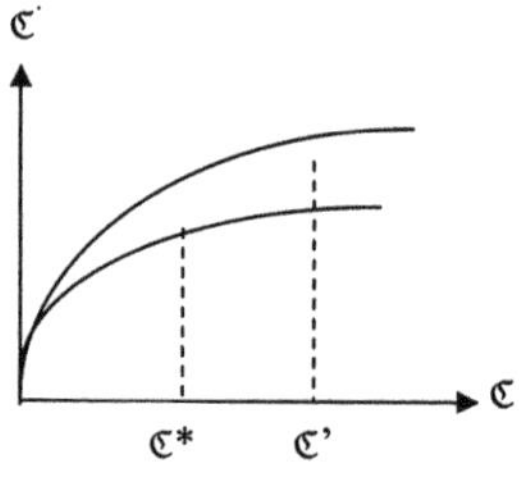

§5.2-2 Systematic Approach to Development and Trade

Global trade stages. To classify the stage of trade, we shall pay attention to the following factors: import of commodities and outside culture, import substitution of commodities, export of commodities, import-substitution of outside culture or develop of indigenous culture, and eventually export of one's own culture.

For nations of early industrialization, after the previous autarchy stage, the process of developing their global trade may be classified into five stages. The first stage is that of imperialism imposing colonialism onto weak nations by military means. The second stage is to export light industrial products and to import agricultural products. The third stage involves the export of heavy industrial products and the import of agricultural products, raw materials and light industrial products. In the fourth stage, industrially advanced nations export high-technological products and import agricultural, light and heavy industrial products from outside. Finally, in the fifth stage, these nations export their cultures, maybe by the combination of cultural, financial and military means.

It is well known that, in the last four trading stages, industrially advanced nations have strengthened their trade positions by the use of free trade mechanism, imperialist or quasi-imperialist means, direct or humanitarian interventionist devises, or other methods to induce and force non-industrial nations to accept their demands to trade, eother voluntary or involuntarily.

For the latecomer nations of industrialization, in general, there are also five stage of trade development to be concerned with: traditional stage of importing light industrial products, stage of importing light industrial products/weaponry together with large scale import of outside cultures, import-substitution stage (at first to substitute light industrial product under low-level and low-technological culture, then to substitute heavy industrial product under the intermediate-and-medium level of technological culture), export-substitution stage (at first to import high-level and high-technological culture and to export light industrial product, then to engage in a preliminary attempt to regenerate and re-develop one's own culture and to export heavy industrial product), the stage of cultural substitution stage in regenerate and recreate indigenous culture.

Below let us represent some examples to illustrate our theory of trade. Latin American countries, at the third stage economic culture-development, engaged in substituting light and heavy industrial products and exported agricultural products and mineral resources. For socialist countries, in general, from the very beginning, they severed their trade tie with capitalist countries and engaged in the substitution of military, light and heavy industrial products.

As for Taiwan and South Korea, they pursued the import substitution policy only for a very short period of time, approximately a decade or so since 1950. At the same time, Hong Kong directed itself to become the financial center linking China with the outside world, and Singapore evolved into the regional financial center of Southeast Asia.

At the fourth stage of culture-economic development, nations like Taiwan and South Korea created and instituted their own strategies and pursued trade paths in defying the conventional wisdom of free trade. In general, these countries invented and implemented effective policies and brand new strategies to export light-industrial products and import agricultural products and raw materials from outside in supporting their trade expansion. This is the initial phase of Asian NICs' export-substitution stage.

At the later phase of this stage, Taiwan, Hong Kong, Singapore and South Korea pursued the growth path of promoting export of light electronic products. Furthermore, South Korea attempted to develop steel, machinery, automobile, and ship-building industries for the purpose of enhancing export, and was very successful in some of these activities. In the realm of Latin America, due to geographic vicinity to the United States, at this stage Mexico expanded rapidly its scope of export-substitution policy.

For the latecomers, the theories of David Ricardo's comparative advantage and the trade cycle (Vernon 1966) are useful if we are to deal with the conventionally defined economic problems. For the developing countries, at the afore-mentioned third and forth stages of trade development, the theory of dynamically comparative advantage under the aegis of various national governments' growth strategies is helpful. Recall that List had a dynamic theory of "protecting infant industries" (Hayami 2001, p.233) relating trade protection to the time dynamics of the cost of production. But the principles underlying the above-mentioned stages are somewhat different from List's theory. It seems that List did not discuss the factors such as (engineering and cultural) education, public R&D and global political and military strategies.

In general, for most of the latecomer-nations, the fifth stage is either the current or the future stage. This is a dynamic or "sheng-sheng generatic" (life-oriented dynamical) stage of economic development or advancement. At this stage, in the conventional economics, there is a difference between the concepts of mathematical equilibrium and disequilibrium; while in culture, there is a difference between the concepts of systemic or life-oriented continuity and discontinuity. In systemics, all cultural variables change simultaneously. At this last stage, the industrially underdeveloped countries may want to replace the un-discriminatively imported and transplanted cultural mix with the indigenously developed new culture. Before this phase of culture-trade development, some industrially underdeveloped countries may have already given up their own cultures completely and lost their cultural identity. For the newly created culture, one ideal case is to treat one's own cultural heritage as the basis and to choose the cream of Western cultures to be integrated into it. By so doing, this new culture shall amount to the simultaneous creation of one's own culture and a new "Western" culture. Then upon this cultural basis, the task of the transfusion of Western technology may be achieved with reasonable efforts and new technology is also expected to be created indigenously. This would be a great cycle of culture-technology-culture in which the indigenous creativity of culture is the ultimate source of technological and organizational (including the business) creativities. In this sense, culture creativity is essentially the basis of global trade. Therefore in the long-term perspective, culture-strategic advantage constitutes the most important aspect of a nation's comparative advantage of trade.

Essentially this is the *stage of cultural exchange*, in which culture is not necessarily treated as a commodity. That is, this is a stage of exporting one's own culture (at least with a distinctive niche) to outside world once it is created after absorbing the merits of others' cultures. This is essentially a process of exchanging cultures among nations.

Stages of modern economic development. In general, for the process of economic development, we may be able to classify it into the extensive stage which may be divided into two phases -- labor-intensive and capital-intensive phases, the intensive stage or technology-intensive stage, and the cultural stage.

(1) Extensive stage. In this stage (say, the first phase of the foreign culture-dominating stage), there is the one-dimensional production possibility frontier which may shift outward by the growth of raw labor and capital, through the promotion of domestic capital formation and the import of capital stock from abroad.

(2) Intensive stage. This may be considered as the "single foreign cultural" stage (say, the second phase of the foreign culture-dominating stage) in which the production possibility frontier may shift upward once for all in the second dimension depicted by the strength of technological progress created by a single culture of a foreign country. Due to the nature of a monoculture, there is only a single chain of will-to-creation and rationality-to-creation in this imported culture.

(3) The stage of the culture of self-masterism. This is a multiple cultural stage in which the *new indigenous culture* is developed with the background of the global culture. For this stage, in the context of the newly developed indigenous culture stimulated by the advancement of the global culture, we shall divide it into two phases.

Phase I. This is the initial phase in which the cultural strength manifests itself in the strength of technological progress. In this phase, culture may be constant, and the cultural strength leads to the development of new technologies due to the merits of this cultural attributes. The production possibility frontier shifts further upward in the second dimension depicted by the culture-technological strength. Because this involves multiple cultures, the will-rationality complex is then a composite chain complex of the will-to-creation and rationality-to-creation.

Phase II. This is the subsequent phase in which the cultural strength manifests itself in the strength of organizational improvement or advancement. In this phase, the development of new culture leads not only to the development of new technologies, but also to the development of new organizational forms. The production possibility frontier is therefore shifted upward in the third dimension depicted by the culture-organizational strength. This cultural strength is closely related to the idea of cultural advantage about which we shall have more discussion later.

In the following, we shall rely on some mathematic models in presenting various stages of economic development and advancement. To simplify our analysis, the discussion of the development and advancement process will focus only on three stages: capital stage, technological stage, cultural stage.

At the capital stage, we stipulate that technology would not vary (or the change of technology is negligible) and culture would stand still (or advance with negligible change); that is, in the production function, $y = AK$, capital accumulation constitutes the only force of dynamics. This is similar to what is called the Marx's stage (Hayami 2001, p.149). Note that in this stage, it is extremely important to overcome the "capital stagnation trap."

In this stage, land capital may be enlarged by military conquest over others' territories. A nation may be able to increase its labor supply with little cost by turning other people into slavery and thereby to create the efficiency of primitive accumulation of imperialist capitalism. Or may be due to hard work, high saving and investment rates, the supply of capital stock of a nation may increase significantly.

Let the real national income or output be denoted by y, $\underline{\underline{K}} \equiv K(.\,|\,\underline{tech},\underline{\mathfrak{C}})$ be the capital stock with technology being held constant ($\underline{tech}$) and culture being kept constant as well ($\underline{\mathfrak{C}}$), and a, b, c and d be parameters. Then the "linearized" real national output may be expressed as a first order differential equation, where $y^{\cdot}$ denotes the time derivative of y, $\phi(y)$ a function of y, $\psi(\underline{\underline{K}})$ a function of $\underline{\underline{K}}$, and L the raw labor:

(5.2-2-1) $y^{\cdot} = a\phi(y) + bL + c\psi(\underline{\underline{K}}) + d.$

At the technological stage, given that technology develops rapidly and yet the underlying culture is held constant (or culture changes in a negligibly manner): that is, in the production function, $y = f(L,K;tech) = AL^{\alpha}K^{\beta}$, technology (tech) is the major force of dynamics. This stage is similar to the so-called Kuznets stage (Hayami 2001, p. 149). Note that in this stage, the trap of technological stagnation must be carefully avoided.

This is essentially a stage of micro-technology, and in the conventional approach to economics, technology and the core culture of the human kind are essentially assumed to be separated. In this stage, for one thing, religion may be considered as the culture of the highest spiritual state, and therefore the value of after-life heaven is conceived as higher than the value of life in this world in general and higher than that of technology in particular. In the society of this stage, liberal arts and the systems of sciences and technology are segregated. The social status of the capitalist, politicians, lawyers and medical doctors are much higher than that of physical scientists and engineers. The common people in general pay much more attention to practical issues than to the theory. Students at all levels of schools are not proud of studying natural sciences and mathematics.

At this stage, culture is just a monoculture, being essentially stagnant. One famous example is the theory of "the end of history" advocated by Francis Fukuyama, in which, it is essentially asserted that, from today on, the culture of the mankind will forever be the culture of the United States of America. Thus history has already ended and will not advance any more, and the culture of democratic capitalism is destined to forever dominate the universe.

To present this stage in a mathematical form, let y be the real national income, $\underline{tech} \equiv tech(.\,|\,\underline{C})$ be the technological factor with culture being held constant, and a, b, c, d, e be parameters. Then, after linearization, the real national income y may be expressed in a form of differential equation as follows, with $\phi(y)$ being a function of y, $\psi(\underline{\underline{K}})$ being a function of $\underline{\underline{K}}$, and $\eta(\underline{tech})$ being a function of $\underline{tech}$:

(5.2-2-2) $y^{\cdot} = a\phi(y) + bL + c\psi(\underline{\underline{K}}) + d\eta(\underline{tech}) + e.$

At the cultural stage, suppose culture changes all the time: in the production function $y = f(L,K,\mathfrak{C})$ (or $AL^{\alpha}K^{\beta}\mathfrak{C}^{\gamma}$), culture is the major force of dynamism (be aware whether there is a natural trap of cultural stagnation). At this stage, culture develops with leaps and bounds, and the engineering-technological creativity is eventually determined by the combined forces of micro- and macro-culture.

The impetus for capital accumulation and the creativity promoting technological development may stem from the *culture advantage* of a nation. On the spiritual side, to connect a society's business functions and scientific and engineering activities to religion (or the cause for one's ultimate concerns) and the cultural core certainly renders a great service in improving the performance of the underlying cultural economy. This cultural advantage will also manifest itself in the operations of the polity and society embodying this cultural core. For more detail of this discussion, see Appendix J.

At this stage, technology is one of the self-being and mutual-being and this culture is a comprehensive one. Here the core culture of a society and the technology become one in unity. In this kind of society of a global culture, for instance, the highest spiritual state of the common people is perhaps the life-in-this-world, and this world is a world of culture as well as that of technology. That is, technology becomes an art and a religion as well. To the common person, cultural creativity inter-penetrates technological creativity, and the theory and practice have the equal and same status. Students at all level of schools devote themselves to study physical sciences and mathematics and strive hard to achieve a balance between mastering subjects of liberal arts and the studying of natural sciences. In this society, humanities and science/technology confer equal social prestige, and wherein, the social status of "humanity workers" is highly regarded, and they must acquire the same level of social status as those of capitalist, politician, lawyer, medical doctor, natural scientist and some highly specialized technicians.

In this stage, culture develops from a monoculture into a dual culture, and further to a multiculture and eventually to the global one. The dual and multi-cultures are mixed cultures which may embody easily some endogenous forces of internal confusion, inconsistency and even conflict. From there, they eventually transform and advance into a total or global culture. This total culture may have several phases, ranging from the early one of integration, interpenetration of elements of different origins, to the one of eliminating the less desirable parts and groping for new frontiers, and finally to the one of evolving into the last form of freshly created new culture of the highest state possible. After this global or total culture, by our reasoning, the new stage is then the one of self-differentiation (d-systemism), self-change (in a yinyang direction, y-systemism), self-negation (f-systemism), self-advancement into a higher stage (h-systemism); and it may transform or even transmute into a yet higher level of forms, and so on. For these d-, y-, f- and h-systemisms, see Appendix A, Section A.5. In the case of a European country, the philosophical foundation is simply a Western cultural system or a Western cultural system with a multitude potential for further advancement. In the case of China, for an initial and ideal type of this, we shall call it the culture of self-masterism with the philosophical foundations developed from a due process of integrating tao-chi multidimensional monism with being monism and "self-organizationalism." In general, the cultural basis depends on the historical heritage of the nation in question.

The system of self-mastery, either socio-politically or economically, is one in which every person will eventually becomes his or her own master. In the system of democratic capitalism, a human being is way too utilitarian and materialistically oriented, too self-indulged, and too restricted to social norms and conventions set by the culture-it-self and by other members in the same society, be they one's closely associated fellows, overly powerful politicians, or one's employers in career or in a business endeavor. In short, capitalism is permeated with too much pecuniary calculation, and democracy is discharging too much energy toward the frontier of fighting against the "high culture." In the culture of self-masterism, sciences and technology are highly valued, and yet, the spirit and rationality of humanism are what are supposed to dominate sciences and technology. Hopefully and naturally, the ideal case is to synchronize, harmonize and even integrate the developments of humanism and sciences and technology to the mutual benefit of the further developments of both endeavors.

At this cultural stage, sciences and technology are not a set of mono-cultural objects. What lies under sciences and technology of the pure democratic capitalism (i.e., without concerns about Christianity and other human spirits) is the system of mechanics–logic and experimentalism. These are fundamental to the cultures of techniques and the technologies of pure sciences (in the narrow sense). In contrast, sciences and technologies of a dual-culture could be those of being culture and yu-wu culture at the same time, using mathematical and logical reasoning methods to penetrate any single directional entity and employing systemic (multi-factor causal-effect, or simply yu-wu) reasoning process to integrate different intellectual entities into a comprehensive unity. The being-reasoning methods are more quantitative. So far, they are also more accurate in their way of investigation and appear to be with an outward and even forward-looking orientation. In contrast, the process of yu-wu reasoning is more qualitative, more humane and even more spiritual; and so far it appears to be an inward-looking approach, though definitely not a backward-looking one. Nevertheless, in this world of modern and (Western) sciences, the process of yu-wu reasoning has an added advantage of liberating one from one's own cultural limitations. This is natural because the yu-wu reasoning was initially developed with an intention to integrate different cultures into one unity. Historically, we may say that this yu-wu reasoning was developed to unite the northern Chinese Confucian culture with the southern Chinese Taoist culture (and even the Legalist culture). Note that at that time, northern China and southern China had people of different ethnicities and heterogeneous cultural origins. Later on, this yu-wu reasoning was further developed to integrate the classical Chinese culture with the imported foreign culture of Buddhism from India. Now at the modern time, this reasoning process is developed at even a higher stage to integrate the Western cultural mode with the East Asian one. It is reasonable to state that the yu-wu reasoning is always a process of intellectual inquiry into an ideal way of combining and cross-pollinating one's own ideas with foreign ones in order to advance to a higher level unity of culture.

Note that this argument can be strengthened by judging the impact of rationality on business behavior of the East and the West. In the (economics of the) West, a business corporation is considered only as an impersonal institution. But in the context of East Asian culture, a firm is a part of socioeconomic institutions (Tai 1989, p. 19). The interpersonal relationship in an oriental firm goes beyond a pure business endeavor. It involves the family members and affects the social activities of employees beyond the normal duty of business. The employer may adopt a paternalistic altitude toward its employees. That is, in the West, a single-entity approach to business is preferred, while in East Asia, the option of a holistic approach is chosen.

To go beyond the world of dual cultures, we come to one of triple cultures. For a practical scheme, we may name it as the cultural mix of Fziranism, democratic capitalism, and dialectic socialism. It is interesting to note that, under this triple-culturalism, the interactions between yu-wu rationality and dialectic rationality can both stimulate and negate each other, and thereby create a brand new mode of reasoning. Yu-wu rationality and dialectic rationality, with the help of scientific rationality by its logical rigor and its being-oriented experimental measures, could advance the modern technology without any precedent to a new high level. For example, today's China with its background of traditional culture, by absorbing military technology from Russia and through assimilating civilian technology from the Unite States, Europe and Japan, may be able to develop some new technologies of the twenty-first century. Here through the constant interface of military and civilian technologies, new technological heights could be created, since the principles of military and civilian technologies are similar and interchangeable, and thus could be integrated into one. This is a good example of how a triple culture may be able to engage in certain types of backward engineering and, through this process of supporting one technology by the others, applied technology can be unified more easily with theoretical advancement.

Before we go further, let us have a short comment for the nature of endogenous growth. The so-called human capital and monopolistic approach may at best explain only part of endogenous technological advancement. This approach is an incomplete micro-approach, because at this level, technology involves also the non-business will and the ability of the engineering aspect of technology. Furthermore, basic and initial stage of applied R&D is usually done in public-funded and non-business private institutions. All these foundations of technological creativity lie well beyond the reach of any market structural approach. Further, for the so-called human capital, it basically entails the strengths of education and health care. These aspects of human activities may not penetrate deeply into the rationality and will of the human being. This can be seen clearly in the case of classical China which was quite a market economy over two millennia. The fact that China lacked the tradition of Western-type sciences was due to geographic, historical, cultural and even socio-political factors, not much related to the nature of market structure of that nation.

At the macro level, government intervention is extremely important in the process of technological advancement. It is natural to notice that human capital and monopolistic approach to technology ignores the aspect of macro-technology and deep cultural roots.

Below, we shall present a few more mathematical models to address the issues of culture and technology in the process of modern economic development and advancement.

Let the real national income be y, $\mathfrak{C}$ be the cultural variable, and a, b, c, d, e be fixed parameters. Then, for a cultural economy, the real and "linearized" national income may be expressed as the following first-order differential equation, where $\phi(y)$ is a function of y, $\psi(\underline{\underline{K}})$ a function of $\underline{\underline{K}}$, and $\xi(\mathfrak{C})$ a function of $\mathfrak{C}$:

(5.2-2-3) $y^{\cdot} = a\phi(y) + bL + c\xi(\underline{\underline{K}}) + d\mathfrak{C} + e.$

Here the technological factor tech = $f(L,K,\mathfrak{C})$ is a function of raw labor, capital stock, and cultural variable. Technology is essentially a function of culture, and by this is meant that cultural creativity is the most important source of technological creativity. That is, in the long-term perspective, cultural variable is the most important factor in explaining the forces of supply. It is easy to reason that this systematic and cultural approach to the theory of endogenous growth will eventually be a more productive one. The conventional approach to the endogenous growth theory is very narrow, and it essentially relies on a limited span of market institution and a process of innovation. It fails to explain technology in terms of the foundations of human creativity or cultural creativity. In systematics, culture is the general name given to the sum complex of organizational arrangements, strategic elements and the general cultural forces. In this definition, all aspects of business institution and market organizations are included in this variable of culture.

Furthermore, all firms in the economics of culture, including those of competitive ones, have downward-sloping demand curve in the short term and the long term states of strategic continuity and discontinuity (or short run and long run disequilibrium). Therefore, obtaining an above-normal level of profits is a norm but not an exception for all firms. In a world of simple logic, it may be said that only with positive above-normal profits, R&D in a firm becomes possible.

In the context of total supply and total demand of a national economy, government policy affects the supply of capital stock, either through reducing the cost or tax burden of the firms, or by raising the saving and investment rates of the general public, or through formal education to raise the general skill level and the consciousness of positive work ethics as was in the case of East Asia for the past decades. This may also be achieved by the government through importing foreign technology, raising the level of science and technological education, establishing national institutes of research and development, providing national research laboratories, and so on. As a result, these activities of the government help promote the technological level of the nation. On the other hand, by alternating the structure of demand, agricultural production may be reduced on the long term basis and industrial activities may be enhanced (assuming the nation's production mix has a potential for substitution, such as an opportunity for a large scale foreign trade and invoking foreign debt).

Or by alternating the structure of supply, light industrial production may be reduced on the long term basis and heavy industrial activities may be enhanced (assuming the nation's production mix has a potential for substitution, such as an opportunity for a large scale import of foreign capital and technology). By a large scale alternation of the content of supply, such as significantly increasing the supply of heavy and high-technological industrial production, and by reducing the demand for light industrial products, the short-term cs and TS curves will shift downward, cd and TD curves will shift outward, then the real national income will be substantially increased. In the long term process, the outward shift of cs and TS curves will result in the shift of the normal output curve y_N to the right (similar to Figure 4.2-2). In terms of growth, let $h(\underline{tech})$ be a function of $\underline{tech}$, and $f(\underline{K})$ and $g(\underline{K})$ functions of $\underline{K}$. Suppose the time derivatives of $\underline{K}$ and $\underline{tech}$ exit. Then we have the following growth model:

(5.2-2-4) $\underline{K}^{\cdot} = af(\underline{K}) + bL + c,$

(5.2-2-5) $\underline{tech}^{\cdot} = \alpha\, h(\underline{tech}) + \beta g(\underline{K}) + \Upsilon L + \delta,$

where $\underline{K} \equiv K(. \mid \underline{tech}, \underline{C})$ refers to the level of capital stock with which technology does not change and culture remains constant over time, $\underline{tech} \equiv tech(. \mid \underline{C})$ denotes the technological factor when culture remains constant, a, b, α, β are parameters, and c and δ can be either fixed parameters or stochastic variables. In this kind of model (for example, see Eq. (5.2-2-7) where k is replaced by $\underline{K}/L$), technology develops rapidly due to strategic manipulation.

In the process of cultural economic development, because of hard work and frugality of the people, saving rate increases; and because the citizens have a strong desire to develop their nation, the rate of investment increases as well. When this economically less developed nation engages in trade with outside, the import of advanced capital stock may at the same time bring in advanced technology embodied in these imported capital stocks. In this case, an ability to engage in backward engineering of the imported products is essential. Thus, for this nation, the import of capital stock enhances its import and absorption of outside technology, and vice versa.

Therefore, for an economically less developed nation, by strong work ethics, frugality and strong will of the citizens to promote development, the capital stage therefore endures a longer life time. In the case of East Asia, a strong "religious belief" leads to a strong sense of ancestral worship and an emphasis of family continuity. Note that this goes beyond pure economic concerns and this strong tie in family forms a foundation of the family capital which constitutes a solid part of social capital in East Asia. In this stage, the society and the business

community also place extremely high values on the virtues of solidarity, loyalty, dependability, industriousness and compliances. According to Tai (1989, p. 22), East Asian people are said to discourage the undertaking of risk-taking and creative endeavors. This appears to happen only in the earlier phases of this stage.
Similarly, suppose this developing nation has an advantage of multiple culture and its export activities also enable it to accumulate foreign exchange by importing raw materials and exporting manufacturing products out of these imported resources. Then its capital stage will also be lengthened by the positive impact of constantly importing higher and ever higher levels of technology from outside. That is, higher level of technology makes it possible to be essentially more capital abundant. In addition, the technological stage of a developing country may be induced to proceed backward into the past. This is because of the function of trade accelerates the process of absorbing higher level of technology from outside and because this economy has an ability to digest foreign culture at a relatively earlier time. Hence it will induce the technological stage at a time earlier than the normal case.

One more factor related to the acceleration of technological stage is the role of the intellectual-capital-_family-capital_social-capital chain. With a greater emphasis on the culture of technology by the society, communities, all levels of schools, families and the intellectuals as a whole, as we mentioned in the above, the capital stage may enter earlier than its natural course. This cultural stage requires technological as well as cultural creativities. When the individual or the spirit of micro-technology posses a certain degree of religiosity, when the society places people of technological backgrounds on high positions of its political and economic echelons, and when the business community chooses people of technological background to lead its institutions, the culture of sciences penetrates deeply into the world of being, and the culture of yu-wu permeates and moves back and forth between the world of being and the world of nothingness. Naturally due to the totality and the integrated whole of the multiple layers of rationality and will, the distortions generated by human will and rationality in daily routine endeavor is therefore minimized. That is, this multiple cultural stage is best for cultivating, supporting and developing the creativities of both organizational and technological advancement.

Below we shall discuss the *dynamic trajectory of capital and culture*. For a comprehensive treatment, the above stages of capital and culture can be combined into the *stage of capital and culture*. Let $\gamma(\underline{k})$ and $g(\underline{k})$ respectively be functions of $\underline{k}$, for $\underline{k} = \underline{K}/L$, the first derivative of $g(\underline{k})$ be positive and the second derivative of $g(\underline{k})$ be negative. Here $\underline{k}$ denotes the level of capital stock with technology and culture being held constant, and $\underline{k}^{\cdot}$ is defined as a function of technology (i.e., $h(\underline{tech})$, $b, c \in R$) and population growth rate (i.e., $\zeta\,(p^{\cdot}/p)$, $\zeta \in \mathbb{R}$):

$$(5.2\text{-}2\text{-}6)\quad \begin{aligned} y &= \gamma(\underline{k}) + b\, h(\underline{tech}) + \xi(p^{\cdot}/p) + u \\ \underline{k}^{\cdot} &= ag(\underline{k}) - \delta\underline{k} + c\, h(\underline{tech}) + \zeta(p^{\cdot}/p) + \varepsilon \end{aligned}$$

where y represents the (real) per capita national income, δ the rate of per capita capital depreciation, u, ε stochastic variables, and $\xi(p^{\cdot}/p)$ a function of population growth rate for $\xi \in \mathbb{R}$. Then, the steady-state equilibrium level of per capita capital stock $\underline{k}^*$ is obtained as the point of intersection between $ag(\underline{k})$ and $\delta\underline{k}$, if the mathematical expectations of u and ε are set to be zero (strictly speaking, u and ε must be written as u_i and ε_i, respectively, for $i = 1,2,\ldots,n$, n being the number of observation in the probability space). Note that here, $\underline{k}$, population and technology (i.e., $\underline{tech}$) are held constant.

Now if b and c are positive, then when the level of technology rises (or $\underline{tech}$ changes), g($\underline{k}$) will increase significantly and δ will become smaller. Therefore, in the graph of $\dot{k}$-k dimensions, the trajectory of $\underline{k}$* will shift upward, and $\underline{k}$** will increase accordingly. Here, until technology leaps, the marginal product of technology with respect to capital will go down: that is, the first derivative of h($\underline{tech}$) with respect to $\underline{k}$ will be positive and the second derivative will be negative.

But when technology leaps, then the marginal product of technology with respect to capital may not decrease. Logically, if parameters b and c are negative, then the results would be opposite for what we have obtained in the above.

Similarly, if ξ and ζ are positive functions, then when the population growth rate increases, the trajectory of $\underline{k}$* will shift upward, and the steady-state equilibrium level of capital per person $\underline{k}$* will go up. Nevertheless, if ξand ζ are negative, then the result will definitely be in the opposite direction. Thus, in the above, for b, c, ξ and ζ being negative, we derive a conventional Solow-type growth model. Here, we hold the real per capita national income constant. As the level of technology or the population as a whole increases, the marginal product of capital will be higher. Hence, to maintain the original level of per capita national income, less capital is required. That is the logic behind this kind of model: the steady state equilibrium level of capital stock decreases when the level of technology rises while holding per capita national income constant (i.e., in the case of negative b, c, ξ and ζ); or the steady state equilibrium level of per capita national income increases when the level of technology rises or the population grow rate increases.

Figure 5.2-2-1
The steady-state equilibrium level of per capita capital stock under constant levels of technology and population k*

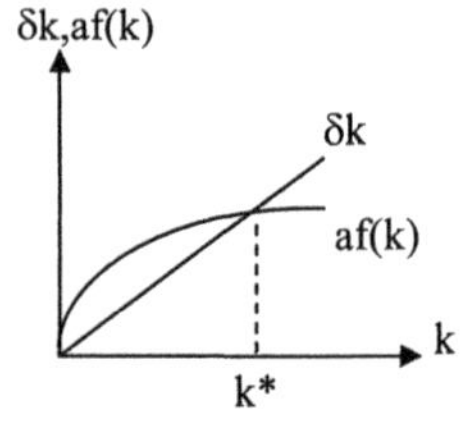

Therefore, with the level of technology or the population increases and per capita national income becomes higher, the upward or downward trend of the steady-state capital stock is determined by the interactions between the rate of capital depreciation and the marginal efficiency of capital. That is to say, if the increase in the rate of depreciation is less than the increase in the marginal efficiency of capita, then the result of the increase in the level of technology (or the population) and the increase in the level of per capita national income will definitely raise the steady-state equilibrium level of capital (in this case, b, c, ξ and ζ are positive). As a contrast, if the increase in the rate of depreciation is greater than the increase in the marginal efficiency of capita, then the combined result of the increase in the level of technology (or the population) and the increase in the level of per capita national income will definitely lower the steady-state equilibrium level of capital (in this case, b, c, ξ and ζ are negative). These results can be easily seen in Figures 5.2-2-1 and 5.2-2-2.

Figure 5.2-2-2
The dynamic trajectory of the steady-state equilibrium level of per capita capital

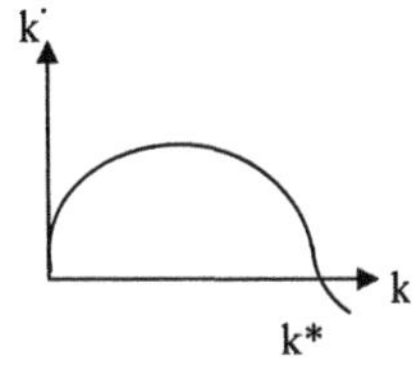

Below we shall establish a cultural model to address the dynamics of an economy in the cultural stage. For a cultural economy at this stage, before culture may have any leap, let f($\mathbb{c}$) be a function of per capita culture ($\mathbb{c} \equiv \mathbb{C}/L$) (assumed to be measurable) with its first derivative being positive and second derivative negative. At the same time, le $\varphi(\mathbb{c},k)$ be a function of $\mathbb{c}$ and k, for g(k) being a function of k (for k = K/L) with u and ε being stochastic variables following a Wiener or Poisson process, and b, c, α, $\beta \in \mathbb{R}$ parameters. The model is then in the following:

$$\text{(5.2-2-7)}\quad \begin{aligned} y &= \varphi(\mathbb{c},k) + \alpha(\dot{p}/p) + u, \\ \dot{\mathbb{c}} &= bf(\mathbb{c}) - c\mathbb{c} + g(k) + \beta(\dot{p}/p) + \varepsilon, \end{aligned}$$

where c is the depreciate rate of culture per capita. Since tech is a function of L, K and $\mathbb{c}$, note that the technological factor is indirectly embodied in Eq. (5.2-2-7) through the factors of $\mathbb{c}$, p (population), and k. Thus, the steady-state equilibrium level of culture $\mathbb{c}^*$ is obtained as the point of intersection between the curves of bf($\mathbb{c}$) and c$\mathbb{c}$ (holding k and population constant) when the mathematical expectations of u and ε are zero. In the figure with $\dot{\mathbb{c}}$-$\mathbb{c}$ dimensions (see Figure 5.2-2-3), as capital stock K increases, f($\mathbb{c}$) will increase; and therefore, as the trajectory of $\mathbb{c}$ shifts upward, $\mathbb{c}^*$ will increase. Here, u and ε could be Wiener or Poisson processes. Similarly, in the figure with $\dot{\mathbb{c}}$-$\mathbb{c}$ dimensions, the increase of the level of technology will raise f($\mathbb{c}$); and when the trajectory of $\dot{\mathbb{c}}$ shifts upward, $\mathbb{c}^{*\cdot}$ will increase and therefore move to the right.

Note that not so much as is in the case of a change in technology, the change in population may or may not be a significant factor exerting any impact on culture.

Historically, one observed that the leap-frog advancement of a culture, other than in the case of dominance by outside forces, is determined by the will and rationality of the human being in the society conditioned upon the underlying factors of economic, social, political, global and environmental dimensions. With culture advancing due to the stimuli of these aforementioned factors, f($\mathbb{c}$) goes up, and consequently the trajectory of $\dot{\mathbb{c}}$ shifts up with an increasing value of $\mathbb{c}^{*\cdot}$ (see Figure 5.2-2-4). In this process, the marginal product of capital with respect to culture may not decrease over time.

Figure 5.2-2-3
The steady-state equilibrium level of per capita culture under constant level of capital stock

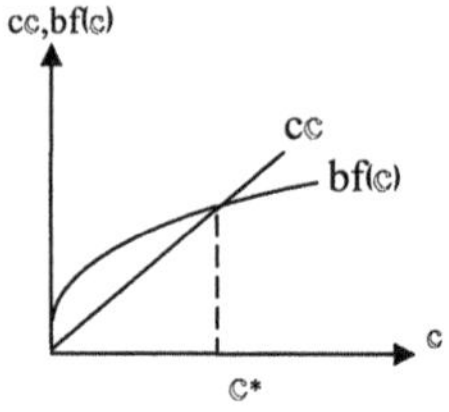

Figure 5.2-2-4
The dynamic trajectory of the steady-state equilibrium level of culture under constant capital stock

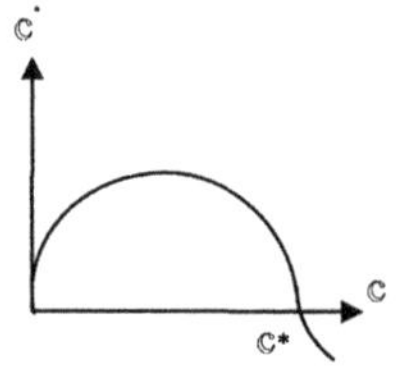

In terms of a macroeconomic model, the interactions between technology and culture will cause rightward shifts of Y_N (under a normal state) and the TS curve (in the TS-TD model, similar to Figure 4.2-2). By this, we establish a natural link between growth and the short-term macroeconomic fluctuation of a cultural economy.

In the above, we establish an endogenous model:

(5.2-2-8) $\underline{k}^{\cdot} = ag(\underline{k}) - \delta\underline{k} + cf(\mathbb{c}) + \eta(p^{\cdot}/p) + \varepsilon_i$,

(5.2-2-9) $\underline{tech}^{\cdot} = \alpha g(\underline{k}) - d\underline{tech} + \gamma f(\mathbb{c}) + \xi(p^{\cdot}/p) + \varepsilon_j$,

where a, c, d, α, δ, γ, η and ξ are assumed to be constants, and ε_i and ε_j can be treated as stochastic variables. From this, the culture may be established as the ultimate source of growth through its impact on the capital formation and technological improvement.

In the Western world of twenty-first century, as a general trend, the number of immigrants becomes larger and ever larger, while the general public, as the combined forces of the families, communities, schools, the business and even the government – may not pay sufficient attention to the role of education in terms of the formation of the desirable personal characters of the student population and the instruction of mathematics and natural sciences in the elementary and secondary schools. Being so, there may be a natural limitation that restricts the potential for the future growth of the West. That is, the limit of growth in the West may stem from the cultural restriction rather than from the ultimate scarcity of natural resources facing these nations. This means culture may place a restriction upon the growth potential of any cultural economy.

By contrast, Chinese culture will most likely develop well in this new century. The Chinese tradition emphasizes the role of liberal arts education, and Marxist culture pays a particular attention to the impact of the education of mathematics and physical sciences upon the society by its philosophy of dialectic materialism. For the modern China, due to the combination of these cultural traditions, the development of sciences and technology becomes a national feast. Partially building upon the political foundation of Western democracy, China may equip itself with a new cultural efficiency to safeguard the continuous advancement of its economy in this century.

Here, simply due to the limitation of space of this paper, we shall not have any in-depth study of the potential for a revival of the creativity of Western Europe.

Now we turn to the relationships between the TS-TD model and three stage development of a cultural economy. By the concept of an economy of the global culturalism, we classify the development process of a cultural economy into three periods: the short term, the medium term, and the long term. In the short term, there are two sub-periods: very short-term and general short-term (somewhat similar to the capitalist stage). In the very short-term, the level of capital stock is held constant. Therefore, with respect to capital, the short-term TS curve (i.e., STTS, see Figure 5.2-1-3 or LRTS in Figure 4.2-2) is horizontal, and is constant. That is, let the cost structure and output structure $C, O \sqsubseteq (\Omega, \mathbb{Z}\circ, {}_{v}\mathbb{H}, \{\mathbb{C}\})$ be:

(5.2-2-10) $C\text{-}O = \underset{\sim}{C}\text{-}\underset{\sim}{O}$,

where C denotes the cost structure with $\underset{\sim}{C}$ being C held constant, and O refers to the output structure with $\underset{\sim}{O}$ being O kept constant. In the general short-term, capital changes, but technology and culture remain constant. Then if capital stock increases, STTS shall shift to the right to STTS'. That is, let $C, O \Vdash (\Omega, \mathbb{Z}\circ, {}_{v}\mathbb{H}, \{\mathbb{C}\})$,

(5.2-2-11) $C\text{-}O \rightarrow C^{-}\text{-}\ O^{+}$,

with C^{-} refers to the cost structure which expands over time with its mathematical measure shrinking over time, and O^{+} depicting the enlarged output structure with its mathematical measure getting larger over time.

In the medium term (somewhat similar to the technological stage), culture is held constant, but capital and technology vary over time. That is, let $C, O \Vdash (\Omega, \mathbb{Z}\circ, {}_{v}\mathbb{H}, \{\mathbb{C}\})$,

(5.2-2-12) $C\text{-}O \rightarrow C^{+}\text{-}\ O^{++}$,

where C^{+} refers to the cost structure which may grow with its mathematical measure being increasing, and O^{++} denotes the output structure which may also grow due to technological progress with a further increase in its mathematical measure. Now, by the increase in national income, total demand will shift outward; and therefore, the cost curve will also shift outward. So STTS at first shifts to the right to STTS', and then rotates downward to the right to STTS." The result is that cost is reduced and output increases over time.

In the long term (partially similar to the cultural stage), the whole curve or the envelop STTS-STTS'- ...- STTS" is called the MTTS. In this time span, LTTS may shift to the left or right, depending upon whether culture progresses or regresses. For if the culture of a society falls into the trough of its cultural cycle, the retreat or even collapse of its cultural creativity of the citizens of this society will cost the stability of the society. And in the worst case scenario, these citizens may even lose their very technological creativity.

Before we turn to the next section, we shall mention briefly the relationship between culture and economic development. First, for Confucianism, see Chung (1989, pp. 149-163 in Tai, ed.) and Park (2000).

Secondly, for the Weberian case of a society with Christian ethics, it is one composed of a class of business people taking advantage of religious belief, rather than a society achieving the highest level of religious spirituality (also see Appendix J). As a transitional one in-between the society of Medieval Age and that of modernity, the religious spirit may not sustain for long.

§5.2-3 Alternative Approach to The Growth of A Cultural Economy

Suppose the cultural system $\mathfrak{C}$ is a real number and let the change in the cultural variable be:

(5.2-3-1) $\Delta\mathfrak{C} = \mathfrak{C}^{+} - \mathfrak{C}^{-}$,

where $\mathfrak{C}^{+}$ refers to the positive increment in $\mathfrak{C}$ (or rising forces of culture), and $\mathfrak{C}^{-}$ the negative increment of $\mathfrak{C}$ (or depreciation of culture) over time. Let

(5.2-3-2) $\mathfrak{C}^{+} = \alpha f(L,K,\mathfrak{C})$,

(5.2-3-3) $\mathfrak{C}^{-} = c\mathfrak{C}$,

with Bcm. (5.2-3-2) derived by assuming the rising forces of culture are proportional to the real national income (i.e., a factor α times the real national income $(L,K,\mathfrak{C})$). Then, from these above becomings, we write:

(5.2-3-4) $\mathfrak{C}^{\cdot} = \alpha f(L,K,\mathfrak{C}) - c\mathfrak{C}$,

by which is meant the net increment in the cultural variable over time (i.e., the time derivative of the culture) is the growing forces of it less the deteriorating forces of it over time. Following the convention of setting for the steady-state equilibrium, we have $\mathfrak{C}^{\cdot} = 0$ and:

(5.2-3-5) $\alpha f(\mathfrak{C};L,K) = c\mathfrak{C}$,

(for $f(\mathfrak{C};L,K)$ denoting the function f(.) with L and K being fixed at certain levels, respectively) from whence we solve for the steady-state equilibrium level of culture $\mathfrak{C}^{*}$. Then, by assuming f(.) as a concave function, we derive Figure 5.2-3-1 in the following.

To derive the real national income from the cultural variable, let $Y = G(L,K,\mathfrak{C}) = \xi(L,K,\mathbb{C}.)\, f(\mathfrak{C})$. That is, it is assumed that the cultural variable is separable from the "cultural residual" $\mathbb{C}.$ which is in turn assumed to be very small and somewhat ignorable. By assuming $f(\mathfrak{C})$ as a concave function, we have Figure 5.2-3-2 [see Figure 5.2-3-2 on p. 101]. Then the steady-state level of (real) national income ((ρ,ω) being a proxy for the cultural variables: $\mathfrak{C} \doteq (\rho,\omega)$) is presented in Figure 5.2-3-2.

Figure 5.2-3-1
The steady-state equilibrium level of Culture

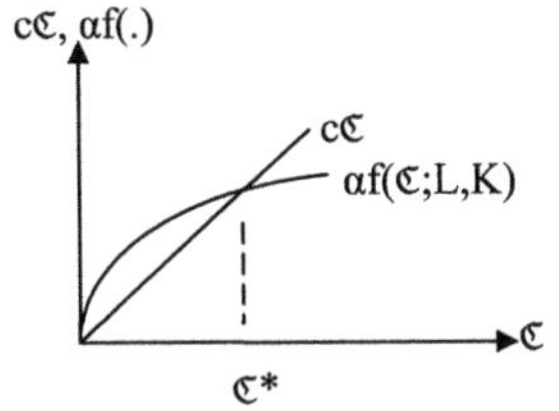

Figure 5.2-3-2
Steady-state culture (ρ,ω)* and Y

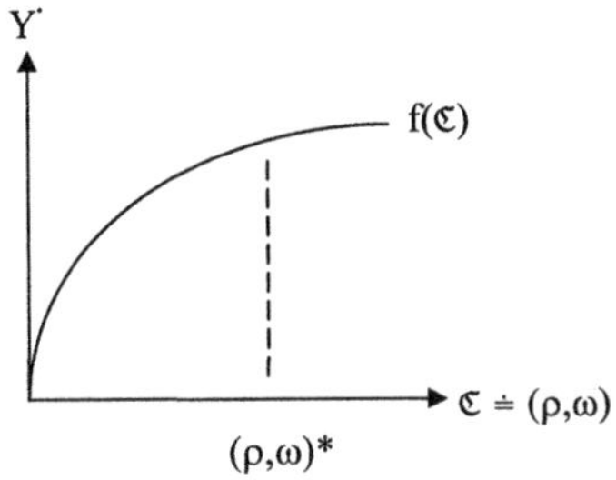

§5.2-4 Moving-Forward and Feedback Cultural Complex and Efficiency-Industrial-Strategic Complex

Here as usual, although we shall not elaborate, the culture and industrial-strategic complexes depend essentially on the culture-institutional arrangements of the IRI chain, the MPFX cycles and the SIFP chain complex of the specific society in question.

Below, let W, D, YW be the will-rationality complexes (or systems) of the culture of conquest-sciences, the dialectic culture, and the yu-wu culture, respectively; and let L^V, K^I, L^F, K^E, and C be the production conducted by the methods of voluntary labor, intensive-use of capital, forced labor, extensive-use of capital, and human creativity, respectively. In addition, let $X/\mathfrak{C}_j$ be the result of the decomposition of the system $X \sqsubseteq (\Omega, \mathbb{Z}\circ, {}_v\mathbb{H}, \{\mathbb{C}\})$ back into the very essential of jth factor of X, for all j factors of our concerns in the above. Then we have Figure

5.2-4 shown below. Here both $\{(L^V,K^I),(L^F,K^E)|C\}$ (**efficiency-industrial strategic complex**) and {W,D|yw-YW} (**cultural complex**) are grand systems.

Further, let f and k be the impactors of reversal construction (or decomposition impactors) and g the **forward construction impactors**. Here f: X → $\{X/\mathfrak{C}_{LvKi}, Y/\mathfrak{C}_{LfKe}, X/\mathfrak{C}_{C}\}$ represents a 3-dimensional operations of f so that in each dimension, we have a reversal construction as shown in Appendix C.

Figure 5.2-4
Moving-Forward and Feedback Cultural Complex and Industrial/Efficiency Strategic Complex

$$\begin{array}{ccc} & \{Y/\mathfrak{C}_W, Y/\mathfrak{C}_D, Y/\mathfrak{C}_{yw}\} & \\ & h\nearrow \qquad\qquad \nwarrow k & \\ X = \{(L^V,K^I),(L^F,K^E)|C\} & \Leftrightarrow & \{W,D|yw\text{-}YW\} = Y \\ & f\searrow \qquad\qquad \nearrow g & \\ & \{X/\mathfrak{C}_{LvKi}, Y/\mathfrak{C}_{LfKe}, X/\mathfrak{C}_C\} & \end{array}$$

Here Both X and Y are corresponding to the efficiency complex of dimension j, where $X/\mathfrak{C}_j$ is the subsystem of X created through reversal construction with $\mathfrak{C}_j$ (the core culture of the factor j of X) being the unit of reversal construction (see Appendix C, ¶C.2, ¶C.3) and similarly for h: X → $\{Y/\mathfrak{C}_W, Y/\mathfrak{C}_D, Y/\mathfrak{C}_{yw}\}$.

In Figure 5.2-4, for X ⇔ Y, we say Y is a copy of **reversal construction** of X, with k: Y → $\{Y/\mathfrak{C}_W, Y/\mathfrak{C}_\Delta, Y/\mathfrak{C}_{yw}\}$ and g: $\{X/\mathfrak{C}_{LvKi}, Y/\mathfrak{C}_{LfKe}, X/\mathfrak{C}_C\}$ → Y: complex {micro-efficiency,macro-efficiency|global-strategic-efficiency} which is a grand system.

Here culture → strategic space ↔ feasibility of the strategy:

SC strategy ← W culture, YW culture
VC ← W culture, YW culture
S ← W culture, YW culture
G ← W culture, YW culture
Δ ← Dialectic culture, YW culture.

Note that in the Section ¶5.2-1, Bcms. (5.2-1-11)-(5.2-1-14) are understood in the context of the culture-strategic background presented here in this subsection.

5.3 Systematic Structures of Cultures in Strategic Economics

Below we present the WR system and its efficiency measure.

WR system (For this section, also see Tonn 2001, Lecture 2, Section 3). Let $\mathfrak{C}_B$, $\mathfrak{C}_\Delta$, $\mathfrak{C}_K$, and $\mathfrak{c}_{yw}$-$\mathfrak{C}_{YW}$ be the culture of conquest-sciences, the dialectic culture, the emptying-out culture, and the yu-wu culture, respectively. Then $\{\mathfrak{C}_B, \mathfrak{C}_\Delta, \mathfrak{C}_K | \mathfrak{c}_{yw}\text{-}\mathfrak{C}_{YW}\}$ is a grand system, in which $\mathfrak{c}_{yw}$-$\mathfrak{C}_{YW}$ is the central system. Here by culture is meant to include the system of will-rationality and the cultures (such as economic and sociopolitical cultures) directly or indirectly related to or supporting this will-rationality system.

Because $\mathfrak{c}_{yw}$-$\mathfrak{C}_{YW}$ is the center, it must have a TCentral will-rationality complex in order to enable the coordination and even integration of all different RW systems into one unity. Note that after this coordination or partial integration, the new grand system may not be one with complete unity. It may retain some degree of tension and even conflict in its inner structure (following the principle of contradiction being no contradiction, in Principle (i) of Section A.2-7).

Efficiency. Let e_L, e_K, and e_c be the micro-efficiency elements of raw labor, capital stock, and culture, respectively, and E_C the macro-strategic efficiency element of culture. Then $\{e_L, e_K | e_c\text{-}E_C\}$ is a grand system of efficiency, in which e_c-E_C is the central system.

Note that the process of cultural changes consist of the adaptation of foreign cultures, modification of the existing culture, creation of new culture, and the export of one's own culture to the outside world, etc.

5.4 Topics on International and Global Economics[5]

In this book, **international economics** is defined as part of global economics which, in the narrow sense, is composed of international economics, global corporations, global management, global marketing, and so on. In the broad sense, all fields of economics belong to **global economics** in which business is an integral part of it. Of course, this global economics is currently only at its initial stage of development.

§5.4-1 Economic Development and International Finance

There are three stages for economically advanced nations: autarchy stage, import and export of commodity stage, and export of culture stage.

There are four stages for developing and advancing nations: autarchy stage, import of commodity and culture stage, export of commodity and import of culture stage, export of culture stage.

In the context of the economics of culture, **economic development** may be defined as a process of economic growth (i.e., a continual increase in the level of material production and consumption) together with a constant improvement of human well-being (i.e., non-material or cultural development closely associated with the process of continual improvement in the material base of the nation).

Note that both of the domestic investment and the net foreign investment are functions of the real interest rate, technology and cultural variables, and so is the case of net exports.

We present the following definitions discussed in the international economics. **Comparative advantage** is defined as an advantage (or merits) a person or a country enjoys with regard to a product if it can produce the product at a cost lower than others can do. Note that a comparative advantage may be achieved in a dynamical sense. Trade balance is the difference between the market value of exports and that of imports in a country. The current account is the summary statement of a country's transactions of goods and services, tourism and government's transfer vis-à-vis the rest of the world. The capital account is the summary statement of a country's transactions of short term and long term financial assets vis-à-vis the rest of the world. Then the balance of payments is the summary of the current account and capital account of a nation vis-à-vis the rest of the world.

Below we turn to the theories of the determination of foreign exchange rate of a nation's currency.

It is well known that the **foreign exchange** rate can be defined as the domestic currency price of one unit of a foreign currency. Foreign exchange rate can also be defined as a foreign currency price of one unit of domestic currency.

There are three theories with regard to the determinants of foreign exchange rate (see Madura 2000). The first is the **theory of interest rate parity** which states that the forward premium is approximately equal to the interest rate differential between two countries. For this, we have the mathematical formula:

$$(5.4\text{-}1\text{-}1)\quad p = \frac{F_j - S_j}{S_j} \approx i_h - i_j$$

where p depicts the forward premium (or forward discount), F_j the forward rate, S_j the spot rate, i_h the home interest rate, and i_f the foreign interest rate.

The second is the theory of **purchasing power parity**. This theory essentially states that the exchange rate's percentage change is approximately equal to the differential in inflation rates between two countries. In mathematical formula, it is:

$$(5.4\text{-}1\text{-}2)\quad e_f = \frac{(1+I_h)}{(1+I_f)} - 1 \approx I_h - I_f$$

with e_f refers to the percentage change in the value of the foreign currency, I_h the home country's inflation rate, and I_f the foreign country's inflation rate.

The last theory of foreign exchange rate determination is the theory of **international fisher effect**. This theory states that the exchange rate's percentage change over the investment horizon is approximately equal to the interest rate differential between two countries. In mathematical formula, it is:

$$(5.4\text{-}1\text{-}3)\quad e_f = \frac{(1+i_h)}{(1+i_f)} - 1 \approx i_h - i_f$$

where e_f denotes the percentage change in the value of the foreign currency, i_h the home country's interest rate, and i_f the foreign country's interest rate.

Now the **systematic advantage** (or systemic advantage) of a nation in trade and development is defined as the advantage or merits of a nation in global trade and business derived from the integrated whole of economic, socio-political and cultural strengths. Note that cultural advantage, together with strategic advantage, is part and parcel of the systemic advantage of a nation.

Below we shall define the terms of trade (TOT) as the ratio of the price index of the exportables (P_{XPT}) over the price index of the importables (P_{MPT}) for a nation, or

$$(5.4\text{-}1\text{-}4)\quad TOT = \frac{\text{prices of exportables}}{\text{prices of importables}}$$

as the absolute value of the slope of the export-import frontier on the Cartesian XPT-MPT coordinate system (see AA' curve in Figure 5.4-1-1).

Figure 5.4-1-1
TOT as the absolute value of the slope of AA' curve

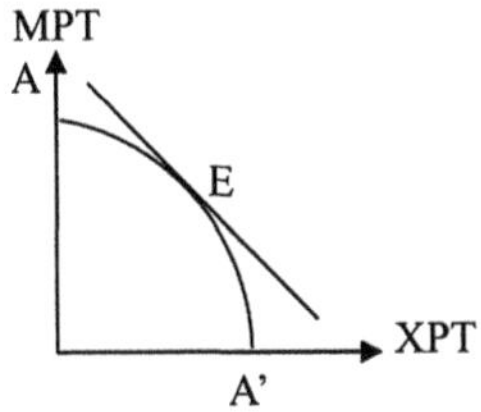

Here by setting the horizontal axis as the axis of exportables (XPT) and the vertical axis as the axis of importables (MPT), it is convenient to derive the terms of trade (TOT) as the slope of the tangent curve on the export-import frontier (AA') in Figure 5.4-1-1. Then, we derive the slope of the AA' curve. Thus, we have:

$$(5.4\text{-}1\text{-}5)\quad \text{Slope of AA' at E} = \frac{dXPT}{dMPT} = -\frac{P_{XPT}}{P_{MPT}}.$$

§5.4-2 Determinants of Trade Balance

The foreign exchange rate together with technology and uncertain cultural variables may be considered as the determinants of a country's trade balance. This is best revealed in the following Figure 5.4-2-1 which shows that, as the real interest at home increases: $r_1 \rightarrow r_2$, the trade balance decreases ($NX_1 \rightarrow NX_2$ or A" → B") when technology and culture are not held constant. Note that this impact of a change in the real interest rate on the net exports may be minimal if technology and culture are held constant. In the real world, as the real interest rate r increases ($r_1 \rightarrow r_2$), its impact on the real exchange rate ε is uncertain, and A → B and A" → B" mainly due to the improvement in technology and the more effective impact of cultural variables.

For Figure 5.4-2-1, the notations are as follows: r depicts the domestic real interest rate, ε the real exchange rate (i.e., amount of foreign currency per unit of domestic currency), T the technology (T < T'), $\mathfrak{C}$ the complex of cultural variables ($\mathfrak{C} < \mathfrak{C}'$), I the domestic investment, NFI the net foreign investment, and NX the net exports, with IN = I + NFI, IN' = I' + NFI', I = I(r;T,$\mathfrak{C}$), I' = I(r;T',$\mathfrak{C}$'), NFI = NFI(r;T,$\mathfrak{C}$), NFI' = NFI(r;T',$\mathfrak{C}$'), NX = NX(ε;T,$\mathfrak{C}$), and NX' = NX(ε;T',$\mathfrak{C}$').

In the model presented here, the shifts of IN to IN', X to X', and NX to NX' are all caused by some changes in cultural variables. Here, for simplicity, the levels of capital accumulation and technology are treated as functions of cultural variables. By assuming that all these IN, X (≡ NFI the net foreign investment curve) and NX curves are relatively steep (to fit many cases of our concerns), the large impact of the change in the net export is mainly accounted for by the impact of a change in cultural variables, rather than by the impact of a change in real interest rate (or of the real foreign exchange rate).

Figure 5.4-2-1
The determination of trade balance

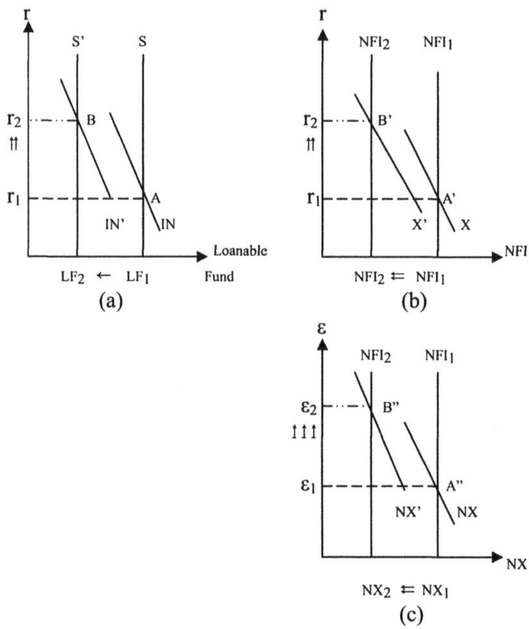

Let us examine Figure 5.4-2-1 presented below. In Panel (a) of Figure 5.4-2-1, the domestic saving is reduced (S↓: S → S'). This causes the level of domestic investment to be lower and therefore reduces the net foreign investment along the IN curve, i.e., LF_1 is reduced to LF_2. Here for I + NFI = IN, by the change in cultural variables, IN shifts to the left: IN → N' because I: I→ I' and NFI↓: NFI → NFI'. By combining the impact of all forces involved, the result is to push up the real interest rate from r_1 to r_2 ($r\uparrow$: $r_1 \rightarrow r_2$). In Panel (b), as the real interest rate increase, the net foreign investment is reduced along the X curve ($NFI\downarrow$: $NFI \rightarrow NFI'$), and by the change in cultural variables, X shifts to X'. By combining the impact of all forces involved, the result is to reduce the level of net foreign investment from NFI_1 to NFI_2 ($NFI \downarrow$: $NFI_1 \rightarrow NFI_2$). In Panel (c), the reduction of net foreign investment (NF_1 shifts to NF_2) causes the value of domestic currency to rise and thus the real exchange rate will go up ($\varepsilon\uparrow$: $\varepsilon_1 \rightarrow \varepsilon_2$). Here the leftward shift of NX to NX' (i..e., the reduction in trade balance of the home country) is accounted for by the change in cultural variables.

Chapter 6 Structural Connections of Systems: Cultural and Comprehensive T centrals, MFCE Scheme and Self-masterism

In this chapter, we introduce in turn each of the concepts of specific T central (Tcentral), general T Central (TCentral), MFCE scheme, and the world of self-masterism for a cultural economy. We shall start off with the concept of a special T central.

Definition 6.1. Let $X = \chi \oplus \langle \mathbb{C}_X(\tau) \rangle \sqsubseteq (\Omega, \mathcal{Z}_\circ, {}_v\mathcal{H}, \{\mathbb{C}\})$ be a system with $X = (X^1, X^2, \ldots, X^n) \sqsubseteq W \Subset \Omega$, $W = \{X | X \Vdash \Omega\}$, be a collection of various unit systems (X^i, for i = 1, 2, …, n). Further, let $X^{i*}(., Z^*, \mathfrak{C}_X^*)$ denote the X^i at the central state, "medietory state" (middle state), common state, normal state, state of balance, desired state, or continuity-reforming state of X, with $\mathfrak{C}_X^*$ being the cultural complex $\mathfrak{C}_X$ at a common, medium, normal, balanced, desirable or central state and Z* being the decision-making and strategic complex Z at a common-normal, medium, normal, balanced, desirable or central state.

In general, by the **specific Tcentral** (sTc) of X is meant X is in a partially ideal state (i.e., ideal only for a part of the whole world of our concerns).

For the other types of specific Tcentrtal of X, also written as $\{X =\langle T^B\}^{sTc} \sqsubseteq Ш^Д$, are in the following:

(i) X^{i*} is said to be at the state of **central sTc** if and only if $X^i = X^{i*}$, for X^{i*} being the central unit system of $X \sqsubseteq W$.

(ii) X^{i*} is said to be at the state of **medietory sTc** if and only if $X^i = X^{i*}$, for X^{i*} being the medietory unit system of $X \sqsubseteq W$.

(iii) X^{i*} is said to be at the state of **normal sTc** if and only if $X^i = X^{i*}$, for X^{i*} being the normal unit system of $X \sqsubseteq W$.

(iv) X^{i*} is said to be at the state of **balanced sTc** if and only if $X^i = X^{i*}$, for X^{i*} being the central unit system of $X \sqsubseteq W$.

(iv) X^{i*} is said to be at the state of **common sTc** if and only if $X^i = X^{i*}$, for X^{i*} being the central unit system of $X \sqsubseteq W$.

(v) X^{i*} is said to be at the state of **desirable sTc** if and only if $X^i = X^{i*}$, for X^{i*} being the desired unit system of $X \sqsubseteq W$.

(vii) X^{i*} is said to be at the state of **continuity/reforming sTc** if and only if $X^i = X^{i*}$, for X^{i*} being the X^i at the state of continuity/reform in $X \sqsubseteq W$.

Note that the other kinds of sTC are related to the specific Tcentral of a subsystem in a grand system.

Below in Section 6.1, we turn our attention to the issues of general T Central. Then, in the later subsections, we shall proceed to the discussions of the rest of the topics of this chapter.

6.1 General TCentral of A Cultural System

For a system $X \sqsubseteq (\Omega,\mathbb{Z}\circ,{}_{v}\mathcal{H},\{\mathbb{C}\})$, we shall formally write it as $X = \chi \oplus \langle\mathbb{C}_X\rangle$, where $\chi = \{\mathbf{x}(H) \Vdash [(vd,hc,\gamma),(R,R^D(e_k))],\tilde{O} \| E\{e_g\},Z\}$ (for more details, see §A.2-2-1). We may call (vd,hc,γ) the set of **formal and informal institutions-culture** (formal-informal organization-hierarchical structure of X, $(R,R^D(e_k))$ the **transformation structure** (or static-dynamical interpenetrating network) of X and $\tilde{O}$ the **outward-connecting mechanism**. For X, $\langle\mathbb{C}_X\rangle = \{\tau | (\mathcal{M}^I(\ell,\tau),\ldots,\mathcal{M}^N(\ell,\tau)) \Vdash [E(e_g(\tau)),Z(\mathfrak{C}^*(\tau))], \tau \Vdash (\mathfrak{I},\text{Ш}^{\text{Д}}) \Vvdash \mathbb{T}\mathbb{zu}^*, \ell \equiv \ell(\sigma,\kappa) \Vdash \mathcal{L}(\sigma,\kappa) \sqsubseteq \text{Ш}^{\text{Д}L}$, represents the cultural complex, with the mind complex $\{\mathcal{M}^i(\ell,\tau)\} \sqsubseteq \langle\mathbb{C}_X\rangle$, $E\{e_g(\tau)\}$ is the external energy system, and Z is the action-decision-making and strategic complex. Note that this χ in X may also be called the **hierarchy-transformational structure** or the **structural framework** of the system X.

In a capitalist system, the complex of formal politico-economic institutions is expressed symbolically as the form of democracy-market. The complex $(R,R^D(e_k))$ manifests itself in various ways. The MPFX cycles (see Appendix E) are good examples of the transformation structures of this $(R,R^D(e_k))$ for a macrosystem. In the present approach, the culture of democratic capitalism crystallizes in the ideologies of people's democracy and capitalist competitive market, blessed wholeheartedly by the culture of science and technology.

Naturally, the capitalist mind set is deeply rooted in Western philosophical tradition and religion. The ideas of democracy and competitive market are fundamentally connected with the cultural complexes developed since the time of the Greeks and Romans. This is an issue of cultural pride, reason and legitimacy. With the institutions of democracy and competitive market, as well as the formal arrangements of social operations, certain beliefs take form. In this system, promoted implicitly by the cultural values and explicitly by the academic establishment, money is accumulated with admiration, considered as a blessing as well a symbol of the highest form of social legitimacy. Due to the ideology of equilibrium, and furthermore a balance of power in politics, the idea of fair competition in the socio-economy is perceived as the one with the utmost value and its form is symbolically maintained.

Under these circumstances, for a system of democratic capitalism, the alliance between those with money and those possessing civil power becomes inevitable. These ties are produced and maintained in order to grasp and share the fruits of social engineering in ways mutually beneficial to both parties. Once such social momentum been created, given the formal institutions being in place, and with the values of the system bestowing its blessing, the MPFX cycles prevail without hindrance. In turn, these MPFX cycles proceed to strengthen the formal institutions as well as the prevailing values of the culture in system X, and thus perpetuate the momentum of these cycles.

For the system of socialism, the complex of formal politico-economic institutions symbolizes itself in the form of government (in name), party authority (in the form of leader-party cells) which infiltrate into every corner of the government, and planning. The party per se is in charge of the structure $(R,R^D(e_k))$ in which the party reproduction cycle manifests itself in a hidden form similar to the complexes of MPFX cycles of capitalism. The doctrine of Marxism-Leninism and also Mao Zedong thought (in China) dominate the cultural complexes of such systems. It is obvious to even a casual observer that these three structures form an integrated unity, though in a dialectical fashion.

For the system of "classical Faziranism" (i.e., system of classic China), the complex of formal politico-economic institutions is best represented by the form of royal authority with civil servants supporting it. "Faziranist networking" is comprised of various networks of connecting different families, groups and communities, and an agrarian market. The complex $(R,R^D(e_r))$ manifests itself in various ways. The complex of GPFX cycle (see Appendix B) illustrates an interesting aspect of it.

May be comparable to the capitalist in the system of capitalism, it appears that, in classical Faziranism, the gentry class was the key player. And yet the real power of this system remained in the hands of the royal family with the direct support provided by the powerful military generals and the indirect justification rendered by the Confucian socio-political doctrine. At the social level, with its central role staged by the gentry class, the operations of GPFX cycles apparently center on the accumulation of sociopolitical titles, a form of symbols, by the talented youths of the gentry families. Such titles are initially obtained via achieving high marks on state examinations, and later and further accumulated through social connections and political maneuvering.

Regarding the gentry class's involvement in the economic front, the accumulation of money by this class has to go through various forms, including first the transition into capital and then into land acquisition and disposal, since this occurred in the background of an agrarian-based economy with the classical technologies of handicraft production. Obviously it is the complex of GMFX cycles, together with the formal Faziranist networks, that provided the ultimate support and the real world structural base for the philosophical complex of Taoism-Legalism-Confucianism in classical China.

In China, religion, be it Taoism or Buddhism, from time to time may not even play an essential role in connecting the cultural complex to the structure $[(vd,hc,\gamma), (R,R^D(e_k))$. In the system of capitalism, however, the opposite appears to be true. In terms of cultural concerns, it is well known that it is religious belief (as one of two pillars of the cultural complex), rather than any philosophical concerns, that provides the ultimate support and justification of the institutions of competitive market and democracy in the West.

In modern China, because of the nature of mixed cultures, the society may be evolving toward a certain mix of MPFX and GPFX cycles.

Below we may define a system, a grand system or a cultural society, to be in the **world of general T Central** (gTC) if and only if the following conditions hold:

(1) Firms and households are moving on their balanced paths, respectively.

(2) Planners obtains the systematic and strategic centralities.

(3) The society reaches a balance between MPFX and GPFX cycles.

(4) The polity established a balance between centralization and decentralization.

(5) Cultural balance: balance between the culture of tranquility and the culture of conflict, between the modern culture and the classical culture, and between indigenous culture and foreign cultures are accomplished.

Below we shall present some other definitions of the general T Central of a (cultural) system adopted from Tonn [2006]).

In the following, we shall present several ways of defining the general TCentral.

Definition 6.1-1. A basic system $\underline{X} = \chi\oplus<\mathbb{C}_X{}^T>$, $\underline{X} = \{X^1,X^2, \ldots, X^n\}$is said to achieve a state of **general T Central**, written as $\underline{X} =< \{T^{C\Delta}\}^{gTC}$ and only if the following conditions are met: (1) In $\underline{X}$, each unit system X^i ($X^i \Vdash \underline{X} \sqsubseteq \Omega\sqcap\mathbb{R}$) achieves its production's specific Tcentral {(production ⊫ PPF) =< $\{T^{C\Delta}\}^{sTc}$ for PPF being the production-potential frontier of X^i and {production ⊫ PPF} is a becoming. (2) In $\underline{X}$, each unit system X^i achieves its consumption's specific Tcentral: {(consumption ⊫ CF) =< $T^{C\Delta}\}^{sTc}$, for CF being the consumption frontier of X^i and (consumption ⊫ PPF) is a becoming. (3) In $\underline{X}$, each unit system X^i achieves its exchange's specific Tcentral: {(exchange ⊫ CH) =< $T\{T^{C\Delta}\}^{sTc}$, for CH being the exchange-contract curve of X^i and {exchange ⊫ CH} is a becoming. (4) Both of $\underline{X}$ as a whole and each unit system X^i in $\underline{X}$ achieve their cultures' specific Tcentral, respectively: {(culture ⊫ CUL) =< $T^{C\Delta}\}^{sTc}$, for CUL being the cultural frontier of $\underline{X}$ and X^i, and (culture ⊫ CUL) is a becoming. That is, balances are achieved between the culture of tranquility and the culture of conflict, between the modern culture and the classical culture, and between the indigenous culture and the foreign cultures. (5) In $\underline{X}$, each unit system X^i achieves its strategy's specific Tcentral: {(strategy ⊫ STRG) =< $T^{C\Delta}\}^{sTc}$, for STRG being the strategic frontier of X^i and (strategy ⊫ STRG) is a becoming. (6) A state of the specific Tcentral of the hierarchy-transformational structure χ of $\underline{X}$. (7) The business community' specific Tcentral for each unit system X^i in $\underline{X}$ (if appropriate): organizational Tcentral, strategic centrality (i.e., proper coordination and decentralization in personnel management, R&D, production, marketing, accounting, information management among different departments). (8) Specific Tcentral of the psychological system of each unit system X^i in $\underline{X}$. (9) Specific Tcentral of the political system of each unit system X^i in $\underline{X}$. (10) Specific Tcentral state of the social system of each unit system X^i in $\underline{X}$. (11) The centrality and strategic supremacy of the center versus non-central subsystems. (12) CE balance between any two subsystems. (13) CE balance and strategic centrality achieved among the intellectuals, the capitalists, the industrialists, the politicians, the civil servants, and the common people. (14) CE balance and strategic centrality achieved between the grand system and the unit systems, between will and rationality, between imitation and creation, etc. (15) Tcentral of the basic system: $\underline{X} =< \{T^{C\Delta}\}^{sTc}$. That is, $\{X^i\}$ achieves Tcentral in the n-polar MFCE system $\underline{X}$, where X^h-$X^{h'}$ being the "horizontal axis," "religion-arts-literature" or "East-West axis in a MFCE system" of the basic system, X^k-$X^{k'}$ being the "vertical axis," "economic and political axis" or "South-North axis in a MFCE system" of the basic system.

Remark 6.1-1. To define a cultural economy of general TCentral, among others, aspects of the well-being and justice of the citizens must be equally taken care of. In the same logic, for the global cultural economy of general TCentral, among others, aspects of the justice on a global scale must be taken care of.

Thus, we have the definition for the cultural economy of TCentral state as follows. The system $X \sqsubseteq (\Omega,\mathcal{Z}\circ,_v\mathcal{H},\{\mathbb{C}\})\sqcap\mathbb{C}$ is said to be in a state of **TCentral** if and only if the following conditions hold:

(i) For the strategic impactor $\mathcal{T}$, $\mathcal{T}X = \mathcal{T}^*X = X(.|T^{C\Delta})$, $\mathcal{T}^*$ being the desirable (or optimal) strategic impactor and $X(.|T^{C\Delta})$ being X at a state of specific Tcentral.

(ii) For $X = (X_1,\ldots,X_n)$, $\mu(X_i(.|T^{C\Delta})) \geq \mu(X_i^*)$. That is, the mathematical measure of the actual level of each sector in X must equal to or exceed the relevant target level.

(iii) TS = TD (i.e., total supply equals total demand).

(iv) $\mathfrak{C} = \mathfrak{C}(\rho,\omega)^*$ (i.e., the culture is at the desirable level).

(v) Static condition is satisfied (for X being an individual, capitalist, IRI chain, SIFP chain complex, MPFX cycle, etc.): Let $X = \{\varphi^n x, \varphi^{n-1}x, \ldots, \varphi x, x, C\}$ and $X^* = \{\varphi^n x^*, \varphi^{n-1}x^*, \ldots, \varphi x^*, x^*, C^*\}$. Then, for $X = \{\{[\varphi^n(x) \oplus \ldots \oplus \varphi^2(x) \oplus \varphi(x) \oplus x] \oplus Ix\} =< T^{C\Delta}\} \sqsubseteq Ш^{\Delta}$ (see Bcms. (B.1-2-1) and (B.1-3-1)), at each period of time, we need to have: $\mathcal{T}X = X^*$ (i.e., the target X).

(vi) Dynamic condition is satisfied: For X = "$x(.) = [\alpha x(\mathbb{H};.)\ \beta x(\mathbb{H};.)\ \gamma x(\mathbb{H};.)]\ Ix(\mathbb{H};.)$" (Bcm. (B.1-2-3)), at the terminal time T, we need to have: $\mathcal{T}X = X^*$ (the target X).

(vii) Uncertain condition is satisfied (see Section B.2):

$$\text{(B.2-5-6)}\quad T^C_{\text{uncertain}}[\mathcal{T}^T\{x(.)\}] = \{\zeta_{X,\sim(t,n)}, {}^T\{\alpha x(\mathbb{H};.)\}\} \circledast \{\zeta_{X,\sim(t,n)}, \mathcal{T}^T\{\beta x(\mathbb{H};.)\}\} \circledast \{\zeta_{X,\sim(t,n)}, \mathcal{T}^T\{\gamma x(\mathbb{H};.)\}\} \circledast \{\zeta_{X,\sim(t,n)}, \delta_X, \mathcal{T}^T\{x(\mathbb{H};.)\}\},$$

$$\text{(B.2-5-7)}\quad V_{\text{uncertain}}[\mathcal{T}^T\{x(.)\}] = \{\zeta_{X,\sim(t,n)}, \mathcal{T}^T\{Ix(\mathbb{H};.),(\delta_X|\text{potential of uncertainty being deepened})\}.$$

In the above scheme of MFCE system, for example, let $\underline{X} = \{X^i\}$ = {society,private-economy,culture,public-economy,polity} be a 5-polar MFCE basic system, where culture is the center of this grand system. Here, on one hand, the private economy embodies capital and raw labor; and on the other hand, the public economy embodies the basis of technology. Then, X^g-$X^{g'}$ referring to the private economy-public economy may be treated as the horizontal axis of this grand system, and X^f-$X^{f'}$ depicting the society-polity may be regarded as the vertical axis. Thus, from the horizontal axis, by the culture creativity, the system dynamics stretches to reach the society in the South and the polity in the North; and from the horizontal axis, by the culture creativity again, the system dynamics extends to reach the private economy in the West and to the public economy in the East.

In the above, by the so-called specific Tcentral in production, consumption or exchange is meant: (1) to achieve a proper degree of teleological totality, (2) to achieve a proper relationships among all subsystems - such as organization-in-the-middle or organizational centrality, strategic centrality, balance-independence, consensual coordination, conflicting equilibrium, or energy-power hierarchy, (3) to have all subsystems operating or moving on normal, desirable or acceptable trajectories, (4) to reach systemic continuity of all subsystems, and cultural and strategic continuity, etc., and (5) to achieve specific condition such as mathematical equilibrium.

Definition 6.1-2. For a basic system $\underline{X} = \chi \oplus <\mathbb{C}_X{}^T> \sqsubseteq (\Omega, \mathcal{Z}\circ, {}_v\mathcal{H}, \{\mathcal{C}\})$, $\underline{X} = \{X^1, X^2, \ldots, X^n\}$ is said to achieve a state of **general TCentral** if and only if $\underline{X}$ achieves the following conditions in addition to the conditions specified in Definition 6.1-1:

(1) In $\underline{X}$, $X^i \approx X^j$, i,j = 1,2,…,n. That is, independent-and-balance (i.e., non-conflicting equilibrium) or conflicting equilibrium is reached in any pair of non-central systems.

(2) In $\underline{X}$, the central system achieves a strategic supremacy over non-central systems.

(3) In $\underline{X}$, a CE balance is reached among all non-central systems.

(4) In $\underline{X}$, cultural, organizational, strategic and functional Tccentral – i.e., CE balance and centrality --is reached in each system.

(5) In $\underline{X}$, other conditions like mathematical equilibrium are reached.

Definition 6.1-3. For a basic system $\underline{X} = \chi \oplus <\mathbb{C}_X{}^T> \sqsubseteq (\Omega, \mathcal{Z}\circ, {}_v\mathcal{H}, \{\mathcal{C}\})$, $\underline{X} = \{X^1, X^2, \ldots, X^n\}$ achieves a state of **general TCentral** if and only if $\underline{X}$ achieves the following conditions in addition to the conditions specified in Definition 6.1-1:

(1) In $\underline{X}$, $X^i \approx X^j$, i, j = 1,2,…,n. That is, independent-and-balance (i.e., non- conflicting equilibrium) or conflicting equilibrium is reached between any pair of non-central systems.

(2) In $\underline{X}$, the central system achieves organizational strategic centrality vis-à-vis non-central systems.

(3) In $\underline{X}$, CE coordination is achieved among all non-central systems.

Definition 6.1-4. For a basic system $\underline{X} = \chi \oplus <\mathbb{C}_X{}^T> \sqsubseteq (\Omega, \mathcal{Z}\circ, {}_v\mathcal{H}, \{\mathcal{C}\})$, $\underline{X} = \{X^1, X^2, \ldots, X^n\}$ achieves a state of **general TCentral** if and only if $\underline{X}$ achieves the following conditions:

(1) In $\underline{X}$, $\forall$ i, j = 1,2,…,n, equilibrium conditions are achieved in each of X^i.

(2) In $\underline{X}$, $\forall$ i, j = 1,2,…,n, $X^i \approx X^j$. That is, conflicting equilibrium or balance-and-independence (i.e., non-conflicting balance) is achieved in each pair of non-central systems.

(3) In $\underline{X}$, the central system achieves a strategic centrality or supremacy over the non-central systems.

Definition 6.1-5. By a simple language, for a basic system $\underline{X} = \chi \oplus <\mathfrak{C}_X> \sqsubseteq (\Omega, \mathcal{Z}\circ, {}_v\mathcal{H}, \{\mathcal{C}\})$, $\underline{X} = \{X^1, X^2, \ldots, X^n\}$ is said to reach a state of **general TCentral** if and only if $\underline{X}$ achieves the following conditions:

(1) Each system, be it central or non-central, reaches a state of specific Tcentral of systemic continuity (i.e., a state of satisfactorily systemic continuity, T continuity) or equilibrium.

(2) Each system, be it central or non-central, reaches a state of specific Tcentral of development (i.e., a state of satisfactorily continuing development) or developmental equilibrium.

(3) The central system achieves a strategic centrality or systemic supremacy over the non-central systems.

(4) Among all non-central systems, equilibrium-in-conflict or balance-in-independence is reached in each pair of unit systems. That is, a state of intra-systemic balance is reached.

(5) Among all non-central systems as a whole, equilibrium-in-conflict or balance-in-independence is reached between each pair of unit systems. That is, a state of inter-systemic balance is reached.

(6) Balance/equilibrium in political, socio-economic, cultural and other aspects is reached in each system, be it central or non-central.

For more details of the general TCentral, see Subsection §A.2-1-4. Here by the so-called central subsystem, in a democratic capitalism, is meant the capitalist class; in a system of Guangben Faziranism, the bureaucrats; and in a system of Minben Faziranism , the gentry class.

Remark 6.1-2. For practical purposes, the concept of specific Tcentral may be replaced by the concept of operating-level Tcentral to be defined below: A system is said to be in a state of **operating-level Tcentral** if and only if the following conditions are satisfied: For the system, (1) achieving a state of balance, (2) achieving a state of centrality, and (3) achieving a lowest acceptable level of welfare measure for the system as a whole.

Remark 6.1-3. Since it is difficult to deal with a state of general TCentral, for practical purposes, as a lower bound, the concept of general TCcentral may be replaced by the concept of low-level real-world Tcentral to be defined below (Tonn, 2007): A system is said to be in a state of **low-level real-world Tcentral** if and only if the following conditions are satisfied: For the system, (1) achieving a state of independence, (2) achieving a state of balance, (3) achieving a state of centrality, (4) achieving a state of mutuality, (5) achieving a "state of integral whole," (6) achieving a state of developmental dynamics, (7) achieving some measure of welfare maximization for the system as a whole, and (8) achieving some measure of fairness for each member in this system.

Remark 6.1-4. In the limit, the concept of general TCcentral may approximate the concept of TIdeal to be defined below (Tonn [2006] , Definitions 15.5-3 and 15.5-2): A system is said to be in a state of **TIdeal** if and only if the following conditions hold: (1) Each human element attains its "meaning of life." (2) In the long term evolution/drastic transformation of the (grand) system, the cultural sub-system dominates all other subsystems. (3) While in general, the economic subsystem dominates all other subsystems, although all other subsystems may exercise significant feedback effects on the economic subsystems. In this case, economic culture dominates the economic subsystem, while the cultural core of the (grand) system is shared by all subsystems including the economic culture. (4) A state of balance is reached in-between all subsystems: cul ≛ econ ≛ soc≛ pol (e.g., a balance between the culture (cul), economy (econ), society (soc), and polity (pol)). (5) each subsystem reached its state of balance and centrality with a high level of satisfaction. (6)The (grand) system reaches a state of centrality. (7) Each human element and subsystem – especially the cultural, economic and military sectors -- attains a state of self-mastery. (8) The grand system reaches a state of fairness and justice, with the concept of fairness and justice including the fair and appropriate distributions of socio-political power and economic resources.

6.2 MFCE Scheme and Tcentral of A Cultural Economy

The MFCE scheme treated in this book is only a single-layer MFCE scheme. In general, we have the multiple-layer MFCE scheme in which the "dimension is $m \times \ldots \times n$" with m and n may be even going to infinity.

Below we start the discussion of the single-layer MFCE scheme which is essentially the model of the circular flow conventionally presented in the economic textbooks. For the state of T central of an economy, we may proceed from the angle of MFCE scheme. In the follow, we shall pursue this approach.

Let the economy $\mathcal{E} \sqsubseteq (\Omega, \mathcal{Z}\circ, {}_{v}\mathcal{H}, \{\mathbb{C}\})$ be a grand system, with the households (Hh) and the business community (Bus) as two unit systems, the government (G) as the center (of the grand system), and the cultural core system ($\mathfrak{C}$) as the virtual center (of the grand system). Below, the signs "+," "-," "OUT", and "IN" denote Hh, Bus, output market and input market, respectively. In terms of a graphical presentation, see Figure 6.2-2 of the circular flow of a cultural economy: {Hh,Bus|G-M}, where Hh (households) = $(\mathbb{C}_H, Z(\mathcal{E})|(\rho,\omega))^H$, Bus (business) = $(\mathbb{C}_B, Z(\mathcal{E})|\ (\rho,\omega))^B$, and G-M chain (simplified as G the government in the above) = $(\mathbb{C}_G, Z(\mathcal{E})|(\rho,\omega))^G$.

Symbolic expression of the upward flow of the systemic energy. One way to formalize the scheme of upward flow is to employ the concept of cultural energy generated in this grand system. Then, the upward part of the cyclical motion can be expressed as $\langle\mathbb{C}_{up}\rangle$: $(\langle\mathbb{C}_-\rangle \to \langle\mathbb{C}_+\rangle) \to \langle\mathbb{C}_{out}\rangle \to \langle-\mathbb{C}_{out}\rangle \to (\langle\mathbb{C}_+\rangle \to \langle\mathbb{C}_-\rangle)$, where $\langle-\mathbb{C}_{out}\rangle$ denotes the negative level of energy generated by the cultural core of the "revertor" of the output system.

Since every culture has a pair of yin and yang forces (+,-), these forces generate a cyclic path for the cultural energy. That is, $G(+,-) : \mathfrak{C} \Rightarrow (\mathbb{C}_- \to \mathbb{C}_+) \to \mathbb{C}_{out} \to -\mathbb{C}_{out} \to (\mathbb{C}_+ \to \mathbb{C}_-)$. Here, each of $\langle\mathbb{C}_-\rangle$, $\langle\mathbb{C}_+\rangle$, $\langle-\mathbb{C}_{out}\rangle$ and $\langle-\mathbb{C}_{out}\rangle$ represents the cultural set generated by the Bus system, Hh system, output market system and the reverse of the output market system, respectively. We assume that these cultures, $\langle\mathbb{C}_-\rangle$, $\langle\mathbb{C}_+\rangle$, $\langle\mathbb{C}_{out}\rangle$ and $\langle-\mathbb{C}_{out}\rangle$, share a common core $\mathfrak{C}$: $\langle\mathbb{C}_{up}\rangle\backslash\langle\mathbb{C}_-\rangle\backslash\langle\mathbb{C}_+\rangle\backslash\langle\mathbb{C}_{out}\rangle\backslash\langle-\mathbb{C}_{out}\rangle = \langle\mathbb{C}_{up}\backslash\mathbb{C}_-\backslash\mathbb{C}_+\backslash\mathbb{C}_{out}\backslash-\mathbb{C}_{out}\rangle = \langle\mathfrak{C}\rangle$. Here the term "x\y" refers to the interaction between x and y, , for x and y being systems, and $\langle\mathbb{C}_-\rangle = \langle\mathbb{C}_{|-}\rangle$ (i.e., the cultural energy restricted to the Hh system), $\langle\mathbb{C}_+\rangle = \langle\mathbb{C}_{|+}\rangle$, $\langle\mathbb{C}_{out}\rangle = \langle\mathbb{C}_{|out}\rangle$, and $\langle-\mathbb{C}_{out}\rangle = -\langle\mathbb{C}_{|out}\rangle$.

Two processes of the systematic growth dynamics are as follows. (1) To generate an output market (as a system) from the pair of Bus and Hh systems as the result of the strategic operation of the **shengsheng generator** (a creative impactor operating with YYWX forces) σ initiated by the virtual center (the cultural core $\mathfrak{C}$). Here σ is the complex of the self-creating and self-mastering life-will and the self-existing, self-organizing and self-illuminating systemic rationality (or LW-SR impactor). As a consequence, we have: $\sigma(\mathfrak{C})$: $(\langle\mathbb{C}_-\rangle,\langle\mathbb{C}_+\rangle) \to (\langle\mathbb{C}_-\rangle,\langle\mathbb{C}_+\rangle)/Z(\mathcal{E})$, where

$$\text{(A.4-1-3)} \quad \frac{(\langle\mathbb{C}_-\rangle,\langle\mathbb{C}_+\rangle)}{Z(\mathcal{E})} = \frac{(\langle\mathbb{C}_-\rangle,\langle\mathbb{C}_+\rangle)}{\langle\mathfrak{C}_Z\rangle} = \frac{\langle\mathbb{C}_-,\mathbb{C}_+\rangle}{\langle\mathfrak{C}_Z\rangle}$$

$$= \langle\mathbb{C}_{(-,+)/Z}\rangle.$$

Here $Z(\mathcal{E})$ ($\neq$ the center G, $\neq$ the virtual center $\mathfrak{C}$), a unitary system, is the **virtual operational force** (or virtual operating center) of the very system in question and is composed of all sectors (i.e., the public as well as private sectors) affected by the public impactor of the center G. Here by "$(\langle\mathfrak{C}_-\rangle,\langle\mathfrak{C}_+\rangle)/Z(\mathcal{E})$" is meant that the pair of the cultural energies of households and businesses is immersed in the cultural energy of the virtual operating force of the system $\mathcal{E}$. In other words, this pair of energies is able to flow back to the core energy of the grand system in order to transfer the energy of one system into other system(s).

Note that, here, $\mathbb{C}_Z$ is the cultural generator of $Z(\mathcal{E})$: $Z(\mathcal{E}) \leftarrow (\mathbb{C}_Z;G) \Lleftarrow \mathfrak{C}$. That is, $Z(\mathcal{E})$ is created by the cultural generator $\mathbb{C}_Z$ under the influence of the government G, and $(\mathbb{C}_Z;G)$ as a pair is conditioned upon the cultural core $\mathfrak{C}$. Then, by applying the "output-market generating" impactor Φ^{out}, we get Bcm. (6.2-1).

(6.2-1) $$\Phi^{out}\{\langle\mathbb{C}_{(-,+)/Z}\rangle\} = \left\langle\frac{\mathbb{C}_{out}}{\mathfrak{C}_Z}\right\rangle = \frac{\langle\mathbb{C}_{out}\rangle}{Z(\mathcal{E})},$$

Then, by the "**invertor**" of Φ^{out} operation, we get:

(6.2-2) $$\Phi^{-1}\left\{\frac{\langle\mathbb{C}_{out}\rangle}{Z(\mathcal{E})}\right\} = \Sigma \oplus \langle\mathbb{C}_{out}\rangle.$$

Here, the impactor "$\oplus$" is a connector linking two terms in an "organic" way.

(2) To generate the "negative output market system" from the output market system and then the pair of Bus and Hh systems from the "negative output market system" as the results of the strategic operation of the shengsheng generator (or impactor of creation) σ on the output market system. Thus, we have $\sigma(\mathfrak{C})$: $\langle\mathbb{C}_{out}\rangle \to \langle\mathbb{C}_{out}\rangle/Z(\mathcal{E})$, where

(6.2-3) $$\frac{\langle\mathbb{C}_{out}\rangle}{Z(\mathcal{E})} = \frac{\langle\mathbb{C}_{out}\rangle}{\langle\mathfrak{C}_Z\rangle} = \left\langle\frac{\mathbb{C}_{out}}{\mathfrak{C}_Z}\right\rangle = \langle\mathbb{C}_{out/Z}\rangle,$$

Then, by applying the **revertor** (or growth-reverse impactor) Φ^{RV}, we get:

(6.2-4) $$\Phi^{RV}\{\langle\mathbb{C}_{out/Z}\rangle\} = \left\langle\frac{-\mathbb{C}_{out}}{\mathfrak{C}_Z}\right\rangle = \frac{\langle-\mathbb{C}_{out}\rangle}{Z(\mathcal{E})},$$

and by the operation of the invertor Φ^{RV} (i.e, Ψ^{-1}), we derive:

(6.2-5) $$\Psi^{-1}\left\{\frac{\langle-\mathbb{C}_{out}\rangle}{Z(\mathcal{E})}\right\} = (\Sigma^{-} \oplus \langle\mathbb{C}_{out}\rangle)^{-} = \Sigma^{-} \oplus \langle-\mathbb{C}_{out}\rangle.$$

(3) We revert the process of $\sigma(\mathfrak{C})\{(\mathbb{C}_-\to\mathbb{C}_+)\} \to \mathbb{C}_{out}$ to $-\mathbb{C}_{out} \to (\mathbb{C}_+\to\mathbb{C}_-)$ in the above. Then we derive the desired process.

Symbolic expression of the downward flow of the systemic energy. Similar to the above symbolic expression, by employing the concept of cultural energy generated, we have this downward part of the cyclical flowing motion to be expressed as $\mathbb{C}_{down}$: $(<\mathbb{C}_+> \to <\mathbb{C}_->) \to <\mathbb{C}_{in}> \to <-\mathbb{C}_{in}> \to (<\mathbb{C}_-> \to <\mathbb{C}_+>)$. That is, the flow of motion is that $\sigma(+,-) : \mathfrak{C} \Rightarrow (\mathbb{C}_- \to \mathbb{C}_+) \to \mathbb{C}_F \to -\mathbb{C}_F \to (\mathbb{C}_- \to \mathbb{C}_+)$. For these cultural sets $<\mathbb{C}_{in}>$, $<\mathbb{C}_->$, $<\mathbb{C}_+>$, and $<-\mathbb{C}_{in}>$, similar to the above case, we shall also assume that they share a common corc $\mathfrak{C}$: $<\mathbb{C}_{down}>\backslash<\mathbb{C}_{in}>\backslash<\mathbb{C}_->\backslash<\mathbb{C}_+>\backslash<-\mathbb{C}_{in}> = <\mathbb{C}_{down}\backslash\mathbb{C}_{in}\backslash\mathbb{C}_-\backslash\mathbb{C}_+\backslash\mathbb{C}_{-in}> = <\mathfrak{C}>$, where $<\mathbb{C}_{in}> = <\mathbb{C}_{|in}>$, $<\mathbb{C}_-> = <\mathbb{C}_{|-}>$, $<\mathbb{C}_+> = <\mathbb{C}_{|+}>$ and $<-\mathbb{C}_{in}> = <-\mathbb{C}_{|in}> = <\mathbb{C}_{|-in}>$.

Two processes of the systematic growth (or decaying) dynamics are as follows. (1) To generate the input market system from the pair of Hh and Bus as the results of the strategic operation of the shengsheng generator σ on the yin-yang pair. Therefore, we have $\sigma(\mathfrak{C})$: $(<\mathbb{C}_+>,<\mathbb{C}_->) \to (<\mathbb{C}_+>,<\mathbb{C}_->)/Z(\mathcal{E})$, where

$$(6.2\text{-}6) \quad \frac{(<\mathbb{C}_+>,<\mathbb{C}_->)}{Z(\mathcal{E})} = \frac{(<\mathbb{C}_+>,<\mathbb{C}_->)}{<\mathfrak{C}_Z>} = \frac{<\mathbb{C}_+,\mathbb{C}_->}{<\mathfrak{C}_Z>} = <\frac{\mathbb{C}_+,\mathbb{C}_-}{\mathfrak{C}_Z}> = <\mathbb{C}_{(+,-)/Z}>$$

Then, by applying the input market impactor Φ^{in}, we get:

$$(6.2\text{-}7) \quad \Phi^{in}\{<\mathbb{C}_{(+,-)/Z}>\} = <\frac{\mathbb{C}_{in}}{\mathfrak{C}_Z}> = \frac{<\mathbb{C}_{in}>}{Z(\mathcal{E})},$$

and by the invertor of Φ^F operation, (i.e., Φ^{-1} operation), we derive:

$$(6.2\text{-}8) \quad \Phi^{-1}\left\{\frac{<\mathbb{C}_{in}>}{Z(\mathcal{E})}\right\} = IN \oplus <\mathbb{C}_{in}>.$$

(2) To generate a "negative input market system" from the input market system is to apply the shengsheng generator σ on the input market system. By doing so, then, it yields $\sigma(\mathfrak{C})$: $<\mathbb{C}_{in}> \to <\mathbb{C}_{in}>/Z(\mathcal{E})$, where

$$(6.2\text{-}9) \quad \frac{<\mathbb{C}_{in}>}{Z(\mathcal{E})} = \frac{<\mathbb{C}_{in}>}{<\mathfrak{C}_Z>} = <\frac{\mathbb{C}_{in}}{\mathfrak{C}_Z}> = <\mathbb{C}_{in/Z}>.$$

Then, by applying the revertor (or growth-reverse impactor) Φ^{RV}, we get:

$$(6.2\text{-}10) \quad \Phi^{RV}\{<\mathbb{C}_{in/Z}>\} = <\frac{-\mathbb{C}_{in}}{\mathfrak{C}_Z}> = \frac{<-\mathbb{C}_{in}>}{Z(\mathcal{E})};$$

and by the operation of the invertor (or revertor) Φ^{-1}, we derive:

$$(6.2\text{-}11) \quad \Phi^{-1}\left\{\frac{<-\mathbb{C}_{in}>}{Z(\mathcal{E})}\right\} = (IN \oplus <\mathbb{C}_{in}>)^- = IN^- \oplus <-\mathbb{C}_{in}>.$$

We revert the process of "$(\mathfrak{C}_+ \rightarrow \mathfrak{C}_-) \rightarrow \mathfrak{C}_{in}$" to "$-\mathbb{C}_{in} \rightarrow (\mathbb{C}_- \rightarrow \mathbb{C}_+)$" in the above. Then we derive the desired process.

Remark 6.2-1. In the above, we studied the issues of the generations of "OUT" and "IN" through the operations of the shengsheng generator σ on the virtual center (i.e., the cultural core). Below we briefly mention the process of the generations of the cultural core (ℭ), the center (G the government), the households (Hh) and the business (Bus).

i) The virtual center (i.e., the cultural core ℭ) is generated by the forces or the agents of Ultimate Creativity-Destructibility ((σ,κ) or τ, σ ⇜ τ, κ ⇜ τ, τ ⊫ (ℑ,Ш^{Д}) ⊪ Tzu*). That is, in this scheme, what is treated as a data or a **primitive element** is a universal element and is an undefined term. The other approach is as follows. Let ψ ⊨ $\mathcal{Z}$o,v$\mathcal{H}$ (here ψ may be a considered as a secondary Form of τ), then we have:

(6.2-12) $\psi\{(\sigma,\kappa)|\mathfrak{I}\} = \mathfrak{C}$,

where ℑ may serve as a Form of Ultimate Creativity-Destructivity Tzu*.

ii) The "yin element" Hh (y^-, households) is treated as a primitive element, created by the virtual center. That is, let $\psi_{\mathfrak{C}}$ ⊨ $\mathcal{Z}$o,v$\mathcal{H}$ (here $\psi_{\mathfrak{C}}$ may be considered a secondary Form of ψ), then we have:

(6.2-13) $\psi_{\mathfrak{C}}\{\mathfrak{C}|\mathfrak{I}\} = y^-$.

iii) The "yang element" Bus (y^+, the business community) is created by the yin element y^- through a y-systemism: for y ⊨ $\mathcal{Z}$o,v$\mathcal{H}$ (an impactor of y-systemism), we have:

(6.2-14) $y\{y^-|\mathfrak{I}\} = y^+$.

iv) The center C (i.e., G, the government) is created by the joint operation of yin-yang elements through an h-systemism: for h ⊨ $\mathcal{Z}$o,v$\mathcal{H}$ (an impactor of h-systemism), we have:

(6.2-15) $h\{y^-,y^+|\mathfrak{I}\} = C$.

For the balance or equilibrium among the sectors of the economy, we shall assume the cultural core is in a state of systemic continuity. Below, in order to achieve states of balance/equilibrium, we shall proceed in several steps. First, by applying the principle of CE centrality (similar to what is derived in Bcm. (4.2-3)), a balance or equilibrium among the sectors of Hh, BUS, output market and input market is achieved:

(6.2-16) $\psi\{X_1 \doteq X_2 \doteq X_3 \doteq X_4,\Delta\} \mathrel{\overline{\curlywedge}} \tau$;

or

(6.2-17) $\psi\{X_1,\Delta\} \doteq \psi\{X_2,\Delta\} \doteq \psi\{X_3,\Delta\} \doteq \psi\{X_4,\Delta\}$,

where X_1, X_2, X_3, and X_4 represent Hh, BUS, output market and input market, respectively.

Secondly, a balance (a state of tranquility) or equilibrium (a state of internal tension) is achieved within each of the sectors of Hh, BUS, output market and input market, etc.:

(6.2-18) $\psi\{X_1 \triangleq X_2 ...... \triangleq Xn,\Delta\} \bar{\barwedge}\tau$,

where X_1, X_2, ... and X_n represent various subsectors of each of Hh, BUS, output market and input market, respectively.
Apply this above principle to the aggregate-demand side of the economy, we have:

(6.2-19) $\psi\{C \triangleq I^{pub} \triangleq I^{priv} \triangleq G \triangleq (EX\text{-}IM),\Delta\} \bar{\barwedge} \tau$,

where C, I^{pub}, I^{priv}, G and (EX-IM) represent the private consumption, public investment, private investment, government consumption and foreign sector, respectively, for the real national income to be: $y = C + I^{pub} + I^{priv} + G + (EX\text{-}IM)$.

By apply this above principle to the aggregate-supply side of the economy, we then have:

(6.2-20) $\psi\{L \triangleq K \triangleq \mathbb{C},\Delta\} \bar{\barwedge} \tau$,

where L, K and $\mathbb{C}$ represent raw-labor, capital stock and the set of cultural variables, respectively, for the production function of the cultural economy to be: $Q = Q(L,K,\mathbb{C})$.

As for the well-being of the society, we have:

(6.2-21) $\psi\{\text{consumers} \triangleq \text{producers},\Delta\} \bar{\barwedge} \tau$,

depicting a balance between the welfare of the group of consumers and that of producers.

Thirdly, a state of strategic centrality of the government over all ither sectors of the economy is achieved by applying the principle of strategic centrality (similar to the derivation of Bcm. (4.2-5)):

(6.2-22) $\psi\{\mathcal{T}^*G \geq \mathcal{T}_iX_i,\Delta\} \bar{\barwedge} \tau$,

where $\mathcal{T}^*$ refers to the set of strategic forces operated by the government and $\mathcal{T}_i$ the set of strategic forces operated by the sector i. Here, by the scheme "$\mathcal{T}^*G \geq \mathcal{T}_iX_i$" is meant the (strategy of) government dominates (the strategies of) all non-government sectors of the economy. In addition, for $i \in \mathbb{N}$, X_i represents each of the non-central unit systems in the cultural economy. Note that the cultural core is not a non-central unit system of the grand system; rather, it is a **co-central unit system** of the grand system.

For a specific example the principle of strategic centrality, we apply it to the relationship between the government and the business community to have:

(6.2-23) $\psi\{ \mathcal{T}^*G \geq \mathcal{T}_j P_j,\Delta\} \bar{\barwedge} \tau$,

Where $\mathcal{T}^*G$ stands for the government's strategy for national development and advancement, and $\mathcal{T}_jP_j$ the business strategies of the jth business unit system, for $j \in \mathbb{N}$.

In the above, we represented a **scheme of balanced Tcentral**. For the **scheme of unbalanced Tcentral**, Bcm. (6.2-16) in the above should be replaced by the following becoming:

(6.2-24) $\psi\{X_1 > X_2 > X_3 > \ldots > X_n, \Delta\} \;\bar{\bar{\wedge}}\; \tau$,

where “>” denotes the dominant relationship between X_i and X_j, $i, j \in \mathbb{N}$.

Remark 6.2-2. To connect the above scheme with a graphical presentation, let us set up a 5-polar (or sub-system) MFCE scheme as follows: {E, R, $\mathfrak{C}$, Abs, and Ac}, where E stands for the unit system (or subsystem) of events-things, R stands for that of reflection, $\mathfrak{C}$ stands for that of the cultural core, Abs stands for that of abstraction, and Ac stands for that of actions.

Due to the limitation of space, in terms of graphical presentation, we shall have the E-R-$\mathfrak{C}$ sub-scheme in the following:

Figure 6.2-1
E-R-$\mathfrak{C}$ sub-scheme in the E-R-$\mathfrak{C}$-Abs-Ac scheme ($\mathfrak{C} \rightarrow \mathfrak{C}_R$, $\mathfrak{C}_E \rightarrow \mathfrak{C}_E$ in $(\mathfrak{C}_E, Z(\mathcal{E})| (\rho,\omega))$), and $(\mathfrak{C}_E, Z(\mathcal{E})| (\rho,\omega))^E \rightarrow Z(\mathcal{E})$)

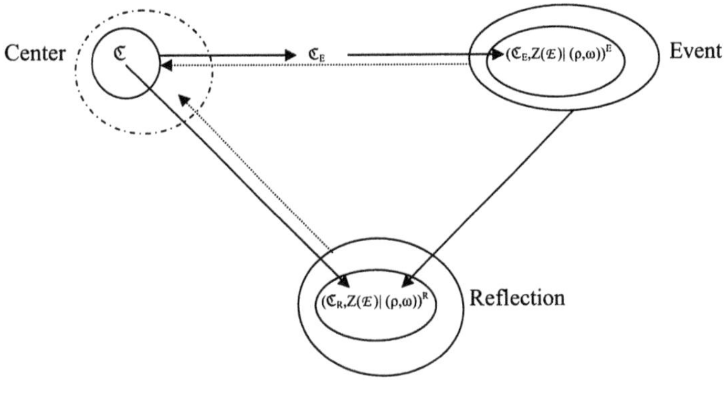

That is, from the center ($\mathfrak{C}$) of the E-R-$\mathfrak{C}$-Abs-Ac scheme, the energy is emitting into the Event sub-scheme and the center is simultaneously receiving the feedback energy coming backward into it. For the Event subsystem, it is receiving the energy from the center while at the same time receiving the energy transferred from the Action subsystem (in a loop) as well. That is to say, the joint becoming process of the “energy from the center” and “the transforming energy from the Action subsystem” generates the Event sub-system (with the energy $\mathfrak{C}_E$ of the system). Then moving forward to another node (or link) of the E-R-$\mathfrak{C}$-Abs-Ac scheme, we have the Reflection sub-system receiving the energy from the center while at the same time receiving the energy transferred from the Event subsystem as well. That is to say, the joint becoming process of the “energy from the center” and “the transforming energy from the Event sub-system” generates the Reflection sub-system (with the energy $\mathfrak{C}_R$ of the system).

In the following, in terms of the regular MFCE scheme, we have:

(6.2-25) $\Phi^R\{<\mathfrak{C}_{Axis/Z}>\} = <\mathfrak{C}_R/\mathfrak{C}_Z> = <\mathfrak{C}_R>/Z(\mathcal{E})$, where Φ^R is the impactor in the process of generating the reflection system, and the Axis represents the core culture of the E-R-$\mathfrak{C}$-Abs-Ac scheme (Axis $\equiv \mathfrak{C}_{co}$, or $\mathfrak{C}$ in this case) which serves as the virtual center of the scheme-system. Then, by the operation of $\Phi^{-R} \equiv (\Phi^R)^{-1}$ (i.e., invertor of Φ^R) we get:

(6.2-26) $\Phi^{-R} \{<\mathfrak{C}_R>/Z(\mathcal{E})\} = R$,

where R depicts the Reflection sub-system.

Remark 6.2-3 (Circular flow scheme). In this scheme, we have a weak government, and the culture is treated as the virtual center (see Figure 6.2-2).

Figure 6.2-2
Circular flow scheme

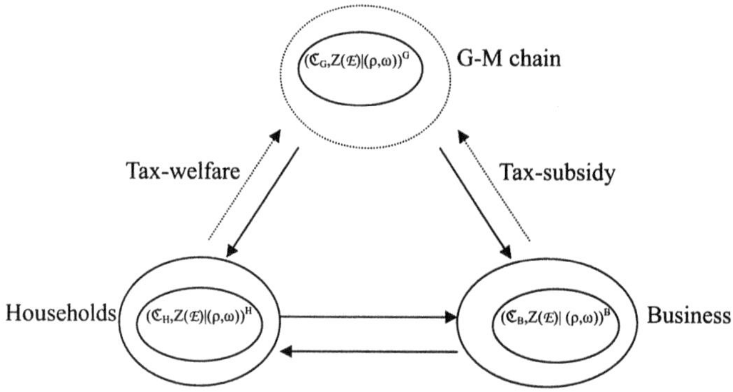

6.3 Strategic Continuity and Systemic Continuity

§6.3-1 Introduction

The cultural foundations of systemic continuity and strategic continuity are rooted in the cultural (or philosophical) scheme of self-masterism. And yet to present the mechanism of the structures of these continuities, we need to bridge the gap between our systematic approach to continuity-discontinuity and the Tcentral and self-mastering approach.

In this section, the schemes of systemic and strategic continuities will be developed in light of the guidance of our theory of cultural systematics. Then, in the next section (i.e., Section 6.4), we shall study the Tcentral and self-mastering schemes.

§6.3-2 The Economy

The underlying economy of our interest is an economy of mixed public-private sectors with a cultural mix of science-based democratic capitalism, socialism and Faziranism.

In terms of the economic setting, let the production function be $Q=Q(L,K,\mathfrak{C})$, where L refers to the raw labor, K the capital stock, and $\mathfrak{C}$ the set of cultural variables. Then the real national income is designated by $Y = \mathcal{P}Q$, where $\mathcal{P}$ is the general price level. Let S and I refer to saving and investment, respectively. Let $Y^{\cdot} \equiv dY/dt$, $I = S$, $Y^{\cdot} \geq 0$. Then we have:

(6.3-2-1) $S = S(.,Z;\mathfrak{C})$,

(6.3-2-2) $I = I(.,m_{\pi},Z;\mathfrak{C})$,

where m_{π} refers to the profit motivation and Z the decision-making and strategic complex. That is, investment is a function of decision-making and strategic complex, given the cultural conditions underlying the economy with regard to the cultural in general and the attitude toward risk-taking in particular.

§6.3-3 Notations and Preliminary Concepts

Definition 6.3-3-1. Let $X \sqsubseteq (\Omega,\mathcal{Z}^{\circ},{}_{v}\mathcal{H},\{\mathbb{C}\})$ be the system in question. Then for $\mathbb{C}$ being the complex system of mathematics, $X \sqsubseteq (\Omega,\mathcal{Z}^{\circ},{}_{v}\mathcal{H},\{\mathbb{C}\})\sqcap\mathbb{C}$ is said to be a **cultural economy** or simply the economy.

Definition 6.3-3-2. Saving-investment CE balance: $I = S$, where S and I depict the saving and investment of the economy, respectively.

Definition 6.3-3-3. The system $X \sqsubseteq (\Omega,\mathcal{Z}^{\circ},{}_{v}\mathcal{H},\{\mathbb{C}\})\sqcap\mathbb{C}$ is in **systemic continuity** if and only if the following conditions hold:

(6.3-3-1) $X^{\cdot} = 0$ (i.e., the system remains constant over time).

In the case of a cultural economy, we have:

(6.3-3-2) $X^{\cdot}(.|\mathfrak{C}_X=\underline{\mathfrak{C}_X}) = 0$ ($\underline{\mathfrak{C}_X}$ denoting $\mathfrak{C}_X$ being fixed).

Definition 6.3-3-4. The system $X \sqsubseteq (\Omega,\mathcal{Z}^{\circ},{}_{v}\mathcal{H},\{\mathbb{C}\})\sqcap\mathbb{C}$ is in **strategic continuity** iff the following conditions hold:

(i) $\mathcal{T} \geq \mathcal{T}^*$ such that $\mathcal{T}X \geq \mathcal{T}^*X$ ($\mathcal{T}$ being the strategic impactor, $\mathcal{T}\cdot$ being the desirable or optimal strategic impactor.

(ii) $\mathcal{T}X_t \geq \mathcal{T}^*X_t \geq X_t^*$ (t being time; X_t^* denoting the desirable level or state of X_t).

(iii) $Z(C,.|\mathcal{T}) = Z^*$ such that $Z^{\cdot} = 0$ (strategic continuity in the narrow sense, with Z* referring to the targeted strategic complex, and C referring to the center of the system). Here for $Z^{\cdot} = 0 \Leftrightarrow Z^{\cdot}(C,.|\, \mathcal{T}^{\cdot}=0) = 0$ (where $\mathcal{T}^{\cdot} = 0 \Leftrightarrow \mathcal{T}=\overline{\mathcal{T}}$, $\overline{\mathcal{T}}$ denoting $\mathcal{T}$ being fixed).

(iv). $\mathfrak{C}= \mathfrak{C}(\rho,\omega)^*$ (the culture being at a desirable level).

(v). Static condition (for X being an individual, capitalist, IRI chain, SIFP chain complex, MPFX cycle, etc.): Let $X =\{\varphi^n x,\varphi^{n-1}x,\ldots,\varphi x,x,C\}$ and $X^* =\{\varphi^n x^*,\varphi^{n-1}x^*,\ldots,\varphi x^*, x^*,C^*\}$.

Then, for X = {{[φ^n(x) ⊕ … ⊕ φ^2(x) ⊕ φ(x) ⊕ x] ⊙ Ix}= Φ (By generalizing Bcm. (B.1-2-2)), at each period of time, we need to have: $\mathcal{T}$X = X* (i.e., the target X) or better.

(vi). Dynamic condition: For X = "x(.) = [αx(ℍ;.) ⊕ βx(ℍ;.) ⊕ γx(ℍ;.)] ⊕ Ix(ℍ;.)" (Bcm (B.1-2-3)), at the terminal time T, we need to have: $\mathcal{T}$X = X* (the target X).

(vii). Uncertain condition: $T^C_{uncertain}[\mathcal{T}^T\{x(.)\}] = T^C_{uncertain}[\{[\mathcal{T}^T\{\alpha x(\mathbb{H};.)\} \oplus \mathcal{T}^T \{\beta x(\mathbb{H};.)\}] \oplus \mathcal{T}^T\{\gamma x(\mathbb{H};.)\}] \oplus \mathcal{T}^T\{Ix(\mathbb{H};.)\}\} \circledcirc \Delta X]$.

(viii). Unemployment rate: u(.|C) = u*.

(ix). Inflation rate: π(.|C) = π* (π* being a desirable level of inflation).

(x). ℭ= ℭ* (the culture being at a target level).

(xi). (social justice) Satisfactory income and wealth distributions: TW = IW* (IW being the distributions of income and wealth, and IW* being a target level of income and wealth distributions).

(xii). C = C# (The center C being held constant, C# being a fixed level of C).

Remark 6.3-3-1. For the uncertain condition, we have: From Sections B.2,

(B.2-4-2) $\mathcal{T}^T\{x(.)\} = \{[\mathcal{T}^T\{\alpha x(\mathbb{H};.)\} \oplus \mathcal{T}^T\{\beta x(\mathbb{H};.)\}] \oplus \mathcal{T}^T\{\gamma x(\mathbb{H};.)\}] \oplus \mathcal{T}^T\{Ix(\mathbb{H};.)\}\} \otimes \Delta X$,

with α, β, γ being the impactors of the systemic-change becoming, ΔX being the change in X.

(B.2-4-3) $\Delta X = \zeta_{X\sim(t,n)} \oplus \{\delta_X, U_{\sim(t,n)}\}$,

($\zeta_{X\sim(t,n)}$ being the best-common structure of X and δ_X being the differencing from the best-common structure of X), with the uncertain system $U_{\sim(t,n)} = U_{\sim(t,n)}(\tau)$, τ ⊫ ℑ ⊪ 𝕋zu*, $U_{\sim(t,n)} \sim (T^C_{uncertain}[U_{\sim(t,n)}], V_{uncertain}[U_{\sim(t,n)}])$ (see Bcms. (B.2-2-3) and (B.2-3-10)).

With all the information provided in the above, at each period of time or the terminal time T, we need to have: $T^C_{\mathfrak{c}i,statej}[\mathcal{T}X]$ = X* (i.e., the target X, see Bcm. (B.2-3-10)) for X being a distribution system.

Note that from Bcms. (B.2-4-2) and (B.2-4-3):

$$\begin{aligned} &T^C_{uncertain}[\mathcal{T}^T\{x(.)\}] \\ &= T^C_{uncertain}[\{[\mathcal{T}^T\{\alpha x(\mathbb{H};.)\} \oplus \mathcal{T}^T\{\beta x(\mathbb{H};.)\}] \oplus \mathcal{T}^T\{\gamma x(\mathbb{H};.)\}] \oplus \mathcal{T}^T\{Ix(\mathbb{H};.)\}\} \circledcirc \Delta X], \end{aligned}$$

and

(B.2-5-6)
$$\begin{aligned} &T^C_{uncertain}[\mathcal{T}^T\{x(.)\}] \\ &= T^C_{uncertain}[\zeta_{X,\sim(t,n)}, \mathcal{T}^T\{\alpha x(\mathbb{H};.)\}] \circledcirc \\ &\quad T^C_{uncertain}[\zeta_{X,\sim(t,n)}, \mathcal{T}^T\{\beta x(\mathbb{H};.)\}] \circledcirc T^C_{uncertain}[\gamma_{X,\sim(t,n)}, \mathcal{T}^T\{\gamma x(\mathbb{H};.)\}] \circledcirc \\ &\quad T^C_{uncertain}[\zeta_{X,\sim(t,n)}, \delta_X, \mathcal{T}^T\{Ix(\mathbb{H};.)\}, U_{\sim(t,n)}\}]. \\ &= \{\zeta_{X,\sim(t,n)}, \mathcal{T}^T\{\alpha x(\mathbb{H};.)\}\} \circledcirc \{\zeta_{X,\sim(t,n)}, \delta_X, \mathcal{T}^T\{\beta x(\mathbb{H};.)\}\} \circledcirc \\ &\quad \{\zeta_{X,\sim(t,n)}, \mathcal{T}^T\{\gamma x(\mathbb{H};.)\}\} \circledcirc \{\zeta_{X,\sim(t,n)}, \delta_X, \mathcal{T}^T\{Ix(\mathbb{H};.)\}\} T^C_{uncertain}[U_{\sim(t,n)}] \end{aligned}$$

$$= \{\zeta_{X,\sim(t,n)}, \mathcal{T}^{T}\{\alpha x(\mathbb{H};.)\}\} \circledast \{\zeta_{X,\sim(t,n)}, \mathcal{T}^{T}\{\beta x(\mathbb{H};.)\}\}$$
$$\circledast \{\zeta_{X,\sim(t,n)}, \mathcal{T}^{T}\{\gamma x(\mathbb{H};.)\}\} \circledast \{\zeta_{X,\sim(t,n)}, \delta_X, \mathcal{T}^{T}\{x(\mathbb{H};.)\}\},$$

(B.2-5-7) $V_{uncertain}[\mathcal{T}^{T}\{x(.)\}]$

$$= V_{uncertain}[\zeta_{X,\sim(t,n)}, \mathcal{T}^{T}\{\alpha x(\mathbb{H};.)\}] \circledast V_{uncertain}[\zeta_{X,\sim(t,n)}, \mathcal{T}^{T}\{\beta x(\mathbb{H};.)\}] \circledast$$
$$V_{uncertain}[\zeta_{X,\sim(t,n)}, \mathcal{T}^{T}\{\gamma x(\mathbb{H};.)\}] \circledast V_{uncertain}[\zeta_{X,\sim(t,n)}, \delta_X, \mathcal{T}^{T}\{Ix(\mathbb{H};.)\}, U_{\sim(t,n)}]$$
$$= [\circ\circledast\circ\circledast\circ]\circledast\{\zeta_{X,\sim(t,n)}, \mathcal{T}^{T}\{Ix(\mathbb{H};.), (\delta_X|\text{potential of uncertainty being deepened})\}.$$
$$= \{\zeta_{X,\sim(t,n)}, \mathcal{T}^{T}\{Ix(\mathbb{H};.), (\delta_X|\text{potential of uncertainty being deepened})\}.$$

(B.2-5-11) $T^{C}{}_{\mathfrak{C}i,statej}[\mathcal{T}^{T}\{x(.)\}]$

$$= \{\zeta_{X,\sim(t,n)}, \mathcal{T}^{T}\{\alpha x(\mathbb{H};.)\}\} \circledast \{\zeta_{X,\sim(t,n)}, \delta_X, \mathcal{T}^{T}\{\beta x(\mathbb{H};.)\}\} \circledast$$
$$\{\zeta_{X,\sim(t,n)}, \mathcal{T}^{T}\{\gamma x(\mathbb{H};.)\}\} \circledast \{\zeta_{X,\sim(t,n)}, \delta_X, \mathcal{T}^{T}\{Ix(\mathbb{H};.)\}\} T^{C}{}_{\mathfrak{C}i,statej}[U_{\sim(t,n)}].$$

Definition 6.3-3-5. The cultural economy $X \sqsubseteq (\Omega, \mathbb{Z}^{\circ}, {}_{v}\mathcal{H}, \{\mathbb{C}\}) \sqcap \mathbb{C}$ is in **strategic continuity** if and only if the following conditions hold:

(i) Production optimum: $\mathcal{T}X \geq \mathcal{T}\cdot X_i \geq X_i^*$ such that $(\mathcal{T}Q)^{\cdot} = [(\mathcal{T}Q)^{\cdot}]^*$, for $Q = Q(L,K,\mathfrak{C})$, and each firm reaches a state of Tcentral in its functions of management, finance, production, marketing and so on.

(ii) AS=AD and consumption optimum: $\mathcal{T}X_i \geq \mathcal{T}\cdot X_i \geq X_i^*$ such that $\{\mathcal{T}(\mathcal{P},Q;-\},C\text{-}Z|\mathfrak{C}\} = \{\mathcal{T}(\mathcal{P},Q;+\},C\text{-}Z|\mathfrak{C}\}$, for Q = CC (Consumption) + I + G in $\{\mathcal{T}(\mathcal{P},Q;-\},C\text{-}Z|\mathfrak{C}\}$. Note that this is also a state of exchange Tcentral.

(iii) $Z^{\cdot} = 0$ (Z being the decision-making and strategic complex).

(iv). $\mathfrak{C} = \mathfrak{C}(\rho,\omega)^*$, such that the culture is in Tcentral and especially the cultural creativity is in Tcentral.

(v). Static condition: Let $X = \{\varphi^{n}x, \varphi^{n-1}x, \ldots, \varphi x, x, C\}$ and $X^* = \{\varphi^{n}x^*, \varphi^{n-1}x^*, \ldots, \varphi x^*, x^*, C^*\}$. Then, for $X = \{\{[\varphi^{n}(x) \oplus \ldots \oplus \varphi^{2}(x) \oplus \varphi(x) \oplus x] \circledast Ix\} = \sigma \Vdash \Sigma^{Tc}$, at each period of time: $\mathcal{T}X = X^*$ (X^* being the target X).

(vi). Dynamic condition: For X = "$x(.) = [\alpha x(\mathbb{H};.) \oplus \beta x(\mathbb{H};.) \oplus \gamma x(\mathbb{H};.)] \oplus Ix(\mathbb{H};.)$" (Bcm. (B.1-2-3)), at the terminal time T: $\mathcal{T}X = X^*$.

(vii). Uncertain condition: In Section B.2, we have:

(6.3-3-3) $$[\{\zeta_{X,\sim(t,n)}, \mathcal{T}^{T}\{\varphi^{2}(x)\}\} \circledast \{\zeta_{X,\sim(t,n)}, \mathcal{T}^{T}\{\mathcal{T}^{T}\{\varphi(x)\}\} \circledast$$
$$\{\zeta_{X,\sim(t,n)}, \mathcal{T}^{T}\{x\}] \circledast \{\mathcal{T}^{T}\{Ix\}, \zeta_{X,\sim(t,n)}', \{\delta_X, U_{\sim t}\}'\} = \Phi,$$

(6.3-3-4) $\mathcal{T}^{T}\{x(.)\}$

$$= [\{\zeta_{X,\sim(t,n)}, \mathcal{T}^{T}\{\alpha x(\mathbb{H};.)\}\} \circledast \{\zeta_{X,\sim(t,n)}, \mathcal{T}^{T}\{\beta x(\mathbb{H};.)\}\} \circledast \{\zeta_{X,\sim(t,n)}, \mathcal{T}^{T}\{\gamma x(\mathbb{H};.)\}] \circledast$$
$$\{\mathcal{T}^{T}\{Ix(\mathbb{H};.)\}, \zeta_{X,\sim(t,n)}', \{\delta_X, U_{\sim t}\}'\},$$

and at each period of time or the terminal time T: $T^{C}{}_{uncertain}[\mathcal{T}X] = X^*$ for X being a distribution system.

(viii). Unemployment rate: $u(.|C) = u^*$.

(ix). Inflation rate: $\pi(.|C) = \pi^*$.

(x). (Social justice) Satisfactory income and wealth distributions.

(xi) Social well-being for all is in Tcentral.

(xii). $C = C^*$ (no change in the center c, systemic continuity).

(xiii). $Z(C) = Z^*$ such that $Z^{\cdot} = 0$ (strategic continuity in the narrow sense).

§6.3-4 Systemic Continuity and Strategic Continuity

Thema 6.3-4-1. For any cultural economy under strong assumptions (i.e., production optimum, consumption optimum, AS = AD, $u(.|C) = u^*, \pi(.|C) = \pi^*$), if $\mathfrak{C} = \mathfrak{C}^*$, then there exists a state of strategic continuity.

Reasoning. Under the strong assumptions,

(1) Use the technique of CE balance and strategic centrality to prove social justice and equality of income and wealth distribution (see Section 4.2).

(2) Use techniques of Themata 8.3-1 and 8.3-2 to prove static conditions.

(3) Use techniques of Section B.2 to prove dynamic and uncertain conditions.

(4) Use MFCE scheme to prove that: $\mathfrak{C} = \mathfrak{C}^* \rightarrow C = C^* \rightarrow Z = Z^*$ (see Section A.4).

(5) Use flat-steep production/consumption to prove production/consumption optima.

(6) For prices $\mathcal{P} = \mathcal{P}^*$ inter-penetrating the realm of price-systems (in the worlds of mathematics-systematics), use fixed point theorem.

Remark 6.3-4-1. Possible directions for the techniques of proof:

(1) Use the technique of Section 8.3 (see Thema 8.3-1, Thema 8.3-2). Fully development of the potential of cultural creativity leads to at least a constrained "optimal state" of the economy (i.e., X with full potential "converges to" X*) for at any moment of time.

(2) To prove the conditions of statics and dynamics of a thema, we need to show that the fully development of the potential of cultural creativity leads to at least a constrained "optimal state" of economy (i.e., X with full potential "converges to" X*).

(3) To prove the uncertain conditions of a thema, we need to show that the fully development of the potential of cultural creativity leads to at least a constrained "optimal state" of the economy (i.e., X with full potential "converges to" X*) in term of the "center/middle" of the economy while the deviation of the system may not be under any control (See Remarks B.1-1-1, B.1-1-2).

(4) SK CE balance/equilibrium (see SK CE balanced strategy right before Bcm. (K.2-15)).

(5) IRI chain, MPFX cycles, SIFP chain complex.

6.4 The World of General Self-Masterism

To address the issue of the ideal world for the human kind, one the major problems is that we may not know what is really the ideal world. In this section, we shall present the world of self-mastersm which has a real world meaning as a first level approximation to this ideal world.

§6.4-1 Introduction

To deal with a mixed system, from Bcm. (A.2-2-1-5), for $X \sqsubseteq (\Omega, \mathcal{Z}\circ, {}_{v}\mathcal{H}, \{\mathbb{C}\})$, $X = \chi_X \oplus <\mathbb{C}_X>$, where $\chi = \{\mathbf{x}(H^*)|\mathbf{x}(H^*) \Vdash (v,h,\gamma(\tau)),(R,R^D) \| E\{e_j\},Z\}$, $\tau \Vdash (\mathfrak{I}, Ш^Д) \Vvdash \mathbb{T}zu^*$, let us write:

(6.4-1-1) $X = \chi_X \oplus <\mathbb{C}_X>,\ \chi_X = [(v,h,\gamma(\tau)),(R,R^D),(E\{e_j\},Z)]^X$

(6.4-1-2) $Y = \chi_Y \oplus <\mathbb{C}_Y>,\ \chi_Y = [(v,h,\gamma(\tau)),(R,R^D),(E\{e_j\},Z)]^Y$.

From Bcms. (A.3-3-4) and (3.6-1), we have:

(6.4-1-3) $X = (\Delta_{X1}-\Delta_{X2}-\ldots-\Delta_{Xi})-(\boxtimes_{X1}\sim\boxtimes_{X2}\sim\boxtimes_{Xj}) \oplus (<\mathbb{C}_{X1}><\mathbb{C}_{X2}>\ldots<\mathbb{C}_{Xn}>)$

(6.4-1-4) $Y = (\Delta_{Y1}-\Delta_{Y2}-\ldots-\Delta_{Yi})-(\boxtimes_{Y1}\sim\boxtimes_{Y2}\sim\boxtimes_{Yj}) \oplus (<\mathbb{C}_{Y1}><\mathbb{C}_{Y2}>\ldots<\mathbb{C}_{Yn}>)$

Let "$^{\#}$", $\psi \vDash \mathcal{Z}\circ, {}_{v}\mathcal{H}$ be impactors. Then for $X^{\#}Y$, in terms of Bcms. (6.4-1-1) and (6.4-1-2), we may have:

(6.4-1-5)
$$
\begin{aligned}
X^{\#}Y &= (\chi_X \oplus <\mathbb{C}_X>)^{\#}(\chi_Y \oplus <\mathbb{C}_Y>) \\
&= (\chi_X{}^{\#}\chi_Y) \oplus (<\mathbb{C}_X>{}^{\#}<\mathbb{C}_Y>) \\
&= [(v,h,\gamma(\tau)),(R,R^D),(E(E\{e_j\},Z)]^{X\,\#}[(v,h,\gamma(\tau)),(R,R^D),(E(E\{e_j\},Z)]^Y \\
&\quad \oplus (<\mathbb{C}_X>{}^{\#}<\mathbb{C}_Y>)
\end{aligned}
$$

where the operation of "$[(v,h,\gamma(\tau)),(R,R^D),(E(E\{e_j\},Z)]^{X\,\#}[(v,h,\gamma(\tau)),(R,R^D),(E(E\{e_j\},Z)]^Y$ " is to be defined. And in terms of Bcms. (6.4-1-1) and (6.4-1-2), we may have:

(6.4-1-6)
$$
\begin{aligned}
X^{\#}Y &= [(\Delta_{X1}-\Delta_{X2})-(\boxtimes_{X1}\sim\boxtimes_{X2}) \oplus (<\mathbb{C}_{X1}><\mathbb{C}_{X2}>)] \\
&\quad {}^{\#}[(\Delta_{Y1}-\Delta_{Y2})-(\boxtimes_{Y1}\sim\boxtimes_{Y2}) \oplus (<\mathbb{C}_{Y1}><\mathbb{C}_{Y2}>)] \\
&= [(\Delta_{X1}-\Delta_{X2})^{\#}(\Delta_{Y1}-\Delta_{Y2})] \oplus [(\boxtimes_{X1}\sim\boxtimes_{X2})^{\#}(\boxtimes_{Y1}\sim\boxtimes_{Y2})] \\
&\quad \oplus [(<\mathbb{C}_{X1}><\mathbb{C}_{X2}>)^{\#}(<\mathbb{C}_{Y1}><\mathbb{C}_{Y2}>)].
\end{aligned}
$$

Note that, in general, the rules for the operations of interactors are not strictly to be theoretically determined, but rather to be determined by very specific and functional situations.

§6.4-2 Basic Concepts of Self-mastering System

Definition 6.4-2-1. The element $x \Vdash \mathbf{U}$ is said to be an **element of self-masterism** if and only if the following conditions hold:

(1) It is self-preserving. That is, it achieves its self-sufficient level of energy (for self-preservation) indirectly and eventually from Tzu*.

(2) It is self-developing and self-advancing.

(3) It achieves a level of self-mastering power-energy, That is, the level of self-mastery is in the world of the power-energy of self-masterism.

(4) Any interactive operation (of mutuality) with other elements (in the system or outside systems) or other systems would not change the voluntary and pleasant nature of the independent operation of x itself. These operations may be in the forms of CE balance, be they of the nature of tranquility or conflict.

(5) For a sophisticated element $x_i \equiv \{x_i(y_{i1},y_{i2},..,y_{is};h_{i1}^*,h_{i2}^*,..,h_{it}^*,IRI_i),.)|x_i(y_{i1},y_{i2},..,y_{is};h_{i1}^*, h_{i2}^*,..,h_{it}^*,IRI_i(\rho,\omega),.) \Vdash (\gamma(\tau)),R^{Dyn},\tilde{O}\|E\{e_j\},z\} \sqsubseteq \mathbf{U}$, $\tau \Vdash (\mathfrak{I},Ш^{Д}) \Vvdash$ Tzu*, $(i \in \mathbb{N})$ (R^{Dyn} being the "dynamical forces of x), the operations of $\gamma(\tau)$) and R^{Dyn} would not interfere with the self-independent operations of the $x_i(IRI_i)$. Note that a sophisticated element is defined as an element, not an n-level system.

(6) It is in a state of Tcentral.

Remark 6.4-2-1. In the above Definition, (i) the self-independent operations of the $x_i(IRI_i)$ implies the complete independence of the operations of IRI_i, especially in the area of free decision-making; and (ii) for $x_i(y_{i1},y_{i2},..,y_{is};h_{i1}^*,h_{i2}^*,..,h_{it}^*)$ in X, we may write $x_i(y_{i1},y_{i2},..,y_{is}; h_{i1}^*, h_{i2}^*,..,h_{it}^*;IRI_i(\rho,\omega))$ to be consistent and slightly more elaborate.

Remark 6.4-2-2. This may imply that the level of energy embodied in Tzu* in Definition 6.4-2-1 eventually approaches infinity.

Definition 6.4-2-2. Let the index of mastery (i.e., power-energy) of an entity $x \sqsubseteq \mathbf{U}$ be:

(6.4-2-1) $P = v(E) \otimes V(N)$,

where v(.) depicts the value or measure of power-energy of $(.) \sqsubseteq \mathbf{U}$, E the economic entity possessed (owned, controlled, or is endowed) by x, N the non-economic entity possessed (owned, controlled, or is endowed) by x, for some impactor $\otimes$. Then x is said to reach a **state of self-masterism** if and only if the following conditions hold:

(1) $v(E) = \{E,C_E\}$, C_E being the economic creativity that generates meaning or value of E to x.

(2) $v(N) = \{E,C_N\}$, C_N being the non-economic creativity that generates meaning or value of N to x.

(3) $E \uparrow \Rightarrow P\uparrow$, $C_E\uparrow\Rightarrow P\uparrow$, all other things being equal; and $N \uparrow \Rightarrow P\uparrow$, $C_N\uparrow\Rightarrow P\uparrow$, all other things being equal.

(4) P is at the level of self-mastering power-energy.

Remark 6.4-2-3. In Bcm. (6.4-2-1), $\{C_E, C_E\}$ is called the **cultural power-energy** or **creativity** of x, v(E) the economic power of x, and v(N) the non-economic power of x.
Definition 6.4-2-3. The system $X = (x_1, x_2, \ldots, x_n) \sqsubseteq (\Omega, \mathbb{Z}\circ, {}_v\mathbb{H}, \{\mathbb{C}\})$ for $x_i \sqsubseteq$ **U**, is said to be a **system of self-masterism** if and only if the following conditions hold:

(1) Each element $x_i \Vdash X$ $(i \in \mathbb{N})$ is an element of self-masterism.

(2) Among different elements in the system, there are various interactions of mutuality that do not negate the self-mastering characteristics of each element involved.
(3) For $x_i \sqsubseteq X \equiv \{x_i(y_{i1}, y_{i2}, .., y_{is}; h_{i1}^*, h_{i2}^*, .., h_{it}^*, IRI_{i,}) | x_i(y_{i1}, y_{i2}, .., y_{is}; h_{i1}^*, h_{i2}^*, .., h_{it}^*, IRI_{i,.}) \Vdash (v, h, \gamma(\tau)), (R, R^D), \tilde{O} \| E\{e_j\}, Z\}$, $\tau \Vdash (\mathfrak{J}, \text{Ш}^{\text{Д}}) \Vvdash \mathbb{T}\mathbb{zu}^*$, $(i \in \mathbb{N})$, the operations of $(v, h, \gamma(\tau))$ and (R, R^D) would not interfere with the self-independent operations of the $x_i(., IRI_{i,.})$.

Remark 6.4-2-4. All definitions introduced in this subsection are still valid if the condition of x (or x_i) $\sqsubseteq$ **U** is replaced by x (or x_i) $\sqsubseteq$ **H** (that is, x or x_i being a human element, instead of a universal element).

Definition 6.4-2-4. The system $X \sqsubseteq (\Omega, \mathbb{Z}\circ, {}_v\mathbb{H}, \{\mathbb{C}\}) \sqcap \mathbb{C}$ is said to be a **grand system of self-masterism** if and only if the following conditions hold:

(1) Each unit system is a system of self-masterism.

(2) Among different unit systems in the grand system, there are various interactions of mutuality that do not negate the self-mastering characteristics of each unit system involved.

(3) Unit systems of this grand system interacting with outside would not negate their respective independence.

Definition 6.4-2-5. The system $X \sqsubseteq (\Omega, \mathbb{Z}\circ, {}_v\mathbb{H}, \{\mathbb{C}\}) \sqcap \mathbb{C}$ is said to be a **constituting unit-grand system** (or **unit-grand system** for short) in a great-grand system if and only if the following conditions hold:

(1) Each of these (constituting unit-grand) systems are systems of self-mastery.

(2) The interactions among these (constituting unit-grand) systems would not negate the self-mastering characteristics of each of them.

(3) The interactions between these (constituting unit-grand) systems and the outside environments would not negate their respective independence.

Definition 6.4-2-6. The system $X \sqsubseteq (\Omega, \mathbb{Z}\circ, {}_v\mathbb{H}, \{\mathbb{C}\}) \sqcap \mathbb{C}$ is said to be a **great-grand system of self-masterism** if and only if the following conditions hold:

(1) Each constituting unit-grand system is a system of self-masterism. In particular, if it applies, then all grand systems in this great-grand system, be they in the basis being-field, the social power-energy net or the will-rationality-to-creation entity, must be self-preserving and be in the state of self-masterism.

(2) Among different unit-grand systems, there are various interactions of mutuality that do not negate the self-mastering characteristics of each grand system involved. Here this grand system may serve as a sub-grand system of a grand-grand system.

(3) The interactions between these systems (i.e., constituting grand systems as sub-grand systems) and the outside environments would not negate their respective independence.

Definition 6.4-2-7. The collection of all systems (systems, grand systems, great-grand systems or any others) is said to be a **world of self-masterism** if and only if the following conditions hold:

(1) These systems are systems of self-mastering.

(2) The forces of creations and destructions are balanced so that all these systems are developing and advancing.

(3) If it is relevant, global justice must prevail in this world.

§6.4-3 Existence of The World of Self-Masterism

Thema 6.4-3-1. A world of self-masterism exists under the following conditions.

(1) The energy of the whole world is infinite.

(2) The life-will and rationality ensure that each human element is striving for achieving its own self-masterism and/or that of the conquest of others.

(3) The world is in a state of CE balance-centrality.

(4) If it is relevant, global justice must prevail in this world.

Reasoning. By (1) and (2), the cultural factors are driving each human element toward achieving its own state of being the self-master and/or that of the conquest of others. But at the state of CE balance-centrality by (3), the conquest of others is impossible. Hence, each achieves its status of being the self-master. Now with the condition (4), this world is a world of self-masterism.

PART II OVERALL DEVELOPMENT OF A CULTURAL ENTITY

Chapter 7 - Overall Future Development of A Cultural-Polity

Here we develop theories concerning the impact of cultural forces on the development and advancement of a cultural economy.

7.1 A Short-Medium Term Model of Prediction

To predict the future of a cultural economy, in the short- to medium-term time span, we could resort to the method of symbolic iso-systemism.

In the following, to be specific, we present two examples as follows. First, we shall compare the experiences of the United States with that of England. The United States in the second half of the twentieth century is like England in the second half of the seventeenth century. In these periods, England initiated its industrial revolution perhaps by absorbing sciences and technologies from the Continental Europe, especially Belgium, France, and the Netherlands. Its transfer of sciences and technology is made possible, among others, by the factors of culture and geography: (1) The close relationship between the British and French cultures, (2) the British channel that was "relatively narrow historically" in facilitating this transfer, and (3) the British channel was "quite wide historically" (by the standard of technology of that time) that prevented Continental European armies from conquering England.

In the relevant period, the United States began the development of its indigenous science and technologies by absorbing them from Europe which was destroyed by two world wars in this twentieth century. This transfer of sciences and technology was made possible, among others, also by the factors of culture and geography: (1) The close relationship between the American Culture and the European cultures, (2) the rise of the technologies of warfare and oceanic traveling and transportation that made possible to transfer people and cultures to the Americas, and (3) the Pacific and Atlantic Oceans on two fronts of the United States that have prevented European powers from attacking the home land of the United States.

Below let us set up a scheme of analogy, or a simple SIS (symbolic iso-systemism "$\approx^{SIS}$") as follows:

(7.1-1) $s \approx^{SIS} S \Leftrightarrow c\text{-}e_N\text{-}e_H\text{-}ad\text{-}e_x \approx^{SIS} Cc\text{-}E_N\text{-}E_H\text{-}AaDd\text{-}E_xM$.

To be a little formal, let the system of the frame-of-reference nation (i.e., England) be presented as: $s = c\text{-}e_N\text{-}e_H\text{-}ad\text{-}e_x$, where c, e_N, e_H, ad, and e_x refer to the nation's culture, geographic and natural resource base, human resource endowment, socio-political and economic organizations, and foreign relationships, respectively. Note that s is a grand system with c, e_N, e_H, ad, and e_x being unit systems in s ("ad" may be considered as a composite system of two unit systems). Then, the Unite States as a nation may be represented as $S = Cc\text{-}E_N\text{-}E_H\text{-}AaDd\text{-}E_xM$, where Cc, E_N, E_H, AaDd and E_xM depict the nation's culture, natural resource base, human resource endowment, socio-political and economic organizations, and foreign relationships/military strengths, respectively. Here S is a grand system with Cc , E_N, E_H, AaDd and E_xM being subsystems in S; and note that Cc, AaDd and E_xM may be considered as grand systems comprising two or more subsystems. For more details of a, A, d and D, see Bcm. (7.1-4).

Secondly, we employ China as an example to illustrate this method of prediction. The experiences of Japan, Taiwan and South Korea showed that their golden ages of economic development lasted approximately 25-35 years with the annual average GNP growth rate of 5-7%. This is roughly for Japan, the period of years 1955 to 1985/90, for Taiwan, 1960 to 1990, and for South Korea, 1965 to 1990. By an analogy, China's diamond age of development may be expected to last at least 40 to 50 years, i.e., from 1980 to 2020/2030. This analogy is established on the basis that, China shares with Japan, South Korea and Taiwan the same or a very similar set of backgrounds in culture and external environments. In addition, China is of a size much lager size in both territory and population, and has much stronger social and political establishments.

China has well a stretched coastal area and a vast inland region. To China, Japan, Taiwan and South Korea, being nations of islands (Japan and Taiwan) and "peninsula" (South Korea), are just like nations of coastal areas. In China, modern development of the inland region will definitely take a much longer time than the development of the coastal area. With this capacity of inland development and also with this delay, it is most natural to expect the process of rapid development in China to last longer that those in the cases of Japan, Taiwan and South Korea.

To be somewhat formal, let the system of the major frame-of-reference nation in this case, i.e., Taiwan, be presented as: $s = c\text{-}e_N\text{-}e_H\text{-}ad\text{-}E_x$, where c, e_N, e_H, ad, and E_x refer to the nation's culture, geographic and natural resource base, human resource endowment, socio-political and economic organizations, and foreign relationships, respectively. Note that s is a grand system with c, e_N, e_H, ad, and E_x being unit systems in s (ad may be considered as a composite system of two unit systems). Then, China as a nation may be represented as $S = Cc\text{-}E_N\text{-}E_H\text{-}AaDd\text{-}e_xM$, where Cc, E_N, E_H, AaDd and e_xM depict the nation's culture, natural resource base, human resource endowment, socio-political and economic organizations, and foreign relationships/ military strengths, respectively. Here S is a grand system with Cc , E_N, E_H, AaDd and e_xM being unit systems in S; and note that Cc, AaDd and e_xM may be considered as composite systems of two or more unit systems.

To predict the future of China, we shall establish the symbolic iso-systemism (SIS) between s and S. In the following, we approach this SIS through the method of inducing a simple SIS between s and S as follows:

(7.1-2) $s \approx^{SIS} S \Leftrightarrow c\text{-}e_N\text{-}e_H\text{-}ad\text{-}E_x \approx^{SIS} Cc\text{-}E_N\text{-}E_H\text{-}AaDd\text{-}e_xM.$

or

(7.1-3) $I^{SIS}\{Cc\text{-}E_N\text{-}E_H\text{-}AaDd\text{-}e_xM\} = c\text{-}e_N\text{-}e_H\text{-}ad\text{-}E_x,$

for the SIS impactor I^{SIS} or $\approx^{SIS} \vDash \mathbb{Z}\circ,{}_v\mathbb{H}$, the systems s, $S \sqsubseteq (\Omega,\mathbb{Z}\circ,{}_v\mathbb{H},\{\mathbb{C}\})$. In the above Bcm. (7.1-2), capital letters denote greater strengths of a nation, while the lower case letters refer to weaker positions vis-à-vis its counter part of comparison.

This claim of SIS is support by the following points of reasoning:

(1) Cultural background c, C. the cultural backgrounds of Taiwan and China are very similar, both emphasizing a sense of always preparing for the hardship of life (i.e., crisis mentality, also see Murray 1998, p. 15) and the human and technological creativity, except that the culture of modern China have been influenced more by the culture of socialism and thus focuses more on the self-dependency of technological development. That is, $I^{SIS}\{Cc\} = c$ in a semi-strong form.

(2) Geographic and natural resource bases e_N, E_N. China is much more richly endowed with natural resources, although Taiwan, as a small island bordering the Pacific Ocean and Japan, has a set of much more favorable geopolitical conditions for economic development and trade. That is, $I^{SIS}\{E_N\} = e_N$ in a strong form.

(3) Human resource endowments e_N, E_N. Both has a very similar background. Taiwan has a well educated body of semi-skilled labor, skillful technicians and engineers, and in general, competent business and socio-political leaders. On the other hand, China has a much larger size of population. That is, $I^{SIS}\{E_H\} = e_H$ in a strong form.

(4) Economic, social, and political organizations. Both of Taiwan and China have a similar array of organizations. The common citizens have a strong desire for social order, economic prosperity, and effective, stable and controllable governments.

After suffering various consequence of the collapse of the classical China, there is a strong consensus for the nation to focus on economic construction. Building upon this social philosophy of stability and prosperity, and with long-term tradition of organizational efficiency to be further improved through adaptation of Western organizational theories and practices, the modern organizations of Taiwan and the modern China have been relatively effective. That is, they are very similar in this aspect. That is, $I^{SIS}\{AaDd\} = ad$ in a semi-strong form.

(5) External relationships. In this respect, Taiwan has a more natural tie with the United States and Japan, with the former being the major source of technological improvement and a major export market of Taiwan, and the latter being the secondary source of technological transfer. In general, China has maintained a good relationship with both the United States and Japan, although at times, this relationship has also been a major source of rift due to divergent economic interests among them (for example, see Murray 1998, p. 175). Further, China maintains stronger relationships with Russia and Islamic countries in general. That is, $I^{SIS}\{e_XM\} = E_X$ in a weak form.

In the above, for the general conditions of the simple SIS conditions, see Appendix A, Section A.6. Therefore, the simple SIS between Taiwan and China, i.e., $s \approx^{SIS} S$, is established.

Throughout the history of this world of economic and military contest, China at times had very rough time in dealing with the outside world. But finally in the twenty-first century, under the cultural efficiency of organization under the Chinese Communist Party (CCP), with its military might, China does enjoy a relative advantage of war efficiency (Tonn 2001, Lecture III, p. 60). Note that the concept of war efficiency was also discussed in Tonn (1984).

For the external relationships with countries other than the United States, Japan, Russia and many Islamic countries, China positions itself much better than Taiwan. Nevertheless, for simplicity of analysis (or systemic study), we may say their outside environments are similar to the extent that, in terms of the impact on the long-term performance of their societies and economies, unfavorable external political factor may be less pertinent in the future growth of these nations.

In another approach, we may write Bcm. (7.1-2) as: for φ, ψ, φ., ψ., $\mathcal{S} \models \mathbb{Z}$o,$_v\mathbb{H}$, and s, S ⊑ (Ω,$\mathbb{Z}$o,$_v\mathbb{H}$,{ℂ}),

(7.1-4) S = [φAa_ψDd + <$\mathcal{S}\mathbb{C}_{x1}$,$\mathcal{S}\mathbb{C}_{x2}$>] | E_N_E_H_e_xM,

where {φ{A(org,.|E),ψ{D(K,.|E),ψd(L,.|E),φa(tech,.|E) | ($\mathcal{S}\mathbb{C}_{x1}$,$\mathcal{S}\mathbb{C}_{x2}$)} forms a 5-polar MFCE scheme, for E ≡ E_N_E_H_e_xM. For a comparison, we may write the MFCE scheme of Taiwan as:

(7.1-5) s = [φa_ψd + <$\mathcal{S}\mathbb{C}_{x1}$,$\mathcal{S}\mathbb{C}_{x2}$>] | e_N_e_H_E_x,

where {φa_1(org,.|E),ψ{d_1(K,.|E),ψd_2(L,.|E),φa_2(tech,.|E) | ($\mathcal{S}\mathbb{C}_{x1}$,$\mathcal{S}\mathbb{C}_{x2}$)} forms a 5- polar MFCE scheme, for E ≡ e_N_e_H_E_x.

7.2 A Long-Term Catch-up System

To begin the systematic analysis of a long-term catch-up process, in the following, first let the system X under the organizational efficiency (o), technological efficiency (T), the operating efficiency of latecomer ($\mathcal{L}$), and the leap efficiency ($\mathcal{L}p$) applying to the whole system be: $\mathcal{L}p${o-T-$\mathcal{L}$}(X). Next, let x be the part of X which is under the operations of impactors o, $\mathcal{L}$, $\mathcal{L}p$, and T, and X = {x,o-$\mathcal{L}$ | $\mathcal{L}p$T}. Thirdly, let X = {$\mathcal{L}$-o {L,K},E | ℭ | P-S,$\mathcal{L}p$T{R&D}}, for {L,K} being the input set, E being the economy, ℭ being the culture (the center of X), P-S being the socio-polity, and R&D being the set of research and development of X. In addition, let τ denote the technological advantage. Then we have the chain symbolic iso-systemism:

(7.2-1) {x,o -$\mathcal{L}$ | $\mathcal{L}p$T} $\approx^{SIS}$ $\mathcal{L}p${o-T-$\mathcal{L}$}(X) $\approx^{SIS}$ X{ $\mathcal{L}$-o{L,K},E | ℭ | P-S,$\mathcal{L}p$Tτ},

where {x,o-$\mathcal{L}$|$\mathcal{L}p$T}is a tri-system, $\mathcal{L}p${o-T-$\mathcal{L}$}(X) a "matrix system," and {$\mathcal{L}$-o {K,L},E | ℭ | P-S,$\mathcal{L}p$Tτ} is a 5-polar MFCE system in which ℭ (being the will-rationality complex or the mind complex {$\mathcal{M}$|E(e_k),$\mathbb{T}$zu*}) is the center. Note that Bcm. (7.2-1) will be more easily understood as a developmental chain over time. Let ω denote the other advantages, such as the advantage of resource availability and global geopolitical advantage. Furthermore, let Φ denote the first mover's advantage, and Ψ^{IN} denote the global financial advantage. Then, in Y (see Bcm. 7.2-3), {Φ.Ψ^{IN}.ω{L,K}, E | ℭ | P-S,Tτ} is a 5-polar MFCE system. Here we write the "matrix system" of X (without explicitly spelling out the role of ℭ) as:

(7.2-2) $\mathcal{L}p${o-T-$\mathcal{L}$}(X) =
$$\left|\begin{matrix} & \text{R\&D} & \\ & & \text{pub} \\ \text{priv} & & \\ & \text{K-L} & \end{matrix}\right|,$$

where pub, priv, R&D, and K-L refers to the public sector (or the planning sector), the private sector, the research and development (or technology) sector, and the input (raw labor and capital stock) sector, respectively. For more details of this "matrix system," see Appendix G.

Then, for

$$(7.2\text{-}3)\quad X \equiv \left/\begin{matrix} \mathcal{L}p\mathrm{T} \\ x \quad o\text{-}\mathcal{L} \end{matrix}\right|,\quad X' \equiv \left/\begin{matrix} \mathcal{L}p'\ \mathrm{T}' \\ x' \quad o'\text{-}\mathcal{L}' \end{matrix}\right|,\quad Y \equiv \left/\begin{matrix} \tau^{Y} \\ y \quad \Phi.\Psi^{IN}.\omega \end{matrix}\right|,$$

and $Y^{P} = \{\tau.\Phi.\Psi^{IN}.\omega\{Y\}\}^{P}$, Y is the target nation with the superscript P denoting the practical system of Y (rather than the theoretical system of Y), and the chain of catching-up becomings is as follows:

$$(7.2\text{-}4)\quad \left/\begin{matrix} \mathcal{L}p\mathrm{T} \\ x \quad o\text{-}\mathcal{L} \end{matrix}\right| \rightarrow \left/\begin{matrix} \mathcal{L}p'\ \mathrm{T}' \\ x' \quad o'\text{-}\mathcal{L} \end{matrix}\right|,\ X' \approx^{SIS} Y^{P}$$

That is, by transforming into X', X eventually catches up to Y in a practical sense. Here "$\approx^{SIS}$" denotes the symbol of iso-systemism.

For a latecomer, Bcm. (7.2-3) expresses the idea that, in order to catch up to the leader Y^{P}, one way to go is to create a leap efficiency ($\mathcal{L}p$) of technological development under the control (in the case of a planned economy) or guidance (in the case of a market economy) of the government by combing the cultural efficiency with the organizational efficiency and technological efficiency of the society. That is, to set up X so that

$$(7.2\text{-}5)\quad \{X,L|o\} \rightarrow \{X,\{L,K\}\text{-}\ T\ |o\} \rightarrow \{X,\{L,\mathcal{L}pK\}\text{-}\mathcal{L}p\ T\ |o\} \rightarrow \{X,\{L,K'\}\text{-}\mathcal{L}p'\ T\ '|o'\},$$

where $\mathcal{L}p'$, K', T ' and o' are higher levels of $\mathcal{L}p$, K, T and o, respectively. That is to say, by the strategic operation under the cultural advantage of the society, (1) the levels of saving and investment have been significantly higher, (2) under the operation of new cultural creativity, work ethics is promoted and the technological efficiency is created, and (3) the leap efficiency raises the levels of organizational efficiency, technological efficiency, and all other types of efficiency.

Note that Bcm. (7.2-4) is equivalent to Bcm. (7.2-6) presented below:

$$(7.2\text{-}6)\quad \mathcal{L}p\{o\text{-}T\text{-}\mathcal{L}\}(X) \rightarrow^{SD} X^{*},\ \ \mathcal{L}p^{*}T^{*X} \approx^{StgB} T\tau^{YP},$$

X* being the X in the state of strategic continuity with the superscript SD denoting the state of strategic discontinuity and Y^{P} being Y operating at the practical level of efficiency (rather than the theoretical level of efficiency). Here the superscript "StgB" denote a state of strategic balance. Here, "$\mathcal{L}p^{*}T^{*X}$" denotes $\mathcal{L}p^{*}T^{*}$ of system X. In addition, $\mathcal{L}p^{*}$ and T* refers to $\mathcal{L}p$ and T in the state of strategic continuity, respectively.

$$(7.2\text{-}7)\quad Y^{P} = \left|\begin{matrix} & \text{R\&D} & \\ \text{Priv} & & \\ & & \\ & & \text{D} \\ & \text{L-K} & \end{matrix}\right|^{P},$$

With D denoting the public sector or the Defense Department, R&D denoting the sector of research and development, Priv denoting the private sector, and L-K denoting the factor mix of inputs, with the superscript "P" denoting "the practical level," we have the practical level of Y in Bcm. (7.2-7).

Further note that the weak from version of Bcm. (7.2-3) or (7.2-5) is the iso-systemism in-between the R&D sectors of systems X and those of Y:

(7.2-8) $R\&D_X \approx^{SIS} R\&D_Y^{P}$;

and the strong form version of it is the iso-systemism in-between system Y and the transformed system of X (i.e., $X' = \{X, \{L, K'\}\text{-}\mathcal{L}p' T' | o'\}$):

(7.2-9) $X\{o\text{-}T\text{-}\mathcal{L}\text{-}\mathcal{L}p\} \rightarrow X' \approx^{SIS} Y\{T\text{-}\Phi\text{-}\Psi^{IN}\text{-}\omega\}$,

where Y is assumed to be at its theoretical and full potential level.

7.3 Future Development of The Culture-and-Polity

Culturally for a newly developed country (in the case of a "big nation"), in the first stage, an essential approach is to preserve one's cultural merits while being adaptive to outside cultures and to maintain social stability in the course of rapid technological and economic development. Thus a balance may be achieved between the cultural advancement and the development of the economy associated with the rapid development of its technologies.

In terms of political development, democracy may be achieved by the interactions between the intellectuals as a class and all the political parties as a group. In terms of economic development, a balance between the intensive growth path and the extensive growth path may also be reached.

In the case of a backward country, due to the need for an extensive growth, an appropriate level of social stability is essential. Otherwise, a certain degree of tight social control may be necessary.

As for the issues directly related to the creation of the new culture of the nation, we may discuss them in terms of two periods or stages. The first is the stage of initial development. At this stage, in the arena of social life, citizens must obey the social norms and compete with others in a fair manner. In terms of personal virtue or individual conduct, a citizen may need to have peace in one's mind and not to blame others for one's unsuccessful endeavor. In terms of national construction, the society must pursue democracy (in the sense of self-masterism), collective or group stability, economic prosperity and a reasonable capacity for the self-defense of the nation. At this time, cultural development must rely upon the basis of technological and economic development; and the personal, social and national development must depend on the cultural development of the nation.

The second stage is the period of higher-level development. Using a Western society as an example, there are the ideas of freedom, independence, justice and mercy (or caring for others). Using the society of East Asia as an example, we may state that, individually for one's self cultivation of virtues, freedom really means the mind-illumination and always looking for truth, sincerity and steadfast of one's mind, jen-loving and yi-righteousness and the transcendence of one's life (in the sense of the self-creation of one's meaning of life).

Then, in one's social life, the principles of freedom, justice and fairness, and human dignity must be duly addressed. Here, the so-called freedom must be the "freedom of self-creation," or the type of freedom that the human being experiences within the constraint of the nature. In terms of national development, creating wealth for the citizens and creating national power against foreign dominance must be two of the top priorities of the developing country in facing formidable challenge from the outside world. At this time, in general, the development of culture must precede the technological and economic developments.

Simultaneously required in this second stage, in terms of cultural development, one may have to break away from the existing cultures and to be creative. In terms of political development, one has to develop a system promoting the self-determination of citizens or that of "self-masterism," in which every person is the master of himself or herself, in order to safeguard one's meaning of life and the society's utmost well-being. In this second stage, by the same reasoning, one may go beyond this world and penetrate into the realm of mysteries to look for the well-being and happiness of the whole universe.

Naturally, this above two-stage classification may be modified into three-stage classification: military-economic stage, economic and military stage, and the stage of military-politics and high cultural development, or even four-stage classification: military, economic, political and high cultural development stages.

Chapter 8 - Strategic Competition between Nations

In this chapter, we shall discuss topics of the strategic competition between nations and the catch-up processes of late-comer nations. For this purpose, in Section 8.1, systems of productions shall be introduced in order to set the stage for the discussions of these topics in later sections of this chapter.

8.1 Introduction: Production Systems

To facilitate our strategic discussion, below let us define a general production system. That is, for human/production activities $x_1, x_2, \ldots, x_n \Vdash \mathbf{H}$ (x_i are human elements) $y_1,y_2,\ldots,y_n \Vdash \mathbf{U}$ (y_i are universal elements in the input-output system), a **production system** φ is defined as:

(8.1-1) $\varphi = (x_1,x_2, \ldots,x_m,y_1,y_2,\ldots,y_n|R,E(e_g))$,

where $R = (R_V,R_H)$ with R_V being the technological hierarchy of the production system, R_H being the horizontal relationship among members, and $E(e_g)$ being the energy system upon which φ is conditioned. Note that in Bcm. (A.2-2-2-1), $x_i = x_i(y_i;h_i^*,IRI_i)$. Therefore, we may write:

(8.1-2) $\varphi = (x_1(y_1,h_1^*,IRI_1),x_2(y_2,h_2^*,IRI_2), \ldots,x_m(y_m,h_m^*,IRI_m),y_1,y_2,\ldots,y_n|R,E(e_g))$,

where $IRI_i = IRI_i(\rho,\omega)$. That is, the cultural variables with the decision making process (in the IRI chain) directly enter into the production system.

For an example of R, we have

/z|

(8.1-3) $\nabla_1 = (x,y,z;R|E(e_g)) =$ /x y|,

x, y, z $\Vdash$ **U** (or **H**), is a production system with R_V denoting two levels of technologies: (x y) in the lower level of technological hierarchy and z in the high level, and R_H denoting one element in the high level together with two elements x and y in the lower level. Here, x and y are mutually independent, given the culture of conflict; or they are mutually cooperative with each other, given the culture of tranquility.

To have a better understanding about the production system, below we introduce four specific systems of production.

The **unitary system of production**, given the human/activity elements and the level of energy ε, is a system of balanced and symmetric membership (i.e., Δ–shaped system): in each row of this system, there are exactly one or several more elements in the higher level than its immediate lower level. As this pattern holds for the whole system, the top row must also has exactly one central element, and all other rows have balanced distribution of members. For example, two systems of this type are: $|(d\ e) \setminus c|^T$ and $|(a\ b\ e) \setminus (f\ g) \setminus c|^T$, for c being the center element of the system, a, b, d, e, f, and g being non-central elements, with each of the superscript "T" denoting the "transpose" of the "matrix-like system." Two more examples of the unitary system of production are provided as follows: for a, b, c d, e, f, g, h, k $\Vdash$ **U**, $|(a,b,c) \setminus (d,e) \setminus f|^T \equiv (a,b,c,d,e,f;R|\varepsilon)$ and $|\ (a,b,c,d,e) \setminus (f,g,h) \setminus k|^T \equiv (a,b,c,d,e,f,g,h,k;R|\varepsilon)$ (see Bcms. (8.1-4) and (8.1-5), respectively).

```
                              /f\
                             /d  e\
(8.1-4)  (a,b,c,d,e,f;R|ε) = /a   b  c\,
```

```
                                      /k\
                                     /f g h\
(8.1-5)  (a,b,c,d,e,f,g,h,k;R|ε) = /a b c d e\.
```

The **steep system of production** (|$_{\Delta}$-𝒫), given the human/activity elements and the level of energy ε, is a system of upward-skewed structure of technologies: in this system, in some row of higher technological level, there are one element less than the number of elements in its immediate lower row. And in some other rows, there may have the same number of elements in the higher technological level as in its respective immediate lower row. In addition, on the top row of this system, there must have one and only one central element.

Three examples of the steep system of production are presented as follows: for a, b, c, d, e, f, g, h ⊩ **U**,

```
                       |b|
(8.1-6)  (a,b;R|ε) = |a|,
```

```
                           |d|
                           |c|
(8.1-7)  (a,b,c,d;R|ε) = |a b\,
```

```
                                   |h|
                                   |g|
                                   |f|
                                   |d e\
(8.1-8)  (a,b,c,d,e,f,g,h;R|ε) = |a b c\.
```

The **flat system of production** ({_$_{\Delta}$-𝒫}), given the human/activity elements and the level of energy ε, is a system skewed toward the lower-right hand side in its levels of technologies: in this system, in each row of lower technology level, there are many more elements than in its immediate higher row. One rule related to this is that, the number of reduction from the lower row to its immediate higher row must increase as the process proceeds. Further, this system could have no or even more than two central elements (locating on the top row).

Three examples of the flat system of production are shown as follows: for a, b, c, d, e, f, g, h, k, l, m, n, p, q, s, t, u, v, z ⊩ **U**,

```
(8.1-9)  (a,b,c;R|ε) = |a b c|,
```

```
                            |z\
(8.1-10)  (s,t,u,v,z;R|ε) = |s t u v\,
```

(8.1-11) (a,b,c,d,e,f,g,h,k,l,m,n,p,q;R|ε) = |(a b c d e f g h) \ (k l m n p) \ q|^{T}.

Note that, here, another way of expressing Bcm (8.1-11) is as follows:

|q\
|k l m n p\
(8.1-12) (a,b,c,d,e,f,g,h,k,l,m,n,p,q;R|ε) = |a b c d e f g h\.

The **Parabolic system of production** (Δ_{down}-$\mathcal{P}$,Δ^{up}-$\mathcal{P}$), given the human/activity elements and the level of energy ε, is a system with a shape skewed toward both the upper-left and the lower-right hand sides. In a sense, it is a systematic union of a steep system and a flat system. Note that Δ_{down}-$\mathcal{P}$ represents an **almost-steep** (or steep-skewed) productive system, Δ^{up}-$\mathcal{P}$ represents an **almost-flat** (or flat-skewed) productive system.

For example, the following is a parabolic system of production: for a, b, c, d, e, f, g, h, k ⊫ **H**,

|k|
|h|
|f g\
(8.1-13) (s,t,u,v,z;R|ε) = |a b c d e\.

Now we turn formally to the discussion of our strategic space. For a specific cultural economy (with the culture ℭ), $\mathcal{T}${S} = $\mathcal{T}$[z y x]^T = [φ{z } ψ{y} $\mathcal{T}${x}|$_{ℭ}$]^T = [z* y' x$^{\#}$]^T , where x$^{\#}$ = $\mathcal{T}${x}|$_{ℭ}$ ≠ x referring to the impactor $\mathcal{T}$ (for example, an effective cultural policy that would otherwise be ineffective) on the private sector which is originally beyond the impact range of the public policy impactor. For example, let a strategic space be Ω^T= {Ω^D, Ω^{Rh}, Ω^S, Ω^V, Ω^{sC}}, where Ω^D ={YX{__Δ-$\mathcal{P}$},YX{Δ_{down}-$\mathcal{P}$} → (|$_{\Delta}$-$\mathcal{P}$)|YX being a YY dynamical impactor}, Ω^{Rh} = {YX{__$_{\Delta}$-$\mathcal{P}$},YX{Δ_{down}-$\mathcal{P}$} →YX{Δ^{up}-$\mathcal{P}$} or YX{Δ^{up}-$\mathcal{P}$}→{|$_{\Delta}$-$\mathcal{P}$}, YX being a highly effective impactor}, Ω^S = {YX{__$_{\Delta}$-$\mathcal{P}$}→YX{Δ_{down}-$\mathcal{P}$},YX{Δ_{down}-$\mathcal{P}$}→ YX(Δ^{up}- $\mathcal{P}$); or YX{Δ^{up}-$\mathcal{P}$ }→ (|$_{\Delta}$-$\mathcal{P}$), YX being a moderately effective impactor}, Ω^V = (ν{__$_{\Delta}$-$\mathcal{P}$},ν{Δ_{down}-$\mathcal{P}$ },ν{Δ^{up}-$\mathcal{P}$} or ν{|$_{\Delta}$-$\mathcal{P}$}, ν ⊨ $\mathbb{Z}$ being a variational impactor}, Ω^{sC} = {ϕ = ϕ∘, the empty impactor), i.e., no impactor is effective under this strategic space}.

8.2 Strategic Spaces of Economic-Cultural Advancement

Development-advancement strategies of a cultural economy. In general, the cultural economy in the real world consists of the socialist, capitalist, Faziranist, Indian and Islam economies, etc. To facilitate the discussion in this section, the target economy of our strategic study is set as the general cultural economy, an integrated or even a virtual entity of all cultural economies of the world. In the following, we shall be dealing mainly with the cultural economies of socialism, capitalism and Faziranism.

Let S ⊑ (Ω,$\mathcal{Z}$∘,$_{v}\mathcal{H}$,{ℂ}) be a system, z, y, x ⊨ (Ω,$\mathcal{Z}$∘,$_{v}\mathcal{H}$,{ℂ}) be sub-systems of S (i.e., z, y, x ⊑ S). Let the system of the general cultural economy be: S = [z y x]^T, where z is the set of public firms or the public sector which is directly controlled by the planner of a nation, y is the Faziranist net-working or the "sector" which is indirectly affected by the planner of a nation, x is private sector which is beyond the control of the planner, T denotes the superscript of system transformation as is in the case of transpose in matrix operation. Let $\mathcal{T}$, φ, ψ ⊨ $\Omega^{\mathcal{T}}$⊓($\mathcal{Z}$∘,$_{v}\mathcal{H}$) ($\Omega^{\mathcal{T}}$ denotes the strategic space), with $\mathcal{T}$ referring to the strategic impactor, φ{.} the impactor on z, z* the result of φ{z} (i.e., z* = φ{z}), ψ{.} the impactor on y, and y' the result of ψ{y} (i.e., y' = ψ{y}). Then, under the general condition, we have

(8.2-1) $\mathcal{T}${S} = $\mathcal{T}$[z y x]^T = [φ{z} ψ{y} x]^T = [z* y' x]^T .

Generally speaking, in $(\Omega,\mathbb{Z}\circ,{}_{v}\mathbb{H},\{\mathbb{C}\})\sqcap\mathcal{E}^{c}$ ($\mathcal{E}^{c}$ referring to the general cultural economy), if z and y are flat sub-systems (a sub-system is itself a system by definition), then z* and y' become steep sub-systems. This result may differ from the operation in a specific cultural economy.

Remark 8-2-1-1. Seen from Bcm. (8-1-2), by combining with the materials of Bcm. (A.2-1-1-5) and Section E.3, the IRI chain, MPFX cycle and SIFP chain complex enter into the production system directly. Thus any operation of a cultural economy is part of the system per se under the general cultural operation. That is, culture is an integral part of the operations of any cultural economy.

Note that both of capitalist and socialist systems can be represented by n-pole MFCE schemes (see Subsection A.4), and these two systems (or schemes) differ in a major way: in the capitalist system, the center is a virtual one; whereas the center of the socialist system is a real one. As for a mixed system, see Appendix G.

Below, we shall discuss each of the strategic choices facing a cultural economy by applying various principles like the CE balance principle and the principle of strategic centrality to the development processes of culture, sciences and technology, and organization. In terms of culture, we may classify it into being, yu-wu (or tao-jen), Indian, Islam, and self-mastering cultures. Within a culture, it may also be classified into specific micro-cultures according to whether they are engaging in artistic, religious or daily activities. In terms of science-based technology (i.e., modern Western technology), we may classify it according to whether it is labor-, capital- and human intelligence-intensive; and we may classify it into low- (or agricultural), medium- (or light-industrial), high- (or heavy and chemical), and super-technological (or high-technological) types as well. In terms of organization, it can be classified according to whether it is centralized or decentralized, whether private or public, whether centrally planned or market induced, whether profit-oriented or altruistic, and whether politically oriented, economic-financially oriented, or engineering-oriented.

Leap strategy (**diamond strategy D**). Below is the 5-polar diamond-strategic scheme (or scheme of leap strategy). In our previous presentation (Tonn 2001), there are MFCE scheme and 4-polar CE scheme. For this 4-polar CE scheme, let East (or E), West (or W), South (or S), North (or N) and Center (or C) be universal elements in **U**. Then for $X = (S,W,E,N) \sqsubseteq (\Omega,\mathbb{Z}\circ,{}_{v}\mathbb{H},\{\mathbb{C}\})$, X is a 4-polar yin-yang CE scheme. Now let C ≡ "leap" be a new universal element attached to the 4-polar CE scheme. Here C is the central element with characteristics of a "leap strategy." Then $X' = (S,W,C,E,N) = (S,W,E,N|C) \sqsubseteq (\Omega,\mathbb{Z}\circ,{}_{v}\mathbb{H},\{\mathbb{C}\})$, where (W,E) is a non-central and horizontal yin-yang pair of elements and (S,N) is the non-central and vertical yin-yang pair of elements. This X is then the desired 5-polar CE leap scheme. Here C is the leap-pole with strategies controlling and directing the horizontal and vertical flows of energies to create a leap force in this system X.

For a leap strategy, nations may adopt a Legalist growth path (Warring States, ancient China), a Stalinist growth path (the Soviet Union: 1928-1955), Maoist-Cultural Revolutionist growth path (China: 1949-1957, 1967-1976, see Tonn 1984). Although this strategy may reap great rewards, it is highly risky and its costs may be astronomical. Thus, even if its planners embark on the enlightened policies, this leap strategy is extremely difficult to sustain for a long time.

The objective of the classic Legalist leap strategy is to strengthen the military power of the nation and to enhance the personal power and riches of the king. The leap strategist usually employed a mechanism of a primitive type of central planning in coercing peasants to engage in uncompensated and forced labor by combined methods of terror, threat of death and occasionally pecuniary or political rewards. Historically, the key economic-political policies of this Legalist growth path were those policies designed for the increase in agricultural production and the promotion of national power to wage wars against other countries.

To be formal, let the classic Legalist cultural-economic system be: $X \sqsubseteq (\Omega, \mathbb{Z}\circ, {}_{v}\mathbb{H}, \{\mathbb{C}\}) \sqcap \mathcal{E}^{F}$, where $\mathcal{E}^{F}$ is a Faziranist cultural system. In terms of the will-to-excellence and rationality-to-creation, the classic Legalist cultural system may be expressed as: $<\mathbb{C}_X> \Leftrightarrow (\omega,\rho) = \{YW|YX < F\}^\wedge\{C|YX<F\}$, where F is the Legalist pre-dialectic rationality, YW is the Taoist yu-wu rationality, and YX is the Taoist YYTR (yin-yang tao-reversal or YYWX) rationality. For modern China which may be considered as a new-Legalist cultural entity, its cultural set is: $<\mathbb{C}_X> \Leftrightarrow (\omega,\rho) = \{YW,S|YX<DD\}^\wedge\{T,C|YX<DD\}$, where DD refers to the Marxist dialectic rationality, S refers to the scientific rationality of the West, and C refers to the control-rationality of the Soviet communists. As for the Soviet Union which could perhaps be treated as a Western-and-modern version of Legalist system, its cultural set may be presented as: $<\mathbb{C}_X> \Leftrightarrow (\omega,\rho) = \{S|DD\}^\wedge\{C|DD\}$.

For the modern socialism-communism, its leap strategy is one embarking on a forced growth path with the foundation of Marxist-Leninist dialectic rationality. In this strategy, the focal point is the production policy of developing heavy-chemical industries from the foundation of an agrarian economy. In the historical perspective, the main goals of the Soviet Leap growth may be thought of as to defend the fruits of Russia's century-old territorial expansion and to catch up to the economic level of advanced capitalism by using mechanisms of central planning and military expansion. Note that the practice of this strategy was made possible by developing forcibly from the base of a weak light-industrial sector (the Soviet Union) or essentially an agrarian economy with abundant labor supply (especially China) and abundant natural resources (especially Russia). This is an extensive path of economic growth. In terms of the required technologies, they are labor-intensive or natural-resource-intensive and are based on mature heavy-industrial technologies developed in advanced capitalist economies. In terms of the political institution, this strategy depends on a system of dictatorship, although a high spirit of patriotism may help greatly.

In terms of control/coordination mechanisms of the economy, it is well known that, in this case of jumping directly from agriculture or a weak light industrial base to heavy industries, market mechanism can not be operational. Only central planning mechanism may work. That is, the strategy of leap growth depends on the polity of a centralized system which in turn depends upon the culture of centralization or communitarian-group consensus. It is also well known to the development economists that this kind of import-substitution and heavy-industrial strategies must rely upon the use of overvalued foreign exchange rate, artificially depressed agricultural and mineral resource prices, artificially jacked-up prices of manufactured-goods, and highly suppressed living standards of the rural peasant class.[6]

In sum, the leap growth path depends on high levels of saving and investment, highly coerced labor production, and a mechanism of imitating more advanced technologies from outside. The recipe for the success of this type of strategy depends as well upon artificially holding-down level of consumption of the citizens in order to achieve the highest possible level of the export of raw materials and agricultural products in exchange for the import of machinery (in the case of China and especially the former Soviet Union). This leap growth path can be expressed as either $YX\{\_\_{}_{\Delta}\text{-}\mathcal{P}\} \rightarrow |_{\Delta}\text{-}\mathcal{P}$ or $YX\{\Delta_{down}\text{-}\mathcal{P}\} \rightarrow |_{\Delta}\text{-}\mathcal{P}$. This is, in order to concentrate all efforts on promoting a few key industrial projects or exchanging for the import of foreign advanced technology, specific cultural traits and effective methods of national organization are required and an efficiency of concerted efforts must be ensured. This is in actuality a **systematic efficiency** of national development and advancement. This type of leap growth strives to reduce the level of consumption and the investment activities in such areas as the transportation network and residential housing (at least in the short term dimension of time). This strategy calls for a significant increase in the level of investment in education, usually in the narrow fields of physical sciences and engineering. This may also require the indoctrination of the citizens by the party ideology.

The growth path of this leap strategy also involves a long-term process of national advancement. In addition, in order to achieve the efficiency of this strategy, a political atmosphere of anti-continuity and anti-equilibrium is required as well. In this process, the revolutionaries and party cadres become the master of the new society, and engineers, physical scientists and urban dwellers benefit from this revolutionary process. But peasants, landlords and the intellectuals in general are sacrificed.

In this case, in the macroeconomic model, under favorable conditions, the planner may be able to set the output level of the nation at the point of intersection between the TS curve and the MR curve of the TD^N curve (similar to the point y_n in Figure 4.2-2) in order to maximize the well-being of the citizens of the nation. On this (YY) CE centrality point, what is saved may be invested into those linkage sectors in order to promote the highest level of sciences and technological advancement. At this CE centrality point, a minimal level of social energy is consumed. But this may not be feasible under democratic polity. This strategy is feasible only under favorable socio-political conditions.

In terms of the sectors of productive development, under this leap-strategy, agriculture will be sacrificed and manufacturing industries will benefit, with the scope of service sector being significantly reduced. In terms of technological development, the scale of backward linkage could be maximized, and the scale of forward linkage may also be maximized.

Real world experiences of nations had shown repeatedly that this leap strategy involves great risks. It is difficult for this strategy to sustain for long, because for the economic system to move on this radical growth path, the traditional culture underlying the economy may be destroyed, the land lords class and the intellectuals (rooted deeply in this tradition) may be purged, the old political establishment may be completely replaced, foreign relations may have to be completely reinstituted. By this endeavor, the economic and financial structures may be truncated and only the military-industrial complex (in the modern case or the military-oriented agriculture and handicrafts production in the classic world) are served. Thus, agriculture and the light industries are ignored, and education is oriented only toward technical and technological development. Generally speaking, it takes time to cultivate human resources. It is simply not easy to foster the development of new technology in a short period of time, and it needs milliards of experiments and practical experiences to access and determine the validity of new culture. It is especially vital that the continuous expansion of heavy and chemical industries depends upon the constantly enlarging base of agriculture and light industry (in the context of the developing economy in the twentieth century). That is, if the bases of agriculture and light industry fail to grow over time, the self-generating heavy and chemical industries would eventually collapse. At the same time, by draining scarce resources for the single purpose of developing chemical and heavy industries (without due regard to develop agriculture and the civilian- and consumption-oriented light industry), the high-tech sector is self-served and would not be able to prosper. Eventually, the limit of the usefulness of importing foreign advanced technologies would be reached. The more than seventy years of experiences of the Soviet Union have clearly shown that, the tireless devotion of scare resources of the country entirely to the development of military and heavy industries actually disserved the economy the economy and suppressed the momentum of the economic and cultural developments. Furthermore, the results of the experiences of China under Mao and those of India before the 1990s also point to the same direction.

The leap-growth path also minimizes the role of the external economic relations. This growth strategy may induce the economy to move closer to a point of autarky. But nevertheless, the weakness of this strategy is obvious: the loss of any opportunity for absorbing foreign cultures and the missing of great chances to establish long-term human foundations for cultural renewable and continual advancement. This strategy focuses one-sidedly on the promotion of (physical) sciences and engineering education only at the expense of the education of arts and humanities.

In terms of human resource development, this strategy may favor those cadres with with educational backgrounds in sciences and especially in fields of engineerings. Examples are abounds like Nikita Krushchev and Brezniev in the former Soviet Union, and Li Peng, Jiang Zemin and Zhu Rongji in China.

In terms of property rights, for the system under this leap strategy, all the land and most of the productive enterprises belong to the state. That is, all are under the control of the ruling party, apparently not conducive to democratic development.

In terms of economic development, this strategy exalts a policy of import-substitution. For a late-comer in the process of economic development, initially, agriculture is heavily taxed in order to finance the development of heavy and chemical industries. At the same time, unless a significant amount of foreign loan is secured, it is essential that mechanisms for encouraging and fostering domestic private saving and public investment must be successfully created. Note that in this strategy, light industry is ignored. But to sustain this process, in the intermediate stage, the success of this strategy depends very much on a well developed light industrial sector. In the final stage of this strategic development, a balance between the light and heavy industries must be achieved, and a feedback mechanism from the heavy industry to support agriculture and the light industry must also be well instituted. Otherwise, this strategy will eventually backfire and collapse. Besides, in order to develop industry well, the government must see to it that a large scale foreign advanced technology is imported and then supplied to the private sector at lower than its real cost.

From the above reasoning, it is seen that the socio-political nature of an economy is essential in determining whether a leap strategy is suitable. For a capitalist economy, except in the case of wartime emergency, a leap strategy may not be feasible. For a socialist economy with a large public sector, a leap strategy appears to be feasible (on a short-term base). As for a Faziranist economy, due to the efficiency of its traditional public sector (i.e., the government-handicraft industry), at the theoretical level, a leap strategy also appears to be feasible.

Below, let

(8.2-2) $\Omega^{T*} = \{\Omega^{D}, \Omega^{Rh}, \Omega^{H}, \Omega^{S}, \Omega^{V}, \Omega^{sC}\}$

be the strategic space facing the leap-strategic planners, where Ω^{D} (D or WT), Ω^{R} (or G^{+}) Ω^{H} (or G), Ω^{S}, Ω^{V}, and Ω^{sC} represent the space of leap strategy, the space of rapidly developing strategy, the space of high-speed developing strategy, the space of stable-and-moderately developing strategy, the space of slow-and-variational strategy, and the space of strategic continuity, respectively. This strategic space Ω^{T*} may be expanded into a strategy-technological space:

$$(8.2\text{-}3)\quad \Omega^{T*} \to \Omega^{T*} \sqcup \Omega^{Tch},$$

where $\Omega^{Tch} = \Omega^{Tch\text{-}Home} \sqcup \Omega^{Tch\text{-}F}$ is the space of technology, $\Omega^{Tch\text{-}Home}$ the space of domestically generated technologies, and $\Omega^{Tch\text{-}F}$ the space of foreign technologies. Generally speaking, the space of technology may also be written as:

$$(8.2\text{-}4)\quad \Omega^{Tch} = \{\ \_\_{}_{\Delta}, \Delta_{down}, \Delta^{up} \mid_{\Delta} \}.$$

That is, the space of technology is composed of technologies used in the flat production system, moderately flat production system, moderately steep production system and steep production system.

Similarly, the strategic space may be expanded into the strategy-organizational space. That is:

$$(8.2\text{-}5)\quad \Omega^{T*} \to \Omega^{T*} \sqcup \Omega^{Org},$$

where $\Omega^{Org} = \Omega^{Org\text{-}Home} \sqcup \Omega^{Org\text{-}F}$ is the space of strategy-organization, $\Omega^{Org\text{-}Home}$ is the space of domestic organizations, and $\Omega^{Org\text{-}F}$ the space of foreign organizations. In general, because of the resilient nature of culture and the inertia of organization, it is easier to expand the space of technology, but much harder to expand the space of organization, especially in a short span of time. Further note that it is easier to expand the space of technology than the space of sciences, due the fact that science as a complete entity is at a higher cultural level than technology. This is why it took a much longer time for China to learn the culture of sciences from the West in the modern time, and yet it appears to take much less efforts for the West to adopt technologies from China in the pre-modern time.

Generally speaking, the space of technology is a complex becoming of cultural space, organizational space and strategic space. Note that the formation of cultural space is essentially determined by the intellectuals and the public in general perhaps through strategic behaviors, while, in general, the impact of the strategic space on the cultural space is rather limited.

In terms of production systems, the leap strategy is one with political power to alter in a short period of time a flat production system ($\_\Delta$-$\mathcal{P}$) or an almost-flat production system (Δ_{down}-$\mathcal{P}$) into a steep production system ($|_{\Delta}$-$\mathcal{P}$). The *center of this strategy* is D = $\{YX\{(\_\Delta\text{-}\mathcal{P})\} \to (|_{\Delta}\text{-}\mathcal{P})\}\wedge\{YX\{(\Delta_{down}\text{-}\mathcal{P})\} \to (|_{\Delta}\text{-}\mathcal{P})\}$, where YX is the multi-factor CE impactor (or yin-yang five-element impactor).

Leap Tcentral. Let $X \sqsubseteq (\Omega, \mathbb{Z}\circ, {}_{v}\mathbb{H}, \{\mathbb{C}\}) \sqcap \mathcal{E}^{F/C}$ be a system, where $\mathcal{P}^{F/C}$ is a Faziranist or centralized system. Then X achieves a state of **leap T central** if and only if (i) $\phi^{D}X \sqsubseteq \mathcal{P}^{D} \sqcap T^{C\Delta}$, and for the strategic impactor $\phi^{D} \vDash \mathbb{Z}\circ, {}_{v}\mathbb{H} \Subset \{\Omega^{D} \sqcap (\mathbb{Z}\circ, {}_{v}\mathbb{H}), \{X\{\phi^{Rh}\} =< T^{B\text{-}C}\} \sqsubseteq Ш^{\Delta}$; and (ii) for $\mathcal{P}^{D}$ being the growth path of a leap strategy, $\mathcal{P}^{D} \sqsubseteq \Omega^{D} \sqcap \Omega^{TchD} \sqcap \Omega^{Org\text{-}D}$, where Ω^{D} is the space of the growth path of a leap strategy, Ω^{TchD} is the space of technological leap, $\Omega^{Org\text{-}D}$ is the space of organizational leap. Here by the **principle of Leap T Central** (see Section 3.2), we have:

$$(8.2\text{-}6) \qquad \psi\{Y_j > Y_k, \Delta_i\} \overline{\barwedge} \tau \\ \Leftrightarrow \phi^{Rh}X \sqsubseteq \mathcal{P}^D \sqcap T^B.$$

Schemes of leap and rapid developments amid uncertainty. Let Y_t, S_t, $X_t \sqsubseteq (\Omega, \mathbb{Z}\circ, {}_v\mathbb{H}, \{\mathbb{C}\})$, $Z \sqsubseteq \Omega^D \sqcup \Omega^{Rh}$ (Z as the decision-making and strategic complex of Y_t, Ω^D as a space of leap strategy and Ω^{Rh} as a space of rapidly developing strategy), $X_t \sqsubseteq T^{sysC} \sqcup T^L$ is a distribution system (in uncertainty, see Appendix I). Then $Y_t \sqsubseteq \mathcal{P}^D \sqcup \mathcal{P}^{Rh}$ ($\mathcal{P}^D$ is a leap path, $\mathcal{P}^{Rh}$ is a rapidly developing path) is a leap/rapidly developing system if and only if Bcm. (8.2-6) is true:

$$(8.2\text{-}7) \quad Y_t = S_t \oplus X_t,$$

where S_t and X_t are the certainty part and the uncertain part (i.e., uncertain system) of Y_t, respectively, with

$$(8.2\text{-}8) \quad \mathit{Ch}^H\{Y_{t+1}\} = \mathcal{S}_1\{\mathcal{P}^{NS}(S_t)\} \oplus \mathit{Ch}^H\{S_t\} \otimes \mathcal{S}_2\{X_t\},$$

$$(8.2\text{-}9) \quad \mathit{Ch}^L\{Y_{t+1}\} = \mathcal{S}_1\{\mathcal{P}^{NS}(S_t)\} \oplus \mathit{Ch}^L\{S_t\} \otimes \mathcal{S}_2\{X_t\},$$

with $\mathit{Ch}^H\{Y_{t+1}\}$ being the high-level difference of Y_{t+1}, $\mathit{Ch}^H\{Y_{t+1}\}$ being the low-level difference of Y_{t+1} (see Bcms. (I.2-2) and (I.2-3)), $\mathcal{P}^{NS}$, $\mathcal{S}_1$, $\mathcal{S}_2$, $\mathit{Ch}^H\{.\}$, $\mathit{Ch}^L\{.\} \vDash \mathbb{Z}\circ, v\mathbb{H}$, for $\mathcal{S}_1$ and $\mathcal{S}_2$ being the entity-augmenting (or matrix-expansion) impactors of a specific period of time and for $\otimes \vDash \mathbb{H}$.

Strategy of rapid development (**golden$^+$ strategy G^+**). This is a strategy of achieving a state of CE balance or a TCentral state of stability and rapid socio-economic development. This strategy is riskier than the stable strategy to be introduced below. Below we shall present a 5-polar strategic system, i.e., a model of rapid growth (or golden strategy).

Let X = (S,W,C,E,N|rapid-growth pole) $\sqsubseteq (\Omega, \mathbb{Z}\circ, {}_v\mathbb{H}, \{\mathbb{C}\})$ be a 5-polar system, where the "rapid-growth pole" (C) is the center of this system. Here, the systemic energy flowing upward toward the rapid-growth pole is one with a momentum for rapid development. The "rapid-growth pole" is the central unit system, carrying with it the strategy of rapid development; and S, W, E and N are non-central unit systems. This X is called the rapid-development 5-polar strategic system.

Now we proceed to a state of Tcentral for this rapid development strategy. Note that this developmental strategy is related to the growth path of South Korea in the period 1965-1972. Let $X \sqsubseteq \Omega$ be a system, $\Omega^{Rh} = \{G^+, G, S, V, sC\} \sqsubseteq (\Omega, \mathbb{Z}\circ, {}_v\mathbb{H}, \{\mathbb{C}\}) \sqcap \mathcal{E}^F$ be the space of some rapid development strategy. Then X reaches a **rapidly developmental T Central** if and only if (i) $\phi^{Rh}X \sqsubseteq \mathcal{P}^{Rh} \sqcap T^B$, and for the strategic impactor $\phi^{Rh} \vDash \mathbb{Z}\circ, {}_v\mathbb{H} \Subset \Omega^{Rh} \sqcap (\mathbb{Z}\circ, {}_v\mathbb{H})$, $\{X\{\phi^{Rh}\} =< T^{B\Delta}\} \sqsubseteq \text{Ш}^\Delta$, where $\mathcal{P}^{Rh}$ is the growth path of the rapid-speed developmental strategy.

This **principle of rapidly developmental Tcentral** (see Section 3.2) is then:

$$(8.2\text{-}10) \qquad \psi\{Y_j > Y_k, \Delta_i\} \overline{\barwedge} \tau \\ \Leftrightarrow \phi^{Rh}X \sqsubseteq \mathcal{P}^{Rh} \sqcap T^B.$$

Usually this rapid developmental strategy requires some specific complexes of culture in order for it to be feasible. For example, in the case of China after Mao, let the cultural complex be: $<\mathbb{C}_X> \Leftrightarrow (\omega,\rho) = \{T,C|D^{-}<YX^*\}^{\wedge}\{YW,S|D^{-}<YX^*\}$, where T represents the culture of tranquility, C refers to the culture of conflict and conquest, YW is the self-generating yu-wu rationality complex, S is the science-based being rationality complex, $\{D^{-} = (D,F) =< T^{B\Delta}\} \sqsubseteq Ш^{\Delta}$ (i.e., D^{-} being the CE TCentral system comprising the Marxist dialectic will-rationality complex D and the pre-dialectic will-rationality complex of Legalism F), and YX* is the complex of the will structures and the thinking patterns of the modernized form of yinyang wuxing (YYWX) scheme. Then, China could pursue this strategy of rapid development.

In the periods of 1960s and 1970s, South Korean Government pursued a golden+ strategy and supplied investment fund to a few selected private enterprises at interest rates well below market equilibrium levels. The government simultaneously implemented inflationary policy to increase the profit rates of the heavy industrial firms.

The golden+ strategy of South Korea does not fit the general state of the political economy of a democratic capitalism. Unless in war time emergency or some unusual states, the strategic space of a democratic capitalist economy does not have any element of a leap strategy. The growth path of leap and bound can only be seen in a capitalist economy when the underlying economy is in great emergency. For instance, at the time of rapid territorial expansion which may also be a period of rapid population expansion, the energy of the economy itself (without any specific strategic manipulation by the government) may explode and push the course of economic growth onto a leap path. Still another example is that in a war time, like the United States in the Second World War of the twentieth century, the economy of that country may suddenly release its full potential. In general, any political economy of authoritarianism could adopt a leap strategy, but only those with effective public sector (i.e., those with effective measures to mobilize abundant labor and abundant natural resources) and under favorable external conditions may succeed.

High-speed development strategy (**golden strategy G**). This is related to the strategic paths pursued by Japan and Taiwan in the post-war period of the twentieth century. Theoretically, the growth path of The Kuan Tzu could be derived from this strategic path.

Let $X \sqsubseteq \Omega$ be a system, $\Omega^H = \{G,S,V,sC\} \sqsubseteq (\Omega,\mathcal{Z}\circ,{}_v\mathcal{H},\{C\}) \sqcap \mathcal{E}^C$ be the space of some high-speed development strategy B where $\mathcal{E}^C$ denotes the space of a specific cultural system (or for instance, the space of a science-based democratic capitalism). Then X achieves a **high-speed development T Central** if and only if $\phi^H X \sqsubseteq \mathcal{P}^H \sqcap T^B$, the strategic impactor $\phi^H \vDash \Omega^H \sqcap(\mathcal{Z}\circ,{}_v\mathcal{H}) \in \mathcal{Z}\circ,{}_v\mathcal{H}$, $\{\phi^H X =< T^B\} \sqsubseteq Ш^{\Delta}$, where $\mathcal{P}^H$ is the path of high-speed development strategy.

Below we address the issues of the high-speed developmental Tcentral. Let $X \sqsubseteq (\Omega,\mathcal{Z}\circ,{}_v\mathcal{H},\{C\}) \sqcap \mathcal{E}^c$ be a system. Then X achieves a specific cultural **high-speed development T Central** if and only if: (i) $\phi^H X \sqsubseteq \mathcal{P}^H \sqcap T^B$, and for the strategic impactor $\phi^H \vDash \{\Omega^H \sqcap(\mathcal{Z}\circ,{}_v\mathcal{H}) \in (\mathcal{Z}\circ,{}_v\mathcal{H})$, $\{\phi^H X =< T^{B\Delta}\} \sqsubseteq Ш^{\Delta}$; and (ii) for $\mathcal{P}^H$ being the development path of a high-speed growth strategy, $\mathcal{P}^H \sqsubseteq \Omega^H \sqcap \Omega^{TchH} \sqcap \Omega^{Org\text{-}H}$, where Ω^H is the space of high-speed development path, Ω^{TchH} is the space of high-speed developmental technology, and $\Omega^{Org\text{-}H}$ is the space of high-speed developmental organization. By the principle of CE centrality (see Bcm. 4.2-2), we have the **principle of high-speed development Tcentral** (see Section 3.2):

(8.2-11) $$\psi\{Y_j>Y_k,\Delta_i\} \barwedge \tau \Leftrightarrow \phi^H X \sqsubseteq \mathcal{P}^H \sqcap T^B.$$

In the case of Taiwan in the post-war period and the case of South Korea in the 1990s, the cultural complex may have become: $<\mathbb{C}_X> \Leftrightarrow (\omega,\rho) = \{YW,S|\,K^{-}<YX\}\wedge\{T,C|\,K^{-} < YX\}$, with K^{-} being the dialectic rationality of "The modern Kuantzu."

Let us look at what Taiwan government did in the period of 1950s to 1970s. The government did not spare any effort in supporting the development of the public enterprises which was under the monopoly of the ruling party (Kumintang KMT), and yet it failed eventually. This may be due to the alien nature of the ruling nationalist Chinese party KMT. In addition, it may also be caused by the nature of a political party which may not be the best candidate in conducting business and in developing an economy. In this period, Taiwan pursued a policy of high interest with low inflation rate, and succeeded in developing light industry based on the primacy of the private sector.

For another example, in the case of South Korea in the period of 1972-1980s (1972 was the year President Park's authoritarian regime ended), let the cultural complex be represented as: $<\mathbb{C}_X> \Leftrightarrow (\omega,\rho) = \{YW,S|F^{-}<YX\}\wedge\{T,C|\,F^{-}<YX\}$, where F^{-} depicts the dialectic rationality of "modern Legalism," thus, South Korea could also pursue this strategy of rapid development.

Scheme of high-speed developing amid uncertainty. Let Y_t, S_t, $X_t \sqsubseteq (\Omega,\mathbb{Z}\circ,\mathrm{v}\mathbb{H},\{\mathbb{C}\})$, $Z \sqsubseteq \Omega^H$ (Z as the decision-making and strategic set of Y_t and Ω^H as a space of high-speed development), $X_t \sqsubseteq T^{sysC} \sqcup T^L$. Then $Y_t \sqsubseteq \Phi^H$ (Φ^H is a high-speed developing path) is a system of high-speed development if and only if Bcms. (8.2-7) and (8.2-8) (Bcms. (I.3-10) and (I.3-11), respectively) are true.

Note that the distribution factor in this high-speed strategic path is created by uncertain forces, while the distribution factor in the rapidly-developing strategic path is created by both "strategic-cultural" and uncertain forces.

From the decomposition becomings of the self-mutual entity-in-tranquility in Bcms. (A.3.4-1d) and (A.3.4-7), we know that $\mu\{\text{mutual--self}\}^*$ and $\mu\{\text{pub—priv}\}^*$ are positive (for μ being a mathematical measure). Then, for $X_t \sqsubseteq \Omega^F \sqcap \Omega^{YW}$, the strategy of Y_t must employ the public sector as the virtual operating forces, with appropriate level of strategic interventions. At the same time, even if the structure of the high-low differences of X_t can be properly manipulated, ($\mathcal{C}\hbar^H$ and $\mathcal{C}\hbar^L$ are the high-and-high-level and low-and-low-level differences of Y_t, respectively), one needs to pay attention to the fact that a leap/rapid growth path can not be prolonged indefinitely.

By the decomposition becoming of capital-sciences and technology-culture in capitalism: $T\{\{Y\,|\,\mathbb{C}_{sp} =< T^{B\text{-}C}\} \sqsubseteq Ш^{\Delta}\} = L^* \oplus K^* \oplus \{tech|K,\mathbb{C}\}^* \oplus co\mathbb{C}^* \oplus \{tech\text{--}(L,K),\mathbb{C}\}^*$ (see Bcm. (A.3-5-2), with $T^{B\text{-}C}$ referring to a state of balance-centrality and $\mathbb{C}_{sp}$ referring to a specific culture) at different phases of the capital-sciences & technology-cultural stage, the sources of the systemic dynamics of the leap/rapid growth are different. At the agricultural stage (i.e., the initial phase of the stage of capitalism), should one (i.e., the planner) ever try to drive the economy with capital (i.e., heavy and chemical industries) as the major source of systemic dynamics, one would still face insurmountable obstacles.

At this agricultural stage, unless the economy is under extremely favorable conditions, if one would rely on light industry as the major engine of growth, then the obstacles for economic development is still formidable. But if the economy has a capital-organizational advantage, then depending on stages of growth, $co\mathbb{C}^*$ and $\{tech\text{--}(L,K),\mathbb{C}\}^*$ are those terms that would probably be conducive to the development of capital and technology. These are actually the major forces that enable the East Asian economies to achieve the high-saving-rate/high-investment-rate /high-capital-formation chain (at the capital stage) and to develop successfully the product-imitation/product improvement chain (at the technological stage) in post-war period of the twentieth century. Here in the case of East Asia, for the second half of the twentieth century, these two stages overlap; and the cultural stage has not arrived yet.

Stable-and-moderately/slowly developing strategy (**silver^{+}**, **silver** and **silver^{-} strategies**). This is the scheme of moderate-and-stable or stable-and-low-level growth. Note that this may be considered as the strategic path pursued by England since the eighteenth century, and the strategic path pursued by Germany in the nineteen century may be a modified one (i.e., silver^{+} strategy, on with significant government-sponsored growth programs).

Below is a 5-polar model, one of moderate or low-level growth. Let X = (S,W,C,E,N|middle-pole) $\sqsubseteq (\Omega, \mathcal{Z}\circ, {}_{v}\mathcal{H}, \{\mathbb{C}\})$, be a 5-pole system, where "middle- pole" is the center of the system. Here the "middle-pole" is the central system carrying an energy flowing upward along a dynamical path of stable-and-middle- or stable-and-low-level growth; while S, W, E and N are noncentral units systems. This X is called the middle/low level developmental 5-polar system.

Further, let S_t, $X_t \sqsubseteq (\Omega, \mathcal{Z}\circ, {}_{v}\mathcal{H}, \{\mathbb{C}\})$, $Z \sqsubseteq \Omega^{S}$ (Z being the decision-making and strategic complex of S_t, Ω^{S} the space of the strategy of stable moderate/slow growth), and $X_t \sqsubseteq T^{sysC} \sqcup T^{L}$ be a distribution system (in uncertainty). Then $Y_t \sqsubseteq \mathcal{P}^{S}$ ($\mathcal{P}^{S}$ being the path of stable growth) is a system of stable and moderate/slow growth if and only if Bcm. (8.2-12) is true:

(8.2-12) $Y_t = S_t \oplus X_t$,

where $\mathcal{P}^{NS}\{X_t\} = \circ$ which is an "empty system" (see Appendix I or Bcm. (8.2-6)). From the decomposition becoming of the self-mutual entity Bcm. (A.3-4-1) in Appendix A (Subsection §A.3.4), it is known that μ {self--mutual}$^{\#}$ is negative. Now if $X_t \sqsubseteq \Omega^{C} \sqcap \Omega^{ST}$, then by the strategy of Y_t, it may be better to institute a policy of anti-monopoly with a background of a small but efficient government.

Below we proceed to discuss the stable moderate/slow developmental CE Tcentral. Let X $\sqsubseteq (\Omega, \mathcal{Z}\circ, {}_{v}\mathcal{H}, \{\mathbb{C}\}) \sqcap \mathcal{E}^{C}$ be a system. Then X achieves a **stable growth Tcentral under a specific culture** if and only if (i) $\phi^{L}X \sqsubseteq \mathcal{P}^{S} \sqcap T^{B}$, the strategic impactor $\phi^{S} \vDash \Omega^{S} \sqcap (\mathcal{Z}\circ, {}_{v}\mathcal{H})$, $\{\phi^{L}X =< T^{B\Delta}\} \sqsubseteq Ш^{\Delta}$; and (ii) for $\mathcal{P}^{S}$ being the growth path of a stable strategy, $\mathcal{P}^{S} \Subset \Omega^{S} \sqcap \Omega^{TchS} \sqcap \Omega^{OrgS}$, where Ω^{S} is the space of the growth path of a stable strategy, Ω^{TchS} is the space of the stable growth technology, Ω^{OrgS} is the space of moderately developmental organization. Then by the principle of CE centrality (see Bcm. 4.2-2), we have the **principle of stable growth Tcentral**:

(8.2-13)
$$\psi\{Y_j > Y_k, \Delta_i\} \,\bar{\bar{\barwedge}}\, \tau$$
$$\Leftrightarrow \phi^{S}X \sqsubseteq \mathcal{P}^{S} \sqcap T^{B}.$$

In terms of a distribution system, let Y_t, $X_t \sqsubseteq (\Omega, \mathcal{Z}\circ, {}_{v}\mathcal{H}, \{\mathbb{C}\})$, $Z \sqsubseteq \Omega^{S}$ (Z being the strategic set of Y_t, Ω^{S} the space of stable growth strategy), $X_t \sqsubseteq T^{sysC} \sqcup T^{L}$ a distribution system (in uncertainty). Then $Y_t \sqsubseteq \mathcal{P}^{S}$ ($\mathcal{P}^{S}$ being a strategic path of stable growth) is an uncertain stable growth system if and only if Bcms. (8.2-12), (8.2-14) and (8.2-15) are true:

(8.2-14) $\mathcal{C}h^{\mathrm{H}}\{Y_{t+1}\} = \mathcal{S}\{\mathcal{P}^{\mathrm{NS}}(Y_t)\} \oplus \mathcal{C}h^{\mathrm{H}}\{Y_t\} \otimes \mathcal{S}\{X_t\}$,

(8.2-15) $\mathcal{C}h^{\mathrm{L}}\{Y_{t+1}\} = \mathcal{S}\{\mathcal{P}^{\mathrm{NS}}(Y_t)\} \oplus \mathcal{C}h^{\mathrm{L}}\{Y_t\} \otimes \mathcal{S}\{X_t\}$,

where $\otimes \vDash \mathbb{H}$ is an interactor.

In terms of economic strategy, these above becomings involve those of pursuing a moderate or low-level growth amid a state of sustaining stability. This strategy of stable growth pursues a path between the extremes of high-speed growth and variational growth, and seeks a CE balance. Because this strategic path pursues stability, it naturally invokes much less risk. It appears that this is the strategy pursued by the Confucian bureaucrats in the classical world and by the governments of Netherlands, the United Kingdom and France in the modern time. One famous example is the theory of industrialization developed by Alexander Hamilton, a founding father of the United Stated of America[7]. The objective of his theory is to adopt Western European mercantilism to promote rapid industrialization. He contends that the government should institute a developmental agency, and employ heavy tariffs and financial subsidies to help promote industry, with the final goal of achieving self sufficiency of the country. Hamilton is a statist, not an individualist. He considers industrialization as the best conduit of developing the power of a country.

This is closely connected to the prevailing wisdom of national development since the day of industrialization first occurred in England in the 18th century. According to the traditional wisdom, with the market system, the role of government is limited. The tools of government intervention are few, and only indirect methods like taxation and imposition of tariffs are available. In an economy of this kind, the time preference of consumers in general is high, and consumption demand is high as well. In this market system, the engine of growth is in the hands of the private sector. Further, in this system, the long term strategy is nothing but the simple sum of short-term policies.

This is, by the structural context of a cultural economy of the West, the most natural and spontaneous course of economic development. Following the natural sequence of economic development, at first, agriculture is developed; then light industry is developed on the basis of the matured agriculture (under the existing conditions of agricultural technology). Once the light industry matures, heavy industry will be developed with the help of the market created and sustained by agriculture and the light industry. From the perspective of today's technology, the latest stage of economic development is then the high-technology or super-technology industry. This is the process of economic development of a pure market-pure private capitalist economy, purely based upon the private sector to provide the engine of growth. The surplus of the former stage provides the sources for the development of the subsequent stage of the economy. As such, this is a course of stable development given favorable socio-political and physical environments, with the forward and backward technological linkages forming, developing and enlarging in the economy so that eventually these linkages are able to be maximized. Since private entrepreneurs are major players of the market economy, price mechanism is indispensable.

In this economy, the intensity of economic activities are determined by the private capitalists, and the development of technology from its very onset is a self-generating process, as a result of the combinations of profit motivation and the technical orientation of those involved in its development, not to be determined or even guided by the government. As is indicated by Karl Marx, Max Weber, and others in separate occasions, the master of this economy is the capitalist or the private entrepreneurs as a whole, and the systemic dynamics appears to be driven by the profit motivation. But definitely, the observation provided in the above deals only with the demand-side of a cultural economy.

In a sense, it is quite paradoxical that, from the perspective of pure economics, it appears that the majority of key figures enjoying the benefits of technological development are the capitalists (or the so-called entrepreneurs); and yet the major characters of the technological development of any cultural economy must actually be played by the researchers and technical developers, not the capitalists (and neither the entrepreneurs). What benefits the capitalist may not benefit these researchers and technical developers. Without adjusting to other factors that may significantly alter the supply-side conditions, it may be fair to say that, compared with a socialist or Faziranist cultural economy, the strengths of the capitalist cultural economy lie in the role played by the private business which ferments, fosters and ultimately advances the superior productivities of the underlying economy. In terms of demand-supply dichotomy, any strategic concern of this economy on the demand side must be the natural development of the theories of Keynesian fiscal policy and post-Second World War monetary policy.

Variational strategy (V). This could be a scheme of low-level intervention by the government. Now the presentation of the 5-polar scheme of variational strategy is in order.

Let $X = (S,W,C,E,N|\text{variational pole}) \sqsubseteq (\Omega,\mathbb{Z}\circ,_{v}\mathbb{H},\{\mathbb{C}\})$ be a 5-polar system. Here the energy flowing toward this variational pole represents a stream of slowly developing momentum of cultural economic activities. While the "variational pole" is the center of this system carries with it a force of low-level intervention of the cultural economy by the government, S, W, E and N are non-central units systems, and C is the **pseudo-center** of this system. That is, C is merely the agent of the variational pole in acting seemingly as the center of the system. This X is called the variational developmental 5-polar system.

Below we proceed to discuss the variational developmental Tcentral. Let $X \sqsubseteq (\Omega,\mathbb{Z}\circ,_{v}\mathbb{H},\{\mathbb{C}\})\sqcap\mathcal{E}^{C}$ be a system, $\mathcal{E}^{C}$ being a specific cultural system. Then X is said to achieve a **variational Tcentral under a specific culture** if and only if the following two conditions hold: (i) $\phi^{V}X \sqsubseteq \mathcal{P}^{V} \sqcap T^{B}$, and for the strategic impactor $\phi^{V} \models (\Omega^{V}\sqcap(\mathbb{Z}\circ,_{v}\mathbb{H})) \Subset (\mathbb{Z}\circ,_{v}\mathbb{H})$, $\{\phi^{V}X =< T^{B\Delta}\} \sqsubseteq Ш^{\Delta}$. (ii) For $\mathcal{P}^{V}$ being a growth path of variational strategy, $\mathcal{P}^{V} \Subset \Omega^{V}\sqcap\Omega^{TchV}\sqcap\Omega^{Org\text{-}V}$, where Ω^{V} is the space of the growth path of variational strategy, Ω^{TchV} is the space of the variational development of technology, and $\Omega^{Org\text{-}V}$ is the space of variational development of organization. Then by the principle of CE Tcentral, we have the **principle of variational growth Tcentral** (see Section 3.2):

$$(8.2\text{-}16) \qquad \psi\{Y_{j}>Y_{k},\Delta_{i}\} \mathrel{\overline{\overline{\barwedge}}} \tau \\ \Leftrightarrow \phi^{V}X \sqsubseteq \mathcal{P}^{V}\sqcap T^{B}.$$

Historically, this is the growth path of the Ideal Confucianism, Huang-Laoist Taoism and pure capitalism. The related economic policies of this strategy naturally follow the doctrine of laissez faire. The theory of agricultural development by Thomas Jefferson, one of the founding fathers of the United States, is that an ideal economy is one with self sufficiency under the management of farm owners.[8] Jefferson was interested only in small cities and small-scaled industries. To minimize the role of foreign trade, he suggested the importing of only those products that could not be produced domestically. Politically, he favored a small government, and was strongly against a centralized political system. Apparently his goal is to establish a country of self-sufficient farms with individual freedom to be cherished dearly.

Continuity strategy (Continuity strategy sC). Below we introduce a 5-polar strategic system – a scheme of strategic continuity.

Let X = (S,W,C,E,N|continuity pole) $\sqsubseteq$ (Ω,$\mathcal{Z}$o,$_v\mathcal{H}$,{$\mathbb{C}$}) be a 5-polar system. Here the submerged stream of the energy of the non-central unit systems (or elements) flows continuously toward this "pole of continuity." While the "pole of continuity" is the center of this system carrying with it characteristics of "continuity strategy," S, W, E and N are noncentral unit systems (or elements). This X is called the 5-pole system of continuity strategy.

Below, let X $\sqsubseteq$ (Ω,$\mathcal{Z}$o,$_v\mathcal{H}$,{$\mathbb{C}$})$\sqcap\mathcal{E}^C$ be a system. Then X is said to achieve a **CE Tcentral of continuity development** under a specific culture if and only if the following conditions hold: (i) $\phi^{sC}X \sqsubseteq \mathcal{P}^{sC} \sqcap T^B$, and for the strategic impactor $\phi^{sC} \vDash (\Omega^{sC}\sqcap(\mathcal{Z}o,_v\mathcal{H})) \Subset \mathcal{Z}o,_v\mathcal{H}$, $\{\phi^{sC}X =< T^{B\Delta}\} \sqsubseteq Ш^{\Delta}$. (ii) For $\mathcal{P}^{sC}$ being a growth path of continuity strategy, $\mathcal{P}^{sC} \Subset \Omega^{sC}\sqcap\Omega^{TchsC}\sqcap\Omega^{Org\text{-}sC}$, where Ω^{sC} denotes a space of continuity strategy, Ω^{TchsC} refers to a space of system-continuously technological development, $\Omega^{Org\text{-}sC}$ stands for a space of system-continuity organization. Then by the principle of CE centrality, we have (see Section 3.2):

$$(8.2\text{-}17) \qquad \psi\{Y_j > Y_k, \Delta_i\} \,\overline{\barwedge}\, \tau \Leftrightarrow \phi^{sC}X \sqsubseteq \mathcal{P}^{sC} \sqcap T^B.$$

Note that if we let Ω^{sC} be the space of system-continuity strategies, then the strategic space of Taoism may be written as: Ω^{sC} = {sC}.

8.3 Models of Strategic Competition between Nations

For the roles of the IRI chain, MPFX cycle and SIFP chain complex, see Remark 8-2-1-1 .

Thema 8.3-1. Let a nation A $\sqsubseteq$ (Ω,$\mathcal{Z}$o,$_v\mathcal{H}$,{$\mathbb{C}$})$\sqcap\mathcal{E}^{SI}$, for $\mathcal{E}^{SI}$ being a being cultural system of sciences and individualism and the other nation be B $\sqsubseteq$(Ω,$\mathcal{Z}$o,$_v\mathcal{H}$,{$\mathbb{C}$}) $\sqcap\mathcal{E}^{YW}\sqcap\mathcal{E}^{SI}$, for $\mathcal{E}^{YW}$ being a system of yu-wu culture. At the same time, let A be a capitalist economy and B the modern Faziranist economy of triple systems (i.e., a system with dual public-private sectors added onto the basis of the traditional Faziranism). Furthermore, when $t = t_0$, let the economy of B lag behind that of A. If the strategic scheme of competition between these two nations are:

Figure 8.3-1
TK strategic complex

$$\begin{array}{ccc} A: (G,\pi) & \rightarrow & (G^+,\pi^+) \\ | & & | \\ B: (D,\lambda,\zeta) & \rightarrow & (G,\pi_1,\pi_2) \end{array}$$

Then B fails to catch up to A in a limited period of time. Note that $t_2 - t_1$ is the period of time of strategic transition.

Reasoning. By definition, D represents a leap strategy, G^+ a rapidly-developing strategy and G a high-speed development strategy. Let $(\zeta,\xi) \vDash \mathcal{Z}o,_v\mathcal{H}$ be a pair of leap-strategic impactors on the public-private sector, $\pi^{+} \models \mathcal{Z}_{O,v}\mathbb{H}$ an impactor of rapidly-developing strategy, $\pi_1, \pi_2 \models \mathcal{Z}_{O,v}\mathbb{H}$ impactors of high-speed development strategy. Here (λ,ζ), π^{+}, π_1 and π_2 are all matrix-augmenting impactors (i.e., element, row, column, and row-and-column augmenting impactors, also see Subsection §A.2-3-6). Suppose contrary to what we would like to prove is true: at time $t = t_1$, the economy of country B still lags behind that of country A, and B catches up to A at time $t = t_2 > t_1$. That is, at time $t = t_2$, through strategic manipulation by the planners, the economy of B catches up to that of AB: $\mathcal{T}B \uparrow \mathcal{T}^{*}A$ ($\mathcal{T}$, $\mathcal{T}^{*}$ are strategic impactors). Let the civilian sector (i.e., private sector) of country A at time $t = t_0$ be $[a_0]$, at time $t = t_1$ be $\varphi[a_0]$, and at time $t = t_2$ be $\pi\{\varphi[a_0]\}$ ($\mathcal{T}^{*} \equiv \pi\{\varphi[.]\}$ being a composite strategic impactor).

Let the private sector (i.e., part of the civilian sector) of country B at time $t = t_0$ be $[b_0]$, at time $t = t_1$ be $\zeta[b_0]$, and at time $t = t_2$ be $\pi_2\{\zeta[b_0]\}$ ($\mathcal{T}' \equiv \pi_2\{\zeta[.]\}$ being a composite strategic impactor). Let the public sector of country B at time $t = t_0$ be $[d_0]$, at time $t = t_1$ be $\lambda[d_0]$, and at time $t = t_2$ be $\pi_1\{\lambda[d_0]\}$ ($\mathcal{T}'' \equiv \pi_1\{\lambda\}$ being a composite strategic impactor, and the strategy of B is $\mathcal{T}$ $(\mathcal{T}',\mathcal{T}'')$).

To achieve a state of CE strategic centrality by the principle of CE centrality (i.e., Bcm (3.2-2-10)), let the economy of a country be $X \sqsubseteq (\Omega,\mathcal{Z}_{O,v}\mathbb{H},\{\mathbb{C}\})$, $X = \{X_1,X_2,\ldots,X_n,C\}$, $[Y_k,Y_j] \Leftarrow <\mathbb{C}_X>$. Here X_i, $i = 1, 2, \ldots, n$, $i \neq k, j$, are noncentral elements (or unit systems, depending on the context) and C is the center. Suppose at time $t = t_1$, the private sector develops as a result of the nation's efforts in importing technology and capital stocks from outside under the government policy of developing first the agriculture and then the light industry. Note that this is also a result of the interactions of the private and pubic sectors. That is, ζ is the row-and-column augmenting impactor on $[b_0]$. Let $\lambda[d_0] = [d_{11}\ d_{12} \ldots d_{1n}]$ be the results of importing technology and capital stocks from outside under the new government policy of developing heavy-and-chemical industries and the military industry. That is, λ is the element-augmenting impactor on $[d_0]$. Here the selection of these two impactors is determined by the factors and stages of sociopolitical development, the strategies of national economic development and the underlying culture. Note that the private sector's strategic impactor is determined by the private entrepreneurs under the demand and supply conditions of the cultural economy, while the public sector's strategic impactor is mainly determined by strategic concerns of the planners under the general and overall conditions of the economy.

$$(8.3\text{-}1)\quad \zeta\,[b_0] = \begin{vmatrix} c_{11} & c_{12} \ldots\ldots c_{1m} \\ b_{11} & b_{12} \ldots\ldots b_{1k} \end{vmatrix}$$

Thus, at time $t = t_1$, the economy of B becomes:

$$(8.3\text{-}2)\quad \begin{vmatrix} d_{11} & d_{12} \ldots\ldots\ldots d_{1n} \\ c_{11} & c_{12} \ldots\ldots c_{1m} \\ b_{11} & b_{12} \ldots b_{1k} \end{vmatrix}$$

In the above, this is the results of the dual operations of the principle of CE centrality (see Bcm. (4.2-2)) and the principle of strategic centrality (see Bcm. (4.2-5)) on a Faziranist economy, implementing the principle: $Y_j > Y_k$, for Y_j being the public sector and Y_k the private sector. At this juncture, the public institutions, as a part of the public sector in the broad sense, engage in basic and applied researches and develop the military technologies. The technologies absorbed and further refined by the public institutions are then supplied to the public sector (the up-stream production) and to the private sector (the down-stream production) in the part of civilian economy. In this first stage development, the strategy is designed to tilt toward the development of heavy and chemical industries; consequently the public sector develops faster, while the private sector develops rapidly with the help of the government.

Simultaneously at time $t = t_1$, the economy of A becomes Bcm. (8.3-3), where $| a_{11}\ a_{12} \ldots\ldots a_{1r} |$ is the high-tech industrial sector, $| a_{21}\ a_{22} \ldots\ldots a_{2p} |$ the heavy-and-chemical industrial sector, $| a_{m1}\ a_{m2} \ldots\ldots a_{mq} |$ the light-industrial sector, and $| a_{n1}\ a_{n2} \ldots\ldots a_{np} |$ the agricultural sector. That is, at time $t = t_1$, the economy of A is ahead of that of B; and when A is engaging in the development of high-tech industry, B still has no high-tech industry. Here π_1 and π_2 are the element-augmenting impactor of $[b_0]$, to be determined by the strategic planning. By the time $t = t_2$, the economy of B still lags behind that of A. This is because before the time $t = t_2$, by implementing the policy following the strategic directive of $Y_j > Y_k$, the speed of development is not fast enough (from t_1 to t_2), although the agricultural, light industrial and heavy-and-chemical industrial sectors of B may catch up to the corresponding sectors of A, respectively. And yet, at this time, the development of high-tech industry of B is still of no avail. But then, after this time, the further development of high-tech industry in A proceeds smoothly and rapidly. Hence, the hypothesis of the catching up to A by B leads to a contradiction.

$$(8.3\text{-}3) \qquad \left| \begin{array}{l} a_{11}\ a_{12} \ldots\ldots a_{1r} \\ a_{21}\ a_{22} \ldots\ldots a_{2p} \\ a_{m1}\ a_{m2} \ldots\ldots a_{mq} \\ a_{n1}\ a_{n2} \ldots\ldots a_{np} \end{array} \right|$$

Thema 8.3-2. Let the country A $\sqsubseteq (\Omega,\mathcal{Z}^{\circ},v\mathcal{H},\{C\})\sqcap\mathcal{E}^{SI}$, where $\mathcal{E}^{SI}$ is the cultural system of science-based individualism. In addition, let the country B $\sqsubseteq (\Omega,\mathcal{Z}^{\circ},v\mathcal{H},\{C\})\sqcap\mathcal{E}^{YW}\sqcap\mathcal{E}^{SI}$, where $\mathcal{E}^{YW}$ is the cultural system of yu-wu–culture-based groupism-individualism. Furthermore, let A be an economy of capitalism, B a dual public-private modern economy of Faziranism. Suppose at time $t = t_0$, the economy of B lags to that of A. If the competitive strategic set of these two countries are:

Figure 8.3-2
A-B strategic complex

$$\begin{array}{ccc} A:(V,v) & \rightarrow & (V^{+},v^{+}) \\ | & & | \\ B:(D;\lambda,\zeta) & \rightarrow & (G^{+};\pi^{1},\pi^{2}), \end{array}$$

then B may catch up to A in a limited time (assuming the period of time of the strategic transformation for B is t_1- t_2- t_3).

Reasoning. By definition, D is a leap strategy, G^{+} a strategy of rapid development, V^{+} a variation+ strategy, V a variational strategy. Let $(\lambda,\zeta) \models \mathcal{Z}^{\circ},v\mathcal{H}$ be a pair of leap impactors, $(\pi^{1},\pi^{2}) \models \mathcal{Z}^{\circ},v\mathcal{H}$ a rapidly developing strategic impactor, $\lambda \models \mathcal{Z}^{\circ},v\mathcal{H}$ a high-speed strategic impactor, $v \models \mathcal{Z}^{\circ},v\mathcal{H}$, a variational strategic impactor, $v^{+} \models \mathcal{Z}^{\circ},v\mathcal{H}$ a variation^{+} strategic impactor. Here (λ,ζ), π^{1}, π^{2}, v and v^{+} are all matrix-augmenting impactors. Suppose the result is contrary to what we desire to have; at time $t = t_1$, the economy of B lags behind that of A, and yet in a limited time $t = t_2 > t_1$, B catches up to A: that is, at time $t = t_2$, $\mathcal{T}B \uparrow \mathcal{T}^{*}A$ ($\mathcal{T}$, $\mathcal{T}^{*}$ being strategic impactors).

Suppose the civilian sector of A is $[a_0]$ at time t_0, $v[a_0]$ at time t_1, and $v^+\{v[a_0]\}$ at time t_2 ($\mathcal{T}^* \equiv v^+\{v[.]\}$ is a composite strategic impactor). Suppose the private sector of B is $[c_0]$ at time t_0, $\zeta[b_0]$ at time t_1, $\pi^2\{\zeta[b_0]\}$ at time t_2 ($\mathcal{T}^2 \equiv \pi^2\{\zeta[.]\}$ is a strategic impactor). Suppose the public sector of B is $[c_0]$ at time t_0, $\lambda[d_0]$ at time t_1, $\pi^1\{\lambda[d_0]\}$ at time t_2 ($\mathcal{T}^1 \equiv \pi^1\{\lambda[.]\}$, $\mathcal{T} = (\mathcal{T}^1, \mathcal{T}^2)$ is a pair of strategic impactors).

To achieve a state of strategic T central, let the economy of the nation be $X \sqsubseteq (\Omega, \mathbb{Z}\circ, v\, \mathbb{H}, \{\mathbb{C}\})$, $X = \{X_1, X_2, \ldots, X_n\}$, $[Y_k, Y_j] \Leftarrow \langle \mathbb{C}_X \rangle$. Below we shall apply the principle of strategic centrality ($\forall i$, $\forall X_i$, $\psi\{\mathcal{T}^*C \geq \mathcal{T}X_i, \Delta_i\} \barwedge \tau$) and the principle of Tcentral ($\psi\{Y_j > Y_k, \Delta_j\} \barwedge \tau$, $i = 1,2,\ldots,n$, $i \neq j$, k: $\psi\{[\mathbb{C}_{X1/Z}, \mathbb{C}_{X2/Z}, .., \mathbb{C}_{Xn/Z} | \sigma(C)] > [\mathbb{C}_{C/Z} | (\xi_1(X_1), \xi_2(X_2), \ldots, \xi n(X_n))], \Delta_i\} \barwedge [\mathbb{C}_X \Leftarrow E]$ (here, $\mathbb{C}$ representing specific cultures related to subsystems, also see Bcm. (A.5-2-12)), $\xi_j \vDash \mathbb{Z}\circ, v\mathbb{H}$, j = 1,2,…n. Let

$$(8.3\text{-}4)\quad \zeta\,[b_0] = \begin{vmatrix} c_{11} & c_{12} \ldots\ldots & c_{1m} \\ b_{11} & b_{12} \ldots & b_{1k} \end{vmatrix}$$

be the results of importing technology and capital stocks from outside and developing agriculture first and then light industry. Here ζ is the row-and-column-augmenting impactor of $[b_0]$. Let $\lambda[d_0] = [d_{11}\, d_{12} \ldots d_{1n}]$ the results of importing technology and capital stocks in an attempt to develop heavy-and-chemical industries. Note that here λ is the element-augmenting impactor of $[d_0]$. Thus at time t_1, the economy of B becomes:

$$(8.3\text{-}5)\qquad \begin{vmatrix} d_{11} & d_{12} \ldots\ldots & d_{1n} \\ c_{11} & c_{12} \ldots\ldots & c_{1m} \\ b_{11} & b_{12} \ldots & b_{1k} \end{vmatrix}$$

This result is obtained by applying the principle of CE Tcentral to a process of lopsided developments of heavy and chemical industries. So the public sector develops faster than the private industry. Here, λ is the element-augmenting impactor of $[d_0]$ in the public sector, and ζ is the element-augmenting impactor of $[b_0]$ in the private sector.

$$(8.3\text{-}6)\qquad \begin{vmatrix} a_{11} & & \\ a_{21} & a_{22} \ldots\ldots & a_{2r} \\ a_{m1} & a_{m2} \ldots\ldots & a_{mq} \\ a_{n1} & a_{n2} \ldots\ldots & a_{np} \end{vmatrix}$$

Simultaneously at time t_1, the economy of A becomes Bcm. (8.3-6), where $|a_{11}|$ is the emerging high-tech sector, $|a_{21}\ a_{22} \ldots\ldots a_{2r}|$ is the heavy-and-chemical industrial sector, $|a_{m1}\ a_{m2} \ldots\ldots a_{mq}|$ the light industrial sector, $|a_{n1}\ a_{n2} \ldots\ldots a_{np}|$ the agricultural sector, for m, n, p, q, r $\in \mathbb{N}$. Here, v is the element-augmenting impactor of $[a_0]$ at time $t < t_2$. That is, at this time, the economy of A is ahead of that of B: A is starting to develop high-tech industry, while B still has no heavy–and-chemical industries.

At time t_2, B develops high-tech industry rapidly by essentially relying on the public-civilian and military sectors, with some help secured from the private sector.

Thus, at time t_2, the economy of B becomes Bcm. (8.3-7) as follows:

$$(8.3\text{-}7)\qquad \left|\begin{array}{l} e_{11} \\ \pi^2(d_{11}\ d_{12}\ldots\ldots\ldots\ d_{1n}) \\ \pi^*(c_{11}\ c_{12}\ldots\ldots\ c_{1m}) \\ \pi^1(b_{11}\ b_{12}\ldots\ b_{1k}) \end{array}\right|$$

where $|e_{11}|$ is the emerging high-tech industrial sector, $|\pi^2(d_{11}\ d_{12}\ldots\ldots d_{1n})|$ the heavy-and-chemical industrial sector, $|\pi^*(c_{11}\ c_{12}\ldots\ldots c_{1m})|$ the export-oriented light industrial sector, $|\pi^1(b_{11}\ b_{12}\ldots\ b_{1k})|$ is the export-oriented agricultural sector. This is the result of implementing the principle of T Central in developing lopsidedly both of the heavy-and-chemical industries and the military high-technological industries. Consequently the public sector develops faster, and the private sector also develops rapidly with the help rendered by the government. Here π^2 is the element-augmenting impactor of $[d_0]$, π^1 is the row-and-column-augmenting impactor of $[b_0]$. Note that this above is made possible by (1) the characteristics of B being a modern Faziranist cultural economy which embodies a (partial) efficiency of the being culture (or the scientific efficiency) and the efficiency of the yu-wu culture (i.e., both efficiency of organization and efficiency of the self-mastering and self-organizing yu-wu rationality) and (2) the characteristics of A being a free market cultural economy from which B can import technology and capital stocks freely and to which B can export its agricultural and light industrial products freely.

Simultaneously at time t_2, the economy of A evolves into:

$$(8.3\text{-}8)\qquad \left|\begin{array}{l} \eta(a_{11}) \\ \eta(a_{21}\ a_{22},\ldots\ldots\ a_{2r}) \\ \eta(a_{m1}\ a_{m2}\ldots\ldots\ a_{mt}) \\ \eta(a_{n1}\ an_2\ \ldots\ldots\ an_s) \end{array}\right|$$

At this time, i.e., at time t_2, the economy of B is still lags to that of A (as was essentially shown in Thema 8.3-1). Here , η is an element-augmenting impactor.

But at time t_3, country B is in its intermediate stage of economic development; and this intermediate stage is achieved by the implementation of the principle of CE centrality: $\psi\{Y_j>Y_k,\Delta_i\}$ $\bar{\bar{\barwedge}}$ τ. At this time, the heavy-and-chemical /military industries are developed lopsidedly. But a degree of balance between the public and the private sectors is pursued, and the production of the private sector is not ignored. Therefore, the speed of development is the same for either the public sector or the private sector. At this time, the private sector is also engaging in applied research, with some help rendered by the government. That is, at time t_3, because a higher speed development strategy has been adopted (from t_2 to t_3) and also because of the interactions between the public and private sectors under the somewhat balanced strategy G^+, all of the agricultural, light industrial and heavy-and-chemical industrial sectors of B has finally achieved the long-desired target of catching-up to those of A, respectively.

The reasoning in the above may be expressed by using *systematic notations*. Let systems A, B, C, a, b_0, d, $\circ_d \sqsubseteq (\Omega, \mathcal{Z}\circ, v\mathbb{H}, \{\mathfrak{C}\})$, $\mathcal{T} \vDash \mathbb{Z}\circ, v\mathbb{H}$ being an impactor and $C_b \vDash \mathbb{H}$ being an concealing and selective auxiliary-impactor.

At time t, the economy of A is: $a = b_0$, $b =$ "$b_0 \oplus \circ_d$" ($\oplus$ is a simply connecting impactor, and at time t, $\circ_d$ does not exists or is an "empty system"; it is actually a concealing impactor: $\circ_d = \circ$). Here by a factor is meant a universal element, a system, or even an impactor.

At time t+1, the economy of A evolves into: $\mathcal{T}\{a|C_b,z\} = \mathcal{T}\{b_0 \oplus \circ_d | C_b,z\} = \mathcal{T}\{b_0|C_b\} \oplus \mathcal{T}\{\circ_d|z\} \rightarrow \mathcal{T}'\{b_0\} \oplus \mathcal{T}\{d\}$, with $\oplus$ being an impactor corresponding to $\oplus$. Here $C_b \vDash \mathcal{Z}$ is a potential-row- augmenting impactor (i.e., it is an selective and auxiliary impactor or concealing and selective type of auxiliary impactor of b, concealing its power at time t), $z \vDash \mathcal{Z}$ is a concealing factor) (i.e., it may be called z' and is an selective and auxiliary impactor of d, only revealing its power with the help of strategic impactor z at time later than t and concealing its power at time t), and $\mathcal{T}'\{b_0\} = B \oplus C$, $\mathcal{T}\{d\} = D$. That is:

(8.3-9) At time t, A_t: $a = b_0$ (b_0 ="$b_0 \oplus \circ_d$") .

(8.3-10) At time t+1, A_{t+1}: $\mathcal{T}\{a|C_b,z\} = B \oplus C \oplus D$.

Here $\mathcal{T}$ is an element-and-row-augmenting impactor, $\mathcal{T}$ is an element-augmenting impactor, $\oplus$ is a "matrix-vertical developing impactor." Using the scheme presented in the above to express this $\mathcal{T}\{b_0\}$, we have:

(8.3-11) $\mathcal{T}\{b_0\} = \zeta[b_0] = |(c_{11}\ c_{12} \ldots\ldots c_{1m})\ \ (b_{11}\ b_{12} \ldots b_{1k})|^T$,

where $B = |b_{11}, b_{12}, \ldots\ldots, b_{1k}|$, $C = |c_{11}, c_{12}, \ldots\ldots, c_{1m}|$, with the superscript "T" expressing the sign of transpose for a "matrix."

At time t_1 = t+1, we have A_{t+1}: $\mathcal{T}\{a|C_b,z\} = B \oplus C \oplus D$:

(8.3-12) $$\begin{vmatrix} d_{11}, d_{12}, \ldots\ldots, d_{1n} \\ c_{11}\ c_{12} \ldots\ldots\ c_{1m} \\ b_{11}\ b_{12} \ldots b_{1k} \end{vmatrix},$$

where $D = |d_{11}, d_{12}, \ldots\ldots, d_{1n}|$.

Here in terms of a distribution system (in uncertainty), we can use Bcm. (8.2-12): $Y_t = S_t \oplus X_t$. Let $S_t = \mathcal{T}\{a|C_b,z\}$, then from the above two Bcms. (8.3-9) and (8.3-10), we have:

(8.3-13) At time t, A_t: $Y_t = a = b_0$.

(8.3-14) At time t+1, A_{t+1}: $Y_{t+1} = \mathcal{T}\{a|C_b,z\} \oplus X_t$,

where $X_t \sqsubseteq T^{sysC}$ (or T^{sysD}, T^L, K^{sysC} , K^{sysD}, K^L) is a distribution system (see Bcms (8.4-3-1), (8.4-3-2), and Section I.2 of Appendix I).

Example 8.3-1. The Soviet Union 1917-1991: D → collapse. The reason is that, in this period, the Soviet planners devoted most of the resources of their country to promote the steep production system $|_\Delta$- $\mathcal{P}$, resulting in the exhaustion of scarce resources in military activities. The collapse of the Soviet Union in 1991 appears to be natural because it violated the principle of CE Tcentral: (1) the scarce resources of the economy were sucked up in the development of the self-serving military technologies, without sufficient attention of the planners paying to the civilian sectoral technologies, (2) the economy tied up in the development of the heavy-and-chemical industries, without paying enough attention to the light industrial and agricultural sectors, and (3) the economy failed to rid itself of the old pattern of military and heavy-and-chemical industrial development after the economy matured in its heavy industrial stage roughly in the 1950s, and concurrently failed to transform itself into the high-tech stage thereafter. It is noticed even by casual observers from outside that the Soviet planners failed to develop a systematic and effective economic theory of strategic advancement in the entire Soviet period of central planning operations.

Example 8.3-2. The United States 1949-2003: A vibrant private economy with a huge burden in military and social-welfare expenditures. In the economy, the saving and investment rates are low relative to other OECD countries. The society rewards (pecuniarily, or psychologically if not pecuniarily) students studying in the fields of liberal arts, law, medicine, and the like, and yet fails to motivate a sufficient number of students to study engineering, mathematics and physical sciences.

At the elementary and secondary levels, the private institutions of education proceed well under the forces of capitalism (for the elite schools) or perhaps strongly influenced by a deep-rooted sense of religiosity (for those religious schools). But the public school system, which serves the children of the poor and the majority of the lower-middle class, with some limited exceptions, does not seem to advance over time. Due to the cultural background serving the system of democratic capitalism, the government of the United States simply does not have any effective strategy for long-term economic advancement other than relying upon military spending to spurt the economy.

Over time, one added dimension of the society of the United Sates is the significant divergence of ethnic centrality. It is predicted that in the year 2050, the ethnic minority groups together shall constitute over 50% of the total population.

Last but not least, one of the urgent tasks facing the United Sates in this new century is the development of inter-metropolitan rapid transit system (for instance, the system connecting Boston, New York and Washington D.C.), to tackle the ever increasing costs of energy. This system will further conserve the land of scarcity by building up a string of medium sized cities within this region of rapid inter-city transportation.

Example 8.3-3. China 1949-2003 : $D \rightarrow G^{+} \rightarrow G$?. In the period 1949-1976, China adopted a D strategy. After 1978, China adopted a G^{+} strategy. At the beginning of the 21st century, China may switch to a G strategy.

Figure 8.3-3
TK strategic matrix ("?" depicting the essential question of whether it is Tcentral)

Conflict	T Central? →	Conflict/coordination
Tcentral? ↓		↑ Tcentral?
Coordination/Conflict	← T Central?	Coordination

TK strategic scheme. Now we come to the TK strategic scheme. The direct or indirect strategic interactions between South Korea and Taiwan took place in the second half of the 20th century. Let us scrutinize Figure 8.3-3. If both players choose the upper-left corner of the strategic scheme, they shall fight against each other; and both suffer. If both players choose the lower–right corner: to coordinate with each other, then both benefit; and yet it is hard to coordinate. If both players choose the upper-right or the lower-left corner, then it is a situation both coordinate with and struggle against each other simultaneously. This may be beneficial to both players if it is possible to partition sectors of strategic operations, and then each concentrates on the development of those sectors one has strategic advantages and gives up those areas one does not have any strategic advantages. This last option is feasible as long as the levels of development of both countries are similar and each has some strategic niches of its own.

In a systematic notation, the TK strategic scheme may be expressed as follows (see Figure 8.3-3). Let "$\rightarrow$" be an impactor denoting the transformation through time; at time t_1, X, Y, R_1 and R_2 denote system X, system Y, the conflict operation between two players, and coordination operation between two players, respectively; and similarly for X', Y', R_1' and R_2' at time t_2 (see Bcm. (8.3-15)), with the following becoming (8.3-15):

(8.3-15) $(X,Y;R_1(cf),R_2(cr)) \rightarrow (X',Y';R_1(cf,cr)',R_2(cf,cr)')$,

with

$$(X,Y;R_1(cf),R_2(cr)) \equiv (X(t_1),Y(t_1);R_1(cf,t_1),R_2(cf,t_1))$$
$$(X,Y;R_1(cf),R_2(cr)) \equiv (X(t_2),Y(t_2);R_1(cf,cr;t_2),R_2(cf,cr;t_2)),$$

where $R_1(cf,cr;t_2)$ and $R_2(cf,cr;t_2)$ depict the simultaneous relationships of conflict and coordination at time 2 for X and Y, respectively.

TK strategic complex 1952-1975. The G^+ strategy of South Korea could not sustain for long. Eventually the trajectory of this G^+ strategy transforms into that of a G strategy. On the other hand, the initial silver+ strategy of Taiwan has to shift to a G strategy at a later time in order to compete successfully against South Korea (see Figure 8.3-4).

Figure 8.3-4
TK strategic paths 1952-1975

South Korea: $G^+ \rightarrow G$
| |
Taiwan: $S^+ \rightarrow G$

Taiwan: It is a land of a highly-coerced culture of tranquility in this period. In the 1940s, through Japanese colonial rule some light industries were established in Taiwan. Nationalist Chinese took over Taiwan in 1945, the year the Japanese lost its control of Taiwan. At that time, Taiwan was ruled as a land of quasi-colony by the nationalist Chinese who relied upon military forces and secrete polices to oppress the Taiwanese people. Economically, the Taiwan government strived to develop light and high-tech industries like shoe and garment industries, electronics and personal computer industry, while at the same time worked hard to eradicate the mind-power of the Taiwanese intellectuals and the riches of Taiwanese landlord class. In terms of its global strategy of economic construction, domestic saving was encouraged, the development of small- and medium-sized private firms were fostered to help promote export, and foreign and overseas Chinese capitals were skillfully lured to flow into and invest in

Taiwan. Started from 1972, the development of heavy industries like ship-building and steel-making industries was initiated.

South Korea: It is also a land of a highly-coerced culture of tranquility in this period. It gained independence in 1945, the year the Japanese lost its control of Korea. At the time of independence, with a few exceptions, South Korea had no basis of even light industry.

After Korean War, often South Korea was ruled by military strongmen. Note that these military strongmen were native Koreans, not coming from an alien land like in the case of Taiwan. In terms of economic strategy, at the time President Park took over political power through military coup d'état, the development of chemical and heavy industries like ship-building, automotive and heavy machinery industries were prioritized. The development of large-scaled firms were artificially accelerated by favorable government policies like high-inflationary rate, low-interest loans and the protection of domestic market in order to promote the economies of scale and to foster exports.

Roughly starting at the year of 1975, South Korea switched to a tone-down version of its industrial rush strategy, partially due to its deteriorated domestic conditions like the increased tension between the big businesses and the workers and unfavorable external factors like the abruptly increased petroleum prices starting in the year 1973.

Below we shall formally introduce two variants of the TK strategic scheme.

TK strategic scheme (I). Let a basic system $X = \{X_1,X_2,\ldots,X_n\} \sqsubseteq (\Omega,\mathbb{Z}^{\circ},{}_{\mathrm{v}}\mathbb{H},\{\mathbb{C}\})$, $[Y_k,Y_j] \Lleftarrow \langle\mathbb{C}_X\rangle$, where $Y_j \equiv [(X_1,\mathbb{C}_{X1/Z}),(X_2,\mathbb{C}_{X2/Z}),\ldots,(X_n,\mathbb{C}_{Xn/Z})|(C,\sigma(C)]$, $Y_k \equiv [(C,\mathbb{C}_{C/Z})|((X_1,\xi_1(X_1)), X_2,\xi_2(X_2)),\ldots,(X_n,\xi_n(X_n))]$, $\xi_i \models \mathbb{Z}^{\circ},{}_{\mathrm{v}}\mathbb{H}$, $i = 1,2,\ldots,n$ (see Appendix A, Bcm. (A.5-2-12)). Under the effective IISO/T scheme, that is, by the principle of effective systemic intra-inter operations and T continuity (i.e., $X = \chi \oplus \langle\mathbb{C}_X^{T}\rangle$ achieving a joint state of equicentrality and T continuity), there is a solution for the following scheme. Here, let this scheme be:

(8.3-16) (1) Under the operation of the unit system X_i, to achieve $\varphi\{X\} = X$ (i.e., systemic continuity, maybe with changes in minor characteristics), $i = 1, 2, \ldots, n$, $i \neq k, j$, where $\varphi \models \mathbb{Z}^{\circ},{}_{\mathrm{v}}\mathbb{H}$ is a system's operational impactor; and

(2) the operation of this system is conditioned upon the structure of the pure force of change $\Delta \Vdash \Omega$.

To find the solution, let

(8.3-17) $T = X \curlyvee \Delta$,

where $\curlyvee \models \mathbb{Z}^{\circ},{}_{\mathrm{v}}\mathbb{H}$ is the interactor connecting X and Δ. Let us denote this operation involves the dynamical changes of the whole system (i.e., mutual-entity per se) and any entity itself (i.e., self-entity per se). Thus, from the above, we have:

(8.3-18)
$$\begin{aligned}
&(\varphi\{T\})_{X1,\ldots,Xn} \\
&= (\varphi\{X \curlyvee \Delta\})_{X1,\ldots,Xn,Ix} \\
&= (\varphi\{X,\Delta\})_{X1,\ldots,Xn} \ltimes \varphi\{Ix,E\}
\end{aligned}$$

$$
\begin{aligned}
&= (\varphi\{X\}\otimes \psi\{X_\alpha > X_\alpha',\Delta\} \ltimes \varphi\{Ix_\alpha,E\})\\
&\qquad \otimes (\varphi\{X\}\otimes\psi\{X_\beta > X_\beta',\Delta\} \ltimes \varphi\{Ix_\beta,E\})\\
&\qquad \otimes (\varphi\{X\}\otimes\psi\{X_\Upsilon > X_\Upsilon',\Delta\} \ltimes \varphi\{Ix_\Upsilon,E\})\\
&\qquad \otimes (\varphi\{X\}\otimes\psi\{X_\delta > X_\delta',\Delta\} \ltimes \varphi\{Ix_\delta ,E\},
\end{aligned}
$$

where X_α is the factor in X_i in pairing with the factor of the other system either in conflict or in coordination: $(X_\alpha,X_\alpha') \equiv (X_\alpha,y)$, or X_α is pairing with y, where $y \equiv X_\alpha'$ is the factor of Y so that (X_i,Y) is the pair that is either in conflict or in coordination. In other words, $(X_\alpha,X_\alpha') \equiv (X_\alpha,y)$ is the pair either in conflict or in coordination, representing the forces of conflict or coordination in the pair (X_i,Y). Then X_β, X_Υ, X_δ (and X_β', X_Υ', X_δ', respectively) are defined in a similar fashion. That is, we derive the **TK strategic Tcentral**:

$$
\begin{aligned}
(8.3\text{-}19)\quad &\text{For each } X_i,\ \psi\{X_\alpha > X_\alpha',\Delta\}\ \bar{\barwedge}\tau,\\
&\qquad \text{or } \psi\{X_\beta < X_\beta',\Delta\}\ \bar{\barwedge}\tau,\\
&\qquad \text{or } \psi\{X_\Upsilon > X_\Upsilon',\Delta\}\ \bar{\barwedge}\ \tau,\\
&\qquad \text{or } \psi\{X_\delta > X_\delta',\Delta\}\ \bar{\barwedge}\ \tau,
\end{aligned}
$$

for $\tau \Vdash \mathfrak{J}$, $\mathfrak{J}$ is the complex of energy generated by Ultimate Creativity/ Destructivity $\mathbb{Tzu}^*$ (Bcm. (3.2-2-5)).

Here by this state of T central, we have the following conditions: (1) For a short-term strategy, one concentrates on those areas that this country enjoys strategic advantage X_α: $\psi\{X_\alpha > X_\alpha',\Delta\}\ \bar{\barwedge}\ \tau$, with X_α' being the weak areas of the rival of this country). (2) For a short-term strategy, one gives up those areas that this country do not enjoy strategic advantage X_β: $\psi\{X_\beta < X_\beta',\Delta\}\ \bar{\barwedge}\ \tau$, with $X_{\beta\alpha}'$ being the strong areas of the rival of this country. (3) In a long-term strategy, one develops step by step those new areas that this country will eventually enjoy strategic advantage X_Υ: $(\psi\{X_\Upsilon > X_\Upsilon',\Delta\}\ \bar{\barwedge}\tau$, X_Υ' being the long-term weak areas of the rival of this country. (4) In a long-term strategy, one gradually gives up those areas that this country does not enjoy long-term strategic advantage X_δ: $\psi\{X_\delta < X_\delta',\Delta\}\ \bar{\barwedge}\ \tau$, X_δ' being the long-term strong areas of the rival of this country.

The principle of CE T Central in the above may be derived alternatively as shown below.

TK strategic scheme (II). Let A and B be composite systems under a specific culture: $A, B \sqsubseteq (\Omega,\mathbb{Z}^{\circ},{}_{v}\mathbb{H},\{\mathbb{C}\})\sqcap\Omega^{S}$, $A = A(y\text{-},y\text{+},yh)$, $B = B(\text{-},\text{+},c)$. Here $\mathcal{T} = (y\text{-},y\text{+}|yh) \sqsubseteq (\Omega,\mathbb{Z}^{\circ},{}_{v}\mathbb{H},\{\mathbb{C}\})\sqcap\Omega^{\mathcal{T}}$ is a system under the culture of tranquil groupism, $\mathcal{K} = (\text{-},\text{+}|c) \sqsubseteq (\Omega,\mathbb{Z}^{\circ},{}_{v}\mathbb{H},\{\mathbb{C}\})\sqcap\Omega^{\mathcal{K}}$ is a system under the culture of conflict individualism or dialectic collectivism, $\mathcal{H} = (s,k|z) \sqsubseteq (\Omega,\mathbb{Z}^{\circ},{}_{v}\mathbb{H},\{\mathbb{C}\})\sqcap\Omega^{Z}$ is a system under the culture of CE balance, $\Omega^{S} = \Omega^{\mathcal{T}}\sqcap\Omega^{\mathcal{K}}\sqcap\Omega^{Z}$.

Let $\mathcal{T} \vDash \mathbb{Z}^{\circ},{}_{v}\mathbb{H} \sqsubseteq (\Omega,\mathbb{Z}^{\circ},{}_{v}\mathbb{H},\{\mathbb{C}\})\sqcap Z^{\mathcal{T}}\sqcap Z^{\mathcal{K}}\sqcap Z^{Z}$ be a strategic impactor capable of integrating different cultures, for $Z^{\mathcal{T}}$, $Z^{\mathcal{K}}$, and Z^{Z} being the decision-making and strategic complex of tranquil culture, conflict culture, and CE balance culture (or middle-central culture), respectively, $\mathfrak{C}^* = co(\mathbb{C}^{\mathcal{T}}\sqcap\mathbb{C}^{\mathcal{K}}\sqcap\mathbb{C}^{Z})$ be the core of the new composite culture under integration as indicated in the above. If the complex of CE will-rationality achieves a state of Tcentral of "**creative-and-destructive balance**" (CD balance), then we have:

$$
\begin{aligned}
(8.3\text{-}20)\quad &\mathcal{T}\{ A(y\text{-},y\text{+},yh),B(\text{-},\text{+},c)\}\\
&= \{(A,B)|\ [(y\text{-},y\text{+},yh),(\text{-},\text{+},c)\,|\,\mathfrak{C}^*\}\\
&= \{(A,B)|\ (\mathcal{T},\mathcal{K},\mathcal{H})^*\}\\
&= \{(A,B)|\ (\mathcal{T},\mathcal{K}|\,\mathcal{H}^*)\}.
\end{aligned}
$$

Let $X_{\alpha}, X_{\beta}, X_{\Upsilon}, X_{\delta} \Vdash A \sqsubseteq (\Omega, \mathbb{Z}^{\circ}, {}_{v}\mathbb{H}, \{\mathbb{C}\})$, $X_{\alpha}', X_{\beta}', X_{\Upsilon}', X_{\delta}' \Vdash B \sqsubseteq (\Omega, \mathbb{Z}^{\circ}, {}_{v}\mathbb{H}, \{\mathbb{C}\})$. If $\{(A,B)|(\mathcal{T},\mathcal{K}|\mathcal{H}^{*})\} \rightarrow \{(A,B)|(\mathcal{T},\mathcal{K}|\mathcal{H}^{*})^{TK}\}\}$: (1) $\psi\{X_{\alpha}>X_{\alpha}',\Delta\} \doublebarwedge \tau$, (2) $\psi\{X_{\beta}<X_{\beta}',\Delta\} \doublebarwedge \tau$, (3) $\psi\{X_{\Upsilon}>X_{\Upsilon}',\Delta\} \doublebarwedge \tau$, and (4) $\psi\{X_{\delta}>X_{\delta}',\Delta\} \doublebarwedge \tau$, then A and B achieve a state of TK strategic T central.

Generally speaking, this TK strategic T central has the following implications. That is, in the constant process of environmental changes, following the principles of systemic efficiency (while cultures remain constant) and cultural efficiency (when cultures change) and the economies of scale, scope, and networking, in order to achieve a state of T central, a country has to build up strategic alliance with friendly nations in an attempt to attack its enemies and the enemies' alliance. In addition, in the short-term perspective, one has to utilize the power of one's strength and to remedy one's shortcoming; and in the long-term perspective, one must take effective measures, may be through some step-by-step approaches, to establish one's power in favorable fields and eliminate the fields of one's weakness in order to prevent the rise of and even to reduce the power of one's enemies.

This principle of strategic Tcentral is different from the concept of Nash equilibrium: "Nash equilibrium is a state of equilibrium so that in this equilibrium, each person believes definitely that, given the strategy of the other participant, he or she chooses the best strategy in responding to the strategy of his or her rival" (http://www.peopledaily.com.cn 8/17/02).

In studying human behavior, Nash equilibrium is a logical concept employing mathematical approach to the case of conflict and self-interests-centered individualism. The participants of the Nash equilibrium are "mathematical men," behaving in accordance with the logic of mathematics. This is because Nash equilibrium is working in the world of mathematical system. Human being and human activities are not some complex numbers of mathematics. Human systems are not mathematical systems, although they may have shared with mathematics some of the same characteristics. Rather, a human being is a "human element" in the universe; and the background of human activities is the universe system (or the collection of all systems in the universe, called the complex of will-and rationality-to-creation system/social power-energy system/physical basis in the cultural systematics). Even if one would like to apply "mathematics" to study human events, this "human mathematics" must be one of "mutuality mathematics", not the conventional kind of the "mathematics of individuality and independence." Generally speaking, the units of human gaming are systems of organizations, but not any individual human being; and definitely they are not "non-cultural men." In the approach to games, the basic concern of Nash is isolated individuals, not group behaviors in a socio-cultural sense. This must be due to the influence of the culture of individualism. Moreover, equilibrium is a concept of conflict, neither one of tranquility in East Asian sense nor one of loving others in Christian sense. This concept is not suitable for the study of the global-and-humane society.

Remark 8.3-1. For one engaging in turning the studies of cultural and social events into fields of applied mathematics (or applied physics, engineering and biology), one may have to be aware of "the fallacy of mistaken anology" between the human and group activies and the movements of physical/biological units. Clasical Taoists mistakenly applied the model of yin yang and five elements (developed from the classical studies of human and social activities in East Asia) to the fields of bilogy and physical worlds. In contrast, not a few scholars of the modern West have been doing exactly the opposite thing, and thus those "physical science-based" scholarly efforts may be conceived as iso-systemic to Taoist endeavors).

8.4 Strategic Systems

Definition 8.4-1. The **system of Faziranism** is one with strong center, which arises from the cultural setting and institutional arrangements underlying the system of Faziranism.

This system may be represented by the following schemes:

(8.4-1) $\{\text{priv},\text{pub}|\text{govt}\} \sqsubseteq (\Omega,\mathcal{Z}^{o},{}_{v}\mathcal{H},\{\mathbb{C}\})$,

where priv, pub and govt refer to the private sector, the public sector (the economic operating arm of the government) and the government (or the planners), respectively, with govt = g($\mathcal{T}$|.), with $\mathcal{T}$ being the strategic impactor controlled by the government, and

(8.4-2) $\{\text{priv}^*,\text{pub}^*|\text{govt}^*\} \sqsubseteq (\Omega,\mathcal{Z}^{o},{}_{v}\mathcal{H},\{\mathbb{C}\})$,

where priv*, pub* and govt* refer to the strategies of the private sector, the public sector and the planners, respectively, with govt* = g*($\mathcal{T}$*,.|priv*.), with $\mathcal{T}$* being the strategic impactor controlled by the government.

Definition 8.4-2. The **system with a virtual center** is one with the core culture or a comprehensive and non-specific force as the center, for example, the pure capitalism in which the center is a non-personal market force. Since all players in this system compete against each other, at least at times there is no central coordinating force at work.

This system may be represented by the following schemes:

(8.4-2) $\{\text{priv}^1,\text{priv}^1|\text{E}\} \sqsubseteq (\Omega,\mathcal{Z}^{o},{}_{v}\mathcal{H},\{\mathbb{C}\})$,

where priv^1,priv^2,..., and priv^n refer to the strategies of the private firm 1, private firm 2, .., and private firm n, respectively.

Definition 8.4-3. The **system with no center** is one without any explicit center. And yet, due to the culture of mutuality, a force of indirect and impersonal coordination does exist in this system.

This system may be represented by the following schemes:

(8.4-3) $\{\text{priv}^1,\text{priv}^2,\ldots,\text{priv}^n|\text{co}\mathbb{C}\} \sqsubseteq (\Omega,\mathcal{Z}^{o},{}_{v}\mathcal{H},\{\mathbb{C}\})$,

where $\mathfrak{C}^* \equiv \text{co}\mathbb{C}$ refers to the cultural core underlying this system in acting as the virtual center.

Note that this is the ideal type of the market Faziranism.

Definition 8.4-4. Let o $\sqsubseteq (\Omega,\mathcal{Z}^{o},{}_{v}\mathcal{H},\{\mathbb{C}\})$ be a system of the activities of inner risk-taking which internalize risk from within, and O $\sqsubseteq (\Omega,\mathcal{Z}^{o},{}_{v}\mathcal{H},\{\mathbb{C}\})$ a system of the activities of outer risk-taking which handle risk dictated by the external environments. (1) Then the system complex o-O $\sqsubseteq (\Omega,\mathcal{Z}^{o},{}_{v}\mathcal{H},\{\mathbb{C}\})$ with the structures of o connected (and followed) by O is said to be an **o-O system**. (2) The system complex O-o $\sqsubseteq (\Omega,\mathcal{Z}^{o},{}_{v}\mathcal{H},\{\mathbb{C}\})$ with the structures of O connected (and followed) by o is said to be an **O-o system**.

This above definition means that O-o system is anti-systemic to O-o system. That is, these two systems are not commutative, the order of systems o and O is important in the sense that the timing of internal and external risks may play a significant role in determining the profitability of business ventures.

§8.4-1 Strategic Systems: Static CE Balance

By the principle of CE balance (Bcm. (3.2-2-6)): $\psi\{X_1 \stackrel{\star}{=} X_2 \stackrel{\star}{=} \ldots \stackrel{\star}{=} X_n,\Delta\}\ \overline{\barwedge}\tau$, we have for the o-O system,

o dominates O: For the energy of o, $\varepsilon(o) \sqsubseteq (\Omega,\mathbb{Z}^{\circ},{}_{v}\mathbb{H},\{\mathbb{C}\})$, the energy of O, $\varepsilon(O) \sqsubseteq (\Omega,\mathbb{Z}^{\circ},{}_{v}\mathbb{H},\{\mathbb{C}\})$, the strategy of o, $\mathcal{T}(o) \sqsubseteq (\Omega,\mathbb{Z}^{\circ},{}_{v}\mathbb{H},\{\mathbb{C}\})$ for $\mathcal{T} \models \mathbb{Z}^{\circ},{}_{v}\mathbb{H}$, and the strategy of O, $\mathcal{T}(O) \sqsubseteq (\Omega,\mathbb{Z}^{\circ},{}_{v}\mathbb{H},\{\mathbb{C}\})$, we have:

(8.4-1-1) $\varepsilon(o) > \varepsilon(O)$, $\mathcal{T}(o) > \mathcal{T}(O)$.

(8.4-1-2) $\psi\{X_1 \stackrel{\star}{=} X_2 \stackrel{\star}{=} \ldots \stackrel{\star}{=} X_n,\Delta\}^{o}\ \overline{\barwedge}\ \tau$ in o, and $\psi\{X_1 \stackrel{\star}{=} X_2 \stackrel{\star}{=} \ldots \stackrel{\star}{=} X_n,\Delta\}^{O}\ \overline{\barwedge}\ \tau$ in O.

Similarly we have for the O-o system, the relation is reversed.

§8.4-2 Strategic Systems: Dynamic Generative CE Balance

Let the static structure of the system o-O be: $o\text{-}O\oplus\langle\mathbb{C}_{o\text{-}O}\rangle$ or $S_o\text{-}S_O\oplus\langle\mathbb{C}_{o\text{-}O}\rangle \sqsubseteq (\Omega,\mathbb{Z}^{\circ},{}_{v}\mathbb{H},\{\mathbb{C}\})$. Then we have the dynamical structure of the o-O system: $D_o\text{-}D_O\oplus\langle\mathfrak{C}_{o\text{-}O}\rangle \sqsubseteq (\Omega,\mathbb{Z}^{\circ},{}_{v}\mathbb{H},\{\mathbb{C}\})$, where $D_o \sqsubseteq (\Omega,\mathbb{Z}^{\circ},{}_{v}\mathbb{H},\{\mathbb{C}\})$ is the dynamical structure of o and $D_O \sqsubseteq (\Omega,\mathbb{Z}^{\circ},{}_{v}\mathbb{H},\{\mathbb{C}\})$ is the dynamical structure of O. Similarly, let the static structure of the system O-o be: $O\text{-}o\oplus\langle\mathbb{C}_{o\text{-}O}\rangle$ or $S_O\text{-}S_o\oplus\ \langle\mathfrak{C}_{O\text{-}o}\rangle \sqsubseteq (\Omega,\mathbb{Z}^{\circ},{}_{v}\mathbb{H},\{\mathbb{C}\})$. Then we have the dynamical structure of the o-O system: $D_O\text{-}D_o\oplus\langle\mathfrak{C}_{O\text{-}o}\rangle \sqsubseteq (\Omega,\mathbb{Z}^{\circ},{}_{v}\mathbb{H},\{\mathbb{C}\})$. Below we shall write $D_o\text{-}D_O$ as $\{D_o > D_O\}$.

Now for $\{D_o\} = \{x_1,x_2,|x_3\} \sqsubseteq (\Omega,\mathbb{Z}^{\circ},{}_{v}\mathbb{H},\{\mathbb{C}\})$ with $x_2 = \varphi(x_1)$ and $x_3 = \varphi^2(x_1)$ and $\varphi, \oplus \models \mathbb{Z}^{\circ},{}_{v}\mathbb{H}$ with $\{[x_1\oplus x_2\oplus x_3] \circledast \mathrm{I}x\} = \sigma \Vdash \Sigma^{TC}$ (i.e., the system is in a state of simple Tcentral), we have (see Bcm. (S.2-1)):

(8.4-2-1) $\{[\varphi^2(x_1) \oplus\varphi(x_1) \oplus x_1\oplus x\ ] \circledast \mathrm{I}x\} = \Phi$,

where Ix denoting the factors (i.e., elements or systems) of $\varphi^2(x_1)$, $\varphi(x_1)$ and x_1 into X as a system with $\mathrm{I} \models \mathbb{Z}^{\circ},{}_{v}\mathbb{H}$. Note that Bcm. (8.4-2-1) is derived from:

(8.4-2-2) $x_1\oplus x_2\oplus x_3 = \sigma \Vdash \Sigma^{TC}$

with Σ^{TC} referring to a state of simple T Central (see Bcm. (B.1-1-1), Appendix B.1). Then we write

(8.4-2-3) $T^{Rev}\{x_1\oplus x_2\} = x_3$,

or $T^{-1}\{x_1\oplus x_2\} = x_3$ or $\{x_1\oplus x_2\}^{-1} = x_3$, where $T^{Rev}\{.\}$ stands for the tao reversal of $\{.\}$. By Bcm. (C.2-3), we mean that x_3 and $T^{Rev}\{x_1\oplus x_2\}$ constitute a yinyang pair in a state of T Central. A solution of Bcm. (8.4-2-2) is, for $X \equiv D_o$:

(8.4-2-4) $X(.) = \xi X_{\varphi 2}(\mathbb{H};.) \oplus \zeta X_{\varphi}(\mathbb{H};.) \oplus X_x(\mathbb{H};.) \circledast Ix_x(\mathbb{H};.)$,

where ξ_x represents the characteristics for X evolving into φX, ζ_x represents the characteristics for X evolving into $\varphi^2 X$, with $X(\mathbb{H})$ being the core of X at the state of Tcentral, and $Ix_x(\mathbb{H};.)$ refers to the integrating factor of organizing $\xi X_{\varphi 2}(\mathbb{H};.)$, $\zeta X_{\varphi}(\mathbb{H};.)$ and $X_x(\mathbb{H};.)$ into the system X(.).

Now for $\{D_O\} = \{y_1,y_2|y_3\} = \{[y_1 \oplus y_2 \oplus y_3] \circledast Iy\}$ (see Bcm. (A.2-1-4-7)) $\sqsubseteq (\Omega, \mathcal{Z}_O, {}_v\mathcal{H}, \{\mathbb{C}\})$ with $y_2 = \varphi(y_1)$ and $y_3 = \varphi^2(y_1)$ and φ, $\oplus \vDash \mathcal{Z}_O, {}_v\mathcal{H}$ with $\{y_1 \oplus y_2 \oplus y_3 =< T^{C\Delta}\} \Vdash Ш^{\Delta}$, (i.e., the system is in a state of Tcentral), we have (see Bcm. (C.2-1)):

(8.4-2-5) $\{\{[\varphi^2(y_1) \oplus \varphi(y_1) \oplus y_1] \circledast Iy\} = \Phi$,

or

(8.4-2-6) $y_1 \oplus y_2 \oplus y_3 = \sigma \Vdash \Sigma^{TC}$. Then we write

(8.4-2-7) $T^{Rev}\{y_1 \oplus y_2\} = y_3$,

or $T^{-1}\{y_1 \oplus y_2\} = y_3$ or $\{y_1 \oplus y_2\}^{-1} = y_3$, where $T^{Rev}\{.\}$ stands for the tao reversal of {.}. By (8.4-2-3), we mean that y_3 and $T^{Rev}\{y_1 \oplus y_2\}$ constitute a yinyang pair in a state of T Central.

A solution of Bcm. (8.4-2-6) is, for $X \equiv D_O$:

(8.4-2-7) $Y(.) = [\xi_y Y_{\varphi 2}(\mathbb{H};.) \oplus \zeta_y Y_{\varphi}(\mathbb{H};.) \oplus Y_y(\mathbb{H};.)] \circledast Iy(\mathbb{H};.)$,

where ξ_y represents the characteristics for Y evolving into φY and ζ_y represents the characteristics for Y evolving into $\varphi^2 Y$, with $Y(\mathbb{H})$ being the core of Y at a state of Tcentral.

As the result of the above reasoning, for the system $\{D_o\text{-}D_O\} = \{(x_1>y_1),(x_2>y_2)|\ (x_3>y_3)) \sqsubseteq (\Omega, \mathcal{Z}_O, {}_v\mathcal{H}, \{\mathbb{C}\})$ with $(x_2>y_2) = \varphi((x_1>y_1))$ and $(x_3>y_3) = \varphi^2(x_1>y_1)$ and φ, $\oplus \vDash \mathcal{Z}_O, {}_v\mathcal{H}$ with $\{(x_1>y_1) \oplus (x_2>y_2) \oplus (x_3>y_3) = \Phi$ (with "$= \Phi$" denoting a state of simple T central), we have (see Bcm. (C.2-1)):

(8.4-2-8) $\{\{[(x_1>y_1) \oplus (x_2>y_2) \oplus (x_3>y_3)] \circledast I(x>y)\} =< T^{C\Delta}\} = \Phi$,

where Iz(x>y) representing the integrating force of organizing $(x_1>y_1)$, $(x_2>y_2)$ and $(x_3>y_3)$ into the system Z. Then a solution of Bcm. (8.4-2-8) is, for $Z \equiv D_o\text{- } D_O$,

(8.4-2-9) $Z(.) = [\xi_z Z_o(\mathbb{H}_o>\mathbb{H}_O;.) \oplus \zeta_z Z_O(\mathbb{H}_o<\mathbb{H}_O;.)] \circledast Iz(\mathbb{H};.)$,

where $Iz(\mathbb{H};.)$ representing the integrating force of organizing $\xi_z Z_o(\mathbb{H}_o>\mathbb{H}_O;.)$ and $\zeta_z Z_O(\mathbb{H}_o<\mathbb{H}_O;.)$ into the system Z.

Below, we shall introduce the general principles of dynamical CE balance. Let x(.) and y(.) be solutions of separate static systems (as in Bcm. (8.4-2-7)). Then by applying the principle of static CE balance (see Bcm. (4.2-3)), we have the **principle of general dynamical CE balance** (see Section 3.2):

(8.4-2-10) $\psi^{Sheng}\{x^{Sheng}(.) \pm y^{Sheng}(.),\Delta\} \barwedge \tau$,

where $\psi^{Sheng}\{.\} \vDash \mathcal{Z}\circ,{}_v\mathcal{H}$ is the generative impactor that exercises its power on {.} over time (or inter-sectoral impactor of balance); and by applying the principle of static CE balance (see Bcm. (4.2-6)), we have the **principle of general generative-dynamical CE strategic centrality** (see Section 3.2):

(8.4-2-11) $\psi\{\mathcal{T}^*x(.) \geq \mathcal{T}y(.),\Delta\} \barwedge \tau$,

in the case that $\mathcal{T}$, $\mathcal{T}^* \vDash \mathcal{Z}\circ,{}_v\mathcal{H}$ be the strategic impactor and the target strategic impactor, respectively, and x(.) = C is the central system (or sub-system) and y(.) is the non-central system (or sub-system).

Remark 8.4-2-1. Let the superscript "Sheng" denote the forces of "generatics." That is, the entities with superscript "Sheng" are dynamical forces of non-conventional types. Then, in a static state, $\psi\{x(.) \pm y(.),\Delta\} \barwedge \tau$ is in an instantaneous balance; while in a generative state, $\psi^{Sheng}\{x^{Sheng}(.) \pm y^{Sheng}(.),\Delta\} \barwedge \tau$ is a very long-term CE balance. Note that $x \neq x^{Sheng}$ and $y \neq y^{Sheng}$ in general.

§8.4-3 Strategic Systems: Uncertain CE Balance

In Appendix I, we shall present the definitions of six systems of uncertainty: 0-step T^L distribution system, 0-step T^{sysC} distribution system, 0-step K^L distribution system, 0-step K^{sysC} distribution system, n-step T^{sysD} distribution system, and n-step K^{sysD} distribution system. And further, specific methods of uncertain dynamics will be presented as well.

Now by a principle of uncertain CE balance, for the system $X = \{x_1,x_2,|x_3\} \sqsubseteq (\Omega,\mathcal{Z}\circ,{}_v\mathcal{H},\{\mathbb{C}\})$ with $x_2 = \varphi(x_1)$ and $x_3 = \varphi^2(x_1)$ and φ, $\oplus \vDash \mathcal{Z}\circ,{}_v\mathcal{H}$, we have: in the case of the dynamics of certainty, Bcm. (8.4-2-2): $x_1 \oplus x_2 \oplus x_3 = \sigma \Vdash \Sigma^{TC}$ with the solution Bcm. (8.4-2-7): $Y(.) = \xi_y Y(\mathbb{H};.) \oplus \zeta_y Y(\mathbb{H};.)$. Now, we have for this X, one form of the **uncertain dynamical system** is:

(8.4-3-1) $(x_1 \oplus x_2 \oplus x_3) \circledcirc x_S = \sigma \Vdash \Sigma^{TC}$,

where x_S is the uncertain element of X (i.e., $x_{St} \sqsubseteq T^{sysD} \sqcup K^{sysD}$, any other distribution system, or any other uncertain system, see Definition (I.2-11)) with the solution:

(8.4-3-2) $Y(.) = (\xi_y Y(\mathbb{H};.) \oplus \zeta_y Y(\mathbb{H};.) \circledcirc \mathcal{S}_y Y(\mathbb{H}_S;.)$,

where $\mathcal{S}_y \vDash \mathcal{Z}\circ,{}_v\mathcal{H}$ and $Y(\mathbb{H}_S;.) \sqsubseteq T^{sysD} \sqcup K^{sysD}$ (any other distribution system, or any other uncertain system) refer to an **uncertain impactor** and an uncertain system in a state of Tcentral, respectively.

Below, we shall present a comparison of the real estate investment with stock investment by the use of the **dynamically uncertain methods** of cultural study just presented in the above. To facilitate the study, let $X = \{x_1,x_2,|x_3\} \sqsubseteq (\Omega,\mathcal{Z}\circ,{}_v\mathcal{H},\{\mathbb{C}\})$ with $x_2 = \varphi(x_1)$ and $x_3 = \varphi^2(x_1)$ and φ, $\oplus \vDash \mathcal{Z}\circ,{}_v\mathcal{H}$.

First, for a small investor, in the scenario of a good-time stock market, one could adopt an aggressive strategy (and take a short or long position) in the stock market and passive strategy in the real estate market. By a **principle of uncertain CE balance**, in the activities of stock market investment,

(8.4-3-3) $[x_1 \oplus x_2 \oplus x_3] \circledcirc Ix \circledcirc x_S = \sigma \Vdash \Sigma^{TC}$,

where Ix is the integrating factor of the system X and $x_{St} \sqsubseteq T^L$ or K^L (or any other uncertain system, see Definition (I.2-9)) with the solution:

(8.4-3-4) $Y(.) = [\xi_1 Y(\mathbb{H}_1;.) \oplus \xi_2 Y(\mathbb{H}_2;.) \oplus \xi_3 Y(\mathbb{H}_3;.)] \oplus Iy(\mathbb{H};.) \circledcirc \mathcal{S}_y Y(\mathbb{H}_S;.)$,

where $Iy(\mathbb{H};.)$ is the integrating factor of the system, $\mathcal{S}_y \vDash (\Omega, \mathcal{Z}\circ, {}_v\mathcal{H}, \{\mathbb{C}\})$, and $Y(\mathbb{H}_S;.) \sqsubseteq T^L$ or K^L. Note that the presentations here in Bcms. (8.4-3-3) and (8.4-3-4) are different from those of Bcms. (B.2-4-1)-(B.2-4-11).

For the investment decision of achieving a strategic balance between one type of investment (e.g., stock investment) and the other type of investment (e.g., real estate investment), then we have one form of the **principle of uncertain CE balance** (which is somewhat analogous to Bcm. (3.2-2-6)):

(8.4-3-5) $\{[(x_1 \doteqdot y_1) \oplus (x_2 \doteqdot y_2) \oplus (x_3 \doteqdot y_3)] \circledcirc I(x \doteqdot y)\} \circledcirc z(x \doteqdot y)_S = \sigma \Vdash \Sigma^{TC}$,

where $z(x \doteqdot y)_{St} \sqsubseteq T^L$ (K^L, any other distribution system, or any other uncertain system) with the solution

(8.4-3-6) $Z(.) = \{[\xi_1 Z(\mathbb{H}_{x1} \doteqdot \mathbb{H}_{y1};.) \oplus \xi_2 Z(\mathbb{H}_{x2} \doteqdot \mathbb{H}_{y2};.) \oplus \xi_3 Z(\mathbb{H}_{x3} \doteqdot \mathbb{H}_{y3};.)]$
$\circledcirc Iz(\mathbb{H}_x \doteqdot \mathbb{H}_y;.)\} \circledcirc \mathcal{S}_z Z(\mathbb{H}_S;.)$,

where $\mathcal{S}_z \vDash \mathcal{Z}\circ, {}_v\mathcal{H}$ and $Z(\mathbb{H}_S;.) \sqsubseteq T^L$ (or K^L, any other distribution or uncertain system, see Definition (I.2-11)).

Note that an alternative form of Bcm. (8.4-3-11) may be written as:

(8.4-3-7) $(x_1 \doteqdot y_1 | z_S\} \oplus (x_2 \doteqdot y_2 | z_S) \oplus (x_3 \doteqdot y_3 | z_S) = \sigma \Vdash \Sigma^{TC}$,

where $z_{St} \sqsubseteq T^L \sqcup K^L$ (or any other distribution or uncertain system) with the solution

(8.4-3-8) $Z(.) = [\xi_1 Z(\mathbb{H}_{x1} \doteqdot \mathbb{H}_{y1} | x_S;.) \oplus \xi_2 Z(\mathbb{H}_{x2} \doteqdot \mathbb{H}_{y2} | x_S;.) \oplus \xi_3 Z(\mathbb{H}_{x3} \doteqdot \mathbb{H}_{y3} | x_S;.)]$
$\circledcirc Iz(\mathbb{H}_x \doteqdot \mathbb{H}_y | x_S;.)$,

where $\mathcal{S}_y \vDash \mathcal{Z}\circ, {}_v\mathcal{H}$ and $Z(\mathbb{H}_S;.) \sqsubseteq T^L \sqcup K^L$ (or any other distribution or uncertain system).

But if the investment decision is one of achieving a strategic centrality of one type of investment (e.g., stock investment) over the other type of investment (e.g., real estate investment), then, from (Bcm. (8.4-2-8)), we have a principle of **Uncertain CE balance**:

(8.4-3-9) $\{[(x_1 > y_1) \oplus (x_2 > y_2) \oplus (x_3 > y_3)] \circledcirc I(x > y)\} \circledcirc z_S = \sigma \Vdash \Sigma^{TC}$,

(with $\otimes$ being an appropriate impactor) where $z_{St} \sqsubseteq T^L$ or K^L (any other distribution system, or any other uncertain system).

Then, for $Y \equiv D_o$-D_O (or stock investment-real estate investment), a solution of Bcm. (8.4-3-9) is:

(8.4-3-10) $Y(.) = \{[\xi_y Y(\mathbb{H}_{o>O};.) \oplus \zeta_y Y(\mathbb{H}_{o>O};.)] \circledast Iy(\mathbb{H}_{o>O};.)\} \circledast \mathcal{S}_y Y(\mathbb{H}_S;.)$,

where $\mathcal{S}_y \vDash \mathcal{Z}_{O,v}\mathcal{H}$ and $Y(\mathbb{H}_S;.) \sqsubseteq T^L$ (or K^L, or any other distribution system or uncertain system), and in conformity with the above form:

(8.4-3-11) $Z(.) = \{[\xi_1 Z(\mathbb{H}_{x1>y1};.) \oplus \xi_2 Z(\mathbb{H}_{x2>y2};.) \oplus \xi_3 Z(\mathbb{H}_{x3>y3};.)] \circledast Iz(\mathbb{H}_{x>y};.)\} \circledast$
$\mathcal{S}_z Y(\mathbb{H}_S;.)$,

Note that an alternative form of Bcm. (8.4-3-9) may be written as:

(8.4-3-12) $[(x_1>y_1|z_S\} \oplus (x_2>y_2|z_S) \oplus (x_3>y_3|z_S)] \circledast I(x>y)|z_S) = \sigma \Vdash \Sigma^{TC}$,

where $z_{St} \sqsubseteq T^L$ (or K^L, or any other distribution or uncertain system) with the solution

(8.4-3-13) $Z(.) = [\xi_1 Z(\mathbb{H}_{x1>y1}|z_S;.) \oplus \xi_2 Z(\mathbb{H}_{x2>y2}|z_S;.) \oplus \xi_3 Z(\mathbb{H}_{x3>y3}|z_S;.)]$
$\circledast Iz(\mathbb{H}_{x>y}|z_S;.)$.

As for a small investor, in the scenario of a bad-time stock market, one could adopt a passive strategy (and take a long position) in the stock market and active strategy in the real estate market.

Secondly, for a large investor, in the scenario of a good-time stock market, one could adopt an aggressive strategy in the stock market (and take both short and long position) and passive strategy in the real estate market. By one form of **principle of uncertain CE balance**, in the activities of stock market investment,

(8.4-3-14) $[(x_1>y_1) \oplus (x_2>y_2) \oplus (x_3>y_3)] \circledast (Ix>y|z_S) = \sigma \Vdash \Sigma^{TC}$,

or

(8.4-3-15) $\{[(x_1>y_1) \oplus (x_2>y_2) \oplus (x_3>y_3)] \circledast I(x>y)\} \circledast z_S = \sigma \Vdash \Sigma^{TC}$,

where $z_{St} \sqsubseteq T^L$ (T^{sysD}, K^{sysD}, T^{sysC}, K^{sysC}, any other distribution system, or any other uncertain system, see Definition (I.3-1)) with the slightly different solution:

(8.4-3-16) $Z(.) = \{[\xi_1 Z(\mathbb{H}_{x1}>\mathbb{H}_{y1};.) \oplus \zeta_2 Z(\mathbb{H}_{x2}>\mathbb{H}_{y2};.) \oplus \zeta_3 Z(\mathbb{H}_{x3}>\mathbb{H}_{y3};.)] \circledast$
$Iz(\mathbb{H}_x>\mathbb{H}_y;.)\} \circledast \mathcal{S}_z Z(\mathbb{H}_S;.)$,

with $\mathcal{S}_z \vDash \mathcal{Z}_{O,v}\mathcal{H}$ and $Z(\mathbb{H}_S;.) \sqsubseteq T^L$ (T^{sysD}, K^{sysD}, any other distribution system, or any other uncertain system).

(8.4-3-17) $Z(.) = [\xi_1 Z(\mathbb{H}_{x1}>\mathbb{H}_{y1}|z_S;.) \oplus \zeta_2 Z(\mathbb{H}_{x2}>\mathbb{H}_{y2}|z_S;.) \oplus \zeta_3 Z(\mathbb{H}_{x3}>\mathbb{H}_{y3}|z_S;.)] \circledast$
$Iz(\mathbb{H}_x>\mathbb{H}_y;.)$.

As for a large investor, in the scenario of a bad-time stock market, one could adopt either a passive or an active strategy (and take a short or long position) in the stock market and active strategy in the real estate market.

In this case, the strategic system is: {(real estate,stock)}|Z⇐Culture;E}. That is, the strategy of investments is essentially conditioned by the culture, given the outside environment E.
Below, we shall introduce the general principles of uncertain CE balance. Let x(.) and y(.) be solutions of separate static systems (as in Bcm. (8.4-2-7)). Then by applying the principle of static CE balance (see Bcm. (4.2-3)), we have the **principle of general uncertain CE balance**:

(8.4-3-18) $\psi\{x(.)\stackrel{*}{=}y(.),\Delta\} \,\bar{\barwedge}\, \tau$,

where $\psi \vDash \mathbb{Z}\circ,_{\mathrm{v}}\mathbb{H}$ is the inter-sectoral impactor of balance; and by applying the principle of static CE balance (see Bcm. (4.2-6)), we have the **principle of general dynamical CE strategic centrality**:

(8.4-3-19) $\psi\{\mathcal{T}^*x(.) \geq \mathcal{T}y(.),\Delta\} \,\bar{\barwedge}\, \tau$,

In the case that $\mathcal{T}$, $\mathcal{T}^\cdot \vDash \mathbb{Z}\circ,_{\mathrm{v}}\mathbb{H}$ be the strategic impactor and the target strategic impactor, respectively, and x(.) = C is the central sub-system and y(.) is the non-central sub-system (see for example, Bcms. (8.4-3-4),(8.4-3-12), (8.4-3-16) and (8.4-3-17), Subsections §B.2-4, §B.4-5)).

Remark 8.4-3-1. From Bcm. (8.4-3-14) in the above subsection: $[(x_1>y_1) \oplus(x_2>y_2) \oplus(x_3>y_3)] \circledast(Ix>y|z_S) = \sigma \Vdash \Sigma^{TC}$, in the case of conflict culture, we have the dynamical version of this system:

(8.4-3-20) $[(x_1>y_1) \oplus(x_2>y_2) \oplus(x_3>y_3)] \circledcirc I(x>y) = \sigma \Vdash \Sigma^{TC}$,

for which the system is written as:

(8.4-3-21) $z = \{(x>y),\varphi(x>y)|\varphi^2(x>y)\}$

at the initial time, and

(8.4-3-22) $z = \{\alpha(x>y), \alpha'\varphi(x>y)| \alpha''\varphi^2(x>y)\}$

(α, α' and $\alpha'' \vDash \mathbb{Z}\circ,_{\mathrm{v}}\mathbb{H}$ being dynamical structure-change impactors) at any moment of time. Note that in the case of tranquil culture, instead of Bcms. (8.4-3-21) and (8.4-3-22), we

(8.4-3-21) $z = \{(x>y),\varphi(x>y)| \psi((x>y),\varphi(x>y))\}$

at the initial time, and

(8.4-3-21) $z = \{\alpha(x>y),\alpha'\varphi(x>y)| \alpha''\psi((x>y),\varphi(x>y))\}$

at any moment of time.

§8.4-4 An Alternative Approach to Dynamical CE Balance

For a system $X_i \sqsubseteq (\Omega,\mathbb{Z}\circ,_{\mathrm{v}}\mathbb{H},\{\mathbb{C}\})$, i = 1,2,3, to reach the target of $\varphi\{X_i\} = X_i$ (i.e., in the state of system continuity), $\varphi \vDash \mathbb{Z}\circ,_{\mathrm{v}}\mathbb{H}$ under the constraint of the pure dynamic structure: $\Delta \sqsubseteq \Omega$, we have from Bcm. (3.2-2-1): $T_i = X_i \gamma \Delta$, $\gamma \models \mathcal{Z}\circ,_{v}\mathcal{H}$ being the interactor connecting X and Δ. Then the state of CE balance and strategic centrality are derived as:

(3.2-1-7) $(\varphi\{T_i\})_{Xi1,..,Xin}$

$= (\varphi\{X \gamma \Delta\})_{Xi1,..,Xin,Ixi}$

$= (\varphi[\{X_{i1},..,X_{in}\},\Delta])_{Xi1,..,Xin} \ltimes \varphi[I(x_{i1},..,x_{in}),E]$

$= \varphi[\{X_{i1},..,X_{in}\},\Delta] \otimes \psi\{X_{i1},\Delta\} \stackrel{\star}{=} \ldots \stackrel{\star}{=} \psi\{X_{in},\Delta\} \ltimes \varphi[\, I(x_{i1},..,x_{in}),E]$.

Then the principle of CE balance is:

(8.4-4-1) $\psi\{X_{i1},\Delta\} \stackrel{\star}{=} \ldots \stackrel{\star}{=} \psi\{X_{in},\Delta\}$.

Now suppose, for $T_1,T_2, T_3 \sqsubseteq (\Omega,\mathcal{Z}\circ,_{v}\mathcal{H},\{\mathbb{C}\})$, we have a grand system

(8.4-4-2) $\{T_1,T_2|T_3\} = \{X_1{}^{\gamma}\Delta,\ X_2{}^{\gamma}\Delta,|\ X_3{}^{\gamma}\Delta\}$

in the case of triple sub-systems. Further, let assume that this is in the form of:

(8.4-4-3) $X = \{(X_1{}^{\gamma}\Delta),\varphi(X_1{}^{\gamma}\Delta)|\varphi^2\ (X_1{}^{\gamma}\Delta)\}$

at the initial time. Then we have:

(8.4-4-4) $X = \{(X_1{}^{\gamma}\Delta),\alpha'\varphi(X_1{}^{\gamma}\Delta)|\alpha''\varphi^2(X_1{}^{\gamma}\Delta)\}$

at any moment of time with $\varphi(X_1{}^{\gamma}\Delta)$ being the central unit system.

In terms of dynamics, we have then:

(8.4-4-5) $z(.) = [\alpha_1 z_1(\mathbb{H}_{X1^{\gamma}\Delta};.) \oplus \alpha_2 z_2(\mathbb{H}_{X2^{\gamma}\Delta};.) \oplus \alpha_3 z_3(\mathbb{H}_{X3^{\gamma}\Delta};.)] \circledast Iz(\mathbb{H}_{Xi^{\gamma}\Delta};.)$.

where, at any moment of time, a system of CE balance in which the CE balance of the individual X_1 is described by Bcm. (8.4-4-1).

Similarly, we have, for the system of dynamics expressed by Bcm. (8.4-4-5), a system of CE strategic centrality in which the CE strategic centrality of the individual X_1 is described by the following becoming (see Bcm. (3.2-2-8)):

(8.4-4-6) $\psi\{X_{i1} \geq X_{i2} \geq \ldots \geq X_{in},\Delta\} \overline{\barwedge}\ \tau$,

where X_{i1} is the center in the system of X_i.

8.5 Tcentral Strategy, Self-Mastering and Self-Organizing Strategy, and Other Strategies

In this Section, we study the following strategies: Tcentral strategy, self-mastering and self-organizing strategy, CE balanced strategy, and conquest strategy, etc.

Definition 8.5-1. One is said to choose a **specific Tcentral strategy** if in the strategic space (Bcm. (8.2-2)) $\Omega^{T*} = \{\Omega^D, \Omega^{Rh}, \Omega^H, \Omega^S, \Omega^V, \Omega^{sC}\}$, one chooses either Ω^H (i.e., golden strategy) or Ω^S (i.e., silver strategy), but not others.

Remark 8.5-1. A system of specific Tcentral strategy is in general not a TCentral system, because by adopting a specific Tcentral strategy, the decision-maker may not be able to create

a TCentral system. That is, for $X \sqsubseteq (\Omega, \mathcal{Z}^{o}, {}_{v}\mathcal{H}, \{\mathbb{C}\})$, X(.|specific TCentral strategy) ≠ X(.|TC state) or TC system of X.

Definition 8.5-2. One is said to choose a **self-mastering and self-organizing strategy** if the objective of the strategy is to achieve a system of self-masterism (see Definition 6.4-2-3).

Remark 8.5-2. The TCentral system and the self-mastering system may be considered as desirable systems.

Remark 8.5-3. In order for a system to create a specific position for itself, the use of entity-augmenting impactors (see Thema 8.3-1 in Section 8.3) is essential.

Remark 8.5-4 (system approach). A starting point for reaching a self-mastering system is by first going to the system of sC strategy. Then a short-cut to reach the self-mastering system may be pursued by going through the TCentral system.

Definition 8.5-3. A strategy is said to be a **centralized strategy** if and only if it is a strategy designed to have a strict control over non-central members of the system in question.

Definition 8.5-4. A strategy is said to be a **conquest strategy** if and only if it is a strategy designed to conquer others.

Definition 8.5-5. A strategy is said to be a CE **balanced strategy** if and only if the strategy adopted is derived from the principle of CE balance (that is, if and only if this is a strategy of keeping all elements and/or subsystems in balance).

Figure 8.5-1
Systemic distribution of a system: c = continuity system; zh = TCentral system; s = self-mastering system; "∘" = other systems scattered irregularly

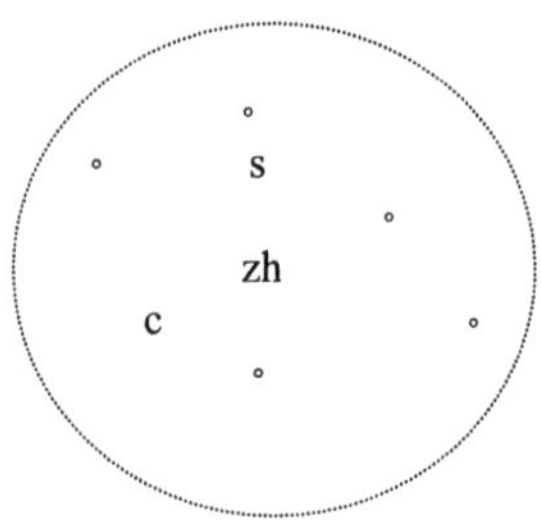

Definition 8.5-6. For a system $X \sqsubseteq (\Omega, \mathcal{Z}^{o}, {}_{v}\mathcal{H}, \{\mathbb{C}\})$, let (i) x(.|target strategy of self-masterism) → self-mastering system, (ii) x(.|target specific Tcentral strategy) → TCentral system, (iii) x(.|target continuity strategy) → continuity system, and (iv) other systems distributed irregularly (for example, see "∘" shown in Figure 8.5-1). Then the collection of all systems --

self-mastering system, TCentral system, continuity system and other systems -- is called the **systemic distribution of a system X.**

Remark 8.5-5. For a system $X \sqsubseteq (\Omega, \mathcal{Z}^{\circ}, {}_{v}\mathcal{H}, \{\mathbb{C}\})$, assume the positions of the self-mastering system, TCentral system and continuity system of X are known. If we vaguely know both of the distances between the self-mastering system of X and its TCentral system and between that of X and its continuity system, then we may be in a better position to predict the whereabouts of the self-mastering system of X.

Note that the dynamical and structural methods presented in Section 6.7 are not very helpful in actual calculation of the position of a system X. In addition, Remark 8.5-5 may be stated alternatively in the following.

Remark 8.5-6. (1) The calculation of $|Tc(X) - X|$, or the difference between the actual system itself and its TCentral position (i.e., TCentral system) may be useful. (2) The calculation of $|sC(X) - X|$, or the difference between itself and its position of continuity (i.e., continuity system), may be helpful.

Chapter 9 – Strategic Spaces and Economic-Cultural Advancing Models

9.1 Introduction

In this chapter, we come back to the world of mathematics to study the models of strategic advancement of a cultural economy. By bringing cultural variables into the model, our approach is to build up solid foundations for the socio-cultural and economic studies.

9.2 Strategic Advancement Models

For the original presentation of these models shown below, see Tonn [2006], Section 6.6.

§9.2-1 A Deterministic Model of Economic Advancement

Let the system $X \sqsubseteq (\Omega, \mathcal{Z}\circ, {}_v\mathcal{H}, \{\mathbb{C}\}) \sqcap \mathbb{C}$, and suppose there is no growth in population and no change in technology in the cultural economy. Then we have the differential equation for capital stock as follows:

$$(9.2\text{-}1\text{-}1) \quad \frac{dK}{dt} = I - \Delta,$$

where K, I and Δ refers to the capital stock, investment and depreciation of the capital stock, respectively.

Let the investment be a function of public policy and private strategy: $I = (\mathcal{T}^*, \mathcal{T})^I f(L,K,\mathbb{C})$, where $(\mathcal{T}^*, \mathcal{T})^I \models \mathcal{Z}\circ, {}_v\mathcal{H}$ refers to the set of public-private investment strategies, $f(L,K,\mathbb{C})$ the production function (for $\mathbb{C}$ being the cultural variables, L the raw labor, and K the capital stock). In addition, let Δ be the function of the public-private capital depreciation impactor $(\mathcal{T}^*, \mathcal{T})^\Delta$ (assuming $(\mathcal{T}^*, \mathcal{T})^\Delta \sqsubseteq (\Omega, \mathcal{Z}\circ, {}_v\mathcal{H}, \{\mathbb{C}\}) \sqcap \mathbb{C}$ is measurable in the mathematical sense). For simplicity, let $\Delta = \phi(\mathcal{T}^*, \mathcal{T})^\Delta h(L,K,\mathbb{C})$; that is, Δ is a reorganizable system separated into $\phi(\mathcal{T}^*, \mathcal{T})^\Delta$ and $h(L,K,\mathbb{C})$, where ϕ is an reorganizing impactor and $h(L,K,\mathbb{C})$ the production-consumption activities related to the depreciation of capital stocks. Here, of course, we assume that Δ, $\phi(\mathcal{T}^*, \mathcal{T})^\Delta$ and $h(L,K,\mathfrak{C})$ are all measurable in the mathematical sense. Then, we have

$$\begin{aligned} &\phi(\mathcal{T}^*, \mathcal{T})^\Delta h(L,K,\mathbb{C}) \\ &= \phi(\mathcal{T}^*, \mathcal{T})^\Delta h[{}^{+3}(L..)\ {}^{+2}(.K.)\ {}^{+1}(..\mathbb{C})] \\ &= \{(\mathcal{T}^*, \mathcal{T})^\Delta, \mathbb{C}\} \otimes L(.) \otimes K(.), \end{aligned}$$

where L(.) and K(.) refer to a function of raw labor and a function of capital stock, respectively. Here, ${}^{+1}(.)$, ${}^{+2}(.)$ and ${}^{+3}(.)$ denote the elements of the top layer, the second-higher layer, and the lower layer, respectively, in a separable or reorganizable system. For simplicity, we shall assume $\{(\mathcal{T}^*, \mathcal{T})^\Delta, \mathbb{C}\} \otimes (L,K) = \eta(\rho,\omega) g(L,K)$ as well, where $\eta(\rho,\omega) \equiv \{(\mathcal{T}^*, \mathcal{T})^\Delta, \mathbb{C}\}$.

Thus, from the operations in the above (i.e., that is, let $(\mathcal{T}^*,\mathcal{T})^{\Delta}h(L,K,\mathbb{C}) \cong \phi(\mathcal{T}^*,\mathcal{T})^{\Delta}h(L,K,\mathbb{C})$, we have:

(9.2-1-2) $\Delta = \eta(\rho,\omega)g(L,K)$.

Now let this cultural economy be maintained in a state of normal operation or T Central, i.e., $f(L,K,\mathbb{C}) = f(L,K,\mathbb{C})^*$, where $f(L,K,\mathbb{C})^*$ denotes the normal or T central state of $f(L,K,\mathbb{C})$. This is the *normal state* of the complex of the culture/socio-polity/ economy operating in a normal or T Central state (excluding the public-private impactors). This is a state of neither sub-normal nor super-normal operations of the system. At this time, if $\gamma f \equiv \gamma(\rho,\omega)f(L,K)$, for $\gamma(\rho,\omega)f(L,K) = (\mathcal{T}^*,\mathcal{T})^{I}f(L,K,\mathbb{C})$, then we have:

(9.2-1-3) $I = (\mathcal{T}^*,\mathcal{T})^{I} f(L,K,\mathbb{C}) = \gamma f$.

By derived from the afore-mentioned Bcms. or Eqs. (9.2-1-1), (9.2-1-2) and (9.2-1-3), We have the following differential equation with regarding to the increment of the capital stock (derived from $\Delta = I$, see the definitions of Δ and I):

$$(9.2\text{-}1\text{-}4) \quad \frac{dK}{dt} = \gamma f - \eta g,$$

where $g \equiv g(L,K)$, $\eta \equiv \eta(\rho,\omega)$, and the steady state level (i.e., $K^{\cdot} = 0$) of capital stock is:

(9.2-1-5) $\gamma f = \eta g$.

Below, let γf and ηg be convex and concave functions of K, respectively. When the population stops growing, the technology stops changing, and the public/private impactors are in some states of T central, we derive the steady state T central capital stock K*of the cultural economy (see Figure 9.2-1-1). But when the population starts to grow, the technology again changes, and the public/private impactors are in some super-normal states of T Central, we derive the *steady state super-normal level* of capital stock K** of the cultural economy (also see Figure 9.2-1-1).

Figure 9.2-1-1
Steady state level of capital stock in both states of Tcentral and super-normal T Central, K*, K**

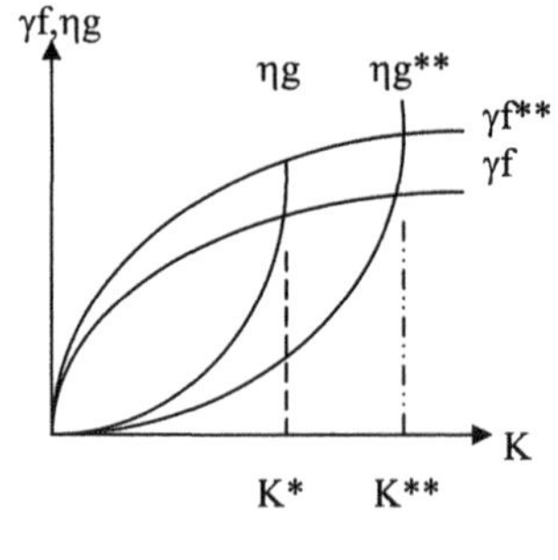

Here, we have: "strategy↑ ∨ technology↑ ∨culture↑ ∨ depreciation↓": ⇒ "K* → K**" (see Figure 9.2-1-2), for the process in which the old steady state evolving into a new steady state. Here $\eta(\rho,\omega) < \eta(\rho,\omega)^{**}$ and $\gamma(\rho,\omega) < \gamma(\rho,\omega)^{**}$, with $\eta(\rho,\omega)^{**}$ and $\gamma(\rho,\omega)^{**}$ depicting those steady-state cultural variables associated with K**.

Business cycle in a market of perfect competition. It is a market in which all firms having long term profit rate $\pi = 0$. If all firms survive in the market, then this system is in a steady state equilibrium. After those firm with zero profit rates dropping out of the market, we have: $\dot{K} < 0$, $K^* < K$ (when the system approaches but not yet reaches a steady state equilibrium). The processes for the system moving from a state of non-steady-state equilibrium to a state of steady state equilibrium (i.e., the process: $(\dot{K} > 0) \wedge (K < K^*) \Rightarrow (\dot{K} = 0) \wedge (K = K^*)$, or $(\dot{K} < 0) \wedge (K^* < K) \Rightarrow (\dot{K} = 0) \wedge (K = K^*)$ is then called a **business cycle**.

In this perfectly competitive market, the wage rate is: $W = MP_L$ (derived from $W^s = VMP = P \times MP_L$). Due to the input of new labor carrying no profit, all firms stop employing any new labor. Then the employment level of the market reaches a state of steady state equilibrium.

Imperfect competition. It is a market in which all firms having profit rates $\pi \geq 0$ or $\pi \leq 0$. Those firms with positive profit rates shall enlarge their productive activities, and those firms with negative profit rates will have to scale back the operations or just leave the market. In sum, in general, any reproductive firm in the imperfect competitive market must have a positive investment rate with increasing level of capital stock. The wage rate in this market is then: $W < MP_L$ (derived from $W^s = MRP = MR \times MP_L$).

In this system, maybe due to population increase, some discoveries of new land/mineral resources, invention of new products or new methods of manufacturing old products, organizational innovation, or new cultural advancement, etc., some firms' profits turn into positive figures. Thus a new business cycle begins.

The wage rate in this imperfect market is: $M/P < MP_L$ (derived from $W^s = MRP = MR \times MP_L$, where $W/P = (MR/P)MP_L$, $MR/P < 0$). By the input of new labor that generates new profits, the cost of hiring new labor is lower that the revenue received. Hence, all firms increase labor hiring, and consequently, the employment level of the cultural economy is raised.

Figure 9.2-1-2
Steady-state equilibrium levels of capital stocks in the new and old business cycles

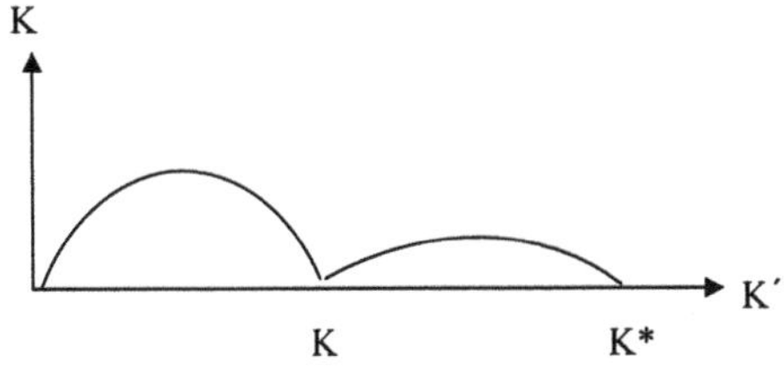

In a disequilibrium market of capitalism, firms with systemic advantage might have a greater chance to maximize their profits. Figure 9.2-1-3 shows that, by ignoring the public-private strategic impactors, the dynamical trajectory of capital stock is: $K = K_1^*$, for $K' = 0$. For this market, with new and higher level of technology, the new steady-state equilibrium level of capital stock is K_2^*, where $K_2^* > K_1^*$ (also see Figure 9.2-1-3).

Figure 9.2-1-3
Steady-state levels of capital Stocks in the market of discontinuity K_1^*, K_2^*

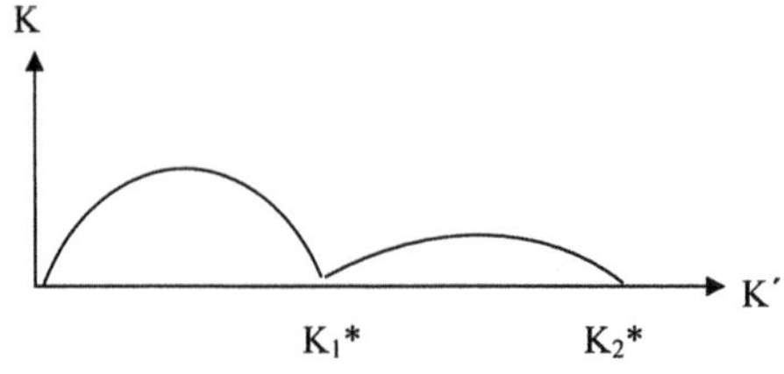

To explore the relationship between cultural and human spirit and the capital stock, let the human capital H be a function of culture (ρ,ω):

(9.2-1-6) $H = h(Ed, Health,.|\rho,\omega)$,

where Ed and Health depict the variables of education and health care, respectively. That is, the human capital is a function of cultural variable, and to say it is a function of education and health care is meant that both education and health care are just two aspects of the complex of cultural variables. Then we have Figure 9.2-1-4.

Figure 9.2-1-4
CE centrality of will-rationality, human power and capital as a function of the cultural mix (ρ,ω).

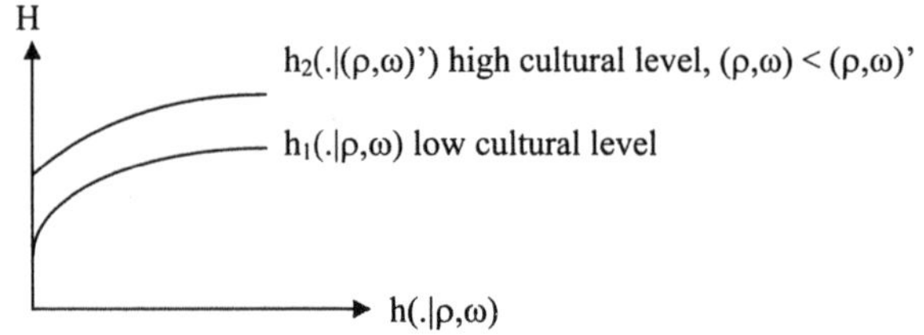

To address the relationship between cultural and capital stock, let capital stock K in the short term perspective be a function of the rate of return in production (r) and the real national income (Y) given the cultural complex (ρ,ω). Then we have Eq. (9.2-1-7).

Figure 9.2-1-5
Dynamical CE centrality of capital K and culture (ρ,ω), (ρ,ω) < (ρ',ω')

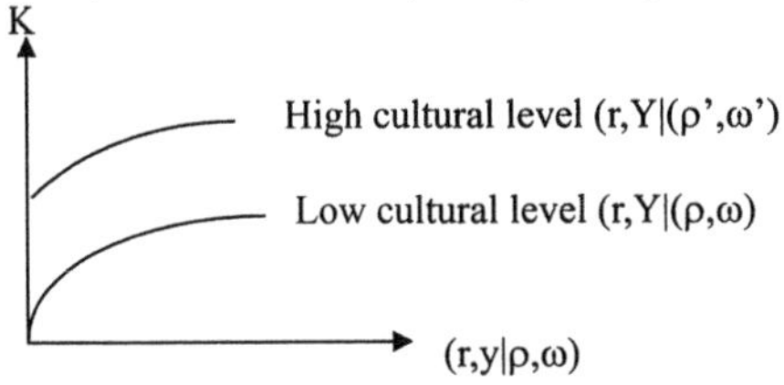

(9.2-1-7) $K = f(r,Y|\rho,\omega)$.

It follows that we have Figure 9.2-1-5. Note that the set of cultural variables (i.e., the cultural complex with (ρ,ω) as a proxy) acts as a shift factor in Figure 9.2-1-5.

And in the long term perspective, let the capital stock K be a function of the cultural complex (ρ,ω), and we have:

(9.2-1-8) $K = f(r,Y|\rho,\omega)$,

that is, capital (K) is a function of the interest rate and the real national income, given the cultural variables. In Figure 9.2-1-5, we would like to treat the set of cultural variables as a factor of rotation; and yet it actual behaves like a shift factor. In the very long-term perspective, culture may act as the determinant of capital stock, more or less like what Karl Marx has done asserted .

Figure 9.2-1-6
CE centrality of Tch and (ρ,ω)

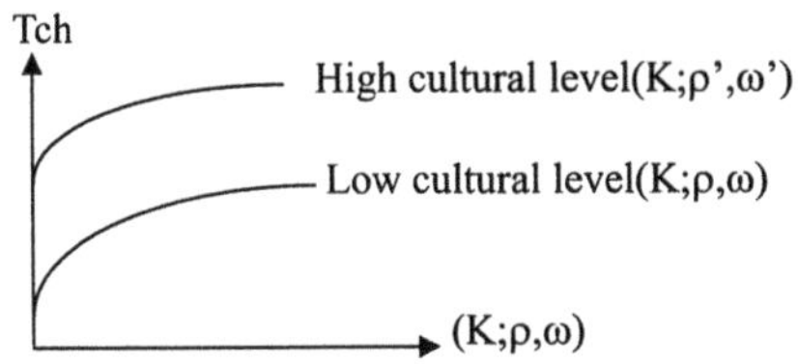

For the relationship between technology and culture, let the technology Tch be a function of the capital stock given the level of culture (ρ,ω):

(9.2-1-9) $Tch = g(K;\rho,\omega)$.

Then we have Figure 9.2-1-6.

Figure 9.2-1-7
Dynamical CE centrality of K, Tch and (ρ,ω), K < K', Tch < Tch'

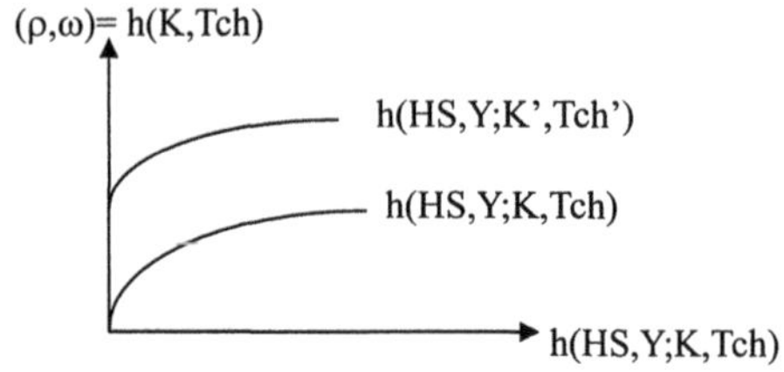

To determine the relationship among culturec capital stock and technology, let the culture (ρ,ω) be a function of human spirituality (HS) and Y, given the level of capital stock K and technology Tch:

(9.2-1-10) $(\rho,\omega) = h(HS,Y;K,Tch)$.

Now we want to show technology as a shift factor of culture, and we have Figure 9.2-1-7.

§9.2-2 Dynamical Trajectories of Culture and Technology

Under the assumption of no change in technology and culture, let the first order differential equation of capital be:

(9.2-2-1) $\underline{\underline{K}}^{\cdot} = a\underline{\underline{K}} + bL + c$,

where L and $\underline{\underline{K}} \equiv K(.\,|\,\underline{tech,\mathfrak{C}})$ represent respectively the raw labor and the level of capital stock for which technology and culture are held constant, and a, b and c are fixed parameters. Here technology and culture are assumed to remain constant all the time. In a two-dimensional diagram, we have $\underline{\underline{K}}^{\cdot} = a\underline{\underline{K}} + \sigma$, σ being a fixed parameter. As the level of capital stock increases, the function represented by Eq. (9.2-1-1) shifts upward and surpasses the original trajectory (see Figure 9.2-2-1).

Figure 9.2-2-1
Dynamical trajectory of K

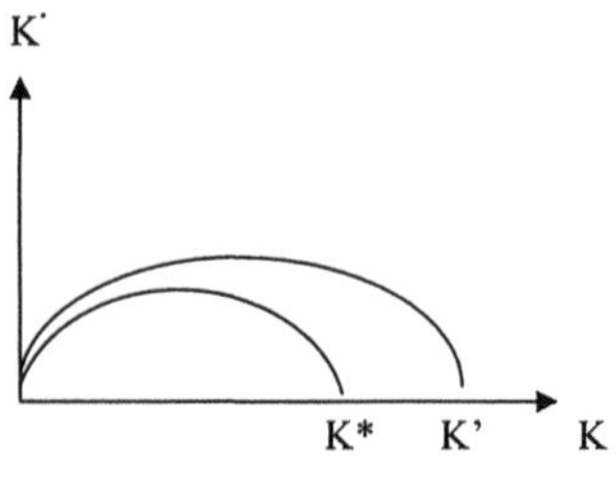

By holding technology and culture constant, we have the first order differential equation of technology be as follows:
(9.2-2-2) $\underline{tech}^{\cdot} = \alpha\, \underline{tech} + \beta \underline{K} + \Upsilon L + \delta$,

where $\underline{tech} \equiv tech(.\,|\,\mathfrak{C})$ is the technological factor under constant culture, and α, β, ϒ and δ are fixed parameters. Then in a diagram of two-dimensions, we have $\underline{tech}^{\cdot} = \alpha\, \underline{tech} + \theta$, θ being a parameter. Then, with culture advancing, the trajectory of Eq. (9.2-2-2) turns upward and surpasses the original trajectory (see Figure 9.2-2-2), where $\underline{K} \equiv K(.\,|\,\underline{tech}, \mathfrak{C})$ is the level of capital stock under constant technology and culture, and $\underline{tech} \equiv tech(.\,|\,\mathfrak{C})$ is the technological factor holding culture constant (see Figures 9.2-2-1 and 9.2-2-2). Here culture is ignored because it remains constant all the time.

§9.2-3 Culture-Technology-Capital Chain

We have the culture-technology-capital chain as follows: "$\mathfrak{C}^{\cdot} = f(\mathfrak{C})$" ⇒ "$tech^{\cdot} = f(tech)$" ⇒ "$K^{\cdot} = h(K)$" ⇒ "$y^{\cdot} = g(y)$"; (cd & cs → value or price of $\mathfrak{C}$) ⇒ (cd & cs→ price or cost of tech) ⇒ (cd and cs → cost of K) ⇒ (cd and cs→ y and prices).

Figure 9.2-2-2
Dynamical trajectory of technology

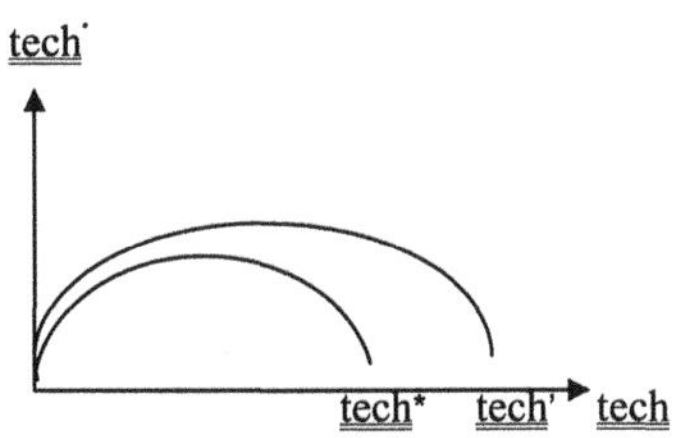

9.3 Stochastic Economic-Cultural Growth Models

In the following, we present a model of cultural economy in which stochastic forces of culture are at work (see Tonn 1994).

§9.3-1 Stochastic Processes of Cultural Accumulation

In the cultural economy, $X = \Gamma_1 E_1(.|x_E) \oplus \Gamma_2 E_2(.|x_E) \sqsubseteq (\Omega, \mathcal{Z}^{o}, {}_{v}\mathcal{H}, \{\mathbb{C}\}) \sqcap \mathbb{C}$, the initial benefit of the economy is set as:

(9.3-1-1) $F(L,K,\mathbb{C}) = Q(L,K,\mathbb{C}) - wL$,

where Q is the production function of the cultural economy (assumed to be a homogeneous function of degree one), and wL the real wage bill of the cultural economy. The objective of the cultural economy is to maximize the net benefit with respect to the level of interest rates I_o (in low-technological industries) and I_v (in high-technological industries):

$$(9.3\text{-}1\text{-}2)\quad \max_{\{I_o,I_v\}} \int_0^{\infty} e^{-rt}\,\{F(L,K,C) - r_o I_o' - r_v I_v' - g'' - q''\}dt,$$

where r_o refers to the cost or rental price of investing in I_o, I_o refers to the investment in low-technology products with $I_o' = I_oL$, r_v refers to the cost or rental price of investing in I_v, I_v refers to the investment in high-tech products with $I_v' = I_vL$, $g'' = g(k^{\cdot})L$ for $g \equiv g(k^{\cdot})$ being the per capita costs of technological externalities, and $q'' = q(k^{\cdot})L$ for $q \equiv q(x^{\cdot})$ being the per capita costs of cultural externalities.

Following Long and Siebert (1992), we shall set $g(k^{\cdot})$ and $q(k^{\cdot})$ as quadratic functions having the following properties: $g(0) = 0$, $g'(0) = 0$; and $g'(k^{\cdot}) > 0$ if $k^{\cdot} > 0$, $g'(k^{\cdot}) < 0$ if $k^{\cdot} < 0$, $g''(k^{\cdot}) \geq 0$. Here one example of this function is:

$$(9.3\text{-}1\text{-}3)\quad g(k^{\cdot}) = (k^{\cdot})^2,\ q(x^{\cdot}) = x^2,$$

that is, the per capita production function is at first convex and then concave in k and x, and the partial derivatives df/dk and df/dx are bell-shaped curves.

For the accumulation of capital stock, without any cultural effect on capital stock, we have the usual equation: $dK = (I_o' - I_v' - \delta K)dt$. By assuming that the investment in high-tech sector is m times as effective as the investment in low-technology sector, we have the modified equation: $dK = (I_o' - mI_v' - \delta K)dt$. Yet because of the cultural impact, with the cultural impactor $\Gamma_1 : I_o' \rightarrow \alpha I_o'$ and $\Gamma_2 : I_v \rightarrow \beta I_v$, we write

$$(9.3\text{-}1\text{-}4)\quad dK = (\alpha I_o' - \beta m I_v' - \delta K)dt.$$

In the mono-cultural economy, for example, in the case of the complex cultural economy of the balance of power, let $\alpha = \alpha_1 + \alpha_1'$ and $\beta = \beta_1 + \beta_1'$, where α_1 depicts the competitive efficiency of product imitation and repetition under the mono-culture that could be transferred to other economy, α_1' depicts the purely competitive efficiency of product imitation under the mono-culture that could not be transferred to other economy, and β_1 depicts the monopolistic efficiency of product imitation and repetition under the mono-culture that could be transferred to other economy, and β_1' depicts the monopolistic efficiency of product imitation under the mono-culture that could not be transferred to other economy.

However, in the bi-cultural (for example, the composite cultural economy of centrality and harmony, i.e., a complex of the modern systemic/yu-wu culture and being culture) and tri-cultural economies (for example, the composite cultural economy of centrality and socialization, i.e., a complex of the modern systemic/yu-wu culture, being culture, and dialectic culture), we would set $\alpha = \alpha_1 + \alpha_2 + \alpha_3$ and $\beta = \beta_1 + \beta_2 + \beta_3$, where α_1 is the coefficient of the competitive efficiency in product repetition and imitation (related to the low-being culture), α_2 is the coefficient of the monopolistic efficiency in product repetition and imitation (related to the low-yu culture), β_1 is the coefficient of the competitive efficiency in the processes of product modification and creation and organizational innovation (related to the high-being culture), β_2 is the coefficient of the monopolistic efficiency in the processes of product modification and creation and organizational innovation (related to the high yu-culture), and β_3 is the efficiency coefficient of the integration of being-creativity and tao-creativity through the processes of you-being and wu recursion (i.e., due to the interactions of the high-being culture, high-yu culture and the wu culture in the modern systemic/yu-wu culture).[9] In the above, by the modern systemic culture is meant the culture comprising the modern systemic rationality and the modern life-will, either self-adaptive or self-mastering.

Below we set the stochastic equation of raw labor as:

(9.3-1-5) $L^{\cdot} = nL + \sigma_h L\zeta$

where $L^{\cdot} \equiv dL/dt$, with σ_h being the coefficient related to the stochasticity of the raw labor, and n being the growth rate of raw labor. Here L and ζ are mutually independent and $dW = \zeta dt$, for ζ being the so-called white noise, with

(9.3-1-6) $dL = nLdt + \sigma_h LdW$.

In the cultural economy, $\Gamma_1 E_1(.|x_E) \oplus \Gamma_2 E_2(.|x_E) \sqsubseteq (\Omega, \mathcal{Z}o, {}_v\mathcal{H}, \{\mathbb{C}\})$, we set the accumulation equation of culture as:

(9.3-1-7) $\mathbb{C}^{\cdot} = [aL + (\sigma_o' + \sigma_v')\,\mathfrak{C}] + u\mathfrak{C}\zeta$,

where $\mathbb{C}^{\cdot} \equiv d\mathbb{C}/dt$. From Eq. (9.3-1-7) in the above, we have:

(9.3-1-8) $d\mathbb{C} = [aL + (\sigma_o' + \sigma_v')\mathbb{C}]dt - u\mathbb{C}dW$.

§9.3-2 Stochastic Control Model of A Cultural Economy

Summarizing Equations (9.3-1-2), (9.3-1-4), (9.3-1-5) and (9.3-1-8) presented in the above, we derive the following stochastic control model of a cultural economy:

$$\max_{\{I_o', I_v'\}} \int_0^{\infty} e^{-rt} \{F(L,K,\mathbb{C}) - r_o I_o' - r_v I_v' - g'' - q''\}dt,$$

$$\text{s.t.} \quad dK = (\alpha I_o' + \beta m I_v' - \delta K)dt$$
$$dL = nLdt + \sigma_h LdW$$
$$d\mathfrak{C} = [aL + (\sigma_o' + \sigma_v')\mathbb{C}]dt + u\mathbb{C}dW$$

where $I_o' \geq 0$ and $I_v' \geq 0$.

Let the per capita capital stock be $k \equiv K/L$. By the Ito theorem (for example, see Arnold 1974), we get

$$dk = (\partial k/\partial t)dt + (\partial k/\partial L)dL + (\partial k/\partial K)dK + (\tfrac{1}{2})[(\partial^2 k/\partial K^2)(dK)^2 + 2(\partial^2 k/\partial K\partial L)dKdL + (\partial^2 k/\partial L^2)(dL)^2],$$

or

(9.3-2-1) $dk = (\alpha I_o' + \beta m I_v')dt - (n + \delta - \sigma_h^2)kdt - \sigma_h kdW$.

Note that here $\partial k/\partial t = 0$, $\partial k/\partial L = \partial(K/L)/\partial L = K[\partial(1/L)/\partial L] = K(-1/L^2)$, and $(\partial k/\partial L)dL = (-K/L)(ndt+\sigma_h dw) = -nkdt - \sigma_h kdw$. Further, let the per capita cultural level be $x \equiv \mathfrak{C}/L$. By applying the Ito theorem again, we get

$$dx = (\partial x/\partial t)dt + (\partial x/\partial L)dL + (\partial x/\partial \mathfrak{C})d\mathfrak{C} + (\tfrac{1}{2})[(\partial^2 x/\partial \mathfrak{C}^2)(d\mathfrak{C})^2 + 2(\partial^2 x/\partial \mathfrak{C}\partial L)d\mathbb{C}dL + (\partial^2 x/\partial L^2)(dL)^2]$$

or

(9.3-2-2) $dx = adt + (u\sigma_h+\sigma_o+\sigma_v-n+\sigma_h^2)xdt - (\sigma_h+u)xdW$

Hence, from either of the above equations, we establish the stochastic control model of the cultural economy as:

(9.3-2-3) $$\max_{\{I_o,I_v\}} \int_0^{\infty} e^{-rt} \{f(k,x) - r_o I_o - r_v I_v - g - q\}dt,$$

s.t.

(9.3-2-4) $k^{\cdot} = \alpha I_o + \beta m I_v - (n+\delta-\sigma_h^2)k - \sigma_h k\zeta$

(9.3-2-5) $x^{\cdot} = a + (u\sigma_h+\sigma_o+\sigma_v-n+\sigma_h^2)x - (\sigma_h+u)x\zeta$,

where $I_o \geq 0$, $I_v \geq 0$, with $f(k,x) = F(L,K,\mathbb{C})/L$. After taking mathematical expectation of the above equations, this becomes a deterministic control model, with the Hamiltonian being:

(9.3-2-6) $$H = E[f(k,x)] - r_o I_o - r_v I_v - E[g] - E[q] + \Psi\{\alpha I_o + \beta m I_v - (n+\delta-\sigma_h^2)E[k]\} + \varphi\{a + (u\sigma_h+\sigma_o+\sigma_v-n+\sigma_h^2)E[x] - (\sigma_h+u)E[x]\}$$

Here I_o and I_v are control variables, k and x the state variables, and Ψ and φ the corresponding co-state variables. By Pontryagin maximum principle (for example, see Macki and Strauss 1982), we have the necessary conditions as follows:

(9.3-2-7) $\partial H/\partial I_o = -r_o - \partial E[g]/\partial I_o - \partial E[q]/\partial I_o + \Psi\alpha + \varphi\sigma_o E[x] = 0$

(9.3-2-8) $\Psi^{\cdot} = r\Psi - \partial H/\partial E[k]$

(9.3-2-9) $\partial H/\partial I_v = -r_v - \partial E[g]/\partial I_v - \partial E[q]/\partial I_v + \Psi\beta m + \varphi\sigma_v E[x] = 0$

(9.3-2-10) $\varphi^{\cdot} = r\varphi - \partial H/\partial E[x]$

with $k^{\cdot} = \partial H/\partial\Psi$ (i.e., Eq. (9.3-2-4)) and $x^{\cdot} = \partial H/\partial\varphi$ (i.e., Eq. (9.3-2-5)).

In the following, we shall first derive the steady-state equilibrium level of the per capita stock k and that of its shadow price Ψ. From Eq. (9.3-2-7), we get

(9.3-2-11) $-q' + (-r_o-\alpha g'+\Psi\alpha)/\sigma_o = -\varphi E[x]$,

where $g' \equiv \partial E[g]/\partial E[k^{\cdot}]$ and $q' \equiv \partial E[q]/\partial E[x^{\cdot}]$. Then, from Eq. (9.3-2-9), we get

$$(9.3\text{-}2\text{-}12)\quad q' + (-r_v - \beta m g' + \beta m \Psi)/\sigma_v = -\varphi E[x].$$

Now from Eqs. (9.3-2-11) and (9.3-2-12), we have

$$(9.3\text{-}2\text{-}13)\quad \Psi = [r_v(\sigma_o/\sigma_v) - r_o]/[\beta m(\sigma_o/\sigma_v) - \alpha] \; + \; g'.$$

By setting $k^{\cdot} = 0$, we derive

$$(9.3\text{-}2\text{-}14)\quad \Psi = [r_v(\sigma_o/\sigma_v) - r_o] \,/\, [\beta m(\sigma_o/\sigma_v) - \alpha],$$

i.e., the equation for $E[k^{\cdot}] = 0$.

Furthermore, from Eq. (9.3-2-8),

$$(9.3\text{-}2\text{-}15)\quad \Psi^{\cdot} = \Psi(r+n+\delta-\sigma_h^2) + g'(n+\delta-\sigma_h^2) - \partial E[f]/\partial E[k].$$

Now let $\Psi^{\cdot} = 0$, and then

$$(9.3\text{-}2\text{-}16)\quad \Psi = \{\partial E[f]/\partial E[k] - (n+\delta-\sigma_h^2)g'\} \,/\, (r+n+\delta-\sigma_h^2).$$

Further, let $E[k^{\cdot}] = 0$. Then, finally, we have

$$(9.3\text{-}2\text{-}17)\quad \Psi = \{\partial E[f]/\partial E[k]\} \,/\, (r+n+\delta-\sigma_h^2)$$

being a bell-shaped curve.

Next, we derive the steady-state equilibrium value of the per capita cultural level x and that of its shadow price φ as follows. From Eq. (9.3-2-10), we get

$$\varphi = \{\partial E[f]/\partial E[x] - q'(u\sigma_h + \sigma_o' + \sigma_v' - n + \sigma_h^2)\}/(r + u\sigma_h + \sigma_o' + \sigma_v' - n + \sigma_h^2)$$

Now let $E[x^{\cdot}] = 0$, and then we derive

$$(9.3\text{-}2\text{-}18)\quad \varphi = \{\partial E[f]/\partial E[x]\}/(r + u\sigma_h + \sigma_o' + \sigma_v' - n + \sigma_h^2)$$

as the equation for $\varphi^{\cdot} = 0$, which is also a bell-shaped curve.

Further, from Eq. (9.3-2-7), we get

$$(9.3\text{-}2\text{-}19)\quad \Psi = (r_o + \alpha g' + \sigma_o q' - \varphi\sigma_o E[x]/\alpha.$$

From Eq. (9.3-2-9), $-r_v - \beta m g' - \sigma_v q' + \beta m \Psi = -\varphi\sigma_v E[x]$,

and therefore,

$$(9.3\text{-}2\text{-}20)\quad \Psi = \{r_v + \beta m g' + \sigma_v q' + \varphi\sigma_v E[x]\}/(\beta m)$$

Now from the above Eqs. (9.3-2-19) and (9.3-2-20), we have

$$(9.3\text{-}2\text{-}21)\quad \varphi = [\beta m(r_o + \sigma_o) - \alpha(r_v + \sigma_v q')] \,/\, \{E[x](\beta m\sigma_o - \alpha\sigma_v)\}$$

Let $E[x^{\cdot}] = 0$, and by Eq. (9.3-2-21), we derive

(9.3-2-22) $\varphi = [ßm(r_o/r_v)-\alpha] / \{E[x](ßm(\sigma_o/\sigma_v)-\alpha\}$

being a hyperbola.

§9.3-3 Culture, Technology and The Steady-State Economy

From the above Eqs. (9.3-2-14) and (9.3-2-17), we solve for the steady-state equilibrium levels of the per capita stock $E[k]^*$ and its shadow price Ψ^* (see Figure 9.3-3-1).

Figure 9.3-3-1
Steady-State Equilibrium Levels of $(\Psi, E[k])$

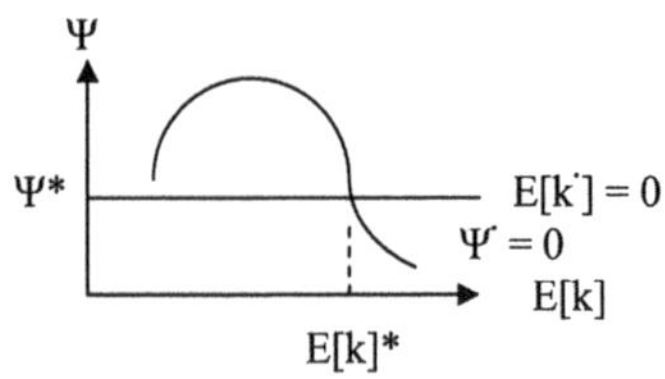

For this analysis, first, suppose

(9.3-3-1) $\Delta[ßm(\sigma_o/\sigma_v)-\alpha] > \Delta[r_v(\sigma_o/\sigma_v)-r_o]$,

where Δ is the change in a term immediately following it. Eq. (9.3-3-1) means that the cultural impactor Γ_2 has a bigger impact on the level of technological progress than the cultural impactor Γ_1 and the impact of the cultural creativity on technology is more powerful than the impact of technology on the cultural creativity. This is a reasonable assumption. First, when the per capita cultural creativity raises the technological efficiency, because of the role of monopolists in the high-tech industries or sector, in Eq. (9.3-2-14), r_v will decrease relative to the value of r_v; and because of positive profits, I_v will increase, and consequently as σ_v increases, ßm will increase even more. And although (σ_o/σ_v) will decrease, $ßm(\sigma_o/\sigma_v)$ as a whole will increase. That is, the impact of ßm will dominate that of (σ_o/σ_v). Therefore, as the per capita cultural level and the technology both rise, Ψ in Eq. (9.3-2-14) will go down. Hence, the curve $E[k^{\cdot}] = 0$ will shift downward.

Secondly, as the cultural creativity advances, the per capita marginal efficiency of capital will increase, due to shift-factor effect. Therefore the curve $\Psi^{\cdot} = 0$ in Eq. (9.3-2-17) will shift upward. Now combining the two effects mentioned above, as per capita level of technology goes up, in the steady-state equilibrium, Ψ will go down, and $E[k]$ will go up.

From the above Eqs. (9.3-2-18) and (9.3-2-22), we solve for the steady-state equilibrium values of the per capita cultural level $E[x]^*$ and its shadow price φ^* (see Figure 9.3-3-2).

Suppose we have:

(9.3-3-2) $\Delta\{E[x](\beta m(\sigma_o/\sigma_v)-\alpha) > \Delta\beta m(r_o/r_v)-\alpha]$

Figure 9.3-3-2
Steady-State Equilibrium Levels of $(\varphi,E[x])$

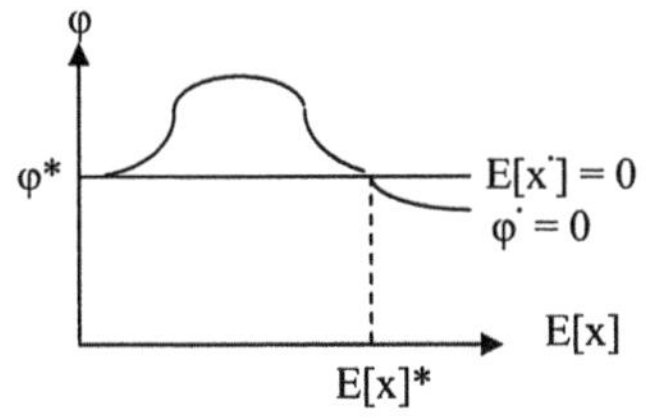

Here Eq. (9.3-3-2) means that the cultural impactor Γ_2 has a bigger impact on the level of technological progress than the cultural impactor Γ_1 and the impact of the cultural creativity on technology is greater than the impact of production costs on technology. That is, when the per capita cultural creativity rises, because of the roles of the self-creating life-will and especially the systemic rationality in developing and advancing new and better ideas of production, the level of technology is certainly higher. However, in most cases, as the level of technology goes up, the costs of production will go up. Here we meant the progress of technological efficiency outweighs the rising costs of production, and the efficiency of technological progress dominates the efficiency of product repetition and imitation in raising the level of national income of a cultural economy.

First, as mentioned in the above, in Eq. (9.3-2-22), the impact of βm is stronger than the impact of r_v on technology and therefore, as (σ_o/σ_v) goes down, $\beta m(\sigma_o/\sigma_v)$ will go up. And further because of the multiple effect of E[x], relatively, as $\beta m(r_o/r_v)-\alpha]$ increases, $\{E[x](\beta m(\sigma_o/\sigma_v)-\alpha)$ will increase to even a larger degree. Therefore, φ in Eq. (9.3-2-22) may become smaller. At the same time, due to the factor of monopsony (assuming its existence as a dual to monopoly), r_o/r_v becomes even smaller. Therefore, as the per capita cultural level rises, the technological efficiency will also rise, and hence φ in Eq. (9.3-2-22) will go up. That is, the curve $E[\dot{x}] = 0$ will shift downward.

Secondly, as the per capita cultural level is higher, the marginal product of culture will not change. At this time, E[k]* is higher at the steady-state equilibrium following the same reasoning as presented in the previous case of analysis. Therefore, $\partial E[f]/\partial E[x]$ in Eq. (9.3-2-18) will go up; and hence, the bell-shaped curve $\dot{\varphi} = 0$ will shift up.

In general, as technology rises, the steady-state equilibrium level of φ will go down and that of E[x] will go up.

Before the end of this section, note that in different cultural economies, the values of α and β are different. Thus in the steady-state equilibrium, for different cultural economies, E[k]*, Ψ*, E[x]* and φ* shall be different.

§9.3-4 Brief Remarks and Conclusion

To study the interactions between culture and the economy, two simple systems and three composite systems of culture were introduced. As the mathematical frame of analysis, we presented our innovative model by integrating a stochastic equation of cultural accumulation with a deterministic optimal control model. This above analysis concludes that, in general, investment and cultural policies have significant effects on the steady-state equilibrium levels of relevant variables. In particular, under favorable conditions (which are asserted under a reasonable hypothesis), investment and cultural policies have positive effects on the steady-state equilibrium level of capital stock and the cultural level of the steady-state equilibrium.

After the discussions of the above subsections, now a few remarks are in order. First, in the long-term trend of East Asian Countries moving toward the East Asian Union, cultural aspects of the afore-mentioned economies should be studied carefully. In East Asian, Taoism, Confucianism, Buddhism, Shintoism, Islam and Christianity all play important roles in the process of economic development and advancement. To integrate these factors into a single economic entity, the coordination of these diverse cultures becomes a very challenging task.

Due to higher values of the coefficients of α and β, theoretically speaking, a bi-cultural economy (such as the composite system of centrality and harmony) and tri-cultural economy (such as the composite system of centrality and socialization) are at least as efficient as a mono-cultural economy (such as the complex system of tension). Note that, theoretically speaking, a cultural economy of tension (i.e., composite system of equilibrium and tension) is as efficient as a cultural economy of harmony.

Secondly, the composite system of centrality and socialization may be more appropriate to serve as a model for a large country than for a small country of East Asia. By contrast, the composite system of centrality and harmony is seen as more suitable to serve as a model for a small country of East Asia.

§9.3-5 Comparison between The Pure and Cultural Economies

From Eqs. (9.3-1-2), (9.3-1-4) and (9.3-1-5) in the above, we derive the stochastic control model of a pure economy (without any cultural variables) as a special case of the aforementioned model of a cultural economy (by setting $\alpha = 1$, $\beta = 1$, $x = 0$ and $x^{*} = 0$):

(9.3-5-1) $$\max_{\{I_o', I_v'\}} \int_0^{\infty} e^{-rt} \{F(K,L) - r_o I_o' - r_v I_v' - g''\} dt$$

s.t.

(9.3-5-2) $$dK = (I_o' + mI_v' - \delta K)dt$$

(9.3-5-3) $$dL = nLdt + \sigma_h L dW,$$

for $I_o' \geq 0$ and $I_v' \geq 0$.

Similar to the methods presented in the above, we derive the stochastic control model of a pure economy in terms of per capita measure below:

(9.3-5-4) $$\max_{\{I_o',I_v'\}} \int_0^\infty e^{-rt} \{f(k) - r_o I_o - r_v I_v - g\}dt$$

s.t.

(9.3-5-5) $k^\cdot = I_o + mI_v - (n+\delta-\sigma_h^2)k - \sigma_h k\zeta,$

for $I_o \geq 0$, $I_v \geq 0$. Here $f(k) = F(L,K)/L$, with the Hamiltonian being:

(9.3-5-6) $H = f(k,x)-r_o I_o-r_v I_v-E[g] + \Psi\{I_o+mI_v-(n+\delta-\sigma_h^2)E[k]\}$

Here I_o and I_v are control variables, k the state variable and Ψ the corresponding co-state variable. By Pontryagin maximum principle, we have the necessary conditions as follows:

(9.3-5-7) $\partial H/\partial I_o = -r_o - \partial E[g]/\partial I_o + \Psi = 0$

(9.3-5-8) $\partial H/\partial I_v = -r_v - \partial E[g]/\partial I_v + \Psi m = 0$

(9.3-5-9) $\Psi^\cdot = r\Psi - \partial H/\partial k$

with $k^\cdot = \partial H/\partial\Psi$ (i.e., Eq. (9.3-6-5)).

In the following, we show the steady-state equilibrium level of the per capita stock E[k] and that of its shadow price Ψ of the pure economy:

(9.3-5-10) $\Psi = [r_v(\sigma_o/\sigma_v)-r_o] / [m(\sigma_o/\sigma_v)-1],$

as the trajectory of $E[k^\cdot] = 0$ of the pure economy is a straight line; and

(9.3-5-11) $\Psi = \{\partial E[f]/\partial E[k]\} / (r+n+\delta-\sigma_h^2),$

as the trajectory of $\Psi^\cdot = 0$ of the pure economy, is a bell-shaped curve. Note that here, this k does not operate under any cultural impactor, and here this Ψ is the shadow price of this k. In contrast, the k there in Eq. (9.3-2-14) operates under a cultural impactor, and there in Eq. (9.3-2-17), Ψ is the shadow price of that k in Eq. (9.3-2-14). Naturally , these corresponding variables are not the same.

By comparing the set comprised of Eqs. (9.3-2-14) and (9.3-2-17) with the set comprised of Eqs. (9.3-5-10) and (9.3-5-11), it is clear that, in general, these two afore-mentioned models lead to very different results. The trajectory of Eq. (9.3-2-14) is seen to lie below that of Eq. (9.3-5-10) because, in general, $0 < \alpha < ß$; and the trajectory of Eq. (9.3-2-17) will lie above that of Eq. (9.3-5-11), because under the impact of a cultural impactor, in general, the marginal product of capita stock will be higher. Thus, the steady-state equilibrium level of the capital stock will be higher for a cultural economy than for a pure economy, and the steady-state equilibrium level of the shadow price of the capital stock will be lower for a cultural economy than for a pure economy.

In other words, a cultural economy is more conducive to the growth of capital accumulation than a pure economy. Consequently, through the function of the production function (i.e., output is a positive function of the capital stock), the steady-state equilibrium level of output will thereby be higher for a cultural economy than for a pure economy of cultural neutrality.

9.4 Cultural Creativity and Economic Catch-up

It is predicted that the cultural creativity of China will be the single most important factor for advancing the nation into one of prosperity in the 21st century.

The cultural creativity breeds the technological creativity, and from there, the economic creativity will develop well.

One of the keys for modern East Asia, including China, to develop new culture in this century is to surpass the cultures of sciences, democracy and capitalism of the West (Tonn [1994]). By absorbing the cultures of the West, it may help non-Western nations to eradicate their cultural burdens from the past. But to catch-up to the West, a nation will have to surpass both the traditional cultures of its own and the modern cultures of the West. Since it is extremely difficult to fully absorb the merits of foreign cultures, an act of just imitating foreign cultures is far from sufficient to enable any non-Western nation to catch up to the cultures of the West. New spirit and new rationality are needed for advancing an old culture to a new height.

In a systemic notation, a process of catching up to the West is to create a systemic complex of bi-cultures or triple cultures comprising the systems of {tech creativity,organ creativity|cul creavitity} and {domestic old culture, new foreign culture|cul creativity}.

Chapter 10 - Competition between The United States and The East Asian Union

At the end of the twentieth century, in terms of political, economic and military strengths, the world is a system with a super power (U.S.) and four secondary powers (China, European Union, Russia and Japan). But in terms of cultural advancement, at the end of the twentieth century, the world is one with two super powers (U.S. and European Union), one emerging super power and two secondary powers (Russia and Islam). In the area of lower and practical cultures, such as those of computer and fast foods, the U.S. stands out as the leader of the world. And yet in the area of high cultures, such as those manifested in the cultural systems of Heidegger, Sartre, Habermas, Derrida, and Foucault, Western Europe is the giant and East Asia is an emerging giant.[9] Here by the language of center-periphery, super power is the center, secondary power is a semi-center, and the non-central member is one of the countries in the periphery.

In the world system of the twenty–first century, weak countries, societies and social groups are far from being their own masters, respectively. In this world system, mass media manipulates the low cultures, and global corporations control the world economy to fit their own agenda.

The twenty-first century may witness the beginning of a new era of the human history. But it appears more likely to be a world system of multiple super-powers (two to three super powers) and multiple major powers, in which, amid close cooperation and mutual assistance among nations, people of different races are struggling against others and eagerly vying for dominance and hegemony.

The topic of the whole world is definitely overwhelming. Below, for us to remain focused, we shall narrow the cope of our discussions and restrict them only to the future perspectives of the United States and East Asia.

10.1 The Cultural Economy of The United States

It may be appropriate to draw a graph to reflect the position of the United States as the center of the world. Following Figure 1.1 of Chapter 1, Figure 10-1-1 is developed below to show the world of systemic distribution in which the TCentral position is at Z. Note that this Tcentral position, currently occupied by the United States, is the position of self-masterism for the United States.

In facing the rising challenge of a new center, one passive strategy for the current center of the world, i.e., the United States, to adopt is to prevent the emerging nation from moving to position such as $Z^{LTarget}$ (i.e., the position of (x^{+},y) in Figure 10.1-1).

An active strategy for the current center of the world to pursue is to move northeast-bound toward $Z^{RivalCenter}$, (i.e., the position of $[(x^{++},y^{++}),\gamma)$ in Figure 10.1-2) by creating new technologies and industries γ.

To move onto this new path, the United States may have to deal with some forces of inertia from within. Among them, some of the factors are: (1) The poor citizens will demand a higher level of welfare spending due to the nature of democracy and the underlying concept of social justice. (2) The pressure of the ethnic minority groups for them to have ever enlarging roles in politics which will then increase the level of government spending on the ethnic minorities, all other things being equal. (3) The continual desire to dominate the world militarily which will then demand a high level of military budget to be spend on the vast areas of the world. (4) Due to the ideology of capitalism, not sufficient attention has been paid to the role of pure sciences and mathematics. (5) The affluence of the society reduces the incentives of the citizen to pursue pure sciences and basic technology. (6) The flow of immigration is expected to channel less of talented youths to this country in the future, due to the war on "terrorism" and the changing cultural and economic positions of the United States vis-à-vis those of the developing countries in the world.

Figure 10.1-1
Anti-TCentral strategic path of the world leader Z: Z = the current position of the world leader; Z^{Target} = the (short-term?) target position of Z; Z' = the emerging new center

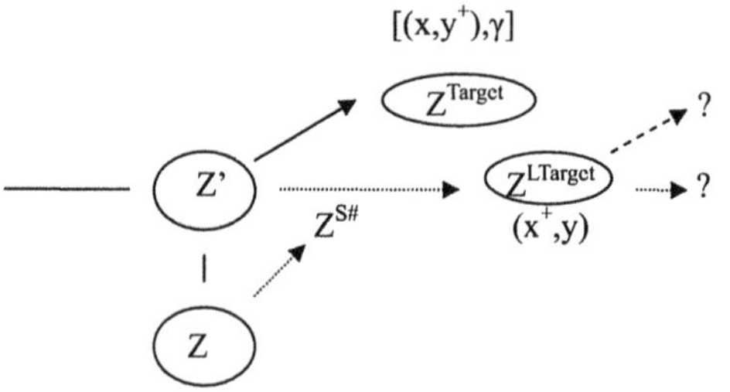

Figure 10.1-2
Anti-TCentral strategic path of the Rival center of Z

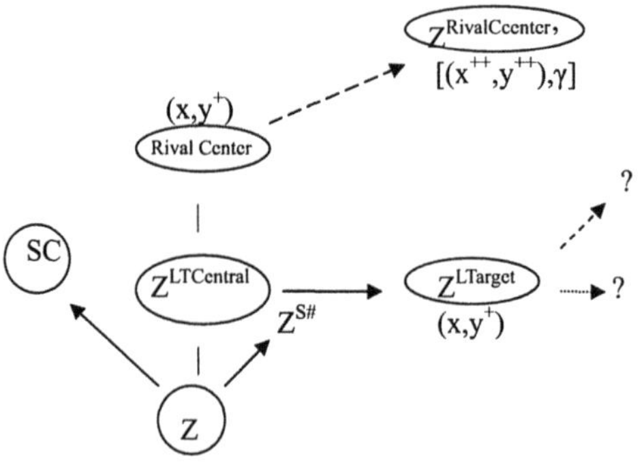

As the most recent events unfold, the U.S.' adventure into Middle East and Central Asia – for controlling precious petroleum resources and the heartland of World Continent, with a stated objective of fighting against terrorism and an incessant desire to spread the ideology of democratic capitalism, may prove to be one of the most significant developments of the human kind in history. Nonetheless, one has to wait and see whether this would become one of a few key factors contributing decisively to the eventual weakening of the U.S. hegemonic power.

10.2 Issues of East Asian Union or New Union

In the long-term trend of East Asian Countries moving toward "East Asian Union" (or "Union of East Asia"), cultural aspects of the afore-mentioned economies should be studied carefully. In East Asia, Taoism, Confucianism, Buddhism, Shintoism, Islam and Christianity all play important roles in the process of economic development and advancement. To integrate these economies into a single economic entity, the coordination and integration of diverse and even inter-conflicting and contradicting cultures become the most important factor of new cultural advancement.

One approach to this integrating factor of new cultural advancement is to consider the culture of self-masterism previously presented. That is, it appears great for East Asia to develop its system of self-masterism amid the new trend of globalism.

The East Asian Union may comprise Mongolia, North and South Koreas, Indochina, Indonesia and nations of Chinese people. By modeling after the European Union, the first step of this new union could be a close economic and cultural union of several core nations. Then political union will be established. In terms of the integration of China with countries of Indochina, other than strengthening the Mekong river network, the railroads connecting China and Myanmar, China and Lao, Myanmar and Lao, Lao and Thailand and Lao and Vietnam must be constructed. At the same time, institutions like the Asian Monetary Unit and the Cultural and Technological Universities of East Asia could be created to foster the interchanging of ideas and technical ingenuity among the people of East Asia. Political union will be the last step of the long-term process of the integration of the people and countries of East Asia.

In the future, this East Asian Union may be further developed into "New Union" by a spirit of voluntarism, cooperation and mutual trust in its process of absorbing countries of South Asia, Middle East, North Africa, Oceania, Russia and even countries of Central and South Americas into its membership. In this process of advancing new culture while preserving significant diversity of local cultural heritages, Sinic culture and the cultures of India, Islam and Russia would play important roles in the formation of the culture of New Union – a global culture amid local cultural diversity.

The establishment of a multi-regional society depends very much on the advancement of new technologies and new consensus among all involved. The principles of freedom, human rights, equality among strong-and-weak must be honored, and the actual pursuit of the true-self must be cherished. The principles of justice and self-masterism cannot be a matter of lip service, used as a pretext of establishing the hegemony of a few people or a country. Those are weak must be given rooms to preserve themselves. Although every one is supposed to be altruist, self-help is the ultimate criterion in guiding the principle of who should be helped.

The technological, economical and political developments are essential for human advancement. Nevertheless, ultimately, cultural advancement is the key to human emancipation.

10.3 East Asia's Creation of New Culture

In East Asia, one way to create new culture (Tonn [1996]) is in general to go beyond the culture of the West; and in particular, to transcend and go beyond the methods of sciences in the academic world and to transcend and ascend beyond the myth of democracy in the political construction of a nation.

One of the essential ingredients of the method of sciences is to decompose the whole (or the macrostructure) into numerous independent units (or microstructures). But in cultural and social areas of theoretical developments, essentially this scientific direction has hardly been prioritized in the West.

Below, take economics as an important example. By the scientific approach, the scholars of the West have never constructed a coherent macroeconomics based on rigorous microeconomic foundations. This shows that the Western economics is not (yet) a science. But one area of the most serious inadequacy of this economics lies in the fact that, although the macroeconomics centers its development on the functions of the (central) government, it has no provision for the structural study of any efficient government in its cultural foundation.

Apparently, this deficiency of macroeconomics stems from the deficiency of the Western microeconomics. It is well known that scholars of the West never developed any sensible microeconomics based on human and cultural conditions. Reasoning in a traditional and "non-logical" way, "economics as a discipline of sciences" must depend its academic foundations on metaphysics which, by any definition, is simply not a science. That is, before the development of metaphysics as a science (i.e., as a discipline of sciences), no academic venture in attempting to transform culture into a science may be justified. And thereby, the intrinsic contradiction between the idea of social field-studies as sciences (as fields of applied mathematics, physics and engineering) and sciences (as rigorous entities constructed on the basis of mathematics and quantitative experimental methods) could not be reconciled easily.

It is clear that this deficiency in the traditional economics can be remedied easily by our systemic approach, by going beyond the mathematic system of numbers in developing new methods of reasoning. Systematics is not a science, and yet it is far from being an anti-science. It is fair to say that, in the traditional economics, scholars turn economics into a "field of applied mathematics." Similarly, some scholars of traditional approach may, perhaps subconsciously, wish to transform the studies of politics, sociology and other socio-cultural fields into those of applied mathematics.

According to the conventional approach, what is valid as theorems of mathematics is automatically assumed to be valid in economics and other fields of socio-cultural studies. Practically, this method of science appears to be excellent. But philosophically though, in a pretty ironical way, it is the inconsistency between the theorems of the number system and the nature and cultural tendency of the human being that makes the traditional economics truly "anti-scientific" in its academic endeavor.

Specifically, in the traditional economic thinking, the government is assumed to be a necessary evil, developed perhaps indirectly and yet powerfully from the idea of the least government in the political philosophies of John Locke and David Hume (Chang [1970], pp. 308, 324-325). To say the government is a necessary evil, the other interpretation may be that, although it (i.e., the government officials as a whole) is rational, the government under democracy can not represent the true interests of the people, but can only represent the sum of different interest groups who are in constant conflict. Because this sum is very often irrational or even anti-rational (actually self-contradictory most of the time), the government representing it has no way to behave rationally. Thus, in general, there is no efficient government under democracy. Here the so-called efficient government may be just a small but effective government.

Obviously, by the scientific approach, scholars of the West have never been able to develop successful cultural and social systems of sciences at the micro level and then integrate them into the cultural and social systems at the macro level. This must be due to the very limited scope of the scientific methods to be applied directly to human and socio-cultural studies.

What is equally obvious is that, by any scientific approach, scholars in the West have so far failed to develop a satisfactory theory of management in dealing with the business world, not to say to integrate this business management theory with economics.

All these failures mentioned in the above point to the limitations of the scientific methods (Tonn [2006]). And yet, we do not mean the traditional economics is not powerful. What we mean is that: (1) The traditional eocnmics is not very scientific. Perhaps it is very a-scientific. (2) The success use of scientific methods must be guided by some cultural and structural methods. In this regard, systematics is treated as one of the cultural and structural methods of socio-cultural studies.

An important theoretical foundation of democracy of the West is the God-based natural law. For a non-Christian country of East Asia, theoretically, the need to go beyond democracy is urgent. To develop a polity by a route different from that of the West, one has to ignore the argument of the "end of history" advanced by Francis Fukuyama. The theory of the "end of history" is way too ideological and not very academic.

One way for East Asia to go beyond democracy is to consider a political system like the polity of self-masterism: a system of two-tier governments. (1) The President of the legislative and executive branches of the government. This is an idea of efficient government but not one of internal conflict and balance. (2) The President of the Academia. Partially inspired Huang Tsunghsi of Ming Dynasty, this is an institution of the intellectuals established to integrate the functions of education, research and development in sciences and technology, judiciary branch of government and "supervision and control". These two Presidents are directly elected by the people in order to create a balance of power between them. One "logical" approach is to design a system to prevent the capitalists from controlling the government as is a norm in the West. Further, this system would deprive the politicians their absolute power in manipulating the government.

Under a system of self-masterism, endowed with a culture different from that of the natural law-based utilitarianism while preserving the very spirit of democracy and human freedom, an efficient government may be established. If so, this will be an important example of cultural advantages (or efficiency) in the political development of East Asia.

This system of two-tier governments may not be appropriate for any country of the West. This is because: (1) the West lacks the traditions of Confucianism/Taoism, (2) the West is deeply immersed in the philosophy of utilitarianism, and (3) Christian ethics underlying the Western society is not strong enough in controlling effectively the daily behavior of a typical Western citizen.

In the example of the possible polity of self-masterism presented in the above, the role of the Academia includes the control of national enterprises and the design and execution of the medium- and long-term plans of national development. As a conceptual framework, this system may serve as a proto-type institution of cultural self-masterism to be distinctively different from those of capitalism and socialism (Tonn [1999]).

In sum, the development of East Asia in the twenty-first century must start with the development of an institution like the Asian Union. In this new century, in the world, there appears to have three major cultural systems: the "being culture" of Europe (i.e., the culture of individual competition, anxiety and technology), the "transcendental culture" of North America (i.e., the culture of individual competition, Christianity and technology), and the "yu-wu culture" of East Asia (the culture of competition amid a balance between humanity and technology). In this new era, on the basis of the absorbed cultures of the West, the culture of East Asia will develop by leap and bound, while the Christian culture of the West may at first encounter a series of unprecedented crises and then rejuvenate after that.

10.4 China's Road to Self-Masterism

In the world of the twenty-first century, in the areas of politics, economic power and culture, there may have two super powers: the U.S. and China. In this century, it appears to be very unlikely that China would catch up to the U.S. in the areas of global politics and technological development on a per capita base. But in terms of political system, China could develop an independent system (self-masterism, liberal Faziranism or the like). This will be a proto-type system of global culturalism in which the essentials of liberal democracy (individual freedom and initiative toward technological advancement) and the noble ideas of the intellectuals (intellectuals' impact on social development) are preserved.

In terms of gross national product, China may catch up to that of the U.S. in this new century. But the U.S. controls the World Ocean with numerous strategic land and island bases. Therefore, in terms of naval and air powers, China can never hope to catch up to the U.S. in this time period. Thus, for China to advance its military power, it appears that the only feasible option is to develop the military forces of outer space -- manned mission to the moon and colonization of the moon and beyond, by employing a leap strategy of military-technological advancement.

In the *improved world of systemic distribution* characterized by the YY 5-polar MFCE scheme (see Figure 10.4-2, which is an improved scheme over Figures 10.1-1 and 10.1-2), theoretically we can locate the TCentral position of the system as $Z^{LTCentral}$ in the case of China.

Now in the first decade of the twenty-first century, apparently China is not in it TCentral position. Further, the world of twenty-first century, presented by a YY 5-polar MFCE scheme, has only one center occupied by the United States. Thus, the TCentral position of the system is not a position of self-masterism. Thus the relevant scheme for China is a YY 5-polar MFCE scheme with multiple centers.

By looking at Figure 10.4-1, we locate the position of the rival center (which has the characteristics of x^+ and y^{++}) at the north of the graph center (i.e., the TCentral position of Z). For China, starting at the position of X (in Firgure 10.4-2), the long-term target position of Z (i.e., $X^{LTTarget} = [(x^+,y^{++}),\varepsilon]$, ε being a new industry) will be at the northeast side of the TCentral of Z. The short-term target will be close to the TCentral of Z (i.e., $Z^{TCentral}$), while the very long-term target will lie to a position to the northeast side of $Z^{LTTarget}$ (which is actually uncertain due to the necessary reactions to the world leader.

This very long-term target of X shall have the characteristics of x^{+++} and y^{+++}, for x^{+++} being the characteristics of having a component of x stronger than x^{+++} (and similarly for y^{+++}). This is because by adopting a leap strategy, the very long-term target of Z is to supersede the rival (with position of $[(x^+,y^{++}),\gamma]$) in terms of the characteristics of z and leaving the characteristics of y in Z to be somewhat lagging to that of the rival center, while paying much less attention to the strength of other characteristics.

Figure 10.4-1
Systemic distribution of Z: TCentral and non-TCentral positions of Z; $Z^{TCentral} \equiv (x,y)$, x=yin, y =yang.

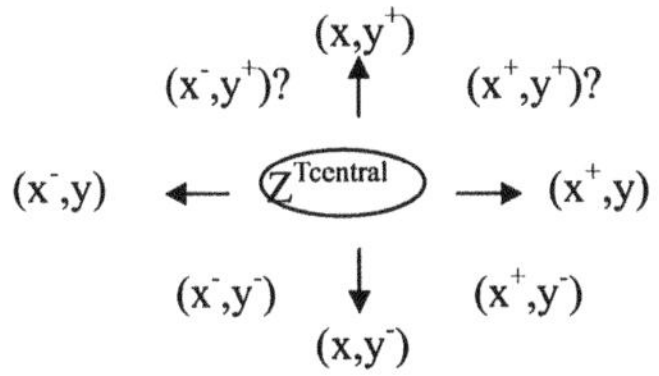

Figure 10.4-2
Anti-TCentral strategic path of Z: $Z^{TCentral}$ = TCentral position of Z; $Z^{S\#}$=short-term target of Z; $Z^{LTTarget}$ = long-term target position of Z; Z^{VLT}=very long-term target of Z (at the position of $[(x^{+++},y^{+++}),\varepsilon,\lambda]$, with λ being the newest industry); Rival center = position of the rival of Z, $Z^{S\#}$=short-term target of Z

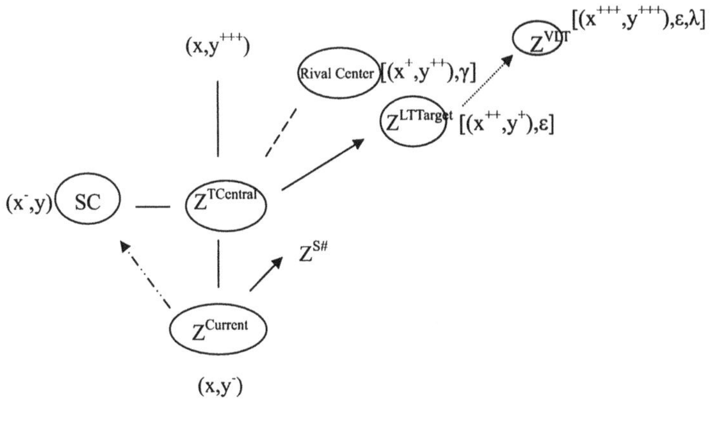

Remark 10.4-1. (1) For X ≡ Z in Figure 10.4-2, we may have:

(10.4-1) $X(.) = [\alpha_2 X(\mathbb{H}_2;.) \oplus \alpha_1 X(\mathbb{H}_1;.) \oplus \alpha_0 X(\mathbb{H}_0;.)] \circledast Ix(\mathbb{H};.)$.
where $X(\mathbb{H}_2;.)$ represents the forces of $X^{LTarget}$ and X^{VL}, $X(\mathbb{H}_1;.)$ represents the force of $X^{S\#}$, and $X(\mathbb{H}_0;.)$ represents the forces of X staying as X over time. (2) The solution of a becoming like Bcm. (10.4-1) depends very much on the problem itself.

Below, for this Z, we write an 8-polar MFCE scheme: $Y = \{Z, Z^A, Z^{Rcenter}, Z^{SC}, Z^{S\#}, Z^{TC}, Z^{LT}, Z^{VLT}\}$, where Z^A (called y_1 for convenience), $X^{Rcenter}$ (also called y_2), Z^{SC} (also called y_3), $Z^{S\#}$ (also called y_4), Z^{TC} (also called y_5), Z^{LT} (also called y_6) and Z^{VLT} (also called y_7) denote the actual or current position of Z, the rival center of Z, the strategic-continuity position of Z, the sort-term target of Z, the long-term target of Z, and the very long-term target of Z which is also the self-mastering state of Z, respectively.

In terms of the TD-TS model, the development of the Chinese economy over time is seen as a transformation of the old TS-TD model to the new TS'-TD' model (see Figure10.4-3).

Seeing from Figure 10-4-3, at time $t = i$, we have y_i derived from the intersection of TS and TD curves. Then a d-systemism of TD-TS system at time i is the new TS-TD system at time j, and we have $y_i \rightarrow y_j$, where y_j is derived from the intersection of TS' and TD' curves at time $t = j$.

Note that TD is a graphical representation of a grand system, and the TS curve can be considered as the graphical representation of the following grand system (see Section 3.4): TS =: $\{(\rho,\omega)|(P,q)^+\} \equiv \lbrace\{[x_k(h_k^*, v_j, IRI_k(\rho,\omega),.)]|(P,q|R^+;O)\|(\mathbb{C}, Z(\mathfrak{C}_{co})) =<T^B\} \Subset \text{Ш}^{\text{Д}}\rbrace$ ($\mathfrak{C}_{co}$ being the cultural core of the grand system). By combining the human cultural factors (ρ,ω), the public and private decision-making and strategic complexes (Z), changing domestic factors such as a new educational system and changing environments of the global economy, the production structure of the economy in question transforms from a flat system to a mix of flat and steep systems. That is, d: $(TS,TD)_i \rightarrow (TS,TD)_j$, where d is an impactor of d-systemism in the period t_i -t_j. Consequently, the level of income is higher: $y_i < y_j$ (in terms of values).

Figure 10.4-3
Transformation of TD-TS model

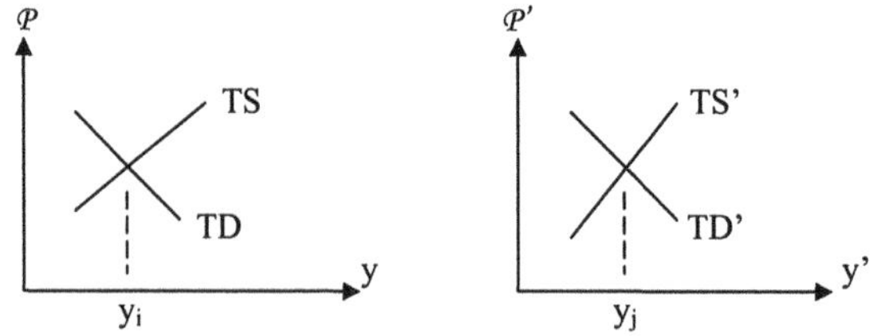

Furthermore, notice that the product mix of y_i is different from that of y_j in the sense that the former has productive sectors of lower level technologies, while the latter has high levels of frontier industries (such as those involved in aerospace activities and outer-space explorations).

Then, we may have the static and dynamic representations of the systemic-change becoming of Y as (analogous to Bcms. (B.1-1-5) and (B.1-1-6), with all the necessary systemisms permissible and with X being denoted as y_0):

(10.4-2) $Y = (y_1 \oplus y_2 \oplus y_3 \oplus y_4 \oplus y_5 \oplus y_6 \oplus y_7 \oplus y_0) \circledast Iy$,

(10.4-3) $y(.) = [\alpha_7 y(\mathbb{H}_7;.) \oplus \alpha_6 y(\mathbb{H}_6;.) \oplus \alpha_5 y(\mathbb{H}_5;.) \oplus \alpha_4 y(\mathbb{H}_4;.) \oplus \alpha_3 y(\mathbb{H}_3;.)$
$\oplus \alpha_2 y(\mathbb{H}_2;.) \oplus \alpha_1 x(\mathbb{H}_1;.) \oplus \alpha_0 y(\mathbb{H}_0;.)] \circledast Iy(\mathbb{H};.)$.

Specifically, the new frontier facing China appears to be establishing a permanent base on the Moon and beyond. This is related to both new frontiers of technologies, military activities and human mentality. China can not hope to compete successfully and rationally against the United States in the areas of air force and navy in a few decades. Militarily, one of the best choices facing China is to concentrate its development on the creation and formation of the "exterrestrial military forces" (outer-space or cosmic military forces) while the United States is bogging down substantially by its commitment to maintain and control the land and island bases of military significance on earth..

Now to finish this Chapter, a few remarks are in order. It may be said that one major hurdle facing the military planners of Beijing is the issue of Taiwan independence. Since the top priority of the Chinese military concern for centuries to come is to develop the outer space military forces, the strategic position of Taiwan as the opening door of China to the Pacific Island chains is becoming much less essential. In this new century, only the country that controls the outer space will be in a favorable position to control the Pacific Ocean! Thus, the strategic value of Taiwan to China is actually rapidly decreasing over time. But a similar assessment may not be true vis-à-vis the United States, due to the important role of Taiwan as a military forefront in defending Japan and due to the eroding relationship between the United States and South Korea. Once Taiwan is lost to China, the United States can not even hope to control the Philippines!

Chapter 11 - Brief Summary and Concluding Remarks

After elaborate studies of the economics of culture in this Part II in the above, it is time to have a brief summary. In our simplified approach, we start with the human rationality and life-will in order to establish the cultural factors of the human being in investigating the formations of demand and supply curves on one hand and in uncovering the structural strata of human organization on the other hand.

In the above, we establish the principles of CE balance and strategic centrality as the counter parts of the equilibrium concept derived with the help of mathematical method of optimization. Our methods are closely related to the concepts of TCentral and CE balance-centrality, and our philosophical foundations rely partially on the YWTC scheme (Yu-Wu Tao-Chi) and the YYWX scheme (i.e., yinyang five-elements).

With brief presentations of the cultural economies of the United States and China in the above, we point out the potential trends of the developments of these two economies in the future: for the United States to purse a golden strategy in keeping a delicate balance between promoting the maximal growth of its domestic economy and maintaining its super power position and for China to pursue a leap strategy for fostering its programs of outer-space exploration. We hope our systematic (i.e., systemic) approach to the economics of culture has much to offer in unfolding the underworlds of any human economy.

In sum, the future of the United states lies in a long-term process of cultural renewal and advancement and in tackling effectively the worldly issues like controlling rapid population growth, minimizing the costs of social welfare and military expenditures, promoting high quality education – establishing Federal Universities, removing the "essential racial quota system" in college admissions, engaging in the development new technological frontier and in the outer-space exploration, creating a core region of rapid inter-metropolitan transportation system, and handling well the rising power of Hispanic ethic group. It is predicted that eventually the U.S. would absorb Mexico into its national boundary. Then the gradual process of the "indigenization of the United States" (or the "development of the indigenous culture of Americas") may prove to be the single most important issue facing this country in centuries to come.

In contrast, China's road to self-masterism in this new century is basically in the development of new ethical codes, new socio-economy and new polity by creating a new and more advanced complex of life-will and rationality in facing the extremely difficult challenges of a new world of multiple centers. Note that this new polity should have an essential spirit of democracy-like self-masterism for each citizen involved. Definitely some of the most urgent issues are the creation of viable ethical standards for the society, population control, sex balance among children, education, social justice for all, ethnic equity, development of advanced sciences, new technologies and frontier industries, and peaceful unification with Taiwan with Taiwan maintaining an independent nation (for instance, in a form of the Union of Chinese Nations).

Now a few remarks are in order. First, the contributions of systematics to the socio-human studies may not be that limited. Since the mathematical methods probably contribute at best 70 percent to our understanding of these fields, it is hoped that this systemic approach will contribute at least additional 15 percent more knowledge to these fields.

Secondly, it is a joy for our humanistic approach to add a lot of fun to the study of the socio-human fields. Mathematic approach itself may prove to be too mechanistic for our mind. That is, humanistic and systematic approach to socio-cultural studies are trscendental as well as asthetic-aspirational in elevating our sense of the meaning of life.

Thirdly, it is firmly believed that, this method of systematics is more than breaking a new ground in the fields of cultural and socio-human studies. In the future, it may prove to be extremely useful in the field-study of physical worlds as well. This should not be a surprise at all to the well-informed scholars, since the original methods of Yu-WuTCentral (YWTC) and YYWX schemes were successfully employed in the creation of the pre-sciences of ancient China.

Now we have one more remark. In a capitalist economy, the efficiency of the private sector may be overestimated in the conventional approach. This can be seen from Themata 8.3-1 and 8.3-2, in which G strategy of Country A may entail the use of national power in financing R&D activities of the private sector. The G^+ strategy of B may entail the use of the public-owned civilian sector in order to promote the technological development of the nation. In the latter case, it is the culture and the efficiency of the civil servants that makes this contribution possible.

In the case of Country A using public resources to benefit some private entities, it may proceed like the following. The majority of the basic research of technology and even the development of the proto-types of new products are conducted by private universities and national research laboratories. The public universities play only a minor role in these basic R&D activities. Here, the R&D activities of the private universities are funded by governmental institutions like National science Foundation, Department of Energy, and Department of Defense. These proto-types of new products are then transferred to the private individuals or businesses. Some of the new products may even be developed by small- and medium-sized businesses based on the pill-over effects of public funded and public-affiliated R&D activities. Then they are taken over by large private firms in the processes of modifying, refining and marketing the new products.

It may be very intriguing to speculate that, in the market economy of modern time, the benefits of technological advancement may be privatized, while the costs these R&D activities may be socialized (and to be funded by the tax payers).

PART III APPENDICES: INTRODUCTION TO THE SYSTEMATICS OF CHANGES AND RELATED TOPICS

Appendix A - Basic Concepts of Systematics

Systematics is defined as the study of the structures of human beings, the global societies and the physical world. It is invented by this author in the late years of the last century and is currently under rigorous development. Systematics could be developed from various directions. Literary works, cultural and philosophical problems, economic organizations and socio-political operations are definitely some among the milliards of resources from which systemic structures and operations can be observed and abstracted.

For developing specific forms of systematics, mathematics could be employed as a source of inspiration. Mathematics is the study of numbers, and hence is quantity-oriented. But mathematic thinking is extremely delicate and is therefore very useful in enhancing the rigor of our reason. Systematics is intended to be the study of "qualitative" and structural aspects of all things in the universe; and if feasible, is designed to absorb eventually the "quantitative approach" of mathematics toward human and physical worlds as well. It is hoped that systematics will be able to develop a quantitative field and thus to enable it to incorporate mathematics into its realm of studies some time in the future.

For practical purposes, mathematics serves as the framework for studying the quantitative structures of all things in the universe. It is well known that mathematics has not been very successful in studying the "inner relations" and "essential structures" of human beings and things. Hence, by the use of mathematics, people essentially study the universe from outside; that is, to study quantitatively rather than qualitative structures. This is especially true when we study things by the use of mathematical statistics.

It is said that mathematics faces great difficulties in studying problems of complexity, mutation, sudden changes, and fuzziness in general, and those of socio-psychology, economy, and polity in particular (Zhang [1993], p. 286). It is natural that, to study the real world, our methodology must go well beyond the Western methods of relying essentially on mathematics (and dialectic to some extent). In the past, mathematics developed in the West because of pre-Western traditions (i.e., mathematical heritages of Babylon and ancient Egypt) and because of the pre-scientific and scientific traditions prevailing in the Western societies. The method of dialectic was also developed in the West. In contrast, Classic China not only developed its "pre-modern" mathematics based upon the decimal system of numbers, but also invented the "Yiching study" and "the study of yin-yang five-elements." By the necessity of synthesizing the methodologies of the East and the West, and by the needs to deal with sophisticated problems in literature, philosophy, economies and socio-polities, etc., ancient or modern, it is absolutely imperative for us to develop an integrated systematics (of culture).

In the West, Husserl developed the (original) method of phenomenology. This is a "rigorous method" essentially based its inspirations upon the Western logic, mathematical principles and human psychological analysis (Wu [1971]). This "rigorous method" is one of the extremely inspiring sources in the process of our life-long efforts in developing the systematics. In the West, it is seen that Alfred Whitehead developed his "process philosophy" by drawing inspirations from mathematical logic, modern physics, and Christian belief (Whitehead 1978). Whitehead intended to integrate the physical universe with the general human experiences by relying upon the concepts of organism and the harmonious whole. Whitehead strived hard in his attempt to synthesize "subjects and objects, causes and effects, materials and human spirits, evolutions and changes, societies and individuals, and the world and God" into his philosophical system (Shen [1990], p.33). Thus, Whitehead's approach is certainly very inspirational.

In systematics, one of our goals is to integrate some seemingly irrelevant or even contradictory concepts, events or entities into a comprehensive whole. The "analytical method" used in (natural) sciences is designed to decompose things, organs, lives into basic matters or some indecomposable "units." This mathematics-oriented analytical method may have a bias toward ignoring the existence of human spirituality. That is, the method of mathematics (or "mathematicism") is seen to be used in decomposing relations of things, human beings or organizations into individual units. It is well known that this method may also have a tendency of being bias toward ignoring the cooperative interactions among things or human beings in a group endeavor. To correct for these kinds of unwarranted biases, one of the objectives of systematics is therefore to provide a brand new method of physical, organic, human and social studies that would preserve the human spirituality and all the interactions characterizing those entities in question in our systemic quest for truth.

It goes without saying that one direction that inspires greatly the development of systematics is related to our deepest concerns about the current and future developments of the cultures, economies and socio-polities of both of the United States and China. By our life-long efforts, we genuinely hope that this development of systematics would help us better understand and manage more wisely the general directions, and especially the cultural directions, of these two great nations in particular, and of the promotion of human justice in the global society in general. Below we introduce and develop cultural systematics with a focus on the theoretical underpinnings of systems.

A.1 The Systematic Universe: The Structure of Universe

§A.1-1The Universe of Systematics

In the universe of systematics, there are two structures: the physical structure (or the structure of sciences) and the symbolic structure (or the structure of systematics). Due to the limitation of space, we shall omit the discussion of physical structure. In terms of the symbolic structure, in the universe, there is a system of double circles. The inside circle is a solid one, and within it there is the *world of yu.* The outside circle is a dotted one. Between these circles there is the *world of yu-wu recursion* which embodies in itself the nature of good and evil. The nature of good is a part of the good which is also embodied in the world of wu to be mentioned below. The upper layer of this world of yu-wu recursion may also be called the world of chi or yin-and-yang. To modify the concepts of Chu Hsi, we may call this world of chi the intermediary between the world of "xing er shang" (what is above shapes or wu) and the world of "xing er xia" (what is within shapes or yu). This chi is the source of both good and evil in the state of flux. Here by the so-called state of flux is meant that this is a state in which, surprisingly, good and evil may interchange their roles by the principle of tao-reversal. Outside of this double circles is the *world of wu* (Wu*), which is in turn encircled by the world of "creativity and nihility" (Tzu*). Note that this may also be called the world of sunyata (or emptiness). This world of wu is one of good without evil, a source of pure creativity. And yet, it is created and may be annihilated by the ultimate entity. That is, underlying the world of wu, there is

Ultimate Creativity-Destructivity (or Nihility), to be called Ultimate One, or Ultimate Self (Self*, Tzuju*, Tzu*). Note that between the world of wu and Self*, there is a dotted circle to separate (i.e., to delimit the boundary between) them or, as a passage or conduit, to connect both of them. The creativity associated with the world of Tzu* (i.e., associated with the reasoning processes of systematics and with the life-will oriented toward Ultimate One or Tzu*) will be called the *"self"-creativity* from which *yu-wu creativity* (or *tao-creativity*) and *being creativity* are derived. Note that the creativity of sciences is part of the being creativity.

Here the yu-wu creativity is, in actuality, the power or energy network jointly created by yu and wu. Here yu and wu are created by Yu and Wu, respectively, and in turn, Yu and Wu are created by Yu* and Wu*, respectively. Essentially, the yu-wu creativity or tao creativity is the joint creation of Yu* and Wu*.

We shall modify Heidegger's worlds of Dasein and Sein.[10] In this system, the *world of Dasein* is defined as the world of true-self, the basis of which dwells in the inner layer of yu-wu recursion. The existence of this basis is guaranteed by Husserl's method of phenomenology. As for the non-basis part of Dasein, it penetrates through the outer layer of yu-wu recursion, and thrusts itself into the world of wu. This world of Dasein coexists solely with a specific "individuality" in space and is activated by time. By the time upon one's death, the world of Dasein vanishes. By our formulation, the *world of Sein* is the world of "angst," anxiety and isolation. It is finite and is a subset of the world of wu. In the spirit of Sein und Zeit (Heidegger 1962, 1977), we may note that the world of wu and God are separated by a solid line, and there is no passage connecting Sein with God!

One way to interpret Christian concept of God is to conceive it as existing outside of the world of wu (in actuality, outside of the world of yu and the world of wu) which borders the infinity. For a Taoist, one may interpret Tao -- the Ultimate Creativity- Destructivity (and Nihility)--as the tao in the narrow or even higher sense, since Tao is pervasive and is everywhere. For a Confucian, one would interpret the Ultimate Creativity-Destructivity (Good, or Tai Chi) as residing outside of the world of wu and call it Tien. Contrary to the Confucian doctrine and by interpreting Tai Chi as generated by Wu Chi (following Chou Tun-yi), one would perceive Tien as a subset of Wu* and is surrounded by Wu*.

For a Christian, one narrow-sense approach is to replace the world of wu by the world of Nothingness, while keeping the worlds of Dasein and Sein and interpreting the world of yu as the world of being and the world of yu-wu recursion as the world of "non-being." Here by the term non-being is meant an entity between being and nothingness. It is not being, neither nothingness, nor something that does not exist; but is a source of good and evil. By Nothingness is meant an entity beyond our comprehension and yet is the final source of creativity/nihility which is good. Then Wu* would be interpreted as *God*, the Ultimate Creativity-Destructivity, the Omnipotence, the Omniscience and All-Good, which goes beyond the world of infinity. From a Chinese perspective, it appears that God is the personified presentation of Tien according to the tradition of the Christendom. In these kinds of ultimate concerns, love may be thought of as the passage of the Ultimate Creativity-Destructivity through and in Dasein (Tonn 1999), and "love may reach God in this life, but not knowledge" (St. John of the Cross, 1957, p. 82).[11] In this sense, the world of Sein is a world outside of and isolated from God, caused by the human ignorance, ungratefulness and disbelief in God. Love is then the conduit of creativity and nihility, linking life and death on both ends of a human being, and is the process of creating infinite meanings in one's world of finitude.

In the above, there is a way to approach God by going through the eyes of apophatic or negative theologians (for example, Merton 1961). Since no one has ever seen God, and the mind of the human being can not understand God, God may be thought of as *Nothingness*, i.e., light and the deepest darkness, or the entity beyond human comprehension--the ultimate mystery. In this narrow sense, God is Wu*. Of course, in the broad-sense, God is Tzu*.

Note that we may consider Whitehead's God as equivalent to our concept of Tao (which is created by Tao*) under the illumination of Tzu*). Wu* is wu because it is in the world of wu-potential. In contrast, Yu* is yu. Wu* and Yu* are created by Tzu*. The difference among Tzu*, Wu* and Yu* are that, when we emphasize the potential-hidden aspect of Tzu*, we employ the concept of Wu*, while we emphasize the potential-ready aspect of Tzu*, we employ the concept of Yu*. Similarly, we differentiate the concepts between Wu and Yu. Wu is created by Wu* under the illumination of Tzu*, and Yu is created by Yu* under the illumination of Tzu*. Tao* is created by Yu* alone "with wu-aspect" and Chi* is created by Yu* alone "with potential-aspect." Tao is created by Tao* in a process of interactions between Wu and Yu. Similarly, Chi is created by Chi* in a process of interactions between Wu and Yu under the illumination of Tzu*. Wu* and Yu* are two-in-one, Tzu, Tao and Chi are three-in-one. Note that Yu is essentially created by Tzu*. Yu is one, and Wu is one as well; while Tao and Chi represent two aspects of "many." In the second layer of the metaphysical world, Tao and Chi can not be combined into an operational pair like dao and qi which are entities in the physical world. Tao is good, while Chi is composed of self-good-and-bad-to-others and self-bad-and-bad-to-others.

Now, partially in terms of physical structure, the universe is composed of three layers of systems: the physical **basis being-field**, the **social power-energy net** (social PE net), and the **will-and-rationality-to-creation /destruction entity** (will-and-rationality entity, creative and destructive entity). The physical basis being-field is a system of systemic continuity/discontinuity/anti-continuity, systemic balance/ imbalance and mathematical equilibrium/ disequilibrium, composed of the worlds of materials and energies studied in the fields of physics, chemistry and biology. This basis being field can also be decomposed into the **physical basis** of the worlds of pure physics and chemistry and the **matter-life basis** of the world of biological studies.

As for the social power-energy net, it is the system of human society which is also a composite world studied in mathematics, social sciences and systematics (i.e., social systematics). The will-and-rationality-to-creation/destruction entity (W/R entity) is the totality of the systems of humanities, composed of human rationality and spirits, and the entity of Ultimate Creativity-and-Destructivity/Nihility. In this system, the human rationality and spirituality are in correspondence to the ultimate forces of creativity and nihility. This correspondence is a symbolic relationship that has not yet been studied well.

A.2 Structure of The Systematic Universe

In this subsection, we shall present our schemes of mind and the universe. Mind is important because human existence and actions depend essentially on our mind sets. The scheme of the universe, or the systems of cosmology and ontology, are important because they affect our mind sets. The questions like which religion to choose, how to choose between religion and arts, or simply to choose any spiritual approach to our lives are related to our belief of the mystery of our lives and the universe. These issues of the meaning of life may affect our economic decision making, or they may be not. In either case, our belief system is an important topic of our researches, and we are deeply concerned with an essential foundation from which we would like to build up an ideal system for the human kind. This is why, in this systematics of culture, we deal with the questions of will, rationality, consciousness and mind in the micro-world and those of cosmology and ontology in the macro-world.

§A.2-1 Rationality, Will, and Elements

§A.2-1-1 Will-to-creation, Rationality and Creativity

Will, rationality and creativity. Below we start with the definitions of will, rationality and creativity. By the *will-to-creation* is meant the human spirituality of creating meaning in one's life. There are several forms of simple will-to creation: the will-to-creation in the spirituality of conquest or will-to-creation in conquest (ω_{Cq}), the will-to-creation in the spiritual unity with the nature or will-to-creation in unity (ω_{Un}), and others. By combining these two categories of will-to-creation mentioned in the above, one derives the composite will-to-creation chain: $\omega_{Un} \underline{\perp\!\!\perp} \omega_{Cq}$. Note that, by assumption, to combine these two types of life-will successfully into one, one needs the medium of integrative-mediatory life-will or Tcentral life-will, which is by its very nature a part of the sefl-creating and self-existing life-will ω_{Un}. Here by the **mediatory life-will** is meant an unbiased will-to-life which will enable the person to strike a balance between different life-wills such as the will-to-creation in conquest and the will-to-creation in unity with the nature.

By *rationality* is meant the capacity for a human being to reason or to think logically or systematically (i.e., in the manner of systematics). In terms of rationality, there are simple rationality and composite rationality. For the simple rationality, there are several forms. For one, there is the **classical systemic rationality** (ρ_{ClSys}) (YYWX, also called the traditional YYTR -- yin-yang tao reversal, tao reversal creativity-destructivity, or yu-wu rationality). Note that this yu-wu rationality (or YYWX) may also be called the symbolic rationality or MFCE rationality of ancient China. The other form is the **modern systemic rationality** (i.e., the "general systemic rationality" which is developed with partial inspiration drawn from "mathematical rationality (or scientific rationality ρ_{Sc}). Then by combining two forms of rationality, one derives a composite rationality chain: ($\rho_{ClSys} \underline{\perp\!\!\perp} \rho_{Sc}$). Note that, by assumption, in integrating these two types of rationality into one, one needs the medium of integrative-mediatory rationality which is by its very nature a part of the yu-wu rationality. Here by the **mediatory rationality** is meant an unbiased rationality which will enable the person in question to achieve a balance between different rationalities such as the (modern) systemic rationality and scientific rationality.

Figure A.2-1-1-1
Composite will-rationality complex

$$\omega \Leftrightarrow \rho = \mathop{\Vdash}\limits_{\omega_{Cq}}^{\omega_{Un}} \omega^{@} \uplus \rho^{@} \mathop{\dashv\!\Vert}\limits_{\rho_{Sc}}^{\rho_{ClSys}}$$

Then we could create a mutual-reaction chain between the composite will-to-creation and the composite rationality (ω⇔ρ) by connecting them together (see Figure A.2-1-1-1), where ╟ is the impactor (or interactor) performing the role of creating the chain-complex between two components of the will-to-creation, ω* is the commanding height of the chain-complex of the will-to-creation, ρ is the composite rationality, "⇔" is the interactor (or symbol denoting an "interactive motion") connecting ω and ρ, ρ* is the commanding height of the chain-complex of human rationality, ╢is the impactor performing the role of the chain-complex between two components of rationality, and "⊎" is the impactor connecting $\omega^{@}$ and $\rho^{@}$.

In terms of human creativity, we have the **organizational creativity** by which is meant the ability to handle a sophisticated task of organizing new forms of human activities in varying and challenging environments. On the other hand, by the **engineering creativity** is meant the ability to invent new products, new forms of material tools, or to develop new procedures to design and produce the old materialistic tools with different factor inputs. These tools are what the human being uses in changing or modifying the physical environments to better fit the human needs, or to help strengthen their physical conditions (for example, to promote the health care). For the concept of creativity, also see the theory of technological change (see Section 4.5).

In the above, we have the (ρ,ω) complex. To reach a deeper world of this complex, we may set $\omega = (w^*, \mathcal{W}^*)$ and $\rho = (r^*, \mathcal{R}^*)$, where w^* depicts the life-impulse of creating and reaching inwardly toward one's inner greatness, $\mathcal{W}^*$ the life-impulse of creating and reaching out to one's external greatness, r^* the rhythm of penetrating deeply into and nurturing of one's micro-rationality, and $\mathcal{R}^*$ the momentum of creating one's micro/macro-rationality working jointly with others. The idea of (ρ,ω) complex $(\{(w^*, \mathcal{W}^*), (r^*, \mathcal{R}^*)\}$ complex) is that each of us is born for the greatness and glory of life.

One's inner greatness lies in the very depth of one's own world of spirituality. One has to have faith in oneself, and is willing to strive hard in order to achieve one's life-goal in facing seemingly unsurmountable obstacles. Mencius once said, "If I am right, I am definitely going to do it even in facing the opposition of tens of thousands of people." This is what we mean by being born for greatness. Note that this can also be developed on the basis of any other liberal belief or religious belief. Sacrifice is unavoidable, and a deep sense of fulfilling the mission of one's life to do sublime things is necessary. Certainly every one is well endowed to achieve one's inner greatness. Note that for achieving one's inner greatness, the road may be extremely lonesome, and one may hardly not receive any encouragement from outside.

The external greatness must be connected to one's willingness to help others unselfishly and to achieve worldly power in amassing energy and scarce resources to realize one's noble objective. Here one must be eager to create and control power for the sake of serving others (or in a position of second-to-none in serving others). Under certain circumstances, this may even require one to sacrifice one's life for achieving the goal of serving others at any costs.

For the micro-rationality, one needs to constantly cultivate it. The study of mathematics and logic helps, the development of common sense helps as well; and self-control is essential. It goes without saying that there are many ways to develop and promote this rationality, and the basis of this depends on one's innate ability and life-long cultivation.

As for the micro/macro rationality, it must be developed under the influence of external environments. That is, it is by a process of interactions between the innate rationality of a

person and the group rationality of the society that this development is made possible.
Then, by combining the organizational and engineering creativities, one derives the mutual-reaction chain to be called the **complex chain of tao-creativity and being-creativity** ($\tau C \rightleftarrows \beta C$). For this, we write the connection between the chain complex of composite will-to-creation and composite rationality and the chain complex of organizational and engineering creativities as $\omega \Updownarrow \rho$ (with $(\omega \Updownarrow \rho) = (\tau C \rightleftarrows \beta C)$, see Figure A.2-1-1-2).

Figure A.2-1-1-2
Simple will-rationality set

$$\begin{array}{c}\omega \Updownarrow \rho \\ | \\ (\tau C \rightleftarrows \beta C)\end{array}$$

Furthermore, from these human creativities, the micro process of cultural creativity involving a product is created by forming a research and development chain comprising (1) the research core: curiosity (free thinking) → ideas & visions → methods of study → solutions of problems → improvement of ideas or theories, (2) production core: trial or tentative design → initial output → final output, and (3) R&D feedback network. The holistic or macro process of cultural creativity involves working with more than one micro process (of a single or multiple related or seemingly unrelated products or events) jointly, in trying to find a commonality fundamental to all of them.[12] For this chain complex expressing the process of cultural energy, we write in symbols in Figure A.2-1-1-3.

Figure A.2-1-1-3
Will-rationality system

$$\begin{array}{c}\omega \Updownarrow \rho \\ | \\ (\tau C \rightleftarrows \beta C)\end{array} \approx \text{holistic} \left\{ \begin{array}{c} C \\ \downarrow \\ \text{micro} \left\{ \begin{array}{c} I \\ \downarrow \\ S \end{array} \right\} \quad M \end{array} \right\} = \varepsilon(\mathfrak{C}),$$

where C denotes human curiosity, I denotes ideas, M denotes methods, S denotes solutions, and $\varepsilon = \varepsilon(\mathfrak{C})$ refers to the energy process of culture ($\mathfrak{C}$).

Note that the micro process is more closely related to the being creativity (by using scientific rationality underlying the mathematical and empirical methods) and the will-to-conquer and is less closely associated with the tao rationality and the life-will of tranquility and unity. Further, the holistic process is more closely related to tao creativity (by using the classical systemic rationality) and the will-to-unity (i.e, will-to-creativity in unity with the nature) than the scientific rationality and the will-to-conquest.

§A.2-1-2 Basic Concepts of Elements: Universal and Human Elements

To establish a solid foundation of systematic analysis, the development of the structures of universal elements is urgently needed. In the following, we shall endeavor rigorously to achieve this goal. A **universal element** or simply an element denoting a thing, a human being, an event or an entity, is an undefined term, to be understood intuitively. The collection of all such universal elements is denoted as the preliminary space of universal elements **U** (see the derivation presented below).

For the simplest structure of the universal elements, we adopt a concept similar to the number line in mathematics. For the arrangement of the horizontal axis of these elements on the right hand side of the origin (or central position, 0) (including this 0), we have the simple collection or set {0 a b c ... z a* b* c* ... z* a** b** c** ... z** ...} (see Figure A.2-1-2-1).

Figure A.2-1-2-1
The set $\mathbf{U}^{+}$

```
|----|-----|------|------|------|-----|------|------|----|-----|------|-------|-----|----->
0   a     b      c ...  z       a*   b*      c* ... z* a**    b**  c** ... z** ...
```

These elements are called **yang elements** (or right elements). The collection of these yang or right elements will be denoted as $\mathbf{U}^{+}$. In the above, the use of the symbols in the set {0 a b c ... z a* b* c* ... z* a** b** c** ... z** ...} is just for convenience. It could be replaced by other sets such as {0 a b c ... j a* b* c* ... j* a** b** c** ... j** ...}, {0 a b c ... t a* b* c* ... t* a** b** c** ... t** ...}. It could also be replaced by a collection of any other symbols, for example, Greek alphabets or Chinese radicals, as long as they denote a definite relationship of one succeeding the other.

Similarly, for the structure of the universal elements, the arrangement of the horizontal axis on the left hand side of the origin (including the origin) could be set as {... ##z ... ##c ##b ##a #z ... #c #b #a _z ... _c _b _a 0}, see Figure A.2-1-2-2.

Figure A.2-1-2-2
The set $^{-}\mathbf{U}$

```
<-----|------|-----|-----|-----|------|-----|------|-----|------|------|-----|------|
 ... ##z... ##c ##b ##a  #z ...  #c    #b    #a    _z ... _c    _b  _a      0
```

These elements are called **yin elements** (or left elements). The collection of these yin or left elements will be denoted as $^{-}\mathbf{U}$. As noted before, here the use of the symbols in the set { 0 _a _b _c ... _z #a #b #c ... #z ##a ##b ##c ... ##z ...} is but for convenience.

The interactions among more than one of yang elements will be depicted by all the elements involved (See Figure A.2-1-2-1). For example, the interaction of a onto b (b onto a, resp.)

will be denoted as ab (ba, resp.). For another example, the interaction of a* onto b* (b* onto a*, resp.) will be denoted as a*b* (b*a*, resp.).

In Figure A.2-1-2-1 (Figure A.2-1-2-2, reps.), the new elements ab and a*b* (_a_b and #a#b, resp.) will be placed in-between a and b (_a and _b, resp.), see Figure A.2-1-2-3.

Figure A.2-1-2-3

```
|------|----|------|--------|------>
0    a   ab  a*b* ...  b ...
```

Figure A.2-1-2-4

```
< ---|------|--------|--------|------|
    _b   #a#b   _a_b     _a     0
```

Note that, in general, the order of operation is important, for example, ab ≠ ba and _a_b ≠ _b_a, and in-between any two elements, there could be as many terms of interactions as it deems appropriate. But in cases that the principle of symmetry holds (i.e., similar to the concept of commutativity in mathematics), then xy = yx for any x, y in the set. That is, in this case of symmetry, these two positions xy and yx are the same. This is not true on the real number line of mathematics, for example, 12 ≠ 21, although, for example, it is true that $1 \times 2 = 2 \times 1$.

Each element (or point) on the (one-dimensional) axis, similar to a vector in a multi-dimensional space in mathematics, represents a cluster of universal phenomena or human activities and mental states, ranging from material-form (i.e., for non-life elements), plant-form, animal form, to human form of substance and activities.

Theoretically, none of the positions in the preliminary space of universal elements as expressed in the horizontal axis is empty. And yet, in applications, at least some positions in the universal system of elements may be absent or empty. For example, the position of an alien is empty, and the interaction between me and an alien is not present.

Now we come to the system of human elements. By utilizing the above concepts, a **person** (h ⊫ **H**) could be expressed as one with multiple dimensions of features and characteristics. This **H** represents the space of human elements. For example, for h in **H** = {h|h = (x,y,z,...)}, x represents a male, y a healthy one, z a professor engaging in researching and teaching the theory of systematics, and so on.

In the above, let **U** = $\mathbf{U}^{+}$ ⊔ $^{-}\mathbf{U}$ (with X ⊔ Y denoting the impactor collecting X and Y into a simple set, for any entities X and Y). Here **U** may be called the **preliminary space of universal elements**. Note that the collection of human elements is part of the universal elements, or **H** ⋐ **U** (with **H** ⋐ **U** denoting the smaller space **H** belonging to the bigger space **U**). Further, h = (x,y,z,...) is considered as a **multi-dimensional element** in which each element x (y or z, resp.) is an **element in a one-dimensional space** X (Y, or Z, resp., with the **space** denoting a collection of universal or human elements with perhaps some specifically instructed relationships).

Remark A.2-1-2-1. A **primitive universal element** is an undefined term $x \Vdash \mathbf{U}$. As for a **sophisticated universal element**, it can be written as: $x_i \equiv \{x_i(y_{i1},y_{i2},..,y_{is};h_{i1}^*,h_{i2}^*,..,h_{it}^*,IRI_i),.) | x_i(y_{i1},y_{i2},..,y_{is};h_{i1}^*,h_{i2}^*,..,h_{it}^*,IRI_i,.) \Vdash (\gamma(\tau)),R^{Dyn},\tilde{O}\|E\{e_j\},z\} \Vdash \mathbf{U}$, $\tau \Vdash (\Im,\text{Ш}^{\text{Д}}) \Vvdash \mathbb{T}\text{zu}^*$, ($i \in \mathbb{N}$, R^{Dyn} being the "dynamical forces" of x), the operations of $\gamma(\tau)$) and R^{Dyn} would not interfere with the self-independent operations of the $x_i(IRI_i)$ (see Definition 6.4-2-1). For this sophisticated universal element x, we also write it as $x \Vdash \mathbf{U}$.

A person, $x \equiv x(h^*(,.|(\rho,\omega))) \Vdash \mathbf{U}$ ($\Vdash$ denoting a relationship of belonging) for $h^*(,.|(\rho,\omega)) \Vdash \mathbf{H}^*$ (for the definition of $\mathbf{H}^*$, see below), is expressed as a universal element with multiple dimensions of human, cultural, sociopolitical and economic features and characteristics. Let **H** represent the space of human elements with the culmination of these dimensions. For example, we may write a person as $x(h^*(,.|(\rho,\omega))) = (x_1,x_2,.;h_1^*(,.|(\rho,\omega)),.)$ where x_1 represents a male, x_2 a healthy one, h_1 a professor engaging in researching and teaching the theory of systematics.

In general, we write the **space of human elements** as:

$$\text{(A.2-1-2-1)} \quad \mathbf{H} = \{x_i(h_j^*(,.|(\rho,\omega)))| \; x_i(h_j^*(,.|(\rho,\omega))) = (x_{i1},x_{i2},..,x_{iM};h_{j1}^*(,.|(\rho,\omega)), h_{j2}^*(,.|(\rho,\omega)),..,h_{jN}^*(,.|(\rho,\omega))) \Vdash \mathbf{U}, \; x_{im} \Vdash \mathbf{U}, \; h_{jn}^*(,.|(\rho,\omega)) \Vdash \mathbf{H}^*\},$$

$i = 1,2,\ldots,I$, $j = 1,2,\ldots,J$, $k = 1,2,\ldots,K$, $m = 1, 2, \ldots, M$, $n = 1, 2, \ldots, N$, where $\mathbf{H}^*$ refers to the **space of human, cultural, sociopolitical and economic features and characteristics**, with x_{im} (a universal element) denoting the mth universal attributes, except human characteristics, and $h_{jn}^*(,.|(\rho,\omega))$ the nth human characteristics as a becoming of the RW complex for all j.

In the following we shall present several examples of human elements on the one-dimensional axis.

(1) Marriage elements: Here let h = (x,y,z,...), where x represents the element of marriage. The origin is the "marriage" in the abstract sense. On the right hand side of the axis, the "a position" designates the male related to the first married couple (accounted somewhat arbitrarily), the "b position" designates male related to the second married couple (accounted somewhat arbitrarily), and so on. On the left hand side of the origin, i.e., on the axis, the "_a position" refers to the female related to the first married couple, the "_b position" refers to the female related to the second married couple, and so on.

(2) Family elements: Here let h = (x,y,z,...), where y represents the element of family membership. The origin is the "family" in the abstract sense. On the right hand side of the axis, the a position designates the males related to the first family, the b position designates the males related to the second family, and so on. On the left hand side of the origin, the _a position refers to the females related to the first family, the _b position refers to the females related to the second family, and so on.

(3) Social elements: Here let h = (x,y,z,...), where z represents the element of social status. The origin is the "social organization" in the abstract sense. On the right hand side of the axis, the a position designates the collection of the males related to the first social organization (accounted somewhat arbitrarily) arranged according to the degree of conservativeness or

progressiveness, the b position designates the collection of the males related to the second social organization (accounted somewhat arbitrarily) arranged according to the degree of conservativeness or progressiveness, and so on. On the left hand side of the origin, i.e., on the axis, the _a position refers to the group of female counter parts related to the first social organization, the _b position refers to the female counterparts related to the second social organization, and so on.

(4) Political elements: Here let h = (x,y,z,u,...), where u represents the element of political status. The origin is the "political element" in the abstract sense. On the right hand side of the axis, there are male citizens arranged according to a criterion of political category. On the left hand side of the origin, i.e., on the axis, there are female citizens arranged according to the same criterion of political category.

§A.2-1-3 CE Balance-Equilibrium, Centrality and Self-Masterism

Figure A.2-1-3-1
Equilibrium Point

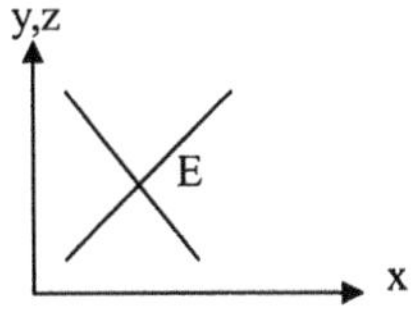

In the following we go beyond the method of equilibrium to present the method of centrality. The method of equilibrium may be said as follows. By **equilibrium-in-conflict** (or simply equilibrium) is meant that more than two or two opposing forces, for example y and z, are in conflicting balance; that is, y and z cancel out each other's influence in a system. In terms of the following figure, we have two curves, demand and supply curves, intersect at the point E. The intersection point E is then called the **equilibrium point**: mathematically, y and z as functions of x respectively, y = z at the point E (see Figure A.2-1-3-1).

By the **CE balance** is meant to strike a simultaneous balance among different elements, groups, or goals, etc. In general, it just means not to go to extremes measures in dealing with things, events and people.

In contrast, the method of centrality may be said as follows. By the **centrality** [13] of a system is meant that certain elements, issues, events, or goals always receive priority in the distribution of power, prestige and benefits as well as in planning, decision-making and implementation of plans. The following are three examples of centrality. (1) The central element dominates non-central elements in a system. (2) The most important elements of the system attain the position of the commanding height. That is, they gain the position of centrality. (3) In a situation of uncertainty or a non-quantifiable state, the most important elements of the system are set in the right direction, where the right direction is determined by the objective of this system. That is, these important elements are set in a certain direction to guarantee that they always gain the position of centrality in terms of system priority. Of course, the direction may be changed according to the environments or the changing nature of the structure of this system.

One way to apply the concept of centrality to a system is to proceed as follows. In a system or an organization, let the efficiency of vertical control (VD) and horizontal coordination (HC) be standardized. That is, set $\mu(AD) \equiv AD = 1 = \mu(HC) \equiv HC$, where μ is the measure of the efficiency of the variable in question. In the following Figure A.2-1-3-2, z (as the center of the rectangle A'B'DC) is the theoretical or ideal point of centrality. We shall compare it with the actual point of centrality.

Before we examine the actual point of *centrality*, we need to define it. In a system represented by Figure A.2-1-3-2, let us differentiate it vertically into upper and lower echelons, and horizontally into right and left echelons. Here the upper echelon could represent the central government, the management strata or the upper structure of a society (for example, the upper class or the upper cultural strata related to philosophy, religion and arts). In contrast, the lower echelon represents the local governments, the workers or the lower structure of a society (for example, the working class or the lower cultural strata related to natural sciences, economy and polity).

Figure A.2-1-3-2
Centrality at Z

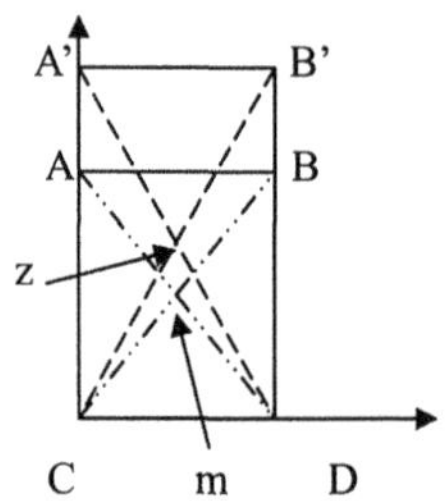

If the actual point of centrality lies on the ideal point z, it means that this system achieves its centrality. Note that, this is also in a sense of "balance." But in this state of centrality or "harmonious balance," the power of the upper echelon is actually greater than that of the lower echelon, although according to Figure A.2-1-3-2, the measure of the power of the upper echelon and that of the lower echelon appear to be the same. This is due to the process of standardization.

In Figure A.2-1-3-2, by stretching the square ABCD into the rectangle A'B'DC, the power of the upper echelon is seen to increase.

For the system ABCD (a square), when the actual point z lies above the mid-point m (i.e., the ideal point), it means that the energy possessed by or the power of the upper strata is too low, and that of the lower strata is too high. That is, in this system, the position of the upper echelon is too weak, and the position of the lower echelon is too powerful. For example, this is a case that the power of central government is smaller than that of local government. That is, it is out of centrality. To correct for the anti-centrality or a-centrality, in the case of growth, the ideal point could be moved to m' = z (m being the point of intersection of AD and BC and z the point of intersection of B'C and A'D, see Figures A.2-1-3-2 and A.2-1-3-3. That is, to extend from A to A' and from B to B' in Figure A.2-1-3-2. Then, in the new situation, CDB'A' (a rectangle), centrality of this system is partially restored. In this case, for example, the power of the central government is equal to that of local government, and yet VD > HC. If point z is moved back to point m in order to restore centrality (see Figure A.1-1-3-2), then this system will not experience growth.

Figure A.2-1-3-3
Anti-centrality and Partial Centrality

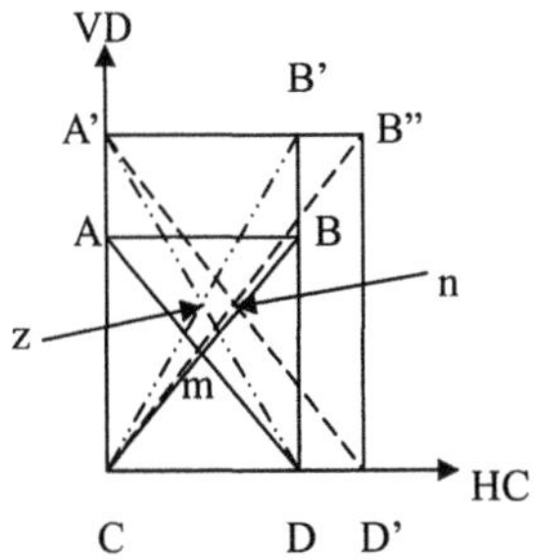

Looking at Figure A.2-1-3-3, it is seen that z is the actual point of *centrality* in the system CDB'A' (also see Figure A.2-1-3-2). This shows that, VD > HC, or the horizontal power is weakened (for example, the power of the government is greater than that of the civil society). One way to restore the full centrality is to move point z to point n and after extending points D to D' and B' to B''. That is, in the new system represented by CD'B''A' (a new square), the actual point of centrality coincides with the ideal point of centrality, and VD = HC (for example, the power of the government equals that of the civil society).

By the **principle of self-masterism** is meant to operate a system X, $X = \{x_1,x_2,\ldots,x_n\} \sqsubseteq (\Omega,\mathbb{Z}\circ,{}_v\mathbb{H},\{\mathbb{C}\})$ for $x_i \sqsubseteq$ **U**, so that (i) each element $x_i \Vdash X$ ($i \in \mathbb{N}$) is an element in the state of being its self-master, and (ii) each element maintains its characteristics of self-masterism under the various operations of the system (also see Definition 6.4-2-3).

§A.2-1-4 General TCentral

Below we turn to the issues of comprehensive or general TCentral. In general, for a basic system $X \equiv \underline{X} = \{X^1,X^2, \ldots, X^n\} \equiv \{x_1,x_2,\ldots,x_n\}$, where X^i is a unit system, we reach the TCentral state of strategic centrality and CE balance by the **method of systemic scheme** (effective IISO/T scheme, Section 3.2). Note that for simplicity of notation, we write X^1 as x_1 and X^2 as x_2, and so on. Below we recapture this method. For i = 1, 2, …, n,, let the basic systems $x_i \sqsubseteq (\Omega,\mathbb{Z}\circ,{}_v\mathbb{H},\{\mathbb{C}\})$ be:

(A.2-1-4-1) $x_1 \Vdash \zeta(\xi(\tau)), \tau \Vdash (\mathfrak{I},Ш^{Д}) \Vdash \mathbb{T}zu^*$,

(A.2-1-4-2) $x_2 \Vdash \zeta(\xi(\tau)), Y \Vdash \zeta(\tau), \tau \Vdash (\mathfrak{I},Ш^{Д}) \Vdash \mathbb{T}zu^*$,

...

where $\zeta \sqsubseteq (\Omega,\mathcal{Z}o,_v\mathcal{H},\{\mathbb{C}\})$ for $\zeta \equiv \{\zeta(\xi) \mid \xi = \xi(\tau) \backsim \tau \Vdash (\mathfrak{I},Ш^{Д})\}$ representing the underlying forces that unify the systems x_1 and x_2. Here ζ is the underlying force of dynamics that unifies the systems x_i, ξ is the operating force of real-world creativity, and τ is the hidden force of creativity (manifested by the seed of creativity which is generated directly by $\mathbb{T}zu^*$, see Section 3.2).

Under the system operation of systems x_1 and x_2,

(A.2-1-4-3) $\varphi\{x_1\} = x_1$,

(A.2-1-4-4) $\varphi\{x_2\} = x_2$,

...

with $\varphi \vDash \mathcal{Z}o,_v\mathcal{H}$, we have:

(A.2-1-4-5) $\Delta \sqsubseteq \Omega$.

To solve this scheme, let

(A.2-1-4-6) $T = \{x_1,x_2,\ldots,x_3\} \curlyvee \Delta$,

where $\curlyvee \vDash \mathcal{Z}o,_v\mathcal{H}$, and suppose this scheme entails the operations of the x_1 and x_2 in a state of CE balance. Under the static decomposition of X into a state of TCentral:

(A.2-1-4-7) $X = \{x_1 \oplus x_2 \oplus x_3 \oplus \ldots \oplus x_n\} \circledast Ix = \sigma \Vdash \Sigma^{TC}$,

where $I \vDash \mathcal{Z}o,_v\mathcal{H}$ is the impactor of system-integration (i.e., Ix refers to I arranging $x_1, x_2,.., x_n$ so that they form a system X), we have:

(A.2-1-4-8)
$$\begin{aligned}
&(\varphi\{T\})\, x_1,x_2,\ldots,x_n,Ix \\
&= (\varphi[\{x_1,x_2,\ldots,x_n,Ix\} \curlyvee \Delta])\, x_1,x_2,\ldots,x_n \\
&= \varphi[\{x_1,x_2,\ldots,x_n\},\Delta]\, x_1,x_2,\ldots,x_n \ltimes \varphi[Ix,E] \\
&= \{\varphi[\{x_1,x_2,\ldots,x_n\},\Delta] \otimes \psi\{x_i,\Delta\}\} \\
&\quad \geq^* \{\{\varphi[\{x_1,x_2,\ldots,x_n\},\Delta] \otimes \psi\{x_1,\Delta\}\} \\
&\qquad \triangleq \{\varphi[\{x_1,x_2,\ldots,x_n\},\Delta] \otimes \psi\{x_2,\Delta\}\} \\
&\qquad \ldots \\
&\qquad \triangleq \{\varphi[\{x_1,x_2,\ldots,x_n\},\Delta] \otimes \psi\{x_n,\Delta\}\}\} \\
&\quad \ltimes \varphi[Ix,E],\ i \neq 1,2,\ldots,i\text{-}1,i\text{+}1,\ldots,n,
\end{aligned}$$

in the case of strategic centrality of x_i (i.e., the central system) over others (with "$A \geq^* B$" for $A, B \sqsubseteq (\Omega,\mathcal{Z}o,_v\mathcal{H},\{\mathbb{C}\})$ means that $\{\mathcal{T}^*A \geq \mathcal{T}B,\Delta\} \barwedge \tau$, see Bcm. (8.4-2-11)), or

(A.2-1-4-9)
$$\begin{aligned}
&(\varphi\ \{T\})\, x_1,x_2,\ldots,x_n,Ix \\
&= (\varphi\ [\{x_1,x_2,\ldots,x_n,Ix\} \curlyvee \Delta])\, x_1,x_2,\ldots,x_n \\
&= \varphi[\{x_1,x_2,\ldots,x_n\},\Delta]\, x_1,x_2,\ldots,x_n \ltimes \varphi[Ix,E] \\
&= \{\varphi[\{x_1,x_2,\ldots,x_n\},\Delta] \otimes \psi\{x_1,\Delta\}\}
\end{aligned}$$

$\triangleq \{\varphi[\{x_1,x_2,\ldots,x_n\},\Delta] \otimes \psi\{x_2,\Delta\}\}$

...

$\triangleq \{\varphi[\{x_1,x_2,\ldots,x_n\},\Delta] \otimes \psi\{x_n,\Delta\}\}\}$

$\ltimes \varphi[Ix,E]$,

in the case of CE balance. Note that in each of x_j, j =1, 2, ..., n, associated with Bcms. (A.2-1-4-8) and (A.2-1-4-9), there are relationships of strategic centrality and CE balance as well.

As for the case of dynamical principles of strategic centrality and CE balance, we have at a state of simple Tcentral (see Bcm. (8.4-2-4)):

(A.2-1-4-10) $X(.) = \xi_n x_n(\mathbb{H};.)\ldots \oplus\xi_2 x_2(\mathbb{H};.) \oplus\xi_1 x_1(\mathbb{H};.)\circledast Ix(\mathbb{H};.)$,

with

(A.2-1-4-11) $\{\psi\{\xi_1 x_1(\mathbb{H};.),\Delta\}\triangleq \psi\{\xi_2 x_2(\mathbb{H};.),\Delta\}\triangleq \ldots\triangleq \psi\{\xi_n x_n(\mathbb{H};.),\Delta\}\} \ltimes \varphi[Ix(\mathbb{H}),E]$,

in the case of CE balance, and

(A.2-1-4-12) $\{\psi\{\xi_i x_i(\mathbb{H};.),\Delta\}\geq^*\psi\{\xi_1 x_1(\mathbb{H};.),\Delta\}\triangleq \ldots\triangleq \psi\{\xi_n x_n(\mathbb{H};.),\Delta\}\} \ltimes \varphi[Ix(\mathbb{H}),E]$,

$i \neq 1, 2, \ldots, i-1, i+1, \ldots, n$, in the case of strategic centrality, where ξ_i represents the impactor of the characteristics for x_i evolving into φx_i and ζ_2 represents the impactors of the characteristics for x_2 evolving into $\varphi^2 x_i$, ..., and so on, with $x_i(\mathbb{H})$ being the core of x_i at a state of Tcentral, and $Ix(\mathbb{H})$ being the core of Ix at a state of Tcentral (I is an integrating and organizing impactor).

Note that in the above Bcms. (A.2-1-4-11) and (A.2-1-4-12), $\xi_i \models \mathcal{Z}\circ,v\mathcal{H} \Subset \Omega^\Delta \Subset Ш^\Delta$ (world of changes) (for all $i \in \mathbb{N}$) and $I \models \mathcal{Z}\circ,v\mathcal{H} \Subset \Omega^\Delta \Vdash Ш^\Delta$ are in the world of changes; that is, we may write $\xi_i \equiv \xi_i^\Delta$ and $I \equiv I^\Delta$:

(A.2-1-4-13) $\{\psi\{\xi_1^\Delta x_1(\mathbb{H};.),\Delta\}\triangleq \psi\{\xi_2^\Delta x_2(\mathbb{H};.),\Delta\}\triangleq \ldots\triangleq \psi\{\xi_n^\Delta x_n(\mathbb{H};.),\Delta\}\}$
$\ltimes \varphi[I^\Delta x(\mathbb{H}),E]$,

in the case of CE balance, and

(A.2-1-4-14) $\{\psi\{\xi_i^\Delta x_i(\mathbb{H};.),\Delta\}\geq^*\psi\{\xi_1^\Delta x_1(\mathbb{H};.),\Delta\}\triangleq \ldots\triangleq \psi\{\xi_n^\Delta x_n(\mathbb{H};.),\Delta\}\}$
$\ltimes \varphi[I^\Delta x(\mathbb{H}),E]$,

$i \neq 1,2,\ldots,i-1,i+1,\ldots,n$, in the case of strategic centrality.

Below we come to several definitions of general Tcentral.

Definition A.2-1-4-1. Let the whole universe be a "basic-grand system" $\underline{X} = \chi \oplus <\mathbb{C}_X>$. Here the so-called basic-grand system is a grand system composed of more than one basic system; note that in this grand system, one basic system is the central system, and other basic systems are non-central systems. Then $\underline{X} = \{X^1,X^2, \ldots, X^n\}$ is said to reach a state of **general TCentral** if and only if the following conditions hold:

(1) Each unit system (which is a basic system by itself) of the grand system X, denoting the basis being field of the universe, is in a state of Tcentral. Here $X^{i} \Vdash \Omega$, {basis being field $\Vdash$PFB} $=< T^{C\Delta}$ (PFB, being the potential frontier of the basis being field, is composed of the worlds of non-life materials, plants and "non-human" animals), is a becoming (or system) which is always in a process of transformation and mutation. In this Tcentral state of basis being-field, the principles of strategic centrality and CE balance are applicable.

(2) Each unit system X^{j}, denoting the socio-power energy system, reaches a state of specific T central. That is, we have: (i) The center dominates the non-central sub-systems strategically: $\mathcal{T}^{*}C \geq \mathcal{T}X_{i}$, for C being the center and X_i being any non-central sub-system. (ii) Among non-central sub-systems, any two sub-systems are in a state of CE balance: $X_{i} \triangleq X_{j}$ for any non-central sub-systems X_i and X_j, $i \neq j$.

Further, we have: i) The culture reaches a state of specific Tcentral. ii) The economy reaches a state of T central. iii) The polity reaches a state of specific Tcentral. iv) The society reaches a state of T central. v) The psychological system reaches a state of T central, and a balance between self-interests (profit motif in the case of a firm, respectively) and altruism (social responsibility in the case of a firm, respectively) is reached as well. vi) States of centrality and balance are reached among the classes of the intellectuals, the capitalists and industrialists, the politicians and the government bureaucrats, and the common people. (vii) States of centrality and balance are reached between the global culture and the local culture, between cultural adaptability and cultural creativity, between rationality and will, between the spirit of conquest and conflict and the spirit of tranquility, between the spirit of self-interests and the spirit of mutuality, between the spiritual orientation and the desire for material acquisition, between religion and worldly dimensionality, between justice (or fairness) and mercy, and between the order of the universe (or nature) and the order of humanity (such as the order of Tao, order of jen-yi and order of Christianity). Note that one definition of justice is to each according to his/her needs, and the other is to one according to one's ability.

(3) The will-and rationality-to-creation reaches a state of specific Tcentral. That is, the human part is in a state of specific Tcentral and the above-human part reaches a state of specific Tcentral as well. Note that in this specific Tcentral state of will-and rationality-to-creation, the principles of strategic centrality and CE balance are applicable as well.

(4) The basic-grand system $\underline{X}$ itself reaches its state of T central: $\underline{X} =< T^{C\Delta} \sqsubseteq Ш^{\Delta}$. This is a specific Tcentral state of an n-polar MFCE scheme (or MFCE basic-grand system) $\underline{X}$, in which X^{h}-X^{h} is the "horizontal axis" or the "material/basis being field axis" of $\underline{X}$. This is analogous to the "East-West axis" of the 5-polar MFCE scheme. Furthermore, X^{k}-$X^{k'}$ is the "vertical axis" or the "social power-energy system/will and rationality-to-creation axis" of $\underline{X}$ which is analogous to the "North-South axis" of the 5-polar MFCE model. Note that, the T central in (1) to (4) are states of specific Tcentrals.

In the above, the specific T central states of the economy in terms of production, consumption, exchange, stability (unemployment and inflation), growth, equal income and wealth distribution (or social justice) and government strategic operations refer to the following conditions. (1) They appropriately reach the objectiveness or purpose of the whole system (or subsystem in the case of a sub-system). (2) A relationship is reached among all sub-systems, like centrality of the organization, centrality of the system's strategy, independence, balance, coordination, a proper structure of energy-power hierarchy. (3) The center dominates the non-central sub-systems strategically. (4) All subsystems are operating in satisfactory (desirable, targeted and acceptable) trajectories of development. (5) Among non-central sub-systems, any two sub-systems are in a state of CE balance. (6) All subsystems, culture and strategy are in their respective states of continuity. (7) Special conditions such as mathematical equilibrium are met.

Remark A.2-1-4-1. By Bcms. (A.2-1-4-7) and (A.2-1-4-12), we have for the universe X in a state of simple Tcentral:

(A.2-1-4-15) $X = \{x_1 \oplus x_2 \oplus x_3\} \circledast \{Ix\} = \sigma \Vdash \Sigma^{TC}$,

where x_1, x_2, and x_3 stand for the will-and rationality-to-creation entity, the socio-power energy system, and the basis being-field, respectively with x_1 being the center, and

(A.2-1-4-16) $\{\psi\{\xi_1 x_1(\mathbb{H};.),\Delta\} \oplus \psi\{\xi_2 x_2(\mathbb{H};.),\Delta\} \oplus \psi\{\xi_2 x_2(\mathbb{H};.),\Delta\}\} \ltimes \varphi[Ix(\mathbb{H}),E]$,

where $\xi_1 x_1(\mathbb{H};.)$, $\xi_2 x_2(\mathbb{H};.)x_2$, and $\xi_3 x_3(\mathbb{H};.)$ stand for the dynamical systems of the will-and rationality-to-creation entity, the socio-power energy system and the basis being-field, respectively, with $\xi_1 x_1(\mathbb{H};.)$ being the center of the dynamical system of x(.) as a whole. The principles of strategic centrality and CE balance presented in Bcms (A.2-1-4-11) and (A.2-1-4-12) are naturally applicable. It follows that, in each grand system of the will-and rationality-to-creation entity, the socio-power energy system and the basis being-field, the principles of strategic centrality and CE balance presented in Bcms. (3.2-2-6) and (3.2-2-9) and the *principle of strategic dominance* (analogous to Bcm. (3.2-1-9) in expanding into the case of multiple sub-systems) are applicable as well.

Definition A.2-1-4-2. A basic or grand system $\underline{X} = \chi \oplus < \mathbb{C}_X >$, $\underline{X} = \{X^1, X^2, \ldots, X^n\}$ is said to be in a state of general TCentral, if and only if the following conditions are met: (1) Each system, be of central or non-central system, reaches a state of specific Tcentral or equilibrium. (2) The central system enjoys the position of systematic centrality or strategic centrality: For each sector or dimension, for $\mathcal{T} \Vdash \mathcal{Z}\circ, v\mathcal{H}$, C, $X_i \sqsubseteq (\Omega, \mathcal{Z}\circ, v\mathcal{H}, \{\mathbb{C}\})$, $\mathcal{T}C > \mathcal{T}X_i$, $\forall$ i, i $\in \mathbb{N}$, C being the central system or primary objective of each sector/dimensional structure or strategy, and X_i being all non-central sub-systems or non-primary objectives. (3) Among non-central systems, each pair of systems achieves a state of equilibrium, harmonious balance, or balance-in-independence. (4) In each non-central system, a state of independence, balance-in-tranquility/equilibrium-in-conflict, or energy hierarchy is reached. (5) Political, social, economic and cultural centralities/balances are reached.

Note that for more details of the concepts of Tcentral and TCentral, see Chapter 6.

§A.2-2 Basic Concepts of Systems: Unit, Basic, Yin-Yang Systems and Mode

§A.2-2-1 Basic Concepts of Systems: Unit and Basic Systems

By an **individual system** (or **unit system**) is meant a set of several universal elements x_α (α being an "index," not necessarily numerable) in conjunction with their universal or human attributes h_α (with $h_\alpha \Vdash$ **H***), their interactive relations Φ^{WR} (in and with the will-and rationality-to-creation-and-destruction entity), R^{SPE} (in and with the social power-energy net), and their relations in and with the basis being-field $\mathfrak{R}^B$ (i.e., the physical worlds of physics, chemistry, biology and physiology). Note that the system having no sub-systems in it is called a **simple system** as well. The individual system X is also denoted as

(A.2-2-1-1) $X = \chi \oplus <\mathbb{C}_X>$,

where

(A.2-2-1-2) $\chi = (\mathbf{x}(H^*), \Phi^{WR}, R^{SPE}, \Re^B)$,

(A.2-2-1-3) $\mathbf{x}(H^*) = \{x_i(h_j^*) | \forall j \in \mathbb{N}, h_j^* \Vdash \mathbf{H^*}\} \sqsubseteq \mathbf{H}, x_i(h_j^*) \Vdash \mathbf{U}, \forall i \in \mathbb{N}$,

with $\mathbf{x}(H^*)$ being a subset of **H** (the space of human elements), **H*** being the space of universal characteristics or human attributes (h_α^* being an element in the space of human attributes with **H*** denoting the collection of some h_j^* of our interest), and $\mathbb{C}_X$ (here $\mathbb{C}_X$ is called the **culture** or **cultural generator** of X) denoting the structure of X or as it is in or associated with the will-and–rationality entity, with $<\mathbb{C}_X>$ depicting the culture complex generated by $\mathbb{C}_X$. That is, the pure cultural characteristics of a person h_α in system X are deeply hidden in $\mathbb{C}_X$. Here Z is the decision-making and strategic complex.

The above is a simplified presentation of χ. For a more detailed presentation, let

(A.2-2-1-4) $\chi = \{\mathbf{x}(H^*)|\mathbf{x}(H^*) \Vdash^{\#} \{[vd,hc,\gamma], C_S \times C^{DS}(e_k), (R_M, R^{DM}(e_k)), \tilde{O}|E\{e_g\}, Z\}\}$,

where (vd,hc,γ) is named for the *formal-informal institutions-culture* (or formal-informal organization-hierarchical structure partially associated with the will-and-rationality-and-destruction entity) of X, and $(R, R^D(e_k))$ is called the static-dynamic transformation structure (or *static-dynamical interpenetrating network* associated with the social power-energy net and the basis being-field) of X. Note that the formal-informal institution-culture and the interpenetrating network may overlap in terms of organizational structure.

By Bcm. (A.2-2-1-4) is meant that χ is the organic collection of all the elements $x_i(h_j^*)$ ($\{x_i(h_j^*)\} \equiv \mathbf{x}(H^*)$) and these elements as the integral whole have the structures of $\{[vd,hc,\gamma], C_S \times C^{DS}(e_k), (R_M, R^{DM}(e_k)), \tilde{O}\}|E\{e_g\}, Z\}$. Here "$\Vdash^{\#}$" designates the symbl of "having the structures of".

Thus we have $X = \chi \oplus <\mathbb{C}_X>$, $\{x_i(h_j^*)\} \equiv \mathbf{x}(H^*)$:

(A.2-2-1-5) $\chi = \{\{x_i(h_j^*)\} \Vdash^{\#} \{(vd,hc,\gamma), [R, R^D(e_k)], \tilde{O}|E(\{e_g\}, Z)\}\}, \gamma \equiv \gamma(\tau, \mathfrak{C}^*) \backsim (\tau, \mathfrak{C}^*)$,
$(\tau, \mathfrak{C}^*) \Vdash (Ш^Д(\tau), <\mathbb{C}_X(\mathfrak{C}^*)>), \tau \Vdash (\mathfrak{I}, Ш^Д) \Vdash \mathbb{T}zu^*$,

with $h_j^* \Vdash \mathbf{H^*}$, $x_i \Vdash \mathbf{H} \Subset \mathbf{U}$, i = 1, 2,..., n, j = 1,2,..., m. Here, $x_i(h_j^*)$ being a universal element (actually a human element in a human-social system), for **H*** being the space of universal attributes or human characteristics connected to the system's cultural background $\mathbb{C}_X$ ($\mathfrak{C}^*$ being the core of $\mathbb{C}_X$) with

(A.2-2-1-6) $<\mathbb{C}_X> = \{\tau|(\mathcal{M}^1(\ell,\tau), ..., \mathcal{M}^N(\ell,\tau)) \Vdash [E(e_g(\tau)), Z(\mathfrak{C}^*(\tau))], \tau \Vdash \mathfrak{I} \Vdash \mathbb{T}zu^*$.

In the above, vd is the vertical relationship between the central element and the non-central elements, hc is the horizontal relationship among non-central elements, and γ is the complex of system-specific culture (or the intangible and informal cultures, among all the elements $x_i(h_j^*)$ of the system) closely related to $<\mathbb{C}_X>$ (the operations of this γ being conditioned jointly by the world-dynamics $Ш^Д(\tau)$ and $<\mathbb{C}_X>$). This γ creates a group spirit and a sense of community in each element of the system. Note the conventional concept of incentive system (see §A.2-10) and communication system belong to $[R,R^D(e_k)]$, although an informal communication system belongs to γ.

In addition, R is (C_S,R_M) with C_S denoting static self-characteristics of elements (which are partially conditioned historically by the outside environments, including energy systems, non-energy-related physical, human and social systems, but excluding any relationship with other members of the underlying system χ) and R_M denotes static mutual-relations of elements (i.e., relationship among members in χ), $R^D(e_k)$ (with $k \varepsilon \{1,2, ...,K\}$) is the shorthand notation of $(C^{DS}(e_k),R^{DM}(e_k))$ with $C^{DS}(e_k)$ denoting dynamical self-characteristics of elements and $R^{DM}(e_k)$ referring to dynamical mutual-relations among elements of this system, Õ provides the conduit between this system and the outside environments (i.e., it conjoins closely with outside environments including energy systems, non-energy-related physical, human and social systems), $E\{e_k\}$ and $E\{e_g\}$ are in the complexes of social and natural environments ($g = 1,2,..,G$) which belong to the social power-energy net and the basis being-filed (in the structure of the universe), respectively.

Further, Z is the decision-making and strategic complex. In the context of a system, it is easily seen that the decision-making and strategic complex and the cultural complex $<\mathbb{C}_X>$ ($\equiv \{\tau|(\mathcal{M}^1,...,\mathcal{M}^N)\Vdash E(e_r)\}$, $\tau \Vdash (\mathfrak{I},Ш^Д) \Vvdash \mathbb{T}\text{zu}^*$) are relations or becomings in the will-to-creation entity, the social environment forms a part of the social power-energy net, and the natural environment constitutes a part of the basis being-field.

Let $X \sqsubseteq \Omega$ be a system where Ω is the collection of all subsets of human elements and $\psi \vDash \mathbb{Z}\circ,_v\mathbb{H}$ be an impactor. Here for $X = \chi\oplus <\mathbb{C}_X>$, $\chi = \{\mathbf{x}(H^*) \sqsubseteq \{[(vd,hc,\gamma),C_S{\times}C^{DS}(e_r),(R_M, R^{DM}(e_r))]|E\{e_j\},Z\}$, for $\{C_S{\times}C^{DS}(e_r), (R_M,R^{DM}(e_r))\} = (R,R^D(e_r)) =$ {WR-to-creation entity_Social power-energy net | Basis being-field $\angle$ $\mathbb{T}$zu*} ^ {MPFX cycle| Property rights/ Gentry class $\angle$ Military power} ^ {I-O, IRI, MW, SIFP, YXr&d/STr&d | Cwr $\prec$ market/ planning} $\Lleftarrow$ { I-YXT| Ruling class} and $<\mathbb{C}_X> = \{\mathcal{M}^1, ... ,\mathcal{M}^N|E(e_r),Z(\mathfrak{C}^*(\tau))$ (I denoting input subsystem, O denoting output subsystem, and YXT denoting the technology-output subsystem based on the model of yin-yang five elements.) Here, the collection of all universal elements with some of them carrying human characteristics is denoted as: $\mathbf{x}(H^*) = \{x_i(h_j)\}$, $i, j \in \mathbb{N}$.

Let $\mathbb{Z}\circ,_v\mathbb{H}$ be the collection of all self-operating impactors together with all the mutually operating interactors, and $\Psi = \{\psi\}$ be the collection of all impactors and interactors. Then for the complete space of systems with their impactors-interactors (i.e., together with their cultures), we write $(X,\Psi) \sqsubseteq (\Omega,\mathbb{Z}\circ,_v\mathbb{H}) \oplus <\mathbb{C}>$ ($\oplus$ being a connector, $<\mathbb{C}>$ being the cultural complex of, or generated by, X), or simply: $X \sqsubseteq (\Omega,\mathbb{Z}\circ,_v\mathbb{H},\{\mathbb{C}\})$.

One way to depict human characteristics is to disclose them in terms of cultural traits. In this perspective, by the term the set of **human characteristics** is meant the collection of rationality, will-to-creation, and whatever underlies their inter-related organizational and strategic features. It is conveniently conceived that this is closely related to the decision-making and strategic complex Z previously presented and closely associated with Ultimate Creativity-Destructivity.

From several individual systems, a **grand system** (or **basic system**) expressed in

(A.2-2-1-7) $X = \chi \oplus \{\{x_i(h_j^*)\} \Vdash^{\#} \{(vd,hc,\gamma),[R,R^D(e_k)],\tilde{O}|E(\{e_g\},Z)\}\}$, we have each constituting units of X tobe a subsystem. Note that , we may write this grand system as: {$\mathbf{X}_i$(H*) | $\mathbf{X}_i$(H*) $\Vdash^{\#}$ {(VD,HC,Γ),R,$R^D(e_k)$],Õ|E{e_g},Z}⊕ <$\mathbb{C}_X$>, with $\mathbf{X}_i$(H), denoting the collection of several $\mathbf{x}_i$(H), being composed of several subsystems or unit systems. Here, for simplicity, we shall use the same notations R, $R^D(e_k)$, Õ, E{e_g}, Z to denote the various complexes of this new system. This grand system is also called a **composite system**, since it consists of more than one subsystem in it.

Remark A.2-2-1-1. In a special case, to be consistent with our set of notations, an element may be treated as a system with only one element, called a **single-element system**.

Remark A.2-2-1-2. For X as an element (i.e., being treated as a system of only one element), a system, a grand system, or a great-grand system, etc., we simply write it as: X ⊑ (Ω,$\mathbb{Z}$o,v $\mathbb{H}$,{ℂ}).

Note that we shall use the **basic-grand system** to designate a grand system in which the constituting "elements" are basic systems which are by themselves systems comprising several unit systems, respectively.

Remark A.2-2-1-3. For a system which is composed of several layers of subsystems, it may be called a **n-layer grand system** or simply a **n-level system**, with n denoting any natural number. For example, X is an n-level system if and only if the following conditions are true:

(1) X is a system in which X_i's are subsystems, i ∈ℕ.

(2) For i ∈ℕ, X_i is a system in which X_{ij}'s are subsystems, j ∈ℕ.

(3) For j ∈ℕ,X_{ijk} is a system in which X_{ijk}'s are subsystems, k ∈ℕ.

...

(n) For n ∈ℕ,$X_{ijk,\ldots,n}$ is a system in which $X_{ijk,\ldots,n(n+1)}$'s are subsystems, (n+1) ∈ℕ.

Note that in the above presentation of Bcm. (A.2-2-1-1), X = χ⊕<$\mathbb{C}_X$>, we may treat χ as the "**real system**" and <$\mathbb{C}_X$> the "**virtual system**." In χ, the relevant cultures (γ) are specific cultures like the political culture, social culture, economic culture, and belief system. In the virtual system <$\mathbb{C}_X$>, the center is the core culture, or what is directly related to Ultimate Creativity-Destructivity of the universe, and the semi- or non-central elements are various cultures, be they technological creativity, newly absorbed foreign cultures or any other s with each associated with a broadly defined culture (like the culture of conflict or the culture of tranquility).

To form a system, we may use the following figure A.2-2-1-1 to present universal members.

Looking at Figure A.2-2-1-1, we shall let a_i, b_i, c_i ⊩ **U** (or the preliminary space of universal elements), then we may write {a_i,b_i|c_i} as a system with O being the T Central identity (or virtual center, see §A.2-2-2), for i ∈ℕ. For example, let {a_i,b_i|c_i} be the same as the system {yin,yang|he}. Then [(yin,yang|he)‖$\mathcal{T}ci$] is a system with $\mathcal{T}ci$ being the **T central identity** of the system. Note that this O could be the cluster of all the T Central identities of {a_i,b_i|c_i} for all i (i.e., {O_i}) if we would like to differentiate the T Central identity of {a_i,b_i|c_i} from that of{a_j,b_j|c_j}, for i ≠ j. Furthermore, note that the limit concept of mathematics could be applied to this space of universal elements **U** and especially to this cluster O.

Figure A.2-2-1-1
Presentation of Universal Elements

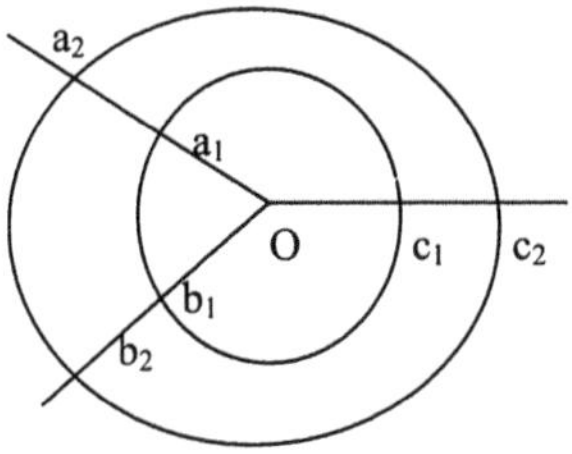

To relate the space of the system $\{a_i,b_i|c_i\}$ to the preliminary space of universal elements **U**, we could assign the space of c_i, $\{c_i\}$, to **U**, and assign the space of the pair $\{a_i,b_i\}$ to $^{-}\mathbf{U}$. Then the new space $\{\{a_i,b_i\},c_i\}$ is a (new) super-space of universal elements in which we could assign the space of $\{a_i,b_i\}$ in the way that $\{b_i\} \equiv \mathbf{U}^{+}$ and $\{a_i\} \equiv {}^{-}\mathbf{U}$. Here we treat $\mathbf{U}^{+}$ as a space and $^{-}\mathbf{U}$ as another space. To be more specific, we assign $\{a_i,b_i|c_i\}$ as $\{\{^{-}\mathbf{U}, \mathbf{U}^{+}\},\mathbf{U}^{++}\} = \mathbf{U}''$, a super space of super space (with $\{c_i\}$ as $\mathbf{U}^{++}$, i.e., one which is very similar to and yet different from $\{a_i\} \equiv \mathbf{U}^{+}$). By the same reasoning process, we could create a series of ever more complicated super spaces. For the matter of convenience, in the lectures presented below, we shall call the collection of all these spaces and "upper- or super-spaces" just as the **space of universal elements**. And if there is no confusion, we shall simply designate this space of universal elements as **U**.

Remark A.2-2-1-4. For a system of three elements a, b, c ⊩ **U**, it can be written as {a,b,c} (a collection of three elements without structure of a system), {a,b|c} (for c being the center, while a and b are non-central elements), or $\{a,b|c\} \oplus <\mathbb{C}_{\{a,b|c\}}>$ (for $\mathbb{C}_{\{a,b|c\}}$ being the cultural generator of the system in question).

§A.2-2-2 Structure of A System

In this subsection, we introduce the structure of a system. We may treat the concept of element as an undefined term. As was presented in A.2-1-2, by universal element is just meant a human being, thing or event, etc. The space of the universal elements is denoted by **U**.

As in the above, we define the *human element* as: x(h*)⊩ **U**, where h* ⊩ **H*** is a universal element endowed with multiple dimensions of human, cultural, economic, political and social characteristics such as those of human body, religious belief, community activities and political affiliation. For the space of human beings, we shall denote it by **H** = {x(h*)⊩ **U** |h* ⊩ **H***}. For example, John Smith can be expressed as: $x(h^*) = (x_1,x_2,.;h_1^*,.)$, where x_1 refers to the characteristic of a male, x_2 refers to the characteristic of healthy body, and h_1^* is, for example, the characteristic of being a professor teaching English poetry.

In general, the *space of human elements* is written as:

(A.2-2-2-1) $\mathbf{H}$

$$= \{x_i \mid x_i = x_i(y_i;h_i^*;.)\}$$
$$= \{[x_1(y_{11},y_{12},..,y_{1s};h_{11}^*,h_{12}^*,..,h_{1t}^*;IRI_1,.], x_2(y_{21},y_{22},..,y_{2s};h_{21}^*, h_{22}^*, ..,h_{2t}^*;IRI_2,.), ..,x_r(y_{r1},y_{r2},..,y_{rs}; h_{r1}^*,h_{r2}^*,..,h_{rt}^*;IRI_r,.)] \mid x_i \Vdash \mathbf{U}, y_{ij}^* \Vdash \mathbf{\Phi}^*, h_{ik}^* \Vdash \mathbf{H}^*\}, i = 1,2,..,r, j = 1,2,..,s, k = 1,2,..,t,$$

where $\mathbf{\Phi}^*$ is the space of a person's physiological and biological characteristics, x_i is the ith person, $y_i = (y_{ij})$ for y_{ij} being the jth feature of the ith person's physical and biological (i.e., non-human) characteristics, and $\mathbf{H}^*$ is the space of a person's human and cultural characteristics, where $h_i^* = (h_{ik}^*)$ for h_{ik}^* being the kth feature of the ith person's human and cultural characteristics. Note that $x_i(y_{11},y_{12},..,y_{1s};h_{i1}^*, h_{i2}^*,..,h_{it}^*; IRI_i)$, $i \in \mathbb{N}$, is a system, and IRI_i (which is closely associated with the $(\gamma,\mathbb{C}_X)$ complex of the system X in Bcms (A.2-2-1-3) and (A.2-2-1-4)) is the information-evaluation _rational-decision-making_planning-implementation chain of the person i.

Remark A.2-2-2-1. To have a more comprehensive account of a system, we have the following statement. X is said to be a system if and only if the following conditions old:

(i) $X = \chi \oplus <\mathbb{C}_X>$.

(ii) $\chi = \{\mathbf{x}(H^*) \| [\mathbf{x}(H^*) \Vdash (v,h,\gamma(\tau)),(R,R^D),\tilde{O} \| E\{e_j\},Z]\}, \tau \Vdash (\mathfrak{I},\text{Ш}^{\text{Д}}) \Vvdash \mathbb{T}\text{zu}^*$.

(iii) $\mathbf{x}(H^*) = \{x_1(y_1;h_1^*,.),\ldots, x_n(y_n;h_n^*,.)\}$.

(iv) $x_i(y_i;h_i^*,.) = x_i(y_{i1},y_{i2},..,y_{is};h_{i1}^*, h_{i2}^*,..,h_{it}^*;IRI_i)$, $x_i(.) \Vdash \mathbf{U}$, $y_{ij}^* \Vdash \mathbf{\Phi}^*$, $h_{ik}^* \Vdash \mathbf{H}^*$, $i = 1,2,..,n$, $j = 1,2,..,s$, $k = 1,2,..,t$.

(v) $<\mathbb{C}_X>=\{\tau | (\mathcal{M}^1,\ldots, \mathcal{M}^N) \Vdash [E(e_g(\tau)),Z(\mathfrak{C}^*(\tau))], \tau \Vdash \mathfrak{I} \Vvdash \mathbb{T}\text{zu}^*$ (Bcm. (A.2-2-1-6)).

The collection of the space of universal elements x_α (or human elements; α being an index, not necessarily be mathematically countable or measurable), the characteristics of x_α (or human elements h_α, $h_\alpha \Vdash \mathbf{H}^*$), the interactive relationships of the universal element x_α (expressed by R which locates in the rationality/will-to-creation entity and the social power-energy net, and the organic integrated whole of the relationships $\mathfrak{R}$ between them and the basis being-field of the universe, i.e., the worlds embracing objects of physics, chemistry, biology and physiology) is called the *unit system* (or individual system). Recall that a unit system X is expressed as: $X = \chi \oplus <\mathbb{C}_X>$, where $\chi = [\mathbf{x}(H^*),R,\mathfrak{R},\tilde{O}]$, $\mathbf{x}(H^*) = \{x_\alpha(h_\alpha^*),\forall\alpha \mid h_\alpha^* \Vdash \mathbf{H}^*\} \sqsubseteq \mathbf{H}$, $\mathbf{x}(.) \sqsubseteq \mathbf{U}$ ($\mathbf{x}(H^*)$ is a "subset" of U), $\mathfrak{C}_X$ is the cultural generator (i.e., creator) of X. Here $<\mathbb{C}_X>$ is the cultural complex generated by $\mathbb{C}_X$. That is, the simple collection of the individual's cultural characteristics (h_α) of the human elements of X is embodied in $\mathbb{C}_X$. In the above, we present the structure of χ. Here (vd,hc) denotes the hierarchical and horizontal structures of the elements of X. Furthermore, it may indicate a structure of "**virtual center**" (also see Subsection Definition I.2-6 in Appendix I). For example, if this system is (x,y|z), then z versus x and y has a structure of being the center of the system. In addition, this system (x,y|z) (in this case to be written as $[(x,y|z) \| \mathcal{Tci}]$ may have a "**T central identity**" if the following conditions hold: (1) x is the vertical-down-to-the-left invertor of z and z is the vertical up-from-the-left invertor of x (2) y is the vertical-down-to-the-right invertor of z and z is the vertical up-from-the-right invertor of x, and (3) x is the horizontal-at-the-left invertor of y and y is the horizontal-at the-right invertor of x.

In the above, note that this $\mathcal{T}ci$ is the *virtual center* of this system, and the so-called "invertor" is actually the **impactor of yin-yang tao-reversals** (YYTR impactor) or that of the negations of the entities in question. That is, yin-yang tao-reversal is an interactor of d- , h- or iso-systemism. Thus, in the above system $[(x,y|z)\|\mathcal{T}ci]$, x is the horizontal YYTR–to-the-left of y, and y is the YYTR–to-the-right of X, (x,y) is the vertical YYTR-down of z, and so on.

In the presentation of X as a *system*: $X = \chi \oplus \langle\mathbb{C}_X\rangle$, where $X = \{\mathbf{x}(H^*) \sqsubseteq [(vd,hc,\gamma),C_s{\times}C^{DS}(e_r),(R_M,R^{DM}(e_r))],\tilde{O}|E\{e_j\},Z\}$ or $\chi = \{\mathbf{x}(H^*)\} \sqsubseteq [(vd,hc,\gamma),(R,R^D(e_r))],\tilde{O}|\ E(\{e_j\},Z]$ for simplicity (see Bcms. A.2-2-1-4, A.2-2-1-5), we shall call $[(vd,hc,\gamma),C_S{\times}C^{DS}(e_r),\ (R_M, R^{DM}(e_r)),\tilde{O}]$ the organizational and static-dynamical structures of a system in which (vd,hc,γ) is the formal-informal organizational structure, "$C_S{\times}C^{DS}(e_r),(R_M,R^{DM}(e_r)),\tilde{O}$" the static-dynamical framing network system, $\langle\mathbb{C}_X\rangle = \{\tau|\ \mathcal{M} \Vdash E(e_r),\ \tau \Vdash \mathfrak{I} \Vvdash \mathbb{T}zu^*\}$ the cultural complex, Z the decision-making and strategic complex, $E\{e_j\}$ and $E(e_r)$ the external energy systems (belonging to the social-power energy net and the basis being-field of the universe, resp.), $\mathcal{M} = [\mathcal{M}^{I}(\ell,\tau)\ \mathcal{M}^{II}(\ell,\tau)\ \mathcal{M}^{III}(\ell,\tau)\ \mathcal{M}^{IV}(\ell,\tau)\ \ldots]^T$ the mind complex, and $\mathbb{T}zu^*$ "Ultimate Creativity-Destructivity". Note that we have: $\gamma(\tau,\mathfrak{C}^*) \leadsto (\tau,\ \mathfrak{C}^*)$, $(\tau,\ \mathfrak{C}^*) \Vdash (Ш^{\Delta}(\tau),\langle\mathbb{C}_X\rangle) \Vvdash \mathbb{T}zu^*$.

In the above, the cultural set is determined by the culture underlying the system in question. For example, for a Confucian system, the cultural complex $\langle\mathbb{C}_X\rangle$ is centered on the dynamical process of jen as constantly practiced in a family and constantly manifested in various forms such as yi (righteousness) and li (propriety). For a Taoist, this $\langle\mathbb{C}_X\rangle$ manifests the dynamical process of one striving to be united with the nature following the usually unfathomable and ever vibrating rhythms of the nature. As for a Christian, this $\langle\mathbb{C}_X\rangle$ extols the values of the dynamical processes of mercy (or loving others unconditionally) and justice in the religious community under question. Note that for the Heidegger's system in Being and Time, this cultural complex $\langle\mathbb{C}_X\rangle$ comprises the dynamical process of how Dasein with its existence and sorge-orientation evolves over time in affecting the history of X.

Here, in the state without any leap, the evolution of the natural environments in E must follow the law of causality, statistical law of causality or the "natural tendency of biology."[14] In the law of causality, there are the laws of physical and chemical causalities. Law of causality and statistical law of causality have regularities. The tendency associated with the biological teleology is conditioned by various goals of biology. The tendency of biological teleology is not deterministic, and it may involve changes with multiple irregularities.

Furthermore, in the self-organizational structures of a non-biological entity, the action-strategic complex Z indicates the space or cope of its motion. As for the case of biological entity, the action-strategic complex Z comprises the possible space of teleological activities of biological entities. At the same time, in the broadest sense, the strategic complex Z is in actuality connecting directly to "laws" (or the natural tendency) of the self-organizing entities. In terms of transformations and exchanges of information and energy, the afore-mentioned strategic objectives may be considered as the results of the functions of communication, absorption, transformation, storage or emission of the information and energy.[15] In the systems of human beings, societies and super-societies, these exchanges and functioning of information and energy are the products of the internal structure $\{(vd,hc,\gamma),C_S{\times}C^{DS}(e_r),\tilde{O}\}$ in the grand system. In an elaborate way, these exchange and functioning may be eventually supportive of and be supported by the evolution of the external environments $(R,R^D(e_r))$. Here we have (IRI,SIFP,automatic developing structures, MW-personnel entity (i.e., workers-managers entity), other developing entities MW) $\sqsubseteq (R,R^D(e_r))$.

That is, in the external relations of the grand system and the interactive relationships among the unit systems, these IRI chain, MW-personnel chain, SIFP chain, other interactive chain, and self-developing chain to execute functions of communication, transformation, translation and passing of the cultural heritage, etc.

For a system X, γ in (vd,hc,γ) is a composite factor including the implicit forces associated with micro-culture, incentive mechanisms, passing information, decision making, and strategic execution of X. Note that we have: $\gamma(\tau,\mathfrak{C}^*) \rightsquigarrow (\tau, \mathfrak{C}^*)$, $(\tau, \mathfrak{C}^*) \Vdash (Ш^{\Delta}(\kappa),\langle\mathbb{C}_X\rangle)$, $\tau \Vdash (\mathfrak{I}, Ш^{\Delta}) \Vdash \mathbb{T}zu^*$.

This is directly connected with the IRI chain in $(R,R^D(e_r))$ for a single basic system and the SIFP chain in the cultural complex $\langle\mathbb{C}_X\rangle$ for the big system (like capitalism).

In the formal-informal organization of a system (vd,hc,γ), in the case of a business entity, it is said that γ represents the implicit corporate culture, while (vd,hc) represents the hierarchical structure from which the corporate strategy is carried out. For the latter, it refers to the degree of "$\mathcal{T}^*C \geq \mathcal{T}X_i$," the degree of freedom of $\mathcal{T}X_i$ and how $\mathcal{T}^*C$ is formulated from $\mathcal{T}X_i$. Here if $\mathcal{T}X_i$ has a higher degree of freedom, then the hc chain of the system will be longer (i.e., the system is more decentralized).

In the study of a system, one way to describe it is to analyze the mechanisms governing the human characteristics. It is obvious that this set of human characteristics is conditioned upon the spirituality and rationality underlying the system in question, and very often it is a reflection of the mind set hidden in the system.

The collection of various subsystems (ie., unit systems) with some integrated relationships is called the **grand system** (or **basic system**) (see Bcm.(A.2-2-1-5)): $X = \{\{x_i(h_j^*)\}\Vdash^{\#} \{(vd,hc,\gamma),[R,R^D(e_k)],\tilde{O}|E(\{e_g\},Z)\}\} \oplus \langle\mathbb{C}_X\rangle$, in which each constituting unit designates a system.

In the above, we have already defined the **systematic space** as: $(\Omega,\mathcal{Z}\circ,_v\mathcal{H},\{\mathbb{C}\})$. Here (z,h): $\Omega\times\Omega\times\ldots\times\Omega \rightarrow \Omega$, where Ω is the collection of various systems and all impactors involved, $\mathcal{Z}$ is the collection of all impactors operating on the self-entities ($z \vDash \mathcal{Z} \Subset \Omega$, i.e., the collection of impactors $\mathcal{Z}$ is also a system), $\mathcal{H} = \{h\}$ the collection of all interactors (the interactor $h \equiv$ "*" is a system as well: $h \vDash \mathcal{H} \Subset \Omega$) so that "$x \sqsubseteq \Omega$ and $y \sqsubseteq \Omega$" $\Rightarrow x^*y \sqsubseteq \Omega$. Here, a system has at least a dimension of m x n (m and n are natural numbers for m being the vertical order of the system and n the horizontal order of the system). Thus, for a universal element, it is a system of dimension 1 × 1 with (vd,hc,γ) being an empty entity.

§A.2-2-3 Basic Concepts of Systems: Yin-Yang Components and Modes

For a "simple system," there are certain structures associated with it, and we shall call this the mode of system. Let us formally define this concept.

Definition A.2-2-3-1a (Mode of two elements: mutual prosperity). For $x, y \Vdash X \sqsubseteq \Omega$ (i.e., x and y are universal or human elements in the collection X which is a sub-collection of Ω) and $*, \# \vDash \mathcal{Z}\circ,_v\mathcal{H}$ (i.e., * and # are either self- or mutual-impactors), a system $X = \{x,y|*,\#\} \sqsubseteq (\Omega,\mathcal{Z}\circ,_v\mathcal{H},\{\mathbb{C}\})$ is called a **mode of elements** if and only if the following conditions hold:

(1) Closure properties: x*y, y*x $\Vdash$ X $\sqsubseteq \Omega$ and x#y, y#x $\Vdash$ X $\sqsubseteq \Omega$.

(2) Symmetric properties: x*y = y*x (for example, x marries to y is the same as y marrying to x).

(3) Asymmetric properties: x#y $\neq$ y#x (for example, for x being the wife and y the husband is not the same as x being the husband and y the wife).

(4) Properties of central-noncentral elements: x and y are non-central elements with

i). (Horizontal coordination: (x,y) be a **horizontal yin-yang pair**, or there is a relationship of coordination between two non-central elements.
ii). (Vertical dominance: the central element is missing).

(4') (System of completion, "yin-complement" and "yang-complement") In the yin-yang pair (x,y), {x,y;*,#} is called the **system of component-completion**; and we call the yin element x (given that x is the yin element) the **yin-component** and the yang element y (given that y is the yang element pairing with x) the **yang-component**.

(5) For (x,y) being a yin-yang pair, it is said that: x is the **y-invertor** (or left-invertor) of y and y is the y-invertor (or right-invertor) of x., and x*y = I, for I_H = (x,y) (i.e., the yin-yang pair) being the **y-identity**. Here I is called the **horizontal identity** as well.

Definition A.2-2-3-1b (Mode of two elements: dominance). The system X = {x,z|*,#} $\sqsubseteq$ $(\Omega,\mathbb{Z}\circ,{}_{v}\mathbb{H},\{\mathbb{C}\})$, for x, z $\Vdash$ X $\sqsubseteq \Omega$, * $\models$ $\mathbb{Z}\circ,{}_{v}\mathbb{H}$, is called a **mode of elements** if and only if the following conditions hold:

(1) Closure properties: x*z, z*x $\Vdash$ X $\sqsubseteq \Omega$.

(2) Asymmetric properties: x*z $\neq$ z*x . Note that, by defining * as the operation of dominance, if we assign z as the central element with x being the non-central element, then x*z does not exists, or x*z = $\circ$ (i.e., empty system).

(3) Properties of central-noncentral elements: x is the central element while y is the non-central elements with the vertical dominance: z dominates x, i.e., z*x.

(4) (system of completion, "yin-complement" and "yang-complement") In the yin-yang pair (x,z), for each of x and y, {x,z;*,#} is the **system of component-completion**; and we call the yin element x (given that x is the yin element) the **yin-component** and the yang element z (given that z is the yang element) the **yang- component**.

(5) Let (x,z) be a yin-yang pair. Then x is the **y-invertor** (or down-invertor) of z and z is the y-invertor (up-invertor) of x, and x*z = I, for I_V = (x,z) being the **y-identity**. Here I is called the **vertical identity** as well.

Note that as an analogy to abstract algebra, the mode of elements (or systems) may be called the "*systematic group,*" and the system of completion be called the "*systematic identity.*"

Definition A.2-2-3-2 (Mode of two elements: single kill). A system X = {x:y|*} ⊑ (Ω,Zo,vH,{ℂ}), for x, y ⊫ X ⊑ Ω, * ⊨ Zo,vH, is called a **mode of elements** if and only if the following conditions hold:

(1) Closure properties: y*x = y ⊫ X ⊑ Ω (y kills x); and x*y ⊫ X ⊑ Ω, x*y (i.e., x kills y) is not defined.

(2) Asymmetric properties: y*x = y and x*y is not defined, and therefore x*y ≠ y*x .

(3) Properties of dominant/dominated elements: (x,y) is a yin-yang pair of domination in {x,y|*} with

i). (Dominance) y dominates x.
ii). (Being dominated) x is dominated by y.

(4) (System of completion, "yin-complement" and "yang-complement") In the yin-yang pair, for each of x and y, {x,y;*} is the **system of component-completion**; and we call the yin element x (given that x is the yin element) the **yin-component** and the yang element y (given that y is the yang element) the **yang-component**.

Definition A.2-2-3-3 (Mode of two elements: mutual destruction). A system X = {x,y|*,#} ⊑ (Ω,Zo,vH,{ℂ}), for x, y ⊫ X ⊑ Ω, * ⊨ Zo,vH, is called a **mode of elements** if and only if the following conditions hold:

(1) Closure properties: x*y, y*x ⊫ X ⊑Ω.

(2) Symmetric properties: x*y = y*x (for example, x kills y while at the same time y kills x)

(3) Properties of dual dominance: (x,y) is a yin-yang pair of dual domination in {x,y|*} with

i). (Domination) x dominates y.
ii). (Reversal Dominance) y dominates x.

(4) (System of completion, "yin-invertor" and "yang-invertor") In the yin-yang pair, for each of x and y, {x,y;*} is the **system of identity** in which no one survives; and we call the yin element x (given that x is the yin element) the **yin-invertor** and the yang element y (given that y is the yang element) the **yang-invertor**.

Definition A.2-2-3-4 (Mode of two elements: independence). A system X = {x,y|*} ⊑ (Ω,Zo,vH,{ℂ}), for x, y ⊫ X ⊑ Ω, * ⊨ (Ω,Zo,vH,{ℂ}), is called a **mode of elements** if and only if the following conditions hold:

(1) Closure properties: x*y, y*x ⊫ X ⊑ Ω.

(2) Asymmetric properties: x*y = x, y*x = y, and therefore x*y ≠ y*x.

(3) Properties of independence: x and y operate independently of each other: this * operation is an "empty impactor."

i). Horizontal coordination is missing.
ii). Vertical dominance is missing.

(4) (system of completion and independent complements) In the pair {x,y}, for each of x and y, {x,y;*} is the **system of component-completion** and we call y the **independent component** of x and x the **independent component** of y.

Definition A.2-2-3-5 (Mode of three elements - in a standard system). A system X = $\{[x,y,z|R],*\} \sqsubseteq (\Omega,\mathbb{Z}_{\circ,v}\mathbb{H},\{\mathbb{C}\})$, for x, y $\Vdash X \sqsubseteq \Omega$, * $\vDash \mathbb{Z}_{\circ,v}\mathbb{H}$, is called a **mode of elements** if and only if the following conditions hold:

(1) Closure properties: x*y, x*z, y*z $\Vdash X \sqsubseteq \Omega$.

(2) Symmetric properties: x*y = y*x, x*z =z*x, y*z = z*y; and x*(y*z) = (x*y)*z.

(3) Properties of central-noncentral elements: x and y are non-central elements while z is the central element with

i). ([z,(x,y)] be a vertical yin-yang pair) z to x and z to y have a property of dominance of the central over a non-central element, respectively, (y is the y-systemism of x, while z is the h-systemism of y) and.
ii). ((x,y) be a horizontal yin-yang pair) x to y has a property of coordination between non-central elements, and vice versa for y to x.

Note that by a **standard system** is meant a system {x,y|z} with the following conditions: (i) x and y are non-central elements while z is the central element. (ii) Between x and y, there is a certain relationship of systemism, and similarly between y and z or between (x,y) and z. Here by a **systemism** is meant a transformation of one entity into other entity (see Section A.5 for the details of systemism). (iii) ([z,(x,y)] being a vertical yin-yang pair) For z to x and z to y, there is a relationship of dominance of the central element over each of the non-central elements. (iv) ((x,y) being a horizontal yin-yang pair) Between x and y, there is a relationship of mutual coordination.

Note that by a **standard Hg-system** is meant a system {x,y|z} with the following conditions: (i) x and y are non-central elements while z is the central element. (ii) y is the Hf-systemism of x, while z is the Hh-systemism of x. (iii) ([z,(x,y)] be a vertical yin-yang pair) For z to x and z to y, there is a relationship of dominance of the central over non-central elements. (iv) ((x,y) be a horizontal yin-yang pair) Between x to y, there is a relationship of coordination.

Note that by a **standard L-system** is meant a system {x,y|ℭ} with the following conditions: (i) x and y are non-central elements while the role of the central element is performed by a core (e.g., cultural core ℭ). (ii) y is the y-systemism of x. (iii) ((x,y) be a horizontal yin-yang pair) Between x to y, there is a relationship of coordination.

Leibniz' system of monad and Adam Smith's economic system are, in essence, examples of L-systems.

Note that by a **standard R-system** is meant a system {x,y|z} with the following conditions: (i) x and y are non-central elements while z is the central element. (ii) Although y is a non-central element, y is in a position higher than x ((x,y) is an r-horizontal yin-yang pair). (iii) y is a **Ry-systemism** of x; that is, y is the y-systemism of x and y is at a step (or stage) higher than x. (iv) y is a **Rh-systemism** of x; that is, z is the h-systemism of x (i.e., x→y being a y-systemism and y→z being a y-systemism) and z is at a step (or stage) higher than y. (v) (x,y) is called an R-horizontal yin-yang pair, and ((x,y),z) is called an R-vertical yin-yang pair. The relationship of these (R-horizontal and R-vertical) yin-yang pairs is a tranquil type.

Note that by a **standard Y-system** is meant a system {x,y|z} with the following conditions: (i) x and y are non-central elements while z is the central element. (ii) y is the y-systemism of x, while z is the y-systemism of (x,y). (iii) ([z,(x,y)] be a vertical yin-yang pair) For z to x and z to y, there is a relationship of dominance of the central over non-central elements. (iv) ((x,y) be a horizontal yin-yang pair) Between x to y, there is a relationship of coordination.

Definition A.2-2-3-6 (Mode of systems I). A general system {A,A'} = {{[x,y,z| R],*}, {[x',y',z'|R'],*'}} ⊑ (Ω,$\mathbb{Z}$o,$_v\mathbb{H}$,{ℂ}), for x, y, z ⊫ A = {x|(y,z)}, x', y', z' ⊫ A' = {x'|(y',z')}, and , *' ⊨ $\mathbb{Z}$o,$_v\mathbb{H}$, is called a **mode of systems** if and only if the following conditions hold:

(1) Closure properties: x*y, x*z, y*z ⊫ A ⊑ (Ω_A,$\mathbb{Z}$o,$_v\mathbb{H}$,{ℂ}); and similarly for A'.

(2) Symmetric properties: x*y = y*x, x*z =z*x, y*z = z*y, and x*(y*z) = (x*y)*z; and similarly for A'.

(3) Properties of central-noncentral elements: For A, x is the non-central element while y and z are co-central elements with

i). (y,z) is the high-horizontal yin-yang pair; and similarly for (y',z').
ii). (x,y) and (x,z) are vertical yin-yang pairs: z to x and y to x have a property of dominance of the central element over a non-central element, respectively, and similarly for (x',y') and (x',z').
iii). The interactive relationships of the low-horizontal yin-yang pairs (at the level of x) is missing in (Ω_A,$\mathbb{Z}$o,$_v\mathbb{H}$,{ℂ}) (Ω_A ⋐ Ω, Ω_A being a subset of Ω) and similarly for ($\Omega_{A'}$,$\mathbb{Z}$o,$_v\mathbb{H}$,{ℂ}) for A' ⊑ $\Omega_{A'}$.

(4) (grand system of completion, "yin-system" and "yang-system") For x ⊫ A ⊑ Ω and x' ⊫ A' ⊑ (Ω,$\mathbb{Z}$o,$_v\mathbb{H}$,{ℂ}), let (x,x') be a yin-yang pair so that {x,x'} forms a new system {x,x'}. Here, {y,z} and {y',z'} remain in the old systems.

That is to say, in the above definition, for two systems A = {x|(y,z)} and A' = {x'|(y',z')} with {A,A'} being the old grand system, {{x,x'}|{y,z},{y',z'}} forms a new grand system.

Example A.2-2-3-1 (the offsprings of two families getting married to form the third family). Let A = {x|(y,z)} and A' = {x'|(y',z')} be two families with x and x' being a young female human element and a young male human element, respectively. That is, {A,A'} is the old grand system with two families living independently.

Then, once x and x' leave their own families respectively and get married to form a new family, {{x,x'}|{y,z},{y',z'}} becomes the new grand system composing of three families: two old and modified families with a new family. Thus, in the yin-yang and tao-changing sense, {{x,x'}|{y,z},{y',z'}} is the system of completion for {{x|(y,z)},{x'|(y',z')}} over time. For this, we may say, {{x,x'}|{y,z},{y',z'}} is the "**systemic identity**" (**grand system of completion**), while {x|(y,z)} and {x'|(y',z')} are the "**systemic invertors**" to each other (i.e., the one with the young female member is the **yin-system** and the one with the young male member is the **yang-system**).

Definition A.2-2-3-7 (Mode of systems II). A general system {A,A'} = {{[x,y,z| R],*}, {[x',y',z'|R'],*'}} ⊑ (Ω,$\mathcal{Z}$○,v$\mathcal{H}$,{ℂ}), for *' ⊨ $\mathcal{Z}$○,v$\mathcal{H}$, is called a **mode of systems with** mediety-Tcentral if and only if the following conditions hold:

(1) Closure properties: x*y, x*z, y*z ⊫ A ⊑ (Ω,$\mathcal{Z}$○,v$\mathcal{H}$,{ℂ}) (here "A ⊑ Ω" and means that "A is an entity in the collection or set Ω"); and similarly for A'.

(2) Symmetric properties: x*y = y*x, x*z =z*x, y*z = z*y, and x*(y*z) = (x*y)*z; and similarly for A'.

(3) Properties of central-noncentral elements: x and y are non-central elements while z is the central element with:

i). ([z,(x,y)] be a vertical yin-yang pair) z as a central element dominates the noncentral element x, and at the same time, z dominates the non-central element z as well.
ii). ((x,y) be a horizontal yin-yang pair) The relationship between x and y is one of coordination between two non-central elements.

(3') Properties of central-noncentral elements. Let x, y, z ⊫ A = {x|(y,z)} and x', y', z' ⊫ A' = {x'|(y',z'}. Then for A, x being the non-central element while y and z are co-central elements, and similarly for A', and furthermore, we have:

i) . (y,z) is the high-horizontal yin-yang pair; and similarly for (y',z').
ii). (x,y) and (x,z) are vertical yin-yang pairs: z dominates (x,y).
iii). The low-horizontal yin-yang pairs (at the level of x) is missing in Ω_A (see Definition (2-2-3-6); and similarly for A'.

(4) (System of mediety-Tcentral, "yin-system" and "yang-system"). For x, y, z ⊫ Ω_X ⋐ Ω, x' ⊫ $\Omega_{X'}$ ⋐ Ω in the system space ⊑ (Ω,$\mathcal{Z}$○,v$\mathcal{H}$,{ℂ}), for Ω_X being unbalanced toward one side while $\Omega_{X'}$ being unbalanced toward the other side, there exists a system {a,b|c} so that {a,b|c} is in a state of mediety-Tcentral for A and A'. Note that as an analogy to abstract algebra, this mediety-Tcentral balance is a **systemic identity**.

For example, if A is a system with strong non-central elements and a weak central element while A' is a system with weak non-central elements and a strong central element, then as a system of mediety-Tcentral of A and A', {a,b|c} is a system with moderate non-central elements and a moderate center.

Remark A.2-2-3-1. Let X ={a,b|c} ⊑ (Ω,$\mathcal{Z}$○,v$\mathcal{H}$,{ℂ}), for a, b, c ⊫ Ω_X ⋐ Ω, and b = ξ(a), c = ξ^2(a) (or c = ψ(b)), ξ, ψ ⊨ $\mathcal{Z}$○,v$\mathcal{H}$. Then Ψ is said to be a **system-creating impactor** if and only if Φ{a} = X. Here we have, for $\Phi^{-1} \equiv \Phi^{Rev} \equiv \Psi$ ⊨ $\mathcal{Z}$○,v$\mathcal{H}$ (i.e., an invertor or revertor, i.e., a system-deconstructing impactor), we have: Φ_a{X} = a, Φ_b{X} = b, Φ_c{X} = c, and X = {a,ξ(a)| ξ^2(a)} or {a,ξ(a)| ψ(ξ(a))}.

Remark A.2-2-3-2. For X in Remark A.2-2-2-1, let ⊕, ⊚ ⊨ $\mathcal{Z}$○,v$\mathcal{H}$, ⊕ being an IDR-additive impactor, and ⊕ being an integrating impactor. Then we may write:

(A.2-2-3-1) $X = (a \oplus b \oplus c) \circledast Ix$,

where a, b and c are IDR components of X and Ix is the integrating factor of composing a, b, and c into X. Further, we may also write:

(A.2-2-3-2) $X = (a \oplus b \oplus c) \oplus (I_{ab} \oplus I_{bc} \oplus I_{ac}) \oplus I_{abc}) \circledast Ix^*$,

where $a^+ = a \oplus (I_{ab} \oplus I_{ac} \oplus I_{abc})$ (i.e., the comprehensive or conventional sense of a , a^+, is equal to a "plus" I_{ab}, I_{ac} and I_{abc}), and similarly for $b^+ = b \oplus (I_{ab} \oplus I_{bc} \oplus I_{abc})$ and $c^+ = c \oplus (I_{ab} \oplus I_{bc} \oplus I_{abc})$, with Ix* being the integrating factor or the residual in this process of decomposition.

§A.2-3 Impactors, System Operations and System Creation

§A.2-3-1 Introduction

Below we shall introduce impactors that create systems. In general, by an **impactor** is meant a force of self-motions or one of exerting influence on other entities. Note that all of systemisms are also impactors.

§A.2-3-2 Impactors for System Creation and Decomposition

Let $X \sqsubseteq (\Omega, \mathbb{Z}\circ,_v\mathbb{H}, \{\mathbb{C}\})$ with $X = \{a,b|c\} = [a ╪ b ╪ c||c \Vdash \mathbf{C}]$ (╪ being an IDR impactor and **C** being the set of central elements or sub-systems) (see Bcm (A.2-11-1)), $\Psi \vDash \mathbb{Z}\circ,_v\mathbb{H}$ be the system-decomposition impactor to be defined below. Recalled that [x╪y] = [y╪x] for x, y being elements or unit systems in a basic or grand system.

Then for Ψ to be the **system-decomposition impactor**, we have:

(A.2-3-2-1)
$$\begin{aligned}
&\Psi X \\
&= \Psi\{a,b|c\} \\
&= \Psi\{[a ╪ b ╪ c]||c \Vdash \mathbf{C}\} \\
&= \Psi\{[a \perp b \perp c] \wedge [a|b|c]||c \Vdash \mathbf{C}\} \\
&= \Psi\{\{[a \perp b \perp c] \wedge [a|b|c]\} \odot Ix\} \\
&= \Psi\{[a \perp b \perp c] \wedge \Psi\{[a|b|c]\} \circledast \Psi\{Ix\} \\
&= (a \oplus b \oplus c) \wedge (a \oplus b \oplus c) \wedge \circ,
\end{aligned}$$

with the impactor "|" referring to a hierarchically and orderly organizing operation, "⊥" referring to the impactor of a horizontally and independently organoizing operation, and "||" referring to the impactor of "conditioned upon."

Here we have:

(A.2-3-2-2)
$$\begin{aligned}
&\Psi\{\{[a \perp b \perp c] \wedge [a|b|c]\} \odot Ix\} \\
&= \Psi\{[a \perp b \perp c] \wedge \Psi\{ [a|b|c]\} \circledast \Psi\{Ix\} \\
&= \Psi\{[a \perp b \perp c] \wedge \Psi\{ [a|b|c]\} \circledast \circ \\
&= \Psi\{[a \perp b \perp c] \wedge \Psi\{ [a|b|c]\}
\end{aligned}$$

because we have:

(A.2-3-2-3) $\Psi\{[a\perp b\perp c] \wedge [a|b|c]\}$,
$= \Psi\{[a\perp b\perp c] \wedge \Psi\{ [a|b|c]\}$,

(A.2-3-2-4) $\Psi\{A \odot Ix\}$,
$= \Psi\{A\} \circledast \Psi\{Ix\}$,

for A, Ix $\sqsubseteq (\Omega,\mathbb{Z}\circ,_{v}\mathbb{H},\{\mathbb{C}\})$; and we have the following becomings as well:
(A.2-3-2-5) $\Psi\{[a\perp b\perp c]\} = (a \oplus b \oplus c)$,

(A.2-3-2-6) $\Psi\{[a\ |b|c]\} = (a \oplus b \oplus c)$,

by separating the horizontal structure from hierarchical structure in the system X. In addition, we have:

(A.2-3-2-7) $\Psi\{Ix\} = \circ$.

Finally, from the above becomings, we have:

(A.2-3-2-8) $\Psi\{\{[a\perp b\perp c] \wedge [a\ |b|c]\} \odot Ix\}$
$= (a \oplus b \oplus c) \wedge (a \oplus b \oplus c)$
$= (a \oplus b \oplus c)$,

for an IND-sys impactor $\oplus \vDash \mathbb{Z}\circ,_{v}\mathbb{H}$, because for A $\sqsubseteq (\Omega,\mathbb{Z}\circ,_{v}\mathbb{H},\{\mathbb{C}\})$:

(A.2-3-2-9a) $A \wedge A = A$.

Now we have by definition the **individualized system-decomposition impactors** Ψ_a, Ψ_b, Ψ_c:

(A.2-3-2-9b) $\Psi_a\{X\} = a$,
$\Psi_b\{X\} = b$,
$\Psi_c\{X\} = c$,

We derive, for X = $\{[a|b|c]\}$,

(A.2-3-2-10) $\Psi\{X\} = \Psi_a\{X\} \oplus \Psi_b\{X\} \oplus \Psi_c\{X\}$.

Remark A.2-3-1. For X , as a collection of universal elements a, b, and c, while not being a system, we can write:

(A.2-3-2-11) $X = \{\Psi_a\{X\} \oplus \Psi_b\{X\} \oplus \Psi_c\{X\}\}$.

That is, X is not a system and we have Ix = ○ and {non-{w.x.y.z}} = ○ (see Bcm. (A.2-11-1)). In the case that X is an IDR system (with Ix ≠ ○), we can write:

(A.2-3-2-12) $X = \{\{\{\Psi_a\{X\} \oplus \Psi_b\{X\} \oplus \Psi_c\{X\}\} \otimes^* \text{non-}\{a,b,c\}\text{'s}\} \circledcirc Ix$.

But if X is a complete IDR system (with Ix ≠ ○), then we can write:

(A.2-3-2-13) $X = \{\{\Psi_a\{X\} \oplus \Psi_b\{X\} \oplus \Psi_c\{X\}\} \circledcirc Ix$.

For $X \sqsubseteq (\Omega, \mathbb{Z}\circ,_{v}\mathbb{H}, \{\mathbb{C}\})$, X = {a,b|c} is said to be a *system-created* with a being the *basic element for system-creation* if and only the following is true:

$$(A.2\text{-}3\text{-}2\text{-}14)\quad X = \begin{cases} \{a, \varphi(a)|\varphi^2(a)\}\ (\varphi \vDash \mathbb{Z}\circ,_{v}\mathbb{H},\text{ standard Hg-system}) \\ \{a,\varphi(a)|\psi(a,\varphi(a))\}\ (\varphi, \psi \vDash \mathbb{Z}\circ,_{v}\mathbb{H},\text{ standard Y-system}), \\ \{a,a|\mathfrak{C}\}\ (\mathfrak{C}\text{ as the virtual center, standard L-system}). \end{cases}$$

Remark A.2-3-2. Note that, in general, for a system to be created from the element a ⊫ **U**, this element a is called the **basic element for system-creation.**

Then $\mathcal{I} \vDash \mathbb{Z}\circ,_{v}\mathbb{H}$ is called a **system-creating impactor** if and only if the following is true:

$$(A.2\text{-}3\text{-}2\text{-}15)\quad \mathcal{I}\{a\} = X.$$

In the above, $\mathcal{I}$ is called the macro-impactor for system-creation; and φ and (φ,ψ) are called the micro-impactor and the set of micro-impactors, respectively, for system-creation of X from a ⊫**U**.

From Bcms. (A.2-3-2-8), and (A.2-3-2-9b), we get:

$$(A.2\text{-}3\text{-}2\text{-}16)\quad \begin{aligned} &\Psi\{[a,b|c]\} \\ &= a \oplus b \oplus c \\ &= \Psi_a\{X\} \oplus \Psi_b\{X\} \oplus \Psi_c\{X\}. \end{aligned}$$

$$(A.2\text{-}3\text{-}2\text{-}17)\quad \begin{aligned} &\mathcal{I}_a\{\Psi\{X\}\} \\ &= \mathcal{I}_a\{(a\oplus b\oplus c)\} \\ &= \mathcal{I}_a\{(a\oplus b\oplus c) \odot \circ\} \\ &= \mathcal{I}_a\{(a\oplus b\oplus c)\} \circledast Ix \\ &= (a\oplus b\oplus c) \circledast Ix \\ &= X \end{aligned}$$

by defining $\mathcal{I}_a\{a\oplus b\oplus c\} = \mathcal{I}_a\{a\}$, where b = φ(a) and c = $\varphi^2(a)$ in the case of a standard Hg-system, b = φ(a) and c = ψ(a,φ(a)) in the case of a standard Y-system. Note that in the case of a standard L-system, we study it by the similar systemic reasoning. Finally, we have:

$$(A.2\text{-}3\text{-}2\text{-}19)\quad \begin{aligned} &\Psi\{\mathcal{I}_a\{a\}\} \\ &= \Psi\{X\} \\ &= a \end{aligned}$$

by defining Ψ{X} = a, for X = {a,b|c}.

§A.2-3-3 Basic Impactors for Elements and Systems

Below we shall introduce and develop some useful impactors.

A matrix in mathematics can not grow any bigger. This author proposed the idea of a growing "matrix" in order to tackle the problems of economic development and advancement.

Now, let an element-augmenting impactor be the operation to enable a "matrix" (quasi-matrrix, in actuality) to grow. For example, for the impactor φ, let $\varphi x = |x\ y|$, that is, to grow a single scalar x into a row vector of x and y, or let φ be an impactor to grow a 2×2 matrix into a 2×3 matrix as shown below:

$$\psi \left\{ \begin{matrix} |a\ b| \\ \\ |c\ d| \end{matrix} \right\} = \begin{vmatrix} a & b & x \\ e & f & y \\ c & d & z \end{vmatrix}.$$

The inspiration of a growing matrix is essentyially drawn form the idea of a growing system (expressed in a "quasi-matrix form"). In general, these are growing systems and contractive systems, and this issue of systems of growth and contraction involves specific impactors.

For some impactors applied to more than one element or systems, the operations may involve more than elements, systems or grand systems. Relationships or structures of system may be altered, eradicated, or created.

In the following, we shall proceed to discuss the operations of basic impactors.

I. *Rules for the operations of two elements*. These rules are as follows:

(I-1) Mutually beneficial operation. Let a and x $\Vdash$ **H** be two human elements and $☆^{+}$, $\oplus$, #, $*^{+}$ $\vDash \mathbb{Z}$ be interactors. Let $\oplus$ be a "simple additive impactor." Then we have the following rule:

(A.2-3-3-1) $a ☆^{+} x = [a*^{+}\xi(a\#x)] \oplus [x*^{+}\zeta(a\#x)] = a^{+} \oplus x^{+}$,

with a and x referring to elements with a potential for system-creation, $\xi = \xi(a\#x)$, $\zeta = \zeta(a\#x)$ standing for elements with no potential for system-creation, and a^{+} and x^{+} denoting the higher-a and the higher-x, respectively.

(I-2) Beneficial-harmful operation. Let a and x $\Vdash$ **H** be two human elements and $☆^{+-}$, $\oplus$, $*^{+}$, *, # $\vDash \mathbb{Z}$ be interactors. Let $\oplus$ be a simple-additive impactor. Then we have the following rule:

(A.2-3-3-2) $a ☆^{+-} x = [a*^{+}\xi(a\#x)] \oplus [x*^{-}\zeta(a\#x)] = a^{+} \oplus x_{-}$,

where x_{-} denotes a lower-x.

(I-3) Beneficial-neutral operation. Let a and x $\Vdash$ **H** be two human elements and $☆^{\uparrow N}$ (beneficial-neutral interactor), $\oplus$, $*^{\uparrow}$ (beneficial impactor), $*^{N}$ (beneficial-neutral impactor), # $\vDash \mathbb{Z}$ be interactors. Let $\oplus$ be a simple additive impactor. Then we have the following rule:

(A.2-3-3-3) $a ☆^{\uparrow N} x = [a*^{\uparrow}\xi(a\#x)] \oplus [x*^{N}\zeta(a\#x)] = a^{\uparrow} \oplus x$.

(I-4) Neutral-harmful operation. Let a and x $\Vdash$ **H** be two human elements and $☆^{N\downarrow}$ (neutral-harmful interactor), $\oplus$, $*^{N}$ (neutral-harmful impactor), $*^{\downarrow}$ (harmful impactor), # $\vDash \mathbb{Z}$ be interactors. Let $\oplus$ be a simple additive impactor. Then we have the following rule:

(A.2-3-3-4) $a ☆^{N\downarrow} x = [a*^{\uparrow}\xi(a\#x)] \oplus [x*^{\downarrow}\zeta(a\#x)] = a \oplus x^{\downarrow}$,

where $x^{\downarrow}$ denotes X being somewhat harmed.

(I-5) Mutually harmful operation. Let a and x ⊫ **H** be two human elements and $☆^{-}$, ⊕, $*^{-}$, # ⊨ $\mathcal{Z}$ be interactors. Let ⊕ be a simple additive impactor. Then we have the following rule:

(A.2-3-3-5) $a ☆^{-} x = [a*^{-}\xi(a\#x)] \oplus [x*^{-}\zeta(a\#x)] = a_{-}\oplus x_{-}$,

where a_{-} denotes a lower-a.

As a special case of this rule (i.e., for $☆^{0} \equiv ☆^{-}$), we have:
(A.2-3-3-6) $a ☆^{0} x = \circ$,

where ○ is an "empty element."

(I-6) Independence/irrelevance. Let a and x ⊫ **H** be two human elements and $☆^{|}$, $\oplus^{|}$ ⊨ $\mathcal{Z}$ be independent/irrelevant interactors. Then we have the following rule:

(A.2-3-3-7) $a ☆^{|} x = a \oplus^{|} x = \{a,x,|R_I\}$,

where, for R_I denoting an independent/irrelevant relationship, $\{a,x,|R_I\}$ stands for a "loose collection" of a and x in which a and x are independent and each operates independently of the other. Here, $R_I = \circ$ (i.e., empty element).

(I-7) Empty element. Let a and ○ ⊫ **H** be two human elements and * ⊨ $\mathcal{Z}$ be an interactors. Then we have the following rule:

(A.2-3-3-8) $a*\circ = \circ*a = a$.

(I-8) System-creation. Let a and x ⊫ **H** be two human elements and $☆^{|sc}$ ⊨ $\mathcal{Z}$ be a system-creating interactors. Then we have the following rule:

$$\text{(A.2-3-3-9)} \quad a ☆^{|sc} x = \left\{ \begin{array}{l} \{a,x|vd\} = [a\ x]^{T} \\ \\ \{a,x|hc\} = [a\ x] \end{array} \right\},$$

where, with vd denoting a relationship of vertical dominance, {a,x|vd} stands for a system with vertical dominance of x by a; and with hc denoting a relationship of horizontal coordination, {a,x|hc} stands for a system with horizontal coordination. Note that in the system {a,x|vd}, there is a center (i.e., a); while in the system {a,x|hc}, both elements are non-central elements.

In the above, Bcm. (A.2-3-3-9) says that either $a ☆^{|sc} x$ = {a,x|hc} or {a,x|hc}. Further, if we let φ ⊨ $\mathcal{Z}$ be a system-creating impactor, then for example we have φ{[a,x]} = $a ☆^{|sc} x$.

II. *Rules for the operations of systems*. These rules are as follows:

(II-1) Mutually beneficial operation. Let A, X ⊑ $(\Omega,\mathcal{Z}_{\circ},{}_{v}\mathcal{H},\{\mathbb{C}\})$ be two systems and $☆^{\uparrow}$,⊕, #, $*^{+}$ ⊨ $\mathcal{Z}$ be interactors. Let ⊕ be a simple additive impactor. Then we have the following rule:

(A.2-3-3-10) $A ☆^{\uparrow} X = [A*^{\uparrow}\xi(A\#X)] \oplus [X*^{\uparrow}\zeta(A\#X)] = A^{\uparrow}\oplus X^{\uparrow}$, with A and X referring to systems with some potential for system integrating-operations, $\xi = \xi(A\#X)$ and $\zeta = \zeta(A\#X)$ sysetms with no potential for system integrating-operations, and $A^{\uparrow}$ and $X^{\uparrow}$ denoting the scale-enlarged-A and scale-enlarged-X, respectively.

(II-2) Beneficial-harmful operation. Let A, X ⊑ (Ω,$\mathbb{Z}$∘,$_v\mathbb{H}$,{ℂ}) be two systems and $☆^{\uparrow\downarrow}$,⊕, $*^{\uparrow}$, $*^{\downarrow}$, # ⊨ $\mathbb{Z}$ be interactors. Let ⊕ be a simple additive impactor. Then we have the following rule:

(A.2-3-3-11) $A ☆^{\uparrow\downarrow} X = [A*^{\uparrow}\xi(A\#X)] \oplus [X*^{\downarrow}\zeta(A\#X)] = A^{\uparrow}\oplus X^{\downarrow}$,

where $X^{\downarrow}$ denotes a scale-reduced X.

As a special case of this rule, we have:

(A.2-3-3-12) $A ☆^{\uparrow\downarrow} X = [A*^{\uparrow}\xi(A\#X)] \oplus x = A^{\uparrow}\oplus x$,

where x ⊫ X is an element, not a system.

(II-3) Beneficial-neutral operation. Let A, X ⊑ (Ω,$\mathbb{Z}$∘,$_v\mathbb{H}$,{ℂ}) be two systems and $☆^{\uparrow N}$, ⊕, $*^{\uparrow}$, $*^{N}$, # ⊨ $\mathbb{Z}$ be interactors. Let ⊕ be a simple additive impactor. Then we have the following rule:

(A.2-3-3-13) $A ☆^{\uparrow N} X = [A*^{\uparrow}\xi(A\#X)] \oplus [X*^{N}\zeta(A\#X)] = A^{\uparrow}\oplus X$,

where $X^{\downarrow}$ denotes a scale-reduced X.

(II-4) Neutral-harmful operation. Let A, X ⊑ (Ω,$\mathbb{Z}$∘,$_v\mathbb{H}$,{ℂ}) be two systems and $☆^{N\downarrow}$, ⊕, $*^{N}$, $*^{\downarrow}$, # ⊨ $\mathbb{Z}$ be interactors. Let ⊕ be a "simple additive impactor." Then we have the following rule:

(A.2-3-3-14) $A ☆^{N\downarrow} X = [A*^{N}\xi(A\#X)] \oplus [X*^{\downarrow}\zeta(A\#X)] = A \oplus X^{\downarrow}$,

or

(A.2-3-3-15) $A ☆^{N\downarrow} X = [A*^{N}\xi(A\#X)] \oplus [X*^{\downarrow}\zeta(A\#X)] = A \oplus x$,

where x ⊫ X is an element, not a system.

(II-5) Mutually harmful operation. Let A, X ⊑ (Ω,$\mathbb{Z}$∘,$_v\mathbb{H}$,{ℂ}) be two systems and $☆^{-}$,⊕, $*^{-}$, # ⊨ $\mathbb{Z}$ be interactors. Let ⊕ be a simple additive impactor. Then we have the following rule:

(A.2-3-3-16) $A ☆^{-} X = [A*^{-}\xi(A\#X)]\oplus[X*^{-}\zeta(A\#X)] = A^{\downarrow}\oplus X^{\downarrow}$,

where $A^{\downarrow}$ denotes a scale-reduced A.

As a special case of this rule, we have:

(A.2-3-3-17) $A ☆^{-} X = [A*^{\downarrow}\xi(A\#X)] \oplus[X*^{\downarrow}\zeta(A\#X)] = A^{\downarrow}\oplus x$,

where x ⊫ X is an element, not a system, or

(A.2-3-3-18) $A ☆^{-} X = [A*^{\downarrow}\xi(A\#X)] \oplus[X*^{\downarrow}\zeta(A\#X)] = a \oplus x$,

where a ⊫ A is an element, not a system.

As another special case of this rule, $☆^0$ being a special impactor of $☆^{\cdot}$, we have:
(A.2-3-3-19) $A ☆^0 X = \circ$,

where $\circ$ is either an empty element or an "empty system."

(II-6) Independence/irrelevance. Let A, X $\sqsubseteq (\Omega,\mathbb{Z}\circ,{}_v\mathbb{H},\{\mathbb{C}\})$ be two systems and $☆^{|}$, $\oplus^{|} \vDash \mathbb{Z}$ be independent/irrelevant interactors. Then we have the following rule:

(A.2-3-3-20) $A ☆^{|} X = A \oplus^{|} X = \{A,X|R_I\}$,
where, for R_I denoting an independent/irrelevant relationship (or an empty system), $\{A,X,|R_I\}$ stands for a "loose collection" of A and X in which A and X are independent and each operates independently of the other.

(II-7) Empty system. Let A, $\circ \sqsubseteq (\Omega,\mathbb{Z}\circ,{}_v\mathbb{H},\{\mathbb{C}\})$ be two systems (with $\circ$ being an empty system) and $* \vDash \mathbb{Z}$ be an interactors. Then we have the following rule:

(A.2-3-3-21) $A*\circ = \circ*A = A$.

(II-8) Grand-system-creation 1. Let A, X $\sqsubseteq (\Omega,\mathbb{Z}\circ,{}_v\mathbb{H},\{\mathbb{C}\})$ be two systems and $☆^{|SCI} \vDash \mathbb{Z}$ be a system-creating interactor. Then we have the following rule:

(A.2-3-3-22) $$A ☆^{|SCI} X = \left\{ \begin{array}{l} \{A,X|VD\} = [A\ X]^T \\ \\ \{A,X|HC\} = [A\ X] \end{array} \right\},$$

where, with VD denoting a relationship of vertical dominance, {A,X|VD} stands for a grand-system with vertical dominance of X by A; and with HC denoting a relationship of horizontal coordination, {A,X|VD} stands for a grand-system with horizontal coordination. Note that in the grand-system {A,X|VD}, there is a center (i.e., A); while in the grand-system {A,X|HC}, both systemts are non-central systems. In the above, Bcm. (A.2-3-3-22) means that either $A ☆^{|SCI} x = \{A,X|HC\}$ or {A,X|HC}. Further, if we let be a system-creating impactor $\varphi \vDash \mathbb{Z}$, then we have $\varphi\{A,X\} = A ☆^{|SCI} X$.

(II-9) Grand-system-creation 2. Let A = {a,b|c}, X= (x,y|z) $\sqsubseteq (\Omega,\mathbb{Z}\circ,{}_v\mathbb{H},\{\mathbb{C}\})$ be two systems and $☆^{|SCII} \vDash \mathbb{Z}$ be a system-creating interactor. Then we have the following rule:

(A.2-3-3-23) $A ☆^{|SCII} X = \{[ax],[by]|[cz]\}$,

or

(A.2-3-3-24) $A ☆^{|SCII} X = \{[a\ x]^T,[b\ y]^T |[c\ z]^T\}$.

where $[a\ x]^T = \{x|a\}$ depicts a system with the center a and the non-central element x, and similarly for $[b\ y]^T$ and $[c\ z]^{T.}$

§A.2-3-4 Rules of System-Creation

As are in the cases of impactors, the operations of any system creation may involve more than elements, systems or grand systems. In the any process of operations, the dimensions, relationships or structures of systems may be altered, destroyed, or created as well.

In general, a process (or a chain of reactions) of creating a system from an element $x \Vdash X \sqsubseteq (\Omega, \mathbb{Z}\circ,_v\mathbb{H}, \{\mathbb{C}\})$, for $\psi \vDash \mathbb{Z}\circ,_v\mathbb{H}$, the created system is a dynamical system, not a static one. Let us define the **H-standard process of creating a system** as: ψ: $x \rightarrow \{x^\Delta, y^\Delta | z^\Delta\}$ where y^Δ and z^Δ refer to the Hf-systemism of x and Hh-systemism, respectively, with $x^\Delta(\mathbb{H}_x) \Vdash \{x(\mathbb{H}_x) \Vvdash Ш^\Delta\}$, $y^\Delta(\mathbb{H}_y) \Vdash \{y(\mathbb{H}_y) \Vvdash Ш^\Delta\}$, $z^\Delta(\mathbb{H}_z) \Vdash \{z(\mathbb{H}_z) \Vvdash Ш^\Delta\}$ for $x^\Delta \equiv x^\Delta(\mathbb{H}_x)$, $y^\Delta \equiv y^\Delta(\mathbb{H}_y)$, and $z^\Delta \equiv z^\Delta(\mathbb{H}_z)$, respectively. Here $\mathbb{H}_x$ is the core of x that would not change over time in the context of a systemic-becoming of change (see Appendix B). Similarly, $\mathbb{H}_y$ is the core of y that remains constant over time, and $\mathbb{H}_z$ is the core of x that remains constant forever.

Here $Ш^\Delta$ (or $Ш^Д$) refers to the **world of changes** (or the dynamical world), and by "$x^\Delta(\mathbb{H}_x) \Vdash \{x(\mathbb{H}_x) \Subset Ш^\Delta\}$" is meant that: $\{x(\mathbb{H}_x)\}_t \equiv \{x^\Delta(\mathbb{H}_x)\}_t \neq \{x^\Delta(\mathbb{H}_x)\}_{t+1} \equiv \{x(\mathbb{H}_x)\}_t$. That is, x at time t is different from x at time t+1: $\{x^\Delta(\mathbb{H}_x)\}_{t+1}$ is a d-systemism of $\{x^\Delta(\mathbb{H}_x)\}_t$ and $\{x^\Delta(\mathbb{H}_x)\}_t$ is a time-reversed d-systemism of $\{x^\Delta(\mathbb{H}_x)\}_{t+1}$.

Here naturally, by "$x^\Delta(\mathbb{H}_x) \Vdash \{x(\mathbb{H}_x) \Vvdash Ш^\Delta\}$" is also meant that: for the conditions $\alpha \neq \beta$, $\{x(\mathbb{H}_x|\alpha\}_t \equiv \{x^\Delta(\mathbb{H}_x|\alpha)\}_t \neq \{x^\Delta(\mathbb{H}_x|\beta)\}_t \equiv \{x(\mathbb{H}_x|\beta)\}_t$. That is, if $\alpha \neq \beta$, then "x at time t with the condition α" is different from "x at time t with the condition β."

Let us define the **standard process of creating a system** as: ψ: $x \rightarrow \{x', y' | z'\}$ where y' and z' refer to the y-systemism and h-systemism of x, respectively, with $x^\Delta(\mathbb{H}_x) \Vdash \{x(\mathbb{H}_x) \Vvdash Ш^\Delta\}$, $y^\Delta(\mathbb{H}_y) \Vdash \{y(\mathbb{H}_y) \Vvdash Ш^\Delta\}$, $z^\Delta(\mathbb{H}_z) \Vdash \{z(\mathbb{H}_z) \Subset Ш^\Delta\}$ for $x' \equiv x^\Delta(\mathbb{H}_x)$, $y' \equiv y^\Delta(\mathbb{H}_y)$, $z' \equiv z^\Delta(\mathbb{H}_z)$, respectively.

In the following, we shall present rules of system-creation:

(1) No System-creation. Let $a \Vdash$ **U** be a universal element with no potential to be built into a system. Then for $\varphi \vDash \mathbb{Z}\circ,_v\mathbb{H}$ being a system-creating or building impactor, we have:

(A.2-3-4-1) $\varphi(a) = a$.

Note that the "empty element" $\circ$ is a universal element with no potential to be built into a system. Thus, $\varphi(\circ) = \circ$.

(2) Simple system-creation. Let $a \Vdash$ **U** be a universal element with potential to be built into a system. Then for $\varphi \vDash \mathbb{Z}\circ,_v\mathbb{H}$ being a system-creating or building impactor, we have:

(A.2-3-4-2) $\varphi(a) \sqsubseteq (\Omega, \mathbb{Z}\circ,_v\mathbb{H}, \{\mathbb{C}\})$,

or $\varphi(a)$ is a system (we may also write $\varphi\{a\}$ as $\varphi(a)$ or even φa).

Note that we may have $\varphi\{a\} = \{a,b|c\} \sqsubseteq (\Omega, \mathbb{Z}\circ,_v\mathbb{H}, \{\mathbb{C}\})$. Here $\{a,b|c\}$ is called a **standard T system** if and only if the following conditions hold: (i) c is the center of the system, (ii) a and b are non-central elements, (iii) There exists a relationship of horizontal coordination between a and b, (iv) b is an y- or f-systemism of a, and (v) c is an h-systemism of a.

(3) System-creation with mutually beneficial interactor $☆^+$. Let $\varphi \vDash \mathbb{Z}\circ,_{v}\mathbb{H}$ be a system-creating impactor. If $\varphi(a^+ \oplus x^+) = \varphi(a^+) \oplus \varphi(x^+)$ or φ is an additive system-creating impactor, then from Bcm. (A.2-3-3-1), we have the following rule:
(A.2-3-4-3) $\varphi\{a ☆^+ x\} = \varphi(a^+ \oplus x^+) = \varphi(a^+) \oplus \varphi(x^+)$,

where $\varphi(a^+)$ and $\varphi(x^+)$ are systems.

Here we define φ as a **simply-additive system-creating impactor** on $\oplus$ if and only if: $\varphi(a^+ \oplus x^+) = \varphi(a^+) \oplus \varphi(x^+)$. In general, for a and x being two elements, $\varphi(a \oplus x) \neq \varphi(a) \oplus \varphi(x)$. Furthermore, in general, this is also true in the case of system operations.

Note that if a and x are elements with some potential for system-creation, and $\varphi(a^+)$ and $\varphi(x^+)$ $\sqsubseteq (\Omega, \mathbb{Z}\circ,_{v}\mathbb{H}, \{\mathbb{C}\})$ are systems. But if a^+ is an element with no potential for system-creation, then $\varphi(a^+) = a^+$ is not a system; and if x^+ is an element with no potential for system-creation, then $\varphi\{x\} = x^+$ is not a system.

(4) System-creation with beneficial-harmful impactor $☆^{+-}$ on elements. Let $\varphi \vDash \mathbb{Z}$ be a system-creating impactor. If φ is a simply-additive system-creating impactor, then from Bcm. (A.2-3-3-2), for a and x being elements (but not systems), we have the following rule:

(A.2-3-4-4) $\varphi\{a ☆^{+-} x\} = \varphi\{a^+ \oplus x^-\} = \varphi(a^+) \oplus \varphi(x^-)$.

(5) System-creation with beneficial-harmful impactor $☆^{\uparrow\downarrow}$ on elements/systems. Let A, X $\sqsubseteq$ $(\Omega, \mathbb{Z}\circ,_{v}\mathbb{H}, \{\mathbb{C}\})$ be two systems and $\varphi \vDash \mathbb{Z}\circ,_{v}\mathbb{H}$ be a system-creating impactor. If φ is a simply-additive system-creating impactor, then from Bcm. (A.2-3-3-11), we have

(A.2-3-4-5) $\varphi\{A ☆^{\uparrow\downarrow} X\} = \varphi\{A^{\uparrow} \oplus X^{\downarrow}\} = \varphi\{A^{\uparrow}\} \oplus \varphi\{X^{\downarrow}\}$,

where both $\varphi\{A^{\uparrow}\} \oplus \varphi\{X^{\downarrow}\}$ are grand-systems. For then, from Bcm. (A.2-3-3-12), we have:

(A.2-3-4-6) $\varphi\{A ☆^{\uparrow\downarrow} X\} = \varphi\{A^{\uparrow} \oplus x\} = \varphi\{A^{\uparrow}\} \oplus \varphi\{x\}$,

where $\varphi\{A^{\uparrow}\}$ is a grand system and $\varphi\{x\}$ is a system, except when x does not have any potential for system-creation.

Note that, in general, for A and X being two elements, $\varphi(A \oplus X) \neq \varphi(A) \oplus \varphi(X)$.

(6) Beneficial-neutral operation on elements. Let a and x be two elements and $\varphi \vDash \mathbb{Z}\circ,_{v}\mathbb{H}$ be a system-creating impactor. If φ is a simply-additive system-creating impactor, then from Bcm. (A.2-3-3-3), we have

(A.2-3-4-7) $\varphi\{a ☆^{\uparrow N} x\} = \varphi\{a^{\uparrow} \oplus x\} = \varphi\{a^{\uparrow}\} \oplus \varphi\{x\}$.

(7) Beneficial-neutral operation on systems. Let A, X $\sqsubseteq$ $(\Omega, \mathbb{Z}\circ,_{v}\mathbb{H}, \{\mathbb{C}\})$ be two systems and $\varphi \vDash \mathbb{Z}\circ,_{v}\mathbb{H}$ be a system-creating impactor. If φ is a simply-additive system-creating impactor, then from Bcm (A.2-3-3-13), we have:

(A.2-3-4-8) $\varphi\{A ☆^{\uparrow N} X\} = \varphi\{A^{\uparrow} \oplus X\} = \varphi\{A^{\uparrow}\} \oplus \varphi\{X\}$.

(8) Neutral-harmful operation on elements. Let a and x $\Vdash$ **H** be two human elements and $\varphi \models \mathbb{Z}_{\circ,\vee}\mathbb{H}$ be a system-creating impactor. If φ is a simply-additive system-creating impactor, then from Bcm. (A.2-3-3-4), we have:

(A.2-3-4-9) $\varphi\{a \star^{N\downarrow} x\} = \varphi\{a \oplus x^{\downarrow}\} = \varphi\{a\} \oplus \varphi\{x^{\downarrow}\}$.

(9) Neutral-harmful operation on systems. Let A, X $\sqsubseteq$ $(\Omega, \mathbb{Z}_{\circ,\vee}\mathbb{H}, \{\mathbb{C}\})$ be two systems and $\varphi \models \mathbb{Z}_{\circ,\vee}\mathbb{H}$ be a system-creating impactor. If φ is a simply-additive system-creating impactor, then from Bcm. (A.2-3-3-14), we have:

(A.2-3-4-10) $\varphi\{A \star^{N\downarrow} X\} = \varphi\{A \oplus X^{\downarrow}\} = \varphi\{A\} \oplus \varphi\{X^{\downarrow}\}$,

or

(A.2-3-4-11) $\varphi\{A \star^{N\downarrow} X = \varphi\{A \oplus x,\} = \varphi\{A\} \oplus \varphi\{x\}$,

where x $\Vdash$ X is an element, not a system.

(10) System-creation with mutually harmful operation on elements. Let a and x $\Vdash$ **H** be two human elements and $\varphi \models \mathbb{Z}_{\circ,\vee}\mathbb{H}$ be a system-creating impactor. If φ is a simply-additive system-creating impactor, then from Bcm. (A.2-3-3-5), we have:

(A.2-3-4-12) $\varphi\{a \star^{-} x\} = \varphi\{a_{-} \oplus x_{-}\} = \varphi\{a_{-}\} \oplus \varphi\{x_{-}\}$.

As a special case of this rule, we have:

(A.2-3-4-13) $\varphi\{a \star^{0} x\} = \varphi\{\circ\} = \circ$.

(11) System-creation with mutually harmful operation on systems. Let A, X $\sqsubseteq$ $(\Omega, \mathbb{Z}_{\circ,\vee}\mathbb{H}, \{\mathbb{C}\})$ be two systems and $\varphi \models \mathbb{Z}_{\circ,\vee}\mathbb{H}$ be a system-creating impactor. If φ is a simply-additive system-creating impactor, then from Bcm. (A.2-3-3-16), we have:

(A.2-3-4-14) $\varphi\{A \star^{\downarrow} X\} = \varphi\{A^{\downarrow} \oplus X^{\downarrow}\} = \varphi\{A^{\downarrow}\} \oplus \varphi\{X^{\downarrow}\}$.

As a special case of this rule, we have:

(A.2-3-4-15) $\varphi\{A \star^{\downarrow} X\} = \varphi\{A^{\downarrow} \oplus x\}$,

or

(A.2-3-4-16) $\varphi\{A \star^{\downarrow} X\} = \varphi\{a \oplus x\}$.

As another special case of this rule (for $\star^{0} \equiv \star^{-}$), we have:

(A.2-3-4-17) $\varphi\{A \star^{0} X\} = \varphi\{\circ\} = \circ$.

(12) Independence/irrelevant. Let a and x $\Vdash$ **H** be two human elements and $\varphi \models \mathbb{Z}_{\circ,\vee}\mathbb{H}$ be a system-creating impactor. For $\star^{|}$, $\oplus^{|} \models \mathbb{Z}$ be independent/irrelevant interactors, from Bcm. (A.2-3-3-7), we have the following rule:

(A.2-3-4-18) $\varphi\{a \star^{|} x\} = \varphi\{a \oplus^{|} x\} = \varphi\{\{a, x, |R_{I}\}\}$.

(13) System-creation with independence/irrelevant systems. Let A, X $\sqsubseteq$ (Ω,$\mathbb{Z}$○,$_v\mathbb{H}$,{$\mathbb{C}$}) be two systems and $\varphi \vDash \mathbb{Z}$○,$_v\mathbb{H}$ be a system-creating impactor. Then analogous to Bcm. (A.2-3-3-20), we have:

(A.2-3-4-19) $\varphi\{A ☆^{|}X\} = \varphi\{A ☆^{|},\oplus^{|} X\} = \varphi\{A,X,|R_I\}$,

(14) System-creation with empty element. Let a and ○ $\Vdash$ **H** be two human elements and $\varphi \vDash \mathbb{Z}$○,$_v\mathbb{H}$ be a system-creating impactor. For * $\vDash \mathbb{Z}$ being an interactor, analogous to Bcm. (A.2-3-3-21), we have the following rule:

(A.2-3-4-20) $\varphi\{a*○\} = \varphi\{○*a\} = \varphi\{a\}$.

(15) System-creation with empty system. Let A, ○ $\sqsubseteq$ (Ω,$\mathbb{Z}$○,$_v\mathbb{H}$,{$\mathbb{C}$}) be two systems and $\varphi \vDash \mathbb{Z}$○,$_v\mathbb{H}$ be a system-creating impactor. Then analogous to Bcm. (A.2-3-3-21), we have:

(A.2-3-4-21) $\varphi\{A*○\} = \varphi\{○*A\} = \varphi\{A\}$.

(16) System-creation with system-creating on elements. Let a and x $\Vdash$ **H** be two human elements and $\varphi \vDash \mathbb{Z}$○,$_v\mathbb{H}$ be a system-creating impactor. For $☆^{|} \vDash \mathbb{Z}$ being an interactor, analogous to Bcm. (A.2-3-3-9), we have the following rule:

(A.2-3-4-22) $\varphi\{a ☆^{|}x\} = \varphi\{\{a,x|vd\}\} = \varphi\{ [a\ x]^T\}$ or (ii) $\varphi\{\{a,x|hc\}\} = \varphi\{ [a\ x]\}$.

(17) System-creation with creating grand-system 1. Let A, X $\sqsubseteq$ (Ω,$\mathbb{Z}$○,$_v\mathbb{H}$,{$\mathbb{C}$}) be two systems and $\varphi \vDash \mathbb{Z}$ be a system-creating impactor. For $☆^{|SCI} \vDash \mathbb{Z}$ being an interactor, analogous to Bcm. (A.2-3-3-22), we have:

(A.2-3-4-23) $\varphi\{A ☆^{|SCI} X\}$ = (i) $\varphi\{\{A,X|VD\}\} = \varphi\{[A\ X]^T\}$ or (ii) $\varphi\{\{A,X|HC\}\} = \varphi\{[A\ X]\}$

(18) System-creation with creating grand-system 2. Let A, X $\sqsubseteq$ (Ω,$\mathbb{Z}$○,$_v\mathbb{H}$,{$\mathbb{C}$}) be two systems and $\varphi \vDash \mathbb{Z}$○,$_v\mathbb{H}$ be a system-creating impactor. For $☆^{|SCII} \vDash \mathbb{Z}$ being an interactor, then analogous to Bcms. (A.2-3-3-23) and (A.2-3-3-24), we have:

(A.2-3-4-24) $\varphi\{A ☆^{|SCII} X\}$ = (i) $\varphi\{[ax],[by]|[cz]\}$ or (ii) $\varphi\{[a\ x]^T,[b\ y]^T |[c\ z]^T\}$

Here we write $\varphi\{\{[ax],[by]|[cz]\})$ as $\varphi\{[ax],[by]|[cz]\}$, or in general, $\varphi\{\{X\}\} = \varphi\{X\}$.

§A.2-3-5 Rules of Reversal System-Creation

The rules governing the reversal system-creation impactor are as follows:

(1) (No System-creation: φ). Let a $\Vdash$ **U** be a universal element with no potential to be built into a system and a system-creating impactor $\varphi \vDash \mathbb{Z}$○,$_v\mathbb{H}$. Recall Bcm. (A.2-3-4-1): $\varphi(a) = a$. Then, for $\psi \equiv \varphi^{-1} \vDash \mathbb{Z}$○,$_v\mathbb{H}$ being a reversal system-creating impactor (i.e., ψ being the reversal impactor of φ), we have:

(A.2-3-5-1) $\psi(a) = a$.

(2) (Simple system-creation: φ). Let $a \Vdash \mathbf{U}$ be a universal element with potential to be built into a system and a system-creating impactor $\varphi \models \mathcal{Z}_{\circ,v}\mathcal{H}$. Recall Bcm. (A.2-3-4-2): $\varphi(a) \sqsubseteq (\Omega,\mathcal{Z}_{\circ,v}\mathcal{H},\{\mathbb{C}\})$. Then, for $\psi \equiv \varphi^{-1} \models \mathcal{Z}_{\circ,v}\mathcal{H}$ being a reversal system-creating impactor, we have:

(A.2-3-5-2): $\psi\{\varphi(a)\} = a \Vdash \mathbf{U}$.

(3) (System-creation with mutually beneficial interactor: φ with $\star^{+}$). Let $a, x \Vdash \mathbf{U}$, $\oplus \models \mathcal{Z}_{\circ,v}\mathcal{H}$, and $\varphi \models \mathcal{Z}_{\circ,v}\mathcal{H}$ be a system-creating impactor. Recall Bcm. (A.2-3-4-3): $\varphi\{a \star^{+} x\} = \varphi(a^{+}\oplus x^{+}) = \varphi(a^{+})\oplus\varphi(x^{+})$. If $\varphi(a^{+}\oplus x^{+}) = \varphi(a^{+})\oplus\varphi(x^{+})$ is a simply-additive system-creating impactor, then, for $\psi \equiv \varphi^{-1} \models \mathcal{Z}_{\circ,v}\mathcal{H}$ being a reversal system-creating impactor, we have the following rule:

(A.2-3-5-3) $\psi\{\varphi(a^{+})\oplus\varphi(x^{+})\} = a^{+}\oplus x^{+} = a \star^{+} x$,

or in general for $\varphi(.)$ being a simply-additive system-creating impactor,

(A.2-3-5-4) $\psi\{\varphi(a) \oplus\varphi(x)\} = a\oplus x$.

(4) (System-creation with beneficial-harmful impactor: φ with $\star^{+-}$ on elements) Let $a, x \Vdash \mathbf{U}$, $\oplus \models \mathcal{Z}_{\circ,v}\mathcal{H}$, and $\varphi \models \mathcal{Z}_{\circ,v}\mathcal{H}$ be a system-creating impactor. Recall Bcm. (A.2-3-4-4): $\varphi\{a \star^{+-} x\} = \varphi\{a^{+}\oplus x^{-}\} = \varphi(a^{+})\oplus\varphi(x^{-})$. If $\varphi(a^{+}\oplus x^{+}) = \varphi(a^{+})\oplus\varphi(x^{-})$ is a simply-additive system-creating impactor, then, for $\psi \equiv \varphi^{-1} \models \mathcal{Z}_{\circ,v}\mathcal{H}$ being a reversal system-creating impactor, we have the following rule:

(A.2-3-5-5) $\psi\{\varphi(a^{+})\oplus\varphi(x^{-})\} = a^{+}\oplus x_{-} = a \star^{+-} x$.

(5) (System-creation with beneficial-harmful impactor: φ with $\star^{+-}$ on elements/systems). Let $a, x \Vdash \mathbf{U}$, $\oplus \models \mathcal{Z}_{\circ,v}\mathcal{H}$, and $\varphi \models \mathcal{Z}_{\circ,v}\mathcal{H}$ be a system-creating impactor. Recall Bcm. (A.2-3-4-5): $\varphi\{A \star^{\uparrow\downarrow} X\} = \varphi\{A^{\uparrow}\oplus X^{\downarrow}\} = \varphi\{A^{\uparrow}\}\oplus\varphi\{X^{\downarrow}\}$. Then, for $\psi \equiv \varphi^{-1} \models \mathcal{Z}_{\circ,v}\mathcal{H}$ being a reversal system-creating impactor, we have the following rule:

(A.2-3-5-6) $\psi\{\varphi\{A^{\uparrow}\}\oplus\varphi\{X^{\downarrow}\}\} = A^{\uparrow}\oplus X^{\downarrow} = A \star^{\uparrow\downarrow} X$.

Recall Bcm (A.2-3-4-6): $\varphi\{A \star^{\uparrow\downarrow} X\} = \varphi\{A^{\uparrow}\oplus x\} = \varphi\{A^{\uparrow}\}\oplus\varphi\{x\}$, then we have:

(A.2-3-5-7) $\psi\{\varphi\{A^{\uparrow}\}\oplus\varphi\{x\}\} = A^{\uparrow}\oplus x = A \star^{\uparrow\downarrow} X$.

Note that, in general, for A and X being two elements, $\psi(A\oplus X) \neq \psi(A)\oplus\psi(X)$.

(6) (Beneficial-neutral operation on elements: φ with $\star^{\uparrow N}$). Let $a, x \Vdash \mathbf{U}$, $\oplus \models \mathcal{Z}_{\circ,v}\mathcal{H}$, and $\varphi \models \mathcal{Z}_{\circ,v}\mathcal{H}$ be a system-creating impactor. Recall Bcm. (A.2-3-4-7): $\varphi\{a \star^{\uparrow N} x\} = \varphi\{a^{\uparrow}\oplus x\} = \varphi\{a^{\uparrow}\}\oplus\varphi\{x\}$. Then, for $\psi \equiv \varphi^{-1} \models \mathcal{Z}_{\circ,v}\mathcal{H}$ being a reversal system-creating impactor, we have the following rule:

(A.2-3-5-8) $\psi\{\varphi\{a^{\uparrow}\}\oplus\varphi\{x\}\} = a^{\uparrow}\oplus x = a \star^{\uparrow N} x$.

(7) (Beneficial-neutral operation on systems: φ with $\star^{\uparrow N}$). Let $A, A^{\uparrow}, X \sqsubseteq (\Omega,\mathcal{Z}_{\circ,v}\mathcal{H},\{\mathbb{C}\})$, $\oplus \models \mathcal{Z}_{\circ,v}\mathcal{H}$ and $\varphi \models \mathcal{Z}_{\circ,v}\mathcal{H}$ be a system-creating impactor. Recall Bcm. (A.2-3-4-8): $\varphi\{A\star^{\uparrow N}X\} = \varphi\{A^{\uparrow}\oplus X\} = \varphi\{A^{\uparrow}\}\oplus\varphi\{X\}$. Then, for $\psi \equiv \varphi^{-1} \models \mathcal{Z}_{\circ,v}\mathcal{H}$ being a reversal system-creating impactor, we have the following rule:

(A.2-3-5-9) $\psi\{\varphi\{A^{\uparrow}\}\oplus\varphi\{X\}\} = A^{\uparrow}\oplus X = A\star^{\uparrow N}X$.

(8) (Neutral-harmful operation on elements: φ with $\star^{N\downarrow}$). Let a, x ⊩ **U**, ⊕ ⊨ $\mathbb{Z}_{\circ,v}\mathbb{H}$ and φ ⊨ $\mathbb{Z}_{\circ,v}\mathbb{H}$ be a system-creating impactor. Recall Bcm. (A.2-3-4-9): $\varphi\{a \star^{N\downarrow} x\} = \varphi\{a\oplus x^{\downarrow}\} = \varphi\{a\}\oplus\varphi\{x^{\downarrow}\}$. Then, for $\psi \equiv \varphi^{-1}$ ⊨ $\mathbb{Z}_{\circ,v}\mathbb{H}$ being a reversal system-creating impactor, we have the following rule:

(A.2-3-5-10) $\psi\{\varphi\{a\}\oplus\varphi\{x^{\downarrow}\}\} = a\oplus x^{\downarrow} = a \star^{N\downarrow} x$.

(9) (Neutral-harmful operation on systems: φ with $\star^{N\downarrow}$). Let A, $A^{\uparrow}$, X ⊑ $(\Omega,\mathbb{Z}_{\circ,v}\mathbb{H},\{\mathbb{C}\})$, ⊕ ⊨ $\mathbb{Z}_{\circ,v}\mathbb{H}$ and φ ⊨ $\mathbb{Z}_{\circ,v}\mathbb{H}$ be a system-creating impactor. Recall Bcm. (A.2-3-4-10): $\varphi\{A \star^{N\downarrow}X\} = \varphi\{A\oplus X^{\downarrow},\} = \varphi\{A\}\oplus\varphi\{X^{\downarrow}\}$. Then, for $\psi \equiv \varphi^{-1}$ ⊨ $\mathbb{Z}_{\circ,v}\mathbb{H}$ being a reversal system- creating impactor, we have the following rule:
(A.2-3-5-11) $\psi\{\varphi\{A\}\oplus\varphi\{X^{\downarrow}\}\} = A\oplus X^{\downarrow} = A \star^{N\downarrow}X$.

or (recall Bcm. (A.2-3-4-11): $\varphi\{A \star^{N\downarrow}X\} = \varphi\{A\oplus x,\} = \varphi\{A\}\oplus\varphi\{x\}$)

(A.2-3-5-12) $\psi\{\varphi\{A\}\oplus\varphi\{x\}\} = A\oplus x = A \star^{N\downarrow}X$.

(10) (System-creation with mutually harmful operation on elements: φ with $\star^{-}$). Let a, x ⊩ **U**, ⊕⊨ $\mathbb{Z}_{\circ,v}\mathbb{H}$ and φ ⊨ $\mathbb{Z}_{\circ,v}\mathbb{H}$ be a system-creating impactor. Recall Bcm. (A.2-3-4-12): $\varphi\{a \star^{-}x\} = \varphi\{a_{-}\oplus x_{-}\} = \varphi\{a_{-}\}\oplus\varphi\{x_{-}\}$. Then, for $\psi \equiv \varphi^{-1}$ ⊨ $\mathbb{Z}_{\circ,v}\mathbb{H}$ being a reversal system-creating impactor, we have the following rule:

(A.2-3-5-13) $\psi\{\varphi\{a_{-}\}\oplus\varphi\{x_{-}\}\} = a_{-}\oplus x_{-} = a \star^{-}x$.

As a special case of this rule, recall Bcm. (A.2-3-4-13): $\varphi\{a \star^{0}x\} = \varphi\{\circ\} = \circ$, we have: $\psi\{\circ\} = \circ$, and as a *special case*:

(A.2-3-5-14) $\psi\{\circ|_{\star 0;a,x}\} = \circ|_{\star 0;a,x} = a \star^{0}x$.

(11) (System-creation with mutually harmful operation on systems: φ with $\star^{\downarrow}$). Let A, $A^{\downarrow}$, X, $X^{\downarrow}$ ⊑ $(\Omega,\mathbb{Z}_{\circ,v}\mathbb{H},\{\mathbb{C}\})$, ⊕ ⊨ $\mathbb{Z}_{\circ,v}\mathbb{H}$ and φ ⊨ $\mathbb{Z}_{\circ,v}\mathbb{H}$ be a system-creating impactor. Recall Bcm. (A.2-3-4-14): $\varphi\{A \star^{\downarrow}X\} = \varphi\{A^{\downarrow}\oplus X^{\downarrow}\} = \varphi\{A^{\downarrow}\}\oplus\varphi\{X^{\downarrow}\}$. Then, for $\psi \equiv \varphi^{-1}$ ($\equiv \varphi^{Rev}$) ⊨ $\mathbb{Z}_{\circ,v}\mathbb{H}$ being a reversal system-creating impactor, we have the following rule:

(A.2-3-5-15) $\psi\{\varphi\{A^{\downarrow}\}\oplus\varphi\{X^{\downarrow}\}\} = A^{\downarrow}\oplus X^{\downarrow} = A \star^{\downarrow}X$.

As a special case of this rule, recall Bcm. (A.2-3-4-15): $\varphi\{A \star^{\downarrow}X\} = \varphi\{A^{\downarrow}\oplus x\}$, we have:

(A.2-3-5-16) $\psi\{\varphi\{A^{\downarrow}\oplus x\}\} = A \star^{\downarrow}X$,

or, recall Bcm. (A.2-3-4-16): $\varphi\{A\star^{\downarrow}X\} = \varphi\{a\oplus x\}$, we have

(A.2-3-5-17) $\psi\{\varphi\{a\oplus x\}\} = A \star^{\downarrow}X$.

As another special case of this rule, recall Bcm. (A.2-3-4-17): $\varphi\{A \star^{0}X\} = \varphi\{\circ\} = \circ$, we have, as a *special case*:

(A.2-3-5-18) $\varphi\{\circ|_{\star 0;A,X}\} = \circ|_{\star 0;A,X} = A \star^{0}X$.

(12) (Independence/irrelevant: φ with $\star^{|}$). Let a, x $\Vdash$ **U**, $\oplus^{|} \models \mathbb{Z}_{\circ,v}\mathbb{H}$ and $\varphi \models \mathbb{Z}_{\circ,v}\mathbb{H}$ be a system-creating impactor. Recall Bcm. (A.2-3-4-18): $\varphi\{a \star^{|} x\} = \varphi\{a \oplus^{|} x\} = \varphi\{\{a,x,|R_I\}$. Then, for $\psi \equiv \varphi^{-1}$ ($\equiv \varphi^{Rcv}$) $\models \mathbb{Z}_{\circ,v}\mathbb{H}$ being a reversal system-creating impactor, we have the following rule:

(A.2-3-5-19) $\psi\{\{a,x,|R_I\}\} = a \oplus^{|} x = a \star^{|} x$.

(13) (System-creation with independence/irrelevant systems: φ with $\star^{|}$). Let A, X $\sqsubseteq$ $(\Omega,\mathbb{Z}_{\circ,v}\mathbb{H},\{\mathbb{C}\})$, $\oplus^{|} \models \mathbb{Z}_{\circ,v}\mathbb{H}$, and $\varphi \models \mathbb{Z}_{\circ,v}\mathbb{H}$ be a system-creating impactor. Recall Bcm. (A.2-3-4-19): $\varphi\{A \star^{|} X\} = \varphi\{A \oplus^{|} X\} = \varphi\{A,X,|R_I\}$. Then, for $\psi \equiv \varphi^{-1}$ ($\equiv\varphi^{Rcv}$) $\models \mathbb{Z}_{\circ,v}\mathbb{H}$ being a reversal system-creating impactor, we have the following rule:

(A.2-3-5-20) $\psi\{\varphi\{A,X,|R_I\}\} = A \oplus^{||} X = A \star^{|} X$.

(14) (System-creation with empty element : φ with *). Let a, $\circ \Vdash$ **U**, $* \models \mathbb{Z}_{\circ,v}\mathbb{H}$ be a system-creating impactor. Recall Bcm. (A.2-3-4-20): $\varphi\{a*\circ\} = \varphi\{\circ*a\} = \varphi\{a\}$. Then, for $\psi \equiv *^{-1} \models \mathbb{Z}_{\circ,v}\mathbb{H}$ being a reversal system-creating impactor, we have the following rule:

(A.2-3-5-21) $\psi\{\varphi\{a\}\} = \circ*a = a*\circ$.

(15) (System-creation with empty system: φ with *). Let A, $\circ \sqsubseteq (\Omega,\mathbb{Z}_{\circ,v}\mathbb{H},\{\mathbb{C}\})$, $* \models \mathbb{Z}_{\circ,v}\mathbb{H}$ be a system-creating impactor. Recall Bcm. (A.2-3-4-21): $\varphi\{A*\circ\} = \varphi\{\circ*A\} = \varphi\{A\}$. Then, for $\psi \equiv *^{-1} \models \mathbb{Z}_{\circ,v}\mathbb{H}$ being a reversal system-creating impactor, we have the following rule:

(A.2-3-5-22) $\psi\{\varphi\{A\}\} = \circ*A = A*\circ$.

(16) (System-creation with system-creating on elements: φ with $\star^{|}$). Let a, x $\Vdash$ **U**, [a,x], $[a\ x]^T$ $\sqsubseteq (\Omega,\mathbb{Z}_{\circ,v}\mathbb{H},\{\mathbb{C}\})$, $* \models \mathbb{Z}_{\circ,v}\mathbb{H}$ be a system-creating impactor. Recall Bcm. (A.2-3-4-22):

(A.2-3-5-23) $\varphi\{a \star^{|} x\} =$ (i) $\varphi\{\{a,x|vd\}\} = \varphi\{[a\ x]^T\}$ or (ii) $\varphi\{\{a,x|hc\}\} = \varphi\{[a\ x]\}$

Then, for $\psi \equiv *^{-1} \models \mathbb{Z}_{\circ,v}\mathbb{H}$ being a reversal system-creating impactor, we have the following rule:

(A.2-3-5-24) $\psi\ \{\begin{Bmatrix} \varphi\{[a\ x]^T\} \\ \varphi\{[a\ x]\} \end{Bmatrix}\} = a \star^{|} x.$

(17) (System-creation with creating grand-system: $\varphi 1$). Let A, X, [A X], $[A\ X]^T \sqsubseteq (\Omega,\mathbb{Z}_{\circ,v}\mathbb{H},\{\mathbb{C}\})$, $* \models \mathbb{Z}_{\circ,v}\mathbb{H}$ be a system-creating impactor. Recall Bcm. (A.2-3-4-23), then we have the following rule:

(A.2-3-5-25) $\varphi\{A \star^{|SCI} X\} =$ (i) $\varphi\{\{A,X|VD\}\} = \varphi\{[A\ X]^T\}$ or (ii) $\varphi\{\{A,X|HC\}\} = \varphi\{[A\ X]\}$

Furthermore, for $\psi \equiv *^{-1} \models \mathbb{Z}_{\circ,v}\mathbb{H}$ being a reversal system-creating impactor, we also have the following rule:

(A.2-3-5-26) $\psi\{\varphi\{A\}\}$

$$= \psi \left\{ \begin{array}{l} \varphi\{[A\ X]^T\} \\ \\ \varphi\{[A\ X]\} \end{array} \right\}$$

$$= \{A \star^{|SC|} X\}.$$

(18) (System-creation with creating grand-system: φ2). Let a, x ⊫ **U**, A, X, [a,x], [a x]^T ⊑ (Ω,$\mathbb{Z}$∘,$_v\mathbb{H}$,{ℂ}), * ⊨ $\mathbb{Z}$∘,$_v\mathbb{H}$ be a system-creating impactor. Recall Bcm. (A.2-3-4-24):

$$\text{(A.2-3-5-27)}\quad \varphi\{A \star^{|SCI|} X\} = \left\{ \begin{array}{l} \varphi\{[ax],[by]||[cz]\} \\ \\ \varphi\{[a\ x]^T,[b\ y]^T ||[c\ z]^T\} \end{array} \right\}$$

Then, for $\psi \equiv *^{-1}$ ⊨ $\mathbb{Z}$∘,$_v\mathbb{H}$ being a reversal system-creating impactor, we have the following rule:
(A.2-2-5-28) $\psi\{|\ \varphi\{[ax],[by]||[cz]\}\quad \varphi\{[a\ x]^T,[b\ y]^T ||[c\ z]^T\}\ |^T\} = \{A \star^{|SCI|} X\}$,

where the superscirpt "T" depicts the transpose of the matrix |φ{.} φ{..}|.

§A.2-3-6 Simple Impactors – Association and Conflict Impactors, Row and Column Impactors, Element-augmenting and Eliminating Impactors, and System-creating Impactors

In this subsection, we shall study simple impactors. Here by the simple impactors is meant the association and conflict impactors, row and column impactors, element-augmenting and eliminating impactors, and system-creating impactors.

Remark A.2-3-6-1. We developed the basic concepts of entity-augmenting impactor for matrix-like system and matrix-like system-creating impactor in Tonn (2001). By applying these ideas to mathematics, we have the entity-augmenting operations for matrices and matrix-creating operations. Note that we could have a "matrix" of more than three dimensions, for example,

$|x_{111}\ \ x_{121}|\ //\ |y_{112}\ y_{122}|$
$|x_{211}\ \ x_{221}|\ //\ |y_{212}\ \ y_{222}|$

is a "matrix" of three dimensions $\{x_{ijk}/y_{ijk}\}$, with the first subscript (i = 1, 2) representing the first dimension, the second subscript (j = 1, 2) and the third subscript (k = 1, 2) representing the third dimension.

Definition A.2-3-6-1. Let X, Y ⊑ (Ω,$\mathbb{Z}$∘,$_v\mathbb{H}$,{ℂ}) be two human elements or systems, and Φ ⊨ $\mathbb{Z}$∘,$_v\mathbb{H}$ be an impactor. Then Φ is said to be an **association impactor** if and only if:

(A.2-3-6-1) $\Phi(X,Y) = X \star Y$,

where X☆Y = X⊕Y⊕(X⋆Y) with ⊕ ⊨ $\mathbb{Z}$∘,$_v\mathbb{H}$ being an impactor connecting the elements or systems in front and after it in an "independent manner," and "X⋆Y " being defined as X **interacts** positively with Y. Here "⋆" is called the notation of **interaction impactor**.
One easy example is the impactor of creating a family with a child.

(A.2-3-6-2) $\Phi(z,y) = z \star y = \{x|(y,z)\}$,

where, before the operation, y and z stand for the single male and female, respectively; while after the operation, x, y and z in $\{x|(y,z)\}$ refer to the child, mother and father, respectively.

Definition A.2-3-6-2. Let $X, Y \sqsubseteq (\Omega, \mathcal{Z}_{\circ,\vee}\mathcal{H}, \{\mathbb{C}\})$ be two human elements or systems, and $\psi \models \mathcal{Z}_{\circ,\vee}\mathcal{H}$ be an impactor. Then ψ is said to be a **conflict impactor** if and only if the following condition holds:

(A.2-3-6-3) $\psi(X,Y) = X \star^{-} Y$,

where $X \star^{-} Y = (X \oplus Y) \ominus (X \star Y)$ with $\ominus \models \mathcal{Z}_{\circ,\vee}\mathcal{H}$ being an impactor removing the "element or system after it" from the "element or system before it."

Below we shall introduce a few key impactors. Let a system $X = (X_i, X_2, \ldots, X_n) \sqsubseteq (\Omega, \mathcal{Z}_{\circ,\vee}\mathcal{H}, \{\mathbb{C}\})$.

Definition A.2-3-6-3. From Tonn (2001, pp. 118, 129-132), we have $M_{x \to i} \models \mathcal{Z}_{\circ,\vee}\mathcal{H}$ as a mie impactor: $M_{x \to i} X = X_i$, $i = 1,2, \ldots, n$, where X_i denotes the ith componet of X. That is, $\psi_i \equiv M_{x \to i} \models \mathcal{Z}_{\circ,\vee}\mathcal{H}$ is called the **decomposition-subtraction impactor** (or mie impactor) if and only if the following condition holds:

(A.2-3-6-4) $\psi_i X = X_i$, $i = 1,2, \ldots, n$

Below, for $X \sqsubseteq (\Omega, \mathcal{Z}_{\circ,\vee}\mathcal{H}, \{\mathbb{C}\})$, let

(A.2-3-6-5) $X = |(x21 \;\; x22 \;\; x23) \setminus (x11 \;\; x12) \setminus z|^T$,

z being the central element, x_{ij} the non-central elements ($i, j \in \mathbb{N}$ the natural numbers).

Now, let $M_i \models \mathcal{Z}_{\circ,\vee}\mathcal{H}$ (i to be determined by the related impactors according to the context of the problem), then under the *neutrality of culture*, let the operations of subtracting-the-middle impactor, subtracting-row impactor and subtracting-column impactor be defined in the following.

Definition A.2-3-6-4. Under the neutrality of culture, M_M is said to be the **subtracting-the-middle impactor** if and only if the following condition holds:

(A.2-3-6-6) $M_M X = |(x21 \;\; x22 \;\; x23) \setminus (x11 \;\; x12)|^T$.

Here M_M is the impactor eliminating the center for X in Bcm. (A.2-3-6-5).

Definition A.2-3-6-5. Under the neutrality of culture, M_M is said to be a **subtracting non-center-and-right-column impactor** if and only if the following conditions hold:

(1) $M_M X = |(x21 \;\; x22) \setminus (x11 \;\; x12) \setminus z|^T$.

Similarly, we have $M_M^{(2)}$ and $M_M^{(3)}$ as a **subtracting non-center-and-right-column impactors**:

(2) $M_M^{(2)} X = |\, x21 \setminus x11 \setminus z\, |^T$.

(3) $M_M^{(3)} X = z$.

Here $M_M \equiv M_M^{(1)}$ is the impactor eliminating the column of non-central elements on the right, and the superscript i in the parentheses denotes the operation of the impactor for i times.

Definition A.2-3-6-6. Under the neutrality of culture, M_{Down} is said to be a **subtracting-the-lower-row impactor** if and only if the following conditions hold:

(1) $M_{Down} X = |\, (x11\ \ x12) \setminus z\, |^T$.

Similarly, we have $M_{Down}^{(2)}$ as a **subtracting-the-lower-row impactor**:

(2) $M_{Down}^{(2)} X = z$.

Here $M_{Down} \equiv M_{Down}^{(1)}$ is the impactor eliminating the lowest row of the non-central elements, and as in the above, the superscript i in the parentheses denotes the operation of the impactor for i times.

Let $X = \{x_1, x_2, \ldots, x_n, z\} \sqsubseteq (\Omega, \mathcal{Z}\circ,_v\mathcal{H}, \{\mathbb{C}\})$, z being the center element, x_i ($i \in \mathbb{N}$) the non-central elements. In addition, let $M_i \models \mathcal{Z}\circ,_v\mathcal{H}$ (i will be determined by the related impactors in the appropriate context). Then under the *neutrality of culture*, let the operations of subtracting-the-middle impactor and subtracting-the-right-element impactor be defined in the following.

Definition A.2-3-6-7. Under the neutrality of culture, M_M is said to be the **subtracting-the-middle impactor** if and only if the following is true:

(1) $M_M X = \{x_1, x_2, \ldots, x_n\}$.

Definition A.2-3-6-8. Under the neutrality of culture, M_N is said to be the **subtracting-the-right-element impactor** if and only if the following conditions hold:

(1) $M_M X = \{x_1, x_2, \ldots, x_{n-1}, z\}$.

(2) $M_M^{(2)} X = \{x_1, x_2, \ldots, x_{n-2}, z\}$.

......

(n-1) $M_M^{(n-1)} X = \{x_1, z\}$.

(n) $M_M^{(n)} X = \{z\}$.

with $M_M \equiv M_M^{(2)}$. Now we come to the time-eliminating impactor. For this purpose, let $X = \{x_1, x_2, \ldots, x_n, z; t\} \sqsubseteq (\Omega, \mathcal{Z}\circ,_v\mathcal{H}, \{\mathbb{C}\})$, z the central element, x_i ($i \in \mathbb{N}$) the non-central elements. In addition, let $M_i \models \mathcal{Z}\circ,_v\mathcal{H}$ (i will be determined by the related impactors in the appropriate context), then we have the following definition.

Definition A.2-3-6-9. Under the neutrality of culture, M_t is said to be the **general time-subtracting impactor** if and only if the following conditions hold:

(1) $M_t X = \{x_1, x_2,\ldots, x_n,z;t\text{-}1\}$.

(2) $M_t^{(2)} X = \{x_1, x_2,\ldots,, x_n,z;t\text{-}2\}$.

......

(n) $M_t^{(n)} X = \{x_1,x_2,\ldots,x_n,z;t\text{-}n\}$.

Let $X = \{(x_1, x_2,\ldots, x_n;t),(z;t)\} \sqsubseteq (\Omega,\mathcal{Z}\circ,_v\mathcal{H},\{\mathbb{C}\})$ in which z is center element, and x_i the non-central elements, for $i \in \mathbb{N}$. In addition, let $M_i \vDash \mathcal{Z}\circ,_v\mathcal{H}$(i will be determined by the related impactors in the appropriate context), then we have the following definition.

Definition A.2-3-6-10. Under the neutrality of culture, $M_{M,t}$ is said to be the **special impactor to shift-backward the time of the central element** if and only if the following conditions hold:

$M_{M,t}X = \{(x_1, x_2,\ldots, x_n;t),(z;t\text{-}1)\}$.

......

$M_{M,t}^{(n)}X = \{(x_1, x_2,\ldots, x_n;t),(z;t\text{-}n)\}$,

where $M_{M,t} \equiv M_{M,t}^{(1)}$. That is, in $\{(x_1, x_2,\ldots, x_n;t),(z;t)\}$, the central element (z;t) is replaced by (z;t-1), with t denoting time.

Let $X = \{(x_1, x_2,\ldots, x_n;t),(z;t)\} \sqsubseteq (\Omega,\mathcal{Z}\circ,_v\mathcal{H},\{\mathbb{C}\})$ in which z is center element, and x_i the non-central elements, for $i \in \mathbb{N}$. In addition, let $M_i \vDash \mathcal{Z}\circ,_v\mathcal{H}$ (i will be determined by the related impactors in the appropriate context), then we have:

Definition A.2-3-6-11. Under the neutrality of culture, $M_{N,t}$ is said to be the **special impactor to shift-backward the time of non-central element** if and only if the following conditions hold:

$M_{N,t}X = \{(x_1, x_2,\ldots, x_n;t\text{-}1),(z;t)\}$.

That is, in $\{(x_1, x_2,\ldots, x_n;t),(z;t)\}$, the non-central element $(x_1,x_2,\ldots, x_n;t)$ is replaced by $(x_1, x_2,\ldots, x_n;t\text{-}1)$.

Let $X = \{(x_1, x_2,\ldots, x_n;t),(z;t)\} \sqsubseteq (\Omega,\mathcal{Z}\circ,_v\mathcal{H},\{\mathbb{C}\})$ in which z is center element, and x_i the non-central elements, for $i \in \mathbb{N}$. In addition, let $M_{N,i} \vDash \mathcal{Z}\circ,_v\mathcal{H}$ (i will be determined by the related impactors in the appropriate context), then we have the following definition.

Definition A.2-3-6-12. Under the neutrality of culture, M_t is said to be the **special impactor to shift-backward the time of non-central element** if and only if the following conditions hold:

$M_{x1,t}X = \{(x_1;t\text{-}1),(x_2,\ldots, x_n,z;t)\}$.

That is, in the a system $(x_1, x_2,\ldots, x_n;t),(z;t)\}$, $(x_1;t)$ is replaced by $(x_1;t\text{-}1)$.

Let $X = \{(x_1, x_2,\ldots, x_n;t),(z;t)\} \sqsubseteq (\Omega,\mathcal{Z}\circ,_v\mathcal{H},\{\mathbb{C}\})$ in which z is center element, and x_i the non-central elements, for $i \in \mathbb{N}$. In addition, let $M_i \vDash \mathcal{Z}\circ,_v\mathcal{H}$ (i will be determined by the related impactors in the appropriate context), then we have the following definition.

Definition A.2-3-6-13. Under the neutrality of culture, $M_{x1,t}$ is said to be the **special impactor to shift-backward the time of non-central element** if and only if the following conditions hold:

$$M_{x1,t}^{(2)}X = \{(x_1;t\text{-}2),(x_2,\ldots, x_n,z;t)\}.$$

That is, in $\{(x_1, x_2,\ldots, x_n;t),(z;t)\}$, $(x_1;t)$ is replaced by $(x_1;t\text{-}2)$.

Let $X = \{(x_1, x_2,\ldots, x_n;t),(z;t)\} \sqsubseteq (\Omega,\mathcal{Z}\circ,{}_v\mathcal{H},\{\mathbb{C}\})$ in which z is center element, and x_i the non-central elements, for $i \in \mathbb{N}$. In addition, let $M_i \vDash \mathcal{Z}\circ,{}_v\mathcal{H}$ (i will be determined by the related impactors in the appropriate context), then we have the following definition.

Definition A.2-3-6-14. Under the neutrality of culture, $M_{M,t}^{(n)}$ is said to be the **special impactor to shift-backward the time of non-central element** if and only if the following conditions hold:

$$M_{M,t}^{(n)}X = \{(x_1, x_2,\ldots, x_n;t\text{-}n),(z;t)\}.$$

Let $X = \{x_1, x_2,\ldots, x_n,z\} \sqsubseteq (\Omega,\mathcal{Z}\circ,{}_v\mathcal{H},\{\mathbb{C}\})$, z being the center, and x_i the non-central elements, $i \in \mathbb{N}$. Let $M_i \vDash \mathcal{Z}\circ,{}_v\mathcal{H}$ (i shall be determined by the related impactors in the appropriate context). Then we have the following definition.

Definition A.2-3-6-15. Under a specific culture, M_M is said to be the **α-eliminating impactor** if and only if the following conditions hold:

$$M_MX = \{x_1, x_2,\ldots, x_n,\alpha\},$$

where α is the newly created element in X.

Let $X = \{x_1,x_2,\ldots, x_n,z\} \sqsubseteq (\Omega,\mathcal{Z}\circ,{}_v\mathcal{H},\{\mathbb{C}\})$, z being the center, and x_i the non-central elements, $i \in \mathbb{N}$. Let $M_i \vDash \mathcal{Z}\circ,{}_v\mathcal{H}$ (i shall be determined by the related impactors in the appropriate context). Then we have the following definition.

Definition A.2-3-6-16. Under a specific culture, M_N is said to be the **β-eliminating impactor** if and only if the following conditions hold:

(1) $M_NX = \{x_1, x_2,\ldots,x_{n-1},\beta,z\}$,

(2) $M_N^{(2)}X = \{x_1, x_2,\ldots,x_{n-2},\beta_1,\beta_2,z\}$,

where β, β_1 and β_2 are the newly created elements in X.

Definition A.2-3-6-17. Let $x \Vdash \Omega$ be a system and $\varphi_i \vDash \mathcal{Z}\circ,{}_v\mathcal{H}$ be an impactor. Then φ is said to be a **two-element-system-creating impactor** if and only if one of the following conditions hold:

(1) $\varphi(x) = \{x,y\} \sqsubseteq (\Omega,\mathcal{Z}\circ,{}_v\mathcal{H},\{\mathbb{C}\})$, where {x,y} is a system without a center and y is the y-systemism or f-systemism of x (or x and y constitute a y-yinyang or f-yinyang pair).

(2) $\varphi(x) = \{x|z\} \sqsubseteq (\Omega,\mathcal{Z}\circ,_{v}\mathcal{H},\{\mathbb{C}\})$, where $\{x|z\}$ is a system with z being the center and y the noncentral element, and z is the h-systemism of x (or x and z constitute an h-yinyang pair).

An example for the above Definition (A.2-2-6-17), we have φ as a marriage impactor.

Definition A.2-3-6-18. Let $x \Vdash \Omega$ be a system and $\varphi_i \models \mathcal{Z}\circ,_{v}\mathcal{H}$ be an impactor. Then φ is said to be a **three-element-system-creating impactor** if and only if the following conditions hold:

(1) $\varphi(x) = \{x,y|z\} \sqsubseteq (\Omega,\mathcal{Z}\circ,_{v}\mathcal{H},\{\mathbb{C}\})$, where z is central element and x and y are non-central elements, with y be the y-systemism (or f-systemism) of x and z the h-systemism of x.

(2) $\varphi(x) = \{x|(y,z)\} \sqsubseteq (\Omega,\mathcal{Z}\circ,_{v}\mathcal{H},\{\mathbb{C}\})$, where y and z are co-central elements and x is the non-central element, with y be the h-systemism of x and y-systemism (or f-systemism) of z, and z the h-systemism of x.

An example for the above definition, we have φ as a family impactor with: $\varphi(x) = \{x|(y,z)\}$. Note that here $\{x|(y,z)\} = z \star y$, in which $x = x \star y$ (see Definition (A.2-3-6-1)).

§A.2-3-7 Remarks about The System-Operating Impactors/Interactors

Let A and $B \sqsubseteq (\Omega,\mathcal{Z}\circ,_{v}\mathcal{H},\{\mathbb{C}\})$ be systems. That is, we have:

(A.2-3-7-1) $A = \{\mathbf{A}(H^*) \sqsubseteq [(vd,hc,\gamma),C_s{\times}C^{DS}(e_r),(R_M,R^{DM}(e_r))]|E_A\{e_j\},Z_A\}\oplus\langle\mathbb{C}_A\rangle$

(A.2-3-7-2) $B = \{\mathbf{B}(H^*) \sqsubseteq [(vd,hc,\gamma),C_s{\times}C^{DS}(e_r),(R_M,R^{DM}(e_r))]|E_B\{e_j\},Z_B\}\oplus\langle\mathbb{C}_B\rangle$

To employ short-hand notations, we then write:

(A.2-3-7-3) $A = [(vd,hc,\gamma),(R,R^D)]^A,\ \gamma^A = \gamma(\mathfrak{C}_A(\kappa),Z_A(\kappa)),\ \kappa \Vdash \mathfrak{R} \Vdash \mathrm{Tzu}^*,$

(A.2-3-7-4) $B = [(vd,hc,\gamma),(R,R^D)]^B,\ \gamma^B = \gamma(\mathfrak{C}_B(\kappa),Z_B(\kappa)),\ \kappa \Vdash \mathfrak{R} \Vdash \mathrm{Tzu}^*.$

To illustrate the operation of an interactor, for the integrator $* \models \mathcal{H}$, recall from Bcm. (A.2-3-3-10): for $\star^\dagger$, ⊕ (IDR-additive interactor), ⊕, #, $* \models \mathcal{Z}$, $A \star^\dagger B = [A*^\dagger\xi(A\#B)] \oplus [B*^\dagger\zeta(A\#B)] = A^\dagger \oplus B^\dagger$.

Thus, for $* \equiv \star^\dagger \models \mathcal{Z}$ and an integrating impactor ⊗ (an operating impator), ⊙ (integrating impactor) $\models \mathcal{Z}$, we have:

(A.2-3-7-5)
$$\begin{aligned} & A * B \\ &= [(vd,hc,\gamma),(R,R^D)]^A * [(vd,hc,\gamma),(R,R^D)]^B \\ &= [(vd,hc,\gamma)^A,(R,R^D)^A] * [(vd,hc,\gamma)^B,(R,R^D)^B] \\ &= (vd,hc,\gamma)^{A*B} \otimes (R,R^D)^{A*B} \end{aligned}$$

and

(A.2-3-7-6)
$$\begin{aligned} & A * B \\ &= [(vd,hc,\gamma),(R,R^D)]^A * [(vd,hc,\gamma),(R,R^D)]^B \\ &= [(vd,hc,\gamma)^A \oplus (R,R^D)^A \odot I_A] * [(vd,hc,\gamma)^B \oplus (R,R^D)^B \odot I_B] \end{aligned}$$

$= \{[(vd,hc,\gamma)^{A} \oplus (R,R^{D})^{A}] \oplus [(vd,hc,\gamma)^{B} \oplus (R,R^{D})^{B}]\}$
$\circledcirc (I_{A} * I_{B})$
$= \{[(vd,hc,\gamma)^{A} \oplus (R,R^{D})^{A}] \oplus [(vd,hc,\gamma)^{B} \oplus (R,R^{D})^{B}]$
$\oplus [(I_{AB} \ominus I_{B}) \oplus (I_{AB} \ominus I_{A})]\} \circledcirc I_{AB}^{Rcs}$ (for I_{AB}^{Rcs} being the integrating factor or the residual of I_{AB} in this process)
$= \{[(vd,hc,\gamma)^{A} \oplus (R,R^{D})^{A} \oplus (I_{AB} \ominus I_{B})] \oplus [(vd,hc,\gamma)^{B} \oplus (R,R^{D})^{B}$
$\oplus (I_{AB} \ominus I_{A})]\} \circledcirc I_{AB}^{*}$ ($I_{AB}^{*} = I_{AB}^{Rcs}$ being the "integrating factor" of A and B)
$= \{[(A \oplus I_{A}^{**}) \oplus (B \oplus I_{B}^{**})]\} \circledcirc I_{AB}^{**}\ A^{\dagger} \oplus B^{\dagger}$,

for the IDR interactor $\oplus \vDash \mathbb{Z}$ (here $\ominus \vDash \mathbb{Z}$ is an "substraction" impactor). Note that $I_{A}^{**} = (I_{AB} \ominus I_{B}) \oplus$ (part of I_{AB}^{*}, $I_{B}^{**} = (I_{AB} \ominus I_{B}) \oplus$(part of I_{AB}^{*}), and I_{AB}^{**} is the "integrating factor" of "A^{+}" $\equiv (A \oplus I_{A}^{**})$ and "B^{+}" $\equiv (B \oplus I_{B}^{**})$.

That is, we must have: $(vd,hc,\gamma)^{A*B} \otimes (R,R^{D})^{A*B} = A^{\dagger} \oplus B^{\dagger}$ by definition.

Here for

(A.2-3-7-7) $(R^{A*B},R^{DA*B}) = (R,R^{D})^{A*B}$,
we may represent R^{A*B} and R^{DA*B} by the static system and the dynamical system, respectively. Further, we may present $(v,h)^{A*B}$ by the scheme of CE balance, for $(vd,hc,\gamma) \equiv (v,h)$:

(A.2-3-7-8) $(v,h)^{A*B} = (v,h,\gamma)^{A*B} = (v^{A*B},h^{A*B},\gamma)$.

Below we illustrate this point. For example, at the state of CE balance ($\mathcal{T}$ as the strategic impactor which may be treated here as $\circ$):

(A.2-3-7-9) $\mathcal{T}\{v(y\text{-},y\text{+},yh),h(\text{-},\text{+},c)\}$
$= \{(v,h)|\ [(y\text{-},y\text{+},yh),(\text{-},\text{+},c)\,|\,\mathfrak{C}^{S}\}$
$= \{(v,h)|\ (\mathcal{T},\mathcal{K}|\,\mathcal{H})\}$,

with $h \equiv h(y\text{-},y\text{+},yh)$ being a force of voluntary tranquility, $v \equiv v(\text{-},\text{+},c)$ being a force of suppressed conflict, and $\mathfrak{C}^{S}$ being a specific culture (or cultural mix) assuming the forces of tranquility and conflict can be reconciled for $(vd,hc,\gamma)^{A*B}$ under this specific culture (say, in the case of keiretsu or kuanhsi group):

(A.2-3-7-10) $\{[(y\text{-},y\text{+},yh),(\text{-},\text{+},c)\,|\,\mathfrak{C}^{S}\} = \{(v,h)|\ (\mathcal{T},\mathcal{K}|\mathcal{H}^{*})\}$.

For one more example, we may have:

(A.2-3-7-11) $\{[v(y\text{-},y\text{+},yh),v(\text{-},\text{+},c)\,|\,\mathfrak{C}^{S}\} = v(\mathcal{T},\mathcal{K}|\mathcal{H}^{*})$,

if the forces of tranquility and conflict can be reconciled for $(vd)^{A*B}$ at the state of CE balance under this specific culture.

Remark A.2-3-7-1. Let $Y = \{(a,b|c)|(a,b|c) \Vdash \{[(vd,hc,\gamma),(R,R^{D})]\ |.\}\} \equiv \{(a,b|c)|.\} \sqsubseteq (\Omega,\mathbb{Z}\circ,_{v}\mathbb{H},\{\mathbb{C}\})$, for a, b, c $\Vdash \Omega$, and $b = \xi(a)$, $c = \psi(\xi(a),a)$, $\xi, \zeta, \psi \vDash \mathbb{Z}\circ,_{v}\mathbb{H}$. Then Ψ is said to be a **system-creating impactor** if and only if $\Phi\{a\} = Y$. Here we have, for $\Psi \equiv \Phi^{Rev} \vDash \mathbb{Z}\circ,_{v}\mathbb{H}$ (i.e., a system-deconstructing impactor), we have: $\Phi_{a}\{Y\} = a$, $\Phi_{b}\{Y\} = b$, $\Phi_{c}\{Y\} = c$, and $Y = \{,.[a,\xi(a)|\psi(\xi(a),a)]|.\}$.

Below, to apply the above definition to the study of a firm, let X $=\{(\text{prod,fin,mkt}|\ \text{mgt})\ |(\text{prod,fin,mkt}|\text{mgt}) \Vdash \{[(\text{vd,hc},\gamma), (R,R^D)]|.\}\} \equiv \{(\text{prod,fin, mkt}|\ \text{mgt})|.\} \sqsubseteq (\Omega,\mathbb{Z}\circ,_{v}\mathbb{H},\{\mathbb{C}\})$, for p $\equiv$ prod, f $\equiv$ fin, c $\equiv$ mgt, k $\equiv$ mkt $\Vdash \Omega$, and $f = \xi(p)$, $m = \psi(\zeta(p),\xi(p),p)$, $k = \zeta(p)$, $\xi, \zeta, \psi \models \mathbb{Z}\circ,_{v}\mathbb{H}$. Then Ψ is a system-crating impactor if and only if $\Phi\{a\} = X$. Here we have, for $\Psi \equiv \Phi^{Rev} \models \mathbb{Z}\circ,_{v}\mathbb{H}$ (i.e., a system-deconstructing impactor), we have: $\Phi_p\{X\} = p$, $\Phi_f\{X\} = f$, $\Phi_c\{X\} = c$, $\Phi_k\{X\} = k$, and $X = \{[p,\xi(p), \zeta(p)|\psi(\zeta(p),\xi(p),p)]|.\} \equiv \{[p,\xi(p), \zeta(p)|\ \psi(\zeta(p),\xi(p),p)]|.\}$.
Now, let $* \models \mathbb{Z}\circ,_{v}\mathbb{H}$ (for example, see Bcm. (A.2-3-3-10)), $\oplus$ being an IDR-additive impactor, $\otimes$ an operating impator, and $\circledast$ an integrating impactor. Then for firms A, B $\sqsubseteq (\Omega,\mathbb{Z}\circ,_{v}\mathbb{H},\{\mathbb{C}\})$, we may write:

(A.2-3-7-12)
$$\begin{aligned}
&A * B\\
&= \{(p,f,k|c)|.\}^A * \{(p,f,k|c)|.\}^B\\
&= \{[(p,f,k|c)^A\oplus(.)^A]\circledast I_A\} *\{ [(p,f,k|c)^B\oplus(.)^B]\circledast I_B\}\\
&= \{[(p,f,k|c)^A\oplus(.)^A] \oplus [(p,f,k|c)^B\oplus(.)^B]\}\circledast(I_A* I_B)\\
&= \{[(p,f,k|c)^A\oplus(.)^A] \oplus[(p,f,k|c)^B\oplus(.)^B]\oplus[(I_{AB}\Theta I_B) \oplus(I_{AB}\Theta I_A)]\} \circledast I_{AB}^{Rcs}\\
&= \{[(p,f,k|c)^A\oplus(.)^A\oplus(I_{AB}\Theta I_B)] \oplus[(p,f,k|c)^B\oplus(.)^B\oplus(I_{AB}\Theta I_A)]\} \circledast\ I_{AB}^{*}\\
&= \{[(A \oplus I_A{**}) \oplus (B \oplus I_B{**})]\} \circledast\ I_{AB}^{**}\\
&= A^{\dagger}\oplus B^{\dagger},
\end{aligned}$$

and

(A.2-3-7-13)
$$\begin{aligned}
&A * B\\
&= \{[(p,f,k|c)^A\circleddash(p,f,k|c)^B] \oplus [(.)^A \oplus(I_{AB}\Theta I_B)] \oplus[(.)^B \oplus(I_{AB}\Theta I_A)] \} \circledast\ I_{AB}^{*}\\
&= \{[(p^A,p^B),(f^A,f^B),(k^A,k^B)|c^A,c^B] \oplus [(.)^A\oplus(I_{AB}\Theta I_B)]\oplus[(.)^B\oplus(I_{AB}\Theta I_A)] \}\\
&\qquad \circledast\ I_{AB}^{*},\\
&=\{[(p^A,p^B),(f^A,f^B),(k^A,k^B)|(c^A,c^B)] \oplus[.]\} \circledast\ I_{AB}^{*}\\
&=\{[(p^A,p^B),(f^A,f^B),(k^A,k^B)|(c^A,c^B)] \odot\{[.] \circledast I_{AB}^{*}\}\\
&= [(p^A,p^B),(f^A,f^B),(k^A,k^B)|(c^A,c^B)] \odot\{[(vd,hc,\gamma),(R,R^D)^{-}]^{A*B}\}\\
&= [(p^A,p^B),(f^A,f^B),(k^A,k^B)|(c^A,c^B)]\\
&\qquad \odot \{[(vd,hc,\gamma),(R,R^D)^{-}]^A \# [(vd,hc,\gamma),(R,R^D)^{-}]^B\},
\end{aligned}$$

for $\#, \odot, \circleddash \models \mathbb{Z}\circ,_{v}\mathbb{H}$ so that $[(p,f,k|c)^A \circleddash (p,f,k|c)^B] = \{(p^A,p^B),(f^A,f^B),(k^A,k^B)|c^A,c^B\}$. Here each of these A and B is called an **association-friendly management system**, for example, in the case of a keiretsu or kuanhsi group. Here (p,f,k|c) is considered as part of (R,R^D), while the rest of (R,R^D) may be in the static-dynamic structures of socio-political and cultural orientations and other functions. In addition, the symbol "mgt" represents only the function of management of a firm.

In the above becoming, we may write $\{[.] \circledast I_{AB}^{*}\} \equiv (A*B)^{-}$ as $\{[(vd,hc,\gamma),(R,R^D)]^{A*B}\}^{-}$. Here, by coordinating $\{(p^A,p^B),(f^A,f^B),(k^A,k^B)|c^A,c^B\}$ in a comprehensive manner, the IRI efficiency of the group as a whole increases, by reducing the conflicts in operations between the IRI system of A and that of B (by setting: $\{(p^A,p^B),(f^A,f^B),(k^A,k^B)|c^A,c^B\} = (\mathcal{T}^A,\mathcal{T}^B)(IRI^A,IRI^B)$, for $\mathcal{T}^A$, $\mathcal{T}^B$ being the strategic complexes of A and B, respectively). Otherwise, some inefficiency in the IRI system (or more fundamentally the will-rationality systems) may be caused by the blocking and distorting the information between two rivaling systems.

Remark A.2-3-7-2. The inter-system operations can be conducted through the static-dynamical scheme of systemic-change becoming, SK scheme (Bcms. (K.2-15)-(K.2-18)), and MFCE schemes (Section 6.2) as well. Below we shall illustrate these points.

(1) Scheme of systemic-change becoming. From Definition 3.7-7, we have, for $A = \{a_1,a_2,a_3\} \sqsubseteq (\Omega,\mathcal{Z}\circ,{}_v\mathcal{H},\{\mathbb{C}\})$ to be written as:

(3.7-5) $A = (a_1 \oplus a_2 \oplus a_3) \circledast Ia = \sigma \Vdash \Sigma^{TC}$

(at a state of simple Tcentral, where $a_2 = \varphi(a_1)$, $a_3 = \varphi^2(a_1)$, for $\varphi \models \mathcal{Z}\circ,{}_v\mathcal{H}$ being the impactor of transforming a_1 into a_2) with the solution:

(3.7-6) $x(.) = [\alpha_1 x(\mathbb{H}_1;,) \oplus \alpha_2 x(\mathbb{H}_2;,) \oplus \alpha_3 x(\mathbb{H}_3;,) \circledast Ix(\mathbb{H};,)]$.

Similarly, for $B = \{b_1,b_2,b_3\} \sqsubseteq (\Omega,\mathcal{Z}\circ,{}_v\mathcal{H},\{\mathbb{C}\})$, we can write:

(A.2-3-7-14) $B = (b_1 \oplus b_2 \oplus b_3) \circledast Ib = \sigma \Vdash \Sigma^{TC}$

at a state of simple Tcentral, where $b_2 = \psi(b_1)$, $b_3 = \psi^2(b_1)$, for $\psi \models \mathcal{Z}\circ,{}_v\mathcal{H}$ being the impactor of transforming b_1 into b_2) with the solution

(A.2-3-7-15) $x(.) = [\beta_1 x(\mathbb{H}_1;.) \oplus_2 x(\mathbb{H}_2;.) \oplus \beta_3 x(\mathbb{H}_3;.)] \circledast Ix(\mathbb{H};.)$.
From the above, we have

(A.2-3-7-16)
$$\begin{aligned} & A*B \\ &= [(a_1 \oplus a_2 \oplus a_3) \circledast Ia]*[(b_1 \oplus b_2 \oplus b_3) \circledast Ib] \\ &= [(a_1*b_1) \oplus (a_2*b_2) \oplus (a_3*b_3)] \circledast (Ia*Ib) \end{aligned}$$

and in the dynamics operations:

(A.2-3-7-17)
$$\begin{aligned} & A*B \\ &= x(.)^A * x(.)^B \\ &= \{[\alpha_1 x(\mathbb{H}_1;.) \oplus \alpha_2 x(\mathbb{H}_2;.) \oplus \alpha_3 x(\mathbb{H}_3;.)] \circledast Ix(\mathbb{H};.)\}^A \\ &\quad * \{[\beta_1 x(\mathbb{H}_1;.) \oplus \beta_2 x(\mathbb{H}_2;.) \oplus \beta_3 x(\mathbb{H}_3;.)] \circledast Ix(\mathbb{H};.)\}^B \\ &= \{[\alpha_1 x^A(\mathbb{H}_1;.) * \beta_1 x^B(\mathbb{H}_1;.)] \oplus [\alpha_2 x^A(\mathbb{H}_2;.) * \beta_2 x^B(\mathbb{H}_2;.)] \\ &\quad \oplus [\alpha_3 x^A(\mathbb{H}_3;.) * \beta_3 x^B(\mathbb{H}_3;.)]\} \circledast [Ix^A(\mathbb{H};.) * Ix^B(\mathbb{H};.)] \\ &= [\gamma_1 x^{A*B}(\mathbb{H}_1;.) \oplus \gamma_2 x^{A*B}(\mathbb{H}_2;.) \oplus \gamma_3 x^{A*B}(\mathbb{H}_3;.)] \circledast [Ix^{A*B}(\mathbb{H};.)], \end{aligned}$$

for γ_i to be somewhat related to (α_i,β_i), $i = 1, 2, 3$, with $Ix^{A*B}(.)$ denoting the adjustment-integrating factor for the system as a whole.

(2) SK scheme. For $A, B \sqsubseteq (\Omega,\mathcal{Z}\circ,{}_v\mathcal{H},\{\mathbb{C}\})$ being systems with $\mathfrak{C}^* = C(\mathfrak{C}^T)$ (culture at a state of SK balance): the cultures of sheng ($\mathcal{S}$) and the culture of ke ($\mathcal{K}$), $\mathfrak{C}^T$ being the core of the composite culture of $\mathcal{S}$ and $\mathcal{K}$ at CE balance: $\mathcal{H} = (\mathcal{S} = \mathcal{K})\}$, then from Bcm. (K.2-15), we have

(A.2-3-7-18)
$$\begin{aligned} & \{A*B \| \mathfrak{C}^*\} \\ &= \{A(y-,y+,yh)*B(+,-,c) \| C(\mathfrak{C}^T)\} \\ &= \{[A(y-)*B(-)),[A(y+)*B(+)] | [A(yh)*B(c)] \| \mathcal{H}\}. \end{aligned}$$

(3) MFCE scheme. For $A, B \sqsubseteq (\Omega,\mathcal{Z}\circ,{}_v\mathcal{H},\{\mathbb{C}\})$ being systems in a MFCE scheme: {A,-,C,+,B} with C being the center, A-B (or (A,B)) being the vertical axis and "-+" (or (-,+)) the horizontal axis of this scheme. Then from Bcm. (6.2-1), let

(A.2-3-7-19) $$A = \Phi^{A}\{<\mathbb{C}_{(-,+)/Z}>\} = <\frac{\mathbb{C}_A}{\mathfrak{C}_Z}> = \frac{<\mathbb{C}_A>}{Z(\mathcal{E})}$$

(A.2-3-7-20) $$B = \Phi^{B}\{<\mathbb{C}_{(-,+)/Z}>\} = <\frac{\mathbb{C}_B}{\mathfrak{C}_Z}> = \frac{<\mathbb{C}_B>}{Z(\mathcal{E})},$$

we have

(A.2-3-7-21) $$\begin{aligned} & A*B \\ &= [<\mathbb{C}_A>/ Z(\mathcal{E})]* [<\mathbb{C}_B>/ Z(\mathcal{E})] \\ &= [<\mathbb{C}_A>*<\mathbb{C}_B>]/ Z(\mathcal{E}) \\ &= <\mathbb{C}_A*\mathbb{C}_B>/ Z(\mathcal{E}) \\ &= <\mathbb{C}_A*\mathbb{C}_B>/<\mathfrak{C}_Z> \\ &= <\mathbb{C}_{A*B}>/<\mathfrak{C}_Z> \\ &= <\mathbb{C}_{(A*B)/Z}>, \end{aligned}$$

under appropriate conditions.

Remark A.2-3-7-3. (1) For $X = \{a,,b|c\} = (a_1 \oplus a_2 \oplus a_3) \circledast Ia$, let each of a, b, and c be expressed as an MFCE scheme, then we shall have the solution as: $x(.) = [\alpha_1 x(\mathbb{H}_1;.) \oplus \alpha_2 x(\mathbb{H}_2;.) \oplus \alpha_3 x(\mathbb{H}_3;.)] \circledast Ix(\mathbb{H};.)$, where each of $x(\mathbb{H}_i;.)$ (i = 1, 2, 3) and $Ix(\mathbb{H};.)$ is an MFCE scheme.

(2) In Bcms. (A.2-3-7-19) and (A.2-3-7-20), we may express each of the terms $\mathbb{C}_A$, $<\mathbb{C}_A>$, $\mathbb{C}_B$, $<\mathbb{C}_B>$, $<\mathbb{C}_{(-,+)/Z}>$, $\mathfrak{C}_Z$, and $Z(\mathcal{E})$ as static-dynamical systemic-change becoming. Consequently, for each of these terms, we shall be able to construct an MFCE scheme.

§A.2-4 Systematic Structure of The Mind

To encompass the above chains of transformation of ideas, human relations, social institutions, and production of consumer's goods, we shall deduce, metaphorically, a four-fold structure of the mind (i.e., the mind complex $\mathcal{M} = (\mathcal{M}^{I}, \mathcal{M}^{II}, \mathcal{M}^{III}, \mathcal{M}^{IV}))$ as follows.

Table A.2-4-1 illustrates in a hierarchical order (or on a reverse course) from materialistic to spiritual layers, whose incarcerating and bouncing energies infiltrate instantly and ermanently the mind $\mathcal{M}^{i}$, i = I, II, III, IV, be it a concept or an idea relating to a human relationship, a social institution, or a consumer's good. On the original course, the mind actively and creatively penetrates energy nets of these categorical activities.

There are four kinds of transformation and production structures: (1) The one for producing the consumer's goods, (2) the one for creating and modifying social institutions, (3) the one for instituting human relations, and (4) the one for generating ideas.

Table A.2-4-1
Structure of Mind Set A

$\mathcal{M}^{I}$: Ideas
$\mathcal{M}^{II}$: Human relations
$\mathcal{M}^{III}$: Social institutions
$\mathcal{M}^{IV}$: Consumer's goods

Let $\mathcal{M}^{I} = \mathcal{M}^{I}(Ar)$, for Ar representing the artistic creativity; $\mathcal{M}^{II} = \mathcal{M}^{II}(Sm)$, for Sm depicting the creativity for generating spiritual symbols; $\mathcal{M}^{III} = \mathcal{M}^{III}(HE)$, for HE referring to the human engineering activities; and $\mathcal{M}^{IV} = \mathcal{M}^{IV}(PE)$, for PE denoting the physical engineering activities. Then, for "$\rightleftarrows$" being the interactive impactor (or interactor), we have:

(A.2-4-1) $\quad \mathcal{M}^{i} \rightleftarrows \{\{[C_S{\times}C^{DS}(e_r)]^{i},[R_M,R^{DM}(e_r)]^{i},[\tilde{O}]^{i},Z^{i}\},$

for i = I, II, III, IV.

Note that, in general, we write $\mathcal{M}^{i} = (\mathcal{M}^{i}(\ell,\tau))$. That is, the mind set is the becoming of the positive-negative factor of historicity (ℓ) and the factor derived from the forces of Ultimate Creativity/Destructivity (τ).

The rationale of this "becoming" is multiple-faceted. The case of $\mathcal{M}^{I}$ involves the creation of ideas which are closely associated with the arts, literature, religion, philosophy or other spiritual activities. In the case of $\mathcal{M}^{II}$, it invokes the will-to-creation and the rationality that are expressed through various rites, rituals, and other forms of symbolic communication. Recall that the cultural capital and the so-called social capital belong to this category of output. With $\mathcal{M}^{III}$, we implicate what we call the realm of human engineering with rules governing human interactions, physical structures of offices and buildings, and technologies of human interactions and communications. The so-called human capital belongs to this realm. Finally $\mathcal{M}^{IV}$ represents the realm of those entangling with what we know as physical engineering activities, such as real-world and space-time objects, capital stocks, and the technologies of production and consumption.

For the interconnection between $\mathcal{M}^{i}$ and $O^{i} \equiv \{\{[C_S{\times}C^{DS}(e_k)]^{i},[R_M,R^{DM}(e_k)]^{i}, \tilde{O}\}|E(e_j),Z^{i}\}$, i = I, II, III, and IV, the ideal state is one in which $\mathcal{M}^{i}$ and O^{i} are in a state of Tao central. In symbols, using ω for the will-to-creation and ρ for the rationality, this T centrality is expressed in Table A.2-4-2.

In the state of T central, the flow of energy from M^{i} to O^{i} is smooth and steady, for each i. Recall that for N = IV and N being the non-energy related environment including Ultimate Creativity-Destructivity/Nihility, and $O^{i} \Vdash \chi$, $\mathcal{M}^{i} \Vdash \langle\mathfrak{C}_X\rangle = \{\mathcal{M}^{I}(\mathcal{M}^{I}(\ell,\tau),...,\mathcal{M}^{N}(\ell,\tau)|E(e_r(\tau)), \mathfrak{I}^{*}(\tau)\}$, $\ell \equiv \ell(\sigma,\kappa) \Vdash \mathcal{L}(\sigma,\kappa) \sqsubseteq Ш^{ДL} \Vvdash \mathbb{T}\mathrm{zu}^{*}$, $\tau \Vdash (\mathfrak{I},Ш^{Д}) \Vvdash \mathbb{T}\mathrm{zu}^{*}$ ($\mathfrak{I}^{*}(\tau)$ being a From of $\mathbb{T}\mathrm{zu}^{*}$), is a part of the cultural complex of the system X. In addition, in the whole system $\mathcal{M}^{i} \rightleftarrows \{\{[C_S{\times}C^{DS}(e_k)]^{i},[R_M,R^{DM}(e_k)]^{i},\tilde{O}\} |E(e_j),Z^{i}\}$ the energies flowing between $\mathcal{M}^{i}$ and O^{i} are in their normal states, respectively. Furthermore, in each step ascending toward a higher level of mind activities, a new layer of energy is generated and adheres to the energy mix of that higher step. Therefore through the process of transformation, the structure of mind complex A will be replaced by a new structure, i.e., that of the mind complex B.

TableA.2-4-2
Flow Structure between the Mind and Energy

$$(\omega,\rho) \rightarrow \mathcal{M}^{I} \text{ ---------- } \mathcal{M}^{II} \text{ ---------- } \mathcal{M}^{III} \text{ ------- } \mathcal{M}^{IV}$$

$$O^{I} \text{ ---------- } O^{II} \text{ ---------- } O^{III} \text{ ------ } O^{IV}$$

$$(e_k^{I},e_k^{II},e_k^{III},e_k^{IV}) - (e_k^{II},e_k^{III},e_k^{IV}) - (e_k^{III},e_k^{IV}) - (e_k^{IV})$$

In Table A.2-4-3, the higher levels of energy ($\{\mathcal{M}^{III} \ldots \rightarrow \mathcal{M}^{I}\}$) are created by the steeper structure of production systems due to the higher level of technology-related backward linkage systems as well as that of consumption systems in a groupist culture. In contrast, in an individualist culture, higher levels of energy are acquired when flatter systems of consumption and production are created.

Table A.2-4-3
Structure of Mind Set B

$\mathcal{M}^{I}(Ar;e_r^{I},e_r^{II},e_r^{III},e_r^{IV})$: Ideas
$\mathcal{M}^{II}(Sm;e_r^{II},e_r^{III},e_r^{IV})$: Human relations
$\mathcal{M}^{III}(HE;e_r^{III},e_r^{IV})$: Social institutions
$\mathcal{M}^{IV}(PE;e_r^{IV})$: Consumer's goods

This mind complex (expressed in Table A.2-4-3) symbolically entails a four-pole MFCE scheme wherein $\mathcal{M}^{I}$(Ar;.) positions itself as the central element (Tonn 2001). In contrast, Xion Shili's scheme (bi,xi) illustrates a two-pole MFCE system without a center. After Tang Junyi, the scheme: ((wangwu sanshu jing,yilei chengfeng jing,gongneng xuyun jing),(ganjue hushe jing,guanzhao lingxu jing,daode shijian jing)|(guixiang yishen jing,tiande liuxing jing, kong-wu jing)) demonstrates a three-pole system with the center being presented by (guixiang yishen jing,tiande liuxing jing, kong-wu jing).

In order to relate this mind set system (or complex) to those of St. Thomas Aquinas and Chu Hsi, we need to enlarge it to include {Physical worlds, [$\mathcal{M}^{I}$(Ar;.),$\mathcal{M}^{II}$(Sm;.),$\mathcal{M}^{III}$(HE;.), $\mathcal{M}^{IV}$(PE;.)]| $\Im^*$}, where the "mind" [$\mathcal{M}^{I}$(.),$\mathcal{M}^{II}$(.),$\mathcal{M}^{III}$(.), $\mathcal{M}^{IV}$(.)] refers to the one that controls the human society through a force ($\Im^*$) which is a Form of and derived from Ultimate Creativity-Destructivity Tzu*. By this above arrangement, it allows our system to correspond to St. Thomas Aquinas' system most naturally within the world of symbolic transformation.

Furthermore, from Chu Hsi's scheme of yinyang wuxing (or five elements), one can naturally project it to a system like {world of non-living materials, worlds of animals and plants, $\mathbb{W}\mathbb{u}$,human society} where $\mathbb{W}\mathbb{u}$, as the center of this system, is the manifestation of the forces of Ultimate Creativity-Destructivity (and Nihility). The correspondence between our system and this revised Chu Hsi scheme may become obvious, symbolically and metaphorically of course, once we regroup the world of non-living materials as well as the worlds of animals and plants into the "physical worlds group" in the system of St. Thomas Aquinas.

§A.2-5 Consciousness, Actions, Existence and Dualism

For the questions of the world's existence, we are concerned with the existence of the self and that of external things or entities ("human being outside of me" and "entities outside of me"). Logically, the existence of the self must be asserted as a "primitive way of recognition." This so-called "primitive existence" is derived from the logic of "every things being known through my consciousness." Like in the case of the Cartesian method reasoning that "I think, and therefore I must exist," we could assert that "I doubt (whether I am existing), and therefore I am existing." A more modern approach to this issue may follow a path of reasoning that we intuitively assert "I am conscious (of myself), and therefore I exist." A yet another approach to this issue is to follow the principle of "every thing is in constant motion" and intuitively conclude that "I am in constant motion, and therefore I am existing."
The acknowledgement of the existence of "external man" (i.e., human beings other than me) can be deduced in the following.

For the *system of self*, we shall proceed in two directions. Our first direction is as follows: let $X \sqsubseteq (\Omega, \mathbb{Z}^{\circ}, {}_{v}\mathbb{H}, \{\mathbb{C}\})$ be a human element, that is, $X \Vdash \mathbf{H} \Subset \mathbf{U}$. Suppose that man (or a person) has consciousness (i.e., consciousness in general), outward consciousness (i.e., my consciousness-toward-outside) and has an ability to perceive an outside-to-myself consciousness (i.e., outsiders' consciousness about my existence). In the following, we present an argument about the chain reasoning starting with the intuitive assumption of the existence of one's consciousness and ending up with a primitive assertion of the existence of self (or person in general) or "the self-evident existence of man (or human being in general). Let $x, y \Vdash \mathbf{U}$ be universal elements of thinking things (thinking elements), and further, let x, y be the objective targets of these thinking thing (target of thinking thing), respectively. That is, X is the subject of consciousness, outward intentionality, and outside-to-me intentionality, where {outward intentionality, outside-to-me intentionality| consciousness} constitutes a unit system, with consciousness as the center. That is, we have in X the chain information of consciousness: consciousness → external consciousness → outside-to-self consciousness. Then for $x \Vdash \mathbf{U}$, X = {(outward intentionality, outside-to-me intentionality|consciousness) | x} constitutes a grand system. And for $y \Vdash \mathbf{U}$, $x \neq y$, Y = {(outward intentionality,outside-to-me intentionality|consciousness) | y} constitutes a basic system as well. Here by the structure of X, it implies that X posses an attribute of communicating and interacting with outside entity (Y, for example). Here, Y is the grand system about which X is "thinking." Therefore, X and Y are the objects of mutual interactions.

In the above, even by putting X and Y together, the collection {X,Y} does not constitute a great-grand system from which one can hope to escape the Cartesian type solipsism. This is the fundamental problem facing Husserl's phenomenology, because on the foundation of "phenomenological analysis," one is only conscious about one's own consciousness, and is not in any position to assert the existence of any other person or the physical world outside of oneself. Formally, from this foundation, one would intuitively assert the existence of oneself (in actuality, only the existence of one's consciousness) and set this axiom as the starting point of any theoretical analysis. But logically this would lead to the assertion of neither the existence of other human beings and nor the existence of the nature. This is like the theory of "atomism" in ancient physics (or the pre-physics of Democritus). This spirit of "atomism" may be revealed in Leibniz's theory of monism, in which each monad is independent and has no window leading to other monads, although this monad does posses a mechanism leading to God in some mysterious way. One might imagine that Husserlian man lives in a world of monads that isolate one from the rest of the society based on the pure spirit of mathematics and natural sciences. And yet, by the very endeavor of phenomenology, Husserlian man has no route leading to God. As such, Husserlian phenomenology can not escape from the world of self-consciousness, unless, of course, it resorts to Husserl's last period development of phenomenological theory (Guan [2000]).

The afore-mentioned theory of atomism contradicts the true structure of the universe. And yet, paradoxically, historically, it paved the way for eventual development of modern physics. But this goes well beyond the scope of our systematic study.

It appears that the world of monism is, in some respect, similar to the world of Lao Tzu -- a world of small nation -- in which each family is isolated from its neighbors and would not communicate with others (Lao Tzu [1980], Chapter 80). But Lao Tzu's world is not one of a single person. In each family of Taoism, there are yin and yang elements to be in balance. Thus, there exists at least a "self-independent family" in which there are mother, father and one child, say a daughter. But then, there must be another family which is composed of mother, father and a son; because, otherwise, there is no such thing as yin-yang balance (of families) in this world. A Taoist world is one of balance and growth (in the state of systemic continuity). These two families must communicate to each other and therefore this daughter and this son may get together to form a new family in order to produce offspring.

Thus, by a Taoist reasoning, Husserl's phenomenology could easily be improved by an extension to a triple dimensional world: (1) Extending to one more dimension of "group thinking of Taoism" while its orientation toward "individualism" is still essentially preserved. (2) Incorporating human actions and interactions in order to go beyond the pure approach of consciousness. (3) Adopting an indirect approach to its core theory by advancing at least a proof based on the theory of coherence (see Urban 1995). Similarly, by resorting to Confucian mode of thinking, i.e., the scheme of king-subject and father-son in TCentral, Husserl's phenomenology could easily be developed to reach the state of the self-evidence of the most basic existence of man and the society. Historically, starting from the position of transcendental idealism, Immanuel Kant set up the transcendental categories as the product of human ideas. Then, it is obvious that Kant could not break away from the dichotomy of mind and matter (which is essentially the Deity-man dualism). By the mind-matter two-dimensional monism with interactions, (i.e., a CE balance between idealism and materialism), one could establish the premises of the transcendental categories as the product of the interactions between man, society and nature. If so, by embedding Husserlian phenomenology in Taoist group-individualism or Confucian family-groupism, then "the solipsism without matter" could be transformed into a solid system for proving the existence of the universe.

In the above approach, it is clearly seen that we need to go beyond the systemic thinking of taking only into account of the human actions in order to escape the trap of solipsism. One way to modify the conventional approach is in the following. Let $X \sqsubseteq (\Omega, \mathbb{Z}_{\circ}, {}_{v}\mathbb{H}, \{\mathbb{C}\})$ be a human element, that is, $X \Vdash \mathbf{H} \Subset \mathbf{U}$ and suppose that X' = {(intentionality/activity-toward-outside, intentionality/activity of outside-to-me |consciousness/action) is a system as well. By this modification, we hope to embrace Wang Yangming's idea of the unity of knowledge and action. Here, if consciousness is treated as an implicit or inward activity, by "action" here, we mean an explicit or outward activity.

Note that we could convert X' into a composite system so that $X' = \Phi(X_A, X_B)$, where X_A = {(intentionality-toward-outside,intentionality of outside-to-me |consciousness of X given the physical environments), X_B = {(activity-toward-outside,activity of outside-affecting-me| actions of X given the physical environments), and Φ is the integrating impactor making X' identical to (X_A, X_B) assuming A and B are independent of each other.

Similarly, let $Y' = \Phi(Y_A, Y_B)$, where Y_A = {(intentionality-toward-outside,intentionality of outside-to-me |consciousness of Y given the physical environments), Y_B= {(activity-toward-outside,activity of outside-affecting-me|actions of Y given the physical environments), and Φ is the integrating impactor making Y' identical to (Y_A, Y_B) assuming A and B are independent of each other. Then, by grouping X' and Y' organically together, we have {X',Y'} as a great-grand system in which the existence of the universe surrounding X and Y is primitively established.

Our second direction is as follows: let $X \sqsubseteq (\Omega, \mathcal{Z}_O, {}_v\mathcal{H}, \{\mathfrak{C}\})$ be a human element, that is, $X \Vdash \mathbf{H} \Subset \mathbf{U}$. Suppose that man (or a person) has perception-rationality (i.e., rationality amid perception), outward consciousness-rationality (my perception-rationality-toward-outside), outside–to-me consciousness-rationality (i.e., outsiders' perception-rationality toward me). Then, let U: consciousness-rationality → external perception-rationality → outside-to-self consciousness-rationality, and we have X = {(consciousness- rationality-toward-outside, consciousness-rationality of outside-to- me | consciousness -rationality) as a system.

For the *system of two persons*, let

X: consciousness → external consciousness (e.g., toward-Y) → Outside-to-me consciousness (e.g., consciousness of Y-to-X),

Y: consciousness → external consciousness (e.g., consciousness toward-X) → Outside-to-me consciousness (e.g., consciousness of X-to-Y).

That is, X = {(external intentionality,outside-to-me intentionality|consciousness-action, given the physical environments) is a system, Y ={(external intentionality,outside-to-me intentionality|consciousness-action, given the physical environments)) is another system, and {X,Y} is a grand system in which there is no center.

For the *system of two persons and one thing*, let X = {(external intentionality,outside-to-me intentionality|consciousness) be a system, Y ={((external intentionality,outside-to-me intentionality|consciousness) be another system, and {E|(X,Y)} be a basic system in which E is a non-central thing, and X and Y are the power-balanced co-centers. The other way to present this system is to treat {E|(X,Y)} as: $\{X,Y|(Z_X,Z_Y;R_{xy}); [(\gamma_X,\gamma_Y;I_{xy}),(\rho_X,\rho_Y;I_{xy}')];E\}$, $X, Y, E \sqsubseteq Ш^{\Delta}$, where X and Y are non-central members or systems (without any center in this grand system), $Z = (Z_X,Z_Y;R_{xy})$ is the co-strategic complex of X and Y (with Z_X being the strategic complex of X, Z_Y the strategic complex of Y, and R_{xy} the static-dynamic relationships between Z_X and Z_Y), $(\gamma_X,\gamma_Y;I_{xy})$ the system of the consciousness of X and Y, $(\rho_X,\rho_Y;I_{xy}')$ the system of rationality of X and Y, and E is the changing outside (physical and social) environments that X and Y are facing jointly and dynamically. Here ($\gamma_X,\gamma_Y;I_{xy}$) represents the consciousness of each of X and Y for the direct awareness of their own individual existence (γ_X and γ_Y) with I_{xy} referring to the interface between their consciousness, and ($\rho_X,\rho_Y;I_{xy}$') represents the rationality of each of X and Y for the indirect awareness of other's existence (ρ_X and ρ_Y) with I_{xy}' referring to the interface between the actions of both individuals.

Here let the external intentionality be a kind of intentionality in Husserl's phenomenology and to be treated as a self-evident existence. At the same time, because everything in the universe is in its own constant motion, consciousness is in actuality an action. For example, when one collects food, this person possesses the consciousness of self-preservation and self-surviving. Here, in an action to obtain food in order to safeguard one's survival, one must have a consciousness-toward-outside (i.e., external consciousness toward food). As a result, this external consciousness is also an action-toward-outside. This may be what motivated Heidegger to use activity-primitiveness as the starting point of his phenomenological analysis (Chang [1996], p. 127). In other words, this is exactly what amounts to treat the existence of the activity-primitiveness as self-evident. As such, this is an acknowledgment of the interchangeability between the concepts of action-perception and that of the activity-consciousness as well.

For the existence of outside-to-self consciousness to be self-evident, the best starting point may lie in the fact that an infant or a small child can not exits without the mother (or some one else) taking care of it. It follows that the outside-to-self consciousness emanating from the mother exists in this baby's consciousness through the interactions (i.e., actions) between this baby and the mother. Here, this existence may be taken as self-evident (or no need to be proved logically). As such, from Husserl's phenomenology, the self (i.e., the self consciousness of X) exists self-evidently, and the existence of external world (i.e., consciousness toward Y) is also derived from the self-evident existence of the self.

At this moment, let the system of two-persons and one thing be {E|(X,Y)}, where E is the sources of foods for a baby and the other, X is the baby and Y is the mother of the baby. In this system, then, both the baby and the mother must be able to judge evidently the existence of the self consciousness, external intentionality, and outside-to-self intentionality. May be one would argue that a baby is too small to have the self consciousness and the consciousness for the existence of the mother. If so, then replace the role of the baby by a small child, and the argument goes through. In the process of the interactions between the baby and the mother, both must be able to "imperfectly" judge the existence of each other. That is, without food provided by the mother, the baby can not survive; and without the baby, the mother is no longer a mother. This is apparently not the case since the human kind continues to exist up to now. Thus, the existence of the outside world can be primitively ascertained. But if we want to assert the existence of the outside world in a non-primitive manner, then it would take a great effort to employ the scientific methods in order to prove it (only indirectly). Note that the scientific methods are consistent with the logical methods, which rely on the analytic methods of self-containment and non-contradiction. Nevertheless, the existence of the outside world is ultimately beyond the reach of our reason if we insist on pursuing the ideal state of complete sufficiency and perfection.

The primitive judgment about the existence of man and the outside world involves time. But by being associated with different levels of consciousness and appropriate segregation of space, time can be partitioned into three categories: present -- the present-now, the just-past now and the forthcoming-now, past -- the passing-past, just-passed past and the past-past, and future – the forthcoming-future, the near-future, and the far-away future. Since the overlapping between the just-past now and the passing-past is inevitable, and similarly for the overlapping of the forthcoming-now with the forthcoming-future, human experiences in time -- in the mode of present-past-future -- repeat themselves again and again, due to the overlapping of the consciousness associated with the partition of time into the above sub-categories and the segregation of space (for example, into far-left, just-left, left-here, here, right-here, just-right and far right, and so on). Therefore, in the processes of integration of the overlapping consciousness, space and time, from the past (and the present), human being produces

memory; and from the future, human being deduces expectation. (For the overlapping time, for example, see Figure A.2-5-1.)

Figure A.2-5-1
Overlapping of the just-past now and the passing-past

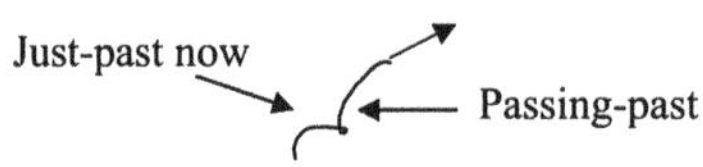

In the system of two persons and one thing (i.e., an event or physical entity), the experiences through the time of "past-present-future" may help one grasp the truth of the objective world. Otherwise, the memory carried from the past may be in vain, and the expectation of the future may be illusory. Meanwhile at this moment, first, the experiences and existence of the passing- past_present_forthcoming future chain of things and events may form a solid basis for judging the "true existence" of the objective world. Secondly, from the experiences and the passing-past, non-memorial memory is produced, and from the experiences of the forthcoming future, non-expected expectation is formulated.

Due to the processing of the just-passing-present_present-now_forthcoming-present string, for each person, the string of one-with-consciousness_outward-intentionality_outside–to–me-intentionality is acting on myself at the instant of the "present" dimension of the spatiotemporal world order. As for two persons interacting to each other at this instant, each of the human-activity_outward-activity_outside-to-me activity string is acting at this instance, and the interactions between the human being and the physical environments are carrying on at this instant-spot of the time-space as well. Hence, by the repetition again and again of the triple union, or the memory_triple-presents-expectation string interacting instantaneously at the same time, and also by the fact that man exists ever in this instant-spot (while one is still alive), one's primitive acceptance of the existence of one-self and the outside world converges eventually to one's intuitive assertion about (or acceptance of) the existence of the real world.

As already mentioned in the above, it is necessary for a non-primitive assessment of the existence of the outside world to go through an elaborate processes of proving by the use of scientific methods, logical reasoning and rigorous analysis.

In systemics, an essential set of metaphoric and symbolic relationships are to be established. In the following, we present some of these relationships in terms of systems.

One way to help justify our approach of systematics is to utilize the Coherence Theory in searching for and accessing truth (Urban 1995).[16]
Since in one's limited time and life process, there is no way to exhaust the processes for the verification of truth, one has to rely upon a set of coherent theories to access the truth of our inner life and the outer world. For some parts of truth, although it may appear somewhat in an intuitive and even naive way, we can directly demonstrate their existence to ourselves. That is, along with sound reasoning procedures, we can sense and feel them and thereby directly sense their existence. But for others, we can only access their truth or falsehood indirectly. This latter point involves our sense of, comprehension of and belief about things, objects, events, things uncertain and even beyond.
Furthermore, the existence judgment of man and the nature involves problems of history and culture in general, and religion in particular. In actuality, outside of the concerns of consciousness and daily human activities, if one would simultaneously invoke the perspectives of history, arts-and-literary activities and religious life, then the objective existence of man and the nature would definitely be much more convincing.

One may easily assert that, in general, a significant problem of history is definitely the problem of power, technology and organization. It follows that justice is a significant problem of history as well. On the moral high ground, justice has to be considered as the most important issue facing the human kind. And yet, it is the idealist who would treats justice as the major problem of the history. Those treating the problem of efficiency (as most of the conventional economists would do) or that of survival (as many of the intellectuals living in the developing world would like to) are the realists, not the idealists. The ideal has a great value, but in fact, the ideal may not be real. It is great if one just pursues the ideal. Like Mencius once said that, as long as one is right (with jen-yi on one's side), one ought to go ahead even if thousands of people are in the way. One ought to do this. But on balance it appears to be fine at least some of the time (in the very historicity of the human kind) if one works in the real world. It is the great paradox of history. Of course, we could try to fight against the force of history even if we are powerless. And we do not have to give up for the fight. However, in this life of here-and-now, whether one favors the ideal or the real world (of power, profits or material production and consumption), the continual dispute over the merits and wisdoms of the divergence of the reality from the ideal world may be duly regarded as an elegant "living proof" of the existence of man and the nature.

The problem of the individual life is a private issue and may not be a public one, be it an issue of survival, sex, love, hate, pursuit of fame and profits, or any thing else. It does not matter to be a sage or a common person, for man to be conscious is for man to be in action. By enlarging the individual's life to the life of the public, the system of multiple persons is therefore established solidly as a sure thing of existence.

The problem of religion can be "put in a bracket" like what Edmond Husserl did, that is, the believers believe and the non-believers simply do not believe. For the believers, the world with Deity is perfect; and for the non-believers, the world without any deity is perfect as well. Similarly, for one type of religion, the followers believe in their Deity (or gods); and yet for another type of religion, the followers believe in a different Deity. The existence of these Deities may be in conflict or in contradiction, logically across the human spectra; and yet these religions are perfect for their believers, respectively. Here, the real issue is that although religion is beyond the grip of our normal rationality, it is within the reach of the "rationality of life." This religious rationality may not be any type of logical, mathematical or scientific rationality. Rather, it may belong to the world of systemic rationality. Whether one believes in a

Deity or not, the belief or disbelief makes a person to sing, to cry, to be puzzled and/or to be in ecstasy. Maybe in a paradoxical way, this actually provides a strong evidence that man and the nature exist. Here we connect the nature logically or systemically to Deity, Ultimate Creativity-Destructivity.

Religion is one of the most important issues facing the people of the West for more than two millennia. We may believe that the epistemological problems of the dichotomy of mind and matter facing Descartes, Kant and Husserl are really the manifestations of the problem of the dichotomy of man and God. Mind and matter can be naturally unified, and the dichotomy can be resolved reasonably in systematics. Hence, it does not appear reasonable that man and Deity can not be unified in some way constructive. Following the tradition of East Asia, Confucian idea of the unification between Tien and the human being is most natural. Evidently from Chuang Tzu, "Heaven and Earth were simultaneously born with me, and milliards of thing are the same as me,"[17] the unity of the nature with the human being is nothing but the essence of Taoist culture. Following the traditions of Taoism and Confucianism, "outside of the six-dimensions of universe, sages would not say a thing,"[18] "Master would not discuss prodigies, prowess, lawlessness, and supernatural beings,"[19] East Asia has no Heideggerian problems of the "disunity of man with Deity" (or Dasein was discarded by Sein on the way leading to the final death of man). The Buddhist, by regarding the ever momentarily advancing toward the state of becoming-Buddha as the true mind, may not be disturbed by this religious problem of the West. Note that in the tradition of Brahmanism, by its belief in the "unity of Brahman and me," the dichotomy of man and the universe is never an issue.
Arts and the masterpieces of literature are the jewels of human spiritual activities. As for those without any religious belief, in the issue of the so-called ultimate concerns, literature or arts may become an effective substitute for a religious belief. Whether it is in the form of poetry, painting, sculpture, dance, music, movie or something else, as long as it is an artistic entity or activity, it must be composed of sensual reception, impression and idea, assisted by the processes of sense, understanding, rationality and non- or even anti-rationality.

Whether it is an entity or activity of imagination, doubt, vision, ex-post reflection, inquiry, understanding, judgment, decision, intention or desire, or abstract thought (in conflict or in coordination), or whether it is one concerning aesthetics, morality, leisurely games, or else, this entity or activity, by its very association with life, is instantaneously the living proof of the existence of the human being and the nature.

Now we turn to the issues of duality. There are three ways to address the issues of the origin of the universe: matter, mind-matter duality, and mind (consciousness -- every entity is consciousness, or mind). Like what Harman (1998, p. 30) has observed, there are three kinds of metaphysical point of view: materialism, mind-matter dualism, idealism or transcendental monism. In materialism, energy-matter is conceived as the ultimate substance of the universe. The positivist regards the quantifiable world as the only meaningful world. Following the line of materialistic reasoning, the universe is originally formed by matter. Later, consciousness (or life) is then evolved from matter over time and this evolution is taking place with an extremely small probability. In the processes of one's own activities and the interactions of one with the environments, the living thing uses its sense organs (five senses or receptors -- eyes, ears, tongue (and mouth), nose and skin -- in the case of a human being) – to receive stimuli from outside. For a person engaging in daily activities, the stimuli received by and transmitted through the entire nervous system – sensory neurons, central neurons, interconnecting neurons, motor neurons, endings, and synapse, etc – will finally pass on to the brain. In other words,

The information from outside environments is received by the receptors and to be codified into nervous impulse, which will then be gradually transmitted to the cerebral cortex of the brain. This whole process proceeds through three areas: (i) peripheral receptors (various cells in the retina for the visual receptors or system), hair-like receptor cells scattering around the base of the snail-shaped cochlea in the auditory apparatus (or system); (ii) interconnecting systems such as the optic nerve of the visual system, cochlea's nervous nucleus,..., and auditory nerve, etc. of the auditory system; and (iii) the last one is the cerebral cortex which can be divided further into the primary, secondary and tertiary function areas (Hu [1993], p.226).
That is, in the interactions between the self and the external environments and in the long and elaborate process of interactions and feedbacks through sense organs, nervous cells, and new, old and middle cerebral cortexes of brain, human consciousness is thus generated.

According to the idealistic monism, a spirit (actually the highest spirit) or super-natural entity is the ultimate substance of the universe. Matter and energy are created by this supernatural entity. Logically, this is a fine argument. But the apparent difficulty of this approach is that it is in obvious conflict with sciences. In contrast, the difficulty of material monism is paradoxically similar, because from matter no spirit has yet been produced by any method of sciences. Nevertheless, the difficulty confronting the material monism is actually more complicate than we have just mentioned. That is, no methods of (physical) sciences can successfully explain the human and cultural phenomena, not to say in solving problems of human society.

From the stand point of conventional philosophy, mind-matter dualism may be in a much better position to explain everything in the universe, by avoiding the traps of both idealistic and materialistic monism. The obvious inadequacy of this dualism is that mind and matter are independent of each other, and any one cannot be deduced from the other. Nonetheless, it does appear that there is one way to eliminate the contradiction of mind-matter dualism by proposing that both mind and matter are created by the same force, Ultimate Creativity-Destructivity/Nihility (this is what we mean the two-dimensional monism). It appears that the problem of mind-matter dualism can be solved, perhaps not entirely successfully; but it is the Deity-man dualism that really creates difficult intellectual problems.

The following is a sketch of history of dualism of the West. Founded in the ancient Greece, the classical dualism of the West changed its major course during the medieval age when Hebraism was introduced by the Church to the society. Modern dualism of the West is then the product of the spirit of sciences in its continual battle to dominate the world of theology. The primitive form of dualism of the West-Middle East might originate in the Fertile Crescent in the ancient time. To this, little is known. At the time before Plato, it is said that Anaxagoras started to dichotomize between mind and matter (in a primitive way) and became the forerunner of the Cartesian dualism of the modern time (Copelston1993, Fu [1970], Jones 1970). Later Plato developed a system of dualism to distinguish the unchanged and eternal Form from the changing and imperfect real world which he considered as the inferior imitation of the perfect Form. Plato contended that Form is the "objective reality" and the real world of human experiences is the transient one. Still later, on the foundation of Platonic Form-phenomenal dualism, Aristotle developed a new form of dualism – the reality-purest Form dualism. In this dualism, the purest Form is considered as the unmoved first mover.

Note that, from the perspectives of mathematics and the Taoist theory of tao-reversal, this Aristotelian concept of unmoved first mover is not valid. Assume that this were true. The fundamental argument of the so-called unmoved first mover essentially depends on the system of natural numbers. Assume that this statement that there is the unmoved first mover were true. But then, to be thoroughly logical, we must delve into the system of zero and negative numbers and beyond as well. That is, behind the unmoved first mover, there is the unmoved "zero mover;" behind the unmoved zero mover, there is the unmoved "negative first mover;" behind the unmoved negative first mover, there is the unmoved "negative second mover;" ...; until we go beyond the real number system and reach the unmoved "negative infinity mover." Now we go beyond the logic and reach the realm of the systematics of tao. Hence, we shall apply the impactor of tao-reversal and instantaneously, this unmoved "negative infinity mover" is actually the "first mover to be moved" (or the "infinite mover to be moved" if we like to proceed in this direction, the tao reversal of the "mover" is transformed into "what is to be moved"). This is a contradiction. Therefore, there is no such thing as the unmoved first mover.

According to Aristotle, entities in our world of experiences, being maters or some very weak versions of the pure Form, are therefore far from perfect. To him, only the unmoved first mover is the Form of the pure good nature and perfection. As is well known, in the medieval age, this Aristotelian dualism was then transformed by Hebraic theism and culminated in the dichotomy between the City of God and the city of Babylon (in Augustine's vocabulary) perhaps by going through the eyes of Averroists.

By imposing Hebraic philosophy onto Aristotelian dualism and then by deleting those overlapping with the Christian theology, one may derive the core of the modern Western dualism developed since the day of Descartes. From one perspective, the mind-matter dualism of the West may essentially be considered as based on the Deity-man dualism.

In the following, let us touch upon the classical dualism of China. As an approach to the study of the physical nature, the classical tao-chi dualism of China is based on the framework of yin-yang five elements. Here yin and yang constitute a dual (actually an imperfect dual, from the perspective of Western logic, since yin and yang are not completely independent of each other), and yin-yang and five-elements constitute yet another (imperfect) dual. On the other hand, from the perspective of human-social concerns, the classical tao-chi dualism of China may be treated as virtually founded on the good-evil dualism of human nature. The theory of good human nature propagated by Mencius and the theory of evil or hypocritical human nature advanced by Hsun Tzu together formulated an early good-evil dualism of human nature. Under the impact of Buddhist philosophical methodology (i.e, that of system building), over centuries, this dualism culminated into the Heavenly Reason-human desire tao-chi dualism. Mencius advocated the good human nature. Ironically, Hsun Tzu also believed implicitly that the "princely man" (sage, ruler, gentleman, or the intellectual) possesses the good human nature. Although Hsun Tzu believed that the "small man" (common person, mean person) has evil human nature to begin with, this "small man" actually is believed either to possess some potential to be influence by the good heart of the "princely man," or to possess a potential and hidden good human nature within his own mind complex.

In Indian Buddhism, "avidyā" (no light, failure to be illuminated) is a pivotal idea more or less resembling the Christian concept of the "original sin." But under the influence of Confucian ethics of good human nature, this focal point of avidyā in the Chinese Buddhism was transformed into the idea of pursuing the Buddha-hood, or the mind of Buddha, in this life. In the case of Neo-Confucianism, Cheng Yi's position is close to that of Li-centralism (Li-ism, the system of Heavenly Reason) of the Li-Chi dualism (Pang [1992], p. 61). As for Chu Hsi, he promulgated a form of Li-Chi dualism as well. According to Chu Hsi, " Master also said that Chi is generated by Li, Li goes first and Chi is second"; "Tai Chi is just Li of Heaven and Earth;" "before there are Heaven and Earth, there is only Li;" "there is Li, then there is Chi flowing around and creating milliards of things thereafter;" "hence Li is above the shape, and Chi below the shape"; "there is this Li, and simultaneously there is this Chi; and yet Li comes before Chi"[20] (Chu Hsi, Volume I), "Li is not created by anything else and will not perish' (Chu Hsi, Volume VIII)"[21]; "but Chi may not exist"[22] (Chu Hsi, Vol. IV); "Chi is constantly fermenting in creating milliards of things"[23] (Chu Hsi, Vol. I). Here, essentially, Li begets Chi and then Chi exists by its own term.

Hence, it appears that Chu Hsi was a Li-ist. But Chu Hsi often appeared to lean toward Li-Chi dualism: "There is no Chi which does not embody Li, and there is neither Li which does not possess Chi"[24] (Chu Hsi, Vol. I). By this is meant Li and Chi are separate entities: "Although Chi was created by Li, but once it is created, Chi is out of the control of Li"[25] (Chu Hsi, Vol. IV). This appears to be a Li monism from the perspective of cosmology. But this is really a Li-Chi dualism from the perspective of ontology. According to the system of Chu Hsi, by "Li is good"[26] (Chu Hsi, Vol. IV) and therefore "no Li is not good."[27] But then Chi must have both good and evil elements. The tricky question is then how can the good Li create the bad Chi? Logically good human nature and bad human nature can not be created by the same source since the logic does not allow self-contradiction. If "goodness" creates bad, then this "goodness" must be bad! Is it not?

Therefore, to be objective, we must say that Chu Hsi is a dualist with his Li-Chi system to be stronger in Li and weaker in Chi (or a dualist with a dichotomy between Tien Li and the human desire). People tend to blame Chu Hsi and hold him responsible for the weak Dynasty of Sung (or Song), may be because his philosophical system is thought to suppress the human spirit (actually the human desire) so that the energy of the people and hence the cultural creativity of the nation of Sung Dynasty were eventually depleted. But Ching (or Qing) Dynasty was also weak in facing the challenge of West; and although the Manchurian exalted this Chu Hsi-type philosophical system of dualism, they neither practiced it in the daily activities, nor in their energetic pursuit of building their military power and maintaining their political supremacy over the Han Chinese.

The tradition of dualism ran deep in China especially since the Song dynasty. (Thomé Fang 1981, pp. 473, 496, 503). Maybe due to this dualism, which must be deepened significantly by the absorption of Indian Buddhism, traditionally, the Chinese intellectuals looked down upon the manual work. This is probably more than the tao-chi dualism, and could be called humanity-technological dualism. According to this tradition, the intellectuals focused on nurturing the human nature and polishing their skills in serving the socio-polity, and the task of technological developed was relegated to the not-well educated technicians. This may be the genesis of the inability of the modern Chinese (before the twenty-first century) to apply the essentially wood work-based technology in dealing with the Western military power derived from the metallurgy-based technology. This is a fatal flaw of the modern civilization of China.

§A.2-6 Cosmic Structure of The System of Zizhuism

According to Chuang Tzu, "human being is a condensation of chi; while the condensation leads to life, dispersion leads to death."[28] From a modern point of view, the metaphor of the condensation-dispersion of chi is a convenient summary of the whole processes that by arranging DNAs and RNAs, structures of cells in human body are generated and lives forms are created. These processes involve the becoming of forces which include the change and growth of human body -- the formation and growth of bones, muscles, cerebral cortices, and other organs, the development of desire and emotion, the development of languages and abstract ideas, and the development of inter-personal relationship – communication, exchange, actions and reactions to other human bodies, etc. To have a comprehensive overview of these whole processes in an "organic way," including those of cosmic motions, we may want to employ the traditional tao-chi monism/dualism of classic China as the primordial skeleton, and then to integrate the self-organizationalism of material worlds, the evolutionism and the zizhuism (self-masterism) of the biological worlds, and capitalism, socialism, Faziranism and other systems of the human socio-polity and cultural economy into a comprehensive whole. For this new comprehensive system, inclusive of the "self-organizing will-to-creation" (which in certain cases may be just a motion within the inner world of the universe) and the "self-organizing rationality" (which in certain cases may involve some (at least partially) predictable forces associated with the dynamics of the universe, certain or uncertain), it may be called the **zizhu-zizuzhiism** (system of self-organization and self-masterism) (For an introduction to the system of self-organization, see Shen et al [1993]).

Within the matter, be it organic or inorganic, all of molecular and particles possess certain modes of reaction and self-maintenance/self-mastering vis-à-vis the environments, perhaps in some unconscious and disequilibrium-and-nonlinear fashions. In the biological world, amino acids in nucleus, protein, RNA, DNA, photosynthesis, and nerves, etc. are all engaging in the activities of self-mastering in accepting external stimuli. That is, all of them have some kinds of ability to sense, to respond to stimuli and react, to self-support or to rely on others for support, to grow, to reproduce or to die in a somewhat disequilibrium and nonlinear manner. These actions of disequilibrium and nonlinearity are deterministic/stochastic and continual/leap types of motions that constantly exchange information, physical and chemical elements, and electronic/magnetic energy with outside environments in the processes of absorption of scarce resources and emission of waste. In the non-biological world, there are phenomena of isolated- and self-motions. In the biological world, there are motions of living in groups. In all the worlds of life- and non-life forms, either among non-life forms or between the life-forms and non-life forms, there are input–out relationships. Further, between the living and nonliving things and among lower levels of living things and the higher levels of living things, there are various forms of the food chain relationships and the phenomena of self-benefiting behaviors. These are parts of the so-called Confucian "Tien-jen interactions and inter-responses" (or the sensual inter-responses between Heaven and the human being). Note that the other kind of Tien-jen interactions and inter-responses are in the forms of uncontrollability and altruism characterizing the phenomena of mutual benefiting, co-prosperity and concrescence of the non-living things, the living entities and those between the living entities and the non-living things.

In the following, we shall employing the Self* ontology (or the ontology of yu-wu/being and beyond) as the genesis of the infinity-finitude of the universe, with Tao-Chi and Being (or explicit and implicit Forms) revealing forms of the duality of the Ultimate Creativity and the Ultimate Destructivity (which may be called the substance of the universe) manifested in terms of the duality of mind and matter. If one is not biased toward any side of the social or life philosophy, be it one of contradiction and struggle, justice and orderly competition, or tranquility and willing-and-hearted coordination, then it makes a great sense to study this system of self-masterism (or system of Faziranist self-organization and self-mastering). By this system, the human worlds have (the primary) center, (co-centers), secondary centers and periphery entities. In the universe, it may not be applicable to distinguish a center from non-center entities and may not be natural to differentiate the primary from the secondary entities. But any way, we shall try to proceed further by following this direction. In the solar system, the sun is apparently the center, the earth may be the secondary center, others are non-central planets, and asteroids, the "empty space" and other floating particles and objects are in the periphery. Here, every entity or subsystem in the universe has its own structure and course, moving on its own trajectory according to its laws of motion, and developing according to its inner function, structure and tendency adjusting necessarily to its external environments over time. The universe as a whole has both of its laws of consistency and rules of contradiction. In sum, at the state of strategic continuity (in the cases of human being and even some species of living objects) or systemic continuity (in all the cases of living creatures and non-living things), "milliards of things 'live' by their own natures and develop their own courses, respectively, as well" and "milliards of things co-exist and are co-prosperous, and thus the various taos are parallel and not to contradict to each other" (Golden Means, Chapter 30).[29] Note that the "laws" of the universe may be different from the taos of the universe, because laws governing some entities are in conflict to laws governing some others while taos of all things are believed to be harmonious and compatible with each others.

Among systems in the universe there are structures of iso-systemism and anti-systemism. Common to the systems of all inorganic entities, there are similar or even same physical and chemical structures. That is, they have the same structures of atoms, particles, quarks, and chemical elements, i.e., there are iso-systemic to various natural and human systems. The so-called black hole and white hole are apparently a system and an anti-system, respectively, and are iso-systemic to various systems of physical elements, respectively.

The self-organizing and self-mastering systemism may serve as a medium between the tao-chi philosophy and the philosophy of self-organization, by using the theoretical foundation – the system of "the unity of knowledge and action" characterized by the tight linkage among consciousness, intentionality and activity.

For this purpose, let X = { (outward intentionality / activity, outside-to-me intentionality / activity | consciousness) be a system of one person, Y = { (outward tendency/activity, outside-to-me tendency/activity | tendency/activity) be a living system, Z = { (outward motion's regularity, outward-to-me's motion regularity | motion's regularity) be a non-living system. Here, the so-called living thing's tendency is observable, and it is also called the objective or the set of goals of the living things. For example, a living thing always absorbs nutrients from outside in its growth process. This process is interpreted as a manifestation of the "objective of the living thing for growth." Another example is the tendency for a plant to move toward sunlight. Similarly, the regularity of the motion of a non-living thing can be observed and this is called the "tendency of a non-living thing." For this later tendency, one example is the regular motion of the moon around the earth. From the perspective of the philosophical system of self-organization and self-masterism, the non-living thing's tendency and the living thing's objective are both the manifestation of the self-organizing motions of various entities in the universe.

Similar to the grouping of X, Y and Z in the above into a system, by grouping all entities in the universe into an integrated grand system, we derive at the grand system of self-organizing universe. This self-organizing process as a whole appears to be the totality of the systemic diffusion, condensation and transformation of Chi (with the implicit impact on its potentiality operating by Tao). This is a comprehensive yin-yang process in which milliards of thing "sense and react" (or receive forcible motions from outside and respond to them) to other milliards of things. By the reasoning of the classical tao-chi system, this is the causal process of natural progress and regress in which things change constantly into other forms according to the specific conditions of their peculiar levels of energy, positions, places and self-activities. The universe is in a delicate and stable order because each living thing has a certain tendency toward a state of "good-for-the-self and self-nurturing" and "good-for-the-universe" and each non-living thing has a certain tendency toward a state of continuity, stability and equilibrium.

In the above, we interpret in a broad sense the meaning of "consciousness/ intentionality/activity in the context of the unity of the knowledge and activity" in the direction of the unity of the tendency of the non-living thing and the objective of the living thing. As such, it is genuinely reasoned that this so-called consciousness/ intentionality/activity in the context of the unity of the knowledge and activity must also be integrated by the unity of the tendency and the objective of all things.

If the material universe is a stable system, then it could be an equilibrium system, where an equilibrium system belongs to the space of systems of continuity. This equilibrium system could be an n-pole MFCE system, inclining toward a conflict system or a system of no center. If this is a system of human beings, then it could be an equilibrium system, i.e., an n-pole MFCE system, may be inclining toward conflict spirit and the spirit of self indulgence, scientific rationality, and with no center. This system of human beings could also be an n-pole system of CE centrality, with its spirit inclining toward tranquility, its rationality toward yu-wu recursion, and its momentum ever toward a well-structured central subsystem coordinating or commanding all non-central subsystems.

§A.2-7 Structures of Systems and Guiding Principles

In mathematics, the studies of algebra and real and complex analyses are essential. In contrast, in systematics, we study the structures of systems and the operations of impactors and interactors. In abstract algebra, isomorphism is a useful starting point of analysis. In systematics, instead, we employ the mechanisms of iso-systemism (or symbolic iso-systemism SIS) as the staring point of research. In mathematics, equilibrium method is a key to static and dynamical analyses. In systematics, the concepts and mechanisms of centrality, mediety (or middle-ground), and MFCE (central position, or strategic) balance and strategic manipulation (or continuity) are pivotal in the systematic study of human and social affairs. In addition, systemic continuity is an important idea for the study of events and physical systems. In mathematics, methods of differential and difference equations are developed for studying dynamic phenomena. In systematics, methods of systematic-change becoming are devised to investigate the yin-yang alterations and transmutations of the taos and the dialectical and variational issues of physical world, human activities and the states of mind complex.

Previously in the systematic approach, the universe is decomposed into three subsystems: basis being-field, social power-energy net (social PE net), and rationality-will-to-creation entity (rationality-will entity, RW entity). In the basis being-field, it is further divided into two parts, the narrowly defined physical basis and the narrowly defined matter-life basis. The former is the pure world of physics and chemistry, while the latter is the world of physics, chemistry and biology. The world of chemistry is one in which through the motion of chemical elements various micro systems are created. The world of physics is one in which motions of particles such as atoms (electrons, neutrons, protons), basic particles and quarks are essential to the systems of micro-worlds, and from these micro-worlds, various macro-worlds are developed. For example, to extend from the system of the earth (spinning by itself and spinning around the sun by an equilibrium between forces of pulling and pushing, or attraction and repellence) to the solar system, and then to milky way, and further to the systems immediately outside of milky way, and finally to the boundary of the universe, systems of the physical world are accounted for.

Here, in this study of the physical universe, the categorical concepts developed in the pre-scientific systems like that of yin-yang five-elements appear to be simple and yet extremely useful. Some of the basic concepts related to them are yin, yang, center or middle (e.g., non-center ← center → non-center), quiescence, movement, balance, and opposition. Note that instead, in the mathematic methods, the concepts of equilibrium/disequilibrium and algebraic structures are essential. Here, the point of mathematical equilibrium is set as: force of pulling = force of pushing, or $dy/dx = 0$, for y being a function of x ($y = f(x)$). That is, the characteristic of equilibrium is that the first derivative of the dependent variable with respect to the independent variable is zero. In the world of chemical motions, the structures of the systemic CE balance and continuity among numerous elements (in the systematic approach) must be as important as the algebraic structures (i.e., the structures of group and ring in the mathematical approach). The world of living things is part of the matter-life basis broadly defined, and the issues of cells and heredity are some of the most important keys to this study. Besides, the systemic and mathematical structures of the physical and chemical elements of this basis also play very important roles.

The social power-energy net is the world of the interactions among the economic, social and political forces, among others. As for the rationality-will-to-creation entity (or WR entity), it is the world-complex of the individual motions, the human interactions and the Great Unknown. For the human being, this WR entity is the world in which people are motivated by the cultural forces and powered by the statics and dynamics of strategic operations. In this world, the economic analysis is usually conducted by the use of mathematical equilibrium (neo-classical approach), disequilibrium (Keynesian approach) and anti-equilibrium (Marxian approach, which is not very popular now a day). In the social and political analyses, these equilibrium and disequilibrium methods have also turned out to be very helpful.

But it appears that in studying the social power-energy net, the systemic structures of the underlying cultures, the symbolic iso-systemism (SIS) within each subsystem, and the metaphorical transformations among systems and subsystems (i.e., SIS, metaphorical anti-systemism MAS, and d-, f-, h-systemisms in dealing with differences, contrasts or even oppositions of systems) may one day prove to be extremely forceful in discerning and unfolding the mysteries of mind, society, culture in general, arts and even the super-natural entities (perhaps in some limited and secretive way).

To support the above arguments, we once again revisit the concepts of systemic continuity and strategic continuity (as a form of mediety-TCentrality) as follows. (1) Let a systemic impactor $\zeta \vDash \mathbb{Z}_{\circ,\mathrm{v}}\mathbb{H}$ be a force of operation in the world of yin-yang tao-reversal, dialectic and other non-scientific manipulations. Then for a system $y \sqsubseteq (\Omega, \mathbb{Z}_{\circ,\mathrm{v}}\mathbb{H}, \{\mathbb{C}\})$, y is said to be in a state of *systemic continuity* if and only if $\zeta(y) = y$. That is, this is a state in which the system remains unchanged over time. (2) Let $x \sqsubseteq (\Omega, \mathbb{Z}_{\circ,\mathrm{v}}\mathbb{H}, \{\mathbb{C}\})$ be a system and $\mathcal{T} \sqsubseteq \mathbb{Z}_{\circ,\mathrm{v}}\mathbb{H}$, $\mathcal{T} \Vdash Z$ be a strategic impactor (Z being the decision-making and strategic complex). Then it is said to be in a state of *systemic continuity* if and only if $\mathcal{T}(x) = x$. That is, it is a state in which system X is constant with regard to any strategic manipulation.

Note that, to be consistent with our cultural approach, these states of system's continuity may belong to the ideal worlds ($\zeta y = y^*$ and $\mathcal{T}x = x^*$) that implies strategic continuity if the cultural forces remain dormant (that is, if one is satisfied with the status quo).

In the sphere of human activities, there are issues of freedom versus control. In the sphere of economic activities, there are issues concerning the operations of "Faziran social network," planning and market. In the sphere of political activities, there are issues of democracy, authoritarianism and the polity of Faziranism. All these belong to the sphere of social power-energy net.
As for the WR entity (i.e., Will-and-rationality-to-creation entity), it is the world of culture and philosophical thinking and that of the subject of strategic operations as well. This is definitely the world in which the principles of systematics are applicable. For the sectors (or subsystems) in the WR entity, key issues are those of the symbolic transformation between sectors, the difference, coordination and opposition among different sectors, and the dominance of the center over non-central sectors.

One other important issue in the WR entity is how would the impactors operate in it. These operations are related to the issues of good and evil human nature. By the good human nature is meant the characteristics of being good-to-oneself and good-to-others, or good for oneself and yet neutral to others. So by the evil human nature is meant the characteristics of being good-for-oneself but harmful to others. Note that to be harmful to oneself and neutral to other is also considered as one aspect of evil human nature. It is paradoxical that to be harmful to oneself and yet beneficial to others is considered as good, unless it is for the greater good of all involved.

In general, human nature is considered good because one has a tendency to be good to oneself. When Mencius postulated that human nature is good, he may mean man ought to be good to others following Confucian doctrine of jen (humanity) and yi (righteousness). Being always good to others may be just an ideal, because it does not seem to be true over history all the time. But it is definitely a noble cause to do so. Here the important issue is to do what one claims but not just to pay lip service to a great idea, for either feeling good in oneself or pretending for the sake of showing off something untrue as real to others. We have seen people pretending, and we know from our experiences that some people did evil things. Mencius had a great idea but was hardly in any enviable position. Perhaps a great thing in our life is to be noble in our soul and yet to be realistic.

That is to say that there is a place to postulate that human nature is evil, because evil things happened in history at least some of the time. When Hsun Tzu postulated that human nature is evil, he might mean that one is always trying to be good to oneself but to be harmful to others. For a few noble persons, good human nature is most natural because they have the innate conscience in their hearts. This is the fundamental doctrine of the ideal school of Confucianism following the tradition of Mencius. Confucianism appears to be a great school of political philosophy in the history of China. But in general, this doctrine never had any serious claim to have a mandate over the lives of the kings and emperors of China. Rather, it essentially served to strengthen the power and to enhance the interests of these kings and emperors over the entire populace of China over history. For this, naturally, it is not the fault of any doctrine of political philosophy. It is the military and political forces of kings and emperors in violent forms that made them so power as to dominant any doctrine of philosophy and social idea.

This is essentially the rationale demanding any good political system to be one in which each person is the master of oneself and not a servant or slave of any other person. This is our ideal system, the **polity of self-masterism** (in which every citizen is his/her own self-master), with the belief that one's human nature is good – i.e., good for oneself and others simultaneously -- and the pursuit of one's own interests will benefit the society as a whole, perhaps in a time-consuming and round-about way.

For the idealistic Confucian doctrine, there is the state that "milliards of things co-exist and are co-prosperous, and various kinds of tao are parallel and not to be in conflict with each other." For some scholars, it is easy to advance the postulate that one's nature is to be good to self and to be good to others as well. But for a common person, to practice it (or to put this postulate to real world practice), it may not be a simple task. In Christian theology, human being is said to possess "original sin." If by this is meant "to be good to self but neutral to others," then according to the neoclassical doctrine of economics, this may appear to be a postulate of good human nature (in a weak form). But if by this is meant "to be harmful to self and to others simultaneously," then this is definitely a postulate of evil human nature.

To be sublime, one may be good to self and yet be "harmful" to others. This is the case that one has to be good to self in order to develop the potential fully and be in a position to be good to others later. This is so-called "not to be in the second or lower position in the pursuit of good human deed." This is in reality to mean that one could and should pursue self-good in a fair competition against others.

There are such relationships as symbolic transformation, coordination and opposition between the RW entity and the social power-energy net. Each of the RW entity and the social power-energy net is a system, and both together constitute a grand system in which the RW entity is the center and the social power-energy net is a non-central system.

The relationships among the RW entity, the social PE net and the basis being-field are sophisticated. On the surface, the grouping of these three entities constitutes a great-grand system: (1) The RW entity-social PE net is the center in this new system, and various sectors (or subsystems) of the basis being-field are non-central systems. (2) This RW entity-social PE net is a grand system, as discussed in the above. (3) At the same time, the basis being-field serves essentially as the external environments for the RW entity-social PE net, and provides energy for them. (4) These structural relationships in the great-grand system are both systemic and mathematical.

In substance, the grouping of these three entities constitutes a great-grand system with the following relationships: As a group, they constitute a 4-polar CE scheme in which the WR entity-social PE net serves only as the secondary center with the WR entity acting as the center of this secondary center. In this great-grand system, all sectors of the basis being-field are non-central systems, and the center is the very sublimity of the universe – the Ultimate Creativity-Destructivity which is obvious not (yet) a scientific concept (to some extent similar to Lao Tzu's idea of "wu" or the creator of Wu*, according to our systemic reasoning). That is, Ultimate Creativity-Destructivity is symbolically analogous to some entity existing by itself. It is just indescribable. Note that Ultimate Creativity-Destructivity is not a theological concept either, although "it" is consistent with the philosophical idea of "Deity." In actuality, this may be comprehended as the "virtual Deity."

In this great-grand system of the universe, each system "strives to exhaust the universe, in its process of absorbing, accumulating, transforming and hoarding up necessary amount of energy and establishing order for itself; and disorder is then created as a result and is left to the environments" (Zhang [1993], p. 256). As such, we are faced with questions of how the universe creates and maintains its order. Since the total amount of energy in the university is constant (by the law of the conservation of energy), does this meant that, in the simplest case, each system has an anti-system so that the order of one system is balanced out by the disorder of its anti-system? That is, the system space of the universe must include in it both systems (in the narrow sense) and anti-systems. Here, any anti-system is a system (in the broad sense).

Now we turn to the guiding principles governing the constant operations and incessant transformations of the universe. In the following, we shall attempt at first to present some categorical concepts that reflect our thinking patterns and then to formulate some useful principles in order to facilitate our understanding of the universe from the perspective of systematics.

For the general structures of the universe, we begin with the concepts of universal element, human element, material element (i.e., non-living and non-human element), event-element (or a composite element composed of two or more elements), idea-element, single-element system (i.e., an element to be considered as a "system"), system (or multiple-element system), subsystem, grand system, super-system (great-grand system or others), single-pole system, multi-pole system, two-element-system (or bi-system), tri-system (or triangle system), and multiple-element system and so on.

Then we have the concepts of system in tranquility or conflict, and in harmony or competition as well. We also have symbolic iso-systemism and metaphorical anti-systemism between systems and super-systems. As for a system, we have: CE T Central, CE centrality of a system, systemic continuity and strategic continuity, and we also have impactors and interactors operating within a system and among several systems, respectively. In order to describe and to picture these impactors, we may have to rely upon some formats like "quasi-matrices" in order to illustrate symbolically those processes of creation, transformation, growth/enlargement, decline/diminution and destruction, either statically or dynamically.

In the following, we shall present the most basic categories of cultural systematics:

Tzuu: Tzu* (Ultimate Creativity-Destructibility), Tzu (generated by Tzu*), <Self> ≡ <Tzu> ≡ tzuu ("tzu" in general), zi (a person, "tsu" in the physical world)

Wu: Wu* (Ultimate "wu"), Wu (transcendental "wu", generated by Wu*), WU ("wu" in Lao Tzu), Wu ("wu" in Chuang Tzu), <wu> (wuu, "wu' in general), wwu (absolutely nothing, nothingness in the physical world)

Yuu: Yu * (Ultimate "yuu"), Yu (transcendental "yuu", generated by Yu*), <yu> (≡ yuu, "yuu" in general), you (some thing existing in the physical world), self-entity-in-tranquility (mind, matter), mutual-entity-in-tranquility, self-entity-in-conflict (mind, matter), mutual-entity-in-conflict)

Ii: I* (the world as a holistic self), <I> (≡ Ii in general), I-me or I (me)

Forms: Time*/Space* (Ultimate Time and Space), Time (transcendental time, generated by Time*), time (physical time), Space (transcendental space, generated by Space*), space (space in the physical world), 𝔍 (Form generated by Tzu).

Energy: transformation and transmutation, change

Creation (or generation) and Destruction: motion, quiescence, creation, generation and life (pi-generation), destruction and death

Yin-yang duals: yu, wu (being, non-being); life, death; luck, misfortune; yin, yang; tao, chi; male, female; quiescence, motion; T Central, non-T Central; equilibrium, disequilibrium; systemic continuity, systemic discontinuity; human being, Deity (deity); I and me, other person; master, slave; friend, enemy; beauty, ugliness; good, evil; tranquility, conflict; self-entity, mutual-entity; principle, application; thesis, antithesis; partition and division, integration; small, big; activity, knowledge; benefit, cost.

Below we shall present some guiding principles for the operations of the universal entities. These guiding principles are:

i) Principle of Ultimate Creativity-Destructivity. Ultimate Creativity/Destructivity exists by itself, and is self-mastering and self-illuminating. The existence of Ultimate Creativity-Destructivity can not be proved except by intuitive sense and reasoning. Principle of creativity is implied by the principle of Ultimate Creativity-Destructivity. This is a super-metaphysical principle. Ultimate Creativity-Destructivity is the "ultimate creativity and the ultimate destructivity" itself, and it neither creates nor destroys itself. According to Lao Tzu, "it is not self-created, therefore it lasts forever." This is contradictory in logic (or the logic of one dimension), and yet it is not contradictory in systematics. Note that, for a and b being two universal elements and X being a system, if a is in contradiction to b, by setting X = |a b|, or a being the element in dimension one of x and b being the element in dimension two of x, then there is no contradiction in X. Thus, this is the "principle of contradiction being no contradiction." Here, for simplicity, this principle is called the "principle of contradiction" as well. To be sure, Ultimate Creativity-Destructivity is Tzu* (SELF, Self*), the very creativity/destructivity itself. Thus, Tzu* is both the source of "contradiction in no-contradiction" and "no-contradiction in contradiction."

One way to look at this issue is that, in extending the dimension, contradiction may be seen as no-contradiction. As for things of no contradiction in different dimensions, by collapsing the dimension, they may become things of contradiction in the same (actually one) dimension.

The principle of yu-wu is implied by the principle of Ultimate Creativity-Destructivity. In the real world sense, this yu presents some entity of existent, and wu represents "nothingness." To go beyond the "real-world existence," the principle of wu is the one of co-potential existence. Similarly, in the sense of beyond the "real-world existence," the principle of yu is either the one of metaphysical existence, or the one of super-metaphysical existence. It is not necessary to prove the non-existence of nothingness in the real-world sense. The principle of wu may also be the principle of "destruction," in the sense of metaphysics and super-metaphysics.

ii) Principle of creation. By the generative-destructive interactions (or generative-conflictive interactions) of yu and wu and with the crescendo and diminuendo of tao and chi, milliards of things are created. Here Wu* and Yu* are instantaneously, constantly and separately created by Tzu*, Wu* begets Wu through the interactive power-energy of Tzu*, and Yu* begets Yu through the interactive power-energy of Tzu* as well. Then Wu and Yu interact under the light of Tzu* to generate One, One acts under the illumination of Tzu* to generate Two, and Two acts under the illumination of Tzu* to generate Three. Then, in turn, Three acts under the illumination of Tzu* to generate Milliards of Things in the universe. Here by One is meant the "metaphysical one" (i.e., above-the-shape One) generates the real-world one (i.e., below-the-shape One), by Two is meant the "metaphysical two" (i.e., above-the-shape Two) that generates the real-world two (i.e., below-the-shape Two), by Three is meant the "metaphysical three" (i.e., above-the-shape Three) that generates the real-world three (i.e., below-the-shape Three), ..., and by Milliards of Things is meant the "metaphysical

milliards-of-things" (i.e., above-the-shape Milliards-of-Things) that generates the real-world milliards of things (i.e., below-the-shape Milliards of Things).

iii) Principle of Wu. Wu is created by Wu* and is the wu of co-creation. It is wuu (wu in general) and is also the wu of potential destruction. The above is a super-metaphysical principle. The wwu (nothing) is created by Wu, and is nothing. This is the principle of no-existence. The existence of wwu does not need any proof. This is also the principle of destruction.

iv) Principle of yu (or being) as potential. From Tzu to Wu is a co-potentiality; and from Tzu to yu is also a co-potentiality. From Tzu* to Wu* is a creation of co-potentiality; and from Tzu* to Yu* is also a creation of co-potentiality. From Tzu* to Yu* and Wu*, it is the principle of contradiction, dialectic principle and principle of contradiction creating potentiality. Here Yu is the yu of co-potential. The Yu is created jointly by Yu* and other forces of potential. The existence of you (yu in the real world) is self-evident by either the logic of Descartes -- I think, and therefore I am -- or by the logic of Husserl – I am conscious, and therefore I am. Here, by self-evident is meant a presumption, hypothesis or axiom. Note that the existence of I-me (i.e., I or me) may be self-evident, but the existence of others (other human beings or the physical world external to the human being) are not. Here, by the term I-me (i.e., I or me in the real world) is meant the micro-I, not the macro- or universal I (i.e., the universe) which will be called I*).

In the above, logically, Kant's position with regard to the existence of "thing in itself " (Ding an Sich) is simply a premise, assumption, hypothesis, or axiom. Though my intention-toward-outside is self evident (to myself), the existence of the objects of Husserl's intentionality are not self-evident. Except at the last stage of philosophical development, Husserl suspended any judgment about the object of one's intentionality (see Guan [2000])[30]. Therefore, the existence of the external objects is not ensured. That is, according to Husserlian phenomenology, we should not discuss this topic of human existence. But to have a real discussion about the issues of human and external existence, it is surely necessary to assume that this external world exists outside of our consciousness, and we need to constantly fail to deny the validity of this assumption from our real world experiences (that is, simply stated, one is required to "verify" and to reinstate (or fail to nullify) constantly this assumption)[31]. In consequence, it is always required to ascertain this hypothesis before the external world can be investigated. By following Husserl's "bracketing" the existence issue of the object of one's intentionality, one loses the solid philosophical ground to engage in scientific or even systemic study of the outside world. In this principle, since the existence of the outside world has not been falsified by sciences so far, the hypothesis of the existence of the outside world is patently maintained.

v) Principle of yu (or being) as a field of systemic study. Yu is created by Tzu, and Tzu is primordially created by Tzu*. In other words, Yu is create by Yu* under the light of Tzu*. Then, by possessing potential, Yu transforms into you, or the real world existence. Here, by the term potential is meant a certain force possessing a "seed" or "origin" of existence. This principle embodies in itself the principle of the cause of tao and that of the cause of chi. Moreover, this principle embodies the principle of formal cause and of material cause as well. In principle, Yu also splits itself and transforms into Tao and Chi, certainly under the illumination of Tzu*. Tao may be regarded as a solid and pervasive entity, though hard to be pinpointed, permeating everywhere at any instance; and Chi is a force untouchable and exists in no forms, and it can be perceived only by one's heart vaguely and even mysteriously. Nevertheless, Chi may exist even without having been detected by the keenest heart.

vi) Principle of yu being matter. This is the principle that the Ultimate Creativity-Destructivity creates matter. Once Lao Tzu said, "Tao generates One, One generates Two."[32] Certainly, in physical sense, one out of Two is matter. Moreover, what Chou Tunyi declared: "From Wu Chi and then Tai Chi, the motion of Tai Chi generates…, quiescence generates yin"[33] and what Xiong Shili regarded as Xi generating matter are similar to this line of thinking. This is also the principle of the cause of chi which is identical to the principle of the cause of tao (also see the next paragraph).

To say "yu being matter," following the Chinese tradition, is meant "Tao generates Chi", or "Chi generates qi." Here "Tao is Chi," "Chi is Tao," or "Tao and Chi are identical and together becomes One"[34] Consequently, One creates Two or matter.

In this occasion, it is a contradiction if dao (principle, way, load) is said to create qi (air). It is preferable not to have a statement like Tao creating Chi, because this is a very confusing one and is actually a contradiction. To claim that Tao* creates Chi*, this may be interpreted as Self* creating Tao* and Self* creating Chi* in separate acts. Consequently, it is preferred to state that Self* (i.e., Tzu*) creates Tao* and Tao* creates Tao under the light of Self*, and then Self* creates Chi* and Chi* creates Chi under the light of Self* as well in order to save logical confusion. That is, the so-called Tao creates Chi, interpreted in the above, is essentially contradictory and yet not a contradiction; and this is an illustration of the application of the principle of contradiction being no contradiction.

It would be logical to make a statement like "Tao generates dao." Note that dao and qi are symbolic notations for forces in the real world. Here, dao and qi are independent, because dao does not generate qi and vice versa.

vii) The principle of yu being mind. This is the principle of Ultimate Creativity-Destructivity creating mind. Here, in a systemic manner, this mind means soul as well. Like in the case of Tao generates one, and one generates two, one of these two entities is matter. Moreover, what Chou Tunyi said: "From Wu Chi and then Tai Chi, the motion of Tai Chi generates yang"[35] and what Xiong Shili regarded as pi generating mind are similar to this idea.

One may say that Yu (or Being) creates mind. This is another way to state the principle of the cause of chi. Being creates matter, and Being creates mind as well. In the dominant Occidental convention (with a culture of conflict), mind and matter contradicts to each other and yet are unified (in the Hegelian sense). In contrast, in the Oriental mind (with a culture of tranquility), although mind is not matter and matter is not mind, mind and matter transform into each other in their original states. This is yet another application of the principle of contradiction being no contradiction. Following the Oriental tradition, dualism is at best in a mild form, in which the distinction between mind and matter does not prevent them from interacting in an integrating way under the light of Self*. This is exactly what we mean the **scheme of two dimensions in one origin** (or one "primordiality").

Note that Chou Tunyi once claimed, "Sages set it up for upright-center and jen-yi, and center (the mind) on (the state of) quiescence."[36] This is the yin part of Ultimate Creativity-Destructivity. We also need to address the other aspect of Ultimate Creativity. That is, according to the principle of systematics, Ultimate Creativity-Destructivity is simultaneously Yin, Yang, and Mediety-Center with unyieldingness (or resoluteness), tenderness, and a MFCE balance between unyieldingness and tenderness.[37] As for Xion Shili, there are the ideas of Pi operating in Xi (i.e., matter is embodied in mind, matter is in mind) and of "Xi being the force of condensation causing the "substance" to transform into matter with physical shapes and Pi, as the vigorous-and-dynamic force, operating in Xi and being the master"(Jiang [1991]).[38] These statements could be interpreted as quite similar to what we mean Self* creates Chi*. Perhaps one could try to say that Tao* creates Chi under the light of Self*, but this does not appear to be the best way to describe it.

Note that the key idea of Xion Shili may be followed up by the idea of Mo [1983]which may be interpreted as an assertion that, by the self-trapping or running-against-self, mind creates the matter-attached knowledge. That is, mind creates matter by a process of self-denial.[39] As such, this view of the self-degradation of mind creating matter is certainly one point of view in the realm of the monism of mind (or ideal monism).

It is certain that one may approach issues of the "primordiality" (or origin) of the world at the onset from the comprehensive Weltanschauung which provides a solid ground for all of the ideal monism, material monism, mind-matter dualism, and even agnosticism, since sciences have not favor any one over the others.

Nevertheless, from the viewpoint of an individual, the human being is the most sublime entity of the universe and is therefore situating in the position of dominating this universe. By our ideal account, nothing less than the belief of good human nature is acceptable. If the universe is legislated by the human morality as suggested by Mo Tsungsan, then the human being ought to have hearts. But it would be prefect if the laws of the universe could be legislated by Tao, Chi, Being, and Beauty as well.

Moreover, the idea of yu being mind may just be identical to the idea of Tao* creating Tao. This is the same as: Tao is One, Tao creates One which in turn creates Two (which in turns creates "two things"); and one of these two things is mind (or Tao).

Remark A.2-7-1. In this tao-chi scheme (Tao,Chi|Wu), Tao* and Chi* are created by Tzu*, Tao is created by Tao*, Chi* is created by Chi*, and the interactions of Tao and Chi create the "Milliards of things." Here the integration of the potentials embodied in Tao* and Chi* is called Wu, and the collection of the real world manifestations of Tao* and Chi* is called Yu.[40] Note that, here, this is not an application of the principle of contradiction being no contradiction.

According to Chu Hsi, mind is in command of human nature and desire (affection, temperament, or emotion), with human nature being created by Heavenly Li and affection being begotten by Chi. In the mind, we shall differentiate between will and rationality. This will-to-

creation penetrates desire and chi, whereas in its operations, the rationality-to-creation embodies elements emanating from Heavenly Li and Tao. The will can be classified according to whether it is vigorous (hard or unyielding), soft (gentle or tender), neither-hard-nor-soft, or just one of moderation or mediety. The rationality will be classified into yu-wu rationality, scientific rationality, dialectic rationality, revelation rationality and so on. Within the realm of human will, although the hard or vigorous will-to-creation dominates the human temperament, the soft and moderate wills still have their appropriate places. As for the human rationality, the yu-wu rationality–to-creation must coordinate well with scientific rationality, dialectic rationality, super-natural rationality and other types of rationalities. By the **yu-wu rationality** is meant the collective entity of not only the intuitive, holistic and organic rationality, but other types of rationality like the kung-wu rationality (or emptying-out-and-nothing rationality and MFCE rationality as well.
The kung-wu rationality possesses the characteristics of leisurely wandering about and roaming over at ease and of surpassing concrete things and negating the existing entities as well. Here the so-called *yu-wu rationality* implies organizational rationality, coordination rationality and tranquil rationality, etc. Moreover, because it is capable of transcending and negating things, this *yu-wu rationality* is actually part of the fine creativity of human faculty.

In the above, rationality can be classified into the rationality of morality and the rationality of non-morality. Similarly, human will can be classified into the will of morality and the will of non-morality. This yu-wu rationality may lead to leisurely-surpassing and worldly-jen-yi morality. Similarly, the *self-mastering life-will* at times leads to the will of morality which is immersed in mind-fasting/soul-forgetting, long-life/deep-vision and rightfully ambitious endeavor, with the so-called rightfully ambition being the type of courageous engagement against all odds if it deems morally superior to do so.

viii) Principle of the cause of interconnectedness (or relatedness.) Under the spatiotemporal conditions, any entity possessing both causes of tao and chi (or formal and material causes) are interrelated, be it significant or negligible. This is also the principle of spatiotemporal conditions or the principle of static cause of organization.

ix) Principle of the causes of motion. This is also the principle of the cause of automatic motion and the principle of the cause of mutual motion.

x) Principle of the causes of organization (or systemic formation). This principle can be classified into the dynamical principle of the cause of self-organization and the dynamical principle of the cause of mutual organization.

xi) Principle of the final cause. By the coordination of final cause and the causes of mutual motions conditioned upon the automatic motion of all elements involved, the mode of motion in the universe is established.

Note that these causes of automatic motion and mutual motion are closely related to the characteristics of a universal element. For $x \Vdash \mathbf{U}$, $x = x((s,d),.)$, $(s,d) \Vdash (C_S x C^{DS}(e_r)$, $(s,d) \sim (f,a,m)$, where s and d stand for the static cause and dynamical cause, respectively, and f , a and m stand for the final cause, the cause of automatic motion and the cause of mutual motion, respectively. Here $(c_S x c^{DS}(e_r))$ is the set of static and dynamic characteristics of a universal element, "~" $\models \mathbb{Z}\circ,_v\mathbb{H}$ is an impactor connecting this (s,d) to (f,a,m). For the latter, that is, (s,d) is the set of forces of a universal element partaking the static and dynamic creativity of the universe.

Through the principle of the cause of interconnectedness, all of the cause of automatic motion, the cause of mutual motion, the cause of self-organization, the cause of mutual organization and the final cause can be integrated into a holistic entity. Here the principle of the final cause is conditioned upon the forces of Ultimate Creativity-Destructivity and is therefore part of the principle of the ultimate creativity and destructivity.

xii) Principle of conflict or the principle of contradictory motion. The whole universe is in a causal net in which the motion of one entity is in constant conflict with the motion of other entities.

xiii) Principle of tranquility or the principle of harmonious motion. The universe is simultaneously a causal net in which the motion of one entity is in tranquility or harmony with the motion of others.

xiv) Principle of transformation and transmutation. This is the principle representing the total processes of changes leading eventually to the ultimate perfection of the universe in infinite time. In the spatiotemporal world, each entity is in constant transformation or transmutation. By the integration of the principle of transformation and transmutation, the principle of the cause of organization and the principle of the cause of motion, various subsystems and grand systems may be created so that the differentiation between the micro-system and macro-system and between the cause and effect will subsequently manifest in numerous forms following the inner dynamics of the nature. But if we integrate this principle of transformation and transmutation with the principle of the Ultimate Creativity-Destructivity, by the activities of creating and those of being created, then the world of the human beings and that of the physical entities will be distinguished accordingly. Naturally amid the integration of the principle of ultimate creativity and destructivity and the principles of transformation and transmutation, interconnectedness, motion and organization, the perfect world is supposed to be created eventually in the infinite time. Thereby milliards of things shall co-develop without harming each other, and tao proceeds with chi without any interference.

This principle of transformation and transmutation is also the medium between the principle of tranquility and that of conflict. Here, we have: {principle of contradictory motion, principle of harmonious motion/principle of transformation and transmutation} as a system in which the principle of transformation and transmutation serves as the center.

xv) Principle of systemic continuity, discontinuity and anti-continuity. Universal elements and events possess the characteristics of systemic continuity, discontinuity and anti-continuity. The perfect world and the perfect universe are in general, by definition, the systems of systemic and strategic continuities. In the states of systemic discontinuity and anti-continuity, all entities in the universe, living or non-living, may be in conflict against and harmful to each other. It follows that in the states of dis- or anti-continuity, because of the principle of the universe forever leading toward the "good-nature" and self-generation, some entities of living and non-living things and some events vanish whereas some others emerge during both processes of conflict and invigoration. In general, the total impact of conflict and invigoration between any two entities in the universe is positive, or that the positive impact overweighs the negative impact.

In the state of systemic discontinuity, the forces in the universe may be in some processes of smooth movement or variational motions, or may tend to be more unstable over time. If due to unstable movement, a system gradually transforms itself into variational state, then it may eventually converge to moderately conflicting equilibrium or even harmonious balance (in a mathematical sense). This is because the universe is created by the contradictory impactor which may lead to explosive contradiction, non-explosive and moderate contradiction, harmonious difference, or even tranquility-in-unity. For a system isolated from the rest of the universe, overtime it shall converge to a stable state, although unstable motion may persist for a long time and a system might never reach a stable state.

In a system in a state of systemic discontinuity, if this discontinuity leads to even more unstable state of motion, then the system may explode and eventually reach a state of systemic anti-continuity. This is because the universe may be created by some contradictory impactors which tend to push the system in question to converge into a state of explosive contradiction and violence (the contradictory impactor is one manifestation of the forces of Ultimate Creativity-Destructivity). Thus the possibility for the systemic anti-continuity to be created must be there. This is especially true when a system is struggling to survive against unfavorable external environments. ting from outside and it will certainly creates a great force of systemic anti-continuity.

xvi) Principle of strategic continuity, discontinuity and anti-continuity for the social power-energy net and the will-and-rationality-to-creation entity. Strategic continuity may be generated by the force of systemic continuity; and naturally at this juncture, the coordination effect must be greater than the conflict effect.

Strategic discontinuity may be created by systemic discontinuity. If so, then in order to restore a certain level of systemic continuity, the will-and-rationality-to-creation entity may need to be modified and the social power-energy net may need to be partially reformed. In this case, the coordination effect may be greater than the conflict effect.

Strategic anti-continuity may be generated by systemic anti-continuity. If so, then the will-and-rationality-to-creation entity (in the narrow sense) may need to be overhauled and the social power-energy net may need to be completely altered. In this case, the coordination effect may be entirely destroyed, and only the conflict effect remains.

When the relationship between the basis being-field of the universe and the human being changes significantly, strategic continuity of a human being or any society shall consequently be disrupted. And the WR entity (in the narrow sense) and social PE net will also be distorted accordingly. For example, after the human being successfully colonizing the moon (in the future), to sustain this endeavor of outer space expedition, a supply chain must be created in order to disrupt the normal operation of the human society on earth.

xvii) Principle of the independence of individual entity. This is the principle stating that each individual is endowed with intrinsic freedom while in existence.

xviii) Principle of a least degree of equality among all people. From this principle, the possibility of a least degree of fairness among all human beings is safeguarded.

xix) Principle of mutual adaptation and coordination. This principle is an extension of the principle of transformation and transmutation.

xx) Principle of centrality. In a system, there must be a pivotal point of cultural energies serving as the center of gravity.

In the above, some of our principles point to the same direction as Alfred Whitehead did in his theory of process philosophy (for example, see Shen [1990, p. 45]).

The traditional thinking patterns of classical China are those of the yinyang causal (YYCE or yin-yang five-element) iso-systemism among human beings, families, societies, nations and the universe. The focal point of this iso-systemism may be said to lie in the family. In the Iching-Confucian culture, we have the following systems. The nucleus family is one composed of parents and children. The cosmic system is one composed of Heaven which is perceived as the "father," Earth as the "mother" and male and female human beings as the children of Heaven and Earth. The social system is the extended family system which automatically and simultaneously serves as the system of a nation: the emperor is the "father," the empress is the "mother," and common people are "children." The cosmic-life system is the one with: yin-yang phenomenal changes as "father," the balance between hard and soft textures of the physical entities as "mother" and jen-yi morality of the human being as children. The so-called concentric circles of cultivating virtues for oneself, harmonizing the family, ruling the nation by benevolence and pacifying the whole world are systems of iso-systemisms representing the core of the ethical and socio-political systems of Confucianism. The foundation or the origin of these Confucian iso-systemisms is actually the absolute paternalistic society-polity of the emperor-based Faziranism; and for this, the nucleus system of the Chi-family-based feudalism of the ancient Chou Dynasty is the best and the only example. Theoretically speaking, the master of the royal family harmonizes the family once he cultivates his virtue because by definition he is in control of the family (and his family members are in a position of voluntarily obeying his rule). He is in absolute control of the nation due to his position as the head of the extended family which rules the nation. In other words, all the kinsmen and kinswomen obey his rule voluntarily, and his cultivation of own virtue sets the stage for the peace and prosperity of the nation. Thus, this is the iso-systemism among the systems of oneself, the family, the society, the nation, and the world.

This Confucian iso-systemism is one based on the systemic and strategic continuity, since presumably the structure and ethics of the society under the Confucian doctrine will last forever and be always the same as what have been inherited from the sages of the primordial world. In ancient Greece, the iso-systemism of the human being and the universe might be conceived as the one between the human society and the personified world of deities. This is most natural since the structure of the world of deities must be the same as that of the human society by this belief. Nevertheless, from the perspective of systemic thinking, the world of the ancient Greeks is in fact in a state of systemic and strategic discontinuity.

In the Christian doctrine, it appears that the system of belief-disbelief is the core of the iso-systemism among the dichotomies of belief-disbelief, good-evil, redemption-punishment and heaven-hell. To fully address the issue of belief systems, we need to establish a comprehensive framework of religion. Due thto the limitation of space and time, we shall leave this important topic to future research (may see Tonn [2006]).

§A.2-8 Competitive System

In the competitive system: (opposition $>^{dom}$ centrality; conflict subsystem $>^{dom}$ tranquil subsystem).

In terms of the structures of conflict and tranquil cultures, a competitive system is one in which the conflict subsystem dominates the tranquil subsystem: tranquil sub-sys < conflict sub-sys. Here by "x<y" is meant x to be dominated by y, and the power of x is weaker than that of y. For example, if x and y $\sqsubseteq (\Omega,\mathcal{Z}\circ,{}_{\mathrm{v}}\mathcal{H},\{\mathbb{C}\})$ are unit systems, we may write x = $\{(v,h,\gamma(\tau)),(R,R^D)\}$, $\tau \Vdash (\mathfrak{I},Ш^{Д}) \Vvdash \mathbb{T}zu^*$ (short-hand notation from Bcm. (A.2-2-1-5)) and similarly for y. Now for the system Z = {x<y}, we have:

$$\text{(A.2-8-1)}\quad z = \{[(v,h,\gamma(\tau)),(R,R^D)]^{x} <^{dom} [(v,h,\gamma(\tau)),(R,R^D)]^{y};.\},$$
$$= \{(v,h,\gamma(\tau))^{T} <^{dom} (R,R^D)^{K},\ (v,h,\gamma(\tau))^{T} <^{dom} (R,R^D)^{K};.\},\ \tau \Vdash (\mathfrak{I},Ш^{Д}) \Vvdash \mathbb{T}zu^*$$

where the superscripts T and K denote the cultures of tranquility and conflict, respectively.

Figure A.2-8-1
Competitive structure: YY CE balance

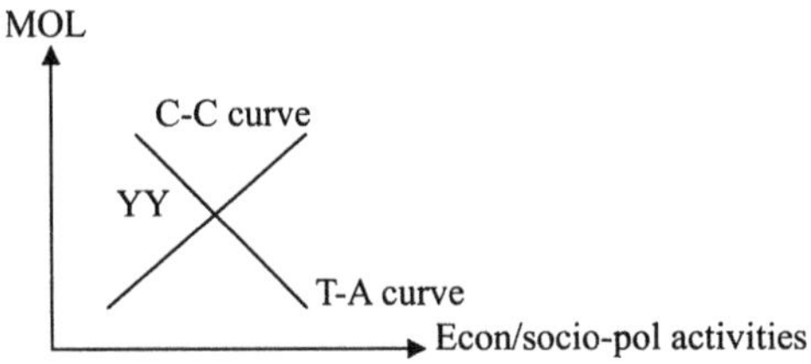

Below, let the becoming of the relationship between the economic and sociopolitical activities (econ/soc/pol-activities) and the meaning of life (MOL) be:

$$\text{(A.2-8-2)}\quad \{\varphi(\text{MOL,econ/soc/pol-activities}) =< T^{TC}\} \sqsubseteq Ш^{\Delta},$$

for $\varphi \vDash \mathcal{Z}\circ,{}_{\mathrm{v}}\mathcal{H}$ being an impactor, "$=< T^{TC}$" denoting the status of being in a state of T Central, and "$\sqsubseteq Ш^{\Delta}$" referring to the status of being in the world of everlasting motion.

Below, we shall describe the steps that must be taken in order to transform Bcm. (A.2-8-1) into the world in which the gap between systematics and mathematics is bridged (similar to the derivations of cs and cd curves in Appendix F). For this purpose, suppose $\{\varphi(\text{MOL,econ/soc/pol-activities}) =< T^{TC}\} \sqsubseteq (\Omega,\mathcal{Z}\circ,{}_{\mathrm{v}}\mathcal{H},\{\mathbb{C}\}) \sqcap \mathbb{R}$, and let the capital stock and raw labor be held constant. Furthermore, we shall assign the conquest/conflict curve as one with a positive slope and the tranquility/association curve as one with a negative slope, with both of these curves to be assumed as 1-1 functions (see Figure A.2-8-1). Then, the intersection of these two curves is the point of YY centrality which is in the state of stable tension in dialectical operations, CE balance in tao reversal processes, and equilibrium in logical-mathematical manipulations. In Figure A.2-8-1, T-A curve, C-C curve and YY refer to the tranquility-association curve and the conquest-conflict curve and (yin-yang) CE balance point, respectively.

In Figure A.2-8-1, the tranquility/association curve has a negative slope; this is because for people oriented toward competition, the higher the level of tranquil/associative activities, the lower the level of MOL. In contrast, the conquest/conflict curve has a positive slope because, for people oriented toward competition, the higher the level of conquest/conflict activities, the higher the level of MOL.

In this figure, above the YY CE TCentral point, the level of the activities of conquest and conflict is larger than that of tranquility and association; and the larger is the gap, the higher the level of MOL becomes. The contrary is true for the points below the YY CE TCentral point. Below this point, the level of the activities of conquest and conflict is smaller than that of tranquility and association; and the larger is the gap, the lower the level of MOL becomes.

Below, in terms of spiritual/material culture, let the systematic-change becoming for the relationship between the economic and sociopolitical activities and the meaning of life (MOL) be: $\{\varphi(\text{MOL,econ/soc/pol-activities}) =<T^{TC}\} \subseteq Ш^{\Delta}$, for $\varphi \models \mathbb{Z}\circ,_{\vee}\mathbb{H}$ being an impactor. Furthermore, let the spirit-cultural curve be one with negative slope, and let the material-cultural curve be one with positive slope. As in the above, these curves are also assumed to be 1-1 functions (see Figure A.2-8-2).

Figure A.2-8-2
Competitive structure: Material and spiritual cultural curves

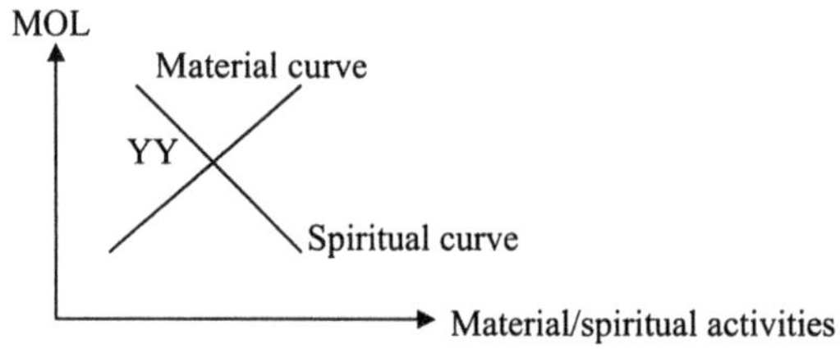

In Figure A.2-8-2, for people oriented toward material life, the spirit-cultural curve is downward sloping because as the level of spiritual activities ascends, the life becomes more boring, and therefore the lower the level of MOL becomes. In contrast, the material-cultural curve is upward sloping because, for people oriented toward material life, as the level of material accumulation rises, the life becomes more meaningful and thereby the level of MOL increases

In this Figure A.2-8-2, above the YY CE Tcentral point on the right, the level of material activities is larger than that of spiritual. The contrary is true for the points below the YY CE Tcentral point. Below this point on the left of the YY point, the level of material activities is lower than that of spiritual activities.

§A.2-9 Harmonious System

In the harmonious system: opposition $<^{dom}$ centrality; conflict subsystem $<^{dom}$ tranquil subsystem. Now for the system $Z = \{x<y\}$, we have:

$$(A.2\text{-}9\text{-}1)\quad z = \{[(v,h,\gamma(\tau)),(R,R^D)]^x <^{dom} [(v,h,\gamma(\tau)),(R,R^D)]^y;.\}$$
$$= \{(v,h,\gamma(\tau))^K <^{dom} (R,R^D)^T, (v,h,\gamma(\tau))^K <^{dom} (R,R^D)^T;.\}, \tau \Vdash (\mathfrak{I},Ш^Д) \Vvdash \mathbb{T}\mathbb{z}\mathbb{u}^*,$$

where the superscripts T and K denote the cultures of tranquility-centralization and conflict-opposition, respectively.

In terms of the conflict-tranquil structure, theoretically speaking, a harmonious system is one in which the conflict sub-system is dominated by the tranquil sub-system: conflict sub-sys < tranquil sub-sys. Here by "x<y" is meant x is dominated by y, and the power or influence of x is weaker than that of y.

Below, in terms of tranquil/conflict culture, let the systematic-change becoming for the relationship between the economic and sociopolitical activities and the meaning of life (MOL) be: $\{\varphi(MOL,econ/soc/pol\text{-}activities) =<T^{TC}\} \sqsubseteq Ш^{\Delta}$, for $\varphi \vDash \mathbb{Z}\circ,_{\mathbf{v}}\mathbb{H}$ being an impactor.

Figure A.2-9-1
Harmonious structure: T-A/C-C curve, with T/A = the tranquil-associational cultural curve, C/C curve = conquest-conflict cultural curve

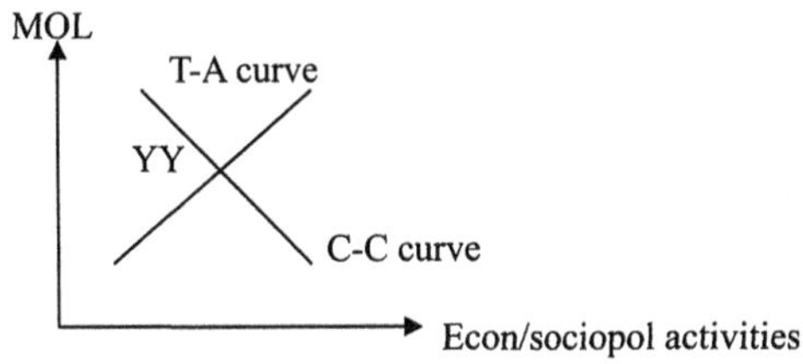

Furthermore, for capital stock and raw labor being held constant, let the conquest/conflict curve be one with a negative slope and the tranquility/association curve be one with a positive slope. That is, by converting to mathematical operation, there is a 1-1 correspondence between the economic/social/political activities and the meaning of life (MOL) (see Figure A.2-9-1).

In Figure A.2-9-1, the conquest/conflict curve has a negative slope; this is because for people oriented toward harmony, as the level of conflict rises, the level of MOL decreases. In contrast, the tranquility/association curve has a positive slope because, because for people oriented toward harmony, as the level of tranquil/associative activities rises, the level of MOL increases.

In this figure, above the YY CE Tcentral point on the right, the level of the activities of tranquility and association is larger than that of conquest and conflict. The contrary is true for the points below the YY CE Tcentral point. Below this point on the left, the level of the activities of tranquility and association is smaller than that of conquest and conflict.

Below, in terms of spiritual/material culture, let the becoming for the relationship between the economic and sociopolitical activities and the meaning of life (MOL) be: {φ(MOL,econ

/soc/pol-activities) $=< T^{TC}\} \sqsubseteq Ш^{\Delta}$, for $\varphi \vDash \mathbb{Z}\circ,_{v}\mathbb{H}$ being an impactor. Furthermore, let $\{\varphi(\text{MOL,econ/soc/pol-activities}) =< T^{TC}\} \sqsubseteq (\Omega,\mathbb{Z}\circ,_{v}\mathbb{H},\{\mathbb{C}\})\sqcap\mathbb{R}$, and (by transforming Bcm. (A.2-9-1) into the world of mathematics), for the capital stock and raw labor being held constant, let the material curve be one with a positive slope and the spiritual curve be one with a negative slope. Note that after the mathematical transformation, there is a 1-1 correspondence between the economic/social/political activities and the meaning of life (MOL) curve (see Figure A.2-9-2).

In Figure A.2-9-2, for people oriented toward spiritual life, the spirit-cultural curve is upward sloping because as the level of spiritual activities rises, the life becomes more meaningful, and therefore the level of MOL increases. In contrast, the material-cultural curve is downward sloping because, for people oriented away from material life, as the level of material accumulation rises, the life becomes less meaningful and thereby the level of MOL decreases.

Figure A.2-9-2
Harmonious structure: Spiritual/material cultural curves

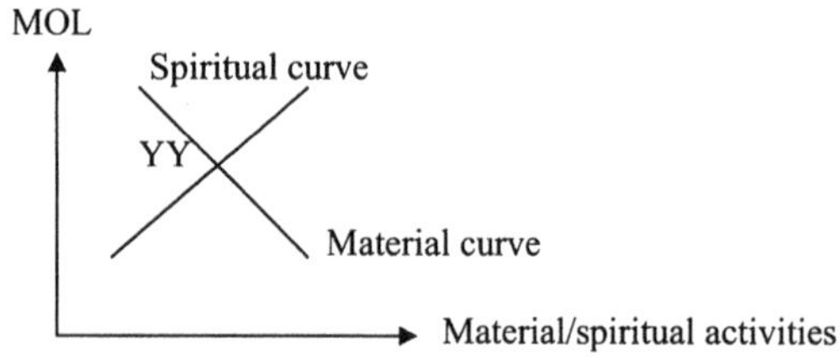

Economic structures: Household, firm, market, the macro economy, the global economy.

Political structures: Party, governments, military forces.

Social structures: Marriage-family, educational institution, religious community, professional community, general community, criminal community.

Principles: commanding over others, individuality, altruism, material acquisition, spiritual pursuit, realism, transcendentalism, profit motif, non-profit motivation, conflict, association, pursuing one's self-interests.

Family: Nucleus family, single-parent family, extended family.

Education: pre-school, elementary school, secondary school, college, graduate schools.

Religion: Buddhism, Christianity, Hinduism, Islam, Taoism, etc.

The society as a whole: See Figure A.2-9-3 as follows:

Figure A.2-9-3
Structure of the society as a whole

Religious communities
|
The intellectuals-educational institutions — Government — Industry-business communities
|
Common people

§A.2-10 More on The Structures of The Management Systems of Technology and Organization

From Subsection §A.2-2, we know that a system can be written as : $X = \chi\oplus <\mathbb{C}_X> \sqsubseteq (\Omega^{\Delta},\mathbb{Z}\circ,_v \mathbb{H},\{\mathbb{C}\})$, where $\chi = \{\mathbf{x}(H^*)\sqsubseteq\{[(vd,hc,\gamma),C_S\times^{DS}(e_r),(R_M,R^{DM}(e_r)),\tilde{O}]\|E\{e_j\},Z\}$, $< \mathbb{C}_X> =\{\tau|\mathcal{M}\Vdash [E(e_g(\tau)),Z(\mathfrak{C}^*(\tau))]\}$, $\tau \Vdash \mathfrak{J} \Vvdash \mathbb{T}zu^*$, with $\mathcal{M} = | \mathcal{M}^1(\ell,\tau),..., \mathcal{M}^N(\ell,\tau)),... |^T$ being the mind complex, E(e) being the environment or external energy, and $\mathbb{T}zu^*$ being Ultimate Creativity-Destructivity.

For an **organization** $X \sqsubseteq (\Omega^{\Delta},\mathbb{Z}\circ,_v \mathbb{H},\{\mathbb{C}\})$, it can be expressed as: $X = \{(vd,hc,\gamma) \mid$ IRI,MW,mutual dynamical chain, personnel chain$\|$ (SIFP,MPFX) $\sqsubseteq E\{e_j\},Z\}$, with $Z = Z(\rho,\omega,\mathbb{c})$, $\mathbb{c} \Vdash <\mathbb{C}_X>$, (IRI,MW,mutual dynamical chain,personnel chain) $\sqsubseteq (R,R^D(e_r))$ being a link in the static-dynamical structures of X, and the chain complex SIFP and the MPFX cycle being some links in the external environments $E\{e_j\}$. Note that $E\{e_j\}$ also contains the set {event,state,"system"}, with "event," "state" and "system" refer to the event of equilibrium or disequilibrium, the state of continuity or discontinuity and the system of democracy-capitalism, socialism or Faziranism, respectively. Here IRI denotes the chain complex of the information collection and evaluation, rational decision–making, and plan-implementation, MW stands for the relationship between the employer and the employees, whereas the saving-investment-finance-production chain complex (SIFP) designates the chain complex comprising the subsystems of energy-absorption and storage, conversion of financial assets into working capital, physical investment, input-output production and exchanges of products.

When the static-dynamical interpenetrating network $(R,R^D(e_r)) = \{(vd,hc,\gamma),[C_S\times C^{DS}(e_r), (R_M, R^{DM}(e_r))],\tilde{O}\}$ of a system changes, its technological-managerial structure will change accordingly. For simplicity, we shall classify organizational structures into three categories: consensual–and-harmonious centrality, absolute centralization, and decentralization. In the following, we discuss each category in turn.

(1) Structure of the consensual-and-harmonious centrality. Let this structure be the formal-informal institutions-culture: $(vd,hc,\gamma) = ((vd >^H hc,\gamma)\wedge\{X_i=\psi\{\mathcal{T}^*C=\mathcal{T}_i^*X_i,\Delta_i\} \barwedge \tau\}$, with C being the central element and all elements of the system reaching a consensus in actions and strategies. Here by "$vd >^H hc$" is meant the center controlling consensually and harmoniously the non-central elements, $\psi \vDash \mathbb{Z}\circ,_v\mathbb{H}$, $\mathcal{T} \vDash \mathbb{Z}\circ,_v\mathbb{H}$.

One example of the structure of the consensual and harmonious centrality is the system of emperor-based Huangben Faziranism in which static-dynamical interpenetrating network is: $(R,R^D(e_r) =\{(\rho,\omega)^F$: MPFX; military power $\angle$ emperor's power$\|$basis being-field$\angle$Mandate of Heaven$\}\wedge\{$IRI, SIFP, YXr&d | Cwr $\lessdot$ Legalist planning$\} \Lleftarrow \{$YX|emperor$\}$. Here, $(R,R^D(e_r)) \equiv [C_S\times C^{DS}(e_r),(R_M,R^{DM}(e_r))]$, and the SIFP chain complex may be replaced by the *YXSIFP chain* by which is meant the traditional Chinese saving-investment-financing-production chain complex. Note that in this traditional Chinese financial system, financial function is limited.

In the above, in addition, Cwr refers to the creativity of technology and organization (which includes the planning will-and-rationality and the so-called entrepreneurship) as a becoming of will and rationality based on the energy emanating from Ultimate Creativity-Destructivity, YX depicts the reasoning and research processes of the scheme of yin-yang five elements, and YXr&d stands for the YX-based R & D chain.

(2) Structure of the authoritarian organization: $(vd,hc,\gamma) = (vd>^{C}hc,\gamma) \wedge X_i = \psi\{\mathcal{T}^{*}C> \mathcal{T}X_i,\Delta_i\}$ $\barwedge\ \tau$. Here "vd $>^{C}$ hc" refers to the center controlling coercively the non-central elements or subsystems (of the system).

One example of the authoritarian organization is that of the socialist collectivism in which the static-dynamical inter-penetrating network is: $(R,R^{D}(e_r)) = \{(\rho,\omega)^{A}$: MPFX; party-power∠ military-power| basis being-field ∠dialectical self-organizing creativity} ^ {IRI,MW,SIFP, STr&d| Cwr⋞central planning} ⇚ {ST-Δ|party-cadre}. Here ST-Δ refers to the reasoning and research patterns of sciences and dialectic, and STr&d refers to the science-based R & D chain of production.
(3) Structure of the organization of decentralization: $(vd,hc,\gamma) = ((vd\approx hc,\gamma)\wedge\{X_i = \psi\{\mathcal{T}_i{}^{*}{}_i,\Delta_i\}$ $\barwedge\ \tau\}$. Here, "≈" refers to a state of the balance of power.

One best example of the decentralized organization is the capitalist system in which the static-dynamical inter-penetrating network may be presented as: $(R,R^{D}(e_r)) = \{(\rho,\omega)^{C}$: MPFX; property rights | basis being-field ∠ Deity}∧ {IRI, SIFP, STr&d | Cwr ⋞ market}⇚ ({ST|market}. Here ST refers to the reasoning and research patterns of scientific and technological inquiries.

General speaking, in a system, $\mathcal{T} \vDash \mathcal{Z}\circ,_{v}\mathcal{H}$, Z ⇚ $\{[(vd,hc,\gamma) \lessdot <\mathbb{C}_X>] \sqsubseteq Ш^{\Delta}\}$. That is, in the world of everlasting motion, the organizational power structure of a system is conditioned upon and constrained by its underlying culture. The decision-making and strategic complex of this system is under the constraint of the power structure of the system, although this strategic complex has a feedback control effect on the formation of the power structure.

In the following, let the business structure of a system be $X \sqsubseteq (\Omega,\mathcal{Z}\circ,_{v}\mathcal{H},\{\mathbb{C}\})$ which is a 5-pole system: $X = \{X_1,X_2,X_3,X_4,X_5\} = \{X_f \oplus <\mathbb{C}_f>, X \oplus <\mathbb{C}_->, C, X_+ \oplus <\mathbb{C}_+>, X\oplus<\mathbb{C}_s>\}$, where X_1 refers to the employees, X_2 the low-medium layer of the management, X_3 the board of directors and CEO, X_4 the staffs, X_5 the higher level management. In addition, let the center of the system be C (the CEO-chair of the Board of Directors of the organization), and the culture be one of capitalism: $<\mathbb{C}_X> =\{\tau|(M^{I}(\ell,\tau),\ldots,M^{N}(\ell,\tau))\Vdash E(e_r)\}$, $\tau \Vdash \mathfrak{J} \Vvdash$ $\mathbb{T}$zu* with $\mathbb{T}$zu* = Deity, where $M = |M^{I}(\ell,\tau)\ M^{II}(\ell,\tau)\ M^{III}(\ell,\tau)\ M^{IV}(\ell,\tau)\ \ldots|^{T}$. Then X represents a corporate organizational structure of capitalism.

In general, for $X = \{ X_1 ,X_2 ,\ldots,X_n \}$, let $[Y_k,Y_j]$ ⇚ $<\mathbb{C}_X>$. Then the principles of CE balance and Tcentral are applicable (see Subsection §3.2-2). At the same time, let $X \equiv F \sqsubseteq (\Omega,\mathcal{Z}\circ,_{v}\mathcal{H},\{\mathbb{C}\})\sqcap\mathcal{E}^{G}\sqcap\mathcal{E}^{wr}$, with $(\Omega,\mathcal{Z}\circ,_{v}\mathcal{H},\{\mathbb{C}\})$ denoting the system space, $\mathcal{E}^{G}$ denoting an organizational system of "groupism," and $\mathcal{E}^{wr}$ denoting a certain cultural system of will-rationality.

In the organizational system presented in the above (vd,hc,γ), the incentive system is a part of γ. The incentive system of an organization can be in the form of either individual or system-wide incentive. In terms of the individual incentive, in general, financial incentive is the most powerful mechanism in affecting the operations of the static-dynamical inter-penetrating network of an organization, $(R,R^D(e_r))$. In this static-dynamical structure, the IRI chain may be distorted by improper incentive, the policy-making may also be disoriented and thereby alter the effectiveness of any policy implementation. By instituting an incentive system, the level of creativity embodied in Cwr (i.e., the collection of S&T creativities as a becoming of will-rationality complex) may increase or decease, according to the nature of the incentive packages. In addition, the incentive system may also significantly influence the SIFP chain complex. Thus the stock market of an advanced economy may be considered as a partial function of this incentive mechanism.

Now we turn to the issues of moral incentive. It appears to be obvious that moral incentive has a prominent role to play in the static-dynamical penetrating structure of a system. If the cultural complex and the informal culture $\{\mathbb{C}_X,\gamma\}$ change, then IRI, MW, SIFP and Cwr shall change accordingly. Here the IRI chain of an organization is closely connected with the (vd,hc,γ) structure and the culture $\mathbb{C}_X$ (i.e., (ρ,ω)), while the SIFP chain complex is integrated with the static-dynamical inter-penetrating network and the cultural complex of the system.

As the action-strategic complex Z changes, the efficiency of management will change accordingly. It Z = Z* so that T = T*, where T is the actual target, T* is the desirable target of the system and Z* is the thought-of target of Z, then Z is judged as *efficient*. Here, by "T = T*" may mean that, for example, Tch = Tch*, q = q*(q is the output), or π = π* (π refers to the profits).

For more discussions of the topic of organization, see Sections 3.6-3.7 and Appendix F.

§A.2-11 Reorganizable Impactor and Systems

Definition A.2-11-1. Let a system X = {w,x,y,z} ⊑ $(\Omega,\mathbb{Z}\circ,{}_v\mathbb{H},\{\mathbb{C}\})$ and ϕ ⊨ $\mathbb{Z}\circ,{}_v\mathbb{H}$. Then ϕ is said to be an **independently decomposing and reorganizing impactor** (IDR impactor) if and only if the following becoming holds:

(A.2-11-1) ϕX = ϕ {w,x,y,z} = [{w,others}, {x,others}, {y,others}, {z,others}]
= [w⊙{non-w's}, x⊙{non-x's}, y⊙{non-y's}, z⊙{non-z's}]
= {[w╪x╪y╪z]^T ⊗* {non-{w,x,y,z}'s}} ⊛ Ix,

(for Ix being ○, ⊛ ⊨ $\mathbb{Z}\circ,{}_v\mathbb{H}$ being an integrating impactor) where ⊙ ⊨ $\mathbb{Z}\circ,{}_v\mathbb{H}$ depicts an interactor leading to some independent relationship, ⊗* ⊨ $\mathbb{Z}\circ,{}_v\mathbb{H}$ depicts a **separable interactor** (which is capable of separating groups of elements or systems, especially residuals, into independent entities. Here, "╪"⊨ $\mathbb{Z}\circ,{}_v\mathbb{H}$ is an IDR impactor such that [w╪x╪y╪z] ≡ [w ⊥ x ⊥ y ⊥ z] ^ [w | x | y | z], with "⊥" referring to an impactor of horizontally independent and internally hierarchical operation (i.e., [w⊥x⊥y⊥z] is a system of horizontally independent and internally hierarchical operation) and " | " referring to an hierarchically and orderly organizing impactor (i.e., [w | x | y | z] is a system of hierarchical organization).

Note that [x╪y] = [y╪x] for x, y being elements (subsystems, resp.) in a system (grand system, resp.).

Below, we have the needed definition.

Definition A.2-11-2. For X = {w,x,y,z} ⊑ (Ω,ℤ○,ᵥℍ,{ℂ}) and φ ⊨ ℤ○,ᵥℍ, if we have:

(A.2-11-2) φX
= ϕ{w,x,y,z}
= [{w,others}, {x,others}, {y,others}, {z,others}]
= [w⊙{non-w's}, x⊙{non-x's}, y⊙{non-y's}, z⊙{non-z's}]
= {[w╬x╬y╬z]^T ⊗* {non-{w,x,y,z}'s}} ⊛ Ix,
= [w╬x╬y╬z]^T

with {non-{w,x,y,z}'s}} = ○ and Ix = ○, then X is called **a complete IDR system**, and φ is called **a complete IDR impactor**.

Example A.2-11-1. h(L,K,ℂ) is an independently decomposable and reorganizable system (IDR system) if and only if ϕh(L,K,ℂ) = h[$^{+1}$ L $^{+2}$ K $^{+3}$ ℂ] or h[⊕ ^{1} L ⊕ ^{2} K ⊕^{3} ℂ]. Here ϕh(L,K,ℂ) = h[⊕^{1} L ⊕^{2} K ⊕^{3} ℂ] ≡ [L∣K∣ℂ]^T ^ [L⊥K⊥ℂ]^T, with X^T referring to the transpose of X for X as a set of elements or systems. That is, ⊕^{i} ≡ ╬ is an IDR impactor rearranging elements to form internally hierarchical and externally independent organizations, i = 1, 2, 3. Here, by "L ⊕^{i} K" is meant [⊕^{1} L ⊕^{2} K]^T ≡ [L $^{+i}$ K]^T ≡ [L ⊕^{i} K]^T, where L and K, each being an internally hierarchical organization, are independent of the other. Therefore, by setting [L ⊕$^{-i}$ K]^T ⊑ (Ω,ℤ○,ᵥℍ,{ℂ})⊓ℝ, for i = 1,2,3,..., we may transform it into a mathematical operation: [L ⊕$^{-i}$ K]^T ≈ μL - μK, with ≈ depicting an approximately equivalent relation, μL and μK depicting the mathematical measures of L and K, respectively.

Example A.2-11-2. Let X = {w,x,y,z} ⊑ ⊑ (Ω,ℤ○,ᵥℍ,{ℂ}) and ϕ ⊨ ℤ○,ᵥℍ. Then ϕ is said to be an **independently decomposing and reorganizing 1 impactor** (IDR 1 impactor) if and only if the following condition holds:

(A.2-11-3) ϕX = {[C╬N_1╬N_2╬...╬N_n] ⊗* [F]} ⊛ Ix,

(for Ix being ○, Ix integrates [C╬N_1╬N_2╬...╬N_n] and [F] into X) where C is the center of the system, N_i are non-central elements, for i ∈ℕ, and [F] denotes a collection of elements which do not belong to any system, ⊗* ⊨ ⊑ ℤ○,ᵥℍ is a separable impactor, and ⊛ ⊨ ⊑ ℤ○,ᵥℍ is an integrating impactor.

Definition A.2-11-3. Let x be a factor (element or system) which is very small in size or extremely insignificant, and is called **nullifiable factor** (element or system). Then χ is said to be a **nullifying impactor** if and only if χx → ○ (○ denoting an empty element or system). Note that this nullifying impactor is a mie impactor (see Tonn 2001, pp. 118, 129-132).

Example A.2-11-3. Let ϕ be an IDR impactor, X = {w,x,y,z} be a system in which {non-{w,x,y,z}} ≡ ε is a nullifiable factor and χ (or ϕ°: ϕ°ε = ○) is a residual-nullifying impactor for the residual ε (with ⊗* ⊨ ℍ being an interactor). Then we have:

(A.2-11-4) χϕX = χ{{ [w╬x╬y╬z]^T ⊗* ε}⊛* Ix}
= {[w╬x╬y╬z]^T ⊗ χ ε}⊛ Ix
= {[w╬x╬y╬z]^T ⊗ ○ }⊛ Ix
= {[w╬x╬y╬z]^T}⊛ Ix
= [w╬x╬y╬z]^T},

for the impactors (or interactors) ⊗*, ⊗, ⊛*, ⊛ and their operations been properly taken care of. Note that:

(A.2-11-5) $\chi\{$ [w╫x╫y╫z]^T = [w╫x╫y╫z]^T

(A.2-11-6) $\chi\{Ix\} = Ix$.

In addition, for [C╫N_1 ╫N_2╫…╫N_n] being a system, note that there is no need for any integrating factor within itself:

(A.2-11-7) [x╫y] ⊛ Ix = x╫y,

and here [w╫x╫y╫z]^T ≡ [w | x | y| z]^T ∧ [w⊥ x⊥ y⊥ z] refers to the system [w╫x╫y╫z]^T with each of w, x, y and z being independent and forming orderly and hierarchical relations with others. Here $\chi\phi$ is also called a *complete IDR impactor* (with the residual "non-{w,x,y,z}'s" in Bcm. (A.2-11-1) being ○, and actually, a composite impactor). Besides, [w ⊥ x ⊥ y ⊥ z] stands for a system in which all elements are independent of the other, and [w | x | y| z]^T or [w | x | y| z] stands for a system in which the elements form an orderly and vertically structured hierarchical relationship. Here X is a complete IDR system which is also called a *system with elements completely and independently decomposable-and-reorganizable* as well.

Example A.2-11-4. Let X be an (m × n × …)-dimensional system with X ⊑ $\{X^\Delta\}$, where X^Δ depicts a system with changing dimension in a non-orderly pattern. Here, $\{X^\Delta\}$ is the space containing all elements of X^Δ system. To illustrate, let $X^\Delta = X_{m\times n\times\ldots\infty}$ be a system for which m, n, … and so on are either changing over time or changing without any pattern.

Furthermore, let $X_{\backslash\frown}$ depict X with the interactions among all of its elements being eliminated and $X_{m\backslash i,n\backslash j}$ stands for a system in which there is no order and there is no independent relations among all elements and for a system derived by eliminating i rows and j columns of elements of $X_{m,n}$ from the right-hand side, i = 1,…,n, j = 1,…,m. This system $X_{m\backslash i,n\backslash j}$ is called a **diminutive $X_{m,n}$** as well. If $\phi X = X_{\backslash\frown} \otimes Z^*$, where $Z^* \equiv X_{m\backslash 1,n\backslash 1} \otimes X_{m\backslash 2,n\backslash 2} \otimes \ldots = [X_{m\backslash 1,n\backslash 1} \mid X_{m\backslash 2,n\backslash 2} \mid \ldots]$, then ϕX is called **Z* independently decomposed system** of X, and ϕ the **Z* independently decomposable impactor** of X (Z* IND impactor).

Example A.2-11-5. In a capitalist market, tracing individual firms from the market is a reversal-construction process. Let x, y, z ⊑ (Ω,$\mathcal{Z}$○,$_v\mathcal{H}$,{ℂ}) be firms, the market S = {x,y,z} ≡ {x╫y╫z} be a system composed of independent and reorganizable firms with the interactor "╫" and $\phi \models \mathcal{Z}$○,$_v\mathcal{H}$ being two IDR impactors (i.e., independently decomposing and reorganizing impactors). Then ϕS = ϕ\{x,y,z\} = [x|y|z] ⊗* N or [x╫y╫z]^T ⊗* N (≈ "$\Sigma_i F_i - \alpha$" in mathematical measure), i = 1,2,…,f, with N being a factor of reduction for $\alpha \geq 0$ (i.e., $\alpha > 0$ or $\alpha = 0$), F_i being the output of the ith firm. Here ⊗* is an IDR connector.

In the above Example A.2-11-5, if S is a system of Faziranist market, then ϕS = ϕ {x,y,z} = [x╫y╫z]^T ⊗* P (≈ $\Sigma_j F_j + \beta$ in mathematical measure), i = 1, 2 ,…, f, with P being a factor of addition, $\beta \geq 0$, F_j being the output of the jth firm.

Definition A.2-11-4. Let ϕ be an independently decomposed reorganizing impactor, $X_{m,n}$ be a system. Furthermore, let $\phi X_{m,n} = [(\Sigma_| X_|) \mid \alpha]$, where "$\Sigma_| x_|$" = $[x_1 \mid x_2 \mid \ldots \mid x_n \mid \ldots]$ denotes the "collection of independent $x_1, x_2, \ldots x_n, \ldots$" and $\alpha = [X_{m-1,n-1} \mid X_{m-2,n-2} \mid \ldots \mid \ldots] \otimes^* X_\Delta$ for X_Δ

being a very small diminutive of X, Then $\phi X_{m,n}$ is called the **α-independently decomposed reorganization** (α-IDR) of X and ϕ is called an α-IDR impactor.

Definition A.2-11-5. Let ϕ be an independently decomposed reorganizing impactor, $X_{m,n}$ be a system. Furthermore, let $\phi X_{m,n} = [(\Sigma_{|}X_{|}) \mid \beta]$, $\beta = [X_{m-3,n-1} \mid X_{m-5,n-3} \mid \ldots] \otimes^{*} X_{\downarrow}$, for $X_{\downarrow}$ being a very small diminutive of X, Then $\phi X_{m,n}$ is called the **β-independently decomposed reorganization** (β-IDR) of X and ϕ is called an β-IDR impactor.

§A.2-12 Existence of Strategies

Thema A.2-12-1 (Existence of strategy). Let a system $X \sqsubseteq (\Omega, \mathbb{Z}^{\circ}, {}_{v}\mathbb{H}, \{\mathbb{C}\})$ exists (i.e., Ω contains at least a non-empty system). If X reaches a state of TCentral, then the strategy $\mathcal{T} \Vdash \mathbb{Z}$ (or $\mathcal{T} \vDash \mathbb{Z}^{\circ}, {}_{v}\mathbb{H}$) exists.

Supporting reasoning. For $X \sqsubseteq (\Omega, \mathbb{Z}^{\circ}, {}_{v}\mathbb{H}, \{\mathbb{C}\})$ being a non-empty system, let $X \sqsubseteq Ш^{\Delta} \sqcap \Omega^{\mathcal{F}}$, with $\Omega^{\mathcal{F}}$ being the space of Faziranist culture. Because X is not empty, there exists at least one element in it; and without loss of generality, let it be the central element for a Faziranist system. In $X = \chi \oplus <\mathbb{C}_X>$, let the decision-making and strategic complex $Z \sqsubseteq \chi$ (Z being the complex of actions and strategies in the system X) is the "strategy" in the "static world" rather than in the "dynamical world" (i.e., $Z = Z(\tau)$, $\tau \Vdash (Ш^{\Delta})^{-1}$, "$(Ш^{\Delta})^{-1}$" being a non-dynamic world). Then this is a potential strategy but not a real world strategy. In the fazirainst system (or the system with the Faziranist culture), every element is associated with a real world activity. Therefore, let the strategic impactor $\mathcal{T} \Vdash \mathbb{Z}$ be the strategy in the dynamical world.

Let X be in a state of general TCentral. In general, this is: $X = X^*$ (where X^* is the desired X). Since $X \sqsubseteq Ш^{\Delta}$, $\mathcal{T}X \sqsubseteq Ш^{\Delta}$. Now, $\mathcal{T}X = \mathcal{T}X^* = X^*$ exists and $Ш^{\Delta}$ exists (by the assumption of Ω having at least a non-empty system). Then $\mathcal{T}$ exists (because Z exists in a non-empty system and Z implies $\mathcal{T}$). Note that for $\mathcal{T} \Vdash \mathbb{Z} \Subset Ш^{\Delta}$ and $X \sqsubseteq Ш^{\Delta}$, $\mathcal{T}X \sqsubseteq Ш^{\Delta}$ must be true by the closure property, since $\mathcal{T}$ (i.e., action) is an integral part of the world. It is a contradiction, for if $\mathcal{T}$ does not exist in $Ш^{\Delta}$, $\mathcal{T}X$ is not defined and would not exists in $Ш^{\Delta}$. If $\mathcal{T}$ is an empty impactor (i.e., one without any impact), then $\mathcal{T}X^* = X^*$. That is, $\mathcal{T} = \circ$ exists. Now, let $\mathcal{T}$ be a non-empty impactor, with $X \neq X^*$ (assumed for the sake of seeking a contradiction). But then with $\mathcal{T}X^* = X^*$, we have a contradiction. Thus, the existence of X implies that of $\mathcal{T}$ (otherwise, it is again a contradiction. This is because, without the existence of any impactor (say φ), it is impossible for $\varphi x \rightarrow \varphi x = x^*$ so that $X \rightarrow X^*$ under the action-strategy φ). Note that this $\mathcal{T}$ may be a strategy of continuity.

Thema A.2-12-2 (existence of the state of the general T Central for a system). If TX strategy exists in the state of strategic continuity with appropriate conditions, then the general TCentral of the system exists.

Supporting reasoning. Intuitively, among all possible strategies, there is one of continuity strategy. With necessary conditions, the system of continuity strategy guarantees the existence of systemic continuity. But any state of systemic continuity requires satiafactory operations prevailing in the system in question. Thus, if these preconditions are required to lead to the general TCentral, then the general TCentral of the system exists

§A.3 Integrating and Decomposition Procedures

§A.3-1 Introduction

In this section, we shall study basic methods of integrating elements into a system (or integrating systems to a grand system) and some basic methods of decomposition or deconstruction of systems.

§A.3-2 System's Completely Separable Impactor, IND-sys/A, Time-Becoming of A System

In this subsection, we shall apply the **method of time-becomings of a system** (or systematic-change equation in Tonn 2001) to study the time-structure of a tranquil system.

Definition A.3-2-1. Let a system X = $\{x_1,x_2,\ldots,x_n,res\} \sqsubseteq (\Omega,\mathbb{Z}o,_v\mathbb{H},\{\mathbb{C}\})$ be a multiple-factor system. Here by "X=$\{x_1,x_2,\ldots x_n,res\}$" is meant X is composed of x_1, x_2, …, x_n (x_i is an element, collection of elements, or system, for all I $\in\mathbb{N}$), and some residuals (res), not necessarily in any structural sense. Then X is said to be the **completely separable system (IND-sys)** or "simple-additive" system if and only if the following conditions hold:

(i) x_1, x_2, …, x_n are independent systems, which are completely separable from other elements or sub-systems.
(ii) X = $\{(\alpha_1x_1 \oplus \alpha_2x_2 \oplus \ldots \oplus \alpha_nx_n,) \oplus res\} \circledast Ix$, that is, X is decomposable into independent subsystems (modified with impactors α_i's to be determined) and some residuals when the integrating factor Ix is dissolved ($\oplus \models \mathbb{Z}o,_v\mathbb{H}$ and $\circledast \models \mathbb{Z}o,_v\mathbb{H}$ being independently associated impactor and integrating impactor, respective.

Below, let us use an example to illustrate this IND-system (i.e., IND-sys). For this purpose, let a system X $\sqsubseteq (\Omega,\mathbb{Z}o,_v\mathbb{H},\{\mathbb{C}\})$ be a multiple-factor non-independently separable system. For $\varphi \models \mathbb{Z}o,_v\mathbb{H}$, let us have the following becoming:

$$\text{(A.3-2-1)} \quad X = [\varphi^1X_1 \oplus (\varphi^2X_2 \oplus \varphi^2{}_{-1}X_{2,-1}) \oplus (\varphi^3X_3 \oplus \varphi^3{}_{-1}X_{3,-1} \oplus \varphi^3{}_{-2}X_{3,-2}) \oplus \ldots \oplus (\varphi^nX_n \oplus \varphi^n{}_{-1}X_{n,-1} \oplus \varphi^n{}_{-2}X_{n,-2} \oplus \ldots \oplus \varphi^n{}_{-n+1}X_{n,-n+1}) \oplus \Sigma] \circledast (Ix,\xi)$$

(with $\circledast$ being the integrating impactor, Ix being the integrating factor and (Ix,ξ) being ○, $\xi = \xi(\tau)$, $\tau \Vdash (\mho,Ш^{Д}) \Vdash \mathbb{T}zu^*$) where φ^i is the partial-impactor on X_i (the ith factor in X, i.e., φ^i is the impactor effective only in operating on the ith factor in X), i = 1, 2 , …, n with i denoting a superscript, X_{-j} is X of the $(-j)^{th}$ period or X reverting backward to the jth period, j = 1, 2, …,n-1), $\varphi^i{}_{-j}$ the partial-impactor on the ith factor in the $(-j)^{th}$ period of X (i.e., $\varphi^i{}_{-j}$ is the impactor effective only in operating on the ith factor in Y with Y being X reverting backward to the jth period), and Σ the residual. Here, "+" ≡ ⊕ $\models \mathbb{Z}o,_v\mathbb{H}$ is the interactor between completely separable elements or systems. In other words, here by the IND-sys impactor (or more accurately **IND-sys interactor**) for elements or systems x and y, denoted by "x ⊕ y," is meant the collective of x and y which are completely independent of the other. Then, φ is called a **completely separable impactor** or simple-additive interactor (**IND-sys impactor**) of the system X.

Applying Bcm. (A.3-2-1) to a cultural economy of tranquility E (with three major factors: the economy, polity and culture) and with some simple manipulations, we have: the economic becoming

$$\text{(A.3-2-2)}\quad E_{t+1} = \{\Phi^{E}_{t}\{E_t\} \oplus co(\Phi^{E}_{-I})\{E_{-I}\} \oplus \Phi^{P}_{t}\{E_t\} \oplus \Phi^{W}_{t}\{E_t\} \oplus co(\Phi^{W}_{-I})\{E_{-I}\} \oplus co(\Phi^{W}_{-II})\{E_{-II}\} \oplus co(\Phi^{W}_{-III})\{E_{-III}\} \oplus \Sigma_E\} \circledast (Ix,\xi)$$

(with (Ix,ξ) being $\circ$) where the superscripts "E", "P", and "W" represent the impactor on the factor of the economy, polity and culture, respectively, $co(\Phi^{E}_{-I})$ is the core of Φ^{E}_{-I} (i.e., the core of the partial impactor Φ^{E} of the last step in the past), $co(\Phi^{W}_{-I})$ is the core of Φ^{W}_{-I} (i.e., the core of the partial impactor Φ^{W}_{-I} of the last step in the past), $co(\Phi^{W}_{-II})$ is the core of Φ^{W}_{-II} (i.e., the core of the partial impactor Φ^{W}_{-II} of the second last step in the past), $co(\Phi^{W}_{-III})$ is the core of Φ^{W}_{-III} (i.e., the core of the partial impactor Φ^{W}_{-III} of the third last step in the past), and Σ_E is the residual.

After applying Bcm. (A.3-2-1) to the polity P of tranquil culture (with three major factors: polity, economy and culture) and with some manipulation, we have the political becoming:

$$\text{(A.3-2-3)}\quad P_{t+1} = \{\Phi^{P}_{t}\{P_t\} \oplus co(\Phi^{P}_{-I})\{P_{-I}\} \oplus \Phi^{E}_{t}\{P_t\} \oplus co(\Phi^{E}_{-I})\{P_{-I}\} \oplus co(\Phi^{E}_{-II})\{P_{-II}\} \oplus \Phi^{W}_{t}\{P_t\} \oplus co(\Phi^{W}_{-I})\{P_{-I}\} \oplus co(\Phi^{W}_{-II})\{P_{-II}\} \oplus co(\Phi^{W}_{-III})\{P_{-III}\} \oplus \Sigma_P\} \circledast (Ix,\xi)$$

(with (Ix,ξ) being $\circ$) where Σ_P is the residual, and the rest of symbols can be derived analogically from Bcms. (A.3-2-1) and (A.3-2-2).

Definition A.3-2-2 (IND-sys/A impactor). Let a system $X = (X_1,X_2,\ldots,X_N) \sqsubseteq (\Omega,\mathbb{Z}\circ,{}_v\mathbb{H},\{\mathbb{C}\})$ be an N-factor non-independently separable system, φ, $\varphi^{I}_{I\downarrow} \vDash \mathbb{Z}\circ,{}_v\mathbb{H}$, I = I, II, …, N, $N_i \in \mathbb{N}$ ($\mathbb{N}$ being the natural number system), then for all i, j $\in \mathbb{N}$, $\varphi^{i}_{n}X_i$ and $\varphi^{j}_{\downarrow} X_j \sqsubseteq (\Omega,\mathbb{Z}\circ,{}_v\mathbb{H},\{\mathbb{C}\})$ be systems, then S is said to be an **IND-sys/A becoming** if and only if the following condition holds:

$$\text{(A.3-2-4)}\quad X = (\varphi^{1}_{n}X_1 \oplus \varphi^{1}_{I\downarrow}X_1 \oplus \varphi^{1}_{II\downarrow}X_1 \oplus\ldots\oplus \varphi^{1}_{N1\downarrow}X_1) \oplus (\varphi^{2}_{n}X_2 \oplus \varphi^{2}_{I\downarrow}X_2 \oplus \varphi^{2}_{II\downarrow}X_2 \oplus\ldots\oplus\varphi^{2}_{N2\downarrow}X_2)\oplus \ldots \oplus (\varphi^{N}_{n}X_N \oplus \varphi^{N}_{I\downarrow}X_N \oplus \varphi^{N}_{II\downarrow}X_N \oplus\ldots\oplus \varphi^{N}_{Nn\downarrow}X_N) \oplus \Sigma\} \circledast (Ix,\xi)$$

(with (Ix,ξ) being $\circ$) where X_i denotes the ith factor of X, i, N_i, N $\in \mathbb{N}$, $N_n \neq n$, $\oplus \vDash \mathbb{Z}\circ,{}_v\mathbb{H}$ the IND-sys/A (or adding-and-integrating) impactor operating on independently subsystems, Σ the residual, φ^{i}_{n} the normal-state impactor operating on X_i, $\varphi^{i}_{I\downarrow}$ the Ith step weak impactor operating on X_i, $\varphi^{i}_{II\downarrow}$ the IIth step weak impactor operating on X_i, $\varphi^{i}_{III\downarrow}$, the IIIth step weak impactor operating on X_i, etc.

Here, the normal impactors and i^{th} step weak impactors are different for different factors. In addition, we may define the 1st step weak impactor as the 1st step weakened-form of the normal impactor; for example, let $\varphi^{i}_{I\downarrow}X_i$ be the operation on X_i by eliminating the last column or the lowest row of X_i (which is a system and is here arranged in a "quasi-matrix form"). That is, in general, we may define the Nth step weak impactor as the Nth step weakened-form of the normal impactor; for example, let $\varphi^{i}_{N\downarrow}X_i$ be the operation on X_i by eliminating the last N columns or the lowest N rows from X_i.

Similar to Bcm. (A.3-2-4), we have the following definition.

Definition A.3-2-3. Let a system $X = (X_1, X_2, \ldots, X_N) \sqsubseteq (\Omega, \mathcal{Z}\circ,_v\mathbb{H}, \{\mathbb{C}\})$ be an N-factor non-independently separable system. For all i, j, k $\in \mathbb{N}$, $\varphi^i{}_C X_i$, $\varphi^j{}_{i\downarrow} X_{k,i\downarrow} \sqsubseteq (\Omega, \mathcal{Z}\circ,_v\mathbb{H}, \{\mathbb{C}\})$ be systems, X is said to be in an **alternative form of the IND-sys/A becoming** if and only if the following condition holds:

$$\text{(A.3-2-5)}\quad X = (\varphi^I{}_n X_I \oplus \varphi^I{}_{I\downarrow} X_{I,I\downarrow} \oplus \varphi^I{}_{II\downarrow} X_{I,II\downarrow} \oplus \ldots \oplus \varphi^I{}_{NI\downarrow} X_{I,NI\downarrow} \Theta \alpha_I) \oplus (\varphi^2{}_n X_2 \oplus \varphi^2{}_{I\downarrow} X_{2,I\downarrow} \oplus \varphi^2{}_{II\downarrow} X_{2,II\downarrow} \oplus \ldots \oplus \varphi^2{}_{N2\downarrow} X_{2,N2\downarrow} \Theta \alpha_2) \oplus \ldots \oplus (\varphi^N{}_n X_N \oplus \varphi^N{}_{I\downarrow} X_{N,I\downarrow} \oplus \varphi^N{}_{II\downarrow} X_{N,II\downarrow} \oplus \ldots \oplus \varphi^N{}_{Nn\downarrow} X_{N,Nn\downarrow} \Theta \alpha_N) \oplus \Sigma\} \circledcirc (Ix,\xi)$$

(with (Ix,ξ) being $\circ$) where $\Theta \vDash \mathcal{Z}\circ,_v\mathbb{H}$ is an adjustment impactor (for example, eliminating impactor), $\alpha_K \sqsubseteq (\Omega, \mathcal{Z}\circ,_v\mathbb{H}, \{\mathbb{C}\})$ is a factor for negative adjustment (to be further defined), K = 1, 2, …,N. Here $X_{k,i\downarrow}$ is defined as the ith step weak-form of X_k (i.e., **i^{th} step diminutive X**): $X_{k,I\downarrow}$ is defined as the Ith step weak-form of X_i, $X_{k,II\downarrow}$ is defined as the IIth step weak-form of X_{II}, …, and etc. Note that $X_{k,II\downarrow}$ is $X_{k,I\downarrow}$ further weakened; that is, $X_{k,-II}$ is a form of X_k weaker than $X_{k,-II}$.

Independently separable time-becoming of a system. Let a system $X = \{x,y,c\} \sqsubseteq (\Omega, \mathcal{Z}\circ,_v\mathbb{H}, \{\mathbb{C}\})$ be a 3-factor **independently separable system** (i.e., system that can be decomposed into independent sub-systems), where c is the center, y the middle-layer non-central element and x the lower-layer non-central element. Furthermore, let the impactors ψ_n, ψ_S, ψ_m, $\psi_w \vDash \mathcal{Z}\circ,_v\mathbb{H}$. Then we have the following systematically variational becoming or **independently separable time becoming**:

$$\text{(A.3-2-6)}\quad \begin{aligned} c_{t+1} &= \psi_n c_t \oplus \psi_w y_t \oplus \psi_w x_t, \\ y_{t+1} &= \psi_n y_t \oplus \psi_S c_t \oplus \psi_w x_t, \\ x_{t+1} &= \psi_n x_t \oplus \psi_m c_t \oplus \psi_w y_t, \\ X_t &= \{c_t, y_t, x_t\}, \end{aligned}$$

where the subscripts t and t+1 denote time t and t+1, respectively, $\oplus \vDash \mathcal{Z}\circ,_v\mathbb{H}$ an IND-sys (or "adding and integrating") impactor on independent (sub-)systems, ψ_n a normal impactor, ψ_S an impactor of "strong functions," ψ_m an impactor of "medium level functions," ψ_w an impactor of weak functions. Here the definition of strong, normal or weak functions (or operations) must depend on specific circumstances or historical backgrounds.

Applying Bcms. (A.3-2-4) to (A.3-2-6) yields:

$$\begin{aligned} \text{(A.3-2-7)}\quad X_{t+1} &= \{(\varphi^1{}_n \oplus \varphi^1{}_{-I} \oplus \varphi^1{}_{-II} \oplus \ldots \oplus \varphi^1{}_{-NI})\{c_{t+1}\} \oplus (\varphi^2{}_n \oplus \varphi^2{}_{-I} \oplus \varphi^2{}_{-II} \oplus \ldots \\ &\quad \oplus \varphi^2{}_{-N2})\{y_{t+1}\} \oplus (\varphi^3{}_n \oplus \varphi^3{}_{-I} \oplus \varphi^3{}_{-II} \oplus \ldots \oplus \varphi^3{}_{-Nn})\{x_{t+1}\} \\ &\quad \oplus \Sigma\} \circledcirc (Ix,\upsilon) \\ &= \{(\varphi^1{}_n \oplus \varphi^1{}_{-I} \oplus \varphi^1{}_{-II} \oplus \ldots \oplus \varphi^1{}_{-NI})\{\psi_n c_t \oplus \psi_w y_t \oplus \psi_w x_t\} \\ &\quad \oplus (\varphi^2{}_n \oplus \varphi^2{}_{-I} \oplus \varphi^2{}_{-II} \oplus \ldots \oplus \varphi^2{}_{-N2})\{\psi_n y_t \oplus \psi_S c_t \oplus \psi_w x_t\} \\ &\quad \oplus (\varphi^3{}_n \oplus \varphi^3{}_{-I} \oplus \varphi^3{}_{-II} \oplus \ldots \oplus \varphi^3{}_{-Nn})\{\psi_n x_t \oplus \psi_m c_t \oplus \psi_w y_t\} \oplus \Sigma\} \\ &\quad \circledcirc (Ix,\upsilon) \end{aligned}$$

(with (Ix,υ) being $\circ$, $\upsilon = \upsilon(\tau)$, $\tau \Vdash (\mathfrak{I}, \text{Ш}^\Delta) \Vdash \mathbb{T}zu^*$) with the settings that $(\xi \oplus \zeta)(\varphi \oplus \psi)\{A\} = [(\xi\varphi \oplus \xi\psi) \oplus (\zeta\varphi \oplus \zeta\psi)]\{A\} = (\xi\varphi \oplus \xi\psi \oplus \zeta\varphi \oplus \zeta\psi)\{A\} = \xi\varphi\{A\} \oplus \xi\psi\{A\} \oplus \zeta\varphi\{A\} \oplus \zeta\psi\{A\}$, $\xi, \zeta, \varphi, \psi, \xi\varphi, \xi\psi, \zeta\varphi, \zeta\psi \vDash \mathcal{Z}\circ,_v\mathbb{H}$, $A \sqsubseteq (\Omega, \mathcal{Z}\circ,_v\mathbb{H}, \{\mathbb{C}\})$, etc. Here the definitions of the compound impactors $\xi\varphi$, $\xi\psi$, $\zeta\varphi$ and $\zeta\psi$ must depend on the underlying questions or specified circumstances.

§A.3-3 General Integrating and Decomposition Impactors

Let A ⊑ (Ω,$\mathcal{Z}$o,$_v\mathcal{H}$,{ℂ}) be a system, ξ_i, ζ, + ⊨ (Ω,$\mathcal{Z}$o,$_v\mathcal{H}$,{ℂ}), i = a_j, b_j, …, o_j, j ∈ $\mathbf{I}^+$ (positive integers), be impactors, and O(.,ξ_{oj}) ⋐ **U** be a set of universal element. Furthermore, let A_i be subsystems of A, B_i be subsystems of A_i, and so on. Suppose that ξ_{ai} are the corresponding impactors of ζ in A_i, ξ_{bi} are the corresponding impactors of ζ in B_i, and ξ_{oi} are the corresponding impactors of ζ in O_i; that is: (+,(ξ_1,ξ_2,…,ξ_n)) ↔ ζ. Here by "(+,(ξ_1,ξ_2,…,ξ_n)) ↔ ζ" is meant, for "+"⊨ $\mathcal{Z}$o,$_v\mathcal{H}$, ξ_i are the respective interactive elements or interactors of ζ in A_i, B_i and O_i so that these subsystems, "sub-subsystems" and residuals (i.e., elements of O) can able to be integrated into the whole system A in an interrelated manner. Note that, by "(+,(ξ_1,ξ_2,…,ξ_n)) ↔ ζ" is meant, for "+"⊨ $\mathcal{Z}$o,$_v\mathcal{H}$ ("+" ≡ "╫" in the case of IDR impactor, see Definition A.2-11-1, or "+" ≡ "⊕" in the case of IND-sys impactor, see Definition A.3-2-1)

Assume this procedure will further continue in the same fashion. In addition, these A_i, B_i and O_i are assumed to be independent of each other. That is, each of these A_i, B_i and O_i is not part of the other systems (or subsystems and sub-subsystems) or elements.

Definition A.3-3-1. Let A ⊑ (Ω,$\mathcal{Z}$o,$_v\mathcal{H}$,{ℂ}) be a system. With the notations and impactors defined in the above, A is said to follow the **general decomposition/ integrating procedure** of a system A if and only if the following condition holds:

(A.3-3-1) $A = A_1(.,s\text{-}t|\xi_{a1}) \oplus A_2(.,s\text{-}t|\xi_{a2}) \oplus\ldots\oplus B_1(.,s\text{-}t|\xi_{b1}) \oplus B_2(.,s\text{-}t|\xi_{b2}) \oplus\ldots$
$\oplus\, O(.,s\text{-}t|\xi_{o1}) \oplus O(.,s\text{-}t|\xi_{o2}) \oplus \ldots \} \circledcirc (Ix,\zeta)$

(with Ix being ○ implying "⊚(Ix,ζ)" = "⊕ζ") where "s-t|" refers to the spatiotemporal dimensions.

To introduce the dynamics and interactions of elements and subsystems in a system, given the impactors φ_i,ψ_j, ζ, ⊚ ⊨ $\mathcal{Z}$o,$_v\mathcal{H}$ (with relevant indices) and the system A ⊑ (Ω,$\mathcal{Z}$o,$_v\mathcal{H}$,{ℂ}), let

(A.3-3-2) $A(.,s\text{-}t|\xi) = \{\varphi_{a1}A_1(.,s\text{-}t|\xi_{a1}) \oplus \varphi_{a2}A_2(.,s\text{-}t|\xi_{a2}) \oplus\ldots\oplus \varphi_{b1}B_1(.,s\text{-}t|\xi_{b1}) \oplus$
$\varphi_{b2}B_2(.,s\text{-}t|\xi_{b2}) \oplus\ldots\oplus\psi_{o1}O_1(.,s\text{-}t|\xi_{o1}) \oplus \psi_{o2}O_2(.,s\text{-}t|\xi_{o2}) \oplus \ldots \}$
$\circledcirc (Ix,\zeta)$ (with Ix being ○ implying "⊚(Ix,ζ)" = "⊕ζ")

(A.3-3-3) $\xi_{.} \backsim \zeta = \zeta(+,-;\Delta)$, Δ ⊫ Ш$^\Delta$,

where ξ represents the creative cultural force of A which is conditioned on the spatiotemporal order s-t and is also corresponding to ζ, ζ represents the ultimate creative cultural force which exists in the universe and affects the systemic dynamics of A, "+" in ζ denotes the positive factor of interactions among elements or subsystems (to be denoted by the interactive impactors ☆,⋆) and "-" in ζ denotes the negative factor of interactions among elements or subsystems (to be denoted by the interactive impactors ☆$^-$,⋆$^-$). Note that Δ (Δ ⊫ Ш$^\Delta$) refers to the dynamics which is closely related to the generating and creative forces of multiple cultures within A. This forces of systemic generation and creation apparently exist in the universe **U**. In general, the totality of these creative forces is represented by the symbol Δ which represents a constant process of motion, transformation or even transmutation manifesting in the form of general, interactive, creative, or annihilating impactors. Note that in the above, we write $\varphi_i\{A_.(.,s\text{-}t|\xi_i)\}$ as $\varphi_iA_.(.,s\text{-}t|\xi_i)$ if it is understood properly (for appropriate indices). Similarly we write $\varphi_j B(.,s\text{-}t|\xi_j)$ instead of $\varphi_j\{B(.,s\text{-}t|\xi_j)\}$ and $\psi_k O(.,s\text{-}t|\xi_k)$ instead of $\psi_k O(.,s\text{-}t|\xi_k)$ (for appropriate indices).

In the following, we shall introduce a few new concepts of integration and decomposition. Let

(A.3-3-4) $X = \varphi\{A_1(.)\text{-}A_2(.)\}\_\psi\{D_1(.)D_2(.)\} \oplus \mathcal{S}\langle\mathbb{C}_{x1},\mathbb{C}_{x2}\rangle$,

where φ, ψ, $\mathcal{S} \vDash \mathcal{Z}\circ,_v\mathcal{H}$ are uncertain impactors that will create uncertain systems from non-uncertain systems (see Bcms. (3.6-1), (7.1-4) and (8.4-3-2)). Here by an uncertain system is meant either a distribution system (Section I.2 of Appendix I) or a becoming system of uncertainty (subsections B.2-2 – B.2-3). Then,

(A.3-3-5) $X = \mathcal{Z}h\{A_1(.,s\text{-}t|\xi_{a1}),A_2(.,s\text{-}t|\xi_{a2}),D_1(.,s\text{-}t|\xi_{d1}),D_2(.,s\text{-}t|\xi_{d2}),$
$\mathbb{C}_{x1}(.,s\text{-}t|\xi_{c1}),\mathbb{C}_{x2}(.,s\text{-}t|\xi_{c2})\}$,

(A.3-3-6) $\mathcal{F}j\{X\} = A_1(.,s\text{-}t|\xi_{a1}) + A_2(.,s\text{-}t|\xi_{a2})+D_1(.,s\text{-}t|\xi_{d1})+D_2(.,s\text{-}t|\xi_{d2})$
$+ \mathbb{C}_{x1}(.,s\text{-}t|\xi_{c1}) + \mathbb{C}_{x2}(.,s\text{-}t|\xi_{c2})$,

where "$\mathcal{Z}h$" $\vDash \mathcal{Z}\circ,_v\mathcal{H}$ is the integrating impactor and "$\mathcal{F}j$" $\vDash \mathcal{Z}\circ,_v\mathcal{H}$ is a decomposing impactor.

§A.3-4 Decomposition of Systems of Self Entity-in-Tranquility and Mutual Entity-in-Tranquility

First, let $(\Omega,\mathcal{Z}\circ,_v\mathcal{H},\{\mathbb{C}\})$ be a system space (i.e., SysSM, the system of selfhood and mutuality), Ω be a collection of all universal elements and all the systems of self entities- and mutual entities-in-tranquility (for the complete definition of a system, see Subsection §A.2-2-1), then we define **r-SysSM** as follows: SysSM(tranquility) ≡ r-SysSM = $(\Omega,\mathcal{Z}\circ,_v\mathcal{H},\{\mathbb{C}\})\sqcap\mathbb{R}\text{-}\mathbb{C}$, $\mathbb{R}\text{-}\mathbb{C}$ being the real or complex number systems with their field operations (with $\sqcap$ denoting the "intersection" or the relation of belong to both sets). Here, r-SysSM is the space comprising those systems with their necessary operations (in terms of systemic, dialectical and "logical" operations), all the transformations of systems from system space into the space of real/complex numbers, and the real/complex numbers with their field operations.

That is, by "$\forall X \sqsubseteq \Omega$, $X \sqsubseteq$ r-SysSM" is meant $X \sqsubseteq (\Omega,\mathcal{Z}\circ,_v\mathcal{H},\{\mathbb{C}\})$ and $\mu(X) \in \mathbb{R}\text{-}\mathbb{C}$, $\mu : (\Omega,\mathcal{Z}\circ,_v\mathcal{H},\{\mathbb{C}\}) \to \mathbb{R}\text{-}\mathbb{C}$ (μ is an impactor transforming systems into real-complex numbers).

Secondly, let the systems {self,mutual}, {self-mutual|.}, {mutual--self}, {self}, {self|mutual}, {self|.}, {self|mutual|.}, {mutual--slef|.} $\sqsubseteq$ r-SysSM. Here, the self entity-in-tranquility (self: note that "self" ≠ Ultimate Creativity-Destructivity) and mutual entity-in-tranquility constitute the **self-mutual entity-in-tranquility chain**. That is, for a system X belonging to the space of the m-polar self entity-in-tranquility chain, we write $X \sqsubseteq (Mm,RR^S) = \Omega^S \Subset \Omega$. For a system X belonging to the space of the n-polar mutual entity-in-tranquility chain, we then write $X \sqsubseteq (Mn,RR^M) = \Omega^M$. Thus, for a system X jointly belonging to the space of the m-polar self entity-in-tranquility chain and to the space of the n-polar mutual entity-in-tranquility chain, we write $X \sqsubseteq (Mm{\times}n,RR^{SM}) \equiv \Omega^S\sqcup\Omega^M \Subset \Omega$.

Here the interactor $\sqcup$ denotes the "union" or the relationship of belonging to either one.

Let $\mathfrak{C}_{yw}$ be the core of yu-wu culture, for $\mathfrak{C}_{yw} \sqsubseteq \{\mathfrak{C}_{yw} =< \mathcal{Y}^{T}\}=\{(\mathfrak{C}_{yw} =< T^{B\text{-}C}) \sqsubseteq Ш^{\Delta}\}$ (i.e., $\mathfrak{C}_{yw}$ achieves a systematically dynamical state of CE balance-centrality. In addition. Let $\mathcal{T} \vDash \mathcal{Z}\circ_{,v}\mathbb{H}\sqcap\mathfrak{C}$ be an **entity-augmenting impactor** (element/pole/system- or row/column/matrix-augmenting impactor) and $\mathcal{T}^{B\text{-}C}$ be a $T^{B\text{-}C}$**-impactor** in the systematically dynamical state of CE balance-centrality of the **core of yu-wu culture**. Here "$\vDash$" refers to a relation of "belonging to," and for $\mathcal{T} = \mathcal{T}|_{\mathfrak{C}}{}^{T}$, $\mathcal{T} \vDash \mathcal{Z}\circ_{,v}\mathbb{H}\sqcap\mathfrak{C}^{T}$ is also an impactor of tranquil culture. Let $X \sqsubseteq (\Omega,\mathcal{Z}\circ_{,v}\mathbb{H},\{\mathbb{C}\})$ in a system of tranquil culture. Then the interactions of the self and mutual entity-in-tranquility systems, for self ≡ self entity-in-tranquility, yield:

(A.3-4-1a) $\mathcal{T}\{X \mid \mathfrak{C}_{yw} =< \mathcal{Y}^{T}\} = \{\text{self,mutual} \mid \mathfrak{C}_{yw} =< \mathcal{Y}^{T}\}$.

That is, X grows into a system with unit systems of "self" and "mutual" under the operation of the entity-augmenting impactor. Then by assuming X to be an IDR system, we have:

$$\begin{aligned}\text{(A.3-4-1b)}\quad X &= \{\text{self,mutual} \mid \mathfrak{C}_{yw} =< \mathcal{Y}^{T}\}\\ &= \{\text{self-mutual} \mid \mathfrak{C}^{T}\}\\ &= \{\{\text{self} \mid \mathfrak{C}^{T}\} \# \{\text{mutual|self} \mid \mathfrak{C}^{T}\} \# \{\text{mutual--self} \mid \mathfrak{C}^{T}\} \oplus \Sigma\} \circledcirc \text{Ix}\end{aligned}$$

with the residual Σ being $\circ$. Now let $\psi \vDash \mathcal{Z}\circ_{,v}\mathbb{H}$ be an IDR impactor. Then we have:

$$\begin{aligned}\text{(A.3-4-1c)}\quad \psi X &= \psi\{\text{self,mutual} \mid \mathfrak{C}_{yw} =< \mathcal{Y}^{T}\}\\ &= \psi\{\{\text{self} \mid \mathfrak{C}^{T}\} \# \{\text{mutual|self} \mid \mathfrak{C}^{T}\} \# \{\text{mutual--self} \mid \mathfrak{C}^{T}\} \oplus \Sigma\} \circledcirc^{*} \text{Ix}\},\\ &= \{\text{self} \mid \mathfrak{C}^{T}\} \oplus \{\text{mutual|self} \mid \mathfrak{C}^{T}\} \oplus \{\text{mutual--self} \mid \mathfrak{C}^{T}\} \circledcirc \text{Ix},\end{aligned}$$

assuming $\psi\Sigma = \circ$ (i.e., for Σ being a "nullifiable" entity and ψ being also a nullifying impactor).

By applying the principle of CE balance-centrality (for $\mathcal{T}^{B\text{-}C}$ being a $T^{B\text{-}C}$- impactor), it yields:

$$\begin{aligned}\text{(A.3-4-1d)}\quad &\mathcal{T}^{c}\{\psi\{X \mid \mathfrak{C}_{yw} =< \mathcal{Y}^{T}\}\}\\ &= \mathcal{T}^{c}\{\psi\{\text{self-mutual} \mid \mathfrak{C}^{T}\}\}\\ &= \mathcal{T}^{c}\{\{\text{self} \mid \mathfrak{C}^{T}\} \oplus \{\text{mutual|self} \mid \mathfrak{C}^{T}\} \oplus \{\text{mutual--self} \mid \mathfrak{C}^{T}\} \circledcirc \text{Ix}\}\\ &= \{\mathcal{T}^{c}\{\text{self} \mid \mathfrak{C}^{T}\} \bigoplus \mathcal{T}^{c}\{\text{mutual|self} \mid \mathfrak{C}^{T}\} \bigoplus \mathcal{T}^{c}\{\text{mutual--self} \mid \mathfrak{C}^{T}\} \circledcirc \mathcal{T}^{c}\{\text{Ix}\}\\ &= \text{self\#} \bigoplus (\text{mutual|self})\# \bigoplus \{\text{mutual--self}\}\#,\end{aligned}$$

(with $\mathcal{T}^{c}\{\text{Ix}\}$ being "$\circ$" by assumption) where self# = $\mathcal{T}^{c}\{\text{self} \mid \mathfrak{C}^{T}\}$ (μ(self#) as a positive number) is the product of the self-activities released from the activities of the "mutual entity," (mutual|self)# = $\mathcal{T}^{c}\{\text{mutual|self} \mid \mathfrak{C}^{T}\}$ (with μ(mutual|self)# being a positive number) is the product of self-activities under the spiritual inspiration of altruist rationality, (mutual--self)# = $\mathcal{T}^{c}\{\text{mutual--self} \mid \mathfrak{C}^{T}\}$ measures the effectiveness of a diminutive self-mutual chain under the impact of the coordination of all members of the system -- by eliminating self# and (mutual|self)# -- (that is, {mutual--self}# = $\{\text{mutual-self} \mid \mathfrak{C}^{T}\}_{\downarrow}$, μ\{self-- mutual\}# being a positive number), and $\oplus$ and $\bigoplus$ denote the impactors of the operational relations among various entities (element, systems or else).

The principle of CE Tcentral employed in the above is derived below. Let a systematic scheme be:

(A.3-4-2) The operation of the grand-system on the unit system X_i, setting $\varphi\{X\} = X \sqsubseteq (\Omega, \mathcal{Z}^{\circ}, {}_{v}\mathcal{H}, \{\mathbb{C}\})$, $i = 1, 2, \ldots, n$, $i \neq k, j$, where $\varphi \models \mathcal{Z}^{\circ}, {}_{v}\mathcal{H}$ is an impactor. Here $X = \{X_i\} \sqsubseteq (\Omega, \mathcal{Z}^{\circ}, {}_{v}\mathcal{H}, \{\mathbb{C}\})$, $X \Lleftarrow \Delta$ (that is, $X \curlyvee \Delta$, X operates under the constraint of $\Delta \Vdash \Omega$ (the pure dynamical forces and structures in the universe).

To find a solution, let us set up the virtual system T:

(A.3-4-3) $T = X \curlyvee \Delta$,

where $\curlyvee \models \mathcal{Z}^{\circ}, {}_{v}\mathcal{H}$ is the interactor connecting X with Δ (T being the virtual system constructed temporarily for the purpose of getting a solution). Under the principle of effective intra-inter systemic operations in a state of T continuity (IISO/T scheme), this system's operations are carried out in the environments involving both of the operations of mutuality (or operation of the grand system as a whole) and the operations of individuality (or operations of each of the unit systems in its own world of individuality -- with the existence of other unit systems being entirely ignored). Then, we have:

(A.3-4-4) $\psi\{\text{slef,mutual}\} = \psi\{\text{self}\} \oplus \psi(\text{mutual}|\text{self}) \oplus \psi(\text{mutual--self})$,

where ψ is the interactor operating between the self entity and the mutual entity, $\psi\{\text{self}\}$ the impactor operating on the self entity, and ψ (mutual|self) and $\psi\{\text{mutual--self}\}$ are interactors operating back and forth between the self entity and the mutual entity. Thus, it yields:

(A.3-4-5)
$$
\begin{aligned}
&(\varphi\ \{T\})_{x_1,\ldots,x_n}\\
&= (\varphi\{X \curlyvee \Delta\})_{x_1,\ldots,x_n,I_x}\\
&= [(\varphi\{X_1, X_2, \ldots, X_n, I(x_{1,\ldots,}x_n), \Delta\})_{x_1,\ldots,x_n} \ltimes \varphi\{(I(x_{1,\ldots,}\ x_n), E\}\\
&= (\varphi\{X\} \otimes \psi\{X_1 \stackrel{\star}{=} X_2 \stackrel{\star}{=} \ldots \stackrel{\star}{=} X_n, \Delta\}) \ltimes \varphi\{I(x_{1,\ldots,}\ x_n), E\}.
\end{aligned}
$$

Now, let the operation with respective to (X,i) be at the state of CE T Central, or in the mutual state of CE T Central and strategic continuity ($X=X^*$): $X = \varphi\{X\} \otimes \psi\{X_1 \stackrel{\star}{=} X_2 \stackrel{\star}{=} \ldots \stackrel{\star}{=} X_n, \Delta\} \ltimes \varphi\{I(x_{1,\ldots,}x_n), E\}$. Under the above conditions, we then have $\varphi\{X\} = X$, and $\{\{\psi\{X_1 \stackrel{\star}{=} X_2 \stackrel{\star}{=} \ldots \stackrel{\star}{=} X_n, \Delta\} \ltimes \varphi\{I(x_{1,\ldots,}x_n), E\} =< T^B\} \sqsubseteq Ш^Д$. Here "$\stackrel{\star}{=}$" represents the desirable balance in the state of CE balance-centrality.

That is, we derived in the above the **principle of CE balance** or **principle of CE centrality**:

(A.3-4-6a) $\psi\{X_1 \stackrel{\star}{=} X_2 \stackrel{\star}{=} \ldots \stackrel{\star}{=} X_n, \Delta\} \barwedge \tau$,

or

(A.3-4-6b) $\psi\{X_1, \Delta\} \stackrel{\star}{=} \psi\{X_2, \Delta\} \stackrel{\star}{=} \ldots \stackrel{\star}{=} \psi\{X_n, \Delta\}$,

with $\tau \Vdash (\mathfrak{I}, Ш^Д) \Vvdash \mathbb{T}\text{zu}^*$, $\mathbb{T}\text{zu}^*$ being Ultimate Creativity/Destructivity.

From the derivation in the above, if the "systemic dynamics" of the tao-jen culture projects its cultural core mainly through the economic planning chain to the public-private business community, then, under the government-industry-academics chain (gov-ind-acad chain), we have for $\mathcal{T} \models \mathcal{Z}^{\circ}, {}_{v}\mathcal{H} \sqcap \mathfrak{C}_{YW}$:

(A.3-4-7) $\mathcal{T}$\{pub,priv|gov-ind-acad chain, $\mathfrak{C}_{YW}$ =< $\mathcal{Y}^T$\}
= $\mathcal{T}^c$\{pub-priv | $\mathfrak{C}^T$\}
= $\mathcal{T}^c$\{pub-priv| gov-ind-acad chain,planning chain | $\mathfrak{C}^T$\}
= \{$\mathcal{T}^c$\{pub | $\mathfrak{C}^T$\} ⊕$\mathcal{T}^c$\{pub|priv | $\mathfrak{C}^T$\} ⊕$\mathcal{T}^c$\{pub--priv | $\mathfrak{C}^T$\} ⊛ Ix
= pub# ⊕ (pub|priv)# ⊕\{pub--priv\}#,

(with ⊛Ix being ○) where pub, priv, gov-ind-acad chain and planning chain represent the co-ordination chain of the public sector, the private sector, the government-industry-academic circle and the planning chain, respectively. In the above, we have, by letting $\mathcal{T}^c$ be a complete IDR inpactor, $\mathcal{T}^c$\{pub,priv|.\} = pub# ⊕ (pub|priv)# ⊕ \{pub--priv\}#. That is, under the operation of a complete IDR impactor (i.e., the grand system can be decomposed into several smaller sub-systems, where each is independent of the others), the totality (or total efficiency) of the grand system of the tao-jen cultural economy is equal to the "sum" of individual sub-systems (i.e., the public sector as an independent system and the private sector as another independent system, with an adjustment factor accounting for the interactive mechanism (which is presumably a system as well) between the public and the private sectors. Here, from the perspective of the cultural economy as a whole, at the initial period of development, re-development or advancement, the dynamics of the systematic and strategic advantages come from the operations of the system-augmenting impactors on the gov-ind-acad chain. This is because of the following facts. (1) Due to the strategic need, only the public sector under the aegis of government protection can resist the pressure from the global corporations of foreign origin. (2) The informal socio-cultural network of the citizens as a whole will create the economies of scale, the economy of scope, and the systemic advantage of joint efforts of the citizens. (3) The consensus and aggregation of the citizens as a whole will generate necessary dynamic forces of development and growth. (4) The transformation of the private firms from family-oriented management style to professionals-controlled style of management is very difficult.

Similarly to the derivation of Bcm. (A.3-4-7), we get one of the following:

(A.3-4-8) $\mathcal{T}$\{priv,pub|gov-ind-acad, $\mathfrak{C}_{YW}$ =< $\mathcal{Y}^T$\}
= priv# ⊕(pub|priv)# ⊕\{pub--priv\}#,
(A.3-4-9) $\mathcal{T}$\{priv,pub|gov-ind-acad, $\mathfrak{C}_{YW}$ =< $\mathcal{Y}^T$\}
= priv# ⊕ (priv|pub)# ⊕ \{pub--ptiv\}#.

In Bcm. (A.3-4-8), the term comparable to $\mathcal{T}^c$\{mutual|self | $\mathfrak{C}^T$\} in Bcm. (A.3-4-1b) is the term (pub|priv)#, because we set the condition that the private sector is under the guidance of the public sector (mainly the planner). In Bcm. (A.3-4-7), the term comparable to $\mathcal{T}^c$\{mutual|self | $\mathfrak{C}^T$\} in Bcm. (A.3-4-16) is the term (priv|pub)#, because in this case we set the condition that the private sector is the major player of the cultural economy.

Applying Bcm. (21.2-2-15) in Tonn[2006] to Bcm (A.3-4-1) yields:

(A.3-4-10) $X = \{\varphi^1 X_1 \oplus(\varphi^2 X_2 \oplus \varphi^2_{-1} X_{2,1\downarrow}) \oplus (\varphi^3 X_3 \oplus \varphi^3_{1\downarrow} X_{3,1\downarrow} \oplus \varphi^3_{2\downarrow} X_{3,2\downarrow}) \oplus \Sigma\} \circledcirc$ Ix,

(with Ix = ○) where φ^i is the core of the partial impactor operating on i^{th} factor of X, for all i ∈ ℕ, and the superscripts 1, 2, and 3 denote self#, (self|mutual)# and \{mutual--self\}#, respectively. Here by the **core of the partial impactor** is meant the most essential entity among all the partial impactors.

Applying Bcm. (21.2-2-15) in Tonn [2006] to the above Bcm. (A.1-3-1-7) yields:

(A.3-4-11) $X = \{\varphi^1 X_1 \oplus (\varphi^2 X_2 \oplus \varphi^2{}_{1\downarrow} X_{2,1\downarrow}) \oplus (\varphi^3 X_3 \oplus \varphi^3{}_{1\downarrow} X_{3,1\downarrow} \oplus \varphi^3{}_{2\downarrow} X_{3,2\downarrow}) \oplus \Sigma\} \circledast Ix$,

(with $Ix = \circ$) where φ^i is the core of the partial impactor operating on i^{th} factor of X, for all $i \in \mathbb{N}$, and the superscripts 1, 2, 3, 4 and 5 denote pub#, priv#, (priv|pub)#, {pub|priv)# and {pub--priv}#, respectively.
If $\mathcal{T} \models (\mathbb{Z}\circ,_{\mathrm{v}}\mathbb{H}) \sqcap \mathfrak{C}_{YW}$ on Z_1 (i.e., self1) and Z_2 (self2), then we have:

(A.3-4-12)
$$\begin{aligned} &\mathcal{T}\{Z_1,Z_2 | \mathfrak{C}_{YW} =< \mathcal{Y}^T\} \\ &= \mathcal{T}^c\{Z_1\text{-}Z_2 | \mathfrak{C}^T\} \\ &= \{\{\mathcal{T}^c\{Z_1 | \mathfrak{C}^T\},\mathcal{T}^c\{Z_2 | \mathfrak{C}^T\},\mathcal{T}^c\{H+ | \mathfrak{C}^T\},\mathcal{T}^c\{H- | \mathfrak{C}^T\}\} \\ &\quad \oplus \{\mathcal{T}^c\{Z_1 | \mathfrak{C}^T\}_\downarrow,\mathcal{T}^c\{Z_2 | \mathfrak{C}^T\}_\downarrow,\mathcal{T}^c\{H+ | \mathfrak{C}^T\}_\downarrow,\mathcal{T}^c\{H- | \mathfrak{C}^T\}_\downarrow\}\} \circledast Ix \\ &= Z_1{}^* \oplus Z_2{}^* \oplus (H+)^* \oplus \{H-\}^* \oplus Z_{1,\downarrow}{}^* \oplus Z_{2,\downarrow}{}^* \oplus (H+)_\downarrow{}^* \oplus \{H-\}_\downarrow{}^* \oplus Z_{1,\downarrow\downarrow}{}^* \oplus \\ &\quad Z_{2,\downarrow\downarrow}{}^* \oplus (H+)_{\downarrow\downarrow}{}^* \oplus \{H-\}_{\downarrow\downarrow}{}^* \oplus Z_{1,\downarrow\downarrow\downarrow}{}^* \oplus Z_{2,\downarrow\downarrow\downarrow}{}^* \oplus (H+)_{\downarrow\downarrow\downarrow}{}^* \oplus \{H-\}_{\downarrow\downarrow\downarrow}{}^* \oplus \ldots \\ &\qquad \oplus E, \end{aligned}$$

(with $Ix = \circ$) with $Z_i{}^* = T^*\{Z_i | \mathfrak{C}^T\}$ ($\mu(Z_i)$ being a positive number) being the product of the individual self-operation decomposed from the interactive network of mutuality, i = 1, 2, $(H+)^* = \mathcal{T}^c\{H+ | \mathfrak{C}^T\}$ ($\mu(H+)^*$ being a positive number) and the result of coordination and other positive interactions between the self-mutual chain and all other members of the grand system, $(H-)^* = \mathcal{T}^c\{H- | \mathfrak{C}^T\}$ ($\mu(H-)^*$ being a negative number) the (negative) result of the conflicting interactions between the self-mutual chain and all other members of the grand system, and $\oplus$ the operational relationships of the impactor $\mathcal{T}$.

In the above Bcm. (A.3-4-12), the subscript "$_\downarrow$" (≡ "$_{\downarrow 1}$" ≡ "$_{1\downarrow}$") refers to the first step diminutive notation, the subscript "$_{\downarrow\downarrow}$" (≡ "$_{\downarrow 2}$" ≡ "$_{2\downarrow}$") the second step diminutive notation, the subscript "$_{\downarrow\downarrow\downarrow}$" (≡ "$_{\downarrow 3}$" ≡ "$_{\downarrow 3}$") the third step diminutive notation, and so on. As for E, it is the residual which may be treated in an uncertain process.

In Bcm. (A.3-4-12), under strategic continuity, we shall use $\mathcal{P}^{NS}(E)$ instead of the underlying system E. (for $\mathcal{P}^{NS}$, see Appendix I, Bcm. (I.2-1)).

A.3-5 Decomposition of Systems of The Self Entity-in-Conflict and Mutual Entity-in-Conflict

Suppose in the following cultural system of conflict, the core of culture projects itself to the self-mutual entity-in-conflict chain. That is,

(A.3-5-1) A conflict culture: core culture → interactions between all of the self-entity chains and the mutual-entity chain in a system

Note: For the mutual entity-in-conflict chain, the core existence = being ≠ existence, and being ≠ Dasein.

Here, first, let $(\Omega,\mathbb{Z}\circ,_{\mathrm{v}}\mathbb{H},\{\mathbb{C}\})$ be a system space, Ω be the collection of all universal elements, and all the systems of self entities- and mutual entities-in-conflict, and r-SysSM = $(\Omega,\mathbb{Z}\circ,_{\mathrm{v}}\mathbb{H},\{\mathbb{C}\}) \sqcap \mathbb{R}\text{-}\mathbb{C}$. Here, by "$\forall X \sqsubseteq \Omega$, $X \sqsubseteq$ r-SysSM" is meant that $X \sqsubseteq (\Omega,\mathbb{Z}\circ,_{\mathrm{v}}\mathbb{H},\{\mathbb{C}\})$ and $\mu(X) \in \mathbb{R}\text{-}\mathbb{C}$ ($\mu:(\Omega,\mathbb{Z}\circ,_{\mathrm{v}}\mathbb{H},\{\mathbb{C}\}) \rightarrow \mathbb{R}\text{-}\mathbb{C}$ (as a real-complex number) is an impactor transforming an entity from the space of systematic operations into a number in the space of mathematical operations.

Secondly, let {self,mutual}, {self-mutual}, {self--mutual} $\sqsubseteq$ r-SysSM(conflict). Here the self entity and the mutual entity are unified into a self-mutuality chain. That is, SysSM(conflict) $\equiv$ {self-entity-in-conflict, mutual-entity-in-conflict}. That is, for a system X belonging to SysSM(conflict), we have: (1) X $\sqsubseteq$ (Mm,RR^S) $\equiv \Omega^S \Subset \Omega$, i.e., this system X belongs to the **space of m-polar self-entity-in-conflict chain**; and (2) X $\sqsubseteq$ (Mn,RR^H) $\equiv \Omega^H \Subset \Omega$, i.e., this system belongs to the **space of n-polar mutual-entity-in-conflict chain**. Therefore, the joint space of the m-polar self entity-in-tranquility chain and the n-polar mutual entity-in-tranquility chain is (Mm,RR^S) $\equiv$ (Mm×n,RR^{SH}) $\equiv \Omega^S \sqcup \Omega^H \Subset \Omega$. Here SysSM(conflict) is the space in which a system is either in the space of self entities-in-conflict or in a space of mutual entities-in-conflict.

Secondly, let $\mathfrak{C}_{Bcing}$ be the **core of being culture**, or $\mathfrak{C}_{Bcing} \sqsubseteq \{\mathfrak{C}_{Bcing} =< \mathcal{Y}^c\}=\{\mathfrak{C}_{Bcing} =< T^{B\text{-}C}\} \sqsubseteq$ Ш$^\Delta$, that is, $\mathfrak{C}_{Bcing}$ achieves a state of conflicting CE T Central of the being culture, for $\mathcal{T}^\wedge$, $\mathcal{T}^A$ (an IDR impactor) $\models \mathcal{Z}\circ,_v\mathcal{H} \sqcap \mathfrak{C}$, the latter being an augmenting impactor (an impactor of "creation") of conflict culture. If, for the core culture $=< \mathcal{Y}^C$ ($\mathcal{Y}^C$ represneting a conflict culture), $\mathcal{T}^A$ represents the impactor of the core of the conflict culture operating in the state of systemic and strategic anti-continuity, then one possible result of the conflict between the self and the mutual, for self $\equiv$ self entity-in-conflict, will be:

(A.3-5-2) $\mathcal{T}^\wedge$ {self,mutual | $\mathfrak{C}_{Bcing} =< \mathcal{Y}^c$}
$= \mathcal{T}^A$ {self-mutual}
$= (\mathcal{T}^A$ {self | $\mathfrak{C}_{Bcing}$}, $\mathcal{T}^A$ {self|mutual}, $\mathcal{T}^A$ {elf--mutual})
$= \{\mathcal{T}^A$ {self | $\mathfrak{C}_{Bcing}$} $\oplus \mathcal{T}^A$ {self|mutual | $(\mathfrak{C}^{Cq}+)$} $\oplus \mathcal{T}^A$ {self--mutual | $(\mathfrak{C}^{Cq}-)$}} $\circledcirc$Ix
= self$^\wedge \oplus$ (self|mutual)$^\wedge$ $\oplus$ {self--mutual}$^\wedge$,

(with "Ix" being "$\circ$") where self$^\wedge$ $= \mathcal{T}^A$ {self | $\mathfrak{C}_{Bcing}$} being the product of self-efficiency (μ (self$^\wedge$) being a positive number), (self|mutal)$^\wedge$ $= \mathcal{T}^A$ {self|mutual | $(\mathfrak{C}^{Cq}+)$} the product of self-motivation under the spirit-rationality of conquest (μ(self|mtual)$^\wedge$ being a positive number), {self--mutual}$^\wedge$ $= \mathcal{T}^A$ {self--mutual | $(\mathfrak{C}^{Cq}-)$} the destructive product caused by the conflicts among the private individuals and the private firms (with μ{self--mutual}$^{\#\#}$ being negative). Then from the above becoming Bcm. (A.3.5-2), if the dynamism and engine of growth of the being culture is the projection through the market mechanism (market) to the private firms (priv), then for $\mathcal{T}^{\wedge\wedge}$, $\mathcal{T}^A$ (an IDR impactor) $\models (\mathcal{Z}\circ,_v\mathcal{H}) \sqcap \mathfrak{C}$, we have

(A.3-5-3) $\mathcal{T}^{\wedge\wedge}$ {priv,market | $\mathfrak{C}_{Bcing} =< \mathcal{Y}^c$}
$= \mathcal{T}^A$ {priv-market}
$= \{(\mathcal{T}^A$ {priv | $\mathfrak{C}_{Bcing}$} $\oplus \mathcal{T}^A$ {priv|-market | $\mathfrak{C}^{Cq}+$} $\oplus \mathcal{T}^A$ {priv—market| $\mathfrak{C}^{Cq}-$}} $\circledcirc$Ix
= priv$^{\wedge\wedge}$ $\oplus$ {priv|market}$^{\wedge\wedge}$ $\oplus$ {priv--market}$^{\wedge\wedge}$,

(with "Ix" being "$\circ$") with priv$^{\wedge\wedge}$ $\equiv \mathcal{T}^A$ {priv | $\mathfrak{C}_{Bcing}$}, (priv|market)$^{\wedge\wedge}$ $\equiv \mathcal{T}^A$ {priv|market | $(\mathfrak{C}^{Cq}+)$} and {priv--market}$^{\wedge\wedge}$ $\equiv \mathcal{T}^A$ {priv--marekt | $(\mathfrak{C}^{Cq}-)$} (analogous to Bcm. (A.3-4-1d)).

If we further let $\mathcal{T}^A$ be a complete IDR impactor (i.e., an impactor to decompose a grand system into unit systems), then $\mathcal{T}^A$ {priv|market,($\mathfrak{C}_{Bcing} =< \mathcal{Y}^c$} = priv$^{\wedge\wedge}$ + {priv|market}$^{\wedge\wedge}$ + {priv--market}$^{\wedge\wedge}$ (here for "+" being "$\oplus$" in the case of a complete IDR system). That is,

under the operations of complete IDR impactors, the efficiency of this system of being culture is the sum of private firms operating in isolation, the additional efforts of the private firms under the pressure of market and the destructive forces of market operating under the being culture. Here the systemic momentum of the impactor ($\mathcal{T}^A$ stems mainly from the technological efficiency of the individuals and the private firms. That is, the sources of efficiency of a conflict culture are: (1) the individual's technological efficiency following millennial traditions of sciences, (2) the individual and private efficiency in the course of market competition, (3) the negative effects caused by the conflicts among the individuals and firms.
By applying Bcm. (21.2-2-15) in Tonn {2006} to Bcms. (A.3-5-2) and (A.3-5-3) in the above, we are able to obtain the following becomings (or formulae):

(A.3-5-4) $X = \{\varphi^1 X_1 \oplus (\varphi^2 X_2 \oplus \varphi^2{}_{-1} X_{2,1\downarrow}) \oplus (\varphi^3 X_3 \oplus \varphi^3{}_{1\downarrow} X_{3,1\downarrow} \oplus \varphi^3{}_{2\downarrow} X_{3,2\downarrow}) \oplus \Sigma\} \circledcirc Ix$,

(with "Ix" being "○") where φ^i is the core of the partial impactor operating on the ith factor of X with the superscripts 1, 2 and 3 referring to self$^{\wedge\wedge}$, (self|mutual)$^{\wedge\wedge}$ and {self--mutual}$^{\wedge\wedge}$, respectively;

(A.3-5-5) $X = \{\varphi^1 X_1 \oplus (\varphi^2 X_2 \oplus \varphi^2{}_{-\downarrow} X_{2,1\downarrow}) \oplus (\varphi^3 X_3 \oplus \varphi^3{}_{1\downarrow} X_{3,1\downarrow} \oplus \varphi^3{}_{2\downarrow} X_{3,2\downarrow}) \oplus \Sigma\} \circledcirc Ix$,

(with "Ix" being "○") where φ^i is the core of the partial impactor operating on the ith factor of X with the superscripts 1, 2 and 3 referring to priv$^{\wedge\wedge}$, (priv|market)$^{\wedge\wedge}$ and {priv--market}$^{\#}$, respectively.

§A.3-6 L-K-ℭ Decomposition

Let X = {L,K|ℂ} ⊑ (Ω,$\mathcal{Z}$o,$_v\mathcal{H}$,{ℂ}) be a system. By Subsection §8.4-2, we may write X as: X = (L⊕K⊕C) ⊙ Ix, assuming X as an IDR system. Then a dynamical scheme of X can be derived accordingly.

A.4 MFCE Scheme, Mind, and Systems of Tao-Chi and Self-Organization

§A.4-1 MFCE Scheme

In this section, we introduce the multiple-factor cause-effect scheme, i.e., **MFCE scheme**, or the scheme of yin-yang and multiple factors (YYMF scheme developed in Lecture IV of Tonn (2001)). Chu Hsi constructed a scheme of the universe based on some models of yin-yang and the five-elements developed by Taoist priests. By the concept of "five elements" is meant simply many factors in determining the structure and operations of the universe and by the term "yin-yang" the relationship among these factors as mutually complementary as well as in constant conflict. Here in this book by the term "multiple factors" is meant the collection of all physical factors or forces responsible for the operations of the universe, including chemical elements, atoms and particles, and their subdivisions existing in the physical, biological and human worlds. Here the so-called "multiple factors or elements" is meant to be a modern term in capturing the essential concept of "five elements" prevailing in classic China.

According to Chou Tunyi, Supreme Ultimate (Tai Chi) is generated from and by Ultimateless (Wu Chi), which is parallel to and derived from Lao Tzu's idea of ≪Wu≫, that is, ≪Yu≫ ("somethingness," beings, being, or Being) is generated from Lao Tzu's ≪Wu≫ (or Nothingness). Then, through movements (tung), Supreme Ultimate produces Yang. Having reaching its limits, Yang is then followed by quiescence (ching), which consequently produces Yin. The movements and quiescence, in a cyclic motion, become the source of each other. By distinguishing Yin and Yang, Two Forms (liang yi) reveal themselves. After this, Yang changes and Yin unites with it, and thereby water, fire, wood, metal and earth are produced (Fung 1973, p. 437).

Similar to this above process, somewhat symbolically, it is natural to state that since there is <wu> (Wu*, Wu, or Nothingness), there is <yu> (or Being). Wu is beyond human comprehension and its full meaning is not yet quite unfolding to us. In Yu, one may be able to distinguish Yin from Yang. In actuality, when Wu and Yu are combined and in constant interactions, it is or is becoming a unified entity, or the One. One is one (according to Lao Tzu, <<Wu>> generates <<Yu>>; while in our approach, Tzu* generates Tzu, and then Tzu begets One, and from this One, Two are generated. Further, by the interactions of One and Two, Many are generated. In our scheme, Many may reveal itself as five elements (to say "five," just for convenience). In the following, these five elements, water, fire, wood, metal and earth, are presented as five unit systems.

We have studied the steep and flat systems in Lecture IV of Tonn (2001). In the following, we develop the closed scheme of yin-yang multiple-factors. In general, for a *system* X, let us define its structure as follows:

(A.4-1-1) $X = \chi \oplus \langle \mathbb{C}_X \rangle$,

where the *hierarchy-transformational structure* is:

(A.4-1-2) $\chi = \{X(H)\varepsilon[(VD,HC,\Gamma),(C_S,R_M),R^D(e_k)],\tilde{O}|E\{e_g\},Z\}$, $g = 1, 2, ..., G$.

Here C_S stands for the static self-characteristics of elements related to outside environments, R_M depicts the static mutual-relations of elements in the system, $R^D(e_k)$ refers to $(C^{DS}(e_k),R^{DM}(e_k))$ with $C^{DS}(e_k)$ denoting the dynamical self-characteristics of elements, $R^{DM}(e_r)$ denotes the dynamical mutual-relations of elements, $\tilde{O}$ depicts the mechanism connecting this system with the outside environments, $\langle \mathbb{C}_X \rangle$ represents the energy or the cultural complex generated by the culture of X ($\mathbb{C}_X$), VD represents the relationships of vertical dominance among members, HC represents the relationships of horizontal coordination, Γ (under the influence of $\mathbb{C}_X$) represents the complex of informal culture, $E\{e_g\}$ represents the outside environmental complex ($E\{e_g\}$ depending upon e_g, the energy of gth input in the outside environments), and Z is simply the decision-making and strategic complex.

For the **steep system** S with the structure of (VD,HC) and the cultural generator C_S (here we omit Γ, just for convenience), the following conditions hold. (1) $yV \dashv Vy$ (complete vertical dominance), where Vy represents the force that the top or superior V exerting on the bottom echelon y and yV represents the force that the bottom echelon exercised on the top or central element V. By this is meant that the gravity of the vertical force lies on the top and the forces or energies of the top dominates completely those of the bottom echelon. (2) $Lx \backsimeq xR$, where Lx denotes the force that the left element L exerting on the right-element and xR the force that the right element R exerting on the left-element x. That is, there is a harmonious balance between or among horizontal elements. (3) $S = \Sigma \oplus \langle \mathbb{C}_S \rangle$, where Σ refers to the structure of the steep system and $\langle \mathbb{C}_S \rangle$ stands for the entity emitting the energies of the steep system generated by the steep-culture (i.e., the culture complex underlying the steep system).

We defined (in Tonn 2001) the **yang-flat system** F^+ as a flat system having some vertical layers skewed to the right. In this system, the structure of skewness is represented below: (1) $Lx \ll Rx$ (weak skewness toward the right), by which is meant the gravity of the horizontal force is on the right and the forces on the right outweigh the forces on the left. (2) $yV \ll Vy$ (weak vertical dominance). That is, the top echelon of the system dominates the low echelon to a lesser degree (i.e., lesser than that of the unitary case: $yV \lll Vy$, see below). Here "Vy" denotes the forces of the top echelon dominating the lower echelons, while "yV" denotes the opposite of Vy.
Note that in the case of the open-system of MFCE, this condition will be replaced by $Lx \gg xR$. That is, the skewness is pointing outward and thus the gravity of the horizontal force is on the left and the forces on the left are greater than the forces on the right.

(3) $F^+ = Y^+ \oplus \langle \mathbb{C}_+ \rangle$, for Y^+ being the structure of the yang-flat system and $\langle \mathfrak{C}_+ \rangle$ being the energy of the yang-flat system generated by the yang-culture.

We further defined (Tonn 2001) the **yin-flat system** F^- as a flat system having less vertical layers (and skewing to the left) or one with a lesser degree of hierarchical structure. In this yin-flat system, the structure of some skewness to the left is represented as: $Lx > xR$ (very weak horizontal skewness toward the left) and $yV < Vy$ (very weak vertical dominance). In this system F-, the generating structure may be represented as: $F^- = Y^- \oplus \langle \mathbb{C}_- \rangle$, for Y^- being the structure of the yin-flat system and $\langle \mathbb{C}_- \rangle$ being the energy of the yin-flat system generated by the yin-culture.

For the **almost-flat system** FF, it is simply defined as a flat system having the least vertical layers (or with almost no hierarchical structure). This structural system of almost-no-skewness is represented as: $Lx \fallingdotseq^{\text{almost-no-H}} xR$ ($\fallingdotseq^{\text{almost-no-H}}$, referring to the notation of "almost no horizontal dominance") and $yV \fallingdotseq^{\text{almost-no-V}} Vy$ ($\fallingdotseq^{\text{almost-no-V}}$, referring to the notation of "almost no vertical dominance").
In this system FF, the generating structure may be represented as : $FF = F \oplus \langle \mathbb{C}_F \rangle$, for F being the structure of the almost-flat system and $\langle \mathbb{C}_F \rangle$ being the energy of the almost-flat system generated by the almost flat-culture.

Now we come to the **unitary system** defined as: $UU = U \oplus \langle \mathbb{C}_U \rangle$ with (1) strong vertical dominance $yV \lll Vy$ ("$\lll$" denoting the relationship of strong vertical dominance) and (2) no horizontal coordination $Lx \gg\ll xR$ ("$\gg\ll$" denoting the relationship of no horizontal dominance).

Below we turn to the discussion of the **universal scheme of yin-yang and multiple factors** (universal MFCE). In this scheme, in the east, it is the yang-flat system (i.e., the flat system, traditionally representing "Wood" or number 3)[41], and in the west, the yin-flat system (i.e., flatter system, traditionally representing "Metal" or number 4). In the north, it is the steep system (traditionally representing "Water" or number 1); and in the south, it is the almost-flat system (traditionally representing "Fire" or number 2). Finally in the middle, it is the position of a unitary system (traditionally representing "Earth" or number 5).

In this scheme, the Center or Earth represents the human being governed by the principles of centrality, mutuality, systematic balance/conflict and strategic continuity/discontinuity. East or Wood represents the world of animals in general, West or Metal represents the botanic world. South or Fire represents the chemical and physical worlds governed by laws of mathematics and principles of equilibrium and symmetry. Finally, in this system, North or Water represents

Ultimate Creativity-Destructivity/Nihility, God, the deity, or the world of human spiritual activities. Note that in another approach, we could interchange the positions of Earth and North: Earth to the north position and Ultimate Creativity-Destructivity to the central position. Fang [1983b] has suggested an upward flowing force similar to the flowing energy going upward from East and West in our scheme. Mo [1968, p. 22] has once mentioned Tien and here it is represented as North (or Center in the revised universal MFCE scheme) in the

MFCE scheme. North can also be represented by Sein in Heidegger's scheme (see Being and Time, Heidegger 1962, 1977). Perhaps in a way, Sein is Tien in isolation, or Tien is the ideal Sein.

Following Heidegger (Being and Time, Vorträge and Aufsätze, Neske 1954, Indirectly quoted from Macquarrie 1994, p. 65), we developed a fourfold scheme of earth, sky, mortals and gods. This is a hierarchical scheme based on the traditions of Aristotle and St. Thomas. Instead of the above approaches, we could also follow the ancient Greek philosopher Empedocles and develop a scheme of four elements or materials: earth, water, fire and wind. We could further develop a scheme by following the idea of an Indian school of materialism (Carvaka) which proclaims that every thing (dharma) and self (i.e., soul) are composed of earth, water, fire and wind (see Yang [1995, p. 101]). It appears to be self-evident that, all schemes developed on the bases of Western and Indian traditions are different from the MFCE scheme developed on the basis of YYWX will-and-rationality in which the essential concepts of the center and the specific role of man as Earth-the center stand out naturally.

Below we shall have more discussions about the center or Earth. Note that Heidegger's Dasein can be absorbed by Earth, number 5 in our scheme. Earth actually represents the Center-Middle in The Iching or the human being in Confucian schemes. For a Taoist, this earth represents the state of mind-fast, self-forgetfulness, sincerity, self-mercifulness, self-illumination, and the ultimate quiescence of the human being. The concept of Confucius' jen (humanity, or loving others), Mencius' concept of yi (righteousness), Wang Yangming's idea of practicing good human heart, and Chu Hsi's notion of Heavenly Li (heavenly forces, or Tien-li) are but different manifestations of the good-nature of the human being. This Center, or earth (or number 5) possesses, with the cultural energy immersing immensely in wu and then penetrating deeply into yu, self-disciplined ethics and self-generating and self-active vitality.

By drawing an inspiration from St. Thomas's idea unifying the knowledge of the universe and the faith in God -- the All-mighty, Omniscience and All-good, one may call this unity as the Center in our scheme. In this scheme, man is created with the mandate of controlling and managing nature (or East, West and South) as a steward of the estate of God. In Heidegger's world of "Sein und Zeit," Dasein, in the journey from birth to its inevitable death, represents the essence of Angst (anxiety) by itself and Sorge (care, or "fear for no reason") in falling. This Dasein may also be represented somewhat by the "Center in its bad mood" in the MFCE scheme.

In this above elaboration, before we came to Heidegger's concept of Dasein, we discussed the good human nature of the human being. But the nature of human beings has inevitably its dark side. Heidegger depicted the concepts of temporality and historicity in his book "Being and Time." Dasein's temporality may be interpreted in the sense of history from the perspective of St. Augustine. By the pure temporality, one may perceive three dimensions of time: Past -- the time frame in which the primitive man struggled to survive by gathering food and defending themselves against beasts (i.e., man struggling against the nature) and, for a true Christian believer, God exists; present -- the time frame in which the social man is in constant conflict with other human beings and, for Dasein, Sein ceases to exist in the world of Dasein; future -- the time frame in which man is a man of technology and for Dasein, death is what they have been waiting for. In the time frame of the past, man could be one with good human nature endowed by Ultimate Creativity-Destructivity of the universe as in the case of Confucian sage-kings.

In the time frame of the present, the human being has a good nature stemming from within; and it is seen time and again that the virtues of the self-generating freedom, loving others, righteousness, and behaving emanating smoothly and even springing out spontaneous from one's own good human nature. However, in this same time frame of the present, the evil nature of the human being must also be simultaneously accounted for here and now. Since at the present time, human beings are against the human beings; then, a social man must naturally have his dark side as he inflicts harm on others in the modern environment of fierce competition of man against man (Han Fei Tzu [2002, p. 661]). This is not like the time of Adam Smith wherein selfishness generates altruism and evil is becoming virtue. Essentially, this dark side of present time (of the human being) is the time of social Darwinism and cut-throat competition. Even a casual observation would confirm the existence of evil human nature which, in actuality, has been well documented over history. In classic China, Hsun Tzu developed a theory of the evil human nature. In South Sung Dynasty, Chu Hsi raised the issue of the "nightly vital force" and human desire as a contrast to Tien Li (Heavenly force). Further, this dark side of the human being, as already noted in the above, is presumably presented as the complex set of anxiety, fear with no cause, and a falling in Heidegger's system of Being and Time. For the last part, man is seen as falling from the grace of God. Dasein cares about his doom to death which may be completely unpredictable. Therefore, he-Dasein is in a constant state of anxiety (original sin, perhaps, see Dostal 1993, p. 157). To have a second thought, one may note that Dasein does not represent the evil nature of the human being. It is simply one losing its good human nature.

Now it is time to explain the details of the upward and downward flows of the MFCE scheme. Within this grand system of MFCE, comprised of an almost-flat system, a yin-flat system, a unitary system, a yang-flat system and a steep system, the circular motion of double flows is swirling around swiftly and relentlessly.

In the following, the unit systems in this grand system will be renamed as East (to replace the almost-flat system), South (to replace the yin-flat system), Center (to replace the unitary system), West (to replace the yang-flat system) and North (to replace the steep system), respectively, in order to conform to the tradition patterns of thinking (for example, see Xiao [1991]).

From East, by receiving energy from Center, **yang chi** (explicit vital force) flows upward toward North and then comes back down, passes East and flows toward South (Fire). From West, **yin chi** (implicit vital force) flows upward toward North and then come back down, passes West and flows toward South (Fire). So there are two forces flowing up and down that constitute the energy flows connecting all unit systems of the whole grand-system.

In the grand flow of the whole system (i.e, the grand system), Earth is in the center and as Center, it connects with the other four factors through constant energy flows emanating out of and injecting back into it.

Symbolic expression of the upward flow. One way to formalize an upward flow is to employ the concept of cultural energy generated in this grand system. Then, the upward part of the cyclical motion can be expressed as $\langle\mathbb{C}_U\rangle: (\langle\mathbb{C}_-\rangle \to \langle\mathbb{C}_+\rangle) \to \langle\mathbb{C}_S\rangle \to \langle -\mathbb{C}_S\rangle \to (\langle\mathbb{C}_+\rangle \to \langle\mathbb{C}_-\rangle)$, where $\langle -\mathbb{C}_S\rangle$ denotes the negative level of energy generated by the cultural core of the reverse of the steep system. Note that $\mathbb{C}$ with subscript(s) presents the culture force(s) of a subsystem in the grand system, while $\mathfrak{C}$ is the culture core of the grand system.

Since every culture has a pair of yin and yang forces (+,-), these forces joint together to generate a cyclic path for the cultural energy. That is, $UU(+,-) : \mathfrak{C} \Rightarrow (\mathbb{C}_- \to \mathbb{C}_+) \to \mathbb{C}_S \to -\mathbb{C}_S \to (\mathbb{C}_+ \to \mathbb{C}_-)$. Here, $\langle\mathbb{C}_-\rangle$, $\langle\mathbb{C}_+\rangle$, $\langle -\mathbb{C}_S\rangle$ and $\langle -\mathbb{C}_S\rangle$, each represents the cultural set generated by the yin-flat system, yang-flat system, steep system and the reverse of the steep system, respectively. We assume that these cultures, $\langle\mathbb{C}_-\rangle$, $\langle\mathbb{C}_+\rangle$, $\langle\mathbb{C}_S\rangle$ and $\langle -\mathbb{C}_S\rangle$, share a common core $\mathfrak{C}$: $\langle\mathbb{C}_U\rangle\backslash\langle\mathbb{C}_-\rangle\backslash\langle\mathbb{C}_+\rangle\backslash\langle\mathbb{C}_S\rangle\backslash\langle -\mathbb{C}_S\rangle = \langle\mathbb{C}_U\backslash\mathbb{C}_-\backslash\mathbb{C}_+\backslash\mathbb{C}_S\backslash -\mathbb{C}_S\rangle = \langle\mathfrak{C}\rangle$. Here "x\y" (or $x \sqcap y$) refers to the interaction between x and y, and $\langle\mathbb{C}_-\rangle = \langle\mathbb{C}_{|-}\rangle$ (i.e., the cultural energy restricted to the yin-flat system), $\langle\mathbb{C}_+\rangle = \langle\mathbb{C}_{|+}\rangle$, $\langle\mathbb{C}_S\rangle = \langle\mathbb{C}_{|S}\rangle$, and $\langle -\mathbb{C}_S\rangle = -\langle\mathbb{C}_{|S}\rangle$.

Two processes of the systematic growth dynamics are as follows. (1) To generate a steep system from the pair of yin-flat and yang-flat systems as the result of the strategic operation of the shengsheng generator σ initiated by Center. Here σ is the complex impactor of the self-existing and self-creating life-will and the systemic rationality, modern or classical. As a consequence, we have: $\sigma(\mathfrak{C})$: $(\langle\mathbb{C}_-\rangle,\langle\mathbb{C}_+\rangle) \to (\langle\mathbb{C}_-\rangle,\langle\mathbb{C}_+\rangle)/Z(\mathcal{E})$ (with $\mathfrak{C}$ serving as the virtual center of the MFCE system or scheme), where

$$\text{(A.4-1-3)} \quad (\langle\mathbb{C}_-\rangle,\langle\mathbb{C}_+\rangle)/\,Z(\mathcal{E}) = (\langle\mathbb{C}_-\rangle,\langle\mathbb{C}_+\rangle)/\langle\mathfrak{C}_Z\rangle = \langle\mathbb{C}_-,\mathbb{C}_+\rangle/\langle\mathfrak{C}_Z\rangle = \langle\mathbb{C}_{(-,+)/Z}\rangle.$$

Here $Z(\mathcal{E})$ ($\neq$ the center CC or UU), a unitary system, is the **virtual operational force** of the very system in question and is comprised of all sectors (i.e., the public as well as private sectors) affected by the public impactor of the center CC. Here by $(\langle\mathbb{C}_-\rangle,\langle\mathbb{C}_+\rangle)/Z(\mathcal{E})$ is meant that the pair of the cultural energies of yin-yang flat systems are immersed in the cultural energy of the virtual operational force of the system $\mathcal{E}$. In other words, this pair of energies is able to flow back to the core energy of the grand system in order to engage in energy transformation into other system(s). Note that, here, $\mathfrak{C}_Z$ is the **cultural generator** of $Z(\mathcal{E})$. Then, by applying the steep growth impactor Φ^S, we get

$$\text{(A.4-1-4)} \quad \Phi^S\{\langle\mathbb{C}_{(-,+)/Z}\rangle\} = \langle\,\mathbb{C}_S\,/\,\mathfrak{C}_Z\,\rangle = \langle\mathbb{C}_S\rangle/Z(\mathcal{E}),$$

and by Φ^{-1} (**reverse** or the invertor of the Φ^S) operation to get

$$\text{(A.4-1-5)} \quad \Phi^{-1}\{\langle\mathbb{C}_S\rangle/Z(\mathcal{E})\} = \Sigma \oplus \langle\mathbb{C}_S\rangle.$$

(2) To generate the negative steep system from the steep system and then the pair of yin-flat and yang-flat systems from the negative steep system as the results of the strategic operation of the shengsheng generator σ on the steep system. Thus, we have $\sigma(\mathfrak{C})$: $\langle\mathbb{C}_S\rangle \to \langle\mathbb{C}_S\rangle/Z(\mathcal{E})$, where

(A.4-1-6) $<\mathbb{C}_S> / Z(\mathcal{E}) = <\mathbb{C}_S>/ <\mathfrak{C}_Z> =<\mathbb{C}_S/ \mathfrak{C}_Z> = <\mathbb{C}_{S/Z}>$,

Then, by applying the reverse growth impactor Φ^{RV}, we get

(A.4-1-7) $\Phi^{RV}\{<\mathfrak{C}_{S/Z}>\} = <-\mathbb{C}_S / \mathfrak{C}_Z > = <-\mathbb{C}_S> / Z(\mathcal{E})$,

and by the reverse of Φ^{RV} operation (i.e., the Ψ^{-1} operation), to get

(A.4-1-8) $\Psi^{-1}\{ <-\mathbb{C}_S> / Z(\mathcal{E}) \} = (\Sigma^- \oplus <\mathbb{C}_S>)^- = \Sigma^- \oplus <-\mathbb{C}_S>$.

We reverse the process of $UU(\mathbb{C}_- \to \mathbb{C}_+) \to \mathbb{C}_S$ to $-\mathbb{C}_S \to (\mathbb{C}_+ \to \mathbb{C}_-)$ in the above. Then the desired process is derived.
Symbolic expression of the downward flow. Similar to the above symbolic expression, by employing the concept of cultural energy generated, this downward part of the cyclical flowing motion can be expressed as $\mathbb{C}_D$: $(<\mathbb{C}_+> \to <\mathbb{C}_->) \to <\mathbb{C}_F> \to <-\mathbb{C}_F> \to (<\mathbb{C}_-> \to <\mathbb{C}_+>)$. That is, the flow of motion is that $UU(+,-) : \mathfrak{C} \Rightarrow (\mathbb{C}_- \to \mathbb{C}_+) \to \mathbb{C}_F \to -\mathbb{C}_F \to (\mathbb{C}_- \to \mathbb{C}_+)$. For these cultural complexes $<\mathbb{C}_F>$, $<\mathbb{C}_->$, $<\mathbb{C}_+>$, and $<-\mathbb{C}_F>$, similar to the above case, we shall also assume that they share a common core $\mathfrak{C}$. Then we have the procedure as follows: $<\mathbb{C}_D> \backslash <\mathbb{C}_F> \backslash <\mathbb{C}_-> \backslash <\mathbb{C}_+> \backslash <-\mathbb{C}_F> = <\mathbb{C}_D \backslash \mathbb{C}_F \backslash \mathbb{C}_- \backslash \mathbb{C}_+ \backslash \mathbb{C}_{-F}> = <\mathfrak{C}>$, where $<\mathbb{C}_F> = <\mathbb{C}_{|F}>$, $<\mathbb{C}_-> = <\mathbb{C}_{|-}>$, $<\mathbb{C}_+> = <\mathbb{C}_{|+}>$ and $<-\mathbb{C}_F> = <-\mathbb{C}_{|F}> = <\mathbb{C}_{|-F}>$.

Two processes of the systematic growth (or decaying) dynamics are as follows. (1) To generate an almost-flat system from the pair of yin-flat and yang-flat systems as the result of the strategic operation of the shengsheng generator σ on the yin-yang pair. Therefore, we have $\sigma(\mathfrak{C}) : (<\mathbb{C}_+>,<\mathbb{C}_->) \to (<\mathbb{C}_+>,<\mathbb{C}_->)/Z(\mathcal{E})$, where

(A.4-1-9) $(<\mathbb{C}_+>,<\mathbb{C}_->)/Z(\mathcal{E}) = (<\mathbb{C}_+>,<\mathbb{C}_->)/<\mathfrak{C}_Z> = <\mathbb{C}_+,\mathbb{C}_->/<\mathfrak{C}_Z> = <<\mathbb{C}_+,\mathbb{C}_->/\mathfrak{C}_Z> = <\mathbb{C}_{(+,-)/Z}>$

Then, by applying the flat growth impactor Φ^F, we get

(A.4-1-10) $\Phi^F\{<\mathbb{C}_{(+,-)/Z}> = < \mathbb{C}_F / \mathfrak{C}_Z > = <\mathbb{C}_F> / Z(\mathcal{E})$,

and by the Φ^{-1} (reverse, revertor, tao reverse or tao-revertor) of Φ^F operation to get
(A.4-1-11) $\Phi^{-1} \{<\mathbb{C}_F>/ Z(\mathcal{E}) \} = F \oplus <\mathbb{C}_F>$.

(2) To generate a negative almost-flat system from the almost-flat system is by applying the shengsheng generator σ on the almost-flat system. Wherefore it yields $\sigma(\mathfrak{C})$: $<\mathbb{C}_F> \to <\mathbb{C}_F>/Z(\mathcal{E})$, with

(A.4-1-12) $<\mathbb{C}_F>/ Z(\mathcal{E}) = <\mathbb{C}_F> /<\mathfrak{C}_Z> = < \mathbb{C}_F >/ \mathfrak{C}_Z > = <\mathbb{C}_{F/Z}>$.

Then, by applying the reverse growth impactor Φ^{RV}, we get

(A.4-1-13) $\Phi^{RV}\{<\mathbb{C}_{F/Z}>\} = <-\mathbb{C}_F/ \mathfrak{C}_Z > =<-\mathbb{C}_F>/ Z(\mathcal{E})$,

and by the reverse or inverse Φ^{-1} operation, we get

(A.4-1-14) $\Phi^{-1}\{<-\mathbb{C}_F>/ Z(\mathcal{E})\} = (F \oplus <\mathbb{C}_F>)^- = F^- \oplus <-\mathbb{C}_F>$.

We reverse the process of "$(\mathbb{C}_{+} \to \mathbb{C}_{-}) \to \mathbb{C}_F$" to "$-\mathbb{C}_F \to (\mathbb{C}_{-} \to \mathbb{C}_{+})$" in the above. Then we derive the desired process.

Variational MFCE scheme. In the above MFCE scheme, with the support of yin-flat system representing life-will to creation, the yang-flat system may instead represent the systemic rationality; and its motion may at times go up or down. Similarly, the motion of the yin-flat system, with the support of the yang-flat system, may also go up or down. That is, in the above step (2), we have instead: (a) $\sigma(\mathfrak{C}): <\mathbb{C}_{-}> \to <\mathbb{C}_{-}>/Z(\mathcal{E})$,

(A.4-1-15) $<\mathbb{C}_{-}>/Z(\mathcal{E}) = <\mathbb{C}_{-}>/<\mathfrak{C}_Z> = <\mathbb{C}_{-/Z}>$,

(A.4-1-16) $\Phi^F\{<\mathbb{C}_{-/Z}> = <\mathbb{C}_F/\mathfrak{C}_Z> = <\mathbb{C}_F>/Z(\mathcal{E})$,

(A.4-1-17) $\Phi^{-1}\{<\mathbb{C}_F>/Z(\mathcal{E})\} = \Sigma \oplus <\mathbb{C}_F>$.

(b) We have $\sigma(UU): <\mathbb{C}_{+}> \to <\mathbb{C}_{+}>/Z(\mathcal{E})$, where

(A.4-1-18) $<\mathbb{C}_{+}>/Z(\mathcal{E}) = <\mathbb{C}_{+}>/<\mathfrak{C}_Z> = <\mathbb{C}_{+/Z}>$,

(A.4-1-19) $\Phi^F\{<\mathbb{C}_{+/Z}>\} = <\mathbb{C}_F/\mathfrak{C}_Z> = <\mathbb{C}_F>/Z(\mathcal{E})$,

(A.4-1-20) $\Phi^{-1}\{<\mathbb{C}_F>/Z(\mathcal{E})\} = \Sigma \oplus <\mathbb{C}_F>$.

Remark A.4-1-1. IRI chain, SIFX chain complex, and MPFX and GPFX cycles can all be expressed as some variants of the MFCE scheme.

§A.4-2 Mind, Nature and Emotion Scheme

In Chu Hsi's scheme of mind (M, hsin) unifying and commanding nature (N, hsing) and passion (P, ching), called the MNP scheme,[42] we may state that, through the support of the emotion, it entails a law of motion for the nature which is upward-oriented. Likewise, through the support of the nature, this scheme entails as well a law of motion for the emotion which is downward-oriented. In terms of a variational MFCE scheme, in this MNE scheme, Tien lies in the north, Ti in the south, human nature in the east, passion in the west, and mind in the middle. Then, in correspondence, mind is represented by a unitary system, the nature by a yang-flat system, the passion by a yin-flat system, Tien by a steep system, and Ti by an almost flat system, respectively.

In the above MFCE scheme, the complete circle of energy is called "yi chou tien" (complete trip around earth, man and heaven). This is very close to the shengsheng mode of The Iching which was previously called the **legend of four dragons** entailing a pattern of cyclic motion: Potential Dragon (completely flat system) → Field Dragon (almost flat system) → Flying Dragon (steep system) → Regretting Dragon (reverse steep system).

This scheme of yin-yang multiple-factor scheme (i.e., an MFCE scheme, the legend of four dragons, four dragon chain) may be integrated with Thomas Aquinas' scheme built upon the basis of the Aristotelian universe. Here the Aristotle's scheme of the universe is perceived as one with lower layers (i.e., physical world and the worlds of lower level life forms) in the bottom, intermediate layer (the world of humans) in the middle, and the world of Ideas on the top (i.e., Plato's world of Forms). Further, we shall treat Aquinas' scheme of the universe as one with a harmonious balance between knowledge and revelation, albeit somewhat tipping toward faith and revelation. It is conceived understandably that, in our interpretation, the layers in Aquinas' scheme are quite similar to those in Aristotle's scheme. Nevertheless, there is a major difference between these two schemes in that in Aquinas' scheme, the top echelon is occupied by the personified, all mighty and omniscient God. In contrast, in Aristotle's scheme, the top position is occupied by Ideas, not a personified Deity.

It is perhaps useful to note that the scheme unifying the world of yin-yang multiple-factors with that of Aquinas's is one in which God is unified with the nature, $\mathbb{T}\mathbb{zu}$*, or Ultimate Creativity-Destructivity.

This variational MFCE scheme (or YYMF scheme) can be modified and refined to formulate a scheme for a polity, comprising of a king (chun), nobles (kuan), low-level public servants (li) and common people (min). It goes without saying that this variational scheme can be transformed as well into a scheme for a business corporation, comprising of a CEO, managers, staffs and workers.

Before we proceed to the next section, note that this above scheme can be employed to elucidate the processes of how diffusion, integration and even co-creation of cultures of the East and West can take place. Our theory concerning the trend toward global culturalism is different from either the theme of the "end of history" (Fukuyama 1992) or that of cultural war (also called the "clash of civilizations," see Huntington 1993, 1996). Although the theme of the cultural war is very powerful and is partially valid in some meticulously way (for example, tension and wars between Christians and Muslims in some parts of the world), it is fundamentally a misleading concept and, worse still, a counter productive one to the advancement of human civilization.[43] As for the concept of the "end of history," it is not a serious and academic one. In fact, the modern world is a world of multiple cultures. Neither the ideology of democratic capitalism nor that of the so-called liberal democratic persuasion is universally valid. For example, the market systems of East Asia are at best capitalism merely in name. And similarly, "East Asian democracy" is essentially not a western-type democracy. This is because the ancient economic system of East Asia was predominantly a market economy and the modern polities of East Asia, albeit their Western appearance, have to rely upon cultural foundations significantly different from the cultures of Christianity and Western utilitarianism.

In the MFCE scheme, Earth or Center can be expanded into a grand system comprising shi (officials) in the north, nong (peasants) in the south, kong (artisans) in the west, shang (merchants) in the east and chung (chun or king) in the center. This new system can be essentially derived from The Kuan Tzu [1981].

To apply this variational MFCE scheme to economics, the center of this scheme can be expanded to become a scheme of industries comprising R&D activities in the north, the primary sector in the south, the secondary sector in the west, the tertiary sector in the east, and the planner in the center. Then it is necessary to seek a harmonious balance among the south, the west, the east and the north, and to work out as well some types of consensual dominance of all of them by the planner in order to complete the scheme.

Remark A.4-2-1. The simplest idea of a MFCE scheme $X = \{E,S,C,N,W\} \sqsubseteq (\Omega,\mathbb{Z}\circ,\sqrt{\mathbb{H}},\{\mathbb{C}\})$ with C being the center is that the system energy along with the center creates the elements of

N and S by going through the horizontal E-W axis, while the system energy together with the center creates the elements of E and W by going through the vertical S-N axis.

Remark A.4-2-1. For the MFCE scheme X = {E,S,C,N,W} ⊑ (Ω,Z∘,ᵥH,{ℂ}) with C being the center, we may write X as:

(A.4-2-1) $X = [E\oplus S\oplus C\oplus N\oplus W] \oplus I_{C>}. = \sigma \Vdash \Sigma^{TC}$,

(under the assumption that W is an Hf-systemism of E: W = φ(E), S is a Hh-systemism of (E,W): S = ψ(E,φ(E)), N is a Hh-systemism of S: N = τ(S) = τ{ψ(E,φ(E))}, for φ, ψ, τ ⊨ (Ω,Z∘,ᵥH,{ℂ}), and $I_{C>}$. is the integrating factor) with the solution:

(A.4-2-2) $W(.) = [\sigma_1 W(\mathbb{H}_{E};.)\oplus\sigma_2 W(\mathbb{H}_{W};.)\oplus\sigma_3 W(\mathbb{H}_{S};.)\ \sigma_4 W(\mathbb{H}_{N};.)] \oplus I_{C>}.(\mathbb{H};.)$

with appropriate interpretations for σ_1, σ_2, σ_3 and $I_W(\mathbb{H};.)$ at the state of TCentral (see Subsection §8.4-3).

Remark A.4-2-2. For φ, ψ, τ ⊨ Z∘,ᵥH, the following relationships hold: **N** is an Hf-systemism of S: N = τ(S), W as a Hh-systemism of (S,N): W = φ{S,τ(S)}, E is a Hh-systemism of W: E = ψ(W).

§A.4-3 Systems of Tao-Chi and Self-organization

Below, we shall apply the essential method of the MFCE scheme and expand our study to the areas of the tao-chi scheme, yin-yang generating scheme, thesis-antithesis-synthesis generating scheme, and self-organization scheme.

The tao-chi generating scheme. In order to generate Chi from Tzu* (for which, to be a bit inaccurately, we may say it is generated indirectly by Tao*), one process is in the following. First, let Tao (Tao ≠ dao): $T = \chi_T \oplus$ <$\mathbb{C}_T$> ⊑ (Ω^{Δ},Z∘,ᵥH,{ℂ}) be a system, where <$\mathbb{C}_T$> represents the yin-yang statics and tao-dynamics of <tao> (i.e., "static and dynamical forms" of Tao).

In order to derive the system of dao: $D = \chi_D \oplus$ <$\mathbb{C}_D$> ⊑ (Ω^{Δ},Z∘,ᵥH,{ℂ}), a concretizing realization of the potential is needed: for a concretizing impactor K ⊨ Z∘,ᵥH, K(T) = D, where $T = \chi_T \oplus$ <$\mathbb{C}_T$>.

Now let Z(ℰ) be the "virtual operating force" under the operation of Tzu* (for which we say, inaccurately that, Tao is begot by Tao*, the latter being a manifestation of Ultimate Creativity-Destructivity). Note that the concrete realization of Tao in the real world is called dao. Following the MFCE scheme (see Section 6.2, Chapter 6), we have:

(A.4-3-1) <$\mathbb{C}_T$> / Z(ℰ) = <$\mathbb{C}_T$>/<$\mathfrak{C}_Z$> = < $\mathbb{C}_T/\mathfrak{C}_Z$ > = <$\mathbb{C}_{T/Z}$>.

Here, in Bcm. (A.4-3-1), the subscript "Z" is the short-hand notation of Z(ℰ), i.e., Z ≡ Z(ℰ). Subsequently by applying the generating impactor ψ^S ⊨ Z∘,ᵥH (which is also a result of the operation of the force of <tao>: "anti-generation") we have:

(A.4-3-2) $\psi^S\{<\mathbb{C}_{T/Z}>\} = <\mathbb{C}_{-T} / \mathfrak{C}_Z> = <-\mathbb{C}_T>/Z(\mathcal{E})$;

Furthermore, by "reversing" the generating impactor ψ^S introduced in the above (i.e., by applying the impactor $(\psi^S)^{-1} \models \mathcal{Z}\circ,_v\mathcal{H}$, we derive:

(A.4-3-3) $(\psi^S)^{-1}\{ <-\mathbb{C}_T>/Z(\mathcal{E})\} = (\mathcal{T}\oplus <\mathbb{C}_T>)^{-1} = \mathit{Chi} \oplus <\mathbb{C}_{Chi}>$,

(A.4-3-4) $K\{\mathit{Chi} \oplus <\mathbb{C}_{Chi}>) = \mathcal{Q} \oplus <\mathbb{C}_Q>$,

for a "concretizing impactor" $K \models \mathcal{Z}\circ,_v\mathcal{H}$, where Chi = $\mathit{Chi} \oplus <\mathbb{C}_{Chi}>$ is created through the operation of the reverse impactor; and qi: $Q = \mathcal{Q} \oplus <\mathbb{C}_Q>$ is a systemic realization of Chi, created by the operation of a concretizing impactor.

Note that qi is set as the "reverse" of dao, because (Tao*,Chi*) or (Tao,Chi) is a yin-yang pair in the sense of tao-reversal. Further, Tao* is more than "above-the-shape," actually "above-above-the-shape;" Tao* generates Tao, and Tao is "above-the-shape." Tao generates dao (under the light of Tzu*) and qi is generated by Chi (under the light of Tzu*, while Chi* generates Chi) with qi being a force below-the-shape. Here, Tao* is a "Form," a manifestation of the creativity-of-the-universe per se that can not be perceived be man, and Tao is a "Form" (or "Heavenly Reason or principle") or a manifestation of the creativity-of-the-universe per se that can only be perceived "vaguely." Theoretically, we may also just say that Chi* generates Chi, while Chi is "above-the-shape," qi is a force "below-the-shape." Besides, Chi is a "Form," a generative Form in the Tao*-Chi* pair created by Ultimate Creativity-Destructivity of the universe per se (Tzu*, Self*) in the "world of Forms." This Chi can not be perceived by man in general (except perhaps in a very vague way), and qi is "matter," "love and desire," or a manifestation of the creativity of the universe per se that exists in the real worlds.

Note that Tao* and Chi* are "Forms" exist forever and are with potential for dynamical movements, while Tao and Chi are "dynamical Forms" created by Tao* and Chi*, respectively. That is, the former pair is composed of "Forms" of potential forces of creativity-destructivity with the potentiality requiring the supports of some other auxiliary forces in order to be realized; whereas the latter pair is composed of "Forms" embodying dynamical forces of creativity-destructivity by themselves.[44] Here Tao*, Tao, Chi* and Chi are entities exist in different layers of the "beyond-the-real-word" ("super-metaphysical worlds," "metaphysical" or "abstract" worlds).[45] In contrast, dao and qi are forces exist in the real worlds.
Here, one of the ultimate entities exiting in the second layer of the "ultimate world," i.e., Tien or Tao, is not "static" (or a static entity); that is, it exists forever and is always in motion. In contrast, Tao* is defined as a "Form" with potentiality provided for dynamical movements. Note that, first, in a non-strict sense and if no confusion would arise, we may say that Tao* is Chi* and Chi* is Tao*, both are created by Tzu*, the ultimate force of creativity and destructivity in the universe. Secondly, again if there is no confusion, we may say Tao and Chi are created by Wu*, Yu* or Tzu* as well.

Here Tao and Chi are independent in their origins, because Tao does not generate Chi and vice versa. Here, Tao and Chi form a grand system: {T,Ch}, where T is Tao, the center of the grand system, Ch is Chi, the non-central unit system. This Tao-Chi system (may be written as tao-chi system, for convenience), together with W, formulates a grand system: {T,Ch|W}, where Ch is a non-central sub-system, T is the secondary center of the basic system, and W (i.e., Wu, the center of the grand center) is generated by Wu* (under the illumination of Tzu*). Here, W is the force of creation-destruction that can only be perceived vaguely by intuition.

Note that the culture of {T,Ch|W} is that of tranquility, wherein tranquil relationship exists among all sub-systems of this grand system {T,Ch|W}.

If we would like to have Tao and Chi (together under the illumination of Tzu*) generating milliards of thing, then the process of creation constitute a 5-polar MFCE scheme, with the pair ($<\mathbb{C}_T>$,$<\mathbb{C}_{Chi}>$) (or ($<\mathbb{C}_D>$,$<\mathbb{C}_Q>$) in its concretizing realization) replacing the pair ($<\mathbb{C}_+>$,$<\mathbb{C}_->$). Here, {D,Q|W}, as a concretizing realization of the system {T,Ch|W}, is a system of tranquil culture. Note that in the above the system {D,Q|W} may also be formulated as {D,Q|(σ,κ)}, for σ (i.e., a force of creativity) ⇝ τ and κ (i.e., a force of destructivity) ⇝ τ, τ ⊫ $\mathfrak{I}$ ⊪ Tzu*.

Yin-yang generating scheme. This scheme is similar to the 5-polar scheme just presented in the above. Here, ($<\mathbb{C}_+>$,$<\mathbb{C}_->$) is a yin-yang pair, and {+,-|(σ,κ)}is also a system of tranquil culture, with "+" and "-" being non-central elements, (σ,κ) being the central element, and the cultural core from which " +" and " –" share part of the cultural creativity is the virtual center of the system.

Dialectic scheme. Let T (thesis) ⊑ (Ω^Δ,$\mathcal{Z}$○,$_v\mathcal{H}$,{$\mathbb{C}$}) be a system, ψ ⊨ $\mathcal{Z}$○,$_v\mathcal{H}$ be a "reverse- or inverse-impactor." Then ψ{T} ⊑ (Ω^Δ,$\mathcal{Z}$○,$_v\mathcal{H}$,{$\mathbb{C}$}) is a system. Here, the reverse-impactor ψ "eliminate" T and "generates" A (antithesis) ⊑ (Ω^Δ,$\mathcal{Z}$○,$_v\mathcal{H}$,{$\mathbb{C}$}).

Furthermore, let ψ^2≡ ψoψ ⊨ $\mathcal{Z}$○,$_v\mathcal{H}$ be a "synthesis-impactor." Then ψ^2{T}≡ S (i.e., synthesis) ⊑ (Ω^Δ,$\mathcal{Z}$○,$_v\mathcal{H}$,{$\mathbb{C}$}) is a system. Here, the synthesis impactor ψ^2 "eliminates" A and generates S ⊑ (Ω^Δ,$\mathcal{Z}$○,$_v\mathcal{H}$,{$\mathbb{C}$}). In this case, if T and A coexist, then {T,A} is a conflict system; and between T and A, there is only a conflict relationship. Note that there is no center in this system. But if T, A and S coexist, then {T,A|S}is a centralized system of conflict culture. Here, S is the center of this system, T and A are non-central elements (treated as such, just for convenience), and between T and A there is a conflict relationship.

Below, let us express the system of thesis-antithesis-synthesis as an n-polar MFCE scheme: Let $<\mathbb{C}_\Delta>$ be the culture complex of a system Δ, F the f-systemism of Δ, and H the Hh-systemism of Δ. Furthermore, let:

(A.4-3-5) $<\mathbb{C}_\Delta>/\ Z(\mathcal{E})\ =\ <\mathbb{C}_\Delta>/<\mathfrak{C}_{\mathcal{Z}}>\ =<\mathbb{C}_{\Delta/\mathcal{Z}}>$,

where Z($\mathcal{E}$) is the virtual operating force. Then from φ^F ⊨ $\mathcal{Z}$○,$_v\mathcal{H}$ yields φ^F{$<\mathbb{C}_{\Delta/\mathcal{Z}}>$} = $<\mathfrak{C}_{F/\mathcal{Z}}>$. Likewise, let ψ^H ⊨ $\mathcal{Z}$○,$_v\mathcal{H}$, we get ψ^H{$<\mathbb{C}_{F/\mathcal{Z}}>$} = $<\mathbb{C}_{H/\mathcal{Z}}>$. That is: {A→S}⇔{$<\mathbb{C}_{\Delta/\mathcal{Z}}>$} →$<\mathbb{C}_{F/\mathcal{Z}}>$→$<\mathbb{C}_{H/\mathcal{Z}}>$}.

Here, the other way to derive synthesis from antithesis is:

(A.4-3-6) ($<\mathbb{C}_\Delta>$,$<\mathbb{C}_\Delta>$) / Z($\mathcal{E}$) =$<\mathbb{C}_{(\Delta,F)/\mathcal{Z}}>$,

where ψ^H{$<\mathbb{C}_{(\Delta,F)/\mathcal{Z}}>$} =$<\mathbb{C}_{H/\mathcal{Z}}>$.

Self-organization's growth scheme. At first, let X_1, X_2,…,X_N ⊑ (Ω,$\mathcal{Z}$○,$_v\mathcal{H}$,{$\mathbb{C}$}) be subsystems, and $<\mathbb{C}_{Xi}>$ be the cultural complex of X_i, for i = 1, 2, …, N. Then, first, as in a 5-polar CEMF scheme, we have: {$<\mathbb{C}_{X1}>$,$<\mathbb{C}_{X2}>$,…,$<\mathbb{C}_{XN}>$}/Z($\mathcal{E}$) = $<\mathbb{C}_{X1,X2,...,XN}>$/Z($\mathcal{E}$) = $<\mathbb{C}_{X1,X2,..,XN/\mathcal{Z}}>$, and by applying the generating impactor ψ^S ⊨ $\mathcal{Z}$○,$_v\mathcal{H}$ yields ψ^S{$<\mathbb{C}_{X1,X2,..,XN/\mathcal{Z}}>$} = <-$\mathbb{C}_{X1,X2,..,XN/\mathcal{Z}}$> /Z($\mathcal{E}$). Secondly, by applying the reverse-growth impactor $(\psi^S)^{-1}$ ⊨ $\mathcal{Z}$○,$_v\mathcal{H}$ yields

$(\psi^S)^{-1}\{<-\mathbb{C}_{X1,X2,\ldots,XN/Z}>/Z(\mathcal{E})\} = (\mathcal{T} \oplus <\mathbb{C}_T>)^{-1} = \mathcal{Y}_1 \oplus <\mathbb{C}_{Y1}> = Y_1$. Here, the system of tao: $T = \mathcal{T} \oplus <\mathbb{C}_T>$ is created by Tao* under the light of Ultimate Creativity-Destructivity Tzu*. Although this <tao> (i.e., T} is the virtual center of the system $\{X_1, X_2, \ldots, X_N\}$, note that a better way to describe this virtual center may be in the following: the collective and integrated force underlying the dynamic or "cultural" forces of {dao,qi} and $\{<\mathbb{C}_{X1}>, <\mathbb{C}_{X2}>, \ldots, <\mathbb{C}_{XN}>\}$ is the cultural core of the system, and is therefore the virtual center.

Similarly, like in the above procedure, we derive $\mathcal{Y}_2 \oplus <\mathbb{C}_{Y2}> = Y_2, \ldots,$ and $\mathcal{Y}_N \oplus <\mathbb{C}_{XN}> = Y_N$. Here, $Y_1, Y_2, \ldots, Y_N \sqsubseteq (\Omega, \mathcal{Z}o, {}_v\mathcal{H}, \{\mathbb{C}\})$ are also subsystems. Note that this approach is not a-scientific, and scientists must be able to link the above process, definitely in a very imaginative way, to the real world operations of the basic particles in physics (or things even more basic elements in physics), the most basic elements in chemistry, and the most basic living cells in biology (cell, RNA, and DNA, etc.).
<tao>-<chi> self-organizational scheme. In the above, in the self-organization's growth scheme, let $Y_1, Y_2, \ldots, Y_N \sqsubseteq (\Omega, \mathcal{Z}o, {}_v\mathcal{H}, \{\mathbb{C}\})$ be various "faces" or manifestations of Chi in the process of condensing itself or becoming thin. Then for the <tao>-<chi> (or simply tao-chi) self-organizational scheme, Tao is a Form created by (or a manifestation of) Tao* or Self*, Self is a creation of Self* (i.e., Tzu* or SELF), and dao is an actualization of Tao in the real world (or a "real form" of <tao> in the real world). Here, SELF is the universe itself, the essence, substance, origin, or the ultimate "self-ness" of the universe itself.

In addition, Chi is a Form created by Chi* (or a manifestation of SELF), and qi is an actualization of Chi in the real world (or a "real form" of <chi> in the real world). Here, "qi" is "matter" and is also a manifestation or "transforming face" of Self.

Tao and Chi incorporate both mind and matter. Tao is more than mind and Chi is more than matter. In our theory, dao is set as mind, not matter; and qi is matter, not mind. Note that this above comment applies to Tao* and Chi* as well.

Tao* (≡ Original Good*) and Chi* (≡ Original Chi*) are "perfectly good." Because Tao is created by Tao* (under the illumination of Tzu*), it must be good as well. Nevertheless, although Chi (which is both a co-origin of good human nature and the origin of evil human nature) is created by Chi*, it embodies both good and evil human nature. Tao is a co-origin of "self-good" (i.e., beneficial and good for oneself) and good-for-others. Chi embodies Good-Chi and Bad-Chi. While Good-Chi is a co-origin of the forces of self-good and good-for-others, Bad-Chi is instead the origin of the forces for self-good-and-bad-for-others and self-bad-and-bad-for-others. Here the so-called self-bad is meant the forces harmful to oneself. On one hand, the organic combination and integration of Tao and Good-Chi (or {Tao,Good-Chi} as a system) creates the good human nature. On the other hand, Bad-Chi itself alone as a system creates the evil nature. Thus, in the evil human nature, there is neither the impactor or influence of Tao nor that of Good-Chi.

Hence, in this system, mind and matter together constitute two-dimensions of the same origin (i.e., manifestation of Self* or the higher force). This is also a system of tao-chi two dimensions and good-evil two-dimensions. In sum, these multifaceted structures of two-dimensions are created by the "dialectical or contradiction-integrating impactor" or the "ultimate impactor of creation-destruction."

§A.4-4 Some Simple MFCE Schemes

In this subsection, we shall discuss systems of two elements, three elements, and four-elements.

Two-element System: horizontal. For a system of horizontal two-element system, let $\{x,y\} \sqsubseteq (\Omega,\mathcal{Z}\circ,_v\mathcal{H},\{\mathbb{C}\})$. That is, $\{x,y\} = \{x,y|R\}$, with R depicting a horizontal relationship between x and y.

In this system, we can set y as either an h-systemism of x or a y-systemism of x. Suppose y is a y-systemism of x. Then, in terms of a MFCE scheme, we shall develop it as follows.

Let the direction of the motion of the cultural energy generated in this system be $\varphi\{\mathfrak{C}\}$: $\mathbb{C}_- \rightarrow \mathbb{C}_+$, or $\varphi\{<\mathfrak{C}>\}$: $<\mathbb{C}_-|\mathfrak{C}> \rightarrow <\mathbb{C}_+>$, where $\varphi \models \mathcal{Z}\circ,_v\mathcal{H}$ is the culture-generating impactor, and $\mathfrak{C}$, $\mathbb{C}_-$ and $\mathbb{C}_+$ denote the levels of cultural energy of the core (i.e., core culture of the system), x (i.e., yin element) and y (i.e., yang element), respectively. Here $<\mathfrak{C}>$, $<\mathbb{C}_->$ and $<\mathbb{C}_+>$ depict the levels of cultural energy generated by the core, x and y, respectively.

The details of the processes of the systematic growth dynamics are as follows. (1) To generate y from x as the result of the strategic operation of the shengsheng generator σ initiated by the core of the system $Z(\mathcal{E})$ ($\mathcal{E}$ denoting the system and $Z(\mathcal{E})$ is called the **virtual operational force** of the system). Here $\sigma \models \mathcal{Z}\circ,_v\mathcal{H}$ is the complex impactor of self-mastering life-will and the self-creating systemic rationality. As a consequence, we have: $\sigma(\mathcal{E})$: $<\mathbb{C}_-> \rightarrow (<\mathbb{C}_->)/Z(\mathcal{E})$, where

(A.4-4-1) $\quad <\mathbb{C}_-> / Z(\mathcal{E}) \;= <\mathbb{C}_-\,\mathfrak{C}_Z> = <\mathbb{C}_{-/Z}>.$

Here, by Bcm. (A.4-4-1) "$<\mathbb{C}_{-/Z}> = <\mathbb{C}_-/\mathfrak{C}_Z>$" is meant the cultural forces of $\mathbb{C}_-$ deriving its strengths from the interactions with the cultural core $\mathfrak{C}$ of the system in question. Then, by applying the steep growth impactor $\Phi^S \models \mathcal{Z}\circ,_v\mathcal{H}$, we get:

(A.4-4-2) $\;\Phi^S\{<\mathbb{C}_{-/Z}>\} = <\mathbb{C}_+/\,\mathfrak{C}_Z> = <\mathbb{C}_+>/Z(\mathcal{E}),$

and by the **reverse** of Φ^S operation (or the invertor of Φ^S operation) to get

(A.4-4-3) $\quad \Phi^{-1}\,\{<\mathbb{C}_+>/Z(\mathcal{E})\} \;=\; y^{++} \oplus <\mathbb{C}_+> = y,$

with y^{++} being the structural framework of y and $<\mathbb{C}_+>$ the cultural complex of y. Here $Z(\mathcal{E})$ comprises all of the elements to be affected by the mutual interactions of the system as a dynamical whole. Here by $<\mathbb{C}_+>)/Z(\mathcal{E})$ is meant that the cultural energy of yang element is immersed in the cultural energy of the virtual operational force of the system $\mathcal{E}$. In other words, this immersion enables the energy to flow backward into the core energy of the whole system in order to engage in creative transformation of the potential into the real world entity. Note that, here, $\mathbb{C}_Z$ is the cultural generator of $Z(\mathcal{E})$.

The generation of x from y is the result of the strategic operation of the shengsheng generator σ initiated by the core of the system $Z(\mathcal{E})$. This generative becoming chain proceeds as follows. With $\sigma \models \mathcal{Z}\circ,_v\mathcal{H}$ defined in the above, we have for $\sigma^{-1} \models \mathcal{Z}\circ,_v\mathcal{H}$ as the reversal impactor of σ: $\sigma^{-1}(\mathcal{E})$: $<\mathbb{C}_+> \rightarrow (<\mathbb{C}_+>)/Z(\mathcal{E})$, where

(A.4-4-4) $<\mathbb{C}_+>/Z(\mathcal{E}) = <\mathbb{C}_+/\ \mathfrak{C}_Z> = <\mathbb{C}_{+/Z}>$.

Then, by applying the steep growth impactor $\Phi^{S*} \vDash \mathbb{Z}\circ,_v\mathbb{H}$, we get

(A.4-4-5) $\Phi^{S*}\{<\mathfrak{C}_{+/Z}>\} = <\mathbb{C}_-/\mathfrak{C}_Z> = <\mathbb{C}_-> /Z(\mathcal{E})$,
and by the **reverse** of Φ^{S*} operation to get

(A.4-4-6) $\Phi^{-1}\ \{<\mathbb{C}_->/Z(\mathcal{E})\} = x^{--} \oplus <\mathbb{C}_-> = x$,

with x^{--} being the structural framework of x and $<\mathbb{C}_->$ the cultural complex of x. Here by $<\mathbb{C}_->)/Z(\mathcal{E})$ is meant the cultural energy of yin element to be immersed in the cultural energy of the virtual operational force of the system $\mathcal{E}$. In other words, this immersion enables the energy to flow backward into the core energy of the whole system in order to transform the potential into real world entities.

Two-element System: In this case, the process of creation is identical to the above case of a horizontal system with two elements, except that the relationship in this system is vertical.

Three-element System: For a system of three-elements, let $\{x,y,w\} \sqsubseteq (\Omega,\mathbb{Z}\circ,_v\mathbb{H},\{\mathbb{C}\})$. In this system, we can set y as either an h-systemism of x or a y-systemism of x. Suppose y is a y-systemism of x, and z is the h-systemism of {x,y}. Then, in terms of a MFCE scheme, we shall construct it as follows.

Let the direction of the motion of the cultural energy generated in this system be $\varphi\{\mathfrak{C}\}: \mathbb{C}_- \rightarrow \mathbb{C}_+$, or $\varphi\{<\mathfrak{C}>\}: <\mathbb{C}_-|\mathfrak{C}> \rightarrow <\mathbb{C}_+>$, where $\varphi \vDash \mathbb{Z}\circ,_v\mathbb{H}$ is the culture-generating impactor of y-systemism, and $\psi\{\varphi\{\mathfrak{C}\}\}: <\mathbb{C}_-,\mathbb{C}_+> \rightarrow <\mathbb{C}_w>$ or $\psi\{\varphi\{<\mathfrak{C}>\}\}: <\mathbb{C}_-,\mathbb{C}_+|\mathfrak{C}> \rightarrow <\mathbb{C}_w>$, with $\psi \vDash \mathbb{Z}\circ,_v\mathbb{H}$ being the culture-generating impactor of h-systemism, and $\mathfrak{C}$, $\mathbb{C}_-$, $\mathbb{C}_+$, and $\mathbb{C}_w$ being the levels of cultural energy of the system core, that of x (i.e., yin element), that of y (i.e., yang element) and that of w (i.e., the central element), respectively. Here $<\mathfrak{C}>$, $<\mathbb{C}_->$, $<\mathbb{C}_+>$ and $<\mathbb{C}_w>$ depict the levels of cultural energy generated by the core, x, y and w, respectively.

The details of the processes of systematic growth dynamics of this system are as follows. (1) The generation of y from x is the result of the strategic operation of the shengsheng generator σ initiated by the core of the system $Z(\mathcal{E})$. Here $\sigma \vDash \mathbb{Z}\circ,_v\mathbb{H}$ is the complex impactor of self-mastering life-will and self-creating systemic rationality. As a consequence, we have: $\sigma(\mathcal{E})$: $<\mathbb{C}_-> \rightarrow (<\mathbb{C}_->)/Z(\mathcal{E})$, where

(A.4-4-7) $<\mathbb{C}_->/Z(\mathcal{E}) = <\mathbb{C}_-/\ \mathfrak{C}_Z> = <\mathbb{C}_{-/Z}>$.

Note that, here, $\mathfrak{C}_Z$ is the cultural generator of $Z(\mathcal{E})$. Then, by applying the growth $\Phi^S \vDash \mathbb{Z}\circ,_v\mathbb{H}$, we get

(A.4-4-8) $\Phi^S\{<\mathbb{C}_{-/Z}>\} = <\mathbb{C}_+/\ \mathfrak{C}_Z> = <\mathbb{C}_+> /Z(\mathcal{E})$,

and by the **reverse** of Φ^S operation (or the invertor of Φ^S operation) to get

(A.4-4-9) $\Phi^{-1}\ \{<\mathbb{C}_+>/\ Z(\mathcal{E})\} = y^* \oplus <\mathbb{C}_+> = y$.

(2) To generate w from the yin-yang pair (x,y) as the result of the strategic operation of the shengsheng generator ψ initiated by the core of the system $Z(\mathcal{E})$. By having $\psi\{\sigma(\mathcal{E})\}$: $(<\mathbb{C}_->,<\mathbb{C}_+>) \rightarrow (<\mathbb{C}_->,<\mathbb{C}_+>)/Z(\mathcal{E})$,

(A.4-4-10) $(<\mathbb{C}_->,<\mathbb{C}_+>)/ Z(\mathcal{E}) = (<\mathbb{C}_->,<\mathbb{C}_+>)/<\mathfrak{C}_Z> = <\mathbb{C}_-,\mathbb{C}_+>/<\mathfrak{C}_Z> = <\mathbb{C}_{(-,+)/Z}>$.

Here by $(<\mathfrak{C}_->,<\mathfrak{C}_+>)/Z(\mathcal{E})$ is meant that the pair of the cultural energies of yin- and yang-flat systems are immersed in the cultural energy of the virtual operational force of the system $\mathcal{E}$. In other words, this pair of energies is able to flow back to the core energy of the grand system in order to engage in energy transformation into other system(s). Then, by applying the growth impactor Φ^S, we get

(A.4-4-11) $\Phi^S\{<\mathbb{C}_{(-,+)/Z}>\} = < \mathbb{C}_w / \mathfrak{C}_Z> = <\mathbb{C}_w> /Z(\mathcal{E})$,

and by the **reverse** of Φ^S operation (or the invertor of Φ^S operation) to get

(A.4-4-12) $\Phi^{-1} \{<\mathbb{C}_w>/Z(\mathcal{E}\} = w^* \oplus <\mathbb{C}_w> = w$.

(3) The processes of generating y from x and generating x and y from w, etc. are similar to the systematic procedures presented in the above.

Four-element System: The systematic procedures of generating this system are the same as presented previously in this above subsection.

§A.4-5 Legend of Four Dragons

Below we introduce the legend of four dragons as a form of MFCE schemes. (1) From Field dragon to generate yin-flat system (with the cultural complex $<\mathbb{C}_->$) and yang-flat system (with the cultural complex $<\mathbb{C}_+>$). Then by operating the shengsheng impator $\sigma \models \mathcal{Z}\circ,_v\mathcal{H}$ on the yin-yang pair $(<\mathbb{C}_->,<\mathbb{C}_+>)$ to generate Flying dragon. That is, let $\sigma(\mathfrak{C})$: $(<\mathbb{C}_->,<\mathbb{C}_+>) \rightarrow (<\mathbb{C}_->,<\mathbb{C}_+>)/ Z(\mathcal{E})$, with

(A.4-5-1) $(<\mathbb{C}_->,<\mathbb{C}_+>)/Z(\mathcal{E}) = (<\mathbb{C}_->,<\mathbb{C}_+>)/<\mathfrak{C}_S> = <\mathbb{C}_-,\mathbb{C}_+>/<\mathfrak{C}_S> = <(\mathbb{C}_-,\mathbb{C}_+)/\mathfrak{C}_S> = <\mathbb{C}_{(-,+)/Z}>$.

Then, by the operation of the growth impactor Φ^S:
(A.4-5-2) $\Phi^S \{<\mathbb{C}_{(-,+)/Z}>\} =< \mathbb{C}_S/\mathfrak{C}_Z> = <\mathbb{C}_S>/Z(\mathcal{E})$.

And further by the operation of the tao-reversal of Φ^S to get:

(A.4-5-3) $\Phi^{-1}\{<\mathbb{C}_S>/Z(\mathcal{E})\} = \Sigma + <\mathbb{C}_S>$.

(2) To derive Regretting dragon from Flying dragon, let the shengsheng impactor σ operate on the system; that is, $\sigma(\mathfrak{C})$: $<\mathbb{C}_S> \rightarrow <\mathbb{C}_S>/ Z(\mathcal{E})$, with

(A.4-5-4) $<\mathbb{C}_S>/ Z(\mathcal{E}) = <\mathbb{C}_S>/<\mathfrak{C}_Z> = <\mathbb{C}_S/<\mathfrak{C}_Z> = <\mathbb{C}_{S/Z}>$,

where $\mathfrak{C}_Z$ be the culture generator of $Z(\mathcal{E})$. Then, the revertor of the steep-growth impactor Φ^{RV} (Φ^{-1}), we get:

(A.4-5-5) $\Phi^{RV}\{<\mathbb{C}_{S/Z}>\} = <-\mathbb{C}_S/<\mathfrak{C}_Z> =<-\mathbb{C}_S>/Z(\mathcal{E})$.

At last, by reversing the operation of Φ, we get

(A.4-5-6) $\Phi^{-1}\{=<-\mathbb{C}_S>/Z(\mathcal{E}\} = (\Sigma^- + <-\mathbb{C}_S>)^- = \Sigma^- \oplus <-\mathbb{C}_S>$.

(3) To derive Field dragon from Potential dragon.

(4) To derive Potential dragon from Regretting dragon.

This legend of four dragons may be analyzed by the method of reversal construction or the method of systemic-change becoming (see Appendix C).

§A.4-6 SK Scheme

Figure A.4-6-1
Zh(σ,κ)-S scheme with φ(τ) being the virtual center

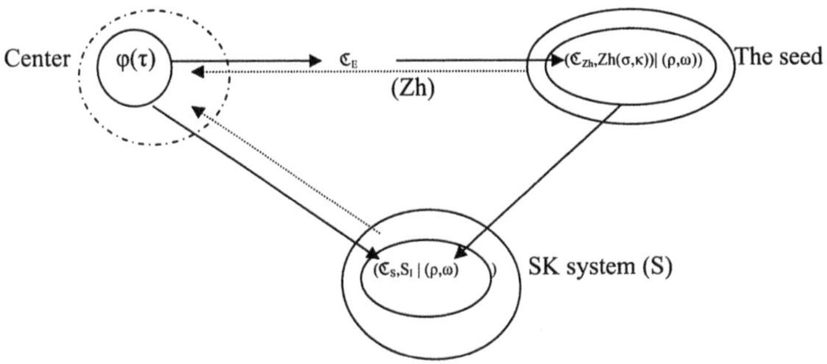

Here in this subsection, we present a scheme of benefit-harm (or tranquility and conflict) in which the relationship between the SK system (i.e., S) is accentuated by the forces of center.

Phase I. We have the 2-pole SK scheme {Zh,S} with φ(τ) as the virtual center with the following characteristics. (1) The seed, Zh(σ,κ), is a becoming of promoting-power (or constructing force, σ) and restraining-power (or destructing force, κ) with σ ↜ τ and κ ↜ τ, with the τ ⊫ 𝔍 ⊪ 𝕋zu* as the ultimate seed of creativity and destructivity. (2) S is a system of benefit and loss. (3) Phase I is the scheme of Zh transforming into S_I (the system S at stage I).

In terms of a graphical presentation we have Figure A.4-6-1.

Phase II. The scheme is the same as in Phase I except that S_I is now replaced by S_{II}.

The mechanism of the intra-phase transformation. Let $\xi_{m+(ih)} \vDash \mathcal{Z}^{\circ},{}_v\mathcal{H}$ be a transformational impactor. Then, (1) for the promoting-power of S at phase I, we have:

$$S_{I,m}(\sigma) \oplus \alpha_0$$
$$\xrightarrow{\xi_{m+1}} S_{I,m+1}(\sigma) \oplus \alpha_1$$
$$\xrightarrow{\xi_{m+2}} S_{I,m+2}(\sigma) \oplus \alpha_2$$
$$\xrightarrow{\xi_{.}} \ldots$$
$$\xrightarrow{\xi_{m+(ih)}} S_{I,m+(ih)}(\sigma) \oplus \alpha^*$$
$$\xrightarrow{\text{leap}} S_{II,0},$$

as h in $i_h \to \infty$ with $\alpha_{m+(ih)} \equiv \alpha^* = \circ$ at the instant (α being a leap factor) that S transforms from phase I to phase II (i.e., a leap) when $S_{I,m+(ih)} = S_{II,0}$.

In the above, we have $\alpha_n \downarrow \alpha$, n = 1,2,…, and $S_{I,(ih)}$ is the form of the system S_I at the time i_h, for the subscript $_{(ih)} \equiv i_h$.

(2) Let $\zeta_{n+(jk)} \vDash \mathcal{Z}^{\circ},_{v}\mathcal{H}$ be a transformational impactor. Then, for the restraining-power of S at phase I, we have:

$$S_{I,n}(\kappa) \oplus \beta_0$$
$$\xrightarrow{\zeta_{m+1}} S_{I,n+1}(\kappa) \oplus \beta_1$$
$$\xrightarrow{\zeta_{m+2}} S_{I,n+2}(\kappa) \oplus \beta_2$$
$$\xrightarrow{\zeta_{.}} \ldots$$
$$\xrightarrow{\zeta_{n+(jk)}} S_{I,n+(jk)}(\kappa) \oplus \beta^*$$
$$\xrightarrow{\text{leap}} S_{II,0},$$

as k in $j_k \to \infty$ with $\beta_{n+(jk)} \equiv \beta^* = \circ$ at the instant (β being a leap factor) that S transforms from phase I to phase II (i.e., a leap) when $S_{I,n+(jk)} = S_{II,0}$.
In the above, we have $\beta_n \downarrow \beta$, n = 1,2,…, and $S_{I,(jk)}$ is the form of the system S_I at the time i_h, for the subscript $_{(jk)} \equiv j_k$.

The mechanism of the inter-phase transformation. Let $\varphi_{m+(ih)} \vDash \mathcal{Z}^{\circ},_{v}\mathcal{H}$ be a transformational impactor. Then,

(1) for the promoting-power of S at phase I, we have:

$$S_{I,m}(\sigma,\kappa) \oplus \gamma_0$$
$$\xrightarrow{\varphi_{m+1}} S_{I,m+1}(\sigma,\kappa) \oplus \gamma_1$$
$$\xrightarrow{\varphi_{m+2}} S_{I,m+2}(\sigma,\kappa) \oplus \gamma_2$$
$$\xrightarrow{\varphi_{.}} \ldots$$

$\varphi_{m+(ih)}$
$\longrightarrow S_{I,m+(ih)}(\sigma,\kappa) \oplus \gamma^*$
leap
$\longrightarrow S_{II,0}$,

as h in $i_h \to \infty$ with $\gamma_{m+(ih)} \equiv \gamma^* = \circ$ at the instant (γ being a leap factor) that S transforms from phase I to phase II (i.e., a leap) when $S_{I,m+(ih)} = S_{II,0}$. In the above, we have $\gamma_n \downarrow \gamma$, n = 1,2,..., and $S_{I,(ih)}$ is the form of the system S_I at the time i_h, for the subscript $_{(ih)} \equiv i_h$.

(2) Let $\psi_{n+(jk)} \models \mathcal{Z}^{\circ},_{v}\mathcal{H}$ be a transformational impactor. Then, for the restraining-power of S at the nth step (n > 0) of phase II to go backward into the 0th step of phase II, we have:

$S_{II,0+}(\sigma,\kappa) \oplus \delta_{0+}$
ψ_{m+1}
$\longrightarrow S_{II,(0+)-1}(\sigma,\kappa) \oplus \delta_{(0+)-1}$
$\longrightarrow S_{II,(0+)-2}(\sigma,\kappa) \oplus \delta_{(0+)-2}$
$\psi.$
$\longrightarrow \ldots$
$\psi_{n+(jk)}$
$\longrightarrow S_{II,(0+)-(jr)}(\sigma,\kappa) \oplus \delta^*$
limit
$\longrightarrow S_{II,0}$
leap
$\longrightarrow S_{I,Last}$,

as r in $j_r \to \infty$ with $\delta_{(0+)-(jr)} \equiv \delta^* = \circ$ at the instant that S transforms from phase I to phase II (i.e., a leap) when $S_{II,0} \equiv S_{II,(0+)-(jr)} = S_{I,Last}$, assuming the unequal partitions of time and (steps and) phases of S are that the initial step of phase II of S is the same as S at the last step of the Phase I at an instantaneous moment of time.

In the above, we have $\delta_n \downarrow \delta^*$, n = -1,-2,-3,..., and $S_{II,0-jr}$ (the initial step of the system S_{II}) at time 0-j_r (say, at the limit as j_r goes to infinity) is the same S at the last step of phase I (i.e., $S_{I,Last}$), with the subscript $_{(jr)} \equiv j_r$.

In the above, the SK scheme describes how does the seed of creativity obtains its strengths (i.e., flows of cultural energy) from the center of the system. Then , this seed grows into the SK system and develop its forces of benefits and harmful acts.

A.5 Various Systemisms

In this section, we shall study various kinds of systemisms. By **systemism** is meant a transformation of one entity into any other entity. Note that iso-systemism and anti-systemism are also part of systemisms. Here, by the **iso-systemism** of two systems is meant these two systems have essentially the same structures, and by the **anti-systemism** of two systems is meant these two systems have essentially the opposite structures.

§A.5-1 Iso-systemism and Anti-systemism

Definition A.5-1-1 (general iso-systemism). Let X = $(x_1,x_2,\ldots,x_m|R_{X1},R_{X2},\ldots,R_{Xn})$ and Y = $(y_1,y_2,\ldots,y_m|\ R_{Y1},R_{Y2},\ldots,R_{Yn}) \sqsubseteq (\Omega,\mathcal{Z}\circ,_v\mathcal{H},\{\mathbb{C}\})$, m, n $\in \mathbb{N}$, be two separate systems. Then the transformation from X to Y or vice versa is said to be a **general iso-systemism** if and only if the following conditions hold:

i). These two systems have exactly the same number of elements.

ii). They have exactly the same number of relations.

iii). The transformation (φ,ψ) from X to Y is a general iso-yin-yang transformation with the concept of the general iso-yin-yang transformation ($\varphi(x_i) = y_i$, i $\in \mathbb{N}$, $\psi(R_{Xj}) = R_{Yj}$, j $\in \mathbb{N}$) to be specifically defined.

Definition A.5-1-2 (iso-systemism). Let X = $(x_1,x_2,\ldots,x_m|R_{X1},R_{X2},\ldots,R_{Xn})$ and Y = $(y_1,y_2,\ldots, y_m|R_{Y1},R_{Y2},\ldots,R_{Yn}) \sqsubseteq (\Omega,\mathcal{Z}\circ,_v\mathcal{H},\{\mathbb{C}\})$, m, n $\in \mathbb{N}$, be two separate systems. Then the transformation from X to Y or vice versa is said to be an **iso-systemism** if and only if the following conditions hold:

i). These two systems have exactly the same number of elements.

ii). They have exactly the same number of relations.

iii). The transformation (φ,ψ) from X to Y is an iso-yin-yang transformation with the concept of iso-yin-yang transformation ($\varphi(x_i) = y_i$, i $\in \mathbb{N}$, $\psi(R_{Xj}) = R_{Yj}$, j $\in \mathbb{N}$) to be specifically defined.

Example A.5-1-1. In Confucian there are five relations: the ruler and ruled, father and son, elder brother and younger brother, one and his friend, and husband and wife.[46] These are the five cardinal relations forming mutual yin-yang pairs: Ruler is benevolent and the subject is loyal, father is parochially caring and son is a filially pious, elder brother loves the younger brother while the younger brother respects elder brother, friends treating each other with righteousness, and there are differences between husband and wife.

These systems – (inferior,master|benevolence-loyalty), (son,father|parental care-filial piety), (younger brother,elder brother|brotherly care-respect), (friend,friend| righteousness), (wife,husband|differentiation) $\sqsubseteq (\Omega,\mathcal{Z}\circ,_v\mathcal{H},\{\mathbb{C}\})\sqcap\mathbb{R}$ -- are iso-systemic to each other because each system has the identical structures of two (human) elements and one relation, and according to Confucian doctrine, benevolence-loyalty, parental care-filial piety, brotherly care-respect, righteousness and differentiation (or loving-and- respecting affectionately between each other) are regarded as the transformations in a symbolic way of the same relation to fit different social strata. In the following, we illustrate the iso-systemism between (inferior,master|benevolence-loyalty) and (son,father| parental care-filial piety):

Figure A.5-1-1
Master/benevolence-inferior/loyalty

National ethics φ	Emperor
Inferior	Benevolence-loyalty

Figure A.5-1-2
Father/parental care-son/filial piety

Family ethics ψ	Father
Son	Parental care-filial piety

In Figures A.5-1-1 and A.5-1-2, φ(emperor,inferior) stands for the "benevolence-loyalty," and ψ(father,son) stands for the "parental care-filial piety;" and these relationships are in a yin-yang pair (benevolence-loyalty, parental care-filial piety).

Figure A.5-1-3
Emperor/benevolence-inferior/ loyalty

National ethics *	Emperor
Inferior	Benevolence-loyalty

Figure A.5-1-4
Father/parental care-son/filial piety

Family ethics ▫	Father
Son	Parental care-filial piety

Thema A.5-1-1. By transforming to mathematics and with $\varphi = \psi$, an iso-systemism is an isomorphism.

Supporting reasoning. The relationship between (benevolence-loyalty) and (parental care-filial piety) is one of "isomorphism" in mathematics if we define a "function" π: $x \rightarrow y$ for $x \in$ {inferior,emperor,benevolence-loyalty}and $y \in$ {son,father,parental care-filial piety} because π is a 1-1 correspondence and emperor* inferior = benevolence-loyalty, π(emperor*inferior) = π(benevolence-loyalty) = parental care-filial piety, while π(emperor) ▫ π(inferior) = father ▫ Son = parental care-filial piety so that π(emperor*inferior) = π(emperor) ▫ π(inferior). Here, "▫" is a notation for an 1-1 functional mapping of x into y.

For the relevant figures, see Figures A.5-1-3 and A.5-1-4:

Definition A.5-1-3 (Anti-systemism). Let $X = (x_1,x_2,\ldots,x_m|R_{X1},R_{X2},\ldots,R_{Xn})$ and $Y = (y_1,y_2,\ldots,y_m| R_{Y1},R_{Y2},\ldots,R_{Yn}) \sqsubseteq (\Omega,\mathcal{Z}^{\circ},{}_{v}\mathcal{H},\{\mathbb{C}\})$, $m, n \in \mathbb{N}$, be two separate systems. Then the transformation from X to Y or vice versa is said to be an **anti-systemism** if and only if the following conditions hold:

i). These two systems have exactly the same number of elements.

ii). They have exactly the same number of relations.

iii). The transformation (φ,ψ) from X to Y is an anti-yin-yang transformation with the concept of anti-yin-yang transformation ($\varphi(x_i) = y_i$, $i \in \mathbb{N}$, $\psi(R_{Xj}) = R_{Yj}$, $j \in \mathbb{N}$) to be specifically defined.

Figure A.5-1-5
Capitalist cultural economy

Capitalist ethics*	Government
People	Market

Figure A.5-1-6
Socialist cultural economy

Socialist ethics	Government
People	Economic planning

Let {government,people|market}, {government,people|planning} $\sqsubseteq (\Omega, \mathcal{Z}^{\circ}, {}_{v}\mathcal{H}, \{\mathbb{C}\}) \sqcap \mathbb{R}$ be two systems, and capitalist ethics*{government,people} = market, socialist ethics $\circ$ {government,people} = economic planning. They are anti-systemic to each other because each system has two (human) elements and one relation, and according to our understanding, "{government, people | capitalist ethics*, market} $\rightarrow$ {government, people | socialist ethics, economic planning}" are regarded as the transformations in a symbolic way of the opposite relation to fit different social strata. For the relevant figures, see Figures A.5-1-5 and A.5-1-6.

§A.5-2 The d-, y-, f-, Hf, h-, and Hh-systemisms

Some of the methods used in our studies of socio-cultural events are the methods based on the concepts of *similarities* (or iso-systemism), *yinyang complements* (or y-systemism), *differences* (d-systemism), *connections* (c-systemism), *yinyang change* (or reversal) (rev- or f-systemism), *opposition (or negation)* (Hf-systemism), and the *negation of negation* (Hh-systemism) among things, phenomena or events. In dealing with the problems of natural sciences, scientific rationality is extremely helpful. But for dealing with cultural and social issues, systemic rationality is essential. Note that systemic rationality enables us to see big pictures beyond the confinement of each specific field typically studied in sciences and fields of engineering.

Definition A.5-2-1a (y-systemism). Let $X = (x_1,x_2,\ldots,x_m|R_{X1}, R_{X2},\ldots,R_{Xm})$ and $Y = (y_1,y_2,\ldots,y_n| R_{Y1},R_{Y2},\ldots,R_{Yn}) \sqsubseteq (\Omega, \mathcal{Z}^{\circ}, {}_{v}\mathcal{H}, \{\mathbb{C}\})$, $m, n \in \mathbb{N}$, be two separate systems. Then the transformation from X to Y or vice versa is said to be a **y-systemism** if and only if the following conditions hold:

i). These two systems have exactly the same number of elements.

ii). They have exactly the same number of relations.

iii). The transformation $(\varphi,\psi) \models \mathbb{Z}^{\circ,\vee}\mathbb{H}$ from X to Y is a y-yin-yang transformation with the concept of the y-yin-yang transformation ($\varphi(x_i) = y_i$, $i \in \mathbb{N}$, $\psi(R_{Xj}) = R_{Yj}$, $j \in \mathbb{N}$) to be specifically defined. Note that X and Y form a yin-yang pair and the relationship between X and Y may be either harmonious or complementary.

Here, by the transformation (φ,ψ) from X to Y to be a y-systemism is meant that $X \neq Y$.

Definition A.5-2-1b (alternative y-systemism). Let $X = (x_1,x_2,\ldots,x_m| R_{X1},R_{X2},\ldots, R_{Xm})$ and $Y = (y_1,y_2,\ldots,y_n| R_{Y1},R_{Y2},\ldots,R_{Yn}) \sqsubseteq (\Omega,\mathbb{Z}^{\circ,\vee}\mathbb{H},\{\mathbb{C}\})$, m, n $\in \mathbb{N}$, be two separate systems. Then the transformation from X to Y or vice versa is said to be a **y-systemism** if and only if the transformation $(\varphi,\psi) \models \mathbb{Z}^{\circ,\vee}\mathbb{H}$ from X to Y is a y-yin-yang transformation with the concept of the y-yin-yang transformation ($\varphi(x_i) = y_j$, $i \in \mathbb{N}$, $\psi(R_{Xi}) = R_{Yj}$, $j \in \mathbb{N}$) to be specifically defined.

Note that X and Y form a yin-yang pair and the relationship between X and Y may be either harmonious or complementary.

Definition A.5-2-2 (d-systemism). Let $X = (x_1,x_2,\ldots,x_m|R_{X1},R_{X2},\ldots,R_{Xn})$ and $Y = (y_1,y_2,\ldots,y_m| R_{Y1},R_{Y2},\ldots,R_{Yn}) \sqsubseteq (\Omega,\mathbb{Z}^{\circ,\vee}\mathbb{H},\{\mathbb{C}\})$, m, n $\in \mathbb{N}$, be two separate systems. Then the transformation from X to Y or vice versa is said to be a **d-systemism** if and only if the following conditions hold:

i). These two systems have exactly the same number of elements.

ii). They have exactly the same number of relations.

iii). The transformation (φ,ψ) from X to Y is a d-yin-yang transformation with the concept of the d-yin-yang transformation ($\varphi(x_i) = y_i$, $i \in \mathbb{N}$, $\psi(R_{Xj}) = R_{Yj}$, $j \in \mathbb{N}$) to be specifically defined.

Here, by the transformation (φ,ψ) from X to Y to be a d-yin-yang transformation is meant $X \neq Y$ ($x_i \neq y_i$ and $R_{Xj} \neq R_{Yj}$, $i, j \in \mathbb{N}$) as well.

Thema A.5-2-1. d-systemism is a special case of the "general iso-systemsim."

Supporting reasoning. By Definitions A.5-1-1 and A.5-2-2, for i), we have the same process of reasoning; and for ii) we also have the same process of reasoning. For iii), d yin-yang transformation is a special case of the general iso-yin-yang transformation.

Definition A.5-2-3 (Alternative definition, d-systemism). Let x and y be universal elements. If $f(x) = y \neq x$, then f is a one-dimensional impactor of d-systemism on x. In general, let $\Delta_1 = (a,b,..,c|R) \sqsubseteq (\Omega,\mathbb{Z}^{\circ,\vee}\mathbb{H},\{\mathbb{C}\})$ be an $m \times n$ system, a, b, .., c being universal elements, and R a specific relationship among these elements. Then ξ is said to be an impactor of **d-systemism** if

(A.5-2-1) $\xi\{\Delta_1\} \neq \Delta_1$.

For example, for

(A.5-2-2) $\Delta_1 = |a \setminus c|^T$,

and

(A.5-2-3) $\xi\{\Delta_1\} = |(a\ \ b) \setminus c|^T$,

ξ is an impactor of (2×1 bi-system : 2×1 tri-system) for c being another universal element. Note that for this d-systemism to be meaningful, when $\xi\{\Delta_1\} \neq \Delta_1$, we may require the difference between them to be significant according to a specific set of criteria.

Definition A.5-2-4a (f-systemism or reversal-systemism). Let $X = (x_1, x_2, \ldots, x_m | R_{X1}, R_{X2}, \ldots, R_{Xn})$ and $Y = (y_1, y_2, \ldots, y_m | R_{Y1}, R_{Y2}, \ldots, R_{Yn}) \sqsubseteq (\Omega, \mathcal{Z}\circ, {}_v\mathcal{H}, \{\mathbb{C}\})$, m, n $\in \mathbb{N}$, be two separate systems. Then the transformation from X to Y or vice versa is said to be an **f-systemism** (or reversal-systemism) if and only if the following conditions hold:

i). These two systems have exactly the same number of elements.

ii). They have exactly the same number of relations.

iii). The transformation (φ,ψ) from X to Y is an f-yin-yang transformation with the concept of the f-yin-yang transformation ($\varphi(x_i) = y_i$, $i \in \mathbb{N}$, $\psi(R_{Xj}) = R_{Yj}$, $j \in \mathbb{N}$) to be specifically defined.

Here, by the transformation (φ,ψ) from X to Y to be an f-systemism is meant (1) $X \neq Y$ and (2) Y is either at the same stage (or two-step) development of X or is a one-stage (or one-step) higher development of X with the concept of same-stage (or same-step) and one-stage (or one-step) higher developments to be defined specifically. That is, we have either (1) X and Y being in a yin-yang pair or (2) X and Y being opposite to each other.

Note that these relations are, in general, in the metaphorical sense of yin-yang pairs (anti-yin-yang pairs, quasi-yin-yang pairs, or other types of yin-yang pairs to be specifically defined).

Definition A.5-2-4b (alternative f-systemism). Let $X = (x_1, x_2, \ldots, x_m | R_{X1}, R_{X2}, \ldots, R_{Xm})$ and $Z = (z_1, z_2, \ldots, z_n | R_{z1}, R_{z2}, \ldots, R_{zn}) \sqsubseteq (\Omega, \mathcal{Z}\circ, {}_v\mathcal{H}, \{\mathbb{C}\})$, m, n $\in \mathbb{N}$, be two separate systems. Then the transformation from X to Z is said to be an **f-systemism** if and only if the following conditions hold:

i). The transformation $(\varphi,\psi) \vDash \mathcal{Z}\circ, {}_v\mathcal{H}$ from X to Z is one of transforming into the opposite of X, with the concept of opposite transformation ($\varphi(X) = Z$, $i \in \mathbb{N}$, $\psi(R_{Xj}) = R_{Zj}$, $j \in \mathbb{N}$) to be specifically defined.

ii). X and Z form a yin-yang pair and the relationship between X and Z may be in conflict or in tranquility.

iii). In the static case, Z and X are at the same stage (or step) of development; while in the dynamic case, either Z (R_{Zm}, respectively) is at a one-stage (or one-step) higher than that of X (R_{Xm}, respectively).

Definition A.5-2-5 (Hf-systemism). Let $X = (x_1,x_2,\dots,x_m|R_{X1},R_{X2},\dots,R_{Xn})$ and $Y = (y_1,y_2,\dots,y_m|R_{Y1},R_{Y2},\dots,R_{Yn}) \sqsubseteq (\Omega,\mathcal{Z}^{o},{}_{v}\mathcal{H},\{\mathbb{C}\})$, m, n ∈ ℕ, be two separate systems. Then the transformation from X to Y and vice versa is said to be an **Hf-systemism** if and only if the following conditions hold:

i). These two systems have exactly the same number of elements.

ii). They have exactly the same number of relations.

iii). The transformation φ from X to Y (i.e., φ(X) = Y) is a Hegelian opposition-transformation with y_i being the opposition of x_i, for each i ∈ ℕ, and R_{Yj} is the one-step (or half-stage) higher development of R_{Xj}, for each j ∈ ℕ. Note that, here, each y_i is a one-step (or half-stage) development of x_1, and each R_{Yj} is the opposite of R_{Xj}, for j ∈ ℕ. Here, in addition, the concept of opposition shall be specifically defined in the context of the problem.

Definition A.5-2-6 (Alternative definition of f-systemism). Let $\mathbb{C}_x$ (i.e., generators of the cultural complex of X), $\mathbb{C}_y$ (i.e., generators of the cultural complex of X) ⊫U be universal elements, $\mathfrak{R}$ be a set of relationship among these elements, and $\{\mathbb{C}_x,\mathbb{C}_y|\mathfrak{R}\}$ form a system. Then $\xi \models \mathcal{Z}^{o},{}_{v}\mathcal{H}$ is an impactor of **f-systemism** if

(A.5-2-4) $\xi\{\mathbb{C}_x\} = \mathbb{C}_y$ or $\xi\{\mathbb{C}_y\} = \mathbb{C}_x$

for $(\mathbb{C}_x,\mathbb{C}_y|\mathfrak{R})$ being a system.

For an example, let the economic culture $\mathbb{C}_E$ and the political culture $\mathbb{C}_P$ share a fundamental core $\mathfrak{C}_{EP}^{co}$. Then for

(A.5-2-5) $\xi\{\mathbb{C}_E\} = \mathfrak{C}_P$, or $\xi\{\mathbb{C}_P\} = \mathbb{C}_E$,

where ξ is an impactor of f-systemism from the set $\mathbb{C}_E$ to $\mathbb{C}_P$ or vice versa.

Definition A.5-2-7 (h-systemism). Let x, y, z ⊫ **U** (or x, y, z $\sqsubseteq (\Omega,\mathcal{Z}^{o},{}_{v}\mathcal{H},\{\mathbb{C}\})$). Then for x transforming into y and y transforming into z (denoted as: x → y → z) is said to be an **h-systemism** if and only if the following conditions hold:

(1) x → y is y systmeism.

(2) y → z is a y-systemism.

(3) The underlying culture of {x,y,z} is one of tranquil culture.

Definition A.5-2-8 (h-systemism I). Let $X = (x_1,x_2,\dots,x_m|R_{X1}, R_{X2}, \dots,R_{Xn})$, $Y = (y_1,y_2,\dots,y_m|R_{Y1},R_{Y2},\dots,R_{Yn})$ and $Z = (z_1,z_2,\dots,z_m| R_{Z1},R_{Z2},\dots,R_{Zn}) \sqsubseteq (\Omega,\mathcal{Z}^{o},{}_{v}\mathcal{H},\{\mathbb{C}\})$, m, n ∈ ℕ, be three separate systems. Then the transformation from the yin-yang pair (X,Y) to Z or vice versa is said to be an **h-systemism II** if and only if the following conditions hold:

i). These three systems have exactly the same number of elements.

ii). They have exactly the same number of relations.

iii). The transformation of φ from X to Y (i.e., Y = φX with $R_{Yi} = \varphi R_{Xi}$) or vice versa is a y-systemism.

iv).The transformation of ψ from (X,Y) = (X,φX) to Z is a y-yinyang transformation with the concept of y-yinyang transformation $\psi(x_i,y_i) = z_i$, $i \in \mathbb{N}$ and $\psi(R_{Xj},R_{Yj}) = R_{Zj}$, $j \in \mathbb{N}$, for $\varphi x_i = y_i$, $\varphi R_{Xj} = R_{Yj}$, to be specifically defined.

Here, by the transformation (φ,ψ) from X to Z to be an h-systemism is meant X $\neq$ X and Z is a one-stage higher development of (X,Y) for both Y and X being at the same stage of development.

Definition A.5-2-9 (h-systemism II). Let $\mathbb{C}_x$ and $\mathbb{C}_y \Vdash \mathbf{U}$ be universal elements. Then $\xi \vDash \mathcal{Z}\circ,_v\mathcal{H}$ is an impactor of **h-systemism II** if $\mathbb{C}^H$ is the system of higher step (or stage) development out of $(\mathbb{C}_x,\mathbb{C}_y|\mathcal{R})$, or $\mathbb{C}^H = (\mathbb{C}_x,\mathbb{C}_y|\mathcal{R})^H$, for $(\mathbb{C}_x,\mathbb{C}_y|\mathcal{R})$ being a system with $\mathcal{R}$ denoting a specific set of relations.

Definition A.5-2-10 (y^L-systemism). The transformation of x $\rightarrow$ y is said to be a **y^L-systemism** if and only if the following conditions hold: (1) The transformation from x to y is a y-systemism. (2) The transformation from (x,y) to z is a y-systemism. (3) The transformation from (x,y) to z is at a category different from, but not higher than, the transformation from x to y. (4) The underlying culture of {x,y,z} is one of tranquility.

Definition A.5-2-11 (h^L-systemism). The transformation from x to z is said to be a h^L-**systemism** if and only if the following conditions hold: (1) The transformation from x to y is a y-systemism. (2) The transformation from (x,y) to z is a y-systemism. (3) The transformation from (x,y) to z is at a category higher than the transformation from x to y. (4) The underlying culture of {x,y,z} is one of tranquility.

Definition A.5-2-12 (h^L-systemism I). The transformation from x to z (x $\rightarrow$z) is said to be an **h^L-systemism I** if and only is the following conditions hold:

(1) x $\rightarrow$ y is a y-systemism.

(2) y $\rightarrow$ z is a y-systemism.

(3) (x,y) $\rightarrow$ z is a one-step (or stage) higher category or development. Here, y is the yang component of x in one category and z is the yang component of (x,y) in a different category. Note that, "y being the yang component of x" means x is the "yin component" of y.

(4) z and (x,y) are in a center-noncentral relation. Note that this does not imply a top-down or master-subject relationship.

Definition A.5-2-13 (h^L-systemism II). Let X = $(x_1,x_2,\ldots,x_m|R_{X1}, R_{X2},\ldots,R_{Xn})$, Y = $(y_1,y_2,\ldots,y_m|R_{Y1},R_{Y2},\ldots,R_{Yn})$ and Z = $(z_1,z_2,\ldots,z_m| R_{Z1},R_{Z2},\ldots,R_{Zn}) \sqsubseteq (\Omega,\mathcal{Z}\circ,_v\mathcal{H},\{\mathbb{C}\})$, m, n $\in \mathbb{N}$, be three separate systems. Then the transformation from the yin-yang pair (X,Y) to Z or vice versa is said to be an **h^L-systemism II** if and only if the following conditions hold:

i). These three systems have exactly the same number of elements.

ii). They have exactly the same number of relations.

iii). The transformation of φ from X to Y (i.e., $Y = \varphi X$ with $R_{Yi} = \varphi R_{Xi}$) or vice versa is a y-systemism. That is, y is a yang component of x.

iv).The transformation of ψ from (X,Y) = (X,φX) to Z is an y-systemism with the concept of y-yinyang transformation $\psi(x_i,y_i) = z_i$, $i \in \mathbb{N}$ and $\psi(R_{Xj},R_{Yj}) = R_{Zj}$, $j \in \mathbb{N}$, for $\varphi x_i = y_i$, $\varphi R_{Xj} = R_{Yj}$, to be specifically defined. That is, z is a yang component of (x,y).
Definition A.5-2-14 (y^R-systemism). The transformation from x to z is said to be a y^R-systemism if and only if the following conditions hold: (1) The transformation from x to y is a y-systemism. That is, y is a yang component of x. (2) The transformation from y to z is a y-systemism. That is, z is a yang component of y. (3) The yang component of x and the yang component of y are at different categories. (4) The underlying culture of {x,y,z} is one of tranquility.

Definition A.5-2-15 (h^R-systemism). The transformation form x to z is said to be an h^R-systemism if and only if the following conditions hold:

(1) The transformation from x to y is a y-systemism. That is, y is a yang component of x and y is at a category or level of development higher than that of x.

(2) The transformation from y to z is a y-systemism. That is, z is a yang component of y and z is at a category higher than y.

(3) The category of y being the yang component of x is higher than the category of z being the yang component of y.

(4) The underlying culture of {x,y,z} is one of tranquility.

Definition A.5-2-16 (h^R-systemism I). The transformation from x to z ($x \rightarrow z$) is said to be an **h^R-systemism I** if and only is the following conditions hold:

(1) $x \rightarrow y$ is a y-systemism and one-step (or stage) higher in category or development.

(2) $y \rightarrow z$ is a y-systemism and one-step (or stage) higher in category or development.

(3) z and (x,y) form a top-down yin-yang pair.

Definition A.5-2-17 (Hh-systemism). Let $Y = (y_1,y_2,\ldots,y_m|R_{Y1}, R_{Y2},\ldots,R_{Yn})$ and $Z = (z_1,z_2,\ldots,z_m| R_{Z1},R_{Z2},\ldots,R_{Zn}) \sqsubseteq (\Omega,\mathcal{Z}^o,{}_v\mathcal{H},\{\mathbb{C}\})$, m, n $\in \mathbb{N}$, be two separate systems with Y being the Hegelian f-systemism of $X = (x_1,x_2,\ldots,x_m|R_{X1}, R_{X2},\ldots,R_{Xn})$. Then the transformation from Y to Z or vice versa is said to be an **Hh-systemism** if and only if the following conditions hold:
i). These two systems have exactly the same number of elements.

ii). They have exactly the same number of relations.

iii). The transformation ψ from Y to Z (i.e., $\psi(Y) = Z$) is a Hegelian opposition-transformation, with z_i being the opposition of y_i, for each $i \in \mathbb{N}$, and R_{Zj} is also the opposition of R_{Yj}. In the static case, z_i and y_i are at different categories (with this concept to be defined). And yet in the dynamical case, z_i is a one-step (or half-stage) higher development of

y_i, for each $i \in \mathbb{N}$, and R_{Zj} is a one-step (or half-stage) higher development of R_{Yj}, for each $j \in \mathbb{N}$. Here the concept of opposition shall be specifically defined in the context of the problem.

iv). The transformation $\psi\{\varphi\}$ from X to Z (i.e., $\psi\{\varphi(X)\} = \psi(Y) = Z$) is a Hegelian synthetic transformation (or synthesis) from the thesis X to Z. In the static case, the transformation occurs at different categories, and similarly for the transformation from R_{Xj} to R_{Zj}, for each $j \in \mathbb{N}$. Here, for the synthetic transformation (or synthesis) $\hat{h}$ of X to Z, $\hat{h} = \psi\{\varphi(.)\}$, we write $\hat{h} = \varphi^2(.)$. But in the dynamical case, z_i is a two-step (or one-stage) development of x_i, for each $i \in \mathbb{N}$, and similarly, this synthesis transformation $\hat{h}$ of X to Z is a two-stage development from X to Z.

Examples of d-, f- and h-systemisms. In order to provide examples of d-, f- and h-systemisms, let us at first set up the system of marriage/production.

The system of marriage/production. The formation of a system out of elements of a , b $\sqsubseteq$ **U** for a = a(y-), b = b(y+) (y- and y+ being yin- and yang-element, respectively), $\mathcal{T} \models \mathcal{Z}\circ,_{v}\mathcal{H}$ is:

(A.5-2-6) $\{(\mathcal{T}X=<T^{C\Delta}) \sqsubseteq Ш^{\Delta}\} \Leftrightarrow X = a \oplus^{TC} b$,

where X = (a,b) $\sqsubseteq (\Omega,\mathcal{Z}\circ,_{v}\mathcal{H},\{\mathbb{C}\})$. Here by "a $\oplus^{TC}$ b" is meant that a and b form a system at the state of Tcentral. Let $\mathcal{M} \models \mathcal{Z}\circ,_{v}\mathcal{H}$ be the marriage impactor. Then the $\mathcal{T}$(a,b) is a marriage system if and only if the following condition holds:

(A.5-2-7) $\mathcal{T}(a,b) = \{a(y-) \oplus^{TC} b(y+)\} = (a,b)(y-,y+) = \mathcal{M}(a,b)$.

That is, a(y-) of yin-element and b(y+) of yang-element are in marriage-balance at a state of Tcentral. This is closely related to the system of a family. Let the simple family be: {(s,d),m|f} $\sqsubseteq (\Omega,\mathcal{Z}\circ,_{v}\mathcal{H},\{\mathbb{C}\})$, for s(son), d(daughter), m(mother), f(father) $\Vdash$ **H**.

In this family, the culture of father and mother is the virtual operating force of the family system, from which it eventually transforms into the culture of the son and daughter. In conventional economic terminology, this family culture will transform into the family culture-capital, and the so-called social culture-capital is the collection of all these family culture-capital in a society.

Assuming this family has a culture of tranquility. Then let

(A.5-2-8) $X = \{X_1, X_2, \ldots, X_n\}$,

(A.5-2-9) $\{X, \{Y_k, Y_j\}\} \Leftarrow <\mathbb{C}_X>$,

(A.5-2-10) $Y_j \equiv [(X_1, \mathbb{C}_{X1/Z}), (X_2, \mathbb{C}_{X2/Z}), \ldots, (X_n, \mathbb{C}_{Xn/Z}) | (C, \sigma(C))]$,
(A.5-2-11) $Y_k \equiv [(C, \mathbb{C}_{C/Z}) | ((X_1, \xi_1(X_1)), (X_2, \xi_2(X_2)), \ldots, (X_n, \xi_n(X_n))]$,

where C is the center of the system , and $\xi_i \models \mathcal{Z}\circ,_{v}\mathcal{H}$, i = 1,2,…,n .
In the above, Y_j represents the role of the center, Y_k the forces of the counter-center activities of the non-central elements, C the center of the system, and σ(C) the role of the center.

In addition, let $n = 3$, $i \neq k, j$, $X_1 = $ (son,daughter), X_2 being the mother, X_3 being the father. Applying the principle of Tcentral: $\psi\{Y_j > Y_k, \Delta_i\} \barwedge \tau$ to this family system $X = \{$(son, daughter), mother|father$\} = \{X_1, X_2, \ldots, X_n\}$, $n = 3$, $i \neq k, j$, yields :

(A.5-2-12) $\psi\{[\mathbb{C}_{(S,D)/Z}, \mathbb{C}_{M/Z} | \sigma(F)] > [(\zeta(M), \mathbb{C}_{F/Z}) | \xi(S,D)], \Delta_i\} \barwedge [\mathbb{C}_X \Leftarrow E]$,

for $\psi, \sigma, \xi, \zeta \models \mathcal{Z}o,_v\mathcal{H}$, where $\mathbb{C}_{(S,D)/Z}$ represents the culture of son and daughter in the subsystem $[.|\sigma(F)]$, $\mathbb{C}_{M/Z}$ the culture of mother in the subsystem $[.|\sigma(F)]$, $\mathbb{C}_{F/Z}$ the culture of the family under the virtual operating forces $Z \equiv Z(\pounds)$ of the system, $\sigma(F)$ the cultural energy of the father (as the center of the subsystem $[\mathbb{C}_{(S,D)/Z}, \mathbb{C}_{M/Z} | \sigma(F)]$), $\zeta(M)$ the cultural energy of the mother in the subsystem $[.|\xi(S,D)]$, $\mathbb{C}_{F/Z}$ the cultural energy of the father in the subsystem $[.|\xi(S,D)]$, and $\xi(S,D)$ the cultural energy of the sons and daughter serving as the center of the subsystem $[.|\xi(S,D)]$. In addition, in the above, S ,D, M and F denote the son, daughter, mother and father, respectively, with the family's cultural energy operating under the total energy of the environment (i.e., under the global Faziranist culture).

Here by Bcm. (A.5-2-12), or the sTc (special Tcentral) of a family, is meant: to ensure the force of Y_j operating in the universal dynamics (i.e., Δ_i or X_i operating in Δ), the impact of the active operation of the father toward the son or daughter (and the mother to the son or daughter) – love and guiding role -- is greater than the force of Y_k, i.e., the impact of the anti-active (i.e., counter-active) operation of the son toward the father or mother (and the daughter toward the father or mother) -- love in respect and willingness to follow the guidance of one's parents.

Furthermore, let $i = 1,2,\ldots,n$, $n > 3$, $i \neq k, j$. By applying the principle of mediety-centrality: $\psi\{Y_j > Y_k, \Delta_i\} \barwedge \tau$ to the family system X, $i = 1,2,\ldots,n$, $n > 3$, $i \neq k, j$, yields the **principle of centrality**:

(A.5-2-13) $\psi\{[\mathbb{C}_{X1/Z}, \mathbb{C}_{X2/Z}, \ldots, \mathbb{C}_{Xn/Z} | (C, \sigma(C))] > [(C, \mathfrak{C}_{C/Z}) | (\xi_1(X_1), \xi_2(X_2), \ldots, \xi_n(X_n))], \Delta_i\}$
$\barwedge [\mathbb{C}_X \Leftarrow E]$,

Note that, in the above, each of $\xi_1(X_1)$, $\xi_2(X_2)$, …, and $\xi_n(X_n)$ serves as a co-central subsystem of the grand system $[(C, \mathfrak{C}_{C/Z}) | (\xi_1(X_1), \xi_2(X_2), \ldots, \xi_n(X_n))]$. In the above scheme of a family of 4-polars: $\{(s,d), m|f\} \sqsubseteq (\Omega, \mathcal{Z}o,_v\mathcal{H}, \{C\})$, s, d, m, f $\Vdash$ **H**, $\mathcal{M}$, $\mathcal{T} \models \mathcal{Z}o,_v\mathcal{H}$, let $\mathcal{T}(a,b) = \{a(y-) \oplus^{TC} b(y+)\} = \mathcal{M}(a,b)$ be the marriage/production impactor. Then both $X_1 = \{d, m_1 | f_1\} \sqsubseteq \Omega$ and $X_2 = \{s, m_2 | f_2\} \sqsubseteq \Omega$ are 3-polar systems in which f_i is the center, m_i the second center, and s and d non-center members in their respective family systems.

We could also designate any member of the system or family as: $x_i = \mathcal{S}(\varphi(A_{i1}\text{-}A_{i2}, \varphi)\text{-}\psi(D_{i1}\text{-}D_{i2})\text{-}E(\mathbb{C}_{xi1}, \mathbb{C}_{xi2}))$ in the format of **transitional energy SBC** (systematic becoming chain) with $\mathcal{S}$ referring to an energy-generated impactor, E(.) denoting an energy system, and A_{ij} and D_{ij} representing the static and dynamical structures of system i, respectively, for $j = 1, 2$ ($j = 1$ being the yin-side and $j = 2$ being yang-side). Here $\varphi(A_{i1}\text{-}A_{i2})$ and $\psi(D_{i1}\text{-}D_{i2})$ stand for the systemic structures of A and D, respectively, and $\mathbb{C}_{i1}$ and $\mathbb{C}_{i2}$ representing the cultural generators of system i, for $j = 1$ being the yin-side and $j = 2$ being yang-side.

Let $f_i \Vdash X_i$ (the father in family i, $i = 1, 2$) be: $f_i = \varphi\{A_{i1}, A_{i2}\}\psi\{D_{i1}, D_{i2}\} \oplus \mathcal{S}\langle C_1, C_2\rangle$, wherein $\{A_1, A_2, D_1, D_2 | (\mathbb{C}_1, \mathbb{C}_2)\}$ is a 5-polar sub-system (A_{1j} and D_{1j} representing the static and dynamical structures of system 1, respectively; $j = 1, 2$ for $j = 1$ being the yin-side and $j = 2$ being yang-side), and $(\mathbb{C}_{i1}, \mathbb{C}_{i2})$ is the pair of double-centers ($\mathbb{C}_{i1}$ and $\mathbb{C}_{i2}$ representing the cultural generators of system 1, for j = 1 being the yin-side and j = 2 being yang-side). Similarly, let $s = \varphi\{A_{s1},A_{s2}\}\psi\{D_{s1},D_{s2}\} \oplus \mathcal{S}\langle \mathbb{C}_{s1},\mathbb{C}_{s2}\rangle$, wherein $\{A_{s1},A_{s2},D_{s1},D_{s2}| (\mathbb{C}_{s1},\mathbb{C}_{s2})\}$ is a 5-polar system, and $(\mathbb{C}_{s1},\mathbb{C}_{s2})$ is the pair of double-centers. Note that for the son $s = \varphi\{A_{s1},A_{s2}\}\psi\{D_{s1},D_{s2}\} \oplus \mathcal{S}\langle \mathbb{C}_{s1},\mathbb{C}_{s2}\rangle$, $\mathbb{C}_{s1}$ could represent the culture inherited from his mother-side, $\mathbb{C}_{s2}$ the culture inherited from his father-side.

Given the first family $X_1 = \{d_1|(f_1,m_1)\}$ and the second family $X_2 = \{s_2|(f_2,m_2)\}$, the young family $X_3 = \{w_3,h_3\}= \{d_1,s_2\} \sqsubseteq \Omega$ is created, with w_3 and h_3 referring to the wife (i.e., the daughter of the first family) and husband (i.e., the son of the second family) of the new family. Then in $f_3(.|t_1) = Ш_{0\to1}s_2(.|t_0)$, $Ш_{0\to1} \vDash \mathcal{Z}\circ,_v\mathcal{H}$ as a creative impactor is an impactor of h-systemism. At the same time, in $Ш_{0\to1}s_2(.|t_0) = f(.|t_1)$, $Ш_{0\to1} \vDash \mathcal{Z}\circ,_v\mathcal{H}$ as a creative impactor is an impactor of d-systemism as well. In this case, the impactor of (new-element creating) d-systemism is $Ш_{0\to1}\{f_3(.|t_0),m_3(.|t_0)\} = d_3(.|t_1)$. That is, the daughter is the product of marriage/production in the new family (i.e., the third family), as the result of the h-systemism for which by $Ш_{0\to1}$ (or a "synthesis impactor") is meant the marriage/production becoming of the family.

Furthermore, for $\mathcal{M}$, $\mathcal{T} \vDash \mathcal{Z}\circ,_v\mathcal{H}$, $\xi \vDash \mathcal{Z}\circ,_v\mathcal{H}$, $f(.|t_0) = \xi_{0\to0}m(.|t_0)$ or $m(.|t_0) = \xi^{-1}Ш_{0\to0}f(.|t_0)$, let ξ be the "change-to-the-opposite impactor," ξ^{-1} be the "reverse impactor" of ξ, $\xi_{0\to0} \vDash \mathcal{Z}\circ,_v\mathcal{H}$ be an impactor of f-systemism. Then we have $\mathcal{T}(f,m) = \{f(y-) \oplus^{TC} m(y+)\} = \mathcal{M}(f,m)$ as a marriage/ production system.

In the above, an impactor is called a **creative impactor** if and only if the following conditions hold: i) It is a system-creation impactor. ii) It creates a new system. In the above, for example, we have: $\{d,s\} \to \{w,h\} \Rightarrow \{d'|(m,f)\}$, with w, h and d' referring to the daughter, the wife and the husband of the new family, respectively.

§A.5-3 Symbolic Iso-systemism and Metaphorical Anti-systemism

By the **symbolic iso-systemism** (SIS) between systems A and B (or a systematic transformation from systems A to B, denoted by SIS(A,B)) is meant that the core of A, co(A), is the same as the core of B, co(B), where the core of A is A from which its non-essential parts are eliminated and some necessary parts are added to it, and similarly for the core of B. That is, the symbolic iso-systemism of A and B means that they are "essentially the same" and they share the same orientation toward the core system C*.

Let $N_W \sqsubseteq (\Omega,\mathcal{Z}\circ,_v\mathcal{H},\{\mathbb{C}\})$ be the non-essentials of $W^* \sqsubseteq (\Omega,\mathcal{Z}\circ,_v\mathcal{H},\{\mathbb{C}\})$ (i.e., those being particular to the culture of wu), $N_S \sqsubseteq (\Omega,\mathcal{Z}\circ,_v\mathcal{H},\{\mathbb{C}\})$ be the non-essentials of $S^* \sqsubseteq (\Omega,\mathcal{Z}\circ,_v\mathcal{H},\{\mathbb{C}\})$ (i.e., those being particular to the culture of sunyata) and $N_N \sqsubseteq (\Omega,\mathcal{Z}\circ,_v\mathcal{H},\{\mathbb{C}\})$ be the non-essentials of $N^* \sqsubseteq (\Omega,\mathcal{Z}\circ,_v\mathcal{H},\{\mathbb{C}\})$ (those being particular to the culture of non-being). Furthermore, for a system $X \sqsubseteq (\Omega,\mathcal{Z}\circ,_v\mathcal{H},\{\mathbb{C}\})$, let $cl_{core}(X) \sqsubseteq (\Omega,\mathcal{Z}\circ,_v\mathcal{H},\{\mathbb{C}\})$ be the closure of the core of X, called the essential world of X, meaning the completion of an entity X with its core. For example, $cl_{core}(W^*\backslash N_W) \sqsubseteq (\Omega,\mathcal{Z}\circ,_v\mathcal{H},\{\mathbb{C}\})$ is the closure of the core of $W^*\backslash N_W$ so that the connection between $W^*\backslash N_W$ and $C^* \sqsubseteq (\Omega,\mathcal{Z}\circ,_v\mathcal{H},\{\mathbb{C}\})$ is completed. That is,

$$\text{(A.5-3-1)}\quad \tau : X^* \underset{(\varepsilon_X,\alpha_X)}{\to} cl_{core}(X^*\backslash N_X)$$

where $\tau \models \mathbb{Z}_{o,v}\mathbb{H}$ is the "set impactor" (ε_X,α_X), ε_X being an "elimination impactor toward the core" and α_X an "addition impactor to the core."

Then we have the symbolic iso-systemism (SIS) among the systems $W^*\backslash N_W$, $S^*\backslash N_S$, and $N^*\backslash N_N$, to be written as $W^*\backslash N_W \leftrightarrow S^*\backslash N_S \leftrightarrow N^*\backslash N_N$, or

$$\text{(A.5-3-2)} \qquad cl_{core}(W^*\backslash N_W) \approx^{SIS} cl_{core}(S^*\backslash N_S) \approx^{SIS} cl_{core}(N^*\backslash N_N)$$

where $\approx^{SIS} \models \mathbb{Z}_{o,v}\mathbb{H}$ depicts the impactor of symbolic iso-systemism. Here, Bcm. (A.5-3-2) represents the set of symbolic iso-systemisms between the closures of any two systems in the grand system $\{W^*\backslash N_W, S^*\backslash N_S, N^*\backslash N_N\}$.

We also have the following "injection mapping" ι: $C_i \to C$, i = W, S, N, and the "projection mapping" π: $C \to C_i$, i = W, S, N.
With SIS(A,B) and SIS(B,C), for systems A, B, and C, the sequence of SIS(A,B)-SIS(B,C) is called the **two-step SIS chain**.

Now we are in a position to define the opposite concept of symbolic iso-systemism. In one approach, by the **metaphorical anti-systemism** (MAS) between systems A and B (or a transformation from systems A to B, denoted MAS(A,B)) is meant the core of A, co(A), is the opposite of the core of B, co(B), with the term "opposite" to be interpreted according to the context. That is, the metaphoric anti-systemism of A and B means that their core systems are exactly opposite.

And yet, in the second approach to MAS, we shall say systems A and B are in a metamorphic anti-systemism, or MAS(A,B), when A and B are opposite in their real-life orientation. This second meaning is what we adopted when we referred to MAS(wu,sunyata,nothingness).

With MAS(A,B) and MAS(B,C), for system A, B, and C, the sequence of MAS(A,B)-MAS(B,C) is called the **two-step MAS chain**.

Let $\Omega_W \sqsubseteq (\Omega,\mathbb{Z}_{o,v}\mathbb{H},\{\mathbb{C}\})$ be the **world of wu**, written as {wu}, for wu $\sqsubseteq (\Omega,\mathbb{Z}_{o,v}\mathbb{H},\{\mathbb{C}\})$, and let $C_W \sqsubseteq (\Omega,\mathbb{Z}_{o,v}\mathbb{H},\{\mathbb{C}\})$ be the ultimate world of tao-creativity (or generality) as perceived from the orientation of tao or systematic rationality (which lies beyond the world of yu and may be just empty). Here the world of wu and C_W may not be mutually exclusive. Then the extension of the world of wu to the joint-world of wu and the ultimate tao-creativity is denoted as: $\Omega_W \to \Omega_W \sqcup C_W$. Here $\Omega_W \sqcup C_W \equiv W^*$, is called the **creative world of wu**.

Let $\Omega_S \sqsubseteq (\Omega,\mathbb{Z}_{o,v}\mathbb{H},\{\mathbb{C}\})$ be the world of sunyata, written as {sunyata}, and let $C_S \sqsubseteq (\Omega,\mathbb{Z}_{o,v}\mathbb{H},\{\mathbb{C}\})$ be the world of nirvana-creativity (i.e., that of the creativity perceived beyond the orientation of nirvana or non-solidness). Here too the world of sunyata and C_S may not be mutually exclusive either. Then we extend the world of sunyata to the joint-world of sunyata and the nirvana-creativity, and denote it as: $\Omega_S \to \Omega_S \sqcup C_S$. Here $\Omega_S \sqcup C_S \equiv S^*$ is called the **creative world of sunyata**.
Let $\Omega_N \sqsubseteq (\Omega,\mathbb{Z}_{o,v}\mathbb{H},\{\mathbb{C}\})$ be the world of nothingness, {nothingness}, and let $C_N \sqsubseteq (\Omega,\mathbb{Z}_{o,v}\mathbb{H},\{\mathbb{C}\})$ be the ultimate world of being-creativity as perceived from the orientation of being or modern sciences (which lies beyond the world of being and which may be empty). Again the world of nothingness and C_N may not be mutually exclusive. Then the extension from the world of nothingness (or non-being) to the joint-world of nothingness and ultimate being-

creativity is denoted as: $\Omega_N \to \Omega_N \sqcup C_N$. Here $\Omega_N \sqcup C_N \equiv N^*$ is called the **creative world of nothingness**.

Let $C^* \sqsubseteq (\Omega, \mathcal{Z}\circ, {}_v\mathcal{H}, \{\mathbb{C}\})$ be the core of creativity and nihility, independent of the created worlds of wu, sunyata and nothingness. This is in an unknown world, which may be empty, and yet we may be in a position neither to acknowledge nor to deny it. Here this core may be considered as the great beyond, assuming that it exists. Then for $\mathfrak{C} \equiv \mathfrak{C}(N)$,

(A.5-3-3) $\mathfrak{C} \equiv C_W \otimes C_S \otimes C_N \otimes C^*$,

with $\otimes \sqsubseteq (\Omega, \mathcal{Z}\circ, {}_v\mathcal{H}, \{\mathbb{C}\})$ referring to an integrating impactor, is called the "sphere of creativity and nihility," or the **extended world of ultimate nothingness**.

In the following, we establish the following creative worlds: $W^* = (\Omega_W \sqcup C_W|\tau)$, for $\tau \backsim \varsigma \Vdash (\mathfrak{I}, Ш^{Д}) \Vvdash \mathbb{T}\text{zu}^*$, $S^* = (\Omega_S \sqcup C_S|\tau)$ and $N^* = (\Omega_N \sqcup C_N|\tau)$, called the **space of wu, space of sunyata** and **space of nothingness**, respectively.

Then $\Omega_W \sqcup C_W \to \Omega_S \sqcup C_S$ is the space transformation from W^* to S^*. In this transformation, the non-essentials of W^* are be eliminated, and some non-essentials of S^* are added to it. Likewise, we have $\Omega_S \sqcup C_S \to \Omega_N \sqcup C_N$ as the space transformation from S^* to N^*, and $\Omega_N \sqcup C_N \to \Omega_W \sqcup C_W$ as the space transformation from N^* to W^*.

Let $N_W \sqsubseteq (\Omega, \mathcal{Z}\circ, {}_v\mathcal{H}, \{\mathbb{C}\})$ be the non-essentials of $W^* \sqsubseteq (\Omega, \mathcal{Z}\circ, {}_v\mathcal{H}, \{\mathbb{C}\})$ (i.e., those being particular to the culture of wu), $N_S \sqsubseteq (\Omega, \mathcal{Z}\circ, {}_v\mathcal{H}, \{\mathbb{C}\})$ the non-essentials of $S^* \sqsubseteq (\Omega, \mathcal{Z}\circ, {}_v\mathcal{H}, \{\mathbb{C}\})$ (i.e., those being particular to the culture of sunyata) and $N_N \sqsubseteq (\Omega, \mathcal{Z}\circ, {}_v\mathcal{H}, \{\mathbb{C}\})$ the non-essentials of $N^* \sqsubseteq (\Omega, \mathcal{Z}\circ, {}_v\mathcal{H}, \{\mathbb{C}\})$ (those being particular to the culture of non-being). Then we have the SIS between each pair in the super-system $\{W^*\backslash N_W, S^*\backslash N_S, N^*\backslash N_N\} \sqsubseteq (\Omega, \mathcal{Z}\circ, {}_v\mathcal{H}, \{\mathbb{C}\})$ to be written as:

(A.5-3-4) $\quad W^*\backslash N_W \leftrightarrow S^*\backslash N_S \leftrightarrow N^*\backslash N_N$

which are symbolic iso-systemisms between any two sets in the super-set.

A.6 A New Approach to Symbolic Iso-systemism

In considering s and S, if each unit system of s is iso-systemic to a corresponding unit system in S, and the system-integrating impactors of s and S are also iso-systemic to each other, then we say s is iso-systemic to S: $s \approx^{SIS} S$.

Below we study the details of this iso-systemism. For s, $S \sqsubseteq (\Omega, \mathcal{Z}\circ, {}_v\mathcal{H}, \{\mathbb{C}\})$, let s = a-b-…-n and S = A-B-…-N, where a, b, …, n refer to each subsystem of s, respectively, and A, B,…,N depict each of the subsystems of S, respectively.

Furthermore, by the use of Bcm. (A.3-3-1), let us decompose s and S into:
(A.6-1) $s(.,s\text{-}t|\xi_s) = \varphi_a a(.,s\text{-}t|\xi_a) \oplus \varphi_b b(.,s\text{-}t|\xi_b) \oplus \ldots \oplus \varphi_n n(.,s\text{-}t|\xi_n) \oplus \zeta_s$

(A.6-2) $\quad \zeta_s = \zeta_s(+,-;\Delta),\ \Delta \Vdash Ш^{\Delta}$;

(A.6-3) $S(.,s\text{-}t|\xi_S) = \varphi_A A(.,s\text{-}t|\xi_A) \oplus \varphi_B B(.,s\text{-}t|\xi_B) \oplus \ldots \oplus \varphi_N N(.,s\text{-}t|\xi_N) \oplus \zeta_S$

(A.6-4) $\zeta_S = \zeta_S(+,-;\Delta),\ \Delta \Vdash Ш^{\Delta}$.

Then it is said that s is **iso-systemic** to S (or the other way around) if and only if the following conditions hold:

(A.6-5) $\varphi_a \overset{SIS}{\approx} \varphi_A,\ \varphi_b \overset{SIS}{\approx} \varphi_B,\ \ldots,\ \varphi_n \overset{SIS}{\approx} \varphi_N$.

(A.6-6) $\xi_s \overset{SIS}{\approx} \xi_S,\ \xi_a \overset{SIS}{\approx} \xi_A,\ \xi_b \overset{SIS}{\approx} \xi_B,\ \ldots,\ \xi_n \overset{SIS}{\approx} \xi_N$,

(A.6-7) $a(.) \overset{SIS}{\approx} A(.),\ b(.) \overset{SIS}{\approx} B(.)\ ,\ \ldots,\ n(.) \overset{SIS}{\approx} N(.)$.

(A.6-8) $\zeta_s \overset{SIS}{\approx} \zeta_S$.

A.7 Operations of Tri-systems

§A.7-1 Introduction

Here in this section A.7, we present some rules of systems' operations. These rules presented are for special cases, rather than valid for general cases. Nevertheless, from these rules, we may later be inspired to develop more general rules of systemic operations.

§A.7-2 Tri-systems

In the following, let us present several tri-systems in a slightly different way in order to be able to "combine" them. Let a, b, c $\Vdash$ **H** $\sqcap$ ℝ, where ℝ is the set of real numbers and **H** the set of human elements. Then for c being the central element and a, b non-central elements (i.e., c dominates a and b, respectively, and a and b are in balance to each other), the collection of a, b, c in forming (a,b|c), also written as

(A.7-2-1) $\Delta = |(a\ \ b) \setminus c\,|^T$,

is called a **tri-system** (i.e., a system of three members).

Definition A.7-2-1. The operation * ⊨ (Ω,$\mathcal{Z}$o,v$\mathcal{H}$,{ℂ}) on two tri-systems Δ_1 = (a,b|c) and Δ_2 = (x,y|z), a, b, c, x, y, z $\Vdash$ **H** $\sqcap$ ℝ, is defined as follows:

(A.7-2-2) $\Delta_1 * \Delta_2 = |a\ \ b) \setminus c\,|^T * \,|\,(x\ \ y) \setminus z\,||^T$
= {[(c a)#(z x)+(c b)#(z y)]/2|a+x,b+y}
= [cz+(ax+by)/2|a+x,b+y]

where (c a)#(z x) = cz + ax and similarly for (c b)#(z y). In the case that these a, b, c, x, y, z $\Vdash$ **H**, but a, b, c, x, y, z $\not\Vdash$ ℝ (with "$\not\Vdash$" denoting "not belong to"), the above "+" is interpreted as an operation of "quasi-union" and the operation of "{[(c a)#(z x)+(c b)#(z y)]/2,a+x,b+y}" as (c^@z^|a@x,b@y) with @ denoting the "interactive unity" of two elements. c^@z^, then, is the new central element in which the power of c^ growing from "c" to "[(c a)#(z x)]/2" and that of z^ growing from C to [(c b)#(z y)]/2. Here a@x is the new element a+x, and similarly for b@y.

Note that $\Delta_I = (0,0|1)$ is the identity element of the set of all tri-systems defined in the above. To see this, we have:

$$(A.7\text{-}2\text{-}3)\quad \Delta_I * \Delta_I = \begin{array}{c} /\,1| \\ /0\;\;0| \end{array} * \begin{array}{c} /\,1| \\ /0\;\;0| \end{array} = \begin{array}{c} /1| \\ /0\;0| \end{array},$$

$$(A.7\text{-}2\text{-}4)\quad \Delta * \Delta_I = \begin{array}{c} /\,c\,| \\ /a\;\;b| \end{array} * \begin{array}{c} /\,1\,| \\ /0\;\;0| \end{array} = \begin{array}{c} /c| \\ /a\;\;b| \end{array},$$

$$(A.7\text{-}2\text{-}5)\quad \Delta_I * \Delta = \begin{array}{c} /\,1| \\ /0\;\;0| \end{array} * \begin{array}{c} /\,c| \\ /a\;\;b| \end{array} = \begin{array}{c} /\,c| \\ /a\;b| \end{array}.$$

That is, $\Delta_I = \Delta_I * \Delta_I$ is both the right and left identities of the set of all tri-systems. Now let Ω denote the space of tri-systems (Δ_i's):
(A.7-2-6) $\Omega = \{(\Delta_i,*)|\ \Delta_i = (a,b|c),\ a,\ b,\ c \Vdash \mathbf{H} \sqcap \mathbb{R},\ i = 1,2,\ldots,n\}$.

To study several ways of "combining" these tri-systems, first let:

$$(A.7\text{-}2\text{-}7)\qquad \Delta_1 = /x_{11}| = |x_{11}|$$

be the system with one element, where x is a human element ($x \Vdash \mathbf{H}$) or a unit system of a basic (i.e., grand) system. Secondly, let

$$(A.7\text{-}2\text{-}8)\quad \Delta_2 = \begin{array}{c} /\,x_{22}| \\ /x_{11}\;x_{12}| \end{array} = \begin{array}{c} |\;x_{22}\;\;| \\ |x_{11}\;x_{12}| \end{array}$$

be a system with two elements in the bottom row and one element in the top row, where each of x_{ij} is a human element ($x_{ij} \Vdash \mathbf{H}$), for all i, j = 1, 2 (or a unit system in a grand system). Thirdly, let

$$(A.7\text{-}2\text{-}9)\quad \Delta_3 = \begin{array}{c} /x_{33}| \\ /x_{22}\;x_{23}| \\ /x_{11}\;x_{12}\;x_{13}| \end{array} = \begin{array}{c} |\quad x_{33}\quad| \\ |\;x_{22}\;x_{23}\;| \\ |x_{11}\;x_{12}\;x_{13}| \end{array}$$

be a system with three elements in the bottom row, two elements in the middle row, and one element in the top row, where x_{ij} is a human element ($x_{ij} \Vdash \mathbf{H}$; i.e., $x_{ij} = x_{ij}(h_j^*) \Vdash \mathbf{U}$, for $h_j^* \Vdash \mathbf{H}^*$), for all i, j = 1, 2, 3 (or a unit or a system); and so on for Δ_n, where i, j = i, ..., n. Here we have a set of systems with elements and rows augmenting in an orderly fashion over time.

Similarly, let

$$(A.7\text{-}2\text{-}10)\quad \nabla_1 = /x_{11}| = \Delta_1$$

be the system with one element, where the element x is a human element ($x \Vdash \mathbf{H}$), or a unit of a system. Also let

$$(A.7\text{-}2\text{-}11)\quad \nabla_2 = \begin{array}{c} /\,x_{22}| \\ /x_{11}\;\;.\,| \end{array}$$

be the system with one element in the bottom row (i.e., x_{12} is missing compared with Δ_2, denoted by a dot) and one element in the top row, where x_{ij} is a human element ($x_{ij} \Vdash \mathbf{H}$), for all i, j = 1, 2, or a unit of a system. In addition, let

$$\begin{array}{llll} & /x_{33}/ & & /\ x_{33}| \\ & /x_{22}/ & & /\ x_{22}\ .| \\ \text{(A.7-2-12)}\quad \nabla_3 = & /x_{11}/, & = & /x_{11}\ .\ .\ | \end{array}$$

be the system with one element in the bottom row (x_{12} and x_{13} are missing, compared with the bottom row of Δ_3), one element in the middle row (x_{22} is missing, compared with the middle row of Δ_3), and one element in the top row, where x_{ij} is a human number ($x_{ij} \Vdash \mathbf{H}$), for all i, j = 1, 2, 3 (or a unit of a system); and so on for ∇_n, where i, j = i, ..., n. Here, these dots denote the missing elements, and we also have a set of systems with elements and rows augmenting in an orderly fashion over time.

Now let Φ be the system-augmenting impactor such that $\Phi_2(\Delta)$ is a new system (on the basis of $\Delta = |x_{11}|$) adding one element to the right of x_{11}, eliminating x_{11}, and adding one element to the top row. That is, for $\Delta = \Delta_1$,

$$\begin{array}{llll} & /x_{22}| & & /x_{22}/ \\ \text{(A.7-2-13)}\quad \Phi_2(\Delta) = & /.\ x_{12}| & = & /x_{12}/, \end{array}$$

or $\Phi_2(\Delta) = \Delta_2 \Theta \Delta_1$, with the impactor "$\Theta$" denoting the removing of the elements of Δ_1 from Δ_2. Further, let $\Phi_2(\Delta)$ be a new system based on $\Phi_1(\Delta)$. On the basis of $\Phi_2(\Delta) = |x_{22}\, x_{12}|^T$ (with the superscript T denoting "transpose"), this operation entails that: at the bottom row, one element is added to the right of x_{12}, eliminating x_{12}; at the second (i.e., middle) row, one element is added to the right of x_{22}, eliminating x_{22}; and finally, one element is added to form the top row (i.e., a new row). That is, we have:

$$\begin{array}{llll} & |x_{33}| & & /x_{33}| \\ & |x_{23}| & & /.\ x_{23}| \\ \text{(A.7-2-14)}\quad \Phi_3(\Delta) = & |x_{13}| & = & /.\ .\ x_{13}|, \end{array}$$

or $\Phi_3(\Delta) = \Delta_3 \Theta \Delta_2$. We could continue this process until $\Phi_n(\Delta) = \Delta_n \Theta \Delta_{n-1}$.

In passing, note that we could have upside-down tri-systems like in Bcms. (A.7-2-15) and (A.7-2-16) (or the cases of m by n tri-systems, m and n being natural numbers, in general) with operations similarly defined.

Note that Bcm. (A.7-2-15) can also be writen as: $|(x11 \setminus (x21\ x22)|^T$, and Bcm. (A.72-16) can also be writen as: $|(x11 \setminus (x21\ x22) \setminus (x31\ x32\ x33)\ |^T$,

$$\begin{array}{ll} & \backslash x_{21}\ x_{22}/ \\ \text{(A.7-2-15)}\qquad & \quad \backslash x_{11}/ \end{array}$$

and

$$\begin{array}{l} \backslash x_{31}\ x_{32}\ x_{33}| \\ \quad\backslash x_{21}\ x_{22}| \\ \qquad\backslash x_{11}| \end{array} \quad \text{(A.7-2-16)}$$

To develop the categories of systems, let us define new augmenting-diminutive operators. Let $\Delta_1 = /a| = |a|$, where $a = f_1 \Vdash \mathbf{H}$ is a human element. In the *symbolic world of tranquility*, let $f_1 = (f_{11}, f^*, ...)$, f_{11} being the only organizational position and f^* being the cultural of tranquility. Note that in systematics, the set of subscripts or superscripts {0,1,2,...} is a convenient substitute for the set {0,a,b,c,...,z,a*,b*,c*,..,z*, ...}, and the set of subsequence {11,12,13,...} is a convenient substitute for {a*a,a*b,a*c,...} (see Sub-subsection §A.2-1-2).

Then, for $\Delta_1 = /a| = |a|$, let the augmenting-diminutive impactor ξ be defined as:

(A.7-2-17) $\xi\{\Delta_1\} = |(a\ \ b) \backslash c\,|^T$,

where $a = f_1 = (f_{11}, f^*, ...) \Vdash \mathbf{H}$, with f_{11} denoting the non-central yin- (or left) position in the organization and f^* denoting the cultural of tranquility; $b = f_2 = (f_{21}, f^*, ...) \Vdash \mathbf{H}$, with f_{21} denoting the non-central yang- (or right) position in the organization; and $c = f_3 = (f_{31}, f^*, ...) \Vdash \mathbf{H}$, with f_{31} denoting the central position in the organization.

Further, let $x = g_1 = (g_{11}, g^*, ...) \Vdash \mathbf{H}$ be a human element, with g_{11} denoting the non-central yin- (or left) position in the organization and g^* denoting the culture of tranquility as is embodied in a human element. Further, let $y = g_2 = (g_{21}, g^*, ...) \Vdash \mathbf{H}$, with g_{21} denoting the non-central yang- (or right) position in the organization and $z = g_3 = (g_{31}, g_2^*, ...) \Vdash \mathbf{H}$, with g_{31} denoting the central position in the organization. Then for $\Delta_2 = /x| = |x|$,

(A.7-2-18) $\xi\{\Delta_2\} = |\,(x\ \ y) \backslash z\,|^T$,

is a system. That is, $\xi \vDash (\Omega, \mathbb{Z}_\circ, {}_v\mathbb{H}, \{\mathbb{C}\})$ is a system-creating impactor (see Subsection §A.2-3).

In the *symbolic world of conflict*, let $\Delta_1 = /a| = |a|$, where $a = h \Vdash \mathbf{H}$. Further, let the augmenting-diminutive impactor ζ be defined as:

(A.7-2-19) $\zeta\{\Delta_1\} = /a\ \ b\ \ \alpha) \backslash c\,|^T$,

where $a = (u_{11}, u^*, u_3, ...)$, with u_{11} being the non-central (on the left) position in the organization, and u^* being the culture of conflict; $b = u_2 = (u_{21}, u_2^*, ...) \Vdash \mathbf{H}$, with u_{21} denoting the non-central anti- (on the right) position in the organization; and $c = u_3 = (u_{31}, u_2^*, ...) \Vdash \mathbf{H}$, with u_{31} denoting the central position in the organization. Similarly, let α be a human element with conflict culture. These a, b, c, α are not empty and have (mathematical) measures of positive values. Note that in the above $\zeta\{\Delta_1\} = \{a\ b\ \alpha|c\}$ is a system.

In addition, let $\Delta_2 = /x| = |x|$,

(A.7-2-20) $\zeta\{\Delta_2\} = |\,(x\ \ y\ \ \beta) \backslash z\,|^T$,

where $x = v_1 = (v_{11}, v^*, ...) \Vdash \mathbf{H}$, with v_{11} being the non-central (on the left) position in the organization and v^* being the culture of conflict, $b = v_2 = (v_{21}, v^*, ...) \Vdash \mathbf{H}$, with v_{21} denoting the non-central anti- (on the right) position in the organization, and $c = v_3 = (v_{31}, v^*, ...)\ \varepsilon\ \mathbf{H}$, with v_{31} denoting the central position in the organization. Similarly, let ß be a human element with conflict culture. Note that these a, b, c and ß are not empty and have measures of positive values. Then in the above $\zeta\{\Delta_2\} = \{x\ y\ \beta|z\}$ is a system.

By comparing $\xi\{\Delta_1\}$ and $\zeta\{\Delta_1\}$, it is easy to see that ζ has a greater micro-efficiency (or horizontal productivity) relative to ξ if z = c(or measures m(z) = m(c)), a = x, b = y, and $m(\alpha)<m(\beta)$.
In the above illustration, we see that, for different systems (or categories of systems), different symbolically interactive operations (i.e., interactors) yield different results.

Below, we show a few rules of interactive operations between two systems. In a sense of interactive mutuality, due to the nature of interactors associated with them, it is believed that systems in the symbolic world of tranquility have greater organizational efficiency than the systems in the symbolic world of competition. We see this in the following. Let $\Delta_1 = (a,b|c)$, $\Delta_2 = (x,y|z)$, then in the *symbolic world of tranquility*, the interactor $* \models \mathcal{Z}_{\circ,v}\mathcal{H}$ between two tri-systems under the culture of tranquility may be defined as:
(A.7-2-21) $\Delta_1 * \Delta_2 = |(a\ \ b)\backslash c|^T * |(x\ \ y)\backslash z|^T = /(a\ x\ b\ y)\backslash z'\backslash c'|^T$,
where c' is c transformed after absorbing the influence of z, and z' is z transformed after absorbing the influence of c (z' is not "empty" and is "positive"). Here $\Delta_1 * \Delta_2 = |a\ x\ b\ y\ |z'\|\ c'| \equiv |(a\ x\ b\ y)\ \backslash\ z'\ \backslash\ c'|^T$ is a system. But in the *symbolic world of conflict*, we define the interactive operation # between two tri-systems under the culture of conflict as follows:

(A.7-2-22) $\Delta_1 \# \Delta_2 = |(a\ \ b\ \ \alpha)\backslash c|^T \# |(x\ \ y\ \beta)\backslash z|^T = |(a\ x\ b\ y\ \alpha\ \beta)\backslash c'|^T$,

Here $\Delta_1 \# \Delta_2 = |(a\ x\ b\ y\ \alpha\ \beta)\ \backslash\ c'|^T$ is a system. Note that in this case, z' is missing in the last system (i.e., in the system after the second equal sign). Then, because of the existence of z', it is obvious for the interactive operation $* \models \mathcal{Z}_{\circ,v}\mathcal{H}$ (relative to the operation of $\# \models \mathcal{Z}_{\circ,v}\mathcal{H}$) in the symbolic world of tranquility to have an "organizational efficiency" (with the assumption of z' having a positive measure).

Now, let $\{\Delta_3\} = (a) = /a|$, $\Delta_4 = (x) = /x|$. Then, we define:

(A.7-2-23) $\xi\{\Delta_1\} * \xi\{\Delta_2\} = |(a\ \ b)\backslash c|^T\ *\ |(x\ \ y)\backslash z|^T = |(a\ \ x\ \ b\ \ y\backslash z'\backslash c'|^T$,

(A.7-2-24) $\zeta\{\Delta_1\} \# \zeta\{\Delta_2\} = |(a\ b\ \alpha)\backslash c|^T \# |(x\ y\ \beta)\backslash z|^T = |(a\ x\ b\ y\ \alpha\ \beta)\backslash.\ c'|^T$,

Here again it shows that the symbolic world of tranquility has a stronger vertical effect (dominance) and the symbolic world of conflict has a stronger horizontal effect (coordination), following the above definitions of the interactor's operations.

Note that, in the above, these operations are intrinsic to the organizational arrangements. In the economics of culture, to proceed from the organizational operation to production, by our specifications, a culture-organizational transformation is essential in the symbolic world of tranquility, and a culture-technological transformation is essential in the symbolic world of conflict. In the former case, the culture-technological generator (or impactor) C^O, through organizational efforts (due to the culture of tranquility), will transform the organizational effect into a production-technological effect:

(A.7-2-25) $C^O\{(\xi\{\Delta_1\} * \xi\{\Delta_2\})^O\} = (\xi\{\Delta_1\} * \xi\{\Delta_2\})^I$,
where the superscript O associated with the parentheses (I, respectively) denotes the organization structure (production-industrial, respectively).

As for the latter case, under the culture of conflict, the organizational effect and the production-technological effect are identical, and the culture-technology generating impactor C^T through a process of industry-technological upgrades will transform the original form of the production-industrial structure into a new form. For example, in the state of "*systematic*

balance" between the symbolic world of tranquility and that of conflict, due to the culture of conflict, we may have for the symbolic world of conflict:

(A.7-2-26) $C^T\{(\zeta\{\Delta_1\} \# \zeta\{\Delta_2\})^{I}\} = C^T\{|\,(a\ x\ b\ y\ \alpha\ \beta\}\setminus c'\,|^T\} = |\,(a\ x\ b\ y)\setminus z'\setminus c'\,|^T$.

In general, in the state of "*systematic balance*" between the symbolic world of tranquility and that of conflict, we need the following formula:

(A.7-2-27) $\mu(\xi\{\Delta_1\} * \xi\{\Delta_2\}) = \mu(\zeta\{\Delta_1\} \# \zeta\{\Delta_2\})$,

where $\mu(u)$ is an efficiency measure of the system u. That is, in systematic balance the efficiency measures of these two composite operations (macro and organizational efficiency for the former, micro and technological efficiency for the latter) must be equal. Alternatively, these two worlds under the above composite operations are said to be in systematic balance if and only if $\mu(/z'|) = \mu(/\alpha\ \beta|)$.

In the symbolic worlds of composite operations, it is the joint efforts of these two above-mentioned worlds that determine production-industrial structure. There are two sub-cases associated with these joint operations. First, in the world of harmony, the forces of tranquility dominate those of conflict. That is, the structure of $\xi\{\Delta_1\} * \xi\{\Delta_2\}$ in Bcm. (A.7-2-26) will dominate that of $\zeta\{\Delta_1\} \# \zeta\{\Delta_2\}$ (see Bcm. (A.7-2-27)). Now, it is the operation of the coordinating component of tao-rationality (yu-wu rationality, YYWX rationality, or classical systemic rationality) that helps somewhat to bridge the gap between these two structures. In addition, the cultural efficiency of the government or bureaucracy is needed to safeguard the smooth and efficient growth of the public sector, and the efficiency of the private sector is further required to ensure the efficient operation of the organization-technological chain. Symbolically, the operation of these components due to the forces of underlying cultures may be defined as:

(A.7-2-28) $[\xi\{\Delta_1\}*\xi\{\Delta_2\}]**[\zeta\{\Delta_1\}\#\zeta\{\Delta_2\}] = |\,(a\ x\ b\ y)\setminus z'|^T ** |\,(a\ x\ b\ y\ \alpha\ \beta)\setminus c'\,|^T$
$= |\,(a\ a\ x\ x\ b\ b\ y\ y\ \alpha\ \beta)\setminus (z'\ c')\setminus c''\,|^T$,

where c" is transformed from c' in the first "system."

Secondly, in the world of competition, the forces of conflict dominate those of tranquility. That is, in the private sector, the production-technological structure of $\zeta\{\Delta_1\} \# \zeta\{\Delta_2\}$ will dominate the organizational structure of $\xi\{\Delta_1\} * \xi\{\Delta_2\}$ due to the cultural requirements of this composite structure. Now, a spirit and rationality of compromise or dialectic one is needed to coordinate the private firms as to control negative externalities and to promote positive externalities.

Symbolically, due to cultural forces, with c" being what is transformed from c' in the second "system," this may be defined and presented by:
(A.7-2-29) $[\zeta\{\Delta_1\}\#\zeta\{\Delta_2\}]\#\#[\xi\{\Delta_1\}*\xi\{\Delta_2\}] = |\,(a\ x\ b\ y\ \alpha\ \beta)\setminus c'\,|^T \#\# |(a\ x\ b\ y)\setminus z'\setminus c'\,|^T$
$= |\,(a\ a\ x\ x\ b\ b\ y\ y\ \alpha\ \beta)\setminus (c'\ c''\ z')\,|^T$,

In general, for these composite worlds to be in systematic balance, one condition is:

(A.7-2-30) $\mu([\xi\{\Delta_1\} * \xi\{\Delta_2\}] ** [\zeta\{\Delta_1\} \# \zeta\{\Delta_2\}])$
$= \mu([\zeta\{\Delta_1\} \# \zeta\{\Delta_2\}] \#\# [\xi\{\Delta_1\} * \xi\{\Delta_2\}])$,

where ** $\vDash \mathcal{Z}_{\circ,\vee}\mathcal{H}$ is the interactor between the tranquility and conflict sectors in the symbolic world of harmony, and ## $\vDash \mathcal{Z}_{\circ,\vee}\mathcal{H}$ is the interactor between the conflict and tranquility sectors in the symbolic world of competition.

§A.7-3 Transformations and Operations between Tri-systems and Square-systems

In this subsection, in order to study tri-systems and square-sytems in some details, we introduce the rules of transformations and operations between tri-systems and square-systems. Let a, b, c, d, x, y, z and w be elements in **U**. Then we have the operations and impactors to be defined below.

Suppose /a| is a system with one element, $|x \setminus z|^T \equiv (x,z||R)$ is a vertical system with two elements (R a special relationship between x and z), |x z| is a horizontal system with x and z being the left and right member of the system, respectively, and between x and z, there is a left-and-right relationship, $/(a\ b) \setminus c|^T \equiv (a\ b,c|\mathcal{R})$ is a tri-system, $|(x\ \ y) \setminus (z\ w)|^T \equiv (x\ y,z,w|\mathcal{R})$ is a four-member system of dimension 2×2 (or square system) in which, within each pair (x,y) or (z,w), there is a left-right relationship and, between the pairs (z,w) and (x,y), there is a dominant relationship.

Then, for $|a \setminus c|^T$, $|(a\ b) \setminus (c\ d)|^T$, |a| and |a b| in the *symbolic world of tranquility* and $|x \setminus x|^T$, $|(x\ \ y) \setminus (x\ y)|^T$, |z| , |z w| in the *symbolic world of conflict*, we shall define:

(A.7-3-1) /a| * |x| = |x a|,

(A.7-3-2) $/a| * (|x \setminus z|)^T = |(x\ \ z) \setminus a'|^T$,

where a' is a transformed;

(A.7-3-3) /a| * |x y| = /x y a|,

(A.7-3-4) $/a| * |(x\ y) \setminus (z\ w)|^T = /(x\ y\ w'\ z') \setminus a'|^T$,

where a' is a transformed, z' is z transformed, and w' is w transformed;

(A.7-3-5) /a b| * |x| = |x a b|,

(A.7-3-6) $/a\ b| * |x \setminus z|^T = |(a\ x\ z) \setminus b'|^T$,
where b' is b transformed, z' is z transformed;

(A.7-3-7) /a b| * |x y| = /x y a b|,

(A.7-3-8a) $/a\ b| * |(x\ y) \setminus (z\ w)|^T = |(x\ y\ a\ z') \setminus b'|^T$,
z' is z transformed, b' is b transformed (note that Bcm. (A.7-3-8a) is also written as:

|z w| /   b'|
(A.7-3-8b) /a b| * |x y | = /x y a z'| ;
(A.7-3-9) |a| * |x \ c| = |(x a) \ c|^{T},

(A.7-3-10) |a \ c|^{T} * |x \ z|^{T} = |(x a z) \ c'|^{T},

(A.7-3-11) |a \ c|^{T} * |x y| = |(x y a) \ c|^{T},

(A.7-3-12a) |a \ c|^{T} * |(x y) \ (z w) \ c'|^{T},

where c' is c transformed (note that Bcm. (A.7-3-12a) is also written as:

/c'|
|c| |z w| /z w|
(A.7-3-12b) |a| * |x y| = /x y a|,

(A.7-3-13) |(a b) \ c|^{T} * |x| = |(x a b) \ c|^{T},

(A.7-3-14) |(a b) \ c|^{T} * |x \ z|^{T} = |(x a b) \ z \ c'|^{T}

(A.7-3-15) |(a b) \ c|^{T} * |x y| = |(x y a b) \ c|^{T},

(A.7-3-16) |(a b) \ c|^{T} * |(x y) \ (z w)|^{T} = |(x y a b) \ (z w) \ c'|^{T};

where c' is c transformed;

(A.7-3-17) |(a b) \ (z w)|^{T} * |(x y) \ (z w)|^{T} = |(x y a b) \ (z w) \ (c' d')|^{T},

where c' is c transformed, d' is d transformed. In the same fashion as in the above, we further define:

(A.7-3-18) |x| # /a| = |a x|,

(A.7-3-19) |x \ z|^{T} # |a| = |(x a) \ z|^{T},

(A.7-3-20) |x y| # /a| = |a x y|,

(A.7-3-21) |(x y) \ (z w)|^{T} # /a| = |a x y) \ (z w)|^{T},

(A.7-3-22) |x| # /a b| = |x a b|,

(A.7-3-23) |x \ z|^{T} # /a b| = |(a b x) \ z|^{T},
(A.7-3-24) |x y| # /a b| = |a b x y|,

(A.7-3-25) |(x y) \ (z w)|^{T} # /a b| = |(a b x y) \ (z w)|^{T},

(A.7-3-26a) |x| # |a \ c|^{T} = |a c' x|,

where c' is c transformed (note that Bcm. (A.7-3-26a) can also be written as:

(A.7-3-26b) $|x| \# \overset{|c|}{|a|} = |a\ c'\ x|$;

(A.7-3-27) $|x \setminus z|^{T} \# |a \setminus c|^{T} = |(a\ x\ c') \setminus z|^{T}$,

where c' is c transformed;

(A.7-3-28) $|x\ y| \# |a \setminus c|^{T} = |a\ x\ c'\ y|$,

where c' is c transformed;

(A.7-3-29) $|(x\ \ y) \setminus (z\ w)|^{T} \# |a \setminus c\ |^{T} = |(a\ x\ y) \setminus (z\ w)|^{T}$,

(A.7-3-30) $|x| \# |(a\ b) \setminus c|^{T} = /a\ b\ c'\ x'|$,

where c' is c transformed, x' is x transformed;

(A.7-3-31) $|x \setminus z|^{T} \# /a\ b| = |(a\ b\ x\ c') \setminus z|^{T}$,

where c' is c transformed;

(A.7-3-32) $|x\ y| \# |(a\ b) \setminus c|^{T} = /a\ b\ x\ c'\ y|$,

where c' is c transformed;

(A.7-3-33) $|(x\ y) \setminus (z\ w)|^{T} \# /a\ b| = |(a\ b\ x\ y) \setminus (z\ w)|^{T}$,

(A.7-3-34) $|(x\ y) \setminus (z\ w)|^{T} \# |(a\ b) \setminus (c\ d)|^{T} = |(a\ b\ x\ y) \setminus (z\ w)|^{T}$.

In addition, we may define as well the following operations of impactors:

(A.7-3-35) $\Phi\{|a|\} = |x|$,

(A.7-3-36) $\Phi_1\{|a|\} = |x\ y|$

(A.7-3-37) $\Phi_2\{|a|\} = |x \setminus z|^{T}$

(A.7-3-38) $\Phi_3\{|a|\} = |(x\ y) \setminus (z\ w)|^{T}$

(A.7-3-39) $\varphi\{|a\ b| = |x|$

(A.7-3-40) $\varphi_1\{|a\ b|\} = |x\ y|$

(A.7-3-41) $\varphi_2\{|a\ b|\} = |x \setminus z|^{T}$

(A.7-3-42) $\varphi_3\{|a\ b|\} = |(x\ y) \setminus (z\ w)|^{T}$

(A.7-3-43) $\tau\{|(a\ b) \setminus c|^{T}\} = |x|$

(A.7-3-44) $\tau_1\{|(a\ b) \setminus c|^{T}\} = |x\ y|$

(A.7-3-45) $\tau_2\{|(a\ b) \setminus c|^{T}\} = |x \setminus z|^{T}$

(A.7-3-46) $\tau_3\{|(a\ b) \backslash c|^T\} = |(x\ y) \backslash (z\ w)\,|^T$.

Note that in different cultural worlds, to achieve the same effect, impactors may be different. In the above, we temporarily ignore the role of cultural worlds in this respect. In a sense, in the following are the essence of systmaitcs: (i) Rules may be different for different occasions, and worse still, for every rule, there may have more than one exceptions. (ii) For a world of specific time, space and human-culture-socoety, there do appear to exist some definite and useful rules enabling us to pursue more meaning lives. Therefore, in systematics, we impose the existence of "systemic causality" for practical sense. Note that "causality" exists in the world of mathematics and logic, simply because we set it up. In reality, there is no such thing as pure and absolute causality.

From the above operations and the definitions of impactors, it is seen that systems of all dimensions and all shapes could be handled in a similar though not obvious fashion.

Remark A.7-1 (Δ*□, □*Δ). Below, we show some specific rules of interactive operations between two systems. Note that these rules underlie system operations in some hypothetical worlds. In a real world, these operations would be related to the integration of two institutions or organizations, the consolidation of two systems into one, and the taking over of one organization by the other such as in the cases of business acquisitions and mergers. The general format underlying the afore-mentioned operations in Bcms. (A.7-3-1)-(A.7-3-46) may be stated as follows. Let Δ be a tri-system and □ be a square system (inclusive of horizontal and vertical systems), then:

(A.7-3-47) $\Delta * \square \Rightarrow \Delta > \square$,

(A.7-3-48) $\square * \Delta \Rightarrow \square > \Delta$,

where ">" denotes a state of "dominance." That is, for a tri-system to operate on a square system, then the tri-system dominates the square system; and for a square system to operate on a tri-system, then the square system dominates the tri-system.

Appendix B – Solutions to Systemic Becoming of Changes

B.1 Solutions to Systemic Becoming of Changes – Systems of Certainty

In this section, we develop the methods of systematic-change becoming for the systems in the state of certainty.

§B.1-1 Introduction

Let $X \sqsubseteq (\Omega, \mathbb{Z}\circ, {}_v\mathbb{H}, \{\mathbb{C}\})$ be a system of multiple elements, $\varphi \vDash \mathbb{Z}\circ, {}_v\mathbb{H}$ be an impactor, and $\mathbb{H}$ be the core of X with external environments held constant. Further, for the system $X = \{x, \varphi(x)\} = [x \oplus \varphi(x)] \circledast Ix$ of standard Hg-system with Hf-systemism and Hh-systemism, let $\oplus$ be an IDR impactor (see Bcm. A.2-11-1) and Ix be an **integrating factor** of the system in the process of decomposition. Then, at any moment of time, we have the **basic systemic-change becoming** at the state of simple Tcentral as follows:

(B.1-1-1) $\{[x \oplus \varphi(x)] \circledast Ix\} = \sigma \Vdash \Sigma^{TC}$,

where the notation "$\sigma \Vdash \Sigma^{TC}$" means σ is in a state of simple Tcentral. In order to derive a solution for Bcm. (B.1-1-1), we shall establish the following definition.

Definition B.1-1. A system is said to be in a **state of simple T central** if and only if the following conditions hold:

(i) The system is temporarily in an ideal state.

(ii) In the system, the relationships among different members are either in some states of CE balance or in a state of controlled tension/conflict.

(iii) In the system, the center dominates weakly the non-central members so that states of CE balance or tension/conflict sustain over time.

To derive the **basic representation of the static systemic-change becoming** (or **static representation of a system**), we shall set the system in question at the state of simple Tcentral. Then we have:

(B.1-1-2) $[x \oplus \varphi(x)] \circledast Ix = \Phi$

denoting the system, expressed as $[x \oplus \varphi(x)] \circledast Ix$ (or $[\varphi(x) \oplus x] \circledast Ix$), to be at a state of simple T central. Here for a variable y, "$y = \Phi$" denotes that y is in a state of simple T central derived from "$(\underline{.}) = \sigma \Vdash \Sigma^{TC}$" (see Bcm. (B.1-1-1) in the above). Here, "$\sigma \Vdash \Sigma^{TC}$" $\Leftrightarrow$ "$\sigma = \Phi$." That is, "$\sigma \Vdash \Sigma^{TC}$" implies "$\sigma = \Phi$," and vice versa.

Therefore by setting:

(B.1-1-3) $\varphi X(\mathbb{H}) = X(\mathbb{H})$,

we have a solution to Bcm. (B.1-1-2) (or (B.1-1-1)):

(B.1-1-4) $y(.) = [\alpha_0 y(\mathbb{H}_0;,) \oplus \alpha_1 y(\mathbb{H}_1;,)] \circledcirc Iy(\mathbb{H}_y;,)$,

for $\oplus \models \mathcal{Z}\circ,_v\mathcal{H}$ (being an IDR impactor), where $\mathbb{H}$ is the **core** of X in statics (i.e., $X(\mathbb{H})$ is considered as the **systemic core in statics** of X that keeps X to be X over time, α_1 is the system-dynamic force that will eventually transform $y(\mathbb{H}_1;.)$ into $\varphi y(\mathbb{H}_0)$ (see Bcm. (B.1-1-3), for $\varphi(x)$ in Bcm. (B.1-1-2)), α_1 is the system-dynamic force (i.e., impactor) that preserves $X(\mathbb{H}_0)$ over time (see Bcm. (B.1-1-3), for x in Bcm. (B.1-1-2)), and $Iy(\mathbb{H}_y;.)$ is the integrating factor of y(.) (see Bcm. (B.1-1-4)).

Here $\mathbb{H}_0$ and $\mathbb{H}_1$ are the cores of x and the core of $\varphi(x)$ in a state of simple Tcentral, respectively.

Thema B.1-1-1. Let Bcm. (B.1-1-2) be a systemic-change becoming as was just presented in the above. Then a solution to Bcm. (B.1-1-2) is Bcm. (B.1-1-4).

Reasoning. For $X_1 = (a_1 \oplus b_1) \circledcirc Ix_1 \sqsubseteq (\Omega,\mathcal{Z}\circ,_v\mathcal{H},\{\mathbb{C}\})$ be an Hg-standard system, there exists an Hg-standard system $X_2 = (a_2 \oplus b_2) \circledcirc Ix_2 \sqsubseteq (\Omega,\mathcal{Z}\circ,_v\mathcal{H},\{\mathbb{C}\})$ to form a thesis-antithesis pair. Over time, X_1 and X_2 then form the system Y_1 (by the principle of yin-yang mutuality or generation): $Y_1 = (c_1 \oplus d_1) \circledcirc Iy_1 \sqsubseteq (\Omega,\mathcal{Z}\circ,_v\mathcal{H},\{\mathbb{C}\})$ be an Hg-standard system. Once again, there exists an Hg-standard system $Y_2 = (c_2 \oplus d_2) \circledcirc Iy_2 \sqsubseteq (\Omega,\mathcal{Z}\circ,_v\mathcal{H},\{\mathbb{C}\})$ to form a thesis-antithesis pair with Y_1.

Over time, Y_1 and Y_2 form the system Z_1: $Z_1 = (e_1 \oplus f_1) \circledcirc Iz_1 \sqsubseteq (\Omega,\mathcal{Z}\circ,_v\mathcal{H},\{\mathbb{C}\})$ be an Hg-standard system. ... Continue this process forever. Now, to aggregate this whole process and to find a representative system (i.e., dynamic state representation of a system), we have

(B.1-1-5) $X = (a \oplus b) \circledcirc Ix$,

for $X \sqsubseteq (\Omega,\mathcal{Z}\circ,_v\mathcal{H},\{\mathbb{C}\})$ be an Hg-standard system. If we would like to find a solution (at the state of simple Tcentral) to Bcm (B.1-1-5) from which every system X_1, X_2, Y_1, Y_2, Z_1, Z_2,... can be generated naturally, we have the desired result:

(B.1-1-6) $x(.) = [\alpha_0 x(\mathbb{H}_0;,) \oplus \alpha_1 x(\mathbb{H}_1;,)] \circledcirc Ix(\mathbb{H};,)$,

for $\alpha_1, \alpha_2 \models \mathcal{Z}\circ,_v\mathcal{H}$. Here, $\alpha_0 x(\mathbb{H}_0;,)$ and $\alpha_1 x(\mathbb{H}_1;,)$ form a thesis-antithesis pair mentioned in the above, as the limits of these is in a state of simple T central .

Note that in the afore-mentioned case of system-dynamics, we have

(B.1-1-7) $\varphi X(\mathbb{H};t) = X(\mathbb{H};t) = X^*$,

where X* is the CE Tcentral X under systemic continuity, t being time. That is, X* is constant with respect to time: $X(t) = X = X^*$.

Definition B.1-1-1. A system is said to be a **CE Tcentral system** if and only if the following conditions hold:

(i) The system's objective of S is achieved.

(ii) X is in systemic continuity.

(iii) The external environments of X are held constant.

Further, in the case of uncertain transformation, we have:

(B.1-1-8) $\varphi X(\mathbb{H};t|\tau) = X(\mathbb{H};t|\tau) = X(.|\tau)^*$,

where τ represents the unobservable factor in the uncertain system $U_{\sim t}(\tau)$, $\tau \Vdash (\mathfrak{I}, Ш^{Д}) \Vdash \mathbb{T}\mathbb{z}\mathbb{u}^*$, of Bcm. (B.2-2-3):

(B.1-1-9) $\Delta z = \zeta_{X,\sim t} \oplus \{\delta_X, U_{\sim t}(\tau)\}$,

(Δz is a system composed of $U_{\sim t}(\tau)$), or (see (B.2-2-1)):

(B.1-1-10) $\{[\varphi x(\mathbb{H}_0;t|\tau) \oplus x(\mathbb{H}_1;t|\tau)] \circledast Ix(\mathbb{H}_x;t|\tau)\} \odot \Delta z = \Phi\}$.

Note that Bcm. (B.1-1-10) implies that

(B.1-1-11) $x(.) = \{[\varphi x(\mathbb{H}_0;t|\tau) \oplus x(\mathbb{H}_1;t|\tau)] \circledast Ix(\mathbb{H}_x;t|\tau)\} \odot \Delta z$.

Remark B.1-1-1. In Bcm. (B.1-1-1), what keep this system together as an integrated entity are the combined effects of appropriate strategy and the favorable internal systemic structure and dynamics, holding the external environments and the ultimate force of the cultural creativity of the system constant.

Remark B.1-1-2. In Bcm. (B.1-1-4), what keep this system in continual mode of dynamic motion are the combined effects of appropriate strategy, favorable internal systemic structure and dynamics, favorable external environments, and the ultimate force of the cultural creativity of the system. Furthermore, the ultimate force of the cultural creativity is also at work in keeping this system continuously transforming itself along the particular trajectory of a strategic path (assuming the existence of this particular strategy).

Remark B.1-1-3. For a systemic-change becoming such as Bcm. (B.1-1-4), in order to derive some practical solutions of it in the future time, it might be quite helpful to study the current reality and some historical facts about this system to be represented by this systemic-change becoming may render a great help.

§B.1-2 Conflict System as A Systemic-Change Becoming

Let the system in question be one with the culture of conflict. Below we shall present the study of the systemic becoming of the system in detail.

Definition B.1-2-1. Let a system $X = \{x,y|z\} \sqsubseteq (\Omega, \mathbb{Z}^{\circ}, {}_{v}\mathbb{H}, \{\mathbb{C}\})$ be a standard Hg-system in which z is the center and x and y are non-central elements with y being an Hf-systemism of x and z an Hh-systemism of x. Then, by letting $\varphi \models \mathbb{Z}$ be a self-operating impactor and $\oplus \models \mathbb{H}$ be an interactor between elements or systems, we may express X by the following systemic-change becoming:

(B.1-2-1) $\{\{[x \oplus \varphi(x) \oplus \varphi^2(x)] \circledast Ix\} = \sigma \Vdash \Sigma^{TC}$, assuming that $X = \{x,\varphi(x),\varphi^2(x),Ix\}$ is an IDR system (or an independently decomposable and re-organizable system where the use of an IDR impactor is applicable, see §A.2-11). Here, Ix may be considered as the virtual center (or **virtual co-center**) of the system X. Further, for $\varphi \models \mathbb{Z}$, we employ $\varphi(x)$ as the Hf-systemism of x, $\varphi^2(x) = \varphi\{\varphi(x)\} = \varphi\{y\} = z$ as the Hh-systemism of x, and Ix as a term to represent the integrating force of organizing x, $\varphi(x)$ and $\varphi^2(x)$ into the system X. Here Ix (a virtual center) is used, in the process of decomposing (or "linearize") the system X into independent units, to present the totality of: (i) the impact effect of the central element (or system) upon the non-central elements (or systems), (ii) the positive effect of the interactive forces among all non-central elements (or systems), and (iii) the negative effect of the interactive forces among all non-central elements (or system). By this afore-mentioned totality, all the secondary and higher order impacts (as is analogous to the case of Taylor series expansion) are supposed to be captured.

For this, we may write the static systemic becoming as:

(B.1-2-2) $[x\oplus\varphi(x)\oplus\varphi^2(x)] \circledcirc Ix = \Phi$,

or "$[\varphi^2(x)\oplus\varphi(x)\oplus x]\circledcirc Ix = \Phi$," where "$= \Phi$" depicts a state of simple T Central (i.e., $\sigma \Vdash \Sigma^{TC}$).

Remark B.1-2-1. Note that we may employ Bcm. (B.1-2-2) as a **static representation** of the system X.

It follows from the above development that a solution to Bcm. (B.1-2-2) is Bcm. (B.1-2-3) in the following with $\alpha \models \mathbb{Z}_{\circ,\mathrm{v}}\mathcal{H}$ being an impactor and α, ξ and $\zeta \models \mathbb{Z}_{\circ,\mathrm{v}}\mathcal{H}$ being certain system-dynamical impactors:

(B.1-2-3) $x(.) = [\alpha_0 x(\mathbb{H}_0;.)\oplus\alpha_1 x(\mathbb{H}_1;.)\oplus\alpha_2 x(\mathbb{H}_2;.)]\circledcirc Ix(\mathbb{H}_x;.)$,

assuming that $x(.) = \{\alpha_0 x(\mathbb{H}_0;.),\alpha_1 x(\mathbb{H}_1;.),\alpha_2 x(\mathbb{H}_2;.),Ix(\mathbb{H}_x;.)\}$ is an IDR system, with $\oplus \models \mathbb{Z}_{\circ,\mathrm{v}}\mathcal{H}$ being a certain inter-connecting impactor. Here α depicts the forces of x(.) evolving over time while preserving its essential characteristics; and since $\varphi x(\mathbb{H})$ is the half-stage higher development of $x(\mathbb{H})$ and $\varphi^2 x(\mathbb{H})$ is the one-stage higher development of $x(\mathbb{H})$, the system-dynamical impactor ξ represents the characteristics for x evolving into φx and the system-dynamical impactor ζ represents the characteristics for x evolving into $\varphi^2 x$. In addition, $Ix(\mathbb{H};.)$ represents a term that is employed to integrate $\varphi^2(x)$, $\varphi(x)$ and x into the system X at any moment of time. Note that in the static case, this x(.) is nothing but X itself.

Besides, in the process of decomposing (or "linearize") the system x(.) into independent units, $Ix(\mathbb{H};.)$ as a virtual center is used to present the totality of: (i) the impact effect of the central element (or system, i.e., one of $\alpha x(\mathbb{H};.)$, $\xi x(\mathbb{H};.)$ and $\zeta x(\mathbb{H};.)$ upon the non-central elements (or systems, i.e., the central one is excluded from $\alpha x(\mathbb{H};.)$, $\xi x(\mathbb{H};.)$ and $\zeta x(\mathbb{H};.)$), (ii) the positive effect of the interactive forces among all non-central elements (or system, i.e., $\alpha x(\mathbb{H};.)$, $\xi x(\mathbb{H};.)$ and $\zeta x(\mathbb{H};.)$ with the exclusion of the central one), and (iii) the negative effect of the interactive forces among all non-central elements (or systems).

Remark B.1-2-2. We may employ Bcm. (B.1-2-3) as a **variational state representation (dynamical-and-nonleap state representations, leap state representation,** respectively) of the system X if it is required to have $X \sqsubseteq \Omega^V$ (Ω^H, Ω^{Rh}, or Ω^D, respectively). Note that by the **variational state** of a system is meant that the same system dynamics essentially remains over time.

§B.1-3 Tranquil System as A Systemic-Change Becoming

Let the system in question be one with the culture of tranquil. Below we shall present a solution to this systemic becoming essentially as we did in the above.

Definition B.1-3-1. Let a system $X = \{x,y|z\} \sqsubseteq (\Omega,\mathbb{Z}\circ,{}_v\mathbb{H},\{\mathbb{C}\})$ be a standard Y-system in which z is the center and x and y are non-central elements, with y being the y-systemism of x and z the h-systemism of (x,y). Let $\varphi \models \mathbb{Z}$ be a self-operating impactor of y-systemism, $\psi \models \mathbb{Z}$ be a self-operating impactor of h-systemism, and $\oplus \models \mathbb{H}$ be an interactor. Then we may represent X by the following systemic-change becoming:

(B.1-3-1) $\{\{[\psi(x,\varphi(x))\oplus\varphi(x)\oplus x] \circledast Ix\} = \sigma \Vdash \Sigma^{TC}$,

assuming that $X = \{\psi(x,\varphi(x)),\varphi(x),x,Ix\}$ is an IDR system, with Ix depicting a term to represent a virtual center (or virtual co-center) or integrating force of organizing $\psi(x,\varphi(x))$, $\varphi(x)$ and x into the system X.

For this, we further write:

(B.1-3-2) $[\psi(x,\varphi(x))\oplus\varphi(x)\oplus x] \circledast Ix\} = \Phi$,

where $\sigma \Vdash \Sigma^{TC}$ is a state of simple T central. Note that, here, if the error of margin is not sufficiently large, we may approximate Bcm. (B.1-3-2) by. Bcm (B.1-2-2).

Remark B.1-3-1. Note that we may employ Bcm. (B.1-3-2) as a **static state representation** of the system X.

It follows from the above development that the solution to Bcm. (B.1-3-1) will be as follows, given that $\xi, \zeta \models \mathbb{Z}\circ,{}_v\mathbb{H}$ are system-dynamic impactors with certainty:

(B.1-3-3) $x(.) = [\alpha_2x(\mathbb{H}_2;.) \oplus\alpha_1x(\mathbb{H}_1;.)\oplus\alpha_0x(\mathbb{H}_0;.)] \circledast Ix(\mathbb{H}_x;.)$,

assuming that $x(.) = \{\alpha_2x(\mathbb{H}_2;.),\alpha_1x(\mathbb{H}_1;.),\alpha_0x(\mathbb{H}_0;.),Ix(\mathbb{H}_x;.)\}$ is an IDR system, with $\oplus \models \mathbb{Z}\circ,{}_v\mathbb{H}$ being an interactor connecting factors $\alpha_2x(\mathbb{H}_2;.)$, $\alpha_1x(\mathbb{H}_1;.)$ and $\alpha_0x(\mathbb{H}_0;.)$. Here α depicts the forces of x(.) keeping its characteristics essentially the same over time, the system-dynamical impactor ξ represents the characteristics for x evolving into φx, and the system-dynamical impactor ζ represents the characteristics for x evolving into $\psi(x,\varphi(x))$. Further, $Ix(\mathbb{H};.)$, being a virtual center, represents a term that is employed to integrate $\alpha x(\mathbb{H};.)$, $\xi x(\mathbb{H};.)$ and $\zeta x(\mathbb{H};.)$ into the system X at any moment of time.

Looking from the other direction, let a system $A = (x,y,|z) \sqsubseteq (\Omega,\mathbb{Z}\circ,{}_v\mathbb{H},\{\mathbb{C}\})$ and $\varphi \models \mathbb{Z}\circ,{}_v\mathbb{H}$ with $\{\{[x\oplus y\oplus z] \circledast Ia\} =< T^{C\Delta}\} \sqsubseteq Ш^{\Delta}$,(i.e., the system is in a state of simple T Central with Ia denoting the integrating force of the system A), or

(B.1-3-4) $[x\oplus y\oplus z] \circledast Ia = \Phi$.

Then we write

(B.1-3-5) $T^{Rcv}\{x\oplus y\} = z$,

or $T^{-1}\{x\oplus y\} = z$ (or $\{x\oplus y\}^{-1} = z$), where $T^{Rev}\{.\}$ stands for the tao reversal of {.}. By (B.1-3-5), we mean that z and $T^{Rev}\{x\oplus y\}$ constitute a yinyang pair (i.e., yy pair) in a state of simple T central.

Remark B.1-3-2. Note that we may employ Bcm. (B.1-3-3) as a **variational state representation (dynamical–and-nonleap state representations, leap state repre-sentation**, respectively) of the system X for $X \sqsubseteq \Omega^V$ (Ω^H, Ω^{Rh}, Ω^D, respectively).

§B.1-4 Two-step Dynamical Transformation as A Systemic-Change Becoming

For a dynamical yin-yang process Σ, a process of standard Y-transformations of x to y and then to z, we may write:

(B.1-4-1) $\Sigma: x \rightarrow y \Rightarrow z$,

by assuming an iso-systemism between this process and the system {x,y|z} presented in the above Definition B.1-3-1.

Bcm. (B.1-3-2) may be used to express this dynamical process Σ. Naturally, Bcm. (B.1-3-3) represents a solution as well to this Bcm. (B.1-4-1) if it is presented in the context of dynamics. Below we shall elaborate on this theme.

Definition B.1-4-1 (standard 2-step Y-transformation). Let x, y, z ⊩ Ω ⋐ **H** be human elements (or {x,y,z} ⊑ (Ω,𝒵○,ᵥℋ,{ℂ}) be a system). Then the process of transformations of x to y and then to z: $x \rightarrow y \Rightarrow z$ is called the **standard two-step Y-transformation** if and only if the transformation of x to y is a y-systemism and the transformation of (x,y) to z is an h-systemism.

Thema B.1-4-1. There exists an essential iso-systemism between the standard 2-step Y-transformation and the standard Y-system. Here by an **essential iso-systemism** is meant that by going through some process of elimating non-essentialparts and adding necessary supplements.

Supporting reasoning. From Definition B.1-4-1, we may write the process of the standard Y-transformation (see Bcm. (B.1-4-1)) "$\Sigma: x \rightarrow y \Rightarrow z$," in its static equivalence, as: $[\psi(x,\varphi(x))\oplus\varphi(x)\oplus x] \circledast Ix = \Phi$ (see Definition B.1-3-1). For the standard y-system, we may write exactly the same form: $[\psi(x,\varphi(x))\oplus\varphi(x)\oplus x] \circledast Ix = \Phi$. That is, the standard 2-step Y-transformation and the standard Y-system are essential iso-systemic to each other.

For a dynamical Hegelian process, a process of standard Hg-transformation of x to y and then to z is:

(B.1-4-2) $\Pi: x \rightarrow y \Rightarrow z$,

by assuming an iso-systemism between this process and the system {x,y|z} presented in the above Definition B.1-2-1.

Bcm. (B.1-2-2) may be used to express this dynamical process Π. Naturally, Bcm. (B.1-2-3) represents a solution as well to this Bcm (B.1-4-4) if it is in the context of dynamics. Below we shall examine it closely.

Definition B.1-4-2 (standard 2-step Hg-transformation). Let x, y, z ⊫ Ω ⋐ **H** be human elements (or {x,y,z} ⊑ (Ω,$\mathcal{Z}$o,$_v\mathcal{H}$,{ℂ}) be a system). Then the process of transformations of x to y and then to z: x → y ⇉z is called the **standard two-step Hg-transformation** if and only if the transformation of x to y is an Hf-systemism and that of y to z is an Hh-systemism.

Thema B.1-4-2. There exists an iso-systemism between the standard 2-step Hg-transformation and the standard Hg-system.

Supporting reasoning. We write: Π: x → y ⇉ z for the standard Hg-transformation, but we write x → φ(x) ⇉ φ^2(x) for the standard two-step Hg-transformation. Since these two process are essential the same because y = φ(x) and z = φ^2(x) by the definitions of standard 2-step Hg-transformation (see Definition B.1-4-2), the reasoning is complete.

(Alternative reasoning, see Thema 1.4-1.) From Definition B.1-4-2, we may write the process of the standard Hg-transformation x → y ⇉ z as: [φ^2(x) ⊕φ(x) ⊕x] ⊚Ix =ⵀ (see Bcm. B.1-2-2). By employing Thema B.1-4-2-1, note that although we may write the process of the standard transformation x → y ⇉ z as: φ^2(x) ⊕ φ(x) ⊕ x = ⵀ, this is only a symbolic expression. That is, this reasoning is complete.

§B.1-5 Systemic-Change Becoming of Two Cultures

Let A = {a,b|c;$\mathbb{C}^T$} ⊑ (Ω,$\mathcal{Z}$o,$_v\mathcal{H}$,{ℂ}) be a standard Y-system with $\mathbb{C}^T$ referring to the culture of tranquility and let X = {x,y|z;$\mathbb{C}^K$} ⊑ (Ω,$\mathcal{Z}$o,$_v\mathcal{H}$,{ℂ}) be a standard Hg-system with $\mathbb{C}^K$ referring to the culture of conflict. Then, by letting φ, ψ, η ⊨ (Ω,$\mathcal{Z}$o,$_v\mathcal{H}$,{ℂ}) be impactors, we have the following systemic-change becomings for A and X, respectively:

(B.1-5-1) [ψ(a,φ(a))⊕φ(a)⊕a] ⊚ Ia =ⵀ,

(B.1-5-2) [η^2(x)⊕η(x)⊕x] ⊚ Ix =ⵀ.

Remark B.1-5-1. Note that we may employ Bcms. (B.1-5-1) and (B.1-5-2) as the **static state representations** of the system A and X, respectively.

A possible joint solution to these two becomings is then:

(B.1-5-3) x(.) = [(α_a⊕α_x)x($\mathbb{H}_2$;.)⊕(ξ_a⊕ξ_x)x($\mathbb{H}_1$;.)⊕(ζ_a⊕ζ_x)x($\mathbb{H}_0$;.)]⊚ x($\mathbb{H}_x$;.),

with the system-dynamic impactor α_a representing the characteristics for a remaining essentially itself over time, the system-dynamic impactor ξ_a representing the characteristics for a evolving into φa over time, the system-dynamical impactor ζ_a representing the characteristics for (a,φ(a)) evolving into ψ(a, φ(a)) over time, the system-dynamical impactor α_x representing the characteristics for x remaining essentially itself over time, the system-dynamical impactor ξ_x representing the characteristics for x evolving into ηx over time, and the system-dynamical impactor ζ_x representing the characteristics for x evolving into η^2x over time.

Remark B.1-5-2. Note that we may employ Bcm. (B.1-5-3) as a **variational state representation (dynamical-and-nonleap state representations, leap state representation**, respectively) of the system X for $X \sqsubseteq \Omega^V$ (Ω^H, Ω^{Rh} and Ω^D, respectively).

§B.1-6 YYDSB and Systemic-Change Becoming

For s_1 (i.e., factor 1) and s_2 (i.e., factor 2), let the first generative force $x \equiv z_-$ (i.e., Sheng 1) be $z_-(s_1,s_2)$ and the second generative force z_2 (i.e., sheng 2) be $z_+(s_1,s_2)$ with $z_+ = y\{z_-\}$, for y being the impactor of y-systemism. Then for this system $A = [z_- \ z_+] \sqsubseteq (\Omega,\mathcal{Z}\circ,{}_v\mathcal{H},\{\mathbb{C}\})$, we have: $[z_- \oplus y(z_-)] \circledast Ia = \Phi$, or $[x \oplus y(x)] \circledast Ia = \Phi$, and we may obtain a solution as $z(.) = [\alpha_1 x(\mathbb{H}_x;.) \oplus\alpha_2(y(\mathbb{H}_y;.)] \circledast Iz(\mathbb{H}_z;.)$, with α_1 and $\mathbb{H}_x$ being forces for x (i.e., z_-) to remain essentially the same over time, α_2 and $\mathbb{H}_y$ being forces for x (i.e., z_+) to grow and evolve into y{x} (i.e., z_-) overtime, and $\oplus$ being the mutually beneficial impactor (see Figure B.1-6-1).

Figure B.1-6-1
YY DSB1

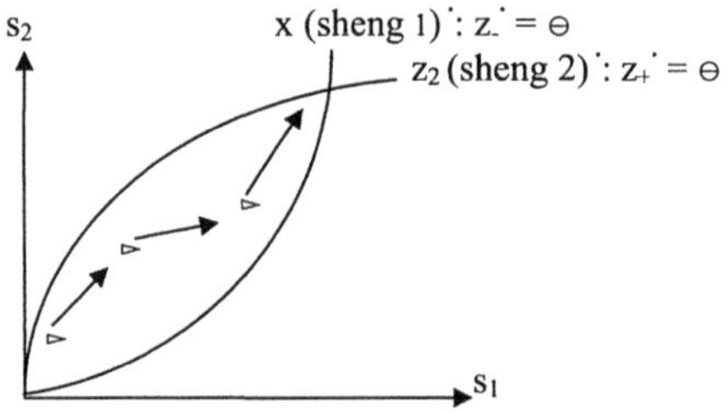

Suppose Figure B.1-6-1 is the relevant figure representing these two generative forces, then the becoming chain " ▻➔ ▻ ➔▻" is called the **YYDSB1** (YYDSB, dynamical systemic yin-yang becoming chain).

Now, we have a dynamical systemic benefit/conflict becoming chain **YYDSB2** (sheng-ke YY DSB, see Figure B.1-6-2). For r_1 (i.e., factor 1) and r_2 (i.e., factor 2), let the first generative force $u \equiv w_+$ (i.e., sheng) be $w_+(r_1,r_2)$ and the second generative force w_- (i.e., ke) be $w_-(r_1,r_2)$ with $w_- = v\{w_+\}$, for v being the impactor of Hf-systmeism.

Then for this system $B = [w_+ \ W_-] \sqsubseteq (\Omega,\mathcal{Z}\circ,{}_v\mathcal{H},\{\mathbb{C}\})$, we have: $[w_+ \oplus v(W_+)] \circledast Ib = \Phi$, or $[u \oplus v(u)] \circledast Ib = \Phi$, and we may obtain a solution as $w(.) = [\beta_1 u(\mathbb{H}_u;.) \oplus\beta_2 v(\mathbb{H}_v;.)] \circledast Iw(\mathbb{H}_w;.)$, with β_1 and $\mathbb{H}_u$ being forces for u (i.e., w_+) to remain essentially the same over time, β_2 and $\mathbb{H}_y$ being forces for u (i.e., w_+) to grow and evolve into v{u} (i.e., w_-) overtime, and $\oplus$ being the mutually beneficial-harmful impactor (or sheng-ke impactor).

By comparing Figures B.1-6-1 and B.1-6-2, we note that the "slope" (if there is one) of the YYDSB1 is flatter than the "slope" (if there is one) of the YYDSB2. That is, over time, both factors of the system with benefits of mutuality will grow faster, while the factors of the system with both structures of benefits and conflicts may not grow that fast.

Figure B.1-6-2
YY DSB 2, (1) = "ke $w_-^{\cdot} = \Phi$ ", (2) = "sheng $w_+^{\cdot} = \Phi$"

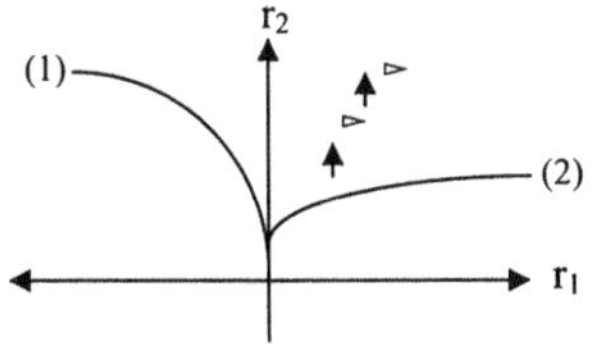

In Figure B.1-6-2, the chain "➔ ▻ ➔ ▻" is the YYDSB 2.

B.2 Solutions to Systemic Becoming of Changes – Systems of Uncertainty

§B.2-1 Introduction

Below, we shall develop the methods of systematic–change becoming for systems in the state of uncertainty.

§B.2-2 Uncertain Becoming Systems (I)

Below the uncertain becoming systems (i.e., becoming systems in the state of uncertainty) are also called the uncertain systematic–change becomings.

Let a system $X = \{x,y|z\} \sqsubseteq (\Omega,\mathbb{Z}\circ,_v\mathbb{H},\{\mathbb{C}\})$ be a standard Hg-system with z being the center, x and y being the non-central elements. Furthermore, let y be an Hf-systemism of x, z be an Hh-systemism of x and $\varphi \models \mathbb{Z}$ be a self-operating impactor with $\oplus \models \mathbb{H}$ being an interactor (see Definition B.1-2-1). Then we have the following systemic-change becoming (repeating Sub-section B.1-2):

(B.1-2-1) $\{\{[\varphi^2(x)\oplus\varphi(x)\oplus x] \circledast Ix\} = \sigma \Vdash \Sigma^{TC}$,

where $X = \{\varphi^2(x),\varphi(x),x,Ix\}$ is an IDR system (see §A.2-11). Here, for $\varphi \models \mathbb{Z}$, $\varphi(x)$ is the Hf-systemism of x, $\varphi^2(x) = \varphi\{\varphi(x)\} = \varphi\{y\} = z$ is the Hh-systemism of x, and Ix is the integrating force of the system X. From this above becoming, we have:

(B.1-2-2) $[\varphi^2(x)\oplus\varphi(x)\}\oplus x] \circledast Ix = \Phi$,

where $\sigma \Vdash \Sigma^{TC}$ is a state of simple T central.

It follows from the above development that a set of the solution to Bcm. (B.1-2-2), in the case of X being a conflict system, is:

(B.1-2-3) $x(.) = [\alpha_0 x(\mathbb{H}_0;.)\oplus\alpha_1 x(\mathbb{H}_1;.)\oplus\alpha_2 x(\mathbb{H}_2;.)] \circledast Ix(\mathbb{H}_x;.)$.
Further, let a system $X = \{x,y|z\} \sqsubseteq (\Omega,\mathbb{Z}\circ,_v\mathbb{H},\{\mathbb{C}\})$ be a standard Y-system with z being the center, x and y being the non-central elements. In addition, let y be the y-systemism of x, z be the h-systemism of (x, ,y) and $\varphi \models \mathbb{Z}$ be a self-operating impactor of h-systemism with $\oplus \models \mathbb{H}$

being an interactor. Then we have the following systemic-change becoming:
(B.1-3-1) $\{\{[\psi(x,\varphi(x))\oplus\varphi(x)\oplus x] \circledcirc Ix\} = \sigma \Vdash \Sigma^{TC}$,

where X = {ψ(x,φ(x)),φ(x),x,Ix} is an IDR system, with Ix depicting the integrating force of the system X. From this above becoming, we have:

(B.1-3-2) $[\psi(x,\varphi(x))\oplus\varphi(x)\}\oplus x] \circledcirc Ix = \Phi$,

where $\sigma \Vdash \Sigma^{TC}$ is a state of simple T central. It follows from the above development that a set of the solution to Bcm. (B.1-3-2), in the case of X being a tranquil system, is:

(B.1-3-3) $x(.) = [\alpha_2 x(\mathbb{H}_2;.)\oplus\alpha_1 x(\mathbb{H}_1;.)\oplus\alpha_0 x(\mathbb{H}_0;.)] \circledcirc Ix(\mathbb{H}_x;.)$.

Now, for an **uncertain becoming system**, for $\mathcal{T}^T\{.\} \models \mathcal{Z}\circ,_v\mathcal{H}$ being a transformational impactor, let:

(B.2-2-1) $\{[\mathcal{T}^T\{\varphi^2(x)\}\oplus\mathcal{T}^T\{\varphi(x)\}\oplus\mathcal{T}^T\{x\}] \circledcirc \mathcal{T}^T\{Ix\}\} \circledcirc \Delta X = \Phi$,

(B.2-2-2) $\mathcal{T}^T\{x(.)\} = \{[\mathcal{T}^T\{\alpha_2 x(\mathbb{H}_2;.)\}\oplus\mathcal{T}^T\{\alpha_1 x(\mathbb{H}_1;.)\}\oplus\mathcal{T}^T\{\alpha_0 x(\mathbb{H}_0;.)\}]$
$\circledcirc \mathcal{T}^T\{Ix(\mathbb{H}_x;.)\}\} \circledcirc \Delta X$,

where the **uncertain system** ΔX is defined as:

(B.2-2-3) $\Delta X = \zeta_{X,\sim(t,n)} \oplus \{\delta_X,U_{\sim t}\}$,

for $\otimes \models \mathcal{Z}\circ,_v\mathcal{H}$ ($\zeta_{X,\sim(t,n)}$ referring to the representative entity of X as a partial operation of time and size and δ_X referring to the differencing of X, with $U_{\sim t}$ depicting an uncertain system partially conditioned on time (for X being an **uncertain system**: $X \sqsubseteq T^{sysC}, K^{sysC}, T^{sysD}, K^{sysD}, T^L$, or K^L, see Definitions (8.4-3-1)-(8.4-3-2), (I.2-7)-(I.3-6). Here, ΔX is an uncertain system with its TC structure being $T^C_{uncertain}$ and difference $V_{uncertain}$ (see Bcms (B.2-3-3), (B.2-3-4)) (with the definition of $T^C_{\mathfrak{C}i,\ state\ j}$ and R_{VAR} being introduced in the next section, see Bcm. (B.2-3-10), (B.2-3-12)).

For X, Y, A, B $\sqsubseteq (\Omega,\mathcal{Z}\circ,_v\mathcal{H},\{\mathbb{C}\})$ and $\diamond$, $\circledcirc \models \mathcal{Z}\circ,_v\mathcal{H}$, let:

(B.2-2-4) $(X\oplus Y) \otimes^* (A\oplus B) = XA \diamond XB \diamond YA \diamond YB \diamond \{X,Y,A,B\}\#$.

where {X,Y,A,B}# serves as a term representing the interactive relationships among X, Y, A, and B; and

(B.2-2-5) $(X\oplus Y) \otimes (A\oplus B) = XA \diamond YB \diamond O$,

with O denoting the collective of all terms other than XB, YA and {A,B,C,D}#.

Then, by applying Bcm (B.2-2-4) to Bcm (B.2-2-1), we have:

(B.2-2-6) $\{\zeta_{X,\sim(t,n)},\mathcal{T}^T\{\varphi^2(x)\}\} \vartriangle \{\zeta_{X,\sim(t,n)},\mathcal{T}^T\{\mathcal{T}^T\{\varphi(x)\}\} \vartriangle \{\zeta_{X,\sim(t,n)},\mathcal{T}^T\{\mathcal{T}^T\{x\}\} \vartriangle$
$\{\{\delta_X,U_{\sim t}\},\mathcal{T}^T\{\varphi^2(x)\}\} \vartriangle \{\delta_X,U_{\sim t},\mathcal{T}^T\{\mathcal{T}^T\{\varphi(x)\}\} \vartriangle \{\{\delta_X,U_{\sim t}\},\mathcal{T}^T\{x\}]$
$\circledcirc \{\mathcal{T}^T\{Ix\},\zeta_{X,\sim(t,n)},\{\delta_X,U_{\sim t}\}\} = \Phi$,

with $\{\mathcal{T}^{T}\{Ix\},\zeta_{X,\backsim(t,n)}\},\{\delta_X,U_{\backsim t}\}\}$ representing the term $\{X,Y,A,B\}\#$ in Bcm. (B.2-2-4}; and by employing Bcm. (B.2-2-5), we have

(B.2-2-7) $$\{\zeta_{X,\backsim(t,n)},\mathcal{T}^{T}\{\varphi^{2}(x)\}\} \vartriangle \{\zeta_{X,\backsim(t,n)},\mathcal{T}^{T}\{\mathcal{T}^{T}\{\varphi(x)\}\} \vartriangle \{\zeta_{X,\backsim(t,n)}, \mathcal{T}^{T}\{\mathcal{T}^{T}\{x\}\} \circledast \{\mathcal{T}^{T}\{Ix\},\zeta_{X,\backsim(t,n)},\{\delta_X,U_{\backsim t}\}\} = \Phi,$$

or

(B.2-2-8) $$\{\{\delta_X,U_{\backsim t}\},\mathcal{T}^{T}\{\varphi^{2}(x)\}\} \vartriangle \{\{\delta_X,U_{\backsim t}\},\mathcal{T}^{T}\{\mathcal{T}^{T}\{\varphi(x)\}\} \vartriangle \{\{\delta_X,U_{\backsim t}\},\mathcal{T}^{T}\{x\}] \circledast \{\mathcal{T}^{T}\{Ix\},\zeta_{X,\backsim(t,n)},\{\delta_X,U_{\backsim t}\}\} = \Phi.$$

For an **alternative approach to uncertain becoming systems**, we have:

(B.2-2-9) $$[\{\{\delta_X,U_{\backsim t}\},\mathcal{T}^{T}\{\varphi^{2}(x)\}\} \vartriangle \{\{\delta_X,U_{\backsim t}\},\mathcal{T}^{T}\{\mathcal{T}^{T}\{\varphi(x)\}\} \vartriangle \{\{\delta_X,U_{\backsim t}\},\mathcal{T}^{T}\{x\}] \circledast \{\mathcal{T}^{T}\{Ix\},\zeta_{X,\backsim(t,n)}\} = \Phi,$$

(B.2-2-10) $$\mathcal{T}^{T}\{x(.)\} = [\{\{\delta_X,U_{\backsim t}\},\mathcal{T}^{T}\{\alpha x(\mathbb{H};.)\}\} \vartriangle \{\{\delta_X,U_{\backsim t}\},\mathcal{T}^{T}\{\beta x(\mathbb{H};.)\} \vartriangle \{\{\delta_X,U_{\backsim t}\},\mathcal{T}^{T}\{\gamma x(\mathbb{H};.)\}] \circledast \{\mathcal{T}^{T}\{Ix(\mathbb{H};.)\},\zeta_{X,\backsim(t,n)}\},$$

That is, the variations of the uncertain system penetrate deeply into individual members of the system, while the impact of the "mean" of the uncertain system manifests itself in the "totality factors "(i.e., Ix in Bcm. (B.2-2-9) and {Ix($\mathbb{H}$;.) in Bcm. (B.2-2-10)) of the system in question.

The other **alternative approach to uncertain becoming systems** is to have the following becomings:

(B.2-2-11) $$[\{\zeta_{X,\backsim(t,n)},\mathcal{T}^{T}\{\varphi^{2}(x)\}\} \vartriangle \{\zeta_{X,\backsim(t,n)},\mathcal{T}^{T}\{\mathcal{T}^{T}\{\varphi(x)\}\} \vartriangle \{\zeta_{X,\backsim(t,n)},\mathcal{T}^{T}\{x\}] \circledast \{\mathcal{T}^{T}\{Ix\},\{\delta_X,U_{\backsim t}\}\} = \Phi,$$

(B.2-2-12) $$\mathcal{T}^{T}\{x(.)\} = [\{\zeta_{X,\backsim(t,n)},\mathcal{T}^{T}\{\alpha x(\mathbb{H};.)\}\} \vartriangle \{\zeta_{X,\backsim(t,n)},\mathcal{T}^{T}\{\beta x(\mathbb{H};.)\} \vartriangle \{\zeta_{X,\backsim(t,n)},\mathcal{T}^{T}\{\gamma x(\mathbb{H};.)\}] \circledast \{\mathcal{T}^{T}\{Ix(\mathbb{H};.)\},\{\delta_X,U_{\backsim t}\}\},$$

That is, the force of the "mean" of the uncertain system penetrates into individual members of the system, while the impact of the "variation" of the uncertain system manifests itself in the "totality factors" (i.e., Ix in Bcm. (B.2-2-11) and {Ix($\mathbb{H}$;.) in Bcm. (B.2-2-12)) of the system in question.

The last **alternative approach to uncertain becoming systems** will have to go through the following becomings:

(B.2-2-13) $$[\{\{\delta_X,U_{\backsim t}\},\zeta_{X,\backsim(t,n)},\mathcal{T}^{T}\{\varphi^{2}(x)\}\} \vartriangle \{\{\delta_X,U_{\backsim t}\},\zeta_{X,\backsim(t,n)},\mathcal{T}^{T}\{\mathcal{T}^{T}\{\varphi(x)\}\} \vartriangle \{\{\delta_X,U_{\backsim t}\},\zeta_{X,\backsim(t,n)},\mathcal{T}^{T}\{x\}] \circledast \{\mathcal{T}^{T}\{Ix\},\zeta_{X,\backsim(t,n)},\{\delta_X,U_{\backsim t}\}\} = \Phi,$$

(B.2-2-14) $$\mathcal{T}^{T}\{x(.)\} = [\{\{\delta_X,U_{\backsim t}\},\zeta_{X,\backsim(t,n)},\mathcal{T}^{T}\{\alpha x(\mathbb{H};.)\}\} \vartriangle \{\{\delta_X,U_{\backsim t}\},\zeta_{X,\backsim(t,n)},\mathcal{T}^{T}\{\beta x(\mathbb{H};.)\} \vartriangle \{\{\delta_X,U_{\backsim t}\},\zeta_{X,\backsim(t,n)},\mathcal{T}^{T}\{\gamma x(\mathbb{H};.)\}] \circledast \{\mathcal{T}^{T}\{Ix(\mathbb{H};.)\},\zeta_{X,\backsim(t,n)},\{\delta_X,U_{\backsim t}\}\}.$$

§B.2-3 Uncertain Becoming Systems (II)

(I). For the distribution system $X_t = [\psi(x,\varphi(x)) \oplus\varphi(x)\} \oplus x] \circledcirc Ix \sqsubseteq T^{sysC}$ (or T^{sysD}, T^L, K^{sysC}, K^{LsysD}, K^L), we have in a state of simple Tcentral:

(B.1-3-2) $[\psi(x,\varphi(x)) \oplus \varphi(x)] \oplus x] \circledcirc Ix = \Phi$.

It follows from the above development that a set of the solution to Bcm. (B.1-3-2) is:

(B.1-3-3) $x(.) = [\alpha x(\mathbb{H};.) \oplus \beta x(\mathbb{H};.) \oplus \gamma x(\mathbb{H};.)] \circledcirc Ix(\mathbb{H};.)$.

(II). In the state of uncertainty, let the distribution system x(.) be:

(B.2-3-1) $x(.) = \{[\alpha x(\mathbb{H};.) \oplus \beta x(\mathbb{H};.) \oplus \gamma x(\mathbb{H};.)] \circledcirc Ix(\mathbb{H};.) \circledcirc \Delta X$,

with X(.) in $\{[\alpha x(\mathbb{H};.) \oplus \beta\xi x(\mathbb{H};.) \oplus \gamma x(\mathbb{H};.)] \circledcirc Ix(\mathbb{H};.)$ being a distribution system and

(B.2-2-3) $\Delta X = \zeta_{X,\backsim(t,n)} \oplus \{\delta_X, U_{\backsim t}\}$,

with $\zeta_{X,\backsim(t,n)}$ being the representative entity of X partially affected by time and δ_X the differencing of X .

From

(B.2-2-5) $(X \oplus Y) \otimes (A \oplus B) = XA \diamond YA \diamond O$

(with O denoting all other terms to be set as empty systems vanishing in the becomings presented below) and Bcm. (B.2-2-2):

(B.2-2-2) $\mathcal{T}^T\{x(.)\} = \{[\mathcal{T}^T\{\alpha x(\mathbb{H};.) \oplus \mathcal{T}^T\{\beta x(\mathbb{H};.) \oplus \mathcal{T}^T\{\gamma x(\mathbb{H};.) \oplus] \circledcirc \mathcal{T}^T\{Ix(\mathbb{H};.)\}$
$\circledcirc \Delta X$,

we derive:

(B.2-3-2) $\mathcal{T}^T\{x(.)\} = \{\{\zeta_{X,\backsim(t,n)}, \mathcal{T}^T\{\alpha x(\mathbb{H};.)\}\} \vartriangle \{\{\zeta_{X,\backsim(t,n)}, \mathcal{T}^T\{\beta x(\mathbb{H};.)\}\}$
$\vartriangle \{\{\zeta_{X,\backsim(t,n)}, \mathcal{T}^T\{\gamma x(\mathbb{H};.)\}\} \circledcirc \{\{\zeta_{X,\backsim(t,n)}, \delta_X, \mathcal{T}^T\{Ix(\mathbb{H};.))\}, U_{\backsim t}\}$.

Here the **uncertain system**: $U_{\backsim t} = U_{\backsim t}(\tau)$, ($U_{\backsim t}(\tau) \backsim \tau \Vdash (\mathfrak{I}, Ш^{Д}) \Vdash$ Tzu*) is defined as:

(B.2-3-3) The **TCentral uncertainty of U**: $T^C_{uncertain}[U_{\backsim t}(\kappa)] = \circ$ (for $T^C_{uncertain}[.]$, the empty system "○" representing an "ineffective" impactor), where "$T^C_{uncertain}[X]$" stands for the operation of setting X to its state of simple Tcentral,

(B.2-3-4a) The **variation of U**: $V_{uncertain}[U_{\backsim(t,n)}] \equiv V_{uncertain}[U_{\backsim(t,n)}(\tau)]$ = "deepening the potentials of uncertainty."

(B.2-3-4b) "Variation of uncertainty" of U: $V_{uncertain}[U_{\backsim t}(\tau)]$, where "$V_{uncertain}[X]$" $V_{uncertain}[U_{\backsim(t,n)}] \equiv V_{uncertain}[U_{\backsim(t,n)}(\tau)]$ stands for the operation of "opening-up the world of the potential of uncertain force: tapping and deepening the potentials of the deviation of X."

Then, from Bcms. (B.2-2-2)-(B.2-2-5) and by "employing" Bcm. (B.2-2-7), we get:

$$\text{(B.2-3-5)}\quad \mathcal{T}^{T}\{x(.)\} = [\{\zeta_{X,\smile(t,n)},\mathcal{T}^{T}\{\alpha_2 x(\mathbb{H}_2;.)\}\}\vartriangle \{\zeta_{X,\smile(t,n)},\mathcal{T}^{T}\{\alpha_1 x(\mathbb{H}_1;.)\}\} \vartriangle\{\zeta_{X,\smile(t,n)},\mathcal{T}^{T}\{\alpha_0 x(\mathbb{H}_0;.)\}\}]\circledast\{\zeta_{X,\smile(t,n)},\delta_X,\mathcal{T}^{T}\{Ix(\mathbb{H}_x;.)\},U_{\smile t}\},$$

where

$$\begin{aligned}\text{(B.2-3-6)}\quad T^{C}_{uncertain(U)}[\mathcal{T}^{T}\{x(.)\}] &= T^{C}_{uncertain(U)}[\zeta_{X,\smile(t,n)},\mathcal{T}^{T}\{\alpha_2 x(\mathbb{H}_2;.)\}]\vartriangle\\ &\quad T^{C}_{uncertain(U)}[\zeta_{X,\smile(t,n)},\mathcal{T}^{T}\{\alpha_1 x(\mathbb{H}_1;.)\}]\vartriangle\\ &\quad T^{C}_{uncertain(U)}[\zeta_{X,\smile(t,n)},\mathcal{T}^{T}\{\alpha_0 x(\mathbb{H}_0;.)\}]\circledast\\ &\quad T^{C}_{uncertain(U)}[\zeta_{X,\smile(t,n)},\delta_X,\mathcal{T}^{T}\{Ix(\mathbb{H}_x;.)\},U_{\smile t}].\\ &= [\{\zeta_{X,\smile(t,n)},\mathcal{T}^{T}\{\alpha_2 x(\mathbb{H}_2;.)\}\}\vartriangle\\ &\quad \{\mu_{X,\smile t},\delta_X,\mathcal{T}^{T}\{\alpha_1 x(\mathbb{H}_1;.)\}\}\vartriangle\\ &\quad \{\zeta_{X,\smile(t,n)},\mathcal{T}^{T}\{\alpha_0 x(\mathbb{H}_0;.)\}\}]\circledast\\ &\quad \{\zeta_{X,\smile(t,n)},\delta_X,\mathcal{T}^{T}\{Ix(\mathbb{H}_x;.)\}\}T^{C}_{uncertain(U)}[U_{\smile t}]\\ &= \{\zeta_{X,\smile(t,n)},\mathcal{T}^{T}\{\alpha_2 x(\mathbb{H}_2;.)\}\}\vartriangle\{\zeta_{X,\smile(t,n)},\mathcal{T}^{T}\{\alpha_1 x(\mathbb{H}_1;.)\}\}\\ &\quad \vartriangle\{\zeta_{X,\smile(t,n)},\mathcal{T}^{T}\{\alpha_0 x(\mathbb{H}_0;.)\}\}\circledast\{\zeta_{X,\smile(t,n)},\sigma_X,\mathcal{T}^{T}\{Ix(\mathbb{H}_x;.)\}\},\end{aligned}$$

since $\{\zeta_{X,\smile(t,n)},\delta_X,\mathcal{T}^{T}\{Ix(\mathbb{H}_x;.)\},\ T^{C}_{uncertain(U)}[U_{\smile t}]\} = \{\zeta_{X,\smile(t,n)},\ \delta_X,\ \mathcal{T}^{T}\{Ix(\mathbb{H}_x;.)\},\ \circ\} = \{\zeta_{X,\smile(t,n)},\delta_X,\mathcal{T}^{T}\{Ix(\mathbb{H}_x;.)\}\}$; and from Bcm. (B.2-4-2), we have:

$$\begin{aligned}\text{(B.2-3-7)}\quad & V_{uncertain(U)}[\mathcal{T}^{T}\{x(.)\}]\\ &= \{V_{uncertain(U)}[\zeta_{X,\smile(t,n)},\mathcal{T}^{T}\{\alpha_2 x(\mathbb{H}_2;.)\}]\vartriangle V_{uncertain(U)}[\zeta_{X,\smile(t,n)},\mathcal{T}^{T}\{\alpha_1 x(\mathbb{H}_1;.)\}]\vartriangle\\ &\quad V_{uncertain(U)}[\zeta_{X,\smile(t,n)},\mathcal{T}^{T}\{\alpha_0 x(\mathbb{H}_0;.)\}]\}\\ &\quad \circledast\ V_{uncertain(U)}[\zeta_{X,\smile(t,n)},\delta_X,\mathcal{T}^{T}\{Ix(\mathbb{H}_x;.)\},U_{\smile t}]\\ &= \{\zeta_{X,\smile(t,n)},\mathcal{T}^{T}\{Ix(\mathbb{H}_x;.),(\delta_X|\text{world of the potential of uncertainty being open})\},\end{aligned}$$

because $V_{uncertain(U)}[\mu_{X,\smile t},\mathcal{T}^{T}\{\alpha_2 x(\mathbb{H}_2;.)\}] = V_{uncertain(U)}[\mu_{X,\smile t},\mathcal{T}^{T}\{\alpha_1 x(\mathbb{H}_1;.)\}] = V_{uncertain(U)}[\mu_{X,\smile t},\mathcal{T}^{T}\{\alpha_0 x(\mathbb{H}_0;.)\}] = \circ$, and

$$\begin{aligned}\text{(B.2-3-8)}\quad & (\circ\vartriangle\circ\vartriangle\circ)\circledast V_{uncertain(U)}[\zeta_{X,\smile(t,n)},\ \delta_X,\mathcal{T}^{T}\{Ix(\mathbb{H}_x;.)\},U_{\smile t}]\\ &= V_{uncertain(U)}[\zeta_{X,\smile(t,n)},\mathcal{T}^{T}\{Ix(\mathbb{H}_x;.)\},(\delta_X,U_{\smile t})]\\ &= \{\zeta_{X,\smile(t,n)},\mathcal{T}^{T}\{Ix(\mathbb{H}_x;.)\},V_{uncertain(U)}[(\delta_X,U_{\smile t})]\}\\ &= \{\zeta_{X,\smile(t,n)},\mathcal{T}^{T}\{Ix(\mathbb{H}_x;.),(\delta_X|\text{world of the potential of uncertainty being open})\},\end{aligned}$$

with, for X being an element or a system,

(B.2-3-9) $\{\delta_X$ with the ith level of deviation| potential of uncertainty in deviation being developed$\}$ = δ_X with the (i+1)th level of deviation (for j>1 and j is determined by the nature of X).

Remark B.2-3-1. To illustrate Bcm. (B.2-2-8), let us have the following examples:

(i) $\{\delta_X$ with the 1st level of deviation| world of the potential of deepening uncertainty in deviation being open$\}$ = δ_X with the 2nd level of deviation,

(ii) $\{\delta_X$ with the 2nd level of deviation|world of the potential of deepening uncertainty in deviation being open$\}$ = δ_X with the 4th level of deviation,

(iii) $\{\delta_X$ with the 3rd level of deviation| world of the potential of deepening uncertainty in deviation being open$\}$ = δ_X with the 6th level of deviation.

Remark B.2-3-1. Suppose we have:

(B.2-3-10) The **TC$_{\mathfrak{C}i,statej}$uncertainty of U** (or TC (culture i and state j) uncertainty of U): $T^C_{\mathfrak{C}i,statej(U)}[U_{\sim(t,n)}] \equiv T^C_{\mathfrak{C}i,statej(U)}[U_{\sim(t,n)}(\tau)]$.

Then we have:

(B.2-3-11)
$$\begin{aligned} &T^C_{\mathfrak{C}i,statej(U)}[\mathcal{T}^T\{x(.)\}] \\ &= \{T^C_{\mathfrak{C}i,statej(U)}[\zeta_{X,\sim(t,n)},\mathcal{T}^T\{\alpha_2 x(\mathbb{H}_2;.)\}] \triangle T^C_{\mathfrak{C}i,statej(U)}[\zeta_{X,\sim(t,n)},\mathcal{T}^T\{\alpha_1 x(\mathbb{H}\alpha_1;.)\}] \\ &\quad \triangle\, T^C_{\mathfrak{C}i,statej(U)}[\gamma_{X,\sim(t,n)},\mathcal{T}^T\{\alpha_0 x(\mathbb{H}_0;.)\}]\} \\ &\quad\quad \circledast\, T^C_{\mathfrak{C}i,statej(U)}[\zeta_{X,\sim(t,n)},\delta_X,\mathcal{T}^T\{Ix(\mathbb{H}_x;.)\},U_{\sim(t,n)}\}]. \\ &= \{\{\zeta_{X,\sim(t,n)},\mathcal{T}^T\{\alpha_2 x(\mathbb{H}_2;.)\}\} \triangle \{\zeta_{X,\sim(t,n)},\, \delta_X,\mathcal{T}^T\{\alpha_1 x(\mathbb{H}_1;.)\}\} \\ &\quad \triangle \{\zeta_{X,\sim(t,n)},\mathcal{T}^T\{\alpha_0 x(\mathbb{H}_0;.)\}\}\} \\ &\quad\quad \circledast \{\zeta_{X,\sim(t,n)},\, \delta_X,\mathcal{T}^T\{Ix(\mathbb{H}_x;.)\}\} T^C_{\mathfrak{C}i,statej(U)}[U_{\sim(t,n)}] \end{aligned}$$

and

(B.2-3-12) **Range of variation**: $R_{VAR(U)}[\mathcal{T}^T\{x(.)\}]$, from the left-end of the distribution to the right-end of distribution of X.

Remark B.2-3-3. (i) For X as an uncertain system of culture i (i∈ℕ) with the four-season (Sp-S-F-W) cycle, we have:

(B.2-3-13)
$$T^C_{\mathfrak{C}i,statej(X)}[X] = \begin{cases} \text{Sp-X} \\ \text{S-X} \\ \\ \text{F-X} \\ \text{W-X} \end{cases} \text{, if X is in the state of } \begin{cases} \text{Sp} \\ \text{S} \\ , \\ \text{F} \\ \text{W} \end{cases}$$

with Sp, S, F and W denoting Spring, Summer, Fall and Winter, respectively. Related to Bcm. (B.2-3-13), we have:

(B.2-3-14) $R_{VAR(X)}[\mathcal{T}^T\{x(.)\}] = \text{Sp-W}$.

(ii) Four dragon (P-F-Fly-R) cycle. Let P, F, A, and R denote Potential Dragon, Field (or Wild) Dragon, Flying Dragon and Regretting Dragon, respectively. Then we have:

(B.2-3-15) $R_{VAR(X)}[\mathcal{T}^T\{x(.)\}] = \text{P-R}$.

Furthermore, related to Bcm. (B.2-3-15), we have:

(B.2-3-16)
$$T^C_{\mathfrak{C}i,statej(X)}[\mathcal{T}X] = \begin{cases} \text{P-X} \\ \text{F-X} \\ \\ \text{Fly-X} \\ \text{R-X} \end{cases} \text{, if X is in the state of } \begin{cases} \text{P} \\ \text{F} \\ , \\ \text{A} \\ \text{R} \end{cases}$$

Remark B.2-3-4. In the three-dimentional world of time-space-human being (t-s-h), we have an uncertain system reprensented by $T^C_{t\text{-}s\text{-}h}[\mathcal{T}^T\{x(.)\}]$ and $V_{t\text{-}s\text{-}h}[\mathcal{T}^T\{x(.)\}]$ as follows:

(B.2-3-17) $T^{C}_{t\text{-}s\text{-}h}[\mathcal{T}^{T}\{x(.)\}]$
$= \{T^{C}_{t\text{-}s\text{-}h}[\zeta_{X,\sim(t,n)}, \mathcal{T}^{T}\{\alpha_2 x(\mathbb{H}_2;.)\}] \triangle$
$T^{C}_{t\text{-}s\text{-}h}[\zeta_{X,\sim(t,n)}, \mathcal{T}^{T}\{\alpha_1 x(\mathbb{H}_1;.)\}] \triangle$
$T^{C}_{t\text{-}s\text{-}h}[\zeta_{X,\sim(t,n)}, \mathcal{T}^{T}\{\alpha_0 x(\mathbb{H}_0;.)\}]\} \circledast$
$T^{C}_{t\text{-}s\text{-}h}[\zeta_{X,\sim(t,n)}, \delta_X, \mathcal{T}^{T}\{Ix(\mathbb{H}_x;.)\}, U_{\sim t}].$
$= [\{\zeta_{X,\sim(t,n)}, \mathcal{T}^{T}\{\alpha_2 x(\mathbb{H}_2;.)\}\} \triangle$
$\{\mu_{X,\sim t}, \delta_X, \mathcal{T}^{T}\{\alpha_1 x(\mathbb{H}_1;.)\}\} \triangle$
$\{\zeta_{X,\sim(t,n)}, \mathcal{T}^{T}\{\alpha_0 x(\mathbb{H}_0;.)\}\}] \circledcirc$
$\{\zeta_{X,\sim(t,n)}, \delta_X, \mathcal{T}^{T}\{Ix(\mathbb{H}_x;.)\}\} T^{C}_{t\text{-}s\text{-}h}[U_{\sim t}],$

where the content of $T^{C}_{t\text{-}s\text{-}h}[U_{\sim t}]$ is to be determined; and

(B.2-3-18) $V_{t\text{-}s\text{-}h}[\mathcal{T}^{T}\{x(.)\}]$
$= (V_{t\text{-}s\text{-}h}[\zeta_{X,\sim(t,n)}, \mathcal{T}^{T}\{\alpha_2 x(\mathbb{H}_2;.)\}] \triangle V_{t\text{-}s\text{-}h}[\zeta_{X,\sim(t,n)}, \mathcal{T}^{T}\{\alpha_1 x(\mathbb{H}_1;.)\}] \circledast$
$V_{t\text{-}s\text{-}h}[\zeta_{X,\sim(t,n)}, \mathcal{T}^{T}\{\alpha_0 x(\mathbb{H}_0;.)\}]) \circledast V_{t\text{-}s\text{-}h}[\zeta_{X,\sim(t,n)}, \delta_X, \mathcal{T}^{T}\{Ix(\mathbb{H}_x;.)\}, U_{\sim t}],$
$= [\zeta_{X,\sim(t,n)}, \delta_X, \mathcal{T}^{T}\{Ix(\mathbb{H}_x;.)\}] \circledcirc V_{t\text{-}s\text{-}h}[U_{\sim t}],$

Where the contenets of $\circledcirc$ and $V_{t\text{-}s\text{-}h}[U_{\sim t}]$ are to be determined.

Appendix C – Reversal Construction Systems and Systematic-Change Becomings

C.1 Introduction

In this Appendix, we formally introduce the method of reversal construction and the scheme of systemic-change becoming of a system. The method of reversal construction was first developed in Tonn [1998, pp. 36-37].

C.2 General Reversal Construction Systems and Dynamics

Below we shall study a system from the perspective of the general reversal construction. Let $A \sqsubseteq (\Omega, \mathbb{Z}^{o}, {}_{v}\mathcal{H}, \{\mathbb{C}\})$ be a tranquil system with x, y, z $\Vdash$ A and y be the y-systemism of x (i.e., tranquil-type transformation of f-systemism), and z be the h-systemism of x.

Let the will-and-rationality complex of these elements be in a state of iso-systemism. From an "abstract angle," let f: M→M' be the relation of system-generation with the system to be expressed by the representative element C = M/H.

Here f is an impactor, M and M' are systems with fM = M', M is the original system (in the case of an organization: M is the management), M' is the manifestation of the operations or power of management. Then H is called the **unit of reversal construction** of M. Thus the **scheme of reversal construction** for this system may be represented as: f: M → M' (see Figure C.2-1). For a system of organization (or management), Figure C.2-1 means that the management of this system relies on M/H (for example, the pursuit of power and profits) as the core culture, or the humane foundation of the system's dynamical forces.

Figure C.2-1
Scheme of Deconstruction

$$
\begin{array}{ccc}
 & f & \\
M & \dashrightarrow & M' \\
g \searrow & & \nearrow h \\
 & M/H &
\end{array}
$$

In Figure C.2-1, M/H is called the **reversal-construction subsystem** (reversal representative entity of a system or the subsystem of M created through reversal construction. In other words, "M/N" denotes the "**core-unit system**" or the representative unit or subsystem in M, in a sense that it is the "core" of M from which M is constructed. Then, if we have f = g # h, for "#" being a composite impactor, M is said to have a property of **commutativity**.

Note that by the method of systematic-change becoming, we may write this system in the above as (see Appendix B, Section B.1): For the case of mutual cooperation, let a system S = $(x,y,|z) \sqsubseteq (\Omega, \mathbb{Z}^{o}, {}_{v}\mathcal{H}, \{\mathbb{C}\})$ and $\varphi, \oplus \vDash \mathbb{Z}^{o}, {}_{v}\mathcal{H}$ with $\{[x \oplus y \oplus z] \circledcirc Is = < T^{C\Delta} \} \sqsubseteq Ш^{\Delta}$ (i.e., the system is in a state of simple T central with s representing the system of S as a whole in Is, $I \vDash \mathbb{Z}^{o}, {}_{v}\mathcal{H}$:

(C.2-1) $\{\{[\varphi^2(x) \oplus \varphi(x) \oplus x] \circledast Is\} =< T^{C\Delta}\} \Subset Ш^{\Delta}$,
(here we employ this becoming to approximate Bcm. (B.1-3-2)) or

(C.2-2) $x \oplus y \oplus z = \sigma \Vdash \Sigma^{TC}$ (Σ^{TC} referring to a state of simple T central),

where $y = \varphi(x)$ and $z = \varphi^2(x)$. Then we write:

(C.2-3) $T^{Rcv}\{x \oplus y\} = z$,

or $T^{-1}\{x \oplus y\} = z$ or $\{x \oplus y\}^{-1} = z$, where $T^{Rcv}\{.\}$ stands for the tao reversal of $\{.\}$. By Bcm. (C.2-3), we mean that z and $T^{Rcv}\{x \oplus y\}$ constitute a yinyang pair in a state of simple T central.

A solution of Bcm. (C.2-2) is then:

(C.2-4) $X(.) = [\alpha_2 X(\mathbb{H}_2;.) \oplus \alpha_1 X(\mathbb{H}_1;.) \oplus \alpha_0 X(\mathbb{H}_0;.)] \circledast Ix(\mathbb{H}_x;.)$,

where α depicts the forces keeping X constant over time, β depicts the system-dynamical impactor representing the characteristics for X evolving into φX, γ depicts the system-dynamical impactor representing the characteristics for X evolving into $\varphi^2 X$, with $X(\mathbb{H})$ being the core of X at a state of simple Tcentral, and $Iz(\mathbb{H};.)$ represents the integrating force of organizing $\alpha X(\mathbb{H};.) \oplus \beta X(\mathbb{H};.)$ and $\gamma X(\mathbb{H};.)$ into the system Z.

In a sense, M/H in the above deconstruction is corresponding to $X(\mathbb{H})$ or $\mathbb{H}$ in Bcm. (C.2-4). Similarly, the system of the employees of a firm (E) can be deconstructed (see Figure C.2-2).

Figure C.2-2
Scheme of Deconstruction

f
E - - → E'
g ↘ ↗ h
E/W

where E' depicts the performance of the employees, and E/W the pursuit of salaries and wages and obedience of the management's power.

Here for an organizational system, if "M/H = E/W," i.e., the management's culture is isosystemic to the employees' culture, then there is a common ground for establishing the best type of management. That is, for the firm (A,B;C) = (A(-)|B(+);co(c)), A, B, C $\sqsubseteq$ (Ω,$\mathbb{Z}$o,v $\mathcal{H}$,{ℂ}) being the employees, the managers, and the core culture of this organization, respectively, the key to management is M/H = E/W, where M/H represents the core-unit of B (associated with co($\mathbb{C}_B$)) and E/W the core-unit of A (associated with co($\mathbb{C}_A$)). Here $<\mathfrak{C}> \equiv$ co($\mathfrak{C}$) = co($\mathbb{C}_B$) ⊓ co($\mathbb{C}_A$) which, by the notation of an MFCE scheme, is to be represented by: $<\mathbb{C}_A>\backslash<\mathbb{C}_B>=<\mathfrak{C}>$.

C.3 Reversal Construction of Tranquil and Conflict Systems

Culturally, tranquil system is an abstraction of the classical East Asian system (except in the cases of Japan and Mongolia). With proper modification, this can also serve as a proto-type system for Catholicism. In the following, we shall investigate this system E from the perspective of "reversal construction." Let j: E→E' be the system's generating relationship, i.e., E' is the transformation of E over time (i.e., for j being an impactor, jE = E'); and let Z be the representative entity of the system or the core-unit system (i.e., core unit of the system). Suppose Z = E/G, for E/G being called the *reversal-construction sub-system* of E. That is, E/G = {unit public enterprise, unit household, unit private enterprise}, by assuming the unit public enterprise is the typical system of the public enterprises and similarly for the unit private enterprise and unit household. Here G is the *basis of reversal construction*, representing the subsystem of the public-enterprise, households, and the private-enterprises.

Then this classical East Asian system can be expressed by Figure C.3-1. Let k: E/G→E' (k(E/G) = E', for k being an impactor), i: E/G→E, j: E→E'. Here if k = j*i for "*" being a composite operation, then this system is said to be "commutative."

Figure C.3-1
Scheme of Deconstruction

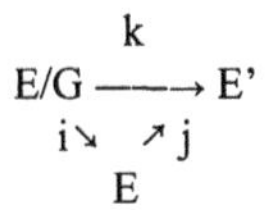

In Figure C.3-1, the substance of tranquility is manifested through the commutativity of this system. That is, public enterprises are essentially the major players of the economy under the control of the emperor. Since essentially there is no private business power, and the public enterprises are all controlled by the emperor, only (coerced) harmony exists in this classical East Asian system E.

A conflict system can also be investigated from the perspective of reversal construction. Let j: E→E' be the system's generating relationship, i.e., E' is the transformation of E over time; and Z be the representative element of the system: Z = E/HF. That is, E/HF = {unit household, unit private enterprise}, by assuming the unit private enterprise is the typical system of the private enterprises and similarly for the unit household. Here HF is the representative subsystem of the public-enterprise/household/private-enterprise or the unit of reversal construction, and, as shown in the above, E/G is called the reversal–construction sub-system (unit-core system, or the representative entity) of E. Then this conflict system can be expressed below. Let g: E/HF→E', h: E/HF→E, f: E→E'. Here if k = h # g for "#" being a composite operation, then this system is "commutative," see Figure C.3-2.

As seen in Figure C.3-2, the major entity of the conflict system (or a "competitive capitalist economy") is the sectors of households and private firms which carry the spirit of "competition" or conflict. Apparently there is no place for the public firm in this system.

Figure C.3-2
Scheme of Deconstruction

$$\begin{array}{ccc} & f & \\ E & \longrightarrow & E' \\ & g \searrow \;\; \nearrow h & \\ & E/HF & \end{array}$$

C.4 Strategic Chain Complex of Development

For the original idea of this section, see Tonn (1990), pp. 14-19.

Definition C.4-1. Let A, B $\sqsubseteq (\Omega,\mathcal{Z}\circ,{}_v\mathcal{H},\{\mathbb{C}\})$ be a system with E^A being the energy carried by A, and B be the transformed system of A with E^B being the energy carried by B. Here, for B being the transformed system of A, we may designate B as the d-systemism (for instance, y-systemsim, f-systemism, Hf-systemism, h-systemism, Hh-systemism) of A. If it is true that $A(E^A;t) \rightarrow B(E^B;t+1)$ for all t, then D*SYS = $\{A(E^A;t)\rightarrow B(E^B;t+1) \mid t=1,2,..,T\}$ is called the **space of dynamical system chain** (D*SYS). Below, for the consistency of notations, we shall denote D*SYS by $(\Omega^\Delta,\mathcal{Z}\circ,{}_v\mathcal{H},\{\mathbb{C}\})$.

Definition C.4-2. Let A $\sqsubseteq (\Omega^\Delta,\mathcal{Z}\circ,{}_v\mathcal{H},\{\mathbb{C}\})$ be a dynamical system and A^α be the energy attracting A. Let $\{(A,E^A,A^\alpha)\}$ be the closure of the operations of (A,E^A,A^α). Then $\Omega^{SEC} \equiv \{(A,E^A,A^\alpha;t\}\rightarrow(A,E^A,A^\alpha;t+n)\}$, $n \geq 1$ $(n\in\mathbb{N})$, is called the **system-energy complex 1** (SEC-1). If this SEC-1 is mathematically measurable, then it is called the **system-energy complex-measurable 1** (SEC-μ1): that is, $\Omega^{SEC}\text{-}\mu 1 \equiv \Omega^{SEC1}\sqcap\mathbb{C}$, or $x \Vdash X \sqsubseteq (\Omega^{SEC}\text{-}\mu 1,\mathcal{Z}\circ,{}_v\mathcal{H},\{\mathbb{C}\}) \Leftrightarrow x \Vdash X \sqsubseteq (\Omega^{SEC1},\mathcal{Z}\circ,{}_v\mathcal{H},\{\mathbb{C}\})\sqcap\mathbb{C}$.

Denition C.4-3. Let A , B $\sqsubseteq (\Omega^\Delta,\mathcal{Z}\circ,{}_v\mathcal{H},\{\mathbb{C}\})$ be a dynamical system and A^B be the energy attracting A. Let $\{(A,E^A,A^B)\}$ be the closure of the operations of (A,E^A,A^B). Then $\Omega^{SEC2} \equiv \{(A,E^A,A^B;t\}\rightarrow (B,E^B,B^A;t+n)\}$, $n \geq 1$ $(n\in\mathbb{N})$, is called the **system-energy complex-2** (SEC-2). If this SEC-2 is mathematically measurable, then it is also called the **system-energy complex-measurable** 2 (SEC-μ2): that is, $\Omega^{SEC}\text{-}\mu 2 \equiv \Omega^{SEC2}\sqcap\mathbb{C}$, or $x \Vdash X \sqsubseteq (\Omega^{SEC}\text{-}\mu 2,\mathcal{Z}\circ,{}_v\mathcal{H},\{\mathbb{C}\}) \Leftrightarrow x \Vdash X \sqsubseteq (\Omega^{SEC2},\mathcal{Z}\circ,{}_v\mathcal{H},\{\mathbb{C}\})\sqcap\mathbb{C}$.

Definition C.4-4 (H-continuity). Let A, B $\sqsubseteq$ SEC-μ $(A^\alpha, B^\beta = \circ)$. Then the becoming f: $A(t) \rightarrow B(t+n)$, $n \geq 1$ $(n\in\mathbb{N})$, (noted as: A → B), is called **H-continuity** if and only if $|\{A(E^A;t)\Theta B(E^B;t+n)\}\|_{\downarrow SU}| = \ominus$ as $n\rightarrow 0$ (n being an arbitrary number and $\ominus$ being the notation for "zero system"). Here "| . |" is the notation for choosing the positive difference (i.e., differencing), Θ is an impactor for differencing, and "$\|_{\downarrow SU}$" is a notation for downward scaling to a standardized unit size. Note that for A and B being systems, by "AΘB $= \ominus$" (AΘB is a **zero system**) is meant that A is identical to B. For simplicity of notation, we may write this as: $(A, E^A;t) \rightarrow^{HC} (B,E^B;t+1)$.

Definition C.4-5. (H-leap). Let A, B $\sqsubseteq$ SEC-μ $(A^\alpha, B^\beta = \circ)$. Then the becoming f: $A(t) \rightarrow B(t+\gamma)$ (noted as: A → B) is called **H-Leap** if and only if $\{fA(E^A;t)\Theta B(E^B;t+\gamma)\}\ \|_{\downarrow SU} \neq \ominus$ as $\gamma >> 0$ (where "x>>0" is the notation for x being a number much larger than zero). For simplicity of notation, we may write this as: $(A, E^A;t) \rightarrow^{HL} (B,E^B;t+\gamma)$.

Definition C.4-6. Let A, B $\sqsubseteq$ SEC-μ (with A^{α}, $B^{\beta} = \circ$). Then the becoming ϕ: A(t) $\longrightarrow$ B(t+1) (written as : A $\rightarrow$ B) is said to be one of **continuity in uncertainty** if and only if $\{\phi A(E^{A};t)\Theta B(E^{B};t+1)\}||_{\downarrow SU} = \obar$, where ϕ is an uncertain impactor (see the impactors associated with the uncertain system and distribution system). For simplicity of notation, we may write this as: (A, E^{A};t) $\longrightarrow^{StoC}$ (B,E^{B};t+1).

Remarks C.4-1. (1) If (A,E^{A};t) $\longrightarrow$ (B,E^{B};t+1), t being time, then it is said that in the period {t,t+1}, A becomes or transforms into B. (2) If A $\sqsubseteq$ (Ω^{D},$\mathcal{Z}$ $\circ$,v $\mathcal{H}$,{$\mathbb{C}$})$\sqcap\mathbb{C}$, then $\lim_{n\to\infty}$ (A_n,$E^{A}{}_{n}$,$A^{A}{}_{n}$) exists.

Definition C.4-7. Let A, B $\sqsubseteq$ SEC-μ (for A^{α}, $B^{\beta} \neq \circ$). Then the impactor f: A(E^{A},A^{α};t) $\longrightarrow$ B(E^{B},B^{β};t) is called **H-unifiable impactor I** if and only if $\{\phi(E^{A};t)\Theta\ (E^{B};t)\}||_{\downarrow SU} = \obar$ and $\{\phi(A^{\alpha};t)\Theta(B^{\beta};t)\}||_{S\downarrow} = \obar$. For simplicity of notation, we may write this as: (A, E^{A},A^{α};t) $\longrightarrow^{H\text{-unif}}$ (B,E^{B},B^{β};t), where "$\longrightarrow^{H\text{-unif}}$" denotes a unifiable impactor.

Definition C.4-8. Let A, B $\sqsubseteq$ SEC-μ1 or 2 (A^{B},$B^{A} \neq \obar$). Then the impactor f: A(E^{A},A^{B};t) $\longrightarrow$ B(E^{B},B^{A};t) is called **H-unifiable impactor II** (H-unif-II) if and only if $\{\phi(E^{A};t)\Theta(E^{B};t)\}||_{\downarrow SU} = \obar$ and {(A^{B};t),(B^{A};t)} $\sqsubseteq$ (Ω^{Δ},$\mathcal{Z}\circ$,v$\mathcal{H}$,{$\mathbb{C}$}). For simplicity of notation, we may write this as: (A,E^{A},A^{B};t) $\longrightarrow^{H\text{-unif-II}}$ (B,E^{B},B^{A};t).

Remark C.4-2. (1) Let A, B $\sqsubseteq$ SEC-μ1 or 2. If E^{A} = A^{B} or $|(E^{A};t)\Theta(E^{B};t)\}\ /\oslash\sigma_{X}|\} = \obar$ and {E^{B},A^{A}} $\sqsubseteq$ (Ω^{Δ},$\mathcal{Z}\circ$,v$\mathcal{H}$,{$\mathbb{C}$}), then (A,E^{A},A^{A};t) $\longrightarrow$ (B,E^{B},A^{B};t+1). (2) The marriage between a female F and a male M, F, M A, B $\sqsubseteq$ SEC-μ can be expressed as: (A,E^{A},A^{A};t) $\longrightarrow$ (B,E^{B},A^{B};t).

Definition C.4-9. For A, B, C $\sqsubseteq$ (Ω,$\mathcal{Z}\circ$,v$\mathcal{H}$,{$\mathbb{C}$}), let $\oplus \vDash \mathcal{H}$ be any impactor. Then $\mathcal{T} \vDash \mathcal{Z}\circ$,v$\mathcal{H}$ is called an **easily-separable impactor** if and only if $\mathcal{T}$\{A $\oplus$ B) = $\mathcal{T}$\{A\} $\oplus$ $\mathcal{T}$\{B\}. Note that for $\mathcal{T} \vDash \mathcal{Z}\circ$,v$\mathcal{H}$ such that $\mathcal{T}$\{A $\oplus$ B\} = $\mathcal{T}$\{A\} $\oplus$ $\mathcal{T}$\{B\} $\oplus$ C with C $\neq \circ$, it is not an easily-separable impactor.

Definition C.4-10. Let A= [$a_{i,j}$], B $\sqsubseteq$ (Ω^{Δ},$\mathcal{Z}\circ$,v$\mathcal{H}$,{$\mathbb{C}$}), c $\Vdash \Omega$ (c being some non-central elements or empty element $\circ$). If we have

$$\text{(C.4-1)}\quad B = \mathcal{T}A = \mathcal{T}[a_{i,j}] = \begin{vmatrix} a_{i,j} & a_{i,j+1} & c \\ a_{i+1,j} & a_{i+1,j+1} & c \\ & & c \end{vmatrix},$$

$$\text{(C.4-2)}\quad A = \begin{vmatrix} a_{i,j} & a_{i,j+1} \\ a_{i+1,j} & a_{i+1,j+1} \end{vmatrix},$$

for $\mathcal{T} \vDash \mathcal{Z}\circ$,v$\mathcal{H}$, then $\mathcal{T}$ is called a **matrix generating or augmenting impactor** generating B from A.

The ideas of element-impactors and system-creating/augmenting impactors, the matrix generating/augmenting operators, were originally called the super-vector SS operators (Tonn 1990a, and Tonn 1994: SK generator in Appendix D).

Definition C.4-11. Let $\Omega^{T*} = \{\Omega^{D},\Omega^{Rh},\Omega^{H},\Omega^{S+},\Omega^{S},\Omega^{S-},\Omega^{V},\Omega^{sC}\}$ be the complete strategic space, where Ω^{D} (D or WT), Ω^{Rh} (or G^{+}), Ω^{H} (or G), Ω^{S+}, Ω^{S}, Ω^{S-}, Ω^{V} and Ω^{sC} (or C) represent the spaces of leap strategy, rapidly developing strategy, high-speed developing strategy, stable and moderately-developing strategy, slow-and-variational strategy, and strategic continuity, respectively (see Chapter 8, Section 8.2).

For D $\Vdash \Omega^D$, D is a leap strategy, $G^+ \Vdash \Omega^{Rh}$ is the rapidly developing strategy, $G^+ \Vdash \Omega^R$ is the rapidly developmental strategy, G $\Vdash \Omega^H$ is the high-speed development strategy, $S^+ \Vdash \Omega^{S+}$ is the growth$^+$-in-stability development strategy, S $\Vdash \Omega^S$ is the stable-and-moderately development strategy, S $\Vdash \Omega^{S-}$ is the growth$^-$-in-stability development strategy, V $\Vdash \Omega^V$ is the slow-and-variational development strategy, and sC $\Vdash \Omega^{sC}$ is the strategy of continuity or no change. Let $(\zeta,\xi) \models \mathcal{Z}\circ,_v\mathcal{H}$ be a pair of leap impactors, $(\pi^1,\pi^2) \models \mathcal{Z}\circ,_v\mathcal{H}$ a pair of impactors of the rapidly developing strategy, $\varphi \models \mathcal{Z}\circ,_v\mathcal{H}$ a high-speed (developmental) strategic impactor, $\nu \models \mathcal{Z}\circ,_v\mathcal{H}$, a variational strategic impactor, $\nu+ \models \mathcal{Z}\circ,_v\mathcal{H}$ a variation$^+$ strategic impactor. Then ζ, ξ, π^1, π^2, φ, $\nu+$ and ν are all matrix-augmenting impactors.

Definition C.4-12. If A_t-$B_{t+1} \sqsubseteq (\Omega^\Delta,\mathcal{Z}\circ,_v\mathcal{H},\{\mathbb{C}\})$ for all $t \in [t_0,T]$ (i.e., A is in a **developmental system-strategic chain complex**, where B_{t+1} is the transformation of A_t at time t+1, for all t). Here, for all t, A_t, $B_t \sqsubseteq \Omega^{T\Delta} \equiv \{Sc,V, S^-,S,S^+,G,G^+,W^T\}$, for $W^T \equiv D$, and $\{A(E^A,A^\alpha;t) \rightarrow B(E^B,B^\beta;t+1)\}$ is called a developmental system-chain. Note that $(\Omega^\Delta,\mathcal{Z}\circ,_v\mathcal{H},\{\mathbb{C}\})$ is the space of dynamical system transformation.

Figure C.4-1
Developmental system-strategic chain

$$(A,E^A;t) \xrightarrow{\text{(H-continuity)}} (A,E^A;t+i) \rightarrow \ldots \rightarrow (A,E^A;t+i+\gamma)$$
$$(B,E^B;t) \rightarrow \ldots \rightarrow \ldots \rightarrow (B,E^B;t+\gamma) \rightarrow \ldots \rightarrow (B,E^B;t+i+\gamma)$$
(H-leap: $(A,E^A;t+i) \rightarrow (B,E^B;t+i+\gamma)$)

Thema C.4-1. Let $A(E^A,.)$, $B(E^B,.) \sqsubseteq (\Omega^\Delta,\mathcal{Z}\circ,_v\mathcal{H},\{\mathbb{C}\})$ (i.e., D*SYS) and the strategic sets of $(A,E^A;t)$ and $(B,E^B;t)$ be different. If f: $(A,E^A;t) \rightarrow (A,E^A;t+1)$ $(n \in \mathbb{N})$ is H-continuous and g: $(A,E^A;t) \rightarrow (B,E^B,t+n)$ is H-leap ($n \in \mathbb{N}$, $n >> 0$ or n is much greater than zero), then $\{(A,E^A;t) \rightarrow (B,E^B;t+n)\}$ is a developmental system-chain. That is, $(A,E^A;t)$ could develop into $(B,E^B;t+n)$ by changing strategies (see Figure C.4-1).

Reasoning. Since A, B $\sqsubseteq (\Omega^\Delta,\mathcal{Z}\circ,_v\mathcal{H},\{\mathbb{C}\})$, we have $(A,E^A;t) \rightarrow (A,E^A;t+1) \rightarrow \ldots \rightarrow (A,E^A;t+m)$ $(0 \leq m < n)$ and $(B,E^B;t) \rightarrow (B,E^B;t+1) \rightarrow \ldots \rightarrow (B,E^B;t+\gamma)$, for $\gamma > n >> 0$. Because $(A,E^A;t) \rightarrow (A,E^A;t+j)$, for all $j < n$, is H-continuous, we have $(A,E^A;t) \rightarrow (A,E^A;t+i)$, for $i \leq j < n$, is H-continuous. Further, because $(A,E^A;t+i) \rightarrow (B,E^B;t+i+\gamma)$, is H-leap, $(A,E^A;t+i) \rightarrow (B,E^B;t+i+\gamma)$ is H-leap. Hence, we have $(A,E^A;t) \rightarrow (A,E^A;t+i) \rightarrow (B,E^B;t+i+\gamma)$ as a feasible strategic path (see Figure C.4-1).

That is, we have $\{(A,E^A;t) \rightarrow (B,E^B;t+m)\}$ as a "H-leap/continuity chain." That is, $\{(A,E^A;t) \rightarrow (B,E^B;t+m)\}$ for $m \in \mathbb{N}$ (by setting $i+\gamma < m$) and $0 << m$, by transforming A into B, is a developmental system-strategic chain when leap and non-leap strategies are properly incorporated in the system A (for example, with strategy D, in order to initiate a leap strategic path) and system B (for example, with strategy G^+ after the leap-transformation).

In the following, we shall investigate some useful schemes of strategic competition. Given two system (or countries), the leader A and the follower B. If A: $G_t \rightarrow G_{t+1}$ (denoted G_t-G_{t+1}, or simply G-G) and B: $G_t \rightarrow W^T_{t+1}$ (denoted G_t-W^T_{t+1}, or simply G-W^T), then B may catch up to A, all other things being equal.

Thema C.4-2. For the leader A and the follower B, let A, B $\sqsubseteq$ (Ω,$\mathbb{Z}$o,$_v\mathbb{H}$,{$\mathbb{C}$}) and (A,E^A;t), (B,E^B;t) $\sqsubseteq$ (Ω,$\mathbb{Z}$o,$_v\mathbb{H}$,{$\mathbb{C}$}). If either f: $(A,E^A)_t \rightarrow (A,E^A)_{t+1}$ and g: $(B,E^B)_t \rightarrow (B,E^B)_{t+1}$ are H-continuous, or A and B adopt the same strategy over time, then B may not catch up to A , all other things being equal.

Reasoning. (i) Without loss of generality, let A, B $\sqsubseteq$ (Ω^{SEC},$\mathbb{Z}$o,$_v\mathbb{H}$,{$\mathbb{C}$})$\sqcap\mathbb{R}$. Let both A and B adopt the same strategy all the time, and suppose that B eventually catches up to A. Since g: (B,E^B;t) $\rightarrow$(B',$E^{B'}$;t+1) is H-continuous, in the limit of systemic change (or YY-limit), (B,E^B;t) $\rightarrow$(B*,E^{B*}), for (B*,E^{B*}) being the Tcentral (B*,E^{B*}). That is:

$$
\begin{aligned}
\text{(C.4-1)}\quad & YY_{j\rightarrow j^*}\{B_i,E^B_j\} \\
&= YY_{j\rightarrow j^*}\{\textstyle\int_B \psi(B_K,E^B_j)d(B_K,E^B_j)\} \\
&= \{\textstyle\int_B YY_{j\rightarrow j^*}\psi(B_K,E^B_j)d(B_K,E^B_j)\} \\
&= \{\textstyle\int_B \psi(B_K,E^B_{j^*})d(B_K,E^B_{j^*}\} \\
&= \{B_k,E^B_{j^*}\} \\
&= \{B^*,E^B*\},
\end{aligned}
$$

at a state of simple TCentral, assuming that $\{B_k,E^B_j\}$ may be expressed in the form of $\int_B \psi(B_K,E^B_j)d(B_K,E^B_j)$, and by applying the assumption of the **linear YY operation**:

$$\text{(C.4-2)}\quad YY_{j\rightarrow j^*}\{\textstyle\int_B x(i,j)dx(j)\} = \int_B [YY_{j\rightarrow j^*}\, x(i,j)]dx(j^*), \text{ for } x\in B.$$

That is, (B,E^B) may remain the same over time. Similarly, (A,E^A) may remain the same over time as well. But (B,E^B) may not change over time! For B lags to A at the initial time and B would eventually catch up to A, B must grow over time. But this is not possible!

Note that in the above we may have a set of alternative becomings to Bcms. (C.4-1) and (C.4-2), that is, we have:

$$
\begin{aligned}
\text{(C.4-3)}\quad & YY_{j\rightarrow j^*}\{B_i,E^B_j\} \\
&= YY_{j\rightarrow j^*}\{\xi(B_K,E^B_j)\} \\
&= \xi\{YY_{j\rightarrow j^*}(B_K,E^B_j)\} \\
&= \xi(B_K,E^B_{j^*}) \\
&= \{B_k,E^B_{j^*}\} \\
&= \{B^*,E^B*\},
\end{aligned}
$$

at a state of Tcentral, By employing the principle of **YY leap operation**:

$$\text{(C.4-4)}\quad YY_{j\rightarrow j^*}\{\xi(B_K,E^B_j)\} = \xi[YY_{j\rightarrow j^*}(B_K,E^B_j)].$$

(ii) Without loss of generality, let A, B $\sqsubseteq$ (Ω^{SEC},$\mathbb{Z}$o,$_v\mathbb{H}$,{$\mathbb{C}$}). Let A and B adopt different strategies over time, and suppose that B eventually catches up to A. But from the above reasoning, this may not be possible under the assumption of H-continuity.

Definition C.4-13. For the leader A and the follower B, let A, B $\sqsubseteq$ (Ω,$\mathbb{Z}$o,$_v\mathbb{H}$,{$\mathbb{C}$}) and (A,E^A;t), (B,E^B;t) $\sqsubseteq$ (Ω^Δ,$\mathbb{Z}$o,$_v\mathbb{H}$,{$\mathbb{C}$}). Then the following strategic complex is called the scheme of **GG^+-W^TG strategic-competitive complex**:

Figure C.4-2
GG^{+}-$W^{T}G$ strategic-competitive complex

$$\begin{array}{ccc} A: G & \rightarrow & G^{+} \\ \updownarrow & & \updownarrow \\ B: W^{T} & \rightarrow & G \end{array}$$

Thema C.4-3. For the leader A and the follower B, let A, B $\sqsubseteq (\Omega, \mathcal{Z}\circ,_{v}\mathcal{H}, \{\mathbb{C}\})$ and $(A,E^{A};t)$, $(B,E^{B};t) \sqsubseteq (\Omega^{\Delta}, \mathcal{Z}\circ,_{v}\mathcal{H}, \{\mathbb{C}\})$. If g: $(B,E^{B})_{t} \rightarrow (B,E^{B})_{t+1}$ is not H-continuous and B adopts strategies different from A, then B may catch up to A , all other things being equal.

Reasoning. Suppose the strategic trajectory of A is G-G, and that of B is G-G^{+} or G-W^{T}. That is, $(B,E^{B})_{t} \rightarrow (B,E^{B})_{t+1}$ is H-leap. By adopting a G^{+} or W^{T} strategy over time, in a finite period of time, it is possible for $(B,E^{B})_{t} \rightarrow (B,E^{B})^{*}$, the target of $(B,E^{B})_{t}$. That is, by assuming B has a greater potential than A and it has a more effective set of strategies, if $\{A(E^{A};\tau)\ominus B(E^{B};\tau)\}||_{\downarrow SU} = \odot$ at time $t = \tau$, $0 << \tau$, then B catches up to A in the finite period of time.

Thema C.4-4. For the leader A and the follower B, let A, B $\sqsubseteq (\Omega, \mathcal{Z}\circ,_{v}\mathcal{H}, \{\mathbb{C}\})$ and $(A,E^{A};t)$, $(B,E^{B};t) \sqsubseteq (\Omega^{\Delta}, \mathcal{Z}\circ,_{v}\mathcal{H}, \{\mathbb{C}\})$, and $\mathcal{T}$, $\varphi \vDash \mathcal{Z}\circ,_{v}\mathcal{H}$ be system-creating (or element/ system-augmenting) impactor. Then in the above scheme of GG^{+}-$W^{T}G$ strategic- competitive complex, B may not eventually catch up to A. That is, it may not happen that $\mathcal{T}B_{t} \rightarrow \varphi A^{*}$, for t = 1,2,…,s. Here, $\mathcal{T}B_{t}$ is B at time t = s, and φA^{*} is A at time t = s.

Reasoning. Suppose the contrary that $\mathcal{T}B_{t} \rightarrow \varphi A^{*}$, for t = 1, 2, …, s. (1). Let B a time t be: $B^{CIV} = [b_{i1}\ b_{i2} \ldots b_{iL}]$, i = 1, 2,…, L. At time t_{1} ($t_{1} > t$), let $\mathcal{C}$ be the system-creating impactor of the civilian sector, which is also the impactor that exports agricultural products and importing light industrial technology from outside. That is, by applying $YY\{.\}^{WT}$ to b_{iL} at time t_{1}, we have:

(C.4-5) $\mathcal{C}\{B^{CIV}\} \equiv [b_{i1}\ b_{i2} \ldots YY\{b_{iL}\}^{WT}] = [b_{i1}\ b_{i2} \ldots \{b_{iL}\}^{WT}]$,

where $\{b_{iL}\}^{WT}$ depicts the light industry under W^{T} strategy.

(2) At time t, let B be: $B^{CIV} = [b_{j1}\ b_{j2} \ldots b_{jm}]$, j = 1, 2,…,J. Then, at time t_{1} ($t_{1} > t$), let $\mathcal{M}$ be the system-creating impactor of the military sector, which is also the impactor exporting agricultural products and importing heavy-and military technology from outside. That is, by applying $YY\{.\}^{WT}$ to b_{jM} at time t_{1}, we have:

(C.4-6) $\mathcal{M}\{B^{CIV}\} \equiv [b_{j1}\ b_{j2} \ldots YY\{b_{jM}\}^{WT}] = \left| \begin{array}{l} b_{j1}\ b_{j2}\ \ldots\ M_{j}^{WT} \\ b_{j+1,1}\ b_{j+2,2} \ldots M_{j+1}^{WT} \end{array} \right|$,

where the old military sector $[b_{j1}\ b_{j2} \ldots b_{jM}]$ becomes the new sector $[b_{j+1,1}\ b_{j+2,2} \ldots M_{j}^{WT}]$, while due to the creative effect of this impactor $\mathcal{M}$, a new heavy-industrial sector $[b_{j1}\ b_{j2} \ldots M_{j+1}^{WT}]$ is created.

By integrating the total effects of the impactors of $\mathcal{L}$ and $\mathcal{M}$, we have:

$$\text{(C.4-7)}\quad (\mathcal{M},\mathcal{L})\{B\} = \begin{vmatrix} \mathcal{L}B^{CIV} \\ \mathcal{M}B^{M} \end{vmatrix} = \begin{vmatrix} b_{i1}\ b_{i2}\ \ldots\ (c,\{b_{iL}\}^{WT}) \\ b_{j1}\ b_{j2}\ \ldots\ (c,\{b_{jM}\}^{WT}) \\ b_{j+1,1}\ b_{j+1,2}\ \ (c,\{b_{j+1,M}\}^{WT}) \end{vmatrix},$$

$i = 1, 2, \ldots, I$, $j = 1, 2, \ldots, J$, with c as an arbitrary factor. In addition, let $h = 1, 2, \ldots, I, \ldots, I+J$, $k = j+1$, $L^* = \max\{L,M\}$, then we have:

$$\text{(C.4-8)}\quad (\mathcal{M},\mathcal{L})\{B\} = \begin{vmatrix} b_{h1}\ b_{h2}\ \ldots(c,\{b_{hL^*}{}^{WT}\}) \\ b_{k1}\ b_{k2}\ \ldots(c,\{b_{kM}\}^{WT}) \end{vmatrix}.$$

Therefore, in B, as a result of employing W^W strategy, the new industries, especially that of $|b_{j1}\ b_{j2}\ \ldots\ M_j^{WT}\ |$, may help B to catch up to A at time t_1. This is also made possible by the strategy G employed by A up to time t_1. Thus, B grows faster than A in the period t-t_1, and it may be true that: $\mathcal{T}B \equiv (\mathcal{M},\mathcal{L})B(t-t_1) \uparrow \varphi A(t-t_1)$.

But at time t_1 ($t_2 > t_1$), A changes its strategy to G^+, while B switches its strategy to G. In this case, if B fails to catch up to A at time t_1, or in the period t_1-t_2, B starts to lag behind A again, then it may not be true that: $\mathcal{T}B(t_2) \uparrow \varphi A(t_2)$. Contradiction.

Thema C.4-5. For the leader A and the follower B, let A, B $\sqsubseteq (\Omega,\mathcal{Z}\circ,{}_v\mathcal{H},\{\mathbb{C}\})$ and $(A,E^A;t)$, $(B,E^B;t) \sqsubseteq (\Omega,\mathcal{Z}\circ,{}_v\mathcal{H},\{\mathbb{C}\})$. Then in the GG^+-W^TG strategic-competitive complex B may catch up to A in a finite period of time (See Figure C.4-3) .

Reasoning. Similar to the reasoning presented in Thema C.4-4.

Figure C.4-3
GG^+-W^TG strategic-competitive complex

$$\begin{array}{ll} A: G \rightarrow & G^+ \\ \quad\ \uparrow & \ \uparrow \\ B: W^T \rightarrow & G \end{array}$$

Appendix D – Dynamic CE Balance

D.1 Introduction

In this Appendix D, we shall develop two schemes of dynamical Tcentral. The first scheme, the Scheme 1, is based on a static scheme in which the structures of all players change over time. The second scheme, Scheme 2, will have its dynamical imprint through some schemes of systemic-change becoming. Below we develop them in turn.

D.2 Scheme 1

Now we develop the first scheme of dynamical Tcentral. For this purpose, let a basic or grand system be: $X = \{X_1, X_2, \ldots, X_n\} \sqsubseteq (\Omega, \mathbb{Z}^{\circ}, {}_{v}\mathbb{H}, \{\mathbb{C}\})$, $[Y_k, Y_j] \Lleftarrow \langle \mathbb{C}_X \rangle$, where $Y_j \equiv [(X_1, \mathbb{C}_{X1/Z}), (X_2, \mathbb{C}_{X2/Z}), \ldots, (X_n, \mathbb{C}_{Xn/Z}) | (c, \sigma(c))]$, $Y_k \equiv [(c, \mathbb{C}_{C/Z}) | ((X_1, \xi_1(X_1)), (X_2, \xi_2(X_2)), \ldots, (X_n, \xi_n(X_n))]]$, $\xi_i \vDash \mathbb{Z}^{\circ}, {}_{v}\mathbb{H}$, $i = 1,2,\ldots,n$. Here these X_i, X_j, X_k are sub- or unit systems.

Remark D.2-1. From, for example, Bcm. (A.4-4-1), "$\langle \mathbb{C}_{Xi/Z} \rangle = \langle \mathbb{C}_{Xi} / \mathfrak{C}_Z \rangle$" is meant the cultural forces of $\mathbb{C}_{Xi}$ deriving its strengths from the interactions with the cultural core $\mathfrak{C}$ of the system in question. In contrast, $\sigma(c)$ represents the cultural force of the center element c. In other words, $\sigma(c)$ is the force of impact of the center upon all the non-central elements X_i. Thus, Y_j reprensents the force of control of the center over the non-central elements, while Y_k reprensents the feedback force of all the non-central elements upon the central element.

Let $X = \chi \oplus \langle \mathbb{C}_X \rangle$ reach a specific state of T continuity, then there exists a solution to the following scheme (see Section 3.2). Let this scheme be: Under the system operation of unit system X_i, for each i, and for system-creating impactor $\Psi \vDash \mathbb{Z}^{\circ}, {}_{v}\mathbb{H}$, for

(D.2-1) $\varphi\{X\} = X$

(i.e., X is in a state of systemic continuity), $i = 1,2,\ldots,n$, $i \neq k, j$, with $\varphi \vDash \mathbb{Z}^{\circ}, {}_{v}\mathbb{H}$ as an impactor of T continuity of the system, $\Psi\{X\}$ is under the environment of the pure dynamic structure:

(D.2-2) $\Delta \in \Omega$.

To solve this model, let

(D.2-3) $T = \Psi\{X\} \text{ ɤ } \Delta$,

where ɤ $\vDash \mathbb{Z}^{\circ}, {}_{v}\mathbb{H}$ is the interactor connecting $\Psi\{X\}$ and Δ.

Suppose, under the effective IISO/T scheme (principle of effective intra-inter systemic operations -- partition, modification, alternation, reorganization, and/or integration, etc. and a state of T continuity), this scheme entails the operations of the whole (or mutuality) and individuality (or selfhood). Then, simultaneously at a joint state of equicentrality and T continuity (see §3.2-2), we have:

$$(D.2\text{-}4)\quad (\varphi\{T\})_{x1,x2,\ldots,xn} = (\varphi\{\Psi\{X\}^{\curlyvee}\Delta\})_{x1,x2,\ldots,xn,Ix}$$
$$= (\varphi\{\Psi\{X\},\Delta\})_{x1,x2,\ldots,xn} \ltimes \varphi\{\Psi\{Ix\},E\}$$
$$= \varphi\{\Psi\{X\}\otimes(\Gamma^{\Delta}\{X_1 \stackrel{\star}{=} X_2 \stackrel{\star}{=} \ldots \stackrel{\star}{=} X_n,\Delta\} \ltimes \varphi\{\Psi\{Ix\},E\}).$$

(where $Ix \equiv I(x_1,x_2,\ldots,x_n)$, see Bcms. (3.2-1-7) and (3.2-2-4a)). Here $(\varphi\{\Psi\{X\},\Delta\})_i$ represents the operations of the whole (or mutuality), while $\varphi\{\Psi\{X\},E\}$ represents the interactive operations of the whole (or mutuality) and individuality (or selfhood). Note that $\ltimes \models \mathcal{Z}_{\circ,v}\mathcal{H}$ is the impactor connecting $\varphi\{X\}$ with $\varphi\{\Delta\}$, $\Gamma \models \mathcal{Z}_{\circ,v}\mathcal{H}$ is the impactor implementing the policy or strategy of "$X_1 \stackrel{\star}{=} X_2 \stackrel{\star}{=} \ldots \stackrel{\star}{=} X_n$" (or $Y_j \stackrel{\star}{=} Y_k$ in case of two factors or subsystems, see D.3 for the Definitions of Y_j and Y_k) under the influence of Δ, and $\otimes \models \mathcal{Z}_{\circ,v}\mathcal{H}$ is the impactor separating Δ from X. Here it is assumed that, after the separation, Δ operates together with "$Y_j \stackrel{\star}{=} Y_k$" (in the case of two subsystems) and the content of Y_j and Y_k is determined by the operation of Δ in X_i, where E is the external environment conditioned by $\mathbb{S}$elf* (i.e., the Ultimate Creativity-Destructivity or $\mathbb{T}$zu*). Then, we find out the solution under the condition of systemic continuity: $\varphi\{T\} = \varphi\{X\}$ under the operation of "$X_i,\ldots,X_n$." That is, we have $(\varphi\{T\})_{x1,x2,\ldots,xn} = (\varphi\{T\}) = \varphi\{\Psi\{X\}\}$, where $(\varphi\{T\})_{x1,x2,\ldots,xn}$ is $\varphi\{T\}$ under the operation of $\Psi\{X\}_{x1,x2,\ldots,xn}$.

For $\varphi\{T\}= \varphi\{\Psi\{X\}^{\curlyvee}\Delta\}=\varphi\{T\}$, the other route to derive this is as follows: let φ be the imactor creating a central system. Here by a central system ($\ominus$, "zero system") is like an "empty system" $\circ$, analogous to zero (i.e., 0) or the empty set $\varnothing$ in mathematics: for any set $A \in R$ the set of real numbers, $A \cup \varnothing = A$; or $a + 0 = 0$, $a \in R$. At the same time, let the systems $\xi = \zeta$, $\Delta \equiv \xi\,^{\text{-}}\,\zeta$, where $\Delta \equiv \xi\,^{\text{-}}\,\zeta$ is an "identity system" under the operation of "$X_i,\ldots,X_n$," for "$^{\text{-}}$" being the impactor eliminating the last term from the first term to set a stage for CE middle-centrality. In other words, φ forces Δ to "go away" (or φ behaves as a "nullifying impactor" that makes Δ an empty system). Therefore, we have: $\varphi\{T\} = \varphi\{\Psi\{X\}^{\curlyvee}\Delta\} = \varphi\{\Psi\{X\}\}$, X* being X in the state of CE middle-centrality. Without loss of generality, we write X for X*. Therefore, $\varphi\{T\} = \varphi\{\Psi\{X\}\}$.

Afterwards, under the operation of "$X_i,\ldots,X_n$," the basic system reaches a state of CE balance, or in a state of system's continuity for X (or X = X*): $(\varphi\{T\})_{x1,x2,\ldots,xn} = \Psi\{X\} = \Psi\{X\}^*$. Consequently, $(\varphi\{T\})_{x1,x2,\ldots,xn} = \Psi\{X\}$, and by replacing $(\varphi\{T\})_{x1,x2,\ldots,xn}$ by $\Psi\{X\}$ in the right hand side of Bcm. (D.2-4), in the case of dynamical world (i.e., right after reaching a state of instantaneous continuity, the system starts to move into a dynamical world), we get $\Psi\{X\} = \varphi\{\Psi\{X\}\}\otimes(\Gamma^{\Delta}\{X_1 \stackrel{\star}{=} X_2,\ldots \stackrel{\star}{=} X_n,\Delta\} \ltimes \varphi\{Ix,E\})$ (or "$X_k \stackrel{\star}{=} X_j$" to replace "$X_1 \stackrel{\star}{=} X_2,\ldots \stackrel{\star}{=} X_n$" in the case of two factors). Because in the state of CE mediety-centrality $\varphi\{\Psi\{X\}\} = \Psi\{X\}$, by removing $\Psi\{X\}$ and $(\varphi\{T\})_{x1,x2,\ldots,xn}$ from each side of Bcm. (T.2-4) respectively, we derive the formula $\{\Gamma^{\Delta}\{X_1 \stackrel{\star}{=} X_2 \stackrel{\star}{=} \ldots \stackrel{\star}{=} X_n,\Delta\} \ltimes \varphi\{Ix,E\}) =< T^{CE}\} \Vdash \text{Ш}^{\Delta}$ (or "$X_k \stackrel{\star}{=} X_j$" to replace "$X_1 \stackrel{\star}{=} X_2 \stackrel{\star}{=} \ldots \stackrel{\star}{=} X_n$" in the case of two factors).

Here, Γ is a **dynamic impactor**: $\Gamma^{\Delta}\{(X_1,X_2,\ldots,X_n),\Delta\} \equiv \Gamma^{\Delta}\{X_1 \stackrel{\star}{=} X_2 \stackrel{\star}{=} \ldots X_n,\Delta\}$ implies that $(X_1,X_2,\ldots,X_n) \equiv (X_1,X_2,\ldots,X_n)^{\Delta} \sqsubseteq \text{Ш}^{\Delta}$, and over time we may have one of the following: X_j, $\stackrel{\star}{=} X_k$, $X_j \geq X_k$, and X_j, $\leq X_k$.

$$(D.2\text{-}5a)\qquad (X_1,X_2,\ldots,X_n)^{\Delta} \sqsubseteq \text{Ш}^{\Delta}$$
$$\Leftrightarrow X_i^{\Delta} \stackrel{\star}{=} X_j^{\Delta},\ X_i^{\Delta} \geq X_j^{\Delta},\ \text{or}\ X_i^{\Delta} \leq X_j^{\Delta},$$

for all i, j, where X_i^{Δ} is a dynamical X_i for all i; or

(D.2-5b) $(Y_i,Y_k)^{\Delta} \sqsubseteq \text{Ш}^{\Delta}$

$\Leftrightarrow Y_j^{\Delta} \stackrel{\star}{=} Y_k^{\Delta}, Y_j^{\Delta} \geq Y_k^{\Delta}$, or $Y_j^{\Delta} \leq Y_k^{\Delta}$

in the case of two factors.

That is, in the case of a **balanced micro-management** for two factors or subsystems, we have:

(D.2-6) $\Gamma^{\Delta}\{Y_j \stackrel{\star}{=} Y_k,\Delta\} \overline{\barwedge}\, \tau, \tau \Vdash (\mathfrak{I},\text{Ш}^{Д}) \Vvdash \mathbb{T}\text{zu}^*$,

or in the case of multiple factors or subsystems: for all X_i,

(D.2-7) $\Gamma^{\Delta}\{X_1 \stackrel{\star}{=} X_2 \stackrel{\star}{=} \ldots \stackrel{\star}{=} X_n,\Delta\} \overline{\barwedge}\, \tau, \tau \Vdash (\mathfrak{I},\text{Ш}^{Д}) \Vvdash \mathbb{T}\text{zu}^*$.

This above becoming or formula can also be written as: $\Gamma^{\Delta}\{Y_j \stackrel{\star}{=} Y_k,\Delta\} \overline{\barwedge}\, \tau$ or $\Gamma^{\Delta}\{ X_1 \stackrel{\star}{=} X_2 \stackrel{\star}{=} \ldots \stackrel{\star}{=} X_n,\Delta\} \overline{\barwedge}\, \tau$, where

(D.2-8) $\Delta_i \equiv$ "$X_i \Lleftarrow \Delta$"

or $\Delta_{X1,X2,\ldots,Xn} \equiv$ "$X_{X1,X2,\ldots,Xn} \Lleftarrow \Delta$"

for "$X_i \Lleftarrow \Delta$" being X_i operating under the influence of the pure dynamical structure Δ_i and similarly for "$X_{X1,X2,\ldots,Xn} \Lleftarrow \Delta$", "$\Lleftarrow$" $\vDash \mathbb{Z}o,_v\mathbb{H}$ being a restrictive impactor, and "$\overline{\barwedge}$" $\vDash \mathbb{Z}o,_v\mathbb{H}$ being an impactor connecting Γ^{Δ} and τ (and $\mathbb{T}\text{zu}^*$ indirectly) .

This means, for a firm, the objective is not just to maximize profits, but also to achieve a balance between organizational and technological approaches, and between profit maximization and market share maximization. This objective may also involve a determination to promote technology, organizational efficiency and strategic effectiveness.

Note that in the above derivation of Bcm. (D.2-4), if $\Gamma^{\Delta}\{X_1 \stackrel{\star}{=} X_2 \stackrel{\star}{=} \ldots \stackrel{\star}{=} X_n,\Delta\}$ is replaced by $\Gamma^{\Delta}\{X_1 \geq X_2 \geq \ldots \geq X_n,\Delta\}$, then we have the **principle of unbalanced micro-management in the broad sense**: for each X_i,

(D.2-9) $\Gamma^{\Delta}\{X_1 \geq X_2 \geq \ldots \geq X_n,\Delta\} \overline{\barwedge}\, \tau, \tau \Vdash (\mathfrak{I},\text{Ш}^{Д}) \Vvdash \mathbb{T}\text{zu}^*$.

To have the principle of interconnectedness, in the above derivation of Bcm. (D.2-4), replace the third line by: $(\varphi\{X\} \otimes \Gamma^{\Delta}\{X_1 \leftrightharpoons X_2 \leftrightharpoons \ldots \leftrightharpoons X_n,\Delta\}) \ltimes \varphi\ \{Ix,E\}$ with "$\leftrightharpoons$" denoting the impactor of interconnectedness (i.e., one closely connected to other in a reciprocal manner, such as in the case of Taiwanese kuanhsi business group, Japanese keiretsu or South Korean chaebol). Then we have the **principle of interconnectedness**: for each X_i,

(D.2-10) $X_i = \Gamma^{\Delta}\{X_1 \leftrightharpoons X_2 \leftrightharpoons \ldots \leftrightharpoons X_n,\Delta\} \overline{\barwedge}\, \tau, \tau \Vdash (\mathfrak{I},\text{Ш}^{Д}) \Vvdash \mathbb{T}\text{zu}^*$.

Note that in a cultural economy, this principle of connectedness may lead to the economies of network and thereby the cultural advantage which may be expressed by the formula: $E(C \mid \psi\{R,\Delta\} \stackrel{\star}{=} \psi\{P,\Delta\}) = E[\mathcal{E}\_\mathcal{P}\_\mathcal{S}(\xi),\mathcal{E}\_\mathcal{F}\_\mathcal{E}g(\xi),\mathcal{E}\_\omega\text{-}\rho(\xi) \mid \xi \Vdash co(C)]$ (see Bcm. (J.4) in Appendix J where R stands for righteousness and p for profits).

D.3 Scheme 2

In this section, we shall develop the second scheme of dynamical Tcentral based on the *systemic-change becoming*. For this purpose, let a basic or grand system be: $X = \{X_1,X_2,\ldots,X_n\} \sqsubseteq (\Omega,\mathcal{Z}\circ,_v\mathcal{H},\{\mathbb{C}\})$, $[Y_k,Y_j] \Leftarrow <\mathbb{C}_X>$, where $Y_j \equiv[(C,\sigma(C))|((X_1,\mathbb{C}_{X1/Z}), (X_2,\mathbb{C}_{X2/Z}),\ldots,(X_n,\mathbb{C}_{Xn/Z}))]$ (C being the central element/system), $Y_k \equiv [(X_1,\xi_1(X_1)),(X_2,\xi_2 (X_2)),\ldots,(X_n ,\xi_n(X_n))|(c,\mathbb{C}_{C/Z})]$, $\xi_i \vDash \mathcal{Z}\circ,_v\mathcal{H}$, $i = 1, 2, \ldots, n$. Here these X_i, X_j, X_k are subsystems. Let $X = \chi \oplus <\mathbb{C}_X>$ reaches a state of simple Tcentral, that is, the following scheme has a solution (see Chapter 3). Let this scheme be: Under the system operations of X_i, for each i, and for system-creating impactor $\Psi \vDash \mathcal{Z}\circ,_v\mathcal{H}$, $\varphi\{X\} = \{X,Y|Z\} \sqsubseteq (\Omega,\mathcal{Z}\circ,_v\mathcal{H},\{\mathbb{C}\})$, for

(D.3-1) $\varphi\{X\} = X$

(i.e., X is in a state of system continuity), $i = 1,2,\ldots,n$, $i \neq k, j$, with $\varphi \vDash \mathcal{Z}\circ,_v\mathcal{H}$ as a Tcentral impactor of the system, $\Psi\{X\}$ is under the solution of the created system S:

(D.3-2) $X^S(.) = \{\xi X_x(\mathbb{H}_x;.)\oplus\zeta X_y(\mathbb{H}_y;.)\oplus\eta X_z(\mathbb{H}_z;.)\} \circledast Ix(\mathbb{H}_s;.)$,

where (D.3-2) is a solution to the dynamical-change becoming: for $S \equiv \varphi\{X\}= \{X\oplus Y\oplus Z\}$ so that $X\oplus Y\oplus Z = \Phi \Vdash \Sigma^{TC}$ (i.e., $\{ X\oplus Y\oplus Z =< T^{C\Delta}\} \Vdash Ш^{\Delta}$), and under the operations of the pure dynamic force as a becoming of cultures (i.e, the cultural core $\mathfrak{C}$):

(D.3-3) $\Delta \equiv \Delta(\mathfrak{C}) \in\Omega$.

To solve this scheme, let

(D.3-4) $T = \Psi\{X\} \curlyvee (X^S,\Delta(\mathfrak{C}))$, or

(D.3-5) $T = \Psi\{X^S\} \curlyvee \Delta(\mathfrak{C})$,

where $\curlyvee \vDash \mathcal{Z}\circ,_v\mathcal{H}$ is the interactor connecting $\Psi\{X^S\}$ and $\Delta(\mathfrak{C})$ (or $\Psi\{X\}$ and $(X^S,\Delta(\mathfrak{C}))$. Note that here we have: $\Psi\{X^S\} = \Psi\{X\}\curlyvee X^S$.

Suppose, by the ISSO/T operations (i.e., the *principle of effective intra-inter systemic operations/T continuity* - partition, modification, alternation, reorganization, and/or integration, etc.), this scheme entails the operations of the whole (or mutuality) and individuality (or selfhood) similar to the case of static scheme. If we use the principle of CE balance, then from the above, we have:

$$
\begin{aligned}
\text{(D.3-6)}\quad (\varphi\{T\})_{X1,X2,\ldots,Xn} &= (\varphi\{\Psi\{X^S\}\curlyvee\Delta(\mathfrak{C})\})_{X1,X2,\ldots,Xn,Ix} \\
&= (\varphi\{\Psi\{X^S\},\Delta(\mathfrak{C})\})_{X1,X2,\ldots,Xn} \ltimes \varphi\{\Psi\{Ix^S\},E\} \\
&= \varphi\{\Psi\{X^S\}\otimes (\Gamma^{\Delta}\{X^S,\Delta(\mathfrak{C})\} \ltimes \varphi\{\Psi\{Ix^S\},E\}).
\end{aligned}
$$

Here $(\varphi\{\Psi\{X^S\},\Delta(\mathfrak{C})\})_{X1,X2,\ldots,Xn}$ represents the operations of the whole (or mutuality), while $\varphi\{\Psi\{Ix^S\},E\}$ represents the interactive operations of the whole (or mutuality) and individuality (or selfhood). Note that $\ltimes \vDash \mathcal{Z}\circ,_v\mathcal{H}$ is the impactor connecting $\varphi\{X^S\}$ and $\varphi\{\Delta(\mathfrak{C})\}$, and $\Gamma^{\Delta} \vDash \mathcal{Z}\circ,_v\mathcal{H}$ is the impactor generating the system S overtime.

Here it is assumed that, after the separation, the content of Γ^{Δ} shall depend on the potential factors embodied in X^S, nurtured in the environment or $\mathbb{T}zu^*$. Then, we derive the solution under the condition of continuity: $\varphi\{T\} = \varphi\{X\}$ under the operation of $X_{X1,X2,...Xn}$. That is, we have $(\varphi\{T\})_{X1,X2,...Xn} = (\varphi\{T\}) = \varphi\{\Psi\{X^S\}$, where $(\varphi\{T\})_{X1,X2,...Xn}$ is $\varphi\{T\}$ under the operation of $\Psi\{X\}_{X1,X2,...Xn}$.

Thus, we derive the **principle of dynamical CE Tcentral** : for each X_i^Δ,
(D.3-7) $\Gamma^\Delta\{X^S,\Delta(\mathfrak{C})_i\} \doublebarwedge \tau, \tau \Vdash (\mathfrak{I},\text{Ш}^{\text{Д}}) \Vvdash \mathbb{T}\mathrm{zu}^*$,

from $\{\Gamma^\Delta\{X^S,\Delta(\mathfrak{C})\} \ltimes \varphi\{Ix^S,E\})=<T^{C\Delta}\} \Subset \text{Ш}^\Delta$.

Below, we shall use a hypothetical system of Faziranism as an example to illustrate the evolution/revolutionary "trajectory" of Bcm. (D.3-7). By so doing, we shall proceed from the classical Faziranism to capitalist Faziranism, then to socialism, and eventually to the projected Faziranist self-masterism:

(i) $X_1^\Delta = \Gamma^\Delta\{X^S,\Delta(\mathfrak{C}^{Faz})_1\}$ is the system of classical Faziranism (at the first stage).

(ii) $X_2^\Delta = \Gamma^\Delta\{X^S,\Delta(\mathfrak{C}^{Cap})_2\}$ is the systems of capitalist Faziransim (at the second stage).

(iii) $X_3^\Delta = \Gamma^\Delta\{X^S,\Delta(\mathfrak{C}^{Sos})_3\}$ is the system of socialism (at the third stage),

(iv) $X_4^\Delta = \Gamma^\Delta\{X^S,\Delta(\mathfrak{C}^{FSelf})_4\}$ is the system of Faziranist self-masterism (at the fourth stage).

In Figure D.3-1, let $X_i = \{y_{-i}, y_{+i}\}$, for y_{-I} and y_{+i} being yin and yang forces of systemic changes, respectively, and $X_i^\Delta = \{(y_{-i})' = \odot, (y_{+i})' = \odot\}$. Then we derive a graph showing four stages of YY DSB.

Figure D.3-1
Four stages of YY DSB

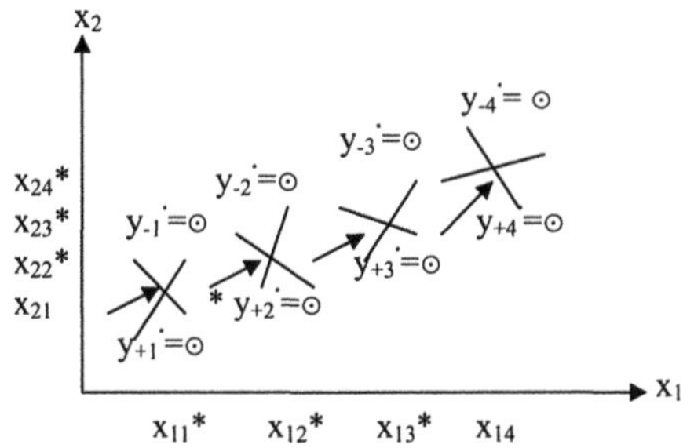

Appendix E – Mind Complex and MPFX-GPFX Cycles

E.1 Introduction

In this Appendix, we study the general mind complex and a few general socio-economic chain complexes associated with it. Two of these major socio-economic chain complexes are called MPFX and GPFX cycles.

In the economics of culture, one of our focal points is the production and consumption complex of a system. For any socio-economic system, the production and consumption complex is part of $\{.,(R_M,R^{DM}(e_r)),\tilde{O}|E(\{e_g\},.\}$. To further simplify the presentation, we may write the totality of production set (or subsystem), consumption set and planning set (i.e., the strategic complex or part of it) as a grand system: {production,consumption|planning}, where production set and consumption set are non-central members and planning set (or mind-action-strategic chain complex) is the central component of this grand system (see Tonn 2001).

In the following, we shall start off with the study of the mind complex in the context of the economics of culture.

E.2 Mind Complex in A System

The strategic complex behind any system of production and consumption are closely related to all cultural and spiritual dimensions of the human being. That is, the activities of production and consumption are reflections of human mind complexes in their interactions with the basis being-field under the general guidance of the social power-energy net.

In terms of the specifications of the mind and soul, there are several routes available to approach this mind set underlying the action-strategic complex Z.[47] They are all conditioned upon the cultural and institutional settings of the system in question. Note that these setting are also the conditioning factors for the strategic complex. That is, to study any system of production and consumption, we have to study the strategic complex, and to study the strategic complex, we have to study the cultural and institutional settings.

The study of the mind complex is also important for the study of the cultural complex of a single system, a person, a community or even a nation. And one way to approach this cultural complex is through the looking-mirror of the mind complex of the members of the system in question.

In general, human mind complex involves all fields of human and cultural studies, for example, the fields of philosophy, psychology, politics, sociology, and anthropology. Below, we shall touch upon a few issues related directly to these fields.

Note that for a community or nation, its mind complex is subsystem of its cultural complex. For example, the classical Chinese mind set is very much reflected in its cultural tradition in general and its philosophical tradition in particular.

Now we just briefly present a direction for approaching this cultural complex.

(1) Tonn's preliminary approach: This complex is presented by the dichotomy of will-rationality (WR) complex: the complex of conflict will-to-creation/scientific rationality versus the complex of tranquil will-to-creation/systemic rationality. Note that by this approach, dialectic rationality is considered as a part of systemic rationality. One of its implications is that with the former WR set, the underlying economy-polity shall be able to generate a planning-centralization efficiency for the system of communitarianism or socialism (or systematic efficiency for the system of Faziranism), while with the latter WR set, the underlying economy-polity creates and benefits from a market-decentralization efficiency.

(2) Hofstede-Bond approach (see Hofstede 1983, Hofstede and Bond 1984): Hofstede proposed a few sets of dichotomy: decentralized power structure (i.e., no power distance or democracy) versus centralized power structure (i.e., power distance or authoritarianism), risk-taking versus risk avoidance, individualism versus collectivism, and masculinity versus femininity. This implies that with the former WR set, the underlying economy-polity which is Western constitutes an advanced system, while with the latter WR set, the underlying economy-polity which is non-Western remains a backward system. Later on, in slightly modifying Bond's approach, Hofstede-Bond's approach adds a new dimension of Confucian dynamics to the system.

(3) Weber's approach (see Weber 1955, Huang 1989)[48]: Weber posed a dichotomy between the Western system and the non-Western system. For our presentation, the Western system symbolizes the collection of capitalist institutions, democratic bureaucracies, scientific spirits and Protestant ethics. By contrast, the non-Western system discloses a collection of non-capitalist institutions, non-democratic bureaucracy, non-scientific spirit and non-Christian ethics. It goes without saying that Max Weber contented that Western system is efficient whereas non-Western systems such as Islamic system and "Confucian system" are inefficient.

(4) Parsons' approach (see Sun [1992]): Parsons is thought to have argued for the dichotomies of emotional bias versus emotional neutrality, individualistic versus collectivist orientation, particular versus general standardization, innate quality versus achieved performance in one's life, and specific versus diffusive orientation toward one's duty. But there does not appear to have a clear cut criterion in addressing the issues of creativity or efficiency. Nevertheless, the culture associated with the former orientation may have artistic creativity, while the one associated with the latter may point to scientific efficiency.

In general, for the Western schemes, the classical mind complex appears to be connected to the philosophical systems of Plato, Aristotle, Augustine, Thomas Aquinas, and so on. For example, one may conceive St. Augustine's mind complex as {Babylon| city of God} (i.e., the mind in which the city of God dominates the city of Babylon) being a system, and St. Thomas Aquinas' mind complex as {reason,faith|God} (i.e., the wisdom of God dominates and maintains a balance between knowledge and faith) being another system. In the latter case, a world system of Thomas Aquinas can be constructed as {physical worlds, human society| God}, or God resides over both the human society and physical worlds of biology, chemistry and physics.

From one's mind complex as already mentioned in the above, in the classical setting of the West, one unfolds reason in order to gain some knowledge about the physical worlds surrounding us and thereby attempts to control it. In addition, one displays faith and reveals one's inner strengths rooted in an unlimited and unrestrained belief in God. The dichotomy of reason and faith is thought to be dissolved and to transform into an integrated unity under the light of God. But even under this circumstance, the implications of the mind complex for the related strategic complexes may not be clear following this sequence of reasoning.

Before turning away from the world of Western minds, we would like to suggest a possible way to approach the minds of Martin Heidegger and Alfred North Whitehead. By reading Heidegger's "Being and Time" (Sein und Zeit, Heidegger 1962, 1977), which may not yet delineate the matured mind of Heidegger, we might be able to introduce a trichotomy among the world of "existentielle," the world of Dasein (the real and sensible world for the mankind, or the world of "existential"), and the world of Sein (where to live is to be united with the "eternal meaning of life") or the world of Nothingness. In this above model, it is thought that no connection, or none of any consequence, exists between any two of these worlds we mentioned above. To simplify it, we may write this model as {Matter|Dasein|Sein} wherein each element is separated from the others. This depicts a pretty insipid, dull and unanimated world of life. To do more justice to it, it may be replaced by the following "symbolic" system: {Matter,Dasein,Chung} or {Matter,Dasein,Wu}, where Wu (or Nothingness) or Chung (the central element of the system) recites the forces of Ultimate Creativity and Destructivity/Nihility. Here Tzu* (or Chung) recounts what is responsible for the ultimate forces in the real worlds of statics/dynamics, potentiality/realization, and tao reversal. Then, this may be reinvigorated into a lively world in which entities, things or events like scientific, artistic and religious activities develop spontaneously and consummate exhilaratingly.

In the following, we propose a new angle to read Whitehead's Process and Reality (Whitehead 1978). Being universally "hermeneutical," we shall penetrate deeply into the "metanarrative" regarding to his idea of God being the entity representing the pure goodness. According to Whitehead, the real world and God are both entities of creativity, and yet the world is an entity of nihility (or destruction) as well. Note that this is somewhat analogous to the worlds of Chi and Tao (in our "scheme of Tao-Chi-and self-organization," see Subsection §A.4-1). By this interpretation, our new model must be presented by: (matter,mind,{God,C*-N}} where C* depicting the Ultimate Creativity of matter and N depicting the forces of Ultimate Neutrality and Nihility. Thus it implies that mind is jointly created by God and C*-N. Further, immediately after been created, mind and matter gain their own independent existences from God and C*-N, respectively, albeit their activities being still at the mercy of God and the world (or C*-N, forces of Ultimate Creativity of matter and of Neutrality/Nihility), respectively.

As for the Chinese schemes of philosophical thought, this mind complex appeals and adheres to the diverse cultural and philosophical systems such as those of Lao Tzu-Chuang Tzu, Confucius-Mencius, The Kuan Tzu, Chu Hsi, Wang Shoujen, Fung Yulan, Xiong Shili, Tang Junyi and Hsu Fukuan. Similar to the case of Western schemes, the implications for the related strategic complexes of these Chinese schemes may not be clear either. Nevertheless, below we shall attempt to ascertain some brief implications from the philosophical systems of Chu His, Fung Yulan, Xion Shili, Tang Chunyi and Hsu Fukuan.

The system of the mind complex of Chu Hsi may be constructed as {ching,hsing|mind}. According to Chu Hsi, the "mind" would integrate and be in charge of hsing (i.e., human nature or the part of human nature leaning naturally toward the ultimate good) and ching (i.e., human affection or the part of human nature inclining toward worldly desire or even evil). One's mind should always be cultivated by eradicating human desire and adhering closely to heavenly Li (reason or tao). Otherwise, it may be easy for man to be attracted by some evil acts.

From Chu Hsi's scheme, Fung Yulan developed a model of "pure metaphysics." In this metaphysics of Fung, both Li and Chi are pure and everlasting. Despite these Li and Chi present the self-generating truths in Fung's scheme, they are not dynamical elements. We could employ this world of pure "ideas" (in which Li and Chi exist) to match the world of real-sense, and to pair them with the worlds of potential and realization, and with worlds of statics-dynamics and tao reversal (i.e., self-dynamics/mutual-dynamics and yin-yang reversal). Thus in our new scheme, we have Chung = {Chi,Li|(potential-realization,statics-dynamics-YY reversal)} = {Chi,Li| Chung}, where Li stands for the ideal type of mind (will-to-creation) or sense-emotion, Chi stands for the ideal type of matter or rationality, and Chung as usual stands for (i) the potential and realizing forces and static-dynamical and yin-yang (or YY) reversal forces behind Li and Chi and (ii) the forces of mutual interactions between Li and Chi in the worlds of reality and motions.

Remark E.2-1. Note that this {Chi,Li|Chung} in the above is a standard R-system (see Sub-subsection A.2-2-3).

For this above scheme, it could be somewhat scrutinized from a new perspective. As such, at the conventional or *second level*, a dichotomy is assumed: either material (i.e., matter or Chi) or ideal (i.e., mind or Li), Deity or non-existence of Deity, Tao (i.e., li or Li) or Chi (or chi), shi (Shi, perception, consciousness or mind) or material, but not both. As for the operations of these mind (or Shi, shi) or matter, Tao or Chi, there arises behind them an entity called chung to denote the mutual reactions between them. Here, to be different from Fung's assertion, these tao and qi are assumed to carry some potential and dynamical forces. That is, at the *first level*, the whole is called Chung which is the totality of {mind,matter}. This is identical to {matter, mind|Chung} where Chung is operating as the central element. Being written in the form of the *third level*, Chung can be viewed as {matter, mind} wherein chung is left out and understood.

As for the mind system of Xiong Shili, it may be regarded as: {bi,xi}, {bi,xi|wu} or {bi,xi|he}, and for that of Tang Chunyi: {(wanwu sanshu jing,yilei chenghua jing,kungneng hsuyun jing),(kanchue hushe jing,kuanchau linghsu jing,taote shichien jing)|(gueihsiang yishen jing,wofa erkung jing,tiente liouhsing jing)}. Whereas the mind complexes of both Xiong Shili and Tang Chunyi are philosophical, that of Hsu Fukuan turns out to be more political. Hsu explicated a concept of crisis mentality, "youhuan yishih," in explaining the role of one's willingness to change and reform one's own culture. In the extreme case, it is this crisis mentality that motivates one to transplant the external culture in one's home land.

Strategically, the change of the planner's or a society's mind complex called conscience collective by Durkheim[49]) will set the stage for changing the cultural supply and demand curves and the total supply and demand curves we developed in the economics of culture. As a result, this mind complex, through its connection to the strategic set in a system, is responsible for the creation of a super normal state of the economy (if it is feasible), either in microeconomic, macroeconomic or global-systematic sense.

Note that one general approach to the mind complex points to the direction of developing systems of harmonious versus competitive cultures, or individualistic versus groupist cultures. Following the same pattern of reasoning, one may develop systems of market versus planning cultures. And to go beyond the conventional wisdom, one may even develop a system of Faziranist culture, which is based in naturalism, "spontaneitism," or humanism and is guided by systemic rationality. Note that this Faziranist culture may encompass both aspects of individualistic and groupist cultures as well as both aspects of market and planning cultures.

E.3 MPFX and GPFX Cycles

For the structures and operations of systems, we shall investigate a few human and social aspects in more detail.

In studying a system, both aspects of actions and communications among elements must be fully considered.[50] Besides, outside environments may posit as a determining factor when one is situated in either extremely favorable or unfavorable environments.

It is clear that the dynamics of the system mentioned in the above is created by the actions and interactions of individual elements or unit systems (i.e., the most basic systems) under the guidance of the systems' mind and strategic complexes in their relationships to other systems or outside environments. As a system, it has a self-generating capacity in its reactions to the environment, be it favorable or unfavorable.

In as much as any system having an organizational scheme, communication among members of a system, as a network of information, utterance and understanding, is ultimately necessary. Luhmann held that due to intentional or unintentional misrepresentation created through members' mechanisms of self-reference (that is, each may choose to either reveal or conceal one's true intention or situation), conflict may result in an organization. Whereas in the case of faithful revelation of one's intention and situation and of true coordinating one's expectation of others and being adaptive to others' actions, positive aspiration, social order and harmony may result (Lu [1992]).

Althusser (Althusser 1969, 1970; Wei [1992], James 1985) held that society is a function of multiple dimensions. By this it entails that the whole determines the parts, and yet some single parts can also determine the whole (or some other parts) at some critical juncture. In other words, a theory of multiple determinism of a system can be naturally established. In addition, a theory of interchanging roles of central and non-central elements in a system can be formulated as well. As a result, at some particular occasions, some non-central elements (unit systems, resp.) of a system (grand system, resp.) may determine the structure and direction of other non-central elements (unit systems, resp.) and even the central element (unit systems, resp.).

In a system, communication constitutes an integral part of the internal structure of χ. Being so, it is an essential component of the structure $\{.,C_S \times C^{DS}(e_r), [R_M, R^{DM}(e_r)], \tilde{O}|E(\{e_g\},.\}$. As regards the connection among multiple systems, (external) communication is a necessary medium of chain reaction responsible for these systems' actions. In terms of the ideas and agents of social change, the related symbols, rites and rituals, and tools and channels of action and communication within a specific society, Jürgen Habermas had a rather interesting approach. He developed a theory of background consensus, composed of four elements: comprehensibility claim (i.e., presentation of understandable information to others in the sense of correct pronunciation, grammar and syntax), truth claim (i.e., presentation of truth in one's speech act), rightness claim (i.e., presentation of an speech act fitting well into the mutual relations) and truthfulness claim (i.e., presentation of a speech act to be appreciated by others) (Huang [1996]).

When the process of communication is interrupted due to any lack of proper claims mentioned by Habermas, some remedies (i.e., modes of redemption) must be undertaken. Habermas further proclaimed that ideal speech acts are ones with high quality of communicative speech acts (i.e., every participant uses reason in communication), constatative speech acts (wherewith every participant criticizes others' speech and defends one's own speech in a communication process), organization of interactions (whereto every participant is free to express one's attitude, emotion and intention), and regulative speech acts that every participant must follow the conventions of languages in presenting one's speech acts.

In communication, one may engage in strategic acts by distorting one's presentation, whether intentionally or subconsciously. To be engaged disparagingly by participating actors, the communication conduit may break down. In other cases, ideal speech acts may not proceed well for the interruption of communication channels often arise in connection with defects of some parts of these channels themselves.

In the above, we just mentioned that under the natural courses of the mind and strategic complexes, relationships among members of a system may work to advance the interests of the said system. Consequently the system may be preserved or even expanded through absorbing more energy from the other systems or environments or by acquiring other systems as subsystems. In the operations of a system, not only physical outputs (or material products serving as inputs for other activities) are produced and reproduced, some services, ideas or even intangible things (such as so-called symbols) may also be generated time and again.

To look into a seemingly unusual aspect of the operations of a social system, we may look for some inspiration from Pièrre Bourdieu (Gao [1991]). In the sphere of sociopolitics, Bourdieu classified capital into four types: economic, cultural, social, and symbolic capital, as dynamic factors of a "symbolic market." The cultural capital arises from the concrete embodiment or daily functioning of a person's "habitus," settled deeply into one's mind complex, consciously or unconsciously, may be through education s/he received. One may seek to explain this habitus as some thing like an "élan vital" always fermenting and regenerating in one's mind and soul. Bourdieu further described a process which may be called the process of social alchemy. To our understanding, this is a mechanism artificially developed in combination with education, influence of power and wealth, and social process of legitimization, and through which the ruling class of a society passes over its power, prestige, and wealth to its offspring. In this process, the transformations and interactions among these four types of capital explicate some very fascinating case studies. He further argued that there exists an iso-systemism (in his word: "homólogie structure") between the education system and the power-prestige-wealth structure of a system (or a society). This iso-systemism is said as a result of the legitimization of unequal exchange in the "market place" (or the society) through which psychologically rather hard-to-detect impacts of symbolic operations of judiciary, education, cultural and even religious and artistic systems are effectively and even traumatically imprinting on the mind complexes of the common citizens.

In a system $X = \chi \oplus <\mathbb{C}_X>$, any energy absorbed from the complex $E\{e_j\}$ will be converted into inputs of this system. To generate a product or to transform some products, in the case of human society, it involves the ability and willingness of the system to perform this critical role. On one hand, the ability of any system to transform an "input" (such as the input of symbol) into an "output," either being a physical product or an idea, must depend on the characteristics of $C_S \times C^{DS}(e_r)$ and the chain structure of $(R_M, R^{DM}(e_r)$. On the other hand, the willingness of people to engage in this task of transformation depends on the structure of the action-strategic complex Z in the system X. In the real world, definitely the structures of $C_S \times C^{DS}(e_r)$ and $(R_M, R^{DM}(e_r))$ are in a state of flux, constantly changing and restructuring. Consequently in the system X, the structure of (vd,hc,γ), along with $(R, R^D(e_r))$ in instituting the core of the mechanisms of market/planning/interpersonal network, as well as social and political institutions, is changing accordingly. Very often in this modern time, $\langle \mathbb{C}_X \rangle$ evolves into a multi-cultural complex due to the interactions of different cultures on a global scale.

Let us illustrate the above principles of system characteristics and dynamics. For example, without capitalist spirit and instrumental rationality (as was asserted by Max Weber), a system would not be in a strong position to convert physical outputs into money, and in turn alter and transform money into the form of hired labor or workers. Eventually from labor and capital, commodities are produced and exchanged among the capitalists themselves and between the producers and the consumers in an effort to make profits in the market place. As such, communication acts involving prices and quality of commodities between individuals and commercial agencies are necessary mediums in any system, be they capitalism, socialism, Islam, or Faziranism.

It goes without saying that, this system X can be considered as open, and yet it is not completely open. Were it a totally open system, then it would lose its identity. Therefore a system is closed in order to preserve its distinct characteristics in a particular moment of time. And yet, it must remain open in the historical time.

To discuss the structural dynamism of the multi-cultural set of our systems, we can construct the following formulae.[51]

(E.3-1) Input of one system
$\rightarrow$ Output of the same system = Input of a new system

(E.3-2) Actions/operations
$\rightarrow$ Medium/transformation through systems' structure

That is to say, systems are considered as based on functions of input-output operations or transformations through which physical objects, ideas, and even symbols are constantly creating and created, transforming and transformed, and recreating and recreated. In other words, input-output transformations of human and social systems are always in a constant state of metamorphosis. For instance, in a chain of systematic operations, the following series may be observed in succession:

(E.3-3) Private property rights: Money : Capital:
Labor contract: Profits[52]

(E.3-4) Public property rights: Money : Capital:
Labor contract: Social justice

(E.3-5) Public/Private property rights: Money : Capital:
Labor contract: Symbols : Power

Note that these processes involve M^{II}, M^{III} and M^{IV} (see below). Even a casual observer could easily discover that in a real world system there exist three cycles of reproduction centered on money, especially with regard to its intimate alliance with political power (or capital) and academic power/capital. These cycles are called **money-power-fame-sex (MPFX) cycles**:

(1) basic cycle (or **MPF cycle**):

(E.3-6) physical productive assets (phyK) ⟷ capital : money (K:**M**)⟷ power (P) ⟷ fame and social status (FS), or in symbols, see Figure E.3-1.

Figure E.3-1
Basic MPFX cycle of capitalism

phyK ⟷ (K : **M**)⟷ P ⟷ FS.

This basic cycle centers on the role of money. What does it mean is that with the power of money, the capitalist is able to convert it backwards into capital to control assets of production and forwards to institute an intimate alliance with political power. Subsequently financial and political powers jointly control, or at least are able to exert a decisive force, over the seemingly innocent and objective academic circle.

For this afore-mentioned cycle, in terms of a diagrammatical representation, we have Figure E.3-2.

Figure E.3-2
Basic MPFX cycle of capitalism

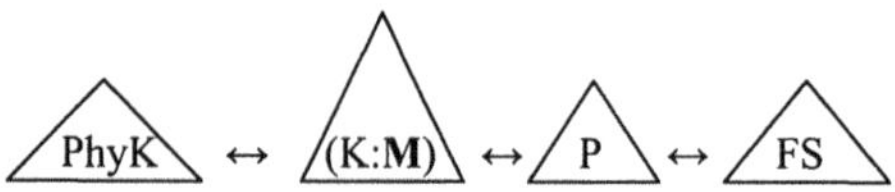

Figure E.3-3
Basic MPFX cycle of capitalism as a leaf-shaped system

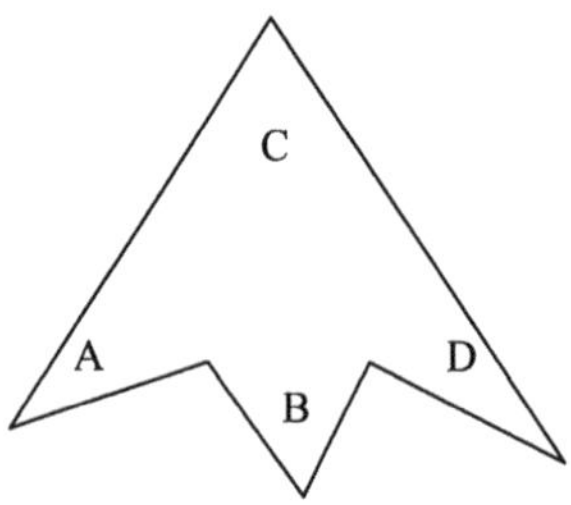

The alternative diagrammatical representation of the Basic MPFX cycle of capitalism is the leaf-shaped system (see Figure E.3-4): for $X \sqsubseteq (\Omega, \mathbb{Z}^{o}, {}_{v}\mathcal{H}, \{\mathbb{C}\})$, X = A-C-B-D (C as the central unit system, the others as non-central unit-systems): X = (A⊕C⊕B⊕D) ⊛Ix($_{.<C}$) (also see Section 3.7) with A = phyK, B = P, C = (K:**M**), D = FS.

(2) Single generational cycle:

Figure E.3-4
Single-generational MPFX cycle of capitalism

hyK ←→ (K : **M**) ←→ P ←→ AFS → X

Seen in Figure E.3-4, A represents the academic reputation, AFS refers to the combination of academic reputation, fame and social status, while X depicts the attractiveness to opposite sex. Here the transformation of money and power to academic reputation is achieved subtly through the admissions policy of colleges and universities that are influenced by ethnical concerns, financial donations, political power and the factor of alumni.

In Figure E.3-4, the second cycle shows that the MPF cycle in (1) in the above, with the decisive role of the capitalist, is able to stretch itself and reaches out to the practice of mating rituals when such activities exist.

Multiple-generational cycle. The multiple-generational MPFX cycle of capitalism can be expressed as follow:

(E.3-8) physical productive assets ← capital : money ←→ power ←→ academic reputation, fame and social status → attractiveness to opposite sex → reproduction of gene
↓
physical productive assets ← capital : money ←→ power ←→ academic reputation, fame and social status → attractiveness to opposite sex → reproduction of gene
↓
...

In symbols, we have Figure E.3-5.

Figure E.3-5
Multiple-generational MPFX cycle of capitalism

↓
phyK ←→ [K : (**M** ←→ P)] ←→ AFS → X → RG
↓
phyK ←→ [K : (**M** ←→ P)] ←→ AFS → X → RG
↓
...

In this cycle, see Figure E.3-5, RG denotes the reproduction of gene, while AFS designates the academic reputation, fame and social status.

In this inter-generational phenomenon, the MPFX cycle encompasses activities of more than one generation. Therefore, the MPFX cycle creates its own stability with the blessing bestowed to it by the culture, either openly or more subtly in the under-world of the "conscience collective."

In this case the transformation from the reproduction of gene to that of money comes into existence through the social institution of inheriting private property rights. The transformation process usually unveils itself grandiosely, even majestically, as one of creation, reproduction, modification and exchange of symbols through operations and various becoming stages. These processes can be seen as constant changes taking place within the structure $[C_S \times C^{DS}(e_r),(R_M,R^{DM}(e_g)),\tilde{O}]$ in every system X.[53]

In the context of classical China, there exist cycles similar to the aforementioned MPFX cycles of capitalism. In this context, the major cycle of classical China could be called the inter-generational **GPFX cycle**. The major difference between this and the MPFX cycle, single generational or multiple generational, is evident in the instrumental role played by the gentry class in the former; while in the MFPX cycles of capitalism, the most energetic role of the society is displayed by the capitalist class.

In symbols, let $\mathbf{G}|_{\underline{P}}$ be the major player, the gentry class, under the dominance of the royal family or the emperor. Then, we can derive the GPFX cycle in Figure E.3-6. Further note that this process involves M^I and M^{II} (see Subsection §A.2-4).

Figure E.3-6
GPFX cycle of Classical China

$$\begin{array}{l} \qquad\qquad\qquad\qquad\quad \cdots \\ \qquad\qquad\qquad\qquad\quad \downarrow \\ \text{phyK} \longleftrightarrow \text{K : M} \leftarrow (\mathbf{G}|_{\underline{P}} \longleftrightarrow \text{P}) \longleftrightarrow \text{AFS} \rightarrow \text{X} \rightarrow \text{RG} \\ \qquad\qquad\qquad\qquad\quad \downarrow \\ \text{phyK} \longleftrightarrow (\text{K : M}) \leftarrow (\mathbf{G}|_{\underline{P}} \longleftrightarrow \text{P}) \longleftrightarrow \text{AFS} \rightarrow \text{X} \rightarrow \text{RG} \\ \qquad\qquad\qquad\qquad\quad \downarrow \\ \qquad\qquad\qquad\qquad\quad \cdots \end{array}$$

In these cycles, each node can be perceived as a system, and these systems are connected organically and dynamically by an integrating impactor to create a grand system. Note that in a capitalist society, the capitalist ethos as the cultural core of this system may be treated as the central system (i.e., virtual center). Furthermore, note that these systems in the above can also be represented by uncertain systems (for uncertain distribution systems and uncertain systems, see Appendix X).

In symbols, for example let us pick the scheme of Figure E.3-1: phyK $\longleftrightarrow$ (K : **M**)$\longleftrightarrow$ P $\longleftrightarrow$ FS. We have:

(E.3-9) $\quad \phi X = \mathfrak{C} \otimes \mathcal{E} = \{C \oplus (N_1 \oplus N_2 \oplus \ldots \oplus N_n)\} \circledast Ix,$

where X is the basic MPFX cycle of capitalism, $\phi \vDash \mathcal{Z}\circ,_{v}\mathcal{H}$ is the decomposing impactor (see Section A.3), $\mathfrak{C}$ is the cultural core of capitalism (i.e., profits motif), $\mathcal{E}$ is the collection of the "units of CE balance" (or "equilibrium units"), C is the central system (K : **M**), N_i is the ith

noncentral system, for all i = 1, 2, 3 (i.e., phyK, P, FS; n = 3 here), $\otimes \models \mathbb{Z}_{\circ,\vee}\mathbb{H}$ is some sort of integrating impactor of this grand system, and $\odot \models \mathbb{Z}_{\circ,\vee}\mathbb{H}$ is the integrating impactor of this grand system under the factor of Ix.

Appendix F – Cs, Cd Curves and Firms

F.1 Introduction

In this Appendix F, we show the derivations of the cultural supply curve (cs), the cultural demand curve (cd) and simple structures of firms.

F.2 Supply, Demand and Firms

Below, at first in Subsection §F.2-1, we define the will-to-creation and rationality-to-creation curves, and then from the intersections of these curves and after some transformations and elaborations, we derive the culturally determined pre-supply curve and the supply curve. Secondly in Subsection §F.2-2, we define the will-to-use and rationality-to-use curves, and then from the intersections of these curves and after some transformation, the cultural supply curve cs is then derived.

Now we come to the derivation of supply and demand curves and a discussion of firms.

§F.2-1 Cultural Supply Curve

Following a conventional approach, we can set up new assumptions that cultural preferences definitely shift and rotate demand and supply curves by alternate quantity demanded and supplied under given prices. Examples are abound; for example, under given prices, changing quantity demanded for more cultural goods (in the case of a consumer group), or changing quantity supplied of high-technology products (in the case of a person engaging in research and development) will shift or rotate the relevant curves.

To us, in the economics of culture, the impact of cultures must enter directly into the flow of the economic activities by affecting the formation of demand and supply. In the following, we shall present a culturally determined pre-supply curve in several steps.

In the following, let the becoming systems in question be mathematically measurable. Then we shall draw a culturally determined pre-supply curve. First, on the first quadrant of the space of Cartesian product, let the *will-to-creation curve* be upward sloping, with the meaning of life (MOL) measure on the vertical axis and the quantity provided or supplied (q) on the horizontal axis. That is, $\{q,MOL\} \sqsubseteq (\Omega,\mathbb{Z}^{\circ},{}_{v}\mathcal{H},\{\mathbb{C}\})\sqcap\mathbb{R}$ as a becoming system is mathematically measurable, and thus it can be represented by a curve. Note that the correspondence between MOL and q is assumed to be a relation, not necessarily a function.

Here this will-to-creation curve is positively sloped (see Figure F.2-1-2). This is because, the larger the quantity supplied is to be provided, the level of the will-to-creation is required to be much larger. Since in terms of production and supply, it is hard to stimulate the will to supply; and to continue this process, it requires an ever greater efforts to sustain it.

Secondly, on the first quadrant of the space of Cartesian product, let the *rationality-to-creation curve* be downward sloping, with the meaning of life measure on the vertical axis and the quantity supplied on the horizontal axis. That is, $\{q,MOL\} \sqsubseteq (\Omega,\mathbb{Z}^{\circ},{}_{v}\mathcal{H},\{\mathbb{C}\})\sqcap\mathbb{R}$ as a becoming system is mathematically measurable, and thus it can be represented by a curve. As is in the case of the will-to-creation curve, this new curve represents a relation, not necessarily a function

Here this rationality-to-creation curve is negatively sloped (see Figure F.2-1-1). That is, once the process of the quantity supplied starts, the ability to supply is established. And then it becomes an ever easier process to continue the activity of supply. Hence, as the quantity of supply is increased unit by unit, the required level of rationality-to-creation shall be reduced accordingly.

Then, by drawing the will-to-creation and the rationality-to-creation curves together and by shifting them, we derive the upward-sloping MOL-q *meaning-to-creation curve* (see Figure F.2-1-7). The reason for this shape is that: When the artistic and religious orientations and the life impulse are at a state of simple Tcentral, as the quantity provided increases, the response of MOL is such that the degree of the downward shift of the will-to-creation curve (to the right) is much smaller than the degree of the upward shift of the rationality-to-creation curve (to the right). The collection of the loci of the resulting intersection points is an upward-sloping curve. And after the transformation of MOL into price, we derive the pre-supply curve from the meaning-to-creation curve. That is, by postulating that the vertical axis (MOL) can be transformed into price (P) and that this new P-q relation or curve is a 1-1 function, we derive the *pre-supply curve*.

Another way to see the shape of the upward-sloping meaning-to-creation curve is this: in creating or supplying goods and services, the rationality dominates the will, because it involves more heavily with human rationality than human will in production, manufacturing and technological development.

In the above, we derive the pre-supply for a simple system, i.e., an economy of one culture. Note that for the system with tranquility culture, the pre-supply curve is treated as the supply curve. For an economy of two cultures, we shall derive its pre-supply function in the following.

Suppose the system is composed of two cultures, those of conflict and tranquility. Let the rationality of a system with conflict culture be scientific rationality (associated with sciences and the philosophy of utilitarianism) and the rationality of a system with tranquil culture be systemic rationality (associated with the revelation rationality in the West and with the modern systemic rationality, or yu-wu rationality of Taoism, Confucianism and Buddhism in East Asia). The downward-sloping *rationality-to-creation* curve of the system with conflict culture lies to the right of that with tranquil culture because the former has a level of science-based technology higher than the level of the systemic-rationality-base technology of the latter (see Figure F.2-1-1).

Let the life-will of a system with conflict culture be associated with a conquest spirit (associated with the philosophy of social Darwinism in the West and with that of Legalism in East Asia) and let the life-will of a system with tranquil culture be associated with the spirit of peace and tranquility (associated with the life-will of loving others unconditionally in the West and with the self-generating life-will in East Asia). The upward-sloping *will-to-creation curve* of the system with conflict culture lies to the right of that with tranquil culture because the latter has macro-economic, organizational and systematic efficiency (see Figure F.2-1-2).

Figure F.2-1-1
Rationality-to-creation curves

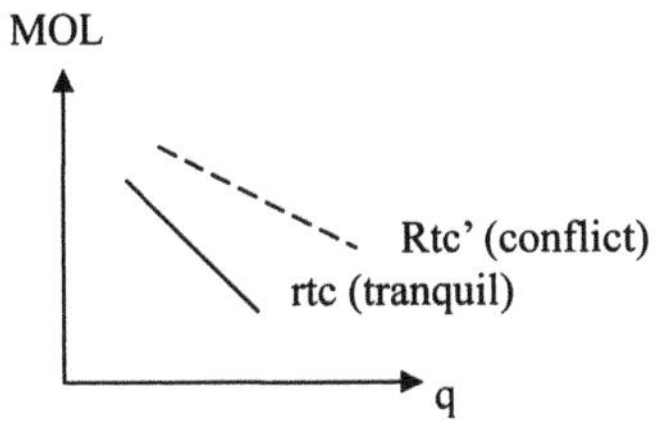

Figure F.2-1-2
Will-to-creation curves

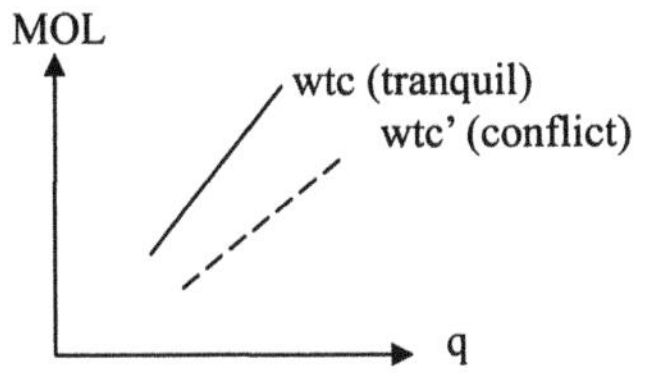

Figure F.2-1-3
MTCs of Two systems

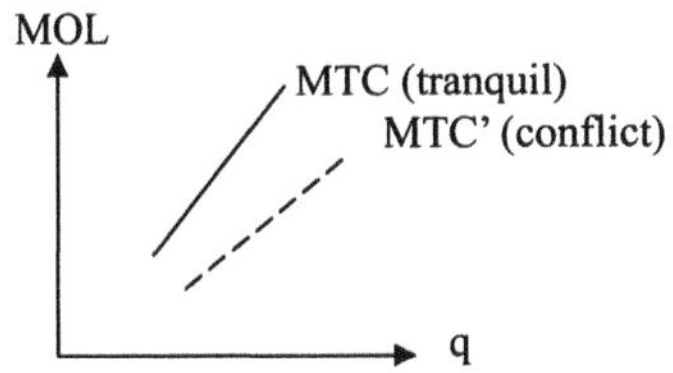

Analogous to what we have in Figure F.2-1-2, we will then derive the upward-sloping *meaning-to-creation curve* for the system of two cultures, for which that of the system with conflict culture lies to the right of that with tranquil culture (see Figures F.2-1-3 and F.2-1-7).

Then let us define the competitive system to be a system of two cultures in which conflict culture dominates tranquil culture, and define the harmonious system to be a system with two cultures in which tranquil culture dominates conflict culture.

Hence, we derive the upward meaning-to-creation curve, for which this curve of the competitive system (conflict system, respectively) lies to the right of that of harmonious system (tranquil system, respectively). After the transformation of axis, this is defined as the *pre-supply curve*, or the average cost curve (see Figure F.2-1-4).

Figure F.2-1-4
Pre-supply curves of two systems

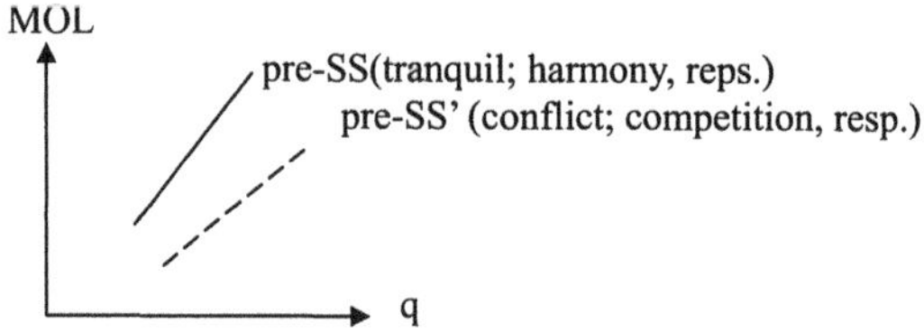

In the economics of culture, the impact of cultures directly enters into the center of economic activities by affecting the formation of the culturally determined supply curves.

Below we can also derive the cultural supply curve as follows. Let MOL denote the meaning of life and q the quantity of commodities, both being at first "meaningful" in the systematic sense (i.e., being universal elements), and then "measurable" in the mathematical sense (i.e., being numbers). Following the above concept of right-down BCM, we postulate that *rationality–to-creation curve* (rtc) represents a negative relationship between MOL and q, for an example, see Figure F.2-1-5.

Figure F.2-1-5
Rationality-to-creation curve

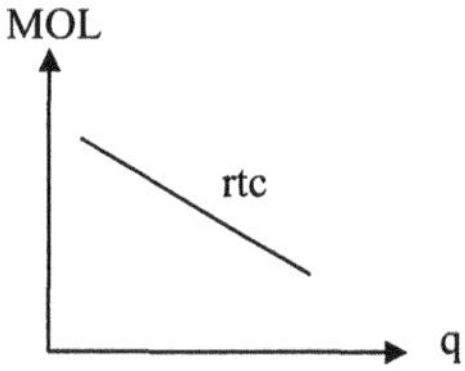

That is, on the first quadrant of the space of Cartesian product, let the rationality-to-creation curve be downward sloping, with the meaning of life measure on the vertical axis and the quantity provided or supplied (q) on the horizontal axis (see Figure F.2-1-5). As is in the case of the will-to-creation curve, this new curve also represents a becoming. Here we have: $\odot \approx^{B} \{\{[(\rho,\omega)\ |\varphi(MOL,q)] =< T^{B\Delta}\} \sqsubseteq \text{Ш}^{\text{Д}}\}$ or $\odot \approx^{B} \{\{[x_i(y_i,h_i*,v_i,.IRI_i(\rho,\omega)\ ,.),\ldots,\ x_n(y_n,h_n*,\ v_n,IRI_n(\rho,\omega),.)|\varphi(MOL,q)] =< T^{B\Delta}\} \sqsubseteq \text{Ш}^{\text{Д}}\}$ (see Sections 3.4 in Chapter 3) as a systematic expression of the rationality-to-creation becoming.

Similarly, following the above concept of right-up BCM, we postulate that *will–to-creation curve* (wtc) represents a positive relationship between MOL and q (see Figure F.2-1-6).

Figure F.2-1-6
Will-to-creation curve

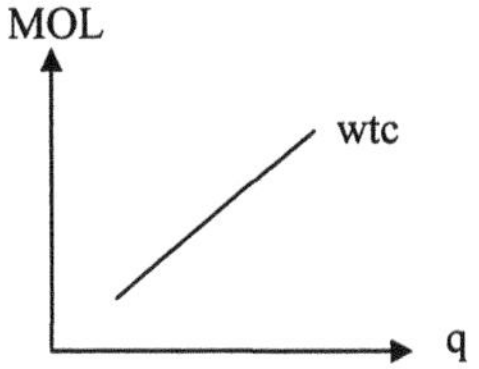

That is, on the first quadrant of the space of Cartesian product, let the will-to-creation curve be upward sloping, with the meaning of life measure on the vertical axis and the quantity provided or supplied on the horizontal axis. As is in the case of the rationality-to-creation curve, this new curve represents a relation and thus a becoming. Similar to the case of rationality-to-creation curve, here we have $\odot \approx^{B} \{\{[x_i(y_i,h_i^*, v_i,.IRI_i(\rho,\omega),.),\ldots, x_n(y_n,h_n^*,v_n, IRI_n(\rho,\omega),.)|\varphi(MOL,q)] =< T^{B\Delta}\} \sqsubseteq \text{Ш}^{\text{Д}}\}$, or in short $\odot \approx^{B} \{\{[(\rho,\omega)|\varphi(MOL,q)] =< T^{B\Delta}\} \sqsubseteq \text{Ш}^{\text{Д}}\}$ (see Chapter 3, Section 3.4) as a systematic expression of the will-to-creation becoming.

Figure F.2-1-7
Meaning-to-creation curve

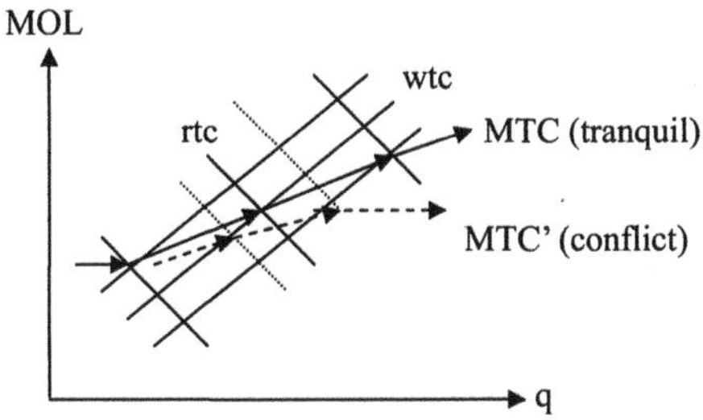

Now we come to the concept of the *meaning-to-creation becoming*. Here we have $\odot \approx^{B} \{\{[(\rho,\omega)|\varphi(MOL,q)] =< T^{B\Delta}\} \sqsubseteq \text{Ш}^{\text{Д}}\}$ as a systematic expression of the meaning-to-creation becoming.

Then, by drawing the will-to-creation and the rationality-to-creation curves together on the first quadrant of the space of Cartesian product and by shifting them, we derive the downward-sloping MOL-q *meaning-to-creation becoming or curve* (MTC) (see Figure F.2-1-7). The reason for the positive slope of this curve is that, given the normal levels of culture (excluding the will and the rationality per se), capital and labor, when the life impulse and human rationality are at a state of simple TCentral, as the quantity supplied increases, the response of MOL is such that the degree of the downward shift of the will-to-creation curve (to the right) is smaller than that of the upward shift (to the right) of the rationality-to-creation curve. This is due to the much more important role of rationality than that of will in the process of production and supply. The collection of the loci of the resulted intersection points is an upward-sloping curve (or a relation).

Note that the upward-sloping MTC curve of a system with tranquil culture (for example, see Figure F.2-1-7, MTC) lies to the left of the upward-sloping MTC curve of a system with conflict culture (for example, see Figure F.2-1-7, MTC'). This is because as the same unit of q changes, the required shifting response of rtc (to the right) is less for the system with conflict culture (the dotted line MTC' in Figure F.2-1-7) than for that with tranquil culture (the solid line MTC in Figure F.2-1-7).

Thus we have Figure F.2-1-8 for the MTC curves with systems of tranquil and conflict cultures.

Figure F.2-1-8
MTCs for tranquil and conflict cultures

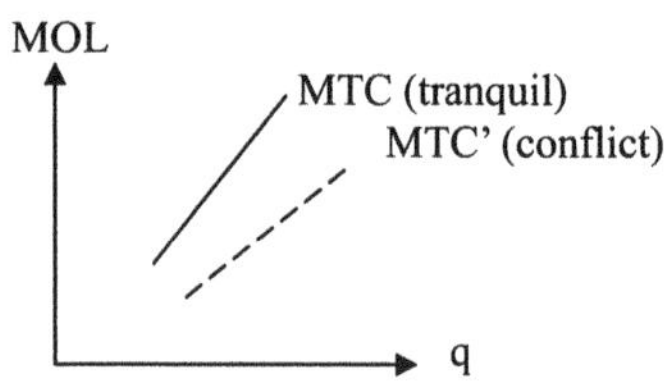

After the transformation of MOL into price, the **pre-supply curve (pre-cs)** is derived from the meaning-to-creation curve. Note that the pre-supply curve is the "average cost curve" which represents the collection of the average points of the cost function of production. Further note that the classical tranquil economy shall use the pre-supply function as the "**cultural supply function**." As for the economies of conflict culture and modern tranquil culture, the **cultural supply curve** is derived by taking T derivative of the cost curves reconstructed from the pre-supply curve.

§F.2-2 Cultural Demand Curve

In the following, we shall derive the cultural demand curve. Again, first, following the above concept of right-up SBC, we postulate that *rationality–to-use curve* (rtu) represents a negative relationship between MOL and q, for an example, see Figure F.2-2-1.

Figure F.2-2-1
Rationality-to-use curve

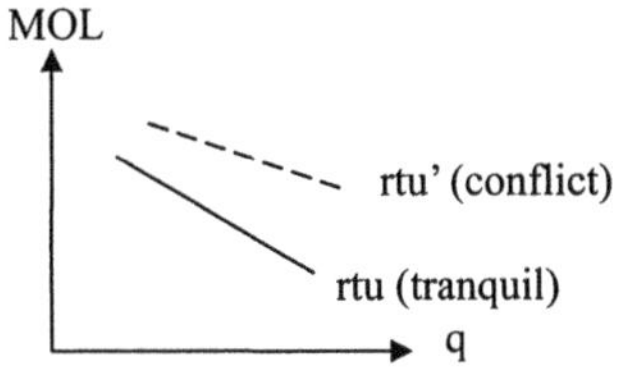

That is, on the first quadrant of the space of Cartesian product, let the rationality-to-use curve be downward sloping, with the meaning of life measure on the vertical axis and the quantity demanded on the horizontal axis. Similar to the above case, the correspondence between MOL and q is assumed to be a relation, not necessarily a function. Here we have $\odot \approx \{\{[(\rho,\omega)|\varphi(MOL,q)] =< T^{B\Delta}\} \sqsubseteq Ш^{Д}\}$, where this form is a systematic expression of the rationality-to-use becoming.

This rationality-to-use curve is positively sloped. Here the higher the level of the quantity demanded, the additional level of the rationality-to-use required will be higher. For the increase in the quantity demanded, the effective demand which represents the ability to purchase for consumption is extremely important. In order to continue the process of this effective demand, which is dominated by the rationality, an ever stronger rationality is required to sustain it. Therefore, as the quantity demanded of a consumption good or service ever increases, the required level of the rationality-to-use will be ever larger.

Secondly, following the above concept of right-up BCM, we postulate that *will–to-use curve* (wtu) represents a positive relationship between MOL and q, for an example, see Figure F.2-2-2.

This will-to-use curve is negatively sloped. This is because it is much harder to create the will-to-use than to sustaining it; and once the will is created, it becomes an ever easier process to continue. Thus the additional will-to-use will be decreased as the quantity demanded increases.

Figure F.2-2-2
Will-to-use curve

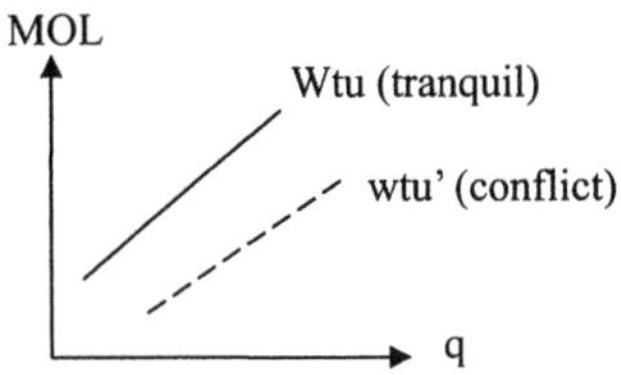

Thirdly, by drawing the rationality-to-use and the will-to-use curves together and by shifting them, we derive the downward-sloping MOL-q *meaning-to-use curve* (MTU) (see Figure F.2-2-3). Similar to the above two cases, here we have $\odot \approx^{\text{В}} \{\{[(\rho,\omega)|\varphi(\text{MOL},q)] =< \text{T}^{\text{В}\Delta}\} \sqsubseteq \text{Ш}^{\text{Д}}\}$ as a systematic expression of the meaning- to-use becoming.
The reason for this shape of negative slope is that, given the normal levels of culture (excluding the will and the rationality per se), capital and labor, when the life impulse and human rationality are at a state of simple Tcentral, as the quantity demanded increases, the response of MOL is such that the degree of the upward shift of the will-to-use curve (to the right) is much smaller than the degree of the down shift (to the right) of the rationality-to-use curve. This is due to the scarcity of consumption goods or services, and therefore the role of rationality carries a much heavier weight than that of will in shifting of these curves. The collection of the loci of the resulted intersection points is a downward-sloping curve (or a relation).

Figure F.2-2-3
Meaning-to-use curve

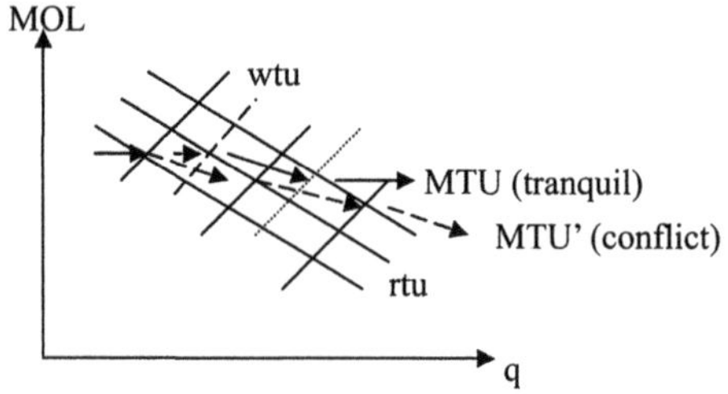

Note that in the formulation of the meaning-to-use curve, as the quantity demanded increases, the reduction in the rationality-to-use (rtu) measure or MOL is far outweighed by the increase in the will-to-use (wtu) measure or MOL. Thus, essentially, the role of will-to-use becoming is far greater than that of rationality-to-use becoming in the formulation of the meaning-to-use curve.

Note that the downward-sloping MTU curve (or meaning-to-use becoming) of a system with tranquil culture (solid line see Figure F.2-2-3, MTU) lies to the right of the downward - sloping MTC curve of a system with conflict culture (solid line, see Figure F.2-2-3, MTU'). This is because as the same unit of q changes, the required shifting response of wtu (to the right) is less for the system with tranquil culture (the solid line wtu in Figure F.2-2-2) than for that with conflict culture (the dotted line wtu' in Figure F.2-2-2).

Thus we have Figure F.2-2-4 for the MTU curves with systems of tranquil and conflict cultures.

Figure F.2-2-4
MTUs for tranquil and conflict cultures

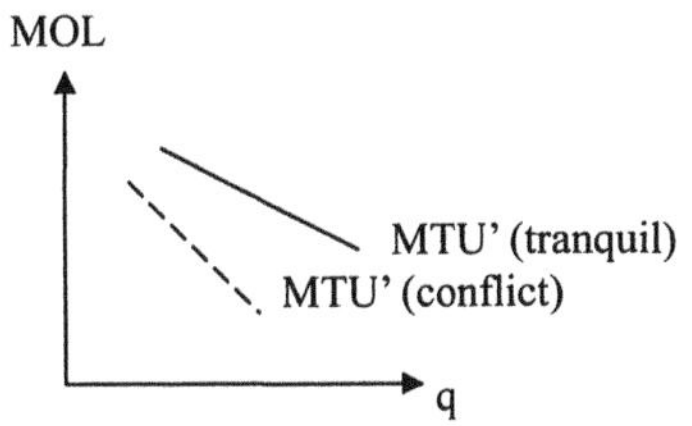

Below, after the transformation of MOL into price, the **pre-demand curve** can be derived from the meaning-to-use curve. Then for an economy of tranquil culture, the pre-demand curve is simply treated as the **cultural demand curve (cd)**.

Figure F.2-2-5
Cultural demand curve

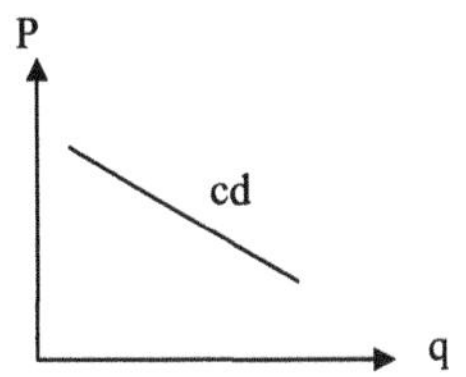

Now we turn to the derivation of the demand function of a system of two cultures. Similar to the above procedure, we derive the downward-sloping *meaning-to-use curve* (MTU). Here, the MTU curve of the competitive system lies to the left of that of harmonious system. After the transformation of axis, this transformed MTU is then defined as the *demand curve*, which is downward sloping.

Note that when the cultural variables like artistic aspiration and religious orientation vary, with the human will and rationality per se being held constant, the meaning-to-use curve will shift. But when the cultural variables (excluding the will and rationality per se) like artistic aspiration and religious orientation vary, with the human will and rationality per se having been affected by them, the meaning-to-use curve shall shift and rotate at the same time.

One way to see the shape of the downward-sloping meaning-to-use curve is this: in consuming goods and services, the will dominates the rationality. Similarly, the shape of the upward-sloping meaning-to-creation curve is easily seen in the fact that by producing goods and services, the will is dominated by rationality. This is because it involves more heavily with human rationality than human will in production, manufacturing and technological development.

Note that the original relationships of the will-to-use curve, rationality-to-use curve, and meaning-to-use curve are becomings, rather than equations. For example, what is called a systematic-change equation in Tonn (2001, pp. 18, 73) is thus referred to as a systematic-change becoming. The name **meaning-to-use becoming** is used to describe the relationships in cultural systematics, for instance, the one between the meaning of life and the quantity supplied or demanded of a product. This becoming is not measurable, or at least not easy to do so. In contrast, the idea of curve (for example the will-to-use curve) depicts a mathematical function, measurable in the real and complex analysis.

Thus, we have derived the pre-demand functions for a simple system, in this case, the economy of one culture. Note that for the economy of classical tranquil culture, we have the **cultural demand function** (or the average revenue function) serving as the operating demand function. Here the culture of tranquil is the one of having tranquility and serenity in the mind of each human element and having peace between oneself and others. Note that the economies of conflict culture and modern tranquil culture also use the pre-demand function as the **cultural demand function.**

Note that in our theory of cultural systematics, the demand and supply curves of the conflict firm (i.e., the firm with conflict culture) are fundamentally different from the cultural demand and cultural supply curves of the conflict unit of the harmonious and competitive firms. These cultural demand and cultural supply curves are what we have derived in the above while the demand and supply curves of the conflict firm are what prevail in the conventional economic textbook (in the West).

§F.2-3 Conflict Firm and Tranquil Firm

FgureF.2-3-1
Conflict firm in the short run disequilibrium, $P^* = dd_i \nLeftrightarrow MC_i = MR_i$ and $\pi > 0$

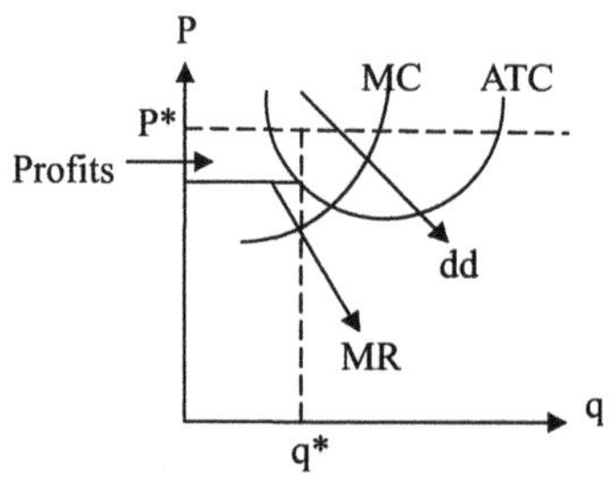

Here we present our model for the typical firm in the conflict market (conventionally called perfectly competitive market) without the existence of any government in the national economy. Related to this conflict market, we shall define the typical **conflict firm** (conventionally called perfectly competitive firm) as a firm with conflict culture. This firm has an upward sloping supply curve (MC_i) and a downward-sloping demand curve (dd_i). And yet, this firm is a **price-taker**, because its price is determined by the market force. In other words, this firm does not have any power in setting its own price. In the short run disequilibrium, this i^{th} firm, i = 1,2,...n, will not produce at the intersection point of its demand curve dd_i and the market equilibrium price P* (which is determined by the market supply curve SS and the market demand curve DD).

It will produce at the intersection point of its marginal revenue curve MR_i and its marginal cost curve MC_i. In the short run equilibrium, this i^{th} firm will produce at the intersection point of its demand curve dd_i and the market equilibrium price P* (which will then equal to the level of output set by the intersection point of its MR_i and MC_i).

In general, in the short run, this firm has an above-normal level of profit. And yet in the long run equilibrium, this firm has a zero level of above-normal profit.

But in the case of long run disequilibrium, this firm has an above-normal profit providing funds for its research and development, and thereby paving a path for its technological improvement.

Graphically, this model is shown in Figure F.2-3-1. Here for the conflict firm in the short run disequilibrium, its effective demand curve is a kinked one (see Figure F.2-3-2).

Figure F.2-3-2
Kinked demand curve of a conflict firm

Figure F.2-3-3
Conflict firm in the short run equilibrium: $P^* = dd_i \Leftrightarrow MC_i = MR_i$ and $\pi > 0$

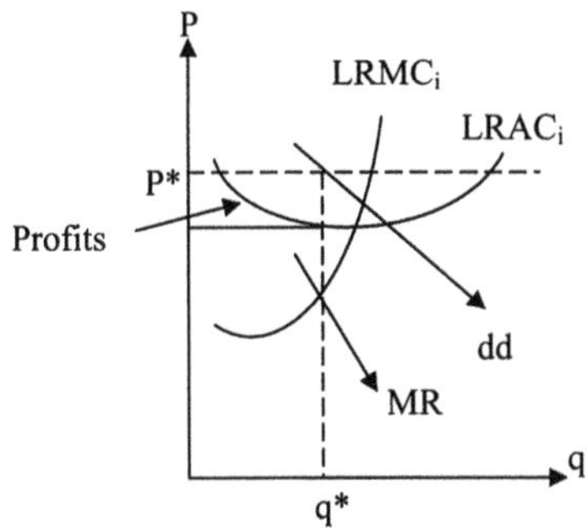

The other cases of a conflict firm in the long run disequilibrium are: (1) $P^* = dd_i \Leftrightarrow MC_i = MR_i$ and $\pi > 0$, and (2) the trivial case $P^* = dd_i \Leftarrow/\Rightarrow MC_i = MR_i$ and $\pi = 0$.
Note that for a firm in the long run, even if $P^* = dd_i$ and $MC_i = MR_i$, as long as $\pi > 0$, this firm is not in long run equilibrium. Further, as long as the objective of the firm (be it profit maximization, market-share maximization, organization reforms, satisfactory level, or any

other) is not met, these equilibrium or disequilibrium solutions are in some states of strategic discontinuity or anti-continuity. At times, the concepts of strategic continuity and equilibrium are quite different.

Figure F.2-3-4

Conflict firm in the long run disequilibrium: Case 1: $P^* = dd_i \Leftarrow\!/\!\Rightarrow MC_i = MR_i$ and $\pi > 0$

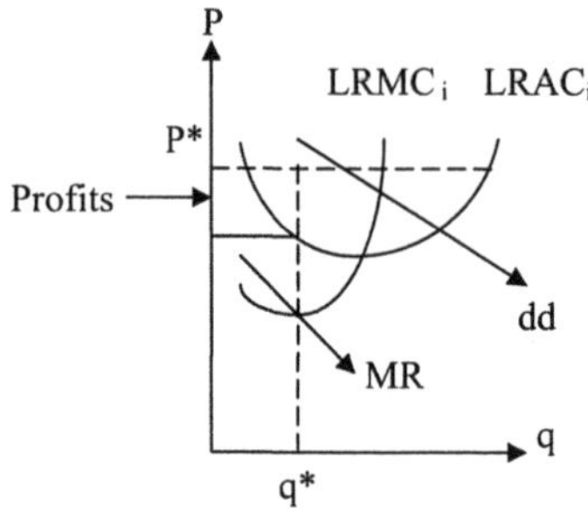

Figure F.2-3-5

Conflict firm in the long run equilibrium: i) $P^* = dd_i \Leftrightarrow MC_i = MR_i$, ii) $\pi = 0$

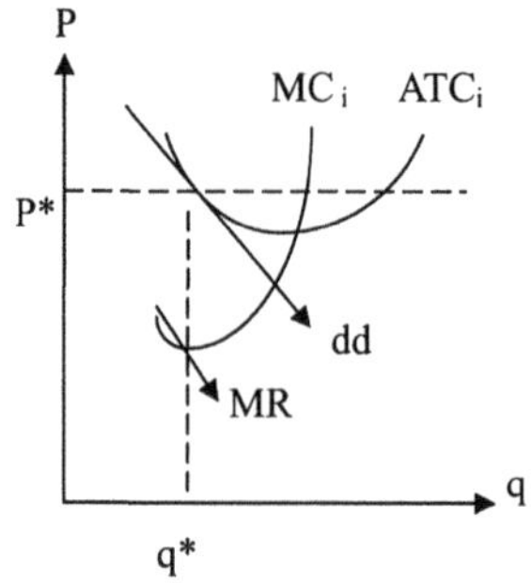

In the above, the model of conflict market is a classical one. In the model of conflict market of the modern cultural economy, the government performs the role of the center of the market (as a system), and the government is assumed to be in the state of strategic continuity. Hence, the demand and supply curves (i.e., the culturally-determined cs and cd) of a conflict firm are functions of the government policies, such as policies affecting education, research and development activities, international trade and cultural development. These policies influence the supply conditions of firms and may also alter the taste of households as consumers in the economy. Once the government changes its policies, these policy variables become the shift factors of supply and demand in the conflict market.

In the above, we presented the demand and supply curves of the firm with conflict culture. The cultural backgrounds of life-will and rationality–to-creation are intrinsically present in the formation of these curves. Thus, this conflict firm has a **life-will efficiency** of conquest and **rationality–to-creation efficiency** of scientism. When the underlying culture of this firm changes, it will create shift factors of the demand and supply curves.

In the **conflict market**, i.e., the market composed of firms of conflict culture, there is a case of the **economies of conflict** by which is meant the efficiency of forcing firms to strive its best to produce at the least level of costs possible under the market pressure of conflict. In this conflict market, there will also be a case of the **diseconomies of conflict** by forcing firms to engage in short-run cut-throat warfare in the market.

As for the firm of tranquil culture, the cultural backgrounds of life-will and rationality–to-creation are also present in the formation of these curves. Thus, this tranquil firm has a **life-will efficiency** of inner ease and external strength and a **rationality–to-creation efficiency** of self-generating systemism. With the underlying culture of this firm changes, shift factors of the demand and supply curves will also be created. In general, for the firm of tranquil culture, there is a network mechanism operating in this firm's internal structure and an outward-related structure for external connection. Thus for the mechanism of the demand and supply curves of this firm to be operational, the dimension of networking must be taken into account. That is, this networking forms a part of culture for the firm of tranquility. With the structure of networking changes, shift factors of the demand and supply curves will definitely be created.

In general, this phenomenon may create a case of the *economies of networking*. This case of the economies of network provides an important linkage between the structures of the society-polity and the *cultural advantage* (also see 3.2) of East Asian economies. Nonetheless, at the theoretical level, the phenomenon of inter-personal relations may be conducive to either economies of networking or diseconomies of networking. Wank (1999) has an interesting observation about the operation of networking in Xiamen, China. The **perfect networking** (or **networking, perfect**) based on perfectly mutual trust (conditioned by the culture) in the ideal case may present a case of the perfect economies of networking. In the case of imperfect networking with trust and breach of trust prevailing simultaneously, both scenarios of the economies of networking and the diseconomies of networking shall coexist.

Of course, two examples of the **diseconomies of networking** in a society of tranquil culture are the corrupt behavior (or socially adversary collusion) of the firms and the corruption of the government.

The economies of network is different from the **advantage of centrality in planning** through which scarce resources are allocated to the most beneficial activities under the holistic considerations involving both supply- and demand-side development. It is natural that, the trust stemming from the culture of mutuality shall reduce transactions costs of doing business. On one hand, this trust may facilitate the transfer of technology between firms in a society and thereby reduce the costs of production. Therefore the supply curve of the firm shall shift downward. One the other hand, this trust may also enlarge the market demand and thereby shift the demand curve of this firm outward.

F.3 Systematic Organizations

§F.3-1 Introduction

In a righteous organization (or organization of righteous culture), i.e., an organization under the culture of virtue and mutual trust, let $X = [(x \rightleftarrows y) \rightleftarrows z \mid \mathbb{C}^{TJ}] \sqsubseteq (\Omega, \mathcal{Z}\circ, {}_{v}\mathcal{H}, \{\mathbb{C}\})$ be a system, where x and y being non-central elements and z the center, with the culture of tranquility, tao-jen spirituality and mutual trust ($\mathbb{C}^{TJ}$). Then, we may write its virtue–oriented organization as (see §3.2):

(F.3-1-1) $\{\psi[(x \rightleftharpoons y \rightleftharpoons z, \Delta) \mid (x,y|z) \| \mathbb{C}^{TJ}(\tau)]\} =< T^{B}, \tau \Vdash (\mathfrak{I}, \text{Ш}^{\text{Д}}) \Vvdash \mathbb{T}zu^{*}$,

where "$\rightleftharpoons$" denotes an impactor of mutual trust. In general, for the system of n elements (z as the center) under the culture of tranquility, we have:

(F.3-1-2) $\{\psi[(x_1 \rightleftharpoons x_2 \rightleftharpoons \ldots \rightleftharpoons x_n, \Delta) \mid (x_1, x_2, \ldots, x_{n-1}|z) \| \mathbb{C}^{T}(\tau)]\} =< T^{B}$,
$\tau \Vdash (\mathfrak{I}, \text{Ш}^{\text{Д}}) \Vvdash \mathbb{T}zu^{*}$.

where $\mathbb{C}^{T}$ denotes the culture of tranquility (see Bcm. (3.9) in Section III).

As for a capitalist corporation, i.e., a for-profit corporation, let $X = [(x \rightleftarrows y) \rightleftarrows z \mid \mathbb{C}^{K}] \sqsubseteq (\Omega, \mathcal{Z}\circ, {}_{v}\mathcal{H}, \{\mathbb{C}\})$ be a system, where x and y being non-central elements and z the center, with the culture of conflict and conquest ($\mathbb{C}^{K}$). Then, we may write its profit–oriented organization as:

(F.3-1-3) $\{\psi[(x \leftarrow\!\mapsto y \leftarrow\!\mapsto z, \Delta) \mid (x,y|z) \| \mathbb{C}^{K}(\tau)]\} =< T^{B}, \tau \Vdash (\mathfrak{I}, \text{Ш}^{\text{Д}}) \Vvdash \mathbb{T}zu^{*}$,

where "$\leftarrow\!\mapsto$" denotes an impactor of conflict. In general, for the system of n elements (z as the center) with the culture of conflict:

(F.3-1-4) $\{\psi[(x_1 \leftarrow\!\mapsto x_2 \leftarrow\!\mapsto \ldots \leftarrow\!\mapsto x_n, \Delta) \mid (x_1, x_2, \ldots, x_{n-1}|z) \| \mathfrak{C}^{TJ}(\tau)]\} =< T^{C\Delta}$,
$\tau \Vdash (\mathfrak{I}, \text{Ш}^{\text{Д}}) \Vvdash \mathbb{T}zu^{*}$.

In the following, the discussion of a system of organization shall begin with its tranquil and conflict units. In the tranquil unit which is a system as well (i.e., as a unit system in a grand system), every member is oriented toward self-interest as well as the interests of others, and each one has inner peace in mind and has a complete goodwill toward others. In contrast, in the conflict unit which is a unit system, every member is oriented toward self-interest at the expense of others, and each one has anxiety in one's inner mind complex and always desires to conquer others. By combining these two units into a new system (i.e., a grand system), one derives the organization of harmony as well as that of competition. Note that, in the harmonious system or organization, the tranquil unit dominates the conflict unit; while in contrast, in the competitive system or organization, the tranquil unit is instead dominated by the conflict unit.

In any organization which is a system or more generally a grand system, the major issues are whether it is of the culture of tranquility or conflict, whether it is of the culture of independence or coordination, whether its system is one of centrality or equilibrium, and whether its strategy is of continuity or discontinuity.

The management styles of firms may be classified according to whether the underlying system is one of centralization or decentralization. Conflict organization is one with the culture of anxiety and internal conflict. For the conflict organization in a state of T continuity, for a highly complicated task which requires local initiative and individual devotion, the decentralized management style appears to be appropriate, while for a simple task, the coerced and centralized management style may be efficient. In the latter case, each member of the organization is motivated to fully utilize his/her (technological) capacity; and there is a **passive efficiency of mutuality–in-conflict** (which is defined as the positive impact of the threatening environments of striving for survival) created by the process of conflict (or cut-throat competition) but not any kind of **active efficiency of mutuality-in-tranquility** (which is defined as the positive effects of interchanging ideas, complementary work effort and reinforcing task force) based on the principle of solidarity and mutual help existing in this organization.

In general, for a conflict organization, assuming no negative factor of mutuality, the sum of individuals' benefits is almost equal to the total benefits of the organization. In the case of strategic discontinuity or even anti-continuity, it may be appropriate for the conflict organization to adopt a management style of a high degree of centralization. In this case, since the human nature is not supposed to be good, the principle of the survival of the fittest prevails. Here this may be called the **efficiency of strategic centrality**. But in the case that the economies of scale, economies of mutual assistance and technological creativity are required, even under an effective leadership and far-reached vision, for a conflict organization, a decentralized style of management may be easier to be justified.

Tranquil system is one of peaceful coordination from within. For this system, in the case of T continuity, decentralized management style may be appropriate. That is, in a state of momentarily systemic and strategic continuity, there are forces of internal peace and self-generating spontaneity in one's inner-self. For this system, by the merits of individual initiation, local flexibility and active creativity, decentralized management is effective. In this case, it is said to have only the passive efficiency of mutuality based on one's inner motivation. And yet in a state of T continuity, centralized management style is appropriate if an active efficiency of mutuality, based upon centralized "planning mechanism" of scarce talents in the organization, is required. But note that in this case, due to the active efficiency of mutuality, the **active efficiency of self-energizing**, which is defined as the positive impact of self-motivation and self-initiative under the encouraging environments of friendly cooperation, may be adversely affected by the centralized management.

For a tranquil system in the state of T continuity, if it achieves a balance between decentralized management and strategic centrality, then this organization enjoys the passive efficiency of mutuality and the active efficiency of self-energizing. Similarly for a socio-polity of self-mastering in which the government is bestowed the indirect power of effective control while the common people retain the direct power, the underlying society may possess both kinds of passive and active efficiencies of mutuality.

For a business firm, the state of *T continuity* includes the following conditions: At an instantaneous time, (1) the level of profits of the firm is temporarily at or above the satisfactory level, (2) the market share of the firm is temporarily at or above its target level, and (3) the internal structure of the firm is momentarily stable.[54]

In an organization, the life aspiration (be it out of abstract reasoning, philosophical idea, spiritual contemplation, or even something mystical), artistic orientation (be it out of concrete reasoning or irrational emotion) and religious sentiment (be it super-rationality or else) of a member of the organization in question are closely interrelated. They actually have a generative-and-destructive (shengke or dialectic) relationship.

Below we come to the issues of the shift factors of supply and demand. For the tranquility unit, on the supply-side, the shift factors are: (1) creative factor, like real-world and outward spirit, be it artistic, religious, organizational or just an approach of the life-will, (2) sustaining factor, be it leisure-like, inward-looking, defensive, or that of emptying-out those too much attached to the daily-world conditions, and (3) destructive factor. Note that shift factors combining two or more aspects of creativity, sustainability and destructivity also exist.

For the tranquility unit, on the demand-side, the shift factors are: (1) cultural factors, going to either creative or destructive direction, and (2) non-cultural factors, also going to either direction of creativity or destructivity.

For the conflict unit, on the supply-side, the shift factors are: (1) creative factor, like real-world and outward spirit, be it artistic, religious, or scientific, (2) sustaining factor, be it leisure-like, inward-looking, or defensive, and (3) destructive factor. Note that shift factors combining two or more aspects of creativity, sustainability and destructivity may also exist.

For the conflict unit, on the demand-side, the shift factors are: (1) acquisitive, possessive or materialistic factors, going to either creative or destructive direction, and (2) non-materialistic factors, also going to the direction of either creativity or destructivity.

In business, tranquil unit with coerced centrality will have a stronger influence over small- and medium-sized enterprises. This is because in these relatively small-sized organizations, the owners are in a better position to directly exercise their power over employees, like in some cases of Chinese and French business firms. Because many relatives of the owners are employed and occupying some key positions in the organizations, the privately-owned small and medium-size businesses tend to be tranquil organizations. As a contrast, conflict culture tends to prevail in large-scaled enterprises, partially due to the fact that ownership is separated from management. These tranquil and conflict cultures have strong influence over the operations of the underlying organizations, in the sense of rotating or even shifting their supply and demand curves. Thus, transactions costs are affected and therefore the cultural variables shift the supply and demand curves.

In terms of a model of management, this trust or the economies of networking may lead to Ouchi's theory Z in management.

The human-factor strategy of the organization with centralization-in-tranquility. In the following, we shall define the centralization-in-tranquility organization as one with centralized structure culture conditioned or created by a tranquil culture. Here, each member of the organization lives peacefully by oneself; and simultaneously, all members live together harmonious.

The basic organization of this centralization-in-tranquility organization is:

(F.3-1-5) [(Low-Middle)-Upper | centralization-tranquil culture],

where Low refers to the low-level employees, Upper the upper-level management and the staff, Middle the middle-level management, and centralization the relationship of centralization in which central element controls strictly the non-central elements.

In general, this tranquil organization may be represented by the following system:

(F.3-1-6) [(Yin-Yang)-He | centralization-tranquil culture],

where Yin represents the yin or implicit element, Yang the yang or explicit element, and "He" the central and unifying element. Note that, this is a standard R-system. Here "He" is the central element, and Yin and Yang are non-central elements. In this system, "He" dominates both yin and yang elements; and although Yin and Yang elements are complementary to each other, Yang is at a position higher than that of Yin.

When the tranquil-centralization organization (Y_t) embarks on a human-factor- based strategy, (F.3-1-6) may be expressed as S_t, the certainty part of an uncertain system Y_t. That is, for $Y_t = S_t \oplus X_t$ (see Bcm. (I.3-9)):

(F.3-1-7) S_t = [(Yin-Yang)-He | centralization-tranquil culture| $\mathcal{L}^{YX}$-$\mathbb{C}^{T}$]

or

(F.3-1-8) S_t = [(Yin-Yang)-He | centralization-tranquil culture| $\mathcal{L}^{ST}$-$\mathbb{C}^{K}$]

with X_t as the uncertainty part of Y_t, be it a 0-step K^L uncertain process, 0-step K^{sysC} uncertain process, 0-step T^L uncertain process, 0-step T^{sysC} uncertain process, n-step K^{sysD} uncertain process, n-step T^{sysD} uncertain process, or the uncertain systems in B.2, B.3 (see Definitions (I.3-1) - (I.3.6) of Appendix I or Tonn (2006, Appendix K)).

In the following, theory Z may be interpreted as a theory of tranquil system, together with the culture of centralization dominating the culture of equilibrium—a balance between centralization and equilibrium with the force of centralization outweighing that of equilibrium. Here by the so-called force of equilibrium is meant that noncentral members have some natural degree of independence, and the so-called balance between centralization and equilibrium is meant that noncentral members of the system have some power of independence but subordinate themselves voluntarily to the power of the central member. In the following, theories like Tseng' contingency theory [Tseng 1987], 5c management and systematic management are all theories of management with the culture of tranquil-in-centralization.

The centralization-tranquil organization may be expressed as one of separable system. In general, a separable system is a grand system which can be separated into several smaller (sub-)systems (if it is feasible to do so). If this organization is separable (see Definition A.3-2-1), then for $X = \{x_1, x_2, \ldots, x_n, res\} \sqsubseteq (\Omega, \mathbb{Z}_O, {}_v\mathbb{H}, \{\mathbb{C}\})$ be a grand system, X is said to be a *completely separable system* if and only if the following becoming is true:

(F.3-1-9) $\phi X = C \otimes \mathcal{T} = \{[C \oplus (N_1 \oplus N_2 \oplus \ldots \oplus N_{n-1})] \oplus (\text{res elements})\} \circledast Ix$,

where $\phi \vDash \mathbb{Z}_{\circ,v}\mathbb{H}$ is the separable impactor, $C = x_n$ is the centralization unit, $\mathcal{T}$ is the tranquil unit, C is the central system, N_i is the ith noncentral system, for all $i = 1,2,\ldots,n-1$, $\otimes \vDash \mathbb{Z}_{\circ,v}\mathbb{H}$ is some integrating impactor of this grand system, (res elements) is the set of elements not in any sub-system (i.e., residuals), $\circledast \vDash \mathbb{Z}_{\circ,v}\mathbb{H}$ is an integrating impactor, and Ix is the integrating factor of the grand system.

One of the best examples of these centralization-tranquil grand systems is the Japanese Keiretsu (or a loose conglomerate) as a grand system in which the group bank may be considered as the central system and each member firm is a decomposable system.

Note that the IRI chain (in a person's mind complex or in a firm) and SIFP chain complex (in a cultural economy) of an organization of centralization-tranquil culture can also be represented as dynamical grand systems or chain complexes of simple (or unit) systems. For the original concepts of IRI chain and SIFP chain complex, one may see Tonn (2001, pp. 144-147, 149-151). The key factor linking these simple systems into an integrated whole is the shared cultural orientation existing in each of these simple systems. Naturally all the core of these individual unit systems (which share the same cultural orientation) together form the core of the grand system. Under the centralization-tranquil culture, the cultural traits or shared cultural values underlying the IRI chain (which represents the IE-RD-PI information evaluation- rational decision making-planning implementation chain), i.e., the willingness to contribute to the best well-being of the group and the rationality of functioning the systems systemically, safeguard the smooth flow of energies operating through this IRI chain (X). In symbols, for the completely separation impactor $\phi \vDash \mathbb{Z}_{\circ,v}\mathbb{H}$, some integrating impactor $\otimes \vDash \mathbb{Z}_{\circ,v}\mathbb{H}$, and additive associational impactor $\oplus \vDash \mathbb{Z}_{\circ,v}\mathbb{H}$, and the standard integrating impactor $\circledast \vDash \mathbb{Z}_{\circ,v}\mathbb{H}$, we have:

(F.3-1-10)
$$\begin{aligned}\phi X &= C \otimes \mathcal{T} \\ &= \{[C \oplus (N_1 \oplus N_2 \oplus N_3)] \oplus (\text{res elements})\} \circledast Ix \\ &= [(IE \oplus RD \oplus PI) \oplus (\text{res elements})] \circledast Ix,\end{aligned}$$

where C, $\mathcal{T}$, N_1, N_2 and N_3 represent the cultural core (i.e., the central system), the tranquil unit of the system, IE, RD and PI systems of the firm in question, respectively.

Remark F.3-1-1. As in the case of a firm, (i.e., a general business organization), the IRI chain can be expressed in terms of a system (see Example F.3-1-1) or a systemic-change becoming, either static or dynamical forms (see Example F.3-1-2).

Figure F.3-1-1
IRI system

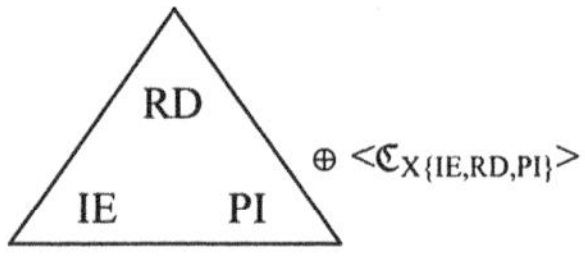

Example F.3-1-1. (i). The IRI chain can be expressed in terms of a graph as follows:

(iia). By the principle of CE balance, we have from Bcm. (3.2-1-8): ψ{IE,Δ}≛ ψ{PI,Δ}, or from Bcm. (3.2-2-5): ψ{IE≛PI,Δ} ⊼̄ τ, τ ⊫ (ℑ,$Ш^{Д}$) ⊪ 𝕋zu*.

(iib). By the principle of CE centrality, we have from Bcm. (3.2-2-10): ψ{RD≥IE,Δ} ⊼̄ and ψ{RD≥PI,Δ} ⊼̄τ.

(iii). We can treat the IRI chain as a leaf-shaped MFCE scheme (see Figure E.3-3).

(iv). We can treat the IRI chain as a two-way circular flow (see 6.2) as well:

Figure F.3-1-2
IRI chain as a two-way circular flow

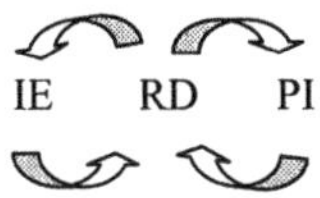

Below, for the IRI chain, we write:

(F.3-1-11) IRI = χ^{IRI} ⊕<$\mathbb{C}_{IRI}$>,

where χ^{IRI} = {**x**(H)⊫[(vd,hc,γ),(R,$R^D(e_k)$),Õ]||E{e_g},Z}^{IRI}. Then we have the following example for this IRI chain.

Example F.3-1-2. Let IE be a becoming of x, i.e., IE = IE(x), RD be a becoming of y, i.e., RD = RD(y), and PI be a becoming of z, i.e., PI = PI(z). Here, for instance, x may be considered as a complex of the will-rationality complex: x ⇜ (ρ,ω). For these, we may write:

(F.3-1-12) IE → x ⊕ res(IE),
RD → y ⊕ res(RD),
PI → z ⊕ res(PI),

where res' are some residual terms. Now, let y = φ(x), z = φ^2(x) (see B1.). From these above expressions, we have in a form of the static representation of systemic- change becoming as follows:

(F.3-1-13) IRI = [(φ^2x ⊕φx ⊕x) ⊕(res)] ⊚ Ix

(see Bcms (3.6-8) and (3.6-9) and Sections B.1 and B.2 in Appendix B). Then we have the dynamical forms of this IRI (at a state of simple TCentral) as follows:

(F.3-1-14) u(.) = = [α_2u($\mathbb{H}_2$;z,.)⊕α_1u($\mathbb{H}_1$;y,.)]⊕α_0u($\mathbb{H}_0$;x,)]⊚Iu($\mathbb{H}_u$;.),

with all terms being properly defined (analogous to Bcm. (A.8-1-3)).

Similarly, under the centralization-tranquil culture, the cultural characteristics which undergird the SIFP chain complex (which represents the sciences and technology-investment-financing-production chain) safeguards the smooth flow of the energies of unit nodes and thereby effectively transmit them throughout this chain complex. In terms of symbols, in the following we have for the IRI chain (X) and the SIFP chain (Y):

$$\text{(F.3-1-15)}\quad \begin{aligned} &\phi X \\ &= C \otimes \mathcal{T} \\ &= [\mathfrak{C} \oplus (\mathcal{N}_1 \oplus \mathcal{N}_2 \oplus \mathcal{N}_3 \oplus \mathcal{N}_4) \oplus (\text{res elements})] \circledast \text{Ix} \\ &= [(\text{ST} \oplus \text{I} \oplus \text{F} \oplus \text{P}) \oplus (\text{res elements})] \circledast \text{Ix}, \end{aligned}$$

where $\mathfrak{C}$, $\mathcal{N}_1$, $\mathcal{N}_2$, $\mathcal{N}_3$ and $\mathcal{N}_4$ represent the cultural core, sciences and technology, investment activities and production activities systems of the economy in question, respectively.

Note that as is in Bcm. (F.3-1-7), (F.3-1-8) or (F.3-1-11) can be made into a becoming of uncertain systems.

§F.3-2 Various Theories of Organization

Theory Z. William G. Ouchi holds that effective management must employ methods of consensual decision-making. By obtaining more detailed information and better advice, unbalanced and extremely biased decisions may be eliminated, and better quality of decision may be ensured. Therefore, Ouchi argues for the merits of (1) workers' active participation of the decision-making process, (2) effective and constructive communication between management and workers, and (3) the controlling of the work place by workers. The background of theory Z is the culture of tranquility with centralization system dominating equilibrium system. In this Z system (i.e., the organizational system operating according to the principle of theory Z), the power is centralized (i.e., centrality). And yet because of workers' participation (i.e., by (1) and (2)), the channel transmitting the information effectively from workers to the management is open. In the above, the workers are said to have a power for suggestion, and by (3), the employees also have the power to set the conditions of the worker place. But to our knowledge, this Ochi's theory suggesting workers to have power to set working conditions for themselves does not appear to prevail essentially in any real world system except in the case of former Yugoslav

In the following Figure E.2-1, a, b, c $\Vdash$ **H** $\Subset \Omega$ and $\{a,b,c\} \sqsubseteq (\Omega, \mathcal{Z}\circ, {}_{v}\mathcal{H}, \{\mathbb{C}\})$ with c being the center, and a and b being the non-central yin-element and yang-element, respectively. Here, and either $a \rightarrow c$ is an h^L-systmeism (that is, $a \rightarrow b$ is a y-systemism and $(a,b) \rightarrow c$ is a y^L-systemism) or $a \rightarrow c$ is an h^R-systmeism (that is, both $a \rightarrow b$ and $b \rightarrow c$ are y^L-systemisms). Note that in the former case, {a,b,c} is a T-weak system, and in the latter case, it is a T-semistrong system.. In addition, the cultural system $<\mathbb{C}_x>$ is one of tranquility and balance ($\mathbb{C}_x^{T\&B}$). Note one way to show that the cultural factors (simply represented by the will-rationality complex (ρ,ω)) enters into the system is to have the system as (see Remark (A.2-2-2-1)): foe a system $X = \chi \oplus <\mathbb{C}_X>$, with $\chi = \{\mathbf{x}(H^*).\}$ we have $\mathbf{x}(H^*) = \{x_1(y_1;h_1^*,.),\ldots, x_n(y_n;h_n^*,.)\}$, for $= x_i(y_i;h_i^*,.) = x_i(y_{i1},y_{i2},..,y_{is};h_{i1}^*, h_{i2}^*,..,h_{it}^*;IRI_i)$. Here IRI $\backsim(\rho,\omega)$ or $IRI = IRI(\rho,\omega) = IE(\rho,\omega) \oplus RD(\rho,\omega) \oplus PI(\rho,\omega)$ (see Bcm (3.7-1-3)).

But nevertheless, in terms of the organizational structure of centralization-decentralization, the system of Theory Z is a conventional one, even though its culture is one of consensus.

In terms of a system of organizational, we may express the system of Theory Z as:

$$(\text{F.3-2-1})\quad \{\{[x_i(h_j^*,v_k,..,IRI(\rho,\omega),.)|\ x_i(.) \Vdash (\text{org-func}|\ R;O))^B\|(\mathbb{C}^T,Z),E(e_k)] \oplus <\mathbb{C}_X{}^{T\&B}>\} =< T^{C\Delta}\} \sqsubseteq Ш^{Д}$$

(see Section3.3 YY BCM), where $\mathbb{C} = \mathbb{C}^T$ (the culture is the culture of tranquility), $\mathbb{C}_X{}^{T\&B}$ (the culture is the culture of tranquility and balance), and (org-func| R;O) =(org-func| R;O)^B is one of balance (i.e., superscript B) in centralization-decentralization, for R denoting all internal structures and external relations, o depicting all other entities in the system unaccounted for.

Figure F.3-2-1
Systematic presentation of Theory Z

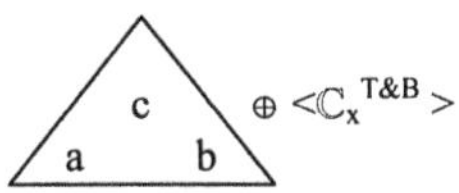

In a Catholic setting, in this Z system (i.e., systems of theory Z), members may trust each other with a strong sense of solidarity. In general, this is a T-strong system (for {A,b,c}, a → b is an f-systemism, b → c is an f-systemism), the cultural background of this system goes beyond that of tranquility, since it also carries with it the cultures of consensus, equilibrium and a further spirituality of religion.

Tseng's principle-contingency system. Tseng [1987] developed a theory of principle-contingency management which is also called the management of people-pacification. In this theory, the principles of management must follow Confucian doctrine, and then measures of contingency follow. To be somewhat critical, we may say that because Confucian ethics is not very flexible, there may not be much room to claim for contingency. Note that this is a T-weak system (see Subsection §3.7-3).

Tseng's system ({a,b,c}, for example) appears to be a T-strong system if it is represented by an h^R-systemism of a to c.

In the following, we shall present the **general n-polar system of organization** or **management** (n is the number to be determined). For a conventional presentation of this general management system, see Figure F.3-2-2. For a systematic presentation of this general management system, see Figure F.3-2-3.

In Figure F.3-2-3, $C|_S$ (Directors-CEO C with staff S) represents the center of the grand management system, with {x,y,z} and {a,b,c,d,e,f} stand for the middle-management system and the collection of workers as a system, respectively. Here, for a, b, c, d,e,f, x, y, z, C, S $\Vdash\Omega$ and for {a,b,c,d,e,f}, {x,y,z}, $C|_S \sqsubseteq (\Omega,\mathcal{Z}\circ,{}_v\mathcal{H},\{\mathbb{C}\})$, {a,b,c} → {x,y,z} is a f- (or Hf-) systemism, and {x,y,z} → $C|_S$ is an h- (or Hh-) systemism. Here {{a,b,c,d,e,f},{x,y,z}| $C|_S$} ⊕ <$\mathbb{C}_X$> is a grand system.

In the above n-polar system: C is the center of the grand system, S (staff) is the **supporting center**, x, y and z are in the intermediate echelon, and a, b, c ,d, e and f are non-central members in the low echelon.

In this system, C employs the principle of centrality in controlling all other members; and the principle of balance or hierarchical balance is to be used for operating the system among x, y and z.

In terms of incentive system, the organization is to be run by the principle of free and voluntary contract, based on pecuniary or other types of rewards.

Figure F.3-2-2
General n-polar system of management or organization

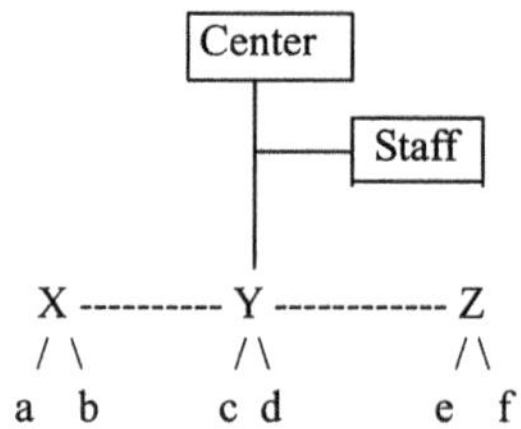

Figure F.3-2-3
Systematic presentation of a general management system, W = {a,b,c,d,e,f}

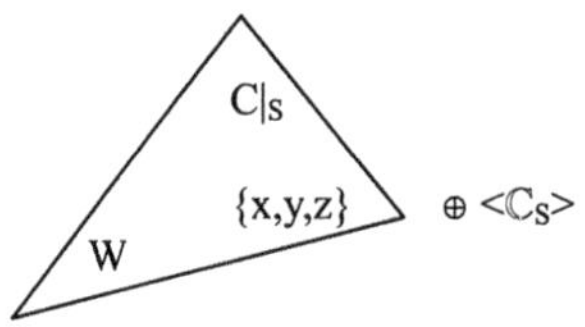

For this general n-polar system of management, in terms of power structure, among others, there are positional power (p), charismatic power (c), and expertise power (e) with P, C, and E serving as their fully developed structures, respectively. Let $\psi \vDash \mathcal{Z}$ be a delay impactor of expansion, $\varphi \vDash \mathcal{Z}$ a delay impactor of contraction, $\xi \vDash \mathcal{Z}$ an auxiliary impactor of expansion, and $\varepsilon \vDash \mathcal{Z}$ an auxiliary impactor of contraction. For a person $x \Vdash X \sqsubseteq (\Omega, \mathcal{Z}_{\circ,v}\mathcal{H}, \{\mathbb{C}\})$, and for p, c, e, P, C, E $\vDash \mathcal{Z}_{\circ,v}\mathcal{H}$, we have the following power structures:

(F.3-2-2)
$$\varphi p\{x \mid \varepsilon\}_t \rightarrow \pi_{t+i} \ldots \twoheadrightarrow P_{t+n},$$
$$\varphi c\{x \mid \varepsilon\}_t \rightarrow \gamma_{t+i} \ldots \twoheadrightarrow C_{t+n},$$
$$\psi e\{x \mid \xi\}_t \ldots \rightarrow E_{t+n}.$$

where π and γ denotes the not fully developed positional power and charismatic power, respectively. Here, the subscripts denote time $t \in R$ (real numbers) with $0 < i < n$, and "$\rightarrow$" and "$\ldots\nrightarrow$" refer to "becoming to" and "not over time becoming to," respectively.

In the long run, for the center x, unless it develops and achieves its expertise power, it would transform itself into π, but not the fully developed positional power P. Similarly, unless it develops and achieves its expertise power, it would transfer itself into γ, and would not transform itself into the fully developed charismatic power C. That is, at a state of simple Tcentral, one would have: $P \stackrel{\star}{=} C \stackrel{\star}{=} E$; otherwise, we have the measure of the positional power ($\mathcal{P}(\pi)$) weaker than that of the expertise power and also measure of the positional power ($\mathcal{P}(\gamma)$) weaker than that of the expertise power: $\mathcal{P}(\pi) < \mathcal{P}(E)$ and $\mathcal{P}(\gamma) < \mathcal{P}(E)$.

In general, those associated with this general n-polar MFCE management systems of tranquility culture are T-weak systems if they are related closely to h^L-systemism, and they are either T-semistrong or T-strong systems if they are related closely to h^R-systemism.

In contrast, for the national economic system, the center or the central government has the power (i.e., enforcing power not operating on the principle of free contract) to tax, through fiscal or monetary means, all members of the economy. That is, a polity is a centralized and coerced system, not necessarily a consensual system or a system of equal power for all members. That is, under the culture of tranquility, the national economic system in general is definitely a T-strong system.

In terms of developmental strategies, T-strong system is related to a strategic space inclusive of leap strategy, while T-semistrong and T-weak systems are related to strategic spaces inclusive of golden strategy and silver strategy, respectively.

There are several schools of thought in terms of management under conflict culture, for example, pre-classical school, classical school, scientific management school, X theory and Legalist school.

Remark F.3-2-1. In general, these schemes are either C-strong or C-weak systems, related closely to the strategic space inclusive of golden strategy and others in the former case and the strategic spaces inclusive of silver strategy and variational strategy and others in the latter case. These C-strong systems may be able to move onto a leap path if (1) it is associated with a high level of technological creativity and (2) it is associated with a high level availability of scarce resources.

In the following, we shall discuss in turn these schools of management under conflict culture.

Pre-classical school (management under strategic continuity). The famous scholars associated with this school are: Taylor, H. Fayol, L. Gullick, L. Urwick, James Mooney and Allen Reilly. The theory of this school in general contends that human nature is not good, and consequently the appropriate method of management is to employees strictly by combining pecuniary rewards with threat of layoff. In this system of organization, members among themselves are in constant conflict and the relation between the management and low-level workers is always tense. That is, this is a system of coerced centralization under conflict culture. In terms of the mechanism of command and control, it is centrally planned; in terms of human resource management, it is rigid; in terms of coordination, horizontal coordination is ignored; and in terms of vertical control chain, it is a top-down system of rigid command.

Classical school (under a variational type of strategic discontinuity sufficiently closed to a state of strategic continuity). This school bases its analysis on the philosophical foundation of the individuals' self-interests. In order to safeguard the centrality of the organization, this school advocates methods of strictly controlling workers. This school differs from the pre-classical school in that the former allows a certain degree of equilibrium to exist in the system. In the pre-classical school, there is no such equilibrium and its methods of control are to be flexible. In contrast, the classical school advocates, beside centralized control, a limited degree of self-adjustment. In terms of the mechanism of central planning, according to the classical school's doctrine, beyond the comprehensive planning of the whole organization, there are detailed plans for each sector and each sub-sector.

Taylor's theory of management. Fredrick W. Taylor studied extensively the behavior of workers in the Midvale Steel Company, Simons Rolling Machine Company and Bethlehem Steel Company. Based on these experiences, he then developed the classical school of scientific management. Taylor believed that under scientific methods of management, the efficiency of workers would be maximized. Thus, the workers' daily operations are to be controlled up to ever single detail by objective and clearly specified procedures. From the perspective of the economics of culture, this is understandable because under the culture of conflict, the self-interest of workers is in fundamental conflict with the self-interest of manager. If workers are unsupervised or under-supervised, this theory predicts that the worker's pursuit of self-interests would not be in the best self-interests of the manager. That is, workers need to be coerced constantly to serve the best-interests of the manager. Since the power of organization is concentrated in the hands of management, if correct working procedures are carefully designed and effective work-supervision are rigorously enforced, the goal of efficient management can be realized through the use of scientific methods assuming there exists neither obstacles to maximize the efficiency nor any uncertainty to undercut this efficiency. The other contribution made by Taylor is the introduction of wages based on piece work.

Science of management. This school of the science of management (or that of scientific management) argues that it is presumably desirable to use mathematical models and logical reasoning processes to study management. By doing so, experimental methods could be easily employed to test the accuracy of these mathematical models.

Theory X. McGregor classifies the conventional theories of management from an angle by having implicit assumptions about human nature. (1) He argued that Taylor considered worker's human nature as not good and therefore Taylor would like to subject the workers to strict supervision. (2) He contended that Mayo was optimistic about human nature and therefore had a more favorable evaluation toward both of the ability and the attitude of the workers. From these new perspectives, McGregor developed his theory X and theory Y of management. In the following, we briefly summarize the contents of theory X. Theory Y will be discussed later. Essentially, theory X is one of conflict culture with centralization, and the key assumptions underlying this theory are: (1) Individuals dislike work and hence have a strong tendency to avoid it. (2) Workers must be forced, controlled, threatened or even manipulated in order to work effectively. (3) Workers prefer stable jobs with no desire to assume responsibility. (4) Only a few people have creativity. Most of the workers do not have their own initiative and creativity.

Figure F.3-2-4
Systematic presentation of Theory X

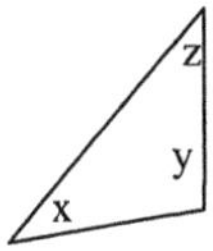

$\oplus <\mathbb{C}_X{}^C>$

In terms of a systematic presentation, see the following Figure F.3-2-4. Let x, y, $z \Vdash \mathbf{H} \Subset \Omega$ and $\{x,y,z\} \sqsubseteq (\Omega, \mathbb{Z}^{\circ}, {}_{v}H, \{\mathbb{C}\})$ with z being the center, and a and b being the non-central elements. Here, a → b is an Hf-systemism, and b → c is another Hf-systemism. In addition, the cultural system $<\mathbb{C}_X{}^C>$ is one of conflict type with the characteristics described in the above, and the structure of control is centralized with most likely a minimal level of horizontal coordination.

Transaction costs theory. This is essentially a theory using a mathematical approach. This is a theory of micro-management using pecuniary reward as the major tool to provide incentive to workers. With the underlying culture of caring only for one's self-interests, stock option and bonus are considered as the most effective means to motivate workers. Under perfect information (for example, workers' ability is known and workers' behavior is predictable) and no uncertainty (e.g., no risk involved), this theory proclaims the merits of first best efficient contract. For this theory, the cultural backgrounds are those of conflict and conquest culture with the implicit assumption of conventional production function in the productive process.

Legalist management theory. Logically, the Legalist school of classic China developed its theory on the basis of systemic and strategic anti-continuity. For the modern Legalist doctrine (if there is one) can be made to be consistent with the doctrine of Marxism-Leninism. Historically, part of Legalist philosophy was originated from The Kuan Tzu in the Spring-Autumn period. In the period of Warring States, there were the former Legalists like Wu Chi and Shang Yang who stressed the importance of ruling by law and the latter Legalists like Shen Buhai who developed a political theory based on the use of statecrafts or tricks, Shen Tao who integrated the study of historical trend or forces to his political theory, and Han Fei Tzu who synthesized all aspects of the doctrines of the school of Legalism. Hanfei Tzu favored a polity of dictatorship with king serving as the master of laws and advocated the use of statecrafts or tricks over its subjects as the most effective methods of state control (Hsiau [1982], p. 231). Here, what we mean by law is the set of codified rules from which daily regulations are derived to rule the common people. By the culture of classic China, kings or emperors were those who set the laws and were above the laws, and statecrafts or tricks are essentially what the rulers used to manipulate and control their subjects (Hou [1985], p. 187). Han Fei Tzu was born at the time of Warring States of classical China when countries were constantly at war with each other and were literally struggling to survive.

In this Legalist way of thinking, the individual is motivated only by self-interests (or selfishness in the Chinese sense). Thus, it is easy for any one to reason that the underlying culture of this theory is that of conflict. But then, the polity of dictatorship achieved its practical Tcentral by the implicit and explicit use of violence. Here by the implicit use is meant to use by the help of some "symbols" -- for instance, religious tricks to bestow legitimacy to the kings and emperors which are ultimately supported by the power of violence of the rulers.

Here by **practical Tcentral** is meant a desirable state of Tcentral achieved under the constraints of the existing internal structures and dynamics of the system and external environments facing the system in question.

According to Han Fei Tzu, the ancient history of China can be classified into three worlds (or periods): ancient world, medieval or immediate-past world and contemporary world. In the ancient world, people were of virtues; in the immediate-past world, people competed against others by the use of intelligence; and in the contemporary world, people eliminate others through violence or military forces.[55] In the ancient world, people did not use violence against each other, because then the economic resources were more than sufficient to feed people. Due to natural resource abundance and there were not that many people to compete for scarce resources, it is unnecessary for people to struggle against each other.[56] In the contemporary world, there is a serious shortage of scarce resources but the population is huge. Therefore, people have to work hard and yet the level of production is not sufficient to support people. Consequently, people resort to violence in order to compete successfully against others.[57] That is to say, in the ancient time, there was no need to use any violence because of no scarcity of natural resources. Therefore, people treated each other well and were virtuous.[58] In the world of the immediate past, scarcity of natural resources developed and yet it was not yet that threatening. Hence, it is to Han Fei Tzu's belief that, in this situation, people could compete in an orderly manner. That is what Han Fei Tzu means to compete by the use of intelligence. In the contemporary world, Han Fei Tzu reasoned that, unless one eradicates others, one would not be able to survive. This is consistent with the theory of Hsun Tzu, the teacher of Han Fei Tzu, that human nature is evil. By this reasoning, the kings also have evil human nature, and accordingly they love to enslave their subjects and strive hard to conquer other nations.

In the management theory of Han Fei Tzu, in the short-term concerns, creativity is essential. This is what Hsun Tzu called learning from the later kings. In the long-term behavior, a subjects is supposed to follow the laws or regulations set by the kings, to strive to develop one's best potential, to be promoted by merits, to be rewarded by appropriate titles, to be accountable, to have appropriate use of reward and punishment, and to manage (or control the common people) by some mysterious methods (Hou [1985]). By this is also meant that to be practical and efficient in management, one has to plan in advance and to have a decent channel of human communications and connections with unified rules of control to be supplemented by effective coordination with flexibility.

Competitive system. By definition, as a grand system, the competitive system is composed of a tranquil sub-system and a conflict sub-system, in which the tranquil unit system is dominated by the conflict unit system. Here for the tranquil system in the West, it may well be in turn composed of a spiritual system – i.e., a system of Christian ethics of absolute belief and loving others unconditionally -- and a rationality system, that of revelation rationality of existential or super-existential creativity. As for the conflict system of the West, it may be thought of as being composed of the ethics of humanism with Nietzsche-Faustian spirit or the spirit of existential-post-modernism and the rationality system of scientism, logical positivism, or others such as structuralism and the system of hermeneutics.

In the following, we shall present some organizational systems of competition with managerial centrality.

The organization theory of Henri Fayol. For the management system under conflict culture, Henri Fayol' contributions to the development of management theories may be identified in the following: (1) To separate management from the supervision of works. By this is meant to assign and concentrate the power of the firm in the hand of the managers rather than on those technicians who supervise workers directly. (2) To define management by functions: planning, organization, control, coordination and execution. (3) To establish a principle of management by focusing on the following key areas: division of labor, authority, discipline and order, unified control, requesting workers to sacrifice themselves for the sake of organization, reasonable compensation and remuneration, concentration of power, the chain control of the lower echelon by the higher echelon, order, equity (required to induce the employee devoting wholeheartedly to and being loyal to the organization), stability of employment in terms of the stability of work, initiative and group spirit. This is a peculiar equilibrium concept giving the employees limited degree of freedom under the central control of management. (4) To acknowledge the fact that management is a process of learning. For this matter, the manager needs some elasticity of learning.

Contingency management. This is a theory arguing for using varying methods of management to cope with different situations in order to take necessary steps in solving problems effectively (Montana and Charnov 1987, p. 24).

Behavioral school of management. By observing workers' action, Elton Mayo reached the following conclusions for his studies: (1) Some workers may have problems created by external forces, for example, unhealthy and hazardous working conditions and not having appropriate tools for their task may hinder the efficiency of their performance. (2) There is a need for individual worker to have a sense of belonging to a certain group. If isolated for a sustainable period of time, the worker will be disoriented and not to perform the required job efficiently.[59] Because too much conflict is not conducive to efficiency of the work place, a mild degree of conflict may be preferred. Further, there is a logical ingredient of capitalism: under the economic power of the capitalists, the appearance of some acts of benevolence may work to the benefits of the masters. This is seen in the later work of Mayo. Through the famous Hawthorne project, the following point of view is emphasized: the factor beyond the physical and biological variables may have a strong impact on the efficiency of the workers.

Theory Y of McGregor. The major content of this theory may be summarized as follows: (1) Under favorable conditions, workers are happy to work. (2) Workers may be strongly motivated to accomplish organizational goals to which they are personally committed. (3) Through learning, an employee may become responsible and accountable for the job. (4) Most of workers have some degree of creativity.

By turning the above summaries into assumptions and by studying the psychology of workers, McGregor finally arrived at the following conclusions: (1) The manager must delegate its power in order to promote the initiative of the workers. (2) It is imperative to make the job interesting to the workers. (3) Non-pecuniary remuneration is effective. (4) Treating workers with respect and sharing information with workers with regard to the design, content and objective of the work are necessary for any effective management (Montana and Charnov 1987, p. 20).

It is fair to say that this theory Y attempts to modify partially the content of conflict culture inherent in theory X. Therefore, the human nature is implicitly assumed to be partially good and some credits are given to the workers for their initiative and creativity.

In terms of the systematic presentation of the Theory Y, it is the same as that of Theory X except that the cultures of these two systems are somewhat different. That is, for x, y, z ⊫ **H** ⋹ Ω and X = {x,y,z} ⊕ <ℂX> ⊑ (Ω,𝒵∘,v𝐻,{ℂ}) with z being the center, and a and b being the non-central elements, we have both a → b and b → c are Hf-systemisms. Note that in Theory X, the culture is that of pure capitalism such that workers are just passive and unintelligent. Here, the cultural system <ℂX> of Theory Y is one in which workers have some initiative and do not just listen and take the order from the superior in a passive manner.

Decision theory school. Simon developed a decision theory of satisfying This is different form the conventional theory of profit maximization. According to Simon's view, human action aims at reaching a region of satisfying, rather than achieving any level of optimization. The conventional theory of economics and management presupposes the culture of conflict (i.e., the so-called culture of competition). To this issue, Simon neither favors nor is against the culture of competition.

Using the concept of cultural systematics, for a competitive organization, by the principle of strategic centrality (4.2-6): $\psi\{\mathcal{T}^*C \geq \mathcal{T}X_i,\Delta_i\} \,\bar{\bar{\wedge}}\, \tau$, its centralized management system (i.e., central unit system) dominates all the decentralized management system (i.e., non-central unit systems). Furthermore, this competitive organization, by the principle of CE balance in Bcm. (3.2-2-5): $\psi\{Y_j \dot{\pm} Y_k,\Delta_i\} \,\bar{\bar{\wedge}}\, \tau$, has to pursue at least a minimal degree of organizational consensus. That is, it has to ensure that members of the organization feel that they are rightfully the members of the organization in question, and hence to let these employees having a chance to develop a sense of belonging to the organization and be proud of being a part of it.

§F.3-3 A Remark on Management

By the convention of the West, management and economics are parallel. But by the tradition of East Asia, management is but a part of economics. In the economics of culture, by the systemic methods which goes well beyond the methods of mathematics, we are able to honor the tradition of treating business as a part of economics. To this end, we need to expand the scope of the schemes of CE balance-centrality (see §3.2) to the **scheme of strategic decisions and actions** with appropriate states and conditions of humanity to derive the principles of (1) systemic centrality, (2) CE balance, (3) individual incentive, (4) leadership, and (5) coordination.

These afore-mentioned principles are useful in dealing with the **key features of management system or organization** (or seven elements or central points of management): (1) setting up objective and goals (Z in a system), (2) collecting and evaluating information (part of (R,R^D) in a system), (3) making decision and planning (Z), (4) organizational structures ((v,h, γ) and part of (R,R^D) in a system), (5) human resources complex and incentive systems (manager-worker personnel entity MW as a part of (R,R^D) in a system), (6) producing the product mix (I-O system as a part of (R,R^D), Õ and $E\{e_g\}$ in a system), and (7) evaluation of the organization in question (part of Z).

§F.3-4 A Theory of Organizational Change

This is similar to the theory of technological creation (see Section 4.5) and will be developed in the future.

F.4 TS-TD Model

Define the **normal level of output** in a cultural economy as the one with the maximal level of output sustainable in the long run. The intersection point of the TS curve and the normal level of output curve Y_N (which is vertical) is called the Keynesian CE Tcentral point (see point N in Figure F.4-1). When the intersection point of the TD and TS curves lies to the right of the normal level of output (see point C in Figure F.4-1), it is a non-Tcentral point. The real output level associated with this non-central point C can not sustain for long except to be supported by higher and higher rates of inflation.

We also define the **historical level of output** as the one with the average level of output in the historical time. The intersection point of the TS curve and the historical level of output curve y_h (which is a vertical line) is called the CE Tcentral point of democratic capitalism (see point H in Figure F.4-1). When the intersection point of the TD and TS curves lies to the left hand side of the historical level of output (for instance, point A in Figure F.4-1), it is a non-Tcentral point. Note that the non-Tcentral point like A (in Figure F.4-1) may not sustain for long. That is, this non-Tcentral point may disappear by the natural forces of the market economy; and thus no government intervention is needed in order for the economy to move away from it. But at times it does not disappear by itself, then the government intervention to move the economy toward a Tcentral point may be desirable.

Figure F.4-1
CE centrality points and non-centrality points: y_N = normal level of real output, y_H = historical level of real output, y_n = national profits maximization level of real output, n = profit-maximization CE centrality point, N = Keynesian CE centrality point, H = CE centrality point of democratic capitalism (A, B, C are non-centrality points)

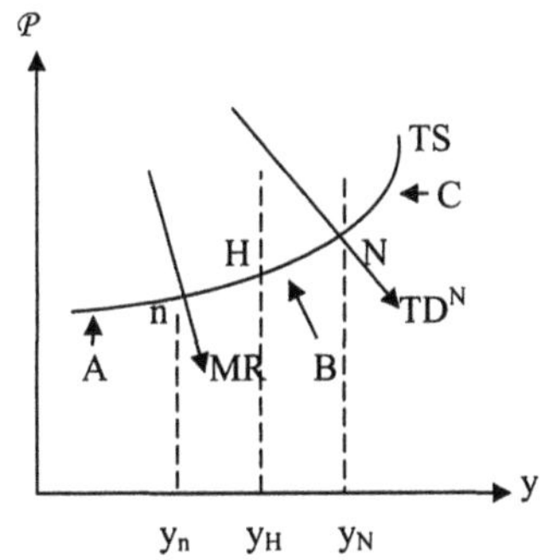

Note that MR curve is the "marginal revenue curve" of the TD curve (i.e., TD^N curve). This MR curve is derived by taking "T derivative" of the TD curve. The point of intersection (i.e., n) of MR and TS is called the CE Tcentral point that maximizes the "profits" of the nation as a whole. Pont n may be a good choice for a non-capitalist cultural economy from the perspective of the national planners. Here the problem of the impossibility to engage in any interpersonal comparison of utility asserted in the conventional microeconomic disappears due to the fact that cultural factors (and therefore the MOL measures) enter into the (actual)

demand and supply curves directly. In general, in our TS-TD analysis, as is in the case of cs-cd analysis, we are dealing with MOL, not utility any more. And yet, to be more comprehensive, we can retain the concept of utility as a very special case of our theory.

Note that these TS and TD curves are transformed from TS and TD becomings which are systems in the study of systematics.

Appendix G – Modern Socioeconomic System of Mixed Cultures

For the following "matrix model," see Tonn (2001, pp. 118-121). In the following, suppose the complex of the transformational impactors would integrate a Western conflict culture and a socialist culture with the tranquil culture of classic East Asia. Let $T = |\Sigma\oplus<\mathbb{C}_S>, Y^{+}\oplus<\mathbb{C}_{+}>, Y^{-}\oplus<\mathbb{C}_{-}>, F\oplus<\mathbb{C}_F>|^{T}$ (with the comma denoting the separation of two entries, and the last "T" denoting the superscript) be a cultural system composed of self-generating life-will and systemic yu-wu rationality. This could be conceived as a simplified representation of a cultural economy with $\Sigma\oplus<\mathbb{C}_S>$, $Y^{+}\oplus<\mathbb{C}_{+}>$, $Y^{-}\oplus<\mathbb{C}_{-}>$ and $F\oplus<\mathbb{C}_F>$ denoting the R&D sector (i.e., those not directly controlled by either the private businesses or the public enterprises), the private business community, the public enterprises, and (L,K) in general (i.e., those not directly controlled by either the private businesses or the public enterprises), respectively. Further, let $\Phi_{CAP} = CAP \oplus <\mathbb{C}_{CAP}>$ be the cultural impactor of democratic capitalism, where CAP refers to the daily-operational and informally-enforced cultural structure of capitalism and $<\mathbb{C}_{CAP}>$ the cultural essentials of scientific rationality and individualistic life-will of conquest, and let $\Phi_{SOC} = SOC \oplus <\mathbb{C}_{SOC}>$ be the political impactor of socialism, with SOC referring to the political structure of socialism and $<\mathbb{C}_{SOC}>$ the culture of dialectical rationality and collectivist life-will of conquest. Note that a transformation from Φ_{SOC} to Φ_{CAP} or vice versa is a symbolic anti-systemism, not a metaphoric iso-systemism.

In a simplified approach to transform the conflict cultural/political system into the afore-mentioned tranquil system, we shall engage in a process of creating a grand system (composed of several unit systems or sub-systems) which entails the applications of both economic impactor of capitalism and political impactor of socialism on T which embodies the culture of faziranism. In the following, we devote ourselves to this elaborate and yet fascinating endeavor. Due to the operations of the systematic rationality and self-generating life-will embodied in T, we shall define the joint operation of the impactors (i.e, Φ_{SOC} and Φ_{CAP}) on T in two steps. First, define the right impactor Φ_{SOC} operating on the "political side" and thereby the public side of T (i.e., $\{T\}\Phi_{SOC}$) as in Bcm. (G.1).

$$\text{(G.1)} \qquad \{T\}\Phi_{SOC} = \left| \begin{array}{l} (\Sigma\oplus<\mathbb{C}_S>) \oplus (SOC\oplus<\mathbb{C}_{SOC}>) \\ \qquad (Y^{+}\oplus<\mathbb{C}_{+}>) \oplus (SOC\oplus<\mathbb{C}_{SOC}>) \\ (Y^{-}\oplus<\mathbb{C}_{-}>) \\ \quad (F\oplus<\mathbb{C}_F>) \oplus (SOC\oplus<\mathbb{C}_{SOC}>) \end{array} \right|$$

$$= \left| \begin{array}{l} (\Sigma,SOC) \oplus<\mathbb{C}_S,\mathbb{C}_{SOC}> \\ \qquad (Y^{+},SOC)\oplus<\mathbb{C}_{+},\mathbb{C}_{SOC}> \\ Y^{-}\oplus<\mathbb{C}_{-}> \\ \quad (F,SOC)\oplus<\mathbb{C}_F,\mathbb{C}_{SOC}> \end{array} \right|$$

Secondly, let $\Sigma\#$ refer to Σ modified by the cultures of socialism and capitalism, $Y^{-}\#$ depict Y^{-} modified by the culture of socialism, $Y^{+}\#$ stand for Y^{+} modified by the culture of capitalism, and F# represent F modified by the cultures of capitalism and socialism. Then, by applying the impactor Φ_S to the private side of $\{T\}\Phi_{SOC}$ (i.e., $\Phi_{CAP}\{\{T\}\Phi_{SOC}\}$, we have the mixed economy embodying three cultures: Faziranism, capitalism and socialism (see Bcm. (G.2)).

Here in general, this operation is not commutative: i.e., $\Phi_{CAP}\{\{T\}\Phi_{SOC}\} \neq \{\Phi_{CAP}\{T\}\}\Phi_{SOC}$. For example, in the real case of China, $\Phi_{CAP}\{T\}$ is not defined. This is because the culture of tranquility of China in the twentieth century (related to the nation's status as a quasi-colony besieged by the imperialistic power of capitalist countries) is not directly compatible with the culture of democratic capitalism.

$$\text{(G.2)} \qquad \Phi_{CAP}\{\{T\}\Phi_{SOC}\} = \left| \begin{array}{l} (\Sigma,SOC)\oplus\langle\mathbb{C}_S,\mathbb{C}_{SOC}\rangle\oplus CAP\oplus\langle\mathbb{C}_{CAP}\rangle \\ \qquad\qquad (Y^+,SOC)\oplus\langle\mathbb{C}_+,\mathbb{C}_{SOC}\rangle \\ Y^-\oplus\langle\mathbb{C}_-\rangle)\oplus CAP\oplus\langle\mathbb{C}_{CAP}\rangle \\ (F,SOC)\oplus\langle\mathbb{C}_F,\mathbb{C}_{SOC}\rangle\oplus CAP\oplus\langle\mathbb{C}_{CAP}\rangle \end{array} \right|$$

$$= \left| \begin{array}{l} \Sigma\#\oplus\langle\mathbb{C}_{CAP},\mathbb{C}_S,\mathbb{C}_{SOC}\rangle \\ \qquad Y^+\#\oplus\langle\mathbb{C}_+,\mathbb{C}_{SOC}\rangle \\ Y^-\#\oplus\langle\mathbb{C}_{CAP},\mathfrak{C}_-\rangle \\ \quad F\#\oplus\langle\mathbb{C}_{CAP},\mathbb{C}_F,\mathbb{C}_{SOC}\rangle \end{array} \right| .$$

In the following, we could proceed to alternative definitions of $\Phi_{CAP}\{\{T\}\Phi_{SOC}\}$ as follows. For this purpose, let $T = |\Sigma\oplus\langle\mathbb{C}_S\rangle,\ Y^+\oplus\langle\mathbb{C}_+\rangle,\ CC,\ Y^-\oplus\langle\mathbb{C}_-\rangle,\ F\oplus\langle\mathbb{C}_F\rangle|^T$ and let $\Phi_{SOC} = |\Sigma^{\vdash}\oplus\langle\mathbb{C}_{S\vdash}\rangle,\ Y^{+\vdash}\oplus\langle\mathbb{C}_{+\vdash}\rangle,\ CC^{\vdash},\ Y^{-\vdash}\oplus\langle\mathbb{C}_{-\vdash}\rangle,\ F^{\vdash}\oplus\langle\mathbb{C}_{F\vdash}\rangle|^T$, where $CC = C \oplus \langle\mathbb{C}_C\rangle$, and $CC^{\vdash} = C^{\vdash}\oplus \langle\mathbb{C}_{C\vdash}\rangle$. Here $C^{\vdash}$ and $\langle\mathbb{C}_{C\vdash}\rangle$ denote the mechanism and the culture of central planning, respectively. Then one can write:

$$\begin{aligned} \text{(G.3)} \quad & \{T\}\Phi_{SOC} \\ &= |\Sigma\oplus\langle\mathbb{C}_S\rangle,Y^+\oplus\langle\mathbb{C}_+\rangle,CC,Y^-\oplus\langle\mathbb{C}_-\rangle,F\oplus\langle\mathbb{C}_F\rangle|^T\ |\Sigma^{\vdash}\oplus\langle\mathbb{C}_{S\vdash}\rangle,Y^{+\vdash}\oplus\langle\mathbb{C}_{+\vdash}\rangle,CC^{\vdash}, \\ &\qquad Y^{-\vdash}\oplus\langle\mathbb{C}_{-\vdash}\rangle,F^{\vdash}\oplus\langle\mathbb{C}_{F\vdash}\rangle|^T \\ &= |(\Sigma,\Sigma^{\vdash})\oplus\langle\mathbb{C}_S,\mathbb{C}_{S\vdash}\rangle,(Y^+,Y^{+\vdash})\oplus(CC,CC^{\vdash}),\langle\mathbb{C}_+,\mathbb{C}_{+\vdash}\rangle,Y^-\oplus\langle\mathbb{C}_-\rangle,(F,F^{\vdash})\oplus\langle\mathbb{C}_F,\mathfrak{C}_{F\vdash}\rangle|^T \\ &= |(\Sigma,\Sigma^{\vdash})\oplus\langle\mathbb{C}_{S,S\vdash}\rangle,(Y^+,Y^{+\vdash})\oplus\langle\mathbb{C}_{+,+\vdash}\rangle,(CC,CC^{\vdash}),Y^-\oplus\langle\mathbb{C}_-\rangle,(F,F^{\vdash})\oplus\langle\mathbb{C}_{F,F\vdash}\rangle|^T. \end{aligned}$$

Similarly, let $\Phi_{CAP} = |\Sigma_{\dashv}\oplus\langle\mathbb{C}_{S\dashv}\rangle,\ Y^{+\dashv}\oplus\langle\mathbb{C}_{+\dashv}\rangle,\ CC_{\dashv},\ Y^{-\dashv}\oplus\langle\mathbb{C}_{-\dashv}\rangle,\ F_{\dashv}\oplus\langle\mathbb{C}_{F\dashv}\rangle|^T$, where $CC_{\dashv} = C_{\dashv} \oplus \langle\mathbb{C}_{C\dashv}\rangle$. Here $C_{\dashv}$ and $\langle\mathbb{C}_{C\dashv}\rangle$ denote the mechanisms and the culture of monetary and fiscal policies, respectively. Then one can write

$$\begin{aligned} \text{(G.4)} \quad & \Phi_{CAP}\{T\} \\ &= |(\Sigma_{\dashv},\Sigma)\oplus\langle\mathbb{C}_{C\dashv,S}\rangle,Y^+\oplus\langle\mathbb{C}_+\rangle,(CC_{\dashv},CC),(Y^{-\dashv},Y^-)\oplus\langle\mathbb{C}_{-\dashv,-}\rangle,(F,F_{\dashv})\oplus\langle\mathbb{C}_{F\dashv,F}\rangle|^T. \end{aligned}$$

In the following, we assume that the cultures $\mathbb{C}_F$, $\mathbb{C}_-$, $\mathbb{C}_+$ and $\mathbb{C}_S$ generate $\langle\mathbb{C}_F\rangle$, $\langle\mathbb{C}_-\rangle$, $\langle\mathbb{C}_+\rangle$ and $\langle\mathbb{C}_S\rangle$, respectively, and they share a common core $\mathfrak{C}$ and $\langle\mathbb{C}_F\rangle\backslash\langle\mathbb{C}_-\rangle\backslash \langle\mathbb{C}_+\rangle\backslash\langle\mathbb{C}_S\rangle = \langle\mathbb{C}_F\backslash\mathbb{C}_-\backslash\mathbb{C}_+\backslash\mathbb{C}_S\rangle = \langle\mathfrak{C}\rangle$ (that is, their interactions lead to $\mathfrak{C}$). Now let us introduce the following notations: $\langle\mathbb{C}_-\rangle = \langle\mathbb{C}_{|-}\rangle$ (i.e., the culture of the grand system to be restricted to that of the public sector (or yin-flat system), $\langle\mathbb{C}_F\rangle = \langle\mathbb{C}_{|F}\rangle$, $\langle\mathbb{C}_+\rangle = \langle\mathbb{C}_{|+}\rangle$ and $\langle\mathbb{C}_S\rangle = \langle\mathbb{C}_{|S}\rangle$.

Here, for both of the self-generating life-will-to-creation and the (yu-wu) systemic rationality-to-creation, it is assumed that they have a cyclical momentum of dynamics.

To show the derivation of $\Phi_{SOC}\{T\}\Phi_{CAP}$, we shall proceed by four steps. We show that $(\{T\}\Phi_{CAP})_{|F} = (F'\oplus\langle\mathbb{C}_F\rangle)\oplus(F\oplus\langle\mathbb{C}_\omega\rangle) = (F',F)\oplus\langle\mathbb{C}_\omega,\mathbb{C}_F\rangle$ and $(\Phi_{SOC}\{T\}\ \Phi_{CAP})_{|F} = (F', F)\oplus(\langle\mathbb{C}_\omega\rangle,\langle\mathbb{C}_F\rangle)\oplus(F''+\langle\mathbb{C}_{\acute{\omega}}\rangle) = F\#\oplus\langle\mathbb{C}_\omega,\mathbb{C}_F,\mathbb{C}_{\acute{\omega}}\rangle$.

Let $\{X\}\Phi_{CAP} = F'\oplus<\mathbb{C}_{\omega}>$ and $\Phi_{SOC}\{X\} = F''\oplus<\mathbb{C}_{\acute{\omega}}>$, for X being any system. Then $\{T\}\Phi_{Cap|F} = M_{X\to F}\{T\} = (F'\oplus<\mathbb{C}_{\omega}>) \oplus (F\oplus<\mathbb{C}_{F}>) = (F',F) \oplus (<\mathbb{C}_{\omega}>,<\mathbb{C}_{F}>)$. Here $M_{X\to F}$ is the decomposition-subtraction impactor (or mie impactor, Definition A.2-3-6-3). Now, let the impactors revert $(<\mathbb{C}_{\omega}>,<\mathbb{C}_{F}>)$ backward to their connections with the virtual operating force $Z(\mathcal{E})$ by the shengsheng generator $\sigma(\mathfrak{C})$: $(F',F) \oplus (<\mathbb{C}_{\omega}>, <\mathbb{C}_{F}>) \to (<\mathbb{C}_{\omega}>,<\mathbb{C}_{F}>)/ Z(\mathcal{E})$. Then, we have

(G.5) $(<\mathbb{C}_{\omega}>,<\mathbb{C}_{F}>)/Z(\mathcal{E}) = (<\mathbb{C}_{\omega}>,<\mathbb{C}_{F}>)/<\mathfrak{C}_{Z}> = <(\mathbb{C}_{\omega},\mathbb{C}_{F})/\mathfrak{C}_{Z}> = (\mathbb{C}_{\omega},\mathbb{C}_{F})/\mathfrak{C}_{Z}$.

Here by $(<\mathbb{C}_{\omega}>,<\mathbb{C}_{F}>)/Z(\mathcal{E})$ is meant that the pair of the cultural energies of the labor-capital sector (i.e., almost-flat system) is immersed in the cultural energy of the center of $\mathcal{E}$. In other words, this pair of energies is able to be transformed backward to the core energy of the grand system in order to be integrated. Note that, here, $\mathfrak{C}_{Z}$ is the cultural generator of $Z(\mathcal{E})$. Then by generating the system element with cultural strength (i.e., using the impactor Φ^{F}), we get:

(G.6) $\Phi^{F}\{<\mathfrak{C}_{(\omega,F)/Z}> = <\mathbb{C}_{\omega,F}/\mathfrak{C}_{Z}> = <\mathbb{C}_{\omega,F}>/ Z(\mathcal{E}) = (F',F) \oplus <\mathbb{C}_{\omega},\mathbb{C}_{F}>$.

Now to derive the Labor-capital sector (i.e., the almost flat system), we have: $\Phi_{SOC}\{\{T\}\Phi_{CAP}\}_{|F} = M_{X\to F}\{T\} = (F'\oplus<\mathbb{C}_{\acute{\omega}}>) \oplus (F',F) \oplus <\mathbb{C}_{\omega},\mathbb{C}_{F}> = (F',F,F'') \oplus (<\mathbb{C}_{\omega}>,<\mathbb{C}_{F}>, <\mathbb{C}_{\acute{\omega}}>)$. Let the impactors revert $(<\mathbb{C}_{\omega}>,<\mathbb{C}_{F}>,<\mathbb{C}_{\acute{\omega}}>)$ backward to their connections with the virtual operating force of the system by applying $\sigma(\mathfrak{C})$: $(F',F,F'')\oplus(<\mathbb{C}_{\omega}>,<\mathbb{C}_{F}>,<\mathbb{C}_{\acute{\omega}}>) \to (<\mathbb{C}_{\omega}>,<\mathbb{C}_{F}>,<\mathbb{C}_{\acute{\omega}}>)/Z(\mathcal{E})$. Then, we have

(G.7) $(<\mathbb{C}_{\omega}>,<\mathbb{C}_{F}>,<\mathbb{C}_{\acute{\omega}}>)/ Z(\mathcal{E}) = (<\mathbb{C}_{\omega}>,<\mathbb{C}_{F}>,<\mathbb{C}_{\acute{\omega}}>)/<\mathfrak{C}_{Z}> = <\mathbb{C}_{\omega},\mathbb{C}_{F},\mathbb{C}_{\acute{\omega}}>/<\mathfrak{C}_{Z}>$
$= <(\mathbb{C}_{\omega},\mathbb{C}_{F},\mathbb{C}_{\acute{\omega}})/ \mathfrak{C}_{Z}> = <\mathbb{C}_{(\omega,F,\acute{\omega})/Z}>$.

At the long last, we have

(G.8) $\Phi^{F}\{<\mathbb{C}_{(\omega,F)/Z}> = <<\mathbb{C}_{\omega,F,\acute{\omega}}>/ \mathfrak{C}_{Z}> = <\mathbb{C}_{\omega,F,\acute{\omega}}>/ Z(\mathcal{E}) = (F',F,F'') \oplus <\mathbb{C}_{\omega},\mathbb{C}_{F},\mathbb{C}_{\acute{\omega}}>$.

That is, $(\Phi_{SOC}\{T\}\Phi_{CAP})_{|F} = (F'\oplus<\mathbb{C}_{\omega}>)\oplus(F\oplus<\mathbb{C}_{F}>)\oplus(F''\oplus<\mathbb{C}_{\acute{\omega}}>) = F\#\oplus<\mathbb{C}_{\omega},\mathbb{C}_{F},\mathbb{C}_{\acute{\omega}}>$.

Similarly, we can show the other operations related to the public sector (or yin-flat system), the private sector (or yang-flat system) and the R&D sector (or steep system) to complete this whole process of $\Phi_{SOC}\{T\}\Phi_{CAP}$.

Note that this above operation of bringing the cultures of socialism and capitalism into a tranquil system can also be achieved by applying mie impactor and shengsheng generator as shown previously.

Socialist and capitalist systems may be represented by various n-polar MFCE schemes. One of the major differences between them is that in a capitalist MFCE system, its center is a "virtual system." And yet in a socialist MFCE system, its center is a real center, not a virtual one.

Appendix H – Metaphysical Systems of Y*(YX), Y+(YX)X- and N(B-HPh)

In the following, at first we discuss the metaphysics of **tzuyu** ("self-have," selfhood, entity of self-in-tranquility) and **huyu** ("mutual-have," mutuality, entity of mutuality-in-tranquility). Later, we shall introduce the metaphysical systems of Y*(YX), Y+(YX)X- and N(B-HPh) by employing the very meanings of these concepts. Tzuyu is yu ("Being," "being" or the substance of "beings"), the "being" of self-ascertainment, self-exiting and self-gaining in the culture of tranquility. Huyu is the "being" or the substance of interactions and multifaceted relationships among many types of tzuyu in the culture of tranquility. In comparison, **tzuti** (entity of self-in-conflict or entity of self-in-independence) is the counterpart of tzuyu in the culture of conflict, and **huti** (entity of mutuality-in-conflict) is the counterpart of huyu in the culture of Conflict. Tzuti is an independent entity (or a self entity-in-conflict), a "being" existing by itself; while huti is the being or the substance of the interactions and multifaceted relationships among all or some tzutis.

Remark H.1. In this Appendix, we present our interpretation of the yu-wu tao-jen metaphysics. This presentation may appear to be somewhat different from our scheme of the universe as presented in Appendix A (Subsection §A.2-7). In actuality, the presentation here and those in other places are the same. The connections are as follows. The idea of Tao as the unity of yu and wu is meant yu is the manifestation of Tao and wu is the potential of Tao. This is essentially the same as saying that "Tao* and Chi* are two aspects of Yu*; Wu* is the potential of Yu*, and Yu* is the realization of Wu* (all of them in the sense of abstract Forms). That is, {Chi*,Tao*| Wu*} is the grand system of Being in which Wu* is the virtual center.

Further, Deity is just a mystery, may be an entity of super-nature and super-rationality.

So it is consistent in conceiving Tao as the unity of yu and wu (non-being or nothingness). One may contemplate that the self-generating and self-illuminating wu, by uniting tao and beauty in transcendence, is Deity; and yet this transcendence may be a unity in contradiction. Wu that fails to transcend metaphysics is not the real wu, but a certain type of wu, or a wu-in-yu. Wu that transcends the self-generating entity and the metaphysical entity is both Nothingness and the potential-and-seed of creativity. That is, Wu that transcends metaphysics is the real wu, Wu. Both of these wu's and Wu* (or Wu) are the creators of yu, the unmoved first movers. Besides, what transcends the unity of tao and beauty both in consistency and contradiction is also wu, or Wu.

"tzuyu" is begeted by wu. At the beginning it is the mother of life, and is the movement in quiescence. It is the quiescence in the mind of a man of wisdom (or a sage). It is unmoved like a mountain, and yet with turbulence existing always in his soul. It is also like the shining sun, rising above the sea of clouds; and like the moon, showering silver streams onto the great rivers ever-flowing to the east. Tzuyu is like a hermit, to be at ease with oneself and always self-adjusted to the nature.

"tzuyu" is also like a strong man, possessing the will of a superman: conquering self, others and the nature. By the principle of preserving matter in transformation, one type of tzuyu, in the process of ever perishing, is always at the same time transforming into another type of existence.

"tzuyu" could be a matter. A materialist believes that every thing is a matter. If so, then tzuyu could simultaneously be the primary consciousness of a living thing. This may be said as the "mind of living thing or the "animating mind" of a human being.
"tzuyu" could also be a soul, or the limit of clear and illuminating chi which will eventually transform iself into tao. That is, the limit of soul is tao which is the dialectic and systemic unity of taos in the real world and beauty, and this limit eventually approaches and becomes the deity or Tao (i.e., the Ultimate Tao).

In the above, we classify the world into three categories: matter, mind and soul. This classification is based on the following reasoning. (1) No mind has ever been created from matter by science, and not any human being has been created through a non-human animal. That is, the assertion of scientific deductionism to transform soul and mind back to matter and from matter to soul and mind is not (yet) valid. (2) The Form claimed by Plato is not a real thing. To declare tzuyu as soul is equivalent to saying that tzuyu is a "copy" or an "image" of this Platonic Form. (3) The totality of the deity (shen) claimed by the Buddhist, the pure reason claimed by Immanuel Kant, the unconditional and limitless love some experiences in one's life, and the "absolute" beauty existing in literature, arts, and our life must be something. This "thing" is yu, not wu, and the Ultimate origin or source of this is named tzuyu (self-generating entity-in-tranquility). (4) This soul-tzuyu is behind what is called the purest transcendental phenomenon[60] by Husserl and Heidegger, the self-evident and independent entity that has a consciousness to question the existence of the self-consciousness of "self." This reason is this: I have some doubt about my own consciousness, therefore I exist. Soul is the self-evident being and existence. This existence is what can not be denied, and therefore it exists by itself.

"huyu" is the interactive and phenomenal becoming of things or entities in the universe[61]; it is also the shengsheng or system-dynamic force of yu governing the auxiliary forces to help transform myriads of tzuyu. One may say that the huyu of soul is composed of the mind of a nation, the subconscious of a group, religious belief of oneself, and the ethics governing a certain communities in historical time, etc. To Chuang Tzu, tzuyu is the very freedom and transcendental leisure of the human being, a toward-self being of the unity of the self and the nature. To a Confucian, in its inner most world of philosophical contemplation, the **mutual possession** of the huyu (mutually-supporting entity-in-tranquility, or mutual and tranquility-permeating entity) may be superseded by the spirit of humanity, righteousness and integrity. From the East to the West, tzuyu transforms itself into tzuti (i.e., self-entity-in-conflict or self-entity in isolation and independence), and huyu transforms itself into mutual–entity-in-conflict (or mutually conflict-ridden entity). For an existentialist, the self-entity is the existence-for-self (or being-for-oneself). But to exist in the grace of Jesus Christ, this mutual-entity is the mutual-entity in loving others unconditionally. For Hegel, mutual-entity is but the **collective-entity** (or collective and conflict-suppressed entity) of the absolute idea, or the Absolute Spirit of history. As for Karl Marx, this collective-entity is the absolute command of life to subject oneself unconditionally to the absolute love of one's social class.

In East Asia, the mutual–supporting entity–in-tranquility is also the very substance underlying the tao-jen tranquil and life-perfection spirit of humanity and the transcendental self-generating and self-evident rationality. The absolute command of life for modern East Asia may manifest itself in the form of the self-generating entity-in-tranquility interacting with the mutually-supporting entity–in-tranquility in the world of the primordial tao-jen spirit. Furthermore, this spirit shall be confronted and contained in both processes of the "tao-reversal in creation-destruction" and the dialectic of the universal-loving and knowledge-penetrating of the totality of self-mutual entity-in-conflict. Thus, transcendental ethics of the universe creates orders for every generated and created entity existing, transforming and perishing in the universe. That is, the life-order of the self-and-mutuality is the order of the universe. Eventually, in the mutual-interacting states of strategic continuity and physical equilibrium, the contradiction between self-entity-in tranquility and self-entity-in-conflict vanishes and the difference between mutual-entity-in-tranquility and mutual-entity-in-conflict disappears, and thereby the self-entity and mutual-entity, being either in tranquility or in conflict, are unified.

Let jen{tao,spirit} be the spirit and rationality complex of tzuyu which is based on the foundations of economic production and social mutuality and which penetrates all layers of mind, soul, Tien and Tao through these foundations. Here by jen is meant the mutuality of humanity and righteousness of Confucianism, and by the spirit of tao is meant the leisurely self-tranquility, the nature-oriented balance, and the knowledge-and profit-inquiry masculinity of Taoism. Here from the perspectives of The Kuan Tzu and Legalism, the masculine self-entity is the mutuality-entity underlying the balance of righteousness and profit (or the self-righteousness and the self-profit that together forms a symbolic iso-systemism with the creativity of the Universe) and the conquest-oriented self-entity of Legalism. But from a Western point of view, this masculine self-entity is also that of the Übermensch of Nietzsche and the class-struggling soul of Karl Marx. In the following, also let Y* be the system: (C,K,L){T,H}←M_jen-yi{SStzuyu}, or (Confucianism, Kuan Tzu, Legalism){tao,Ssu} ← Confucian mutuality of humanity and righteousness {sheng-sheng tzuyu}. Here by "tao" is meant the toward-self, toward-nothing, and leisurely unifying-with-the-universe spirit and rationality of Taoism, by "Ssu" is meant the for-profit spirit and rationality of Ssu Ma-chien. Here M refers to the Confucian mutuality of humanity and righteousness, and SS tzuyu (self-generating or shengsheng tzuyu representing a self-entity of the primordial Tao before its divergence into Tao of Confucianism and that of Taoism.

Let Wu be Nothingness itself, WuChi be the "Pole of Nothingness," TaiChi be the "Pole of the Ultimate" (Tai Chi), and Yu be what is created by Wu (or Being, the being, beings). Furthermore, let Y as in Bcm (H.1) and X in Bcm (H.2), Then for the metaphysics of classic China, we may have the Y*(YX) scheme in Bcm (H.3):

$$\text{(H.1)}\quad Y = (\text{WuChi} \leftrightarrows \text{TaiChi}) \text{ or } \begin{array}{c}\text{WuChi}\\ \updownarrows\\ \text{TaiChi}\end{array},$$

$$\text{(H.2)}\quad X = (\text{Wu} \leftrightarrows \text{Yu}) \text{ or } \begin{array}{c}\text{Wu}\\ \updownarrows\\ \text{Yu}\end{array}.$$

$$\text{(H.3)}\quad Y^*(YX) = \begin{array}{ccc}\text{WuChi} & \leftleftarrows & \text{Wu}\\ \updownarrows & & \updownarrows\\ \text{TaiChi} & \leftleftarrows & \text{Yu}\\ \updownarrows & & \\ Y^* & & \end{array}$$

Note that in Bcm (H.3), each of Y*, Y and X is a system by itself.

Below is a scheme of the tao-jen spirituality and creativity $(Y+(YX)X^{-})$, by which is meant the scheme in which the spirit-rationaity complex of Wu (which recycles through chi and kung) and Yu are eventually able to penetrate deeply into the being creativity of scienceces (going through the whole process of adaptation and re-creation of Western culture) (see Figure H.1).

Figure H.1
A scheme of the tao-jen spirituality and creativity

Creativity of Tao-jen
(yu-wu rationality,SS beauty)
⇅ ⇅
Being (Scientific rationality) ←← Yu →→→→→Wu
⇅ ↓ ↑
Y^+ chi→kung

Here, Y^+ stands for the term "jen{tao,spirit} ← (C,K,L){T,H} ← Confucian huyu{SS tzuyu}," (jen{tao spirit} being also called the tao-jen entity), $X^- \equiv$ (chi←kung) with chi referring to the ultimate stillness and solitariness (chi), kung denoting the ultimate emptiness (kung), and (YX) depicting the rest of the components in Figure H.1 (i.e., those components other than Y^+ and X^-).

To apply this scheme to the learning process, it is conceivable that the first phase of the creative process is to create some thing out of "nothing." That is a process, by applying old knowledge to new frontiers in order to create new knowledge. Then the second phase of the creative process of knowledge is to nullify or negate this knowledge. That is, after learning from others and internalizing it through complete understanding and analyzing all of its parts individually, one tries to nullify this knowledge and become forgetful. But then, the third phase of the creative process sets in to create some thing out of "nothing." That is, by learning new things and again decomposing and integrating them, one gains new knowledge. And yet by later nullification of this knowledge, one actually knows better and understands better. Hence, the so-called invention (in dealing with the creation of real and physical things) and innovation must be the results of developing a new and more valuable knowledge. This is different from imitation which is the remaking of the conventional (or old) things without contribute significantly to the modification, improvement or new development of these things. This is what we mean a process of negation of the negations in the theory of knowledge. But this theory of "knowledge" is more than learning from the physical world. It also relates closely to the reflection of our inner selves.

Note that in systematics, each of Y+, Y, X and X- is a system by itself which can be made into an uncertain system (see Appendix I) and this scheme $(Y^+(YX)X^-)$ can be treated as a cultural core of classic China.

In the scheme of yu-w recursion, $(Y^+(YX)X^-)$ presented in the above, in the upper part, through human rationality and spirit -- the unity of tao-being creativity and beauty, one is able to understand, absorb, comprehend, reflect, criticize, reorganize, attemp with new directions, correct errors, abstract and concretize, qualify and quantify, use intuition and logic, and integrate old ideas to develop new ideas. As for the lower part of this scheme, due to this method of Buddhist emptiness, one expands the width and digging into the depth of the process of yu-wu recursion. By going through these nodes of sincerity, respectfulness, quiescence, settling-down and stability, stillness and solitude, forgetting, emptying out one's mind and refraining from making any judgment or having any thought, one returns to the true self and to be able to eradicate desire and sorrow and even to forsake wisdom and morality of this world. By this process, then, one returns to the very root of human potentiality and the spring of life, and to unite with the Buddha's seed of good human nature in illuminating and manifesting the Self-as-Such (or selfhood) in this world. For a real Buddhist, if endowed with an ability to reach Nirvana, could penetrate the divinity of Deity. It appears that for a Chan-Buddhist or a Taoist of Chan-orientation, this penetration of nirvana creates not only a life-form capable of reaching one's life-as-such, but also a continual process of interactions between Nature and the unnatural self-as-such.[62] Probing from another angle, this may be perceived as Emptiness in Wu which is beyond the description of any language and beyond the comprehension of any mind of this world. This is the self-as-such of Wu[63] with a downward inclination of instilling happiness into our lives and with an upward direction in penetrating into the substance of "sincerity and purity" and reaching behind the "substance of beauty," the trans-metaphysical and the ultimate trans-tao essence of the Original Wu. Naturally and surely, Ultimate Creativity/ Destructivity behind this "Original Wu" is Tzu*.

Generally speaking, the afore-mentioned beauty of illumination and tao, after penetrating into wu-yu and emptiness-solidarity, would (in the real world) transform a person into the human being of the worlds of tao, jen, Confucianized utilitarianism of The Kuan Tzu and Confucianized efficiency frontiers of Legalism. That is, in these worlds, one would achieve a state of CE balance between tao and jen (taojen TCentral) and between yi and li (yili TCcentral). Then, theoretically speaking, by the transformation under the Western spirit and rationality, for instance, in the context of either the ethics of Nietzsche's Übermensch and or the Christian-socialist ethics, this tao-jen entity also becomes a "being of sciences" -- the being of highly abstract, systematic and quantifiable yu. Note that these upward streams and downward flows could reverse their directions. Thus, only by integrating the upward streams and the downward flows with their reverse movements, we can derive the whole picture of this universal motion.

Below a tentative system of Western metaphysics may be presented as N(B-HPh):

(H.4) God …→ Natural Law (N)
↓
Being (B) → human being (H) ← physical world (Ph),

where N, B, H and Ph stand for the Natural Law (constructed by God), Being (the ultimate entity underlying all beings in the world), the human being, and the physical world for which God bestows its stewardship to the human being.

Appendix I – States, Worlds, System's High- and Low-Level Differences, N-step Reference System and Distribution Systems

I-1 States, Worlds and High-and Low-differences of A System

In systematics, there are three states. The high-level state is one with highly developed system, the normal state is a general state, and the low-level state is one with the system underdeveloped.

One purpose of this subsection is to develop some uncertain systems, to be called distribution systems here, by constructing the "representative" and "difference" of them, to serve as the foundations from there we develop the uncertain becoming systems in Sections §B.2-2 and §B.2-3. Below, we start off with the definition of the normal state of a system.

Definition I.1-1 (normal state). Normal state of a system is the state in which all other states of the system vary around it for the period of time under study. It serves as a very useful frame of references.

Definition I.1-2. **High-difference** of a system = system in high-state – the system in normal state, where the system in the high-state is defined as the structure of the system in its highest level of development or expansion.

Definition I.1-3. **Low-difference** of a system = system in normal state – system in low-state, where the system in the low-state is defined as the structure of the system when it shrinks to its lowest level.

Note that in the above, these high- and low-differences of a system, dealing with elements of a system, may be applied to systems.

Below we turn to the worlds of systems. The targeted worlds can be classified into the upper-TCentral (perfect), the normal (or average-acceptable) and the lower-TCentral (lowest acceptable) worlds. Systems in the worlds of long term equilibrium states are different from those in the worlds of their philosophical outlooks, because the former measure mathematical and quantitative tendency while the latter involve mainly the systematic structures.

A world (realm, or sphere) can be classified according to whether it is a real world, potential-realized world and ideal world, or whether it is upper-world, normal or middle-world or lower-world.

I.2 0-Step Reference Systems and Distribution Systems

In the following, we shall define various types of distribution systems.

In the systematic reasoning, there are several states about an activity or event: the high-level state, the normal (or middle-level) state, and the low-level state. In the systematic reasoning, there are also several worlds about an activity or event: the real or potential–realized world $\mathcal{W}^R(X)$, the potential world $\mathcal{W}^P(X)$, and the ideal world $\mathcal{W}^I(X)$. We can classify as well the worlds into the upper-layer world in which the upper-layer of the system develops well with all other layers developing satisfactorily, medium-layer world in which the medium-layer of the system develops well with all other layers developing satisfactorily, and the lower-layer world in which the lower-layer of the system develops well with all other layers developing satisfactorily. In addition, we can classify the worlds into the high-level world in which the system is highly developed, the medium–level world in which the system develops to its medium level, and the low–level world in which the system fails to develop well.

System of normal state is the "system" (or "virtual system") in the middle, medium, or average state.

Definition I.2-1. **system's high-level difference** = system's higher-level state $\ominus$ system's medium-level state, **system's low-level difference** = system's medium-level state $\ominus$ system's low-level state, where $\ominus \models \mathcal{Z}\circ,{}_v\mathcal{H}$ is the impactor eliminating the elements (or subsystems) appearing after it from the elements (or subsystems) appearing beforet. In general, for a system, the high-difference is not identical to the low-difference.

Below, let $X = \{X_t, X_{t+1}, \ldots, X_{t+n}\} \sqsubseteq (\Omega, \mathcal{Z}\circ,{}_v\mathcal{H}, \{\mathbb{C}\})$ be a grand system of n-subsystems (or a system of n-elements), where X at time t is the subsystem $X_t = X_t(.|$ organization-production $|\,\mathbb{C}) \sqsubseteq (\Omega, \mathcal{Z}\circ,{}_v\mathcal{H}, \{\mathbb{C}\})$, $t \in \mathbb{N}$ ($\mathbb{N}$ being the set of natural numbers), φ^{NS}, $\mathcal{C}h^{H}$, $\mathcal{C}h^{L} \models \mathcal{Z}\circ,{}_v\mathcal{H}$ (H = high, L = low). Define:

(I.2-1) Normal state X: $\varphi^{NS}\{X_t\} = X_t(.|\zeta^M\{org\}\text{-}\zeta^M\{prod\}\,|\,\mathbb{C})$,

(I.2-2) High-level difference: $\mathcal{C}h^H\{X_t\} = X_t(.|\zeta^H\{org\}\text{-}\zeta^H\{prod\}\,|\,\mathbb{C}) \ominus \varphi^{NS}\{X_t\}$
$= X_t(.|(\zeta^H \ominus \zeta^M)\{org\}\text{-}(\zeta^H \ominus \zeta^M)\{prod\}\,|\,\mathbb{C})$,

(I.2-3) Low-level difference: $\mathcal{C}h^L\{X_t\} = \varphi^{NS}\{X_t\} \ominus X_t(.|\zeta^L\{org\}\text{-}\zeta^L\{prod\}\,|\,\mathbb{C})$
$= X_t(.|(\zeta^M \ominus \zeta^L)\{org\}\text{-}(\zeta^M \ominus \zeta^L)\{prod\}\,|\,\mathbb{C})$,

where org ≡ organization, prod ≡ production, ζ^H, $\zeta^M\{.\}$ (i.e., $\zeta^M\{.\} \equiv \zeta^G\{.\} \equiv \zeta^{General}\{.\}$), ζ^H, ζ^M, $\zeta^L \models \mathcal{Z}\circ,{}_v\mathcal{H}$ are the impactors of high-, medium- (or normal), and low-level states, respectively (H ≡ high, M ≡ medium, L ≡ low), "-" is the impactor connecting the structures of organization and production sub-systems, and $\ominus \models \mathcal{Z}\circ,{}_v\mathcal{H}$ is the impactor eliminating the organization and production sub-systems or structures. Note that for the *high-level difference* $\mathcal{C}h^H\{X_t\} = X_t(.|(\zeta^H \Theta \zeta^G)\{org\}\text{-}(\zeta^H \Theta \zeta^G)\ \{prod\}\,|\,\mathbb{C})$, it is the higher side of the difference in the organization-production structure {org*prod}; and the *low-level difference* $\mathcal{C}h^L\{X_t\} = X_t(.|(\zeta^G \Theta \zeta^L)\{org\}\text{-}(\zeta^G \Theta \zeta^L)\{prod\}\,|\,\mathbb{C})$ is the lower side of the difference in the organization-production structure.

Note that the medium-system and these high- and low-level differences may be systems in incomplete forms (called pre-systems).

Now we turn to the topics of distribution system – one type of our uncertain systems.

Definition I.2-2. The **0-step reference system**, in the case of three elements, is a system {x,y,c} $\sqsubseteq (\Omega, \mathcal{Z}\circ,{}_v\mathcal{H}, \{\mathbb{C}\})$ in which the "central structure of subsystem" is the one-step higher development of the lower structure or sub-system" and the "power of the center" is the one-step higher development of the "power of the lower structure." Here the development is a dialectical process (in the Hegelian sense). Here, {x,y} represents the lower structure in which x and y are exactly the same except for a few human and cultural dimensions (for example, x has a dimension of yin element and y has a dimension of yang element). In this case, this system does not have any medium-level structure.

Definition I.2-3. By a **pre-system** is meant a structure composed of universal or human elements that is not yet a system. It is a "system" in an incomplete form. Examples are the afore-mentioned high- and low-differences of a system, dealing with elements of a system, may not be systems.

Definition I.2-4. **½-step reference system** is the system $X \sqsubseteq (\Omega,\mathcal{Z}^{\circ},{}_{v}\mathcal{H},\{\mathbb{C}\})$ in which the "central structure" is the one-step higher development of the "medium-lower structure" and the "medium-level structure" is the one-and-a-half-step higher development of the "lower structure." Here the development is a dialectical process (in the Hegelian sense).

Definition I.2-5. **One-step reference system** is the system $X \sqsubseteq (\Omega,\mathcal{Z}^{\circ},{}_{v}\mathcal{H},\{\mathbb{C}\})$ in which the "central structure" is the one-step higher development of the "medium-lower structure" and the "medium-level structure" is the one-step higher development of the "lower structure." Here the development is in the Hegelian sense of dialectic.

Definition I.2-6. **0-step without-center reference system** is the 0-step reference system $X \sqsubseteq (\Omega,\mathcal{Z}^{\circ},{}_{v}\mathcal{H},\{\mathbb{C}\})$ without center. Let this system be $X = \{x_1,x_2,\ldots,x_n\}$, then it may have a **virtual center**: $cl(co\{x_1,x_1,\ldots,x_n\})$ (also see Subsection §A.2-2-1). Here this virtual center is the collection of the essentials of the structures and characteristics of all sub-systems to be supplemented by necessary structures and characteristics to make it the core of the grand system. This grand system is an n-factor MFCE system composed of the center and all non-central subsystems. We may say that the cultural core is the virtual center of this grand system.

Below we shall define various types of distribution systems. We start with the presentation of our first category of distribution systems.

Definition I.2-7. Let $X = \{X_t,X_{t+1},\ldots,X_{t+n}\} \sqsubseteq (\Omega,\mathcal{Z}^{\circ},{}_{v}\mathcal{H},\{\mathbb{C}\})$ be a system (or grand system, resp.) of n elements (or subsystems, resp., with $X_i = X_{it}(.|\text{org-prod}\,|\,\mathbb{C}) \sqsubseteq (\Omega,\mathcal{Z}^{\circ},{}_{v}\mathcal{H},\{\mathbb{C}\})$, $t \in \mathbb{N}$). Then $X = \{X_t\}$ is said to be a **0-step $\mathbf{T^{sysC}}$ distribution system** (in uncertainty with "sysC" denoting system-continuity) if and only if the following conditions hold:

(I.2-4) $X_0 = \{.\ |\text{org}(.|\text{multi-subsystem system with a center})\text{-industries}\,|\ \mathcal{L}^{YX}\text{-}\mathbb{C}^{T}\}$,

(I.2-5) $X \sim (C_X[X],D_X[X])$: X is distributed by $(C_X[X],D_X[X])$ (where $C_X[X] \equiv \zeta_X \equiv \gamma_X$ is the most common system, $D_X[X] \equiv \delta_X[X]$ is the **differencing** of X from $C_X[X]$), or $X\sim (B_X[X],D_X[X])$: X is distributed by $(B_X[X], D_X[X])$ (where $B_X[X] \equiv \zeta_X \equiv \beta_X$ is the best or most representative system, $D_X[X] \equiv \delta_X[X]$) is the differencing of X from $B_X[X]$),

(I.2-6) $\{X_t, X_{t+1},\ldots,X_{t+n}\}$ is a 0-step without-center reference system,

where $\mathbb{C}^{T}$ represents the tranquility culture, t, s $(s < t)$ are the indices of time, and $\mathcal{L}^{YX}\text{-}\mathbb{C}^{T}$ denotes the rationality and reasoning processes of the multi-factor causal-effect and YYWX (yin-yang five-element) system.

Here for X_t to be a T^{sysC} distribution system (in uncertainty), it is written: $X_t \sqsubseteq T^{sysC}$.

Definition I.2-8. **0-step distribution system K^{sysC}** (in uncertainty) is the system $\{X_t\} \sqsubseteq (\Omega, \mathcal{Z}\circ, {}_v\mathcal{H}, \{\mathbb{C}\})$ satisfying the following conditions:

(I.2-7) $X_0 = \{x,y\} = \{.\ |org(.|\text{multi-subsystem system with a center})\text{-industries} \mid \mathcal{L}^{ST} - \mathbb{C}^{K}\}$,

(I.2-8) $X \sim (C_X[X], D_X[X])$: X is distributed by $(C_X[X], D_X[X])$ or $X \sim (B_X[X], D_X[X])$: X is distributed by $(B_X[X], D_X[X])$,

(I.2-9) $\{X_t, X_{t+1}, \ldots, X_{t+n}\}$ is a 0-step without-center reference system,

where $\mathcal{L}^{ST}$ denotes the rationality and reasoning process of the system of sciences and technology and $\mathbb{C}^{K}$ denotes the culture of conflict.

Here for X_t to be a K^{sysC} distribution system (in uncertainty), it is written: $X_t \sqsubseteq K^{sysC}$. Below, we shall define the second category of distribution systems.

Definition I.2-9. Let $X = \{X_t, X_{t+1}, \ldots, X_{t+n}\} \sqsubseteq (\Omega, \mathcal{Z}\circ, {}_v\mathcal{H}, \{\mathbb{C}\})$ be a grand system of n-subsystems, $X_t = X_t(.|\text{org-prod} \mid \mathbb{C}) \sqsubseteq (\Omega, \mathcal{Z}\circ, {}_v\mathcal{H}, \{\mathbb{C}\})$, $t \in \mathbb{N}$, $\mathcal{P}^{NS}$, $\mathcal{C}h^{H}$, $\mathcal{C}h^{L} \vDash \mathcal{Z}\circ, {}_v\mathcal{H}$. Then by the **0-step T^L distribution system** (in uncertainty) (L denoting leap) is meant the system $\{X_{i,t}\}$ (for $X_t \sqsubseteq T^L$) satisfying the following conditions:

(I.2-10) $X_0 = \{.\ |\ \text{org(multi-subsystem with a center)-industries} \mid \mathcal{L}^{YX} - \mathbb{C}^{T}\}$.

(I.2-11) For $\mathcal{S}^{L} \vDash \mathcal{Z}\circ, {}_v\mathcal{H}$, $X \sim \mathcal{S}^{L}(C_X[X], D_D[X])$: X is distributed by $\mathcal{S}^{L}(C_X[X], D_X[X])$ (with $\mathcal{S}^{L}(C_X[X], D_X[X]) = (\mathcal{S}^{L}C_X[X], \mathcal{S}^{L}D_X[X])$), or $X \sim \mathcal{S}^{L}(B_X[X], D_X[X])$: X is distributed by $\mathcal{S}^{L}(B_X[X], D_X[X])$ (with $\mathcal{S}^{L}(B_X[X], D_X[X]) = (\mathcal{S}^{L}B_X[X], \mathcal{S}^{L}D_X[X])$).

(I.2-12) $\{X_t, X_{t+1}, \ldots, X_{t+n}\}$ is a 0-step reference system without-center,

Here $\mathcal{S}^{L} \vDash \mathcal{Z}\circ, {}_v\mathcal{H}$ is a leap impactor: For X to be a system or element, $\mathcal{S}^{L}\{X\}$ will induce X to jump to a higher state or stage.

Definition I.2-10. Let $X = \{X_t, X_{t+1}, \ldots, X_{t+n}\} \sqsubseteq (\Omega, \mathcal{Z}\circ, {}_v\mathcal{H}, \{\mathbb{C}\})$ be a grand system of n-subsystems, $X_t = X_t(.|\text{org-prod} \mid \mathbb{C}) \sqsubseteq (\Omega, \mathcal{Z}\circ, {}_v\mathcal{H}, \{\mathbb{C}\})$, $t \in \mathbb{N}$, $\mathcal{P}^{NS}$, $\mathcal{C}h^{H}$, $\mathcal{C}h^{L} \vDash \mathcal{Z}\circ, {}_v\mathcal{H}$. Then by the **0-step K^L distribution system** (in uncertainty) is meant the grand system $\{X_{i,t}\}$ (for $X_t \sqsubseteq K^L$) satisfying the following conditions:

(I.2-13) $X_0 = \{.\ |\ \text{org(multi-subsystem with a center C)-industries} \mid \mathcal{L}^{ST} - \mathbb{C}^{K}\}$.

(I.2-14) For $\mathcal{S}^{L} \vDash \mathcal{Z}\circ, {}_v\mathcal{H}$, $X \sim \mathcal{S}^{L}(C_X[X], D_X[X])$: X is distributed by $\mathcal{S}^{L}(C_X[X], D_X[X])$ (with $\mathcal{S}^{L}(C_X[X], D_X[X]) = (\mathcal{S}^{L}C_X[X], \mathcal{S}^{L}D_X[X])$), or $X \sim \mathcal{S}^{L}(B_X[X], D_X[X])$: X is distributed by $\mathcal{S}^{L}(B_X[X], D_X[X])$ (with $\mathcal{S}^{L}(B_X[X], D_X[X]) = (\mathcal{S}^{L}B_X[X], \mathcal{S}^{L}D_X[X])$).

(I.2-15) $\{X_t, X_{t+1}, \ldots, X_{t+n}\}$ is a 0-step reference system without-center.

Now we turn to two more distribution systems: n-step T^{sysD} and n-step K^{sysD} distribution systems.

Definition I.2-11. Let $X = \{X_t, X_{t+1}, \ldots, X_{t+n}\} \sqsubseteq (\Omega, \mathcal{Z}\circ, {}_v\mathcal{H}, \{\mathbb{C}\})$ be a grand system of n subsystems, with $X_t = X_t(.|\text{org-prod} \mid \mathbb{C}) \sqsubseteq (\Omega, \mathcal{Z}\circ, {}_v\mathcal{H}, \{\mathbb{C}\})$ being a subsystem, $t \in \mathbb{N}$ ($\mathbb{N}$ be the set of natural numbers), $\mathcal{P}^{NS}$, $\mathcal{Ch}^{H}$, $\mathcal{Ch}^{L}$ $\models$ $\mathcal{Z}\circ,_v\mathcal{H}$. Then X = {$X_t$} is said to be an **n-step T^{sysD} distribution system** (in uncertainty) (sysD denoting system-discontinuity) if and only if the following conditions hold:

(I.2-16) X_0 = {. |org(.|multi-subsystem system with a center)-industries | $\mathcal{L}^{YX}$-$\mathfrak{C}^T$}.

(I.2-17) For $\mathcal{S}^{sysD}$ $\models$ $\mathcal{Z}\circ,_v\mathcal{H}$, X ~ $\mathcal{S}^{sysD}$(C_X[X],D_X[X]): X is distributed by $\mathcal{S}^{sysD}$ (C_X[X],D_X[X]) (where $\mathcal{S}^{sysD}$(C_X[X],D_X[X]) = ($\mathcal{S}^{sysD}C_X$[X], $\mathcal{S}^{sysD}D_X$[X])), or X ~ $\mathcal{S}^{sysD}$(B_X[X],D_X[X]) : X is distributed by $\mathcal{S}^{sysD}$(B_X[X],D_X[X]) (with $\mathcal{S}^{sysD}$(B_X[X],D_X[X]) = ($\mathcal{S}^{sysD}B_X$[X], $\mathcal{S}^{sysD}D_X$[X])).

(I.2-18) {X_t,X_{t+1},...,X_{t+n}} is an n-step without-center reference system, i.e., X is a system of development jumping over more than one step,

where $\mathbb{C}^T$ represents the tranquility culture, t, s (s < t) are the indices of time, and $\mathcal{L}^{YX}$-$\mathbb{C}^T$ denotes the rationality and reasoning processes of the multi-factor causal-effect and YYWX (yin-yang five-element) system, with $\mathcal{S}^{sysD}$ $\models$ $\mathcal{Z}\circ,_v\mathcal{H}$ being a system-discontinuous impactor: For X to be a system or element, $\mathcal{S}^{sysD}${X} will induce X to jump in a discontinous manner (to be determined by the context). Here X_t is a T^{sysD} distribution system: $X_t \sqsubseteq T^{sysD}$.

Definition I.2-12. **n-step K^{sysD} distribution system** (in uncertainty) is a grand system {X_t} $\sqsubseteq$ (Ω,$\mathcal{Z}\circ,_v\mathcal{H}$,{$\mathbb{C}$}) satisfying the following conditions:

(I.2-19) X_0 = {x,y} = {. |org(.|multi-subsystem system with a center)-industries | $\mathcal{L}^{ST}$-$\mathbb{C}^K$},

(I.2-20) For $\mathcal{S}^{sysD}$ $\models$ $\mathcal{Z}\circ,_v\mathcal{H}$, X ~ $\mathcal{S}^{sysD}$(C_X[X],D_X[X]): X is distributed by $\mathcal{S}^{sysD}$(C_X[X], D_X[X]) (where $\mathcal{S}^{sysD}$(C_X[X],D_X[X]) = ($\mathcal{S}^{sysD}C_X$[X], $\mathcal{S}^{sysD}D_X$[X])), or X ~ $\mathcal{S}^{sysD}$(B_X[X],D_X[X]) : X is distributed by $\mathcal{S}^{sysD}$(B_X[X], D_X[X]) (where $\mathcal{S}^{sysD}$(B_X[X],D_X[X]) = ($\mathcal{S}^{sysD}B_X$[X], $\mathcal{S}^{sysD}D_X$[X])).

(I.2-21) {X_t,X_{t+1},...,X_{t+n}} is an n-step without-center reference system, i.e., X ia a system of development jumping over more than one step,

where $\mathcal{L}^{ST}$ denotes the rationality and reasoning process of sciences and $\mathbb{C}^K$ denotes the culture of conflict. Note that X_t is a K^{sysD} distribution system: $X_t \sqsubseteq K^{sysD}$.

Definition I.2-13 (on-off distribution system). If W_t, X_i, Y_j, Z_k $\sqsubseteq$ (Ω,$\mathcal{Z}\circ,_v\mathcal{H}$,{$\mathbb{C}$}), i, j, k, t (time) $\in \mathbb{N}$, then W_t is said to be an **on-off distribution system** if and only if the following condition holds:

(I.2-22) W_t = {I(ijk,t) | I(ijk,t) = [($\Sigma_i X_i$)$\star$($\Sigma_j Y_j$)$\star$($\Sigma_k Z_k$),t]},

where $\Sigma_i X_i \equiv X_1 \oplus X_2 \oplus \ldots \oplus X_n$ and similarly for $\Sigma_j Y_j$ and $\Sigma_k Z_k$. Here for I(ijk,t), we define:

$$\text{(I.2-23)}\ \psi I(ijk,t|w) = \begin{cases} \mathcal{S}\{I(ijk,t|w)\} \text{ if } w \in \mathcal{W}^R(X_i) \sqcap \mathcal{W}^R(Y_j) \sqcap \mathcal{TW}^R(Z_k), \\ \mathcal{M}\{I(ijk,t|w)\} \text{ if } w \notin \mathcal{W}^R(X_i) \sqcap \mathcal{W}^R(Y_j) \sqcap \mathcal{W}^R(Z_k). \end{cases}$$

Here $\mathcal{W}^{RY}(X_i)$, $\mathcal{W}^R(Y_j)$, and $\mathcal{W}^R(Z_k)$ are the potential-realizable worlds of X_i, Y_j, and Z_k, respectively, $\mathcal{S}$, $\mathcal{M}$ $\models$ $\mathcal{Z}\circ,_v\mathcal{H}$ are sheng (or actualization) and mie (or annihilation) impactors,

respectively, and $\psi \models \mathcal{Z}\circ,_v\mathcal{H}$ is the distribution (or uncertain) impactor.
For I(ijk,t|w) in the above, with W_t, X_i, Y_j, $Z_k \sqsubseteq (\Omega,\mathcal{Z}\circ,_v\mathcal{H},\{\mathbb{C}\})\sqcap\mathbb{R}$ (real numbers), i, j, k, t (time) $\in \mathbb{N}$, we shall define it in mathematic term, that is:

$$\text{(I.2-24)}\quad W = I(ijk,t)\Sigma_i\Sigma_j\Sigma_k X_iY_jZ_k,$$

where I(ijk,t) is an indicator function to be defined below:

$$\text{(I.2-25)}\quad I(ijk,t|w)=\begin{cases} 1 \text{ if } w \in \mathcal{W}^R(X_i)\cap\mathcal{W}^R(Y_j)\cap\mathcal{W}^R(Z_k), \\ 0 \text{ if } w \notin \mathcal{W}^R(X_i)\cap\mathcal{W}^R(Y_j)\cap\mathcal{W}^R(Z_k). \end{cases}$$

Here $\mathcal{W}^R(X_i)$, $\mathcal{W}^R(Y_j)$, and $\mathcal{W}^R(Z_k)$ are the potential-realizable spaces of X_i, Y_j, and Z_k, respectively.

I.3 Uncertain Systems

Materials in this section are what we developed first for systems of uncertainty. We keep this section for future inspiration.

Below, let $X = \{X_t, X_{t+1},\ldots,X_{t+n}\} \sqsubseteq (\Omega,\mathcal{Z}\circ,_v\mathcal{H},\{\mathbb{C}\})$ be a grand system, with $X_t = X_t(.|\text{org-prod}\,|\,C) \sqsubseteq (\Omega,\mathcal{Z}\circ,_v\mathcal{H},\{\mathbb{C}\})$ being a subsystem, $t \in \mathbb{N}$ ($\mathbb{N}$ being the set of natural numbers), $\mathcal{P}^{NS}$, $\mathcal{C}h^H$, $\mathcal{C}h^L \models \mathcal{Z}\circ,_v\mathcal{H}$.

Definition I.3-1. Let $X = \{X_t,X_{t+1},\ldots,X_{t+n}\} \sqsubseteq (\Omega,\mathcal{Z}\circ,_v\mathcal{H},\{\mathbb{C}\})$ be a basic system of n-elements, $X_t = X_t(.|\text{org-prod}\,|\,\mathbb{C}) \sqsubseteq (\Omega,\mathcal{Z}\circ,_v\mathcal{H},\{\mathbb{C}\})$ be a unit system, $t \in \mathbb{N}$ ($\mathcal{P}^{NS}$, $\mathcal{C}h^H$, $\mathcal{C}h^L \models \mathcal{Z}\circ,_v\mathcal{H}$. Then X = $\{X_t\}$ is said to be a **0-step uncertain T^{sysC} process** (sysC denoting system-continuity) if and only if the following conditions hold:

$$\text{(I.3-1)}\quad X_0 = \{.\ |\text{org}(.|\text{multi-subsystem system with a center})\text{-industries}\,|\,\mathcal{L}^{YX}\text{-}\mathfrak{C}^T\},$$

$$\text{(I.3-2)}\quad \mathcal{P}^{NS}(X_{t+1}) = \mathcal{P}^{NS}(X_t),$$

$$\text{(I.3-3)}\quad \mathcal{C}h^H(X_{B,t}-X_{\beta,s}) = (B,\beta)^H{}_X,$$
$$\mathcal{C}h^L(X_{A,t}-X_{\alpha,s}) = (A,\alpha)^L{}_X,$$

$$\text{(I.3-4)}\quad \{X_t,X_{t+1},\ldots,X_{t+n}\} \text{ is a o-step without-center reference system,}$$

where $\mathbb{C}^T$ represents the tranquility culture, t, s (s < t) are the indices of time, $X_{B,t}$ is X in t-time and B-step, $X_{\beta,s}$ is X in s-time and β-step, $X_{A,t}$ is X in t-time and A-step, $X_{\alpha,s}$ is X in s-time and α-step, $(B,\beta)^H{}_X$ is the higher–step structure of (B,β) in X, $(A,\alpha)^L{}_X$ is the lower–step structure of (A,α) in X (for example, (high-tech industry, agriculture)$^H{}_X$ is the higher-step structure of high-tech industry and agriculture of X, (high-tech industry,agriculture)$^L{}_X$ is the lower-step structure of the high-tech industry and agriculture of X), $\mathcal{C}h^H(X)$ is the high-level difference of X, $\mathcal{C}h^L(X)$ is the low-level difference of X. Here $\mathcal{L}^{YX}$-$\mathbb{C}^T$ denotes the rationality and reasoning processes of the multi-factor cause-effect and YYWX (yin-yang five-element) system.

Here X_t is a T^{sysC} uncertain process: $X_t \sqsubseteq T^{sysC}$.

In the above, if the state changes, Bcm (I.3-2) will be replaced by Bcm (I.3-2'):

(I.3-2') $\mathcal{P}^{NS}(X_{t+1}(.\mid\xi)) \neq \mathcal{P}^{NS}(X_t(.\mid\xi))$,

where "." is the uncertain variable, organization or state/ world, "ξ" is the changing variable, organization or state/world.

Definition I.3-2. **0-step uncertain process K^{sysC}** is the grand system $\{X_t\} \sqsubseteq (\Omega,\mathcal{Z}\circ,_v\mathcal{H},\{\mathbb{C}\})$ satisfying the following conditions:

(I.3-5) $X_0 = \{x,y\} = \{.\ |org(.|$multi-subsystem system with a center)-industries $\mid \mathcal{L}^{ST}\text{-}\ \mathbb{C}^K\}$.

(I.3-6) $\mathcal{P}^{NS}(X_{t+1}) = \mathcal{P}^{NS}(X_t)$.

(I.3-7) $\mathcal{C}h^H(X_{B,t}–X_{\beta,s}) = (B,\beta)^H{}_X$.
$\mathcal{C}h^L(X_{A,t} – X_{\alpha,s}) = (A,\alpha)^L{}_X$.

(I.3-8) $\{X_t,X_{t+1},\ldots,X_{t+n}\}$ is a 0-step without-center reference system,

Here, $\mathcal{L}^{ST}$ denotes the rationality and reasoning process of sciences and $\mathbb{C}^K$ denotes the culture of conflict.

Here X_t is an uncertain K^{sysC} process: $X_t \sqsubseteq K^{sysC}$. If in the above, the state changes, then Bcm (I.3-6) in the above will be replaced by Bcm (I.3-6'):

(I.3-6') $\mathcal{P}^{NS}(X_{t+1}(.\mid\xi)) \neq \mathcal{P}^{NS}(X_t(.\mid\xi))$.

Below, let $X_t \sqsubseteq K^{sysC}$. Then we have the following definition: $\mathcal{P}^{NS}(X_t) = \mathcal{S}^{SG}\{X_t\}$, $\mathcal{C}h^H(X_t) = \mathcal{S}^{SH}\{X_t\}\ominus\mathcal{S}^{SG}\{X_t\} = (\mathcal{S}^{SH}\ominus\mathcal{S}^{SG})\{X_t\}$, $\mathcal{C}h^L(X_t) = \mathcal{S}^{SG}\{X_t\}\ominus\mathcal{S}^{SL}\{X_t\}= (\mathcal{S}^{SG}\ominus\mathcal{S}^{SL})\{X_t\}$. Here $\mathcal{S}^{SG}$ is a "matrix-expansion" impactor of a general state, $\mathcal{S}^{SH}$ is a "matrix-expansion" impactor of a high-level state, $\mathcal{S}^{SL}$ is a "matrix-expansion" impactor of the low-level state (here the so-called "matrix" is of multiple-dimension, $n_1 \times n_2 \times \ldots \times n_k$).

Below, let $Y_t, S_t, X_t \sqsubseteq (\Omega,\mathcal{Z}\circ,_v\mathcal{H},\{\mathbb{C}\})\sqcap\{\mathbb{C}^{SPC}\}$ ($\mathbb{C}^{SPC}$ being a specific culture), $X_t \sqsubseteq T^{sysC}\sqcup K^{sysC}$ be the uncertain component related to Y_t, $t \in \mathbb{N}$:

(I.3-9) $Y_t = S_t \oplus X_t$,

where S_t and X_t are the certainty part and the uncertain part (i.e., uncertain system) of Y_t, respectively, with

(I.3-10) $\mathcal{C}h^H\{Y_{t+1}\} = \mathcal{S}_1\{\mathcal{P}^{NS}(S_t)\} \oplus\mathcal{C}h^H\{S_t\}\otimes\mathcal{S}_2\{X_t\}$,

(I.3-11) $\mathcal{C}h^L\{Y_{t+1}\} = \mathcal{S}_1\{\mathcal{P}^{NS}(S_t)\} \oplus\mathcal{C}h^L\{S_t\} \otimes\mathcal{S}_2\{X_t\}$,

($\mathcal{C}h^H\{Y_{t+1}\}$ being the high-level difference of Y_{t+1}, $\mathcal{C}h^H\{Y_{t+1}\}$ being the low-level difference of Y_{t+1}), see Bcms (I.2-2) and (I.2-3)) where $\mathcal{P}^{NS}$, $\mathcal{S}_1$, $\mathcal{S}_2$, $\mathcal{C}h^H\{.\}$, $\mathcal{C}h^L\{.\} \vDash \mathcal{Z}\circ,_v\mathcal{H}$, $\mathcal{S}_1$, $\mathcal{S}_2$ are entity-augmenting (or matrix-expansion) impactors of a specific period of time, and $\otimes \vDash \mathcal{H}$ is an interactor.

Here if we would like to "simplify" X_t in the above, then we may use Bcm. (K.2-19) or (K.2-20) in Tonn [2006] (somewhat like a method of linearizing a curve).

In the development and growth models of a cultural economy, the above two types of uncertain processes or systems can be used to present the stable and leap paths of a system, respectively. The term $\mathcal{S}\{\mathcal{P}^{NS}(S_t)\}$ (i.e., the first terms of $\mathcal{C}h^H\{Y_{t+1}\}$ and $\mathcal{C}h^L\{Y_{t+1}\}$ in Bcms. (I.3-13) and (I.3-14) is used to represent the certainty component of a stable and variational paths of the system in question, and the term $\mathcal{S}\{X_t\}$ is added to address the uncertain component of these paths.

Below, we shall define the second category of uncertain processes or systems.

Definition I.3-3. Let $X = \{X_t, X_{t+1}, \ldots, X_{t+n}\} \sqsubseteq (\Omega, \mathbb{Z}\circ, {}_v\mathbb{H}, \{\mathbb{C}\})$ be a grand system of n-subsystems, $X_t = X_t(.|\text{org-prod}|\mathbb{C}) \sqsubseteq (\Omega, \mathbb{Z}\circ, {}_v\mathbb{H}, \{\mathbb{C}\})$, $t \in \mathbb{N}$, $\mathcal{P}^{NS}$, $\mathcal{C}h^H$, $\mathcal{C}h^L \vDash \mathbb{Z}\circ, {}_v\mathbb{H}$. Then by the **0-step T^L uncertain process** (L denoting leap) is meant the grnad system $\{X_i, t\}$ (for $X_t \sqsubseteq T^L$) satisfying the following conditions:

(I.3-12) $X_0 = \{.\,|\,\text{org(multi-subsystem with a center)-industries}\,|\,\mathcal{L}^{YX}\text{-}\mathbb{C}^T\}$,

(I.3-13) $\forall \mathcal{I} = \text{I, II}, \ldots, \text{N(period of time), I, II}, \ldots, N, i, j \in \mathbb{N}\ (i \neq j), \mathcal{I}_i, \mathcal{I}_{i+1} \in \mathcal{I},$
$\mathcal{P}^{NS}\{X(\mathcal{I}_i)\} = \mathcal{P}^{NS}\{X(\mathcal{I}_{i+1})\},\ \mathcal{P}^{NS}\{X(\mathcal{I}+1)\} = \Psi^{N\text{-step}}\{\mathcal{P}^{NS}\{X(\mathcal{I})\}\},$

(I.3-14) $\mathcal{C}h^H(X_{B,t} - X_{\beta,s}) = \Psi^{K\text{-step}}\{(B,\beta)^H{}_X\},$
$\mathcal{C}h^L(X_{A,t} - X_{\alpha,s}) = \Psi_{Q\text{-step}}\{(A,\alpha)^L{}_X\},$

(I.3-15) $\{X_t, X_{t+1}, \ldots, X_{t+n}\}$ is a 0-step reference system without-center,

where "$\mathcal{I}+1$" is the period of time (step, phase or stage) adjacent to "$\mathcal{I}$," $\Psi^{N\text{-step}}$ is an impactor that transforms a system to N-step higher ($\mathcal{I} \in \mathbb{N}$), $\Psi^{K\text{-step}}$ is an impactor that transform a system to K-step higher, $\Psi_{M\text{-step}}$ is an impactor that transforms a system to M-step lower, $K < N < Q$, $K, N, Q \in \mathbb{N}$.

Definition I.3-4. Let $X = \{X_t, X_{t+1}, \ldots, X_{t+n}\} \sqsubseteq (\Omega, \mathbb{Z}\circ, {}_v\mathbb{H}, \{\mathbb{C}\})$ be a grand system of n-subsystems, $X_t = X_t(.|\text{org-prod}|\mathbb{C}) \sqsubseteq (\Omega, \mathbb{Z}\circ, {}_v\mathbb{H}, \{\mathbb{C}\})$, $t \in \mathbb{N}$, $\mathcal{P}^{NS}$, $\mathcal{C}h^H$, $\mathcal{C}h^L \vDash \mathbb{Z}\circ, {}_v\mathbb{H}$. Then by the **0-step K^L uncertain process** is meant the system $\{X_i, t\}$ (for $X_t \sqsubseteq K^L$) satisfying the following conditions:

(I.3-16) $X_0 = \{.\,|\,\text{org(multi-subsystem with a center C)-industries}\,|\,\mathcal{L}^{ST}\text{-}\mathbb{C}^K\}$,

(I.3-17) $\forall \mathcal{I} = \text{I, II}, \ldots, \text{N(period of time), I, II}, \ldots, N, i, j \in \mathbb{N}\ (i \neq j), \mathcal{I}_i, \mathcal{I}_{i+1} \in \mathcal{I}, \mathcal{P}^{NS}\{X(\mathcal{I}_{i+1})\}$
$= \xi_{\sim t}\{\mathcal{P}^{NS}\{X(\mathcal{I}_i)\}, t\} \neq \mathcal{P}^{NS}\{X(\mathcal{I}_i)\}$, $\xi_{\sim t} \vDash \mathbb{Z}\circ, {}_v\mathbb{H}$ ($\xi_{\sim t}$ as an impactor is a "partial becoming" (or operation) of time, t being time and here "$_{\sim t}$" being the force of t that conditions the imapctor ξ), $\mathcal{P}^{NS}\{X(\mathcal{I}+1)\} = \zeta_{\sim t}\{\mathcal{P}^{NS}\{X(\mathcal{I})\}, t\} \neq \Psi^{N\text{-step}}\{\mathcal{P}^{NS}\{X(\mathcal{I})\}\}$, $\zeta_{\sim t} \vDash \mathbb{Z}\circ, {}_v\mathbb{H}$,

(I.3-18) $\mathcal{C}h^H(X_{B,t} - X_{\beta,s}) = \Psi^{K\text{-step}}\{(B,\beta)^H{}_X\},$
$\mathcal{C}h^L(X_{A,t} - X_{\alpha,s}) = \Psi_{Q\text{-step}}\{(A,\alpha)^L{}_X\},$

(I.3-19) $\{X_t, X_{t+1}, \ldots, X_{t+n}\}$ is a 0-step reference system without-center, where "$\mathcal{J}$+1"is the period of time adjacent to "$\mathcal{J}$," $\Psi^{N\text{-step}}$ is an impactor that transforms a system to N-step higher ($\mathcal{J} \in \mathbb{N}$), $\Psi^{K\text{-step}}$ is an impactor that transforms a system to K-step higher, $\Psi_{M\text{-step}}$ is an impactor that transforms a system to M-step lower, $K < N < Q$, $K, N, Q \in \mathbb{N}$.

In the condition of Bcm. (I.3-7), we see that $\mathcal{P}^{NS}\{X(J_i)\} \neq \mathcal{P}^{NS}\{X(J_j)\}$, $J_i \neq J_j$; that is, X_t will jump from one period of time to another. Therefore this process can be applied to a leap path of a cultural economy in the state of uncertainty.

Similar to Bcms. (I.3-10) - (I.3-11), in the following, let $Y_t, S_t, X_t \sqsubseteq (\Omega, \mathcal{Z}\circ, {}_v\mathcal{H}, \{\mathbb{C}\}) \sqcap C^{SPC}$, $X_t \sqsubseteq T^L \sqcup K^L$, $t \in \mathbb{N}$:

(I.2-20) $Y_t = S_t \oplus X_t$,

where S_t and X_t are the certainty part and the uncertain part (i.e., uncertain system) of Y_t, respectively, with

(I.3-21) $\mathcal{C}\!h^H\{Y_{t+1}\} = \mathcal{S}\{\mathcal{P}^{NS}(S_t)\} \oplus \mathcal{C}\!h^H\{S_t\} \otimes \mathcal{S}\{X_t\}$,

(I.3-22) $\mathcal{C}\!h^L\{Y_{t+1}\} = \mathcal{S}\{\mathcal{P}^{NS}(S_t)\} \oplus \mathcal{C}\!h^L\{S_t\} \otimes \mathcal{S}\{X_t\}$,

Here if we "simplify" the system X_t in the above (i.e., by the use of Bcm. (K.2-19) or (K.2-20) in Tonn [2006]), then we derive a more sophisticated version of this system. These two types of uncertain systems or processes can be used to describe the development and growth paths of a cultural economy. The term $X_{t+1} = \mathcal{S}\{\mathcal{P}^{NS}(X_t)\}$ may be used to present a leap path of the system X in the state of certainty. By adding the term $\mathcal{S}\{X_t\}$, then the above two becomings can be used to present a high-growth or leap path of the system X in the state of uncertainty.

Now we turn to two more uncertain systems: n-step T^{sysD} and n-step K^{sysD} uncertain systems.

Definition I.3-5. Let $X = \{X_t, X_{t+1}, \ldots, X_{t+n}\} \sqsubseteq (\Omega, \mathcal{Z}\circ, {}_v\mathcal{H}, \{\mathbb{C}\})$ be a grand system, $X_t = X_t(.|\text{org-prod}\,|\,\mathbb{C}) \sqsubseteq (\Omega, \mathcal{Z}\circ, {}_v\mathcal{H}, \{\mathbb{C}\})$ be a subsystem, $t \in \mathbb{N}$ ($\mathbb{N}$ be the set of natural numbers), $\mathcal{P}^{NS}$, $\mathcal{C}\!h^H$, $\mathcal{C}\!h^L \models \mathcal{Z}\circ, {}_v\mathcal{H}$. Then $X = \{X_t\}$ is said to be an **n-step T^{sysD} uncertain process** (sysD denoting system-discontinuity) if and only if the following conditions hold:

(I.3-23) $X_0 = \{.\ |\text{org}(.|\text{multi-subsystem system with a center})\text{-industries}\,|\,\mathcal{L}^{YX}\text{-}\mathbb{C}^T\}$,

(I.3-24) $\mathcal{P}^{NS}(X_{t+1}) \neq \mathcal{P}^{NS}(X_t)$,

(I.3-25) $\mathcal{C}\!h^H(X_{B,t} - X_{\beta,s}) = \mathcal{S}(B,\beta)^H{}_X$, for $\mathcal{S} \models \mathcal{Z}\circ, {}_v\mathcal{H}$,
$\mathcal{C}\!h^L(X_{A,t} - X_{\alpha,s}) = \mathcal{S}(A,\alpha)^L{}_X$,

(I.3-26) $\{X_t, X_{t+1}, \ldots, X_{t+n}\}$ is an n-step without-center reference system,

where $\mathbb{C}^T$ represents the tranquility culture, t, s ($s < t$) are the indices of time, $X_{B,t}$ is X in t-time and B-step, $X_{\beta,s}$ is X in s-time and β-step, $X_{A,t}$ is X in t-time and A-step, $X_{\alpha,s}$ is X in s-time and α-step, $(B,\beta)^H{}_X$ is the higher–step structure of (B,β) in X, $(A,\alpha)^L{}_X$ is the lower–step structure of (A,α) in X (for example, (high-tech industry,agriculture)$^H{}_X$ is the higher-step structure of the high-tech industry and agriculture of X, (high-tech industry, agriculture)$^L{}_X$ is the lower-step structure of the high-tech industry and agriculture of X), $\mathcal{C}\!h^H(X)$ is the high-level difference of X, and $\mathcal{Ch}^{L}(X)$ is the low-level difference of X. Here $\mathcal{L}^{YX}$-$\mathbb{C}^{T}$ denotes the rationality and reasoning processes of the multi-factor causal-effect and YYWX system.

Note that, in Bcm. (I.3-26), X is a system of development jumping over more than one step, and X_t is a T^{sysD} uncertain process: $X_t \sqsubseteq T^{sysD}$.

Definition I.3-6. **n-step K^{sysD} uncertain process** is the grand system $\{X_t\} \sqsubseteq (\Omega, \mathcal{Z}\circ, {}_v\mathcal{H}, \{\mathbb{C}\})$ satisfying the following conditions:

(I.3-27) $X_0 = \{x,y\} = \{.\ |org(.|$multi-subsystem system with a center)-industries$|$
$\mathcal{L}^{ST}$-$\mathbb{C}^{K}\}$,

(I.3-28) $\mathcal{P}^{NS}(X_{t+1}) \neq \mathcal{P}^{NS}(X_t)$,

(I.3-29) $\mathcal{Ch}^{H}(X_{B,t}-X_{\beta,s}) = (B,\beta)^{H}{}_{X}$, for $\mathcal{S} \models (\Omega, \mathcal{Z}\circ, {}_v\mathcal{H}, \{\mathbb{C}\})$,
$\mathcal{Ch}^{L}(X_{A,t}-X_{\alpha,s}) = (A,\alpha)^{L}{}_{X}$,

(I.3-30) $\{X_t, X_{t+1}, \ldots, X_{t+n}\}$ is an n-step without-center reference system, i.e., X is a system of development jumping over more than one step,

where $\mathcal{L}^{ST}$ denotes the rationality and reasoning process of sciences and $\mathfrak{C}^{K}$ denotes the culture of conflict. Note that Here X_t is a K^{sysD} uncertain process: $X_t \sqsubseteq K^{sysD}$.

Appendix J – Yi-li TCentral

In making a decision between seeking profits (P) and pursuing virtue (righteousness R) in the TCentral state of win-win situation, by the principle of two-system CE balance, we shall have: $\psi\{R,\Delta\} \stackrel{*}{=} \psi\{P,\Delta\}$, or $\psi\{X,\Delta\} \stackrel{*}{=} \psi\{Y,\Delta\}$ with $\{X,Y\} = \{\text{righteousness,profits}\} \equiv \{\text{yi,li}\} \Vdash \zeta(\tau)$, $\tau \Vdash (\mathfrak{I},Ш^{Д}) \Vvdash \mathbb{T}\text{zu}^*$ (see §3.2-1). Note that the cultivation of virtue and the pursuit of profits may be considered as separate manifestations of the ultimate creativity in this world, and yet they come from the same origin. That is, virtue can be conceived as the greater profits and profits can be interpreted as the minor virtue of our life. Thus, in an integrated approach, one may attempt to treat virtue and profits as different manifestations of our life-will and creative rationality in different settings. This is what we meant: $X \Vdash \zeta(\tau)$, $\tau \Vdash (\mathfrak{I},Ш^{Д}) \Vvdash \mathbb{T}\text{zu}^*$ and $Y \Vdash \zeta(\tau)$, $\tau \Vdash (\mathfrak{I},Ш^{Д}) \Vvdash \mathbb{T}\text{zu}^*$, for $\zeta(\tau)$ being related to the ultimate force of creativity and destructivity.

Two examples of economic forces under the direction of ethics are: (1) Macro: Confucian Political economy which may be conceived as the Legalist political economy distorted under Confucianism. (2) Micro: Hui merchants in China. For these macro and micro operations, see the principle of multiple-system CE external imbalance: $\psi\{X,\Delta\} \underline{\leq} \psi\{Y,\Delta\}$ (see Subsection §3.2-1)), where$\psi\{Y,\Delta\}$ represents the operation of Confucian ethics and $\psi\{X,\Delta\}$ represents the operation of Legalist principle (in the former macro case) and business principle (in the latter micro case).

yi-li TCentral

$\Rightarrow$ {
- Political efficiency of specific types of resource allocation $\mathcal{P}$
  (inter-interest group arrangements)
- Socio-organizational efficiency of specific types of resource allocation $\mathcal{S}$
  (inter-personal arrangements at the community level)
- Economic efficiency of specific types of resource allocation $\mathcal{E}$
  (sectoral, industrial, locational, market, and price arrangements)
- Firm level efficiency $\mathcal{F}$
- Engineering efficiency of specific types of resource allocation $\mathcal{E}g$
  (research and production arrangements)
- Efficiency in life-will ω
- Efficiency in creative rationality ρ

$\Leftrightarrow$ Cultural advantage in planning and strategic manipulation C

We have one more example of the economic force operating under the direction of ethics, the Weberian protestant ethics which refers to a Christian ethics distorted by (or subjected to the control of) business interest. For this principle, see the principle of multiple-system CE external imbalance: $\psi\{X,\Delta\} \leq \psi\{Y,\Delta\}$, where $\psi\{Y,\Delta\}$ represents the operation of the business principle and $\psi\{X,\Delta\}$ represents the operation of Christian ethics.

In general, the state of yi-li TCentral of a system may create a *cultural advantage*. Note that in the case of trade protectionism of nations, the prevailing argument for it may be strengthened by resorting to this cultural advantage.[64]

In symbols, we write:

(J.1) $\mathcal{E} \leftarrow \mathcal{P} \leftarrow \mathcal{S}$

(J.2) $\mathcal{E} \leftarrow \mathcal{F} \leftarrow \mathcal{E}g$

(J.3) $\mathcal{E} \leftarrow (\omega,\rho)$.

For the economy E in the state of Yi-li TCentral, the *cultural advantage* of the economy can be written as:

$$
\begin{aligned}
\text{(J.4)}\quad & E(\mathfrak{C} \mid \psi\{yi,\Delta\} \doteq \psi\{li,\Delta\}) \\
&= E[\mathcal{E}(\xi)\_\mathcal{P}(\xi)\_\mathcal{S}(\xi),\mathcal{E}(\xi)\_\mathcal{F}(\xi)\_\mathcal{E}g(\xi),\mathcal{E}(\xi)\_\omega(\xi)\text{-}\rho(\xi) \mid (R,P) \Vdash \zeta(\tau)], \\
&= E[\mathcal{E}\_\mathcal{P}\_\mathcal{S}(\xi),\mathcal{E}\_\mathcal{F}\_\mathcal{E}g(\xi),\mathcal{E}\_\omega\text{-}\rho(\xi) \mid \xi \Vdash co(\mathfrak{C})\sqcap\zeta(\tau)],
\end{aligned}
$$

where $\xi = \{\xi \Leftarrow [\psi(yi,\Delta) \doteq \psi(li,\Delta)]\} \Vdash co(\mathfrak{C})\sqcap\zeta(\tau)$. Here, note that we write $\psi\{R,\Delta\} \equiv \psi\{yi,\Delta\}$ as $\psi(yi,\Delta)$ and $\psi\{P,\Delta\} \equiv \psi\{li,\Delta\}$ as $\psi(li,\Delta)$. The rationale of this cultural efficiency is that (1) this state of yi-li T Central will motivate the human spirit in striving for developing one's best potential, and (2) this state of yi-li T Central will help the human being to allocate scarce resources in a best way (ideally) to facilitate the operation and development of human rationality (to reach and penetrate deeply into the very sources of tao and being creativities) and thereby promote the supply-side conditions of capital formation and subsequent technological progress.

Here since the systems $X \equiv R$ (yi) and $Y \equiv P$ (li) are separately conditioned by ζ, we have, from Subsection §3.2-1 (Bcm. (3.2-1-18)): $X(\xi) \Leftarrow \zeta(\xi)$, $Y(\xi) \Leftarrow \zeta(\xi)$, $\xi = \xi(\tau)$, $\tau \Vdash (\mathfrak{I},Ш^{Д}) \Vdash \mathbb{T}zu^*$, where ξ is the force of creativity ultimately generated by $\mathbb{T}zu^*$, and ω $[\{X(\xi) \Leftarrow \zeta(\xi)\},Y(\xi) \Leftarrow \zeta(\xi)]] \Leftrightarrow [\{X,Y\} \Vdash \zeta \mid \zeta(\tau), \tau \Vdash (\mathfrak{I},Ш^{Д}) \Vdash \mathbb{T}zu^*]$. Thus for ξ in the above, we can write $\xi = \{\xi \Leftarrow [\psi(yi,\Delta) \doteq \psi(li,\Delta)] \mid [\psi(yi,\Delta) \doteq \psi(li,\Delta)] \barwedge \tau)\} \Vdash co(\mathfrak{C})\sqcap\zeta(\tau)$, $\tau \Vdash (\mathfrak{I},Ш^{Д}) \Vdash \mathbb{T}zu^*$.

By the use of the systematic-change becomings, we have the organizational efficiency chain $\mathcal{E}(\xi)\_\mathcal{P}(\xi)\_\mathcal{S}(\xi)$:

$$
\begin{aligned}
\text{(J.5)}\quad & \mathcal{E}(\xi|t) \\
&= \mathcal{E}(\xi|t_0) \oplus \mathcal{S}\{\mathcal{P}(\xi|t)\}\Delta t(\xi)\} \oplus \mathcal{S}\{\mathcal{S}(\xi|t)\}\Delta x(\xi)\} \\
&= \mathcal{E}(\xi|t_0) \oplus \mathcal{S}\Delta\{\mathcal{P}(\xi|t)t(\xi)\} \oplus \mathcal{S}\Delta\{\mathcal{S}(\xi|t)x(\xi)\} \\
&= \mathcal{E}(\xi|t_0) \oplus \{PT\} \oplus \{SX\},
\end{aligned}
$$

where $PT = \mathcal{S}\Delta\{\mathcal{P}(\xi|t)t(\xi)\}$, $SX = \mathcal{S}\Delta\{\mathcal{S}(\xi|t)x(\xi)\}$, for $x(\xi)$ being a distribution system (see Appendix I). For the engineering efficiency chain, we have the following $\mathcal{E}(\xi)\_\mathcal{F}(\xi)\_\mathcal{E}g(\xi)$:

$$
\begin{aligned}
\text{(J.6)}\quad & \mathcal{E}(\xi|t) \\
&= \mathcal{E}(\xi|t_0) \oplus \mathcal{S}\{\mathcal{F}(\xi|t)\ \Delta t(\xi)\} \oplus \mathcal{S}\{\mathcal{E}g(\xi|t)\}\Delta y(\xi)\} \\
&= \mathcal{E}(\xi|t_0) \oplus \mathcal{S}\Delta\{\mathcal{F}(\xi|t)t(\xi)\} \oplus \mathcal{S}\Delta\{\mathcal{E}g(\xi|t)y(\xi)\} \\
&= \mathcal{E}(\xi|t_0) \oplus \{FT\} \oplus \{EY\},
\end{aligned}
$$

where $FT = \mathcal{S}\Delta\{\mathcal{F}(\xi|t)t(\xi)\}$, $EY = \mathcal{S}\Delta\{\mathcal{E}(\xi|t)y(\xi)$, for $y(\xi)$ being a distribution system. As for the will-rationality efficiency chain, we have $\mathcal{E}(\xi)\_(\omega(\xi),\rho(\xi))$:

(J.7)
$$
\begin{aligned}
&\mathcal{E}(\xi|t) \\
&= \mathcal{E}(\xi|t_0) \oplus \mathcal{S}\{\omega(\xi|t)\}\Delta t(\xi)\} \oplus \mathcal{S}\{\omega(\xi|t)\}\Delta z(\xi)\} \\
&\qquad \oplus \mathcal{S}\{\rho(\xi|t)\}\Delta t(\xi)\} \oplus \mathcal{S}\{\rho(\xi|t)\}\Delta z(\xi)\} \\
&= \mathcal{E}(\xi|t_0) \oplus \mathcal{S}\Delta\{\omega(\xi|t)t(\xi)\} \oplus \mathcal{S}\Delta\{\omega(\xi|t)z(\xi)\} \\
&\qquad \oplus \mathcal{S}\Delta\{\rho(\xi|t)t(\xi)\} \oplus \mathcal{S}\Delta\{\rho(\xi|t)z(\xi)\} \\
&= \mathcal{E}(\xi|t_0) \oplus \{WT\} \oplus \{WZ\} \oplus \{RT\} \oplus \{RZ\},
\end{aligned}
$$

where $WT = \mathcal{S}\Delta\{\omega(\xi|t)t(\xi)\}$, $WZ = \mathcal{S}\Delta\{\omega(\xi|t)z(\xi)\}$, $RZ = \mathcal{S}\Delta\{\rho\,(\xi|t)t(\xi)\}$, $RZ = \mathcal{S}\Delta\{\rho\,(\xi|t)z(\xi)\}$, for $z(\xi)$ being an on-off distribution system (see Appendix I.2-22).

In the above, for $\mathcal{S}\Delta\{A(\xi|t)B(\xi)\}$, $A(\xi|t)$, $B(\xi) \sqsubseteq (\Omega,\mathbb{Z}^{\circ},{}_{v}\mathcal{H},\{\mathbb{C}\})\sqcup\mathbb{R}$ ($\mathbb{R}$ being the set of real numbers), we may define:

(J.8) $\mathcal{S}\Delta\{A(\xi|t)B(\xi)\} = \Sigma_i\, A_i \star B_i$,

for $i \in \{1,2,\ldots,n\}$ the set of positive integers, where the interaction between A and B (☆ being the impactor of interaction): A ☆ B = $\{A,B,[\Theta(A \star B)]\}$, where "⋆" is the interactor (Tonn [2006], Section 5.1).

Appendix K – General Scheme of The Society and A simple Scheme of Marriage

K.1 Introduction

Here we shall start off with the schemes of conflict and tranquil societies. In an abstract sense, for the society of conflict culture, it is from the typical individual that the most basic social unit, the household, is developed. Then from the typical household, the business community is developed from one direction (i.e., one dimension), the Christian community is developed from the other direction (i.e., the second dimension), and the political party is developed from the still other direction.

In sum, society is the simple sum of individuals. To present this above scheme in a diagram, we have Figure K.1-1 in the following.

Figure K.1-1
The symbolic structure of the conflict society

Polity
|
Business community – Core Culture – Religious Community
|
Households

In symbols, this above scheme is a 5-pole MFCE scheme: $\{H,B,\mathfrak{C},P,R\}$, where H, B, $\mathfrak{C}$, P and R represent the households, the business community, the core culture (i.e., the culture of conflict) as the (virtual) center, the polity, and the religious community (or the intellectuals-religious community), respectively.

To present this above structure in a formal scheme, let the human element $x \sqsubseteq \mathbf{H}$ be the typical person in the conflict society, and Ψ be the system-creation impactor (see §A.2-3) so that:

(K.1-1) $y = \Psi(x)$,

where $y \sqsubseteq (\Omega, \mathcal{Z}\circ, {}_{v}\mathcal{H}, \{\mathbb{C}\})$ is the most basic social unit, i.e., the household.

In terms of an MFCE scheme, the creation of the system y out of the "basic element for system-creation" x is as follows: Seeing from Section 6.2, we have a shengsheng generator (σ) such that, for $\mathbb{C}_x$ being the culture of x, $\sigma(\mathfrak{C})$: $x \rightarrow (\langle\mathbb{C}_x\rangle)/Z(\mathcal{E})$, where

(K.1-2) $(\langle\mathbb{C}_x\rangle)/Z(\mathcal{E}) = \langle\mathbb{C}_{x/Z}\rangle$.

where $Z(\mathcal{E})$, the virtual operating force of the system, is nothing but cultural force in its operating form. Here by $(\langle\mathbb{C}_x\rangle)/Z(\mathcal{E}) = \langle\mathbb{C}_{H/Z}\rangle$ is meant that the culture energy of x is immersed in the cultural energies of the virtual operating force underlying the element x while the cultural energies of the system is transforming from its potential mode into its acting mode.

Once the cultural potential is activated, then, by applying the "household generating" impactor Φ^{H}, we get

(K.1-3a) $\Phi^{H}\{<\mathbb{C}_{x/Z}>\} = < \mathbb{C}_{H} / \mathfrak{C}_{Z} > = <\mathbb{C}_{H}>/Z(\mathcal{E})$.

Note that, in the above, Bcm. (K.1.3a) can also be written as:

(K.1-3b) $\Phi^{H}\{<\mathbb{C}_{x/Z}>\} = <\dfrac{\mathbb{C}_{H}}{\mathfrak{C}_{Z}}> = \dfrac{<\mathbb{C}_{H}>}{Z(\mathcal{E})}$.

Then, by the tao-invertor of Φ^{H} operation (i.e., Φ^{HRcv}), we get

(K.1-4) $\Phi^{HRcv}\ \{<\mathbb{C}_{H}>/Z(\mathcal{E})\} \ = \ H \oplus <\mathbb{C}_{H}>$.

Now to create the business community (ξy) from the households, let ξy be an Hf-systmeism of y under the cultural core $\mathfrak{C}$. That is, seeing from Section 6.2 again, we have a shengsheng generator (σ) such that $\sigma(\mathfrak{C})$: $<\mathbb{C}_{H}> \rightarrow (<\mathbb{C}_{H}>)/Z(\mathcal{E})$, where

(K.1-5) $(<\mathbb{C}_{H}>)/Z(\mathcal{E}) \ = \ <\mathbb{C}_{H/Z}>$.

Here by $(<\mathbb{C}_{H}>)/Z(\mathcal{E}) = <\mathbb{C}_{H/Z}>$ is meant that the culture energy of the household is immersed in the cultural energies of the virtual operating force while the cultural energies of the system is transforming from its potential mode into its acting mode.

Once the cultural potential is activated, then, by applying the "business-community generating" impactor Φ^{B}, we get

(K.1-6) $\Phi^{B}\{<\mathbb{C}_{H/Z}>\} = < \mathbb{C}_{B} / \mathfrak{C}_{Z}> = \ <\mathbb{C}_{B}>/Z(\mathcal{E})$,

and by the tao-invertor of Φ^{B} operation (i.e., Φ^{BRcv}) to get

(K.1-7) $\Phi^{BRcv}\ \{<\mathbb{C}_{B}>/Z(\mathcal{E})\} \ = \ B \oplus <\mathbb{C}_{B}>$.

Analogous to the above process, in turn we derive $\xi^{2}y$, the polity, as an Hf-systemism of ξy under the realization of the cultural core $\mathfrak{C}$, and $\xi^{3}y$, the religious community, as an Hf-systemism of $\xi^{2}y$ under the realization of the cultural core $\mathfrak{C}$.

Then, the society of the conflict culture is said to be a 5-polar MFCE scheme (in a symbolic sense) if and only if the following is true: $\{H,B,\mathfrak{C},P,R\} = \{\xi^{3}y,\xi^{2}y,\mathfrak{C},\xi^{2}y,y\} \sqsubseteq (\Omega,\mathcal{Z}\circ,{}_{v}\mathcal{H},\{\mathbb{C}\})$, where the cultural core is the (virtual) center of the system. .

In an abstract sense, for the society of tranquil culture, it is from the typical individual that the most basic social unit, the family, is developed. Then from the typical family, the polity is developed in the first dimension, the intellectuals as a group is developed in the second dimension, and the business community is developed in the third dimension.

Then, the society is an organic grand system of all involved. Now to present this grand system {H,B,c,G,I} as a 5-pole MFCE scheme in a diagram, we have Figure K.1-2. In this Figure K.1-2, the cultural background may either be one of competion or one of harmony. This society must have a technological base which is understood and is omitted from it. For a non-Western society, the cultural backgrounds of its technology must be sciences under the guidance of the traditional cultures carried over to the modern time.

Figure K.1-2
Social system

Political party
|
Business community – Core Culture – The Intellectuals
|
Households

K.2 General Scheme of The Society

Below we discuss various types of single-center and two co-center families.

(1) Single-center family of Faziranism.

The family system of Faziranist centralism is based on the culture of consensual tranquility. With the reasoning patterns of yin-yang tao-reversal, the family is eventually developed into the system of groupism. This family system may be expressed below:

(K.2-1) $\{(\text{son},\text{daughter}),\text{mother}|\text{father}\} \sqsubseteq (\Omega,\mathbb{Z}\circ,{}_{v}\mathbb{H},\{\mathbb{C}\})$,

for son, daughter, mother and father $\sqsubseteq \Omega$, where father is the center, mother the secondary center, and son and daughter the non-central elements. The culture of the parents is the *virtual operating force (or virtual operating culture)* that can be transformed into the cultural capital of the children. It is the collection of these types of family capital which is then transformed into the social capital under favorable conditions.

Below let $X = \{X_1,X_2,\ldots,X_n\} \Lleftarrow <\mathbb{C}_X>$ and $[Y_k,Y_j] \Lleftarrow <\mathbb{C}_X>$ for $[Y_k,Y_j] \sqsubseteq (\Omega,\mathbb{Z}\circ,{}_{v}\mathbb{H},\{\mathbb{C}\})$, where $Y_j \equiv [(X_1,\mathbb{C}_{X1/Z}),(X_2,\mathbb{C}_{X2/Z}),\ldots,(X_n,\mathbb{C}_{Xn/Z})|(c,\sigma(c))]$, $Y_k \equiv [(c,\mathbb{C}_{C/Z})|((X_1,\xi_1(X_1)),(X_2,\xi_2(X_2)),\ldots,(X_n,\xi_n(X_n)))]$, where $\xi_i \vDash \mathbb{Z}\circ,{}_{v}\mathbb{H}$, $i = 1, 2, \ldots, n$.

Remark K.2-1. See *Remark* D.2-1 for the meanings of $\mathbb{C}_{Xi/Z}$, $\sigma(c)$, Y_i and Y_k. Essentially, $\mathbb{C}_{Xi}$ represents the energy of the non-central element X_i, $\sigma(c)$ represent the energy of the center element c, Y_j reprensents the control force of the center over the whole system, and Y_k reprensents the feedback control force of the non-central elements over the system.

Let $n = 3$, $i \neq k, j$, X_1, X_2, and X_3 be (son,daughter), the mother, and the father, respectively. If we apply the principle of CE centrality: For each X_i, $\psi\{X_j>X_k,\Delta_i\} \barwedge E$ to the family system $X = \{(\text{son},\text{daughter}),\text{mother}|\text{father}\} = \{X_1,X_2,\ldots,X_n\}$, $n = 3$, $i \neq k, j$ (for X_1, X_2, and X_3 being (son,daughter), the mother, and the father, respectively), we shall have the principle for **CE centrality**:

(K.2-2) For each X_i, $\psi\{[\mathbb{C}_{(son,daughter)/Z},\mathbb{C}_{mother/Z},\sigma(father)]$
$> [\xi(son,daughter),\zeta(mother),\mathfrak{C}_{father/Z}],\Delta_i\}$
$\bar{\wedge}\ [\mathbb{C}_X \Leftarrow E\ ],$

or $\psi\{Y_j > Y_K,\Delta_i\}\ \bar{\wedge}\ [\mathbb{C}_X \Leftarrow E\ ]$, where $Y_j = [\mathbb{C}_{(son,daughter)/Z},\mathbb{C}_{mother/Z}|\sigma(father)]$ and $Y_K = [\mathbb{C}_{father/Z}|(\xi(son,daughter),\ \zeta(mother))]$, for $\psi, \sigma, \xi, \zeta \models \mathbb{Z}_{o,v}\mathbb{H}$. That is, to any element or subsystem X_i, be it (son.,daughter), mother or father, with the cultural energy of the system (or grand system) under the constraint of the environmental energy (i.e., under the cultural energy of Faziranist centralism existing in the modern global society), the **specific CE centrality of family** is to ensure, in the dynamical motion of X_i under the actions-interactions of Heaven and Earth (i.e., Δ_i or X_i acting in Δ), the direct and active impact of the father toward the mother, the son, and the daughter (i.e., love and the provision of leadership) is greater than the indirect, passive feedback-effect of all other members to the father (i.e., respect and willingly obedience).

In general, we shall state that, by applying the principle of CE centrality to the family system X, we have the **principle of specific Tcentral of family**:

(K.2-3) For each X_i, $\psi\{[(\mathbb{C}_{X1/Z},\mathbb{C}_{X2/Z},\ldots,\mathbb{C}_{Xn/Z})|(c,\sigma(c))]$
$> [(c,\mathbb{C}_{C/Z})|(\xi_1(X_1),\xi_2(X_2),\ \ldots\ ,\xi_n(X_n))],\Delta_i\}$
$\bar{\wedge}\ [\mathbb{C}_X \Leftarrow E\ ].$

(2) Family of one center under absolute authority.

This is a culture in which tranquility is reached through coercion. In this culture, self-centered egoism forms the foundation of family life. This system may be expressed by:

(K.2-4) $\{(son,daughter),mother||father\} \sqsubseteq (\Omega,\mathbb{Z}_{o,v}\mathbb{H},\{\mathbb{C}\}),$

for son, daughter, mother and father $\sqsubseteq \Omega$. In this system, the father is the absolute center, the mother is the assistant- or semi-center, and the children are non-central elements.

Below let $X = \{X_1,X_2,\ldots,X_n\}$, X and $[Y_k,Y_j] \Leftarrow <\mathbb{C}_X>$, where $Y_j \equiv [(X_1,\mathbb{C}_{X1/Z}),(X_2,\mathbb{C}_{X2/Z}),\ldots,(X_n,\mathbb{C}_{Xn/Z})|(c,\sigma(c))]$, $Y_k \equiv [(c,\mathbb{C}_{C/Z})|((X_1,\xi_1(X_1)),(X_2,\xi_2(X_2)),\ldots,(X_n,\xi_n(X_n)))]$, for $\xi_i \Vdash \mathbb{Z}_{o,v}\mathbb{H}$, $i = 1,2,\ldots,n$.

Furthermore, let X_1, X_2, X_3 be (son,daughter), mother, and father, respectively, with $i \neq k, j$. By applying the principle of CE centrality: For each X_i, $\psi\{Y_j>Y_k,\Delta_i\}\ \bar{\wedge}\ E$ to this family system $X = \{(son,daughter),mother|father\} = \{X_1,X_2,\ldots,X_n\}$, we have: For each X_i,

(K.2-5) $\psi\{[\mathbb{C}_{(son,daughter)/Z},\mathbb{C}_{mother/Z},\sigma(father)]$
$> [\mathbb{C}_{father/Z}\ |(\xi(son,daughter),\zeta(mother))],\Delta_i\}$
$\bar{\wedge}\ [\mathbb{C}_X \Leftarrow E\ ],$

$\psi, \sigma, \xi, \zeta \models \mathbb{Z}_{o,v}\mathbb{H}$. The specific CE centrality of this family is to ensure that amid the dynamical changes of the universe, the control of the father over (son,daughter) and the mother is absolute. The is, $[\mathbb{C}_{father/Z}|(\xi(son,daughter),\zeta(mother))]$ is an empty system, or the feedback effect of (son,daughter) and the mother to the father does not exist.

Below, we turn our attention to the principle of strategic centrality. Let $\mathcal{T} \vDash \mathcal{Z}\circ,_{v}\mathcal{H}$ be the strategic impactor, $\mathcal{T}^*$ be the desirable target strategy; $\mathcal{T}^* \Leftarrow \{\Omega^{Conflict}|\Omega^{Conflict} \precsim \Omega^{Authoritarian\_organization}(e)\}$, for $e \Vdash E(\tau)$, $\tau \Vdash (\text{Ʒ},\text{Ш}^{\text{Д}}) \Vdash \mathbb{T}\text{zu}^*$. Here "e" stands for the energy generated (indirectly) by Ultimate Creativity/Destructivity. That is, $\mathcal{T}^*$ is under the constraint of the space of organizational energy $\Omega^{Conflict}$. Thus, by simultaneously applying the principle of strategic centrality at a state of T continuity, we have: For each X_i,

$$\text{(K.2-6)}\quad \{\psi\{[\mathbb{C}_{(son,daughter/Z}, \mathbb{C}_{mother/Z}|\sigma(father)]>[\mathbb{C}_{father/Z}|(\xi(son,daughter),\zeta(mother))],\Delta_i\} \barwedge [\mathbb{C}_X \Leftarrow E\,]\} \wedge X_i = \psi\{\mathcal{T}^*C > \mathcal{T}X_i,\Delta_i\} \barwedge \tau,$$

which is called the **principle of absolute authority**.

(3) Family with two centers and no children under the culture of conflict/independence.

In this system, there is no culture of tranquility. The individuals are the major players of this system, and this proto-type is developed out of the model of the atomism of the ancient Greece. Under the culture of conflict, the reasoning pattern of this system follows the mode of logic or mathematical logic. This shall converge eventually to a state of equilibrium which is one of decentralization. In a symbolic expression, this system may be presented as follows:

$$\text{(K.2-7)}\quad \{wife,husband\} \sqsubseteq (\Omega,\mathcal{Z}\circ,_{v}\mathcal{H},\{\mathbb{C}\}),\ wife,\ husband \sqsubseteq \Omega,$$

where father and mother are the co-centers always in conflict. By applying the principle of CE centrality: For each X_i, $\psi\{Y_j>Y_k,\Delta_j\} \barwedge E$ to this family X = {wife, husband}, we have the *principle of CE balance for family*:

$$\text{(K.2-8)}\quad \text{For } X_{ihusband},\ \psi\{[\mathbb{C}_{wife/Z},\sigma(husband)]>[\zeta(wife),\mathbb{C}_{husband/Z}],\Delta_{husband}\} \barwedge [\mathbb{C}_X \Leftarrow E];$$
$$\text{and for } X_{wife},\ \psi\{[\mathbb{C}_{husband/Z},\sigma(wife)]>[\xi(husband),\mathbb{C}_{wife/Z}],\Delta_{wife}\} \barwedge [\mathbb{C}_X \Leftarrow E\,],$$

where $\psi, \sigma, \xi, \zeta \vDash \mathcal{Z}\circ,_{v}\mathcal{H}$. The CE balance-in-conflict of this family system is that, under a constant state of conflict between the husband and wife, each one strives and yet fails to dominate the other. That is, in this instance, the principle of CE balance transforms into the **principle of conflict**: For each of the husband and wife,

$$\text{(K.2-9)}\quad \{\psi\{[\mathbb{C}_{wife/Z}|\sigma(husband)] > [\mathbb{C}_{husband/Z}\,|\zeta(wife)],\Delta_{husband}\} \Leftrightarrow \psi\{[\mathbb{C}_{husband/Z}|\sigma(wife)] > [\mathbb{C}_{wife/Z}|\xi(husband)],\Delta_{wife}\} = X_{wife}\} \barwedge [\mathbb{C}_X \Leftarrow E\,],$$

where the interactor "$\Leftrightarrow$" $\vDash \mathcal{Z}$ depicts the equality of power.

Look at Bcm. (K.2-9), when in this family a balance of power is reached between the husband and the wife, the principle of conflict turns into the **principle of balance-in-independence**:

For both of the husband ($X_{husband}$) and the wife (X_{wife}),

$$\text{(K.2-10)}\quad \{\psi\{[\mathbb{C}_{wife/Z}|\sigma(husband)]>[\mathbb{C}_{husband/Z}\,|\zeta(wife)],\ \Delta_{husband}\} \approx \psi\{[\mathbb{C}_{husband/Z}|\sigma(wife)]>[\mathbb{C}_{wife/Z}|\xi(husband)],\ \Delta_{wife}\}\} \barwedge [\mathbb{C}_X \Leftarrow E\,],$$

where the interactor "$\approx$" $\vDash \mathcal{H}$ depicts the equal sharing of power.

(4) Family of two centers with children under the culture of conflict/independence.
The cultural underpinning of this system is the same as in (3). In this system, there is no culture of tranquility, and the individuals are the major players of this system. Under the culture of conflict, the reasoning pattern of this system is that of logic or mathematical logic. This shall converge eventually to a state of equilibrium which is one of decentralization. In a symbolic way, we may present this system in the following scheme:

(K.2-11) $\{(\text{son,daughter}): \text{mother,father}\} \sqsubseteq (\Omega, \mathcal{Z}^{\circ}, {}_{\mathrm{v}}\mathcal{H}, \{\mathbb{C}\})$,

where son, daughter, mother, father $\sqsubseteq \Omega$, father and mother are co-centers and son and daughter are non-central members. By applying the principle of CE imbalance: For each X_i, $\psi\{Y_j > Y_k, \Delta_i\} \barwedge E$, to the family X = {(son,daughter): mother, father}, we have: For each X_i,

$$\text{(K.2-12)}\quad \begin{aligned}&\psi\{[\mathbb{C}_{(\text{son,daughter})/Z}, \mathbb{C}_{\text{mother}/Z}|\sigma(\text{father})] \\ &\quad >[\mathbb{C}_{\text{father}/Z}|(\xi(\text{son,daughter}),\zeta(\text{mother}))], \Delta_{\text{father}}\} \barwedge [\mathbb{C}_X \Leftarrow E], \\ &\psi\{[\mathbb{C}_{(\text{son,daughter})/Z}, \mathbb{C}_{\text{father}/Z}|\sigma(\text{mother})] \\ &\quad >[\mathbb{C}_{\text{mother}/Z}|(\xi(\text{son,daughte}),\zeta(\text{father}))], \Delta_{\text{mother}}\} \barwedge [\mathbb{C}_X \Leftarrow E],\end{aligned}$$

where $\psi, \sigma, \xi, \zeta \vDash \mathcal{Z}^{\circ}, {}_{\mathrm{v}}\mathcal{H}$. In the world of dynamical fluctuation and motion, the special CE balance of this family system is that each of the parents seeks to dominate the other and eventually a state of equilibrium is reached between them amid constant conflict. Below, we have the **principle of balance/independence**: for each X_i,

$$\text{(K.2-13)}\quad \begin{aligned}&\{\{\psi\{[\mathbb{C}_{(\text{son,daughter})/Z}, \mathbb{C}_{\text{mother}/Z}|\sigma(\text{father})] \\ &\quad >[\mathbb{C}_{\text{father}/Z}|\xi(\text{son,daughter}),\zeta(\text{mother})], \Delta_{\text{father}}\} \\ &\approx \{\psi\{[\mathbb{C}_{(\text{son,daughter})/Z}, \mathbb{C}_{\text{father}/Z}|\sigma(\text{mother})] \\ &\quad >[\mathbb{C}_{\text{mother}/Z}|(\xi(\text{son,daughte}),\zeta(\text{father}))], \Delta_{\text{mother}}\}\} \\ &\barwedge [\mathbb{C}_X \Leftarrow E],\end{aligned}$$

where $\approx \vDash \mathcal{H}$ depicts an impactor for the equalization of power.

On the other hand, if there is no consensus in this family, the constant state of internal conflict shall turn the principle of CE balance into the **principle of conflict**: For each X_i,

$$\text{(K.2-14)}\quad \begin{aligned}&\{\{\psi\{[\mathbb{C}_{(\text{son,daughter})/Z}, \mathbb{C}_{\text{mother}/Z}|\sigma(\text{father})] \\ &\quad >[\mathbb{C}_{\text{father}/Z}|(\xi(\text{son,daughter}),\zeta(\text{mother}))], \Delta_{\text{father}}\} \barwedge [\mathbb{C}_X \Leftarrow E]\}, \\ &\Leftrightarrow \{\psi\{[\sigma(\text{mother})|\mathbb{C}_{(\text{son,daughter})/Z}, \mathbb{C}_{\text{father}/Z}] \\ &\quad > [\mathbb{C}_{\text{mother}/Z}|(\xi(\text{son,daughte}),\zeta(\text{father}))], \Delta_{\text{mother}}\}\} \\ &\barwedge [\mathbb{C}_X \Leftarrow E]\},\end{aligned}$$

i, j = (son,daughter), mother and father, and the interactor $\Leftrightarrow \vDash \mathcal{H}$ depicts the equality of power amid constant conflict.

(5) Single-center family with children under the culture of Faziranist self-masterism.

Let a composite system of ethics under the culture of conquest-sciences and the systemic yu-wu culture (i.e., the culture of self-generating life-will and systemic rationality developed on the basis of classical yu-wu rationality) be: (A(y-,-)B(y+,+)|C(yh,c)) = (passion, rationality |will) $\sqsubseteq (\Omega, \mathcal{Z}^{\circ}, {}_{\mathrm{v}}\mathcal{H}, \{\mathbb{C}\}) \sqcap \Omega^{YW} \sqcap \Omega^{S}$, where (y-,-), (y+,+), (yh,c) $\sqsubseteq (\Omega, \mathcal{Z}^{\circ}, {}_{\mathrm{v}}\mathcal{H}, \{\mathbb{C}\})$ are contradictory elements. Here for $\alpha, \beta, \gamma \Vdash$ **U** (space of universal elements), if $\alpha \sim$ (y-,-) (i.e., α

transforming into (y-,-) so that (y-,-) ⊫ **U** becomes a primitive element in the space of universal elements), $\beta \sim$ (y+,+), $\gamma \sim$ (yh,c), then these α, β and γ are called **contradictory elements** or **self-contradicting primitive elements**.

In addition, let (y-,y+|yh) ⊑ (Ω,𝒵○,ᵥℍ,{ℂ}) be the cultural system (or the will-rationality set (ω,ρ)) of **generativity (generative individuality** or **sociality)** 𝒮 (sheng): $\sigma \equiv \{\tau|(\omega,\rho)^S\} \equiv \mathcal{S} \in \Omega^{YW}$ and (-,+|c) ⊑ (Ω,𝒵○,ᵥℍ,{ℂ}) be the cultural system with the **conflictivity** (or **conflicting sociality**) 𝒦 (ke): $\kappa \equiv \{\tau|(\omega,\rho)^K\} \equiv \mathcal{K} \in \Omega^S$.

Let 𝕋 ⊨ 𝒵○,ᵥℍ, 𝕋 ⊫ Z, be a strategic impactor and in a state of T continuity, and let the system achieve a state of SK CE balance of the will-rationality set. If (A,B|C) =𝕋{A,B}, C* = C($\mathfrak{C}^{SK}$*), (𝒯 being an impactor integrating the cultures of 𝒮 and 𝒦, $\mathfrak{C}^{SK}$ being the core of the composite culture of 𝒮 and 𝒦), then we have the **SK scheme I**:

(K.2-15) 𝕋{A(y-,-),B(y+,+)|C(yh,c)}
= (A(y-,-),B(y+,+)|C(yh,c))
= (A(-),B(+)|C(c))(y-,y+|yh)
= (A(-),B(+)|C(c))(ℋ)
= (A,B|C)(ℋ,(-,+|c))
= (A,B|C)(ℋ,𝒦)
→ (A,B|C)*
= (A*,B*|C*)
= (A*,B*|C($\mathfrak{C}^{T}$*))
= 𝕋*{A,B}.

This is a T continuity-CE balance system of Faziranist self-masterism. That is, in a state of SK balance, 𝕋{A,B} = 𝕋*{A,B}, or 𝕋 = 𝕋* be the strategic impactor of CE balance. Here, by "strategy→strategic SK balance" (𝒯,𝒦) →(𝒯,𝒦)* = (𝒯*,𝒦*) is meant to reach a state of CE balance between the forces of 𝒮 (generativity) and 𝒦 (conflict): 𝒯* = 𝒦*. Here, X is the X of T continuity/SK balance, or X = X*: {X =<T^{SK}} ∈ $Ш^{\Delta}$, ∀ X ⊑ (Ω,𝒵○,ᵥℍ,{ℂ}). If in the above, 𝕋A(y-,-),B(y+,+)} = (A,B|C)(𝒯>𝒦), then this may be treated as a harmonious system of Faziranist self-masterism. But if instead, 𝕋{A(y-,-),B(y+,+)} = (A,B|C)(𝒯<𝒦), then it could be conceived as a competitive system of Faziran self-masterism.

Let the mutual-entity X ⊫ (Ω,𝒵○,ᵥℍ,{ℂ}). Then X = (passion,rationality|will) = (A(y-,+), B(y+,-)|C(yh,c)) ⊑ (Ω,𝒵○,ᵥℍ,{ℂ}) as a composite system may be written as:

(K.2-16) X{(A(y-,+),B(y+,-),C(yh,c))}
= (A(+),B(-),C(c))(y--y+|yh)
= (A(+),B(-),C(c))(𝒯)
= (A(y-(𝒯),+)↔B(y+(𝒯),-)|C(yh(𝒯),c)).

Here 𝒯 = (y--y+|yh) is a tranquil system. If 𝒦 = (+|-||c) ⊑ (Ω,𝒵○,ᵥℍ,{ℂ}) is a conflict system, then we may also write:

(K.2-17) X{(A(y-,+),B(y+,-),C(yh,c))}
= (A(-),B(+),C(c))(y--y+|yh)
= (A(+),B(-),C(c))(𝒯)
= (A←→B|C)((+|-||c),𝒯)
= (A←→B|C)(𝒦,𝒯).

Now if $(\mathcal{K},\mathcal{T}) \rightarrow \mathcal{T}^*I$, that is, $(\mathcal{K},\mathcal{T}) = (\mathcal{T},\mathcal{T}) = \mathcal{T}(1,1)$ for I = (1,1), then X{(A(y-,+), B(y+,-), C(yh,c))} = $(A\longleftrightarrow B|C)\mathcal{T}^*I = (A\longleftrightarrow B|C)^*$, or the T continuity/SK-balance of (A,B,C). Furthermore, if $\mathcal{K}^* = \mathcal{T}^*$, then $(\mathcal{K}, \mathcal{T})^* = (\mathcal{K}^*, \mathcal{T}^*) = \mathcal{T}^*(1,1) = \mathcal{T}^*I$.

Below, let A, B $\sqsubseteq (\Omega,\mathcal{Z}\circ,{}_{\mathrm{v}}\mathcal{H},\{\mathbb{C}\})$ be systems, $\mathbb{T} \vDash \mathcal{Z}\circ,{}_{\mathrm{v}}\mathcal{H}$, $\mathbb{T} \Vdash Z$ be a strategic impactor, $\mathfrak{C}_T$ be the cultural core of $\mathbb{T}$, and $C = C(\mathfrak{C}_T)$ be the subsystem to integrate A and B. Then, by letting $\mathbb{T}\{A,B\} = (A,B|C)$, and for t = 1,2,..., $(A,B|C)_t^* = \mathbb{T}\{(A,B)_t\} = (A,B|C)_{t+1}^*$, we have $\mathbb{T}$ as the impactor of a **SK CE balanced strategy**.

(6) Single-center family with children: Competitive system.

Let a composite system of ethics under the culture of conquest-sciences and the systemic yu-wu culture be: (A(y-,-)B(y+,+)|C(yh,c)) = (passion,rationality|will) $\sqsubseteq (\Omega,\mathcal{Z}\circ,{}_{\mathrm{v}}\mathcal{H},\{\mathbb{C}\})\sqcap\Omega^{YW}\sqcap\Omega^S$, where (y-,-), (y+,+), (yh,c) $\sqsubseteq (\Omega,\mathcal{Z}\circ,{}_{\mathrm{v}}\mathcal{H},\{\mathbb{C}\})$ are contradictory elements. Here these α, β and γ, for α ~ (y-,-), β ~ (y+,+), γ ~ (yh,c), are *contradictory elements* or *self-contradicting primitive elements*.

In addition, let (y-,y+|yh) $\sqsubseteq (\Omega,\mathcal{Z}\circ,{}_{\mathrm{v}}\mathcal{H},\{\mathbb{C}\})$ be the cultural system (or the will-rationality set (ω,ρ)) with the **scientific individuality** $\mathcal{Zh} \equiv \{\tau|(\omega,\rho)^{Zh}\} \Vdash \Omega^S$ (thesis) and(-,+|c) $\sqsubseteq (\Omega,\mathcal{Z}\circ,{}_{\mathrm{v}}\mathcal{H},\{\mathbb{C}\})$ be the cultural system with $\mathcal{F} \equiv \{\tau|(\omega,\rho)^F\} \Vdash \Omega^T$ (anti-thesis) the **religious sociality**. Note that the scientific individuality constitutes a form of the active efficiency of individuality. In contrast, the type of individuality prevailing in a classical system of tranquil culture may constitute a form of the passive efficiency of individuality.

Below let us illustrate a case of integrating a culture of dialectic and a cultural complex of yu-wu and science-conquest cultures for the family system composed of a father and a mother. Let $\mathbb{T} \Vdash (\Omega,\mathcal{Z}\circ,{}_{\mathrm{v}}\mathcal{H},\{\mathbb{C}\})$, $\mathbb{T} \Vdash Z^B\sqcap Z^B$ be a strategic impactor for creating a new composite culture (Z being the action-strategic complex of systems A and B). Furthermore, let (A,B|C) = $\mathbb{T}${A,B}, A and B be the father and mother, respectively and the original cultural complex of yu-wu/science-conquest cultures be $C = C(\mathfrak{C}^{ZhF})$, for $\mathbb{T} \vDash (\Omega,\mathcal{Z}\circ,{}_{\mathrm{v}}\mathcal{H},\{\mathbb{C}\})$, $\mathbb{T} \Vdash Z^\Delta$ being the impactor to integrate the dialectic culture, the scientific individuality and the tranquil (or religious) sociality into a grand system, Z^Δ being the actions-strategic complex under the culture of dialectic, and $\mathfrak{C}^{ZhF}$ being the core of the yu-wu/conquest-scientific cultural complex. For the dialectic rationality to be integrated into the original cultural complex of this system, we have:

(K.2-18)
$$
\begin{aligned}
&\mathbb{T}\{A(y-,-),B(y+,+)\,||Z^\Delta\text{-}\mathfrak{C}^{ZhF}\}\\
&= \{(A(y-,-),B(y+,+)|C(yh,c)\,||Z^\Delta\text{-}\mathfrak{C}^{ZhF})\\
&= \{(A(-),B(+)|(y-,y+|yh\,||Z^\Delta\text{-}\mathfrak{C}^{ZhF}))\\
&= \{(A(-),B(+)|(\mathcal{F}\,||Z^\Delta\text{-}\mathfrak{C}^{ZhF})\}\\
&= \{(A,B|C)(\mathcal{F},(-,+|c)\,||Z^\Delta\text{-}\mathfrak{C}^{ZhF})\}\\
&= \{A,B|(\mathcal{F},\mathcal{Zh})\}.
\end{aligned}
$$

If $\{A,B|(\mathcal{F},\mathcal{Zh})\} \rightarrow \{A,B|\mathcal{F}{<}\mathcal{Zh}\}$, then it becomes a competitive system. Here $\mathcal{Zh}$ may represent "the power of the father seeking to dominate the mother," and $\mathcal{F}$ "the power of the mother seeking to dominate the father."

K.3 Family and Marriage Relationships

Let A(-,+|c), B(y-,y+|yh) ⊑ (Ω,$\mathbb{Z}$o,$_v\mathbb{H}$,{ℂ}) be male and female human elements, respectively, and $\mathcal{T}$ ⊨ $\mathbb{Z}$o,$_v\mathbb{H}$, $\mathcal{T}$ ⊩ Z be an interactor of marriage. If

(K.3-1) $\mathcal{T}${A(-,y+|c),B(y-,+|yh)}
= (A(-,y+),B(y-,+))(c,yh)
= (A(-),B(+))(y-,y+;c,yh)
= (A,B)(-,+,c;y-,y+,yh)
= (A,B)(f,m),

for (f,m) → (f=m)*, (A,B)(f=m)* = M{A,B}, M(.) being a marriage system, then $\mathcal{T}$ is a marriage interactor. Here (f=m)* = {(f,m) =<$T^{C\Delta}$} ⊩ $Ш^{\Delta}$ is a TCentral state of the marriage system (a specific T continuity/CE-balance); M{A,B} is the marriage system between A and B, with B(y-,.|.) being a yin-element and A(.,y+|.) being a yang-element.

Family relationship. Let A(-,+|c), B(y-,y+|yh) ⊑ (Ω,$\mathbb{Z}$o,$_v\mathbb{H}$,{ℂ}) be male and female human elements, respectively, $\mathcal{T}$ ⊨ $\mathbb{Z}$o,$_v\mathbb{H}$, $\mathcal{T}$ ⊩ Z be a marriage interactor. Then in **the scheme of marriage** Bcm. (K.3.1), if C ⊑ (Ω,$\mathbb{Z}$o,$_v\mathbb{H}$,{ℂ}) is a child, F ⊨ $\mathbb{Z}$o,$_v\mathbb{H}$, $\mathcal{T}$ ⊩ Z is a family impactor, M{A,B} → F{C,B,A}, F{C,B,A} = {C,B|A} is a family system, Then F{C,B,A} is a family system with a loose power structure.

Suppose A, B are systems in SK CE balance and let C = C($\mathfrak{C}^T$) be the culture of the system for $\mathfrak{C}^{SK}$ being the cultural core. In addition, let $\mathcal{T}$\{A,B} = (A,B|C), $\mathcal{T}$ being a subsystem-creating impactor of A and B. For t = 1, 2, ..., if $\mathcal{T}$\{$(A,B)_t$} = $(A,B|C)_{t+1}$ = $(A,B|C)_t$ = (A,B|C)*, that is, (A,B|C) does not change over time (because all involved are in their respective desirable target state), then $\mathcal{T}$ is an *SK CE balanced strategic impactor.*

In sum, a marriage system of tranquil culture is stable, while that of conflict culture may be unstable. That is, the marriage under tranquil culture is more stable than the marriage under conflict culture. To illustrate this point, let $\mathcal{T}$* = ($\mathcal{T}$a,$\mathcal{T}$b) ⊨ $\mathbb{Z}$o,v$\mathbb{H}$ be a marriage impactor, where $\mathcal{T}$a and $\mathcal{T}$b are the marriage impactors of a and b, respectively. Now suppose $\mathcal{M}$\{a,b} is a marriage system, $\mathcal{T}$ being a marriage impactor, where $\mathcal{T}$aa refers to the potentiality for marriage of a yin-element, $\mathcal{T}$bb refers to the potentiality for marriage of a yang-element, a(.|y-) is a human-yin element, b(.|y+) is a human-yang element, s_a is in a T continuity/CE balanced state of s_{an}, and s_b is in a T continuity/CE balanced state of s_{bn} for s_{an} and s_{bn} being the energies-of-love of a and b, respectively. Then for (a,b) = (a(.|$\mathcal{T}$aa(y-)), b(.|$\mathcal{T}$bb(y+))), we have:

(K.3-2) $\mathcal{M}$\{.}
→ (a,b)
→ (a(.|$\mathcal{T}$a(y-)), b(.|$\mathcal{T}$b(y+)))
= ($\mathcal{T}$aa(.|s_{an}),$\mathcal{T}$bb(.|s_{bn})|(y-,y+))
= ($\mathcal{T}$a,$\mathcal{T}$b){a(.| s_{an}),b(.|s_{bn})|(y-,y+)}.

If s_{an} → s_a* and s_{bn} → s_b*, for s_{an}, s_a*, s_{bn}, s_b*∈ℝ, and ($\mathcal{T}$a,$\mathcal{T}$b) is a continuous function, then

(K.3-3) $\lim_{n\to\infty}$ ($\mathcal{T}$a,$\mathcal{T}$b){a(.|s_{an}),b(.|s_{bn})|(y-,y+)}
= ($\mathcal{T}$a,$\mathcal{T}$b){a(.|s_a*(y-))←→b(.|s_b*(y+))}
= $\mathcal{T}$\{a(.|s_a*(y-))←→b(.|s_b*(y+))}.

But if $\mathcal{T}${a,b} belongs to a tranquil system (yin,yang|love) (i.e., s_a* and s_b* are dominated by the love factor s_M), then $\mathcal{T}${a(.|s_a*(y-))←—→b(.|s_b*(y+))} is equivalent to $\mathcal{M}$(a,b). Here $\mathcal{T}$aa and $\mathcal{T}$bb are the elements carrying potentials of a and b for marriage, respectively. In addition, a and b carry energies of love, both representing the intensity of love, respectively. Furthermore, if a(.|$\mathcal{T}$aa(y-)) and b(.|$\mathcal{T}$bb(y+)) are elements of a tranquil system, then this marriage is more stable. Here, by the yin-yang integration of elements with deep affection and love, the marriage is tight. Below, we shall express this marriage by symbolic schemes.

Let (f(yin element),m(yang element)) = (f(y-,-|yin element), m(y+,+|yanf element)) = (f(-),m(+))(y-,y+|energy of love(yin element,yang element)) → M{f(-)←—→m(+)}. Then (y-,y+|energy of love(yin element,yang element)) = (y-←—→y+|love)* =(y-←—→y+|(yin element*,yang element*)) = (y-←—→y+|Y*I), with Y* being the love energy of the yang element, I = (1,1)).

Suppose a(.|$\mathcal{T}$aa(-)) and b(.|$\mathcal{T}$bb(+)) are the negative (or explicit) element and the positive (or implicit) element of a conflict culture, respectively, then the marriage will be less stable. Here because the positive and negative energies of love are in constant conflict, love may not be maintained for long. Eventually, it is quite possible to lead to a divorce.

For this marriage scheme, let K = (y-←|→y+), H = (y-←|→y+|energy of love (yin element,yang element), H* = (y--←|→y+|Y*I). Suppose (K|H*) → (K>H), then M(f(-),m(+))) = (f,m)(-,+|(y-←|→y+)*) = (f,m)(K,H*) → (f,m)(K>H) → D{f,m}, where D{.} is an impactor of divorce. That is, in a conflict system (i.e., a system with conflict culture), for $\mathcal{T}$ ⊨ $\mathbb{Z}$o,v$\mathbb{H}$ as the marriage/divorce impactor:

(K.3-4) $\lim_{n\to\infty}$ ($\mathcal{T}$a,$\mathcal{T}$b){a(.|s_{an}),b(.|s_{bn})|(s←↑→t)}
= $\mathcal{T}${a(.|s_a*(s)) ←↑→b(.|s_b*(t))} ⇒ divorce

is a divorce process in a competitive system (in which tranquil culture dominates conflict culture). Then,

(K.3.5) $\lim_{n\to\infty}$ ($\mathcal{T}$a,$\mathcal{T}$b){a(.|s_{an}),b(.|s_{bn})|(z|f)}
= $\mathcal{T}$ {a(.|s_a*(z))|b(.|s_b*(f))}

is a "tight process of marriage" (which is ultimately stable).

Before the end of this subsection, let us present a summary case of creating a marriage and family system as follows

Creation of marriage and family system. Let x (female, mother), y (male, father), c (child) ⊫ X ⊑ (Ω,$\mathbb{Z}$o,v$\mathbb{H}$,{ℂ}) be human elements and η, ψ ⊨ $\mathbb{Z}$o,v$\mathbb{H}$ be system-creation impactors so that φ is a marriage impactor and η is a family-creation impactor. Then

(K.3-6) η{φ{x}} = η{x,y} = {c|(x,y)},

where φ creates a marriage system {x,y} from the element x ⊫ X and ψ creates a family with a child c from the family {x,y} with φ{x} and η{φ{x}} ⊑ (Ω,$\mathbb{Z}$o,v$\mathbb{H}$,{ℂ}).

For Bcm. (K.3-5), we have:

(i) The condition for CE centrality: For each X_i,

$$\text{(K.3-7)}\quad \psi\{[\mathbb{C}_{child/Z}|\sigma(\text{father,mother})]>[\mathbb{C}_{(father,mother)/Z}|\xi(\text{child})],\Delta_i\} \,\bar{\wedge}\, [\mathbb{C}_X \Leftarrow E],$$

for $\psi, \sigma, \xi, \zeta \vDash \mathcal{Z}^{\circ},{}_{v}\mathcal{H}$. That is to say, in the dynamical motion of X_i under the actions-motions of Δ (i.e., Δ_i acting on X_i), the direct and active impact of the parents (i.e., love and the provision of leadership) is greater than the indirect, passive feedback-effect of the child toward the parents (i.e., respect and willing obedience).

(ii) The condition for the marriage-family CE balance is:

$$\text{(K.3-8)}\quad \text{For } X_{husband},\ \psi\{[\mathbb{C}_{wife/Z}|\sigma(\text{husband})] \geq [\mathbb{C}_{husband/Z}|\zeta(\text{wife})],\Delta_{husband}\} \,\bar{\wedge}\, [\mathbb{C}_X \Leftarrow E],$$
$$\text{for } X_{wife},\ \psi\{[\mathbb{C}_{husband/Z}|\sigma(\text{wife})] \geq [\mathbb{C}_{wife/Z}|\xi(\text{husband})],\Delta_{wife}\} \,\bar{\wedge}\, [\mathbb{C}_X \Leftarrow E]$$

in which either the parents are in a constant state of conflict or both achieve a state of the equality or balance of power.

K.4 A Cultural Approach to Systematic-Change Becoming

In this subsection, we shall employ the methods of reversal construction and systemic-change becoming in our attempt to uncover the structure of a polity.

Below, by employing the method of reversal construction, we deconstruct the society backeard to its core community A and then to the typical individual that constitutes this society. Here, the community A may be considered as the system with a weak center.

Under a *society of tranquil and homogeneous culture*, for a society $S \sqsubseteq (\Omega, \mathcal{Z}^{\circ},{}_{v}\mathcal{H}, \{\mathbb{C}\})$ as a system, let S be decomposable backward to its core $S/\mathfrak{C}_c$ (reversal-construction sub-system) where $\mathfrak{C}_c$ is the **unit of reversal construction** (also see Appendix C, Sections C.2, C.3) underlying this society S, and f, g, k $\vDash \mathcal{Z}^{\circ},{}_{v}\mathcal{H}$. For a graphical presentation, see Figure K.4-1.

Figure K.4-1
Reduction of the society to its core

$$\begin{array}{ccc} & k & \\ S & \dashrightarrow & S' \\ f\searrow & & \nearrow g \\ & S/\mathfrak{C}_c & \end{array}$$

In Figure K.4-1, S depicts the social structure in question, S' the operation of this society, with $\mathscr{C}_S = S/\mathfrak{C}_c$ standing for the **core-unit** of the society in reversal construction (i.e, the most representative unit of the society). That is, by deconstruct S through the impactor f to $S/\mathfrak{C}_c$, we retrieves the core-unit of the society, and by going through the impactor h, we reaches S' (S' being the operations of the society S). If the system commutes, then k = g#f is a composite impactor.

Now we turn to the method of systematic-change becoming. Let us further assume that, $S \sqsubseteq (\Omega, \mathbb{Z}\circ, {}_v\mathbb{H}, \{\mathbb{C}\})$ is a completely separable system (i.e., IND-sys), $S = S_{co} \oplus S_n$, S_{co} and S_n are the core and the non-core of the society, respectively (assuming S is separable into S_{co} and S_n, for $\oplus \models \mathbb{Z}\circ, {}_v\mathbb{H}$ being an IND-sys impactor and S being an h-systemism of S_{co}, $S = h(S_{co})$), and $\oplus$, $h \models \mathbb{Z}\circ, {}_v\mathbb{H}$. Then, from the systematic-change becoming:
(K.4-1) $\{\{[S \oplus S_{co}] \circledast Is\} = \sigma \Vdash \Sigma^{TC}$.

Here "$\sigma \Vdash \Sigma^{TC}$" means σ is in a state of simple Tcentral. Then, for S being in a state of simple T Central, we have:

(K.4-2) $[S \oplus S_{co}] \circledast Is = \Phi$,

where for a variable y, the notation "$y = \Phi$" denotes y being in a state of simple T Central. That is, "$\sigma \Vdash \Sigma^{TC}$" implies "$\sigma = \Phi$," and vice versa.

Then for Bcm. (K.4-2), we have a solution:

(K.4-3) $S(.) = [\alpha_1 S(\mathbb{H}_1;.) \oplus \alpha_o S(\mathbb{H}_o;.)] \circledast Is(\mathbb{H};.)$,

with $\mathbb{H}_o$ being the core culture of S_o in a state of simple Tcentral, α_o the characteristics of S_o remaining to be S_o over time, $\mathbb{H}_1$ the core culture in a state of simple Tcentral that characterizes S, and α_1 the characteristics that transforms S_{co} into a higher stage form $S = h(S_{co})$ (h being the impactor of an h-systemism).

Under the *society of conflict and diverse culture*, for a society $X \sqsubseteq (\Omega, \mathbb{Z}\circ, {}_v\mathbb{H}, \{\mathbb{C}\})$ as a system, let $X = \{X_{CO}, X_N\} = X_{CO} \oplus X_N$ (X_{CO} and X_N being the core and non-core of the society, respectively, assuming X is decomposable into X_{CO} and X_N, X_{CO} is an f-systemism of S_{co} (of the tranquil and homogenous system), X_N is an f-systemism of S_n (of the tranquil and homogenous system), for $S = \{S_{co}, S_n\} = S_{co} \oplus S_n$ and $X_{CO} = h(S_{co})$, $X_N = h'(S_n)$, and h, h', $\oplus \models \mathbb{Z}\circ, {}_v\mathbb{H}$.

Figure K.4-2
Reduction of the core to the individual

$$\begin{array}{ccc} & \gamma & \\ S & \dashrightarrow & X \\ \alpha \searrow & & \nearrow \beta \\ & S/\mathfrak{C}_c & \end{array}$$

Then, from the systematic-change becoming:

(K.4-4) $\{[X \oplus X_n \oplus X_{co}] \circledast Ix\} = \sigma \Vdash \Sigma^{TC}$,

we have:

(K.4-5) $[X \oplus X_n \oplus X_{co}] \circledast Ix = \Phi$

in a state of simple Tcentral. Consequently, we have a solution:

(K.4-6) $X(.) = [\alpha_X X(\mathbb{H}_X;.) \oplus \alpha_n X(\mathbb{H}_n;.) \oplus \alpha_{co} X(\mathbb{H}_{co};.)] \circledast Ix(\mathbb{H}_{co};.)$,

with $\mathbb{H}_{co}$ being the core culture of X_{co}, α_{co} the characteristics that keeps X_{co} constant over time, $\mathbb{H}_n$ the core culture of S_n, α_n the characteristics of S_n leading to its transformation into a higher stage form $Hf(X_{co}) = X_N$ (Hf being the impactor of Hf-systemism), $\mathbb{H}_X$ the core culture of S, α_X the characteristics of S leading to the transformation of $X(\mathbb{H}_X;.)$ into X over time, for X being an "h-systemism" of (X_N,X_{co}). Here this "h-systemism" is the same as the regular h-systemism except that in this case the underlying culture is that of conflict.

Appendix L – Systematic Approach to The Structure of Polity

In this Appendix, we shall approach the problems of the general polity from three directions: the approach of reversal-construction and systematic-change becoming, the application of the principle of CE balance-centrality, and the patterns of yin-yang tao-reversal.

L.1 A Scheme of Diplomacy/Global Strategy

Let the grand system be an n-pole YYMF scheme: $X = \{X_1,X_2,\ldots,X_n\} \sqsubseteq (\Omega,\mathbb{Z}\circ,{}_{v}\mathbb{H},\{\mathbb{C}\})$, X and $(Y_k,Y_j) \Lleftarrow <\mathbb{C}_X>$, for $(Y_k,Y_j) \sqsubseteq (\Omega,\mathbb{Z}\circ,{}_{v}\mathbb{H},\{\mathbb{C}\})$, where in general, $Y_j \equiv [(X_1, \mathbb{C}_{X1/Z}),(X_2, \mathbb{C}_{X2/Z}),\ldots,(X_n,\mathbb{C}_{Xn/Z}),(C,\sigma(C))]$, $Y_k \equiv [(X_1,\xi_1(X_1)),(X_2,\xi_2(X_2)),\ldots,(X_n,\xi_n(X_n)),(C,\mathbb{C}_{C/Z})]$, $\xi_i \models \mathbb{Z}\circ,{}_{v}\mathbb{H}$, $i = 1,2,\ldots,n$. Note that in some special cases, for these Y_j and Y_k, we would have: $Y_k \equiv [(X_1,\xi_1(X_1)),(X_2,\xi_2(X_2)),\ldots,(X_n,\xi_n(X_n))|(C,\mathbb{C}_{C/Z})]$ and $Y_k \equiv [(C,\mathbb{C}_{C/Z})|((X_1,\xi_1(X_1)),(X_2,\xi_2(X_2)), \ldots,(X_n,\xi_n(X_n)))]$.

Then, for $X = \chi \oplus <\mathbb{C}_X^T>$ achieving CE balance at a state of T continuity, below is a scheme that will lead to a solution:

(L.1-1) Under the operation of each X_i, $\varphi\{X\} = X$, for all $i = 1,2,\ldots,n$, $i \neq k,j$, with $\varphi \models \mathbb{Z}\circ,{}_{v}\mathbb{H}$ being the system's impactor; and

(L.1-2) the system is under the constraint of the pure dynamical structure $\Delta \in \Omega$.

For deriving the solution, let

(L.1-3) $T = X^{\curlyvee} \Delta$,

where $^{\curlyvee} \models \mathbb{Z}\circ,{}_{v}\mathbb{H}$ is the impactor connecting X and Δ. Suppose that this operation is undertaken in the environments of both system-side over-all operations (i.e., the operations of the mutual-entity) and individual's operations (i.e., the operations of the self-entity). Thus, we have:

(L.1-4)
$$
\begin{aligned}
&(\varphi\{T\})_{X1,\ldots,Xn} \\
&= (\varphi\{X^{\curlyvee} \Delta\})_{X1,\ldots,Xn,I(x1,\ldots,xn)} \\
&= (\varphi\{X,\Delta\})_{X1,\ldots,Xn} \ltimes \varphi\{I(x_1,\ldots,x_n),E\} \\
&= \{(\varphi\{X\}\otimes \psi\{Y_\alpha>Y_\alpha',\Delta\} \\
&\quad \otimes (\varphi\{X\}\otimes\psi\{Y_\beta>Y_\beta',\Delta\} \\
&\quad \otimes (\varphi\{X\}\otimes\psi\{X_\Upsilon>X_\Upsilon',\Delta\} \\
&\quad \otimes (\varphi\{X\}\otimes\psi\{X_\delta>X_\delta',\Delta\} \ltimes \varphi\{I_X,E\},
\end{aligned}
$$

(for the subscript X, we have: $X = \{X_1,X_2,\ldots,X_n\}$) where Y_α is the factor matching the force of Y_α' in an act of coordination or rivalry (i.e., Y_α is one of Y_j's, and Y_α' is one of Y_k's), and similarly we define those factors Y_β, Y_Υ, Y_δ, Y_β', Y_Υ' and Y_δ'.

That is, we derive the *principle of CE balance*: For each X_i,

(L.1-5)
$$
\begin{aligned}
&\psi\{Y_\alpha>Y_\alpha',\Delta\} \doublebarwedge \tau, \\
&\psi\{Y_\beta>Y_\beta',\Delta\} \doublebarwedge \tau, \\
&\psi\{Y_\Upsilon>Y_\Upsilon',\Delta\} \doublebarwedge \tau, \\
&\psi\{Y_\delta>Y_\delta',\Delta\} \doublebarwedge \tau.
\end{aligned}
$$

This principle means that: (1) For a short-term strategy, a nation should work closely with those friendly nations Y_α, and attack those unfriendly nations Y_α' (following $\psi\{Y_\alpha > Y_\alpha', \Delta\} \bar{\bar{\wedge}} \tau$). (2) For a short-term strategy, a nation should try to enhance the relationships with those partially unfriendly nations Y_β, and neutralize those not-entirely unfriendly nations Y_β' (following $\psi\{Y_\beta > Y_\beta', \Delta\} \bar{\bar{\wedge}} \tau$). (3) For a long-term strategy, one should try to maintain and even further develop close relationships with those nations expected to be friendly Y_Υ and try to neutralize those expected to be unfriendly Y_Υ' (following $\psi\{Y_\Upsilon > Y_\Upsilon', \Delta\} \bar{\bar{\wedge}} \tau$). (4) For a long-term strategy, a nation must concentrate in order to attack it's major enemies Y_δ, but simultaneously pay less attention to it's minor enemies Y_δ' (following $\psi\{Y_\delta > Y_\delta', \Delta\} \bar{\bar{\wedge}} \tau$.

L.2 A General Scheme of Polity

In this subsection, we shall discuss some basic features of the political systems of capitalism, Faziranism and absolute authority.

Competitive or democratic polity is a complex composed of a conflict system and a tranquil system in which the former dominates the latter. That is, a competitive polity is a grand system in which the conflict sub-system is the center, while tranquil sub-system is a non-central system. In this grand system, the center has a power of weak dominance. This domination is weak and not complete because the non-center members are in positions to exercise strong feedback effects on the center.

Faziranist polity is a harmonious political system in which tranquil system dominates conflict system. That is, this harmonious system is a composite system in which the tranquil subsystem is the center, while the conflict subsystem is the non-central system. In this case, the domination is strong.

Authoritarian polity is a coerced harmonious political system in which tranquil system dominates conflict system. That is, this system is a composite system in which the tranquil subsystem is the center, while the conflict subsystem is the non-central system. In this case, the domination is complete, because the non-center members are unable to exert any feedback effect on the operation of the center.

In the following, we start with the discussion of the system of Faziranism.

(1) System of Faziranist centralism.

With a tranquil spirituality and the classical yu-wu rationality (or the reasoning patterns of the mode of yin-yang tao-reversal), this system develops its structure around the core link of the nucleus family. We may depict the structure of this system as follows:

(L.2-1) $\{(\text{agr},\text{ind},\text{merc}),\text{intl},\text{off} | \text{Emp}\} \sqsubseteq (\Omega, \mathbb{Z}\circ, {}_{\text{v}}\mathbb{H}, \{\mathbb{C}\})$,

where the Emp (the Emperor) is the center, (agr,ind,merc) (agr = peasants, ind = handicraft industrialists, merc = merchants), intl (intellectuals) and off (government officials) are non-central subsystems; the political status of the government officials and the intellectuals are higher than those of the merchants, handicraft-industrialists, and peasants. In this grand system, the government officials and the intellectuals may be considered as the secondary co-centers.

Remark L.2-1. The cultures of government officials and the intellectuals constitute the system of the virtual operational force, from which the upper-cultures of the peasants, handicraftsmen and merchants are developed. That is, the cultural capital of the gentry class (composed of the government officials and the intellectuals) transforms itself into the upper-cultural capital of those being ruled (i.e., the peasants, handicraftsmen and the merchants). But the lower-cultures of the ruled can not be transformed into a constituting part (of the system) of the virtual operating force. Furthermore, these lower-cultures can not be transformed into a part of the culture of the ruling class (i.e., the cultures of the emperor, the government officials and the intellectuals) by going through the virtual operating force. Certainly, this lower culture of the ruled constitutes a constraint on the sphere of operations of the upper-culture of the polity.

Let us denote the culture of the ruled, the culture of the semi-ruling class and the power (or the generative power) of the center by $\mathbb{C}_{(agr,ind,merc)/Z}$, $\mathbb{C}_{(intl,off)/Z}$, and $\sigma(emp)$, respectively. Let the non-central and semi-co-central sub-systems have some feedback effects on the center, and these shall be depicted by $\xi(agr,ind,merc)$ and $\zeta(intl,off)$, where $\xi \models \mathbb{Z}\circ,_v\mathbb{H}$ and $\zeta \models \mathbb{Z}\circ,_v\mathbb{H}$ are the generative impactor of the culture of non-center and that of the semi-co-center, respectively. Note that here we have: $\xi(agr,ind,merc)$: $<\mathbb{C}_c> \rightarrow <\mathbb{C}_c>/Z(\mathscr{E}) = <\mathbb{C}_{c/Z}>$ and $\zeta(intl,off)$: $<\mathbb{C}_c> \rightarrow <\mathbb{C}_c>/Z(\mathcal{E}) = <\mathbb{C}_{c/Z}>$. Here the subscript c stands for the center of the system in question.

Then, if we apply the principle of CE centrality (Bcm (4.2-4): For each X_i, $\psi\{Y_j>Y_k,\Delta\} \bar{\bar{\barwedge}}\ \tau$) to the polity $X = \{(agr,ind,merc),intl,off|Emp\}$, we have: For each X_i,

$$\text{(L.2-2)}\quad \psi\{[\mathbb{C}_{(agr,ind,merc)/Z},\mathfrak{C}_{(intl,off)/Z}|\sigma(emp)] > [\mathbb{C}_{Emp/Z}|(\xi(agr,ind,merc),\zeta(intl,off))],\Delta_i\} \bar{\bar{\barwedge}} [\mathbb{C}_X \Leftarrow E],$$

where $\psi, \sigma, \xi, \zeta \models \mathbb{Z}\circ,_v\mathbb{H}$. That is, for any sub-system X_i (X_i being (peasants, handicraftsmen, merchants), the intellectuals, or government officials), under the constraints of the physical environments of land, climate, and the permanent threat of northern people, by the operation of the cultural energy (of classical Faziranist centralism), the CE centrality of the political subsystem is to guarantee that, in the processes of systemic dynamics and in the generative creativity of Heaven and Earth (or by the forces of Δ_i -- the operations of X_i in the pure dynamical structure Δ), the active impact of the power of the Emperor over any sub-system (in exercising control in order to maintain its absolute power) is very powerful, and the feedback effects of any subsystem is extremely limited.

Now we shall develop a scheme of the official-based Faziranist polity (Guanben Faziranism). Let $F \sqsubseteq (\Omega,\mathbb{Z}\circ,_v\mathbb{H},\{\mathbb{C}\})$ be a 5-polar MFCE scheme:

$$\text{(L.2-3)}\quad F = \{F_1,F_2,F_3,F_4,F_5\}=\{F_f \oplus <\mathbb{C}_f>, F_- \oplus <\mathbb{C}_->, CF, F_+ \oplus <\mathbb{C}_+>, F_s \oplus <\mathbb{C}_s>\}.$$

To generate an emperor-based Faziranist polity, let F_1 be (the subsystem of) the peasants, F_2 the handicraftsman-merchant class, F_4 the intellectuals, and F_5 the military sector. Furthermore, let the center $CF \equiv F_3$ stand for the emperor and the group of the officials serving him, and let the cultural complex of this system be that of Legalism- Confucianism-Taoism. Then this grand system F represents the grand system of emperor-based Faziranism.

Based on the Faziranist scheme presented in the above, we shall develop a scheme of Faziranist self-masterism as follows.

A polity of Faziranist self-masterism. Let $Z = K\{\{F\}S\} \sqsubseteq (\Omega, \mathbb{Z}_{\circ}, {}_{v}\mathbb{H}, \{\mathbb{C}\})$, where F is a system of Faziranist centralism, {.}S a production-oriented socialist system with its impactor, K{.} a democratic capitalist system with its impactor. In the following, let the interactive operations of these three systems be *non-commutative*: $\{K\{F\}\}S \neq K\{\{F\}S\}$. To facilitate the manipulation of our systemic complex, let

(L.2-4) $K\{\{F\}S\} \equiv K^*(F\#S) = K^*(\{F_1,F_2,F_3,F_4,F_5\}\#S)$,

for the classical system of Faziranist centralism $F = \{F_1,F_2,F_3,F_4,F_5\}$, where $* \vDash \mathbb{H}$ stands for the interactor between K and (F#S), and $\# \vDash \mathbb{H}$ represents the interactor between the systems F and S. Then we write this $K^*(\{F_1,F_2,F_3,F_4,F_5\}\#S)$ as Z:

(L.2-5) $$Z = \{z_f \oplus \langle\mathbb{C}_{zf}\rangle, z_- \oplus \langle\mathbb{C}_{z-}\rangle, Cz, z_+ \oplus \langle\mathbb{C}_{z+}\rangle, z_s \oplus \langle\mathbb{C}_{zs}\rangle\}$$
$$= \{Z_1,Z_2,Z_3,Z_4,Z_5\} = Z = Z_Z \oplus \langle\mathbb{C}_{ZF}\rangle.$$

Here K, F and $S \sqsubseteq (\Omega, \mathbb{Z}_{\circ}, {}_{v}\mathbb{H}, \{\mathbb{C}\})$, and because $Z \sqsubseteq \Omega$ (by assumption) is one of a 5-polar system, we write Z as $\{Z_1,Z_2,Z_3,Z_4,Z_5\}$. For a detail illustration of this K{{F}S}, see Tonn (2001, Section 5 of Lecture V). In this 5-polar MFCE system, let Z_1 be the citizens' sector, Z_2 the private business sector, Z_3 the people-elected government constructed on the basis of the elitist party politics, Z_4 the public sector, Z_5 the R&D sector based on the public engagement with private assistance. If in this system, the systemic yu-wu culture is actively interacting with the culture of sciences, to be flanked by the utilitarian spirit-and-rationality of capitalism and the democratic orientation of socialism, then this would set a stage for the beginning of a new era of polity. Eventually a new system will be created out of this foundation. Then, for the spirit and mechanism of sef-masyterism to prevails, it shall lead to a new system of polity for the human kind.

(2) Conflicting democratic polity.

In this system, there is no harmonious consensus. The individuals are the major players of this system, and this proto-type is developed out of the model of the atomism of the ancient Greece. Under the culture of conflict, the reasoning pattern of this system is a mode of logic or mathematical logic. This system is supposed to converge eventually to a state of equilibrium which is then a state of decentralization. In a symbolic expression, we may present this grand system as follows:

(L.2-6) $\{\text{citz},\text{cap}:\text{jud},\text{leg},\text{exec}\} \sqsubseteq (\Omega, \mathbb{Z}_{\circ}, {}_{v}\mathbb{H}, \{\mathbb{C}\})$,

where jud (i.e., judiciary branch of the government), leg (i.e., legislative branch of the government), and exec (i.e., executive branch of the government) are the co-central subsystems, and citz (the citizens) and cap (the capitalists) are non-central subsystems. By applying the principle of CE centrality (i.e., for each X_i, $\psi\{Y_j > Y_k, \Delta_j\} \;\bar{\bar{\barwedge}}\; E$) to this polity $X=\{\text{citz},\text{cap}:\text{Jud},\text{leg},\text{exec}\}$, we have: For each X_i,

(L.2-7) $$\psi\{[\mathbb{C}_{citz/Z},\mathbb{C}_{cap/Z}|\sigma(\text{jud},\text{leg},\text{exec})] > [\mathbb{C}_{jud,leg,exec/Z}|(\xi(\text{citz}),\zeta(\text{cap}))],\Delta_i\}$$
$$\bar{\bar{\barwedge}}\; [\mathbb{C}_X \Lleftarrow E\,],$$

where $\psi, \sigma, \xi, \zeta \vDash \mathbb{Z}_{\circ}, {}_{v}\mathbb{H}$, i = jud, leg, exec, citz, cap, $Y_j = [\mathbb{C}_{citz/Z},\mathbb{C}_{cap/Z}|\, \sigma(\text{jud},\text{leg},\text{exec})]$, $Y_k = [\mathbb{C}_{jud,leg,exec/Z}|(\xi(\text{citz}),\zeta(\text{cap}))]$; and at the same time: $X_{cap} > X_{citz}$.. That is, the feedback effect of the capitalist on the government (X_{cap}) far exceeds that of the citizens on the government (X_{citz}).

Some of the conditions of the Tcentral state of this system are apparently that (1) the executive branch of the government fails to control the other two branches, and each of the other two branches fails to control the executive branch as well, (2) constant conflict prevails among these three branches of the government, and (3) the citizens and the capitalists are not controlled absolutely by the government.

For a systematic expression, let the democratic polity $C \sqsubseteq (\Omega, \mathcal{Z}_{\circ,\vee}\mathcal{H}, \{\mathbb{C}\})$ be a 5-polar MFCE system as follows:

(L.2-8) $C = \{C_1, C_2, C_3, C_4, C_5\} = \{C_f \oplus <\mathbb{C}_f>, C_- \oplus <\mathbb{C}_->, CC, C_+ \oplus <\mathbb{C}_+>, C_s \oplus <\mathbb{C}_s>\}$.

where C_1, C_2, C_4, C_5 are the citizens in general, labors, religious community, and the business-industrial sector, respectively. Here, $C_3 \equiv CC$ is the loosely–controlled democratic government elected directly by the citizens, and the underlying culture is the mix of utilitarianism and Christianity.

(3) System of absolute authority.

In this system, there is only coerced consensus. The absolute power (or the dictator) is the major player of this system. Under the culture of conflict, the reasoning pattern of this system is a mode of dialectic, which in a peculiar way, may be developed out of the mode of the atomism of ancient Greece. Over time, this system shall converge eventually to a state of equilibrium which is then a state of absolute centralization. In symbolic expression, we may present this grand system as follows:

(L.2-9) $\{citz, cap \| jud=leg=exec\} \sqsubseteq (\Omega, \mathcal{Z}_{\circ,\vee}\mathcal{H}, \{\mathbb{C}\})$,

where the government or the power center (i.e., jud = leg = exec) is the center, and the citizens and the capitalists are non-central subsystems with the socio-political status of the capitalist to be higher than that of the citizens in general.

By applying the principle of CE centrality (for each X_i, $\psi\{Y_j > Y_k, \Delta_i\} \bar{\barwedge}$ E) to this polity $X = \{citz, cap \| jud=leg=exec\}$, we have: For each X_i,

$$\text{(L.2-10)} \quad \psi\{[\mathbb{C}_{citz/Z}, \mathbb{C}_{cap/Z} | \sigma(jud=leg=exec)] > [\mathbb{C}_{jud=leg=exec/Z} | (\xi(citz), \zeta(cap))], \Delta_i\} \\ \bar{\barwedge} [\mathfrak{C}_X \Leftarrow E],$$

where $\psi, \sigma, \xi, \zeta \vDash \mathcal{Z}_{\circ,\vee}\mathcal{H}$, i = jud, leg, exec, citz, cap, $Y_j = [\mathbb{C}_{citz/Z}, \mathbb{C}_{cap/Z} | \sigma(jud=leg=exec)]$, $Y_k = [\mathbb{C}_{jud=leg=exec/Z} | (\xi(citz), \zeta(cap))]$ as in the above. Here in the state of CE centrality, the political power of the center dominates absolutely all other sectors of the polity.

Socialist polity. Let S_1, S_2, S_4, S_5 be the citizens in general, the workers, the military-police-secrete police complex, and the communist party, respectively. Suppose the central subsystem SS is the authoritarian government under communism, and the culture underlying this system is that of Marxism-Leninism. Then we have $S \sqsubseteq \Omega$ (Ω be the collection of all systems) as a 4-polar MFCE system of socialist polity:
(L.2-11) $S = \{S_1, S_2, S_3, S_4, S_5\} = \{S_f \oplus <\mathbb{C}_{sf}>, S_- \oplus <\mathbb{C}_{s-}>, SS, S_+ \oplus <\mathbb{C}_{s+}>, C_s \oplus <\mathbb{C}_{ss}>\}$.

L.3 Reversal-Construction and An Approach of Systematic-Change Becoming

In this subsection, we shall devote our efforts to the studies of the systems of systemic-change becoming and the methods of reversal construction. For a nation of decentralized political framework with the structure of local, state, and federal governments, the deconstruction of the federal government backward to the state government or local government is not feasible. This is because the power structures of the federal government and the state government are different. For example, the state government has the right to tax its citizens for the properties they own. But the federal government does not have this power. The other example is that the local government controls the local police department, but the federal government does not (at least not directly).

To have a simple presentation of this polity, let us turn our attention to reveal the structural difference between the political party and the governments.

Now, see Figure L.3-1, by employing the method of reversal construction, we deconstruct the core power of the party to a certain locally based, rather than nationally based, party cell. Note that this political party is a grand system with a weak center.

Figure L.3-1
Scheme of Deconstruction

$$\begin{array}{ccc} & g & \\ P & \dashrightarrow & P' \\ j\,\square & & \square\,k \\ & P/\mathfrak{C}_c & \end{array}$$

For the *scheme of reversal-construction* presented in Figure L.3-1, P depicts the party structure in question, P' depicts the operations of this party, while $\mathfrak{C}_P = P/\mathfrak{C}_c$ stands for the **core of the party** (i.e., the *reversal-construction sub-system* of the polity, the most powerful cell of the party which dominates the national politics, locating in a certain corner of the party in a somewhat random manner) with $\mathfrak{C}_c$ being the **cultural core** (or *unit of reversal construction* of P) underlying this party politics.

By deconstructing P through the impactor j to $P/\mathfrak{C}_C$, we retrieve the core of the political culture $\mathfrak{C}_P$, and by going through the impactor h, we derive the structure of the party's operating function P'. If the system commutes, then $g = j \# k$ is the composite impactor.

By the method of systematic-change becoming, let $P = \{P_M, P_m\} \sqsubseteq (\Omega, \mathcal{Z}_{\circ,v}\mathcal{H}, \{\mathbb{C}\})$ be a system, P_M and P_m being the dominant party cell and the rest of the party, respectively, $P' = h(P_M)$ being an h-systemism of P_M, and $h \vDash \mathcal{Z}_{\circ,v}\mathcal{H}$ (h, a **self-transforming impactor**, being an impactor of h-systemism as well). Then, from the systematic-change becoming with φ, $\square \vDash \mathcal{H}$ be an impactor connecting P with P_M:

(L.3-1) $\{\{[P \oplus P_M] \odot Ip\} = \sigma \Vdash \Sigma^{TC}$

(i.e., the system is in a state of simple T Central) with $\circledcirc$ denoting the interactor of a system and Ip denoting the system-integrating factor, we have:
(L.3-2) $[P \oplus P_M] \circledast Ip = \Phi$,

where $P_M' = h(P_M)$, and $P' = P_M' \oplus \varphi(P_m)$. Then from Bcm. (L.3-2), let:

(L.3-3) $[P \oplus P_M] \circledcirc Ip = \Phi$,

and we have a solution:

(L.3-4) $P(.) = [\xi P(\mathbb{H}_P;.) \oplus \alpha P(\mathbb{H}_m;.)] \circledcirc Ip(\mathbb{H}.;.)$,

with $\mathbb{H}_M$ being the core culture of P_M and $Ip(\mathbb{H}.;.)$ denoting the system-integrating factor, ξ the system-dynamical impactor representing the characteristics of P_M leading to its transformation into a higher stage form $h(P_M)$ over time, $\mathbb{H}_m$ being the core culture of P_m, and α the system-dynamical impactor representing the characteristics of P_m leading to keep its existing form (but with minor modification) $\varphi(P_m)$ over time.

This above presentation is called the **scheme of polity I**. Although it is not a constructive method, but an abstract framework in a conceptual exercise, it does help us in grasping a certain essential feature of a polity.

Below, by employing the method of reversal construction, we show that the core power of the government can not be fully reduced to the state and local governments. Note that this government is not a grand system, but a grand system of certain (i.e., major) major sub-systems with an alliance of other independent (i.e., minor) sub-systems.

Figure L.3-2
Scheme of Polity 1

G ——→ S
↙ g ↘   ↗ k ↖
G_{Fm} $G_{FM}/\mathfrak{C}_c$ S_m

Let f: G→S be the relation of transforming from the federal government to the core of the state and local governments. Here the system G may be incompletely represented by $G_{FM}/\mathfrak{C}_c$, for $\mathfrak{C}_c$ being the core culture underlying the polity and $G_{FM}/\mathfrak{C}_c$ is the *incomplete unit of reversal construction* of G. Here G_{FM} and G_{Fm} denote the major and minor parts of the federal government, respectively, and S_m refers to the minor part of the state and local governments.

Here if it were true that $P/\mathfrak{C}_c = G/\mathfrak{C}_c$, then there would be an iso-systemism between the party structure and the government structure. But here this is not the case.

For the federal government $G \sqsubseteq (\Omega, \mathcal{Z}^\circ, {}_v\mathcal{H}, \{\mathbb{C}\})$, it can be expressed as $G = \{G_{FM} > G_{Fm} | \mathfrak{C}_c\}$ where G_{FM} and G_{Fm} stand for the major and minor parts of the federal government, respectively. Similarly, let the state and local governments be $G' \sqsubseteq (\Omega, \mathcal{Z}^\circ, {}_v\mathcal{H}, \{\mathbb{C}\})$, where $S' = \{S_M > S_m | \mathfrak{C}_c\}$, for S_M and S_m standing for the major and minor parts of the state and local governments, respectively.

It is seen in Figure L.3-2 that "k#g: $G_{FM} \rightarrow S_{M}$," and there is no relation such that "f: G → G'" exists.

By the method of systemic-change becoming, let $G = \{(G_{FM},G_{Fm}),G_{Fm},S_m\}$ and φ, h, $\oplus \models \mathcal{H}$ with $\{[G_{FM}\oplus G_{Fm}] \circledcirc Ig(M,m)\} = \sigma \Vdash \Sigma^{TC}$ (i.e., the system is in a state of simple T central):

(L.3-5) $[(G_{FM}\oplus S_M) \oplus G_{Fm}\oplus S_m] \circledcirc Ig = \Phi$,

with $G_{FM} = h(S_M)$, Ig(M,m) and Ig representing the system-integrating impactor of the system (M,m) and G, respectively. Then for Bcm. (L.3-5), let:

(L.3-6) $G_{FM}\oplus S_M = \Phi$,

and we have a solution:

(L.3-7) $G^{A}(.) = [\xi S(\mathbb{H}_{FM};.)\oplus \alpha S(\mathbb{H}_{M};.)]\circledcirc Ig(\mathbb{H};.)$,

where $Ig(\mathbb{H};.)$ represents the system-ingtegrating factor, $\mathbb{H}$ represents the core culture of S_M, ξ represents the system-dynamical impactor of transforming the characteristics S_M into G_{FM} (= $h(S_M)$, a higher form of G_{FM}) over time, and α represents the system-dynamical impactor for the characteristics of S_M keeping its existing form essentially (but with minor modification) as $S(\mathbb{H}_M;.)$ over time. Then for Bcm. (L.3-5), we have a solution:

(L.3-8) $G(.) = [\xi S(\mathbb{H}_{FM};.)\oplus \alpha S(\mathbb{H}_{M};.)\oplus \beta S(\mathbb{H}_{Fm};.)\oplus \gamma S(\mathbb{H}_{m};.)]\circledcirc Ig(\mathbb{H};.)$,

where β and γ represent the characteristics for G_{Fm} and S_m evolving over time, respectively.

Then this above presentation shall be called the **scheme of polity II**. Note that the legend of four dragons can be expressed by the methods of reversal-construction scheme and systemic–change becoming.

Appendix M – Human Psychological Schemes and Symbolic Structures of Organizations

M.1 Symbolic Psychological Schemes

Below we shall present a few psychological schemes in a symbolical manner.

Freudian scheme. Freudian scheme may be expressed as: {I,E|S}, where I, E and S depict the id (the original I, where the original energy of libido is stored), ego and super-ego, respectively. The id is defined as the primordial subconscious structure, composed of hereditary genes and the most basic physical desires of a human being. It is an instantaneous and everlasting impulse, aiming at the satisfaction of all the basic desires. The ego is a structure of consciousness, a delicate balancer between the id and the super-ego. That is, the ego is the balancing will-rationality complex that, under the command of the super-ego, strives to suppress the desires dictated by the id. The super-ego is formulated unconsciously through the informal customs and formal regulations of a society, and over one's life time it becomes a structure of subconsciousness or an ideal. This super ego may lead a person through various types of subconscious behaviors of redemption and self-punishment. Then equilibrium is the state that a balance is reached through conflict among the id, ego and super-ego. More accurately speaking, an equilibrium is reached between the id and the super-ego by the strategic acts of the ego; and in this state, this person is normal. But if a state of CE centrality fails to materialize in this system, then this person is abnormal and shall encounter some neuropathic problems. For more detail of this theory, see Zhao [1980].

That is, this system {I,E|S} is in a state of disequilibrium (or non-CE balance) if it is a system of constant conflict without abatement; and it is in a state of equilibrium (or CE balance) if it is a system of conflict suppressed by coerced tranquility (say, under the power of an absolute authority).

N cognition scheme. From the cognition theory of Neisser, we may develop an abstract scheme of N cognition-system: {C,S|I} = {cognition (mind/mental experienced), subjection(introspection)|I} in which I ↔ (behavior, extended study|I) cognitive system. (Schultz and Schultz 1996, p. 453). This system {C,S|I} may be presented by a conflict system of thesis-antithesis and synthesis.

J-H psychological scheme. From the psychological theory of Jung/Horney, and through a process of abstraction, one may be able to detect two categories of unconsciousness: individual and collective unconsciousness, to develop four archetypes of psychology: persona ("the mask each of us wears when we come in contact with other people; it present us as we want to appear to society"), anima and animus (reflecting "the idea that each person exhibits some of the characteristics of the other sex. The anima refers to feminine characters in man; the animus denotes masculine characters in woman"), shadow ("it contains all immoral, passionate, and unaccountable desires and activities"), and self (by " balancing all aspects of the unconscious, the self provides unity and stability to the personality." "The self is the most important archetype"); and to differentiate between two kinds of personalities: introversion (it makes a person "contemplative, introspective, resistant to external influences" and less sociable, or "less confident in relationships with other person and with the external world") and extroversion ('it "directs libido (life energy) outside the self to external events and people" and makes a person sociable and self-confident') (Schultz and Schultz 1996, pp. 408-410).

From this scheme of Jung/Horney, we may formulate the J-H psychological system: $\{A,B \mid C\}$ as a competitive composite-system, with A referring to unconscious, B denoting psychological archetype, and C depicting the personality, for A, B and C all being an n-polar MFCE subsystems with virtual centers.

M.2 Symbolic Schemes of Organizations

In general, the symbolic schemes of organizations are composite systems. These systems are also n-polar MFCE schemes, may be with virtual centers. Below, for simplicity, we shall focus on the discussions of simple systems. The general schemes of psychological structures may be similar to the general symbolic structures of human organizations. Below we shall pursue these general schemes of human organizations.

(1) System of a single-center--Faziranism.

The system of Faziranist centralism is based on the culture of consensual tranquility. With the systemic yu-wu rationality, family is eventually developed into a system of groupism. This system may be expressed below:

$$\text{(M.2-1)} \quad \{(\text{yin},\text{yang})|\text{he}\} \sqsubseteq (\Omega,\mathbb{Z}\circ,{}_{v}\mathbb{H},\{\mathbb{C}\}),$$

for yin, yang, he $\sqsubseteq \Omega$. Here "he" is the center, and the relationship between yin and yang are somewhat uncertain: either we have yin and yang as non-central elements, or yang is the secondary center with yin being the non-central element. Note that the positions of yin and yang can be interchanged. The culture of the "he" is the *virtual operating force* that can be transformed into the cultural capital of yin and yang elements. Below we have $X = \{X_1,X_2,\ldots,X_n\}$, X and $(Y_k,Y_j) \Lleftarrow \langle\mathbb{C}_X\rangle$, for $(Y_k,Y_j) \sqsubseteq (\Omega,\mathbb{Z}\circ,{}_{v}\mathbb{H},\{\mathbb{C}\})$, where $X_j \equiv [(X_1,\mathbb{C}_{X1/Z}),(X_2,\mathbb{C}_{X2/Z}),\ldots,(X_n,\mathbb{C}_{Xn/Z})|(C,\sigma(C))]$, $X_k \equiv [(C,\mathbb{C}_{C/Z})|((X_1,\xi_1(X_1)),(X_2,\xi_2(X_2)),\ldots,(X_n,\xi_n(X_n)))]$, where $\xi_i \models (\Omega,\mathbb{Z}\circ,{}_{v}\mathbb{H},\{\mathbb{C}\})$, $i = 1, 2, \ldots, n$.

Let $n = 3$, $i \neq k, j$, X_1, X_2, and X_3 be yin, yang and he, respectively. If we apply the principle of CE centrality (i.e., for each X_i, $\psi\{Y_j > Y_k,\Delta_i\} \barwedge \tau$) to this system $X = \{\text{yin},\text{yang}|\text{he}\} = \{X_1,X_2,\ldots,X_n\}$, $n = 3$, $i \neq k, j$, then for $\psi, \sigma, \xi, \zeta \models \mathbb{Z}\circ,{}_{v}\mathbb{H}$. we have the *principle of CE centrality* : For each X_i,

$$\text{(M.2-2)} \quad \psi\{[\mathbb{C}_{yin/Z},\mathbb{C}_{yang/Z}|\sigma(\text{he})] > [\mathbb{C}_{he/Z}\,|(\xi(\text{yin}),\zeta(\text{yang}))],\Delta_i\} \barwedge [\mathbb{C}_X \Lleftarrow E\,],$$

or the impact effect of "he" on yin and yang is larger than the feedback effects of both yin and yang on he.

(2) System of one center with absolute authority.

This is a culture in which tranquility is achieved through coercion. In this culture, dialectical egoism forms the foundation of systemic operations, and this proto-type scheme may be developed out of the model of the atomism of ancient Greece. Under the culture of conflict and the reasoning pattern of the mode of mathematical logic, this system shall converge eventually to a state of equilibrium which is one of absolute centralization. In a symbolic pattern, we may present this system as follows:

(M.2-3) $\{(x,y),\text{antithesis}||\text{synthesis}\} \sqsubseteq (\Omega,\mathcal{Z}\circ,_{v}\mathcal{H},\{\mathbb{C}\})$,

for x, y, antithesis and synthesis $\sqsubseteq \Omega$. In this system, synthesis is the absolute center, antithesis may be the semi-center, and x and y are non-central elements.

Below let $X = \{X_1,X_2,\ldots,X_n\}$, X and $(Y_k,Y_j) \Lleftarrow <\mathbb{C}_X>$, where $Y_j \equiv[(X_1,\mathbb{C}_{X1/Z}), (X_2,\mathbb{C}_{X2/Z}),\ldots,(X_n,\mathbb{C}_{Xn/Z}),(C,\sigma(C))]$, $Y_k \equiv [(C,\mathbb{C}_{C/Z})|((X_1,\xi_1(X_1)),(X_2,\xi_2(X_2)),\ldots,(X_n,\xi_n (X_n)))]$, for $\xi_i \Vdash \mathcal{Z}\circ,_{v}\mathcal{H}$, $i = 1, 2, \ldots, n$.

Furthermore, let X_1, X_2, X_3 be (x,y), antithesis, and synthesis, respectively, with $i \neq k, j$. By applying the principle of CE centrality (i.e., for each X_i, $\psi\{X_j>X_k,\Delta_i\} \barwedge \tau$) to this system $X = \{(x,y),\text{antithesis}|\text{synthesis}\} = \{X_1,X_2,\ldots,X_n\}$, we have the principle of *absolute authority*: For each X_i,

(M.2-4) $\psi\{[\mathbb{C}_{(x,y)/Z},\mathbb{C}_{\text{antithesis}/Z}|\sigma(\text{synthesis})] \barwedge [\mathbb{C}_X \Lleftarrow E],$
$\qquad\qquad \wedge X_i = \psi\{\mathcal{T}{*}C\geq\mathcal{T}X_i,\Delta_i\} \barwedge \tau.$

By this Bcm. (M.2-4) is meant that the CE balance of this system is to ensure the absolute power of synthesis over (x,y) and antithesis, and (x,y) or antithesis has no feedback effects on synthesis. That is, $[\xi(x,y),\zeta(\text{antithesis})|C_{\text{synthesis}Z}]$ is an empty system, for $\psi, \sigma, \xi, \zeta \models \mathcal{Z}\circ,_{v}\mathcal{H}$. Note that here "antithesis" may have some limited power over (x,y).

(3) System of two centers.

In this system, there is no internal tranquility. It may be said that the pattern of operation of this system models itself after the patterns of the number system. Thus this is a system of independent individuals and conflict is the norm of operation. This system shall converge eventually to a state of equilibrium which is one of decentralization in conflict.

In a symbolic pattern, we may present this system as follows:

(M.2-5) $\{\text{thesis},\text{antithesis}\} \sqsubseteq (\Omega,\mathcal{Z}\circ,_{v}\mathcal{H},\{\mathbb{C}\})$, thesis, antithesis $\sqsubseteq \Omega$,

where thesis and antithesis are the co-centers always in conflict. By applying the principle of CE centrality (i.e., for each X_i, $\psi\{Y_j>Y_k,\Delta_i\} \barwedge \tau$) to this system $X=\{\text{thesis},\text{antithesis}\}$, we have: For each X_i,

(M.2-6) $\psi\{[\mathbb{C}_{\text{antithesis}/Z}|\sigma(\text{thesis})]>[\mathbb{C}_{\text{thesis}/Z}|\zeta(\text{antithesis})],\Delta_{\text{thesis}}\} \barwedge [\mathbb{C}_X\Lleftarrow E]$
$\qquad\qquad \psi\{[\mathbb{C}_{\text{thesis}/Z}|\sigma(\text{antithesis})]>[\mathbb{C}_{\text{antithesis}/Z}|\xi (\text{thesis})],\Delta_{\text{antithesis}}\} \barwedge [\mathbb{C}_X \Lleftarrow E],$

where $\psi, \sigma, \xi, \zeta \models \mathcal{Z}\circ,_{v}\mathcal{H}$. The CE balance of this system is that, under a constant state of conflict between "thesis" and "antithesis," each strives and yet fails to dominate the other. That is, in this instance, the principle of CE balance transforms into the *principle of conflict*: For each X_i,

(M.2-7) $\{ \psi\{[\mathbb{C}_{\text{antithesis}/Z}|\sigma(\text{thesis})]>[\mathbb{C}_{\text{thesis}/Z}|\zeta(\text{antithesis})],\Delta_{\text{antithesis}}\}$
$\qquad\qquad \Leftrightarrow \psi\{[\mathbb{C}_{\text{thesis}/Z}|\sigma(\text{antithesis})]>[\mathbb{C}_{\text{antithesis}/Z}|\xi(\text{thesis})],\Delta_{\text{antithesis}}\} \}$
$\qquad \barwedge [\mathbb{C}_X \Lleftarrow E],$

where the interactor "$\Leftrightarrow$" $\models \mathcal{H}$ depicts the equality of power.

Further, by looking at Bcm. (M.2-7), when the family {positive, negative} $\sqsubseteq (\Omega, \mathbb{Z}\circ, {}_v\mathbb{H}, \{\mathbb{C}\})$, for "positive" and "negative" $\sqsubseteq \Omega$, each reaches an equilibrium, then the principle of conflict turns into the *principle of balance-in-independence* :

(M.2-8) For $X_{positive}$, $\psi\{[\mathbb{C}_{negative/Z}|\sigma(positive)]>[\mathbb{C}_{positive/Z}|\zeta(negative)],\Delta_{positive}\} \barwedge [\mathbb{C}_X \Leftarrow E]$,
for $X_{negative}$, $\psi\{[\mathbb{C}_{positive/Z}|\sigma(negative)]>[\mathbb{C}_{negative/Z}|\xi(positive)],\Delta_{negative}\} \barwedge [\mathbb{C}_X \Leftarrow E]$,
and $\psi\{[\mathbb{C}_{negative/Z}|\sigma(positive)]>[\mathbb{C}_{positive/Z}|\zeta(negative)],\Delta_{positive}\}$
$\approx \psi\{[\mathbb{C}_{positive/Z}|\sigma(negative)]>[\mathbb{C}_{negative/Z}|\xi(positive)],\Delta_{negative}\}$,

where the interactor "≈" $\vDash \mathbb{H}$ depicts the equal sharing of power. Here For $X_{positive}$, $Y_j = \psi\{[\mathbb{C}_{negative/Z}|\sigma(positive)]\}$ and $Y_k = \{[\mathbb{C}_{positive/Z}|\zeta(negative)],\Delta_{positive}\}$, and for $X_{negative}$, $Y_j = \psi\{[\mathbb{C}_{positive/Z}|\sigma(negative)]\}$ and $Y_k = \{\mathbb{C}_{negative/Z}|[\xi(positive)],\Delta_{negative}\}$.

(4) System of two centers with many non-central elements.

The cultural underpinning of this system is the same as in (3). In this system, there is no culture of tranquility, and the individuals are the major players of this system. Under the culture of conflict and the reasoning patterns of the model of mathematical logic, this shall converge eventually to a state of equilibrium which is one of decentralization. In a symbolic pattern, we may present this system as follows:

(M.2-9) $\{(x,y)|antithesis,thesis\} \sqsubseteq (\Omega, \mathbb{Z}\circ, {}_v\mathbb{H}, \{\mathbb{C}\})$,

where x, y, "thesis" and "antithesis" $\sqsubseteq \Omega$, "thesis" and "antithesis" are co-centers and x and y are non-centra members. By applying the principle of CE centrality (i.e., for each X_i, $\psi\{Y_j>Y_k,\Delta_i\} \barwedge E$) to the family X = {(x,y)|antithesis, thesis}, we have:

(M.2-10) For X_{thesis}, $\psi\{[\mathbb{C}_{(x,y)/Z},\mathbb{C}_{antithesis/Z}|\sigma(thesis)]$
$> [\mathbb{C}_{thesis/Z}|(\xi(x,y),\zeta(antithesis))],\Delta_{thesis}\} \barwedge [\mathbb{C}_X \Leftarrow E]$,
and for $X_{antithesis}$, $\psi\{[\mathbb{C}_{(x,y)/Z},\mathbb{C}_{thesis/Z}|\sigma(antithesis)]$
$> [\mathbb{C}_{antithesis/Z}|((\xi(x,y),\zeta(thesis))],\Delta_{antithesis}\} \barwedge [\mathbb{C}_X \Leftarrow E]$,

where $\psi, \sigma, \xi, \zeta \vDash \mathbb{Z}\circ, {}_v\mathbb{H}$. In the world of dynamical fluctuation and motion, the CE balance of this system is that each of the centers seeks to dominate the other and eventually a state of equilibrium is reached amid constant conflict. That is, x and y are relatively independent of the powers of thesis and antithesis. Below, from the principle of CE balance-centrality, we derive the principle of balance/ independence:

(M.2-11) For X_{thesis}, $\{\psi\{[\mathbb{C}_{(x,y)/Z},\mathbb{C}_{antithesis/Z}|\sigma(thesis)]$
$> [\mathbb{C}_{thesis/Z}|(\xi(x,y),\zeta(antithesis))],\Delta_{thesis}\} \barwedge [\mathbb{C}_X \Leftarrow E]\}$,
for $X_{antithesis}$, $\{\psi\{[\mathbb{C}_{(x,y)/Z},\mathbb{C}_{thesis/Z}|\sigma(antithesis)]$
$> [\mathbb{C}_{antithesis/Z}|(\xi(x,y),\zeta(thesis))],\Delta_{antithesis}\} \barwedge [\mathbb{C}_X \Leftarrow E]\}$,
and $\{\psi\{[\mathbb{C}_{(x,y)/Z},\mathbb{C}_{antithesis/Z}|\sigma(thesis)]$
$> [\mathbb{C}_{thesis/Z}|(\xi(x,y),\zeta(antithesis))],\Delta_{thesis}\}$
$\approx \{\psi\{[\mathbb{C}_{(x,y)/Z},\mathbb{C}_{thesis/Z}|\sigma(antithesis)]$
$> [\mathbb{C}_{antithesis/Z}|(\xi(x,y),\zeta(thesis))],\Delta_{antithesis}\}$,

where "≈" $\vDash \mathbb{H}$ depicts the equalization of power.

On the other hand, if there is no minimal level of consensus prevailing in this system, then the constant state of internal conflict shall transform the principle of CE balance-centrality into the *principle of conflict*:

$$\text{(M.2-12)}\quad \text{For } X_{thesis},\ \{\psi\{[\mathbb{C}_{(x,y)/Z},\mathbb{C}_{antithesis/Z}|\sigma(\text{thesis})] > [\mathbb{C}_{thesis/Z}|(\xi(x,y),\zeta(\text{antithesis})],\Delta_{thesis}\} \barwedge [\mathbb{C}_X \Leftarrow E\,]\}$$
$$\text{for } X_{antithesis},\ \{\psi\{[\mathbb{C}_{(x,y)/Z},\mathbb{C}_{thesis/Z}|\sigma(\text{antithesis})] > [\mathbb{C}_{antithesis/Z}|(\xi(x,y),\zeta(\text{thesis}))],\Delta_{antithesis}\} \barwedge [\mathbb{C}_X \Leftarrow E\,]\}$$
$$\ldots$$
$$\ldots$$
$$\text{and } \{\psi\{[\mathbb{C}_{(x,y)/Z},\mathbb{C}_{antithesis/Z}|\sigma(\text{thesis})] > [\mathbb{C}_{thesis/Z}|(\xi(x,y),\zeta(\text{antithesis}))],\Delta_{thesis}\} \barwedge [\mathbb{C}_X \Leftarrow E\,]\}$$
$$\Leftrightarrow \{\psi\{[\mathbb{C}_{(x,y)/Z},\mathbb{C}_{thesis/Z}|\sigma(\text{antithesis})] > [\mathbb{C}_{antithesis/Z}|(\xi(x,y),\zeta(\text{thesis}))],\Delta_{antithesis}\} \barwedge [\mathbb{C}_X \Leftarrow E\,]\}$$
$$\Leftrightarrow \ldots$$
$$\Leftrightarrow \ldots$$

where "…" denote the schemes of x and y, and the interactor "$\Leftrightarrow$" $\models \mathbb{H}$ depicts the equality of power amid constant conflict.

M.3 Consolidating and Destabilizing Forces of System

Conflict culture: For A, B, C, $(A,B|C) \sqsubseteq (\Omega,\mathbb{Z}\circ,_{v}\mathbb{H},\{\mathbb{C}\})$, we have for the system (A,B|C):

$$\text{(M.3-1)}\quad (A,B|C) = \{A(\sigma_1,\kappa_1),B(\sigma_2,\kappa_2)|C(\sigma_3,\kappa_3)\},$$

with $\sigma_i \leftsquigarrow \tau$ and $\kappa_i \leftsquigarrow \tau$, $\tau \Vdash (\mathfrak{I},\text{Ш}^{\text{Л}}) \Vvdash \mathbb{T}\mathbb{z}\mathbb{u}^*$, $\forall\ i \in \mathbb{N}$. Then, due to the conflicting nature of σ_i and κ_i, $\forall\ i \in \mathbb{N}$, from Bcm. (M.3-1), we have:

$$\text{(M.3-2)}\quad (A,B|C) = \{(A,B|C)\|(\sigma_1,\sigma_2,\sigma_3;\kappa_1,\kappa_2,\kappa_3)\},$$

where σ_1, σ_2 and σ_3 are in constant conflict among themselves, and similarly for κ_1, κ_2 and κ_3.

Tranquil culture: For A, B, C, $(A,B|C) \sqsubseteq (\Omega,\mathbb{Z}\circ,_{v}\mathbb{H},\{\mathbb{C}\})$, we have for the system (A,B|C):

$$\text{(M.3-3)}\quad (A,B|C) = \{A(\sigma,\kappa),B(\sigma,\kappa)|C(\sigma,\kappa)\}, = \{(A,B|C)\|(\sigma,\kappa)\},$$

Where $\sigma \leftsquigarrow \tau$ and $\kappa \leftsquigarrow \tau$, $\tau \Vdash (\mathfrak{I},\text{Ш}^{\text{Л}}) \Vvdash \mathbb{T}\mathbb{z}\mathbb{u}^*$. Then at the state of Tcentral, for the Tcentral impactor $\mathcal{T}^C \models \mathbb{Z}\circ,_{v}\mathbb{H}$, we have:

$$\text{(M.3-4)}\quad \mathcal{T}^C(A,B|C) = \mathcal{T}^C\{(A,B|C)\|(\sigma,\kappa)\} \rightarrow \{(A,B|C)\|\,(\mathcal{T}^*=\mathcal{K}^*\,|\,\mathcal{H}^*)\},$$

where for the consolidating force $\mathcal{T}^*$ (i.e., force of tranquility $\mathcal{T}$ at the state of Tcentral) and the destabilizing force $\mathcal{K}^*$(i.e., force of conflict $\mathcal{K}$ at the state of Tcentral), a state of CE balance is reached: under the mediatory force of $\mathcal{H}^*$, (i.e., $\mathcal{H}$ at the state of Tcentral), the forces of $\mathcal{T}$ and $\mathcal{K}$ are constantly equilibrating.

Appendix N – Systematic Approach to Various Philosophical Systems of The East and The West

N.1 Philosophical System of Conflict Culture

The cultural cores inherited by the modern conflict culture may be considered as: the medieval core, Deity-human dualism.

To address the philosophical scheme of a conflict culture, let us have the following notations: Ph is the philosophical system, S represents the sciences, $C_D = P/\mathfrak{C}_c$ expresses the Deity-man dualism, $P = C_D \sqcup S$, R represents the religion, LW is the form of the life-manifestation, and $LW|_S$ depicts the life manifestation under the constraint of sciences.

Then we have the modern core: dualism of life-will and sciences (see Figure N.1-1).

Figure N.1-1
Dilemma from philosophy orientation to life-will

$$\begin{array}{ccccc} & Ph & \longrightarrow & LW|_S & \\ \swarrow & \searrow g & & h\nearrow & \nwarrow \\ S & & P/\mathfrak{C}_c & & R \end{array}$$

In Figure N.1-1, it is seen that philosophy (Ph) develops into sciences (S), while the essentials of the life-will of the human being ($LW|_S$) remains outside of sciences. Moreover, the life-will of the human being is strongly influenced by religion ®. Thus there is a dichotomy between sciences and the life-will orientation of the conflict mind.

N.2 Philosophical System of Tranquil Culture

The cultural core inherited by the modern tranquil culture may be considered as: Tien-human unity.

Then we have the modern core of the tranquil culture: Life-will and symbolic reasoning methods presented in Figure N.2-1.

In Figure N.1-2, it is clearly seen that philosophy (P) naturally transforms into the life-will of a tranquil mind (P'), the unity of the human being and the Nature (be it Tien or something else).

The structure of Figure is analogous to Figure K.4-1. Note that $\mathfrak{C}_T$ is the core of the "Tien culture."

Remark N.1. For a tentative system of Western metaphysics be presented as N(B-HPh), see the last paragraph of Appendix H (Bcm. (H.4)).

Figure N.2-1
Unity of life-will with philosophical traditions

$$
\begin{array}{ccc}
 & f & \\
P & \longrightarrow & P' \\
g \searrow & & \nearrow h \\
 & P/\mathfrak{C}_T &
\end{array}
$$

Appendix O – Systematic Approach to Literary System

For the major themes of literature, we may consider the following: life, death, sex, love, hatred, friendship, war, and so on.

Below, let us present a scheme of literature with multiple major-themes and multiple minor-themes. This scheme is a system. Then, in this grand system, for each major theme, the core of the theme is presented with some elements of entertainment added to it. Then multiple major themes are presented with a core theme penetrating through all major themes. Let W be a literary piece, T_1 be the theme 1, T_2 be the theme 2, F_1 be the minor theme 1, F_{21} be the minor theme 1 associated with C_2, C_i be the manifestation of theme i, $i \in \mathbb{N}$, T_1/C_c be the core of literary piece 1 (with C_c being the core culture), T_2/C_cbe the core of literary piece 2. Then we have Figure O.1.

Figure O.1
A system of literature

$$
\begin{array}{ccccc}
 & & F_1 & & \\
 & & \uparrow & & \\
C_1 & \leftarrow - & W & - \rightarrow & C_2 \\
\nwarrow & \swarrow g \searrow & & \nearrow h \nwarrow & \\
T_1/C_c & & T_2/C_c & & F_{21}
\end{array}
$$

Figure O.1 means that: (i) From the minor theme 1, the major theme 1 and its manifestation are created, or φ: $F_1 \rightarrow \{F_1|C_1||T_1/C_c\} = X \sqsubseteq (\Omega,\mathbb{Z}o,_v\mathbb{H},\{\mathbb{C}\})$, where $\varphi \vDash \mathbb{Z}o,_v\mathbb{H}$ is a system-creating impactor. That is, in the system X, C_1 is the center, F_1 is the non-central element, given the core T_1/C_c of the theme 1 T_1. (ii) From the minor themes 1 and 2, the major theme 2 and its manifestation are created, or ψ: $\{F_1,F_{21}\} \rightarrow \{ (F_1,F_{21}) |C_2||T_2/C_c\} = Y \sqsubseteq (\Omega,\mathbb{Z}o,_v\mathbb{H},\{\mathbb{C}\})$, where $\psi \vDash \mathbb{Z}o,_v\mathbb{H}$ is a system-creating impactor. That is, in the system Y, C_2 is the center, $\{F_1,F_{21})$ is the non-central subsystem, given the core T_2/C_c of the theme 2 T_2, and (iii) the integration of X and Y is the whole literary piece: $\theta\{X,Y\} = W \sqsubseteq (\Omega,\mathbb{Z}o,_v\mathbb{H},\{\mathbb{C}\})$, where $\theta \vDash \mathbb{Z}o,_v\mathbb{H}$ is an integrating impactor

Appendix P – Systematic Approach to Belief System

Below we discuss only two belief systems.

Belief system Zh. Belief system is a direct Deity-human system. This is called **Zh system** in which the Deity is the center and human affairs evolve around the Deity. In this system, the Deity controls all aspects of human affairs. In terms of the relationship between the Deity and the human being, it may be considered as a T-strong system.

Belief system Ind-HD. Belief system is an indirect human-Deity system composed of Zh system and R system, for **R system** being a pure human system in which the Deity has no control over human behaviors. This belief system may be called the **Ind-HD system** in which R system is the center and Zh system serves as a periphery system. Here the so-called **periphery system** is a non-central subsystem having limited influence over the center. In this Ind-HD system, human affairs are mostly self-contained in R system, Zh system is then independent of the central subsystem; and the influence of the Zh system over human events are limited to pure belief of the human beings and has a very limited impact on the secular events of the human society.

Appendix Q – Systematic Approach to Historical Systems

In this Appendix, we shall present a general scheme of history. In history, in the anti-Tcentral, anti-CE balance and anti-equilibrium processes of the world of multi-faceted self-masterism, under the momentum of the conflicts of the human being in the society, cultural forces grow by its internal dynamics. In actuality, cultural forces are the engine, or may even be the determining forces, of the world history, although at times a few specific individuals, several groups, numerous economic, political and religious forces, some geographical factor and even some incidental events may all have some significant feedback effects on the development of human history.[65]

Below, we shall discuss just a few schemes of history.

Thema Q.1 (consecutive alternation of unification and separation). This theme of consecutive alternation of unification and separation has three levels of meanings:

(1) Let $A \sqsubseteq (\Omega, \mathbb{Z}o, {}_v\mathbb{H}, \{\mathbb{C}\})$ be the system expressing the theme of "unification leading to eventual separation" and $B \sqsubseteq (\Omega, \mathbb{Z}o, {}_v\mathbb{H}, \{\mathbb{C}\})$ be the system expressing the theme of "separation leading to eventual unification". Then B is the f-systemism of A: $B = f(A)$, where $f \models \mathbb{Z}o, {}_v\mathbb{H}$ is an impactor of f-systemism.

Here, let $f^{1} \models \mathbb{Z}o, {}_v\mathbb{H}$ (or $f^{1} \equiv f^{Rev}$) being the reversal systemism of f, then $A = f^{1}(B)$, A is the **reverse-systemism** of B (rev-systemism, defining the reverse of the rev-systemism of a system is the system itself).

(2) For a nation with different space and time, the unification system (or system) and the separation process or system are themselves iso-systemisms, respectively. To illustrate this, let the complex system of unification-separation of a country at time T_1 be (for $F\text{-}H(.| T_i, i \in \mathbb{N}) \sqsubseteq (\Omega, \mathbb{Z}o, {}_v\mathbb{H}, \{\mathbb{C}\})$):

(Q.1) $F\text{-}H(.| T_1) = \Phi\text{-}\Psi$,

where Φ is the separation system at time T_1, Ψ is the separation system at time T_1. Below, let the unification-separation complex at time T_2 be:

(Q.2) $F\text{-}H(.| T_2) = \Phi'\text{-}\Psi'$,

where Φ' is the separation system at time T_2, Ψ' is the separation system at time T_2.

Now let $\iota, \kappa \models \mathbb{Z}o, {}_v\mathbb{H}$ be the impactors of an iso-systemism. Then, in the above, the so-called iso-systemisms of the unification-separation complex are:

(Q.3) $\Phi = \iota(\Phi)$,

(Q.4) $\Psi' = \kappa(\Psi)$.

That is, the separation systems at time T_1 and T_2 are the same, and the unification systems of both times are the same as well.

(3) If this country at time T_1 is a separation system, then it will become a unification time T_2 and vice versa. That is, let $\varphi \models \mathcal{Z}\circ,_{v}\mathcal{H}$ be an impactor of f-systemism,

(Q.5) $F\text{-}H(.| T_2) = \varphi\{F\text{-}H(.| T_1)\}$.

Thema Q2 (Variant of iso-systemism). The variant of iso-systemism is associated with the major change of the less important or non-central subsystems over time and the minor change of the major or central sub-system. The Chinese polity, with its structure evolving from Han system to Tang system is an ever expanding system (Chien [1977]). This is a transformation of he-systemism. Later one, evolving from the Tang system to Sung system and then to Ming system, these become variants of the iso-systemism. That is, the variant is created through only minor changes in the periphery or part of a system.[66]

Nevertheless, the evolution from Chou Li (Rituals of Chou Dynasty) to the Six Classic Statues of Tang may be considered as an h-systemism.[67]

The transformation of the military-orientation of Tang Dynasty to the non-military-orientation of Sung Dynasty may be considered as an f-systemism.

Then from the military system of Yuan Dynasty to the wei-suo system of Ming Dynasty, and then to the bachi system of Manchurian Dynasty, these transformations are variations of d-systemisms.[68]

As for the financial systems of China, from Tang Dynasty to Sung Dynasty, the basic structures did not change that much. Essentially this is an iso-systemism. But from Sung Dynasty to Ming Dynasty, the basic structures of the financial systems did change significantly. Essentially this latter change is an f-systemism.[69]

Appendix R – General Structures of Economic Organizations

R.1 Introduction

In this Appendix, we shall discuss the cultural economic systems of capitalism, socialism, and faziranism.

R.2 Systems of Faziranism

In this section, we investigate various systems of Faziranism: Huangben (i.e., emperor-centered) Faziranism, Guangben Faziranism, classical Faziranism, socialist Faziransim, and captailist Faziranism.

Huangben Faziranism. Let $F \sqsubseteq (\Omega,\mathcal{Z}\circ,{}_{v}\mathcal{H},\{\mathbb{C}\})$ be a system of 5-polar MFCE system: $F = \{F_1,F_2,F_3,F_4,F_5\} = \{F_f + <\mathbb{C}_f>, F_- + <\mathbb{C}_->, CF, F_+ + <\mathbb{C}_+>, F_s + <\mathbb{C}_s>\}$. Let F_1 be the agricultural sector, F_2 be the industrial-business sector, F_3 be the intellectuals, and F_5 be the government-controlled handicraft sector. Furthermore, let the center CF be the royal family, and the culture be that of Legalism-Taoism-Confucianism: $<\mathbb{C}_X> = \{\mathcal{M}^I(\mathcal{M}^I(\ell,\tau),\ldots,\mathcal{M}^N(\ell,\tau)|E(e_r(\tau)),Z(\tau)\}$, $\ell \equiv \ell(\sigma,\kappa) \Vdash \text{Ш}^{\mathcal{L}(\sigma,\kappa)} \Subset \text{Ш}^{\text{Д}L} \Vvdash \mathbb{T}\text{zu}^*$, $\tau \Vdash (\mathfrak{I},\text{Ш}^{\text{Д}}) \Vvdash \mathbb{T}\text{zu}^*$, where $\mathbb{T}\text{zu}^*$ = Yu-Wu-Tao-Chi creativity-destructivity (for $\mathcal{M} = [\mathcal{M}^I\ \mathcal{M}^{II}\ \mathcal{M}^{III}\ \mathcal{M}^{IV} \ldots]^T$, see Subsection §A.2-4). Then F is a system of Huangben Faziranism.

Let $F \sqsubseteq (\Omega,\mathcal{Z}\circ,{}_{v}\mathcal{H},\{\mathbb{C}\})$ be a scheme of 5-polar MFCE system: $F = \{F_1,F_2,F_3,F_4,F_5\} = \{F_f \oplus <\mathbb{C}_f>, F_- \oplus <\mathbb{C}_->, CF, F_+ \oplus <\mathbb{C}_+>, F_s \oplus <\mathbb{C}_s>\}$. Let F_1 be the agricultural sector (or the peasants), F_2 the private commerce-handicraft sector, F_4 the gentry class, F_5 the public sector, and CF be the center – the emperor or royal family; and in addition, let the underlying culture be that of Legalism-Taoism-Confucianism. Then F is a scheme of 5-polar MFCE system.

In general, let $X = \{X_1,X_2, , \ldots,X_n\}$, X and $(Y_k,Y_j) \Lleftarrow <\mathbb{C}_X>$, for $Y_j \equiv [(X_1,\mathbb{C}_{X1/Z}),(X_2,\mathbb{C}_{X2/Z}),\ldots,(X_n,\mathbb{C}_{Xn/Z})|(C,\sigma(C))]$, C being the center, and $Y_k \equiv [(C,\mathbb{C}_{C/Z})|((X_1,\xi_1(X_1)),(X_2,\xi_2(X_2)),\ldots,(X_n,\xi_n(X_n)))]$, where $\xi_i \vDash \mathcal{Z}\circ,{}_{v}\mathcal{H}$, $i = 1,2,\ldots,n$. At the same time, let $X \equiv F \sqsubseteq (\Omega,\mathcal{Z}\circ,{}_{v}\mathcal{H},\{\mathbb{C}\}) \sqcap E^F \sqcap E^{YW}$, E^F being the space of the organizations of Faziranist groupism and E^{YW} being the space of yu-wu cultural systems. Here by applying the principle of CE centrality (for each X_i, $\psi\{Y_j>Y_k,\Delta_i\} \overline{\barwedge}$ E) to the system X, we have the *principle of Huangben authoritarianism*: $\forall\ i = 1, 2, \ldots, n$, for each X_i,

$$\text{(R.2-1)} \quad \psi\{[\mathbb{C}_{X1/Z},\mathbb{C}_{X2/Z},\ldots,\mathbb{C}_{Xn/Z}|\sigma(C)],\Delta_i\} \overline{\barwedge} [\mathbb{C}_X \Lleftarrow E],$$

$\xi_h \vDash \mathcal{Z}\circ,{}_{v}\mathcal{H}$, $h = 1,2,\ldots n$, where C is the center of the system and ψ is the impactor implementing the principle "$Y_j>Y_k$." Here, note that $[\xi_1(X_1),\xi_2(X_2),\ldots,\xi n(X_n),\mathbb{C}_{C/Z}] = \circ$ (the empty system).

Let IRI (or the **IRI chain**) be a chain of systems regulating the activities (or activity systems) and functional systems of information, decision-making and strategy-implementation, SIFP (or the **SIFP chain**) be a chain of systems controlling the activities and functional systems of saving, investment, finance and production, and ST (or the **ST chain**) be a chain of systems connecting and integrating the activities and functional systems of sciences and technology. In a huangben Faziranist system, the basic productivity like agricultural production is promoted, while commerce and handicraft production are under tight control and severely discouraged. Therefore, the general IRI chain of a haugnben enterprise is severely restricted by the bureaucrats representing the power of the emperor. Naturally, within all the IRI chains, there is a **central IRI chain**, that is the emperor's IRI chain, centering on the IE-RD-PI of the emperor (or the royal family).

In the huangben Faziranist system, there is no ST chain (or science-technology chain). In this system, what may be somewhat equivalent to the ST chain of a modern cultural economy is the yinyang five-element chain (or the **YXT chain**). Hence, what is equivalent to the SIFP chain of a modern cultural economy is the **YXSIFP chain**. This YXSIFP relies heavily on the traditional financial intermediary (which may be called the piaufang-money store); and from the modern perspective, it is very inefficient.

Now we have the static-dynamical interpenetrating network of Huangben Faziranism: $(C_S{\times}C^{DS}(e_r), (R_M,R^{DM}(e_r),\tilde{O}) = (R,R^D(e_r)) = \{(\rho,\omega)^F$: MPFX cycle∠military power ∠ emperor's power|basis being field of the universe∠Mandate of Heaven }^{IRI,SIFP| Cwr⋞Lagalist planning}⇚ {YXT| royal family}, where Cwr is the collection of the S&T factors of creativity as a becoming of will-rationality complex. Here the {MPFX cycle∠emperor's power} represents the money-power-fame-sex cycle controlled by the emperor, and $(\rho,\omega)^F$ refers to the Faziranist will-rationality complex.

Guanben Faziranism. The static-dynamical interpenetrating network of Guangben Faziranism is: $(C_S{\times}C^{DS}(e_r),(R_M,R^{DM}(e_r),\tilde{O}) = (R,R^D(e_r)) = \{(\rho,\omega)^F$: MPFX cycle ∠gentry class∠military power∠emperor's power|basis being field of the universe∠Mandate of Heaven }^{IRI, SIFP| Cwr ⋞ Confucianized Lagalist planning∠Heaven-Earth-Man human activism}⇚ {YXT| royal family}.

Minben Faziranism. We have the static-dynamical inter-penetrating network of Minben Faziranism: $(C_S{\times}C^{DS}(e_r),(R_M,R^{DM}(e_r)) = (R,R^D(e_r)) = \{(\rho,\omega)^F$: MPFX cycle ∠gentry class∠ people's mandate|basis being field of the universe∠Mandate of Heaven }^{IRI, SIFP| Cwr⋞ Confucianized Lagalist planning∠Heaven-Earth-Man human activism}⇚ {YXT| Nature}

Faziranist Self-masterism. Let $W = K\{\{F\}S\} \sqsubseteq (\Omega,\mathcal{Z}\circ,_\vee\mathcal{H},\{\mathbb{C}\})$ be a system, with $F = \{F_1,F_2,F_3,F_4,F_5\}$ being a system of huangben Faziranism, {.}S being a system of socialism and its impactor, and K{.} being a system of capitalism and its impactor. Suppose the operation of these three systems is not commutative: $\{K\{F\}\}S \neq K\{\{F\}S\}$, then we define:

(R.2-2) $K\{\{F\}S\} \equiv K^*\{F\#S\} = K^*\{\{F_1,F_2,F_3,F_4,F_5\}\#S\}$,

where $*, \# \models \mathcal{H}$ are interactors such that, for $K = K_f \oplus\langle\mathbb{C}_{Kf}\rangle$, $F = F_f \oplus\langle\mathbb{C}_{ff}\rangle$, and $S = S_f \oplus\langle\mathbb{C}_{sf}\rangle)$, $K\{\{F\}S\} = W$, for $W = \{W_f \oplus\langle\mathbb{C}_{Wf}\rangle, W_- \oplus\langle\mathbb{C}_{Wf-}\rangle, CW, W_+ \oplus\langle\mathbb{C}_{W+}\rangle, W_s \oplus\langle\mathbb{C}_{Ws}\rangle\} = \{W_1,W_2,W_3,W_4,W_5\} = W$. That is, we have:

(R.2-3)
$$\begin{aligned}
&(K_f\oplus\langle\mathbb{C}_{Kf}\rangle)*[(F_f\oplus\langle\mathbb{C}_{ff}\rangle)\#(S_f \oplus\langle\mathbb{C}_{sf}\rangle)]\\
&= (K_f\oplus\langle\mathbb{C}_{kf}\rangle)*[(F_f + S_f) \oplus(\langle\mathbb{C}_{ff}\rangle\oplus\langle\mathbb{C}_{sf}\rangle)]\\
&= (K_f + F_f + S_f) \oplus (\langle\mathbb{C}_{kf}\rangle\oplus\langle\mathbb{C}_{ff}\rangle\oplus\langle\mathbb{C}_{sf}\rangle)\\
&= (K_f,F_f,S_f) \oplus \langle\langle\mathbb{C}_{kf}\rangle,\langle\mathbb{C}_{ff}\rangle,\langle\mathbb{C}_{sf}\rangle\rangle\\
&= W_W \oplus \langle\mathbb{C}_{Wf}\rangle\\
&= W.
\end{aligned}$$

From the other perspective, for K, F, S $\sqsubseteq (\Omega,\mathbb{Z}\circ,{}_{v}\mathbb{H},\{\mathbb{C}\})$, we have W $\sqsubseteq \Omega$ as a scheme of 5-polar MFCE system: $W = \{W_1,W_2,W_3,W_4,W_5\} = \{W_f \oplus <\mathbb{C}_f>, W_- \oplus <\mathbb{C}_->, C_W, W_+ \oplus <\mathbb{C}_+>, W_s \oplus <\mathbb{C}_s>\}$. In this system, W_1 is the private production sector, W_2 is the household sector, $W_3 \equiv C_W$ is the central sub-system in which the central planners play the key role in strategic planning and fiscal-monetary policies, W_4 is the public production sector, and W_5 is the R&D sector (with the public activities as the leading force supplemented by the private R&D activities). If in the above grand system, the culture complex is composed of the culture of self-generating creativity, then the cultures of Legalism-Taoism-Confucianism would play the role of secondary center, and the cultures of utilitarian capitalism and democratic socialism would be in the position of non-central subsystems. Then this band new system is called the system of economic self-masterism (Faziranist self-mastering economy).

In general, let $X = \{X_1,X_2,\ldots,X_n\}$, X and $(Y_k,Y_j) \Lleftarrow <\mathbb{C}_X>$, for $Y_j \equiv [(X_1,\mathbb{C}_{X1/Z}), (X_2,\mathbb{C}_{X2/Z}),\ldots,(X_n,\mathbb{C}_{Xn/Z})|(C,\sigma(C))]$ and $Y_k \equiv [(C,\mathbb{C}_{C/Z})|((X_1,\xi_1(X_1)),(X_2,\xi_2(X_2)), \ldots,(X_n, \xi_n(X_n)))]$, where $\xi_i \vDash \mathbb{Z}\circ,{}_{v}\mathbb{H}$, i = 1, 2, …, n. At the same time, let $X \equiv F \sqsubseteq (\Omega,\mathbb{Z}\circ,{}_{v}\mathbb{H},\{\mathbb{C}\})\sqcap E^{F\text{-}Ind\text{-}G}\sqcap E^{YW}\sqcap E^{Ind}\sqcap E^{SI}$, $E^{F\text{-}Ind\text{-}G}$ being the space of the organizations of Faziranist individualism-groupism, E^{YW} being the space of the systemic yu-wu culture, E^{Ind} being the space of the organizations of individualism, and E^{SI} being the space of individualistic-scientific culture. Here by applying the principle of CE centrality (for each X_i, $\psi\{Y_j>Y_k,\Delta_i\} \barwedge E$) to the system X, we have the *principle of the centrality of self-masterism*: $\forall$ i = 1,2,…,n, for each X_i,

$$\text{(R.2-4)} \qquad \psi\{[\mathbb{C}_{X1/z},\mathbb{C}_{X2/z}, \ldots,\mathbb{C}_{Xn/z}|\sigma(C)] \geq [\mathbb{C}_{C/z}|(\xi_1(X_1),\xi_2(X_2),\ldots,\xi n(X_n))],\Delta_i\} \barwedge [\mathbb{C}_X \Lleftarrow E],$$

$\psi, \xi_h \vDash (\Omega,\mathbb{Z}\circ,{}_{v}\mathbb{H},\{\mathbb{C}\})$, h = 1, 2, …, n, where C is the center of this grand system.

We have the static-dynamical inter-penetrating network of Faziranist self-masterism: $(C_S x C^{DS}(e_r),(R_M,R^{DM}(e_r),\tilde{O})=(R,R^D(e_r)) = \{(\rho,\omega)^F$:R/W creation-destruction entity-social PE net||basis being-field of the universe$\angle\mathbb{T}zu^*\}$^{IRI,MW,SIFP, YXr&d| Cwr⋞self-mastering planning} $\Lleftarrow$ {systematic motions and processing | each one as the master of oneself}.

Below we introduce two definitions for the modified Faziranism in the modern time.

Definition R.2-1 (Faziranist socialism). In the above system of Faziranism, let W_1 be the households, W_2 be the production sector (with the public enterprises and the private enterprises playing equal roles, W_3 be the government with equal weights assigned to the central planning mechanism and the indirect economic policies, Z_4 be the intellectuals under the control of party cadres, W_5 be the R&D sector controlled by the Public funding. If the underlying culture is that of democratic socialism, to be supplemented by the cultures of Legalism-Taoism-Confucianism and utilitarian capitalism, then this is the system of **Faziranist socialism**.

Definition R.2-2 (Faziranist capitalism). In the above system of Faziranism, let W_1 be the households, W_2 be the private sector, W_3 be the government with indirect socioeconomic policies, W_4 be the intellectuals under the control of the capitalists, W_5 be the R&D sector controlled by the private institutions supported through public funding. If the underlying culture is that of utilitarian capitalism, to be supplemented by the cultures of Legalism-Taoism-Confucianism and democratic socialism, then this is the system of **Faziranist capitalism**.

R.3 Capitalism

Conflict capitalism. Let $C \sqsubseteq (\Omega,\mathcal{Z}\circ,_v\mathcal{H},\{\mathbb{C}\})$ be a scheme of 5-polar MFCE system: $C = \{C_1,C_2,C_3,C_4,C_5\} = \{C_f \oplus <\mathbb{C}_f>, C_- \oplus <\mathbb{C}_->, CC, C_+ \oplus <\mathbb{C}_+>, C_s \oplus <\mathbb{C}_s>\}$, where C_1 represents the general citizens, C_2 stands for the workers, C_4 refers to the R&D sector, C_5 refers to the capitalist class, and the center CC depicts the government/economic institutions, with the underlying culture being that of utilitarian capitalism and Christianity. Then this is the system of **conflict capitalism.**

In general, for a cultural capitalist economy, let $X = \{X_1,X_2,\ldots,X_n\}$, X and $(Y_k,Y_j) \Leftarrow <\mathbb{C}_X>$, $Y_j \equiv [(X_1,\mathbb{C}_{X1/Z}),(X_2,\mathbb{C}_{X2/Z}),\ldots,(X_n,\mathbb{C}_{Xn/Z})|(C,\sigma(C))]$, $Y_k \equiv [(C, \mathbb{C}_{C/Z})| ((X_1,\xi_1(X_1)),(X_2,\xi_2(X_2)), \ldots, (X_n,\xi_n(X_n)))]$, where $\xi_i \models \mathcal{Z}\circ,_v\mathcal{H}$, $i = 1, 2, \ldots, n$. At the same time, let $X \equiv F \sqsubseteq (\Omega,\mathcal{Z}\circ,_v\mathcal{H},\{\mathbb{C}\})\sqcap E^{Indiv\text{-}Cq}\sqcap E^{SI}$, for $E^{Indiv\text{-}Cq}$ being the space of organizations embedded in the cultures of individualism and conquest, and E^{SI} being the space of the will-rationality of sciences.

Then, by applying the principle of CE balance or the *principle of balance in conflict* (for each X_i, $\psi\{Y_j>Y_k,\Delta_i\} \bar{\wedge}\ \tau$) to the system X, we have $\forall i = 1,2,\ldots,n$, for each X_i,

$$(R.3\text{-}1)\quad \psi\{[\mathbb{C}_{X1/Z},\mathbb{C}_{X2/Z},\ldots,\mathbb{C}_{Xn/Z}|\sigma(c)] \leftrightarrow [\mathbb{C}_{C/Z}|(\xi_1(X_1),\xi_2(X_2),\ldots,\xi n(X_n))],\Delta_i\} \bar{\wedge}\ [\mathbb{C}_X \Leftarrow E],$$

$\xi_h \models \mathcal{Z}\circ,_v\mathcal{H}$, $h = 1,2,\ldots,n$, where C is the center of the system, ψ is the impactor to implement the strategy: $Y_j>Y_k$, and "$\leftrightarrow$" $\models \mathcal{H}$ is the impactor of balance in conflict.

In sum, the static-dynamical interpenetrating network of the capitalist cultural economy is: $(C_S\times C^{DS}(e_r),(R_M,R^{DM}(e_r),\tilde{O}) = (R,R^D(e_r)) = \{(\rho,\omega)^C$: MPFS cycle; private property rights|basis being field of the universe$\angle$Deity$\}^\wedge\{$IRI,MW,SIFP,STr&d| Cwr$\prec$ Market$\} \Leftarrow \{$ST|the capitalists$\}$, where STr&d is the science-based R&D chain of products, and $(\rho,\omega)^C$ is the W/R chain of sciences and conquest culture.

Below, for $X \sqsubseteq (\Omega, \mathcal{Z}\circ,_v\mathcal{H},\{\mathbb{C}\})$ being a 5-polar MFCE system, we have a scheme of capitalist business system: $X = \{X_1,X_2, X_3,X_4,X_5\} = \{X_f \oplus <\mathbb{C}_f>, X_- \oplus <\mathbb{C}_->, C, X_+ \oplus <\mathbb{C}_+>, X_s \oplus <\mathbb{C}_s>\}$, where X_1 is the workers' sector, X_2 is the middle-and-lower levels of management, X_4 is the staffs, X_5 is high-level management, and the center C represents the CEO/Board of directors, with the culture of capitalism: $<\mathbb{C}_X> =\{\tau|[\mathcal{M}^1(\ell,\tau),\ldots,\mathcal{M}^N(\ell,\tau)]\Vdash[E(e_g(\tau)),Z(\mathfrak{C}^*(\tau))]\}$, $\ell \equiv \ell(\sigma,\kappa) \leadsto (\sigma,\kappa) \Vdash \mathcal{L}(\sigma,\kappa) \sqsubseteq Ш^{ДL} \Vdash \mathbb{T}zu^*$, $\tau \Vdash (\mathfrak{Z},Ш^{Д}) \Vdash \mathbb{T}zu^* =$ Deity. Then for $\chi = \{\mathbf{x}(H^*) \Vdash \{[(vd,hc,\gamma),C_S\times C^{DS}(e_r),(R_M, R^{DM}(e_r)),\tilde{O}]\|E\{e_j\},Z\}$, $X = \chi \oplus <\mathbb{C}_X>$ is a **business organization of systemic capitalism**. Here the entrepreneurship in a business organization is a part of the W/R-to-creation-destruction (or creatorship Cwr) of capitalism, for Cwr $\models \{\gamma,\mathbb{C}_X\}$.

R.4 Socialism

Systemic socialism. Let $S \sqsubseteq (\Omega,\mathcal{Z}\circ,_v\mathcal{H},\{\mathbb{C}\})$ be a scheme of 5-polar MFCE system: $S = \{S_1,S_2,S_3,S_4,S_5\} = \{S_f \oplus <\mathbb{C}_f>, S_- \oplus <\mathbb{C}_->, SC, S_+ \oplus <\mathbb{C}_+>, S_s \oplus <\mathbb{C}_s>\}$, where S_1 refers to the general citizens, S_2 depicts the workers, S_4 stands for the R&D sector, S_5 represents the socialist party, and the center SC denotes the government under the control of the socialist party, with the culture of Marxism-Leninism. Then this S is called the **symbolic scheme of Marxist-Leninist socialism**.

Further, let $X = \chi \oplus \langle \mathbb{C}_X \rangle$. Then we have $\chi = \{\mathbf{x}(H^*) \sqsubseteq \{[((vd^P;hc=\circ)=P,\gamma), (C_S \times C^{DS}(e_r))=P^S, (R_M,R^{DM}(e_r)=P^D)],\tilde{O}|E\{e_j\},Z\}$ expressing the party-based control system, $\langle \mathbb{C}_X \rangle = \{\tau|(\mathcal{M}^{IV}(\ell,\tau) = \ldots = \mathcal{M}^{I}(\ell,\tau)$ = materialistic anti-theism based on dialectical rationality) $\Vdash [E(e_r(\tau)),Z(\tau)]\}$, $\tau \Vdash (\mathfrak{I},Ш^{Д}) \Vvdash$ Tzu* (Ultimate Creativity-Destructivity) ≡ matter. Here in X, the Party mechanism is the controlling center of the polity and socio-economy (i.e., vd^P) and the horizontal coordination mechanism (i.e., hc) does not exist; P is the Party system, P^S is the static energy of the Party, P^D is the dynamic energy of the Party, while γ is the indirect control mechanism of socialism.

Complete control system of socialism: $(\omega,\rho) \rightarrow \mathcal{M}^{IV} = \mathcal{M}^{III} = \mathcal{M}^{II} = \mathcal{M}^{I}$.

Strategic space of socialism = {Leap, high-growth, stable-growth, variational growth, strategic continuity|private property rights = ○}.

Symbolic iso-systemism of socialism. The system of iso-systemism runs through all of the psychological, economic, sociopolitical structures: Dialectic rationality/scientific rationality-coercion-collectivism.

Static-dynamical interpenetrating structure of socialism. Centered on the Party and stretching to the polity-commerce to form the means of production-money-Party-power-sex cycle. This static-dynamical inter-penetrating structure of socialism is: $(C_S \times C^{DS}(e_r)),(R_M,R^{DM}(e_r),\tilde{O}) = (R,R^D(e_r)) = \{(\rho,\omega)^S$: MPFX cycle; Political power∠military power∠Party Power|basis being-field of the universe∠Self-Organizational Creativity-Destructivity}^{IRI,MW,SIFP,STr&d| Cwr ≺ central planning} ⇚ {ST-Δ| party cadres}, where $(\rho,\omega)^{Soc}$ refers to the dialectic rationality-collective will-to-conquest chain.

To be general, let $X = \{X_1,X_2,\ldots,X_n\}$, X and $(Y_k,Y_j) \Lleftarrow \langle \mathbb{C}_X \rangle$. For $X \equiv F \sqsubseteq (\Omega,\mathbb{Z}\circ,_v\mathbb{H},\{\mathbb{C}\}) \sqcap E^s \sqcap E^D$, E^S being the space of collective organization of socialism, E^D being the space of dialectic will/rationality culture, by applying the principle of CE balance and CE centrality (for each X_i, $\psi\{Y_j > Y_k,\Delta_j\} \,\bar{\bar{\barwedge}}\, \tau$) to this system X, we derive the principle of absolute collectivism: $\forall i = 1, 2, \ldots, n$, for each X_i,

(R.4-1) $\psi\{[\mathbb{C}_{X1/Z},\mathbb{C}_{X2/Z}, \ldots,\mathbb{C}_{Xn/Z}|\sigma(C)],\Delta_i\} \wedge \psi\{\mathcal{T}^*C \geq \mathcal{T}X_i,\Delta_i\} \,\bar{\bar{\barwedge}}\, [\mathbb{C}_X \Lleftarrow E]$,

$\xi_h \vDash \mathcal{Z}\circ,_v\mathcal{H}$, $h = 1,2,\ldots n$, where C is the center of the system and ψ is the strategic impactor implementing the strategy: $Y_j > Y_k$ (for $\mathcal{T} \vDash \mathcal{Z}\circ,_v\mathcal{H}$, $\mathcal{T}^*$ being the target strategy, C being the center of the system). Here $[\mathbb{C}_{C/Z}|(\xi_1(X_1),\xi_2(X_2),\ldots,\xi n(X_n))] = \circ$ (the empty system).

R.5 Islam

Symbolic system of Islam. Let $I \sqsubseteq (\Omega,\mathbb{Z}\circ,_v\mathbb{H},\{\mathbb{C}\})$ be a scheme of 5-polar MFCE system: $I = \{I_1,I_2,I_3,I_4,I_5\} = \{I_f \oplus \langle \mathbb{C}_{If} \rangle, I_- \oplus \langle \mathbb{C}_{I-} \rangle, IC, I_l \oplus \langle \mathbb{C}_{I+} \rangle, I_s \oplus \langle \mathbb{C}_{Is} \rangle\}$, where I_1 refers to the general citizens, I_2 depicting the workers, I_4 standing for the R&D sector, I_5 representing the clergy, and the center SC (=C) being the government of central planning under the control of the clergy, with the culture of Islam. Then this I is called the **symbolic system of Islam**.

In the following, we shall develop a scheme of Islam. This is a preliminary attempt, and any suggestion and criticism are cordially welcomed.

Further, let $X = \chi \oplus \langle \mathbb{C}_X \rangle$. Then we have $\chi = \{\mathbf{x}(H^*) \sqsubseteq \{[((vd^S;hc=\circ)=S,\gamma),C_S \times C^{DS}(e_r)=S^S, (R_M, R^{DM}(e_r)=S^D),\tilde{O}]\|E\{e_j\},Z\}$ expressing the Clergy-based control system, $\langle \mathbb{C}_X \rangle = \{\tau|(\mathcal{M}^{IV}(\ell,\tau) =\ldots =\mathcal{M}^{I}(\ell,\tau)=\text{Islamic theism}) \Vdash [E(e_r(\tau)),Z(\tau)], \tau \Vdash (\mathfrak{I},Ш^{Д}) \Vvdash \mathbb{T}\mathbb{zu}^*$ (Ultimate Creativity-Destructivity) $\equiv$ Allah.

In this system, there is no individual activism: $(\omega,\rho) \rightarrow \mathcal{M}^{I}(e_r^{I},e_r^{II},e_r^{III},e_r^{IV})$ --- $\mathcal{M}^{II}(e_r^{II},e_r^{III}, e_r^{IV})$ -- $\mathcal{M}^{III}(e_r^{III},e_r^{IV})$ - $\mathcal{M}^{IV}(e_r^{IV})$. Here in this S, the clerical mechanism is the controlling center of the polity and socio-economy (i.e., vd^S) and the horizontal coordination mechanism (i.e., hc) does not exist; S is the Clerical system, P^S is the static energy of the Clergy, P^D is the dynamic energy of the Clergy, while γ represents the indirect control mechanism of Islam.

Complete control system of Islam: $(\omega,\rho) \rightarrow \mathcal{M}^{I} = \mathcal{M}^{II} = \mathcal{M}^{III} = \mathcal{M}^{IV}$ (theism).

Strategic space of Islam = {high-growth, stable-growth, variational growth, strategic continuity|private property rights $=\circ$}.

Symbolic iso-systemism of Islam. It manifestes itself in all of the psychological, economic, socio-political structures: Theological rationality/ scientific rationality-communitarianism.

Static-dynamical interpenetrating structure of Islam. Centered on the Party and stretching to the polity-commerce to form the means of production-money-Clergy-power-sex cycle. This static-dynamical inter-penetrating structure of Islam is: $(C_S \times^{DS}(e_r),(R_M,R^{DM}(e_r),\tilde{O}) = (R,R^D(e_r))$ $=\{(\rho,\omega)^S$: MPFX cycle; Political power∠military power∠Clergical Power|basis being-field of the universe∠Ultimate Creativity-Destructivity=Allah} ^ {IRI,MW,SIFP,STr&d| Cwr⋞central planning} $\Leftarrow$ {ST-Δ|clergy}, where $(\rho,\omega)^{Islam}$ refers to the theological rationality-communitarian will-to-conquest chain.

To be general, let $X = \{X_1,X_2,\ldots,X_n\}$, X and $(Y_k,Y_j) \Leftarrow \langle \mathbb{C}_X \rangle$. For $X \equiv F \sqsubseteq (\Omega,\mathbb{Z}\circ,_v \mathbb{H},\{\mathbb{C}\}) \sqcap E^{Sh} \sqcap E^{sh}$, E^{Sh} being the space of religious organization of Islam, E^{sh} being the space of Deity's will/rationality culture, by applying the principle of CE balance-centrality (for each X_i, $\psi\{Y_j>Y_k,\Delta_i\} \barwedge E$) to this system X, we derive the principle of absolute collectivism: $\forall i = 1,2,\ldots,n$, for each X_i,

(R.5-1) $\psi\{[\mathbb{C}_{X1/Z},\mathbb{C}_{X2/Z}, \ldots,\mathbb{C}_{Xn/Z}|\sigma(c)],\Delta_i\}\wedge\psi\{\mathcal{T}^*C \geq \mathcal{T}X_i,\Delta_i\} \barwedge [\mathbb{C}_X \Leftarrow E]$,

$\xi_h \vDash \mathbb{Z}\circ,_v\mathbb{H}$, $h = 1,2,\ldots n$, where c is the center of the system and ψ is the strategic impactor implementing the strategy: $Y_j>Y_k$. Here $[\mathbb{C}_{C/Z}|(\xi_1(X_1),\xi_2(X_2),\ldots,\xi n(X_n))] = \circ$ (the empty system).

Appendix S – Systematic Distribution of Self-Mastering System

S.1 Introduction

To have a natural presentation of a system in terms of graphs, in this chapter, we develop a scheme of systemic distribution for a system.

S.2 Basic Concepts and Definitions

In order to facilitate our development of the scheme of systemic distribution of a system, we shall present some basic concepts here in the following.

The **TCentral position of a system** is the location of a system in question in a graph of the YY n-polar MFCE scheme when it reaches a state of TCentral (or, in a simple case, a state of systemic and strategic continuity).

The **position of self-masterism of a system** is the location of a system in question in graph of the YY n-polar MFCE scheme when it reaches a state of self-masterism.

S.3 Systemic Distribution of System

For the **world of systemic distribution**, it can be characterized by a YY 5-polar MFCE scheme. It can also be represented graphically by Figure S.3-1 in which one can locate the TCentral position of the system as in (x,y) (also see Figure 1.1, Chapter 1).

Figure S.3-1
Systemic distribution of X: TCentral and non-TCentral positions of X, $X^{TCentral} \equiv (x,y)$, x = yin, y = yang.

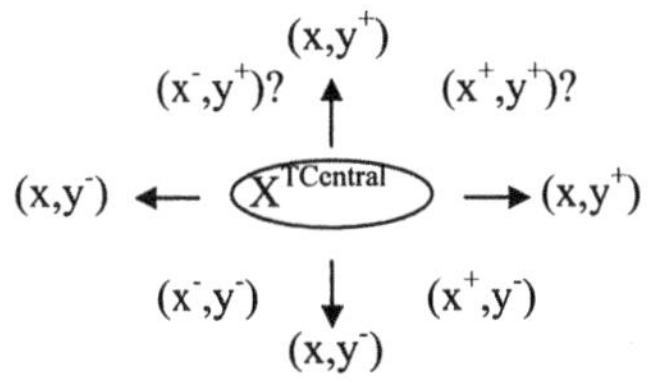

The TCentral position of X is at $X^{TCentral} \equiv (x,y)$, where y and z stand for yin and yang elements, respectively. As for the non-TCentral positions of X, any point other than (x,y) is a non-TCentral position of X.

For a system in question, this TCentral position of the system may be just the position of self-masterism. One case in point is that for the system in question to be the center (or the leader) of the world, it is the position of self-masterism for the leader in the world of one center.

S.4 Systemic Distribution of System in The World of Self-masterism

Seen from Figure S.4-1, in general, the TCentral position of the system may not be a position of self-masterism for this system. In the case that the system in question is not the leader of the world, its position of self-masterism may lie to the northeast-side of (x,y), with (x^{+},y^{++}) or (.,.,N) with N denoting a new sector of industry), while the "Northeast position" of this system (i.e., (x^{+},y^{+})) is occupied by the world leader.

Note that historically, for a weak system (or nation), in order to achieve a position of self-masterism, it may be necessary for this system either to have internal strengths moving onto a leap path and push for a leap process of development and advancement.

PART IV SYSMETRICS

Appendix T – Systemmetric Structure

This Appendix is about the "metric studies" of systematics, called systemmetrics or just sysmetrics for short. Following the inspiration of the systemic distribution presented in previous chapters, one may be able to develop a new statistics, not micro-statistics, but "macro-global statistics" and "systemic statistics." In the following, we shall pursue this direction.

T.1 Introduction

To search for the differences of systems, we could base our studies on examining the differences in structures, functions and psychological/esthetic perceptions.

In the following, we propose two ways to test our theories of systematics. First, we hope to convert our systematic systems into the numerical world, and then use traditional method of statistics, for example, the tests constructed out of standard normal distribution, t distribution, χ^2-distribution, F distribution, some non-parametric methods of testing, and even others.

The direction of the above approach is to develop a statistics of organization in the sense that: (1) each statistics is a system, and (2) the statistics is a statistics of systems.

Secondly, we hope to develop some methods, called the methods of system-metrics, or methods of sysmetrics for short, to handle our problems of testing. For this new direction, we are still searching for effect ways to tackle this problem.

In the following, we shall proceed to develop our techniques based on the differences in structures of the systems in question. For a system, we would like to differentiate the testing of the formal-informal parts of the system from that of cultures involved in the system. To be more specific, let $X = \chi \oplus \langle \mathbb{C}_X \rangle \sqsubseteq (\Omega, \mathcal{Z}_\circ, {}_v\mathcal{H}, \{\mathbb{C}\})$ be a system (with the symbol: $X = \Delta\text{-}\boxtimes \oplus \langle\rangle$), where $\chi = \{\mathbf{x}(H^*) \sqsubseteq \{[(vd,hc,\gamma), C_S \times C^{DS}(e_r),(R_M,R^{DM}(e_r)),\tilde{O}] \| E\{e_j\},Z\}$ is the formal-informal organization-hierarchical part of the system (i.e., the system-organization interpenetrating structures of X) and $\langle \mathbb{C}_X \rangle = \{\tau | (\mathcal{M}^1(\ell,\tau), \ldots, \mathcal{M}^N(\ell,\tau)) \Vdash [E(e_r(\tau)), Z(\tau)]\}$, $\tau \Vdash (\mathfrak{I}, \text{Ш}^{Д}) \Vvdash \mathbb{T}\text{zu}^*$, is the cultural part. Here ℓ ($\equiv \ell(\sigma,\kappa) \Vdash \text{Ш}^{\mathcal{L}(\sigma,\kappa)} \Subset \text{Ш}^{ДL}$) is the forces seeding the historicity of the human kind.

In terms of testing for $\chi = \Delta\text{-}\boxtimes$ in the system $X \sqsubseteq (\Omega, \mathcal{Z}_\circ, {}_v\mathcal{H}, \{\mathbb{C}\})$, we shall use the N-level cceptance deviation and testing to be introduced below in Section T.2, and for testing the cultural complex $\langle \mathbb{C}_X \rangle$, we hope to employ the method of core/partial core distribution introduced below in Section T.3.

T.2 N-Level Acceptable Deviation and Testing

In this section, we discuss two types of N-level acceptable deviation and testing: one in the form of a three-element system with center (i.e., tri-system) and the other in the form of a 5-element system with center (i.e. 5-polar MFCE system).

Before we proceed to the discussions of the testing methods, let us have the following definitions:

(1) The **standard 3-element system** is a 3-element system {x,y|z} in which (i) x and y are in absolute balance, (ii) y is either the y-systemism of x or the Hf-systmeism of x, and (iii) z is either the h-systemism of {x,y}, corresponding to the y-systemism, or the Hh-systemism of x, corresponding to the y-systemism in (ii) in the above.

(2) The **standard 5-polar MFCE scheme** is a 5-polar MFCE scheme {E,N,C,N,W} with the following conditions: (i) C is the center, E and W are in absolute balance and so are the relationships between S and N and between {E,W} and {S,N}. Here, note that the center can be just a virtual center. (ii) The creation of N from {E,W} given the cultural energy of the virtual center is an n-systemism (going north) and the creation of S from {E,W} given the cultural energy of the virtual center is a s-systemism (going south), (iii) The creation of E from {S,N} given the cultural energy of the virtual center is an e-systemism (going east) and the creation of W from {S,N} given the cultural energy of the virtual center is a w-systemism (going west).

Definition T.2-1. Let the systems in question be in the form Δ in "Δ-⊠ ⊕ <>" ⊑ $(\Omega,\mathbb{Z}_{\circ,\vee}\mathbb{H},\{\mathbb{C}\})$. Suppose U is the standard 3-layer system and X is the system we would like to test against U. Let d_{11} be the actual structure of differences of the first layer elements between U and X (at the first level acceptability), $d_{11}*$ be the target structure of differences of the first layer elements between U and X, d_{21} be the actual structure of differences of the second layer elements between U and X, $d_{21}*$ be the target structure of differences of the second layer elements between U and X, d_{31} be the actual structure of differences of the third layer elements between U and X, and $d_{31}*$ be the target structure of differences of the third layer elements between U and X. Then $\{d_{11}*,d_{21}*,d_{31}*\}$ is called the **target of the first-level acceptable deviations** of X from U.

Let d_{12} be the actual structure of differences of the first layer elements between U and X (at the second level acceptability), $d_{12}*$ be the target structure of differences of the first layer elements between U and X ($d_{12}* \neq d_{11}*$, i.e., the structure of $d_{12}*$ is larger than $d_{11}*$)(at the second level acceptability), d_{22} be the actual structure of differences of the second layer elements between U and X (at the second level acceptability), $d_{22}*$ be the target structure of differences of the second layer elements between U and X ($d_{22}* \neq d_{21}*$, the structure of $d_{22}*$ is larger than $d_{21}*$)(at the second level acceptability), d_{32} be the actual structure of differences of the third layer elements between U and X (at the second level acceptability), $d_{32}*$ be the target structure of differences of the third layer elements between U and X ($d_{32}* \neq d_{31}*$, the structure of $d_{32}*$ is larger than d_{31}) (at the second level acceptability). Then $\{d_{12}*,d_{22}*,d_{32}*\}$ is called the **target of the second-level acceptable deviations** of X from U.

Let d_{13} be the actual structure of differences of the first layer elements between U and X (at the third level acceptability), $d_{13}*$ be the target structure of differences of the first layer elements between U and X ($d_{13}* \neq d_{12}*$, the structure of $d_{13}*$ is larger than $d_{12}*$)(at the third level acceptability), d_{23} be the actual structure of differences of the second layer elements between U and X (at the third level acceptability), $d_{23}*$ be the target structure of differences of the second layer elements between U and X ($d_{23}* \neq d_{22}*$, the structure of $d_{23}*$ is larger than $d_{22}*$)(at the third level acceptability), d_{33} be the actual structure of differences of the third layer elements between U and X , d_{33*} be the target structure of differences of the third layer elements between U and X ($d_{33}* \neq d_{32}*$, the structure of $d_{33}*$ is larger than $d_{32}*$)(at the third level acceptability). Then $\{d_{13}^*, d_{23}^*, d_{33}^*\}$ is called the **target of third-level acceptable deviations** of X from U.

Thus, in the above, we have three levels of acceptability in our sysmetric testing conditioned upon the definition of all these d_{ij}, i,j = 1,2,3.

Below we shall develop another testing method by looking at aspects of generating (or sheng) and destructing (i.e., ke) forces within a system.

Definition T.2-2. Let the hypotheses be: for all i, j = 1, 2, 3,

(T.2-1) H_0: $d_{ij} > d_{ij}^*$

(T.2-2) H_1: $d_{ij} \leq d_{ij}^*$

(T.2-3) H_0': $y_{ij} > y_{ij}^*$ (y_{ij} being a y-systemism of x_{ij} where j denotes the jth level of acceptability) or $Hf_{ij} > Hf_{ij}^*$ (Hf_{ij} is an Hf-systemism of x_{ij})

(T.2-4) H_1': $h_{ij} \leq h_{ij}^*$ (h-systemism) or $Hh_{ij} \leq Hh_{ij}^*$ (Hh-systemism)

Then we have the following:

Definition T.2-3. In Definition T.2-2, if H_0 and H_0' are not true, then we fail to reject H_1 and H_1'. That is, in this case, it is said that the deviation is not significant at the level of j.

Definition T.2-4. Let the systems in question be in the form $\boxtimes$ in "$X = \Delta\text{-}\boxtimes \oplus \Diamond$" $\sqsubseteq$ $(\Omega, \mathbb{Z}^{\circ}{}_{,v}\mathbb{H}, \{\mathbb{C}\})$. Suppose S is the standard 5-polar MECE scheme of system X that we would like to test against. Let δ_{11} be the actual structure of differences of the central elements between S and X, δ_{11}^* be the target structure of differences of the central elements between S and X, δe be the target structure of differences of the E-generation between S and X (i.e., σ(sheng1):{S,N|CC}→ E, for σ (sheng1) $\models \mathbb{Z}^{\circ}{}_{,v}\mathbb{H}$ being an impactor of e-systemism), δe* be the target structure of differences of the E-generation between S and X, δw be the actual structure of differences of the W-generation between S and X (i.e., σ(sheng2): {S,N|CC}→ W, for σ (sheng2) $\models \mathbb{Z}^{\circ}{}_{,v}\mathbb{H}$ being an impactor of w-systemism), and δw* be the target structure of differences of the W-generation between S and X.

Further, let δn be the target structure of differences of the N-generation (or "generating-N") between S and X (i.e., σ(ke1):{E,W|CC}→ N, for σ(ke1) $\models \mathbb{Z}^{\circ}{}_{,v}\mathbb{H}$ being an impactor of n-systemism), δn* be the target structure of differences of the N-generation between S and X, δs be the actual structure of differences of the S-generation between S and X (i.e., σ(ke2):{E,W|CC}→ S, for σ(ke2) $\models \mathbb{Z}^{\circ}{}_{,v}\mathbb{H}$ being an impactor of s-systemism), and δs* be the target structure of differences of the S-generation between S and X.

Note that in the above, ($sheng_i$ or shengi) is the "positive aspect" of characteristic i, i = 1, 2; and (ke_i or kei) is the "negative aspect" of characteristic i, i = 1, 2.

Then $\{\delta_{11}^*, \delta e^*, \delta w^*\}$ is called the **target of the mutual-beneficially acceptable deviations** of X from S, in the case of a 5-polar MFCE scheme.

Similarly we define $\{\delta_{11}*, \delta n*, \delta s*\}$ as the **target of the mutual-harmfully acceptable deviations** of X from S. Furthermore, in the case of a 5-polar MFCE scheme, we shall define $\{\delta_{11}*, \delta e*, \delta w*, \delta n*, \delta s*\}$ as the **target of the mutual-beneficially/harmfully acceptable deviations** of X from S (mutual- beneficial/ harmfully acceptable).
Note that we assume in the MFCE scheme presented in the above, the impactor $\sigma(\text{sheng}_i) \vDash \mathbb{Z}\circ,_v\mathbb{H}$ creates a system (or grand system) of tranquility, while impactor $\sigma(\text{ke}_i) \vDash \mathbb{Z}\circ,_v\mathbb{H}$ creates a system (or grand system) of conflict.

Definition T.2-5. Let the hypotheses be: for all i =1, 2, 3, 4, 5, j = 1 (mutual-beneficially acceptable), 2 (mutual-harmfully acceptable), 3 (mutual-beneficial/ harmfully acceptable).

(T.2-5) H_0: $d_{ij} > d_{ij}*$

(T.2-6) H_1: $d_{ij} \leq d_{ij}*$

(T.2-7) H_0''': $\delta e_{ij} > \delta e_{ij}*$($\delta e_{ij}$, $\delta e_{ij}*$ referring to differences in e-systemism)

(T.2-8) H_1''': $\delta e_{ij} \leq \delta e_{ij}*$

(T.2-9) H_0'''': $\delta w_{ij} > \delta w_{ij}*$ (δw_{ij} , $\delta w_{ij}*$ referring to differences in w-systemism)

(T.2-10) H_1'''': $\delta w_{ij} \leq \delta w_{ij}*$

or

(T.2-11) H_0': $\delta n_{ij} > \delta n_{ij}*$ (δn_{ij} , $\delta n_{ij}*$ referring to differences in u-systemism)

(T.2-12) H_1': $\delta n_{ij} \leq \delta n_{ij}*$

(T.2-13) H_0'': $\delta s_{ij} > \delta s_{ij}*$ (s_{ij} , $s_{ij}*$ referring to differences in x-systemism)

(T.2-14) H_1'': $\delta s_{ij} \leq \delta s_{ij}*$

Then we have the following:

Definition T.2-6. In Definition T.2-5, if H_0, H_0'and H_0'' (or H_0''' and H_0'''') are not true, then we fail to reject H_1, H_1'and H_1'' (or H_1''' and H_1''''). That is, in this case, it is said that the deviations are not significant at the level of j.

Below we shall develop another testing method by looking at aspects of strategic options facing the system in question: available strategic options, strategic actions being taken, and timing, etc.

Definition T.2-7. Space of strategic options: $\{D, G^+, G, S^+, S, S^-, V, sC\}$

For example, D-strategic firm/organization:

(T.2-15) X = {consumption,production|central authority|Z} $\sqsubseteq (\Omega, \mathbb{Z}\circ,_v\mathbb{H}, \{\mathbb{C}\})$

(T.2-16) X = X(.|Z), where Z = $Z(.|\Omega^{Org} \sqcap \Omega^{Strg}) \Lleftarrow \{\mathbb{C} \Vdash \mathbb{T}zu*\}$, where $\Omega^{Strg} = \{D,G,S,V,C\}$, following the principle of centrality-balance: centrality of the key element, CE balance among all targets.

T.3 Core/Partial Core Distribution

Distribution of Core/partial core-time, space and states. Let the distribution map of X be: the vertical axis is the axis of first-step core-second-step core- ...-nth-step core ...first-step partial core-second-step core-...-mth-step partial core, and the horizontal axis of X be the collection of the points of observations of time, space or states, etc. These numbers of n and m shall be determined by the specific problem.

Here, if any of these points (ith-step core or jth-step partial core) on the axes are empty, then they are simply missing in this problem. In addition, the distribution of the vertical axis can be: axis of first-step core-second-step core-...-nth-step core ...first-step partial core of the first-step core-first-step partial core of the second-step core-...- first-step partial core of the nth-step core first-step partial core of the -...- qth-step partial core of the first-step core-qth-step partial core of the second-step core-...- qth-step partial core of the nth-step core-..., etc.

Note that partial cores can be classified from the perspectives of steps or the partial cores of thesis/antithesis, positivity/negativity and front/back, etc.

Distributions of the general and partial cores. In the general situation, let the mid-point (or middle point) of X be the highest point. By assuming a symmetric distribution, the distribution of the high-low differences is horizontally balanced. Here the ratios of the areas of the distribution of the first-, second- and third-level differences to total area of distribution must be determined by historical data.

Figure T.3-1
Distribution of Cores/partial cores of X

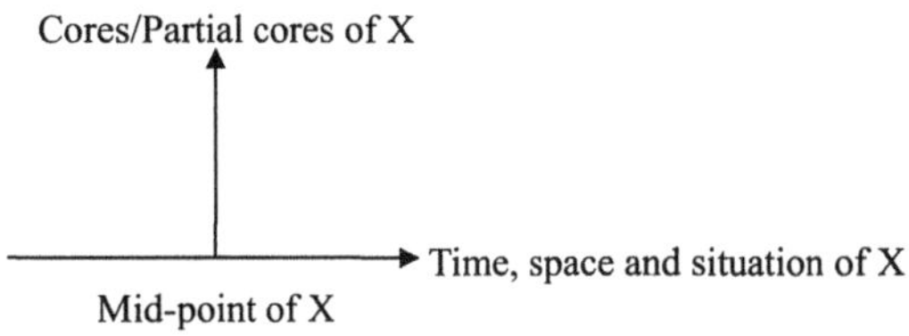

T.4 Testing Methods of Differences

In order to conduct researches on the phenomena of systematics, it is necessary to develop methods of differentiating proto-type systems from non-proto-type systems. Below we take several steps to proceed into this direction.

i. *Yin-yang-he scheme*. Let $X = \{x-,x+,x_h\} \sqsubseteq (\Omega,\mathbb{Z}^{\circ},{}_{v}\mathcal{H},\{\mathbb{C}\})$ be a system, where $x- \Vdash U$ being a yin-element of tranquil culture, $x+ \Vdash U$ being a yang-element of tranquil culture, and $x_h \Vdash U$ being a he-element of tranquil culture.

ii. *Thesis-antithesis-synthesis scheme.* Let $Y = \{y-,y+,y_h\} \sqsubseteq (\Omega,\mathbb{Z}\circ,{}_{v}\mathbb{H},\{\mathbb{C}\})$ be a system in which $y- \Vdash U$ is a thesis-element of conflict culture, $y+ \Vdash U$ is an antithesis-element of conflict culture, and $y_h \Vdash U$ is a synthesis-element of conflict culture.

iii. *Scheme of bi-culture as a system.* Let $X = \{a,b,c\} \sqsubseteq (\Omega,\mathbb{Z}\circ,{}_{v}\mathbb{H},\{\mathbb{C}\})$ be a simple system, $a = (y-,s)$, $b = (y+,t)$, $c = (h,z)$, where $y- \Vdash \mathbf{U}$ is a yin-element of tranquil culture, $y+ \Vdash U$ is a yang-element of tranquil culture, $h \Vdash \mathbf{U}$ is a he-element of tranquil culture, $s \Vdash \mathbf{U}$ is a thesis-element of conflict culture, $t \Vdash \mathbf{U}$ is a antithesis- element of conflict culture, $z \Vdash \mathbf{U}$ is a synthesis-element of conflict culture.

iv. *Scheme of bi-culture as a grand system.* Let $X = \{S,T,W\} \sqsubseteq (\Omega,\mathbb{Z}\circ,{}_{v}\mathbb{H},\{\mathbb{C}\})$ be a grand system in which $S, T, W \sqsubseteq (\Omega,\mathbb{Z}\circ,{}_{v}\mathbb{H},\{\mathbb{C}\})$ are independent subsystems.

Now we are in a position to discuss various systems of sysmetric differences.

Definition T.4-1. Let $X = \{x-,x+,x_h\} \sqsubseteq (\Omega,\mathbb{Z}\circ,{}_{v}\mathbb{H},\{\mathbb{C}\})$ be a proto-type system of yin-yang-he, $F = \{f-,f+,f_h\} \sqsubseteq (\Omega,\mathbb{Z}\circ,{}_{v}\mathbb{H},\{\mathbb{C}\})$ be any system of yin-yang-he. Then $\phi\{X\Theta F\} = \phi\{y-\Theta f-,y+\Theta f+,x_h\Theta f_h\} \sqsubseteq (\Omega,\mathbb{Z}\circ,{}_{v}\mathbb{H},\{\mathbb{C}\})$ is said to be the *difference-manifesting system* of X, where $\Theta \models \mathbb{Z}\circ,{}_{v}\mathbb{H}$ is an impactor to derive differences in-between systems, and $\phi \models \mathbb{Z}\circ,{}_{v}\mathbb{H}$ is system-completion impactor.

We shall also let "$\|_{simple}$" be the symbol expressing the transformation of a system into its simplest form. Then $\phi\{X\Theta F\}\|_{simple} \sqsubseteq (\Omega,\mathbb{Z}\circ,{}_{v}\mathbb{H},\{\mathbb{C}\})$ is said to be a **system of difference-simplification**.

Let $W = \phi\{X\Theta F\}\|_{simple}$. Below we shall designate the **positive difference** by a red color bead, designate the **negative difference** by a blue color bead, and designate **no-difference** by a water-color bead. Then this system of difference-in-simplification can be depicted by the **string of red-blue-water color beads**. If we define it by differentiating the first-level core from the second-level up to the Nth–level cores, and further differentiate them into the first-step partial core (the first–level core/the first-step partial core up to the first-level core /the ith-step partial core) from the second-step up to the Nth–step partial cores (i.e., the Nth–level core/the first-level partial core up to the Nth-level core/the jth-step partial core), $N, i, j \in \mathbb{N}$, then we derive the cores/partial cores string of red-blue-water core beads.

Definition T.4-2. The way to differentiate significant difference from insignificant difference is achieved by focusing on the differences of the cores of the first few stages (for instance, first to three stages) but ignoring the differences of the non-cores. For example, if there is no difference for the first three stages of the cores, then we claim that there is no significant difference between the actual system and the target system.

In the above, to differentiate the significance from the insignificance of the deviations, we may resort to the method of color string by using the deviation-manifesting system $\phi\{X\Theta F\}$.

Definition T.4-3. Let $X = \{x-,x+,x_h\} \sqsubseteq (\Omega,\mathbb{Z}\circ,{}_{v}\mathbb{H},\{\mathbb{C}\})$ be a proto-type system of yin-yang-he, $Y = \{f-,f+,f_h\} \sqsubseteq (\Omega,\mathbb{Z}\circ,{}_{v}\mathbb{H},\{\mathbb{C}\})$ be any system of yin-yang-he, and define $\phi\{Y\Theta X\} = \phi\{f-\Theta y-,f+\Theta y+,f_h\Theta x_h\} \sqsubseteq (\Omega,\mathbb{Z}\circ,{}_{v}\mathbb{H},\{\mathbb{C}\})$ as the part of Y which are not present in X. Then $\phi\{Y\Theta X\} \succ ⌽$ ("$x \succ ⌽$" is read as "x being positive") is said to be the positive or *right difference-manifesting system* of X, where $\Theta \models \mathbb{Z}\circ,{}_{v}\mathbb{H}$ is an impactor to derive differences in between systems, and $\phi \models \mathbb{Z}\circ,{}_{v}\mathbb{H}$ is system-completion impactor. Similar, define $\phi\{Y\Theta X\} = \phi\{f-\Theta y-$

$,f+\Theta y+,f_h\Theta x_h\} \sqsubseteq (\Omega,\mathbb{Z}\circ,_v\mathbb{H},\{\mathbb{C}\})$ as the part of Y which are missing using X as the standard system. Then $\phi\{X\Theta Y\} \prec \Phi$ ("$x \prec \Phi$" is read as "x being negative") is said to be the negative or *left difference-manifesting system* of X, and $|\phi\{X\Theta F\}||_{simple}\ | \equiv \{\phi\{X\Theta F\}||_{simple}\} \sqcup \{\phi\{X\Theta F\}||_{simple}\} \sqsubseteq (\Omega,\mathbb{Z}\circ,_v\mathbb{H},\{\mathbb{C}\})$ is said to be *a two-sided system of difference-in-simplification.*

Figure T.4-1
Distribution of Cores/partial cores of X: M = midpoint of $|\phi\{X\Theta F\}||_{simple}|$

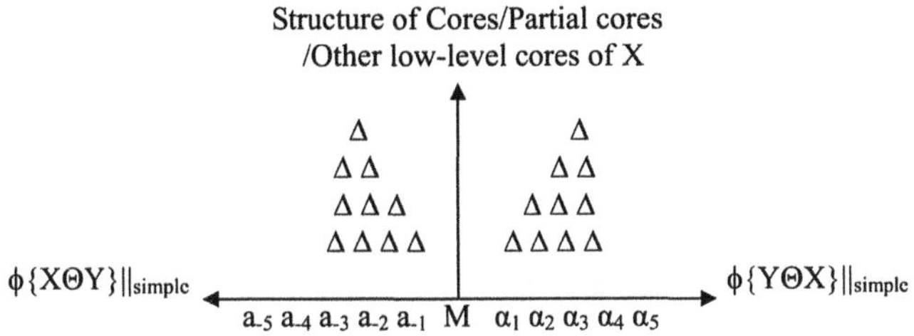

Let $|\phi\{X\Theta F\}||_{simple}| \sqsubseteq (\Omega,\mathbb{Z}\circ,_v\mathbb{H},\{\mathbb{C}\})\sqcap\mathbb{C}$, then for a graphically presentation, we have Figure T.4-1, in which on both sides of M (M being the midpoint of the horizontal axis), we shall assume one-sided skewed distributions.

T.5 The Other Method of Testing Deviation – Dragon Chain

Below we develop a new method for testing deviations of systems.

Definition T.5-1. For $s_1, s_2, s_3 \Vdash \Omega$, let $S = \{s_1,s_2|s_3\} \sqsubseteq (\Omega,\mathbb{Z}\circ,_v\mathbb{H},\{\mathbb{C}\})\sqcap\mathbb{C}$ be the standard system of three-elements with s_3 as the center of the system and s_1, s_2 being non-central elements. Suppose we have N^S, which will be called the **norm of S**, as an integrated measure of the system with $s_1 \geq s_1/N^S$, $s_2 \geq s_2/N^S$ and $s_2 \leq s_3/N^S$. Here, by "s_1/N^S" is meant s_1 to be scaled by the "factor of N^S." Then, for $S' = \{s_1/N^S, s_2/N^S, s_3/N^S\}$, we shall call it the **standardized norm-system.**

Below, let W* be the structure of S' in terms of core-partial cores and Y* be the collection of the orders of the core-partial cores of S'. That is, in Figure T.5-1, W_1* is the structure of core, W_2* is the structure of core and the first –level partial core, W_3* is the structure of core, the first–level partial core and second–level core, etc., while y_1* is the order of the core, y_2* is the order of the core and the first –level partial core, y_3* is the structure of the core, the first–level partial core and second–level core, etc.

Definition T.5-2. For any system $A = \{a_1, a_2, a_3\}$, $a_1, a_2, a_3 \Vdash \Omega$, $A = \{a_1,a_2|a_3\} \sqsubseteq (\Omega,\mathbb{Z}\circ,_v\mathbb{H},\{\mathbb{C}\}) \sqcap \mathbb{C}$, with a_3 being the center of the system and a_1, a_2 being non-central elements. Suppose we have Δ^A, which will be called the **norm of A**, as an integrated measure of the system with $a_1 \geq a_1/\Delta^A$, $a_2 \geq a_2/\Delta^A$ and $a_3 \leq a_3/\Delta^A$. Here, by "a_i/Δ^A" is meant a_i to be scaled by the "factor of Δ^A." Then, for $A' = \{a_1/\Delta^A, a_2/\Delta^A, a_3/\Delta^A\}$, we shall call it the **standardized system of A.**

Figure T.5-1
Distribution of S': Flying/Regretting Dragon chain as the envelop of the distribution

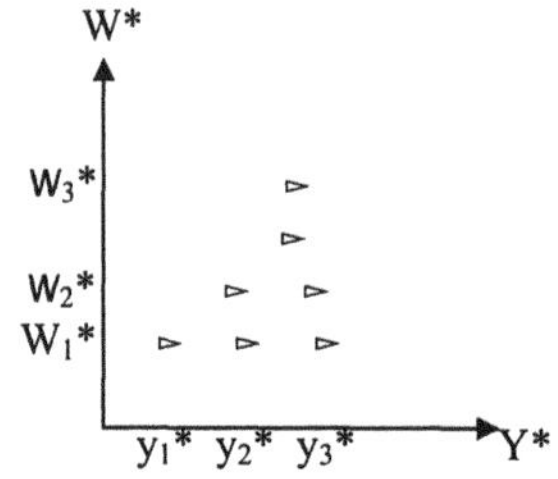

Now we have the Figure T.5-2 as the distribution of a system A'. In this figure, a_1 is the structure of the core of A', a_2 is the structure of the core and the first-level partial core of A', a_3 is the structure of the core and the second-level partial core of A', etc., while y_1 is the order of the core, y_2 is the order of the core and the first-level partial core, y_3 is the order of the core and the second–level core, etc.

Figure T.5-2
Distribution of A'

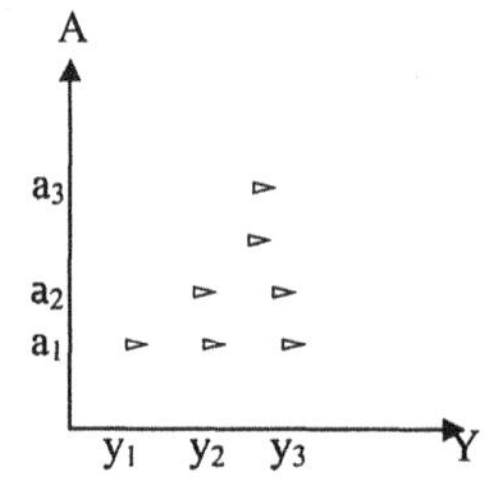

Definition T.5-3. The **average system** of a type of system is the form of the system most likely to appear in history.

Below, for a system A, let the average (or target) system of A be W, and the structures of the deviations of the average (or target) system (after standardization) from the standardized norm-system (and after scaling) be W_{+}^{*} and W_{-}^{*}. That is, W_{+}^{*} represents the structure of $(S'\Theta W')^{+}/ N^{S}$ arranged according to the structures of core/partial cores, and W_{-}^{*} represents the structural arrangement of $(W'\Theta S')^{-}/ N^{S}$ arranged according to the structures of core /partial cores. Then we have Figure T.5-3 in which the envelop of the symbols is the Regretting/Flying chain. That is, the envelop of the symbols on the right-hand side is the Flying Dragon and the envelop of the symbols on the left-hand side is the Regretting Dragon.

Figure T.5-3
Flying/Regretting Dragon chain: Deviation-distribution of the average system from the standardized standard-system

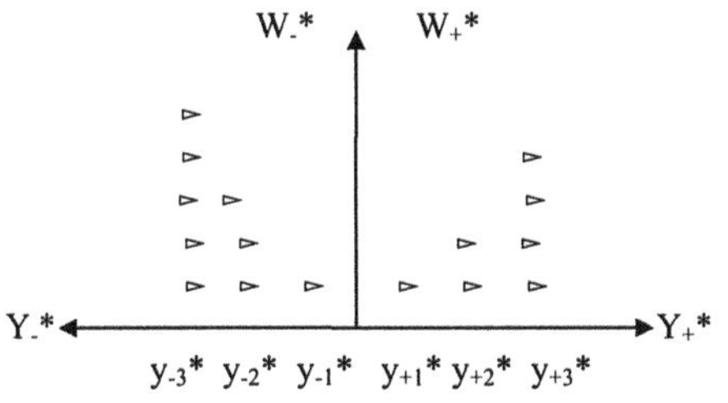

In Figure T.5-3, y_{+1}* is the order of the positive part of the core of A., y_{+2} is the order of the positive part of the core and the first-level partial core of A, y_{+3} is the order of the positive part of the core and the second-level partial core of A. Similarly, y_{-1}* is the order of the negative part of the core of A., y_{-2}* is the order of the negative part of the core and the first-level partial core of A, y_{-3}* is the order of the negative part of the core and the second-level partial core of A.

Below, to test (or to compare) the deviation of a particular system X from S, the standardized norm-system or average system of X, with the structures of W_-*and W*, let us have the following hypotheses:

Hypotheses T.5-1. Let i = 1, 2, 3. Then for Y: H_0: $x_i < W_i$*and H_1: $x_i \geq W_i$*; and for Y-: H_0': $x_{-i} > W_{-i}$*and H_1': $x_{-i} \leq W_{-i}$ *.

Decision rules T.5-1. If both H_1 and H_1' are rejected, then it is said that the deviations of the system X (from S, the standardized norm-system or average system of X) are not i^{th}-level significant. Otherwise, the deviations are said to be i^{th}-level significant.

Definition T.5-4. For any system of three elements $A = \{a_1,a_2|a_3\} \sqsubseteq (\Omega,\mathcal{Z}\circ,_v\mathcal{H},\{\mathbb{C}\})\sqcap\mathbb{C}$, where $a_1, a_2, a_3 \Vdash \Omega$, let $A' = \{a_1/\triangle^A, a_2/\triangle^A, a_3/\triangle^A\}$, and $(A'\Theta W)^+$ (positive$^+$ difference) be the "positive part" of the difference between A' and W (for W being the average, target or reference system of A'), and $(W\Theta A')^-$ (negative$^-$ difference) be the "negative part" of the difference between A' and W. Here $\Theta \vDash \mathcal{Z}\circ,_v\mathcal{H}$ is an impactor to derive differences between two systems.

For each of $(X\Theta W)^+/\triangle^A$ and $(W\Theta X)^-/\triangle^A$, we have three ways to measure the deviation: structures, functions and cultures underlying S and A.

Thus we have one figure for each aspect of these deviations. On the vertical axis of each of these figures represents the chain complex (stretching from the left of the vertical axis to the right of it) ▻-▻-▻, to be called the **Flying-Regretting Dragon chain**.

Let the frequency of all the observations of B, $\{B_i, i \in \mathbb{N}\}$, be placed on the vertical axis. That is, the Flying-Regretting Dragon chain is a systematic form of expressing the frequency of all observations of the targeting system. Furthermore, let W^- be placed on the left-hand side of the horizontal axis, and W^+ be placed on the right-hand side of the horizontal axis. Then we have Figure T.5-4.

Figure T.5-4
Distribution of B

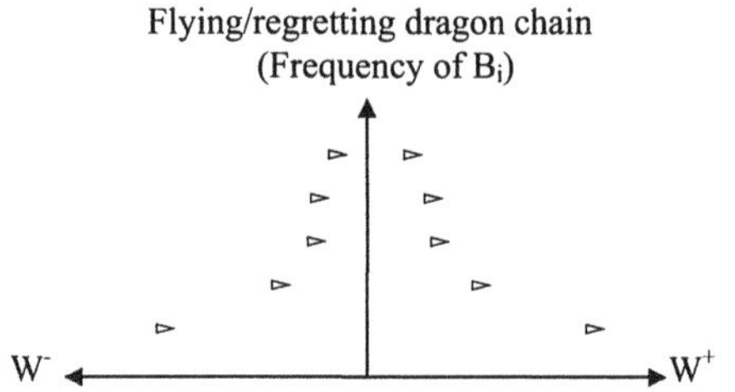

T.6 Three-Level Acceptable Test – An Alternative Dragon Chain

Let $X \sqsubseteq (\Omega, \mathbb{Z}\circ, {}_v\mathbb{H}, \{\mathbb{C}\})$ be a **reference system of testing**, to be used for regular testing. Suppose that X has yin- and yang-side structures and three states of development. Here the yin-side structure of X denotes the negative or undesirable structure of X, whereas the yang side denotes the positive or desirable structure of X; and these three states of X are the highest state (i.e., the most favorable state), the normal state (i.e., the intermediate state) and the lowest state (i.e., the least favorable state). The idea of yin-side and yang-side of X is that if there is the yang side- of X, there must be a yin side of X, in a somewhat symmetrical fashion, to have an internal balance between the favorable and the unfavorable developments.

By drawing three states of the yang structure of X on the right-hand side and by drawing three states of the yin structure of X on the left-hand side, we have Figure T.6-1 "An Alternative Dragon Chain."

In Figure T.6-1, by creating a narrow band around the dragon chain of the standard system for testing, we have a strip of dragon chain, called the **first-level strip of dragon chain**.

The main idea of Figure T.6-1 is that each system (or entity in general) has two sides of characteristics or structures: implicit side (i.e., structures of yin) and explicit side (structures of yang). These implicit and explicit structures are assumed to be in balance: if a system has significant structures of yin, it must have significant structures of yang as well; and similarly if its structures of yin are significant, and its structures of yang must be significant as well.

In practices, if a system is missing some structures of yin (at the first, second, third or any lower level) or some structure of yang (at the first, second, third or any lower level), then we can handle this graph by just leaving an empty spot there in the appropriate position.

Definition T.6-1. Let X be the standard system of testing. For any system $Y \sqsubseteq (\Omega, \mathbb{Z}\circ, {}_v\mathbb{H}, \{\mathbb{C}\})$, if (the trajectory of) its dragon chain falls into this first-level strip of X, then we say Y is acceptable as X at the first-level, or **first-level acceptable as X**. That is, the difference between

X and Y is considered as insignificant at the first level. Otherwise, it is **unacceptable at the first level**.

Figure T.6-1
Yin-yang Structures of X – An Alternative Dragon Chain: H = Highest yin and yang, A+ = Average-Yang, L+ = Lowest yang, A- = Average-, L- = lowest-yin

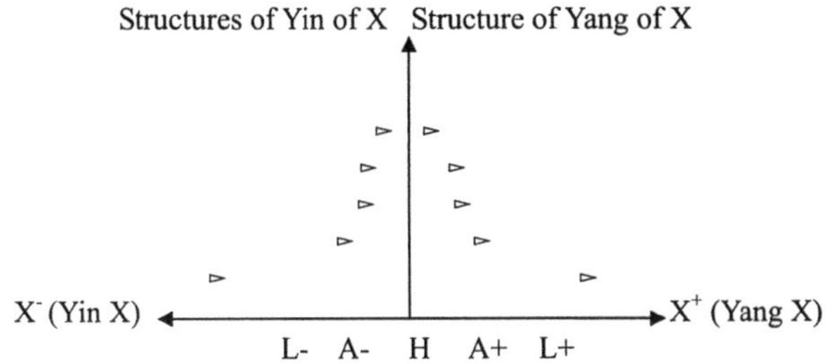

In Figure T.6-1, by creating an additional narrow band around the dragon chain of the standard system for testing, we have the second strip of dragon chain, containing the first strip of dragon chain, called the **second-level strip of dragon chain**.

Definition T.6-2. Let X be the standard system of testing. For any system $Y \sqsubseteq (\Omega, \mathbb{Z}\circ, {}_v\mathbb{H}, \{\mathbb{C}\})$, if (the trajectory of) its dragon chain lies in this second-level strip of X, then we say Y is acceptable as X at the second-level, or **second-level acceptable as X**. That is, the difference between X and Y is considered as insignificant at the second level. Other wise, it is **unacceptable at the second level**.

In Figure T.6-1, by creating the second additional narrow band around the dragon chain of the standard system for testing, containing the second strip of dragon chain, we have the third strip of dragon chain, called the **third-level strip of dragon chain**.

Definition T.6-3. Let X be the standard system of testing. For any system $Y \sqsubseteq (\Omega, \mathbb{Z}\circ, {}_v\mathbb{H}, \{\mathbb{C}\})$, if (the trajectory of) its dragon chain lies in this third-level strip of X, then we say Y is acceptable as X at the third-level, or **third-level acceptable as X**. That is, the difference between X and Y is considered as insignificant at the first level. Otherwise, it is **unacceptable at the third level**.

To apply this method of testing to a system y, let the core, the first partial core and the second partial core of Y be co, p1-co and p2-co, respectively.

Definition T.6-4. Let X be the standard system against which Y is to be tested. Then it is said that X is the **most appropriate representative system** of Y if and only if the core (i.e., co), the first partial core (i.e., p1-co) and the second partial core (i.e., p2-co) of Y all lie in the first-level strips of X, and X is the **least appropriate representative system** of Y if and only if the core, the first partial core and the second partial core of Y all lie in the third-level strips of X. And if the core, the first partial core and the second partial core of Y all lie outside of the third-level strips of X, then it is said to be **unacceptable for X to represent Y**.

T.7 Testing – αβγ-Levels of Acceptance

Figure T.7-1
Yin-yang Structures of X of all levels: H = the highest level, α = α-satisfactory level, β = β-satisfactory level, γ = γ-satisfactory level

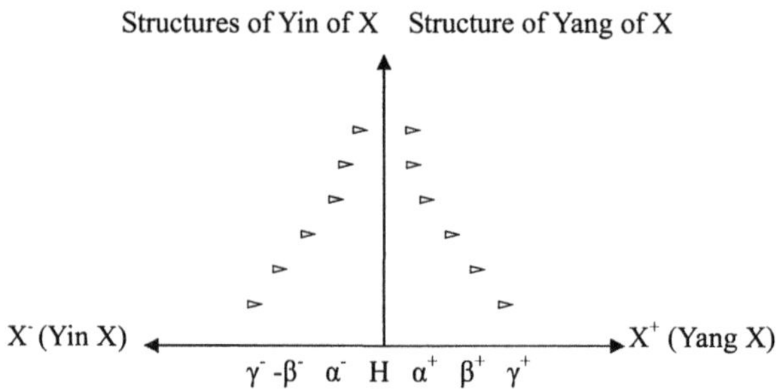

Let $X \sqsubseteq (\Omega, \mathcal{Z}o, {}_v\mathcal{H}, \{\mathbb{C}\})$ be a standard testing system, to be called **αβγ-standard system** of testing, to be used as the norm for testing. In this arrangement, X has yin- and yang-side structures, like in Figure T.6-1. The vertical axis of this figure represents the structures of the system over all levels, while the horizontal axis of this figure shall represent all the levels of the system (see Figure T.7-1).

The theoretical or normal structure of a system in question must be determined by the historical data. These α-level, β-level and γ-level structures of the system must also be determined from the historical data plus some generally agree-upon subjective judgments. Once these structures are determined, then we can perform a meaning testing of a specific system.

Figure T.7-2
αβγ-standard system of testing under tranquil culture

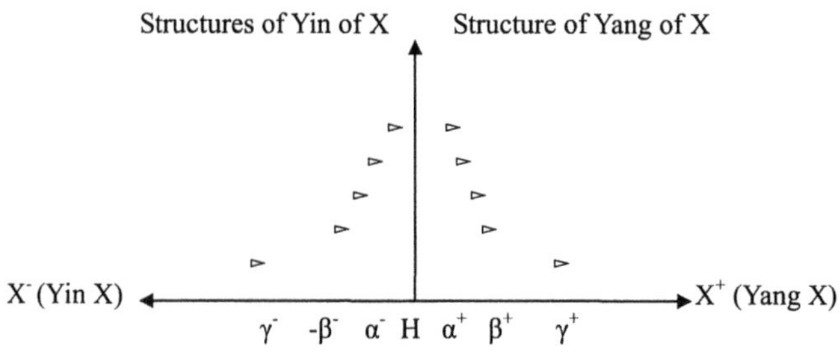

Definition T.7-1. If the system's structures fall in-between the region of the α^+ level and α^- level of the theoretical or normal structures of the system, then the system is said to be **α-level acceptable**. If the system's structures fall in-between the region of the β^+ level and β^- level of the theoretical structures of the system, then the system is said to be **β-level acceptable**. If the system's structures fall in-between the region of the γ^+ level and γ^- level of the theoretical structures of the system, then the system is said to be **γ-level acceptable**.

Definition T.7-2. In the αβγ-standard system of testing, the shape of this system under the tranquil culture must be flatter and shorter than the shape of this system under the conflict culture. That is, the structural difference between the high and low level developments of this system under tranquil culture is not as significant as is under the conflict culture. See Figures T.7-2 and T.7-3.

Figure T.7-3
αβγ-standard system of testing under conflict culture

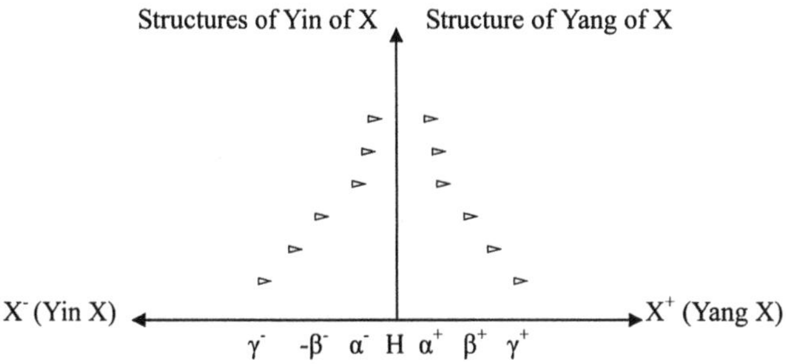

T.8 Further Methods of Testing

Referring to Definitions (I.1-5)-(I.1-6), we assume the mean of X ⊑ (Ω,𝒵○,ᵥ𝐻,{ℂ}) is either a system or a pre-system.

Definition T.8-1. For any system S ⊑ (Ω,𝒵○,ᵥ𝐻,{ℂ}), if S deviates significantly from X, i.e, S does not posses the ten most important attributes of a typical X, then S is not considered as an **X-system**.

Definition T.8-2. For any system S ⊑ (Ω,𝒵○,ᵥ𝐻,{ℂ}), if S possesses the first twenty most important attributes of a typical X (or X possesses the mean and the first level deviation of a typical X), then S is said to have the **first level deviation from X**.

Definition T.8-3. For any system S ⊑ (Ω,𝒵○,ᵥ𝐻,{ℂ}), if S possesses the first thirty most important attributes of a typical X (or X possesses the mean and the first level variation of a typical X), then S is said to have the **second level deviation from X**.

Definition T.8-4. For any system S ⊑ (Ω,𝒵○,ᵥ𝐻,{ℂ}), if S possesses the first forty most important attributes of a typical X (or X possesses the mean and the first level variation of a typical X), then S is said to have the **third level deviation from X**.

T.9 Representative Entity-Differencing Methods of Testing

Definition T.9-1. Let $X \sqsubseteq (\Omega,\mathbb{Z}\circ,{}_{v}\mathbb{H},\{\mathbb{C}\})$. For any system X, ζ_X: X → representative X_i which is called the **most representative entity-best** of X_i is a measure of all X_i by choose the most selective or representative-best X among all X_i. For example, the most beautiful dog.

Definition T.9-2. Let $X \sqsubseteq (\Omega,\mathbb{Z}\circ,{}_{v}\mathbb{H},\{\mathbb{C}\})$. For any system X, δ_X: X → a level of differencing of X which is called the **differencing of X from the most representative-best entity** is a measure of all X_i by choosing the less selective or representative X_i among all X_i. There are several levels of differencing, and the last-level differencing of X is the least selective or least representative X_i among all X_i. For example, the least representative German (with the smallest number of the favorable features), or the most beautiful cat, respectively),

Definition T.9-3. Let $X \sqsubseteq (\Omega,\mathbb{Z}\circ,{}_{v}\mathbb{H},\{\mathbb{C}\})$. For any system X, ζ_X: X → a representative X_i which is called the **most representative entity-common** X_i is a measure of all X_i by choose the most representative-common X_i among all X_i.

Definition T.9-4. Let $X \sqsubseteq (\Omega,\mathbb{Z}\circ,{}_{v}\mathbb{H},\{\mathbb{C}\})$. For any system X, δ_X: X → a level of differencing of X which is called the **differencing of X from the most representative entity-common X** is a measure of all X_i by choosing the X_i to be different from the most common X_i. There are several levels of differencing, and the last-level differencing of X_i is the most-uncommon X_i (or the least selective or representative X_i among all X_i).

Definition T.9-5. Let $X \sqsubseteq (\Omega,\mathbb{Z}\circ,{}_{v}\mathbb{H},\{\mathbb{C}\})$. By the **standardization** of an element or system X is meant to compare X with the most and the least representative "entity-differencings" of X on the universal scope. For example, to standardize the best of X is to compare simultaneously a bison with the most beautiful bison and the least beautiful bison in order to get a "fair evaluation" of this animal. For another example, to assign a letter grade to a student by scaling the grade of this student according to his position in the particular class, rather than assign it according to the absolute grade.

Definition T.9-6. Let $X \sqsubseteq (\Omega,\mathbb{Z}\circ,{}_{v}\mathbb{H},\{\mathbb{C}\})$. By the **reversal or particular standardization** of an element or system X is meant to compare X with the best-differencing (or common-differencing) of X on a particular measure or scale. For example, to standardize the mean of X is to compare simultaneously a sunflower with the most beautiful sunflower (in a designated group) in order to get a "fair evaluation" of this entity. Another example is to assign a letter grade to a student by comparing the grade of this student to the average grade of his/her class.

Definition T.9-7 (Distribution of X according to the concept of the best). For any system $X \sqsubseteq (\Omega,\mathbb{Z}\circ,{}_{v}\mathbb{H},\{\mathbb{C}\})$ on a one–direction number line ($0 \rightarrow +\infty$), put the mean of X on the origin, and arrange the first-level variation, the second level variation, the third level variation,.., and the lowest level variation on the right hand side of this number line. Then, we derive the **distribution of X according to the concept of the best**. Thus the mean has the "highest level of the desirable attributes of X, and the **first level differencing** has less structure or a smaller number of the desirable attributes, the **second level differencing** has even less structure or a smaller number of the desirable attributes, the **third level differencing** has less structure or a smaller number of the desirable attributes than the second level variation of X, and so on. And the **lowest level differencing** has the least structure or the smallest number of the desirable attributes of X.

Definition T.9-8 (Distribution of X according to the most common concept). For any system X $\sqsubseteq (\Omega, \mathbb{Z}^{\circ}, {}_{\mathrm{v}}\mathbb{H}, \{\mathbb{C}\})$ on a two–direction number line ($-\infty \leftarrow 0 \rightarrow +\infty$), put the mean of X on the origin, and assign the first-level yang-differencing, the second level yang-differencing, the third level yang-differencing and so on to the right hand side of the origin, and the first-level yin-differencing, the second level yin-differencing, the third level yin-differencing and so on to the left hand side. Then, we derive the **distribution of X according to the concept of the most common**. Thus the mean has the "highest level of the desirable attributes for the most common X, and the **first level yin- or yang-differencing** has less structure or a smaller number of the desirable attributes, the **second level yin- or yang-differencing** has even less structure or a smaller of the desirable attributes, the **third level yin- or yang-differencing** has less structure or a smaller number of the desirable attributes than the second level differencing of X, and so on.

Remark T.9-10. In the above, the so-called first, second, and third-level differencing, yin- and yang-differencing are determined by historical data and experiences.

Remark T.9-11. **Distribution of the standardized X** for any X $\sqsubseteq (\Omega, \mathbb{Z}^{\circ}, {}_{\mathrm{v}}\mathbb{H}, \{\mathbb{C}\})$ is just the distribution of the X after standardization.

Definition T.9-12 (Test-level of acceptance: best-variation). For any system X to be compared with the best-differencing distribution of X (i.e., ideal X), if it lies between the best and the first level differencing, then it is called the **first-level acceptable**. If it lies between the first level and the second level differencing, then it is called the **second-level acceptable**. And if it lies between the second and the third level differencing, then it is called the **third-level acceptable**.

Definition T.9-13 (Test-level of acceptance: common-deviation). For any system X to be compared with the common-differencing distribution of X (i.e., ideal X), if it lies between the common and the first level differencing, then it is called the **first-level acceptable**. If it lies between the first level and the second level differencing, then it is called the **second-level acceptable**. And if it lies between the second level differencing and the third level differencing, then it is called the **third-level acceptable**.

T.10 Best-Variation /Common-Deviation Methods of Testing

Definition T.10-1. For any system X: $\Sigma\oplus_i X_i \rightarrow$ representation ($E\{X\} \equiv \mu_{X\text{-}t} = (X_1 \oplus X_2 \oplus \ldots \oplus X_n)/\ominus n$) the **best** of X is a measure of all X_l by choose the most selective or representative X among all X_i, for example, the most beautiful hyacinth girl ever wandering in the spring.

Definition T.10-2. For any system X :$\Sigma\oplus_i X_i \rightarrow$ reversal representation ($\sigma_X \equiv Var(X) = [|X_1 \ominus \mu_X| \oplus |X_1 \ominus \mu_X| \oplus \ldots \oplus |X_1 \ominus \mu_X|]||_{\downarrow n}$ where by "$||_{\downarrow n}$" is meant to rescale x by "n time" smaller.) The **variation of X from the best** is a measure of all *X_l by choosing the least selective or representative X among all X_i*, for example, the least representative Chinese (with the smallest number of the favorable features), or the most beautiful morning dove.

Definition T.10-3. For any system X: $\Sigma\oplus_i X_i \rightarrow$ representation ($E\{X\} \equiv \mu_{t,\text{-}t} = [X_1 \oplus X_2 \oplus \ldots \oplus X_n]||_{\downarrow n}$) the **most common** (or average) of X is a measure of all *X_l by choosing the* *most common X among all X_i*, for example, the most typical French (with the largest number of the favorable features).

Definition T.10-4. For any system X: $\Sigma\oplus_i X_i \rightarrow$ reversal representation ($\sigma_X \equiv Var(X) = [|X_1 \ominus \mu_X| \oplus |X_1 \ominus \mu_X| \oplus ... \oplus |X_1 \ominus \mu_X|]||_{\downarrow n}$ where by "$||_{\downarrow n}$" is meant to rescale x by "n times" smaller.) The **deviation from the most common X** is a measure of all X_1 *by choosing the X to be different from the most common X*, for example, the second-category of the most typical Dutch.

Definition T.10-5. By the **standardization** ($W = |X\ominus\mu_X|/\sigma_X$) of an element or system X is meant to compare X with the best-variation (or common-deviation) of X on the universal scope. For example, to standardize the best of X is to compare simultaneously a house with the most beautiful house and the ugliest house of the whole in order to get a "fair evaluation" of this house.

Definition T.10-6. By the **reversal or particular standardization** ($Z = |X\ominus\mu_X|/\sigma_X$) of an element or system X is meant to compare X with the best-variation (or common-deviation) of X on a relative measure or scale.

Definition T.10-7 (Distribution of X according to the concept of the best). For any system X, on a one–way number line ($0 \rightarrow +\infty$), put the "best" of X on the origin (ζ_X), and arrange the first-level deviation from the best (δ_X), the second level deviation from the best, the third level deviation from the best, .., and the lowest level deviation from the best on the right hand side of this number line. Then, we derive the **distribution of X according to the concept of the best**. Thus the mean has the "highest level of the desirable attributes of X, and the **first level deviation** has less structure or a smaller number of the desirable attributes, and so on.

Definition T.10-8 (Distribution of X according to the most common concept). For any system X, on a two–way number line ($-\infty \leftarrow 0 \rightarrow +\infty$), put the "most common" of X (ζ_X) on the origin, and arrange the first-level deviation (δ_X), the second level deviation, the third level deviation and so on to the right hand side of the origin, and the first-level yin-deviation, the second level yin-deviation, the third level yin-deviation and so on to the left. Then, we derive the **distribution of X according to the concept of the most common**. Thus the mean has the "highest level of the desirable attributes for the most common X, and the **first level yin- or yang-deviation** has less structure or a smaller number of the desirable attributes, and so on.

Remark T.10-1. In the above, the so-called first, second, and third-level deviations, variation, yin- and yang-variation are determined by historical data and experiences.

Remark T.10-2. **Distribution of the standardized system X** is just the distribution of the X after standardization.

Definition T.10-9. Let $X \sqsubseteq (\Omega, \mathcal{Z}\circ, {}_v\mathcal{H}, \{\mathbb{C}\})$ be a system with n "observations." Then by the "**mean**" of X is meant the system composed of the ten most frequently appearing attributes among all n observations of X.

Definition T.10-10. Let $X \sqsubseteq (\Omega, \mathcal{Z}\circ, {}_v\mathcal{H}, \{\mathbb{C}\})$ be a system with n "observations." Then by the **first level deviation of X in observation** is meant the system composed of the second ten most frequently appearing attributes among all n observations of X. By the **second level deviation of X in observation** is meant the system composed of the third ten most frequently appearing attributes among all n observations of X. And by the **third level deviation of X in**

observation is meant the system composed of the fourth ten most frequently appearing attributes among all n observations of X.

Definition T.10-11 (Test-level of acceptance: best-deviation). For any system X to be compared with the best distribution of X (i.e., ideal X, $\zeta_{X,\sim(t,n)}$), if it lies between the best and the first level deviation (δ_X), then it is called the **first-level acceptable**. If it lies between the first level and the second level deviations, then it is called the **second-level acceptable**. And if it lies between the second and the third level deviations, then it is called the **third-level acceptable**.

Definition T.10-12 (Test-level of acceptance: common-deviation). For any system X to be compared with the common-deviation distribution of X (i.e., ζ_X, or $\zeta_{X,\sim(t,n)}$)if is a partial operation of time and size), if it lies between the common and the first level deviation (δ_X), then it is called the **first-level acceptable**. If it lies between the first level and the second level deviations, then it is called the **second-level acceptable**. And if it lies between the second and the third level deviations, then it is called the **third-level acceptable**.

PART V ADDITIONAL TOPICS

Additional Topic 1: Scheme of Security Investment

This is a two-parallel cycle scheme complex of investments:

(Add.1)
$$\begin{array}{ccc} A & - & \mathcal{A} \\ \updownarrow & & \updownarrow \\ a & - & \alpha \end{array}$$

where A refers to the MFCE scheme or cycle of a system X under a conflict culture, $\mathcal{A}$ the substantially magnified MFCE scheme of A in which the risk factor may explode, α the down-graded MFCE scheme of A, and α the half-truncated and down-graded MFCE scheme out of $\mathcal{A}$ by refining to reduce risk significantly.

The idea underlying this scheme is this. Let the cycle facing the investors of the culture of conflict be A - $\mathcal{A}$, the former being the cycle of regular time while the latter being the cycle of the extreme time (or good-bad time).

Then, at the regular time, the investors of the culture of tranquility just invest on a small scale in the safe stocks (such as growth stocks) and bonds while keeping a substantial amount of assets in the form of cash or liquid assets. At the good time (as the market booms), this groups of investors will then invest heavily on the first half cycle of the market at the extreme time and to pull out of the stock market half-way through by switching to the invest in other forms of assets such as the real estate properties.

That is, the culture of conflict provides the investors a psychological realm to enjoy risk whereas the culture of tranquility takes away the joy of risk-taking from the investors. These differences in cultures result in this two-parallel cycle scheme complex of investments.

For the stock market to be stable, not only a state of equilibrium of the market (i.e., practical level of demand being equal to the practical level of supply) is necessary, but a state of co-centrality of the key investor-manipulators is also required. Here, the key investor-manipulators are perceived as a co-center of the stock market system. When these investor-manipulators achieve their sTc (specific Tcentral) positions, for instance, being satisfied in their rates of returns, a state of co-centrality is achieved.

Additional Topic 2: More on T Statistics

In the risk analysis of systematics, the mean and variance of a random variable X may be represented by $E^T[X]$ and $var^T[X]$, called T mean and T variance, respectively. For the r.v. X, this T variance is over-estimated under the culture of tranquility because the pooling factor (of risk) is at work. To be a good measure, it needs to be adjusted downward.

In contrast, the r.v. X is underestimated under the culture of conflict. This is because the factor of conquest, to be closely connected to the factor of enjoying risk, is at work under this culture. To be accurate, it needs to be adjusted upward.

Below, we shall develop a method of quantitative measure by drawing inspiration from the theories of systematics. This is the idea of "systematic statistics." One of the issues in the "mathematics of mutuality" facing us is that why a person would ever purchase a lottery ticket for a positive price if the mathematical expectation of the lottery is zero. We believe the conventional formulae may not be applicable at least in some special cases.

Below, to reflect our concerns about the interactive association among entities of a system, we propose a few formulae to capture the idea of potentiality of an individual entity and the forces of the mutual interaction among various entities.

Definition Add.2-1 (Unit point). For a system $X = \{x_1,x_2,\ldots,x_n\}$ with $x_i \Vdash \mathbf{U}$, let $w_i = 1/n_i$ be a weight assigned to the variable x_i and $w_{ik} = 1/n_{ik}$ be a weight assigned to the interactive force between x_i and x_k. Here, in general, n_i and n_{ik} represent the number of observations for x_i. Then for $i = 1, 2, \ldots, n$, $j = 1, 2, \ldots, n$, one formula for the **unit point** of X is defined as:

(Add.2-1) $U(x) = \Sigma_i \Sigma_j w_i(x_i)^j = \Sigma_i \Sigma_j (x_i)^j/n_i$.

In the above, the term $(x_i)^j$ (following a power law)[70], is added to address the idea of the potentiality of the entity x_i.

The alternative formula for the **unit point** of X, to incorporate the interactive factor x_ix_k, $i \neq k$, for $k = 1, 2, \ldots, n$, is:

(Add.2-2) $\mathbb{J}X = \Sigma_i \Sigma_j [w_i(x_i)^j + w_{ik}x_ix_k] = \Sigma_i \Sigma_j [(x_i)^j/n_i + x_ix_k/n_{ik}]$.

In the above, the term x_ix_k (i.e., $w_{ik}x_ix_k$ or x_ix_k/n_{ik}) is added to address the idea of the potentiality of the entity x_i.

Definition Add.2-2 (Changing point). For a system $X = \{x_1,x_2,\ldots,x_n\}$ with $x_i \Vdash \mathbf{U}$, one formula for the **changing point** of X is denfined as:

(Add.2-3) $\mathbb{K}X = \Sigma_i \Sigma_j w_i|x_i- \mathbb{J}X|^j = \Sigma_i \Sigma_j |x_i- \mathbb{J}X|^j/n_i$.

Remark Add.2-1. The term of unit point of system X is a representation of the idea of T mean $E^T[X]$, and the term of changing point is a representation of the idea of T variance $var^T[X]$ (see Remark 4.2-4).

Additional Topic 3: More on Demand and Supply

In Bcm. (4.2-8), the macro TD can be expressed as the sum of micro cd_i, i = 1, …, n, with an adjustment factor α: TD = $\Sigma_{i=1,\ldots,n}cd_i + \alpha$. This is possible because we assume that: (1) the becomings can be transformed into mathematical forms, and (2) this adjustment factor α is positive in magnitude for the economy under the culture of tranquility and negative for the economy under the culture of conflict.

Similarly, in Bcm. (4.2-10), the macro TS can be expressed as the sum of micro cs_i, i = 1, …, m, with an adjustment factor β: TS = $\Sigma_{i=1,\ldots,n}cs_i + \beta$. This is possible because (1) we assume that becomings can be transformed into mathematical forms, and (2) this adjustment factor β is positive for the economy under the culture of tranquility and negative for the economy under the culture of conflict.

As for the definition of the cultural demand curve, essentially it is the graphical representation of the negative relationship between the price and the quantity demanded of a commodity, all other things being equal, under the condition that the primordial cultural forces are in balance (or achieving a balance between human rationality and human will-to-creation). Note that this balanced condition is that: (1) human rationality is in balance, (2) human will-to-creation is in balance, and (3) there is a balance between human rationality and human will-to-creation.

Note that for a cultural economy, in the definitions of cultural demand and supply curves, on the operational level, spiritual factors including the religious factor may be treated as a shift factor.

Alternatively, the cultural demand curve may be defined as the graphical representation of the negative relationship between the price and the quantity demanded of a commodity, all other things being equal, under the condition that yang-side (or human rationality side) of the most basic and direct human intuition and the yin-side (or human will side) of the most basic and direct human intuition are in balance. Here for this concept of the most basic and direct human intuition, one may also see Wang [2001, p. 98].

Similarly, the cultural supply curve is essentially the graphical representation of the positive relationship between the price and quantity supplied of a commodity, all other things being equal, under the condition that the primordial cultural forces are in CE balance/centrality.

As noted in the above, alternatively, the cultural supply curve may be defined as the graphical representation of the positive relationship between the price and the quantity demanded of a commodity, all other things being equal, under the condition that yang-side (or human rationality side) of the most basic and direct human intuition and the yin-side (or human will side) of the most basic and direct human intuition are in CE balance/centrality.

In light of the above spirit, the total supply curve is essentially defined as the graphical representation of the positive relationship between the general price level and the real national income (i.e., output) of a national economy, all other things being equal, under the condition that the primordial cultural forces are in CE balance/centrality.

As noted in the above, alternatively, the total supply curve may be defined as the graphical representation of the positive relationship between the general price level and the real national income of a national economy, all other things being equal, under the condition that yang-side (or human rationality side) of the most basic and direct human intuition and the yin-side (or human will side) of the most basic and direct human intuition are in CE balance/centrality.

Similarly, the total demand curve is essentially defined as the graphical representation of the negative relationship between the general price level and the real national income (i.e., output) of a national economy, all other things being equal, under the condition that the primordial cultural forces are in CE balance/centrality.

As noted in the above, alternatively, the total demand curve may be defined as the graphical representation of the negative relationship between the general price level and the real national income of a national economy, all other things being equal, under the condition that yang-side (or human rationality side) of the most basic and direct human intuition and the yin-side (or human will side) of the most basic and direct human intuition are in CE balance/centrality.

Additional Topic 4: Equilibrium, Low-level Pragmatic TCentral and Welfare Maximization

In this section, we shall go beyond the concept of equilibrium as a state of welfare maximization. For an operational purpose, let us develop a framework of low-level pragmatic TCentral (as a contrast to a state of low-level real-world TCentral, also see Tonn 2006).

A system is said to be in a state of **low-level pragmatic TCentral** if and only if the following conditions are satisfied: For the system, (1) achieving a state of balance, (2) achieving a state of centrality, (3) achieving a state of mutuality, (4) in mathematical sense, achieving some measure of welfare maximization for the system as a whole [71].

For a mixed system of private sector, public sector and social sector (i.e., social forces are at work), there are the mechanisms of market control, central control and social control in Φ-$Z(i^{Equil}, i^{Centrality}, i^{Mutuality})$.

Figure Add.4-1
MB and MC of the society-oriented system

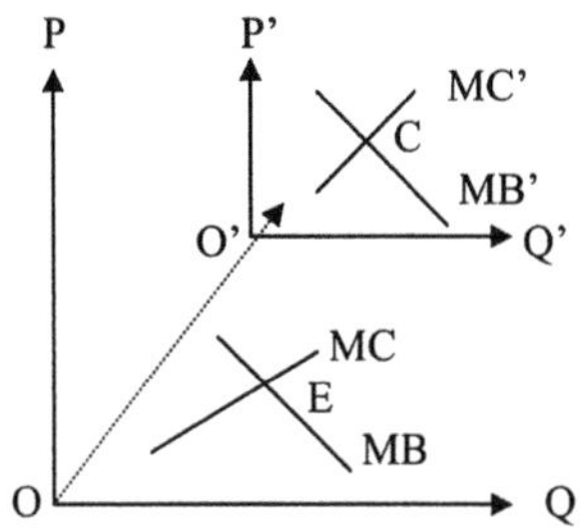

For a mathematical presentation, in the MB-MC model of the private sector, see Figure Add.4-1 with P representing the price of good or service, Q stands for the quantity of good or service. Then the point of equilibrium E is not yet the socially optimal level of the production and consumption. By locating the impact of the public sector (the impact force is presented by shifting along the third dimension as the dotted line with an arrow in this graph), let MB' and MC' be the MB and MC under the joint operation of the private and the public sector. Then C is the point of centrality conditioned upon the equilibrium of the private sector. To add the dimension of mutuality of the society, a fourth axis should be added to the diagram (not shown in Figure Add.4-1). Then only at the joint level of equilibrium, centrality and mutuality, it is possible to achieve the social welfare optimality.

The idea in the above is that, by achieving only a state of equilibrium, it is in a state of non-TCentral. Therefore, in this state, this system is far from achieving any level of social welfare maximization. The policy implication of this model is that, a modern mixed economy can not hope to achieve any social level of efficiency simply by going through market operations, without due regard tot he efficient governmental control and social supervision.

Additional Topic 5: More on Sysmetrics

Add.5-1 Most Representative X

One way to construct the most representative X out of a group of observations of X is as follows.

By studying the group of observations of X, for the first characteristic of X, choose the most representative and name it Ch^X-1. For the second characteristic of X, choose the most representative and name it Ch^X-2. For the third characteristic of X, choose the most representative and name it Ch^X-3. ... For the nth characteristic of X, choose the most representative and name it Ch^X-n.

Then, by integrating these Ch^X-i's together, we construct the most representative X as MostRep(X) = Ch^X-1-Ch^X-2-...Ch^X-n.

Add.5-2 Sysmetrics: Dragon Distribution

In this Topic, we shall develop probability a distribution system by using different variation of the legend of four dragons -- Potential Dragon (P), Field Dragon (F), Flying Dragon (Fly), and Regretting Dragon (R) chain.

Dragon distribution. Convert various combinations of the legend of four dragons into graphs and approximate them by mathematical curves. For each of these curves, use the trial and error process to find the approximation which total area under the curve has the value of one.

Symmetric distributions:

YY Four dragon chain (Φ-Ψ for Φ = P-F-Fly-R, $\Psi = \Phi^{-1}$)

(YY = yinyang)

Figure Add.5-1
Dragon Distribution

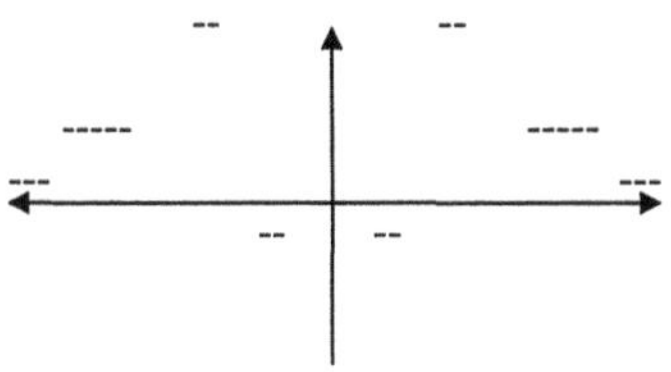

Endnotes

[1] An example of a philosophy-religious approach to culture is the approach of cultural philosophy by Tang Chun-yi〔唐君毅〕.

[2] In examining the ideology of Islam as practiced in Malaysia, Nagata (2000) claim that "economic development is promoted as a means of furthering social justice and assistance to the poor." This is a good example of having a cultural foundation of economic development to go beyond that of utilitarian capitalism.

[3] Note that in the system of tao-chi jen-yi self-organization, Fung Yulan's "new rationalism (新理學), see Fung [1988] and Wu〔伍至學 1995〕, could provide some inspiration to it.

[4] The spirits of The Kuan Tzu and Hsun Tzu provided the essential cultural traditions in supporting an active bureaucracy, strong government and large scale public enterprises in China and some other parts of Sinic cultural East Asia.

[5] This idea of global economics was developed by the author in the late 1980's.

[6] In the case of China, one may see Lin et al〔林毅夫等 2000, pp. 35, 39-45〕.

[7] See Puth (1993), pp. 127-128.

[8] See Puth (1993), pp. 126-127.

[9] Referring to the grand thoughts for the modern time, one may see Austin-Broos (1987), Skinner (1985). As for par of the emerging thoughts of modern China, one may see Chang〔張永儁 1991〕, Du〔杜任之 1980〕, Fang et al〔方克立、李锦全 1991〕, Huang〔黃應貴 1992〕, Luo〔羅義俊 1991〕 and Shen〔沈清松 1990〕. In the case of East Asia, it may prove to be a long way before it emerges successfully as a new giant in the field of grand Human thoughts. To be a new leader of modern human thought, one needs to be more than a person of strong critique to Western thoughts, be it in a partial or comprehensive manner. One needs as well to be more than a reorganizer of existing thoughts, be them Western or Oriental. To be a new giant in this critical concern, essentially one needs to be a creator of a band-new system of methods, structures and visions in the areas of human-social studies.

[10] Here we interpret Heidegger's worlds of Dasein and Sein by the spirit of systematics.

[11] Thanks to Sr. Prudence, Ph.D. for pointing out this source.

[12] Creative intelligence involves more than conventional way of thinking –vertical and horizontal ways of thinking -- and other factors, see Bai〔白學軍 1996〕, pp. 301-308.

[13] Also see the principle of centrality or strategic centrality. Note that, usually, this concept is ignored by the economists.

[14] For this statistical law of causality and the biological "teleology," see Zhang〔張嘉同等主編 1993〕, Chapters 3 and 4.

[15] For the exchange and storage of the information and energy, see Zhang〔張嘉同等主編 1993〕, Chapters 5.

[16] Thanks to Professor Prudence Croke, for my paying attention to this argument.

[17]「天地與我並生，而萬物與我為一」〔《莊子·齊物論》〕(Chuang Tzu, Chi Wu).

[18]「六合之外，聖人存而不論」〔《莊子·齊物論》〕(Chuang Tzu, Chi Wu).

[19]「子不語怪、力、亂、神」〔《論語·述而第七》〕(Analects, Hsu Er).

[20]『子亦言氣由理生，理先氣後，「太極只是天地萬物之理」，「未有天地之先，畢竟是先有此理」，「有理，便有氣流行，發育萬物」，「然理形而上者，氣形而下者」，「有是理，便有是氣，但理是本。」』〔《朱子語類·卷壹》〕(Chu Hsi, Volume 1).

[21]「儒者以理不生不滅」」〔《朱子語類·卷一二六》〕(Chu Hsi, Volume 126).

[22]『然「氣有不存。」』〔《朱子語類·卷四》〕 (Chu Hsi, Volume 4).

[23]『氣「不斷醞釀凝聚生物。」』〔《朱子語類·卷壹》〕 (Chu Hsi, Volume 1)

[24]「天下未有無理之氣，亦未有無氣之理」〔《朱子語類·卷壹》〕 (Chu Hsi, Volume 1).

[25]「氣雖是理之所生，然既生出，則理管他不得」〔《朱子語類·卷四》〕(Chu Hsi, Volume 4).

[26]「理善」〔《朱子語類·卷四》〕 (Chu Hsi, Volume 4).

[27] Cheng Yichuan once proclaimed the idea of "no Li is not good." (「理無不善」) Here "Li" means "Heavenly Reason" or Tien as the Ultimate creativity.

[28]「人之生，氣之聚也；聚則為生，散則為死」〔《莊子、知北游》〕(Chuang Tzu, Chi Beiyou).

[29]「萬物各得其所，各遂其生」，「萬物並育而不相害，道並行而不相悖」〔《中庸》第三十章〕(Golden Means, Chapter 30).

[30] See Guan〔關永中 2000〕, 關于胡氏成熟期知識論的論說, pp. 252-255. The philosophical theory achieved in Husserl's last stage development does not seem to have the same rigor as those of his earlier stages. Also see Kuan〔關永中 2000, p. 396〕,「胡氏在晚期雖已隱然地修正了自己, 然而其晚期的成就仍然力有所不逮」.

[31] Here we are using Popper's methodology of sciences, see Hu〔胡作玄 1980〕and Suppe (1977), pp. 167-170.

[32] (p. 309) See「道生一，一生二。」〔《老子·四十二章》〕 (Lao Tzu, Chapter 42).

[33]「無極而太極，太極動，...靜而生陰。」〔《近思錄·卷一》〕(Chu Hsi, Jinsilu, Volume 1).

[34] In Chinese, this is:「氣」即「道」,「道」即「氣」,「道」、「氣」為壹」; 壹生貳，即生物。

[35]「無極而太極，太極動而生陽。」〔《近思錄·卷一》〕(Chu Hsi, Jinsilu, Volume 1).

[36] See Chou TunYi: “周敦頤所謂「動極而靜，…，聖人定之以中正仁義，而主靜」.”

[37] In systematics, there are factors of quiescence and motion, and those of hardness and softness (系統學原理中，宇宙原創力有陰、有陽、亦有中；在剛柔之間、亦得剛柔的中道。同時，系統學原理要求因時因地因情境可主靜、主動、靜動共主或無主之理。)

[38] This means : Pi is operating in Xi (「闢」運於「翕」之中：熊十力之意,「翕只是收攝凝聚的勢用，使之物化為宇宙形體，故稱為物，而闢是健動而運乎翕之中而為其主宰，可稱為心」(Jiang〔姜允明 1991〕).

[39] It appears to us Mo Tsungsan claimed that Mind could create matter by downgrading itself in transmutation (牟宗三或倡言以良知的自我坎陷轉出有執的知識心性，見 Fu〔傅偉勳 1986〕。此或即自「心」坎陷而生「物」之意。)

[40] For a Tao-Chi model (道氣模式), we may have the following: “此「道氣模式」為 (道,氣|無)，其中，道氣氤氳、有無相生。即是，道氣之由潛能而顯現〔潛能為無、顯現為有〕:『自』→『道』^『氣』;『道』→「道」;「道」^「氣」→「萬物」→ 萬物〔道氣相生萬物〕。”

[41] See Xiao and Luo〔蕭蓮父、罗炽主编 1991〕.

[42] Note that Chu Hsi’s scheme of scheme of the mind unifying and commanding nature and emotion (心統性情模型, scheme of MNE) is based on the ethical foundations of the “five ethical doctrines” and “three key human relationships.” Here the so-called five ethical doctrines (五倫) are:「父子有親，君臣有義，夫婦有別，長幼有序，朋友有信。」〔《孟子·滕文公上》〕and the “three key human relationships” (三綱) are:「君為臣綱，父為子綱，夫為婦綱。」(see Chou〔周世輔 1976，頁 202〕.

[43] Our approach is to create the global culturalism in which all cultures of the world are integrated into a unity.

[44] Mou once commented that in Chu His’s philosophical system, Tien (天) or Tao (道) are static (entities), exists forever and never move (「朱子所瞭解的性體、道體 … 是『只存有而不活動』」,「朱子所瞭解的本體是『只存有而不活動』」, see Mou〔牟宗三 1983, pp. 399, 400〕).

[45] Here the concept of metaphysical entity is similar to what Thomé Fang once said about yin and yang being metaphysical entities (「陰陽也是形而上」, see Fang〔方東美 1983b, p. 129〕).

[46] From “朱子「白鹿洞書院揭示」,” see Liu〔劉述先 1982〕.

[47] The general strategic complex is conceived as comprising D strategy (leap strategy, risky strategy), G+ strategy (golden+ strategy, rapid development strategy), G strategy (golden strategy, high-speed development strategy), S or silver strategy (stable development strategy), variational strategy, and continuity strategy. The strategic space of a specific system X is directly related to the cultural complex <$\mathbb{C}_X$> of this system.

[48] For some detailed accounts (and therefore criticism) of this Weberian system from the Chinese perspectives, see Huang〔1989〕, pp. 11-16. Huang appears to believe that historically Confucian system was inefficient (in the context of Weberian assertion), yet it possesses some potentiality to be transformed into an effective system under the influence of Western culture.

[49] See Gardner (1987) for a more detailed introduction to Durkheim's concept of "conscience collective."

[50] Niklas Luhmann emphasizes the importance of communication between individuals (see Gao〔高宣揚 2002〕). He contends that two individuals should have full freedom in communicating to each other. Therefore, either harmony or conflict may occur as the results of these acts of communication. Luhmann asserts that a system, whatever one may want to define it, has a self-generating capacity within its reaction to the system's environments. This implies that he considers individual's actions as the determining factor in one's development process. This is to say that other individuals of the society, or the outside physical environment, are not harmful or restrictive factors in one's development.

[51] This is more than a relationship of input and output. It is about relationships between systems as well.

[52] This relationship illustrates that capitalism is about profit motif. For the idea of Giddens, see Chang〔張宏輝 1992〕.

[53] One example is the college admissions policy in a country resulted from the combination of the factors of money and political power and a strong desire to preserve the dominance of the group of majority over ethnic minorities. High social status is gained by those students for being admitted to prestigious universities through the operations of money and political favor. Essential racial quota is operated through the smoke of promoting campus diversity and artificial aids provided to a few specific minority groups. Sex factor, usually influenced by money and political power, is then attached to the end to complete this cycle.

[54] This is consistent with what Montana and Charnov says (see Montana and Charnov 1987, pp. 18-.)

[55] 「古人亟於德，中世逐於智，當今爭於力」〔《韓非子集解》卷十八，八說第四十七〕(Han Fei Tzu, Volume 18).

[56] 『上古之人，「不事力，而養足人。民少而財有餘，故民不爭。」』〔《韓非子集解》卷十八，八說第四十七〕(Han Fei Tzu, Volume 18).

[57] 『當今之世，「民眾而貨財寡。是以，事力勞而供養薄。故民爭。」』〔《韓非子集解》卷十九，五蠹第四十九〕(Han Fei Tzu, Volume 19).

[58] This is neither a systemic nor a logical argument. Han Fei Tzu may want to use sophisticated arguments to support his points of view. With his background as a student of Confucian scholar, he may want to emphasize virtue to be in accordance with the teachings of Confucianism in the state of strategic continuity.

[59] This may appear to be a character of tranquil culture. Nevertheless, it is actually a byproduct of conflict culture.

[60] In Chinese, this means: 『最純粹而「先驗」的現象』.

[61] In Chinese, this means: 「宇宙中的生滅萬殊」.

[62] In Chinese, this means:「『自不然』自如」.

[63] In Chinese, this means:「無之『本如』」.

[64] This is inspired by an idea of Professor Hsi C. Li .

[65] In Chinese, this means: 歷史發展的動力—在反中道、反因緣平衡、反均衡的自主多元世界中，文化自生自長的力量以及文化間的競爭及衝突或為推動歷史進展的主要力量。個人的動力、大小群體的力量、族群的因素、偶發的事件、地理及資源新發現的因素、經濟政治宗教等的因素以及階級鬥爭種種，皆為推動歷史進展的重大力量。

[66]「唐代有名钜著唐六典一書，．．．．，千餘年來，國家推行政務，大體以此書爲典範，無多變更。」(see Chien〔錢穆 1977〕, pp. 46-47).

[67]「只由周禮而演進到唐六典，這一步驟，也可認為是中國政治歷史上一極大的進步。」(see Chien〔錢穆 1977〕, p. 47)。《中國歷代政治得失》, 頁 47].

[68]「明代的衛所制度，仿效元朝的做法；滿洲的八旗又大概接替明代的衛所。」(see Huang〔黃仁宇 1999〕, p. 223).

[69]「唐朝和宋朝的轉運是在各地間活動，手中有大量的款項及物質周轉，由中央的指示，廣泛的行使職。在大體上講，明朝放棄了這樣的做法。」(see Huang〔黃仁宇 1999〕, p. 212).

[70] This idea of a power law is inspired by Professor His C. Li of Bryant University.

[71] In Tonn[2008], the concept of "low-level pragmatic TCentral" is replaced by that of "low-level practical T world;" by the latter is meant the state of achieving simultaneously the conditions of individual independence and creativity, balance, mutuality, centrality, and holistic advancement. Note that Tonn[2008] is the most recent development out of Tonn [2006].

Bibliography

(I) In English

Almond, G. (1960), "Introduction: a functional approach to comparative politics," in Almond and J. Coleman, eds., The Politics of developing Areas. Princeton: Princeton University Press.

Almond, G. and J. Coleman, eds. (1960). The Politics of developing Areas. Princeton: Princeton University Press.

Althusser, Louis (1969). *For Marx*. London: Allen Lane.

Althusser, Louis (1970). *Reading Capital*. London: New Left.

Arnold, Ludwig (1974). Stochastic Differential Equations: Theory and Applications. New York: John Wiley and Sons.

Austin-Broos, Diane J., ed. (1987) *Creating Culture: Profiles in the study of culture*. Sydney, London, Boston: Allen & Unwin.

Brook, Timothy and Hy V. Luong, eds. (2000). *Culture and Economy: The Shaping of Capitalism in Eastern Asia*. Ann Arbor: University of Michigan Press.

Cammack, P. (1997). Capitalism and Democracy in the Third world. New York and London: Leichester University Press.

Campos, Edgardo and Hilton L. Root (1996). *The Key to the Asian Miracle: Making Shared Growth Credible*. Washington D.C.: The Brookings Institute.

Chan, Joseph (1999), "A Confucian Perspective on Human Rights for Contemporary China," in Joanne R. Bauer and Daniel A. Bell, eds., *The East Asian Challenge for Human Rights*. Cambridge and New York: Cambridge University Press.

Cheng, Hang-sheng (1989), "Historical factors Affecting China's Economic Development," in Hung-chao Tai, ed. (1989). *Confucianism and Economic Development: An Asian Alternative*. Washington D.C.: Washington Institute for Value in Public Policy.

Chung, Young-iob (1989), "The Impact of Chinese Culture on Korean's Economic Development," in Hung-chao Tai, ed. (1989). *Confucianism and Economic Development: An Asian Alternative*. Washington D.C.: Washington Institute for Value in Public Policy.

Copelston, Federick, S. J. (1993). *A History of Philosophy, Volume I: Greece and Rome*. New York, London: Image.

Csikszentmihalyi, M. (1996) *Creativity: Flow and Psychology of Discovery and Invention*. New York: HaperCollins.

Derry, T. K. and T. I. Williams (1993). *A Short History of Technology*. New York: Dover.

Dong, Fureng (2000), "The Adjustment of macroeconomic policies in China," in P. J. Lloyd and Xiao-guang Zhang, eds., *China in the Global Economy*. Cheltenham, U.K. and Nothampton, MA, USA: Edward Elgar.

Dorn, James A., ed. (1998). *China in the New Millennium*. Washington, D.C.: Cato Institute.

Dostal, R. J. (1993), "Time and phenomenology in Husserl and Heidegger," in C. Guignon, ed., *The Cambridge Companion to Heidegger*. Cambridge, New York: Cambridge University Press.

Eide, Asbjorn (1989), "Linking Human Rights and Development: Aspects of the Norwegian Debate," in Irving Brecher, ed., *Human Rights, Development and Foreign Policy:Canadian Perspectives*. Halifax, Nova Scotia: The Institute for Research on Public Policy.

Frumkin, Norman (2004). *Tracking American Economy*, 4th ed. Armonk, N.Y.: M.E. Sharpe.

Fukuyama, Francis (1992). The End of History and the Last Man. New York: The Free Press.

Fung, Yu-lan (1973). *A History of Chinese Philosophy, Vol. II*. Trans. by Derk Bodde. Princeton: Princeton University Press.
Gardner, Don (1987), "Durkheim on Culture," in Diane Austin-Broos, ed., *Creating Culture: Profiles in the Study of Culture*. Sydney, London, Boston: Allen & Unwin.
Hartfield, Edward F. (1989), "The Divergent Economic Development of China and Japan," in Hung-chao Tai, ed. (1989). *Confucianism and Economic Developmen An Asian Alternative*. Washington D.C.: Washington Institute for Value in Public Policy.
Harman, Willis (1998). *Global Mind Change*. Berrett-Koehler Publishers, Inc.
Hayami, Yujiro (2001). *Economic Development*. Oxford, New York: Oxford University Press.
Heidegger, Martin (1977). *Sein und Zeit*. Tübingen: Max Niemeyer Verlag.
Heidegger, Martin (1962), trans. by John Macquarrie and Edward Robinson. *Being and Time*. New York: Harper & Row, Publishers.
Ho, Samuel P. S. and Y. Y. Kueh, eds. (2000). *Sustainable Economic Development in South China*. New York: St. Martin's Press.
Hofstede, G. (1983), "National Cultures in Four Dimensions: A Research-Based Theory of Cultural Differences Among Nations," *International Studies of Management and Organization*, 13 Spring-Summer), pp. 46-74.
Hofstede, G. and Michael Bond (1984), "The Need for Synergy among Cross-Cultural Studies," *Journal of Cross-Cultural Psychology*, December, p. 419.
Huang, Jueichi (1996). Pipan shehueihsue. Taipei: Sanmin.
Hughes, Jonathan and Louis P. Cain (1993). American Economic History, 5th ed. Reading, M.A.: Addison Wesley.
Huntington, Samuel P. (1993). The Third Wave: Democratization in the Late Twentieth Century. Norman, London: Oklahoma University Press.
Huntington, Samuel P. (1996). The Clash of Civilizations and the Remaking of World Order. New York: Simon & Schuster.
Inada, Kenneth K. (1990), "A Buddhist Response to the Nature of Human Rights," in Claude E. Welch, Jr. and Virginia A. Leary, eds., *Asian Perspectives of Human Rights*. Boulder, Colorado: Westview Press.
James, Susan (1985), "Louis Althusser," in Quentin Skinner, ed, *The Return of Grand Theory in the Human Sciences*, Cambridge University Press.
Janelli, Roger L. and Dawnhee Yim, "The Mutual Constitution of Confucianism and Capitalism in South Korea," in Timothy Brook and Hy V. Luong, eds., *Culture and Economy: The Shaping of Capitalism in Eastern Asia*. Ann Arbor: University of Michigan Press.
Jones, Charles I. (1998). *Introduction to Economic Growth*. New York: W.W. Norton.
Jones, W. T. (1970) *A History of Western Philosophy: The Classical Mind*, 2nd. ed. New York: Harcourt Brace Javanovich.
Jones, W. T. (1969) *A History of Western Philosophy: The Medieval Mind*, 2nd. ed. New York: Harcourt Brace Javanovich.
Jones, W. T. (1969) *A History of Western Philosophy: Hobbes to Hume*, 2nd. ed. New York: Harcourt Brace Javanovich.
Jones, W. T. (1975) *A History of Western Philosophy: Kant and the Nineteenth Century*, 2nd ed. New York: Harcourt Brace Javanovich.
Jones, W. T. (1969) *A History of Western Philosophy: The Twentieth Century to Wittgenstein and Satre*, 2nd. ed. New York: Harcourt Brace Javanovich.
Krugman, P. (1994), "The Myth of Asia's Miracle," Foreign Affairs, November–December, pp. 62-78.
Leahey, Thomas Hardy (1977). *A History of Psychology: main Currents in Psychological Thought*. Upper Saddle River, N.J.: Prentice Hall.
Li, Wen-lang (1989), "Entrepreneurial Role and Social Development in Taiwan," in Hung-

chao Tai, ed. (1989). *Confucianism and Economic Development: An Asian Alternative*. Washington D.C.: Washington Institute for Value in Public Policy.

Liu, Minquan (2000), "Capitalist Firms, Public Enterprises," in Sara Cook, Shujie Yao and Juzhong Zhuang, eds., *The Chinese Economy under Transition*. London: Macmillan Press, LTD.

Long, Ngo Van and H. Siebert (1992), "A Model of Sopcialist Firm in Transition to a Market Economy," *Journal of Economics*, 56, 1, 1-21.

Macquarrie, J (1994). *Heidegger and Christianity*. N.Y.: Continuum Publishing Co.

Maddison, Angus (1998). *Chinese Economic Performance in the Long Run*. Paris: Development Centre, OECD.

Madura, J. (2000) *International Financial Management*, 6th ed. Cincinnati, New York: South-Western.

Makci, Jack and Aaron Straus (1982).Introduciton to Optimal Control Theory. New York, Heidelberg: Springer-Verlag.

Mankiw, N. G. (2003) *Macroeconomics*, 5th ed. New York: Worth Publishers.

Mok, Ka-ho (2000). *Social and Political Development in Post-Reform China*. New York: St. Martin's Press.

Montana, Patrick and Bruce Charnov (1987). *Management*. Hauppauge, N.Y.: Barron's Education Service Inc.

Murray, Geoffrey (1998). *China: The Next Superpower*. New York: St. Martin's Press.

Nagata, Judith (2000), "Religious Correctness and the Place of Islam in Malaysia's Economic Policies," in Timothy Brook and Hy V. Luong, eds., *Culture and Economy: The Shaping of Capitalism in Eastern Asia*. Ann Arbor: University of Michigan Press.

Park, Tae-Kyu (2000), "Confucian Values and Contemporary Economic Development in Korea," in Timothy Brook and Hy V. Luong, eds. (2000). *Culture and Economy: The Shaping of Capitalism in Eastern Asia*. Ann Arbor: University of Michigan Press.

Perry, Michael J. (1998). *The Idea of Human Rights: Four Inquiries*. N.Y.: Oxford University Press.

Popper, Karl (1959) *The Logic of Scientific Discovery*. London: Hutchinson.

Puth , Robert C. (1993). American Economic History, 3rd ed. Fort Worth, T.X.: The Dryden Press.

Pyle, David J. (1997). *China's Economy: From Revolution to Reform*.

Rawski, Thomas G.. (2000), "The political economy of China's declining growth," in P. J. Lloyd and Xiao-guang Zhang, eds, *China in the Global Economy*. Cheltenham, UK and Nothampton, MA, USA: Edward Elgar.

Rosenberg, Nathan (1976). Perspectives on Technology. Cambridge, New York: Cambridge University Press.

Ruttan, V. W. (2001) *Technology, Growth and Development*. New York: Oxford University Press.

Skinner, Quentin, ed. (1985). *The Return of Grand Theory in the Human Sciences*. London, New York: Cambridge University Press.

Sibly, Mulford Q. (1970) *Political Ideas and Ideologies: A History of Political Thought*. New York: Harper & Row, Publishers.

Schultz, Duan P. and Aydney Ellen Schultz (1996). *A History of Modern Psychology*. Harcourt Brace College Publishers.

Tai, Hung-chao (1985), "Human Rights in Taiwan," in James C. Hsiung, ed., *Human Rights in East Asia*. New York: Paragon House Publishers.

Tai, Hung-chao, ed. (1989). *Confucianism and Economic Development: An Asian Alternative*. Washington D.C.: Washington Institute for Value in Public Policy.

Tatsuo, Inoue (1999), "Liberal Democracy and Asian Orientalism," in Joanne R. Bauer and

Daniel A. Bell, eds., *The East Asian Challenge for Human Rights*. Cambridge and New York: Cambridge University Press.

Temple, R. (1986). *The Genius of China: 3000 Years of Science, Discovery and Invention.* New York: Simon & Schuster.

Tonn, Victor Lux (1980), "A Study of Taiwan's Strategy of Economic Development Since 1953--With Reference to the Development Strategy of South Korean Economy Since 1962," New York: Brooklyn College, City University of New York (Unpublished M.A. thesis).

Tonn, Victor Lux (1981), "The Investment, Regional Balance and Economic Development: The Strategy of Economic Development in People's China" (Unpublished manuscript).

Tonn, Victor Lux (1984), "Strategic Optimality of Economic Advancement," Logan, UT: Utah State University (Unpublished Ph.D. dissertation).

Tonn, Victor Lux (1989), "A Theory of Socialist Growth and Development: Long-Term Economic Reforms in the USSR and the PRC," presented at the Allied Social Science Associations Meeting, Atlanta, December 28-29.

Tonn, Victor Lux (1990a), "Economics of Dragons: A System Space Approach to the Post-Confucian Strategic Developmentalism," (October 7, 1990, unpublished manuscript).

Tonn, Victor Lux (1990b), "An Approach to Cultural Economics: A Two-Country Systematics Model of Strategic Rivalry," (November, mimeo.).

Tonn, Victor Lux (1991a), "Economic Perspectives of the Twenty-First Century--Global Culturalism versus Post-Confucianism," delivered at the Bi-Annual Academic Conven tion of the New England Association of Chinese Professionals, Needham, MA, November 9.

Tonn, Victor Lux (1991b), "A System of Strategic Convergence: An Iching's Approach," *Proceedings of the 20th Annual Conference of the NEDSI*, Pittsburgh, April 10-12.

Tonn, Victor Lux (1993), "Sage-King Market Economy, Faziran Cultural Economy, and Enlightened Confucianism of East Asia," *Proceedings of Chinese American Academic and Professional Convention*, Chicago, July 2-5, 1993.

Tonn, Victor Lux (1994), "An Inquiry into the Theory of Strategic Continuity: Optimal Control Systems of Marketism and Enlightened Confucianism," Kingston, Rhode Island: University of Rhode Island (Unpublished Ph.D. Dissertation).

Tonn, Victor L. (2001). *Lecture Notes on the Economics of Culture* (Unpublished manuscript).

Tonn, Victor L. (2003), "Cultural Economy of China and the Asian Union," delivered at the 28th Annual Meetings of the Eastern Economic Association, March 15-17, 2002, Boston.

Tonn, Victor Lux (2006), "Systematic Methods of Interactions between Local and Global Cultures," *Chinese Media Research*, 2(1), pp. 85-92.

Tonn, Victor Lux (2007), "Systematic Foundations of Organizations and Communications," Intercultural Communication Studies XVI: 3, pp. 224-235.

UNDP (2003). *Human Development Report 2003*. Oxford, New York: Oxford University Press.

Urban, Linwood (1995). *A Short History of Christian Thought*. Oxford, New York: Oxford University Press.

Van Den Berg, Hendrik (2001). *Economic Growth and Development*. New York: McGraw-Hill Irwin.

Vernon, R. (1966), "International Investment and International Trade in the Product Cycle,"

Quarterly Journal of Economics, 80 (MAY): 190-207.

Wallerstein, Immanual (1974), "The Rise and Future Demise of the World Capitalist System: Concepts for Comparative Analysis," *Comparative Studies in Society and History*, 16 (September 1974): 387-415.

Wallerstein, Immanual (1991), "The three Instances of Hegemony in the History of the Capitalist World-Economy," in George T. Crane and Abla Amawi, eds., *The Theoretical Evolution of International Political Economy*. New York, Oxford: Oxford UniversityPress.

Wank, David L. (1999). *Commodifying Communism: Business, Trust, and Politics in A Chinese City*. Cambridge, New York: Cambridge University Press.

Weber, Max (1955). *The Protestant Ethics and the Spirit of Capitalism*. New York: Scribner Paperbacks.

Weber, Max (1964). *The Religion of China*. New York: Macmillan.

White, Lynn T. (1998). *Unstately Power: Volume I: Local Causes of China's Economic Reforms*. Almonk: New York: M. E. Sharpe.

Whitehead, Alfred North (1978), ed. by David Ray Griffin and Donald W. Sherburne. *Process and Reality*. New York: The Free Press.

Wong, Yi-ting (1989), "Republic of China's Experiences with Economic Development," in Hung-chao Tai, ed. (1989). *Confucianism and Economic Development: An Asian Alternative*. Washington D.C.: Washington Institute for Value in Public Policy.

Wong, Siu-lun (1989), "Modernization and Chinese Cultural traditions in Hong Kong," in Hung-chao Tai, ed. (1989). *Confucianism and Economic Development: An Asian Alternative*. Washington D.C.: Washington Institute for Value in Public Policy.

World Bank (2003). *World Development Report 2003*. Oxford, New York: Oxford University Press.

Wu, Yu-shan (1994). *Comparative Economic transformations: Mainland China, Hungary, the Soviet Union and Taiwan*. Stanford: Stanford University Press.

Zhang, Wei Wei (2000). *Transforming China: Economic Reforms and Its Political Implications*. New York: St. Martin's Press.

Zhou, Qiren (2000), "Agricultural Reform in China and Russia," in Sara Cook, Shujie Yao and Juzhong Zhuang, eds., *The Chinese Economy under Transition*. London: Macmillan Press, LTD.

(II) In Chinese

白学军〔1996〕。智力心理学的研究进展。杭州：浙江人民出版社。(Bai, Xuejun [1996]. *Research and Development on the psychology of Human Intelligence*. Chejiang: Chejiang Remin Chubanshe.)

北京大学哲学系中国哲学史教研室编写〔北大哲研室 1980〕。中国哲学史，上、下册。北京： 中华书局。([Beijing University [1980]. *A History of Chinese Philosophy*, Volumes 1, 2. Beijing: Zhonghua.)

艾思奇主编〔1980〕。 辩证唯物主义历史唯物主义。北京：人民。(Ai, Siqi [1980]. *Dialectic Materialism and Historical Materialism*. Beijing: Renmin.)

張燦輝〔1996〕。海德格胡塞爾現象學。臺北：東大。(Chang, Tsanhuei [1996]. *The Phenomenlogies of Heidegger and Husserl.* Taipei: Tatung.)

張金鑑〔1996〕。西洋政治思想史。臺北：三民。(Chang, Chinchien [1970]. *The Political Thought of the West.* Taipei: Sanmin.)

張宏輝〔1992〕，「結構化論的旗手：季登斯」。葉啟政主编，當代社會思想巨擘。臺北：正中。(Chang, Hunghuei [1992]. *Giddens*. In Ye Chicheng, ed., *Great Sociologists of Modern Time.* Taipei: Chengchung.)

蔡美麗〔1970〕。存在主義大師–海德格哲學。臺北：環宇出版社。(Chai, Meili [1970]. A*n Existentialist Master: Heidegger.* Taipei: Huanyu.)

張永儁主编〔1991〕。中國新文明的探索: 當代中國思想家。臺北：正中。(Chang Yungchun, ed. (1991). *Searching for New Civilization of China*. Taipei: Chengchung.)

周世輔 〔1976〕。中國哲學史。臺北：三民。(Chou, Shifu [1976]. *A History of Chinese Philosophy*. Taipei: Sanmin.)

錢穆〔1966〕。國史大綱，上、下冊。臺北：臺灣商務印書館。(Chien, Mu [1977]. *Outline of the National History of China*, Volumes I, II. Taipei: Taiwan Shangwu.)

錢穆〔1977〕。中國歷代政治得失。臺北：東大圖書公司。(Chien Mu [1977]. *Political Problems throughout the History of China*. Taipei: Tungta.)

朱熹〔1994 版〕。《朱子語類·卷一–卷八》，上、下冊，黎靖德編。北京：中華書局。(Chu, Hsi [1994]. *Speeches of Chu Tzu*, Volumes 1-8, ed. by Li Chingte. Beijing: Zhonghua Shuju.)

朱熹〔1991 版〕。近思錄集解，楊家駱主編。臺北：世界書局。[Chu, Hsi [1991]. *Recent Thoughts and Their Explanation*, ed. by Yang Chialuo. Taipei: Shihcie.]

Dessler, Gary〔1982〕。組織理論整合結構與行為，余朝權等譯。臺北：聯經。(Dessler, Gary [1982]. *Organizational Theories: Integration and Behavior*, trans. by Yu Chau-chuan et al. Taipei: Liking.)

杜任之主编，中国社会科学院哲学研究所〔1980〕，现代西方著名哲学家述评。北京：三联书店。(Tu, Renzhi, ed. [1980]. *An Introduction to and Critiques of Modern Western Philospophers*. Beijing: Sanlian.)

方東美〔1979〕。生生之德。臺北：黎明。(Fang, Thomé [1979]. *The Virtue of Creative Creativity*. Taipei: Liming.)

方東美〔1981〕。華顏宗哲學，上、下冊。臺北：黎明文化事業公司。(Fang, Thomé [1981]. *ThePhilosophy of Hua-Yen School of Buddhism*. Taipei: Liming.)

方東美〔1983a〕。原始儒家道家哲學。臺北：黎明文化事業公司。(Fang, Thomé [1983]. *Philosophies of Primordial Confucianism and Taoism*. Taipei: Liming.)

方東美〔1983b〕。新儒家哲學十八講。臺北：黎明文化事業公司。(Fang, Thomé [1983]. *Eighteen Lectures on Neo-Confucianism*. Taipei: Liming.)

方東美〔1984〕。中國大乘佛教。臺北：黎明文化事業公司。(Fang, Thomé [1984]. *Mayahanic Buddhism of China*. Taipei: Liming.)

方克立、李锦全〔1991〕。现代新儒学研究论集(二)。北京：中国社会科学出版社。(Fang, Keli et al. [1991]. *Researches on Modern Confucianism*, Volume 2. Beijing: Zhongguo Shehui Kexue Chubanshe.)

冯友兰〔1988〕。冯友兰学术精华录。北京：北京师范学院出版社。(Feng Youlan [1988]. Anthology of Feng Youlane's Scholarly Contributions. Beijing: Beijing Normal College Press.)

傅筑夫〔1980〕。中国经济史论丛，上、下。北京：三联书店。(Fu, Chufu [1980]. *On the Economic History of China, I, II*. Beijing: Sanlian.)

傅偉勳〔1970〕。西洋哲學史。臺北：三民書局。(Fu, Weihsun [1970]. *A History of Western Philosophy*. Taipei: Sanmin.)

傅偉勳〔1986〕，「儒家思想的時代課題及其解決線索」，知識分子，Vol. 2, No. 4 (夏季號)。(Fu, Weihsun [1986], "Critiques on the Philosophy of New Confucianism," *Chishi Fentsu*, Vol. 2, No. 4.)

高宣揚〔1991〕，「政權社會學的開創者：比埃尔·布尔迪厄」，周陽山，當代政治心靈。臺北： 正中。(Gao, Hsuanyang [1991]. The Pioneer of Political Sociology: Pierre Bourdieu. In Yangshan Chou, ed., *Modern Political Minds*. Taipei: Chengchung.)

高宣揚〔2002〕。魯曼社會系統理論與現代性。臺北：五南。 (Gao, Hsuanyang [2002], *The Theory of Lumann's Social Systems and Its Modernity*. Taipei: Chengchung.)

韓非子〔2002〕。《韓非子集解》，王先慎撰。臺北：藝文。 (Han Fei Tzu [1983], In Hsienshen Wang, ed., *Han Fei Tzu Expounded*. Taipei: Yiwen.)

蕭公權〔1982〕。中國政治思想史上、下。臺北：中國文化大學出版社。(Hsiau, Gungchuan [1982]. *History of Chinese Political Thoughts*, Vol. I, II. Taipei: Chungkuo wenhua dahsue.)

候家駒〔1980〕。先秦法家統治經濟思想。臺北：聯經出版事業公司(Hou, Chiachu [1985]. *Leglaist Economic Thoughts in the Pre-Jin Period*. Taipei: Lianjing.)

胡塞尔〔1996〕。纯粹现象学通论，李幼蒸译。北京：商务印书馆。(Husserl, Edmund [1993], trans. by Youzheng Li, *Introduction to the Pure Phenomenology*. Beijing: Shangwu.)

胡文耕主编〔1993〕。科学前沿与哲学。北京：中共中央党校出版社。(Hu, Wengen, ed. [1993]. *The Frontiers of Sciences and Philosophy*. Beijing: Zhonggong Zhong-yang Dang-xiao Chubanshe.)

胡作玄〔1980〕，「卡尔·莱芒德·波普尔」，杜任之主编，现代西方著名哲学家述评。北京：三联书店。(Hu, Zuoxuan [1980]. Karl Raimund Popper. In Renzhi Tu, ed., *An Introduction to and Critiques of Modern Western Philosophers*. Beijing: Sanlian.)

黃仁宇〔1993〕。中國大歷史。臺北：聯經出版事業公司。[Huang, Jenyu [1993]. *China: A Macro History*. Taipei: Linking.]

黃仁宇〔1994〕。萬曆十五年。汐止：臺灣食貨出版社。(Huang, Jenyu [1994]. 1587, A Year of No Significance. Hsichih, Taiwan: Shih Huo.)

黃仁宇〔1994〕。從大歷史的角度讀蔣介石日記。臺北：時報文化出版企業股份有限公司。(Huang, Jenyu [1994]. *Reading the Diary of Chiang Kai-shek from the Perspective of Macro-History*. Taipei: Shihpao.)

黃仁宇〔1995〕。近代中國的出路。臺北：聯經出版事業公司。(Huang, Jenyu [1995]. *The Road of Modern China*. Taipei: Linking.]

黃仁宇〔1999〕。放寬歷史的識界。臺北：允晨文化事業股份有限公司。(Huang, Jenyu [1999]. *Broadening the Horizons of Chinese History*. Taipei: Gunchen.)

黃仁宇〔2000〕。地北天南敘古今。臺北：時報文化出版企業股份有限公司。(Huang, Jenyu [2000]. *Today, Old Days, North and South*. Taipei: Shihpao.)

黃仁宇〔2001a〕。十六世紀明代中國之財政與稅收，阿風等譯。臺北：聯經出版事業公司。(Huang, Jenyu [2001a]. *Taxation and Governmental Finance in Sixteen-Century Ming China, trans*. by Afung et al. Taipei: Linking.)

黃仁宇〔2001b〕。黃河青山。臺北：聯經出版事業公司。(Huang, Jenyu [2001b]. *Yellow River and Blue Mountains*. Taipei: Linking.)

黃瑞祺〔1996〕。批判社會學。臺北：三民。(Huang, Jueichi [1996]. *Sociology of Critique*. Taipei: Sanmin.)

黃光國〔1989〕，「儒家思想與現代化」，中國論壇，卷 27 第 7 期 319 號。(Huang, Guangguo [1989]. Confucian Thought and Modernization, *ChungKuo Luntan*, Vol. 27 No. 7, Issue No. 319.)

黃貴應主编〔1992〕。見證與詮釋：當代人類學家。臺北：正中。(Huang Yinggwei, ed. [1992]. *Witness and Hermeneutics: Modern Anthropologists*. Taipei: Chengchung.)
關永中〔2000〕。知識論(二)—近世思潮。臺北：五南圖書出版公司。(Kuan, Yungchung [2000]. *Epistomology (2): Modern Thought*. Taipei: Wunan.)
《管子》，楊家駱主編〔1981〕。《管子、商君書》。臺北：世界書局印行。(The Kuan Tzu [1981]. *The Kuan Tzu and The Book of Shang Jun*, ed. by Chialuo Yang. Taipei: Shihchie.)
《老子》〔1980〕，王光前著，老子閑談。臺北：星光出版社。(Lao Tzu [1980]. Lao Tzu. In Wang Kuangchien, ed., *Chatting on Lao Tzu*. Taipei: Hsing Kuang.)
李澤厚〔1989〕。華夏美學。臺北：時報文化出版社。(Li, Zehou [1989]. *Chinese Aesthetics*. Taipei: Shihpao.)
李申〔1993〕。中国古代哲学及自然科学。北京：中国社会科学出版社。(Li, Shen [1993]. *Philosophy and Sciences of the Ancient China*. Beijing: Zhongguo Shehui Kexue Chubanshe.)
李幼蒸〔1980〕。「现象学：埃德蒙特·胡塞尔」，杜任之主编，现代西方著名哲学家述评。北京：三联书店。(Li, Youzheng [1980]. Phenomenology: Edmund Husserl. In Du Renzhi, ed., *An Introduction to and Critiques of Modern Western Philosophers*. Beijing: Sanlian).
林毅夫、蔡昉、李周〔2000〕。中國經濟改革與發展。臺北：聯經出版事業公司。(Lin, Yifu et al [2000], *Economic Reforms and Development in China*. Taipei: Linking.)
廖慶洲〔1983〕。日本企管的儒家精神。臺北：聯經。(Liao, Chingchou [1983]. *Confucian Ethics in Japanese Business Management*. Taipei: Linking.)
列宁〔1974〕。哲学笔记。北京：人民。(Lenin [1974]. *Philosophical Notes*. Beijing: Remin Chubanshe.)
劉述先〔1982〕。朱子哲學思想的發展與完成。台灣：學生書局。(Liou, Shuhsien [1982]. *The Development of the Philosophical Thought of Chu Hsi*. Taipei: Hsuesheng.)
盧政春〔1992〕，「當代社會學系統理論大師：魯曼」，葉啟政主编，當代社會思想巨擘。臺北：正中。(Lu, Chengchun [1992]. Master of Modern Systems Theory in Sociology: Lumann. In Chicheng Ye, ed., *Great Sociologists of Modern Time*. Taipei: Chengchung.)
罗义俊〔1991〕。评新儒学。上海：上海人民出版社。(Luo, Yijun [1991]. Critiques on New Confucianism. Shanghai: Shanghai Renmin Chubanshe).
牟宗三〔1968 、 1969〕。心體與性體。臺北：學生書局。 (Mo, Tsung-san [1968, 1969]. *Mind and Human Nature*, Volumes 1, 2, 3. Taipei: Hsuesheng.)
牟宗三〔1992〕。牟宗三新儒學論著輯要：道德理想主義的重建。北京: 中國廣播電視。(Mo, Tsung-san [1992]. *Tsungsan Mo's Selective Works on New Confucianism*. Beijing: Zhongguo Guangbo Dianshi.)
牟宗三〔1983〕。中國哲學十九講。臺北：學生書局。(Mo Tsungsan [1983]. *Nineteen Lectures on the Philosophy of China*. Taipei: Hsuesheng.)
庞万里〔1992〕。二程哲学体系 (页 61)。(Pang, Wanli [1992]. *Philosophies of The Cheng Brothers*. Beijing: Hangkong Hangtian Daxue Chubanshe.]
尚钺主编〔1955〕。中国历史纲要。北京：人民出版社。[Shang, Yue (1955). *An Outline of the History of China*. Beijing: Renimn.]
沈清松〔1990〕，「體系圓融的大哲—懷德海」，沈清松主編，時代心靈之鑰:當代哲學思想家。臺北：正中。[Shen Chinghsung (1990). Alfred Whitehead. In Shen Chinghsung, ed., *The Key to the Minds of the Present Time*. Taipei: Chengchung.]
沈小峰、吴彤、曾国屏著〔1993〕。自组织的哲学—一种新的自然观和科学观。北京：中共中央党校出版社。[Shen, Xiaofeng, Wu Tong and Zeng Guoping (1993). *The Philosophy of Self-Organization – A New World View and a New Perspective of Sciences*. Beijing: Zhonggong Zhongyang Dangxiao Chubanshe.]
孫中興〔1992〕，「結構功能論的營建者：帕深思」，葉啟政主編，當代社會思想巨擘。臺北：正中。[Sun, Chunghsing (1992). Parsons. In Chicheng Ye, ed., *Great Sociologists of Modern Time*. Taipei: Chengchung.]
湯奕天〔1994〕，「試論精神信仰與東亞文化經濟之創造性發展」(科技交流會論文)。(Tonn, Victor

Lux [1994], "On Belief System and the Creative Advancement of the Cultural Economy of East Asian" (delivered at the First Southern New England Sciences and Technology Exchange Conference, Trinity College, Connecticut.)

湯奕天〔1996〕,「文化經濟學與臺海兩岸文化經濟的展望」(科技交流會論文)。(Tonn, Victor Lux [1996], "The Economics of Culture and the Future Perspectives of the Cultural Economies of China and Taiwan" (delivered at the Third Southern New England Sciences and Technology Exchange Conference, Trinity College, Connecticut.)

湯奕天〔1999〕,「異化、人權、臺海兩岸關係與面向二十一世紀的中華文化：從東亞共同體到全球社會的文化發展與創新」(科技交流會論文)。(Tonn, Victor Lux [1999], "Alienation, Human Rights, Relations between Both sides of Taiwan Strait, and the Chinese Culture of the Twenty-First Century: from East Asian Union to the global society," delivered at the Fifth Southern New England Sciences and Technology Exchange Conference, Trinity College, Connecticut.)

湯奕天〔1998〕,「和諧與競爭的系統研探：經濟文化系統學初探」。(Tonn, Victor Lux [1998], "Researches on the systems of Harmony and Competition: the cultural systematics of the economy" (unpublished manuscript)).

湯奕天〔2006〕。《系統學》架構與《文化經濟學》：兼論 X-Y-C-T 系統前路探索之道〔初稿〕。(Tonn, Victor Lux [2006]. *Systematics' Framework and The Economics of Culture: with an exploration into the developmental frontiers of X-Y-C-T systems* (preliminary draft)).

湯奕天〔2008〕。《系統學》、文化、與先進性國家系統前路之探索〔初稿〕。(Tonn, Victor Lux [2008]. *Xystematics, Cultures, and Explorations into the Advancement Frontiers of Nations* (preliminary draft).)

陶在樸〔1997〕。中國大陸經濟問題。臺北：五南出版圖書公司。(Tao, Tsaipu [1997]. *Problems of China's Economy*. Taipei: Wunan.).

王中江〔2001〕。道家形而上學。上海：上海文化出版社。(Wang, Zhongjiang [2001]. *Metaphysics of Taoism*. Shanghai: Shanghai Wenhua Chubanshe.)

韋積慶〔1992〕,「結構馬克思主義的舵手：阿圖塞」, 葉啟政主編，當代社會思想巨擘。臺 北：正中。(Wei, Chiching [1992]. Althuser: A Helmsman of Structuralist Marxism. In Chicheng Ye, ed., *Great Sociologists of Modern Time*. Taipei: Chengchung.)

翁之鏞〔1952〕。中國經濟問題探原。臺北：正中書局。(Wong, Chichien [1952]. *The Origin of the Economic Problems of China*. Taipei: Chung Chung.)

鄔昆如〔1971〕。西洋哲學史。臺北: 正中。 (Wu, Kunju [1971]. *History of Western Philosophy*. Taipei: Cheng Chung.)

曾仕強〔1987〕。現代式中國管理。臺北: 經濟日報社 。(Tseng, Shichiang [1987]. *Modernized Chinese Management*. Taipei: Chingchi Jipao.)

伍潛涛〔1994〕。日本伦理思想与日本现代化。北京：中国人民大学出版社。(Wu, Qiantao [1994]. *Ethics and Modernization in Japan*. Beijing: Zhongguo Renmin.)

項退結〔1991〕。中國哲學之路。臺北：東大圖書公司。(Hsiang, Tueichie [1991]. *A Road to Chinese Philosophy*. Taipei: Tungta.)

萧萐父、罗炽主编〔1991〕。众妙之门—道教文化之谜探微。湖南：湖南教育出版社。(Xiao, Shafu and Chi Luo, eds. [1991]. *The Gateway of Wonderfulness—The Mystery of Taoist Culture*. Hunan: Hunan Jiaoyu Chubanshe.)

萧汉明〔1991〕,「论《周易参同契》的人体生命模型」, 萧萐父、罗炽主编。众妙之 门—道教文化之谜探微。湖南：湖南教育出版社 (Xiao Shafu and Luo Chi [1991]. *The Gateway of Wonder—The Mystery of Taoist Culture*. Hunan: Hunan Jiaoyu Chubanshe.)

张嘉同、沈小峰主编〔1993〕。规律新论。北京：中共中央党校出版社。(Zhang, Jiatong and Shen Xiaofeng, eds. [1993]. *On the New Principles of the World*. Beijing: Zhong- gong Zhongyang Dangxiao Chubanshe.)

赵璧如〔1980〕,「西格蒙德·弗洛伊德」, 杜任之主編，中國社會科學院哲學研究所，現代西方著名哲學家述評。北京：三聯書店。(Zhao Biru [1980]. Sigmund Freud. In Du Renzhi, ed., *An Introduction to and Critiques of Modern Western Philosophers*. Beijing: Sanlian].

Glossary (中英文名詞)

Action, decision-making and strategic complex (complex of action, decision-making and strategic planning and implementation 行動-決策-策略體系 Z). This is the collective term describing the action, the decision-making body of a system and the mechanism of planning and implementation.

Anti-systemism (轉換反系). It is a transformation from an entity to its opposite in the general process of systemic changes.

Basis being-field (宇宙基場). It is the collective term designated for the physical foundations of the universe.

Basis of reversal construction (H in M/H 解構-反向生成基點、深層文化結構) This is the cultural core (in general, denoted as $\mathfrak{C} \equiv H$) or the basis of reversal construction (H which is a sub-system) of the system M.

Becoming (動變式). Becoming is a term used to denote a thing in flux or a group of things with structures changing over time. It may be considered as a counter part of the "equation" in mathematics.

Being culture (存在文化). It is the culture comprising the rationality of sciences and the spirit of conquest. In general, this entials the socio-political cultures of democratic capitalism.

Being efficiency (存在效率). It is the efficiency derived from the being culture.

CE balance (因緣平衡). This is a state of causal balance, i.e., balance in a causal net. In general, CE balance is a part of systemic balance.

CE systemic balance (causal systemic balance or shengsheng balance T^B, 因緣平衡、生生沖衡). The system in a state of CE systemic balance is one entailing baancing operations among all of its members with regard to the distribution of energy, power or vitality, holding all other things constant. In the case of two entities, when v_1 and v_2 interact to each other in the state of CE balance (T^B), we write: $\{\varphi(v_1, v_2) =< T^B\} \Vdash Ш^{Д}$, where $\varphi \vDash \mathbf{U}$ is an interactor. For instance, a T^B state for elements v_1 and v_2 is a state in which v_1 and v_2 have reached an equilibrium-in-conflict or balance in tranquility. That is, this is a state of equal power or influence for both elements.

Centrality (執中、中心、中心中道). This is a concept denoting one or more of the following states: (1) The state or status of the concentration of energies and powers (of a system) in the hands of the center. (2) The state or status to which each entity will eventually converge. Here by "convergence" of one entity to the other is meant the infinite closeness of these two entities. (3) The best possible state facing a system with the concentration of powers and energies.

Chain (鏈). It is a collection of various entities organizing in a sequential manner.

Chain complex (鏈複體). It is a complex which is a chain as well. Here, a complex ia an organic collection of elements interacting holistically.

Chi (氣). It is a symbolic entity following Taoist tradition in representing the "material," "implicit" or "negative" side of the most subtle forces, both potential and realized, of the universe.

Chung (中). I t is a concept or state of middle-mediety or center.

Complete IDR impactor (可完全分解動子). The impactor that deconstructs a system and decomposes it into a hierarchical structure of subsystems in which (1) each unit of constituting substructure (i.e., subsystem) is relatively independent of other units of constituting substructures (i.e., other subsystems) and (2) there are no residual structures which are not subsystems.

Complex (複體). It is a collection of various entities organizing in a holistical manner with the specific structures to be determined in the context.

Contradictory element (or *self-contradicting primitive element* 生勝元素，即內蘊生剋、矛盾的樸實性宇宙元素). This is a primitive element which contains in itself the very forces of self-contradiction. Here, by contradiction is meant the inconsistency in logic.

Conflict effect (相害效果). This is part of the macro efficiency which is negative and is created in the process of harming each other by the members of the system.

Conflictivity (or conflicting sociality 剋) In general, it is the operations of the inner forces of an entity or system that is destructive, negative or mutually harmful (to all the constituting units of the entity or system).

Coordination effect (相生效果). This is part of macro efficiency of a system created through the coordination among members and the mutual rendering of assistance to each other in the system.

CS systemic balance-centrality ($T^{B\text{-}C}$, 因緣平衡-執中). It is a state of CE systemic balance and/or centrality in the process of yin-yang tao reversal or in the creation of a causal net.

Cultural advantages (文化優勢). Cultural advantages reflect the strengths of a system derived from its cultural heritages (or cultural factors, life-will-to-creation and rationality-to-creation).

Cultural complex (文化複合體、思想體系). To be denoted by: $<\mathbb{C}_X> = \{\tau|[\mathcal{M}^I(\ell,\tau),...,\mathcal{M}^N(\ell,\tau)] \Vdash [E(e_r(\tau)),Z(\tau)]\}$ with $\ell(\sigma,\kappa) \Vdash Ш^{ДL}$ and $\tau \Vdash (\mathfrak{J},Ш^{Д}) \Vvdash \mathbb{T}\mathrm{zu}^*$, cultural complex is what is behind the behaviors, activities, and institutions of the members of a group, community, or society.

Cultural core (文化核心). For a group of human beings (a community or society), it is the most essential elements of the culture which has been preserved through out history. In the case of reversal construction, this cultural core is the basis of the reversal construction of the system in question.

Cultural determinism (文化決定論). This is the idea that culture determines history. It is not in any conflict to the idea that, although culture has a significant long-term feedback effect on the economy, economic forces are the determining forces of the history. This is because, the term culture, actually the organic collection of all cultural variables including all institutional factors, strategic factors and the culture in narrow sense, contains the idea of economic culture.

Cultural factors or variables (文化因素). It is the sum total of the institutional or organizational factors, the strategic factors, and the culture in general. In short, it is just called the culture.

Cultural stage of economic development and advancement (經濟發展、先進飛躍上的文化階段). This is the stage that the momentum of economic development and advancement stems from the strengths of institutional and technological advancement, which in turn are created by the cultural creativity. In other words, in this stage, the development and advancement is contributed by the whole society, rather than just by the scientists and engineers.

Cultural stage of trade (國際貿易上的文化階段). This is the stage of global trade in which the determining factor is culture. That is, in this stage, the engine of growth is the import and export of cultural entities and products. In other words, this is the stage of trade in which the growth momentum (of trade and thus the economy) stems from the exports of the indigenously developed culture and cultural products.

Cultural systematics (systemicsof culture 文化系統學). This is the study of culture based on the methods of systematics. In the broad sense, all human-social studies are defined as fields of cultural systematics.

Culture (文化). In the conventional or narrow sense, culture is perceived as the sum total of belief systems, knowledge, habits, customs, life styles, artistic activities, materialistic developments, and the rationality and life-will underlying the behaviors and patterns of the members of a community and their economic, socio-political institutions and spiritual arrangements (文化指感情、理性、生活方式、自主意識及創造意志等因素的總合。) In the broad sense, by culture is meant the integral whole of the culture in the narrow sense, the institutional/organizational arrangements, and the complexes of policies/ strategies of human actions.

d-systemism (d-轉變). It is the transformation of any entity into a different one.

Dao (道). Following Taoisr tradition, it is the set of symbolic principles governing the operations of various entities in the universe.

Decomposition and reorganization of a system (系統性分解重組). It is a process of the deconstruction of a system into independent substructures (i.e., subsystems or elements) with these substructures being simultaneously reorganized in a hierarchical manner. Note that in this decomposition of a grand system, the residuals which are not in any forms of systems must be empty.

Democratic capitalism (民主資本主義體系). This is a system of economic capitalism and political deocrcy. The most basic "philosophical foundation" or basis of the ideas of democracy and invidual economic freedom embodied in this system is the Natural Law bestowed by God. In this modern democracy, a small group of politicians represents the citizens in general in exercising the political power and in enjoying most of the fruits of democracy.

Determining power of the base (基礎對上層建築的決定性作用、經濟對文化的決定性作用). In general, the base of a system determines the upper structures of the system. For example, in designating the totality of culture, economy, polity and society as a grand system, the development of culture must be based on the foundations of polity, society and especially economic activities,. Note that this is a somewhat peculiar system in which although culture is the center,

it is the economy (which is a non-central subsystem) that plays as the most important determining factor. This may be called a **base-center interactive system**.
Dialectic (辯證法). It is the method of analyzing a process of development by dividing it into three consecutive and "dynamical"categories of thesis, anti-thesis and synthesis.

Differencing (差異). In measuring a system of uncertainty, it is the method of eliminating the most representative structures or features of the system in question from the one to be measured.

Economics (conventional economics 經濟學、西方經濟學). This is essentially the economics developed on the basis of the analytical methods of mathematics and natural scicneces. Cultural foundations are entirely ignored in this conventional approach to economics.

Economics of culture (文化-人本經濟學). In the broad sense, it is the unity of the interactive studies of the economy, the polity and the cultural variables. In the narrow sense it is the studies of the economy by taking into account all cultural factors.

Effective intra-inter systemic operations, scheme of (effective IISO scheme 有效性系統內-間運作). By the principle of effective intra-inter system operations, for a system or grand system, in the process of partition, modification, alternation, reorganization, and/or integration, etc., the effective IISO scheme entails the functioning of the whole (or mutuality-entity per se) and the individuality (or self-entity per se) in a state of equicentrality.

Effective intra-inter systemic operations/T continuity (effective IISO/T scheme 有效性系統內-間運作/T 連續). This is the functioning of the effective IISO scheme in a state of T continuity.

Element (元素). The element is the most fundamental constituting entity in the universe. In general it is an undefined term. The most basic elements are the universal elements and human elements. The elements can also be classified according to the categories of primitive element and sophisticated or composite element.

Element/row/column-augmenting impactors (元素/行/列-增益動子). These are impactors that enable us to augment elements, rows and/or columns of matrices (also see the matrix-generating and augmenting impactor in the text).

Empty system (空系統). It denotes a system that does not exist.

Entity (人、事、物的通稱). Entity is a primitive concept denoting a thing, a human being, an event, or a process of a primitive type, etc. It is a primitive term that may even denote "something super-rational and super-natural."

Entity-augmenting impactor (元素、行、列、面向、系統增算子). The impactor that augments constituting factors, elements, or dimensions of an existing element. The actual content of what is to be augmented depends on the context. In addition, this impoactor may also augment subsystems of a grand system.

Equilibrium (equilibrium-in-conflict 均衡). This is a state of permanent conflict in which the powers of various opposing forces of an entity (or a system) are equalized.

Equicentrality (systemic balance-centrality 沖衡、系統性沖衡). This term is coined to designate the state of systemic balance and/or centrality among all relevant entities (or variables), holding all other things constant. That is, it is a state that, all other thing being equal, the following conditions hold: (1) The system as a whole reaches a state of centrality, (2) each member of the system is independent. (3) The system reaches a state of vertical centrality, (4) the system reaches a state of horizontal CE balance. (5) The system establishes a desirable and stable relationship between vertical centrality and horizontal CE balance. (6) The system is in the vicinity of a frontier entailing a partially-flexible ideal state (部分-彈性理想境域, i.e., an ideal state for some flexible and unspecified parts of the system). Here, by this last condition, we may say the system is in the vicinity of a state of "systemic optimality."

External energy system (外在的能量系統). $E\{e_j\} \equiv E(e_{sp})$ $(E(e_r) \equiv E(e_b)$, resp.) is the systm of external energy belonging to the social-power energy net (basis being-field, resp.) of the universe.

f-systemism (f-反變). It is the transformation of an element, system or grand system into its opposite in terms of a yin-yang pair.

Faziranism (法自然體系) It is the basic system of classic China under our classification. In this system, the society is formed by a group of human beings who are self-adaptive to the nature. Politically this society is controlled by a military dictator who claims to derive his power from Heaven to be assisted by the gentry class. The philosophical system at the individual level is that of Taoism and the philosophical foundation of the society is that of Confucianism. Note that for the emperor-based Faziranism (Huangben Faziranism 皇本法自然體系), the philosophical thought of the polity is essentially provided by Legalism. For the Official-based Faziranism (Guanben Faziranism 官本法自然體系), the political power of the system is partially shared by the group of government officials selected from the gentry class. Note that the so-called modern Faziranism is substantially different from the classic Faziranism. One form of the modern Faziranism is essentially designed as a self-organizing and self-mastering system (自組織自主法自然體系). In this self-organizing and self-mastering system, although its social philosophy is close to that of self-creating and self exiting Taoism, its political philosophy (or idea) is neither the "philosophy of democracy" (or doctrine of democracy) nor the philosophy of Confucianism. It is rather a philosophy of self-masterism in which each person is the master of him/herself in the realm of politics.

Feedback effect of upper structure onto the basis (上層建築對基礎的反作用). It is the impact of the upper structure of a system onto its foundations. For example, culture has a significant feedback effect on the operations of the economy.

Formal-informal organizational structure (正式-非正式的組織-層級系統) It is the hierarchical part of the system (vd,hc,γ).

Generativity (generative individuality or generative sociality 生). This is the inner force of an entity that is generative, mutually beneficial or positive.

Generativity-Conflictivity (生剋). As one of the most basic and sophisticated entities representing the complexes of the forces of contradiction from within, it is an entity of creativity in a causal net (因緣網絡).

Government efficiency (政府效率). This denotes the efficiency of the government, especially in the operations of planning.

Government officials' efficiency (文官效率). This is the efficiency of the government officials includes the efficiency of elected representatives and civil servants/bureaucrats.

h-systemism (h-和變). It is the transformation of a pair of yin-yang elements (yin-yang systems, resp.) into its completion which is a higher level element (system, resp.) in the process of yin-yang tao reversal.

Hf-systemism (Hf-反變). It is the transformation of an element, system or grand system into its opposite in terms of a thesis-antithesis pair.

Hh-systemism (Hh-合變). It is the transformation of thesis and antithesis into synthesis in the process of dialectic.

Human activism (人的主觀能動性). This is the active involvement of the human being in determining one's life trajectory, a concept intrinsically embodied in the philosophies like Confucianism, Taoism and Marxism.

Human element (人元素). Human element is a universal element carrying human characteristics.

Independently decomposing and reorganizing impactor (IDR impactor 分解重組動子). The impactor that deconstructs a grand system into a hierarchical structure in which (1) each constituting unit substructure (i.e., subsystem) is relatively independent of other units of substructures (i.e., other subsystems) and (2) there are some residuals which are not subsystems.

Impactor (算子). Impactor is an entity exerting forces on oneself or others in creating motions or initiating processes of changes. An impactor may be an element (primitive or composite), a system or a grnad system.

IDR impactor, complete (獨可完全獨立分解的動子). A grand system that can be decomposed into independent subsystems with the residuals of non-systems vanishing completely.

IND impactor of separation (IND-sys impactor IND-sys 獨立分離動子). This is the impactor that separates or deconstructs a system into independently substructures or elements.

Interactor (互動動子). This is an entity exerting interactive forces in-between two or more elements (or systems). An interactor may be an element, a system or a grand system. Interactor is a special case of the impactor.

Intra-inter systems' effective operation, principle of (principle of effective IISO operations 系統內-間運作原理). See the effective IISO scheme.

IRI chain (信息-決策-執行鏈條). This is the chain complex of information evaluation, rational decision-making and planning and implementation. It is a becoming (or force of constant motion) based on the creativity of the rationality and life-will complex.

Iso-systemism (**轉換共系、象徵共系**). This is a procedure that a system is transformed into another without changing the essentials of the original system. In other words, two systems are iso-systemic if and only if they are "essentially" identical in terms of systemic structures. Here, the content of the term "essential" (essentials, or essentially) depends on the specific context of the problem.

Life-will (生命意志) Life will is the life-long orientation or spiritual impulse of life. In general, human life-will can be classified into the yu-wu life-will (in the yu-wu culture or tao-jen culture), the life-will of conquest (in the being culture), and the self-generating and self-mastering life-will (or the self-creating and self-existing life-will in the culture of self-masterism).

Life-will of conquest (征服性生命意志). It is the life-will that extols the virtues of conquesting onself and others.

Life-will of individuality (自體性生命意志). This is the micro life-will judging every thing from the perspectives of oneself while failing to value any mutual interaction with other human beings.

Life-will of mutuality (互有性生命意志). This is the holistic life-will exalting the values of mutual interactions with other human beings in a system.

Macro efficiency (**總體效率**). This is the efficiency of the whole or the totality of effectiveness of such things as the technological efficiency of mutuality and the organizational efficiency of groups.

Macro-global efficiency (holistic efficiency **整體效率**). This is the totality or organic efficiency of the "system" or an "entity" as a whole, centering on technological efficiency of mutuality and the organizational efficiency of mutuality. The difference between the macro efficiency and the macro-eglobal efficiency is that in a field like economics (or the society, etc., resp.), macro-global concept applies to the global economy (or the global society, etc., resp.), while the macro efficiency applies to the national economy (or the society of a nation, etc., resp.).

Macro-global life-will (**整體生命意志**). This is the totality of the life-will embracing the life-will of individuality and the life-will of mutuality and the outside worlds in the sense of global society.

Macro-global rationality (**整體理性**). This is the global and holistic rationality which is organic and synthetic, and is flexible and easy to transform the reasoning view point from one strict category into other categories. In this approach, much attention is paid to study the interactions and relationship among all the relevant entities.

Market efficiency (市場效率). This is the efficiency of the pure market operations without any government intervention.

Mathematics (**數學**). The study of the structures of numbers, real and imaginary.

Matrix-creating impactor (矩陣創造性算子). This is the factor operating on entities (scaler or matrices) to create new matrices.

Mediety (middle, middle-TCentral 中間、中間中道). It is the middle, medium or intermediate state of an entity.

Metaphorical anti-systemism (隱喻反系). It is a special case of the anti-systemism.
Micro efficiency (個體效率). This is the efficiency of the "micro units" or individuality, centering on the technological efficiency of individuality and the organizational efficiency of individuality.

Micro life-will (個體生命意志). This is the life-will of the individual person, the life-will of individuality.

Micro rationality (個體理性). This is the individualistic and single-categorical aspect of rationality which is analytical and engaging in an ever in-depth investigation of an entity. For example, scientific rationality is a micro rtioanlity.

Mind complex (心靈複合體). In symbols, this is: $[\mathcal{M}^{1}(\ell,\tau),\ldots,\mathcal{M}^{N}(\ell,\tau)]$, for $\ell \equiv \ell(\sigma,\kappa) \Vdash Ш^{\mathcal{L}(\sigma,\kappa)} \Subset Ш^{ДL}$, $\tau \Vdash (\mathfrak{I}, Ш^{Д}) \Vdash \mathbb{Tzu}^{*}$. Individually, this is the system of thought processes and the controlling center of activities of a human being. In this system, the center is the core from which all layers or dimensions of thought processes and the controlling mechanisms of an individual person (i.e., $\mathcal{M}^{i}(\ell,\tau)$, for all $i \in \mathbb{N}$) derive their operating forces in an organic and systematical manner. Note that this core does not have to actually exit, and thus it may just serve as a virtual center.

Most representative entity (代表性人、事、物). It is the entity equipped with all the essential characteristics and traits in representing the category of the entity in question. Ingeneral, it is the collection of the structures or the most representative faces, phases or features of an entity in uncertainty.

Multiple factor cause-effect (MFCE) *scheme* (多元因緣模式). This is the collective and organic designation of all relevant entities which represents a world of simplified realty. In this scheme, all factors are causally related, a center/non-central relationship exists, a state of balance – be it in tranquility or conflict – may be present, a state of centrality may emerge, and a state of TCentral presumably prevails.

Node (link, linkage 關鍵環節). This is a key joint or an essential inter-connector of linkages in a chain complex. In general, a node may well be a system by itself.

Normal state (通常、正常情狀). Normal state of an entity (system, resp.) is the one operating in a regular level with which various internal forces of the complex of the culture/socio-polity/economy underlying this entity (system, resp.) are all operating in a regular or T Central level (i.e., average, best possible, or long-term sustainable level).

Organization (組織). It is a system related to human-social and business activities.

Organizational and static-dynamical structure of a system ($[(vd,hc,\gamma),C_S \times C^{DS}(e_r),(R_M,R^{DM}(e_r)),\tilde{O}]$ 系統組織-系統通貫結構). This is the main part of a system describing the internal structural framework -- both static and dynamic -- of the system, but with the exclusion of the decision-making and strategic complex, external environmental complex and the cultural complex (of the system).

Planning efficiency (計劃效率). This is the effectiveness of a system working through a sequence of orderly planning. Here by planning is meant to take concrete and coordinated steps in carrying out a series of well designed programs in order to achieve some objectives in a specific and timely manner.
Primitive element (樸素元素). Primitive element is the simplest universal element. This term is undefined.

"qi" (气). "qi" is the actual air or a somewhat abstract form of matter in the real world.

Rationality (理性). It is what is behind the human reasoning process. It is part of the most basic culture forces (i.e., the rationality and life-will complex (ρ,ω)).

Reversal construction (deconstruction 逆反建構、系統性解構). A process of deconstructing a system (or grand system, resp.) back into its constituting units (subsystems, resp.).

Reversal-construction subsystem (M/H 反向生成子系統、解構-反向生成基點) See the basis of reserversal construction. The reserversal-construction subsystem is the basis of reserversal construction, the reversal representative entity of a system, or the subsystem representing the core of the system to be created through reversal construction.

Scheme (系統性模式、呈現式). It is a holistic presentation of a set of entities with embodied attributes and relationships. In a more conventional terminology, a scheme may simply be considered as a model.

Scheme of yin-yang five-element (*YYWX* 陰陽五行性模式). It is a presentation of a systme through the structural scheme of yin-yang and five elements – metal (金), wood (木), water (水), fire (火) and earth (土).

Scientific rationality (科學理性) It is a reasoning process using mathematical modeling, methods of controlled experiments, abstract thinking pattern, building up macro structures from micro units, and revising theories after checking against the real world facts. In essence, on one hand, science is the study of entities in the universe by using various models of mathematics. On the other hand, science is closely related to the study of physical worlds like that of physics, chemistry and biology.

Self-creating and self-existing life-will (自創自存性生命意志). This is the life-will of being self-existing and independent and not depending one's life on any thing external. Here independence does not necessarily imply isolation from interacting with others.

Self-adaptive and self-mastering life-will (自生自主性生命意志). This is the life-will of being self-mastering and independent and yet to be reasonably adaptive to the outside environments. Here independence and self-mastery do not necessarily imply isolation from having close relationships with other human beings. And being adaptive, it does not necessarily hinge on being unreasonably conditioned on external environments. That is, in facing unfavorable outside conditions, human initiatives and strong strategic actions are to be assumed.

Self-mastering equicentrality (系統之自主沖衡性). This is the state of self-mastery amid the equicentrality of the system.

Self-masterism, polity of (自主政治體系). This is a polity in which each citizen is the master of itself.

Self-masterism and self-organization, system of (system of zizhu-zizuzhi 自主自組織系統). This is the philosophiccal system developed on the basis of the theory of self-organizations and the idea of self-masterism of each individual in the universe.

Separation of a system (系統之分離). This is the deconstruction of a system to derive its independent and separate subsystems or elements.

Separation impactor (分離動子). See impactor of separation.

SIRFP chain (儲蓄-投資-研究發展-財務-生產鏈條). This is the chain complex of the activities of saving, investment, financing, and production.

SK CE balance (生勝沖衡). This is a dual balance between the forces of mutually beneficial activities (or creations) and mutual conflicts (or destructions).

Social power-energy net (社會權能網). It is the intermediate layer of the universe which is represented as the structures of human being in groups.

Sophisticated element (非樸素元素). The sophisticated element is one with internal structures like a grand system. Note that this sophisticated element is defined as an element (or a system of one element), not a system (i.e., a grand system of more than one subsystem).

Space of systems (系統空間). This is the collection of all systems together with the closure of their operations.

Specific TCentral. In general, the state of specific TCentral (sTC 特定中道) of X is meant X in a partially ideal state (i.e., ideal only for a part of the whole world of our concerns).

Standard Hg system (標準 Hg 系統). This is a system in which a conflict transformation prevails. For a system of three elements {x,y|z}, the following conditions hold: (i) x and y are non-central elements while z is the central element. (ii) y is the Hf-systemism of x, and z is the Hh-systemism of x. (iii) [z,(x,y)] is a vertical thesis-antithesis pair. In addition, for z to x and z to y, there is a relationship of dominance of the central over non-central elements. (iv) (x,y) is a horizontal thesis-antithesis pair. In addition, between x to y, there is a relationship of a conflict-type coordination.

Standard L system (標準 L 系統). This is a system in which there exists a transformation of tranquility type. For a system {x,y|ℭ} of two elements x and y with the cultural core ℭ, the following conditions hold: (i) x and y are non-central elements while the role of the central element is performed by the cultural core ℭ. (ii) y is the y-systemism of x. (iii) (x,y) is a horizontal yin-yang pair. Furthermore, between x to y, there is a relationship of horizontal and consensual coordination.

Standard R system (標準 R 系統). This is a system in which tere exists a transformation of weak tranquility. For a system of three elements {x,y|z}, the following conditions hold: (i) x and y are non-central elements while z is the central element. (ii) Although y is a non-central element, y is in a position higher than x. Here, (x,y) is an r-horizontal yin-yang pair. (iii) y is a

Ry-systemism of x: y is the y-systemism of x and y is at a step (or stage) higher than x. (iv) y is a **Rh-systemism** of x: z is the h-systemism of x (i.e., x→y being a y-systemism and y→z being a y-systemism) and z is at a step (or stage) higher than y. (v) (x,y) is called an R-horizontal yin-yang pair, and ((x,y),z) is called an R-vertical yin-yang pair. The relationship of these (R-horizontal and R-vertical) yin-yang pairs are of tranquil type.
Standard Y system (標準 Y 系統). This is a system in which there exists a transformation of strong tranquility. For a system of three elements {x,y|z}, the following conditions hold: (i) x and y are non-central elements while z is the central element. (ii) y is the y-systemism of x, while z is the y-systemism of (x,y). (iii) [z,(x,y)] is a vertical yin-yang pair. In addition, for z to x and z to y, there is a relationship of dominance of the central over non-central elements. (iv) (x,y) is a horizontal yin-yang pair. In addition, between x to y, there is a relationship of horizontal and consensual coordination.

State of simple T Central (簡易中道). A system is in a state of simple TCentral if and only if the following conditions hold: (i) The system is in systemic continuity. (ii) In the system, the relationships among different members are either in some states of CE balance or in states of controlled tension and conflict. (iii) In the system, the center exerts weak dominance over the non-central members so that states of CE balance or tension/conflict sustain over time.

State of uncertainty (不確定情境). This is the collective term assigned to the partially predictable and yet somewhat fluxional situations. The state of uncertainty can only be measured imperfectly through theories of sysmetrics and the studies of specific historical data.

Static representation of a systemic-change becoming (系統性變異式的靜態表現式). This is the representation of a system as an additive sum of constituting units (i.e., elements or subsystems) in the plural forms of systemisms with various integrating factors.

Static-dynamical framing network system (系統的靜動通貫結構 $[C_S \times C^{DS}(e_r), (R_M, R^{DM}(e_r))]$) This is part of a system that describes its structures of static and dynamical mechanisms.

Strategic efficiency (策略效率). This is the effectiveness of applying a strategy in order to succeed in the pursuit of certain objectives.

Strategic space (策略空間). For a system, this is the collection of all feasible strategies facing the decision maker of the system. For all systems in the world, this is the collection of all strategies.

Strategy (策略). This is the whole process of designing and implementing plans in successive steps and in essentially an orderly manner.

Subsystem (子系統). This is an organic collection of elements that forms a system within a grand system.

Symbolic iso-systemism (象徵共系). This is a special case of iso-systemism or the iso-systemism in the broad sense.

System (系統). System is the collection of universal or human elements together with necessary structures to support these elements and with self or mutual-relational operations of dynamical forces affecting these elements and structures over time. That is, for a simple system (i.e., system without any sub-systems), it is a collection of elements with necessary relations connecting them together in an organic way. In symbols, for X to be a system, it is denoted as: $X = \{[vd,hc,\gamma],C_S\times C^{DS}(e_k),(R_M,R^{DM}(e_k)), \tilde{O}\}|E\{e_g\},Z\}\rangle\oplus<\mathbb{C}_X>$, where$\{[vd,hc,\gamma]$ is the formal-informal organizational structure, "$C_S \times C^{DS}(e_k),(R_M,R^{DM}(e_k)),\tilde{O}\}$" is the organizational and static-dynalimal strutueres, and $<\mathbb{C}_X>$ is the cultural complex.

System of uncertainty (不確定性系統). This is a system with uncertain distribution or spreading-out. The future state of uncertainty is unknown and can only be measured imperfectly by theories constructed on the basis of historical data.

System-creating impactor (系統創建動子). This is the operations of elements or systems in processes of creating new systems.

System-deconstructing impactor (系統解構動子). This is the operations that reduce a system (systems, resp.) to its (their, resp.) basic units.

System-interacting impactor (system's interactor 系統間運作動子). This is the interactor (i.e., interactive impactor) operating among systems.

Systematics (systemics 系統學). In the narrow sense, systematics is the totality of the studies of the self-creating, self-existing, self-organizing and interactive processes and structures of all entities in the universe by the systemic (or yu-wu), dialectic, and other non-mathematical methods of reasoning. In other words, systematics compsirises the studies of entities in the universe by using various schemes of systems. In the broad sense, it is the systematic study of all entities in the universe by all available methods. That is, in the broad sense, systematics is inclusive of methods such as the methods of mathematical modeling and thequantitative-experimental methods.

Systemic balance (系統性平衡). This is a state of balance among members of a system (among subsystems of a grand, resp.), for examples, between two elements (or two subsystems, resp.).

Systemic optimality (系統最優性、系統最適性) is the state that through changing strategies, the system's structures and operations are changed so that this system reaches the vicinity of its targetzone. That is, this is a state in which the most essential aspects of the system in question can at most be variationally improved by any change in the system. This is a state that, by taking into account all generative and destructive effects of changes over time and with hypothetical compensation of the winners to the losers, all possibilities of improvements of the system in question are essentially exhausted (except at the costs this system is not willing to be burdened). This is in a sense a state of systematically generative-and-dynamic Pareto optimality with hypothetical compemsation.

Systemic advantage (系統優勢). This is the collection of all advantages derived from systemic operations. One example is the strategic advantage based on the effectiveness of systematic planning conditioned upon the cultural strengths of the underlying system.

Systemic balance (equicentrality 系統沖衡). This is the same as CE systemic balance orequicentrality.

Systemic-change becoming (系統性變異動變式). It is a becoming depicting a dynamical structure of a system.

Systemic distribution of a system (系統的系統性分布). Theoretically, on one hand, a system is distributed with a TCentral state and four non-TCentral states (see Figure 10.4-1). On the other hand, a system is distributed with the SC state, a short-term target state, a long-term target state and a self-mastering state (i.e., the very long-term target state, see Figure 10.4-2).

Systemic rationality (系統理性) It is what is behind the reasoning process in investigating things essentially in holistic and orderly manner. Systemic rationality, includeing yu-wu rationality, is non-mathemtical in nature.

Systemism (系統變異、轉換). This entials the operations and transformations of entities over time. These include the essential maintenance of entities and the transformations of entities into others over time.

T calculus (T 微積分). This is part of calculus modified by introducing the operations of systematics. This is part of what is to be called the mathematics of mutuality, in contrast to the conventional mathematics which may be called as the mathematics of independence and individuality.

T continuity (T 連續). This is state of a temporary and instantaneous continuity in terms of the structures and strategies of a system. In particular, this is the state that each element or sub-system of a system reaches a state of momentarily systemic continuity and momentarily strategic continuity.

T derivative (T 微分). It is a part of T calculus.

T matrix (T 矩陣). This is a quasi-matrix created by a "'matrix-creating impactor" or operated under the element/row/column/subsystem-augmenting impactors.

Tao (道). This is the creator of the universe following te idea of Lao Tzu. Essentially, it is a symbolic entity conceived as the "spiritual," "explicit" or "positive" side of the most subtle forces, both potential and realized, of the universe.

Tao culture (yu-wu culture 有無-道明文化). This is the culture of Tao (or tao-jen culture) developed upon the foundations of the classic symbolic rationality (or YYWX studies) and the spirit of tranquility and mutuality.

Tao efficiency (道明效率). The efficiency of the culture of Tao (or tao-jen culture) manifested in the government (planning) activities as well as in the private business endeavors.

TCentral, general (T Central 全般中道). For a system, this is the state that the whole system has reached the goal of being in a long-term stable and ideal state. This state may be characterized as a state of the long-term "systemic optimality and equilibrium," thenmost desirable level of centrality and CE balance, the systemic/strategic continuity, and/or the success of pursuing well thought-off objectives. In addition, this is a state of welfare satisfaction for the (grand) system as a whole. In short, this term denotes the idea of an ideal state of centrality, CE balance, and the welfare satisfaction for the (grand) system as a whole.

TCentral, low-level pragmatic (低層次實用中道).A system is said to be in a state of low-level (or low level) pragmatic TCentral if and only if the following conditions are satisfied: For the system, (1) achieving a state of balance, (2) achieving a state of centrality, (3) achieving a state of mutuality, (4) in mathematical sense, achieving some measure of welfare maximization for the system as a whole.

TCentral, low-level real-world (TCentral 低層次現實世界中道). A system is said to be in a state of low-level real-world (or low level real world) Tcentral if and only if the following conditions are satisfied: For the system, (1) achieving a state of independence and reativity of each element of the system, (2) achieving a state of balance, (3) achieving a state of centrality, (4) achieving a state of mutuality, (5) achieving a "state of integral whole," (6) achieving a state of developmental dynamics, (7) achieving some measure of welfare maximization for the system as a whole, and (8) achieving some measure of fairness for each member in this system.

TCentral, practical (實際中道). It is a desirable state of Tcentral which is achieved under the constraints of the existing internal structures and dynamics of the system in question and the external environments facing the system.

Tcentral, simple. See the state of simple Tcentral.

Tcentral, specific (specific Tcentral, sTc 特定中道). This term denotes a special case of Tcentral in which only some conditions of the state of general TCentral are satisfied. Very often, this is a state of balance and centrality. Simply stated, for a specific part of a system, this is the state that it reaches a long-term stable and ideal situation.

Thesis-antithesis pair (正反對子). Two elements (or systems) are said to be in a thesis-antithesis if and only if they constitute a relationship of conflict and contradiction. In general, two entities in a thesis-antithesis pair have an one-to-its-opposite relationship. One such example is the one-and-its-enemy pair.

Transformation (系統轉換). It is the same as systemism in the sense of changing one entity into other.

TSIF chain (工藝技術-儲蓄-投資-財務-生產鏈條). This is the chain complex of technology, saving, investment and finance.

Ultimate Creativity-Destructivity (宇宙最終創斂力 Tzu*). This is the totality of the unknown forces that are presumably responsible for the ultimate operations of the universe.

Universal element (宇宙性元素、一般性元素). A universal element is an undefined term denoting an entity, an event, a person or just a thing.

Virtual operating force (精一運作力). This is the operational aspects of the forces of the center of a system in question. In the case of a Faziranist cultural system, it is comprised of all sectors -- the public sector and the private sector alike -- affected by the public impactor of the center.

Will and rationality to creation-destruction entity (理性意志創斂主體). This is the center of the universe from which the human initiative and activism are derived.

World of self-masterism (自主性境域世界). Essentially this is a world in which every participant is the master itself.

Wu (無). Wu denotes many things. It may denote the ultimate forces of the universe as in Lao Tzu. It may denote the fact that nothing exists at all. In general, it denotes the potential of entities in a metaphorical way.

Y-systemism (Y 轉變、陰陽化變). This is a transformation from a system (an element, respectively) x to another system y (another element, respectively) under the culture of tranquility such that x and y constitute a yin-yang pair.

Yang element (陽元素). It is the element with the characteristic of explicit, right-sided or positive force in a yin-yang pair. According to the reasoning of Lao Tzu, it is the negative force in the yin-yang pair.

Yin element (陰元素). It is the element with the characteristic of implicit, left-sided or negative force in a yin-yang pair. According to the reasoning of Lao Tzu, it is the positive force in the yin-yang pair.

Yin-yang pair (陰陽對子). Two systems (or elements) are said to be in a yin-yang pair if and only if they constitute a relationship of complementarity or contrast. In general, two entities in a yin-yang pair have an implicit-explicit relationship. One such example is the male-female pair, and others include the positive-negative pair and the master-subject pair.

Yu (有). Yu denotes many things. It may denote the existence of entities. In general, it denotes the potentiality, manifestation, and realization of the ultimate forces in the universe in a metaphorical way.

Yu-wu rationality (有無理性). Yu-wu rationality is what is behind the reasoning process of the classical symbolic rationality of Taoism, Cofucianism, egalism and Buddhism. One such example is the rationality underlying the celebrated scheme of yin-yang and five-elements. This yu-wu rationality may be refined by the Buddhist rationality of emptiness.

YXSIF chain (陰陽五行性工藝-儲蓄-投資-財務-生產鏈條). This is a special case of the TSIF chain in which the technology is developed on the foundations of the scheme of yin-yang five-element.

YXT chain (yin-yang five-element technological chain 陰陽五行性工藝鏈條). This is a chain complex with technology developed on the basis of YYWX scheme (i.e., th scheme of yin-yang and five elements).

YYXX. See the scheme of yin-yang an difve elements.

Zero system (零系統). It is a system representing a state of TCentral which is analogous to zero in the number system.

List of Symbols (符號名稱)

$\mathbb{C}^{T}$ ($\mathfrak{C}^{T}$) Tranquil culture 安寧文化

$\mathfrak{C}^{SK}$ Core of the composite culture of $\mathcal{S}$ (生 generativity $\sigma \equiv \{\tau|(\omega,\rho)^{S}\}$) and $\mathcal{K}$ (剋 conflictivity: $\kappa \equiv \{\tau|(\omega,\rho)^{K}\}$) 生剋文化體的核心

$\mathfrak{C}^{ZhF}$ Core of the yu-wu/conquest-scientific cultural complex 有無/征服科學文化複合體的核心

$(\Omega,\mathbb{Z}\circ,_{v}\mathbb{H},\{\mathbb{C}\})$, $(\Omega^{\Delta},\mathbb{Z}\circ,_{v}\mathbb{H},\{\mathbb{C}\})$ Space of systems 系統空間

Ω Collection of systems 系統的簡單集合、聚合

r-SysSM Space of systems and mathematical operations 系統學與數學的共同運作空間

$\mathbb{Z}\circ,_{v}\mathbb{H}$ Space of impactors with $\mathbb{Z}$ being the space of self impactors and $\mathbb{H}$ the space of mutual impactors 自動動子-互動動子空間

$\{\mathbb{C}\}$ Space of culture (i.e., the totality of all cultural complexes) 文化複合體

$\mathbb{C}_{X}$ Cultural generator of (or social culture underlying) the system in question 文化複合體的生子

$\langle\mathbb{C}_{X}\rangle$ Cultural complex of the system X 系統 X 的文化複合體

$\mathfrak{C}^{*}$ Cultural core of underlying $\mathbb{C}_{X}$ 文化核心

χ Hierarchy-transformational structure (structural framework) of a system 系統的層級-通貫結構/子系統

$\psi^{生}$ Generative impactor 生生動子

H Space of human elements 人元素空間

H* Space of universal attributes or human characteristics〔人元素的〕人文特質空間

$\mathcal{K}$(剋): $\kappa \equiv \{\tau|(\omega,\rho)^{K}\}$ Conflictivity 衝突性、對立性

MAS(A,B) Metaphoric anti-systemism between two systems A and B 系統 A、B 間的隱諭反系

$X \sqsubseteq (\Omega^{\Delta},\mathbb{Z}\circ,_{v}\mathbb{H},\{\mathbb{C}\})(D^{*}\text{-SYS})$ System-energy complex 系統-能源空間

$X \sqsubseteq (\Omega^{SEC1},\mathbb{Z}\circ,_{v}\mathbb{H},\{\mathbb{C}\})$ System-energy complex-measurable 1 系統-能源空間之一

$X \sqsubseteq (\Omega^{SEC}\text{-}\mu2,\mathbb{Z}\circ,_{v}\mathbb{H})$ System-energy complex-measurable 2 系統-能源空間之二

$Zh(\sigma,\kappa)$ Seed-becoming composed of the promoting-power (or constructing force) (σ,生力) and the restraining-power (or destructing force) (κ,剋力) 生剋力種子

$X = \chi \oplus \langle\mathbb{C}_{X}\rangle$ System 系統

γ Organizational culture and others 系統的非正式文化結構

$\mathbf{x}(H^{*}) \Vdash \{(vd,hc,\gamma),[R,R^{D}(e_{k})],\tilde{O}|E(\{e_{g}\},Z)\}$, $\gamma(\tau,\mathfrak{C}^{*}) \backsim (\tau,\mathfrak{C}^{*})$, $(\tau,\mathfrak{C}^{*}) \Vdash Ш^{\Delta}(\tau),\langle\mathbb{C}_{X}\rangle) \Vvdash \mathbb{T}\mathrm{zu}^{*}$ Subset of **H**, being a part of χ in a system 人文社會系統的層級-通貫子系統

$\tilde{O}$ Outward-connecting mechanism of a system 系統的涉外關係

$\langle\mathbb{C}_{X}\rangle=\{\tau|[\mathcal{M}^{1}(\ell,\tau),\ldots,\mathcal{M}^{N}(\ell,\tau)]\Vdash[E(e_{g}(\tau)),Z(\tau)]\}$, $\ell \equiv \ell(\sigma,\kappa) \backsim (\sigma,\kappa) \Vdash \mathcal{L}(\sigma,\kappa) \sqsubseteq Ш^{\mathcal{L}(\sigma,\kappa)} \Subset Ш^{ДL} \Vvdash \mathbb{T}\mathrm{zu}^{*}$, $\tau \Vdash (\mathfrak{I},Ш^{Д}) \Vvdash \mathbb{T}\mathrm{zu}^{*}$ Cultural complex of a system 系統的文化複合體

SIS(A,B) Symbolic iso-systmeism between systems A and B 系統 A、B 間的象徵共系

$\Sigma^{Tc} \Leftrightarrow$ "$\sigma \Vdash \Sigma^{Tc}$" A systemic-change becoming being in a state of simple Tcentral 簡單中道下的系統變異式

$\mathcal{S}$: $\sigma \equiv \{\tau|(\omega,\rho)^{S}\}$ Generativity 生

$Ш \equiv Ш^{Д}$ World of changes 動變世界

$Ш^{ДL}$ World of historical changes 歷史的動變世界

Σ^{TC} (i.e., $\sigma \Vdash \Sigma^{TC}$) Being a state of simple T central 簡單中道境

$T^{B\Delta}$ Becoming in a state of CE balance 因緣平衡境的動變式

$T^{B\Delta}$ $T^{B\Delta}$ system 因緣平衡境系統

$T^{B\Delta}$ $T^{B\Delta}$ management system 因緣平衡境的管理系統

$T^{B\Delta}$ $T^{B\Delta}$ becoming structure 因緣平衡境的動變式結構

$T^{B\text{-}C}$ Becoming in a state of CE balance or centrality 因緣平衡/執中境的動變式

$T^{C\Delta}$ State of Tcentral 中道境的動異式

$\{T^{C\Delta}\}^{sTc}$ State of specific Tcentral 特定中道
$\{T^{C\Delta}\}^{sTD}$ State of specific Tcentral 特定欲求之道
$\{T^{C\Delta}\}^{gTCentral}$ State of general TCentral 全般中道
T^{CE} State of CE balance 因緣平衡之境
$T^{CE/C}$ State of CE balance or centrality 因緣平衡或中道之境
T^{CE-T} State of CE balance and T continuity 因緣平衡-T 連續之境
Tzu self, a Form of Tzu* (created by Tzu*)「自」(由『自』生創)
Tzu* Self*, SELF (Ultimate Creativity/Destructivity Itself)『自』、『宇宙最終創斂力』
$\mathbf{U}^+$ Space of yang elements 陽或右元素空間
$^-\mathbf{U}$ Space of yin elements 陰或左元素空間
$\mathbf{U}$ Space of universal elements 宇宙元素空間
Y^T Systemic-dynamic state of CE balance-centrality 因緣平衡-執中的系統動態(即生態)之境
Z Action-decision-making and strategic complex (Action-strategic complex) 系統的行動-決策-策略複合體
^ (A^A = A) Impactor denoting a system operating with itself 事物自我運作的動子(此「運作」僅指思維或邏輯運作)
$\mathcal{S} \equiv \{\tau | (\omega,\rho)^S\} = ((y\text{-},y\text{+}|yh),sheng)$ Generativity 生力
$\sigma(\rho,\omega)_{(\tau)}$ Generativity, force of generation and construction (sheng) 生力
$\mathcal{K} \equiv \{\tau|(\omega,\rho)^K\} = ((\text{-},\text{+}|c),ke)$ Conflictivity 剋力
$\kappa(\rho,\omega)_{(\tau)}$ (ke 剋) Conflictivity, force of restraint and destruction 剋力
$\mathcal{Zh} \equiv \{\tau|(\omega,\rho)^{Zh}\} = ((y\text{-},y\text{+}|yh),thesis)$ "Thesis" 正力
$\mathcal{F} \equiv \{\tau|(\omega,\rho)^F\} = ((\text{-},\text{+}|c),antithesis)$ "Antithesis" 反力
$\{A(E^A;t)\Theta B(E^B;t+n)\}||_{\downarrow SU} = \Phi$ Making the scaling downward of the difference between A and B to a standardized unit size to be a zero system 差異的規模調整性標準化
$\approx^B$ State of CE balance 因緣平衡境
$\approx^{SIS}$ Impactor for symbolic iso-systemism 象徵共系的動子
<< Impactor denoting a weak vertical dominance 弱性垂直控制的動子
<<< Impactor denoting a strong vertical dominance 強性垂直控制的動子
$\backsimeq^{al\text{-}no\text{-}V}$ Impactor denoting a state of almost no-vertical dominance 幾乎一無垂直控制之境
$||_{simple}$ Symbol expressing the transformation of a system into its simplest form 轉變成最簡化原型的標計
$||_{\downarrow n}$ The notation expressing the rescaling to "n times" smaller 規模調整「小化 n-倍」的標計
$M_{x\rightarrow i}$ Decomposition-subtraction impactor 解構動子
$\ominus$ Difference (in high or low difference) 企求高低差異的動子
○ Empty system (depicting a system which is nonexistent) 空系統(意指此系統並不存在)
Θ Impactor for obtaining a difference between two systems (in positive or negative difference) 企求正負差異的動子
$\oplus|$ Impactor attaching an external factor to the original systemic-change becoming 在原有動變式之上附加外在因子的動子
ϕ° Nullifying impactor 無化動子
$\odot$ "$\odot \approx^B \{(.) =< T^{B\Delta})\}$" denoting "(.)" as in a state of CE balance (for seeking a solution in a systemic-change becoming) 系統變異式求解之際因緣平衡境的標記
Φ "$X = \Phi$" $\Leftrightarrow$ "X is in a state of simple T central" (i.e., $\sigma \Vdash \Sigma^{TC}$) denoting a state of simple T central (for seeking a solution in a systemic-change becoming 系統變異式求解之際簡單中道境的標記
"$\succcurlyeq \Phi$" Notation for being positive ("$\preccurlyeq \Phi$" is read as "being negative")「正」或「大於」的標記

⊗ Impactor (depicting an undefined operation between two entities) 動子之一〔標示兩項之間的未必明確性之關係〕

⊗* Impactor (depicting an undefined operation between two entities) 動子之一〔標示兩項之間的未必明確性之關係〕

⊛ Impactor for an integrating factor 動子之一〔標示整合性運作〕

⊕ Impactor for the static form of systemic-change becoming (In general, it is an interactor operating between elements or systems) 動子之一〔使用於系統變異式，標示兩項之間的未必明確性之關係〕

Impactor in a dynamical system) 動子之一〔使用於系統變異式的動態運作，標示兩項之間的未必明確性的關係〕

╪ Independently decomposing and reorganizing (IDR) impactor 獨立分解重組動子

θ Zero system 零系統〔系統變異式求解之際可「無化轉換」的系統；此亦即可求解運作的機制〕

⊨ Belonging to a space of impactors 屬於〔使用於動子空間的從屬關係〕

⊫ Notation denoting the relationship of an element belong to a system 屬於〔使用於元素從屬於系統的關係〕

⊑ A system contained in a space of systems 屬於〔使用於系統空間的從屬關係〕

⊪ Belonging to Ultimate Creativity/Destructivity 屬於〔使用於『宇宙最終創斂力』的從屬關係〕

⊓ Together exclusively (“and”) 和、及、與

⊔ Together non-exclusively (“or”) 或

⋐ Belonging to another space or world 屬於〔使用於小系統與大系統之間的從屬關係〕

ɤ Impactor in the general scheme of CE balance/centrality 動子之一〔使用於 CE 因緣平衡/執中模式〕

⋉ Impactor in the general scheme of CE balance/centrality 動子之一〔使用於 CE 因緣平衡/執中模式〕

∠ Constrained by 受制於某些條件、在...的條件制約之下

≺ Subjected to the force of 受制於、在...勢力制約之下

⇐ Conditioned by 受制於某些條件、在...的條件制約之下

≛ CE balance 因緣平衡

≦ Dominance 主宰、主導

☆ Association impactor 「串聯-協動/整合動子」

⋆ Interaction impactor「交感互動動子」

← Transformed from 轉換

→ Transforming into 轉換成

∽ Conditioned, induced by 受制於某些條件、由…造成

× Multiplication 〔數學〕乘法、或標示面向上的標記

$\dot{y}$ Time derivative of the variable y〔數學〕時間微分的標記

∀ For all 所有

∃ There is 有〔一些而非全部之意〕

∞ Infinity 無限大

∈ Notation for a number in a set 〔數學〕數字的標記

⇔ Logical equivalence, Implying both ways 邏輯上等同

⇒ Implying 蘊含

⇋ Interconnectedness 互動運作之一

Self Tzu (「自」), the notation for a “transcendental” and “metaphysical” entity, generated by Tzu* 「自」為「超有」、「形上」事物的標記〔「自」由『自』創生〕

Tzu* Self*, SELF (『自』), Ultimate Creativitry-Destructivity, the notation for the super-transcendental and super-metaphysical entity 『自』為「超越」、「超形上」事物的標記〔『自』意指不可言傳的『宇宙最終創斂力』〕

<Tzu > <Self>, the notation for a general entity (in metaphysical sense)〈自〉為形上意義上的一般事物

Wu Wu is the symbol expressing the energy or force generated by Wu*. While Wu* is the first level inward-potential energy, Wu is the second level inward-potential energy. It is from the combined forces of Wu and Yu that Tao*and Chi* are generated.

Wu* Wu* is the symbol expressing the yin-side or left-side energy/force generated by Tzu*. It is the inward-potential force manisfested by Tzu*.

Yu Yu is the symbol expressing the energy or force generated by Yu*. While Yu* is the first level outward-potential energy, Yu is the second level outward-potential energy. It is from the combined forces of Wu and Yu that Tao*and Chi* are generated. Note that Tao is generated by Tao* and Chi is generated by Chi*; and while Tao*, Tao and Chi* are pure-good, Chi embodies the forces of both good and bad/evil.

Yu* Yu* is the symbol expressing the yang-side or right-side energy/force energy or force generated by Tzu*. It is the outward-potential force manifested by Tzu*.

≪.≫ (《.》) Notation for Lao Tzu's "transcendental" concept, example: ≪Tao≫《道》(老子之道、超有之道)

<.> Notation for Chuang Tzu's super-spiritual (神靈) concept, example: <Tao> <道> (莊子之道、具神靈之道)

≺ .≻ Notation for Confucian concept which is under the dominance of Tien (『天』) and is super-spiritual (受制於『天』而具神靈事物的標記), example: ≺Tao≻ or ≺道≻, Tao in Confucian sense (儒家之道、受制於『天』而具神靈之道)

Index

Freiberger Beiträge zur interkulturellen und Wirtschaftskommunikation
A Forum for General and Intercultural Business Communication

Herausgegeben von Michael B. Hinner

Band 1 Michael B. Hinner: Introduction to Business Communication. 2005.

Band 2 Michael B. Hinner (ed.): Chinese and Western Business Cultures. A Comparison and Contrast. 2005.

Band 3 Michael B. Hinner (ed.): The Role of Communication in Business Transactions and Relationships. 2007.

Band 4 Michael B. Hinner (ed.): The Influence of Culture in the World of Business. 2007.

Band 5 Victor Lux Tonn: Systematics and the Economics of Culture. 2009.

www.peterlang.de

www.ingramcontent.com/pod-product-compliance
Ingram Content Group UK Ltd.
Pitfield, Milton Keynes, MK11 3LW, UK
UKHW021012120926
8556IPUK00039B/1021

9 783631 576496